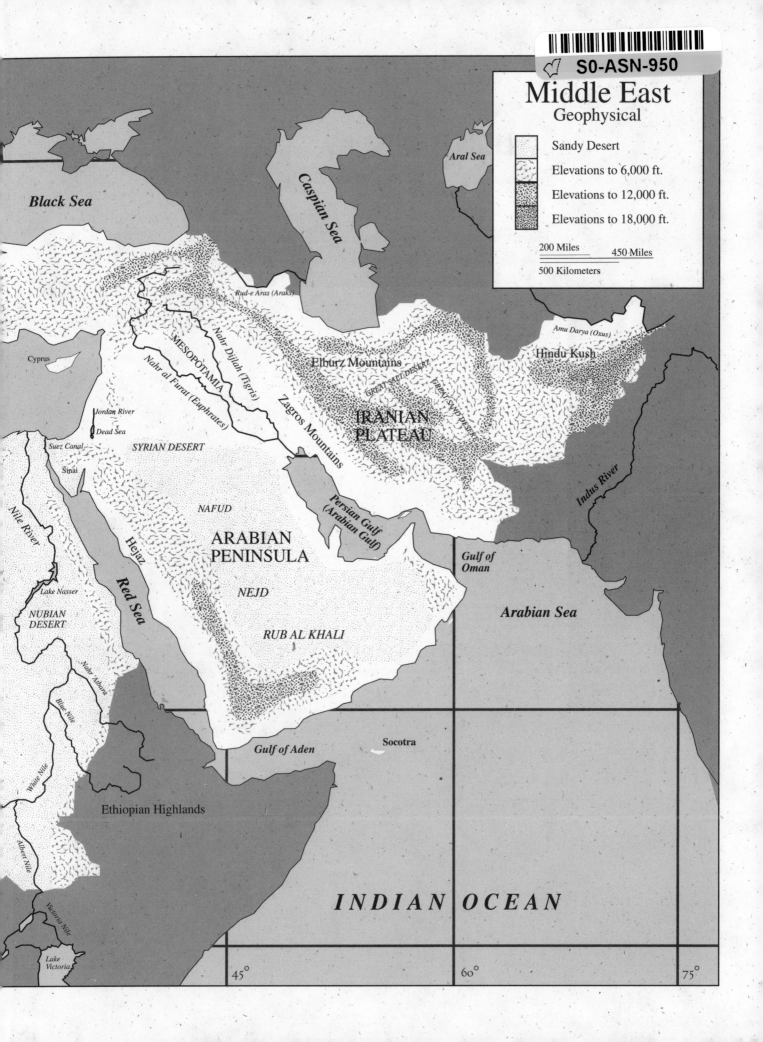

Middle East
Geophysical

S0-ASN-950

	Sandy Desert
	Elevations to 6,000 ft.
	Elevations to 12,000 ft.
	Elevations to 18,000 ft.

200 Miles   450 Miles
500 Kilometers

Black Sea

Caspian Sea

Aral Sea

Rud-e Aras (Araks)

Amu Darya (Oxus)

Cyprus

MESOPOTAMIA

Nahr Dijlah (Tigris)

Nahr al Furat (Euphrates)

Elburz Mountains

Hindu Kush

GREAT SALT DESERT

GREAT SAND DESERT

IRANIAN PLATEAU

Zagros Mountains

Jordan River

Dead Sea

Suez Canal

Sinai

SYRIAN DESERT

NAFUD

Persian Gulf (Arabian Gulf)

Indus River

Nile River

Hejaz

ARABIAN PENINSULA

Gulf of Oman

Red Sea

Lake Nasser

NUBIAN DESERT

NEJD

RUB AL KHALI

Arabian Sea

Nahr Atbara

Blue Nile

White Nile

Gulf of Aden

Socotra

Ethiopian Highlands

Albert Nile

Victoria Nile

INDIAN OCEAN

Lake Victoria

45°   60°   75°

ENCYCLOPEDIA
OF THE
MODERN
MIDDLE EAST

ENCYCLOPEDIA
OF THE
MODERN
MIDDLE EAST

VOLUME 3

Edited by

Reeva S. Simon
Philip Mattar
Richard W. Bulliet

MACMILLAN REFERENCE USA
SIMON & SCHUSTER MACMILLAN
NEW YORK

SIMON & SCHUSTER AND PRENTICE HALL INTERNATIONAL
LONDON   MEXICO CITY   NEW DELHI   SINGAPORE   SYDNEY   TORONTO

Copyright © 1996 by Simon & Schuster, Reeva S. Simon,
Philip Mattar, and The Middle East Institute of Columbia
University

Simon & Schuster Macmillan
1633 Broadway
New York, NY 10019-6785

PRINTED IN THE UNITED STATES OF AMERICA

printing number

1   2   3   4   5   6   7   8   9   10

LIBRARY OF CONGRESS CATALOGING-IN-PUBLICATION DATA

Encyclopedia of the Modern Middle East / edited by Reeva S. Simon,
    Philip Mattar, Richard W. Bulliet.
        p.   cm.
        Includes bibliographical references (p.   ) and index.
        ISBN 0-02-896011-4 (set : lib. bdg. : alk. paper). — ISBN
0-02-897061-6 (v. 1 : lib. bdg. : alk. paper). — ISBN 0-02-897062-4
(v. 2 : lib. bdg. : alk. paper). — ISBN 0-02-897063-2 (v. 3 : lib.
bdg. : alk. paper). — ISBN 0-02-897064-0 (v. 4 : lib. bdg. : alk.
paper).
        1. Middle East—Encyclopedias.   2. Africa, North—Encyclopedias.
I. Simon, Reeva S.   II. Mattar, Philip, 1944–   .   III. Bulliet,
Richard W.
DS43.E53   1996
956′.003—dc20   96-11800
                                                             CIP

ENCYCLOPEDIA
OF THE
MODERN
MIDDLE EAST

L

Laabi, Abdellatif [1942–]

Moroccan poet and novelist.

Laabi was born in Fez, Morocco, to a Muslim family. He obtained a B.A. in French literature and taught French at the Lycée Mulay Idris. He was arrested in 1972 and released from prison on July 18, 1980. Laabi received strong support from friends and intellectuals all over the world while in prison. He continued to write poetry during this period and received many literary prizes. He describes his prison years in a series of poems and letters titled *Chroniques de la citadelle d'exil* (Paris, 1983).

Laabi founded the journal *Souffles,* with Mohammed Khair-Eddine and Mustafa Nissaboury, in 1966. The Arabic counterpart of this journal was called *Anfas.* He contributed to more than one literary genre. His collection of poems *Le règne de barbarie, et d'autres poèmes* (Paris, 1980) marks the beginning of his poetic and literary writings. His works reveal an interest in the human being and a strong commitment to the Palestinian cause. Much of his writing can be described as revolutionary.

Laabi's long-term goal was to sever the strong link to Western culture, in order to end the cultural alienation of the Maghribi writer. Yet he also sought renewal through the elimination of antiquated and unsuitable traditions. His preprison poetry was characterized by a violent anger most certainly provoked by the repressive policy of the time. The writings published in *Souffles* reflect a similar attitude. His postprison poetry shows signs of greater wisdom, maturity, and depth of reflection.

Although primarily a poet, Laabi has published two novels, *L'œil et la nuit* (Casablanca, 1969) and *Les rides du lion* (Paris, 1989). He also has written plays, *Le baptême chacaliste* (Paris, 1987) and *Exercices de tolérance* (Paris, 1993). He sought to eliminate the dividing line between literary genres.

Laabi translated extensively from Arabic into French: the poems of the Moroccan Abdallah Zrika, published as *Rires de l'arbre à palabre* (Paris, 1982); an anthology of Palestinian poetry, *La poésie palestinienne de combat* (Honfleur, 1970); Mahmud DARWISH's poetry, as *Rien qu'une autre année* (Paris, 1983); *Soleil en instance* (Paris, 1986), by the Syrian novelist Hanna Mina; a collection of poetry by the Iraqi Abd al-Wahhab al-BAYATI, *Autobiographie du voleur de feu* (Paris, 1987); a collection of poems by the Palestinian Samih al-Qassim, *Je t'aime au gré de la mort* (Paris, 1988).

Laabi explained his positions, ideology, and prison experience in a series of conversations with Jacques Alessandra, published under the title *La brûlure des interrogations* (Paris, 1985). Through its question-and-answer approach the book gives a useful assessment of the literary scene in Morocco as well as an insight into Laabi's writings and thought.

BIBLIOGRAPHY

GONTARD, MARC. "La Littérature marocaine de langue française." *Europe* (June–July 1979): 102–116.

JAKOBIAK, BERNARD. "*Souffles* de 1966 à 1969." *Europe* (June–July 1979): 117–123.

MEMMI, ALBERT, ed. *Ecrivains francophones du Maghreb: Anthologie.* Paris, 1985.

Aida A. Bamia

Labaki, Naum   [1920–   ]

Lebanese journalist and diplomat.

Born in Baabdate, Lebanon, Labaki completed his elementary and secondary schooling at the College de la Sagesse and later completed studies in political economy. He is a Maronite Catholic; his father (also Naum) served as president of the Representative Council under the French mandate. Labaki had a prolific career as a journalist first at the *Revue du Liban* (1941) and then with other French-speaking publications such as *L'Orient-La Syrie* (1942), *L'Orient* (1945–1949), and *Le Soir* (1950–1965). Labaki occupied several ambassadorial positions, and in November 1969 he became public information adviser to the presidency of Lebanon.

BIBLIOGRAPHY

Who's Who in Lebanon, 1970–1971. Beirut, 1971.

George E. Irani

Labor and Labor Unions

Depending on the country, trade unions in the Middle East are nonexistent (in some cases, illegal), state-controlled, or independent.

Formal trade-union structures in the Middle East grew out of European imperialism and colonialism—especially from the extension of capitalist markets and the introduction of mechanized production. From a relatively undeveloped division of labor with a guild form of collective action, the labor force now comprises a clearly articulated division of labor, new means of production, and workers who own nothing but their labor power. This process occurred relatively quickly in each locality but at very different times. The critical period was from the beginning of the twentieth century until shortly before World War I. After World War II, Middle Eastern economies became relatively closed, socialist, or quasi-socialist. Trade unions played secondary roles and have often been subordinated to state policies.

During the late years of the Ottoman Empire (in Anatolia and the Arab provinces) and the Qajar dynasty (in Iran), peasant production predominated. Urban areas accounted for little more than 15 percent of the economy. Industry was largely artisanal (skilled manual labor), based on simple instruments of production. The division of labor within productive enterprises was slight. Competition with European production often destroyed the domestic artisanal and craft producers. Thus in Iran and Egypt, integration into the world capitalist market decimated the ranks of artisans and guild producers. Something similar occurred in Tunisia, although there foreign domination began in the late 1800s. In Iraq, there appears to have been little private property in the late Ottoman period.

Direct colonial control, where it existed, provided property rights of a capitalist type and the political power European capitalists needed to introduce manufactured goods from outside the Middle East into local markets. Trade unions arose in the context of European colonial domination and thus invariably engaged not only in local social conflict but in the political struggles over control of the various states.

Foreign capitalists used access to political power and to external sources of capital to take advantage of cheap local raw materials and labor in most of the Arab world (but this was somewhat less true of the relatively more independent states of Turkey and Iran). In Palestine, the Arabs were gradually dominated by the European-backed Jewish settlers. In Tunisia, French control allowed the Europeans to command both the agricultural and the mineral sectors. In Iran and Iraq, foreigners (Europeans and Americans) provided the capital for developing the petroleum industry, and intense conflict over the role of the state occurred repeatedly.

European capitalists often introduced foreign (European) labor into the region at higher wages than local laborers could command. They also brought in local workers from various sections of the countryside to work in factories; their employees thus had little in common and were easily manipulated. In Palestine, this interplay of nationalist politics and social conflict was particularly acute because the socialist institutions of the Zionist labor movement (see LABOR ZIONISM) often acted to exclude Palestinian Arabs from particular labor markets; the General Federation of Labor in Eretz Yisrael (HISTADRUT)—unlike Arab, Turkish, or Persian trade unions—created the foundations of a labor economy to support Zionist nationalism as well as to protect the rights of workers. Exceptionally, Histadrut thus had a dual role, as investor as well as trade union, insofar as Histadrut controls the Hevrat Ha'Ovidim firm with its many subordinate companies. Elsewhere, the struggle of workers against capital was often per-

TABLE 1

Trade Union Organization and Strength in Middle East Countries

Country	Status	Number of Unions	Population	Workforce	Union Members
Algeria	Single compulsory		24,290,000	5,425,000	1,000,000
Bahrain	No formal trade unions	12 joint comms.	678,000	204,000	
Egypt	Single compulsory	23 sectoral feds.	51,730,000	13,879,000	
Iran			54,203,000	14,361,000	
Iraq	Single compulsory		18,279,000	4,775,000	
Israel	Noncompulsory monopoly		4,520,000	1,727,000	
Jordan	Plural	19	3,879,000	915,000	
Kuwait	Single compulsory	13	2,048,000	772,000	27,000
Lebanon	Plural	18 federations	2,675,000	856,000	250,000
Libya	Single compulsory	18	4,380,000	1,007,000	275,000
Mauritania	Single compulsory	36	1,969,000	640,000	
Morocco	Plural	13 federations	24,432,000	7,365,000	1,000,000
Oman	Unions illegal		1,448,000	388,000	
Qatar	Unions illegal		422,000	170,000	
Saudi Arabia	Unions illegal		14,435,000	3,811,000	
Sudan	Unions semi-legal		24,492,000	7,640,000	
Syria	Single compulsory	179	11,719,000	2,899,000	223,000
Tunisia	Dominant non-compulsory	198	7,910,000	2,446,000	455,000
Turkey	Plural	800	56,741,000	22,772,000	1,750,000
United Arab Emirates	None		1,547,000	744,000	
Yemen	Single compulsory		11,271,000	2,400,000	
Total			330,754,000		

Figures for trade union membership, population, and size of the workforce refer to the mid- and late-1980s. They are not strictly comparable and only provide order-of-magnitude comparisons.

ceived as a national struggle and was co-opted into the struggle of nationalist politicians.

Early on, two important political currents guided the labor movement. Marxist intellectuals from outside the working class brought the ideas of class struggle and "scientific socialism" into the working class and often (but not always) also recruited workers into Leninist political parties. Workers hostile to the dominance of the liberal professionals in their movement also created their own independent unions.

In the Maghrib (North Africa), and especially in Tunis, the struggle for independence reached a heroic climax with the creation of a separate labor-union structure, the UNION GÉNÉRALE DES TRAVAILLEURS TUNISIENS (General Union of Tunisian Workers; UGTT). It was led by Ferhat HACHED rather than French communists in 1946. Elsewhere in the Arab world, leaders of the trade union move-

ment associated with the nationalist left allied themselves with political elites. After gaining independence, they extended the power of the state over the economy by nationalizing firms and creating a corporate trade union structure. State investments created large public sectors in most countries, and it is the workers in the public sector who usually make up the bulk of trade union members.

Those countries in the Middle East with unions generally have a single, often compulsory, trade union structure. Countries with single-, state-, or ruling-party-controlled federations are Djibouti, Kuwait, Libya, Mauritania, Somalia, Syria, and Yemen. Iraq's public sector employees were part of the state-controlled union federation until 1987, when the law was changed to exclude them so the state could cut its public-sector wage bill. Foreign nationals there, mainly Egyptians, are reported to be underpaid and mistreated. In these countries and in Egypt (where the Egyptian Trade Union Federation is formally separate from the state and the ruling National Democratic Party), strikes by public-sector employees are illegal, and collective bargaining between workers and employers as equals is absent. The mid-1980s saw a renewal of protests and strikes in Egypt, especially in the public sector, as the government retreated from its social-welfare commitments.

Israel's Histadrut, although founded in 1920 in British-mandated Palestine, now controls significant economic resources through its associate institutions—thus remaining the state's sole trade union. Since 1953, Israeli Arabs have been accepted as members. Palestinians in the West Bank and Gaza lack strong unions; both the Israeli government and the Palestinian nationalist movement are uncertain about the long-term effects of unions, and, in the pre-1993 Israel–PLO accord atmosphere, union creation was difficult. In Lebanon and Jordan, autonomous and plural trade union federations exist—in Lebanon, they continued to operate during the civil war.

In Tunisia, an independent trade-union federation with historic links to the ruling Neo-DESTOUR party has operated independently and sometimes in antagonism to the state. The union federation was engaged in a massive wave of strikes in January 1977. In Morocco and Algeria, multiple trade union federations exist independently of the state, and high unemployment coupled with low economic growth have produced labor unrest.

In Bahrain (where worker arbitration committees exist), Oman, Qatar, Saudi Arabia, and the United Arab Emirates, trade unions are illegal. Persistent reports exist of the arrests and executions of workers attempting to form unions in the eastern oil-rich provinces of Saudi Arabia, which also have large Shiʿite populations. In Sudan, trade unions were outlawed after the 1989 coup but have slowly been returned to semi-legal status.

In Turkey, the trade union movement was not integrated into the state, and plural union movements remained, the most important of which is the CONFEDERATION OF TURKISH TRADE UNIONS (Türk-Iş). Although dominant, Türk-Iş faces competition from several other trade unions, notably DISK (The Confederation of Revolutionary Trade Unions, which was banned after the 1980 coup) and Islamic and Turkish nationalist confederations (Haqq-Iş and MISK, respectively).

Trade unions in Iran have infrequently functioned freely since the 1950s. Between the 1953 coup and the 1979 Iranian revolution, the state actively intervened in trade-union affairs. After the revolution, there was (in addition to unions) an experiment in a broader form of workers' councils, known as *shura*. In 1983, the labor minister of the Islamic Republic of Iran failed to win passage of a restrictive new law. Most unions and the shura system were dissolved in 1985, and the government appears to have accepted the principle that workers and owners enter into individual contracts rather than collective agreements.

In the precolonial period, unions were often weak but provided workers with some independent voice in regard to the state and firm owners; in the postcolonial period, the material conditions of workers and their families have been more profoundly affected by decisions of central political authorities than by union struggles. If privatization continues to affect Middle Eastern economies, "wildcat" struggles by workers are likely to increase and the role of unions as independent actors may resume.

BIBLIOGRAPHY

BATATU, HANNA. *The Old Social Classes and the Revolutionary Movements of Iraq.* Princeton, N.J., 1978.

BAYAT, ASSEF. *Workers and Revolution in Iran.* London, 1987.

BEININ, JOEL, and ZACHARY LOCKMAN. *Workers on the Nile.* Princeton, N.J., 1987.

BIANCHI, ROBERT. *Interest Groups and Political Development in Turkey.* Princeton, N.J., 1987.

COULAND, JACQUES. *Le mouvement syndical au Liban 1919–1946.* Paris, 1970.

GALLISOT, RENÉ. *Mouvement ouvrier, communisme et nationalismes dans le monde arabe.* Paris, 1978.

GOLDBERG, ELLIS. *Tinker, Tailor and Textile Worker.* Berkeley, Calif., 1986.

KRAIEM, MUSTAFA. *La classe ouvrière tunisienne et la lutte de libération nationale.* Tunis, 1984.

SHALEV, MICHAEL. *Labour and the Political Economy in Israel.* New York, 1992.

SRAIEB, NUREDDINE. *Le mouvement ouvrier maghrébin.* Paris, 1985.

Ellis Goldberg

Labor Party

The major social-democratic party of Israel since its formation in 1968 through a merger of MAPAI, Rafi, and Ahdut ha-Avodah Poʿalei Zion.

Israel's Labor party (ILP) (Mifleget ha-Avodah) has never stood for election on its own but rather has been the major partner in the Alignment, which was formed in 1969 with MAPAM. Labor, in various manifestations, was in power from the foundation of the state in 1948 until its defeat by the Likud under Menachem Begin in 1977, with the exception of two periods (1967–1969 and 1984–1988) when it shared power with the Likud in a NATIONAL UNITY GOVERNMENT. It returned to full power in the election of 1992. As the senior member of the Labor Alignment in each Knesset since the ILP's formation, it received 80–85 percent of the Alignment's seats. Its leaders, Israel's most prominent social-democratic figures, were also prime ministers when the Alignment was in power: Levi Eshkol (1968–1969), Golda Meir (1969–1973), Yitzhak Rabin (1974–1977), Shimon Peres (1977–1992), Rabin (1992–1995), and Peres (since 1995).

The ILP's programs are broadly liberal in foreign policy and moderate socialist in domestic policy. In regard to the Palestinians, it has long been willing to negotiate with only minimal preconditions, generally preferring a settlement through a Jordanian–Palestinian confederation. But Labor has also joined other Israeli parties in insisting that Israeli security be the first priority. It rejects the idea of annexation of the West Bank and Gaza but insists that the status of Jerusalem is not negotiable. The party also strongly advocates complete equality for the Arabs of Israel. On domestic affairs, the ILP stands for a mixed economy, central economic planning, an extensive network of government-run social services, and close cooperation with the HISTADRUT but also a large role for the private sector. On the important issue of the role of religion, it accepts the status quo: an agreement that religious affairs will be under the jurisdiction of the Orthodox rabbinate and that rules about such matters as public transportation on the Sabbath will remain as they were at the time of the founding of the state. However, the party would also like to see Jewish religious pluralism and more rights for the Reform and Conservative movements.

The history of the ILP has often been stormy, providing an arena for conflicts among its numerous strong personalities. Among these conflicts was the rivalry between Rabin and Peres, often over questions of who was responsible for ILP election setbacks and for the failures of some government policies. In 1977 Rabin's difficulties over an allegedly illegal bank account belonging to his wife were considered by some as one of the causes of the Alignment's defeat by the Likud under Begin. In turn, many attribute subsequent electoral defeats to the "colorless" Peres, citing his replacement by Rabin as an important factor in the Alignment's decisive electoral victory in 1992. In an important reform of internal Israeli political party organization in 1968, the ILP broadened the selection process for Knesset candidates through primary elections, a practice that has since then been adopted by some other Israeli parties as well.

BIBLIOGRAPHY

ARANOFF, MYRON J. *Power and Ritual in the Israel Labor Party.* Armonk, N.Y., 1993.

Walter F. Weiker

Labor Zionism

One of the main ideologies and political currents within the Zionist movement; the dominant political philosophy of Israel, 1948–1977.

From the beginning of the twentieth century, Labor Zionism dominated the political philosophy of the Jews who went to resettle in Palestine, both during the British mandate and then as the philosophical banner of the dominant political party in the new State of Israel until the parliamentary elections of 1977. Its leaders are considered the founding fathers of the Jewish state, the architects of its most distinctive social and economic institutions.

Two powerful ideologies of the nineteenth century—NATIONALISM and socialism—were synthesized into several labor Zionist expressions. Even before the establishment of the first Zionist organizations, Moses Hess published, in 1862, *Rome and Jerusalem,* which advocated a socialist Jewish commonwealth in Palestine as the only solution to the plight of the Jewish masses in the Diaspora, especially those of Russia, Eastern Europe, and the Middle East. As a member of the League of Communists, along with Karl Marx and Friedrich Engels, Hess became one of the first Jewish writers to discuss the collective existence of the dispersed Jews in terms of the socioeconomic conditions of capitalism and to put forth the idea of a political and economic revolution as the solution to the so-called Jewish problem.

For Labor Zionism, the core of the Jewish problem was not that Jews existed in Christian and Islamic host countries, but that only a small proportion of Jews were farmers or workers in the mainstream of their adopted societies. Most were scholars and teachers of Jewish studies or merchants and traders on a small or large scale. The explanation for this distorted occupational structure was rooted in modern European history with its legislation that excluded Jews in most countries from joining guild-dominated trades or from owning land (the Austro-Hungarian Empire was an exception). According to Labor Zionist views, most Jews had been denied the possibility of engaging in productive labor—and therefore their socioeconomic structure was fatally distorted. Although there were Jewish artisans, merchants, and farmers throughout the Diaspora, Labor Zionism assumed there were too few to create an agricultural and craft base for a new Jewish society. For that reason, the framework of ordinary class analysis had to be reworked to account for the plight of European Jewry. In socialist doctrine, class struggle arises from the relations of production—but Jewish socialists saw that most Jews needed to gain access to "the conditions of production," to land, natural resources, and channels of trade.

Without a country of their own, Jews had to acquiesce to those with economic and political power; consequently, they were also forced to discharge functions that other groups refused. In Russia, for example, Jews were routinely called upon to fill pioneering roles in new territories of the Pale and to develop economies—but they were evicted by edict when the economies matured and competitors for their positions emerged from the national majority. Not only did such circumstances produce uncertainty, they also posed enormous dangers. Each expulsion was accompanied by an ideology of degradation that justified the destruction of Jewish property and lives. The ideology of Jew hatred became so internalized that Jews in these circumstances came to accept their powerlessness as natural and unchangeable. Anti-Semitism thus affected them with regard to their economic options, political position, social status, and self-conception. Since socialism postulated class struggle as the means to final and full human liberation, not being able to participate in the process, such Jews could not expect to benefit from the outcome.

In the nineteenth century, the educated youth of Russia and Eastern Europe proved a receptive audience for socialism. Educated and assimilated Jewish youth also became socialists, but some were Jewish nationalists as well—they became Labor Zionists. In 1905, two small Zionist labor parties were founded by Eastern European Jewish youths who went to Palestine. They both advanced the idea of socioeconomic normalization and emphasized that in their own national society Jews would assume all economic roles—not just the restricted and vulnerable occupations of the Diaspora. Although the ultimate aim was to create in Palestine a Jewish working class, the immediate concern was to find or create employment in a land that had no industrial base. The only jobs at first were on farms owned by Jews—earlier immigrants or those from the religious community of Jerusalem whose own economic base was insecure were sustained by philanthropic external financial aid. On these farms Jews had to compete with local Arabs who were willing to work for low wages. Jewish farmers had first to be convinced to employ Jews instead of Arabs—even if costs were higher and profits lower. The immigrant Jews themselves had to be persuaded to work for lower wages than they might have expected.

One of the political parties, Po'alei Zion (Workers of Zion) tried to organize craftsmen into unions and initiated strikes in protest against the conditions of employment in the Jewish farming colonies. A small group from this party also turned its energies toward self-defense. Some Labor Zionists had founded guard units in Eastern Europe to protect Jewish communities there during pogroms. They and their defense concepts were transported to Palestine and expanded; their members were hired as guards on Jewish farms.

The second labor party, Ha-Po'el Ha-Tza'ir (The Young Worker) was formed just weeks before Po'alei Zion. Assuming a capitalist development in Palestine, Ha-Po'el Ha-Tza'ir nevertheless traced its intellectual roots to Russian populism (rather than Marxism), rejected most of the socialist doctrine, and shunned the very word socialism. It had no ties to the international workers' movement, opposed strike actions, and rejected the utility of class struggle. It romanticized the idea of labor—but called to Jews to return to the soil, to drain swamps, to build roads. It also established the first KIBBUTZ, Degania, and was involved with the founding of the first MOSHAV, Nahalal.

The political changes triggered by the Russian Revolution and the end of World War I facilitated the spread of Labor Zionism from 1917 to the early 1920s. The dissolution of the Ottoman Empire and the changed boundaries of Austria-Hungary and Russia stimulated many Jews to leave for the new British mandate territory of Palestine, where the Labor Zionists pressed for the rapid immigration and settlement of Jewish workers. Many adherents, taking matters into their own hands, crossed war-torn borders to enter Palestine without regard to the established policies of either the WORLD ZIONIST ORGANIZATION (WZO) or Palestine's mandate government. Coming of age in the midst of the traumatic conditions of war, revolution, and counterrevolution in Eastern Europe, these Labor Zionists also experienced the postwar pogroms that were unleashed by the Ukrainians and the Poles.

Economic and political circumstances in Palestine forced both political parties to readjust their strategies and activities. The proposals for cooperative settlement on the land that were advanced by the leadership of the WZO provided employment, although the new agricultural settlements challenged the socialist emphasis on industrial development. Both parties also had to find ways to justify their cooperation with the bourgeois Zionist leadership and their policies.

In Palestine, there were powerful incentives to unify the labor movement after World War I. In 1920, the HISTADRUT (the General Federation of Labor) was founded—which brought into a unified framework all Labor Zionist political parties and undertook, on their behalf, a broad range of political, economic, and cultural activities.

One segment of the Labor Zionist movement founded in Vienna (1916) was Ha-Shomer Ha-Tzaʻir (The Young Guard). Its members were youth educated for kibbutz life in Palestine, and it retained its distinctive structure and ideology although it also joined the Histadrut. It founded agricultural collectives, and its vision of liberation owed as much to Freud as to Marx.

For the settlers in Palestine, the careful balancing between Labor Zionist ideology and practicality—the need to revise policies because of changing circumstances—often involved a deviation from socialist principles. Many Labor Zionists, concluding that such adjustments foreclosed all hope for realizing socialism in their time, left their political parties, and some even left Palestine. The evolving political parties were sometimes fractured by the strains of accommodating to political reality. Sometimes, however, circumstances generated strong impulses to unity. In 1930, the MAPAI political party was founded, unifying AH-DUT HA-AVODAH and Ha-Poʻel Ha-Tzaʻir; MAPAI led the labor movement in Palestine on a course of constructive socialism, seeking class goals plus a democratic Jewish nation. It also cooperated with the nonsocialist movements that accepted some social-democratic principles. These principles had been promoted by Berl Katznelson, but their implementation was executed by the party's pragmatic leader, David Ben-Gurion. Those who did not accept Ben-Gurion's pragmatism in dealing with the British mandate authorities in 1935 joined Zeʻev Jabotinsky and formed the REVISIONIST MOVEMENT. Other disagreements led to the formation of other parties, but Ben-Gurion of MAPAI proclaimed the new State of Israel in 1948, and MAPAI provided all early prime ministers, Histadrut secretaries-general, and Knesset (legislature) speakers and presidents but one.

BIBLIOGRAPHY

AVINERI, SHLOMO. *The Making of Modern Zionism.* New York, 1981.

FRANKEL, JONATHAN. *Prophesy and Politics: Socialism, Nationalism, and the Russian Jews, 1862–1914.* Cambridge, U.K., 1981.

Donna Robinson Divine

Lacheraf, Mostefa   [1917–   ]

Algerian intellectual, minister, and ambassador.

Lacheraf was born in Sidi Aissa in northern Algeria. His father was a Muslim magistrate. Lacheraf was educated then taught at the lycée (school) in Mostaganem and then at Paris's prestigious Lycée Louis-le-Grand. He joined the Messali al-HADJ movement, MOUVEMENT POUR LE TRIOMPHE DES LIBERTÉS DÉMOCRATIQUES (Movement for the Triumph of Democratic Liberties) but left it in 1952. Subsequently as a member of the FRONT DE LIBÉRATION NATIONALE (FLN; National Liberation Front), he was seized along with Ahmed Ben Bella, Hocine AIT Ahmed, Mohamed Khider, and Mohamed Boudiaf in the infamous French skyjacking of an Air Maroc airplane in October 1957. Lacheraf escaped from a French clinic in 1961. After independence, he helped draft the TRIPOLI PROGRAMME (1962). He later served as ambassador to Argentina and Mexico. He was an adviser to President Houari Boumédienne, who appointed Lacheraf as minister of national education (April 1977). Lacheraf's ministry was very controversial since he questioned the pragmatism of Algeria's official ARABIZATION POLICIES. He urged a more bilingual approach. In 1982, Lacheraf was appointed as Algeria's permanent delegate to UNESCO. His most famous work is *L'Algérie: Nation et Société* (1965, 1969).

BIBLIOGRAPHY

DÉJEUX, JEAN. *Dictionnaire des auteurs maghrébins de langue française.* Paris, 1984.

Phillip C. Naylor

Lacoste, Robert   [1898–1989]

Resident minister of Algeria from 1956 to 1958.

Robert Lacoste was a socialist who served as resident minister during the ALGERIAN WAR OF INDEPENDENCE under the Mollet, Bourgès-Maunoury, and Gaillard Fourth Republic governments. He supported repression, which included torture, thereby eroding civilian control, in order to keep ALGERIA under French control. Lacoste also promoted accelerated social and economic programs, highlighted by his efforts to "Algerianize" the administration. He increased Algeria's departments (to twelve) and drafted the LOI CADRE (enabling or framework law) designed to enhance internal autonomy and Muslim representation. He was a fervent advocate of France's involvement in the Suez War of October 1956. Lacoste later served in the French senate from 1971 to 1980.

BIBLIOGRAPHY

HORNE, ALISTAIR. *A Savage War of Peace: Algeria, 1954–1962,* 2nd ed. New York, 1987.

Phillip C. Naylor

Ladino

Various forms of Judeo-Spanish spoken and written by the Sephardim—Jews who came to the Ottoman Empire and the Maghrib (North Africa) after their expulsion from Spain in 1492.

Ladino is also called Spanyol or Judezmo; in Northern Morocco, it is called Haketía. It is at base Old Castilian (Spanish, a Romance language). Like all Diaspora Jewish languages, it is written in Hebrew characters and has a significant Hebrew and Aramaic vocabulary. It also—depending upon the region—has assimilated loanwords from Arabic, Greek, Turkish, Italian, and French.

Ladino was the language of Jewish merchants throughout much of the Islamic Mediterranean region from the sixteenth through nineteenth centuries. Except for folk songs and ballads (*cantígas* and *romances*) and some rabbinical writings, there was only a limited Ladino literature until 1730, when Jacob Culi published his popular encyclopedic *Me'am Lo'ez* in Istanbul. In the nineteenth and early twentieth centuries, Ladino became the primary medium of modern learning among Jews in the Ottoman Empire. Hundreds of novels and plays were translated from French, Hebrew, and Yiddish writers. There was a flourishing Ladino press in Turkey, Greece, the Balkans, Palestine, and Egypt.

The language policies of the post–World War I Republic of Turkey, the destruction of much of Balkan Jewry during World War II, and the migration of most of North African and Levantine Jews to Spain, South America, France, and Israel has led to the near disappearance of Ladino as a living language.

BIBLIOGRAPHY

LIDA, DENAH. "Ladino Language and Literature." In *Jewish Languages: Theme and Variations,* ed. by Herbert H. Paper. Cambridge, Mass., 1978.

Norman Stillman

Lado Enclave

Colonial territory in Sudan, connecting the Congo and Nile rivers.

The Lado Enclave was a remnant of the ambitions of King Leopold of Belgium to link his personal empire (the Congro Free State) with the Nile, whose waters flowed to the Mediterranean Sea. He appeared to have achieved his goal in 1894 when Great Britain ceded to him the BAHR AL-GHAZAL, which gave access to the Nile, in a futile attempt to prevent French encroachment on the vital Nile waters. Leopold yielded to French pressure to abandon the Bahr al-Ghazal but demanded his rights under a treaty with Great Britain to retain a small enclave called Lado, which would connect the two great waterways of Africa, the Congo and Nile rivers. Because the Congo Free State and the Lado Enclave were the personal fiefs of King Leopold and not of Belgium, whose government had no desire to acquire the enclave at the expense of Britain's hostility, they passed into history upon the death of Leopold on December 17, 1909. By a treaty signed between Belgium and Great Britain in 1906, the enclave was incorporated into the Anglo–Egyptian Condominium.

Robert O. Collins

Lahad, Antoine   [1929–   ]

Lebanese leader of the Israeli-backed South Lebanon Army.

A Christian from Dayr al-Qamar, Antoine Lahad graduated from the Lebanese Military Academy in 1952. He eventually reached the rank of major-general in the Lebanese army. In January 1984, following the death of Sa'ad Haddad, the founder and leader of the Israeli-funded, -equipped, and -trained South Lebanon Army, Antoine Lahad was enticed out of retirement to become the new head of the militia. Under his leadership, the militia was expanded and upgraded, and its dependence upon Israeli support intensified.

BIBLIOGRAPHY

HIRO, DILIP. *Lebanon: Fire and Embers.* New York, 1992.

Guilain P. Denoeux

Lahouel, Hocine   [1917–   ]

Algerian nationalist.

Lahouel joined Messali Hadj's Etoile Nord-Africaine (ENA) (North African Star) in 1930. He was a leader in the PARTI DU PEUPLE ALGÉRIEN (PPA) (Algerian People's Party) and was an editor of *El Ouma.* After World War II, Lahouel was torn between supporting the *Organisation Spéciale* (OS) (Special Organization) paramilitary operation or the imperfect electoral process. He became secretary-general of the MOUVEMENT POUR LE TRIOMPHE DES LIBERTÉS DÉMOCRATIQUES (MTLD) (Movement of the Triumph of Democratic Liberties) in 1950 and was a leading centralist when the organization split. He joined the FRONT DE LIBÉRATION NATIONALE (FLN) (National Liberation Front) in 1955 and represented it in Indonesia and Pakistan. In 1965 he became president of the National Textile Society. Lahouel received political attention again, however, when he cosigned an antigovernment manifesto in 1976 entitled "New Appeal to the Algerian People."

BIBLIOGRAPHY

STORA, BENJAMIN. *Dictionnaire biographique des militants nationalistes algériens.* Paris, 1985.

Phillip C. Naylor

Laicism

See Gökalp, Ziya; Kemalism

Lajevardi, Qasem   [1921–   ]

Iranian industrialist.

Born to one of the prominent commercial and industrialist families of Iran, Qasem Lajevardi received his master's in business administration from Columbia University and, from 1944 onward, was active in Iranian commerce and industry. He was instrumental in attracting Japanese businessmen to Iran and was a member of the board of directors of the Iran Japan Bank. He also founded the Behshahr Industrial Company, the first successful agrobusiness enterprise in Iran. Member of the Chamber of Industries and Mines, Lajevardi owned several factories throughout Iran that produced shortening, textiles, and soap. He left the country after the Iranian revolution in 1979.

BIBLIOGRAPHY

Iran Who's Who. Tehran, 1972.

Neguin Yavari

La Marsa Convention

The document that formally established the French protectorate over Tunisia.

The La Marsa Convention was signed in June 1883 and ratified by the French Chamber of Deputies in April 1884. The force behind the convention was Paul CAMBON, resident general in Tunisia from 1882 to 1886. The convention provided for a French loan to the bey, allowing him to settle his debts to other European states and thereby bringing an end to the International Financial Commission. With these measures, France won control over the Tunisian economy and, with the protectorate in place, the political affairs of Tunis as well.

BIBLIOGRAPHY

ABUN-NASR, JAMIL. *A History of the Maghrib in the Islamic Period.* London, 1987.

Matthew S. Gordon

Lampson, Miles   [1880–1964]

British diplomat, later Lord Killearn.

Appointed in 1933 as high commissioner to Egypt, Lampson headed the British delegation that negotiated the Anglo–Egyptian Treaty of 1936. Upon its ratification he became ambassador, although he continued to wield the power of a high commissioner in domestic politics until he left Cairo (1946).

In that status he exercised his authority during World War II, despite Egypt's nominal independence. The British, apprehensive of King Farouk's pro-Axis sympathies and fearful of Gen. Erwin Rommel's impending invasion of Egypt, were intent on installing a government of the WAFD, headed by Mustafa al-Nahhas Pasha. On 2 February 1942, Lampson issued an ultimatum to Farouk to appoint Nahhas as prime minister. Farouk complied, thereby averting a showdown. However, the ultimatum and its outcome alienated the Egyptian officer corps, which in 1952 overthrew the monarchy.

BIBLIOGRAPHY

MANSFIELD, PETER. *The British in Egypt.* New York, 1971.

Jean-Marc R. Oppenheim

Lamrani, Muhammad Karim   [1919–   ]

Moroccan politician and business leader.

Educated in Morocco and France with a degree in economics, Lamrani served as an economic adviser to Hassan II in the 1960s. Lamrani went on to various prominent offices, including vice-chairman, then president, of the Casablanca Chamber of Commerce; director of the national airline, Royal Air

Maroc; and director general of the Sharifian Office of Phosphates. Hassan II appointed Lamrani as prime minister on three occasions—in 1971, 1972, and 1983. Unaffiliated with any major political formation, Lamrani effectively served as a mediator between the crown and opposition parties. As prime minister, Lamrani was a champion of the private sector of the Moroccan economy.

BIBLIOGRAPHY

Who's Who in the Arab World, 1978–1979.
ZARTMAN, I. WILLIAM, ed. The Political Economy of Morocco. New York, 1987.

Matthew S. Gordon

Land Code of 1858

Extension of Tanzimat reforms to agricultural property and taxation.

The Ottoman Land Code of 1858 (Turkish, *Arazi Kanunnamesı*) was an extension of the TANZIMAT reforms to the areas of agricultural property and taxation. Aimed at increasing tax revenues while replacing local rule by notables with centralized administration, the code reaffirmed prior laws pertaining to land, updated some old terminology, and introduced two major innovations that, by permitting individuals to possess large areas of land, completely transformed the relationship of people to land in many parts of the Ottoman Empire during the last half of the nineteenth century.

Classical Ottoman land-tenure legislation made a fundamental distinction between the right to cultivate land (*tasarruf*) and the absolute ownership of land (*raqaba*). The two main categories of land were *mülk* and *miri*. The owners of *mülk* land combined the right to cultivate with absolute ownership; this land was largely confined to orchards adjacent to villages and constituted a small proportion of land in the empire. *Mülk* land comes closest to private property as understood in the West. *Miri* land was owned by the state; the actual cultivators of the land were essentially tenants of the state, although they were entitled to pass on the right of cultivation to their heirs. *Miri* land consisted of arable land upon which crops were sown and constituted the vast majority of agricultural land in the empire.

Taxes on agricultural lands were a primary source of income for the Ottoman state. By the late fourteenth century, a system of revenue collection was established called the *timar* system. Large grants of land were given to military officers who collected the land tax and used it to procure and equip military forces to fight the empire's wars. Until the 1800s,

this system was gradually replaced by one called *iltizam* (tax farming). Wealthy individuals, often government officials, would bid at open auction for the right to collect taxes. An agreed-upon proportion of taxes would be transferred to the government, and the tax farmer could keep the rest. While initially tax farms were granted for limited periods of time, in a further development, they were granted for life, and even became inheritable. These grants were known as *malikane*. A consequence of *malikane* was that tax farmers increased their autonomy from the state and often became local rulers (*ayan*). The *ayan* did not challenge the state's claim to ownership of land, but they did prevent the state from collecting taxes, enhancing their own power. In the early nineteenth century, *ayan* from the western provinces of the empire were briefly able to impose their will on the sultan. But this supremacy was short-lived, and by 1815, Sultan MAHMUD II had reestablished the dominant position of the central state.

Mahmud II's successful campaign to reassert state control over the *ayan* created a need for a new system to administer the state's vast tracts of land while preventing reemergence of the ayan political challenge. LAND REFORM was taking place throughout the Middle East. The distinguished historian Ahmed Cevdet Paşa, who served on the commission that drafted the code, stated that the radical administrative and financial changes created by the Tanzimat reforms of the first half of the century produced the need for new regulations of landed property. In addition, the growing need of the state for revenue demanded new forms of land tenure and taxation that would enhance cultivation of existing lands and encourage the reclamation of dead lands, while guaranteeing state collection of tax revenues. Finally, both merchants and farmers inside the empire and European countries were pressuring the sultan to pass reforms that would rationalize the government. Part of this rationalization would be accomplished by guaranteeing the property rights of the sultan's subjects. The 1858 Land Code was a response to these multiple needs.

The passage of the code was preceded by several reforms. In 1846, a ministry of agriculture was established to stimulate agricultural production. Efforts were made to sedentarize nomadic tribes, both to provide laborers for the cultivation of cotton and to subject them to taxation. Tax exemptions offered villages for performing public services such as road building were abolished; new state agencies would perform these services. The agricultural tax, which previously had fluctuated between 10 and 50 percent of the product was fixed at 10 percent; this tax was called the *üşür*. In 1847, the government prepared a system of land registration; land would be registered in a centralized government office, the *defterhane,* and owners would be given deeds of ownership.

The Land Code was characterized by marked continuity with the classical fifteenth- and sixteenth-century QANUNs regulating agrarian property rights. The fundamental distinction between *tasarruf* and *raqaba* was retained, and land continued to be divided into five categories: *mülk, miri,* WAQF (tax-exempt land devoted to supporting religious establishments), *metruk* (land designated for the public activities of villages, such as the village threshing floor), and *mevat* (dead and unclaimed land). The preponderance of land continued to be owned by the state. The Land Code reiterated basic legal doctrine on the means of acquiring land through possession and cultivation of land for a ten-year period, the condition that land uncultivated for a three-year period became *mahlul* (lapsed ownership), and the means of inheriting land. The code liberalized the right of bequeathing land, in the hope that keeping land within one family would lead to greater efforts to improve land.

Despite its conservative nature, the Land Code did contain two crucial innovations that would alter the nature of land ownership in much of the Middle East. The first innovation was the obligation of landowners to register their land with the government and receive formal deed to the land. This measure was not designed to prevent absentee ownership; indeed, the code specifically stated that legal ownership of land took precedence over actual occupation and cultivation. Thus, whereas previously the *ayan* had possessed the right to collect taxes, now those who did not cultivate land could still possess land and become taxpayers. The code was thus concerned with determining the legal status of the taxpayer, suggesting that the drafters of the code perceived the new legislation as a revenue-raising instrument. The code did, however, prohibit any individual or several individuals from gaining title to occupied villages in their entirety. Nevertheless, the second innovation found in the code permitted individuals to own vast tracts of land; beginning in 1858, the state could issue deeds to formerly unoccupied lands. This was designed to increase the area of land under cultivation. When these two innovations were combined, it meant that individuals could now own very large tracts of land on paper.

The major consequence of the 1858 Land Code was the separation of the taxpayer/owner from the cultivator in many parts of the empire. Before the code's passage, peasants had leased land from the state, and powerful individuals had acted as intermediaries who collected taxes from the actual cultivator; after the code's passage, powerful individuals could legally own land that they leased to peasants. It is frequently asserted that this outcome was precisely the opposite of what was intended by the Ottoman government. Inefficient administration of the law, it is contended, allowed powerful individuals to register in their own names lands previously held by peasants. This occurred because peasants depended on local notables for protection; because peasants were afraid that registration of land would be followed by conscription or increased tax burdens; because peasant indebtedness to moneylenders led to forfeiture of deeds to land; because peasants were too ignorant to comprehend land registration; or because bedouin shaykhs used their authority within the tribe to usurp all the land of their tribesmen.

More recent scholarship has contested this view, arguing that the consequences of the Land Code differed from region to region in the empire and that peasants were willing to participate in and benefit from the new system. In Palestine, for example, in the hilly country surrounding Jerusalem, peasants did register land in their own names, and a survey of property records did not find a single case of a city notable or moneylender registering land. On the coastal plains, however, city notables were able to take advantage of the government's new policy of selling deeds to unclaimed lands. Large-scale landlords took possession of vast tracts of land, still mostly unoccupied or unclaimed. Similarly, in Anatolia large estates were formed on wasteland, often located in swampy plains and in the Kurds' tribal lands to the east. In areas of established peasant settlements in central Anatolia and on the coasts, peasant ownership continued to be the predominant form of land tenure.

In other regions, large estates were created. In Mesopotamia (now Iraq), Ottoman governors, seeking the cooperation of tribal shaykhs, permitted them to register tribal lands as their personal property, creating large estates. In Syria, powerful local families had obtained *malikane* grants and ruled almost unchecked from the eighteenth century. By 1858, the distinction between *mülk* and *miri* land had been considerably blurred. Thus, the Land Code seems to have accelerated, not caused, the creation of large estates. The major mechanism for estate formation in Syria seems to have been peasant indebtedness and default to moneylenders. As a result, by the start of the twentieth century, large landholdings had been created and many peasants reduced to the status of tenant farmer or sharecropper. In Syria, as in other regions of the empire where peasants lost ownership of land, estate formation did not mean the creation of unified, plantation-like farms; instead, absentee landowners negotiated arrangements with individual peasants, who continued to farm small plots of land.

Although a great deal of research remains to be done, these divergent consequences of the Land Code mitigate against drawing any overly generalized conclusions about its results. If in Syria and Iraq urban notables and tribal shaykhs were able to wrest ownership of land from peasants, in Palestine and Anatolia large estates were created primarily through the sale by the state of wasteland that needed to be reclaimed. The capacity of peasants in parts of Palestine and Anatolia to obtain legal possession of their land suggests that peasants were not automatically unwilling to register their land; it would seem to be the case that in many regions, they were unable to do so.

It is not clear that the creation of large estates constitutes the failure of the 1858 Land Code. If a primary purpose of the code was to raise state revenues, it was a success: Between 1887 and 1910, a period when the territory of the empire was shrinking, the revenue collected from the agricultural tax increased from 426 million to 718 million piastres.

BIBLIOGRAPHY

BAER, GABRIEL. "The Evolution of Private Landownership in Egypt and the Fertile Crescent." In *The Economic History of the Middle East, 1800–1914,* ed. by Charles Issawi. Chicago, 1966.
GERBER, HAIM. *The Social Origins of the Modern East.* Boulder, Colo., 1988.
HAIDER, SALAH. "Land Problems of Iraq." In *The Economic History of the Middle East, 1800–1914,* ed. by Charles Issawi. Chicago, 1966.
KARPAT, KEMAL H. "The Land Regime, Social Structure, and Modernization in the Ottoman Empire." In *Beginnings of Modernization in the Middle East: The Nineteenth Century,* ed. by William R. Polk and Richard L. Chambers. Chicago, 1966.
SLUGLETT, PETER, and MARION FAROUK-SLUGLETT. "The Application of the 1858 Land Code in Greater Syria: Some Preliminary Observations." In *Land Tenure and Social Transformation in the Middle East,* ed. by Tarif Khalidi. Beirut, 1984.
WARRINER, DOREEN. "Land Tenure in the Fertile Crescent." In *The Economic History of the Middle East, 1800–1914,* ed. by Charles Issawi. Chicago, 1966.

David Waldner

Land Day

Strike by Palestinians to protest confiscation of Arab land in Israel (March 30, 1976).

After Israel's government announced plans to confiscate Arab land in February 1976, the National Committee for the Defense of Arab Lands, the first political organization claiming to represent the entire Palestinian population of Israel, called for a strike and named it Land Day. In the Galilee region, where the appropriations were to take place, villagers clashed with Israel's troops, leading to six Arab deaths, and numerous arrests and injuries. These incidents were similar to demonstrations at KAFR KASIM twenty years before.

The strike demonstrated the political strength of Rakah, the Communist party of Israel, which had organized the demonstrations and had created the Committee. Land Day was declared a Palestinian national holiday in 1992 and is celebrated annually with demonstrations and a general strike by Palestinians residing in Israel, the West Bank, and the Gaza Strip.

BIBLIOGRAPHY

KIMMERLING, BARUCH, and JOEL S. MIGDAL. *Palestinians: The Making of a People.* New York, 1993.

Lawrence Tal

Land of Israel Movement

Israeli political pressure group formed to assure the retention of all lands won in the 1967 war.

Founded after the ARAB–ISRAEL WAR OF 1967, the Land of Israel Movement (LIM) drew its members from many sources, including Labor Zionists, Revisionists, intellectuals, academics, persons with military background, and religious figures. It did not attempt to win Knesset seats, but some of its members, such as Abraham Yoffe and Moshe Shamir, were elected through other parties. Because LIM seldom worked outside of the spheres of publicity and writing, its role faded when more extreme organizations, such as Gush Emunim and Tehiyah, came on the scene.

Walter F. Weiker

Land Reform

Measures designed by government action for a relatively equitable redistribution of agricultural land.

The distribution of property rights in land is a fundamental determinant of production and distribution, as well as a key indicator of the relationship between society and the state. In the Middle East, there have been three phases of land reform, the governmental redistribution of property rights in land: the early phase (nineteenth century), when centralizing states and/or colonialism and expanding market opportunities often concentrated property rights in relatively few hands; a second phase (1945–1975), after World War II and before the petroleum boom of 1973–1985, when independent states expropriated the largest (often colonial) farms—redistributing land usually as private property to middle-class or smaller farmers—and substituted state monopolies for private marketing networks; a third phase may be discerned during the 1980s as states retreated from direct detailed intervention in agriculture.

The critical variable in the first phase was the strength of the state. States always sought to remove intermediaries between themselves and the peasantry but were often too weak to do so. For example, in the Ottoman Empire during the nineteenth century, in Thrace and those areas of Anatolia close to Istanbul, small-scale farming became the norm. By contrast, in the more remote areas of the empire, such as Eastern Anatolia, Çukyrova, or Syria, the need to rely on local intermediaries for administration permitted the conversion of many tax-collecting rights into private property, thereby creating a highly skewed distribution of land. In some cases, a zealous local governor could play a central role: Midhat Paşa prevented the emergence of large landholding in much of Ottoman Iraq at the time when the opposite process was unfolding in neighboring areas of the empire.

European colonialism changed land-tenure patterns throughout the Middle East. In the Maghrib (North Africa), the process of invasion and settler colonialism resembled the Spanish conquest in the Americas: the best farmland was seized by the colonists, who forced the indigenous population onto marginal land on the fringes of cultivation or dispossessed them. Consequently, a small number of European farmers held land in large farms, while the Muslim majority throughout the countryside held small farms in poor areas. For example, on the eve of independence, nearly 25 percent of all farmland in Algeria was held by *colons* (colonists) in farms of some 250 acres (100 ha) or more. Similar patterns prevailed throughout the region.

The nineteenth century Muslim conquest actually generated the same result, as in Egypt from 1805 to 1838, when Muhammad Ali Pasha ruled; after 1838 the British forced him to abandon his system of state monopoly of land—which often had been distributed to his family members, court followers, and other government favorites. By 1914, some 43 percent of Egypt's farmland was held in large farms of over 50 acres (20 ha).

Indirect colonial rule also fostered an uneven distribution of land. During the British mandate over Iraq, the administration permitted tribal leaders (shaykhs and aghas) to register vast tribal areas for Arabs and Kurds in their own names, thereby creating one of the region's (and the world's) most unequal land distributions: by 1953, 1.7 percent of the landholders had 63 percent of the land; 75 percent of the population was landless.

Although various mechanisms were used to exploit the large estates, sharecropping was most common in the lands of the former Ottoman Empire,

while the estates of Egypt and the Maghrib usually relied on more direct management by the landowner or his representative. These latter systems were often characterized by a two-tier labor system, with a small number of resident year-round employees, and a much larger number of seasonal wage laborers hired, for example, at harvest time. These distinctions had consequences for the second phrase of land reform, after World War II. Throughout the region, rural conditions deteriorated as population pressure on increasingly scarce land forced rents up and wages down. Local landlords also enjoyed wide local political and social power.

The second phase of land reform, after World War II, found regional governments attacking such local (and national) power holders. For all the differences in ideology between Arab nationalism or the shah of Iran in the twentieth century and late-nineteenth-century Ottoman sultans, they were alike in their drive to destroy local power holders and to eliminate intermediaries between the central government and the peasantry. Given their greater technological and organizational powers, the later reformers were more successful. The countries experiencing significant land reform during this phase were Egypt, Syria, Iraq, Algeria, Tunisia, Iran, and the People's Democratic Republic of Yemen.

Egypt. The region's first modern land reform was attempted here, and subsequent Arab nationalist reforms (in Iraq and Syria) sought to copy it. The reform moved in stages, in which the legal limitation of ownership size was progressively lowered from two hundred *feddan* (1.038 acres) in 1952 to one hundred in 1961 to fifty in 1969. Large farms, especially those of the deposed (in 1952) King Farouk and his family, largely disappeared in the wake of the reform; only some 12 percent of the total cultivated area was directly redistributed, however, because much of the rest was sold by large estate holders. Egypt was then transformed into a country of predominantly small farms; farms under five feddan covered roughly 55 percent of the area in 1964 and 66 percent in 1975, with nearly all the remainder in farms smaller than fifty feddan. By the early 1980s, the share of small (less than five feddan) farms had fallen to 52 percent of the land area, roughly the same level as in 1964. About 75 percent of this change was the result of the consolidation of the very smallest farms (less than one feddan). At the same time, farms over fifty feddan began to be tolerated again, and such farms covered about 12 percent of the area in 1982, still well below the 21 percent of 1961.

Those who received land, whether in the official reform or as the result of the "distress sales" of the wealthy, were rarely the poorest rural people. Those purchasing land, of course, had to have some resources, and most of them were members of the rural middle class. Direct beneficiaries of the land reform were the year-round workers of the estates, not landless seasonal workers. The reform also controlled rents and, by making it nearly impossible to evict tenants, ceded de facto property rights to them. Output did not fall as a result of the reform; the government created a system of cooperatives, which took over the marketing functions of the expropriated landlords. The government used these cooperatives to (1) manipulate the terms of trade facing the farmers and (2) transfer resources out of the agricultural sphere.

Syria and Iraq. Both attempted to follow the Egyptian example. Here, however, very different conditions prevailed. In particular, these countries lacked the rural support that Egypt enjoyed. Accordingly, although the Syrian and Iraqi governments found it relatively easy to expropriate land, they found it difficult to redistribute it and to take over the marketing function. Unsettled political conditions in both countries during the 1960s also strongly contributed to this result, as did the varied agroecologies of both countries (in contrast to Egypt, where virtually all land was irrigated). Consequently, output fell considerably. Only in the 1970s were the Ba'thist governments able to redistribute land and to create fully functioning cooperatives.

Algeria. European colonial farmers abandoned their farms in large numbers at the time of independence (1962), and the year-round resident workers took them over—in many cases spontaneously. They then tried to manage them collectively (so-called autogestion). A second phase of land reform began in January 1972, when the government took over land owned by tribes, communes, and religious endowments (*habous*); it then attempted to expropriate all private farmland owned by absentees or that exceeded the area a farm family could directly exploit. Although the reform covered some 7.5 million acres (3 million ha), there were both considerable evasion and some difficulties in redistributing expropriated land to poorer farmers. Nevertheless, perhaps 30 percent of the rural population benefited from the 1970s reforms.

Tunisia. Reform here went through three stages. From 1956 to 1960, holders of usufruct rights (legal rights to use and profit from property belonging to another) were transformed into owners. In 1961, the state began to acquire land formerly held by European colonialists, and a "cooperativization" program was launched, aimed at transforming those farms into cooperatives by incorporating the surrounding small farmers. Many of the farmers resisted this program; poor investment policies, the cessation of World Bank funding, social conflict, and uncertainty about property rights all took their toll on agricultural production. By the end of 1969, however, cooperativization was abandoned, and the Algerian government increasingly relied on the private sector throughout the economy.

Iran. Beginning in 1962, landlords were required to sell to the government any land in excess of "one village"; holders of cultivation rights (*nasagh*) were to repay the government in ten annual installments. About 25 percent of peasant households received some land in this first phase. A second phase gave landlords options, such as forming "corporations" with their former tenants and distributing shares rather than land, leasing land for cash, and so on. This phase affected just under 50 percent of peasant households. Allowing for various statistical problems, it is still fair to assert that nearly all *nasagh* holders received some cultivation rights thanks to the reform. The "farm corporation" concept, however, was unpopular with peasants; it often led to small farmers selling out to larger ones. Further, landless agricultural workers were excluded from the reform, and many, perhaps most, of the recipients of land received too little to support a family. The reforms also adversely affected the land and water rights of Islamic charities. During the 1970s, the shah's government became increasingly obsessed with promoting large farms and agribusinesses, especially in Khuzistan. These were mostly unsuccessful and survived only thanks to massive state subsidies. After the IRANIAN REVOLUTION (1979), in the early days of the Islamic republic, considerable amounts of land changed hands as Pahlavi officials were expropriated, peasants occupied land, and local officials took advantage of opportunities. A long debate in the *majles* (legislature) has since ensued about the legality of some of these transfers and the desirability of further land reform. The uncertainty thus created has harmed agricultural investment and output growth.

(Former) People's Democratic Republic of Yemen. In 1968, land reform was implemented after independence. Previously, most farmers were tenants; the rulers, merchants, and religious institutions owned most of the land. Land was redistributed to private farmers, some 65 percent of whom were organized into cooperatives. About 23 percent of all cropped land was held as state farms.

Since about 1980, Middle East governments have increasingly withdrawn from direct management of agriculture—relaxing controls and encouraging private farming. In large part, this is the result of unhappiness with the sluggish performance of state farming. Expanding reliance on the private sector in both farm production and marketing, as well as on reduced regulation of farm prices, is visible today in virtually all countries in the region.

Alan R. Richards

Landsmannschaften

Jewish immigrant benevolent associations.

These groups were formed by Jews in North and South America and Israel according to place of origin of members, to assist their persecuted *landsleit* (hometown brethren) overseas and to ease their emigration and immigration. In the New World, such groups multiplied exponentially until World War I, began to decline after 1930, and largely disappeared by the 1960s. In Israel such organizations developed welfare institutions, mutual aid societies, and even several short-lived political parties.

Zev Maghen

Lansdowne, Henry Charles Keith Petty Fitzmaurice   [1845–1927]

British politician.

Becoming fifth marquess in 1866, Lord Lansdowne held posts in various Liberal administrations in Britain and was governor-general in Canada (1883–1888) and viceroy in India (1888–1894). As war secretary (1895–1900) and foreign secretary (1900–1905) under prime ministers Lord Salisbury, Arthur Balfour, and Henry Campbell-Bannerman, Lansdowne negotiated the Anglo–French Entente of 1904, which, among other things, settled Anglo–French differences over Egypt and Morocco. In Morocco's crisis of 1905, Lansdowne acknowledged French supremacy in that country and supported France against Germany. Involved in the diplomatic intrigues surrounding the proposed Baghdad Railway, Lansdowne, Balfour, and many Cabinet members were in favor of supplying funding for the project, but in the face of anti-German public opinion, they were forced to drop the proposal.

BIBLIOGRAPHY

ANDERSON, M. S. *The Eastern Question.* London, 1966.
TAYLOR, A. J. P. *The Struggle for Mastery in Europe.* New York, 1971.

Zachary Karabell

Laraki, Ahmad   [1931–   ]

Moroccan diplomat and minister.

Laraki earned a medical degree in Paris and in 1957/58 joined the ministry of foreign affairs in Morocco. He served as permanent representative to the United Nations from 1957 to 1959 and as ambassador to Spain, Switzerland, and the United States from 1962 to 1967. Appointed as prime minister in 1969, Laraki weathered rising discontent in Morocco, particularly over economic problems and government corruption, as well as an attempt on the life of Hassan II in 1971. In August 1971, Laraki was replaced by Muhammad Karim Lamrani. From 1971 to 1974, he headed the ministry in charge of medical affairs. In 1974 Laraki was appointed to head the ministry of foreign affairs, an office he held until 1977.

BIBLIOGRAPHY

RINEHART, ROBERT, et al. *Morocco: A Country Survey.* Washington, D.C., 1985.
Who's Who in the Arab World, 1993–1994.

Matthew S. Gordon

Latakia

Major Syrian seaport.

On the Mediterranean Sea, it was known in Greek as Laodicea after the name of the mother of Seleucus Nicator (301–281 B.C.E.), who built it. A fertile coastal plain stretches around Latakia. According to the 1982 administrative divisions of Syria, the prov-

A town square in Latakia, Syria. (Laura Mendelson)

ince of Latakia included 4 *mintaqas* (sections) based on Latakia, Jabala, al-Haffa, and al-Qardaha, 13 *nahiyas* (subdivisions) based on 13 towns, 501 villages, and 590 farms. The population of the city of Latakia in the 1980 census was 196,791; in 1987, its inhabitants numbered 281,000.

Abdul-Karim Rafeq

Latife

Ottoman humor magazine.

Latife was published between March 22 and June 12, 1875, by Zakarya Beykozluyan. *Latife's* short life span was due to editorial, not political, problems.

David Waldner

Latrun

Site of important battles of the Arab–Israel War of 1948.

The village of Latrun is situated in Israel, midway between Jerusalem and Tel Aviv, on strategic heights commanding the roads connecting Jerusalem with the north and west of the country. During the ARAB–ISRAEL WAR of 1948, Latrun was fiercely contested by Israeli and Arab forces, both of which sought to control the vital roads.

Because of its historic significance, Jerusalem was a prize to both sides. Jordan's Arab Legion, which occupied Latrun, captured Jerusalem's Jewish quarter on May 28, 1948. Because Latrun controlled the roads by which Israel's forces could resupply Jerusalem, the legion was able to cut off that city, laying siege to Jewish west Jerusalem.

Israel's forces tried to capture Latrun four times between May 26 and July 16, 1948, sustaining many casualties. While eventually breaking through to Jerusalem, they never captured Latrun and regard this as one of their worst military failures during the 1948/49 war.

BIBLIOGRAPHY

COLLINS, LARRY, and DOMINIQUE LAPIERRE. *O Jerusalem!* New York, 1972.
HERZOG, CHAIM. *The Arab–Israeli Wars: War and Peace in the Middle East from the War of Independence through Lebanon.* New York, 1982.

Michael R. Fischbach

La Tunisie Martyre

Manifesto of the Tunisian nationalist movement.

Written by two leading Tunisian nationalists, Abd al-Aziz THAALBI, the founder of the DESTOUR political party, and Ahmad Sakkah, this manifesto was published in Paris in 1921. It presented the key demands and premises of the fledgling Tunisian movement for nationalism. At its heart was the claim that, prior to the French occupation (1881), a viable Tunisian state had been in place, complete with its own constitution, representative assembly, open press, and healthy economy. On the basis of those earlier institutions, a new and independent Tunisia would be established.

BIBLIOGRAPHY

MICAUD, CHARLES. *Tunisia: The Politics of Modernization.* New York, 1964.
Tunisia: A Country Survey. Washington, D.C., 1988.

Matthew S. Gordon

Lausanne, Treaty of (1912)

With the Treaty of Ouchy, this treaty concluded the Tripolitan War between Italy and the Ottoman Empire.

Signed at Lausanne, Switzerland, on October 18, 1912, the treaty established de facto control by Italy over Tripoli and Cyrenaica, then parts of Libya, though the sultan did not actually renounce the Ottoman Empire's claims to these provinces. This agreement followed the treaty of peace signed on October 5 at Ouchy, Switzerland, and ended the Tripolitan War of the Turkish–Italian War (1911–1912).

BIBLIOGRAPHY

HUREWITZ, J. C., ed. *The Middle East and North Africa in World Politics.* New Haven, Conn., 1975.

Zachary Karabell

Lausanne, Treaty of (1923)

Renegotiation of harsh treaties ending World War I resulted in a more favorable treatment of Turkey.

Defeat in World War I resulted in a series of harsh treaties for the losing powers. For the Ottoman Empire, the Treaty of SÈVRES, signed by the government of Sultan Mehmet VI Vahidettin on August 10, 1920, stripped Turkey of its European territory except for a small area around Constantinople (now Istanbul); demilitarized the straits between the Black and Mediterranean seas, opened them to ships of all nations, and placed them under an international commission; established an independent Armenia and an autonomous Kurdistan in eastern Anatolia; turned over the region around İzmir to the Greeks; restored the capitulations; and placed Turkish finances under foreign control. By separate agreement, some parts of Turkey left to the Turks were assigned to France and Italy as spheres of influence.

Unlike the other losing powers, however, the Turks were able to renegotiate these harsh terms. This was the result of the decline of the sultan's power, the rise of the nationalists under Mustafa Kemal Atatürk, and the defeat of the Greeks in their attempt to expand their power in Turkey. The latter placed Turkish forces near those of the British in the area of the Straits and led to an armistice at Mudanya in October 1922 at which the Allied powers restored Constantinople and the Straits to Turkish authority and called for a peace convention to renegotiate the terms laid down at Sèvres. The Allies invited both governments contesting power in Turkey, that of the sultan and that of the nationalists under Kemal, to a conference at Lausanne, Switzerland. The hope was that the competing representatives would weaken the Turkish position. This precipitated Kemal's decision to separate the positions of sultan and caliph, abolishing the former, exiling Mehmet VI, and giving the residual powers of caliph to his cousin, Abdülmecit II. Thus, when the conference at Lausanne began in November 1922, Kemal's Ankara government was the sole representative of Turkey.

İsmet Paşa, later İsmet İnönü in honor of his two victories over the Greeks at İnönü, led the Turkish delegation as the newly appointed foreign minister. He was determined to reestablish Turkish sovereignty and negotiate as an equal with the British, French, and Italians at the conference. The Allies, led by the British Lord George Curzon, were determined to maintain their dominant position in the eastern Mediterranean. İsmet found himself treated as a supplicant rather than the representative of a government with recent victories. Unable to compete with the sophisticated debate of the Allied diplomats, İsmet responded with his own unique tactics. He feigned deafness, contested every point however minor, read long prepared statements, delayed debate by consultations with his colleagues, and periodically insisted on deferring discussion pending instructions from Ankara. These tactics led to a break of negotiations for two months beginning in February 1923

but ultimately resulted in significant Turkish gains from the conference.

The Lausanne Conference resulted in seventeen diplomatic instruments. Turkey recognized the loss of its Arab provinces, no longer an issue for a Turkish government committed to nationalism rather than a multinational empire. An independent Armenia and an autonomous Kurdistan disappeared. Capitulations for European powers were no longer demanded, and although Turkey did agree to minor financial burdens and tariff restrictions, there were to be no reparations. The Greeks lost their zone around İzmir, and no other powers retained zones of influence. Turkish territory in Europe expanded, but control over Mosul in Iraq and Alexandretta in Syria remained with the British and French respectively. Finally, the conference recognized Turkish sovereignty over the Straits, although there were some concessions in the form of a demilitarized zone and an international commission to supervise transit through the Straits. In short, İsmet achieved virtually all that nationalist Turkey under Kemal's leadership desired.

BIBLIOGRAPHY

BALFOUR, PATRICK, and LORD KINROSS. *Ataturk, a Biography of Mustapha Kemal, Father of Modern Turkey.* New York, 1964.
LEWIS, BERNARD. *The Emergence of Modern Turkey.* London, 1961.

Daniel E. Spector

Lavon, Pinhas

Member of the Knesset and Israeli government minister.

Born in East Galicia in 1904, Lavon studied law at Lvov University, was active in ha-Shomer ha-Za'ir, and emigrated to Palestine in 1929. Lavon was active in the kibbutz movement and in 1938 to 1939 was secretary of MAPAI. He was elected to the Histadrut executive in 1942 where he worked to bring the teachers and religious workers into the trade union. A member of the Knesset (1949–1961), Lavon also served as minister of agriculture (1950–52), minister without portfolio (1952), and minister of defense (1953–54) during Ben-Gurion's retirement. After his resignation from the government in 1955 due to the LAVON AFFAIR, he served as general secretary of the Histadrut until 1961 when he was replaced due to the political controversy that ensued through the early 1960s in connection with the affair.

Reeva S. Simon

Lavon Affair

*Effort by Israel's intelligence services to sabotage
Egyptian–American relationships that led to the fall
of the Ben-Gurion government.*

The Lavon Affair began in late 1953 when a group of
Egyptian Jewish spies, organized by MOSSAD and
Aman (the intelligence branch of the Israel Defense
Forces [IDF]), attempted to destroy U.S. information services, implicate Egypt as the culprit, and damage U.S.–Egyptian relations. It finished (1961–1963)
with the end of David BEN-GURION's long career. It
also created a serious crisis between the Defense Ministry and the security services.

The years from 1953 to 1955 were critical for
Israel's defensive security systems due to Gamal Abdel Nasser's assumption of power in Egypt in 1954,
the failures of Egypt–Israel rapproachment (1953–
1954), Iraq's acceptance of Western aid as a member
of the Baghdad Pact (1954), and what was perceived
by Israel's hard-liners as a favorable attitude of the
United States and the West toward Egypt's "progressive" government.

Ben-Gurion, unable to gain support for his policy
of retaliation against Egypt, came to hold a minority
position in his cabinet; he resigned under pressure.
His replacement as defense minister was Pinchas Lavon, whose expertise was mainly in political party
and trade union politics. Hoping the office would
catapult him into the prime ministership, Lavon decided to recommend and accept recommendations
of aggressive border retaliation policies. Unfortunately for Lavon, due to intrigues in Aman, he was
implicated in the Egyptian fiasco.

It has now been established that Lavon had little or
nothing to do with giving the order for the Egyptian
operation, which failed utterly. Nevertheless, in
1954, Lavon was forced to resign, and was replaced
as defense minister by Ben-Gurion. By 1960, Lavon
sought exoneration from Ben-Gurion, who was
again prime minister. However, Ben-Gurion refused
to exonerate him, believing that only a judicial institution had this power.

On 25 December 1960, the cabinet committee that
had been assigned to investigate the Lavon Affair concluded (1) that Lavon did not "give the order" for the
sabotage action, which was executed without his
knowledge and authorization; (2) that the committee
could not determine exactly what the working relationships were in the Defense Ministry in 1954; and
(3) that it accepted the attorney general's report that
certain documents presented to a previous committee
(1954) were false. These findings precipitated a struggle between Ben-Gurion and his cabinet, which accepted the commission's report; the struggle ended
with Ben-Gurion's resignation in 1963.

BIBLIOGRAPHY

PERLMUTTER, AMOS. "Institutionalization of Civil–
Military Relations in Israel: The Ben-Gurion Legacy
and Its Challengers." *Middle East Journal* (Autumn
1968): 415–432.

———. *Military and Politics in Israel: Nation-Building and
Role Expansion.* London, 1969.

TEVETH, SHABTAI. *The Unhealing Wound: General Harkavi
and the Lavon Affair.* Tel Aviv, 1995.

Amos Perlmutter

Law, Modern

*Modernization of law in the Middle East entailed
reforming or abandoning the heritage of Islamic
(Shari'a) law as set forth in juristic treatises.*

Centralized legal systems, in which lawmaking is
monopolized by governments of nation-states and
uniform law applies throughout the national territory, are now in place in the Middle East or, in a
few countries, in the process of evolving. The
adoption of modern legal systems has led to the
suppression of formerly vital local and customary
legal systems. Modernization of legal systems has
also obviated the need to provide special, exterri-
torial status for members of powerful foreign communities, which had insisted on getting exemptions
from the premodern legal systems of Middle Eastern countries.

Modernization of Middle Eastern law involved
Westernization, since the models for the new laws
were European and the lawyers and other legal professionals who staffed the modernized legal systems
were trained either in Europe or along European
lines. Westernizing reforms were most often imposed
from above by members of autocratic Westernized
ruling elites or under the auspices of European powers. The borrowings from European legal systems
and Westernization of legal education were politically sensitive, since they came to be associated with
subjugation to European powers and were seen by
conservatives as a betrayal of Islamic tradition. Governments' fear of offending religious sentiment accounts for some of the slowness and unevenness of
the modernization process and also for the compro-
mises that permitted islands of SHARI'A law to survive
in all systems outside of Turkey, the only country to
completely secularize its law. Except in Turkey, sort-
ing out what were the appropriate roles for secular
law versus Islamic law proved a major dilemma in
the drafting of constitutions. In most Middle Eastern
countries, constitutional provisions have been
adopted making Islam the state religion and referring
to Islamic law as "a" or "the" main source of law.

After consistent movement toward even greater secularization, in the 1970s and 1980s a countertrend favoring the rollback of secularizing reforms gained momentum as various forces campaigned for Islamization, the reinstatement of Islamic law. In countries where Islamization policies were implemented, there were selective enactments of *Shari'a* rules, which were inserted in systems that had been and remained substantially Westernized. Contemporaneously, Middle Eastern governments had to face mounting pressures for political liberalization and demands for enhanced guarantees for the rule of law, the independence of the judiciary, and respect for international human rights principles.

Leaving aside their occasional Islamic components, modern laws in the Middle East have been shaped by the same forces that led to the adoption of the civil law systems of continental Europe in almost all countries around the world, save those that had been dominated by Britain. British colonization or the exercise of British mandatory or protectorate authority in the Middle East did lead to some transplants from the common law in areas like Aden (later part of South Yemen), Bahrain, Palestine (and areas incorporated after partition in the state of Israel), and Oman, whereas the common law had little long-term impact on the legal systems of Iraq, Jordan, and Kuwait. Over the period of the 1899–1956 Anglo–Egyptian Condominium in the Sudan, the British system was transplanted to that country. In contrast, France's prestige in Egypt, which first encountered French culture during the Napoleonic invasion of 1798–1801, led to a lasting French impact on Egyptian legal culture that survived the 1882–1954 British occupation. Notwithstanding occasional transplants from the common law, civil law, mostly of French derivation, now predominates throughout the Middle East, and the occasional remnants of common law seem unlikely to survive. For example, in 1987 Bahrain broke from British tradition, choosing to enact a commercial code derived from Egyptian and Kuwaiti models, which were French in inspiration.

The contemporary legal systems of Middle Eastern countries share the basic features of French law, such as relying on comprehensive and systematic statements of the law in codes as formal sources of law, maintaining a sharp distinction between public and private law and between commercial and private law, and using the inquisitorial mode of procedure in criminal cases. Characteristics of the French judicial system such as separate administrative court hierarchies and the parquet/prosecutor's office are also found. In contrast, the substantive legal provisions in Middle Eastern codes often have no counterparts in continental European law, corresponding instead to governmental policies, local custom, or Islamic principles. Various codifications of *Shari'a* law were enacted into law, and many secular codes refer to principles of Islamic law or custom as supplementary sources of law.

Although a few states substantially modernized their laws in the nineteenth century, in most areas of the Middle East legal modernization did not begin in earnest until the early twentieth century. It was delayed in countries like Afghanistan, Bahrain, Kuwait, Oman, Saudi Arabia, the states comprising the United Arab Emirates, and Yemen until the middle of the twentieth century. In general, the countries that began legal modernization earliest subsequently made the greatest progress toward secularizing their laws. Modern law was typically adopted first in constitutions, criminal law, procedural rules, and matters involving contracts and commerce. *Shari'a* law remained controlling longest in personal status matters, although even in this area it was for the most part ultimately reformed and/or systemized in codes. Saudi Arabia has remained the most resistant to modernization, never having made a formal break with the premodern Islamic system of jurists' law but having followed a steady course of supplementing juristic treatises by gradually introducing governmental "regulation" in areas important for administration and economic development.

The Ottoman Empire began modernization of law in the mid-1800s, undertaking many codification projects, some of which remained influential long after the colllapse of the empire. Modernization began with attempts to codify Islamic criminal laws in 1840 and 1851, which were followed by the adoption of two French-inspired codes, a penal code in 1858 and a penal procedure code in 1879. An Ottoman constitution was adopted in 1876 and amended in 1909. Inspired by French models, a commercial code (later borrowed by Saudi Arabia in 1931) was enacted in 1850, and commercial procedure codes were enacted in 1861 and 1880. The most famous monument of the Ottoman legal modernization process was the Majalla (Mecelle), issued between 1869 and 1876. This was an attempt to rework principles found in treatises of jurists of the HANAFI school, the official school of law in the Ottomans' domains, to make a modern code of obligations. In addition to substantive rules on civil and commercial transactions and on procedures and evidence, the Majalla was composed of statements and general principles of law designed to guide the application and interpretation of its provisions. The Majalla survived in states carved out of the former Ottoman territories until their eventual adoption of French-based codes, as occurred in Iraq in 1951, in Jordan in 1966, in Kuwait in 1980, in Lebanon in

1932, in Libya in 1954, and in Syria in 1949. The substantive provisions of the Majalla still exert an influence, inspiring many provisions of the 1951 Civil Code of Iraq and the 1985 Code of Civil Transactions of the United Arab Emirates. The Ottoman Family Law of 1917 was another historical experiment with crafting a modern statute out of *Shari'a* rules, using the innovative technique of combining principles of family law from different SUNNI schools of law.

Egypt, which during the nineteenth century became largely independent of Ottoman control, began enacting modern codes in 1874. The most important phase of Egyptian legal history was overseen by the distinguished jurist Abd al-Razzaq al-Sanhuri (1895–1971). An expert in European and Islamic law, he played a major role in drafting the influential Egyptian Civil Code of 1948 (effective in 1949). This essentially French code, which allowed the *Shari'a* to be used as a supplementary source of law, provided the model for the civil codes subsequently adopted in Iraq, Jordan, Kuwait, Libya, and Syria and indirectly influenced the 1984 Sudanese Civil Transactions Act. Italian law shaped Egypt's 1937 criminal code. Like many Middle Eastern countries, Egypt had a checkered constitutional history, having assayed constitutions in 1923, 1930, 1956, 1958–61 (when Egypt and Syria were united in the United Arab Republic), 1964, and 1971.

Long French political domination of North Africa disseminated French legal culture in that region. When Algeria was a French colony, 1830–1962, it was integrated in the French legal system. Algeria enacted new codes after independence in which French influence persisted. In 1984 it adopted a code of family law reinstating premodern *Shari'a* rules and reinforcing the patriarchal structure of the family. Faced with popular pressures for legal reform, in 1989 Algeria adopted a new constitution that diluted the militant socialist character of the 1976 constitution and reflected demands both for strengthened human rights guarantees and for changes that would give the constitution a more Islamic character. In 1861 Tunisia had become the first Middle Eastern country to enact a constitution. As a French protectorate, 1881–1956, Tunisia enacted in 1906 a code of obligations and contracts, which combined elements of French and Islamic law, and in 1913 it adopted a penal code. After independence, Tunisia amended old codes and enacted new ones, the most significant being its 1956 Personal Status Code, constituting the most progressive interpretation in Arab law of Islamic legal requirements in the area of family law. Morocco, a French protectorate 1912–1956, enacted in 1913 its Code of Obligations and Contracts, which was similar to the 1906 Tunisian code. Morocco enacted some French-inspired codes after

independence, but it retained many rules of traditional *Shari'a* law in its 1958 Personal Status Code and incorporated aspects of Islamic criminal law in provisions of its 1962 Penal Code.

Some Middle Eastern countries followed distinctive paths of legal development.

Iran adopted a constitution in 1906, which was amended in 1907. An Iranian Civil Code was enacted in the period 1927–1937 that combined elements of Twelver SHI'ISM law with French and Swiss law. French law provided the models for other codifications undertaken by Iran in the 1930s. The progressive Iranian Family Protection Act of 1967, amended in 1975, was abrogated after the Islamic IRANIAN REVOLUTION of 1978–1979. Since the revolution, Iran has officially endorsed Islamization, adopting a constitution in 1979 that placed an Islamic jurist at the apex of the scheme of government and established Islamic principles as the supreme law of the land. Westernized legal professionals and Western-style legal training were replaced; Shi'a clerics and Shi'a jurisprudence were given a preeminent role in the legal system. However, there was no return to the old system of jurists' law: Iran's parliament retained its lawmaking authority, and French legal influences were not obliterated.

Turkey was reconstituted in 1921 as a nation-state out of the ruins of the Ottoman Empire, which had been dismembered by European powers after its defeat in World War I. Turkey's legal development was determined by Kemal ATATÜRK (1881–1938), the military leader who became Turkey's first president. With an unqualified commitment to Westernize Turkey, Atatürk pursued in the 1920s a program of complete secularization of law, which led to the abandonment of Islamic law even in personal status matters. In 1928 Islam lost its status as the state religion. Turkey imported European codes in the 1920s that were variously taken from German, Italian, and Swiss sources. The Turkish constitutions of 1921, 1924, 1961, and 1982 have differed in many respects, but Turkey's governments have continued to uphold the principle of secularism.

Israel emerged in 1948 as a Jewish state with a legal system in which there coexisted elements deriving from the Ottoman law of prepartition Palestine, Jewish law, and Western law, the latter being an unusual hybrid of common law and civil law elements.

Upon achieving independence in 1951, Libya largely divested itself of Italian law, which had been imposed after it was colonized by Italy in 1912. Egyptian influences on the new legal system were initially strong, but after the 1969 revolution Libya pursued a separate course of radical legal changes that were dictated by the theories of its leader, Muammar al-QADDAFI.

In many Middle Eastern countries law remained a contentious issue, and clashes over the direction of legal development were implicated in some civil wars. Before a Marxist regime seized power in 1978, premodern Islamic law and customary law prevailed in Afghanistan, where only modest modernization measures such as a 1955 commercial code modelled on Turkey's and a 1965 commercial code modelled on Egypt's had been attempted. Socialist and secularizing policies vigorously pursued after 1978 by successive Marxist regimes were one of the causes of the civil war that was carried on between Marxist forces and groups defending Afghan tradition and premodern Islamic law. In Lebanon, where the legal system had been shaped by the dominant Christian elite, communal tensions between Christians and Muslims led in 1975 to the outbreak of civil war and presaged eventual adjustments in the legal system to appease the Muslim majority. After Sudanese independence in 1956 the ingrained common law system was besieged from two sides. Some Sudanese wanted changes that would harmonize Sudanese law with the civil law systems of other Arab countries like Egypt, whereas fundamentalist groups called for Islamization. Programs for enacting *Shariʿa* rules into law that were pursued intermittently by governments beginning in 1983 prolonged the civil war between the Muslim North and non-Muslim South.

Laws have had to be rewritten in many countries to accommodate various projects to unify Middle Eastern countries, most of which have proved short-lived. In 1990 the unification of the northern and southern parts of Yemen, designed to be completed in 1992, involved meshing the more traditional legal heritage of the northern part, which had only begun legal modernization in the 1970s, and the southern part, which after obtaining independence from Britain in 1967 had adhered to Marxist policies that had affected its laws. The establishment of the United Arab Emirates, formed under a 1971 constitution, was followed by the adoption of many federal laws, which included a penal code of 1988 with many provisions inspired by the *Shariʿa*.

Shifts in economic philosophies affected laws. After independence, many Middle Eastern countries subscribed to Marxist ideologies and socialist policies. Pursuant to these, laws were enacted nationalizing industry and commerce, expanding the role of the state in planning and running the economy, and dismantling protections for private property. By the 1980s, the emerging trend in most countries was one of turning away from socialism and undertaking substantial legal reforms designed to achieve privatization and economic liberalization, which necessitated borrowings from business laws and regulatory schemes in Western market economies.

Middle Eastern countries varied in the degree to which they sought integration in the increasingly internationalized post–World War II legal environment. For example, they followed differing policies regarding submission to dispute resolution institutions such as the International Court of Justice and international arbitration, and they also have disparate records of ratifying major international treaties. In general, however, the trend has been in favor of closer integration in the internationalized legal order.

BIBLIOGRAPHY

Sources that are comprehensive, reliable and up-to-date on the general topic of modern law in the Middle East are wanting. The national reports in the multivolume set of the *International Encyclopedia of Comparative Law* (The Hague, various dates) are useful even though varying in length and sometimes very out-of-date. Many entries in the multivolume set *Constitutions of the Countries of the World* edited by ALFRED BLAUSTEIN and GISBERT FLANZ (Dobbs Ferry, N.Y., various dates), which provides updated materials on constitutional developments, include useful essays on modern legal history. An excellent but now dated study is JESWALD SALACUSE's *An Introduction to Law in French-Speaking Africa*, vol. 2: *North Africa* (Charlottesville, Va., 1975). An important examination of the role of the modern legal profession in modernizing law is FARHAT ZIADEH's *Lawyers, Liberalism, and the Rule of Law in Modern Egypt* (Stanford, Calif., 1968). A variety of materials relevant for modern law in the Middle East is presented in HERBERT J. LIEBESNY's *The Law of the Near and Middle East: Readings, Cases & Materials* (Albany, N.Y., 1975).

Ann E. Mayer

Law in the Service of Man

Palestinian human rights organization.

Law in the Service of Man was established by several Palestinian lawyers in the West Bank in 1979, as an affiliate of the Geneva-based International Commission of Jurists, with the goal of upholding the legal rights of Palestinians in the territories occupied by Israel in 1967. Law in the Service of Man conducts research and publishes information relating to international law and the legal aspects of the Israeli occupation. It also provides legal services for local residents and maintains a library.

BIBLIOGRAPHY

SHEHADEH, RAJA. *Occupier's Law: Israel and the West Bank.* Rev. ed. Washington, D.C., 1988.

Michael R. Fischbach

Law of Return

Law that allows Jews to immigrate and become Israeli citizens.

The Law of Return (Khok HaShuut) was enacted by the Israeli Knesset on July 5, 1950. It provides that "any Jew is entitled to immigrate to ERETZ YISRAEL" and acquire a certificate and status of "*oleh,*" conferring (after the passage of the Nationality Law of 1952) automatic citizenship. The Law of Return gives legal expression to Zionism's conception of Israel as both haven and homeland of world Jewry, codifying the guarantee in Israel's Declaration of Independence that "the State of Israel will be open to Jewish immigration and the Ingathering of the Exiles." Jews excluded from this privilege are those deemed by the interior minister to be "acting against the Jewish people" or to constitute a threat to public health or national security (in 1954 these exceptions were augmented by a provision denying access to any whose criminal past was likely to endanger public welfare, later used in 1970 to bar Meyer Lansky's entry). A further clause grants retroactive citizenship to all Jews who arrived prior to the issuance of the law. Acquisition of citizenship by non-Jews is dealt with in the Nationality Law.

The question "Who is a Jew?" under the Law of Return had occasionally preoccupied the government and the courts, and increasingly the various "denominations" within Judaism. An addendum to the law defines a Jew as "anyone born of a Jewish mother or who has converted to Judaism, provided he professes no other religion." Orthodox Jewish parties have persistently and so far unsuccessfully attempted to amend the definition to read "converted . . . according to Jewish law."

Zev Maghen

Lawrence, Thomas Edward   [1888–1935]

British soldier and adventurer, known as Lawrence of Arabia.

Thomas Edward Lawrence, who later changed his surname to Shaw was born in Wales and raised in Scotland, France, and England. He was the illegitimate son of Sir Thomas R. T. Chapman (a.k.a. Thomas Lawrence). After attending Oxford, an interest in Crusader castles and biblical archeology took him to Syria. During World War I, Lawrence became an adviser to the British-supported ARAB REVOLT led by the Hashimites against the Ottoman Empire. He was the first British officer in the field of combat and served longer than any other.

When the war ended, Lawrence accompanied Faisal I ibn Husayn to the PARIS PEACE SETTLEMENTS at Versailles, but with Britain's support for French control of Syria—which Faisal believed to be promised to him—he became convinced of his guilt in what he felt was British betrayal of the Arab cause. Accordingly, he abandoned public life; however, the sensationalized portrayal of his wartime adventures by journalist Lowell Thomas made this impossible. In fact, Lawrence himself published epic accounts of the Arab revolt in *Seven Pillars of Wisdom* (1926) and its abbreviated version, *Revolt in the Desert* (1927).

The British public convinced itself that Lawrence was a storybook hero. The image of triumph in the simple, noble, clean, struggle in the desert stirred a generation otherwise disillusioned by the carnage in the trenches of the Western Front.

BIBLIOGRAPHY

WILSON, JERRY. *Lawrence of Arabia.* London, 1989.

Benjamin Braude

Lawzi, Ahmad   [1925–   ]

Jordanian politician.

Al-Lawzi has held numerous political positions in Jordan, including chief of the royal court, finance minister, and prime minister/defense minister in 1972/73. He has also served as a parliamentarian in both the chamber of deputies and the senate, over which he has presided as president since January 1984.

BIBLIOGRAPHY

ABU GHIDA, RASHID, ADNAN BA'YUN, and ILYAS SAM'AN. *Man huwa?* (Who's Who?). Amman, 1988.

Abla M. Amawi

Laz

Ethnic group in Turkey.

The Laz live on the Black Sea, near the Georgian border with Turkey. A 1983 study found about 44,000 living in Turkey, and all were Muslims. As early as the 1870s, the Ottoman Empire had planned to make them Turkish speakers, but many continued to speak a Kartvelian-family language, Laz, related to Georgian. Because Laz was largely an unwritten language, it was traditionally written using the Georgian alphabet (a version of Cyrillic).

BIBLIOGRAPHY

Cambridge Atlas of the Middle East and North Africa. New York, 1987.

WEEKES, RICHARD V. *Muslim Peoples.* Westport, Conn., 1984.

Elizabeth Thompson

Lazma

In Iraq, an allotment of tilled land.

In river-irrigated areas of Iraq, peasant tribesmen who tilled an individual plot of land regularly assumed a prescriptive right to that land. Called a *lazma,* it was a subdivision allotted to an individual tribesman by the tribe or subtribe that controlled the area under cultivation, even though the tribe did not formally own the land.

Jenab Tutunji

League of Arab States

This foremost pan-Arab organization provides the institutional expression for the aspiration of Arab unity.

The League of Arab States, also known as the Arab League, is composed of twenty-two independent Arab states that have signed the Pact of the League of Arab States. Palestine is included as an independent state as provided in the Annex Regarding Palestine. The multipurpose League of Arab States seeks to strengthen relations between member states; enhance member-state cooperation and the protection of Arab independence and sovereignty; and support Arab interests in general. It promotes economic, social, political, military, and development cooperation among its members.

The league is an international governmental organization with permanent headquarters in Cairo, Egypt. It was temporarily moved to Tunis, Tunisia, in 1979 but returned to Cairo in 1990. Branch headquarters are being built in Tunis. The league has not realized perfect Arab unity as desired by some Arab nationalists. From its inception, however, some states considered the only workable organization to be one of sovereign states and rejected federalists or unionist proposals. Since the league's pact, or charter, emphasizes the importance of sovereignty of the member states, the league serves the mutual interests of its members and also reflects the differences.

History. The League of Arab States was founded March 22, 1945, with the signing of the pact by seven Arab states. Sixteen additional states joined, but Yemen (Aden) and Yemen (San'a) merged in 1990 to form the People's Democratic Republic of Yemen.

While the league was formed after World War II, the process that led to its creation is a function of the development of Arab nationalism, which predates the twentieth century. Arab nationalism grew dramatically after World War II. Mustafa al-Nahhas, Nuri al-Sa'id, and King Abdullah ibn Husayn are credited with being early architects of the league in the 1940s. The British initiated, in part, the preparatory talks leading to its creation. In the fall of 1944, seven Arab states met in Alexandria, Egypt, to discuss the creation of a "Commonwealth of Arab States." On October 7, 1944, Egypt, Iraq, Lebanon, Syria, and Transjordan signed the ALEXANDRIA PROTOCOL, which envisioned a league of independent states, rather than a union or federation. The main points of the protocol were subsequently incorporated into the league, as was an appendix stressing Palestinian independence. The initial members of the league were Egypt, Iraq, Lebanon, Saudi Arabia, Syria, Transjordan (now Jordan), and Yemen (San'a).

The league's general structure has remained intact since its formation, but the scope of its activities has expanded dramatically, especially in nonpolitical fields. The organization consists of a council, special committees, and a secretariat-general. In addition, the league has become an umbrella organization responsible for the numerous specialized agencies, unions, and other institutions that were created to promote Arab interests.

Organization. The pact established a council as the league's principal organ. It is composed of the representatives of each member state, with each state having one vote. Unanimous decisions of the council are binding on all members. Majority decisions are binding only on those members that have accepted them, except that majority decisions are enforceable for certain specific matters relating to personnel, the budget, administrative regulations, and adjournment. The council implements league policies and pursues league goals. It meets twice a year, in March and September, but extraordinary meetings can be called at the request of two members.

Special committees have been established to support and represent the council. The league's current committees include: Political Committee, Culture Committee, Communications Committee, Social

Committee, Legal Committee, Arab Oil Experts Committee, Information Committee, Health Committee, Human Rights Committee, Permanent Committee for Administration and Financial Affairs, Permanent Committee for Meteorology, Committee of Arab Experts on Cooperation, Arab Women's Committee, Organization of Youth Welfare, and Conference of Liaison Officers.

The secretariat-general—consisting of the secretary-general, assistant secretaries-general, and other principal officials of the league—is responsible for administrative and financial activities. The secretary-general is appointed to a renewable five-year term by the council, with the approval of a two-thirds majority of league members. The secretary-general has the rank of ambassador.

The office of the secretary-general was held by Egyptians during the first three decades of the league: Abd al-Rahman al-Azzam (1945–1952); Abd al-Khaleq Hassouna (1952–1972); and Mahmoud Riad (1972–1979). A Tunisian, Chadli Klibi, held the post from 1979 until 1990 when he resigned during the controversy surrounding the Gulf Crisis. Dr. Ahmad Ismat Abd al-Majid, an Egyptian, was unanimously elected secretary-general in May 1991.

In 1950, the Treaty of Joint Defense and Economic Cooperation complemented the league pact and provided for the establishment of the Joint Defense Council and the Permanent Military Commission. An Economic Council was set up under the treaty in 1953. An Arab Unified Military Command was formed in 1964. In 1976 an Arab Deterrent Force was sent to Lebanon under league auspices. Numerous specialized agencies and other bodies have been established to promote the interests of the league and are considered part of the league.

Financing. The League of Arab States is financed by an assessment of charges made to each member. The secretary-general prepares a draft budget and submits it to the council for approval before the beginning of each fiscal year. The council then fixes the share of the expenses or dues to be paid by each member state. This share may be reconsidered if necessary.

The league reportedly experienced significant difficulties in the collection of member-state dues in the aftermath of the Gulf crisis. Its 1991 budget was over 27 million U.S. dollars, with the largest share being assessed to Saudi Arabia, 14 percent; Kuwait, 14 percent; Libya, 12 percent; Iraq, 10 percent; Egypt, 8.5 percent; Algeria, 8 percent; the United Arab Emirates, 6.5 percent; and Morocco, 5 percent. Bahrain, Kuwait, Libya, Morocco, and Yemen had reservations concerning their share of

the league budget. Also, a number of states are late in their payments or have not paid for years. According to Article 15 of the league's bylaws, approved in 1973, members could be denied voting rights if their delinquent dues total more than their total assessment of the current year and the two preceding years.

Policy. The League of Arab States has had a significant impact on the Middle East and on its members. While it has not been a stepping stone to political unity for the Arab, it has fostered Arab cooperation in many fields. Cooperation on political questions has been more difficult. In fact, political conflicts in the Arab world are frequently reflected in the league. Governmental diversity is protected in the league pact, which requires each member to respect the systems of government of other members. The pact also requires states to abstain from action calculated to change the systems of government in other members.

The East–West rivalry (of 1945 to 1991) served to draw political lines within the league between clients of the United States or the USSR. Despite the wealth of some of its members, the league is more closely aligned to the South in the North–South conflict, sometimes acting as a bloc for the South in the United Nations.

The league has actively sought to bolster Arab security, but its efforts are limited by inter-Arab rivalries. It has facilitated the peaceful settlement of disputes between its members, as between Morocco and Mauritania; between groups within member states, as in Lebanon or Somalia; and between members and outside parties, as between Libya and the United States. The league has acted as a regional alternative to the United Nations in this regard.

The league has been united in its support for Palestine vis-à-vis Israel, but major divisions continue to exist over the best way to deal with Israel. Egypt's treaty with Israel (the CAMP DAVID ACCORDS) resulted in its suspension from the league from 1979 to 1989. Members were also divided over the FAHD PLAN; over the leadership of the PALESTINE LIBERATION ORGANIZATION (PLO); and over the Iran–Iraq War. More recently, sharp divisions emerged over Iraq's invasion of Kuwait and the subsequent Gulf Crisis.

Membership. The League of Arab States consists of twenty-two independent states: Algeria, Bahrain, Comoras, Djibouti, Egypt, Iraq, Jordan, Kuwait, Lebanon, Libya, Mauritania, Morocco, Oman, Palestine, Qatar, Saudi Arabia, Somalia, Sudan, Syria, Tunisia, United Arab Emirates, and Yemen. Any independent Arab state is theoretically entitled to become a member, but a request for membership must be made through the permanent secretariat-general of the league and submitted to the council.

Satellite Organizations. Numerous specialized organizations and other institutions that promote Arab cooperation and protect Arab interests in a wide array of fields fall under the league umbrella. These include, among others: the Academy of Arab Music; Administrative Tribunal of the Arab League; Arab Bank for Economic Development in Africa; Arab Bureau of Narcotics; Arab Bureau for Prevention of Crime; Arab Bureau of Criminal Police; Arab Center for the Study of Arid Zones and Dry Lands; Arab Civil Aviation Council; ARAB FUND FOR ECONOMIC AND SOCIAL DEVELOPMENT; Arab Fund for Technical Assistance to Africa and Arab Countries; Arab Industrial Development Organization; Arab Labour Organization; Arab League Educational, Cultural, and Scientific Organization; Arab Maritime Transport Academy; Arab Monetary Fund; Arab Organization for Agricultural Development; Arab Organization for Standardization and Metrology; Arab Organization of Administrative Sciences; Arab Postal Union; Arab Satellite Communications Organization; Arab States Broadcasting Union; Arab Telecommunications Union; Council of Arab Economic Unity; Council of Arab Ministers of the Interior; Inter-Arab Investment Guarantee Corporation; ORGANIZATION OF ARAB PETROLEUM EXPORTING COUNTRIES; and the Special Bureau for Boycotting Israel.

Prospects. After the Gulf crisis, relations between member states of the league are again improving. Dr. Ismat Abd al-Majid, league secretary-general, promises to reunify the Arab ranks. The uncertainties unleashed by the Gulf crisis offer new challenges to the Arab world that require cooperation. The league and the aspiration of Arab unity promise to be central to the creation of a new world order, as does the reality of inevitable divisions in the Arab ranks. Arab cooperation in nonpolitical areas promises to continue under the league's aegis and to promote not only better relations among Arabs, but also between Arabs and outside states and organizations.

BIBLIOGRAPHY

TAWFIQ Y. HASOU offers a critical, but realistic view of the League of Arab States and Gamal Abdel Nasser in *The Struggle for the Arab World: Egypt's Nasser and the Arab League* (Boston, 1985). HUSSEIN A. HASSOUNA, son of a league secretary-general, provides a wealth of first-hand information on the league's role in regional disputes from a predominantly legal perspective in *The League of Arab States and Regional Disputes: A Study in Middle East Conflicts* (Dobbs Ferry, N.Y., 1975). A scholarly work on the politics of the league is ROBERT W. MACDONALD's *The League of Arab States: A Study in the Dynamics of Regional Organization* (Princeton, N.J., 1965). ISTVAN S. POGANY is critical of Syria's dominant role in the Arab Deterrent Force in *The Arab League and Peacekeeping in the Lebanon* (Aldershot, U.K., 1987). The importance of a comprehensive solution to the Arab–Israel conflict and a league secretary-general's frustration over Anwar al-Sadat's treaty with Israel are vividly portrayed in MAHMOUD RIAD's classic, *The Struggle for Peace in the Middle East* (New York, 1981). SIRAG G. ZAMZAMI exhibits Arab nationalist sentiment in his criticisms of the league's failure to achieve unity in "The Origins of the League of Arab States and Its Activities within the Member States: 1942–1970," doctoral thesis (Claremont Graduate School, 1978). *The Arab League: British Documentary Sources 1943–1963,* ed. by ANITA BURDETT (1995), offers a rich ten-volume research collection of documents in facsimile.

Charles G. MacDonald

League of Nations

Organization established after World War I to provide a forum for mediation of conflicts and a structure for cooperation among nations.

Before World War I, treaties and conferences were the vehicles for conflict resolution and for international cooperation. After the beginning of World War I, many observers began to think in terms of a permanent structure to manage international order. In May 1916, U.S. President Woodrow Wilson gave impetus to this movement by calling for a league of nations, and advocates in other countries began to support such an organization. As the war drew to its end, the idea of a league of nations gained momentum, and both the United States and Britain supported the drafting of a covenant for such an organization as part of the peace conference convened at Versailles, France. The result was the Covenant of the League of Nations, signed on 28 June 1919, as part of the Treaty of Versailles. It was to enter into effect on 20 January 1920.

The covenant was a document of about 4,000 words, consisting of a preamble and 26 articles. It established the League of Nations as a loose confederation of states with very limited powers. The league eventually consisted of about sixty states; the United States was not among them because it had not ratified the Treaty of Versailles. It consisted of two deliberative bodies that met in Geneva, Switzerland. The Assembly was made up of representatives from all member nations, each nation having one vote. The Council, with eight members (later fifteen) was the stronghold of the major international powers.

Perhaps the most useful part of the League was the Secretariat, a body of some 750 people of various nationalities organized under the secretary-general into sections dealing with league functions related to armaments and to political, legal, economic, and informational matters. Also part of the league was the Permanent Court of International Justice, a body of judges elected by the Assembly and the Council; during the life of the league it rendered more than thirty decisions and twenty-five advisory opinions, most of which were considered technically competent and fair. The league also included a variety of institutions dealing with international matters ranging from labor to the drug trade, as well as supervision of mandates over territories granted to the major powers under auspices of the league.

Like its successor—the United Nations, formed after World War II—the league was effective only as long as the major powers wished it to be so. Its supervision of the Middle Eastern mandates granted to Britain and France never seriously threatened the control of either nation over those territories, and they were free to organize the mandates as they saw fit; the separation of Lebanon from the Syrian mandate and of Transjordan from the Palestinian mandate serve as examples of the power of France and Britain, respectively, over their mandates. The league decision in 1926 to award Britain continued control over Mosul and its oil resources as part of the mandate for Iraq was another example of its inability to render decisions against the interests of major powers. (However, Turkey was promised 10 percent of the oil revenues from Mosul.)

The influence of the league declined in the 1930s as it proved unable to deal effectively with the aggression of Japan in eastern Asia and of Italy in Ethiopia, and with the rearming of Nazi Germany. Decisions against these nations led to their withdrawal from the league. The league was dissolved in favor of the United Nations in 1946.

[See also: Britain and the Middle East; France and the Middle East; Italy in the Middle East; Mandate System; United Nations and the Middle East.]

BIBLIOGRAPHY

HALL, H. DUNCAN. *Mandates, Dependencies, and Trusteeship.* Mill River, N.Y., 1948.

WALTERS, F. P. *History of the League of Nations.* Oxford, 1952.

Daniel E. Spector

Lebanese Academy of Fine Arts

Educational institution granting degrees in engineering, interior design, and fine arts.

The academy has two branches, one in Sin-el-Fil where the language of education is French and the other in Balamand where courses are taught in English. It offers courses in civil engineering, fine arts, interior design, advertising, and sound engineering.

George E. Irani

Lebanese Arab Army

Muslim military group in Lebanon.

The Lebanese Arab Army was formed in 1975 by a group of Muslim officers and soldiers who defected from the army of Lebanon and accused its Maronite leadership of collaboration with Maronite right-wing militias. Supported by the Palestine Liberation Organization (PLO) (the al-Fath movement in particular), it succeeded in overrunning military barracks controlled by the army of Lebanon. The Lebanese Arab Army's role came to an end in the spring and early summer of 1976, when its forces (along with PLO forces and forces loyal to the Lebanese National Movement) clashed with the army of Syria, which was supporting the coalition of Maronite-oriented right-wing militias.

As'ad AbuKhalil

Lebanese Civil War (1958)

Uprising against the government.

Fifteen years after Lebanon became officially free of French mandatory control, it assumed its role as an independent republic on the basis of an unwritten national pact, whose symbolic and practical importance is difficult to exaggerate. In May 1958, the nation of 1.1 million people, whose political institutions reflected the balance of power between its confessional communities, exploded in civil war.

Rooted in a series of interlocking factors of domestic, regional, and international origin, the primary causes of the war were domestic in nature. They were shaped by the policies of the presidential regime of Camille CHAMOUN (1952–1958), whose personal ambitions capped a domestic politics and foreign policy that greatly exacerbated existing divisions in a state whose civil and national consciousness were less developed than its successful mercantile character.

President Chamoun's ambition to succeed himself in office contributed to the existing political tensions and was widely viewed as one of the major catalysts of civil strife. The Lebanese government claimed that civil insurrection was a function of external intervention organized by Egypt and Syria, in the UNITED ARAB REPUBLIC (UAR). But the war that was sparked by the assassination of the journalist, Nasib Matni, on May 8, 1958, was rooted in pre-existing grievances that involved questions of political access; confessionalism and class; group identity and national consensus; and the major discontent of political elites displaced by corrupt elections in 1957, as well as the dissatisfaction of those constituencies deprived of significant representation.

Opposition groups that included an array of established political figures, some of whom would come to office in the post-Chamoun regime for the first time, opposed the president's perpetuation in office, and, in some instances, his foreign policy as well.

Under the Chamoun regime, Lebanon threw its support to the conservative Arab coalition and became a staunch advocate of U.S. policy and the Eisenhower Doctrine of 1957. That stance identified Lebanon with the anti-Nasserist and anti-Arab nationalist forces in the region. The intensification of domestic tensions exploded with the Nasib Matni assassination, and President Chamoun was challenged by the opposition. The Lebanese government's response was to blame civil strife on interference by the UAR and to charge it with the attempt to undermine Chamoun regime and state. These charges came before the League of Arab States (Arab League) and the United Nations, which assigned a task force to investigate charges of massive infiltration by foreign forces in Lebanon. It was on the basis of this same charge that President Chamoun had requested assistance from the United States. With the military coup in Iraq on July 14, an event that shook the Western powers, the United States responded on July 15 with military intervention in Lebanon, while Great Britain gave protective cover to the Jordanian regime. The United States remained in Lebanon overseeing the election of a new president, Fu'ad Chehab, an event which marked the beginning of a new phase in the nation's development. Many would argue, however, that the fundamental roots of this first civil war had not been satisfactorily resolved.

BIBLIOGRAPHY

AGWANI, M. S. *The Lebanese Crisis, 1958*. London, 1965.
QUBAIN, FAHIM. *Crisis in Lebanon*. Washington, D.C., 1961.

Irene Gendzier

Lebanese Civil War (1975)

Domestic conflict in Lebanon, 1975–1990

There is no consensus among scholars and researchers on what triggered the Lebanese Civil War. The strike of fishermen at Sidon in February 1975 could be considered the first important episode that set off the outbreak of hostilities. That event involved a specific issue: the attempt of former President Camille CHAMOUN (also head of the Maronite-oriented National Liberal Party) to monopolize fishing along the coast of Lebanon. The injustices perceived by the fishermen evoked sympathy from many Lebanese and reinforced the resentment and antipathy that were widely felt against the state and the economic monopolies. The demonstrations against the fishing company were quickly transformed into a political action supported by the political Left and their allies in the Palestine Liberation Organization (PLO). The state tried to suppress the demonstrators, and a government sniper reportedly killed a popular figure in the city, Ma'ruf Sa'd, who was known for his opposition to the government and his support for the Palestinians.

The events in Sidon were not contained for long. The government began to lose control of the situation in April 1975, when a bus carrying Palestinians was ambushed by gunmen belonging to the PHALANGE party. The party claimed that earlier its headquarters had been targeted by unknown gunmen. The attack against the bus in Ayn al-Rummana marked the official beginning of the Lebanese Civil War. Initially, the war pitted Maronite-oriented right-wing militias (most notably the Phalange party and the National Liberal party) against leftist and Muslim-oriented militias (grouped together in the Lebanese National Movement) supported by the PLO. The eruption of military hostilities produced a heated political debate on whether the army of Lebanon, led by a right-wing Maronite commander, should be deployed to end the fighting. Most Muslims and leftists opposed any use of the army, which was seen as anti-Palestinian; most right-wingers called for its immediate deployment.

The characterizations of the combatants in the civil war often obscure the nature of the conflict. Many Lebanese still see the civil war as the product of a conspiracy hatched by outsiders who were jealous of "Lebanese democracy and prosperity." The civil war should be viewed as a multidimensional conflict that at its roots is a classical civil strife with the domestic parties determining the course but rarely the outcome of the fighting. Over the course of Lebanese history external parties have insisted on preventing the Lebanese from proceeding unrestrained in their civil strife. Had the Lebanese been allowed to continue fighting without external restraints, some sects in Lebanon would have been eliminated long ago. This is not to say that the external parties—notably Syria, Iraq, Iran, and Israel—have not contributed to the intensification of the conflict whenever it suited their interests. All of these states have had proxy militias operating in Lebanon.

The roots of the civil war are a set of issues, some having to do with domestic politics and others with foreign policy. It is fair to say that the system of sectarian distribution of power that had been sponsored by France since 1920 led to the increasing frustration of Muslims, who grew demographically but not politically. In 1975 the political system continued to assume that the figures of the 1932 census—the only census in Lebanon's history—which showed the Maronites to be the single largest sect in the country, had not changed. However, it was widely known that the Shi'ites had long been the single largest sect, although their political representation was small. The ceremonial post of speaker of Parliament was reserved for the Shi'ites, whereas the presidency was reserved for Maronites, and the prime ministership for Sunnis. The Shi'ites included a disproportionate number of poor people, and, to add to their misery, predominated in the area of southern Lebanon that in the 1960s became an arena for Israel–Palestinian conflict. The state of Lebanon, which always avoided provoking Israel, simply abandoned southern Lebanon. Many of the people there migrated to the suburbs of Beirut which are known as "poverty belts." The young Shi'ite migrants, who had not participated in the prosperity of prewar Beirut, joined many Lebanese and Palestinian organizations.

The Sunnis had grievances, too. The office of the prime minister was marginalized by the strong presidency of Sulayman FRANJIYYA, who was elected in 1970. In 1973, when Prime Minister Sa'ib SALAM could not fire the commander in chief of the army after a commando raid launched from Israel that targeted three high-ranking PLO leaders, the issue of the powers of the prime minister emerged as a symbol of the sectarian/political imbalance in the country. Socioeconomic dissatisfaction plus political resentment produced an unstable political system.

The presence of Palestinians in Lebanon was another thorny issue. The state decided to crack down on their armed presence in Lebanon while rightwing militias were being armed and financed by the army. Many leftists and Muslims wanted the state to support the Palestinians and to send the army to protect southern Lebanon against raids from Israel. The PLO, on the other hand, was tempted to take advantage of the domestic turmoil to shore up support for its cause and to undermine the military power of the Army, which had long harassed Palestinians.

The first phase of the Lebanese Civil War did not end; it merely came to a temporary halt as a result of regional and international consensus. When it was becoming clear that the PLO and its Lebanese allies were about to overrun predominantly Christian areas, Syria intervened militarily in Lebanon and, with support from Israel, the United States, and France, fought the Palestinians and their Lebanese allies. The fighting stopped for a while, although southern Lebanon continued to be an arena for the conflict between Israel and the Palestinians, as well as the armed militias, who were present throughout Lebanon. By 1978, Syria's relations with Maronite-oriented parties had worsened, and the rise of Bashir JUMAYYIL as head of the LEBANESE FORCES—the coalition of rightwing fighting groups—caused a change in the course of the civil war. Israel became a close ally of the Lebanese Forces, and Syria's regime decided to sponsor the leftist–Palestinian coalition. In the spring of 1978, Israel's army invaded Lebanon in order to end any military presence in southern Lebanon, except that of the pro-Israel militia. Although international opprobium forced Israel southward, and although UN forces were deployed in southern Lebanon to pacify the region, Israel continued to occupy part of southern Lebanon, calling the strip of land "the security zone."

The civil war took another turn in 1982, when Israel invaded Lebanon again; this time Israeli's forces reached Beirut. Israel took advantage of the deteriorating security situation throughout the country and expected that popular frustration with the misconduct of members of the PLO, and Syrian and Lebanese troops, would provide positive climate for its all-out military intervention. The invasion claimed the lives of some 20,000 Lebanese and Palestinians. Israel also wanted to influence the 1982 presidential election; Bashir Jumayyil was elected president but was assassinated a few days later. His assassination was the pretext that the Lebanese Forces gave for their mass killing of Palestinian civilians in the SABRA AND SHATILA REFUGEE CAMPS. Amin Jumayyil, the next president, supported the signing of an Israel–Lebanon peace treaty in May 1983. Lebanon's opposition, coupled with Syria's rejection on the pro-Israel, pro-United States orientation of Jumayyil, resulted in the eruption of hostilities throughout the latter's administration. When Jamayyil's term ended in the summer of 1988, he appointed the Maronite commander in chief of the army, Gen. Michel Aoun, as interim president. His appointment was rejected by many

Lebanese, and Aoun launched a "war of national liberation" against Syria's army in Lebanon. His shells, however, fell on innocent Lebanese living in areas under Syria's control. The beginning of the end of the civil war came in October 1989, when Lebanese deputies gathered in the city of Ta'if in Saudi Arabia. The meeting produced a document of national accord. It was impossible to implement, however, until General Aoun's forces were defeated in October 1990, when Syria's troops attacked his headquarters and he was forced to seek refuge in France. President Ilyas Hrawi was elected in 1989, and the territorial integrity of Lebanon has been partially restored, although Israel still occupies a strip in southern Lebanon.

As'ad AbuKhalil

Lebanese Crises of the 1840s

Druze versus Christian sectarian violence.

The London Treaty of 1840 ended the Egyptian occupation of Mount Lebanon (1831–1840). Soon afterwards the Ottomans dismissed the local governor, Bashir II, whose collusion with the Egyptian ruler Muhammad Ali had discredited him with the local population. The years of Egyptian manipulation of sectarian politics produced a backlash under the Ottomans in the Druze versus Christian conflicts at Dayr al-Qamar in 1841. Bashir III, the last Chehab emir, was replaced in 1842 by a direct governor, Umar Pasha al-Nimsawi (the Austrian). Continued civil strife and European pressure led the Ottomans to establish a system of two sub-governorates in Mount Lebanon (*qa'im-maqamiyatayn*) divided on religious lines. Despite further sectarian clashes in 1845 at Mukhtarah, Jazzin, and Dayr al-Qamar, the tottering new system survived until 1860 when the MUTASARRIF system finally ended Mount Lebanon's autonomy.

BIBLIOGRAPHY

KHALAF, SAMIR. *Persistence and Change in Nineteenth Century Lebanon.* Beirut, 1979.

Tayeb El-Hibri

Lebanese Forces

Lebanese political-military organization.

The Lebanese Forces (LF) emerged in 1976 under the leadership of Bashir JUMAYYIL. At that time var-

ious Lebanese Christian militias had joined forces to destroy the Palestinian refugee camp at Tall al-Za'tar. In August 1976, a joint command council was established to integrate those militias formally and to achieve a degree of political independence from the traditional Maronite (Christian) political leaders. Jumayyil took control of the military wing of his father's PHALANGE party and then proceeded to incorporate other Christian militias. Those that resisted were forcibly integrated. In 1978, Jumayyil subjugated the Marada Brigade, the militia of former president Sulayman Franjiyya, killing Tony Franjiyya, his son, in the process. In 1980, the Tigers' militia of Camille Chamoun was absorbed.

By the early 1980s, the LF controlled East Beirut and parts of Mount Lebanon, and Jumayyil became its "commander." He did not confine the LF to combat; he also created committees within its structure responsible for health, information, foreign policy, education, and other matters of public concern. Jumayyil established links with Israel, and he consistently battled with Syrian forces.

The LF began to decline in 1982, when President-elect Bashir Jumayyil was assassinated. After numerous succession struggles, Elie HOBEYKA—notorious for his role in the 1982 bloodshed in the SABRA AND SHATILA REFUGEE CAMPS—assumed the leadership of the LF. When Hobeyka signed the Syrian-sponsored Tripartite Declaration in December 1985, against the wishes of president Amin Jumayyil, early in 1986 LF chief of staff Samir Geagea launched an attack on Hobeyka and took over the LF. Although Geagea was able to take advantage of the mood of frustration and despair among the Christain masses, Israel, his chief backer, was less interested in his cause than it had been—although it continued to supply his forces with money and arms.

After the appointment of General Michel AOUN as interim president by Amin Jumayyil, Lebanon's army tried to disarm the LF but failed to eliminate its political and military power. The defeat of Aoun by Syrian troops in 1990 led Geagea to try to impose himself as the overall Maronite leader. His attempt to become president of the Phalange party failed, and George Sa'ade remained the head of that predominantly Maronite party.

Geagea promised to allow Lebanon's army to confiscate weapons and ammunition belonging to his militia, according to the terms of the TA'IF accord. He promised to transform his militia into a political party and obtained a license toward that end. Lebanon's army, however, accused his forces of obstruction and discovered large amounts of hidden supplies and weapons. In early 1994, when a bomb exploded in a church in East Beirut, Lebanese authorities uncovered a terrorist ring that answered to Geagea personally. The government found evidence linking him to a series of bombs, car bombs, and assassinations. He was arrested and tried; the LF received a deadly blow and is unlikely to reemerge in the foreseeable future.

BIBLIOGRAPHY

TACHAU, FRANK. *Political Parties of the Middle East and North Africa.* Westport, Conn., 1994.

As'ad AbuKhalil

Lebanese Front

A coalition of major Christian conservative parties, which became an important player in the 1975 civil war in Lebanon.

Established in 1976, the Lebanese Front included the NATIONAL LIBERAL PARTY of the former president, Camille Chamoun; Sulayman FRANJIYYA, the president of Lebanon when the Lebanese Civil War began in 1975; Pierre JUMAYYIL, head of the Phalange—the front's major military power; the Guardians of Cedars; the Permanent Congress of the Lebanese Orders of Monks; al-Tanzeem of Dr. Fuad Shemali; the Maronite League headed by Shaker Abu Suleiman; and other independent personalities such as Dr. Charles Malik, Fuad Boustani, and Edward Honein.

In August 1976, the coalition established a military branch, known as the LEBANESE FORCES, which could mobilize 30,000 troops. At the beginning of 1978, Franjiyya became critical of the open collaboration between Israeli government officials and front leaders Chamoun and Jumayyil. Franjiyya was also against the Camp David peace accord negotiations between Egypt and Israel (approved by other front members) but championed a close relationship with Syria. In May 1978, Franjiyya resigned from the front. It was subsequently wracked with dissent and disintegrated.

The Lebanese Front charter had stressed the need to maintain the unity of Lebanon, to reestablish the authority of the law, and to respect private enterprise in the economic sector.

BIBLIOGRAPHY

AL-MONTADA REPORTS. *The Lebanese Conflict, 1975–1979* (Dossier 2). Beirut, 1979.

George E. Irani

Lebanese–Israeli Armistice

See Israeli–Lebanese Armistice

Lebanese National Movement (LNM)

A coalition of Islamic and leftist Lebanese parties and groups.

Established in 1975, the Lebanese National Movement (LNM) advocated, among other objectives, the solidarity of Lebanon with the Palestinians, the adoption of a proportional system of elections, and the elimination of political and administrative sectarianism. During the Lebanese Civil War, the LNM joined forces with the Palestine Liberation Organization (PLO) and was headed by Kamal Jumblatt. After his assassination in 1977, his son Walid Jumblatt took over and, in October 1982, announced the dissolution of the LNM.

BIBLIOGRAPHY

KHALID, WALID. *Conflict and Violence in Lebanon, Confrontation in the Middle East.* Cambridge, U.K., 1979.

George E. Irani

Lebanese University

University located in Beirut.

The Lebanese University, established in 1952, is under the jurisdiction of the Ministry of Education. It was founded to allow Lebanese from lower income groups to receive a university education, which for decades had been the monopoly of those who could afford private (and expensive) universities. It has two main branches—one in East Beirut and the other in West Beirut—and smaller branches in the provinces of the north, the south, and the Biqa' valley. University faculties (departments) include law, political science and management, engineering, literature and humanities, education, social sciences, fine arts, journalism and advertising, business administration, and agriculture. The language of instruction is Arabic; study of one foreign language is required by all faculties.

Although the Lebanese University has filled a gap and has catered to a sector of the population that had been virtually left out of the private educational system, holders of degrees from the Lebanese University are regarded as inferior job applicants, compared with holders of degrees from the American University of Beirut or Saint Joseph University. The state apparatus also favors graduates of the two private universities.

The Lebanese University's lack of endowment, forces it to be totally dependent on state funding, which is not always forthcoming. Classes are overcrowded, and there are no admissions standards. Staff and faculty are underpaid, which forces many of them to seek outside employment as well. Furthermore, the large student body enables some students to show up only for final exams.

Like other institutions, the university was affected by the LEBANESE CIVIL WAR of 1975. Many professors were forced to take a political stance, and some were pressured by armed students to change their grades. Some of the buildings of the university were occupied by militias, and others were heavily damaged.

BIBLIOGRAPHY

COLLELO, THOMAS, ed. *Lebanon: A Country Study,* 3rd ed. Washington, D.C., 1989.

As'ad AbuKhalil

Lebanon

An independent Arab country located on the eastern end of the Mediterranean Sea.

A small country of 4,105 square miles, with a maximum length (north to south) of 135 miles, Lebanon is bordered by Syria and Israel, both of which have invaded Lebanon's territory. There is no current reliable census of Lebanon's population (the last official census was conducted in 1932); in 1994 it is estimated to be around 3 million. The sectarian composition of the population remains a contentious issue because political power has been distributed according to a formula that favors the MARONITES (Christians), who

in the 1932 census constituted the largest religious group in the country. The demographic profile of the population has changed dramatically since 1932, with the SHI'ITE Muslims becoming more prominent because of their high birth rate. Some estimates put the Shi'ites at 45 percent of the population; and most authorities agree that Muslims (including all sects) are now the majority.

The historical myth of Lebanon, which has been challenged by the Lebanese historian Kamal Salibi, is predicated on the belief that Lebanon has always been a haven for persecuted minorities, its rugged mountains providing shelter for heterodox groups from throughout the Middle East. Lebanonese ultra-nationalists claim that Lebanon has been in existence since before Phoenician times. The late historian Philip Hitti suggested people have been residing in what is today Lebanon for thousands of years. Lebanon as a political entity is a twentieth-century phenomenon, the product of the division between Britain and France of the spoils of World War I. Central Lebanon, known as Mount Lebanon, was occupied by Maronites, Druze, and Shi'ites. Those groups have lived together yet apart, separated by geographic lines of demarcation and by fear and suspicion. Lebanon cannot continue to exist as a political entity in the absence of the minimum degree of social-national cohesion.

For much of the period between 1516 and 1918, Lebanon was quasi-independent. This relative autonomy is exaggerated by those who claim that the Lebanese state has been in continuous existence for thousands of years. The region in question, Mount Lebanon, was governed by a local prince (from the Ma'nid and, later, from the Chehab dynasties) who was in turn under the jurisdiction of a sultan of the Ottoman Empire. The political independence of the local ruler depended on the relative power of the government in Istanbul at a given time and on the degree of external intervention in Lebanese affairs. During the earlier part of the period in question, the Druzes were the politically ascendant group. In the nineteenth century, however, the ruling Chehabi dynasty converted to Maronite Christianity, and the Maronites began moving into areas that had been exclusively Druze-inhabited. The power of the Maronite Church, which was taking advantage of the consequences of TANZIMAT, was also increasing.

In 1840 Mount Lebanon was divided into a southern district (Druze) and a northern district (Maronite). Druze–Maronite clashes occurred throughout the century, and a major conflict in 1860 left the Druzes militarily victorious and the Maronites politically victorious (due to support by European powers). The war resulted in the establishment of a

Ruins at Baʿalbak. (© Mark Dennis)

European commission to oversee the situation. After negotiation with the Ottoman government, it was decided that Lebanon should be ruled by a non-Maronite, non-Lebanese Christian citizen of the Ottoman Empire. The governor (MUTASARRIF in Turkish) would be assisted by a council of representatives from the various sects, with the Maronites constituting the largest group. The regime established in 1861 continued until World War I.

During World War I, Lebanese of all religions were executed for anti-Turkish activities. After the war, France would not allow the "protected" Maronites, who called France *al-Umm al-Hanun* (The Tender Mother), to be placed in an inferior position in Lebanon. Before the beginning of the French MANDATE SYSTEM, Lebanese Maronites launched a strong propaganda campaign, characterized by Christian evangelical zeal, in Egypt (where members of the Maronite elite resided) and in France. The campaign led to the creation of Greater Lebanon, which included Mount Lebanon, southern Lebanon, Tripoli and the North, the Biqaʿ region, and the Beirut region. The addition of those areas was motivated not by considerations of national harmony but by calculations of economic viability. The predominantly Muslim population of the annexed areas was not consulted, and many staunchly opposed what appeared to be a Western-engineered attempt to sever ties between Lebanon and the larger, surrounding Muslim Arab nations.

In 1926 the French mandate authorities urged the elected Lebanese representatives to draft a new constitution. The constitution affirmed the political, diplomatic, economic, and legal supremacy of the French government. Article 95 confirmed the sectarian foundation of Lebanese politics by stipulating that governmental posts shall be distributed "equitably" between the sects. This in effect established a system that had as its basic unit not the individual citizen but the sect. The 1932 census revealed that the Maronites were the most numerous sect; consequently the highest government posts were reserved for them.

Although official and quasi-official Lebanese historiography claims there was an "independence movement" in the country, British–French rivalries in the Levant helped bring about the independence of Lebanon in 1943. Bishara al-KHURI, the foremost Maronite politician and first president after independence, and Riyad al-SULH, the foremost Sunni politician and first prime minister after independence, were the architects of Lebanon's National Pact. This unwritten document became, in the words of Maronite Phalange leader Pierre Jumayyil, more important than the written laws of the country. It stipulated that the Christians (for whom the Maronites spoke, according to the agreement) would not seek protection or alliance with France, and the Muslims (for whom the Sunnis spoke) would respect the sovereignty of Lebanon and renounce dreams of unity with Syria or any other Arab country. The National Pact also de-

Ruins at Baʿalbak. (Richard Bulliet)

Cedars and snow-covered slopes of Lebanon, 1954. (D.W. Lockhard)

creed that the presidency of Lebanon would be held by a Maronite, the speakership of parliament by a Shi-'ite, and the prime ministership by a Sunni. It is still regarded as a social contract, though most Lebanese were not consulted about its provisions.

The country was governed by a small group of wealthy politicians who monopolized power within their sects. Political competition, when it occurred, was between members of the economic/political elite and not between average citizens. The first president, Bishara al-Khuri (1943–1952), disregarded the minimum standards of honesty and integrity. His cronies and relatives enriched themselves, and he had the parliament (which was chosen in the scandalously fraudulent 1947 election) amend the constitution so that he have a second term as president. In 1952 a large bloc of parties and politicians formed a front to force his ouster. After his resignation, Camille CHAMOUN was elected president.

The rule of Chamoun was marked by what many considered to be violations of the National Pact. Although he had been identified with pan-Arab politics, he closely aligned Lebanon with the West during his presidency, particularly on anticommunism and anti-Nasserism. His opposition to Gamal Abdel Nasser, the president of Egypt, provoked many Lebanese who admired the Egyptian leader. Following the example of his predecessor, Chamoun rigged the 1957 elections to ensure a subservient parliament that would allow him a second term. In 1958 the Lebanese civil war broke out, and the United States dispatched the Marines to protect the Chamoun regime.

The most important politician in contemporary Lebanese history was president Fu'ad CHEHAB (1958–1964). This former commander in chief of the Leb-

anese army remains the only politician in the history of Lebanon to have an "ism" associated with his name. Chehabism, the ideology of limited political and economic reforms, was based on the realization that the social and political unrest in Lebanon had socioeconomic roots. Chehab worked to reorganize the Lebanese administration structure, in an attempt to stem the corruption that had been rampant since independence. His regime, however, did not go far enough in its reforms, and Chehab, who distrusted the politicians, ruled through his trusted military aides. Rule by the military establishment was inconsistent with the constitution's promises of freedom; the army used heavy-handed tactics against all who opposed the regime.

Chehab was succeeded by his follower Charles HILU (1964–1970). Hilu quickly disillusioned his former mentor and associated himself with the right-wing factions like the Phalange party, of which he was a founder. He preserved the rule of the Deux-ième Bureau (military intelligence) because he lacked a political power base. His weak response to internal instability led to the election of Sulayman FRANJIYYA (1970–1976), an ultranationalist who favored strong support for the army in light of the growing power of the Palestine Liberation Organization (PLO) in Lebanon. Franjiyya sought to use the army to crush the PLO as King Hussein did in Jordan. The army was too weak to succeed, and Israel was increasingly exposing the impotence of Lebanon against continued military actions by Israel in Lebanon that did not distinguish between Lebanese and Palestinian targets or between civilian and military targets. Franjiyya urged the army to arm and train members of Maronite militias in Lebanon, which he wanted to use in his war against the Palestinians. During his presi-

View of the Mount Lebanon mountain range. (Richard Bulliet)

Beirut with Mount Lebanon in the background, 1954.
(D.W. Lockhard)

dency there were numerous clashes between the PLO and the Lebanese army aided by right-wing militias. Franjiyya's autocratic rule brought calls for a more meaningful partnership between the president and the prime minister.

Much has been written about the civil war, but there is no consensus about its origins. Lebanese often emphasize the external causes of what befell the country; they seem reluctant to place any blame for the protracted conflict on themselves. The civil war allowed various external forces to intervene openly in Lebanese affairs. Syria and Israel both exploited the conflict for their own purposes. In 1976 Syria intervened in the war to save the right-wing militias from what seemed an inevitable defeat by the leftist–PLO alliance. It did not want Lebanon to turn into a radical arena that could drag Syria into an unwanted confrontation with Israel.

The presence of Syrian forces in Lebanon made possible the election of Ilyas SARKIS as president in 1976, and Israel began its de facto occupation of part of southern Lebanon. The relationship of the PLO and its Lebanese allies with Syria began to improve as soon as right-wing militia leader Bashir JUMAYYIL (then commander of the Lebanese Forces) solidified his alliance with Israel and initiated a campaign against Syria's forces in Lebanon. The latter responded with heavy bombardment of East Beirut, the site of Lebanese Forces' headquarters. In the South, Israel formed a militia to further its goals. In 1978, Israel launched a full-scale invasion of Lebanon and was later forced to withdraw to a narrow strip that it called its Security Zone. The United Nations dispatched troops to serve as a buffer between the PLO forces and Israel's forces.

In 1982, Israel launched its biggest invasion ever. Its forces advanced all the way to Beirut and brought about the election of Bashir Jumayyil as president. The PLO came under pressure to withdraw its forces from Lebanon. Jumayyil was assassinated before he officially assumed his responsibilities, and pro-Israel forces killed the Palestinians and Lebanese in the SABRA AND SHATILA REFUGEE CAMPS in revenge for Jumayyil's assassination. Amin JUMAYYIL (1982–1988) succeeded his brother Bashir as president and began a rule by the Phalange party. In 1983 the security situation deteriorated further when Druze and Maronite militias engaged in one of the most ferocious battles of the Lebanese civil war. The Druze militia was able to evict Christians from areas under its control.

The rule of Amin Jumayyil divided the country more sharply than before, and most Muslims boycotted his government. In 1988, minutes before the expiration of his term, he appointed Gen. Michel Aoun (the Maronite commander in chief of the army) as interim president. Aoun cracked down against the Lebanese Forces and declared a war of "national liberation" against Syria's forces in Lebanon. The war did not bear political fruits for him, although it generated enthusiasm among the Maronite masses. In 1990, when world attention was focused on Iraq's invasion of Kuwait, Syria's forces entered Lebanon and destroyed the force commanded by Aoun, who fled to France.

The civil war theoretically ended with the defeat of Aoun and the establishment of the authority of the governmnet of President Ilyas Hrawi. The support of Syria and Saudi Arabia for the new administration revived hopes for badly needed financial aid to war-torn Lebanon. President Hrawi and Prime Minister Rafiq al-HARIRI solidified the rule of the Lebanese government and disarmed the militias in the country except for the Party of God, which continues to wage a war of national resistance against Israel's occupation of southern Lebanon. Whether the war has ended completely or whether a truce at last prevails in Lebanon is a question that requires knowledge of the future.

BIBLIOGRAPHY

AJAMI, FOUAD. *The Vanished Imam: Musa al Sadr and the Shia of Lebanon.* Ithaca, New York, 1986.

COLLELO, T., ed. *Lebanon: A Country Study.* 3rd ed. Washington, D.C., 1989.

HALAWI, M. *A Lebanon Defied.* Boulder, Colo., 1992.

KEDDIE, NIKKI and JUAN R. I. COLE, eds. *Shi'ism and Social Protest.* New Haven, Conn., 1986.

KRAMER, MARTIN. *The Moral Logic of Hizballah.* Tel Aviv, 1987.

NORTON, A. R. *Amal and the Shi'a: Struggle for the Soul of Lebanon.* Austin, Tex., 1987.

As'ad AbuKhalil

Lebanon, Mount

A rugged mountain range that constitutes the geographical core around which modern-day Lebanon was established in 1920.

Mount Lebanon extends from the hinterland of Tripoli in the north to that of Sidon in the south. Because of its geographical isolation and rugged landscape, it historically attracted minorities in search of a haven from persecution. MARONITES moved into the area in the seventh century, and they continue to this day to form the majority of its population. South of the Beirut–Damascus highway, Mount Lebanon is predominantly populated by DRUZE. Smaller Greek Orthodox and Greek Catholic communities also inhabit the area.

Over the centuries, Mount Lebanon developed its own traditions and a distinct identity. Under Ottoman rule (1516–1916), it enjoyed considerable political autonomy. Governance of the area was in the hands of an indigenous emir, who paid nominal allegiance to the Ottoman sultan and oversaw a political structure dominated by a few powerful local families. Following intercommunal hostilities and the mass killing of Christians by Druze in 1860, European countries, particularly France, pressured the authorities in Istanbul to formally grant the area autonomous status in the Ottoman Empire. The so-called Règlement Organique of 1861, guaranteed by the Great Powers, thus established Mount Lebanon as a self-governing province headed by a Christian governor. This development paved the way for the subsequent creation of the modern state of Lebanon in 1920, when the French mandatory power added parts of GREATER SYRIA to Mount Lebanon. Today Mount Lebanon refers to one of the five administrative provinces (governorates) into which Lebanon is divided.

BIBLIOGRAPHY

ZAMIR, MEIR. *The Formation of Modern Lebanon.* Ithaca, N.Y., and Beirut, 1985.

Guilain P. Denoeux

Lebanon Mountains

A chain of mountains in Lebanon.

The Lebanon mountains, which extend from the northeast of Lebanon to the southwest, are mentioned in the Bible and gave the name to what is now Lebanon. They are a legendary site for ultranationalists who glorify the terrain that has provided shelter for persecuted minorities throughout history. The Leb-anon mountains have been the scene of savage fighting between the DRUZE and MARONITES (who form the majority of the inhabitants of the area) in the nineteenth and twentieth centuries. The last episode of heavy fighting between them occurred in 1983.

As'ad AbuKhalil

Lebanon News Agency

The official news agency of Lebanon.

The Lebanon News Agency is part of the Ministry of Information and presents the official position of the government of Lebanon. It publishes bulletins in Arabic, English, and French, most of them dealing with meetings at the presidential palace, the office of the prime minister, and the parliament. The agency disseminates information on the activities of the various ministries and reports on cabinet meetings. The credibility of its news releases is often suspect because of the agency's close association with the government. It now has strong competition from various independent (local and international) news agencies. The current director of the agency (Rafiq Shalala, formerly of the newspaper *al-Nahar*) has tried to improve the quality of its publications, but they remain of limited value.

As'ad AbuKhalil

Lebanon State Railways

A rail network of 179 miles (289 km), established in 1961.

Lebanon's Railway and Public Transportation Authority is an independent entity managed by a board of administration that includes a government representative. It falls under the jurisdiction of the Ministry of Public Works and Transportation, the Ministry of Finance, and the Civil Service Council.

In addition to carrying passengers, Lebanon's state railways have transported such cargo as cement, fuel oil, phosphates, frozen meats, live animals, and other merchandise. In 1974, the value of the merchandise carried by the rail system was equivalent to the weight carried by 58,000 trucks. More than 80,000 passengers were carried to and from the Arab countries and Europe. During the civil war, when the railway was used under dangerous conditions to ship fuel for the electric plants of Jieh (south Lebanon) and Zouk (central Lebanon), the rail system suffered from several acts of plunder, looting, and vandalism.

George E. Irani

Leff

Arabic word for "wrapped" or "layered."

Leff is used especially in the Maghrib (North Africa) to refer to a political coalition, not necessarily kin-based, whose members come to each others' assistance in disputes with members of other coalitions. The equivalent Arabic term in the *Mashriq* (the Arab world from Egypt eastward) and in some parts of the Maghrib is *saff*.

Laurence Michalak

Legislative Council, Palestine

A 1923 British proposal for Palestinian self-government on which Arabs and Jews could not agree.

The League of Nations entrusted Palestine to Great Britain, which conquered the territory in December 1917, as a mandate, one of whose terms called for the "development of self-governing institutions." As a first step in that direction, the high commissioner of Palestine, Sir Herbert Samuel, formally proposed in August 1922 to the country's Muslim, Christian, and Jewish communities the establishment of a legislative council. The council was to be composed of twenty-three members: eleven appointed British members, including the high commissioner, and twelve elected Palestinian members: eight Muslims, two Christians, and two Jews. However, the British denied the council legislative authority over such central issues as Jewish immigration and land purchases in order to safeguard its Balfour policy of support for the Jewish national home. To allay Arab concerns regarding Jewish immigration, the elected members were to form a standing committee to advise the Palestine government on immigration issues.

Palestinian leaders argued that participation in the council would be tantamount to acceptance of the British mandate and Balfour policy, which they opposed. They considered unfair the allocation of only 43 percent of the seats to Palestinians, who constituted 88 percent of the population. And they objected to the limitations placed on the power of the council. A campaign against the proposed council by the Palestine Arab Executive and the Supreme Muslim Council was a potent factor in the Palestinian boycott of the council elections in February 1923. The Jews accepted the proposal despite their objections to the allocation of only two seats to Jews, which, they argued, would have reduced them to a minority role and would have meant that the concerns of the Jewish people as a whole would have

been ignored. The poor election turnout caused the high commissioner to shelve the proposal.

The idea was revived when a new high commissioner, Sir John Chancellor, took over in late 1928, but it was derailed by the Western (or Wailing) Wall disturbances of 1929, only to reemerge as a proposal in the Passfield WHITE PAPERS of 1930. Although the new proposal was identical to the 1922 proposal, the Palestinians this time did not oppose it, but the Jews rejected their minority role in the council and sought a parity formula that would recognize the numbers and the economic role of world Jewry. Intermittent discussions continued until 1935. By then the proposed composition of the council had expanded to twenty-eight, of whom fourteen were to be Muslims and Christians (five nominated), eight Jews (five nominated), five British officials, and one a nominee representing commercial interests. Arabs were divided over the proposal, while Jews were strongly opposed to it. This opposition prompted the British government to once again suspend its implementation.

BIBLIOGRAPHY

LESCH, ANN MOSELY. *Arab Politics in Palestine, 1917–1939: The Frustrations of a Nationalist Movement.* Ithaca, N.Y., 1979.

PATAI, RAPHAEL, ed. *Encyclopedia of Zionism and Israel.* 2 vols. New York, 1971.

PORATH, Y. *The Emergence of the Palestinian-Arab Nationalist Movement, 1918–1929.* London, 1974.

Philip Mattar

LEHI

See Lohamei Herut Yisrael

Leibowitz, Yeshayahu   [1903–   ]

Israeli chemist, philosopher, and social critic.

Born in Riga, Latvia, Yeshayahu Leibowitz was educated at the University of Berlin and Basle University. He was professor of biochemistry at Hebrew University and editor of the *Hebrew Encyclopedia.* He is most widely known for his iconoclastic views and outspoken opinions. As a philosopher, he is best known as an interpreter of Maimonides, whom Leibowitz stanchly portrayed as an ardent theocentrist. As a rationalist and an opponent of mysticism, Leibowitz denied any sacred character to the State of Israel and its agencies. He was a religiously observant Jew who adamantly insisted on the separation of religion and state, including the dissolution of the government-supported rabbinate. He believed that Halakhah, Jewish religious law, developed when there was no Jewish state and has become so firmly set that it is incapable of being adapted to the new circumstance of statehood. He was loudly critical of the tendency to mystify the Six-Day War, and he totally opposed Israel's occupation/administration policies. His rationalism also served as the basis of his opposition to the tendency to view the Western Wall as a holy Jewish shrine.

BIBLIOGRAPHY

LEIBOWITZ, YESHAYAHU. *Judaism, Human Values, and the Jewish State.* Cambridge, Mass., 1992.

Chaim I. Waxman

Le Journal d'Egypte

Egyptian newspaper.

Established in 1936, the French-language morning newspaper has a circulation of about seventy-two thousand. By the mid-1990s, under editor in chief Muhammad Rashad, it boasted the largest circulation of any foreign-language daily newspaper in Cairo.

Michael R. Fischbach

Lemsine, Aicha [1942–]

Pseudonym for Aicha Laidi, an Algerian novelist and essay writer.

Lemsine, born in the Nemencha, Algeria, to a Muslim family, is married to Algeria's ambassador to England; they live in London. Her first novel, *La Chrysalide* (Paris, 1976), is a romantic account of women of two generations; the first battles polygamy and the second displays her emancipation by becoming pregnant out of wedlock. In *Ciel de Porphyre* (Paris, 1978) the author chooses the Algerian war of independence as a setting for the initiation of a young woman into the resistance. The book is, however closer to a mystery novel. Lemsine's third book, *Ordalie des Voix* (Paris, 1983), consists of interviews with Arab women on their role in society.

BIBLIOGRAPHY

ACHOUR, CHRISTINE. *Anthologie de la littérature algérienne de langue française.* Paris, 1990.

Aida A. Bamia

Lend-Lease Program [1941–1945]

Provided U.S. military aid to the Allies in World War II.

Lend-lease was a program that, from 1940, enabled President Franklin D. Roosevelt to extend aid to any country whose fate he felt was vital to U.S. defense—for the sake of national security. Not until March 1941 did the U.S. Congress passed the Lend-Lease Act. It provided for military aid to the World War II Allies, under the condition that equipment extended would be returned or paid for after the war. In practice, lend-lease became the main wartime U.S. aid program of the Roosevelt administration. Little was returned, and even less was paid for. Coordinated first by Harry Hopkins and then by Edward Stettinius, the lend-lease programs conveyed the equivalent of some $3 billion in aid to the Middle East and the countries of the Mediterranean.

Lend-lease for the Middle East was administered primarily through Cairo, Egypt, and Tehran, Iran. Both Egypt and Iran were occupied by the Allies— Iran from the autumn of 1941 to 1945. In 1942, the United States supplied its ally, the USSR, via the Persian/Arabian Gulf and Iran; therefore, Iran became eligible for lend-lease. Although lend-lease was supposed to aid only democratic countries in the struggle against the Axis, petroleum-rich Saudi Arabia was also included in the program by February 1943. The lend-lease program was terminated in August 1945.

BIBLIOGRAPHY

RUBIN, BARRY. *Paved with Good Intentions.* New York, 1980.
YERGIN, DANIEL. *The Prize.* New York, 1991.

Zachary Karabell

Leskofcali Galip [1829–1867]

Ottoman poet.

Born in Nicosia (Levkosia), Cyprus, Leskofcali Galip was the son of an exiled Rumelian *ayan.* He came to Constantinople (now Istanbul) in 1846 and by 1851 had entered the civil service. He composed in a classical style similar to his contemporaries, Naili and Fehim. A collection of his works, *Divan,* was published in 1916.

David Waldner

Lesseps, Ferdinand de   [1805–1894]

French entrepreneur and promoter of building a canal to connect the Mediterranean and the Red seas.

After consular service for France at Lisbon and Tunis, de Lesseps became the French consul in Alexandria, Egypt, where he befriended Muhammad Ali Pasha's son, Sa'id. De Lesseps was appointed consul at Cairo from 1833 to 1837 and, after serving in other countries, resigned from diplomatic service in opposition to the Second Republic of France. In 1854, when Sa'id became khedive (ruler), de Lesseps returned to Egypt. Despite the findings of scientists who accompanied Napoléon Bonaparte during his occupation of Egypt (1798–1801) that a canal could not be built from the Mediterranean Sea to the Red Sea, de Lesseps (not an engineer) had become convinced of the feasibility of the project. He hoped to use his friendship with Sa'id to promote his plan. De Lesseps quickly convinced Sa'id to back him, in part by persuading Sa'id that his name would be immortalized as the builder of the SUEZ CANAL. In 1856, de Lesseps organized an international commission to study the technical aspects of the project. He also set up a company that would be financed by selling shares to the Egyptian and European governments. The Egyptian government provided labor through conscription, and construction took from 1859 to 1869. De Lesseps is remembered as the inspired leader who did whatever was necessary to get the canal built.

BIBLIOGRAPHY

GOLDSCHMIDT, ARTHUR, JR. *Modern Egypt: The Formation of a Nation-State.* Boulder, Colo., 1988.

David Waldner

Le Tunisien

Tunisian nationalist and reformist newspaper founded by Ali Bash-Hamba in 1907.

The first French-language newspaper published by Tunisians, its aim was to sway French public opinion in France and Tunisia toward Tunisian nationalism. A weekly, the paper appeared for five years, until its closing by the French colonial administration in March 1912, when the French protectorate officially began. Of its regular contributors, perhaps the two most important were Ali Bash-HAMBA and Abd al-Jalil Zaoush, both liberal, if elitist, reformers.

BIBLIOGRAPHY

MICAUD, CHARLES. *Tunisia: The Politics of Modernization.* New York, 1964.
Tunisia: A Country Survey. Washington, D.C., 1988.

Matthew S. Gordon

Levantine

A noun or an adjective that defines the non-Muslim populations and cultures of the modern Middle East.

The term *levantine* is French in origin—*levantin*—and implies a geographic reference to the sun rising—*soleil levant*—in the east, or *levant*. The French probably coined the expression as France, in the sixteenth century, was the first Christian national state to exchange diplomatic recognition with the Ottoman Empire located in the eastern Mediterranean littoral. By the early 1800s, English travel literature referred to the lands of the Ottoman Empire as the Levant. Indeed, in the 1990s the London-published international business weekly *The Economist* still refers to their reporters based in Cyprus as their Levant correspondents.

From the 1500s to the 1850s, Levantine traditionally meant a European resident of the Levant involved in European–Ottoman trade. By the end of the nineteenth century, the label was significantly broadened to include a European born in the Levant whose parentage included Greek or Armenian blood. Moreover, Levantine was by then applied to Syro-Lebanese Christians, Sephardic Jews, Maltese, Cypriots, Armenians, and Greeks, all minorities in the Muslim East, living and doing business in the large trading centers of the Ottoman Empire. The term almost always indicated an urbanized commercial bourgeoisie whose members were usually rich and influential merchants, and who were different, due to their Westernized education and culture, from the petty bourgeoisie in the provincial towns and the villages of the hinterland.

Historically, the development of a Levantine bourgeoisie was the result of significant trade with Europe and reflected the growing cultural interaction that both preceded and paralleled imperial ties between Europe and the lands of the Ottoman Empire. The Westernization of Levantines was the result of commerce, travel, emigration, and attendance at the foreign missions' schools that dotted the eastern Mediterranean by the mid 1800s. Believing in progress, Levantines saw Europe as the leader of a progressive world and easily accepted its values. They formed a mercantile elite whose cultural anchors transcended local and regional boundaries, and whose perspective was fixed on Europe. Consequently, there arose a natural affinity between these modernizing groups, regardless of their ethnonational backgrounds, in different parts of the Middle East. Levantines were individuals who were never Muslims nor usually Arab Christians, whose origins were somewhere in the eastern Mediterranean and whose primary language and culture, except for Syro-Lebanese Christians, were not Arabic. Because Levantines were conversant in a number of foreign languages and local dialects, many became the indispensable interpreters and translators of the foreign consulates throughout the Levant.

As non-Muslims, members of these minorities usually acquired the protection of European powers in order to benefit from the privileges afforded foreigners under the CAPITULATIONS. Centuries of insecurity under Mamluk or Ottoman rule had conditioned them to try to obtain the protection of European powers which, in most cases, were only too willing to extend it. This phenomenon had begun as early as the seventeenth century in Lebanon with the Maronite Christians, who received French protection inside the Ottoman Empire.

By the 1900s, "Levantine" had acquired a negative moral coloration. Sir Evelyn Baring, British agent and consul-general in Egypt from 1883 to 1907, adhered to the traditional definition but emphasized the southern European origin of those to whom the term applied. He further included a pejorative nuance that had recently been attached to the term: "Levantines . . . suffer in reputation by reason of qualities which are displayed by only a small minority of their class . . . among this minority are to be found individuals who are tainted with a remarkable degree of moral obliquity." Other writers were more specific and referred to Greek or Armenian money lenders or to "sellers of strong waters to Muslims in most cities of Western Asia."

This pejorative implication appeared to gain ground. An impressive publication that served as a guide to British investors in Egypt, discussing Alexandria as a summer resort, informed its readers that the city became the temporary home of "businessmen from the capital unable to get over to Europe and a certain class of Levantines who invariably return to Cairo richer than they left."

Thus, the evolution of the term "Levantine" encompassed both ethno-cultural identity as well as moral judgment. From applying to a European born and living in the eastern Mediterranean, it came to include either an Eastern Christian or another member of a non-Arab minority whose business dealings were ethically tainted, to the point of implementing the profit motive even while on vacation.

The metamorphosis of the term probably reflected a change in the attitudes of Europeans towards the East. By the end of the nineteenth century, European Arabists believed that Eastern civilization was "purer, more spiritual and more wholesome" than Western civilization and that European greed and viciousness were destroying the Arab East. To such Europeans, Levantines were the carriers of Western and European greed and viciousness, since it was through them—Christian brothers of the Europeans and, to a lesser extent, Jews—that it flowed into Eastern and Arab society.

By the 1920s, "Levantine" and "Levantinism" also acquired political nuances commensurate with the seismic effects of World War I on the region. Various authors used the terms to describe the political crisis affecting Turkish society; the expression ascribed Turkey's defeat in World War I to the fact that Turks from Istanbul had "become Levantiny". Writing in the postcolonial mid-1950s, Elie Kedourie, an Iraqi Jew by birth and an incisive student of Middle Eastern politics and society, maintained that by the 1940s the Levant was perceived as much a region of the spirit as a region of the globe and that the spread of Levantinism was the characteristic malady of Islamic and Arab society.

Albert Hourani, an Arab Christian and a perceptive student of Middle East history, writing shortly after World War II, maintained that Levantinism was a symbol of national and ethnocultural dispossession. He further ascribed to it philosophical aspects of the human condition, a sort of postwar *mal de siècle,* by stating: ". . . to be a Levantine is to live in two worlds or more at once without belonging to either; to be able to go through the external forms which indicate the possession of a certain nationality, religion or culture without actually possessing it. It is no longer to have a standard of one's own, not to be able to create but only able to imitate. . . . It is to belong to no community and to possess nothing of one's own. It reveals itself in lostness, pretentiousness, cynicism and despair." Undoubtedly affected by the postwar atmosphere of frustrated nationalist self-assertion, Hourani cast Levantines as a group adrift without the contemporary concerns of national self-realization. However, his alarm underlines the concerns of Arab Christian minorities caught in the dilemma of decolonization: the fear of rejection by the Arab Muslim majority.

The twentieth century political definitions of Levantinism encompass the notion that people and cultures can be divided into genuine and hybrid with the implication that the former are clearly superior to and more desirable than the latter. They present an arbitrary division of historical phenomena driven by ideology and containing ahistorical value judgments. To apply this perspective to the Middle East overlooks the fact that the area has historically absorbed a number of vastly diverse cultures, languages, customs, and values. While some of these cultures had a stronger influence than others, they all contributed to the region's heterogeneity. Thus, an understanding of Middle East history must include an assessment untainted by ideological prisms but comprising a perspective that includes the experience and the contributions of its diverse populations.

BIBLIOGRAPHY

CROMER, LORD. *Modern Egypt.* London, 1908.
HOURANI, ALBERT. *Minorities in the Arab World.* Oxford, 1947.
———. *Syria and Lebanon: A Political Essay.* Oxford, 1946.
KEDOURIE, ELIE. *England and the Middle East: The Destruction of the Ottoman Empire, 1914–1921.* London, 1956.
OPPENHEIM, JEAN-MARC RAN. *Twilight of a Colonial Ethos: The Alexandria Sporting Club, 1890–1956.* Ph.D. diss., Columbia University, 1991.

Jean-Marc R. Oppenheim

Levin, Hanoch   [1943–   ]

Israeli playwright and storyteller.

Levin was born and grew up in a poor section of Tel Aviv. He began writing satirical plays while still a student. Levin's work is avant-garde, minimalist, and controversial. His *Malkat Ha-Ambatya* (1970, Queen of the Bathtub), a satire on Israeli society after the Arab–Israel War of 1967 created an uproar, and performances had to be canceled.

Salient features of his plays are a pessimistic view of life in general and of human relationships in particular. His plays include: *Solomon Grup* (1969), *Hefetz* (1972), and *Ya'akobi Ve-Leidental* (1972). The latter was widely performed both in Israel and abroad. Many of his plays were first staged at the Cameri, Tel Aviv's municipal theater, and in 1988 Levin was appointed its in-house playwright.

Ann Kahn

Levin, Shmaryahu   [1867–1935]

Zionist orator, propagandist, and advocate.

After serving in the Duma (Russian parliament), in 1906, Levin left Russia. In Germany, he gained support for founding the Haifa Technion (1908). During World War I he mobilized the support of American Jews for the Zionist cause. A strong supporter of Chaim Weizmann within the Zionist movement, Levin settled in Palestine in 1924.

Martin Malin

Levin, Yizhak Meir   [1894–1971]

Merchant, banker, Jewish leader, and communal activist.

Levin was born in Poland and descended from a family of Gerer Hasidim. He was a leader of and active participant in AGUDAT ISRAEL, a worldwide Orthodox Jewish organization and a political party in Israel, from its inception in Poland following World War I. Levin was elected to the organization's world presidium in 1929 and headed its delegation to Palestine in 1935.

Escaping Nazi-occupied Poland, he reached Palestine in 1940, where he worked for the rescue of Jews stranded in Europe. In 1947, he was placed in charge of the Israeli branch of Agudat Israel. As a party member, he was elected to the first Knesset (parliament), serving as minister of social welfare until 1952, when he resigned over the issue of drafting women into the army, to which he was thoroughly opposed. He remained a member of the Knesset until his death.

Ann Kahn

Levinger, Moshe   [1935–   ]

Leader of Gush Emunim, a Zionist settlement movement in Israel's administered territories.

Levinger was born in Jerusalem and was active in the religious Zionist youth movement B'nai Akiva. He became a disciple of Rabbi Zvi Yehuda KOOK, founder of GUSH EMUNIM, while studying at his yeshiva in Jerusalem.

He became the leader of the effort to reestablish and intensify Jewish settlement in Hebron, where he and his family were among the first Jewish residents since the 1929 mass killing of the city's Jews. As the leading promoter of political messianism, he established the first Jewish settlement there in 1968, coercing the Israeli government into designating housing units, which led to the establishment of nearby Kiryat Arba in 1970.

Although he was the ideological leader of Gush Emunim, his influence waned after 1984, when the movement became institutionalized and he persisted in his staunch mystical political messianism. In 1989, he was convicted and imprisoned for shooting and killing a Palestinian.

Chaim I. Waxman

Levontin, Zalman   [1856–1940]

Zionist leader.

Born and educated in Russia, he later became a businessman and banker. Levontin was a close associate of Theodore Herzl and a founding member of the Zionist settlement of Rishon L'tzyon. Levontin was the director of the Jewish Colonial Trust in 1901; he moved to Palestine, where he founded the Anglo-Palestine Bank (which later became the Bank Leumi L'Yisrael).

Bryan Daves

Levy, David   [1937–   ]

Israeli political leader.

Born in Morocco, David Levy has held either an elected or an appointed office since 1965. Since 1969, he has been a member of the Israeli Knesset and is currently the deputy leader of the Likud faction of the Knesset. From 1977 to 1992, he served as a government minister and as a deputy prime minister. He made a bid for the Likud leadership in the 1992 election.

Bryan Daves

Liberal Constitutionalist Party

Egyptian political party founded by former Prime Minister Adli Yakan (October 1922).

Members of the party, mainly landowners and intellectuals, were former members of the WAFD who came to oppose Sa'd Zaghlul because of his intransigence and demagogery. The program of the party, written by Ahmad Lutfi al-Sayyid, called for an independent Egypt, constitutional rule, the protection of civil rights and free speech, and social justice. The party defended the 1922 declaration of independence granted by Britain, which many nationalists considered inadequate, and supported the 1923 constitution, which it had helped to draft. In the late 1920s and early 1930s, the party alternated between allying with the Wafd against Britain and joining with Britain in forming anti-Wafd governments. The news-

paper of the party was *al-Siyasa* (Politics). The party was banned by the Revolutionary Command Council in 1953.

BIBLIOGRAPHY

GOLDSCHMIDT, ARTHUR, JR. *Modern Egypt: The Formation of a Nation-State.* Boulder, Colo., 1988.
AL-SAYYID MARSOT, AFAF LUTFI. *Egypt's Liberal Experiment, 1922–1936.* Berkeley, Calif., 1977.

David Waldner

Liberal Party

An Israeli centrist party formed in 1961 by members of the General Zionists and Progressives.

The Liberal party is primarily interested in furthering the cause of a strong private sector in the economy with minimal government interference. In 1965 it joined the HERUT PARTY in forming an electoral list called Gahal, causing one of its wings to split off to become the Independent Liberals. The Liberal party continues to exist as an independent entity within the LIKUD. In the Begin cabinet of 1977 one of Liberal's leaders, Simha EHRLICH, served as finance minister; two other Liberals, Yitzhak MODA'I and Moshe Nissim, held the same post in the National Unity government of 1984. Another Liberal leader, Arie Dulzin, served for some time as chairman of the World Zionist Organization.

Walter F. Weiker

Liberal Socialist Party

Egyptian political party, originally the right-wing faction of the Arab Socialist Union.

When President Anwar al-Sadat issued the Party Law of 1977, the Liberal Socialist party began to participate in elections under the leadership of Mustafa Kamil Murad. Its platform calls for decreased state control of the economy, for foreign investment in Egypt, and for political liberalization. The party also advocates the implementation of religious law in order to appeal to the religious right. Liberal Socialists supported Sadat's foreign policy and his peace initiatives with Israel. Murad accompanied Sadat on his trip to Jerusalem in 1977. The party sent twelve deputies to parliament in 1976 but suffered defections to the New Wafd party and to Sadat's National Democratic party. In the 1984 elections, the party received no seats in parliament. In 1987, it entered an alliance with the Muslim Brotherhood and the Socialist Labor party that received 17 percent of the vote. The party publishes a newspaper, *al-Ahrar* (The Liberals).

BIBLIOGRAPHY

HINNEBUSCH, RAYMOND. *Egyptian Politics Under Sadat: The Post-Populist Development of an Authoritarian-Modernizing State.* Cambridge, U.K., 1985.
SAID ALY, ABDEL MONEM. "Democratization in Egypt." *American Arab Affairs* 22 (1987): 11–27.

David Waldner

Liberation Party

Political party of Lebanon.

The Liberation party was founded in 1952 on the West Bank by Taki al-Din NABAHANI. It was an Islamic fundamentalist party that competed with the Muslim Brotherhood for support among the masses.

As'ad AbuKhalil

Liberation Rally

Political party formed by Egypt's Revolutionary Command Council following the January 1953 ban on all existing political parties.

The Liberation Rally was intended to mobilize popular support for the new regime—the FREE OFFICERS who had overthrown the government of King Farouk in a military coup in 1952—by coopting student leaders and workers. The Liberation Rally called for the unconditional withdrawal of the British from the Suez Canal zone, self-determination for Sudan, the establishment of a socialist welfare state, PAN-ARABISM, and the installation of a constitution guaranteeing civic liberties. The rally became associated with Gamal Abdel NASSER in his struggle for supremacy with General Muhammad Naguib, who was supported by the Muslim Brotherhood. Following a clash between the Liberation Rally and the Muslim Brotherhood on the campus of Cairo University in January of 1954, Nasser began to mobilize his support in the Rally against Naguib. After Naguib and his supporters were purged from the government, the Liberation Rally was dissolved.

BIBLIOGRAPHY

GOLDSCHMIDT, ARTHUR, JR. *Modern Egypt: The Formation of a Nation-State.* Boulder, Colo., 1988.

David Waldner

Liberty, USS

U.S. ship attacked by Israel.

On the afternoon of 8 June 1967, the electronic surveillance ship USS *Liberty* was about fourteen nautical miles north of al-Arish, Egypt, gathering intelligence data. It was attacked by three combat aircraft, and subsequently by three motor torpedo boats, belonging to Israel; one of the latter launched a torpedo that demolished the *Liberty*'s communications room and killed twenty-five technicians. A Mayday message from the *Liberty* drew rescue aircraft from the carrier *America,* and Israel stopped the attack. In all, thirty-four crew members of the *Liberty* were killed, and 164 were wounded.

Since the outbreak of hostilities, the *Liberty* had lain outside Egyptian territorial waters, off the Sinai coast north of Port Said and al-Arish, monitoring Egypt's and Israel's radio and radar transmissions.

Israel's attack on the *Liberty* has never been satisfactorily explained, since the ship was displaying the American flag very prominently, and the attack continued even following identification. Although an inquiry chaired by Rear Admiral Kidd found no evidence that the attack was premeditated, military experts have concluded that it could not reasonably be attributed to error, and that Israel must have felt that the information being gathered by the *Liberty* could be sufficiently damaging to its interests that it accepted the risk of incurring the anger of the United States.

Two plausible explanations are (a) that Israel was "cooking" (intercepting and altering) messages between Egypt and Jordan, in hopes of drawing Jordan into the war so that Israel could occupy the West Bank, and (b) that Israel wanted to conceal the true extent of its dramatic victory, so as to delay the imposition of a cease-fire. Israel paid $7 million in damages to the families of the U.S. crewmen but has never admitted culpability.

BIBLIOGRAPHY

DUPUY, TREVOR N. *Elusive Victory: The Arab-Israeli Wars 1947–1974.* Dubuque, Iowa, 1992.
LILIENTHAL, ALFRED M. *The Zionist Connection: What Price Peace.* New York, 1979.

Jenab Tutunji

Libya

Formerly a jamahiriya (a state governed by the masses), today the North African Arab republic of Libya is ruled by strongman Muammar al-Qaddafi.

Libya's population is about 4 million (1990), distributed over 680,000 square miles (1.76 million sq. km)

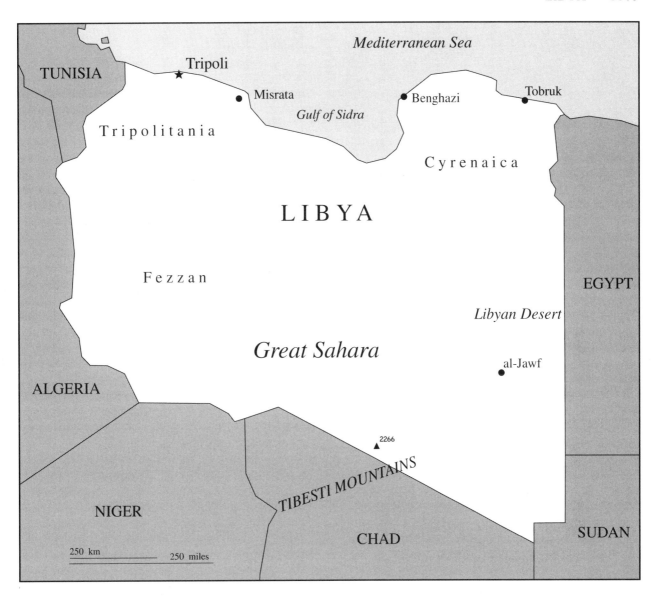

on the northern coast of Africa, bordered to the north by the Mediterranean Sea, to the west by Tunisia and Algeria, to the south by Niger and Chad, and to the east by Sudan and Egypt. The capital city, TRIPOLI, and the other principal urban centers, MISURATA, BENGHAZI, and Derna (or Darnah) are on the coast; several large oases, including Sabha (or Sebha), provincial capital of the southern region of FEZZAN, and Kufrah in the southeast, were major trading centers of the trans-Saharan caravan trade, but they are now principally administrative centers. The population clusters along the coast, where two ranges of hills—Jabal al-Gharb in the western province, Tripolitania, and JABAL AL-AKHDAR in Cyrenaica, the eastern region—divide the narrow coastal plain from the arid plateaus and deserts to the south.

Climate and Resources. Except along the coast, the climate of the country is severe, with wide extremes of temperature, particularly in the mountains and deserts. There is scanty rainfall; even along the coast, the timing of the annual average of eight inches (20 cm) of rain is unpredictable.

As a result, less than 2 percent of the country's surface is arable, and only another 4 to 5 percent is suitable for raising livestock. Much of the country's wealth historically derived from animal husbandry and from the trans-Saharan and coastal trade rather than from agriculture. In the late 1950s, large quantities of petroleum were discovered, and by 1968, oil exports accounted for more than 50 percent of gross domestic product (GDP). Since then, oil has represented some 65 percent of GDP. In 1989, Libya had the highest per capita income in Africa, 5,310 U.S. dollars, and one of the highest population growth rates in the world at 4 percent. Thanks to oil, the government provides very generous welfare benefits to Libyan citizens, and the economy relies

Rail line running along the Mediterranean coast at Benghazi. (Charles Issawi)

heavily on foreign workers; in recent decades more than half a million foreign nationals, mostly Egyptians and Tunisians, have found employment there.

Population and Culture. Libya has a largely homogeneous population, both ethnically and religiously. Virtually all the citizens are Arabs practicing Sunni Islam. Small communities of Berbers, many of whom are followers of Ibadi Islam, still reside in the western hill villages, but nothing remains of the once substantial Jewish community (most of which moved on to Israel). Libya is not home to any major educational or cultural institutions; apart from some locally venerated saintly families, the people of the area traditionally looked to Tunisia and Egypt for their religious teachers and legal authorities. Despite the contemporary urbanization of the country—over two-thirds of the population live in Tripoli and Benghazi alone—the importance of pastoral nomadism in recent history is evident in the continued social and political significance of kinship and tribal ties. Although women are being educated in increasingly large numbers, they ordinarily marry while in their late teens and are not expected to work outside the home.

Government. The Libyan government structure was designed by the ruler, Muammar al-QADDAFI, who holds no formal position of authority but serves as head of state. As he conceives it, Libyans rule themselves without the intervention of elections, politicians, or political parties, through a system of local and national committees and congresses that deliberate, administer, and supervise the affairs of the country on their behalf. By most accounts, the BASIC PEOPLE'S CONGRESSES and committees do fulfill governmental functions at local levels, but in national, particularly foreign, policymaking, Qaddafi and his immediate advisers are believed to make virtually all important decisions.

History. At the beginning of the nineteenth century, today's Libya was three loosely administered provinces of the Ottoman Empire, ruled by the local QARAMANLI DYNASTY in Tripoli. In 1835, disturbed by local unrest, the Ottoman central government overthrew the dynasty, and thereafter Libya was ruled directly from Istanbul.

Although never a rich province, Libya prospered during the second Ottoman era. As the Ottoman order spread throughout the territory, many nomads settled in coastal villages; local agricultural production and trade increased. The Sanusiyya, a religious brotherhood with political aspirations, saw its substantial trading interests flourish in Cyrenaica and the Sahara.

By the end of the nineteenth century, however, Italy had won European acquiescence in its occupation of Libya, and in 1911 Rome launched its long-anticipated invasion. The Ottoman government mounted a major war effort to oppose the Italian encroachment but was soon forced to withdraw, preoccupied by unrest and nationalism in the Balkans. Local Libyan leaders took up the cause of resistance, however, and the Italians faced an armed insurgency until well into the 1930s, only to lose the province a mere decade later in the North African campaigns of World War II. Libya was then governed by British and French military administrations until the country was granted independence by the United Nations at the end of 1951.

The upheavals occasioned by the precipitous withdrawal of the Ottoman administration, the protracted Italian conquest, and the devastating battles for control during World War II left Libya one of the poorest countries in the Middle East. The population was nearly halved by famine, war casualties, and emigration. At independence, illiteracy rates were well over

A corniche at Benghazi. (Charles Issawi)

80 percent, the per capita income was no more than twenty-five U.S. dollars a year, the country's major export was scrap metal scavenged from World War II battlefields. Thus, the British played a large role in establishing and sustaining the government.

The leader of the Sanusiyya brotherhood, IDRIS AL-SAYYID MUHAMMAD AL-SANUSI, had spent the years between the two world wars in exile in Cairo, where he came to know the British authorities, who sponsored him as the king of the new country. Despite Tripolitanian qualms about Idris's partiality for Cyrenaica, provincial leaders acquiesced in his accession to ensure the country's unity and independence. In the early years, the British subsidized Libya's operating budget while the king's clientele and local tribesmen staffed the administration.

The export of commercial quantities of oil in the early 1960s coincided with the heyday of Arab nationalism. A new generation of politically active Libyans argued that the monarchy's close ties with Britain and the United States were now both economically unnecessary and politically undesirable. Moreover, the administration proved unequal to the task of allocating the new wealth, and the government foundered in corruption and mismanagement. On September 1, 1969, a 27-year old captain, Muammar al-Qaddafi, and a small group of his friends and fellow military officers engineered a bloodless coup; the king abdicated as his government collapsed.

At the outset, the new regime appeared to be a typical Arab nationalist military government, with an additional religious (Islamic) coloring, reflecting both Qaddafi's personal piety and the regime's efforts to appeal to the followers of the deposed Sanusi leader. The British and U.S. military bases were closed, the remaining Italian residents were expelled, alcohol was forbidden, nightclubs and churches were closed, and Qaddafi called his fellow rulers to join him in establishing a unified Arab state.

By the mid-1970s, however, with the publication of the first volume of Qaddafi's GREEN BOOK, the Libyan regime began to develop its distinctive profile. Disappointed with the failure of other Arab rulers to heed his calls for immediate and unconditional unity and with the average Libyan's apparent lack of revolutionary fervor, Qaddafi concentrated on domestic affairs, proclaiming a cultural revolution at home. By 1977, Qaddafi had resigned all his official positions, the GENERAL PEOPLE'S CONGRESS had been established, the country's administration given over to the system of committees and congresses outlined in the *Green Book,* and Libya had been declared the first JAMAHIRIYA, or state of the masses.

In part because of accompanying economic reforms—retail trade was abolished as exploitative, wage earners were declared partners in their enter-prises, rent was outlawed and houses given to their occupants—opposition to the new edicts grew quickly. The regime reacted harshly. In the early 1980s, "revolutionary committees" were established to ensure the revolutionary enthusiasm of the Libyan people, and it was these committees that carried out the assassination of Libyan opposition figures abroad.

By then, the regime had grown disenchanted with Arab leaders and devoted itself to exporting the Libyan revolution throughout the world. As a result, Qaddafi found himself in disputes not only with his neighbors but with the Western powers, particularly the United States. Accusing Qaddafi of having harbored terrorists and sponsored terrorism throughout the world, the Reagan administration bombed Tripoli and Benghazi in April 1986 in hopes of reforming (if not removing) the Libyan leader.

Yet, despite both its international isolation and the economic difficulties precipitated by the fall of oil prices in the mid-1980s, it was not until the collapse in 1991 of its international patron, the Soviet Union, that the Qaddafi regime began to show signs of moderating its opposition to the international status quo. A period of discernable domestic relaxation marked the late 1980s, as private retail trade was reintroduced and political prisoners were released. This trend slowed, however, when having been accused of complicity in the December 1988 terrorist bombing of a transatlantic flight, Pan Am 103, Libya was subjected to United Nations–sponsored economic sanctions in 1991 for failing to extradite the two men indicted for the action.

BIBLIOGRAPHY

ANDERSON, LISA S. *The State and Social Transformation in Tunisia and Libya, 1930–1980.* Princeton, N.J., 1986.
DAVIS, JOHN. *Libyan Politics: Tribe and Revolution.* Berkeley, Calif., 1987.
EVANS-PRITCHARD, E. E. *The Sanusi of Cyrenaica.* London, 1949.
KHADDURI, MAJID. *Modern Libya: A Study in Political Development.* Baltimore, 1963.
WRIGHT, JOHN. *Libya: A Modern History.* London, 1981.

Lisa Anderson

LICA

The abbreviation for the League against German Anti-Semitism, Association Formed by all Jewish Works and Institutions in Egypt.

LICA (Ligue contre l'Antisémitisme Allemand, Association Formée par Toutes les Oeuvres et Institutions Juives en Egypte) was founded in April 1933 as part of the mass protests organized by the Cairo B'nai

B'rith against rising German anti-Semitism. Among the leading founders was Léon CASTRO, lawyer, journalist, and Wafd party activist.

In September 1933, the organization joined the International League against German Anti-Semitism (also abbreviated as LICA), which had recently been formed in Amsterdam, the Netherlands, with Castro as its vice-president. About the same time, a youth section, LISCA (Ligue Internationale Scolaire contre l'Antisémitisme; International Student League against Anti-Semitism) was founded in Egypt. By 1935, LICA counted about 1,500 members, and LISCA had about 650.

LICA organized an active campaign in Egypt's Hebrew- and European-language press. It also undertook a boycott of German goods and films. The boycott was most successful in barring German films from Egyptian theaters and in affecting the sale of a number of German products. Egyptian and British officials fearing possible disorders and financial repercussions, however, intervened to halt the boycott, which continued unofficially thereafter on an individual level.

BIBLIOGRAPHY

KRÄMER, GUDRUN. *The Jews in Modern Egypt, 1914–1952.* Seattle, 1989.

Norman Stillman

Lifschitz, Uri   [1936–   ]

Israeli painter.

Born at Kibbutz Givat ha-Sheloshah, Lifschitz is a leading representative of the "new figuration" in Israeli art. His paintings combine abstractionism and expressionism—superimposed on an abstract background are grotesque, contorted figures contoured in black.

In 1971, 1973, and 1978 he worked in Spain, where he was inspired by the works of Goya and Velasquez. He has received many awards, among them the Marc Chagall Fellowship and the Kolb Prize in Tel Aviv; he has exhibited widely in Israel and, to a lesser extent, in Europe.

Ann Kahn

Ligue Tunisienne pour la Défense des Droits de l'Homme [LTDH]

Tunisian human rights organization.

The Tunisian League for the Defense of Human Rights (LTDH) was founded in May 1977. All ma-

jor political groups were represented on its executive committee, with the preponderance being members of the Parti Socialiste Destourien (Destour Socialist party; PSD). Its makeup indicated that it was more of a political body.

By 1982 the LTDH had 1,000 members in 24 local chapters. By 1985, it had 3,000 members in 33 sections, and four years later it had 4,000 adherents in 40 sections (there were still 40 chapters as of December 1993).

In 1985 the LTDH decided it needed a charter to define precisely what it stood for and to prevent any one group within it from seizing control and dictating its political position. Members decided that the United Nations Universal Declaration of Human Rights (UDHR) would be adopted as the model but modified to fit Tunisian conditions. Internal debates focused on the adaptations of the articles on the rights to change one's religion and to marry a non-Muslim, and the rights of illegitimate children.

After 1980 the LTDH began to expand its activities from purely political cases to human rights for those in prison, those who alleged torture by the police and government authorities, members of socioeconomic groups, women and children, and those who alleged ethnic discrimination. It encountered government opposition because of its scrutiny of preventive detention, torture, and other human rights abuses committed by the authorities.

In March 1992, the National Assembly passed a law that sought to tame the LTDH and bring it under PSD control or effect its dissolution by June 15. Refusing to comply, the LTDH dissolved itself. The ensuing international outcry led the regime to reconsider the law. On March 26, 1993, under pressure from President Zayn al-Abidine Ben Ali, the court authorized temporary resumption of the league's operations. According to a report by the Driss Commission in April 1993, prison abuses had declined, and security personnel had received training to ensure their respect for human rights.

As of 1995, the president of the league is Moncef Marzouki; its secretary-general is Taoufik Bouderbala.

BIBLIOGRAPHY

AMNESTY INTERNATIONAL. "Tunisia: Prolonged Incommunicado Detention and Torture." March 1992.
DWYER, KEVIN. *Arab Voices: The Human Rights Debate in the Middle East.* Berkeley, Calif., 1991.
LAWYERS COMMITTEE FOR HUMAN RIGHTS. "The Mass Trial of Islamists before Military Courts in Tunisia." New York, August 21, 1992.

Larry A. Barrie

Likud

An Israeli electoral bloc established in 1973.

Originally, Likud consisted of several independent parties: the HERUT PARTY, the LIBERAL PARTY, the Free Center, State List, and part of the LAND OF ISRAEL MOVEMENT. Much of the emphasis of its program has been on extension of Israeli sovereignty to the territories conquered in the ARAB–ISRAEL WAR OF 1967. It also called for improvement of the social and economic conditions of disadvantaged communities known as Oriental Jews (EDOT HA-MIZRAH).

Taking advantage of public disenchantment with the LABOR PARTY in 1977, Likud won forty-three Knesset seats and formed a coalition government led by Menachem Begin, which continued until 1984. In that year, neither Likud nor the Labor Alignment bloc won enough to form a coalition without the other. The two joined in a NATIONAL UNITY GOVERNMENT in which Likud leader Yitzhak Shamir held the office of prime minister for half of the electoral period, and the blocs divided other government offices. In 1988, Likud and other right-wing and religious parties improved their showing, and Shamir again led the government until the Labor victory of 1992. During its years in power, Likud strongly resisted surrendering sovereignty over the Palestinian territories and made little progress in reducing the role of the government in the economy. One of Likud's problems has been the presence in it of several strong individuals and their factions, including Shamir, former Chief of Staff Ariel Sharon, and Moroccan leader David Levy—all of whom have tried vigorously to become dominant. In 1993, the Likud chairmanship was won by Binyamin Netanyahu, former ambassador to the United Nations and brother to the hero of the Israeli raid on Entebbe. He defeated his former rivals as well as younger figures like Ze'ev Begin, with a spirited campaign based on American-style politics and effective use of the media, even though it was an election confined to party members.

Walter F. Weiker

Lilienblum, Moses Leib   [1843–1910]

Russian Zionist writer and philosopher.

Lilienblum received an Orthodox education and was a recognized scholar of the Talmud. His major activity was as a publicist and social critic. For most of his early career, he advocated normalization of Jewish life in Russia and closer association with that country's non-Jews, as well as an evolutionary concept of religious practice, in the spirit of HASKALA (enlightenment). As political difficulties increased in Russia, he also demanded equal rights. After the pogroms in the late 1870s, however, he became an ardent Zionist and one of the first Russian writers to campaign for the return of Jews to Palestine. One of his main associations was the HIBBAT ZION movement. In addition to these political activities, Lilienblum was a renowned literary critic. His approach has been described as anti-aesthetic pragmatism, stressing the usefulness of art to society and that "the Jewish people wanted to live for the sake of life and not for any purpose beyond life." His influence was based on the great simplicity as well as the logic of his writings.

Walter F. Weiker

Liman von Sanders, Otto   [1855–1929]

German general in World War I.

One of the most important German officers in the Eastern Theater, Liman von Sanders was appointed commander of the Ottoman First Army in 1913. With Mustafa Kemal, he led Ottoman forces at GALLIPOLI in 1915. In 1918 he was made commander of Ottoman forces in Syria, where he slowed the advance of the ARAB REVOLT and the British expeditionary force. His memoirs of the war, *Five Years in Turkey,* were published in 1927.

BIBLIOGRAPHY

FROMKIN, DAVID. *A Peace to End All Peace.* New York, 1989.

Zachary Karabell

Lira

The monetary unit of Turkey, Syria, and Lebanon.

The lira is equivalent to 100 *kurush* or piastres. It was originally the name of an Italian silver coin and is still the monetary unit of Turkey.

[*See also:* Qirsh]

Marilyn Higbee

Lisan al-Hal

Lebanese daily newspaper published in Arabic since 1877.

Lisan al-Hal, founded by Khalil Sarkis in October 1877, has been published continuously ever since.

After Lebanon became independent from France in 1945/46, the paper had no significant political role. It was so overwhelmed by competition from other newspapers that it decided to publish at noon. The noon edition of the paper was popular not because of any original reporting—in fact, most of its items were taken from newspapers that appeared earlier in the day—but because it was sold during the midday rush hour. It also hired famous writers, such as the poet Sa'id AKL, to write regular columns.

As'ad AbuKhalil

LISCA

The abbreviation for the International Student League against Anti-Semitism

LISCA (Ligue Internationale Scolaire contre l'Antisémitisme) was founded in Egypt in September 1933 as the Jewish students' section of LICA (Ligue contre l'Antisémitisme Allemand; League against German Anti-Semitism). LICA had been formed earlier that year in the wake of Egyptian Jewry's protest against Nazi anti-Semitism. By 1934, LISCA's membership had grown to about 650.

Both LICA and LISCA included members who were sympathetic to ZIONISM, but unlike the mainstream liberals who formed the backbone of LICA, LISCA attracted a considerable number of activist youth with Marxist leanings. Rivalries and clashes developed between the Zionists and the Marxists. In Alexandria, in August 1935, a group of the latter led by Raymond Castro, son of Léon Castro, one of the founders of LICA, broke away to form its own association, Jeunesse contre l'Antisémitisme (Youth against Anti-Semitism; JICA). The non-Zionist JICA adopted as its motto "Liberty, Fraternity, Peace."

BIBLIOGRAPHY

KRÄMER, GUDRUN. *The Jews in Modern Egypt, 1914–1952.* Seattle, 1989.

Norman Stillman

Litani Operation

The 1978 Israeli invasion of Lebanon.

Following a Palestine Liberation Organization (PLO) assault on the Mediterranean coast of Israel that killed thirty-seven Israelis, twenty thousand troops of the Israel Defense Forces (IDF) in March 1978 occupied south Lebanon to the Litani river. An estimated two thousand Lebanese and Palestinians were killed during the invasion, intended to clear the region of PLO guerrillas.

The IDF occupied a stretch of territory thirty-seven miles (60 km) long and three to six miles (5 to 10 km) wide for more than three months, thereafter ceding it as a buffer zone to UNIFIL (United Nations Interim Force in Lebanon) peacekeeping forces and an Israeli-supported Christian Lebanese militia headed by Sa'd HADDAD. The Litani operation served as a model for Israel's 1982 invasion of Lebanon (the Arab–Israel War of 1982).

BIBLIOGRAPHY

FISK, ROBERT. *Pity the Nation.* New York, 1990.
SCHIFF, ZE'EV. *A History of the Israeli Army.* New York, 1985.

Elizabeth Thompson

Litani River

River in Lebanon.

Flowing entirely within Lebanon, the Litani rises in the Biqa' valley and flows south between the Leba-

The Litani river and surrounding countryside near Beaufort, Lebanon. (D.W. Lockhard)

non mountains to the west and the anti-Lebanon mountains to the east until Nabatiya, where it turns sharply to the west crosses Lebanon and empties into the Mediterranean Sea.

The major Litani development plan, initiated in the 1950s, was concluded in 1966; it includes the Qar'un reservoir and the Awali hydroelectric power station, which utilizes the water diverted via a tunnel. Hydropower and domestic use receive priority over irrigation, and Shi'ite farmers in the south resent this, fearing diversion of all the water to the north.

After 1971, the growth in southern Lebanon of the Palestine Liberation Organization (PLO)—by refugees from the Jordanian Civil War—resulted in a rise in hostilities in that border area with Israel. These led in 1978 to Operation Litani by Israel and the 1982 ARAB–ISRAEL WAR. The fear exists in Lebanon that Israel will divert the Litani to join the Jordan River system, but Israel has replied that this is politically unfeasible.

BIBLIOGRAPHY

NAFF, THOMAS, and RUTH C. MATSON, eds. *Water in the Middle East, Conflict or Cooperation?* Boulder, Colo., 1984.

Sara Reguer

Literature, Arabic

Arabic literature of the nineteenth and twentieth centuries broke new stylistic ground.

Arabic literature has its roots in pre-Islamic odes, enshrining prosodic and thematic conventions that remained unchallenged centuries after the ethos of desert life had ceased to be widely applicable. The emergence of historic Islam in the seventh century C.E. and, above all, the dogma that the Qur'an is the actual word of God and its miraculous eloquence gave the language of that period an all but hallowed character—which was perpetuated in writing although displaced by local uninflected vernaculars in everyday Arabic speech.

The literary tradition was therefore tinged with a conservative and puristic quality that gave it uncommon homogeneity and continuity. Its conservativeness also insulated it from daily concerns, so that the uneducated majority turned instead to regional folk literatures that were ignored or even despised by the establishment. Nevertheless, changes did occur. One was a growing taste for verbal ornaments, such as the paronomasia and the double entendre. What modern Arabs inherited from the immediate past, therefore, was the literature of a conservative elite, in which correctness, convention, and linguistic virtuosity were prized above content or originality.

By the 1800s, the encroachments of Europe brought new perceptions to Arab intellectuals, who came to admire the very power used against them and sought the knowledge that made it possible. By the 1870s, especially in Egypt and the Levant, a new westward-looking elite had emerged. From it came the producers and consumers of the new literature.

The conscious adaptation of literary standards to changed conditions was gradual. The earliest Arab intellectuals with extensive opportunity to get to know Europe, such as the perceptive Rifa'a al-Rafi al-TAHTAWI and the more mercurial Faris (later, Ahmad Faris) al-SHIDYAQ, were aware that Europeans had different concepts of literature than Arabs did, but they deemed them inferior. And yet a new form of writing was coming into being, which was evident wherever there was a need to convey information (as in the books of these very travelers). It was fostered in translations, even nonliterary ones, where Arabic had to accommodate notions never before expressed; and it was important to a new Middle Eastern profession—born of an imported technology—journalism.

The new direction was strikingly illustrated in the career of Abd Allah al-Nadim (1845–1896), the fiery orator of the Urabi rebellion. He was well established as a master of finely bejeweled rhymed prose, but when he took to journalism, he faced up to the need to reach a wide public. He experimented, briefly, with writing an occasional piece entirely in the vernacular; but the choice he deliberately made was to use a vocabulary as close as possible to that of everyday speech without deviating from the rules of classical Arabic grammar. Others have since wrestled with the strains and anomalies of writing in the Arabic idiom that no one speaks and, indeed, the colloquial has gained a large measure of acceptance in the theater and a more grudging one in the dialogue of novels and short stories. But al-Nadim's practice has prevailed among prose writers for at least eighty years, with only a few in the last generation allowing themselves liberties with the syntax as well.

The transformation was not merely stylistic; by the 1870s, admiration of Europe's successes in science and technology was extended, by a loose association, to political, social, and philosophic endeavors as well. The adoption of European aesthetic norms could not lag far behind. By the turn of the twentieth century, direct and unadorned prose was widely recognized as not only functional but also literarily desirable. Because the learned were few, the principal medium of dissemination was the periodical press, so some major literary works were serialized *before* appearing in book form.

With little to encourage specialization in any one genre, the recognized stylists found their main vehicle in short prose pieces, such as the moralistic essays and tearful narratives of Mustafa Lutfi al-Manfaluti (1876–1924). Indeed, the first half of the twentieth century was dominated by immensely prolific and versatile writers, among whom were Taha HUSAYN and Abbas Mahmud al-AQQAD. They were virtually all secularist and liberal sociopolitically, and romantic in their literary inclinations. Although few set out their aesthetic principles systematically, they accustomed their generation to seek neither formalism nor virtuosity in literature but sincerity and emotion. Experience and maturity, the events of World War II, the subsequent decline of Britain and France, and above all, the challenges of independence in tandem with the turmoil of the Palestinians caused the next generation to turn away from romanticism. The keynote of postwar Arabic writing has been political commitment and realism, strongly tinged with socialism.

The prose style of the West fostered genres previously unknown in Arabic literature. In particular, narratives had suffered from their status as folk art, so that the only form to have gained acceptance was the maqama—a short piece that usually recounted, in highly ornate prose, some petty fraud perpetrated by an amiable rogue. By the end of the nineteenth century, there was a growing public demand for short stories and novels of the European type. The demand was readily met by translations, adaptations, or imitations. The short story proved particularly suitable to the needs of journals and an excellent medium for the piecemeal propagation of new ideas and perceptions. In its Arabic garb, it was brought to a high level of sophistication, as early as the 1920s, by such authors as Mahmud Taymur (1894–1973).

The novel was a more difficult form, especially in the absence of an Arabic tradition. Translations and adaptations apart, a pioneering attempt at a long narrative was made by Muhammad al-Muwaylihi (1858–1930) in *Hadith Isa ibn Hisham* (The Discourse of Isa ibn Hisham), where a resurrected pasha has a series of adventures, offering opportunities to comment on social changes. The fact that it borrows the name of the narrator, and, in places, the style of its only classical predecessor has caused it to be labeled an extended maqama; but the purpose it serves is different, and its link to the novel form is tenuous.

Jurji Zaydan, the indefatigable owner and editor of the journal *al-Hilal*, published more than a score of romances, each twined around some episode of Islamic history—but invention in them is minimal. The first novel of recognized merit rooted in contemporary Arab life was *Zaynab*, the story of a village girl married against her will; it was written by Muhammad Husayn HAYKAL in 1910/11 and first published anonymously. No others of consequence were published until the 1930s, when several writers with already established reputations, such as Taha Husayn, Mahmud Taymur, and Ibrahim Abd al-Qadir al-Mazini (1890–1949), turned to the novel. Greater progress was made under the banner of realism, notably by Najib MAHFUZ, the first Arab to devote most of his energies to one genre. His abundant, varied, and highly competent production earned him the Nobel Prize for literature in 1988.

Even more than the novel, the theater was hindered by the absence of any regional precedent, except as folk art, and by resistance to the use of the Arabic colloquial—even between unlearned characters and before mixed audiences. Yet drama made a comparatively early start; the first performance was *The Miser*—a play which, although not a translation, owed a great deal to the great French comedic playwright Molière (1622–1673). It was produced in Beirut (Lebanon) in 1847 by Marun al-Naqqash (1818–1855). His company, and several others that branched out of it or imitated it, found acceptance in Egypt—but their activities were looked upon as mere entertainment. In fact, although some writers established in other genres also tried to write plays, no Arab acquired a reputation as a playwright until the 1930s, when Tawfiq al-HAKIM, who had had experience as a hack writer for a theatrical company, returned from a period of study in Paris determined to give drama a recognized place among literary arts. His long career, marked by productivity and versatility even into old age, has brought him fame and inspired an impressive group of new playwrights.

In contrast to the newly imported genres, Arabic poetry had a long and rich tradition; its progress to modernity has, consequently, followed a somewhat different course. In the first three quarters of the nineteenth century, poets perpetuated the highly ornate style of their immediate predecessors. When the times called for a less ornamental and more purposeful poetry, the practice of the most talented was to turn not to European models but to the example of early poets from an equally dynamic age. By the turn of the century, a school now known as the neoclassical quickly attained a high level of accomplishment, emulating the grandiloquent odes of Abbasid poets but addressing the public issues of the day. Its leading exponents were Ahmad SHAWQI and Muhammad Hafiz IBRAHIM.

Resonant as they were, their voices were not the only ones to be heard. Others favored more radical initiatives and the expression of more personal emotions. From afar, from outside the Arab heartlands, Syrian Christian émigrés to the Americas, headed by Khalil GIBRAN, echoed a type of poetry long accepted in the West. Not least influential were the leading critics—al-Aqqad and Taha Husayn—who harried the neoclassicists for not equaling the subtleties of the British poet Shelley or the French poet Lamartine. The leanings of these various groups were unmistakable, and after the death of Ahmad Shawqi and Hafiz Ibrahim, the romanticism already evident in prose became evident in poetry as well.

Another new note was sounded in 1949, when two Iraqis—Badr Shakir al-SAYYAB and Nazik al-MALA'IKA—almost simultaneously published their first experiments with free verse. The adoption of lines of uneven length with muted rhymes irregularly arranged, or with no rhymes at all, was the most radical departure ever from classical Arabic poetry. No less significant is that the movement grew—and has continued to grow—out of perceptions shared with Western poets of international stature, chief among whom initially was T. S. Eliot (1888–1965). Most revolutionary of all has been its purpose; for it has given rise to a host of committed poets often able to give tongue to their predicaments as individuals and, at the same time, as Arabs and as humanists. Contributors to all genres are now at one in viewing themselves as individuals sharing in a distinctive experience but informed by a universal consciousness.

BIBLIOGRAPHY

BADAWI, MUSTAFA. *Modern Arabic Drama in Egypt*. Cambridge, U.K., 1988.
BRUGMAN, J. *An Introduction to the History of Modern Arabic Literature in Egypt*. Leiden, Neth., 1984.
CACHIA, PIERRE. *An Overview of Modern Arabic Literature*. Edinburgh, 1991.
JAYYUSI, SALMA KHADRA. *Trends and Movements in Modern Arabic Poetry*. Leiden, Neth., 1977.

Pierre Cachia

Literature, Arabic, North African

North African writers convey their ideas in French and Arabic in a variety of literary genres.

The three countries of the MAGHRIB—ALGERIA, MOROCCO, and TUNISIA—share more than common geographic boundaries. They succumbed to some of the same foreign invasions in the past and fell victim to the same colonial power in modern times: France. Colonial rule in the countries of the Maghrib differed only in its strength and its duration, Algeria having endured the longest and most traumatizing occupation.

The French army landed on the coast of Algeria in 1830 and completed its occupation of the country in 1881. Tunisia was conquered in 1880, and in 1912 Morocco was colonized. Algeria was a French province from 1848 until it achieved independence in 1962; the other two remained protectorates until 1956.

In Algeria, Arabic lost its efficacy long before French was declared the official language in 1938. Algerians conceded the fact that the language of the colonizer was the language of bread. However, being the language of Islam, Arabic maintained its place in the lives of the people, even for the Berbers, who spoke various dialects. It became primarily the language of religious teaching and practice.

Culturally, Morocco and Tunisia experienced French colonialism in a more subdued manner because they had centers of Arabic learning—the al-Qarawiyyin in Fez and the Zaytuna in Tunis—that safeguarded and continued an existing cultural tradition. Many schools opted for bilingual instruction, so Arabic was on a par with French.

The linguistic situation in the Maghrib shaped the lives of the population and provoked heated polemics between the partisans of French and those of Arabic, particularly in Algeria. Although it remains an issue on the cultural scene due to the growing number of writers expressing themselves in French, it has lost its political connotation.

The three countries of the Maghrib are similar in the role assumed by traditional Muslim centers, the ZAWIYAS. Jealous of their power over the population and intent on playing a role in the political arena, the religious authorities in those centers placed themselves in an ambiguous position in relation to the French. The French used them to legitimize their presence and gain the support of the local population. Aided by widespread illiteracy, the zawiyas maintained their control until they were challenged by the reformists known as the SALAFIYYA MOVEMENT, who were increasingly alarmed by the interference of the colonial administration in the religious affairs of their countries. The Algerian Reda HUHU ridiculed the official imams appointed by the colonial authorities and even spoke of an "official Islam," in contrast to the "people's Islam," in his *Ma Himar al-Hakim* (Conversations with al-Hakim's Donkey).

Following in the footsteps of the Salafiyya of the Mashreq, Maghribi intellectuals such as Allal al-FASI (1910–1974) in Morocco, Abd al-Hamid BEN BADIS in Algeria, and Mohammad al-Fadel Ben Ashour (1909–1970) and Mohammad al-Taher Ben Ashour

(1879–1973) in Tunisia, confronted the leaders of the zawiyas. Their aim was to prove the compatibility of Islam and modernity, and the absence of a contradiction between progress, even in a Western context, and Islam. Their position appealed to the Maghribi youth. Opening up to the West, however, did not occur without a price, even for the French-educated Maghribis. The cultural encounter between East and West provoked sparks that burned many devotees. The clash of the two civilizations was successfully dramatized by the Moroccan Driss CHRAIBI, the Algerian Moulaoud MAMMERI (1917–1989) in his novel *Le Sommeil du Juste* (1955; The Sleep of the Just), and the Tunisian Albert MEMMI (b. 1920). The latter endured hardships as a Tunisian Jew caught between family traditions, colonial policy, and Nazi ideology, which he related in his novel *La Statue de Sel* (1953; The Statue of Salt).

Maghribi writers writing in French appear to be finally reconciled with their native culture and at ease in their entity. Those such as the Algerian Habib Tengour (b. 1947), the Tunisian Abdelwahhab MEDDEB (b. 1946) and the Moroccan Taher ben Jelloun (b. 1944) dug in their Arab Islamic history and their folk heritage in search of subject matter for their works. Independence has, in a certain way, liberated the writers from a guilt feeling vis-à-vis the French language. The 1980s witnessed an explosion of literary production in the Maghrib: in the various literary genres, in prose and in verse, in Arabic and French.

Particularly prominent in this trend are the women writers. They are slowly filling a space that for many years was dominated by the lone presence of the Algerian novelist Assia DJEBAR (b. 1936). Approaching the women's world from a romantic angle, her writings have shed much of the traditional sentimentalism. With her last two novels, *L'Amour, la Fantasia* (1985) and *Ombre Sultane* (1987), she achieved a new depth by mixing history and fiction. Algeria's long list of women writing in French includes established names such as Leila SEBBAR, Aicha LEMSINE, and Anna Greki (1931–1966), and new names such as Hawa Djabali (b. 1949) and Miriam Ben (b. 1928). Women writing in Arabic, on the other hand, have relied more on poetry to express themselves. Some of the early poets, such as Ahlam Mustaghanmi (b. 1953), are now silent, but new voices such as Zeinab al-A'waj are being heard. In Tunisia, Hélé Béji contrasted traditional and modern cultures in her first novel, *L'Oeil du Jour* (1985). Novelists writing in Arabic have preceded her, such as Hind Azzouz (b. 1926), Nadjia Thamer (b. 1926), Arusiyya Naluti (b. 1950), and the poet Zoubeida Béchir (b. 1938). In Morocco, Khanatha Bannounah (b. 1940) has con-

tributed four collections of short stories and two novels, *al-nar wa al-Ikhtiyar* (1968; Fire and Choice) and *Al-Ghad wal'-Ghadab* (1981; Anger and the Further).

The boundaries of the Maghribi writers have expanded tremendously, both geographically and culturally. Consequently, it is impossible to ignore the growing presence of Maghribi literature outside the countries of the Maghrib, both in Europe and in the Americas. Many writers live and work outside the Maghrib, a situation that exposes them to various cultures. The Tunisian Mustafa TLILI brings his American experience to his novels, and the writings of a Tunisian residing in Canada, Hédi Bouraoui (b. 1932), reveal a rich canvas on which multiple Western cultures intertwine with Maghribi folklore.

It is important to stress the role that private publishing houses in the Maghrib have played in the promotion of literature. They have freed aspiring young writers from the financial constraints and the delays caused by a bureaucracy.

Algeria. To counteract the impact of French culture, the ASSOCIATION OF ALGERIAN MUSLIM ULAMA was founded in 1931 by Abd al-Hamid Ben Badis (1889–1940). Its motto was "Algeria is my country, Islam is my religion, and Arabic is my language." The Association contributed to the revival of the Arabic language and the launching of a significant literary movement through its schools and its press. Well-known literary figures such as Ahmad Reda Huhu and Zuhur Wanisi (b. 1936) either taught in the schools of the Association or studied there. Both fiction and poetry were published in their two papers, *Ash-Shihab* (1925–1939) and *Al-Basa'ir* (1935–1956). It is fair to say that modern Arabic literature in Algeria was born in the shadow of the association.

While fiction in Arabic was in an early stage and limited to short stories, fiction in French made its first appearance in the period between the two world wars. However, the most significant novel, *Le Fils du Pauvre,* by Mouloud Feraoun (1913–1962), was not published until 1950. Its author stated that his motivation to write was his desire to present a true portrait of the Algerian people, in reaction to Albert Camus's novels dealing with life in Algeria. Although the early novels were more ethnographic in character, the tone became increasingly political as most writers set out to define and defend their national cause. They voiced the people's aspiration to freedom, described the social ills, and condemned France's repressive colonial policy. The nascent literary movement coincided with the heightened political consciousness of the Algerians through their participation in the Etoile Nord Africaine, a party established in 1925 by Maghribis in France.

The Algerian War of Independence (1954–1962) was another literary catalyst. It became the topic of choice for novelists, short story writers, poets, and playwrights, especially after independence. Few, however, succeeded in reproducing the tragic and momentous events of the struggle without writing documentary-type works. The most original novel on the subject is Mohammed DIB's (b. 1920) *Qui se Souvient de la Mer* (1962). Writers dwelt on the war years, using incidents mainly to incriminate the parasites and the false nationalists who exploited the ideals of the revolution and the memory of the martyrs. Rachid BOUDJEDRA (b. 1941) pointed the finger at the new leadership and their coconspirators, the religious authorities, in his novel *La Répudiation* (1969).

The literature written in French gained momentum in the decade following independence while Arabic lagged behind. It took Arabic literature more than a decade after independence to establish itself as a viable partner for that in French. The latter was not expected to survive for long after independence, in view of Algeria's Arabization policy. The prediction did not materialize, but the advocates of the two languages engaged in heated polemics on the merits of one over the other. Although the debates subsided in virulence, the linguistic choice of the Maghribi writers remains a common question for debate. The two literary trends pursue parallel paths with few encounters. The only writer to cross the language barrier is, so far, Rachid Boudjedra. His novel *Al-Tafakkuk* (1982; The Dismantling) began the trend of writing novels in Arabic and translating them into French.

As time passed, writers' interest shifted to various themes, some social, others personal or philosophical. Minority groups such as the Berbers used their writings to promote their heritage. The most committed writer of the postindependence period was Mouloud Mammeri. Meaningful works also were published by the novelist Nabil Fares (b. 1940). Before them, the Amrouche family—Jean el-Mouhouv (1906–1962); his mother, Fadhma (1882–1967); and his sister, Marguerite-Taos (1913–1976)—endeavored to safeguard the Berber folk heritage.

One of Algeria's most prolific writers, and one of its greatest, who shifted his attention to other topics following independence, is Mohammed Dib. Between his well-known trilogy, *Algeria* (*La Grande Maison,* 1952; *L'Incendie,* 1954; and *Le Métier à Tisser,* 1957), and his latest novel, *L'Infante Maure* (1994), the author traversed a path that led him from a direct approach and straightforward style to the depths of abstraction. Dib was among those writers who believed that the role of writers as advocates for the national cause was over with their country's achieving independence. Another who began writing in

the colonial period and continues today is the poet Noureddine Aba (b. 1921). Since Algeria's independence he dedicated his efforts to other Arab causes, particularly to the Palestinian problem. Two of his poetic plays, *Montjoie Palestine* (1970; Palestine, My Joy) and *Tel El-Zaatar S'est Tu à la Tombée de la Nuit* (1981; Tel El-Zaatar Fell Silent at Night) concern the latter. Many of the younger poets writing in Arabic have expressed a great affinity with the ordeal of the Palestinian people.

The younger generation of writers, those who did not experience the war years, manifested a particular concern with the political leadership's handling of the political, financial, and social affairs of the country. Writers such as Taher DJAOUT, Rachid MIMOUNI, and the poet Hamid Skif (1951) did not mince their words in criticizing the government.

Other angry voices were heard around the Mediterranean in the mid-1980s. They are those of the second generation of Maghribi immigrants, mainly Algerians living in France (and in Belgium), known as Beurs. They decried their feelings of loss and their search for identity in violent texts that reflected deep frustration. Although some novels have achieved notoriety—such as Farida Belghoul's (b. 1958) *Georgette* (1986), Sakina Boukhedenna's (b. 1959) *Journal* and *Nationalité: Immigré(e)* (1987), and Mehdi Charef's (b. 1952) *Le Thé au Harem d'Archi Ahmed* (1983; *Tea in the Harem,* 1989), most of the Beurs remain the authors of a single book. Their movement, however, is significant for its global nature.

Morocco. Morocco's modern literary history is in many aspects similar to Tunisia's. Its proximity to the Iberian Peninsula, however, has added an extra dimension to its culture. The Arab Islamic heritage of Andalusia and the flight of many Andalusians, both Muslims and Jews, to Morocco, at the reconquest of Spain, acted as a historical and cultural link with this part of Europe. Because French occupation came late to Morocco and as a result of the political organization of the territory, French culture did not deeply or easily infiltrate the educational foundations of the country. It was also counteracted by the Arab Islamic cultural activities centered in Fez.

The two writers who dominated the colonial period and wrote in French, Driss Chraibi and Ahmad SEFRIOU, did not promote French ideals. The former denounced the traumatic impact of Western civilization and the hardships of the emigrant workers in France. Sefriou, on the other hand, revived the folk literature of his country, thus drawing the line between his world and the Western world. Whereas Sefriou pursues the same path today, Chraibi has become, in his latest novels, an advocate of the Berber cause. Another writer, Mohammad Khair Ed-dine (b. 1941) has shown strong connections with his country in spite of his vagabond life and the many years he spent outside Morocco. A younger novelist, Taher Benjelloun (b. 1944), has achieved fame and has won the Prix Goncourt for his novel *La Nuit Sacrée* (1987). This event crowned a long list of novels innovative in style and form.

Parallel to an important literary movement in French, Morocco counts an impressive array of distinguished writers expressing themselves in Arabic: Mohammad Ezzeddine Tazi (b. 1948) and Mohammad Zafzaf (b. 1946), to name only two. Many among them, such as al-Miloudi Shaghmoum (b. 1947) and Abdessalam al-Boqqali (b. 1932) are bilingual and have used their multiculturalism to produce original works reflecting the new trend in the European novel. A few, such as Mohammad Aziz al-Habbabi (b. 1922), write in both Arabic and French. Many of the novels written in the middle of the century were historical, stressing the authors' pride in their past.

Poetry is a particularly popular genre in Morocco among those writing in Arabic and in French. The imprisonment of Abdellatif LAABI for his daring critical works shows the efficacy of this literary genre.

Traditional in form and patriotic in content at its beginning, Moroccan literature has taken a more personal and philosophical trend since the mid-1970s, with a tendency for renewal and experimentation in form and style.

Tunisia. The history of Tunisia's culture differs from that of its neighbor, Algeria. Tunisia benefited from the activities of the Zaytuna mosque-university and the Sadiqi college; both were instrumental in preserving and promoting Arabic culture. The country's close contacts with the Mashriq were another asset in its rich literary activities. Tunisian writers contributed to the NAHDA, the literary revival in the Arab world. The most significant input came from the poet Abu al-Qasim al-SHABBI.

The majority of the Tunisian writers expressed themselves in Arabic. During the period between the two world wars, writers benefited from the journal *Al-Alam al-Adabi* (1930–1952; The Literary World), which encouraged members of the young generation. The most famous group of this period, known as Jama'at Taht al-Sur (Below the Wall Group), counted such established authors as Ali al-DOU'AJI and Ahmad al-Mes'adi. A similar role was assumed by the journal *Al-Fikr* (1955–1986) in the second half of the century.

Tunisia had very few writers in French during the colonial period. The best known among them was Albert Memmi, now residing in France. Surprisingly, their numbers have soared in the last two decades. Although writing in French, they borrow heavily from their Arab Islamic heritage. A few, such as Salah Garmadi (1933–1982) and Taher Bakri (b. 1951), are bilingual poets.

Arabic literature in Tunisia, especially fiction, continues to flourish. It is a field for innovation and experimentation both in style and in form. The national and patriotic types of the early period gave way to a broader variety of subjects; the tone also became less moralizing. It is not unusual to find writers contributing to more than one literary genre, producing novels, short stories, and plays. The theater, too, has had revival in Tunisia through the efforts of Izziddin al-Madani (b. 1938). Thanks to the numerous cultural festivals held in Tunisia, many plays are performed.

Of the three countries of the Maghrib, Tunisia has the largest number of women writing in Arabic. Although the mere fact of their writing is a reflection of change in society, they do not always promote complete emancipation. Slowly but progressively their tone has become more daring. Raising certain questions is in itself a revolutionary stand. Subjects such as birth control and abortion, discussed by Hind Az-zouz (b. 1926) in *Fid al-Darb Al-Tawil* (1969; On the Long Road), are a novelty. Some, such as Fatima Slim (b. 1942), observe the loss of the old values in a changing society. The most uninhibited is Laila ben Mami (b. 1944), author of *Sawma'a Tahtariq* (1968; The Burning Hermitage), who believes in sexual freedom for the artist.

The image of the modern woman also is defined by men writers. Generally, most novelists of the late 1960s and 1970s called for a bigger role for women in society. In the novel *Wa Nasibi min al-Ufuq* (1970; My Share of the Horizon), Abdel Qader ben Shaikh (b. 1929) calls for the emancipation of women, the easing of parents' control, and the relaxing of social traditions. Mustafa al-Farsi (b. 1931) takes a similar position in *Al-Mun'araj* (1969; The Curve). Women, as reflected in literature, suffered from a changing society and the consequences of their efforts to balance the claims of a traditional upbringing with those of a modern world in which they wanted to prove themselves. The situation claimed some victims in the period of transition—for example, the characters drawn by Natila al-Tabayniyy (b. 1949) in *Shay'un Si Nafsika* (1970; Something within Yourself)—but an irreversible trend was set for future generations.

Some contemporary writers have achieved recognition for their innovative techniques and timely topics while remaining close to the people's problems. Such is the case of Mohammad al-Hadi ben

Saleh (1945), who portrayed the bread riots in his novel *Sifr al-Naqla wa al-Tasawwur* (1988; The Book of Transfer and Imagination).

Poetry, too, responded to the people's concerns, as shown in the poems of Mohammad al-Habib al-Zanad (b. 1946) in his collection *Al-Majzum bi lam* (1970; The Form Tense). Fadila al-Shabi (b. 1946) believes in the free expression of the poet in his work, without outside guidance. Another poet, Samira al-Kasrawi (b. 1957), is preoccupied with the political situation in the Arab world, as is obvious in her books, *Balagha Shi'riyyah fi al-Rafd wa al-Huriyyah wa al-Rasas* (1982; Poetic Eloquence in Rejection, Freedom, and Bullets) and *Malhamat Al-Mawt wa al-Milad fi Sha'bi* (1983; The Epic of Death and Life for My People). Thus, although it is possible to trace the general trend in Tunisian literature, the assessment of individual writers poses problems; many remain the authors of a single book or are still searching for the most suitable form for their ideas.

Aida A. Bamia

Literature, Armenian

A uniquely rich body of written work.

The Armenian language is the last surviving indigenous tongue of the Anatolian peninsula. It is related to the Thraco-Phrygian branch of Indo-European but preserves many words for geographical features and flora from the language of Urartu (8th century B.C.E.). The Armenians subsequently entered the cultural orbit of Iran (6th century B.C.E.–7th century C.E.). In the fourth century, Armenia became the first Christian state (see CHRISTIANS IN THE MIDDLE EAST). In the fifth century, Saint Mesrop (or Mashtots) devised an alphabet for the language, and the large translation, theological, and historiographical literature that came into being very soon afterward was composed in a clear and vigorous dialect, extremely rich in Parthian Iranian loan-words, which had probably been for centuries the vehicle of a sophisticated oral literature. This "literary" (*grabar*) dialect was employed until the late nineteenth century for many formal purposes; it is still used in the liturgy of the Armenian Church (whose founder and patriarchs were, for nearly a millennium, from the same princely Parthian Arsacid family). The histories of the Armenians by Agathangelos, Movses Khorenatsi, Lazar Parpetsi, and Pawstos; the *History of the War of Vardan* by Eghishe; and Eznik Koghbatsi's *Refutation of Sects* are among the major works of this Early or Classical Armenian literature. In the sixth century, a large body of terminology was rendered analytically

from Greek; the resulting "Hellenophilic" works, although technically precise, were often obscure.

This hastened the evolution of written forms of the vernacular (*ashkharhabar*), which, in the centuries of the Arab caliphate, the infiltration into Anatolia by the Turks, and continued Persian (now Muslim) influence, absorbed thousands of Arabic, Turkish, and New Persian loan-words. The lyric poetry of Frik, Hovhannes Tlkurantsi, Kostandin Erznkatsi, and Mkrtich Naghash is composed in this Middle Armenian, as are law codes, chronicles, and medical texts, magical books, and the like. A number of writers, particularly churchmen, composed important works in Classical Armenian. A notable example is the tenth-century mystic Saint Gregory of Narek, whose book of prayers, the *Matean voghbergutean* (Book of Lamentation) until recent years was found in every Armenian home, next to the Psalter and Gospel. Saint Nerses Shnorhali, "the Graceful," (died 1173) composed luminous hymns and doxologies, many preserved in the daily liturgy. Perhaps the last representative of Middle Armenian is the bard Sayat Nova (Hunger of Melodies), who died in 1795. Although there are still such *ashughs* (minstrels, literally "lovers") praising the "beloved" with the Oriental imagery of the rose and nightingale, Christian Armenians in the nineteenth century turned toward their European, especially Russian, coreligionists, and this orientation changed both the language and form of their literature.

Russia liberated the city of Yerevan from the Persians in 1827. Twenty years later, the event was described by Khachatur Abovyan in *Verk Hayastani* (The Wounds of Armenia), the first modern novel in contemporary vernacular Armenian. The year Abovyan wrote the book, Marx issued his Communist Manifesto—and the Armenian translation, published at Constantinople in 1867 (then the capital of the Ottoman Empire) was the first in any Asian language. (The Armenian word for a workers' council, *khorhurd,* from a Parthian term adopted around the time of Jesus, was actually used before the corresponding Russian word and institution, *soviet*.) In the Ottoman and Persian empires, Armenian Socialists agitated for reform and wrote novels of social protest and ethnographical content: Perch Proshyan was the direct successor to Abovyan in this genre, followed by Mikayel Nalbandyan. From Persian Armenia came the Freemason and publicist Raffi (Hakob Melik-Hakobyan), whose novel *Kaytser* (Sparks) condemned the emasculating role of the clergy in national life. (His fellow Armenian and Freemason, Mirza Malkom Khan, was prominent in the Iranian constitutional movement.) Gabriel Sundukyan wrote plays whose themes were similar to those of Russian playwright Anton Chekhov (1860–1904). Armenians living in areas under Russian influence generally wrote in a literary dialect perfected at Tiflis (now Tbilisi); Turkish Armenians like Ghevond Alishan, Krikor Zohrab, Bedros Tourian, and Hagop Baronian wrote in the equally polished vernacular *ashkharhabar* of Constantinople. Baronian's satires of the middle-class manners of the Ottoman capital city are still enjoyed. An Armenian poet of modern Istanbul, Zahrad, writes sharp, haiku-like verses reminiscent of Nazim Hikmet. The historically determined division between "Eastern" and "Western" Armenian—which are mutually comprehensible—persists.

Armenian history in the twentieth century was dominated by two catastrophic events: (1) the massive killing of Armenian civilians in 1915, perpetrated by Turkey, in which nearly 35 percent of the nation perished and 90 percent of the territory of historical Armenia was laid waste; and (2) the Bolshevik coup d'état of 1917 in Russia. The mass killing of 1915 created a vast diaspora, which has produced writers such as the American Armenian William Saroyan and the British Armenian Michael Arlen. Lyric and epic poets like Avedik Isahakyan and Hovhannes Tourmanyan made their peace with the Soviet regime. The visionary poet Yeghishe CHARENTS supported it, but later became its victim, along with many thousands of Armenian intellectuals whose number included the brilliant regional writers, Vahan Totovents, Hagop Mntsuri, and Gurgen Mahari, who had "returned" to their fatherland. In the years after Stalinism, the most brilliant poet to emerge, a great literary scholar as well, was Paruyr Sevak (died 1971), whose epic poem *Anlreli zangakatun* (The Never-Silent Belltower) celebrates the life of the ethnologist and musicologist KOMITAS Vardapet, who witnessed the 1915 massive loss of Armenian lives, went mad, and died many years later without regaining his sanity. Although Soviet Armenians were denied access to much of world literature, and the distinction between themselves and the Armenians of the diaspora was unnaturally accentuated, there is every sign, particularly since the restoration of Armenian independence in 1990, that Armenian literature is developing as a single national entity, in contact with the development of new genres throughout the world.

James R. Russell

Literature, Hebrew

A long and varied tradition that includes innovative techniques and more conventional approaches, a focus on the individual as well as on nationalist concerns.

Modern Hebrew literature began in late eighteenth-century Prussia, surrounded by Yiddish and German. It developed and came of age in central and eastern Europe, centuries after Hebrew ceased being a spoken language. Only after World War I and the destruction of many Jewish cultural centers in Europe did Palestine and later Israel become the focus for Hebrew belles lettres, this time in a Hebrew-speaking milieu.

The year 1784, when *Ha-Me'asef,* the first Hebrew periodical, appeared, serves as a period marker for the beginning of modern Hebrew literature. Its founder, Moses Mendelssohn, a German Enlightenment philosopher, was the leader of the Jewish Enlightenment, or *Haskalah,* which advocated the modernization of Jewish religious and social life. The writers of the Haskalah chose to write in Hebrew not only because it was known to many readers, but also because Hebrew was the only remnant of Jewish independence.

For almost a century, Hebrew literature was committed to the Haskalah movement. From Germany, it spread to Polish Galicia and later to Russia. Poetry was the dominant genre until the mid-nineteenth century. While romanticism was raging in Europe, Hebrew poetry was neoclassical, universalistic, and mimetic. It didactically reinterpreted biblical stories, failing to develop a genuinely poetic idiom. Nevertheless, Haskalah literature revolutionized culture by extracting the literary creation from its religious and communal framework and revived, despite its limitations, the poetic language and universal themes of the Hebrew Bible.

This poetry's most powerful voice was Judah Leib Gordon, who retold biblical and historical stories with dramatic intensity, satirized Jewish life with wit, and empathized with the plight of Jewish women. Micah Joseph Lebensohn's highly charged romantic poems were more individualistic.

The first popular novel was *Ahabat Zion* (Love of Zion, 1853) by Abraham Mapu. Its pastoral view of nature and biblical theme and language reflect Haskalash taste. In 1865, Mapu attempted to depict contemporary life, but not until the work of Mendele Mokher Seforim later in the century did the form mature and acquire new literary and linguistic models. Mendele stands at the crossroads between Haskalah and the period of nationalism and social realism. He manipulated postbiblical materials—Mishnah, the Talamud, and prayer—to create an innovative prose style.

The year 1881, with its wave of pogroms in Russia, marks the shift from Haskalah assimilationism to the Zionist credo of auto-emancipation. The newly established school of Hibbat Zion (Love of Zion) produced national poetry, replete with sentimental and hyperbolical avowals of love for mother Zion and her miserable children, the Jewish people, as well as romantic poetry.

The philosopher of the new nationalist movement and the editor of its periodical, *Ha-Shiloach,* was AHAD Ha-Am, who saw Zion as the future spiritual and cultural center of the Jewish people. He believed that the non-spoken Hebrew of his time could articulate concepts, not emotions, and that the literature should concentrate on Jewish issues exclusively. The challenge to both Ahad Ha-Am's stifling prescription and Mendele's realism and style came from Isaac Leib Peretz, David Frischmann, and the neoromantic Micha Joseph Berdyczewski who all maintained that Hebrew literature was like all others. The individual's subterranean energies motivate Berdyczewski's works of lyrical prose and his style. He believed that national renaissance and vitality would come only with releasing the irrational creative spark and rejecting the restraint of traditional Judaism's intellectualism.

Modern consciousness burst into Hebrew literature in the 1890s through Berdyczewski's fiction and Hayyim Nahman Bialik's verse. Writers began experimenting with modernist techniques. With Bialik, for the first time in Hebrew literature, the "I" of the individual became the central entity, and poetry became the arena of the self. Bialik's verse, like that of the Bible, is both a powerful lyrical expression and a rich essence of the Jewish culture that produced it. From 1892 to 1917, Bialik was dedicated to the idea of national revival. He searched for a meaningful Jewish identity while anguished by a loss of faith.

Saul Tchernichovsky expanded the horizons of Hebrew poetry through his admiration of Hellenic beauty and mastery of classical form. Like Berdyczewski, he broke the constricting bounds of Hebrew literature and the Jewish framework and aspired to express the totality of existence.

Many of the writers of this period started in Europe and continued in Ottoman-ruled Eretz Yisrael, or Palestine. Works of this second Aliyah period were often dominated by questions of identity and by the pendulum of despair and hope reflecting the crisis of immigration. Yosef Hayyim BRENNER's seemingly fragmented, unrefined prose reflects the tortured inner worlds of his intellectual, uprooted, antiheroes and their existential struggles. In his quest for truth and realism, he improvised a semblance of spoken Hebrew and slang. Uri Nissan Gnessin's novellas of alienation and uprootedness, written in a lyrical, figurative prose, are among the first stream-of-consciousness narratives in world literature.

But the towering figure of Hebrew fiction was Shmuel Yosef AGNON, the 1966 Nobel laureate. Zionist philosophy was only one component of Agnon's complex artistic and spiritual oeuvre, which merges Jewish sources with European traditions. Agnon tells the story of the Jews in the modern age: faith and heresy, exile and redemption, Holocaust, uprootedness and belonging. But the Jewish condition is also a reflection of the human condition: tragic fate; nightmarish, at times surrealistic existence; social disintegration; and loss of identity. Like Agnon, Hayyim HAZAZ, the expressionist, wrote in a style different from the spoken language about Jewish life in Europe and Eretz Yisrael.

At the heart of Hebrew literary activity at the time of the British mandate was poetry. With Bialik's hegemony challenged in the 1920s, minor, deviant voices were heard: Rachel, whose lean, intimate diction, musical lyricism, and unfulfilled pioneer and personal dreams won her the public's unmatched love; Esther RAAB, the poetically untamed individualist; David Vogel, the lyrical minimalist; and Avraham Ben Yizhak.

The most vocal revolutionary was Avraham Shlonsky, the editor of *Ktubim* and later *Turim.* Classicist style, layered language, and nationalist preoccupations were overthrown by Russian and French symbolism and postsymbolism, futurism, and German neoromanticism and expressionism as modernism swept through Hebrew verse. Shlonsky's symbolist poetics, subconsciously motivated images and *melos* (tune) abound with intellectual insight. With linguistic virtuosity, he articulated his war-weary generation's despair, exposing urban alienation or describing, like his fellow pioneers Isaac Lamdan, Rachel, and Uri Zvi GREENBERG, the struggle and infatuation with a new landscape.

In Shlonsky's close leftist circle were Natan ALTERMAN and Leah Goldberg. Alterman's maiden collection, *Stars Outside* (1938), nourished more than a generation of poets with its captivating rhythms, carnivalesque imagist world, and oxymoronic metaphors. He later wrote engaged poetry but strictly separated his lyrical and public verse. An unofficial national spokesman, Alterman wrote a column in the labor daily *Davar* in which he took active part in the struggle for independence and for Jewish immigration against British rules. Goldberg refused to write ideological poetry. Well versed in world literature, she often used complex traditional forms to create her own modernist verse.

In his poetics of form, Yonatan Ratosh favored Shlonsky's school, but ideologically he belonged to Vladimir Ze'ev JABOTINSKY's nationalist camp. Believing in a shared cultural heritage for the entire

Middle East, Ratosh founded the Canaanite movement and created idiosyncratic verse suffused with prebiblical mythology and vocabulary.

Expressionism shone through the poetry of Greenberg, the ultranationalist who prophesied the Holocaust and Jewish sovereignty. Drawing from personal and national landscapes and vocabularies, his Whitman-like verse captures raw feeling and pain, messianic and historical visions.

While European Jewry was approaching its demise, the first generation of native Hebrew speakers was coming of age in Eretz Yisrael. Its writers, nicknamed Dor Ba-Arez (A Generation in the Land), made their debut in 1938 with a story by S. Vizhar. They were associated with Zionist socialism and its aspirations, and their realist-positivist works reflect the collective experiences of the new Jew: kibbutz, youth movement, Haganah and the War of Independence in 1948. The individual character and inner turmoil and the shadow side of society are often neglected or suppressed in short stories and novels by Nathan Shaham, Aharon Meged, Moshe Shamin, and Yigal Mossinsohn. But their readers, awed with heroism and struck by the idea of national redemption, received them warmly. Yizhar's introspective, lyrical prose is distinguished in its depiction of mood and contemplation, its renditions of sensory impressions and landscape, and its narrator's wartime ethics and empathy for the Arabs.

Poets of the time, such as Haim Guri, Ayin Hillel, and Nathan Yonathan, expressed an intimate, physical attachment to their local space. They adopted Alterman's poetics, and the values landed in his poems—loyalty, friendship, and the eternal bond between the dead and the living—helped them integrate the traumas of the 1948 battles. Poems from Guri's *Flowers of Fire* became sacred texts, read alongside Alterman's in memorials for the fallen in war. Somewhat different from this generation's unified voice were Aba Kovner and Amir Gilboa who lamented their destroyed European homes.

With the establishment of the state and the waves of immigrants changing the land's character, some writers wrestled with their disillusion through historical novels with reference to present discontent. Others, like Benyamin Tammuz and David Schachar, nostalgically depicted childhood and bygone days.

Generation of the State poets of the 1950s and 1960s unbridled the nationalist agenda's long hold on Hebrew literature. Free, ironic poetics, influenced by modernist English, American, and German works usurped symbolist poetics and nationalist norms. This group believed that poetry ought to focus on the individual's experience not the collective; it rejected pathos and transcendentalism in favor of the concrete

and existential and lowered the diction in favor of everyday discourse and freer form. Natan ZACH, the spokesman of this school, attacked Alterman and his disciples and foregrounded previously marginalized poets like Vogel and the American Hebrew imagist Gabriel Preil. With poetic genuis and originality, Zach's critically acclaimed free verse realized the new principles. Yet, his friend Yehuda AMICHAI's poetry was more easily accepted, due in part to Amichai's ability to merge poetic and linguistic traditions. Amichai's antiwar lines like "I want to die in my bed" expressed this generation's yearnings, while his conceit-like metaphors and whimsical combinations of colloquial and classical Hebrew revolutionized Hebrew verse. David Avidan's linguistic inventiveness was at the forefront of this school. Dan Pagis, who survived a concentration camp, conveyed a sense of horror in his enigmatic verse. Dahlia Ravikovitch delved into the psyche's depths. Her intense, at times desperate verse elegantly reintroduced archaisms and myths to the poetry without surrendering spoken language and syntax.

Fiction of the 1950s and 1960s followed poetry's lead in its challenge to Zionist prescriptions. It focused on the individual's psychological world or on universal, existential themes. The confessional, erotic novel *Life as a Fable* (1958) by Pinhas Sadeh reflected the turn inward and away from realism. Early stories by Amos oz and Avraham B. Yehoshua are metaphorical and allegorical. Amichai's surrealist novel, *Not of This Time, Not of This Place,* uncovers suppressed wishes for an alternative existence. Amalia Kahana-Carmon's works explore life's mysteries and delve into intense, personal analysis reminiscent of Virginia Woolf. Aharon Applefeld's characters wander through inner and outer nightmares of the Holocaust.

After the Arab–Israel War of 1973, the myth of the new Jew was shattered. Hebrew literature's role as the arena for examining the national state of affairs was partly reinstated: Collective tensions were again realized through individual destinies. Post-1973 literature depicts the Israeli condition in relation to changes in social values, the Arabs, immigration and absorption, Jewish roots, the Diaspora, and the Holocaust. Questions of Jewish and Israeli existence occupy late works of veteran 1948 authors, but also others. The Generation of the State abandoned its abstract, schematic universalism and returned to concrete Israeli life, understanding symbolic layers of its texts. Yehoshua's late family novels, for example, are rich with realistic detail and make original and unpopular political, national, and historical philosophical statements. Oz lowered his diction and substituted fantasy with realistic, semi-autobiographical works. The renewed interest in the tangible brought late blooming to Yizhak Ben Ner, Yeshayahu Koren, Yehudit Hendel, Shulamit Hareven, Yaacov Shabti, and Yehoshua Kenaz. Shabtai painstakingly forges the decline of his pioneer parents' Tel Aviv milieu. His *Past Continuous* follows the protagonist's stream of associations in a style unprecedented in Hebrew literature. Kenaz's patient, almost painful realism depicts social and psychological states with authenticity and linguistic mastery. Longing for a declining Eretz Yisrael translates into a bittersweet return to childhood for Ben Ner, Shabtai, and Meir Shalev. Others, like Kenaz, Ruth Almog, and David Grossman, look back with anger. In many of their works, however, the pained personal story is loaded with social and national meaning.

The many writers active in the 1970s and 1980s belong, then, to a number of literary generations. But despite the supposed centrality of male-authored works wrestling with the Zionist undertaking and all its reverberations, subversive narratives crystallized. Although only a few novels and short stories by women had been published previously, in the 1980s there was a proliferation of woman authors. Kahana-Carmon argued that mainstream Hebrew literature, an offspring of synagogue culture, indoctrinated Jewish readers to expect a male national spokesman, while intimate matters of the soul were relegated to the women's gallery of the synagogue, or rather the margins of literature. Dvora Baron was the only woman whose prose won critical acclaim before the 1950s. Hendel, Hareven, Naomi Frenkel, Rachel Eytan, Kahana-Carmon, and later Almog broke through in the interim. But the female voice, often undermining conventional conceptions of women and family institutions, conquered a well-deserved place only in the 1980s.

Prose fiction of the late 1980s and early 1990s was characterized by postmodernist pluralism. Opposing styles coexisted: conventional artistic measures; buds of religious or mystical writing; self-referential experiments with genre, language, theme, and typography. Orli Castel-Bloom's stories and novels shatter myth, reality, and text with lean language as she undermines any existence of truth. Yuval Shimoni internalized fiction and the connections between signifier and signified, while Yoel Hoffman's unpaged works in numbered paragraphs, surrounded by empty spaces or miniature pictures, are dotted with German, translated in the margins. He blends Far Eastern with Western philosophy and blurs the boundaries between languages, sexes, the self and the universe.

Unlike prose, poetry opened itself to a wide prism of possibilities in the 1970s, but its public role was diminished. In the spirit of post-structuralism, this generation of poets had no use for common poetics. Yair Hurvitz wrote romantic symbolist verse, with high diction, and strove to unite opposites. Meir Wieseltier's modernist poetry is biting, almost vulgar, with social, political, and existential emphases. Yona Wallach smashed all borders of psyche and language, theme and form. Her poetry "unravels the unconscious like a fan" and allows words to flow without social, cultural, or literary inhibitions or taboos. Older poets who became central were Zelda and Avoth Yeshurun, whose poetry dismembers reality. Aharon Shabtai created a personal mythology drawn from Greek classics. In her "Data Processing" series, Maya Bejerano drowns chaos in a psychic, rhythmical associative stream.

The war in Lebanon and the Intifada in the late 1980s led to a reawakened interest in political and protest poems. Various contemporary issues—including erotic and homosexual themes, and imagery drawn from the modern media—came to prominence in the 1990s.

BIBLIOGRAPHY

ALTAR, ROBERT. *Hebrew and Modernity.* Bloomington, Ind., 1994.

COHEN, JOSEPH. *Voices of Israel: Essays on and Interviews with Yehuda Amichai, A. B. Yehoshua, T. Carmi, Aharon Applefeld, and Amos Oz.* Albany, N.Y., 1990.

FUCHS, ESTHER. *Encounters with Israeli Authors.* Marblehead, Mass., 1982.

On Jerusalem: Selections in Prose and Verse. Jerusalem, 1979.

WIRTH-NESHER, HANNA. *What Is Jewish Literature?* Philadelphia, 1994.

YUDKIN, LEON. *Escape into Siege: A Survey of Israeli Literature Today.* Boston, 1974.

Nili Gold

Literature, Persian

Since the Iranian Revolution, Persian literature has become more and more relevant to contemporary politics, society, and day-to-day living.

The first nine centuries of imaginative literature in the Persian language constituted an aesthetically rich, premodern tradition. Beginning with Rudaki (died 940/1) and others in Greater Khorasan, Persian literature enjoyed a golden or classical age, which extended to Persian poet Hafez (or Hafiz) (c. 1320–c. 1390) four centuries later. It featured elaborate poetic praise of the court; narrative epics and romances; a sparkling tradition of love lyrics, which eventually combined romantic and gnostic elements; and Sufi lyric and narrative verse. In Persian prose there were significant court, religious, and Sufi writings, from chronicles and romances to biographies of saints. Some hold that classical Persian literature outshines premodern literatures in Arabic, Hebrew, and Turkish, the other great Middle Eastern literary traditions.

But, as rich as premodern Persian literature was, the twentieth century has arguably constituted an equally exciting chapter in the Persian literature of Iran. From the beginning of the century, imaginative literature emerged from court patronage, Sufi brotherhoods, and Twelver Shi'ite environs to address a general Iranian audience. Iranian writers began then to comprise a new class of intellectuals, independent of crown or turban.

Prose developed and matured more quickly than verse in this fast-paced century, starting with journalistic writing by Constitutionalists (1905–1911), such as that by Ali Akbar DEHKHODA (1879–1956). In a preface to *Once upon a Time* (Berlin, 1922), M. A. JAMALZADEH argued that literature in straightforward, living prose was a key to education and enlightenment for Iranians. His six stories in that volume, the first collection of Persian short stories ever, introduced realism, local color, and popular language into one medium of Persian writing.

In the 1920s, Nima Yushij (1895–1960) began experimenting with traditional forms and content in Persian poetry. Earlier, Constitution-era poets had introduced the notion and images of "nation" into poetry to parallel the three traditional subjects of address: God, king, and beloved. Like Jamalzadeh in prose, those poets had thought that poetry should serve as a voice for education and social progress and reform. Nima, however, experimented with individuating the lyric speaker and eschewing didactic intent; his quatrain-sequence poem called *Legend* (1922) and other poems in the 1920s heralded the new sensibility.

The 1930s marked the first age of preeminence of prose in Persian literature, a situation that held true to the end of the century. Sadegh HEDAYAT (1903–1953) played the chief role in this development. His four collections of short stories from 1930 to 1942 and enigmatic, surrealistic novella called *The Blind Owl* (1937, 1941) were initiating texts, the latter demonstrating how a new Persian literary language could create atmosphere and voice surrealism.

The Iranian short story grew to maturity in the 1940s and after. The period from the Allied Occupation of Iran and the abdication and exile of Reza Shah Pahlavi (ruled 1921–1941) to the American-orchestrated coup d'état that brought down the short-lived government of Mohammad Mossadegh (1882–1967) in August 1953 was special for literature because no government censorship interfered with or controlled literary expression. From the establishment

by Naser al-Din Shah Qajar (ruled 1848–1896) of an office of censorship in 1885—with the exception of the first two years of the constitution (1906–1908), the so-called "Twelve Years of Freedom" (1941–1953), and the revolution years (1977–1979)—Persian literary artists labored under constraints of censorship throughout the twentieth century. This has meant, except for the 1941–1953 period, that Iranian prose fiction, lyric verse, and drama have had to resort to indirection and symbolism when dealing critically with the Iranian present.

In the 1940s, Sadeq CHUBAK (1916–   ), Ebrahim Golestan (1922–   ), Jalal AL-E AHMAD (1923–1969), and others joined Hedayat and Bozorg ALAVI (1904–   ), who had published his first collection of short stories in 1934, to give Iranian audiences realistic, naturalistic, social realist, and other fictional modes and stances, paving the way for later generations of short-story writers who contributed to magazines and published collections of stories to the end of the century. Chief among them was the prolific Gholamhosayn Sa'edi (1935/6–1985).

In the 1950s the Iranian novel likewise gained a foothold and led to works of maturity in the 1960s and after. Alavi's *Her Eyes* (1952), Beh'azin's *The Serf's Daughter* (1952), and Al-e Ahmad's *The School Principal* (1958) dealt critically with the Reza Pahlavi and early Mohammad Reza PAHLAVI eras. Of the three, only Al-e Ahmad's indictment of the educational system at the local elementary school level in *The School Principal* was not banned by the government.

From the 1960s, Iranian novels became central to Iranian literary life. Chubak published *Tangsir* (1963) and *The Patient Stone* (1966). Hushang GOLSHIRI (1937–   ) published *Prince Ehtejab* (1968/9); with a stream-of-consciousness narrative point of view and a condemnation of monarchy and aristocracy, which some critics think is Iran's best novel. In 1969, Simin DANESHVAR (1921–   ), who had been the first Iranian woman to publish a collection of short stories with the *The Extinguished Fire* in 1948, published *Savushun* (The Mourners of Siyavosh), which became Iran's best-selling novel of all time, reportedly selling over 150,000 copies by the 1990s.

The 1940s and 1950s also witnessed the blossoming of new or modernist Persian verse. Nima had begun publishing verse again in 1938, and by the 1940s his experiments and achievements with untraditional verse forms, new sensibilities, and an individuated lyric speaker had attracted the attention of Ahmad SHAMLU (1925–   ), Mehdi Akhavan-e Sales (1928–1990), and other major figures in the next generation of modernist poets.

In response, traditionalists maintained devotion to classical forms, diction, and didacticism, while using such for contemporary issues. Conversative readers still outnumbered those receptive to modernist verse, pointing to the achievements of traditional poets Mohammad Taqi Bahar (1886–1955) and Parvin E'tesami (1907–1941), or accepting the moderate modernism of Faridun Tavallali (1919–1985) and others who maintained quatrain sequence forms and traditional imagery and figures of speech, while hinting at modern issues. By the 1970s, however, the traditionalists were in retreat or in the minority, although the debate over past versus present in Persian poetry remains an issue in Iranian literary circles.

In the 1950s and 1960s, modernist Persian poetry achieved great things. Shamlu approached free verse in his forceful works that supported his causes. Akhavan-e Sales breathed fresh air into traditional meters and Iranian myths and history as texture for his poetry. Two of his poems typify the modernist outlook. One called "Winter" (1956) presents a speaker with nowhere to go on a cold evening except to the local tavern run by an Armenian. But it is so late that the tavern is closed. The alienated speaker, who has seen the cold breaths of himself and others as walls between people and who presumably cannot trust his Muslim brethren, would appear to imply that Iran was experiencing a spiritual and social winter, as well as undergoing an actual winter season. The second poem, called "The Ending of the *Shahnameh*" (1957), is a tour de force that depicts a harp playing a tune of yesteryear, specifically a dream of Iran before the Arab Muslim invasion in the middle of the seventh century. The speaker tells the harp to change the tune, to forget the glorious but irretrievable past. This poem voices nostalgia and pessimism typical of secular-minded, literary Iranians.

From the mid-1950s to the end of 1966, Forugh FARROKHZAD (c. 1934–1967) added a dimension and voice to modern Persian poetry that Persian literature had previously lacked: a female speaker and female concerns. Her verse, dealing with a lyric speaker's growth and concerns as an individual, as a poet, and as a woman, represents a culmination of Nima'ic modernism. Another trend appears in the poetry of Sohrab Sepehri (1928–1980), that of the nature poet and, in his case, with neo-Sufic or pantheistic implications.

By the mid-1970s, modernist Persian poetry had proceeded to a standstill. Although a new generation of poets had joined the fray and modernist poetry was produced in abundance into the 1990s, no new poets joined the highest ranks of the earlier poets or took their place.

Nader Naderpur (1929–   ), a popular poet from the mid-1950s and the most prominent moderate modernist, crossed the moderate line in the 1980s

after opting for self-exile in Paris and then Los Angeles. Voicing the alienation and anger of Iranians abroad opposed to the Islamic Republic, Naderpur's characterizations of life in Iran of the 1980s and 1990s and his depictions of feeling unintegrated into life in the West strike familiar chords for many Iranians in similar circumstances. Another poet in exile, Esma'il Kho'i (1938–   ), who had been involved and philosophical as an almost first-rank modernist before the revolution, seemed to gain poetic timbre through his suffering in exile in London.

Circumstances and censorship during the Pahlavi era muted or silenced literary voices. During the first two decades of the Islamic Republic, establishment pressure and censorship seemed designed merely to coerce writers to avoid sexual imagery and direct questioning of Islam but not to silence them. In consequence and also because of a decrease in other entertainment after the revolution and because of a natural growth in readership that would have taken place under any successor regime to the Pahlavis, Persian literary activity, especially prose fiction, became a profession for the self-employed writer for the first time in Iranian history. Novelists, short-story writers, and some essayists became able to support themselves through writing as of the 1980s. Moreover, Iranian novels began to compete for readership for the first time with Western novels in translation.

Among landmark works in Iranian prose fiction after the revolution are: Esma'il Fasih's *Sorayya in a Coma* (1984), Shahnush PARSIPUR's *Tuba and the Meaning of Night* (1989) and *Women Without Men* (1990), and Reza BARAHENI's *Song of the Slain* (1983) and *Secrets of My Land* (1987). With their negative depictions of Iranian *savak* (secret police) and American intelligence and military figures, Baraheni's fictions signal a post-Pahlavi literary trend of denunciation of America-supported Pahlavi era life.

But one novel stands by itself: Mahmud DOWLATABADI's *Klidar* (1983), a tragic saga of mid-twentieth century tribal and village life in 3,700 pages, which brought its author status as the leading writer of fiction in the Islamic Republic period. Just as Ali Mohammad Afghani's *Ahu Khanom's Husband* (1961) had earlier encouraged Iranians to think that the Persian language had the resources to serve as the vehicle for any sort or length of prose fiction, Dowlatabadi's *Klidar*—the title refers to a Kurdish village area in Khorasan—convinced readers of the richness of the everyday rural Iranian experience and of descriptive Persian prose, even though Dowlatabadi attempts nothing experimental in his story.

Of all prerevolution species, Iranian drama suffered most in the 1980s. While it was still a new medium in the late Pahlavi period or a medium to which few Iranians had direct exposure, it had grown by leaps and bounds, with the prolific Sa'edi the best-known playwright. Stage dramas also had turned into television dramas and, as was the case of several important short stories and novels, had became screenplays for the New Wave cinema of the 1970s. By the mid-1980s Iranian cinema was thriving again but without plots, themes, and texture that romantic love stories and women not in traditional Islamic garb would provide. Iranian stage drama, meanwhile, found a haven in the West, where local Iranian communities in major cities enthusiastically supported touring companies. Prominent among them was Parviz SAYYAD's, based in Los Angeles. Through the 1980s, Sayyad staged plays featuring his earlier folk character Samad, first off to the Iran–Iraq war front and then back from the front. Another play presented the imaginary trial regarding the 1978 torching of Abadan's Rex Cinema, killing hundreds of patrons inside. Sayyad's one-man show in the early 1990s, presenting himself and Samad in witty conversation, alternately one on video and the other live, provided sophisticated culture-specific entertainment and introspection on the nature of modern Iranian artistic expression.

A medium that survived the revolution both at home and abroad was the Persian essay from autobiographical academic writing. Socially and politically involved, originally Western in inspiration, the Persian literary essay came of age in the four decades of the twentieth century. Writers then exhibited signature styles and concerns, a far cry from the beginning of the century when a florid, Arabic-laden style and a rhetorical eye to the past prevailed. Jamalzadeh decried that situation in his preface to *Once upon a Time.* Shahrokh Meskoob's conversational style in *Iranian Nationality and the Persian Language* (Paris, 1981) and Al-e Ahmad's brusque and sometimes angry voice in *Weststruckness* (1962, 1964), *Lost in the Crowd* (1966), and *A Stone on a Grave* (1964, not published until 1981) are examples of modern Persian essay writing.

BIBLIOGRAPHY

In addition to representative works by twentieth-century Iranian authors in translation listed in entries under writers' names elsewhere in these volumes, the following anthologies of English versions of works are available: *An Anthology of Modern Persian Poetry,* compiled and translated by AHMAD KARIMI-HAKKAK (1979); *Classics of Persian Literature: An Anthology of Literature in Translation from the Tenth through the Twentieth Centuries,* compiled and edited by MICHAEL HILLMANN (forthcoming, 1994/5); *Iranian Drama: An Anthology,* compiled and edited by M. R. GHANOONPARVAR and JOHN GREEN (1989); *Modern Persian Drama: An Anthology,* compiled and translated by GISELE KAPUSÇINSKI (1987); *Modern Persian Short Stories,* compiled and translated by MINOO S. SOUTHGATE (1980); *Stories from Iran . . . 1921–1991,* compiled by HESHMAT MOAYYAD (1991); *Stories by Iranian Women since the Revolution,* compiled and translated by SORAYA SULLIVAN (1991); and *Theatre of Diaspora: Two Plays,* by PARVIZ SAYYAD (1992).

Michael C. Hillmann

Literature, Turkish

National literature that began during the Tanzimat period of the Ottoman Empire.

Halide Edip ADIVAR, Nazim HIKMET, Sait Faik ABASIYANIK, Fazıl Hüsnü DAĞLARCA, Nüsret Aziz NESIN, Yaşar Kemal, and, more recently, Orhan Pamuk are writers whose works are known outside of Turkey. As more translations appear—the latest is a postmodernist novel titled *Gece* (*Night*), by Bilge Karasu—an increasing number of works are being recognized as having universal appeal. The literature represented evolved in the second half of the nineteenth century with a group of writers who were members of the bureaucratic intelligentsia. Committed to the Tanzimat reforms, they sought to bring change to literature as well, making it a vehicle for influencing sociopolitical thinking and cultural in general. At its inception, therefore, modern Turkish literature has set both didactic and aesthetic goals: to be an art form and source of enjoyment, but also to be engaged.

The pioneers of modernism—İbrahim ŞINASI (1826–1871), NAMIK KEMAL (1840–1888), and Ziya Paşa (1825–1880)—were familiar with European literatures and had lived in Europe. They witnessed the central role literature played there, a role lacking in Turkey, where two distinct literary traditions (elitist and popular) split society. The first, following Arab-Persian classical Islamic tradition and seeking artistic perfection rather than social reality, gave priority to poetry (*divan şiiri*); was rigid in verse form, meter, and rhyme patterns, highly sophisticated in rhetoric and imagery; and employed language saturated with Arabic and Persian loanwords largely unintelligible to the masses. The second was based on Turkish folk traditions of form, content, and style in both poetry and prose, and linked the Turks to their Central Asian heritage. In general it was denigrated by the small, educated class. Religiously inspired works, many of them mystic, were important in both traditions.

In the 1860s the Şinasi-Namık Kemal-Ziya Paşa school took the first steps toward modernity. Through translation and adaptation (primarily from French), then original composition, they introduced Western-style poetry and fiction, and wrote the first Turkish plays designed for the modern stage. They also turned to journalism—the *Tasvir-i Efkar* (Description of ideas) was the principal forum for introducing their works—and accustomed readers to editorials, essays, and literary criticism propagating such concepts as fatherland, patriotism, nation, justice, freedom, and constitutional government. They did not completely reject the past, but gave old poetic forms new elements of content and style, using language more comprehensible to the expanding, middle-class reading public. This movement surged again under the republic, resulting in the romanization of the alphabet and measures to produce an öz türkçe (pure Turkish), both of which had a great effect on literature.

These writers lauded proreform statesmen and satirized traditionalists. They targeted social customs like arranged marriages and moralized against the harem system, marital infidelity, prostitution, and inhuman treatment of slaves. Namık Kemal's play *Vatan yahut Silistre* (Fatherland or Silistria, 1873) caused antiregime demonstrations, and he spent many years in exile as a result. He and his colleagues put reform before creative art, and in articles and prefaces to their works stressed the didactic and social role of literature. Abdülhak Hamit Tarhan (1852–1939) and RECAIZADE MAHMUD EKREM (1847–1914), in contrast, showed increasing concern with aesthetics. Ekrem, a teacher, published his lectures, which displayed his knowledge of Western literature and concern for liberating Ottoman poetic style, and was led into a literary battle with MUALLIM NACI, represented (somewhat unjustly) as the prime defender of the old style. Ekrem also influenced the literary school that flourished in the 1890s, the Edebiyat-ı Cedide (New Literature) or Servet-i Fünun (Wealth of Sciences), the latter title of the journal serving as its main platform. Its leading poets, TEVFIK FIKRET (1867–1916) and CENAP SEHABETTIN (1870–1934), spoke lyrically of love and nature in a Turkish inspired by the language of the *divan* poets. Fikret also wrote very provocative antiregime poems.

In fiction, building on the pioneer efforts of Ahmet (1844–1912), the leading prose writer, Halit Ziya UŞHAKLIĞIL (1866–1945) brought to his novels a more developed literary realism and psychological analysis. His two collections of prose poems show an inclination for artistry that set a trend followed by his contemporary Mehmet Rauf (1875–1931), and still finds the occasional follower today.

Although the 1908 constitutional period brought hope to writers after the repressive control of Abdülhamit II, further Ottoman decline and Europe's antagonism engendered permission and anti-Western outbursts among writers of the Fecr-i Ati (Dawn of the Future) group that formed in 1909. Meanwhile, a current of Nationalism gained strength, poets such as Mehmet Emin YURDAKUL (1869–1944) proclaim-

ing pride in being a Turk and turning to the folk tradition for verse form, meter, and language. The presence in the empire or émigré Turks from Russia fanned consciousness of belonging to a wider "Turanian" nation, and groups of scholars and writers, including Yusuf Akçuroğlu (1876–1935), Mehmet Fuat KÖPRÜLÜ (1890–1966), and Ziya GÖKALP (1876–1924), promoted study of the early history and culture of the Turks. The most important group was Genç Kalemler (Young Pens), formed in 1910, which stressed language reform. Despite strong romanticism, the short stories of its leader, Ömer Seyfettin, represent a breakthrough in the strongest in modern Turkish literature.

World War I and the War of Independence, culminating in the demise of the Ottoman Empire and the founding of the Turkish Republic, presented writers with a fresh panorama of people, places, and events to observe and depict, even greater possibilities for artistic choice through emphasis on Westernization, and an ever-increasing array of readers. Novelists of the older generation, such as Halide Edip Adıvar (1884–1964), the first important activist woman writer; Yakup Kadri Karaosmanoğlu (1889–1974), and Reşat Nuri Güntekin (1889–1956), represent an important advance in both narrative and character analysis, their works depicting the weaknesses of late Ottoman society, the inner conflicts of its people, the surge of patriotism during the War of Independence, and the new roles of women.

In poetry, three prominent poets adhered to the classical meter and verse form: Yahya Kemal Beyatlı (1884–1958), a neoclassicist who expressed his nationalism by nostalgically recalling Ottoman splendors; Ahmet Haşim (1885–1933), a symbolist steadfast in an art for art's sake approach, painting dreamlike vignettes of nature in its most tranquil moments; and Mehmet Akif ERSOY (1873–1936), who, although also choosing the classical traditions, wrote in a language very close to prose and spoken Turkish.

Of the many ideologies to which the Turks were exposed from the early days of the Republic, communism captivated Nazim Hikmet (1902–1963), the major poet of the century. Having been imprisoned for many years, he fled Turkey in 1951 and spent his remaining years behind the Iron Curtain. He fashioned Turkish free verse, and his works (prison poetry, love lyrics, social or political declamation, long narrative verse) display a striking fluidity of language and a new depth of human understanding. Only Fazıl Hüsnü Dağlarca (b. 1914), with the breadth of his aesthetic view and intellectual delving into the metaphysical, approaches his stature.

Of prime importance has been the development of realist village literature. Urban-born nineteenth-century and early twentieth-century writers seldom focused on Anatolia and its rural population. With the center of government moved to Anatolia, and especially after the introduction of a two-party system, the villager became a focus of attention for fiction writers, who now included those born in villages or closely familar with village life. Yaşar Kemal writes of the plight of the peasants in the Taurus Mountains and Çukurova Plain. Other writers have followed the villagers in their migration to country towns or big cities. In recent years an increasing number of works have drawn attention to the problems facing Turks who have migrated to Germany and other European countries since the late 1960s. Among other writers who depict the "little man" with deep understanding are Nüsret Aziz Nesin (b. 1915) and Sait Faik Abasiyanik, who has over 100 short stories set in Istanbul, nearly half of them on the island of Burgaz, revealing the life of the fisherfolk on the Sea of Marmara.

Poets also turned to the "common man." In 1941, Ornan Veli (1914–1950), Oktay Rifat (1914–1988), and Melih Cevdet Anday (b. 1915) published a collection of poems, *Garip* (Strange), calling for poetic realism untrammeled by rules and dictates, unadorned and in colloquial speech, concerned with and attempting to communicate with the man in the street. In the mid-1950s Anday joined the Second New Movement, a group including Ilhan Berk (b. 1916), Cemal Süreya (1931–1990), and Edip Cansever (1928–1986), who turned to obscurantism, writing poetry that was abstract and abtruse, in some cases almost totally incomprehensible.

Women were rarely mentioned among the writers of the Ottoman Empire before the nineteenth century. Their number increased after the Tanzimat, when a new generation of well-educated women emerged who understood French and were familiar with the works of both the French Romantics and the new Ottoman writers. Best known is Fatma Aliye Hanım (1862–1936), elder daughter of Ahmed Cevdet Paşa. The first Turkish woman novelist, her publications also included translations of French, articles, works on history, and a newspaper for women. Halide Edip Adıvar served as a model for women from the early days of the Republic, both as a writer and as an activist. Women have turned to fiction rather than poetry. Güiten Akın (b. 1933), for example, a poet who has won many awards, is the only women represented in *The Penguin Book of Turkish Verse*. In contrast, the surge of enthusiasm for the short story in the 1970s, the Füruzan phenomenon, is credited to the stories published by Füruzan (Selçuk; b. 1935), a young writer of village background who deals especially with the exploitation of villagers in the cities.

In the mid-1990s women continue to participate fully on the Turkish literary scene. Both male and female writers continue to explore the wealth of their heritage and new avenues of expression.

BIBLIOGRAPHY

EVIN, AHMET Ö. *Origins and Development of the Turkish Novel*. Minneapolis, Minn., 1983.

HALMAN, TALAT SAID. *Contemporary Turkish Literature: Fiction and Poetry*. Rutherford, N.J., 1982.

———. "Turkish Literature: Modes of Modernity." *Literature East and West* 17, no. 1 (March 1973).

———, ed. *Modern Turkish Drama*. Minneapolis, Minn., 1976.

MENEMENCIOĞLU, NERMIN, and FAHIR İZ, eds. *The Penguin Book of Turkish Verse*. New York, 1978.

RATHBURN, CAROLE. *The Village in the Turkish Novel and Short Story, 1920–1950*. The Hague, 1972.

REDDY, NILÜFER MIZANOĞLU, trans. *Twenty Stories by Turkish Women Writers*. Bloomington, Ind., 1988.

Kathleen R. F. Burrill

Liwa

Basic unit of Ottoman provincial government.

Equivalent to the term SANJAK, a liwa was a subdivision of a VILAYET and comprised one or more smaller districts called KAZAS. The governor of a liwa was called *mir liwa* and was traditionally granted the title of *bey*. The term *liwa* was abandoned by most states after the Ottoman Empire disbanded, although Iraq used it until 1974.

The Iraqi army has continued to use the secondary meaning of the term, for an army brigade. *Amir al-liwa* is a brigadier in the Iraqi army, a term also used by the Egyptian army until 1939.

BIBLIOGRAPHY

SHAW, STANFORD J. *History of the Ottoman Empire and Modern Turkey*, vol. 1. New York, 1976.

Elizabeth Thompson

Liwa, al-

Egyptian National party newspaper, 1900–1912.

Founded on January 2, 1900, by Mustafa KAMIL, *al-Liwa* (the Banner) was the journalistic house organ for the NATIONAL PARTY of Egypt. Initially set up because Mustafa and other Nationalists were finding *al-Mu'ayyad,* under Shaykh Ali Yusuf, increasingly reluctant to print their articles, *al-Liwa* soon emerged as the most popular Arabic language daily in Egypt, because of its strident attacks against British rule and its pan-Islam advocacy. As the National party grew and sought European aid, Mustafa Kamil and Khedive Abbas Hilmi II decided to publish English and French editions of *al-Liwa,* but these papers lasted only from 1907 to 1909. After Mustafa's death in 1908, Ali Fahmi Kamil (his older brother) became its editor but was soon succeeded by Abd al-Aziz Jawish (1872–1929), whose attacks on the Egyptian cabinet and its British advisers led in 1909 to the revival of the 1881 Press Law, enabling the government to warn, suspend, and later to ban this paper. A lawsuit between some heirs of Mustafa Kamil and the Nationalists led to a decision in 1910 to place *al-Liwa* under sequestration, causing the party to create *al-Alam* and then *al-Sha'b* as its mouthpiece. Restored to Ali Fahmi Kamil in 1912, *al-Liwa* soon antagonized the government for printing a speech by National party president Muhammad Farid. It was finally suppressed on September 7, 1912.

BIBLIOGRAPHY

GOLDSCHMIDT, ARTHUR. *The Memoirs and Diaries of Muhammad Farid, an Egyptian Nationalist Leader (1868–1919).* San Francisco, 1992.

HAMZA, ABD AL-LATIF. *Adab al-maqala al-suhufiya fi Misr, V: Mustafa Kamil, sahib al-Liwa.* Cairo, 1952.

MARKAZ WATHAIQ WA TARIKH MISR AL-MUʿASIR. *Awraq Muhammad Farid, I Mudhakkirati baʿd al-Hijra.* Cairo, 1978.

Arthur Goldschmidt, Jr.

Lloyd George, David   [1863–1945]

British statesman; prime minister of Britain during World War I.

David Lloyd George, 1st Earl of Dwyfor, was born in Manchester, England, and became a solicitor. He was a Liberal party member of parliament from 1890 and, during World War I served as minister of munitions (1915/16). In 1916, he became secretary of state for war and then replaced Lord Asquith as prime minister. He served as prime minister from 1916 to 1922, directing Britain's war policies to victory in 1918 and then dictating the peace settlements.

On December 4, 1916, the Asquith cabinet resigned; Lloyd George formed a war cabinet (December 7–10), and Lord Balfour replaced Sir Edward Grey at the Foreign Office, during which time the BALFOUR DECLARATION (1917) was written, asserting that Jews might have a national home in PALESTINE. Lloyd George led the British delegation at the 1919 Paris peace conference, where he disregarded U.S. President Woodrow WILSON's Fourteen Points, as well as Britain's wartime promises of self-determination to the Hashimite leaders of the ARAB REVOLT. He was responsible, directly or indirectly, for the postwar settlement that saw Britain with League of Nations mandates over Iraq, Palestine, and Transjordan—as awarded at the SAN REMO CONFERENCE in 1920. He also arranged for France to have mandates over Syria and Lebanon, although Amir Faisal (who had fought alongside T. E. Lawrence [of Arabia]) had already established a kingdom in Syria in 1920. Consequently, Faisal was made King of Iraq by the British.

Lloyd George supported Greece in its attempt to annex part of the former western Ottoman Turkey, since the Ottoman Empire was cut up by the victors; in part, because of the failure of this policy and the defeat of the Greeks by Atatürk, Lloyd George was defeated at the polls in 1922. He authored *War Memoirs* (1933–1936) and *The Truth about the Peace* (1938).

BIBLIOGRAPHY

Dictionary of National Biography, 1941–1950. London, 1959.

FROMKIN, DAVID. *A Peace to End All Peace.* New York, 1990.

Zachary Karabell

Loder Memorandum

British experts' recommendation that the problem of the border between Egypt and Libya be discussed with the Egyptian government.

Written on December 29, 1919, by the British boundary expert J. de V. Loder, the memorandum addressed the issue of the Egyptian–Libyan border. Britain's colonial secretary, Lord Milner, and Italy's foreign minister, Tommaso Tittoni, had been discussing the problem for months without resolution. Loder recommended that the matter be discussed with Egypt's government before any decision was made.

BIBLIOGRAPHY

HUREWITZ, J. C., ed. *The Middle East and North Africa in World Politics.* New Haven, Conn., 1979.

Zachary Karabell

Lohamei Herut Yisrael

Israel freedom fighters (LEHI).

Often described as an underground organization for national liberation that fought for the withdrawal of the British from Palestine and the immediate establishment of a Jewish state on both banks of the Jordan. LEHI is also described as a terrorist organization upholding a nationalistic ideology. It was founded in 1940 as the result of a split from IRGUN ZVA'I LE'UMI (IZL) in protest against the renewed military cooperation between the IZL and elements of the British army in Palestine and the discontinuation of its anti-British operations. LEHI defined the British mandate as "foreign rule" and reached the conclusion that its struggle was not only against the British mandate but against "British imperialism" in general. During the years 1940 to 1944, it resorted to methods of individual terror against British policemen and soldiers, and tried to reach an agreement with Nazi Germany in the hope of ousting Britain from Palestine. The great majority of the local Jewish population including the REVISIONIST MOVEMENT and the IZL were opposed to its methods; consequently, it was an ostracized and persecuted organization without public backing. In February 1942, LEHI found itself in a situation of crisis, after its commander, Avraham STERN was shot to death in his hiding place by the Criminal Investigation Division (CID). It was rehabilitated under the leadership of Yitzhak SHAMIR and Natan YELLIN-MOR. In 1943, LEHI carried out a series of terrorist actions against heads of the British administration, which failed. In November 1944, however, members of LEHI assassinated the British minister resident in Cairo, Walter Edward Guinness, Lord Moyne. This act led the YISHUV and the Haganah to initiate operations to liquidate the underground organizations (a move directed in particular against the IZL).

After the Labour Party gained power in Britain, LEHI played an active and important role in creating the joint framework of the Haganah, the IZL, and LEHI in the RESISTANCE MOVEMENT; and carried out a series of attacks against British and Arab targets—alone and together with the IZL.

In May 1948 LEHI, which numbered about 800 fighters, was disbanded. Most of its members joined the Israel Defense Forces (IDF). In April 1948, LEHI men took part in the attack on the Arab village Dayr Yasin; and later assassinated the United Nations mediator, Count Folke Bernadotte (September 17, 1948) in Jerusalem. The organization was declared illegal by Ben Gurion and was forcibly dismantled. Its members set up a political party—Fighters for the Freedom of Israel—that won one seat in the elections for the first Knesset. Several of its members continued to be active in a terrorist organziation that operated in Israel during the 1950s, and others published the periodical *Sulam* (the Ladder).

The ideology of LEHI underwent various changes during the years of its existence. In Stern's time, it was based on national-messianic principles, but after 1944, it developed socialistic elements as well as a pro-Soviet orientation (including attempts at negotiations with representatives of the communist bloc). These latter changes were aimed at both gaining the cooperation of various elements in the Labor Party and in the hope of achieving the national objectives: sovereignty over all areas of historical Palestine as an expression of the immanent and transcendental essence and mission of the Jewish people. At the end of this period, in 1948, the ranks of LEHI were split along ideological lines: those of a right-wing persuasion constituting a radical-national faction; those of a left-wing persuasion; and others that advocated the establishment of a Palestinian state alongside Israel.

BIBLIOGRAPHY

BELL, J. BOWYER. *Terror out of Zion: Irgun Zva'i Le'umi, LEHI, and the Palestine Underground, 1929–1949.* New York, 1977.

GINOSSAR, PINHAS. *LEHI Revealed, 1929–1949.* New York, 1977.

HELLER, JOSEPH. *LEHI/Ideology and Politics, 1940–1949.* Jerusalem, 1989. In Hebrew.

ILAN, AMITZUR. *Bernadotte in Palestine, 1948.* New York, 1989.

Yaacov Shavit

Loi Cadre

French legislative initiative (1957–1958) during Algerian war of independence (1954–1962).

Premier Maurice Bourgès-Maunoury staked his government's political life on the Loi Cadre, which attempted to resolve the contradiction of acknowledging Algeria's "personality" while keeping it integral to France. The French government charged Resident Minister Robert LACOSTE with the task of drafting the document for administrative reform. Its provisions divided Algeria into eight to ten autonomous territories linked by a federal organ. The single electoral college increased Muslim political participation but also recognized ethnic interests (e.g., the KABYLIA). The Loi Cadre aimed to sap the strength of Algerian nationalism. The *pieds-noirs* (European settlers in Algeria) viewed it suspiciously. The National Assembly repudiated the reform and Bourgès-Maunoury's ministry. Though a redrafted Loi Cadre eventually passed during Félix Gaillard's ministry, the extension of *pied-noir* power in the planned territorial assemblies impaired its reforming intent. When Charles DE GAULLE came to power, his government discarded this initiative, though it supported the concept of a single electoral college before eventually pursuing an agonizing decolonization.

BIBLIOGRAPHY

HORNE, ALISTAIR. *A Savage War of Peace: Algeria, 1954–1962,* 2d ed. New York, 1987.

Phillip C. Naylor

London, Treaty of (1871)

Pact restoring Russian access to the Black Sea.

Articles XI–XIII of the 1856 Peace of Paris restricted Russian access to the Turkish Straits and forced a demilitarization of the Black Sea. Czar Alexander II (1855–1881) never accepted this defeat of Russian interests, and in 1870, he finally found an opportunity to amend the galling Black Sea clauses. With the French faring badly in the Franco–Prussian War, in October 1870 Alexander instructed his foreign minister, Prince Aleksandr Gorchakov, to announce that Russia no longer wished to abide by Articles XI–XIII. The French agreed to an international conference to discuss the proposed Russian revision. The conference opened in London in January 1871, and an agreement was reached by March. The Treaty of London annulled the Black Sea naval rearmament. However, in compensation, the sultan of the Ottoman Empire was given greater latitude to close the straits in times of war.

BIBLIOGRAPHY

ANDERSON, M. S. *The Eastern Question.* London, 1966.
HUREWITZ, J. C., ed. *The Middle East and North Africa in World Politics.* New Haven, Conn., 1975.

Zachary Karabell

London, Treaty of (1913)

Pact securing Italian claims in the Middle East.

Signed on April 26, this treaty paved the way for Italy's entry into World War I on the side of the Entente (France and Britain). In return for its support, Italy was promised territory in the Balkans and Anatolia as well as the right to annex Libya, which it had occupied in 1914, and the Dodecanese Islands, part of Greece and formerly, when taken by Italy in 1912, part of the Ottoman Empire.

BIBLIOGRAPHY

ANDERSON, M. S. *The Eastern Question.* London, 1966.
HUREWITZ, J. C., ed. *The Middle East and North Africa in World Politics.* New Haven, Conn., 1975.

Zachary Karabell

London Conference

Conference on Palestine (1939).

In May 1938, Malcolm MACDONALD was appointed colonial secretary. The WOODHEAD COMMISSION reported that the partition, which had been proposed by the PEEL COMMISSION REPORT, was not a viable option for Palestine. On November 7, 1938, Britain's cabinet proposed convening a conference that would bring together Jews and Arabs—including representatives of Egypt, Iraq, Saudi Arabia, Transjordan, and Yemen, as well as exiled Palestinian members of the Higher Arab Committee.

In preparation, the Arabs (except the Transjordanians) met at Cairo in January 1939 and agreed on a joint position. On February 5, Jewish delegates gathered in London to form the Palestine Discussion Conference Committee. Chaim WEIZMANN defined Jewish aims as "large-scale immigration . . . government assistance for the resettlement of refugees . . . development and organization of the Jewish defense forces in Palestine" (Rose, p. 183).

The London (St. James's) conference opened on February 7, 1939. Because the Arabs refused to speak to the Jewish delegation, the conference ran in two channels. The Arabs outlined the position agreed upon in Cairo, demanded an end to the mandate, and argued that the HUSAYN–MCMAHON CORRESPONDENCE took precedence over the BALFOUR DECLARATION because it constituted a prior commitment. The Arabs insisted on an independent Arab state in Palestine, particularly in view of the three-year-old rebellion by dispossessed fellahin; the Jews would not budge from their traditional refusal to curtail immigration, becoming even more adamant after Germany annexed Austria in 1938.

At the final session, on March 15, MacDonald put forward Britain's proposals: After ten years, a Palestinian state, possibly a federation with Arab and Jewish cantons, would be established. A National Assembly would be charged with drafting a constitution. Since the Arabs would have a majority in the assembly, legal guarantees would be included for a Jewish national home. During the first five years, 75,000 Jewish immigrants would be absorbed, of whom 25,000 would be refugees. Subsequent immigration would depend on Arab consent.

The conference officially ended on March 17, when Weizmann informed MacDonald of Jewish rejection of Britain's terms. Britain resumed contacts with the Arab states at Cairo four days later. Tentative agreement was reached for Palestinians to be gradually appointed to the Executive Council, and to sit as department heads alongside the British incumbents, until all departments were headed by Palestinians; at that time the Executive Council would be transformed into a cabinet.

On May 17, Britain published the white paper based on the terms loosely agreed to at Cairo. It conditionally agreed to the establishment of an independent state in Palestine at the end of ten years if relations between Arabs and Jews at the time would "make good government possible." Palestinian heads of departments would be appointed once peace was established, and Jewish immigration would be limited to 75,000 over the next five years.

The effect of the white paper was short-lived. The provisions concerning immigration and land sales were implemented by the high commissioner. When Winston Churchill came to office as prime minister in May 1940, he postponed the implementation of the provisions pertaining to the gradual assumption of governmental positions by the Palestinians.

BIBLIOGRAPHY

COHEN, MICHAEL J. Palestine: Retreat from the Mandate. The Making of British Policy, 1936–45. New York, 1978.
HIRST, DAVID. The Gun and the Olive Branch: The Roots of Violence in the Middle East. London, 1977.
PORATH, YEHOSHUA. The Palestinian Arab National Movement: From Riots to Rebellion, 1929–1939. London, 1977.
ROSE, NORMAN A. The Gentile Zionists: A Study in Anglo–Zionist Diplomacy, 1929–1939. London, 1973.

Jenab Tutunji

Empire, Prussia, Russia, and Austria to a treaty redefining the international status of the Straits of the Bosporus and the Dardanelles. Under its terms, no foreign warships, except small vessels on diplomatic missions, were to pass the straits while the Ottoman Empire was at peace.

In a separate protocol, a graduated series of penalties was laid out if Muhammad Ali, viceroy of Egypt, and his son, Ibrahim Pasha, refused to retreat from Syria. Consequently, Britain's navy bombarded Beirut and Acre, landing troops. This threat to cut off Egyptian supply lines forced the Egyptians to retreat south of the Sinai. On July 13, 1841, the 1840 London Convention was reaffirmed, this time with French adherence. As France had been Muhammad Ali's patron, this second London Convention was a clear defeat for France. Muhammad Ali lost everything for which he had gambled, retaining only the hereditary viceroyship of Egypt, south of the Sinai desert.

BIBLIOGRAPHY

WEBSTER, SIR CHARLES. The Foreign Policy of Palmerston, 1830–1841, 2 vols. New York, 1969.

Arnold Blumberg

Long–Berenger Agreement

Agreement that awarded France the former German share of Mesopotamian oil.

One of the many issues facing the victorious Entente after World War I was Middle Eastern oil, and on April 8, 1919, Walter Long of Great Britain and Senator Henri Berenger of France agreed that France would eventually obtain Germany's former share of 25 percent of the oil in Mesopotamia (now Iraq). The terms of this agreement were later included in the SAN REMO Conference of 1920.

BIBLIOGRAPHY

HUREWITZ, J. C., ed. The Middle East and North Africa in World Politics. New Haven, Conn., 1979.

Zachary Karabell

London Convention

International agreement to keep warships out of the Bosporus.

On July 15, 1840, British Foreign Secretary Lord Palmerston obtained the adherence of the Ottoman

L'Orient

French-language daily newspaper founded in Beirut in 1924.

Soon after its creation, *L'Orient* became the foremost French-language newspaper in Lebanon. Under the French mandate, it supported Emile Eddé, whereas its main competitor, the daily *Le Jour* (founded by Michel Chiha) backed Bishara al-Khuri. In 1970, the two papers merged to become *L'Orient–Le Jour*. *L'Orient–Le Jour* provides excellent coverage of both local and international news. Its independent but generally pro-West orientation caters to a predominantly Christian readership, especially to Greek Orthodox readers. Published in Beirut, the newspaper has a circulation that was estimated at 23,000 in 1992.

BIBLIOGRAPHY

MCFADDEN, TOM J. *The Daily Press in the Arab States.* Columbus, Ohio, 1953.
RUGH, WILLIAM A. *The Arab Press.* Syracuse, N.Y., 1987.

Guilain P. Denoeux

Lotz, Wolfgang [1921–]

Israeli espionage agent in Egypt, 1960–1965; dubbed "the champagne spy" for his extravagance.

Born in Mannheim, Germany, Lotz moved with his mother to Palestine after Hitler's rise to power, changed his name to Ze'ev Gur-Aryeh, and fought in the Haganah and Israel Defense Forces (IDF). Sent to infiltrate Egypt's military and political circles posing as an ex-Nazi and race-horse breeder, Lotz befriended high-echelon officers and transmitted invaluable information, until caught in 1965 and sentenced to life in prison. Freed in a POW exchange after the Arab–Israel War (1967), Lotz eventually tired of civilian life in Israel and moved to West Germany, then to California.

Zev Maghen

Lovers of Zion

See Hibbat Zion

Lowther, Sir Gerald [1858–1916]

British diplomat.

Lowther was minister of Tangier, Morocco, (1904–1908) and then ambassador at Constantinople (now Istanbul), seat of the Ottoman Empire, (1908–1913) where he witnessed the upheavals of the Young Turk Revolution and watched with some skepticism as

they attempted to reconcile the opposing tendencies of Turkish and Ottoman nationalism.

BIBLIOGRAPHY

LEWIS, BERNARD. *The Emergence of Modern Turkey.* New York, 1968.

Zachary Karabell

Luke, Harry [1884–1969]

British civil servant in the Middle East.

Luke was British chief commissioner in Georgia, Armenia, and Azerbaijan, then assistant governor of Jerusalem (1920–1924). He served on the commission investigating the JAFFA RIOTS in 1921 and was chief secretary in Palestine (1928–1930). In August 1929, as acting high commissioner, Luke permitted activist Jewish youth to march to the Wailing Wall. Jews were attacked, and riots broke out a few days later. Unable to restore order, Luke asked for reinforcements from Jordan and Egypt and turned public security over to the Royal Air Force. He served as lieutenant governor of Malta (1930–1938), then as governor of Fiji and high commissioner of the western Pacific (1938–1942). Among his published books are *A Handbook of Palestine* (1922) and *The Handbook of Palestine and Trans-Jordan* (1934).

Jenab Tutunji

Luqman, Muhammad Ali

Arabic literary and cultural leader.

Muhammad Ali Luqman was from an (Isma'ili) Adeni (South Yemen) merchant family of North Yemeni origins, which prospered under the British and became an important part of the Arab "establishment." Luqman was associated with the first Arabic-language newspaper published in Aden (1940), *Fatat al-Jazira* (Youth of the Peninsula). He also participated in the Arab Reform Club, a literary and cultural organization of the period, and later the Aden Association.

Manfred W. Wenner

Lurs

Luri-speaking tribal people of western Iran.

Lurs are found in three areas in and adjoining the Zagros mountains of western Iran-Luristan in the north, Bakhtiari in the center, and Kuhgiluyeh in the south. They are an Indo-European tribally organized people who speak Luri, a language related to Persian (according to some, a dialect of Persian). Lurs are a people classified primarily by language; they have never been united politically, and they are not an organized ethnic group or national minority (unlike the KURDS, for example). They border on the territories of Kurds, Arabs, and Turks and are economically and socially intermixed with these peoples. In terms of ISLAM, almost all Lurs follow Shi'ism. A small number follow Ali Allahi or BAHA'I. In 1990, there were about a million Lurs. Before the 1920s, most Lurs were nomadic pastoralists. Since then, as nomadism became less tenable, most have practiced a mixed economy of sheep-and-goat pastoralism and agriculture. In the 1990s, most Lurs lived in small villages and towns.

BIBLIOGRAPHY

BLACK-MICHAUD, JACOB. *Sheep and Land: The Economics of Power in a Tribal Society.* Cambridge, England, 1986.

FAZEL, GHOLAMREZA. "Lur." In *Muslim Peoples: A World Ethnographic Survey,* 2nd ed., ed. by Richard V. Weekes. Westport, Conn., 1984.

Lois Beck

Lutfi, Ahmet   [1815–1907]

Ottoman chronicler and bureaucrat.

Lutfi wrote the official chronicle of the TANZIMAT, called *Tarih-i Lütfi* (Lutfi's History), a principal source for the history of the period. His text often provides humorous insight into the human side of reforms, such as the trouble men had with the silk tassels on their fezzes. He also served as the *kazasker* of Rumelia and as a member of the council of state.

BIBLIOGRAPHY

SHAW, STANFORD J. and EZEL KURAL SHAW. *History of the Ottoman Empire and Modern Turkey,* vol. 2. New York, 1977, pp. 445, 494.

Elizabeth Thompson

Lutfi al-Sayyid, Ahmad

See Sayyid, Ahmad Lutfi al-

Luti

A term of Persian use.

Luti originally refered to a member of chivalrous brotherhoods in the late nineteenth- and early twentieth-century Iran. It has gradually come to acquire negative implications, such as vagabondry and drunkardness. It is hypothesized that the etymology of the term refers to the biblical tribe of Lot, thus implying an inclination towards pedophilia.

Neguin Yavari

Luxor

Upper Egyptian commercial and tourist center.

This town on the east bank of the Nile river in Upper Egypt is called al-Uqsur in Arabic. It is noted for its ancient temple and its proximity to Karnak, Thebes, and the tombs of the pharaohs, queens, and nobles on the opposite (west) bank of the Nile. It is the site of numerous Coptic churches and monasteries. With the coming of Islam, it became the site of mosques, notably that of al-Hajjaj, built above the

Pharaonic statue at a Luxor temple. (Mia Bloom)

Hieroglyphic inscriptions at the Karnak Temple in Luxor. (Mia Bloom)

Temple of Luxor. Its 1986 population was estimated at 147,900.

BIBLIOGRAPHY

PORTMAN, IAN. *Luxor.* Cairo, 1989.

Arthur Goldschmidt, Jr.

Luz, Kadish   [1895–1972]

Israeli labor leader and third speaker of the Knesset.

Born in Bobruisk, Byelorussia, he studied economics, agriculture, and sciences at Russian and Estonian universities. Luz served in the Russian army during World War I. After the Bolshevik revolution, he assisted Joseph Trumpeldor in founding the HE-HALUTZ ZIONISM youth movement, then immigrated to Palestine where he worked at land reclamation and road building. He became a leader of the kibbutz movement and the Histadrut, and from 1951 was a MAPAI member of the Knesset, Israel's parliament. Luz was minister of agriculture (1955–1959) and speaker of the Knesset (1959–1969).

Zev Maghen

Lyautey, Louis-Hubert Gonzalve
[1854–1934]

French officer and colonial governor of Morocco during the French protectorate, 1912–1925.

Born in Nancy, France, Lyautey was one of the generation of army officers who had been affected by Germany's defeat of France in the Franco-Prussian War (1870–1871). As did many others, he tried to compensate through the colonial adventure. First in Tonkin (French Indochina), then in Madagascar, under General Joseph S. Gallieni's command, he experimented with a doctrine of colonization after the British model—which respected the culture and institutions of the colonized populations more than the French system had.

At the beginning of the twentieth century, when he served in Algeria, first in the southern territories and then as chief of the division based in Oran, he drew a negative image from the colonial system as it was instituted there. Above all, he wanted to keep the original Algerian model from extending into Morocco when that country came under French control. Since the conquest of Morocco was not easy, his theses became attractive to the French government at the beginning of the French protectorate in 1912; they were already preparing for the oncoming conflict with Germany, now called World War I (1914–1918), and wanted to maintain their resources and troops in Europe.

After Lyautey's appointment to Morocco in 1912, he succeeded in freeing the commercial and religious center of Fez from the *makhzen* (mercenary) system of the tribal peoples. He regained the lowlands and the main cities, which traditionally were under their control. Then he had to get Sultan Mulay Hafid, who would not cooperate, to abdicate and put his brother Mulay Yusef on the throne.

Lyautey was a monarchist, and he admired Napoléon Bonaparte's methods of administration in early nineteenth-century Egypt. He wanted to follow them and to get the support of a legitimizing authority, which would help him subdue Morocco without his own submission to strict controls from Paris. Therefore he tried to maintain the Moroccan monarchy while making sure that it would not present a source of future problems. Under such conditions, the new sultan was allowed to keep the major Islamic prerogatives of Moroccan sovereignty: to be a caliph and an imam.

On March 30, 1912, when Lyautey signed the FES TREATY, establishing the French protectorate over Morocco, which was going to define the relationships between the two countries until 1956, he was

given the mission to reform the structure of the colonial administration. He would succeed in doing
so by joining to the traditional services of the makhzen at the central and local levels a parallel French
hierarchy. Without any resistance on the part of
the sultan, Lyautey would create the laws and regulations by edict, which would guarantee the "administrative legal, educational, economic, financial
and military reforms the French government will
judge have to be introduced on Moroccan territory"
(Article 1 of the Fes Treaty). Lyautey would then
be able to establish a quick modernization, using
only a few competent civil servants. At the beginning, this plan was widely accepted. He would also
be able to place most of the country under the formal
authority of the makhzen by using traditional ways of
negotiating with the tribes and by limiting his need
for force.

His opposition to both parliamentary and political
control by France led him to preserve the autonomy
of Morocco so that, in the long run, he might exert
a larger hidden power. The romantic idea of a feudal
system constituted the basis for his debatable policy.
As a tolerant Roman Catholic, he was open toward
and respectful of Islam; since he was attracted to
marginal people (those living neither within one system nor the other), he thought they might help him
understand this country's essence—outside official
circles. Adept at understanding cultural differences
and hierarchical controls, he came to consider the
possible development of two distinct but parallel societies that might save old cities and architecture but
also lead in education. It was a separated system (akin
to a "mild" apartheid) because he refused to introduce into Morocco the French system that prevailed
in Algeria, based on colonization by poor whites. He
then had to turn to private bankers, especially the
Banque de Paris et des Pay-Bas, but he was unable or
unwilling to avoid the expropriation of the richest,
most fertile lands for the benefit of French settlers.
Although he cared about the sultan's interests, he did
not or could not prevent the basic elements of a
future berber policy to take root.

Under the authority of the protectorate, Lyautey
practiced a direct administration policy and benefited
from it, because of the fiction of Moroccan sovereignty. In keeping the sultan, he confined him to an
outdated traditionalism. Meanwhile, Lyautey's colonial *officiers des affaires indigènes* (officers in charge of
native affairs) had been taught his ruling philosophy,
and they used the pashas and the Arab shaykhs as
intermediaries, to keep things under control. His system did not leave much space for the development
of a Moroccan elite, which he became aware of toward the end of his mission. From 1920, he worried

about the future of the country and considered formulas that would allow an easy withdrawal of French
control.

His authority was shaken by the beginning of the
rebellion of Rif leader ABD AL-KARIM, who in 1921
began fighting against the Spanish in their sector of
Morocco. By April of 1925, Abd al-Karim had
turned to fight the French. A French-Spanish force
was organized against him in July and in September,
under World War I hero French Marshal Henri-
Philippe Pétain; the Rifians were driven back. Toward the end of September, Lyautey resigned, and
he left Morocco for France in October. He was replaced by a civilian resident and by Marshal Pétain as
the military leader. Lyautey left as the legendary
leader who had safeguarded the sultan's monarchy,
the reputation of the country in international affairs,
and its resources and finances through development
of its phosphate mining company. He left as the
launcher of its modernization.

He was to end his life in France as an antirepub-
lican, supporting the extreme right—an admirer of
Italian dictator Benito Mussolini. He was suspected,
not long before his death, to have encouraged the
aborted coup against the French parliament on February 6, 1934, launched by the Croix de Feu (Cross
of Fire, a French fascist organization).

BIBLIOGRAPHY

JULIEN, CHARLES-ANDRÉ. *Le Maroc face aux impérialismes,
1415–1956.* Paris, 1978.
RIVET, DANIEL. *Lyautey et l'institution du protectorat français
du Maroc, 1912–1925.* Paris, 1988.

Rémy Leveau

Lyazidi, Ahmad Muhammad

Moroccan nationalist leader and politician.

Educated at the al-Qarawiyyin Madrasa (school attached to a mosque), Lyazidi joined with many Moroccan students in embracing the reformist ideas of
the SALAFIYYA MOVEMENT. In the 1920s Lyazidi
helped establish one of several student groups that
became the nucleus of the nationalist ISTIQLAL PARTY.
Jailed several times by the French for his political
activity, Lyazidi continued to serve as a leader of the
Istiqlal into the early period of Moroccan independence. In the postindependence era, he held the offices of minister of commerce and then, in 1958,
minister of defense. In the latter capacity, he oversaw
the suppression of the RIF revolt. Lyazidi resigned
in 1959.

BIBLIOGRAPHY

ASHFORD, DOUGLAS. *Political Change in Morocco*. Princeton, N.J., 1961.

SPENCER, WILLIAM. *Historical Dictionary of Morocco*. Metuchen, N.J., 1980.

Matthew S. Gordon

Lydda

Town in Israel.

Located southeast of Jaffa and ten miles from the Mediterranean coast, Lydda is the site today of Ben-Gurion Airport and the center of Israel's aircraft industry. Its 1980 population was about forty thousand, almost entirely Jews. Most of the town's more than ten thousand Palestinian Arabs were forcibly evacuated by the Israel Defense Forces during the 1948 ARAB–ISRAEL WAR.

An ancient bibilical town, Lydda was known through the nineteenth century as an intermediate center for caravans and for its magnificent Byzantine basilica over the tomb of St. George. Under Ottoman Empire rule, it was part of the Jerusalem *sanjak* (district) and an important center for soap and olive oil manufacture. In the 1930s, it became one of the most important railroad junctions in the Middle East, with lines connecting Jaffa, Jerusalem, and Cairo. The airport opened in 1937.

BIBLIOGRAPHY

KHALAF, ISSA. *Politics in Palestine: Arab Factionalism and Social Disintegration, 1939–1948*. Albany, N.Y., 1991.

Elizabeth Thompson

Lyttleton, Oliver [1893–1972]

British businessman and diplomat.

After a successful career as a businessman and member of Parliament, Lyttleton became president of the Board of Trade (1940) and then minister in Cairo, Egypt, during World War II. In this capacity he pressured France to negotiate with Syria and Lebanon. He also aided Sir Miles Lampson in coercing King Farouk to dismiss Ali Mahir as Egyptian prime minister. Lyttleton later served as colonial secretary (1951–1954).

BIBLIOGRAPHY

LENCZOWSKI, GEORGE. *The Middle East in World Affairs*. 4th ed. Ithaca, N.Y., 1980.

Zachary Karabell

M

Ma'abarah

A neologism referring to the residential camps for immigrants to Israel in the early 1950s.

The transit or residential camps were established by the new government of ISRAEL (founded in 1948) to house temporarily the masses of immigrants. In flimsy shelters, tents, canvas lean-tos, and tin shacks, living conditions were harsh. During the mid-1950s, the Israeli government built permanent housing and the *ma'abarot* (plural of *ma'abarah*, in Hebrew) were changed into new, poor towns or city districts.

Shlomo Deshen

Ma al-Aynayn [1840–1910]

Important figure in the religio-political history of Mauritania and southern Morocco.

Ma al-Aynayn (also known as Shaykh Muhammad Mustafa ibn Muhammad Fadil al-Qalqami) was the son of Muhammad Fadil, founder of the Fadiliyya Sufi brotherhood, a religious scholar and leader among the nomadic populations of northern MAURITANIA. Like his father, Ma al-Aynayn was head of the Fadiliyya, a noted scholar, and political leader. A prolific author, he is credited with over 140 books on a wide variety of topics.

A close ally and adviser of the sultans of Morocco from 1859, Ma al-Aynayn cooperated in the extension of Moroccan authority into the Western Sahara. Under Sultan HASSAN I and his successor Abd al-Aziz, he organized resistance to imperialist incursions into the western Sahara by France and Spain.

At his death in 1910 he was succeeded by his son AHMAD HIBAT ALLAH, known as "El Hiba."

BIBLIOGRAPHY

CARO BAROJA, JULIO. "Un santon sahariano y su familia." *Estudios saharianos.* Madrid, 1955.
MARTIN, BRADFORD G. *Muslim Brotherhoods in Nineteenth-Century Africa.* Cambridge, U.K., 1976.

Edmund Burke III

Ma'alot

Urban community in Upper Galilee, Israel.

Founded in 1956 to replace two *ma'abarot* (temporary housing communities) of mostly North African Jewish immigrants, in 1963 Ma'alot was united with the nearby Arab village of Tarshiha. The town's population of some 7,000 works largely in industry. In 1974, members of Nayif HAWATMA's Democratic Front for the Liberation of Palestine killed 21 Jewish schoolchildren at Ma'alot's *Netiv Meir* school.

Zev Maghen

Ma'ariv

Daily newspaper published in Tel Aviv.

Ma'ariv was founded in 1948 by a group of journalists as an afternoon paper, following their departure

,from another newspaper, *Yedi'ot Aharonot*. The splinter group was headed by Ezriel Carlebach, who became the paper's first editor.

For many years, *Ma'ariv* garnered the largest readership of any paper in Israel. Over the years its fortunes have waned considerably. Under its present editor, Dan Margalit, *Ma'ariv* defines itself as broad based, apolitical, and with an appeal to both secular and religious Israelis.

Ann Kahn

Maccabi

International Jewish sports organizations.

Named for the Judean heroes who fought Antiochus in the second century B.C.E., the Maccabi World Union began in 1895 with the formation of clubs like the Israel Gymnastics Club in Istanbul and others in Bucharest, Berlin, and Saint Petersburg. By World War I, membership in the Turkish Maccabi was two thousand.

Although not ideologically a Zionist movement, the Maccabi was part of the phenomenon of a rising Jewish national consciousness during the late nineteenth and first half of the twentieth centuries. Maccabi clubs became important institutions in British-mandated Palestine, Egypt, Lebanon, Syria, and Libya. There was a popular Maccabi club in Baghdad during the late 1920s, but it ceased to be officially active as anti-Zionist Arab nationalism turned virulent. Along with groups such as the Union Universelle de la Jeunesse Juive (Universal Union of Jewish Youth), Jewish Scouts, cultural associations, and modern Hebrew-language schools, the Maccabi helped to foster a feeling of solidarity among Middle Eastern and North African Jewry with their coreligionists worldwide, as well as sympathy for Zionism.

BIBLIOGRAPHY

STILLMAN, NORMAN A. *The Jews of Arab Lands in Modern Times.* Philadelphia, 1991.

Norman Stillman

MacDonald, Malcolm [1901–]

British secretary of state for dominion affairs (1935–1938), colonial secretary (1935, 1938–1940).

The son of Prime Minister James Ramsay MACDONALD, Malcolm was the link between the Jewish Agency and Britain's cabinet following the publication of the WHITE PAPER of 1930 that restricted the immigration of Jews to Palestine. He was partly responsible for the letter written by his father to Chaim Weizmann that, through a change in emphasis, opened Palestine to the immigration of Jews.

When MacDonald became colonial secretary for the second time, however, in view of the rebellion of Palestinian Arabs (1936–1939) and the looming threat of world war, he tried to stabilize the situation by placating the Arab states. He opposed partition of Palestine and organized the LONDON (St. James's) CONFERENCE of 1939. This resulted in the white paper of 1939, which set limits on Jews' immigration and land sales, and held out the promise of an independent (federal) state in Palestine. He made immigration by Jews after a five-year period dependent on Arab consent and the creation of an independent state dependent on Jewish consent. He was opposed by the Zionists.

BIBLIOGRAPHY

BILL, JAMES, and CARL LEIDEN. *Politics in the Middle East.* Boston, 1979.

Jenab Tutunji

MacDonald, Ramsay [1866–1937]

Prime minister of Great Britain (1924, 1929–1935).

MacDonald is best known in connection with the Middle East as the author of the MACDONALD LETTER (1931), sent to Chaim WEIZMANN, which overrode the WHITE PAPER of 1930 and served as the legal basis for administering Palestine until the white paper of 1939.

From January to October 1924, MacDonald was Britain's first Labour prime minister. He again became prime minister in 1929. The onset of the Great Depression precipitated a crisis in 1931, and MacDonald was persuaded to head an all-party national government until 1935. In that year he was replaced by Stanley Baldwin.

The white paper of October 1930 presented the findings of two commissions. The SHAW COMMISSION report of 1930 concerned the investigation of an outbreak of violence between Arabs and Jews in 1929, and the mass killing of Jews in HEBRON and SAFED. It found that the deeper cause of the violence was the uprooting of Arab villagers from the lands they had cultivated for generations, as a result of land sales to Jews.

The HOPE-SIMPSON COMMISSION was appointed to study the matter. Its report, completed in October 1930, found that a significant portion of the Arab rural population was on the verge of destitution. It recommended that the immigration of Jews should be assessed not only in terms of the absorptive capacity of the YISHUV but also in terms of its economic impact on the Arab rural population. It recommended a land development scheme primarily to aid displaced Arab farmers and suggested greater controls on immigration.

The Zionists were outraged, perceiving this as undermining the terms of the mandate. Weizmann maintained that the obligation of the mandatory power was to the Jewish people as a whole, not just the 170,000 Jews already in Palestine. To protest, on 20 October, Weizmann resigned the presidency of the JEWISH AGENCY, which served as a liaison with Britain's government.

The government came under very strong pressure from Zionists, as well as from established British political figures and political parties. To placate Weizmann, MacDonald issued a letter addressed to him as head of the Jewish Agency, and submitted it to the Council of the LEAGUE OF NATIONS. The letter was also recorded as an official document and dispatched to the high commissioner of Palestine as an instruction of the cabinet.

While reiterating the principle that Britain's mandate involved a double undertaking to the Jewish as well as the non-Jewish population of Palestine, the letter reaffirmed responsibility for establishing a national home for the Jewish people in Palestine. It spoke in positive terms of the obligations of the government to facilitate Jewish immigration under suitable terms, subject to the abstract proviso that "no prejudice should result to the rights and position of the non-Jewish community." The negative impact of immigration on Arab farmers was displaced from the central position it had occupied. No reference was made to the proposed development scheme or to another proposal for the creation of a Legislative Council.

MacDonald's letter also precipitated an Arab rebellion during the years 1936 to 1939, an outcome the authors of the Shaw and Hope-Simpson reports had been trying to avoid.

BIBLIOGRAPHY

GEDDES, CHARLES L., ed. *A Documentary History of the Arab–Israeli Conflict.* New York, 1991.
HIRST, DAVID. *The Gun and the Olive Branch: The Roots of Violence in the Middle East.* London, 1977.
PORATH, YEHOSHUA. *The Palestinian Arab National Movement: From Riots to Rebellion.* Vol. 2, *1929–1939.* London, 1977.
ROSE, NORMAN A. *The Gentile Zionists: A Study in Anglo-Zionist Diplomacy, 1929–1939.* London, 1973.

Jenab Tutunji

MacDonald Letter

Policy statement from Britain's Prime Minister Ramsay MacDonald to Chaim Weizmann, to clarify British policy in Palestine after the Passfield White Paper.

The Passfield WHITE PAPER of October 1930 was seen by Chaim WEIZMANN and others as antagonistic to the goals of Zionism in Palestine, then under British mandate. Indeed, Weizmann had tendered his resignation as a result, along with other leading members of the Jewish Agency.

Ramsay MACDONALD's letter of February 1931, conciliatory in tone, noted that the white paper did not amount to a change in policy for Britain, which continued to favor a national Jewish home. It went on to say that Jewish immigration had had a positive effect on the development of Palestine and could continue; the British government had no intention of stopping it, though it did wish to take into account Palestine's economic absorptive capacity. As to state lands, MacDonald said that while the White Paper found it necessary to make them available to landless Palestinians, it referred only to those who became landless as a result of Jewish settlement.

Weizmann subsequently issued a statement saying that the MacDonald letter reestablished the basis for British–Zionist cooperation.

BIBLIOGRAPHY

Encyclopaedia of Zionism and Israel.
HERTZBERG, ARTHUR. *The Zionist Idea.* New York, 1984.

Benjamin Joseph

MacMichael, Harold   [1882–1969]

High commissioner of Palestine (1938–1944).

MacMichael favored abandoning the PEEL COMMISSION's partition plan, temporary suspension of land sales to Jews, and limiting immigration of Jews for a few years. He initially opposed implementing the provisions of the WHITE PAPER for gradual Palestinian Arab self-government, then shifted his position.

MacMichael recommended that Britain terminate the mandate and the JEWISH AGENCY, and under various scenarios, set up either a small, independent Jewish state or one with dominion status, and allowing local autonomy for an Arab state while Britain retained control over the holy places. His recommendations were not accepted.

When there was a controversy about establishing a Jewish army, MacMichael recommended that the recruitment program for the Jewish settlement police and special constabulary be expanded; he feared, however, that a Jewish army in Palestine could be turned against the mandate or used to back up postwar Zionist demands. In August 1944, MacMichael was the target of an unsuccessful assassination attempt by Jewish extremists.

BIBLIOGRAPHY

LENCZOWSKI, GEORGE. *The Middle East in World Affairs,* 4th ed. Ithaca, N.Y., 1980.

Jenab Tutunji

Madani, Abassi al-   [1931–   ]

Leader and official spokesman of the Islamic Salvation Front (Front Islamique du Salut; FIS), Algeria's largest Islamic opposition political party.

After joining the National Liberation Front (FLN) in 1954, Madani spent seven years in prison during the War of Independence. In 1978 he received a Ph.D. from the University of London and later became a professor at the University of Algiers. Active in Algeria's Islamic movement in the 1980s, he was a founding member of the FIS in 1989. He was arrested by the government in June 1991 and remains in prison as of 1996.

Bradford Dillman

Madani, Abdullah al-

Journalist and member of both the Constitutional Assembly and the National Assembly in Bahrain.

A religiously trained Shi'ite, al-Madani represented a rural district in BAHRAIN. He was elected to the Constitutional Assembly in 1972 and 1973. In both assemblies, he was the leader of the conservative (Shi'a) religious bloc—the other two blocs being the bourgeois nationalists and the reformists (leftists). During his service, he started a weekly magazine, *al-Mawaqif,* which he edited and published. He was conservative on social-Islamic issues but liberal on political issues. His editorials in *al-Mawaqif* probably made him some enemies; he was assassinated in the late 1970s.

BIBLIOGRAPHY

NAKHLEH, EMILE. *Bahrain: Political Development in a Modernizing Society.* Lexington, Mass., 1976.

Emile A. Nakhleh

Madani, Ahmad   [1929–   ]

Iranian politician, admiral.

Ahmad Madani earned a doctorate and pursued a career in the navy but was purged by the government of Mohammad Reza Shah PAHLAVI because of his political activities. He was a leading member of the now defunct Iran party, which was led by Shahpur BAKHTIAR, prime minister in the provisional government formed in 1979 after the IRANIAN REVOLUTION. In 1979, Madani was appointed, in the capacity of special government envoy, to arbitrate disputes in the southern provinces of Sistan and Baluchistan; he also was made governor-general of Khuzistan and became defense minister of Iran as well. In 1980, he was a runner-up in the first presidential elections. After his unsuccessful bid for the presidency, he was elected the parliamentary deputy from Tehran, but his opponents, relying on documents captured during the takeover of the U.S. embassy, accused him of pro–CENTRAL INTELLIGENCE AGENCY and antirevolutionary activities. Fearing for his life, Madani decided to flee the country rather than appear before the parliament's credentials committee. Once abroad, he launched an antigovernment movement.

BIBLIOGRAPHY

BAKHASH, SHAUL. *The Reign of the Ayatollahs.* New York, 1984.

Neguin Yavari

Madani al-Glawi   [1866–1918]

Quasi-feudal governor of the High Atlas mountains; ally both of Moroccan sultans (1888–1912) and of the French protectorate government until his death.

Madani ibn Muhammad al-Mazwari al-Glawi exploited an alliance with Sultan HASSAN I of MOROCCO in 1893 to expand the family domain in the central High Atlas mountains and the plains of Marrakech. His political skills made him a key figure in the period of the MOROCCAN QUESTION (1900–1912). At first loyal to Sultan ABD AL-AZIZ IBN AL-HASSAN, he subsequently helped depose him in favor of his brother ABD AL-HAFID. He served the latter as grand vizier from 1908 until his dismissal in 1911. For his role in suppressing the rebellion of El Hiba (AHMAD HIBAT ALLAH) in 1912, he was granted exceptional powers as pasha of Marrakech by the French protectorate government.

After his death in May 1918, he was succeeded by his younger brother al-Hajj TUHAMI AL-GLAWI.

BIBLIOGRAPHY

BURKE, EDMUND, III. *Prelude to Protectorate in Morocco: Pre-colonial Protest and Resistance, 1860–1912*. Chicago, 1976.

MONTAGNE, ROBERT. *Les berbères et le makhzan dans le sud du Maroc.* Paris, 1930.

PASCON, PAUL. *Capitalism and Agriculture in the Haouz of Marrakech.* London, 1986.

Edmund Burke III

Madrasa

Arabic word for an Islamic college and, more specifically, a center for religious and legal studies.

The *madrasa* originated in Eastern Iran in the tenth century and spread to major urban centers throughout the Middle East by the late eleventh century. The architect of the madrasa as a state-sponsored institution of higher education was Nizam al-Mulk (died 1092 C.E.), the prime minister of the Seljuk empire. These residential colleges were designed by the ruling elite both as a training ground for state bureaucrats and as a SUNNI ISLAM response to the propaganda of Ismaili SHI'ISM already being generated at al-AZHAR, the theological learning center founded by the Fatimid dynasty in Cairo in 969 C.E. As part of a Sunni Muslim religio-political agenda, the madrasa spread throughout the Islamic world. The madrasa system augmented already extant mosque-centered training sites for the study of religion and law. Unlike these centers, the madrasa forged links between the ULAMA, the religious scholars who directed Islamic education, and the ruling government authorities whose financial support made their control of the madrasa possible.

The madrasa system of education was linked to the MOSQUE, which traditionally had been the place of instruction for Muslims in the QUR'AN and in the HADITH—the traditions that preserved the words and deeds of the Prophet Muhammad. The madrasa combined the site for education with student residences. Libraries and sometimes hospitals would adjoin the madrasa. Financial support for the educational institution was generated by the state in the form of a charitable endowment called WAQF. The revenue on these endowments paid for the maintenance of the buildings, student stipends, and instructors' fees.

The course of instruction at a madrasa included the Qur'an, tradition, ARABIC language, theology, arithmetic, geometry, astronomy and, often, medicine; however, the study of Islamic law (SHARI'A) provided the core of the madrasa's rigorous curriculum. Initially, madrasas were founded to provide specialized instruction in one of the four Sunni legal schools. In time, legal instruction in one or more of the Sunni legal schools might be offered in a single madrasa.

The method of instruction relied heavily on memorization—of the Qur'an and as many traditions as possible. Once these preliminaries were accomplished, students were trained in the technicalities of the law, divergent legal opinions, and the disputed questions that distinguished their law school from the other Sunni legal schools. After four or more years of study, an instructor determined whether an individual student could be licensed to teach law and given a diploma, a signed certificate called an *ijaza*. Any Muslim male could join a madrasa, but the number of students per teacher was usually limited to twenty. Only male students studied at madrasas; Muslim women were not allowed to study Islamic law. Major Sunni madrasas were founded at Medina, Cairo, Tunis, and Fez. Al-Azhar remains the most famous Sunni theological center in the Arab world; it underwent a series of curriculum reforms in the early twentieth century which made the director of that institution the prime link between the Egyptian government and the country's traditional religious elite. Shi'a madrasas in Iran include those of Mashhad and Qom and, in Iraq, Najaf, and Karbala.

In the nineteenth century, the Ottoman Empire founded schools influenced by European models to train their military officers, bureaucrats, and doctors. Similar professional schools were also created in Egypt and Tunisia during this period to offer instruction to those Muslims in government service forced to contend with the European colonial presence in the Middle East. These non-Islamic educational institutions created new urban nationalist elites. In the twentieth century, the breakup of the Ottoman Empire and the formation of Arab states hastened educational reform; secular schools of higher education undermined the madrasa system in the Sunni Muslim world. State-sponsored higher education throughout the Middle East promoted new secular avenues of social mobility and professional prestige for male and female Muslim students in areas such as medicine and engineering. Shi'a madrasas flourish in Iran since the Ayatollah Khomeini's IRANIAN REVOLUTION of 1979 reestablished Islamic rule.

BIBLIOGRAPHY

HUSAYN, TAHA. *The Stream of Days: At the Azhar.* Tr. by H. Wayment, 2nd ed. London, 1948.

MAKDISI, GEORGE. *The Rise of the Colleges: Institutions of Learning in Islam and the West.* Edinburgh, 1981.

MOTTAHEDEH, ROY. *The Mantle of the Prophet: Religion and Politics in Iran.* New York, 1985.

Denise A. Spellberg

Madrid Conference

International conference convened by Morocco's sultan in 1880.

The delegates to the conference, held in Madrid, Spain, considered alleged abuses of the extraterritorial privileges accorded by treaty to European governments and their formally designated agents—known as protégés—in Morocco. Sultan HASSAN I of Morocco convened the conference. Always a flash point of dispute, the protégé system was subject to abuse, especially through the sale by European consular agents of patents of protection, which gave their Moroccan possessors widespread legal privileges and exemptions as the duly authorized agents of European governments or firms. These included exemption from taxes, military conscription, and local legal obligations.

The Madrid Conference also took up other issues, including the right of foreigners to own land in Morocco. Although a final declaration, known as the Madrid Convention was signed on July 3, 1880, by those attending—from the leading European powers and the United States—the abuses continued and the conference was for all practical purposes a failure.

BIBLIOGRAPHY

BOWIE, LELAND. *The Impact of the Protégé System in Morocco, 1880–1912.* Athens, Ohio, 1970.
BURKE, EDMUND, III. *Prelude to Protectorate in Morocco: Precolonial Protest and Resistance, 1860–1912.* Chicago, 1976.
PARSONS, F. V. *The Origins of the Moroccan Question, 1880–1900.* London, 1976.

Edmund Burke III

MAFDAL

See National Religious Party

Magen David Adom

The National emergency medical, ambulance, blood, and disaster service of Israel.

Magen David Adom (MDA) was founded on June 7, 1930, as a first aid society for the city of Tel Aviv with about 20 volunteers, an ambulance, and a first aid hut. Today MDA serves the entire population of Israel with 5,000 volunteers, 900 employees (physicians, medics/paramedics, ambulance emergency medical technicians, and blood bank and fractionation experts and technicians), and 700 ambulances.

In 1950 MDA's duties and responsibilities were legally defined in the Magen David Adom Law in which MDA was recognized as the organization entrusted to carry out in Israel the functions assigned to a National Red Cross Society under the Geneva Conventions. MDA has failed to gain recognition in the League of Red Cross Societies (which accepts the RED CRESCENT and the RED LION AND SUN) because of Arab and communist-bloc intervention. The issue remains unresolved despite support of the American Red Cross, which is exerting pressure for acceptance by the International Red Cross.

MDA supplies all of the blood used for transfusions by Israel's armed forces and for more than 85 percent of the country's blood requirements. It also supplies first aid instruction.

Miriam Simon

Maghrib

Arabic term for northwest Africa in general, and for Morocco in particular.

In its broadest meaning, the Maghrib (also Maghreb) refers to Morocco, Algeria, Tunisia, and, occasionally, Libya. The region is characterized by fertile plains and the Atlas mountain range near the Mediterranean and Atlantic coasts, and sweeping desert in its hinterland.

The term *maghrib* comes from the Arabic word meaning "west" or "place of sunset." The Arabs conquered the region between 643 and 711 C.E., and ruled it through semi-autonomous kingdoms and tribes. From the ninth to the fourteenth century, the Maghrib produced impressive Islamic realms with robust trade economies tied to Saharan caravan routes. In the sixteenth century, the Ottoman Empire conquered the coasts of present-day Tunisia and Algeria, while the interior desert regions and Morocco remained autonomous, free from imperial rule.

France colonized the Maghrib between 1830 and 1912, and from that period, French was commonly spoken in addition to Berber and Arabic. Morocco and Tunisia achieved independence with little violence in 1956, while Algeria fought the bitter ALGERIAN WAR OF INDEPENDENCE from 1954 until 1962 to achieve its freedom. Libya, once a colony of Italy, was next governed by France and Britain, and became independent in 1951.

BIBLIOGRAPHY

LAROUI, ABDULLAH. *The History of the Maghrib.* Princeton, N.J., 1977.

Elizabeth Thompson

Magic Carpet Operation

Airlift of Jews to the new State of Israel from the southern Arabian peninsula.

Operation Magic Carpet was the popular name given to Operation on Wings of Eagles, the airlift that, between December 16, 1948, and September 24, 1950, brought most of the ancient Jewish communities of the southern Arabian peninsula to the new State of Israel. The evacuees included about 43,000 Yemenites, more than 3,000 Adenis, and nearly 1,000 Habbanis (from HADRAMAWT).

This dramatic operation was run by the Jewish Agency with assistance from the American Joint Distribution Committee. The planes for the airlift came from a specially formed U.S. charter airline, the Near East Air Transport Company. During the height of this exodus, in the fall of 1949, as many as eleven planes flying around the clock carried people from the departure point in the British protectorate of Aden to Lod Airport in Israel. Many of the Yemenite refugees trekked hundreds of miles over rough terrain, in many cases entirely on foot, to reach the Hashid transit camp in Aden to await evacuation.

BIBLIOGRAPHY

BARER, SHLOMO. *The Magic Carpet.* New York, 1952.

Norman Stillman

Magnes, Judah [1877–1948]

Rabbi and first president of the Hebrew University.

Judah Magnes was an ordained Reform rabbi and served in that capacity for four years at the Temple Emanuel in New York City. In 1903, he became chairman of the Jewish Self-Defense Association and later was one of the founders of the AMERICAN JEWISH COMMITTEE and the AMERICAN JEWISH CONGRESS.

An avowed pacifist, Magnes feared that the establishment of a Jewish state would lead to bloody conflict with Arabs, and therefore he advocated the creation of a binational state. He founded Brit Shalom to convince the YISHUV leadership and the British mandatory authorities of the merits of a binational state. He also founded the Ihud movement to foster Jewish–Arab understanding in Palestine.

BIBLIOGRAPHY

BRINNER, WILLIAM H., and MOSES RISCHIN, eds. *Like All the Nations? The Life and Legacy of Judah L. Magnes.* Albany, N.Y., 1987.

Bryan Daves

Mahabad Kurdish Republic

See Kurdistan

Mahalla

In Morocco and Tunisia, the movable camp of the ruler and his entourage.

In Arabic, *mahalla* is literally "a place where one makes a halt." Until the early twentieth century, the often annual progress of a royal mahalla served to reaffirm sovereignty over the ruler's regions, levy taxes, and quell dissidence.

BIBLIOGRAPHY

ARNAUD, LOUIS. *Au temps des mehallas, ou le Maroc de 1860 à 1912.* Casablanca, 1952.

Dale F. Eickelman

Mahalla al-Kubra, al-

Egyptian city in the Nile delta.

Mahalla al-Kubra is a city of about 350,000 people, located near the center of the Nile delta, some sixty miles (96.5 km) north of Cairo, in the province of Gharbiya. The climate is, like much of Egypt along the Mediterranean, relatively wetter than that of Cairo, with humidity averaging about 60 percent. Winter temperatures range from 43–66F° (6–19C°), while summer ranges from 63–88F° (17–31C°).

The delta is the great cotton-growing area of Egypt, and the principal industry of Mahalla is cotton-textile production, as it has been for much of the twentieth century. Mahalla is, in fact, the center of the Egyptian TEXTILE INDUSTRY, but rice and flour mills are also important. The area has been associated with textiles for a long time, since silk weaving became important there in the Middle Ages. In 1927, Egypt's Bank Misr created the Misr Spinning and Weaving Company there—a giant modern industrial plant and one of the three largest industrial undertakings in Egypt (the other two being a sugar refinery in Giza province and a textile firm in Alexandria). In the 1980s, textile production accounted for about 35 percent of Egypt's industrial production.

BIBLIOGRAPHY

DAVIS, ERIC. *Challenging Colonialism.* Princeton, N.J., 1983.
GOLDBERG, ELLIS. *Tinker, Tailor and Textile Worker.* Berkeley, Calif., 1986.

Ellis Goldberg

Mahalle Schools

Provincial schools in the Ottoman Empire.

Most of the public schools in the OTTOMAN EMPIRE were built and funded by local governments. These governments often organized councils to build the schools, hoping that they would stimulate economic development. Most *mahalle* schools offered elementary-level education, although curricula varied. With the 1869 Regulation for Public Instruction, the central government organized provincial councils to distribute state funds and encourage standardization of curricula and examinations at the local schools.

The number of students in mahalle schools rose from 242,017 boys and 126,454 girls in 1867 to 640,721 boys and 253,349 girls in 1895, roughly one-third of all children of elementary school age. There were only 35,731 students in the RÜŞDIYE SCHOOLS (funded by the central government), and nearly 400,000 in foreign and MILLET SYSTEM elementary schools.

BIBLIOGRAPHY

SHAW, STANFORD J., and EZEL KURAL SHAW. *History of the Ottoman Empire and Modern Turkey.* Vol. 2. New York, 1977.

Elizabeth Thompson

Mahasin, As'ad   [1909–   ]

Syrian politician and diplomat.

Born in 1909 to Sa'id Mahasin, a barrister and government minister, As'ad Mahasin was educated in France and earned a doctorate of laws. He joined his father's law practice in 1939. He was appointed minister of justice by Adib Shishakli in 1953. As an Independent, he served Premier Sabri al-Asali as minister of finance in 1957. He became Syria's ambassador to France and Morocco from 1958 to 1961; to Italy from 1961 to 1962. Mahasin returned from this post to become minister of foreign affairs in 1962.

BIBLIOGRAPHY

Who's Who in the Middle East, 1967–1968.

Charles U. Zenzie

Mahdavi-Kani, Mohammad Reza
[1931–   ]

Iranian political and religious figure.

Mohammad Reza Mahdavi-Kani was born in Kan, a village now part of the Tehran municipality. He began his theological studies in Tehran and continued them in Qom in 1947. Among his mentors in Qom, the most notable was Ayatollah Khomeini, who appointed him, before the revolution, to the Council of the Islamic Revolution. In September 1981, when former Prime Minister Bahonar was assassinated, he became the interior minister for a period of two months. He represented Ayatollah Khomeini in various positions and governmental organizations: as the Islamic canonist member of the Guardian Council, as a member of the Constitution Review Panel, and as a member of the Supreme Council of Cultural Revolution. He is the incumbent secretary-general of the Tehran Militant Clergy Association.

Farhad Arshad

Mahdawi, Fazil Abbas al-   [1915–1963]

Iraqi army colonel with a bachelor's degree in law; a cousin of Prime Minister Abd al-Karim Kassem.

Mahdawi was born in Baghdad to a poor family. He became known for his role as head of the special military court, commonly called the people's court. Established by Abd al-Karim KASSEM, the court was infamous for its unorthodox and demagogic procedures. From 1958 to 1962, the court tried leaders of Iraq's monarchical regime (1958–1959), members of the BA'TH party who had tried to assassinate Kassem (1959), and army officers who attempted a coup against Kassem (1959). Mahdawi was executed, along with Kassem, by the officers who staged a successful coup against his regime in February 1963.

BIBLIOGRAPHY

KHADDURI, MAJID. *Republican Iraq.* London, 1969.

Louay Bahry

Mahd-e Ulya, Malek Jahan Khanum
[1805–1873]

Wife of Mohammad Shah Qajar, third monarch of Persia's Qajar dynasty, and mother of Naser al-Din Shah, the fourth monarch. She became known as Mahd-e Ulya upon her son's accession to the throne in 1848.

Mahd-e Ulya was the daughter of Soleyman Khan E'tezad al-Dowleh Qajar Qovanlu; her mother was the daughter of FATH ALI SHAH, second monarch of Persia's QAJAR DYNASTY. Her marriage to Mohammad Shah, third monarch of the Qajar dynasty, in 1819 united the two branches of the Qajar tribe, as decreed by Agha Mohammad QAJAR, the founder of the dynasty. In addition to her son, she had a daughter, Malekzadeh Khanum, who married Mirza Taqi Khan AMIR KABIR, who later became premier for her brother the shah. Mahd-e Ulya was well educated, knew Arabic, was an accomplished calligraphist, and was well versed in literature.

Mahd-e Ulya was entrusted with the affairs of state at the end of her husband's life, until the crown prince could reach the palace in Tehran from Tabriz, the traditional seat of the heir to the throne. She had ruled successfully and continued to be involved in politics after her son became shah but was displeased by her daughter's husband, Amir Kabir, who was trying to enact modern reforms as premier. Court intrigues caused Amir Kabir to lose the trust of the young shah, and he was dismissed, then exiled, and later put to death.

Mahd-e Ulya has been blamed for this action and remains an unpopular historical figure because of her association with the death of one of Persia's most remarkable ministers.

BIBLIOGRAPHY

AVERY, PETER. *Modern Iran.* London, 1965.
WATSON, R. G. *A History of Persia from the Beginning of the Nineteenth Century to the Year 1858.* London, 1866.

Mansoureh Ettehadieh

Mahdi

Arabic term for the redeemer or messiah.

In Arabic, the term *al-mahdi* means "the guided one." For Islam, the term developed through the medieval thought of SHI'ISM into a concept charged with genealogical, eschatological (referring to the end of the world), and political significance. By the eighth century, the mahdi would be characterized as a descendant of the Prophet Muhammad, whose appearance as the redeemer, or messiah (from Hebrew *mashiah,* the anointed), presaged the end of the world and all earthly political and religious corruption.

Today, in Iraq and Iran, the Shi'a branch of Islam is represented by Twelver Shi'ites, who believe in the return of the hidden twelfth descendant of Muhammad as the mahdi. Until he reappears, Twelver Shi'ites believe that only their *majtahids* (an elite group among their religious learned) have the power as the mahdi's intermediaries to interpret the faith.

The concept of the mahdi is not central to the beliefs of SUNNI ISLAM, but it has popular appeal. In 1881, Muhammad AHMAD (died 1885) claimed to be the mahdi and led an uprising in the Sudan that outlasted him and was not put down by the British until 1898.

BIBLIOGRAPHY

SACHEDINA, ABDULAZIZ A. *Islamic Messianism.* Albany, N.Y., 1980.

Denise A. Spellberg

Mahdist State

Independent government formed in the northern Sudan from 1885 to 1898.

The Mahdist state was established in the SUDAN in January 1885 by Muhammad AHMAD ibn Abdallah, the self-declared mahdi (the expected divine leader of ISLAM), after he routed the Turko–Egyptian government and armed forces. He died June 22, 1885, and was succeeded by ABDULLAHI Muhammad Turshain, who ruled as Khalifa al-Mahdi (successor of the Mahdi) until 1898. Abdullahi, the Mahdi's closest lieutenant since 1881, commanded the army, treasury, and daily administration during the rebellion. A member of the Ta'aisha tribe, he led the troops of the *baqqara* (cattle-herding) nomads of the western provinces of Kordofan and Darfur.

Khalifa Abdullahi transformed a tribally based, religious-nationalist uprising into a centralized bureaucratic state that controlled most of the northern Sudan. From 1885 to 1891, his rule was contested by the Ashraf (relatives of the Mahdi) and their supporters in the tribes that originated in the Nile valley (*awlad al-balad*). The Khalifa, whose troops controlled the capital of Omdurman and the corn-growing Gezira, prevented the Mahdi's kinsman Khalifa Muhammad Sharif ibn Hamid from being named ruler and deposed most of the military and administrative leaders of the awlad al-balad army. The Khalifa also feared losing control over the baqqara forces and even his Ta'aisha tribe and therefore, in March 1888, ordered them to march to the capital and serve as his standing army. There, the Ta'aisha had to be placated by massive supplies of food and gold, and their presence exacerbated the Khalifa's rift with the awlad al-balad. When the Ashraf attempted a final rebellion in November 1891, the Khalifa destroyed their military and bureaucratic power.

Natural calamities in 1889/1890 led to famine and epidemics, which were exacerbated by the limited administrative capacities of the government and the food requirements of the troops. The exodus of the tribal forces also reduced grain and cattle production in the west while overburdening the Nile valley. Meanwhile, the Khalifa regularized the operations of the state treasury and reintroduced the taxes and administrative methods of the Turko–Egyptian period. Moreover, he organized a 9,000-person bodyguard, commanded by his son Uthman Shaykh al-Din.

Called the Mulazimiyya, that half-slave force super-seded the Ta'aisha tribe as the principal military support for the regime. The Khalifa thus isolated and destroyed any alternative power centers and consolidated his control over the state apparatus.

The territorial limits of the Mahdist state encompassed most of today's northern Sudan. Its control of the Nile river route through the south was tenuous: it only ruled Bahr al-Ghazal in 1885/86, and Belgian and French expeditions began to penetrate the south in the mid-1890s. The Khalifa controlled Darfur from 1887 to 1889, but the border region with Ethiopia remained contested and British troops controlled Suwakin port on the Red Sea. Seesaw battles with Ethiopia helped to open the way for Italy to consolidate control over Eritrea and to capture grain-rich KASSALLAH, and for Britain to capture the Tukar region south of Suwakin.

The Mahdi had envisioned that his revolution would spread throughout the Muslim world. But the Khalifa's effort to march on Egypt was crushed at the battle near Tushki on the Egyptian frontier, August 3, 1889. (The Khalifa had sent messages inviting Britain's Queen Victoria, the sultan of the Ottoman Empire, and the khedive of Egypt to submit to the Mahdiyya.) The Khalifa then focused on consolidating his administration at home, rather than attempting to spread the message abroad.

The Mahdist state fell in 1898, not as a result of internal disintegration, but at the hands of the superior power of the Anglo–Egyptian army led by Lord Horatio Herbert KITCHENER. His forces entered the Sudan in early 1896 from Egypt and constructed a railway system as they moved south. In April 1898, three thousand Sudanese died in the battle at Atbara; eleven thousand died in the battle of Karari, north of Omdurman, on September 2, 1898, which marked the end of the Mahdist state. The Khalifa escaped to the west, dying in the battle of Umma Diwaykarat, near Kosti, November 24, 1899.

The Mahdist movement was based on a blend of religion, social discontent, and antiforeign sentiment. In its short timespan, the Mahdist state became bureaucratized and lost its religious aura. Although the tribes resented taxes and the controls imposed by government, the increasingly complex administration and judiciary stabilized the regime and enabled it to rule over wide expanses for its thirteen years.

[See also: Ansar, al-; Khartoum]

BIBLIOGRAPHY

HOLT, P. M., and M. W. DALY. The History of the Sudan. Boulder, Colo., 1979.

SHEBEIKA, MEKKI. The Independent Sudan. New York, 1959.

Ann M. Lesch

Mahfuz, Najib   [1911–   ]

Egyptian Muslim author of fiction; winner of the Nobel Prize for literature, 1988.

Najib Mahfuz (also Naguib Mahfouz) was born in Cairo, December 11, 1911. He writes in Arabic and publishes under his two given names, without adding his father's, which was Abd al-Aziz. His father was a minor government official, who sent Najib to be educated in secular state schools. Najib studied philosophy at Cairo University but began a writing career without completing his degree. He also joined government service, working until his retirement in 1971.

After translating James Baikie's *Ancient Egypt* into Arabic in 1932 and publishing a volume of his own short stories in 1938, he planned a long series of historical novels set in Pharaonic times, but between 1939 and 1944, he wrote only three. The second, *Radubis* (1943), concerning a young pharaoh who loses the support of his people, was considered a veiled attack on Egypt's King FAROUK.

Between 1945 and 1957, Najib Mahfuz produced a series of realistic novels set in the lower-middle-class quarters of Cairo, with which he was most intimately acquainted. Three of these, each named after a street in Old Cairo but together known as *The Cairo Trilogy,* follow the fortunes of successive generations of one family between the two world wars. Together they depict, vividly and convincingly, urban social reality and intellectual development in a key period of Egypt's modern history. They established him as the foremost novelist of the Arab world.

Another turning point occurred in 1959, when he published a series in the daily newspaper *al-Ahram,* entitled *Awlad Haratna* (literally, The Children of Our Quarter, but translated by Philip Stewart as *Children of Gebelawi* [London, 1981; rev. ed., Washington, D.C., 1991]). This was ostensibly another Cairo novel, but it soon revealed itself as an allegory on the role played in human progress by the three great Semitic religions and by science as their successor. Its publication as a book has not been allowed in Egypt, but it was printed in Lebanon in 1967.

Thereafter, Najib Mahfuz varied his production with short stories, short plays, articles, and film scripts, but his main output remained novels. These are often boldly experimental in form. Several are multilayered, and all show increasing sophistication and manifest commitment to social and political ideologies, with a deepening philosophical import.

The first Arab writer to have devoted most of his energies to one literary genre, he has brought the Arabic novel to a high level of accomplishment, pioneering—notably in *Al-Liss wa al-Kilab* (The Thief and the Dogs; 1961)—such modern techniques as the stream-of-consciousness method. He has also proved himself a thinker of depth and integrity. The allegorical character of many of his later works has lent itself to widely divergent interpretations. Various tendencies have been read into his work, ranging from secularism to mysticism. He has freely acknowledged his indebtedness to the early Fabian socialist Salama MUSA, and although he later showed some scepticism about the sufficiency of reason as the arbiter of human affairs, there are no indications that he favors the revival of the traditional values of Islam or that he has ever departed from a broad humanism.

Najib Mahfuz has over fifty titles to his credit, more than a dozen of which are available in translation. He was awarded the Nobel Prize for literature in 1988.

[*See also:* Literature, Arabic]

BIBLIOGRAPHY

PELED, MATTITYAHU. *Religion, My Own: The Literary Works of Najib Mahfuz.* Fredericton, N.B., 1983.
SOMEKH, SASSON. *The Changing Rhythm: A Study of Najib Mahfuz's Novels.* Leiden, 1973.

Pierre Cachia

Mahir, Ahmad   [c. 1886–1945]

Egyptian politician; prime minister, 1944–1945.

Ahmad Mahir was one of the most important figures in the early history of the WAFD party in Egypt, which under the leadership of Sa'd ZAGHLUL came to prominence in Egyptian politics after World War I and the Egyptian Revolution of 1919. Son of Muhammad Mahir, Egypt's under-secretary of state for war, and brother of Ali Pasha Mahir, he attended Cairo University for a doctoral degree in law and economics.

Implicated in the November 1924 assassination of Sir Lee STACK, the British governor-general of the Sudan, but acquitted of all charges, Mahir occupied several ministerial positions in Wafd governments before being expelled from the party in January 1938, along with Mahmud Fahmi al-NUQRASHI, as a result of an internal party dispute. The two then founded the Sa'dist party (named for Sa'd Zaghlul). Mahir served

as prime minister of Egypt from October 1944 to February 1945. During the preliminaries to the San Francisco conference at which the United Nations was to be founded, Mahir, believing that Egypt's future interests lay in participation, advocated a declaration of war against the Axis. On February 24, 1945, he was assassinated while presenting this proposal to the Egyptian parliament.

BIBLIOGRAPHY

DEEB, MARIUS. *Party Politics in Egypt: The Wafd and Its Rivals 1919–1939.* London, 1979.

Roger Allen

Mahir, Ali   [1882–1960]

Egyptian politician.

While Ali Mahir and his younger brother, Ahmad Mahir, were both prominently involved in the politics of Egypt during the turbulent years between the two world wars, their careers took quite different paths. Ali was educated in the law and an early associate of Sa'd Zaghlul and the WAFD (Egyptian independence party) in the years following Egypt's anticolonial uprising in 1919 (Egypt had become a British protectorate). Following the squabble between Zaghlul and Adli Pasha in 1921, Mahir dissociated himself from the Wafd. In 1922, Britain had been forced to declare Egypt a sovereign state but reserved rights to the Suez Canal and to defend Egypt. With a Machiavellian instinct for political intrigue and survival, Mahir managed to occupy a large number of political positions in the ensuing decades, including service on three occasions as prime minister of Egypt.

Mahir was closely associated with the palace, being appointed chief of the royal cabinet in 1935. His services were always at the king's disposal whenever there was a need to express royal displeasure at outside pressure, most especially when the British were involved. Mahir's terms as prime minister were short. He served in the post for a few months in 1936 but was dismissed during the constitutional discussions that followed the death of King Fu'ad and the succession of King FAROUK. Equally brief was his premiership from 1939 until June 1940, when his palace affiliations and King Farouk's preference for the Axis powers (Germany and its allies) led to British demands that Mahir be dismissed.

Following World War II, Ali Mahir continued to play his role as one of the *eminences grises* of Egyptian political life. It was hardly surprising that, following the uprisings in Cairo in January 1952, Mahir was one of several politicians asked to serve as prime minister in the period leading up to the July Revolution. It was Mahir who conveyed to King Farouk the command of the Revolutionary Council (chaired by General Muhammad Naguib) that the king abdicate. Following Farouk's abdication and departure for Italy in June 1953, Mahir continued to play a role as chairman of a constitutional commission. Its work was never completed, being overtaken by the rapid developments of the ensuing months—the abolition of the monarchy and the proclamation of a republic under General Naguib, who turned it over to Gamal Abdel Nasser.

BIBLIOGRAPHY

DEEB, MARIUS. *Party Politics in Egypt: The Wafd and Its Rivals 1919–1939.* London, 1979.

Roger Allen

Mahmoud, Ahmad   [1930–   ]

Iranian novelist.

Ahmad Mahmoud is the pen name of Ahmad E'ta, a native of Khuzistan. Leftist political activity during his youth led to his imprisonment in the 1950s. In 1974, he gained fame with his first novel, *Hamsayeha* (The Neighbors), which depicts the aftermath of the 1953 coup d'état in Khuzistan. Mahmoud is one of the most prominent "Southern" writers, along with Sadeq Chubak. His work is called "workers' literature."

BIBLIOGRAPHY

MOAYYAD, HESHMAT, ed. *Stories from Iran: A Chicago Anthology, 1921–1991.* Washington, D.C., 1991.

Pardis Minuchehr

Mahmud, Muhammad   [1877–1941]

Egyptian prime minister, 1920s and 1930s.

Born into a family of wealthy landowners in Upper Egypt and educated at Oxford University, England, Muhammad Mahmud was one of the original members of the WAFD (Egyptian independence party); along with Sa'd Zaghlul, he was banished by the British to Malta following the anticolonial uprising in March 1919. In 1922, after Britain declared Egypt a sovereign state, he split from the Wafd and assumed a leadership role in the LIBERAL CONSTITUTIONALIST PARTY. Mahmud was appointed prime minister in

June 1928 and ruled without a parliament under a "law-and-order" slogan. During the 1930s, he and his party steered a middle course between the government of Isma'il SIDQI and the opposition Wafd party.

In 1937, when the young King Farouk dismissed the Wafdist cabinet of Mustafa al-Nahhas Pasha, Muhammad Mahmud became prime minister for a second time, with a cabinet made up of minority, anti-Wafdist parties. His resignation in August 1939 was attributed to ill health but was, in fact, a consequence of political intrigues involving Ali MAHIR and the king's posture toward the Axis powers (Germany and its allies) at the beginning of World War II.

BIBLIOGRAPHY

DEEB, MARIUS. *Party Politics in Egypt: The Wafd and Its Rivals 1919–1939.* London, 1979.

Roger Allen

Mahmud, Nur al-Din   [1897–?]

Soldier and Iraqi prime minister.

Born in Arbil (also Erbil or Irbil) in what is today northern Iraq, Nur al-Din Mahmud had a career in the Ottoman and Iraqi armies. Faced with serious disturbances in Baghdad in November 1952, Mahmud, then chief of staff, requested authority to declare martial law; he was appointed prime minister on November 23, and eighteen people were killed by Iraqi troops the next day. Mahmud resigned as prime minister on January 29, 1953.

Peter Sluglett

Mahmud II   [1785–1839]

Ottoman sultan, 1808–1839.

Mahmud, youngest of twelve sons of Sultan Abdülhamit I, ascended the throne on 28 July 1808, through a chain of accidental events. An armed coup led by the provincial ruler, Mustafa BAYRAKDAR, was intended to restore the deposed Sultan Selim III (1789–1807). During the military operation, however, Selim was killed, Mustafa was deposed, and Mahmud, the only legitimate candidate of the Ottoman dynasty, was declared sultan. Until he ascended the throne, Mahmud had spent his life in seclusion.

During the first months of Mahmud's reign, real power was wielded by Bayrakdar, who had himself appointed grand vizier. In mid-November 1808,

Bayrakdar's government was overthrown by the janissaries of Constantinople (now Istanbul), who then set up a reign of terror and once again began to interfere in state affairs. The anarchy that had prevailed in the capital since the fall of Selim III in May 1807 left the political elite hopelessly divided and demoralized. Mahmud, demonstrating strong leadership and dedication to traditional values, gradually assembled a coalition of religious and political leaders desiring the reestablishment of orderly government. Throughout his reign he endeavored to strengthen the court's position by subordinating all other political forces.

War with Russia, which had begun in 1806, was concluded with the Treaty of Bucharest (28 May 1812), by which the Ottomans ceded Bessarabia to Russia. Meanwhile, Mahmud had initiated a policy designed to restore central authority over the provinces, and when the war ended, this became his primary concern. By 1820 he had reasserted Constantinople's control over most of the provincial centers in Anatolia as well as Thrace, Macedonia, and the Danube districts. Local rulers were replaced by governors appointed from Constantinople.

The Serbs had twice risen in rebellion (1804–1813, 1815). Under Russian pressure, Mahmud agreed to grant them complete autonomy (1829). In February 1822, after almost two years of warfare, the government defeated and executed the rebellious Tepedelenli Ali Pasha, the most powerful *a'yan* (local ruler) in Albania and Greece. This drawn-out conflict aided the Greeks, who rose up in arms in March 1821. The Ottoman forces subdued the Greek uprising in Macedonia and Thessaly but could not advance into the Peloponnesus, and a stalemate ensued. Mahmud appealed to MUHAMMAD ALI, the governor of Egypt, for assistance, promising to cede to him the governorships of Crete and the Peloponnesus in return for his services. In February 1825 Egypt's newly formed, European-style army landed in Greece. The Ottomans renewed their attacks, and by April 1826, with the fall of the key fortress of Missolonghi, the Greek position became desperate.

Since early in his reign Mahmud had been cautiously introducing significant improvements in the military, especially in the artillery and the navy. In the spring of 1826, with his authority restored at the capital and in many provinces, and with the Greek uprising appearing close to extinction, Mahmud decided that the time had come for more comprehensive reforms. The first project was reorganizing part of the janissary corps as an elite unit of active soldiers called Eşkinciyan. Mahmud enlisted the support of the religious and bureaucratic elites as well as the janissary officers themselves. Nevertheless, on the

night of 14 June the janissaries rose up in arms. Mahmud mustered loyal troops, and on 15 June, the rebellion was crushed with considerable bloodshed. Two days later an imperial decree abolished the Janissary Corps.

It is difficult to exaggerate the impact that the suppression of the janissaries had on Ottoman society and in Europe. In an effort to gain universal approval, the regime called the incident "the Beneficial Affair" (Vaka-i Hayriye). The Eşkinciyan project was abandoned in favor of a more ambitious plan calling for the formation of an entirely new army organized and trained on Western models. The new force was named the Trained Victorious Troops of Muhammad (Mu'allem Asakir-i Mansure-yi Muhammadiye; Mansure, for short).

Meanwhile, the plight of the Greeks elicited European intervention. Britain, Russia, and France offered mediation. When the Ottomans objected, the three powers sent their fleets to Greece, where on 20 October 1827, inside the harbor of Navarino, they destroyed an Ottoman Egyptian fleet. This was followed, in May 1828, by a Russian offensive. The Russian army captured Adrianople (now Edirne) on 20 August 1829 and threatened to advance on Constantinople. The war was concluded by the Treaty of Adrianople (14 September 1829). The Ottomans ceded to Russia the Danube delta in Europe and the province of Akhaltsikhe (Ahisha) in Asia. In addition they were required to pay Russia a sizable indemnity and to recognize the autonomy of Serbia, Moldavia, Wallachia, and Greece under Russian protection. Later, in negotiations among the European powers, it was determined that Greece should become an independent monarchy. In July 1832, Mahmud accepted these terms.

Military defeat and the apparent failure of the government's attempts to reform the army rekindled unrest and rebellion in far-flung provinces, especially in Bosnia, Albania, eastern Anatolia, and Baghdad. The government was generally successful in suppressing these uprisings by employing the new disciplined troops, who proved effective as an instrument of coercion and centralization.

Meanwhile, Muhammad Ali sought compensation for his losses in Greece and demanded that Mahmud cede to him the governorship of Syria. When this was rejected, Egypt's army invaded Syria (October 1831), defeated three Ottoman armies, marched into Anatolia, occupied Kütahya (2 February 1833), and was in a position to march on Constantinople. Mahmud sought help from the great powers, but only Russia dispatched a naval force to defend Constantinople (February 1833). This induced Britain and France to offer mediation, resulting in the Peace of

KÜTAHYA (8 April), which conferred on Muhammad Ali the governorship of Syria and the province of Adana. Meanwhile, Russia's paramountcy in Constantinople was underscored by the Treaty of Hünkâr-Iskelesi (8 July), a Russian–Ottoman defensive alliance. The treaty alarmed other powers, especially Britain, which decided to help the Ottomans free themselves of their dependence on Russia.

Despite military disasters and political setbacks, during the 1830s Mahmud proceeded with his reform measures. He continued to focus on centralization of government and greater efficiency in its work. In 1835 he reconstituted the entire administration into three independent branches: the civil bureaucracy (*kalemiye*), the religious–judicial hierarchy (*ilmiye*), and the military (*seyfiye*). Their respective heads—the grand vizier, the *şeyhülislam*, and the *ser asker*—were considered equal and were responsible directly to the sultan. The aggrandizement of the court, now the seat of all power, was mainly at the expense of the grand vizier's office. Traditionally the grand vizier was considered the sultan's absolute deputy (*vekil-i mutlak*) and, as such, the head of the entire government. To underscore the reduction of his authority, in 1838 the grand vizier's title was officially changed to chief deputy, or prime minister (*baş vekil*). At the same time his chief assistants were given the title of minister (*nazir*, later *vekil*). Consultative councils were established to supervise military and civil matters and to propose new legislation. The highest of these, the Supreme Council for Judicial Ordinances (Meclis-i Vala-yi Ahkam-i Adliye), established in 1838, acted as an advisory council to the sultan.

The military, which during Mahmud's last years was allocated about 70 percent of the state's revenues, continued to be the focal point of reform. Most significant was the gradual extension of the authority of the commander in chief (*ser asker*) of the Mansure corps over other services and branches. His headquarters (*bab-i ser asker*) gradually came to combine the roles of a ministry of war and general staff, and was in charge of all land forces. The navy continued to operate independently under the grand admiral, whose administration comprised a separate ministry.

In May 1835, an Ottoman expeditionary force occupied Tripoli in Africa, claiming it back for the sultan. In the following years, Ottoman fleets appeared several times before Tunis, but were turned back by the French navy. The continued occupation of Syria by Muhammad Ali could not be tolerated by the autocratic Mahmud. In the spring of 1839, believing that his army had sufficiently recovered and that a general uprising in Syria against Egypt's rule was imminent, Mahmud precipitated another crisis. On 24 June the Egyptians decisively routed the Ottoman army at Nizip. Mahmud died on 1 July, probably before learning of his army's defeat.

During Mahmud's reign, the Ottoman Empire continued to weaken in relation to the West. Its dependence on Europe increased, and it continued to suffer military humiliation and territorial losses. Yet within the reduced confines of his realm, Mahmud's achievements were considerable. He resurrected the sultan's office, and reformed and rejuvenated the central government. He arrested the disintegration of the state and initiated a process of consolidation. In spite of his intensive reform activities, Mahmud was inherently dedicated to traditional values. He did not attempt to alter the basic fabric of Ottoman society, but rather to strengthen it through modern means. He generally succeeded in integrating the old elites into the new institutions. This was in keeping with his strong attachment to the ideal of justice in the traditional Ottoman sense. The sobriquet he selected for himself, Adli (the Just or Lawful), is an indication of the cast of his mind. Though he may not have intended it, Mahmud's reforms produced basic change and launched Ottoman society on the course of modernization in a final and irrevocable manner.

BIBLIOGRAPHY

BERKES, NIYAZI. *The Development of Secularism in Turkey.* Montreal, 1964.
LEVY, AVIGDOR. "The Officer Corps in Sultan Mahmud II's New Ottoman Army, 1826–1839." *International Journal of Middle East Studies* 2 (1971): 21–39.
———. "Ottoman Attitudes to the Rise of Balkan Nationalism." In *War and Society in East Central Europe During the 18th and 19th Centuries*, ed. by B. K. Kiraly and G. E. Rothenberg. Vol. 1. New York, 1979.
———. "The Ottoman Ulema and the Military Reforms of Sultan Mahmud II." *Asian and African Studies* 7 (1971): 13–39.
SHAW, STANFORD J., and EZEL KURAL SHAW. *History of the Ottoman Empire and Modern Turkey.* Vol. 2. New York, 1977.

Avigdor Levy

Mahmud Durrani   [1765–1829]

Emir of Afghanistan, 1800–1803, 1809–1818.

Mahmud Durrani was one of twenty-one sons of Afghan Emir Timur Shah (1773–1793) and the second oldest. Mahmud was governor of Herat, and in 1800 he successfully fought his half brother Zaman Shah for the Kabul throne. Content to leave the governing to BARAKZAI ministers, Mahmud was ousted by another half brother, Shah Shuja, the seventh son of Timur. Mahmud was imprisoned but escaped to Kandahar in 1809 and regained the Kabul throne in 1813. Once again driven from power in 1819, he retired to Herat, where he died in 1829; according to some reports the cause of death was malaria, but others suggest that he was poisoned by his ambitious son Kamran.

Mahmud's reign marked the beginning of internal conflict and civil war, which was to continue throughout the nineteenth century, until the reign of Abdur Rahman (1880–1901). During this period, much of the territory originally belonging to Afghanistan was lost. Mahmud was a weak leader who preferred to enjoy the perquisites of royalty rather than tending to affairs of state.

BIBLIOGRAPHY

FLETCHER, ARNOLD. *Afghanistan: Highway of Conquest.* Ithaca, N.Y., 1965.

Grant Farr

Mahmudiyya Canal

Artificial waterway in Egypt.

Built between 1817 and 1820 at the command of Muhammad Ali, viceroy of Egypt, this navigation canal connected Alexandria with the delta village of al-Atf and hence with Bulaq, the port city of Cairo. Its construction cost 35,000 purses (7.5 million French francs). Possibly as many as 300,000 peasants were conscripted to dig it during the period of concentrated work in 1819, costing between 12,000 and 100,000 casualties. Owing to the Nile floods, the canal has been dredged often, and annual improvements have been made since its construction. It also provided some summer irrigation and some of Alexandria's drinking water supply.

BIBLIOGRAPHY

RIVLIN, HELEN ANNE B. *The Agricultural Policy of Muhammad Ali in Egypt.* Cambridge, Mass., 1961.

Arthur Goldschmidt, Jr.

Mahmud Nedim   [1818–1883]

Ottoman administrator and grand vizier.

The son of a provincial administrator, Mahmud Nedim was born in Constantinople (now Istanbul) and was trained as a scribe at the Sublime Porte. At the age of sixteen, he entered the civil service working for the Imperial Council. Appointed governor of Sidon

in 1855, he moved on to be governor of Syria and of İzmir before returning to Constantinople in 1858, when he replaced Fuad Paşa as minister of foreign affairs. Although originally a protégé of MUSTAFA REŞID, Nedim was favored by Sultan Abdülaziz who used him to counter modernizing bureaucrats promoting the Tanzimat reforms. Ali Paşa engineered Nedim's downfall in 1860, after which he went into a period of voluntary exile as governor of Tripoli. In 1867, with the support of the YOUNG OTTOMANS, Nedim returned to Constantinople and became a member of the Supreme Council, then minister of justice, and minister of the navy (1867–1871). When Ali died in 1871, Abdülaziz attempted to gain control over the cabinet by appointing Mahmud Nedim Paşa grand vizier, a position he held only until the end of July 1872, when he was replaced by his rival, Midhat Paşa. Nedim held the position of grand vizier again between August 25, 1875, and May 11, 1876.

David Waldner

Mahmud of Sulaymania   [1878–1956]

Kurdish leader.

Born to a prestigious family of Islamic shaykhs in Barzinja (Ottoman Kurdistan, later Iraq), Mahmud Barzinji became the main adversary of Britain's efforts to integrate the KURDS of the *vilayet* (province) of Mosul into Iraq. Proclaiming himself king of Kurdistan in the city of Sulaymaniye, he led several revolts from 1918 to 1930—first against the British then against the new Iraqi monarchy.

BIBLIOGRAPHY

EDMONDS, C. J. *Kurds, Turks and Arabs.* London, 1957.

Chris Kutschera

Mahmut Şevket

See Şevket, Mahmut

Maimon, Yehudah Leib Hacohen
[1875–1962]

Religious Zionist leader, author, and first Israeli minister of religious affairs.

Maimon was born in Markuleshti, Bessarabia, Russia. His parents supported the Lovers of Zion movement and he was exposed to classic religious Zionist writing from an early age. He studied in the yeshivas

(Jewish religious schools) of Lithuania, developing extensive ties with other religious Zionists. One of his associations was with Rabbi Isaac Jacob Reines, founder of the Mizrachi party within the World Zionist Organization, and Maimon rose to leadership there. He immigrated to Palestine in 1913, was arrested and imprisoned, then expelled by the Turks in 1915. He returned to Palestine in 1919, by permission of the British, after spending some years in the United States.

Along with Rabbi A. I. Kook, Maimon established the chief rabbinate in Palestine. In 1935, he was elected Mizrachi representative to the executive of the Jewish Agency. Maimon then founded the Mossad Harav Kook educational institute and publishing house, where he edited the periodical *Sinai*. As Israel's first minister of religious affairs, 1948–1951, he set policy regarding a number of major public religious issues. Maimon also authored many books on religious Zionism and major rabbinic figures.

BIBLIOGRAPHY

BAT-YEHUDAH, GEULAH. *Harav Maimon bedoratav* (Rabbi Maimon in His Generations). Jerusalem, 1979.

Chaim I. Waxman

Maiwandwal, Mohammad Hashim
[1919–1973]

Afghan prime minister, 1965–1967.

Maiwandwal was born in 1919 and educated in Kabul at Habibia High School. He was the editor of several newspapers, including the well known *Anis*. He was appointed prime minister by Zahir Shah in 1965, during the period of constitutional monarchy. When Daud came to power in 1973, Maiwandwal was imprisoned. He reportedly died during torture, although government officials announced that he had committed suicide.

BIBLIOGRAPHY

ADAMEC, LUDWIG. *Historical Dictionary of Afghanistan.* Metuchen, N.J., 1991.

Grant Farr

Majali, Hazza' al-   [1918–1960]

Jordanian prime minister.

As a member of a very influential clan from the Karak area of southern Jordan, Hazza' al-Majali had a strong popular base in Jordan but was viewed as a threat by Palestinians. He was asked by King Hussein ibn Talal to form a government in December 1955 that would push through Jordan's participation in the BAGHDAD PACT. However, he was forced to resign a few days later as a consequence of violent demonstrations against joining. He was known to be strongly pro-regime and encouraged cooperation with the West, particularly the United States, Britain, and Germany, who were supporting Jordan at the time both financially and technically. Yet Majali was considered to be progressive for his times because of his activism in parliament. As a member of parliament in 1953, he helped found the National Socialist party, consisting of thirteen members of parliament. He led them in lively opposition to then Prime Minister Tawfiq Abd al-Huda, forcing him to call for new elections in 1954 rather than face a no confidence vote. He quit the party, however, after Sulayman al-Nabulsi had joined and transformed it into a left-leaning, pro-Nasser party. Majali was assassinated on August 29, 1960, fifteen months into his term as prime minister. During his term, he had earned a reputation for taking firm measures against communism and subversive activities.

BIBLIOGRAPHY

MUSA, SULAYMAN. *A 'lam min al-Urdun: Hazza al-Majali, Sulayman al-Nabulsi, Wasfi al-Tall.* Amman, 1959.

Jenab Tutunji

Majarda Valley

See Medjerda Valley

Majles

The most common word for parliament in Arabic, Persian, and Turkish.

Majles (also *Majlis* or *Meclis*), from the Arabic verb *jalasa*, "he sat," literally denotes a sitting or session. In medieval usage, the term was used quite broadly to designate everything from a class in religion to a reception held by a caliph. Some of these usages continue. Tribal shaykhs and members of ruling families in the Arabian peninsula, for example, commonly hold formal, quasi-public receptions for acquaintances or common citizens. The primary purpose of these assemblies is to manifest hospitality and openness rather than to transact business.

In one of the term's earliest modern usages, Khedive Isma'il of Egypt promulgated in 1866 a set of regulations for a MAJLES SHURA AL-NUWWAB *al-misriyya*, "Consultative Assembly of Egyptian Representatives." The word *shura* derived from the practice of consultation in the earliest Muslim community in Medina, and in particular from the assembly of six leaders presided over by the Caliph Umar's son that nominated Uthman as the third caliph in 644. Though the term MAJLES AL-SHURA is today used for elected legislative assemblies, e.g., in the Islamic Republic of Iran, it is also used for appointed consultative bodies with a purely advisory capacity, as in Saudi Arabia. More conventional Ottoman usages in the nineteenth century included the *Meclis-i Hass* (Privy Council), the *Meclis-i Dar-i Şura-yi Askeri* (Council for Military Affairs), and the *Meclis-i Vala-i Ahkam-i Adliye* (High Council for Judicial Ordinances).

The Ottoman parliament of 1876 was called *Meclis-i Umumi*, "General Assembly," and that instituted by the Turkish republic in 1920, *Türkiye Büyük Millet Meclisi*, "Grand National Assembly of Turkey." The first Iranian parliament of 1906 was called *Majles-e Shura-ye Melli*, "National Consultative Assembly." For parliamentary terminology and history in other countries, see individual country articles.

BIBLIOGRAPHY

"Madjlis." *Encyclopaedia of Islam*, new edition, vol. 5, pp. 1031–1082.

Richard W. Bulliet

Majles al-Shura

National assembly of Iran.

Majles al-Shura-ye Melli, meaning national assembly or parliament, was introduced as a concept to the Middle East in the nineteenth century as a result of increased contact with the West. The history of a representative institution in Iran dates to the constitutional revolution of 1905–1911, when a *Majles al-Shura* was introduced. A senate was added to the national assembly in 1950, in the reign of Mohammad Reza Pahlavi. It is important to note that except for a brief period from its inception to the end of World War I, and again from 1951 to 1953 under the premiership of Mohammad Mossadegh when the oil nationalization bill was passed, the Majles in monarchical Iran did not enjoy a significant degree of autonomy, and exercised little initiative in the nation's political life. Women gained suffrage in 1963, and twenty-four assemblies met from 1906 to 1978.

After the revolution of 1979, the Majles al-Shura-ye Melli was renamed the Majles al-Shura-ye Eslami (Islamic Assembly) and has generally played a more prominent role in political affairs. The new Majles opened on May 28, 1980 with the current president of Iran, Hashemi Rafsanjani, as its speaker, and impeached the then president, Abolhasan Bani Sadr, on June 21, 1981. The speaker of the Majles in the 1990s was Ayatollah Ali Akbar Nateq-e Nuri.

BIBLIOGRAPHY

BAKHASH, SHAUL. *The Reign of the Ayatollahs*. New York, 1984.

ZONIS, MARVIN. *The Political Elite of Iran*. Princeton, N.J., 1971.

Neguin Yavari

Majles Shura al-Nuwwab

Egypt's first quasi-representative assembly.

Established in 1866 by a decree from Khedive Isma'il of Egypt, the *majles* was intended to be a consultative council that would advise him on administrative matters. But he may have been driven by his growing financial straits to co-opt the landowning notables to raise taxes. Its seventy-five members, barred from government posts while they held office, were elected for three-year terms. Timid at first, they grew more assertive as they gained experience and often passed resolutions for administrative reforms. However, they met for only three months at a time and were not even convened in 1872, 1874, and 1875.

While its role was subordinated to the other deliberative bodies, the Privy Council and the Council of Justice, which were smaller and made up of powerful government officials, the *majles* emerged as one of the standard-bearers of Egyptian nationalism in the era of the URABI revolution. In part, this happened because the Egyptian landowners were, along with the peasants, victims of Isma'il's mismanagement and the financial stringencies adopted by Tawfiq and the DUAL CONTROL.

BIBLIOGRAPHY

HUNTER, F. ROBERT. *Egypt under the Khedives, 1805–1879*. Pittsburgh, 1984.

LANDAU, JACOB M. *Parliaments and Parties in Egypt*. Tel Aviv, 1954.

SCHÖLCH, ALEXANDER. *Egypt for the Egyptians!* London, 1981.

Arthur Goldschmidt, Jr.

Makarios II   [1870–1950]

Greek Cypriot cleric; archbishop of Cyprus, 1947–1950.

Born Makarios Myrianthefs to a Greek-speaking Greek Orthodox family in the village of Prodromos on Cyprus, Makarios was elected archbishop of Cyprus in 1947, a position he held until his death. He is known as Makarios II in order to distinguish him from two other archbishops of Cyprus: Makarios I, who served from 1854 to 1856, and MAKARIOS III, who served from 1950 to 1977. He was educated at the Theological School of the Orthodox Ecumenical Patriarchate on the Turkish island Heybeli, at the University of Athens, and at Oxford University. Elected bishop of Kerynia, Cyprus, in 1917, he supported the Greek Cypriot movement for union with Greece. After being elected archbishop of Cyprus in 1947, he organized the referendum in 1950 whereby the Greek Cypriots made known their sentiment for union with Greece.

Alexander Kitroeff

Makarios III   [1913–1977]

Greek Cypriot cleric; archbishop of Cyprus, 1950–1977; president of Cyprus, 1960–1977.

Makarios, whose full name was Mihail Christodoulou Mouskos, was born to a Greek Orthodox peasant family in Paphos, CYPRUS. After serving as a novice at the Kykko monastery, he studied theology at the University of Athens and at Boston University in the United States. He was ordained a priest in 1946 and within two years became bishop of Citium on Cyprus. In 1949, he became president of the Greek Cypriot Ethnarchy, a body that administered the civil prerogatives the Orthodox Church of Cyprus had gained in the Ottoman era and retained through British occupation since 1878. Under his leadership, the ethnarcy organized a referendum in January 1950 that resulted in an overwhelming Greek Cypriot vote in favor of union with Greece. That year, Makarios was elected archbishop of the Greek Orthodox Church of Cyprus, following the death of Archbishop Makarios II.

The new archbishop initiated a series of ecclesiastical reforms but was especially concerned with promoting the cause of Cyprus's union with Greece through the United Nations, thereby formulating the issue in anticolonialist terms. Despite Greece's initial reluctance to take up the issue and Britain's even greater opposition to relinquishing its control over the island, the Cyprus question was discussed at the United Nations in 1951, thanks to Makarios's efforts and the support he received from the nonaligned nations. A year after the outbreak of an anti-British guerilla struggle on Cyprus, directed by the Greek Cypriot organization of EOKA in 1955, the British authorities, suspecting Makarios of being involved

with the guerillas, deported him to the Seychelles. After the EOKA struggle subsided, Makarios was obliged to accept a British plan that gave Cyprus independence rather than union with Greece. He returned to Cyprus in 1960 and was elected president of the Republic of Cyprus.

Through his association with the nonaligned movement, Makarios acquired an international stature far greater than might seem commensurate with the small size of Cyprus. Continued strife between the Greek Cypriot majority and the Turkish Cypriot minority on the island became a divisive element threatening his status. Caught between Greek and Turkish Cypriot extremists, Makarios worked toward preserving the sovereignty and territorial integrity of Cyprus, which was threatened not only domestically but externally by British and U.S. proposals designed to divide the island in various ways in order to diffuse ethnic strife. The conflict culminated in July 1974 when extremist nationalist Greek Cypriots, aided by the dictatorship that ruled Greece, tried to overthrow and assassinate Makarios. He escaped abroad and at the end of the year returned to Cyprus, which by then, however, was a divided island, since Turkey, in retaliation against the coup attempt, had invaded Cyprus and occupied over a third of it. Until his death in August 1977, Makarios worked hard to arrive at a compromise with the Turkish Cypriots, but his efforts were not rewarded.

BIBLIOGRAPHY

VANCZIS, P. N. *Makarios: Life and Leadership.* London, 1979.

Alexander Kitroeff

Makarius III   [1872–c.1945]

114th Coptic patriarch of Egypt, 1944–1945.

Although Makarius spent only eighteen months in office and one-third of that time in exile, he is renowned as one of the great visionaries of the modern Coptic church (see COPTS). As metropolitan or archbishop of the province of Asyut in Central Egypt for forty-seven years, Makarius had promoted education and charitable causes throughout his diocese. He established the first two Coptic elementary schools, one exclusively for boys and another for girls; more than thirty other schools for poor children; and dozens of benevolent societies. So greatly was Makarius esteemed throughout his province that he was nominated for and won the Coptic papacy. Only one other bishop had been elected patriarch; heretofore, monks had made up the field of candidates. Makarius sought to improve relations with the Ethiopic Orthodox Church, which had demanded greater autonomy from the Coptic Church, but the council convened by Makarius in 1945 refused to accede to the Ethiopians' requests. Makarius's proposal of various reforms in financial matters and educational and welfare programs for the entire country also met with opposition from both many provincial bishops and from various members of the Coptic Community Council, the preeminent organization for Coptic laity that had an entrenched hostility to the clergy. Brought together in a rare alliance, both the bishops and the council members resented Makarius's proposed reforms, which would have taken away their control of provincial finances and put them partly under each other's control and partly under the patriarch's jurisdiction. During the ensuing controversy, Makarius exiled himself to a monastery near the Red Sea. He died not long after his return to Cairo, before he had been able to realize many of his plans.

BIBLIOGRAPHY

MEINARDUS, OTTO. *Christian Egypt: Faith and Life.* Cairo, 1970.
SHOUCRI, MOUNIR. "Macarius III." In *The Coptic Encyclopedia*, vol. 5. New York, 1991.

Donald Spanel

Makawi, Abd al-Qawi

Exiled politician of South Yemen.

Makawi—a local employee of A. Besse and Co. in Aden, whose flourishing career as an anti-British nationalist politician in the 1960s was eclipsed by the triumph of the NATIONAL FRONT FOR THE LIBERATION OF SOUTH YEMEN (NLF) as successor to British rule in South Yemen—has been in exile from the mid-1960s to the 1990s, though he continues to make statements about Yemen's politics.

Robert D. Burrowes

Makhmalbaf, Mohsen [1957–]

Iranian film director and writer.

Mohsen Makhmalbaf, born in Tehran, is one of Iran's foremost film directors. He also is a novelist and a screenplay writer. He was jailed from 1974 to 1978 because of plays that he wrote as a high school student showing sympathy for the Islamic cause. In 1986, however, he left the Islamic Propaganda

Organization, a government agency, turning a new chapter in his career as an independent filmmaker. Apart from several awards won in Iranian festivals, Makhmalbaf's *The Bicycle Rider* won the best film award from the Rimini Festival in Italy in 1989. His *Hello Cinema* was shown, to wide critical acclaim, at the Locarno Film Festival in Switzerland in 1995.

Neguin Yavari

Makhus, Ibrahim

Syrian politician.

Syrian-born and holding a doctorate, Ibrahim Makhus was appointed vice president of Dr. Zouayen's cabinet in 1965. A member of the regional directorship of the Ba'th party, he served as foreign minister from 1965 to 1968. As leader of the peasant union (1968–1969), he tried to consolidate its political power against the military wing of the Ba'th party, eventually losing out to the latter.

BIBLIOGRAPHY

Who's Who in the Middle East, 1967–1968.

Charles U. Zenzie

Maki

See Communist Party, Israel

Makki, Hasan Muhammad

Yemeni government official.

Makki came from a prominent family from the Red Sea port of Hodeida and was educated in Italy. Despite his relatively advanced and leftist political ideas and posture, Makki managed to hold high government office in North Yemen much of the time in each of the regimes since the 1962 revolution, as well as since the unification of the two Yemens in 1990. He was prime minister, president of San'a University, and foreign minister, while serving many times as deputy prime minister—the post he held during the first years of the unified Republic of Yemen.

Robert D. Burrowes

Makram, Umar [?–1811]

Political organizer and leader of Cairo's sharifian notables (Naqib al-Ashraf).

An active politician, Makram was a leading figure in Cairo both as head of the notables and as an efficient organizer of the Cairene masses. He organized the artisans of Cairo into a militia to oppose the 1798 invasion and occupation by France. Following his opposition in 1809 to the plan of Egypt's ruler, Muhammad Ali Pasha, to tax the landholdings of the religious elite, Makram was removed from his office and sent into exile.

BIBLIOGRAPHY

AL-SAYYID MARSOT, AFAF LUTFI. *Egypt in the Reign of Muhammad Ali.* Cambridge, U.K., 1984.
WUCHER KING, JOAN. *Historical Dictionary of Egypt.* Metuchen, N.J., 1984.

David Waldner

Maktum, Hamdan ibn Rashid al-

United Arab Emirates' minister of finance and industry.

Hamdan ibn Rashid is the second son of the late ruler of Dubai, Shaykh Rashid ibn Sa'id al-Maktum. Early in 1960 he was appointed chairman of the municipality, the health department, and the department of health and medical services. In fact, Dubai municipality has wide responsibilities and maintains the infrastructure of the modern city. Shaykh Hamdan has been the minister of finance and industry since December 1971 in the federal cabinet of the UNITED ARAB EMIRATES and has remained chairman of the municipality and Department of Information in Dubai. His brother, Shaykh Maktum ibn Rashid al-MAKTUM, is ruler of Dubai and prime minister of the United Arab Emirates.

Today Dubai's media are highly developed. Its radio station started in 1970 and its television transmissions in 1974. There are currently six channels. The daily newspaper *al-Bayan* began in 1979, as did the magazine of *Sports and Youth.*

Shaykh Hamdan is the patron of al-Nasr Sports Club, shows an interest in local camel racing and international horse racing, and has plans for an international festival of long distance sailing-dhow racing. On January 4, 1995, he was appointed deputy ruler in Dubai.

BIBLIOGRAPHY

Persian Gulf Gazette and Supplements, 1953–1972. London, 1987.
Persian Gulf Historical Summaries, 1907–1953. London, 1987.

M. Morsy Abdullah

Maktum, Maktum ibn Rashid al-

Ruler of Dubai; prime minister of United Arab Emirates 1971–1979 and the early 1990s.

Maktum ibn Rashid was declared the crown prince of DUBAI in 1958. He was the right-hand man of his father, the great Rashid (Shaykh Rashid ibn Sa'id al-MAKTUM) in creating modern Dubai. From February 1968 he shared for three years in the efforts to establish the new federation, the UNITED ARAB EMIRATES, and on December 2, 1971, he was appointed the first prime minister. In 1979, when his father took the office of head of the cabinet, he became his deputy.

On his father's death on October 7, 1990, Shaykh Maktum was proclaimed ruler of Dubai. Two weeks later, he was again appointed prime minister and joined the Supreme Council of the United Arab Emirates. Shaykh Maktum's extreme generosity and justice make him a popular personality. He inherited a heavy responsibility in executing his father's plan to develop Dubai into the new Hong Kong of the Middle East, and has, in the process, consolidated the federal government.

BIBLIOGRAPHY

Persian Gulf Gazette and Supplements, 1953–1972. London, 1987.
Persian Gulf Historical Summaries, 1907–1953. London, 1987.

M. Morsy Abdullah

Maktum, Muhammad ibn Rashid al-

Minister of defense, United Arab Emirates.

Shaykh Muhammad ibn Rashid, trained at Sandhurst Military College in England, is a member of Dubai's al-MAKTUM family. He has been head of the police force in Dubai since the 1960s and minister of defense in the federal cabinet of the United Arab Emirates since February 1972. He is also the patron of al-Ahli Sport and Cultural Club, with active interests in local camel and international horse racing. On January 4, 1995, he was proclaimed crown prince in Dubai.

BIBLIOGRAPHY

Persian Gulf Gazette and Supplements, 1953–1972. London, 1987.
Persian Gulf Historical Summaries, 1907–1953. London, 1987.

M. Morsy Abdullah

Maktum, Rashid ibn Sa'id al- [?–1990]

Ruler of Dubai, 1958–1990; prime minister of the United Arab Emirates, 1979–1990.

Shaykh Rashid is one of the important figures in the contemporary history of the UNITED ARAB EMIRATES, the builder of modern DUBAI. Although he ruled officially from 1958, he was the real power in the emirate even a decade earlier. Rashid was skilled in economics and modernization techniques. He was able, in his own way, to realize the aspirations of the reform movement in Dubai, which emerged in 1938.

Since 1968, petroleum and the port's income helped Shaykh Rashid to develop Dubai into what is called the Hong Kong of the Middle East. When in 1968 the British declared that they would withdraw from their protectorate in the Gulf by 1971, Rashid cooperated with Shaykh Zayid, ruler of Abu Dhabi, and with the other rulers of the TRUCIAL COAST states to proclaim the United Arab Emirates on December 2, 1971. Shaykh Rashid was elected vice-president in 1971 and became the prime minister in April 1979. He served until his death in October 1990.

BIBLIOGRAPHY

ABDULLAH, M. MORSY. *The United Arab Emirates.* London, 1978.
HEARD BEY, FRAUKE. *From Trucial States to United Arab Emirates.* New York, 1982.
REICH, BERNARD, ed. *Political Leaders of the Contemporary Middle East and North Africa.* New York, 1990.

M. Morsy Abdullah

Maktum Family, al-

Head of Al Bu Falasa tribe and a member of the Banu Yas federation, the ruling family of the Dubai emirate.

The founder, Maktum ibn Buti, seceded from Abu Dhabi in 1833 and established himself independently in DUBAI. The rulers of the family were well known for their skill in diplomacy and their interest in trade. The most prominent of them were Rashid ibn Maktum (1886–1894) and Maktum ibn Hashr (1894–1906), during whose reign the Dubai port flourished, particularly in 1902, after the British–Indian Steam Navigation Company made it a port of call. As a result of his encouragement, the rich immigrant merchants from the Lingeh port on the Persian coast came to reside in Dubai. In 1938, because of a reform movement in the emirate, the Dubai municipality was established during the rule of Sa'id ibn Maktum (1912–1958). His son Rashid created and

ruled (1958–1990) modern Dubai, becoming vice-president of the UNITED ARAB EMIRATES when it was formed in 1971 and prime minister in 1979.

BIBLIOGRAPHY

HEARD BEY, FRAUKE. *From Trucial States to United Arab Emirates.* New York, 1982.
REICH, BERNARD, ed. *Political Leaders of the Contemporary Middle East and North Africa.* New York, 1990.

M. Morsy Abdullah

Mala'ika, Nazik al- [1923–1992]

Iraqi poet and literary critic.

Born in Baghdad to a rich and prominent family noted for its literary members—her mother was the poet Salma Abd al-Razzaq, Umm Nizar al-Mala'ika, the first Iraqi poet to call for women's rights—Nazik al-Mala'ika was educated at Baghdad Higher Teachers Training College. In 1950, she went to Princeton University for studies of comparative and English literature. Upon her return to Iraq, she took up teaching positions at the Universities of Basra and Mosul, and later at the University of Kuwait. Her poetry, exhibiting a mastery of language and technique, is dominated by love of nature, excessive emotionalism, melancholy, and a highly subjective mood and tone; it is basically an extension of the romantic trend of the 1920s and 1930s. Likewise, al-Mala'ika's conception of poetry and the role of the poet is a romantic one, considering the poet as a preacher of beauty and a visionary, sensitive rebel who endures the suffering of humankind. Although she wrote a handful of political poems, she generally avoided involvement in political poetry.

Al-Mala'ika's most important contribution to modern Arabic poetry was connected with the free verse (*al-shi'r al-hurr*) movement, which rejected the traditional conventions of Arabic poetry. Influenced by former experiments of Arab poets and by English poetry, she was one of the first Arab poets to write in the new style. The essential concept of free verse is the reliance on free repetition of the basic unit of conventional prosody—that is, the use of an irregular number of feet (*taf'ila*), instead of a fixed number. The poet varies the number of feet in a single line according to the need. This new form, which was connected also with al-Mala'ika's compatriot Badr Shakir al-Sayyab (1926–1964), found acceptance throughout the Arab world. Which of these two poets first used this new form has been the subject of keen controversy, and claims of priority have been made by each of them. This issue was complicated because both poets published their first collections of poems in the new form—(al-Mala'ika's *al-Kulira* (Cholera) and al-Sayyab's *Hal Kana Hubban?* (Was It Love?)—in December 1947. In the introduction to her second collection, *Shazaya wa Ramad* (Splinters and Ashes, 1949), al-Mala'ika revealed her dissatisfaction with the limitations of traditional Arabic poetry, propounding her views on the purpose and artistic supremacy of the new form.

The most influential of her critical works is *Qadaya al-Shi'r al-Mu'asir* (Issues of Contemporary Poetry, 1962), a literary study of free verse—its nature, form, and the controversies surrounding it. Later, al-Mala'ika came to feel that the new generation of Arab poets interpreted the form of free verse with too much license, and she advocated a more careful approach to what seemed to her a chaotic use of the form. In her introduction to the fourth edition of *Qadaya al-Shi'r al-Mu'asir*, which appeared in 1978, she emphasized the reliance of the new form on Arabic poetic heritage. She also expressed strong opposition to the prose poem (*qasida al-nathr*) advocated by the Syrian poet Ali Ahmad Sa'id (Adunis, b. 1930) and other members of the *shi'r* group, who wished, according to al-Mala'ika, to cut Arabic poetry from its traditional roots and values.

Her collections of poetry also include: *Ashiqa al-Layl* (1947; Lover of Night); *Qarara al-mawja* (1957; The Bottom of the Wave); *Shajara al-Qamar* (1967; The Moon Tree); and *Ma'sa al-Haya wa-Ughniya li al-Insan* (1970; The Tragedy of Life and a Song for Man). The first edition of her collected works was published in two volumes in 1970 by Dar al-Awda in Beirut under the title *Diwan Nazik al-Mala'ika*. Her publications also include studies on theoretical and critical aspects of modern Arabic poetry. Among them are *Muhadarat fi Shi'r Ali Mahmud Taha* (1965; Lectures on the Poetry of Ali Mahmud Taha), in which she explains how the combination of Taha's music and sensual tendency influenced many young poets writing in Arabic during the 1940s. The second edition was published with a new introduction under the title *Al-Sawma'a wa al-Shurfa al-Hamra: Dirasa Naqdiayya fi Shi'r Ali Mahmud Taha* (1979; The Monk's Cell and the Red Balcony: A Study of the Poetry of Ali Mahmud Taha). Another book of hers is *Al-Tajzi'iyya fi al-Mujtama al-Arabi* (1974; The Fragmentation in Arab Society).

BIBLIOGRAPHY

JAYYUSI, S. K. *Modern Arabic Poetry: An Anthology.* New York, 1987, pp. 329–338.
———. *Trends and Movements in Modern Arabic Poetry.* Leiden, 1977.

MOREH, S. *Modern Arabic Poetry, 1800–1970.* Leiden, 1976, pp. 196–215.

Reuven Snir

Malaria

Disease caused by a parasite, Plasmodium falciparum, transmitted by anopheles mosquitos to humans through blood feeding.

Malaria has a high mortality rate among infants and children. Affected adults become weakened and lethargic, particularly after recurrences of fever. Stagnant water provides an environment that increases mosquito populations, making transmission to humans more likely. Since the 1950s, mosquito control programs have dramatically decreased malaria incidence. The last serious epidemics occurred from 1942 to 1944 in Egypt, affecting some 250,000 people.

Jenab Tutunji

Malcolm, John   [1769–1833]

British soldier in India; diplomat and historian of Iran.

Malcolm was born in Burnfoot, Scotland. He joined the Indian army at the age of twelve and rose to the rank of major general. He was sent as envoy by the viceroy of India to FATH ALI SHAH QAJAR of Persia (now Iran) in 1800 and concluded agreements aimed at curbing French influence there and Afghani aggression on India. Two further missions in 1808 and 1810 were less successful, because by then ambassadors from the British government outranked Malcolm. Returning to India, he wrote his two-volume *History of Persia* (1815).

BIBLIOGRAPHY

YAPP, M. E. "Two British Historians of Persia." In *Historians of the Middle East*, ed. by Bernard Lewis and P. M. Holt. Oxford, 1961.

John R. Perry

Malik

Arabic word for king or monarch, derived from the root "to possess."

"Malik" is often used as both a surname and a forename in the Middle East, for instance by Dr. Charles

Malik of Lebanon or Malik ibn Anas, the famous medieval theologian of Islam.

Zachary Karabell

Malik, Charles Habib   [1906–1990]

Lebanese academic, philosopher, and diplomat.

Born February 11, 1906, to a Greek Orthodox family from Koura in Lebanon, Malik was schooled at the American Tripoli Boy's High School then attended the American University of Beirut, Harvard University, and the University of Freiburg. Throughout his academic career, Malik taught philosophy, mathematics, and physics at the American University of Beirut, where he was also dean. During the 1958 Lebanese civil war, Malik was president of the 13th session of the General Assembly of the United Nations. Foreign minister (1956–1958) during the presidency of Camille Chamoun, Malik alienated many Lebanese politicians because of his pro–United States and pro–Western stands. He accused Egypt, Syria, and the Palestinians of fomenting trouble in the Land of Cedars.

During the 1975/76 Lebanese civil war, Malik joined a coalition of conservative Christian leaders known as the LEBANESE FRONT. In several statements and publications, Malik expressed his full awareness of the tragedy of the Palestinian people, but he was very distrustful of the intentions of Muslim leaders in Lebanon. Malik feared that Lebanon as a land of Christian–Muslim coexistence was bound to be destroyed by outside interferences, mainly from Syria and radical Palestinian forces. Malik authored several books and publications and was awarded honorific titles and degrees.

BIBLIOGRAPHY

HELMICK, RAYMOND G. "Internal Lebanese Politics: The Lebanese Front and Forces." In *Toward a Viable Lebanon,* ed. by H. Barakat. Washington, D.C., 1988.
QUBAIN, FAHIM I. *Crisis in Lebanon.* Washington, D.C., 1961.

George E. Irani

Maliki Law School

One of the four approaches (called schools) to Sunni Muslim law.

The Maliki Law School was named after the traditionalist and lawyer Malik ibn Anas (died 795) of Medina (in today's Saudi Arabia). Malik's active ca-reer fell at a time when the prophetic *sunna* (record of the utterances and deeds of the Prophet) had not yet become a material source of the law on equal footing with the Qur'an and when *hadith* (prophetic traditions) were still relatively limited in number. In his legal reasoning, therefore, Malik made little reference to prophetic traditions and more often resorted to the *amal* (normative practice) of Medina in justification of his doctrines. As expressed in his *Muwatta,* in which he recorded the customary Medinese doctrine, Malik's reliance on traditions as well as his technical legal thought lagged behind those of the Iraqis.

Once the transition from the geographical to the personal schools took place, Malik became the eponym of the former Hijazi or Medinan school. This may be explained by the fact that Malik's writings represented the average doctrine of that geographical area, coupled perhaps with the high esteem in which he was held as a scholar.

Like the namesake of the HANAFI LAW SCHOOL, but unlike the founder of the SHAFI'I LAW SCHOOL, Malik did not provide his school with a developed body of legal doctrine. It was left for his successors, chiefly in the ninth and tenth centuries, to articulate a legal system particular to the school. Among the most important positive law works of the school are: *al-Mudawwana al-Kubra* by Sahnun (died 854); *al-Risala* by Ibn Abi Zayd al-Qayrawani (died 996); *al-Tahdhib,* an authoritative synopsis of *al-Mudawwana,* by Abu Sa'id al-Baradhi'i (died probably after 1039); *al-Bayan,* a commentary by Ibn Rushd (died 1126) on *al-Utbiyya* of al-Utbi (died 869); *Bidaya al-Mujtahid wa Nihaya al-Muqtasid* by Ibn Rushd al-Hafid (died 1189); *al-Mukhtasar* by Sidi Khalil (died 1365); *al-Mi'yar al-Mughrib wa al-Jami al-Mu'rib* by al-Wansharisi (died 1508), one of the most important FATWA collections in the school. Further, in writing on legal theory (*usul al-fiqh*), the Malikis were not as prolific as their Hanafi and Shafi'i counterparts. Three of their most distinguished legal theoreticians are: Ibn Khalaf al-Baji (died 1081), the author of *Ihkam al-Fusul;* al-Qarafi (died 1285), whose main work on the subject is *Sharh Tanqih al-Fusul,* a commentary on the work of the Shafi'i jurist and theologian Fakhr al-Din al-Razi; and Abu Ishaq al-Shatibi (died 1388), who elaborated in his *Muwafaqat* one of the most innovative legal theories that is highly regarded by modern legal reformers.

Since early medieval Islam, Malikism succeeded in spreading mainly in the Maghrib (North Africa) and Muslim Spain, being now the dominant doctrine in all Muslim African countries. In Egypt, it has traditionally shared influence with Shafi'ism. Maliki presence may also be found today in Bahrain and Kuwait.

BIBLIOGRAPHY

BAKIR, AHMAD. *Histoire de l'école malikite en orient jusqu'à la fin du moyen âge*. Tunis, 1962.
BERQUE, J. *Essai sur la méthode juridique maghrébine*. Rabat, 1944.

Wael B. Hallaq

Malki, Adnan al-   [?–1955]

Syrian military officer.

When Adib Shishakli returned to Damascus in December 1952, Lieutenant Colonel Adnan al-Malki presented the president with some political demands. Upon Shishakli's apparent acceptance of the demands, al-Malki produced a list of their proponents, who were subsequently arrested. A progressive and charismatic nationalist leader who was greatly respected by the Ba'th party, al-Malki was reinstated as deputy chief of staff of the army after Shishakli's downfall. He was assassinated by a member of the Parti Populaire Syrien on April 22, 1955. Until his death, al-Malki was instrumental in securing the Egyptian defense pact of March 1955, leading the fight against a pact with Iraq.

[*See also:* Jadid, Ghassan]

BIBLIOGRAPHY

SEALE, PATRICK. *The Struggle for Syria: A Study of Post-War Arab Politics, 1945–1958*. London, 1958.

Charles U. Zenzie

Malkom Khan, Mirza   [1833–1908]

Persian diplomat, political philosopher, and advocate of modernization.

The son of Mirza Ya'qub, an Armenian from Jolfa who had converted to Islam, Malkom (also Malkam, Malkum) studied in Paris, where he became familiar with French social and political theories, especially those of Auguste Comte. On his return to Persia, he was employed as a translator for the European teachers of the Dar al-Fonun, the modern school of higher learning inaugurated in 1851 by Persia's modernizing premier, AMIR KABIR.

In 1857, Malkom wrote the first of his many pamphlets, entitled *Ketabcheh-ye Ghaybi* (The Invisible Booklet), in which he discussed the urgent need for modern reforms for Persia, if it were to survive as an independent nation. He also organized the

Faramush-Khaneh (House of Oblivion), a pseudo-masonic (secret) organization, which incurred the suspicion of the Naser al-Din Shah. Malkom was exiled in 1861 and went to Baghdad. There he was befriended by Mirza Hoseyn Khan, the Persian ambassador to the Ottoman Empire, who agreed with him about modernization and reforms and who obtained his pardon from the shah. Malkom was then made a counselor in the Persian embassy in Istanbul in 1864, during the early modernization period of Ottoman Turkey, called the TANZIMAT. In 1871, Mirza Hoseyn was recalled to Tehran and appointed minister of justice, then prime minister. Malkom was appointed minister to Britain.

From London, Malkom continually addressed the shah and his ministers about the need for modernization reforms. His arguments were not always original, but they were simply argued, easily understood, and effective—he criticized the government, but spared the shah. Some of his suggestions were attempted, but the experiment did not last, since the shah grew tired of the complications of change and the ongoing rivalry at court. He lost interest in all this and became more tyrannical toward the end of his reign.

While Malkom was in London, the shah took three trips to Europe, visiting London each time, where several important concessions were granted to European and British companies. Malkom was involved in their transactions and had the opportunity to benefit financially each time. In 1889, the shah granted a lottery concession to an English company, which came under attack when he returned to Persia, and the concession was canceled. Malkom, however, who knew this, did not reveal the cancellation until he had sold out his own shares.

This unethical situation cost him his position, his title, and his salary. In 1890, he began to publish a pamphlet entitled *Qanun* (The Law) in London. In it his arguments turned to criticism, then outright attack, not even sparing the shah. He also mentioned secret societies that were working for reform and suggested that the natural leaders of the people were by right the *ulama* (body of mollas), and that they should lead the movement. It has since been suggested that these secret societies were not actually organized but that Malkom was saying they should be. *Qanun* was smuggled into the country and enjoyed a widespread popularity, making its mark on a generation that was soon to become involved in the CONSTITUTIONAL REVOLUTION.

After the assassination of Naser al-Din Shah in 1896, Malkom was restored to favor and was appointed minister to Italy. He lived to see the beginning of the Constitutional Revolution in 1906.

Despite a lifetime of argument in favor of reform, his role in the lottery concession continues to sully his name. Notwithstanding such criticism, his influence on the shah, the politicians of his day, and the modernization of Persia cannot be denied.

BIBLIOGRAPHY

ALGAR, HAMID. *Mirza Malkum Khan: A Study in the History of Iranian Modernism.* Berkeley, Calif., 1973.
BAKHASH, SHAUL. *Iran: Monarchy and Reform under the Qajars, 1858–1896.* London, 1978.

Mansoureh Ettehadieh

Malta

Five-island nation situated in the Mediterranean Sea.

Consisting of 122 square miles (316 sq. km) spread over five islands—Malta, Gozo, Comino, Cominotto, and Filfla (the latter two barren rocks)—the independent nation of Malta is located between Libya, Tunisia, and Italy, about 60 miles (97 km) south of the southeastern tip of Sicily and three times as far from Tunisia. Its capital, Valletta, is home to 9,196 of its 400,000 citizens. It has been independent since 1964 and a republic since 1974; its previous status as part of the British Empire dated from 1799 when British troops expelled a Napoleonic garrison

A street in the Maltese town of Suema, decorated for a feast. (Pierre Cachia)

that had seized control from the Knights of the Hospital of St. John the year before. The Treaty of Paris of 1814 confirmed British possession.

The Arab attacks launched from Tunisia by the Aghlabid dynasty in the ninth century conquered Sicily and eventually spread to Malta after the defeat of the Byzantine garrison in 869. Arab occupation was firmly established, and Arabic gradually became the language of the island's population. The population remained predominantly Roman Catholic, as it is today, but a Muslim population gradually grew and was permitted to remain after the Norman conquest until Frederick II expelled it in 1249.

The OTTOMAN EMPIRE drove the crusading order of the Knights of St. John from its headquarters on the island of Rhodes in 1522. In response, in 1530 the Holy Roman Emperor Charles V, to whom the vicissitudes of feudal rivalry and inheritance had granted Malta, gave the island to the order as its permanent seat. The knights beat back Ottoman invasions in 1565 and 1614 and became firmly established as Malta's rulers. They also engaged in the reciprocal piracy and sea raiding that plagued the western Mediterranean in the eighteenth and early nineteenth centuries and produced many Muslim prisoners and slaves, some of whom staged an abortive rebellion in 1722.

The Maltese language is Semitic in structure but heavily influenced by Italian vocabulary (in the comparable way that English, which is based on Anglo-Saxon, has a large admixture of French words). In ancient times, Punic—the Semitic language of the Phoenicians, who established a maritime empire based on Carthage in Tunisia—was spoken in Malta. Contrary to a once popular theory, however, no features of the modern Maltese language can be

Mgarr church. (Pierre Cachia)

traced back to Punic or to any pre-Punic indigenous tongue. Latin and Byzantine Greek lexical items are also scarce. Although virtually unattested in written documents before the fifteenth century, Maltese evidently derives from the North African Arabic brought by the Arab invaders six centuries earlier. Classical Arabic is attested in poetry by Maltese poets and on tombstones as late as the twelfth century, but spoken Maltese developed progressively into a distinct dialect. It gained recognition as a language in its own right in 1933 and was declared the national language in 1964. It is the only Semitic language written in Latin characters. Literature began to be written in the Maltese language in the late nineteenth century, and the substantial output of poetry, novels, and plays reflects tendencies in European literature over the past century more than it does the tendencies of Arabic literature.

An approximate doubling of the population between 1800 and 1900 contributed to substantial migration, mostly to North Africa and Egypt, where Maltese immigrants had an advantage in learning the local language and came to form a significant part of the Levantine community of port cities like Alexandria. By 1900, Maltese agricultural production had fallen well below the needs of the island population, and remittances from these overseas workers had become an important factor in the colony's balance of trade.

Until 1979, Valletta provided a base of crucial importance for the British navy. Admiral Sir Andrew Cunningham, the British commander in chief in the Mediterranean from 1939 to 1943, observed in his book *A Sailor's Odyssey:* "Malta was really the linchpin of the campaign in the Mediterranean. As the island served as the principal operational base for the surface ships, submarines and aircraft working against the Axis supply line to North Africa, its maintenance had a direct bearing on the progress of the battle in Cyrenaica, a fact that is not always appreciated." This strategic association with Great Britain and its wartime allies contributed to Malta's strong economic and political orientation toward Europe after independence.

Since the closing of Malta's military bases in 1979, the country's economy has relied on tourism and manufacturing, and the nation is looking forward to admission into the European Community. Yet the ties forged by generations of overseas workers, with Libya in particular, continue to affect Malta's foreign affairs. Its government is headed by a prime minister who is answerable to a house of representatives consisting of sixty-five members, and its major political parties include the Nationalists and the Malta Labor party.

BIBLIOGRAPHY

BLOUET, BRIAN. *The Story of Malta.* 1967.
SETH, RONALD. *Malta.* New York, 1988.

Richard W. Bulliet

Maluf, Rushdi

Lebanese newspaper columnist.

Maluf, a member of a literary family from Zahla, is best known for his column in the daily *al-*NAHAR in the 1970s. His literary style established him as the founder of a unique school of journalism in Lebanon that emphasized classical Arabic forms of expression.

As'ad AbuKhalil

Mamluks

Rulers in Baghdad from 1749 to 1831.

The Mamluks emerged under Hasan Pasha (1704–1724) and his son Ahmad Pasha (1724–1747), both *wali* (provincial governor) of Baghdad. Hasan Pasha's intent was to strengthen his personal base of power by creating a group of disciplined military and civil functionaries committed uniquely to him and not to the government at Istanbul or the Arabs of Baghdad. A page corps was formed, originally recruited from local families but later composed almost exclusively of slaves (mamluks) imported from the Caucasus and Georgia. These slaves were instructed in reading and writing, but also horsemanship and swimming, a combination of martial and bureaucratic virtues making them superior to Turks and Iraqis as civil servants. Their training emphasized a sense of interdependence and "esprit de corps." They were made to feel that they owed their privilege to their master and to the Mamluk institution. They dominated the power elite, but as an alien force, and were merciless to any suspected rival to their authority. A close disciplined fraternity, and the only effective civil and military organization within the country, the Mamluks provided their pashas with the power of an independent monarch. Nevertheless, Mamluk pashas at no time renounced allegiance to the sultan of the Ottoman Empire. They defended Iraq from the Wahhabis and Persians but did not war on neighbors within the empire.

The first Mamluk pasha, Sulayman Abu Layla (1750–1762), came to power two years after the death of Ahmad Pasha, following an unsuccessful attempt by the Sublime Porte (the Ottoman government) to check Mamluk power by naming nonlocal candidates as pasha of Baghdad. He was followed by Ali Agha (1762–1764) whose obscure Persian birth may have contributed to his fall. The reign of Umar Pasha (1764–1775), while peaceful, was feeble and characterized by ever-lessening authority. His deposition by the sultan introduced in interregnum (1775–1780) during which a number of mostly alien pashas (Abdi Pasha, 1775; Abdullah Pasha, 1775–1777; Hasan Pasha 1778–1780) reigned briefly and without much influence. Sulayman Agha (1780–1802), known as "the Great," restored the dominance and institutions of the Mamluks with such success that his period is known as the zenith of the Mamluk era. His immediate successors, Ali Pasha (1802–1807), Sulayman the Little (1808–1810), Abdallah Pasha (1810–1813), and Sa'id Pasha (1813–1817), all died violently after brief reigns. The last of the Mamluk rulers, Da'ud Pasha (1817–1831), confronted Ottoman resolve, ignited by his failure to provide suitable remissions in the desperate circumstances of the sultan's war with Russia, to end the century-long independence of Iraq and to bring the province once again firmly into the imperial fold. Plague and flooding helped weaken the Mamluk regime and Da'ud ultimately capitulated to the sultan in 1831. He and his family were exiled to Bursa. He was subsequently recalled to service and held a number of important posts throughout the empire before dying in 1851.

BIBLIOGRAPHY

LONGRIGG, STEPHEN HEMSLEY. *Four Centuries of Modern Iraq.* Oxford, 1925.
NIEUWENHUIS, TOM. *Politics and Society in Early Modern Iraq: Mamluk Pashas, Tribal Shaykhs and Local Rule between 1802 and 1831.* The Hague, 1982.

Albertine Jwaideh

Mammeri, Moulaoud   [1917–1989]

Algerian novelist and poet.

Moulaoud Mammeri was born in Taourirt-Mimoun in Great KABYLIA. He attended school in Paris and eventually became a professor at the University of Algiers. He wrote four novels: *La Colline Oubliée* (1952); *Le Sommeil du Juste* (1955); *L'Opium et le Bâton* (1965); and *La Traversée* (1982). Mammeri, like other celebrated members of the "Generation of 1954" (i.e., Mohammed DIB, Mouloud FERAOUN, Kateb YACINE, and Malek HADDAD), wrote about the effect of colonialism and decolonization on Algerian society. Mammeri particularly promoted Berber

ethnicity (e.g., *Les Isefra, Poèmes de Si Mohand ou Mhand* [1969]; *Poèmes Kabyles Anciens* [1980]), which contributed to disturbances in Kabylia in 1980. Mammeri was also a playwright (e.g., *Le Foehn* [1982]). He died in an automobile accident.

BIBLIOGRAPHY

MORTIMER, MILDRED. *Journeys through the French African Novel.* Portsmouth, N.H., 1990.

Phillip C. Naylor

Manama

Capital and largest city of the State of Bahrain.

Located on the north coast of Bahrain island, and now connected by causeway to Muharraq on the adjacent island, it was a commercial and pearling center coveted by the Sassanids, Hormuzis, and Persians. In 1782, it fell to the KHALIFA FAMILY, under whose control it grew into a key transshipment point for trade between India and the Persian/Arabian Gulf. With Bahrain's signing of the 1820 General Treaty of Peace with Britain, the city's merchants flourished. By the early twentieth century, Manama had become cosmopolitan, with substantial Persian, Indian, and Gulf Arab communities; it was also the site of the British Political Agency for Bahrain and, after 1946, the British residency in the Gulf. With its sister city, Muharraq, Manama houses more than 70 percent of Bahrain's inhabitants. Its population in 1981 was about 122,000—some 35 percent larger than it was in 1971, when the State of Bahrain was declared independent. Bahrain's largest port, Mina Sulman, is at the southern end of the city, next to the former British naval base at al-Jufayr.

BIBLIOGRAPHY

CLARKE, ANGELA. *The Islands of Bahrain.* Manama, Bahrain, 1981.

Fred H. Lawson

Manama–Muharraq Causeway

Roadway connecting Bahrain's two largest islands.

This four-mile-long (6.4 km) causeway links Manama, Bahrain's capital, with the city of Muharraq and the Bahrain international airport, located on the adjacent island. The other two Bahraini causeways connect Muharraq with Jazirat al-Azl—an islet that is the site of the drydock and ship-repair industry—and Bahrain island with Saudi Arabia.

BIBLIOGRAPHY

The Gulf Handbook, 1978. London, 1978.

Emile A. Nakhleh

Manar, al-

Cairene magazine.

Al-Manar (The Lighthouse, or Minaret) was published in Cairo by Muhammad Rashid Rida from 1898 until his death in 1935. A few scattered issues came out thereafter until 1941. *Al-Manar* propagated the views of the reform SALAFIYYA MOVEMENT, of which Rida's mentor, Muhammad Abduh, was the central figure. The Salafiyya worked to revive Islam by shedding medieval accretions and returning to the pristine age of early Islam. Rida wrestled with the challenges of Western imperialism and secularism during the period between the two world wars. He tried to revive the caliphate after Turkey abolished it in 1923. He was also active in the cause of ARAB NATIONALISM. By the end of his life, Rida was less at odds with conservatives at al-Azhar than Abduh had been.

BIBLIOGRAPHY

KERR, MALCOLM H. *Islamic Reform: The Political and Legal Theories of Muhammad Abduh and Rashid Rida.* Berkeley, Calif., 1966.

Donald Malcolm Reid

Mandaeans

Gnostic baptist community based in Iraq and Iran.

The Mandaeans of today live as their ancestors did, along the rivers and waterways of southern Iraq and Khuzistan, Iran. The Mandaeans (from *manda*, knowledge) practice a religion that has affinities with Judaism and Christianity. Known by their neighbors as *Subbi* (baptizers), they perform repeated baptism (*masbuta*) on Sundays and special festival days. Two small rites of ablution that require no priest, *rishama* and *tamasha*, are performed by individual Mandaeans. All rituals take place on the riverbank.

Mamoon A. Zaki

Mandate System

The system established after World War I to administer former territories of the German and Ottoman empires.

Until World War I, the victors of most European wars took control of conquered territories as the spoils of victory. This was especially true of the colonial territories of defeated European powers, as the victors sought to expand their own empires. World War I marked a significant break in this tradition. While Britain, France, Italy, and Japan still retained imperial aspirations, other forces tempered these goals. The United States emerged as a world power committed to an anti-imperial policy, one that sought to consider the national aspirations of indigenous peoples as well as the imperial agendas of the victors. The November 5, 1918, pre-armistice statement of the Allies, moreover, affirmed that annexation of territory was not their aim for ending the war.

The result was the mandate system of the League of Nations, established by the treaties ending World War I. Under this system, the victors of World War I were given responsibility for governing former German and Ottoman territories as mandates from the League. The ultimate goal was development of each mandate toward eventual independence. This goal was tempered, some would argue, by the fact that mandates were awarded with full consideration of both public and secret agreements made during the war. For the Middle East, the SYKES–PICOT AGREEMENT of 1916 and the BALFOUR DECLARATION of 1917 helped structure the division of Ottoman territories between France and Britain.

Article 22 of the League's covenant required that the conditions of mandates vary with the character of each territory. This resulted in the establishment of three classes of mandate. Class A mandates were those to be provisionally recognized as independent until they proved able to stand on their own. Class B mandates were those further from qualifying for independence and for which the mandatory powers took on full responsibility for administration and promotion of the material and moral welfare of the inhabitants. Class C mandates were those whose best interests were to be served by integration into the territories of the mandatory power, with due consideration being given to the interests of the inhabitants.

The Ottoman territories in the Middle East became Class A mandates. Based on World War I agreements, Britain was given responsibility for Iraq and Palestine (later Palestine and Transjordan); France got Syria (later Syria and Lebanon). These were to be supervised by the Permanent Mandates Commission consisting originally of members from Belgium, Britain, the Netherlands, France, Italy, Japan, Portugal, Spain, and Sweden, to which representatives from Switzerland and Germany were later added, and a representative from Norway took the place of the Swedish representative. Although the

non-mandatory powers constituted a majority, the commission never followed an aggressive policy against the interests of the mandatory powers. This was manifest by the fact that Britain and France restructured their mandates by the time the formal system came into place in 1924. Britain split the Palestinian mandate into Palestine and Transjordan, giving a special role in the latter to Sharif Husayn's son, Abdullah, as emir of Trans-Jordan to deter his further pursuit of territorial goals in Syria. France split its mandate in Syria into Syria and Lebanon to enhance the position of Uniate Christians in Lebanon and as part of its overall strategy of sponsoring communal differences to solidify its position of eventual arbiter of all disputes in the area. The British mandate for Iraq remained intact, despite the fact that its population diversity invited similar divisions.

Although few would have predicted it in the early 1920s, all of the Class A mandates achieved independence as provided under the conditions of the mandates. The first was Iraq in 1932, although Britain retained significant diplomatic and military concessions. Syria and Lebanon followed in 1941 as World War II was getting under way. In March 1946, just before the formal dissolution of the League of Nations and transfer of its assets to the United Nations, the Treaty of London granted independence to Transjordan as the Kingdom of Jordan. Only Palestine was left to the United Nations under its trusteeship program, and in 1947, Britain presented this thorny problem to the UN General Assembly for resolution. The result was approval of a plan for the partition of Palestine into two Arab and Jewish states and an international city of Jerusalem. Subsequent events precluded implementation of this plan, but since 1949, Israel has been a member of the United Nations.

BIBLIOGRAPHY

LENCZOWSKI, GEORGE. *The Middle East in World Affairs,* 3rd ed. Ithaca, N.Y., 1962.
WALTERS, F. P. *A History of the League of Nations.* London, 1952.

Daniel E. Spector

Manifesto of the Algerian Muslim People

Document that urged Algerian autonomy within the French Union.

Ferhat Abbas, in collaboration with other Algerian leaders, drafted the Manifesto of the Algerian Muslim People during February and March 1943. It contains an analysis of the Algerian condition followed by a program of reform that marks a major stage in the progression of Algerian protest from assimilationism to separatism.

BIBLIOGRAPHY

KADDACHE, MAHFOUD. *Histoire du nationalisme algérien: Question nationale et politique algérienne, 1919–1951.* Algiers, 1981.

John Ruedy

Manoogian, Vazgen [1946–]

Armenian political activist; prime minister of Armenia, 1990–1991.

Manoogian was born in Yerevan, Armenia, and received his higher education at Yerevan State University. He studied mechanical mathematics and pursued a degree at Lomonosov University in Moscow. While in Moscow he organized an Armenian cultural club. He was expelled from Moscow for demonstrating in front of the Turkish embassy on April 24, 1966, in a commemorative protest of the Armenian genocide. He completed his doctorate in Novosybirsk, and began teaching at his alma mater in Yerevan.

Manoogian also returned to political activism in Yerevan, and with like-minded academics he founded the Anania Shirakatsi club. The group was named for the renowned Armenian scientist-mathematician of the Middle Ages. The club attracted members who later emerged as figures in the Karabagh Movement. Manoogian's involvement in the Karabagh Movement came through his friendship with Igor Muradian, one of the earliest advocates of the unification of Karabagh and Armenia.

In February 1988 Manoogian became a member of the so-called Karabagh Committee which led popular rallies in Armenia to press the Soviet government, then under Mikhail Gorbachev, to respond to the appeals of the Armenians of Mountainous Karabagh. Manoogian was arrested on December 10, 1988, along with other members of the Karabagh Committee. Released in May 1989, he set out to organize the ARMENIAN NATIONAL MOVEMENT (ANM) by drafting the program of the ANM. When the ANM formally came into being in November 1989, Manoogian was elected a member of its governing council and gained recognition as its principal strategist.

In May 1990 Manoogian was elected to parliament in Soviet Armenia, which in August of that same year saw a peaceful transfer of power from the Communist party to the ANM. At that time the

Armenian parliament elected Manoogian prime minister, thus placing him at the head of the first non-Communist government of Armenia while the country was still nominally part of the Soviet Union. In September 1991 Manoogian resigned his post—the first free presidential elections were to be held in Armenia and a rival leading figure of the ANM, Levon Ter-Petrossian, won at the polls.

Manoogian withdrew from the ANM and established the National Democratic Union (NDU) and the Center for Strategic Studies. He was elected chairman of the NDU, from which position he resigned when he was invited in August 1992 to join the Ter-Petrossian administration as state minister of defense and military industry. In a January 1993 cabinet reshuffle after the appointment of Hrant Bagratian as prime minister, Manoogian was appointed to the Council of Ministers as acting minister of defense and served through August 1993. He returned to private life and to teaching at Yerevan State University, while remaining active in the NDU and the research center he founded.

Rouben P. Adalian

Mansaf

Popular Middle Eastern lamb dish.

A bedouin dish particularly popular in Jordan and Saudi Arabia. It is a combination of lamb and yogurt served with rice. Mansaf is often prepared at festivals or in honor of guests.

BIBLIOGRAPHY

DER HAROUTUNIAN, ARTO. *Middle Eastern Cookery.* London, 1983.

Zachary Karabell

Mansur, Hasan Ali   [1923–1965]

Iranian prime minister.

Hasan Ali Mansur was born in 1923 and was assassinated in 1965 by Muhammad Bukhara'i. A young Muslim militant, Bukhara'i was angered by the capitulation of Iranian jurisdiction in cases involving American nationals as a consequence of an unpopular bill submitted to the parliament by Prime Minister Mansur earlier that year. Hasan Ali Mansur's father, Rajabali Mansur al-Molk, had been prime minister of Iran several times. Founder of the technocrats' IRAN NOVIN PARTY and prime minister after

the referendum in 1963 that launched the WHITE REVOLUTION, Hasan Ali Mansur conducted his premiership as a mandate for change; after a short period, however, most of his economic and political projects were proven to be reckless. It is widely believed that Mohammad Reza Shah Pahlavi wearied of Mansur's political ambitions and was relieved by his death.

Neguin Yavari

Mansura, al-

Egyptian delta city.

Al-Mansura is located near Damietta, Egypt, in the delta. Founded by the Ayyubid dynasty as a fortified camp in 1219, it served as a buttress against Crusader expansion in 1221 and again in 1250, when the Mamluks scored a significant victory over Louis IX of France. It has been the administrative capital of Daqhaliyya province since 1526. Although predominantly Muslim, there have been some Copts in the city since the seventeenth century. Its population was estimated at 357,800 in 1986.

BIBLIOGRAPHY

Europa World Yearbook, 1994, vol. 1. London, 1994, p. 1024.

Arthur Goldschmidt, Jr.

Mansur al-Molk, Rajabali   [1895–1975]

Iranian statesman; prime minister, 1939–1941, 1950–1951.

Father of Prime Minister Hasan Ali Mansur, Rajabali Mansur al-Molk studied political science in Iran and afterward joined the ministry of foreign affairs. He was appointed deputy minister in 1919, when the Anglo–Iranian treaty was ratified whereby Great Britain presumably reaffirmed Iran's independence but in effect sought to impose a protectorate on Iran. After holding several cabinet positions, he served as prime minister from 1939 to 1941, the year Iran was occupied by the Allied forces. In 1942, he was governor of Khorasan, and in 1946, after the fall of the Soviet-backed republic in Azerbaijan, he was installed as governor there (see AZERBAIJAN CRISIS). In 1950, he again became prime minister and, in 1953, was appointed ambassador to Turkey and to the European office of the United Nations.

Neguin Yavari

Mansure Army

Ottoman army organized in 1826.

Established by the same proclamation that abolished the Janissery Corps, the new army's formal name translated as the Trained Victorious Soldiers of Muhammad. It soon recruited 12,000 troops, initially organized largely along the lines of the former NIZAM-I CEDIT and headed by a commander called SERASKER. The Mansure army was headquartered at a palace in Bayezit (Istanbul), combining the functions of military headquarters and war ministry until the end of the empire. As serasker, Mehmet Paşa Koja HUSREV introduced French military organization into the Mansure and by 1830 expanded it to 27,000 troops, including the former cavalry. All remaining Ottoman fighting corps were incorporated into the Mansure in 1838, when the army's name was changed to the Ordered Troops.

BIBLIOGRAPHY

SHAW, STANFORD J., and EZEL KURAL SHAW. *History of the Ottoman Empire and Modern Turkey.* Vol. 2. New York, 1977.

Elizabeth Thompson

Manufactures

Goods made from raw materials, originally by hand; also those made by machinery.

In antiquity and into the Byzantine Empire, the Middle East was the center of Western civilization and the region from which a wide variety of goods were first made and traded. The settled farming society allowed time for handicrafts, between crop work, and for market days and market towns. Regional trade became established by land caravan, by riverboats, and by coastal vessels that sailed the Mediterranean, the east coast of Africa, and beyond Arabia, into the Indian Ocean.

The ancient Near East was the seat of civilizations that traded with one another—luxury goods for the urban elite and utilitarian items for both urban dwellers and for rural agricultural, herding, and artisan folk. Specialty products included textiles, metals, glassware, pottery, chemicals, and, later, sugar and paper. By the fourteenth and fifteenth centuries, however, Europe had progressed to the point that it was exporting to the Middle East not only high technology goods, such as clocks and spectacles, but refined types of textiles, glassware, and metals. During the following centuries the flow from Europe to the Middle East increased; by the nineteenth century,

Europe overwhelmed the region with goods produced cheaply and abundantly by the machinery of the Industrial Revolution, including the railroads and steamships that transported them. The Anglo–Ottoman treaty of 1838 (called the Convention of Balta Liman) fixed import duties to the Ottoman Empire at a low 8 percent. These factors drove thousands of Middle Eastern craftsmen and artisans out of business, but some managed to retain their shops and others found employment in the new textile factories of the late nineteenth century.

World War I exposed the region's lack of industry and, with the achievement of total or partial independence, the various governments began to take measures to encourage development. Around 1930, the COMMERCIAL AND NAVIGATION TREATIES regulating tariffs lapsed, and most countries regained full fiscal autonomy. They immediately raised tariffs to favor local industry. They also promoted manufacturing in various other ways, such as encouraging people to buy national goods and giving such goods preference for government purchases. Moreover, they set up special banking, such as the Sümer and Eti banks in Turkey and the Agricultural and Industrial banks of Iran and Iraq, to promote manufacturing and mining; they also channeled credit through existing banks, such as Bank Misr in Egypt. Local entrepreneurs also became more active in the economic field, including manufacturing. In Egypt, the Misr and Abboud groups set up various industries, and in Turkey, the Iş Bank promoted development. In Palestine, where some European and Russian Jewish immigrants brought with them both capital and skills, some set up factories or workshops in a wide variety of fields.

It is difficult to estimate the rate of industrial growth: In Turkey, between 1929 and 1938, net manufacturing production increased at 7.5 percent a year and mining advanced at about the same pace. In Egypt, the rate of growth was slightly lower and in the Jewish sector of Palestine distinctly higher. In Iran, between 1926 and 1940, some 150 factories were established with a paid-up capital of about 150 million U.S. dollars and employing 35,000 persons. Nevertheless, industry still played a minor role in the basically agricultural Middle Eastern economy. By 1939, employment in manufacturing and mining was everywhere less than 10 percent of the labor force, and in most of the countries it was closer to 5 percent. Industry's contribution to gross domestic product (GDP) was put at 8 percent in Egypt, 12 in Turkey, and 20 in the Jewish sector of Palestine; in the other countries it was lower. Industry still depended on imports of machinery, spare parts, raw materials, and technicians—and there were no ex-

TABLE 1

Manufacturing Industry in 1970, 1983, 1987

	Value Added (millions of U.S. dollars)			Distribution of Value Added (percent)				
	1970	1983	1987	Food Beverages Tobacco	Textiles Clothing	Machinery & Transport Equipment	Chemicals	Other
Egypt	—	8,950	—	20	26	13	9	32
Iran	1,501	11,596	—	12	21	15	4	48
Iraq	325	—	—	14	9	10	16	50
Israel	—	—	—	12	8	32	8	39
Jordan	32	—	552	22	3	1	7	67
Kuwait	120	—	1,902	10	7	4	6	73
Oman	—	—	464	—	—	—	—	—
Saudi Arabia	372	—	6,068	—	—	—	—	—
Syria	—	—	2,341	24	10	3	15	48
Turkey	1,930	—	15,863	17	15	15	11	43
United Arab Emirates	—	—	2,155	14	1	—	—	84
North Yemen	10	—	578	—	—	—	—	—

Sources: World Bank. *World Development Report, 1990,* Table 6. *World Development Report, 1986,* Table 7.

ports of manufactured goods. A wide range of light industries, including textiles, food processing, building materials, and simple chemicals, had developed in Egypt, Turkey, Iran, Palestine, and, to a smaller extent, in Lebanon, Syria, and Iraq. In addition, Turkey had the beginnings of heavy industry—iron, steel, and coal. Petroleum production and refining had become important to Iran, Bahrain, and Iraq. Several countries were meeting most of their requirements of such basic consumer goods as textiles, refined sugar, shoes, matches, and cement.

World War II gave great stimulus to Middle Eastern industry. Imports were drastically reduced and Allied troops provided a huge market for many goods. The Anglo–American Middle East Supply Center helped by providing parts, materials, and technical assistance. By 1945, total output had increased by some 50 percent. With the resumption of trade, from 1946 to 1950, many firms were hit by foreign competition, but the governments gave them tariff and other protection, so output continued to grow at about 10 percent per annum from 1946 to 1953. This rate was maintained, and in some countries (like Iran) exceeded through the 1970s, but in the 1980s it fell off sharply because of such factors as

the Iran–Iraq War, the Sudanese and Lebanese civil wars, and the 1980s fall in oil prices.

Table 1 shows a breakdown of the structure of Middle Eastern industry. The main branches are still textiles (including garments); food processing (sugar refining, dough products, confectionery, soft drinks, beer); tobacco; building materials (cement, bricks, glass, sanitary ware); and assembly plants for automobiles, refrigerators, radio and television sets, and so forth, with some of the components produced locally. Important new industries have also developed—notably chemicals—including basic products, fertilizers, and various kinds of plastics; basic metals and metal products; and many types of machinery. A particularly rapidly growing branch is petrochemicals, using gases produced in the oil fields or in refineries. Only in petrochemicals, textiles, and food processing does the region's share approach or exceed 5 percent of world output. Similarly, only in phosphates and chromium is the region's share of mineral production significant.

Israel, however, has a large diamond-cutting industry and is a significant exporter of precision instruments. It is also a large exporter of arms, as is Egypt; in the late 1980s each country exported more than 1 billion U.S. dollars worth of weapons; they ranked third and fourth, respectively, among third-world exporters, and twelfth and fifteenth, among world exporters of arms. The ARAB BOYCOTT has, of course, restricted some of Israel's economic pursuits within the region as well as with some international TRADE.

Today, manufacturing plays an important part in the Middle East's economy, accounting in many countries for 15 to 20 percent of GDP. Industry, in the broader sense, which includes mining (and therefore oil), construction, electricity, water, and gas as well as manufacturing, generally constitutes over 30 percent of GDP. In the major oil nations it is 60 percent or more, usually employing 20 to 30 percent of the labor force (including immigrant labor).

With rare exceptions, industries still export very little and survive through government protection. Productivity is low; for example, gross annual value added in 1974 was only worth 4,000 to 5,000 U.S. dollars in most countries (compared to $20,000 in West Germany). This is particularly marked in the more capital-intensive industries, such as steel, automobiles, and aircraft. In the late 1970s, in the Turkish state-owned steel mill in Iskenderun, a ton of steel took 72 worker-hours, compared with 5 in the United States and 7 in Europe; in Egypt, annual output per worker in the automobile industry was one car, compared with 30 to 50 in leading Japanese firms. In the more labor intensive industries, such as textiles, however, physical output per worker is about 30 to 50 percent of European output. Here, very low wages offset low productivity and enable the Middle East to compete. In 1980, hourly wages in the textile industry were equal to 1 U.S. dollar in Syria and Turkey and 40 cents in Egypt, compared to 8.25 U.S. dollars in Western Europe.

Low productivity in the Middle East is caused by many factors. First, capital investment per employee is low, although governments have poured large amounts into industry; in the late 1970s the share of manufacturing, mining (including oil), and energy was over 40 percent of total investment in Egypt, Iraq, and Syria, and 30 percent in Iran. In the Gulf region's petrochemical industry, however, capital intensity is high and up-to-date machinery is used. Second, industry is greatly overstaffed; many governments compel firms to take on more workers—to relieve unemployment or for other political purposes. Third, the poor health, education, and housing of workers adversely affect their productivity—but conditions are improving. Fourth, there has been much bad planning, with factories being located far from suitable raw materials or good transport.

General conditions are also unfavorable for industrial development. The region is, on the whole, poor in raw materials. Wood and water have become very scarce. Minerals are generally sparse, remote, and often low grade. Most agricultural raw materials are of poor quality, lacking the uniformity required for industrial processes. The protection given to manufacturers of producers' goods (e.g., metals, chemicals, sugar) creates a handicap for industries that use their products. The main exceptions are natural and refinery gas, which are available almost free of cost, and raw cotton, which is of fine quality. The small size of the local market makes it impossible to set up factories of optimum size and the general underdevelopment of industries prevents profitable linkages among industries; both factors raise unit costs. Although the infrastructure has greatly improved, it still does not serve manufacturing adequately; for example, the frequency of power failures led many firms to install their own generators and transport costs remain high. A dependence on imported machinery, spare parts, and raw materials, although declining, is still great—hence, when a shortage of foreign exchange curtails imports, factories work below capacity, further raising unit costs.

Middle East industry also suffers from a lack of competition. Because of the small size of the local market and the high degree of protection, firms often enjoy a quasi-monopoly—and behave accordingly. Finally, a great shortage of industrial skills exists at both the supervisory and foreman levels. Even more serious is the shortage of managers; this is compounded where the government has nationalized the bulk of industry—as in Egypt, Iran, Iraq, Sudan, and Syria. Here market discipline has been replaced by bureaucratic control, so efficiency has been sharply reduced.

On the whole, then, manufacturing does not make the contribution to the Middle East's economy commensurate with either the efforts or the capital invested in it. Conditions may be expected to improve, however, as the society and the economy continue to develop and as some measure of peace takes hold.

BIBLIOGRAPHY

ALIBONI, ROBERT. *Arab Industrialization and Economic Integration.* London, 1979.
ECONOMIST INTELLIGENCE UNIT. *Industrialization in the Arab World.* London, 1986.
HERSHLAG, Z. Y. *Contemporary Turkish Economy.* New York, 1988.
ISSAWI, CHARLES. *An Economic History of the Middle East and North Africa.* New York, 1982.
TURNER, LOUIS, and JAMES BEDORE. *Middle East Industrialization.* Fainborough, U.K., 1979.
UNITED NATIONS. *The Development of Manufacturing in Egypt, Israel, and Turkey.* New York, 1958.

Charles Issawi

MAPAI

The principal Israeli socialist party, 1930–1968.

Under the spiritual inspiration of Berl KATZNELSON, MAPAI (Mifleget Po'alei Eretz Yisrael; Party of the Workers of the Land of Israel) became the main ideological and political vehicle for the Jewish labor movement during the Yishuv period. Its central program focus was uniting socialist and national goals. To do that, however, it was necessary to work with nonsocialist parties and to accede to some of their premises.

MAPAI's chief political leader from the mid-1930s to 1963 was David BEN-GURION. A leading pragmatist, he was frequently disputed by party elements that were more ideological. In 1935, for example, there was strong internal dissent over a proposed agreement with the Revisionist leader, Vladimir Ze'ev Jabotinsky. In 1963, Ben-Gurion resigned from MAPAI over the LAVON AFFAIR. In 1965, MAPAI became a partner in the formation of the Labor Alignment, and in 1968 that organization in turn joined with the Rafi party to form the Israel LABOR PARTY. The 1965 election was the last one in which MAPAI ran candidates under its own name. During its existence, MAPAI's membership supplied all but one of Israel's prime ministers, all but one of the state's presidents and Knesset speakers, and all secretaries-general of the Histadrut.

BIBLIOGRAPHY

ARONOFF, MYRON J. *Power and Ritual in the Israel Labor Party.* Armonk, N.Y., 1993.

Walter F. Weiker

MAPAM

Israeli Marxist-Zionist political party.

Founded in 1948, MAPAM (Mifleget Po'alim Me'u-hedet; United Workers Party) followed a Moscow-led policy until the death of Josef STALIN. Thereafter, it concentrated much more on less worldwide matters. Combining the goals of LABOR ZIONISM with a refusal to dispossess Israeli-Arabs, it received considerable criticism when it accepted Arab members. Starting immediately after 1967, MAPAM opposed the establishment of Israeli settlements on the WEST BANK and strongly urged negotiations with the Palestinians. It was also among the quickest and most vigorous objectors to the ARAB–ISRAEL WAR OF 1982.

After 1969 MAPAM became a member of the Labor Alignment. There were vigorous arguments within MAPAM over whether the Alignment's ideology was so mild that MAPAM's very principles were being violated, but those favoring continued membership prevailed until 1984 when the Alignment took part in the formation of the NATIONAL UNITY GOVERNMENT in which Likud was a partner

MAPAM has been represented in every Knesset, though at a steadily smaller level. From nineteen seats in the first Knesset of 1948, it declined to eight or nine in the 1960s and to five to seven seats in the Alignment lists. In 1992 MAPAM joined with Shinui and the Civil Rights Movement to form MERETZ, which became Labor's main coalition partner.

MAPAM's socioeconomic program is the most socialist of any Israeli party. It is also one of the strongest proponents of equality for Israeli Arabs. It does not, however, advocate class struggle in orthodox Marxist terms.

BIBLIOGRAPHY

ROLEF, SUSAN, ed. *Political Dictionary of the State of Israel.* New York, 1987.

Walter F. Weiker

Ma'pilim

Hebrew, "the daring ones"; a term applied to clandestine Jewish immigrants to Palestine during the British mandate.

Britain's policy of restricting the number of Jews entering Palestine—especially after the WHITE PAPER of 1939—was countered by active resistance and an intensification of illegal immigration.

In 1938, an underground organization, Mosad le-Aliyah Bet, was formed to assist the large number of Jews fleeing persecution in Europe both before and after the Holocaust. Many of the ma'pilim, in attempting to reach the shores of Palestine, were intercepted by the British and sent to internment camps in Cyprus. The most renowned group was the 4,515 passengers on the refugee ship *Exodus* whose fate turned world sentiment against the British. The struggle ended with the establishment of the State of Israel in 1948.

Ann Kahn

Maqarin Dam

Dam on the Yarmuk river.

Proposed in the 1950s, the Maqarin (colloquially, Magarin) dam was to span the YARMUK RIVER between Syria and Jordan. No action was taken toward its construction, however, until 1988, when the two governments decided upon a joint project. Renamed Sadd al-Wahda (the Unity Dam), it will hold some 300 million cubic yards (225 million cu. m) of water. Jordan will pay for construction while Syria will gain use of much of the resulting electricity that is generated. The construction continues to be on hold until Israel, Jordan, and Syria agree on partitioning the waters of the Yarmuk. In 1988, when Israel and Jordan held discussions, Syria refused to participate.

BIBLIOGRAPHY

The Middle East and North Africa 1991, 37th ed. London, 1991.

NYRUP, RICHARD F., ed. *Jordan: A Country Study.* Washington, D.C., 1980.

Michael R. Fischbach

Marabout

A Muslim saint or holy person in North Africa.

Marabout (Arabic *murabit,* literally, "the tied one") refers in North Africa to saints or holy persons, living or dead, reputed to serve as intermediaries in securing Allah's blessings (Arabic *baraka*) for their clients and supporters. The term also refers to their shrines. In earlier centuries, marabouts "tied" tribes to Islam and mediated disputes. Although *marabout* remains current in French usage, most North Africans today use the term *salih,* "the pious one," which does not imply that Allah has intermediaries, a notion at odds with Qur'anic doctrine. Unlike Roman Catholicism, Muslims have no formal procedures for recognizing saints, although North African Muslims associate specific "pious ones" with particular regions, towns, tribes, and descent groups. Many shrines are the site for local pilgrimages and annual festivals. Jewish communities in Morocco and Israel have similar practices, calling such a holy person *tzaddik* (or *saddiq*).

BIBLIOGRAPHY

EICKELMAN, DALE F. *Moroccan Islam: Tradition and Society in a Pilgrimage Center.* Austin, Tex., 1976.

WEINGROD, ALEX. "Saints and Shrines, Politics, and Culture: A Morocco-Israel Comparison." In *Muslim Travellers: Pilgrimage, Migration, and the Religious Imagination,* ed. by Dale F. Eickelman and James Piscatori. Berkeley, Calif., 1990.

Dale F. Eickelman

Maratghi, Mustafa al-   [1881–1945]

Egyptian religious leader and politician.

Al-Maratghi served as head of al-Azhar in 1928/29 and from 1935 until his death in 1945. A supporter of the Muslim reformer Muhammad ABDUH, al-Maratghi used his post at al-Azhar to defend the political institutions of Islam and fight against secular nationalist leaders.

Al-Maratghi had played a pivotal role in the Cairo Caliphate Congress of May 1926. The congress discussed the restoration of the caliphate, the office of political and spiritual leader of the Muslim world, which had been abolished by Mustafa Kemal (Atatürk) in 1924. Al-Maratghi supported the candidacy of Egypt's King Farouk for the caliphate but was opposed by forty teachers from al-Azhar, who argued that the caliphate could not be brought to Egypt as long as the country was occupied by Britain. Meanwhile, Egyptian public opinion was more concerned with the parliamentary elections taking place that month. The congress produced no results. In 1930, al-Maratghi participated in efforts to forge a coalition between the Wafd and the Liberal Constitutionalist parties in opposition to the government of Isma'il SIDQI, the prime minister.

BIBLIOGRAPHY

GERSHONI, ISRAEL, and JAMES P. JANKOWSKI. *Egypt, Islam, and the Arabs: The Search for Egyptian Nationhood, 1900–1930.* New York, 1986.

AL-SAYYID MARSOT, AFAF LUTFI. *Egypt's Liberal Experiment, 1922–1936.* Berkeley, 1977.

WUCHER KING, JOAN. *Historical Dictionary of Egypt.* Metuchen, N.J., 1984.

David Waldner

Mardam, Jamil   [1894–1960]

Syrian politician.

Born in Damascus to a landowning bureaucratic Sunni Muslim family, Mardam was active in the Arab national movement from its beginnings in late Ottoman days. He helped to organize al-FATAT and the first Arab Nationalist Congress and was a member of a Syrian Arab delegation to the Paris Peace Conference of 1919. When the Great Syrian Revolt (1925–1927) erupted, Mardam took part in it, seeking, like other Damascene and Druze leaders, not the overturn of the French-controlled system of rule but the modification and relaxation of that rule in a manner that would restore the influence of Syrian notables over local politics. The French had already undercut that influence in various towns as well as in the JABAL DRUZE. In this regard, Mardam was the principal strategist of the policy of "honorable cooperation" with the French, which stated that popular opposition to French presence should not be allowed to disrupt the delicate negotiations between the French and the leadership of SYRIA's independence movements.

This policy tarnished the reputation of Mardam and his supporters and forced them to look beyond Syria's frontiers for political support. In an attempt to rehabilitate their reputation and PAN-ARABISM, they turned their attention to PALESTINE, creating in 1934 the Bureau for National Propaganda, a political body devoted to the dissemination of information on Palestine and other critical Arab issues.

Mardam was a founder of the NATIONAL BLOC, a broad-based group established in 1927 to spearhead the independence struggle in Syria. He also was one of its most active members at the leadership level in Damascus, where the Bloc's headquarters were based. During the French mandate, Mardam was elected a deputy in Syria's National Assembly in 1932, 1936, and 1943 and served as minister from 1932 to 1933, 1936 to 1939, and 1943 to 1945. After full independence was achieved, he served as prime minister from December 1946 to December 1948, as well as minister of the interior in 1947 and minister of defense in 1948.

The growth of action-oriented political organizations in Syria after the ARAB-ISRAEL WAR of 1948 (the Communists, the MUSLIM BROTHERHOOD, and the BA'TH), damaged the prospects of the National Bloc (renamed the NATIONAL PARTY in 1943) in the new local and inter-Arab rivalries that governed political life in Syria throughout the 1950s. In the end, the discrediting of the old guard who led the National Bloc rendered the political fortunes of Mardam bleaker and bleaker, thus forcing him out of politics.

BIBLIOGRAPHY

KHOURY, PHILIP. *Syria and the French Mandate: The Politics of Arab Nationalism, 1920–1945.* Princeton, N.J., 1989.

Muhammad Muslih

Mardom Party

A government-sponsored political party, created in Iran in 1957 as an opposition party.

As a result of pressure for democracy and in the hope of giving the appearance of a two-party system, the Mardom party was established as an "opposition" party under Muhammad Reza Shah Pahlavi's rule in Iran in 1957. Its founder, Amir Asadollah ALAM, was a large landlord, a former prime minister, and a close associate and confidant of the shah. The party's official platform included such issues as raising the standard of living for farmers, workers, and government officials, as well as facilitating the acquisition of land by the farmers. Together with the "official" government party, the Nationalist party or Hezb-e Melliyun, however, the Mardom party came to have a reputation for being a government organ, the Nationalist being known as the "yes" party and the Mardom as the "yes, sir" party. In 1975, the Mardom party was dissolved when the shah decided to revert to a one-party system and started the RASTA-KHIZ party. Many people point to the establishment and dissolution of the Mardom party, both government-inspired, as indications of Mohammad Reza Shah Pahlavi's failure in developing Iran's political system.

BIBLIOGRAPHY

ABRAHAMIAN, E. *Iran between Two Revolutions.* Princeton, N.J., 1982.
WILBER, D. N. *Iran: Past and Present.* 4th ed. Princeton, N.J., 1958.

Parvaneh Pourshariati

Mareth Line

A defensive position in Tunisia.

The Mareth Line was designed by the French to protect Tunisia's southeastern flank against an Italian invasion from Libya. Thirty-five kilometers (22 miles) long, it was named for Mareth, a small town southeast of Gabès. In November 1942, following the defeat of Gen. Erwin Rommel's Afrika Korps at al-Alamayn by British forces under Field Marshal Bernard Montgomery, the Germans rushed reinforcements and equipment to Tunisia. The Mareth Line was the southern key to German defenses.

Breaking through the Mareth Line became a major objective of Allied forces. In March 1943, the British Eighth Army—together with forces from France and New Zealand—assaulted the Mareth Line. An outflanking maneuver by New Zealand troops forced General Jürgen von Armin to withdraw his forces to Enfidaville, near the Cape Bon peninsula.

BIBLIOGRAPHY

NELSON, HAROLD D. *Tunisia: A Country Study.* Washington, D.C., 1988.

Larry A. Barrie

Ma'rib

Ancient town of North Yemen, enjoying new life because of oil.

Until recent years, Ma'rib was the uninviting, all-but-abandoned government center and garrison of the large, sparsely populated province of the same name. The town is located on the eastern reaches of North Yemen, on the edge of the arid Ramlat al-Sabatayn desert. Ma'rib was for centuries before the time of Christ the capital of the rich and powerful trading kingdom of Saba, the kingdom once ruled by Bilqis (or Balkis), the Queen of Saba (SHEBA). The fabled Ma'rib dam spanned the nearby valley, and its monumental remains as well as those of the vast irrigation system it supplied are much in evidence today. The gradual abandonment of these works early in the Christian era forced the emigration of most of the area's sizable population. The sleepy town that remained over the following centuries was all but abandoned after heavy bombardment during the YEMEN CIVIL WAR in the 1960s. Since the mid-1980s, however, the town has undergone a major renewal as the center closest to the important oil exploration, production, and refining operations in the Ma'rib/al-Jawf basin; this has also given the town and its environs new military significance. Financed by the ruler of Abu Dhabi, whose ancestors migrated from the area, the construction of a new dam at Ma'rib in the 1980s has made possible a significant revival of irrigated agriculture in the area.

Robert D. Burrowes

Mariette, Auguste   [1821–1881]

French Egyptologist.

Mariette founded the Egyptian Antiquities Service in 1858 and the EGYPTIAN MUSEUM, thereby slowing the indiscriminate destruction and export of pharaonic antiquities to Europe. His workers in archeology excavated scores of monuments: the Serapeum of the Apis bulls at Saqqara was his most famous discovery. French control of the Antiquities Service was to last until 1952, when the Egyptian monarchy and colonialism ended and a republic was declared.

BIBLIOGRAPHY

DAWSON, WARREN R., and ERIC P. UPHILL. *Who Was Who in Egyptology,* 2nd ed. London, 1972.

Donald Malcolm Reid

Marine Barracks Bombing, Lebanon

A bombing that caused the deaths of 241 U.S. Marines in the Lebanese Civil War.

Following the Israeli invasion of Lebanon in 1982 and the Palestinian massive loss of life at the Sabra and Shatila refugee camps on the outskirts of Beirut, the administration of President Ronald Reagan dispatched peacekeeping troops to Lebanon in the framework of the Multinational Force (MNF). The MNF was composed of U.S., French, British, and Italian contingents tasked with shoring up the regime of President Amin Jumayyil, brother of the assassinated Bashir Jumayyil. The presence of U.S. Marines in West Beirut polarized animosities between Christians and Muslims in Lebanon, and the American contingent became the target of hatred and distrust.

Lebanese Muslims, especially Shi'ites living in the slums of West Beirut and around the airport—where the marines were headquartered—saw the MNF not as a peacekeeping force but as another faction in the Lebanese war. U.S. troops particularly were seen as perpetuating Maronite Catholic rule over Lebanon. Muslim feelings against the American presence were exacerbated when missiles lobbed by the U.S. Sixth Fleet hit innocent bystanders in the Druze-dominated Shuf mountains. On October 20, 1983, a Shi'a Islamic Jihad member drove a truck loaded with 12,000 pounds of TNT into the lobby where the U.S. contingent was stationed and blew himself up, thereby killing 241 servicemen. In 1984, the Reagan administration withdrew the U.S. contingent from Lebanon.

BIBLIOGRAPHY

FRIEDMAN, THOMAS L. *From Beirut to Jerusalem.* New York, 1989.
PINTAK, LARRY. *Beirut Outtakes: A TV Correspondent's Portrait of America's Encounter with Terror.* Lexington, Mass., 1988.

George E. Irani

Maritime Peace in Perpetuity, Treaty of

Treaty signed in 1853 between Great Britain and the rulers of the lower Gulf shaykhdoms.

Superseding treaties of 1820 and 1835 that had ended attacks on maritime commerce, the Treaty of Maritime Peace in Perpetuity obliged the British to enforce maritime peace and protect the TRUCIAL COAST shaykhdoms against external threats. It thereby gave formal permanency to the trucial system.

BIBLIOGRAPHY

PECK, MALCOLM C. *The United Arab Emirates: A Venture in Unity.* Boulder, Colo., 1986.

Malcolm C. Peck

Marja' al-Taqlid

Important Shi'a position of authority.

Marja' al-taqlid, or authority chosen to be emulated by believers, is one of the main pillars of Shi'a theosophy in the period after the occultation of the twelfth imam, the last of the infallible leaders of the Twelver Shi'a community. Twelver Shi'ism holds that the death of the eleventh imam, Hasan al-Askari in 873, marked the beginning of the minor occultation, when Shi'ites throughout the Islamic Empire were left without a member of the progeny of the first imam, Ali ibn Abi Talib, son-in-law and nephew of Muhammad, the prophet of Islam, to rule over them. Before his major occultation, the Twelfth Imam appointed four special assistants, the last of whom died in 939 C.E. Shi'a biographical compilations generally take Abu Ja'far Mohammad Koleyni (d. 940), one of the first compilers of Shi'a traditions, to be the first marja' al-taqlid after the occultation. In the medieval period, however, the office was not well defined. That task was undertaken by Shaykh Mohammad Hasan Esfahani Najafi, known as Sahb al-Javaher (d. 1849). All in all, seventy-seven marja' al-taqlid existed from 940 to 1995 (different sources provide slightly different tabulations), forty-nine of whom were Persians and the rest Arabs.

The marja' al-taqlid serves as one of the highest *ulama* (clergy) in Shi'ism, whose words and deeds serve as a guide for those members of the community unable to exert independent judgement *(ijtihad)*. As such, the position has come to enjoy substantial political clout in the modern period, especially since believers throughout the world provide the marja' al-taqlid with considerable donations in the form of religious tithes. In fact, one of the qualifications of a marja' is his ability to attract donations and raise enough money to finance the education of religious students. There are six conditions for the marja' al-taqlid, accepted unanimously by Shi'a theologians, namely maturity *(bulugh)*, reasonableness *(aql)*, being of the male sex *(dhukurrat)*, faith *(iman)*, justice *(edalat)*, and legitimacy of birth. It should be borne in mind though, that these are general principles for the selection of a marja' al-taqlid, and no specific process has ever been formalized. Except for a brief period of centralization in nineteenth-century Iran, engineered by Shaykh Morteza Ansari (d. 1864), clerical decen-

tralization is an integral part of the Shi'a hierarchy. Another defining characteristic of the marja' al-taqlid, which again distances it from the papacy, is that designation to the position is entirely at the discretion of the believers themselves. The marja' al-taqlid is not appointed by an official body resembling a council of *ulama*.

The sanctity of the office has increased its political clout in the modern period. In 1963, when Ayatollah Ruhollah Khomeini was arrested by the government of Mohammad Reza Pahlavi, the entire Shi'a world rallied behind him and pressured the Shah into releasing him. With the Iranian revolution of 1979 and the establishment of the governance of the jurist *(velayat-e faqih)*, which designates a single leader *(vali-ye faqih)* for Shi'ites throughout the world, the office of marja' al-taqlid has acquired an ambiguous position, somewhat rivaling that of the vali-ye faqih. Today there are several important marja' al-taqlid in the Shi'a world. Since the death of Ayatollah Khomeini in 1989, the position has been shared between ayatollahs Kho'i (d. 1993), Araki (d. 1994), Sistani, Rowhani, Khamene'i, Montazeri, and Qommi.

BIBLIOGRAPHY

ENAYAT, HAMID. *Modern Islamic Political Thought.* Austin, Tex., 1982.
HAIRI, ABDUL-HADI. *Shi'ism and Constitutionalism in Iran.* Leiden, 1977.

Neguin Yavari

Mark VIII

108th Coptic patriarch of Egypt serving from 1796 to 1809.

The papacy of Mark VIII is remembered more for the great historic event that occurred during his tenure—the Napoleonic expedition to Egypt (1798–1801)—than for his accomplishments. The prosperity enjoyed by the Coptic laity throughout Mark's career resulted from individual ambition not from the patriarch's initiative. Even construction of the Cathedral of St. Mark (dedicated to the archbishop's namesake) at al-Azbakiyya was the work of two influential citizens, not the patriarch.

Likewise, a Coptic military unit was more effective than Mark in dealing with Muslim tensions. Under the French, many COPTS held high political and military positions and were handsomely rewarded for their loyalty. The Islamic majority could not tolerate the double disgrace of so many European Christians descending upon Egypt and their subsequent favoritism shown not only to the Copts but also to all other non-Muslims living in Cairo (Syrians, Greeks, and Jews). Several brutal assaults on the Copts in Cairo occurred during the French occupation and even thereafter. The famous Coptic Legion commanded by the illustrious General Ya'qub was created to counter this persecution.

In spiritual matters Mark achieved some distinction. He maintained an active correspondence with the Coptic parishes throughout Egypt and sent an important pastoral letter to Ethiopia. Because the church of St. Mark in "Babylon," the Coptic quarter of Cairo, had been destroyed during the Islamic rampages, the patriarch built a new church dedicated to his namesake.

BIBLIOGRAPHY

SHOUCRI, M. "Mark VIII." In *The Coptic Encyclopedia*, ed. by A. S. Atiya. New York, 1991.

Donald Spanel

Marmara, Sea of

See Straits, Turkish

Marmara University

Public university in Istanbul, Turkey.

The university was established in 1982 by incorporating several independent schools and colleges, including a school of business and economics and a teacher-training college that was founded in 1883. Marmara University now comprises the faculties of science and letters, law, economics, and business administration, dentistry, pharmacology, theology, fine arts, and medicine, as well as three faculties of education, one specializing in technical education; school of journalism and mass communication and two vocational schools are also included in the university. English is used in instruction in some fields, most prominently in medicine, electronics, and other branches of engineering, and various of the social sciences; French is used in the program of public administration. In 1990 the university had twelve hundred teaching staff and nineteen thousand students (eight thousand female). Its state-funded 1991 budget amounted to 158.5 billion Turkish lire, of which 49 billion was earmarked for capital investment. The university was named for the sea of Marmara, on which it is located, near the Turkish Straits.

Marmara University is a typical example of the 1982 solution to a problem which had been festering in Turkey for the previous decade or so—different types of higher education, especially teacher-training colleges and vocational schools; some of them originally established by investors for profit but later closed or taken over by the state, had proliferated alongside universities. The uneven status of graduates of these different academic institutions was confusing both to students and prospective employers. In the 1982 reorganization, all such institutions were incorporated into existing or newly established universities. In this case, the result was a decentralized university, with many faculties and schools located throughout the city. Recently Marmara University has been developing a new campus in Göztepe on the Asian side of Istanbul in an attempt to gain a stronger focus and identity.

BIBLIOGRAPHY

Higher Education in Turkey. UNESCO, European Centre for Higher Education. December 1990.
World of Learning. 1990.

I. Metin Kunt

Maronites

An indigenous church of Lebanon and its largest Eastern-rite church.

The communion between the Maronite church and the Roman Catholic church was established in 1182, broken thereafter, and then reestablished in the sixteenth century. The union allowed the Maronites to retain their own rites and canon laws and to use Arabic and Aramaic in their liturgy, as well as the Karashuni script with old Syriac letters. There is still debate about the origins of the Maronites. Some trace them to Yuhanna Marun of Antioch in the seventh century; others trace them to Yuhanna Marun, a monk of Homs in the late fourth and early fifth centuries. The word *maron*, or *marun*, in Syriac means "small lord."

In the late seventh century, following persecutions from other Christians for their heterodox views and rituals, the Maronites migrated from the coastal regions into the mountainous areas of Lebanon and Syria. During the Ottoman era the Maronites remained isolated and relatively autonomous in these areas, although in recent times this autonomy has been greatly exaggerated for ideological and national reasons. The Maronite community underwent socioeconomic changes in the nineteenth century when the Maronite church wielded tremendous economic and political power and the peasants within the community grew increasingly dissatisfied with the uneven distribution of the community's wealth.

The peasants revolted in 1858 against the large landowning families, but the church quickly engaged them in sectarian agitation. The peasants' revolt soon degenerated into a communal war between DRUZE and Maronites. This conflict came to characterize much of the history of nineteenth-century Lebanon as the ruling families of the two communities split over the question of the credibility of the Chehabi dynasty, among other political and economic issues. Land ownership, distribution of political power, and the question of safe passage of one community's members in the territory of the other remained thorny issues in their relationship. The conflict was internationalized in 1860 when France, the historic "protector" of the Maronites, sent a military expedition to the area.

The relationship of the two groups was not decisively settled in 1920 with the establishment of the mandate system, but the carnage of the previous century seemed to have ended. The Druzes, however, only seemed to accept the political dominance of the Maronites, who were favored by the French authorities. Their dissatisfaction centered on their desire for a continuous, albeit inferior, political representation.

The Maronite sect has been directed and administered by the patriarch of Antioch and the East. Bishops are generally nominated by a church synod from among the graduates of the Maronite College in Rome. In 1994 Mar Nasrallah Butrus Sufayr was the Maronite patriarch.

Besides the Beirut archdiocese, nine other archdioceses and dioceses are located in the Middle East: Aleppo, Ba'albak, Cairo, Cyprus, Damascus, Jubayl al-Batrun area, Sidon, Tripoli, and Tyre. Parishes and independent dioceses are also found wherever Maronites reside in large enough numbers: in Argentina, Brazil, Venezuela, the United States, Canada, Mexico, the Ivory Coast, and Senegal. There are four minor seminaries in Lebanon (al-Batrun, Ghazir, Ayn Sa'ada, and Tripoli) and a faculty of theology at Holy Spirit University at al-Kaslik, which is run by the Maronite monastic order. The patriarch is elected in a secret ceremony by a synod of bishops and confirmed by the pope in Rome.

It is estimated that there are 416,000 Maronites in Lebanon (including an unknown number abroad), who make up 16 percent of the population. Historically, most Maronites have been rural people, like the Druze—although, unlike the Druze, they are scattered throughout the country, with a heavy concentration in Mount Lebanon. The urbanized Maronites reside in East Beirut and its suburbs. The Maronite sect has been traditionally awarded— thanks to French "protection" and support—the highest posts in government, and its status within the

socioeconomic hierarchy of Lebanon has been, in general, higher than that of other sects. Lebanese nationalism has been associated over the years with Maronite sectarian ideologies, so much so that most non-Maronite Lebanese tend to feel uneasy with the notion of Lebanese nationalism because it has come to signify the Lebanese political system with its Maronite dominance.

The Maronites, like other sects in Lebanon, have suffered from the civil war and its consequences. While many Maronites were active as combatants, much of the civilian population of the Maronite community paid a price—like all other civilians in Lebanon—for the recklessness of the warring factions. Many Maronites were displaced as a result of battles and forced expulsions. Many (there are no reliable figures) have chosen to emigrate, going to Europe, the United States, Canada, and Australia in search of peace and prosperity. Maronite leaders continue to warn of the dangers of the diminution in the demographic weight of the Maronite community. The Lebanese political reforms of Ta'if in 1989 did not necessarily undermine the political dominance of the Maronite community. In fact, the sectarian designation of governmental seats was juridically solidified in those reforms, and the presidency was kept for Maronites only. Nevertheless, the increasing powers of the council of ministers curtailed some of the previous arbitrary powers of the president. But the implementation depended, and will continue to depend, on the personal and political impact of politicians, in terms both of their popularity within their own communities and the external support they receive from various regional and international powers.

BIBLIOGRAPHY

MOOSA, MATTI. *Maronites in History*. New York, 1986.
SALIBI, KAMAL S. *Maronite Historians of Medieval Lebanon*. New York, 1959.

As'ad AbuKhalil

Marrakech

Second largest city in Morocco; one of the four imperial cities of precolonial Morocco, established about 1060 C.E.

Located in the Hawz, an agricultural plain bounded to the south and east by the High Atlas mountains, and watered by the Tansift river, Marrakech is situated in a natural site of great potential. In opposition to Fez, the Arab capital of Morocco, Marrakech is a BERBER metropolis, which drew population from the

Minaret of Kutubiya mosque in Marrakech. (Richard Bulliet)

Berber-speaking groups of the nearby central High Altas mountains.

The city was founded by Yusuf ibn-Tashfin (1060–1106), first ruler of the Almoravid dynasty (1055–1157), under whom Marrakech became the base for the conquest of Morocco, portions of the Maghrib, and Andalusia. Extensive irrigation works were undertaken at this time, but little remains of the architecture of the Almoravid period.

Conquered by the Almohads (1130–1269) in 1147, Marrakech became the capital of an empire that at its height extended from Tunisia to the Atlantic, and from the Sahara to Andalusia. The Almohads were the effective builders of the city, constructing the Kutubiya mosque, one of the finest examples of Hispano-Moorish architecture, together with the ramparts, a fortress complex, and extensive bazaars and gardens. The celebrated philosopher, doctor, and savant Ibn Rushd (known in the West as Averroes, 1126–1198) lived in Marrakech, where he wrote several of his best-known works.

Marrakech went into a prolonged decline during the reign of the Marinids (1244–1578), whose capital was at Fez. Under the Sa'dians (1510–1603), who made it their capital in 1554, Marrakech once again became an imperial city. Numerous important palaces were constructed at this time, and the irrigation system of the surrounding Hawz plain was revived.

The Alawi dynasty (1603–present) has continued this tradition. The city continued to benefit from its position as a crossroad of trade between the mountains, the pre-Saharan steppe, and the fertile plains of central Morocco. Under Sultan Hassan I and his successors Abd al-Aziz ibn al-Hassan and Abd al-Hafid, Marrakech was drawn increasingly into the world capitalist market. In the period of the MOROCCAN QUESTION (1900–1912), European business interests in collaboration with local urban notables and Berber lords based in the city began to acquire substantial holdings in the Hawz plain and the surrounding area.

Under the French protectorate (1912–1956), effective authority was conceded to Madani and Tuhami al-Glawi, who ruled much of southern Morocco as pashas of Marrakech and imperial viceroys. In this period, the city became a major agricultural entrepôt and center of light manufacturing. There was considerable investment in irrigation technologies and agriculture, and the population of the city increased from 70,000 in 1912 to 145,000 in 1921 to 215,000 in 1952.

Since Moroccan independence in 1956, Marrakech has continued to grow. Its population in 1990 was about 750,000 people. It is a center of tourism and an agricultural marketplace for southern Morocco, with a university and important cultural installations.

Snake charmer in open market at Marrakech. (Richard Bulliet)

BIBLIOGRAPHY

DEVERDUN, GASTON. *Marrakech des origines à 1912.* 2 vols. Rabat, 1959, 1966.

JULIEN, CHARLES-ANDRÉ. *History of North Africa,* trans. by John Petrie. London, 1970.

PASCON, PAUL. *Capitalism and Agriculture in the Haouz of Marrakech.* London, 1986.

PICKENS, SAMUEL. *Les villes impériales du Maroc.* Courbevoie, France, 1990.

Edmund Burke III

Marriage and Family

The institutions, patterns, and practices of marriage and the family play a key role in Middle Eastern society.

Some observers note that marriage and family form the heart of society. No single set of ideological notions and social practices are found in this vast region, although it is possible to describe some general patterns. Some regional (e.g., North Africa), state, and community-wide practices and notions can also be discerned. Any local set of patterns can be explained in large part by historical, ethnic, religious, and socioeconomic factors. For example, the forms of marriage and the family found among Turkish-speaking QASHQA'I nomadic pastoralists in southwestern Iran can be explained by interconnected and overlapping factors relating to the Middle East (patrilineality, notions of honor and shame), Islamic law and ideology (inheritance rights), central Asian Turkish speakers (notions of hearth and home), the practices and demands of nomadic pastoralism (a diversified economy needing the full labor participation of all men, women, and children), and national-minority status (kinship idioms used in political organization).

Performer at an Egyptian wedding. (Mia Bloom)

Modern wedding in Iran. Note the traditional symbols on the table. (Sandra Batmanglich and the University of Chicago)

Ideology may beat odds with actual practice in marriage and the family. For example, rural agriculturalists in Syria may explain their local social groups in terms of the principles of patrilineality. But, in reality, ties of marriage, the maternal lineage, economics, and friendship may be equally if not more important. As another example, tribespeople in Somalia may assert the historical accuracy of their lengthy genealogies to explain their political affiliations. However, investigation reveals that genealogies are manipulated, even constructed, to correspond to current political realities. People's notions and practices of kinship, marriage, and the family—while corresponding to a degree to certain wider historically based patterns —are constantly evolving to reflect and respond to changing political, economic, and social conditions.

The Middle East has undergone rapid change in the twentieth century. For the people there, certain ideological notions have a sustaining quality in the face of

Bridal party at Siwa, Egypt. (D.W. Lockhard)

change and contain the seeds of continuity with the past. For example, in many regions, women who now have access to advanced formal education and careers continue to face societal restrictions concerning their contacts outside the home and kinship group. These same women may be aided by certain customary notions of propriety, so that if they abide by local codes concerning modest dress (the "veil"), they can travel outside the home and enter a workplace where non-kinsmen and other strangers are also employed. Anthropologists and sociologists unravel these kinds of complexities as they describe and analyze patterns of kinship, marriage, and the family in the Middle East.

Marriage brings together two families in an expanding network of relationships. For some Middle Easterners, marriage between close relatives, even first cousins (especially patrilateral parallel cousins, the children of two brothers), is the preferred form and serves, among other functions, to maintain property within the kinship group. Generations of close-kin marriage create dense social ties for people, who become related to one another by overlapping patrilineal, matrilateral, and marriage bonds. Marriage between kinship groups serves political, economic, and social functions. Each nuclear or extended family arranges different kinds of marriage alliances to accomplish both general and specific purposes. Marriage between a young man and his mother's brother's daughter, for example, serves to draw his mother's kin group closer to her and her children.

Marriages are arranged by many people, often women during the initial stages and the senior men of each family in the final stages. The payment of bridewealth cements the relationship between the two families. The bride's parents may spend the entire bridewealth, plus their own resources, on her dowry. Marriage ceremonies are almost always large, expensive, and joyous affairs involving the groom's wider kinship and residential groups and sometimes the bride's as well. A party from the groom's family collects the bride and brings her to the ceremonies, usually at the home of the groom's parents. Accompanied by her dowry goods, she is usually concealed from view by layers of clothing. The bride often lives with the groom and his family (patrilocal residence), but the trend throughout the Middle East, especially for the urban middle and upper classes, is for a new residence for the groom and bride (neolocal residence). The groom's and bride's families remain in close contact and visit frequently. It is often reported that sons are preferred to daughters and that special ceremonies mark the birth of boys but not girls. Girls eventually marry and leave their parents, so the argument goes, but boys remain with their parents to care for them in their old age.

In a world increasingly buffeted by rapid change beyond the control of individuals, the home and family provide sanctuary, a place for privacy and protection. Bonds of obligation and trust unite people over time, and relationships within families are often intense. Families and kin groups are brought together by births, marriages, deaths, religious and other rituals, and the affairs of daily life. Many personal relationships beyond the home and family are expressed in the language of family relationships. A political patron is called "uncle," for example.

A combination of local customs, interpretations of Islamic law, and other religious laws as well as laws of individual states offer women and men different kinds of rights. Although one of the stereotypical notions of the Middle East is POLYGAMY (more precisely, polygyny), its rates have always been low, and they are decreasing rapidly almost everywhere, primarily for economic and social reasons. A few nation-states have banned polygyny outright, but some other states have

Two children of Siwa, Egypt, wearing traditional garb. (D.W. Lockhard)

restricted its practice, particularly by giving a wife certain protective legal rights against her husband taking additional wives without her permission.

Rates of divorce vary widely across the region, from as high as 60 percent of marriages to as low as 1 percent. Divorce rates are said to be increasing, in tune with the pressures of rapid social change and its impact on family life. The age of marriage for both men and women is rising because of new laws raising the legal age and new opportunities in education and employment for both sexes.

Widespread economic change, especially trends toward modernization and Westernization, have affected customary notions of marriage and the family. New studies on the impact of the modern media (particularly movies and television, especially family-based dramas) in Egypt and Turkey, for example, demonstrate the role of Western models in influencing customary patterns of marriage, the family, and gender roles.

The institutions and practices of marriage and the family are also related directly to politics in the Middle East, for people in power use their kinship and family networks to form reliable alliances. In heatedly competitive contexts, family members are often believed to be more loyal and dependable than others. Marriages between families serve important political functions by allying families with otherwise possibly conflicting interests.

[See also: Women]

BIBLIOGRAPHY

BECK, LOIS. Nomad: A Year in the Life of a Qashqa'i Tribesman in Iran. Berkeley, Calif., 1991.

GEERTZ, CLIFFORD, HILDRED GEERTZ, and LAWRENCE ROSEN. Meaning and Order in Moroccan Society: Three Essays in Cultural Analysis. New York, 1979.

MUNSON, HENRY, JR. The House of Si Abd Allah: The Oral History of a Moroccan Family. New Haven, Conn., 1984.

TAPPER, NANCY. Bartered Brides: Politics, Gender and Marriage in an Afghan Tribal Society. Cambridge, U.K., 1991.

Lois Beck

Marshall, George C. [1880–1959]

U.S. Secretary of State.

As U.S. Army chief of staff from 1939 to 1945, Marshall was the architect of the Western Allied victory in Europe and the Pacific during World War II. He became U.S. secretary of state from 1947 to 1949 under President Harry Truman. In this capacity, he initiated the so-called Marshall Plan for the economic recovery of post-war Europe by the infusion of massive Amer-

ican aid through the Organization for European Economic Cooperation. On Middle East issues, Marshall differed with Truman on the question of Palestine, opposing immediate independence for Israel because Israel would be too weak militarily to fight the expected war and would thus end up relying too heavily on the United States for protection. He also observed that U.S. recognition of Israel would alienate the Arab states, which had important oil reserves. Ultimately, Truman disregarded Marshall's advice and recognized the new State of Israel on May 14, 1948.

BIBLIOGRAPHY

LENCZOWSKI, GEORGE. The Middle East in World Affairs, 4th ed. Ithaca, N.Y., 1980.

Jenab Tutunji

Marsh Arabs

Inhabitants of the vast marshlands in southern Iraq.

The Marsh Arabs live in one of the great marsh areas of the world, a 20,000-square-mile (52,000 sq. km) area triangulated by Kut on the Tigris, al-Kifl on the Euphrates, and Basra on the Shatt al-Arab. A significant number may be non-Semitic in origin, perhaps descendants of the ancient Sumerians, although they have mixed with other peoples through time. Called Marsh Arabs by some owing to their language, social structures, and religion, others designate them Ma'dan to reflect that their way of life is dependent on the water buffalo. Nomads of the marshes, relying on a variety of canoes for transport, they follow buffalo herds as their desert counterparts follow camels or sheep. Most are cultivators, reed gatherers, or buffalo breeders. Traditionally they lived in villages in island settlements, on floating platforms, or on man-made reed islands. Today, their structures are of brick and concrete. Roads and causeways connect major settlements facilitating social improvements, especially in education and health.

BIBLIOGRAPHY

THESIGER, WILFRED. The Marsh Arabs. New York, 1964.

Albertine Jwaideh

Martel, Damien de

French high commissioner in Lebanon.

Martel, the successor of Henri Ponsot as French high commissioner in Lebanon, served from 1933 until 1939. Previously he had been the ambassador to Japan.

As'ad AbuKhalil

Ma'ruf, Muhammad

Syrian military officer.

Muhammad Ma'ruf, an officer in the army intelligence division, became chief of the military police after Colonel Sami al-Hinnawi's coup of August 14, 1949. He was a major target in Adib Shishakli's December 1949 countercoup. With a group of exiled National Social party officers and politicians, Ma'ruf was a key figure in the planning of a pro-Shishakli coup in the spring of 1956. Major Ma'ruf was indicted for his involvement on December 22, 1956. His allegiance shifted to Shishakli (his former captor) because of the prospect for a united Fertile Crescent, a goal he had worked for under previous regimes.

BIBLIOGRAPHY

SEALE, PATRICK. *The Struggle for Syria: A Study of Post-War Arab Politics, 1945–1958.* London, 1958.

Charles U. Zenzie

Ma'rufi, Abbas [1957–]

Iranian writer and editor.

Ma'rufi was born in Tehran and graduated from Tehran University's Faculty of Fine Arts, in dramatic arts. His writings develop a psychoanalytic look into the problems of individuals, adopting a very clear and flowing narrative style. He has published several collections of short stories and, in 1989, his novel, *Samphoni-ye Mordegan* (The Death Symphony) brought him popularity. Ma'rufi edits the literary journal *Gardoon* and has published several novels. He resides in Tehran.

Pardis Minuchehr

Masada

The purported conviction of some Israelis that it is preferable for Israel to go down in defeat rather than concede any land to its Arab neighbors.

The Masada complex derives its name from the ancient fortress site whose occupants committed mass suicide in 73 C.E. rather than surrender to Roman forces. Those who advocate an intransigent negotiating stance argue that self-destructive threats will reduce the actual possibility that Israel will ever be required to cede any territories.

BIBLIOGRAPHY

GONEN, JAY. *A Psychohistory of Zionism.* New York, 1975.

Jon Jucovy

Masharka, Zuhayr

Syrian vice president.

In the Ba'th party congress held in April 1975, he was a member of the regional command. In 1978, Masharka was appointed minister of education in the Halabi government. In 1980, he was elected deputy regional secretary of the Ba'th party. In 1984, he was nominated vice president for party affairs during the cabinet changes headed by Abd al-Ra'uf al-Kasim.

George E. Irani

Mashhad

City in northeast Iran, Khorasan province.

Lying in the center of one of the richest agricultural regions of the country, near the Turkmenistan and Afghanistan borders, Mashhad was long known as an important trade center on the caravan routes from Tehran to India. The modern city of Mashhad (place of martyrdom) is the outgrowth of the ancient city of Tus, the birthplace of al-Ghazzali and the poet Ferdowsi. It contains the burial place and shrine of the eighth imam, Ali Reza, who is believed to have been poisoned, as well as the tomb of Harun al-Rashid. Although the ancient city of Tus never recovered from its destruction at the hands of the Mongols in 1220 and Miran Shah in 1320, its importance to Shi'a Islam was not lost on later generations of Iranian kings; Abbas I (1571–1629) the Safavid king added to the shrine of the imam and encouraged pilgrimage to the city. Nader Shah (1736–1747) made it his capital, and in the nineteenth century, Fath Ali Shah Qajar built the law courts and library and expanded the shrine. Its population in 1986 was 1,463,568.

Cyrus Moshaver

Masira Island

Island in the Arabian Sea, off Oman's south coast.

Masira's jagged rock hills rise from the island, which is some forty miles (64 km) long by four to ten miles (6.4–16 km) wide. Vegetation and land animals are scarce, but bird and sea life, notably nesting sea turtles, are abundant. Before the changes that came with World War II, a population of about 2,000 Janaba lived there in palm-frond huts. They subsisted on fishing, seafaring, combing shipwrecks, and exporting turtle shells, shark fins, and fish. During the 1940s, the British built an air base, and later, a powerful radio installation. In 1977, the air base reverted to Omani control and Sultan Qabus introduced modernization, which included housing, schools, and a clinic. In 1980, the United States was granted limited access to the air base for warehousing military equipment. Masira provided major logistical support to the allied coalition's campaign leading to and during the Gulf War of 1990/91.

BIBLIOGRAPHY

DE GAURY, GERALD. "A Note on Masirah Island." *Geographical Journal* 123 (1957): 499–502.

Robert G. Landen

Masjid

See Mosque

Masmoudi, Muhammad   [1925–   ]

Tunisian diplomat.

Masmoudi was educated in Tunis and at the Law Faculty in Paris. In 1956, he took part in the delegation from TUNISIA that signed the protocols formalizing independence from France (which held a protectorate from 1881). Despite uneven relations with President Habib BOURGUIBA, he held various government posts, including ambassador to France (1965–1969). As minister of foreign affairs (1970–1974), he led an effort to forge ties with Libya, which culminated in a short-lived merger in 1974. With its collapse, Masmoudi was removed from office; shortly thereafter he went into exile, returning in 1977. His ties to Libya put him at the center of controversy in 1984, when he briefly accepted a United Nations post from Libya, a position he was forced to reject by Bourguiba.

BIBLIOGRAPHY

HAHN, LORNA. *North Africa: Nationalism to Nationhood.* Washington, D.C., 1960.
PERKINS, KENNETH. *Tunisia: Crossroads of the Islamic and European Worlds.* Boulder, Colo., 1986.

Matthew S. Gordon

Maspero, Gaston   [1846–1916]

French Egyptologist.

Maspero studied at the Ecole Normale, Paris. As professor of Egyptian Philology and Archeology at the Collège de France, he succeeded Auguste MARIETTE, the founder and director of the Egyptian Antiquities Service and the Egyptian Museum. Maspero served from 1881 to 1886 and from 1899 to 1914, overseeing archeology throughout Egypt. He began editing the immense catalog of the Egyptian Museum and published more than any other Egyptologist.

BIBLIOGRAPHY

DAWSON, WARREN R., and ERIC P. UPHILL. *Who Was Who in Egyptology,* 2nd ed. London, 1972.

Donald Malcolm Reid

Matawirah Tribe

One of four major tribal confederations into which the Alawite community of Syria is divided.

The other three ALAWITE confederations are the Khayyatin, the Haddadin, and the Kalbiyya. Each of these confederations is made up of a number of clans, each of which carries a specific name. A case in point is the Numaylatiyya clan, which is part of the Matawirah tribe.

BIBLIOGRAPHY

KHURI, FUAD. "The Alawis of Syria: Religion, Ideology and Organization." In *Syria, Society, Culture, and Polity,* ed. by Richard Antoun and Donald Quataert. New York, 1991.

Abdul-Karim Rafeq

Matin-Daftari, Hedayatollah   [1929–   ]

Iranian resistance leader.

Born in Tehran, Matin-Daftari was a student at Cambridge University during the height of the Iranian

National Resistance led by Mohammad Mossadegh (1947–1951). He returned to Iran in 1956 and later joined the National Front that was formed in 1961. The Shah's SAVAK arrested him several times, but it is assumed that his father's close relations with the Shah provided him with some leeway and he was freed on each occasion. In 1969, assisted by a group of attorneys, Matin-Daftari founded the Lawyer's Group of the Iranian Bar Association. His activities during and after the 1979 revolution primarily focused on issues concerning human rights and the defense of political prisoners. After the revolution, he initiated a split in the National Front and helped to found the NATIONAL DEMOCRATIC FRONT (NDF). In exile, he continues his active campaign against the Islamic Republic in cooperation with MOJAHEDIN-E KHALQ's National Resistance Council.

BIBLIOGRAPHY

BEHROUZ, K. *Iran Almanac and Book of Facts 1987*, 18th ed. Tr. by S. Kalantari. Tehran, 1987, pp. 417–418.

Farhad Arshad

Matrah

Port city of Oman.

Originally a fishing village, after the sixteenth century Matrah became the hub of Oman's domestic commerce and home of a cosmopolitan merchant community. Today the site of Oman's largest port, Matrah lies adjacent to Musqat, the sultanate's capital. It is essentially being absorbed into the burgeoning capital urban complex.

Fishermen with nets by the roadside in Matrah, Oman. (Richard Bulliet)

BIBLIOGRAPHY

HAWLEY, SIR DONALD. *Oman and Its Renaissance,* rev. ed. London, 1984.

Robert G. Landen

Matruh

Province in Lower Egypt.

Matruh (also Marsa Matruh or Mersa Matruh) is in Egypt's Western desert, on the Mediterranean coast, having a land area of 81,896 square miles (212,112 sq. km) and a 1986 population of some 173,000. Its capital city, Matruh, had a population in 1986 of 42,347 and is located at 31° 21′ N, 27° 14′ E.

BIBLIOGRAPHY

Europa World Yearbook, 1994, vol. 1. London, 1994, p. 1024.

Arthur Goldschmidt, Jr.

Maude, Frederick Stanley [1864–1917]

British soldier.

Maude entered the military in 1884, fought in the South African wars (1899–1902), and became commander of the 13th Division at the Dardanelles in 1915 after the outbreak of World War I. He was ordered to take his troops to Mesopotamia (the area between the Tigris and Euphrates rivers) to relieve the Anglo–Indian forces in the MESOPOTAMIA CAMPAIGN besieged at Kut al-Amara. On February 22, 1917, he drove the Ottoman army from the town and then planned the advance that culminated in the fall of Baghdad on March 11, 1917.

Shortly after this, the so-called Maude Declaration (actually written by Sir Mark Sykes) announced to the people of Baghdad that Britain intended to grant them self-determination. Maude died of cholera in 1917.

BIBLIOGRAPHY

FROMKIN, DAVID. *A Peace to End All Peace.* New York, 1989.

Zachary Karabell

Mauritania

Constitutional republic located in northwest Africa.

The Islamic Republic of Mauritania covers an area of 398,000 square miles (1,030,700 sq. km) and is bordered by Western Sahara and Algeria in the north,

Mali in the east, Mali and Senegal in the south, and the Atlantic Ocean in the west. The population in 1990 was about two million (UN estimate). Nouakchott, the capital and largest city, has more than 400,000 people. The second-largest city is Nouadhibou, a maritime commercial center in the north, with a population of about 70,000. Mauritania has twelve administrative regions plus the district of Nouakchott.

Climate and Resources. Mauritania has three major geographic and climatic areas. The northern Sahara region is more than 65 percent of the country. Covered by arid plains, plateaus, and sand dunes, it receives almost no rainfall and is subject to severe fluctuations in temperature. To its south is the Sahil, a wide area consisting of steppes and meadows. On Mauritania's southern border is the Senegal river region, a narrow strip of cooler temperatures and rainfall that supports considerable plant life.

The national economy has suffered from a lack of natural resources. Climatic conditions limit agriculture to the Senegal river region, where millet, sorghum, rice, and dates are grown. In the Sahil, livestock raising supports much of the rural population. Iron ore, gypsum, and copper constitute the only major mineral deposits. In 1990, Mauritania mined over 11 million tons of iron ore, all of which was exported. In the 1980s, offshore fishing grew rapidly, making fish the country's chief export. The small manufacturing sector is based largely on fish processing. Food and capital goods account for the bulk of imports.

Population and Culture. Approximately 66 percent of the population are Maures of Arab, Berber, and black

African descent who speak Arabic. The remaining population is ethnically black African—composed of Haluparen, Fulbe, Soninké, and Wolof (speakers of Pulaar, Soninké, and Wolof). Almost all Mauritanians are Sunni Muslims.

History. In the early 1800s, emirs and Islamic religious leaders controlled the area that is now Mauritania. France gradually expanded its military and economic presence from Senegal into Maure areas. Between 1901 and 1912, France gained control of all major regions of Mauritania and declared it a protectorate, ruling indirectly through traditional leaders. After World War II, nationalist parties became active. Under the leadership of Mokhtar Ould DADDAH and his Mauritanian Regroupment party, Mauritania declared its independence from France in 1960. Since 1978, it has been ruled by successive military leaders. Since independence, Mauritania has faced severe problems with national unity, desertification (enlargement of desert areas), and economic stability.

Based on the new 1991 constitution, the government is to be headed by a president elected by universal suffrage, who appoints a prime minister and a constitutional council. The legislature is to be composed of the National Assembly with seventy-nine members and the Senate with fifty-six members. The constitution guarantees the right of political parties to form. Until these changes are fully instituted, the government will continue to be controlled by the Military Council for National Salvation, a military body whose president, Maouiga Ould Sid TAYA, has been the head of state since 1984.

BIBLIOGRAPHY

BAUDEL, PIERRE ROBERT, ed. "Mauritanie: Entre arabité et africanité." *Revue du Monde Musulman et de la Méditerranée* 54 (1989).

U.S. LIBRARY OF CONGRESS. FEDERAL RESEARCH DIVISION. *Mauritania: A Country Study,* 2nd ed., ed. by Robert E. Handloff. Washington, D.C., 1990.

Bradford Dillman

Mawla

See Molla; Mulai

Maysalun

Site of armed combat between French and Arab forces immediately prior to the French mandate over Syria.

Khan Maysalun, a quiet market town on the highway between Beirut and Damascus just east of Alayh, won notoriety as the site of the 24 July 1920 clash between French troops and the armed forces of the Arab government in Damascus. The outcome eventuated in France's taking control of Syria for the ensuing quarter century.

British imperial troops occupied the cities of central Syria as soon as the Ottoman garrisons evacuated them in September 1918. With British acquiescence, an Arab government quickly established itself in Damascus, and Arab nationalists announced the creation of a similar administration in Beirut on 1 October. But when British forces entered Beirut a week later, the nationalist government was disbanded and French military governors took charge of Beirut, Saida, and Tyre in the name of implementing the League of Nations mandate. The Arab leader in Damascus, FAISAL I IBN HUSAYN, nevertheless toured Lebanon the following month and received an enthusiastic welcome from the populace in each city he visited. On 21 November, he returned to Beirut on his way to the Versailles peace conference.

While Faisal was in Europe, Britain and France negotiated the boundaries separating their respective zones of control in Syria, according to the terms of the wartime Sykes–Picot agreement. The division of Syria into British and French zones was confirmed at Versailles, over strenuous objections from the United States. By the next summer, it was clear that Britain intended to withdraw its troops from central Syria, prompting Faisal to press the British government to take over the mandate for the region. Britain refused to do this, and on 1 November 1919, while the emir was once again in Europe, British commanders in the Syrian interior turned over their positions to forces loyal to Faisal, while those in Lebanon relinquished their garrisons to French units. In the Biqa' valley, Lebanese Christians attacked Syrian outposts, providing French commanders with a pretext to move into the area in force at the end of the month.

Faisal returned to Syria in mid-January 1920 and attempted to salvage his reputation, which had been badly tarnished during the months of fruitless negotiations with the French. He acquiesced in the General Syrian Congress's decision to declare Syria independent that March and accepted the title of monarch of the new unified kingdom of Syria. Not only did Britain, France, and the United States refuse to recognize Syrian sovereignty, but the authorities in Beirut responded to the declaration by proclaiming Lebanese independence under the mandatory authority of the French. Syria then set up a ministry of war under the leadership of Yusuf al-Azma, and King Faisal delivered a series of strongly worded speeches reaffirming the country's independence. Meanwhile,

French troops pulled out of Cilicia and took up positions along the Lebanon–Syria border.

On 9 July 1920, the French military command in Beirut issued an ultimatum to the Arab government in Damascus, demanding immediate acceptance of the mandate throughout central Syria. Publication of the ultimatum sparked rioting in Damascus and Aleppo, but the Syrian cabinet reluctantly agreed to its terms on 20 July and dispatched a telegram to inform the French of its decision. The next morning, the Third Division of the Armée du Levant, made up of Senegalese, Moroccan, and Algerian battalions, advanced from Shtura and Zahia toward Damascus and on 23 July encamped outside Khan Maysalun. An Arab force of some six hundred regular troops and two thousand volunteers led by al-Azma attacked the encampment at dawn the following day and were routed before noon. The Third Division pursued the retreating Arabs and marched into Damascus unopposed on 25 July. Three days later, the French commander ordered Faisal to leave for British-controlled Palestine, and the mandate era began. Maysalun became a symbol of heroic Arab resistance, in the face of insurmountable odds, to European domination.

BIBLIOGRAPHY

AL-HUSRI, ABU KHALDUN SATI. *The Day of Maysalun: A Page from the Modern History of the Arabs.* Tr. by Sidney Glazer. Washington, D.C., 1966.

Fred H. Lawson

Mazar-e Sharif

Northern Afghan city.

Mazar-e Sharif is a city in Northern Afghanistan with a population of approximately 70,000. The city is the provincial capital of Balkh and near the ancient Bactrian city of Balkh. "Mazar-e Sharif" means "holy tomb," and locals believe that Caliph Ali (656–661) is buried there, although Najaf, Iraq, is generally accepted as Ali's actual burial place. The city is Afghanistan's largest northern city and a major marketing and trading center for the northern area. The people in the area are largely Uzbek, but the city contains major Tajik and Turkoman populations as well.

During the resistance war (1978–1992) the city was a major stronghold of the Marxist government because of its close proximity to the Soviet Union and its flat terrain, which made it easy to defend against guerilla activities. Since the Marxist government fell in 1992, the city has seen fighting between the Tajiks led by Ahmad Shah Mas'ud and the Uzbeks under the command of General Doestam.

BIBLIOGRAPHY

ADAMEC, LUDWIG. *Historical Dictionary of Afghanistan.* Metuchen, N.J., 1991.

Grant Farr

Maziq, Husayn

Leader of the Cyrenaican Barassa tribe.

In the 1950s, Husayn Maziq was *wali* (governor) of Cyrenaica and foreign minister under the premiership of Mahmud Bey Muntasir (1951–1954). He became premier in March 1965 but was forced to resign in June 1967 by popular pressure, because of his decision to resume oil shipments to the West and because of Libya's refusal to participate in the 1967 Arab–Israel War. His premiership was characterized as "benign" but marked by financial, political, and social opportunism. In 1969, his family was linked to the Shalhi family by marriage. Husayn Maziq eventually fled into exile when the Qaddafi regime came to power; he was accused of participating in the abortive July 1970 coup attempt against the new regime.

BIBLIOGRAPHY

WRIGHT, JOHN. *Libya: A Modern History.* London, 1982.

George Joffe

Mazza

An assortment of foods served as appetizers, accompaniments to main dishes, or a complete meal.

A feature of Middle Eastern cuisine from Morocco to Persia, mazza is usually served with a beverage, and may be simple or elaborate. Typically, it consists of nuts, fresh vegetables and herbs, cheeses, salads and dips, savory pastries, and "miniature foods" (smaller versions of main dishes, including grilled meats, vegetable dishes, and beans).

Jenab Tutunji

McMahon, Henry   [1862–1949]

Britain's high commissioner in Egypt, 1914–1916.

During Sir Henry McMahon's tenure as high commissioner, he was responsible for mobilizing war matériel from Egypt for Britain's efforts in World War I. McMahon is best known for his role in the negotiations with Sharif Husayn of Mecca that led to the 1916 Arab Revolt against the Ottoman Empire. These negotiations are contained in the Husayn–McMahon correspondence. The extent of the territorial concessions that McMahon pledged for an independent Arab state continues to be a subject of debate.

BIBLIOGRAPHY

WUCHER KING, JOAN. *Historical Dictionary of Egypt.* Metuchen, N.J., 1984.

David Waldner

Meah She'arim

A section of Jerusalem established in 1874 as an Orthodox quarter outside the Old City.

Inhabited almost exclusively by ultra-Orthodox Jews, Meah She'arim boasts a population of 5,400 and houses hundreds of yeshivas and synagogues; it is also the center of Orthodox anti-Zionist ideology and activity. The neighborhood is highly picturesque, and upon crossing into it, one can sense having entered the domain of an almost autonomous ethno-religious culture. Many of its inhabitants view their turf as their own, and some view all strangers with suspicion. Its streets are closed to vehicular traffic on the Jewish Sabbath; breaches of that closure are occasionally met with violent reactions. Women are enjoined to dress modestly.

BIBLIOGRAPHY

FRIEDMAN, MENACHEM. *Ha-hevra ha-haredit* (The Haredi [Ultra-Orthodox] Society: Sources, Trends and Processes). Jerusalem, 1991.
HEILMAN, SAMUEL. *Defenders of the Faith: Inside Ultra-Orthodox Jewry.* New York, 1992.

Chaim I. Waxman

Mecca

The third largest city in Saudi Arabia and the holiest site in Islam.

Usually referred to as al-Mukarrama (the honored), Mecca (also Makka) lies near the Red Sea about 40 miles (60 km) east of Jidda in the barren foothills below the Hijaz escarpment. The climate is extremely hot and arid. The population of Mecca, today numbering some 750,000, is greatly mixed in origin, consisting of the descendants of pilgrims who settled in it over the centuries, so that virtually all the ethnic groups of ISLAM may be found represented there. However, the religion and culture of Islam unite the inhabitants, the overwhelming majority of whom speak Arabic. A ban on non-Muslims entering the city and its environs further accentuates its uniform Islamic character.

The site of the original revelation of Islam to the Prophet Muhammad, Mecca's chief practical significance is as the place toward which Muslims face in their daily worship. But above all, Mecca is the location of the annual Muslim HAJJ (pilgrimage), which is required of every Muslim once in one's lifetime if one can afford it. The focus of attention in it is God's Holy House, the KA'BA, an empty cubical structure built of stone blocks and mostly dating in its present form to 692, though the QUR'AN states that Abraham first built it. Though Muslims do not believe God resides in the Ka'ba, the building symbolizes God's oneness and thus is the focal point of Muslim worship. The Ka'ba and its surroundings, including the entire city of Mecca and beyond in an irregular circle running as much as 14 miles (22 km) from the building, constitute a sacred enclosure (haram) belonging to God, inside of which certain rules apply, such as the prohibition of fighting, cursing, hunting, and uprooting plants. During the pilgrimage, the city population more than doubles. Even today, serving the needs of pilgrims remains the most important source of livelihood for the city.

Despite its continuing religious significance, Mecca lost its political importance in the seventh century (the first century of Islam), when the capital of the caliphate first moved to Medina and later even outside Arabia altogether. Thus Mecca became a provincial backwater ruled by governors appointed from afar. But as central authority weakened, local sharifs claiming descent from the Prophet Muhammad were able to assert their control and remain substantially in power from about 965 to 1916, but never with full independence. From 1517, the sharifs fell under the suzerainty of the Ottoman Empire but remained effective local rulers, sharing power with the Turkish governors of Jidda. From 1916 to 1924, Mecca was part of the short-lived Kingdom of the Hijaz proclaimed by the last sharif but then was incorporated into Saudi Arabia. The Saudi government has made many improvements, including two gigantic expansions of the Great Mosque surrounding the Ka'ba.

Mecca's abiding importance, aside from its role as a religious shrine, has been as a meeting ground for ideas in Islam, since many prominent Muslims have passed through it on the pilgrimage, though few have settled permanently. Thus, partly through the pilgrimage, Wahhabi ideas were disseminated east and west by Muslims as diverse as Shah Wali Allah al-Dihlawi and the Sanusis of Libya. Most recently,

Mecca's significance was underlined by the occupation of the Great Mosque by Mahdist rebels in 1979.

BIBLIOGRAPHY

GAURY, GERALD DE. *Rulers of Mecca.* London, 1951.
"Makka." In *Encyclopedia of Islam.* 2nd ed.
SABINI, JOHN. *Armies in the Sand: The Struggle for Mecca and Medina.* London, 1981.

Khalid Y. Blankinship

Meclis-i Vala

Ottoman court established in 1838, also known as the Supreme Council of Judicial Ordinances.

Created by MUSTAFA REŞID Paşa, Meclis-i Vala (Court of High Officials) was entrusted with designing the TANZIMAT reform program. Consisting initially of a chairman and five members, it superseded all other consultative bodies, and for fifteen years was the main legislative organ of the empire. Members were handpicked to ensure compliance with tanzimat goals. The council was the highest appeals court for criminal cases and cases of government officials accused of violating the law.

In 1854, because of its overwhelming workload, the council's legislative functions were transferred to the new High Council of the Tanzimat (Meclis-i Ali-i Tanzimat). The two councils were rejoined in 1861, then divided in 1867 into the Council of State (Şurayi Devlet) and Council of Judicial Regulations (Divan-i Ahkam-i Adliye).

BIBLIOGRAPHY

DAVISON, RODERIC H. *Reform in the Ottoman Empire 1856–1876.* Princeton, N.J., 1963.
LEWIS, BERNARD. *The Emergence of Modern Turkey.* New York, 1961.
SHAW, STANFORD J., and EZEL KURAL SHAW. *History of the Ottoman Empire and Modern Turkey.* Vol. 2. New York, 1977.

Elizabeth Thompson

Mecmua-i Ebüzziya

Ottoman literary journal.

Published by EBÜZZIYA TEVFIK, a disciple of Namık Kemal, *Mecmua-i Ebüzziya* was a fortnightly literature review. Between 1887 and 1894, 159 issues of the journal appeared. An organ for Ottomanist ideas, the journal criticized the idea of Turkish nationalism, arguing that this would lead to the disintegration of the empire.

David Waldner

Mecmua-i Fünün

Ottoman journal.

Published by the Ottoman Society of Science, *Mecmua-i Fünün* (Journal of Science) appeared monthly between 1862 and 1867. Modeled on the eighteenth-century French encyclopedias, it was an organ for the dissemination of a western model of science. Through its discussions of positivist science and philosophy, *Mecmua-i Fünün* acted as a forum for Ottoman intellectuals. The journal briefly reappeared in 1883, but was swiftly closed by the censor.

David Waldner

Medani, Tewfiq al-   [1899–1983]

Secretary-general of the Algerian Association of Reformist Ulama, ambassador, and historian.

Born in Tunis, he studied at Zaytuna University and became a cofounder of the DESTOUR PARTY. His pro-nationalism activities provoked his expulsion from Tunisia to Algeria where he contributed profoundly toward reviving Arabic study and a national identity. His works include *Book of Algeria* (1931), an introduction to the country for youth that was implicitly nationalist, and *The War of Three Hundred Years Between Algeria and Spain* (1968). He wrote the play *Hannibal* and was editor-in-chief of *al-Basa'ir.*

Besides his cultural role, Medani also played an important political role. In 1952 he became secretary general of the Algerian Association of Reformist Ulama (body of mullahs) and integrated that organization within the revolutionary FRONT DE LIBÉRATION NATIONALE (FLN). He was later chosen minister of cultural affairs (1958) in the Gouvernement Provisoire de la République Algérienne (GPRA). He became minister for *habous* (religious foundations) in Ahmed Ben Bella's first two governments. He later served as ambassador to Iraq and Pakistan. He retired in order to devote time to his scholarship, which included editorial work for the Centre National D'Etudes Historiques (National Center for Historic Studies) and its journal *al-Tarikh* (History).

BIBLIOGRAPHY

DÉJEUX, JEAN. *La littérature algérienne contemporaine.* Paris, 1975.

STORA, BENJAMIN. *Dictionnaire biographique des militants nationalistes algériens.* Paris, 1985.

Phillip C. Naylor

Meddeb, Abdelwahhab   [1946–   ]

Tunisian novelist and poet.

Meddeb was born in Tunis and studied literature, art history, and archeology in Tunisia and in Paris. He subsequently taught history of architecture at the Ecole des Beaux Arts in Paris. Although he writes in French, his books are rich with references to Arabic texts and contain many quotations in Arabic, revealing not only his knowledge of the language but also his familiarity with Arabic literature and civilization. Meddeb's first novel, *Talismano* (1979), shows his constant concern with the past in addition to his personal interaction with and reaction to his Arab–Islamic culture.

The interest of Meddeb's writings lies, to a large extent, in his original handling of language and his experimentation with words. His point of departure is the bilingual situation in the Maghrib, which gives the writer access to two cultures and languages, and an opportunity to juggle them and, possibly, combine them. The starting point in his novel *Phantasia* (1989) is the human body. Meddeb conceives of writing as an act of perpetual creation, the result of an inner inspiration. The book is built on a cross reference to the Muslim mystic Ibn al-Arabi, around whom Meddeb later wrote a collection of poems, *Tombeau d'ibn Arabi* (1988). The classical Arabic religious and cultural heritage inspired Meddeb's latest book, *Suhrawardi, Chihab al-Din Yahya: Récits de l'Exil Occidental* (1993).

BIBLIOGRAPHY

DÉJEUX, JEAN. *Dictionnaire des auteurs maghrébins de langue française.* Paris, 1984.

JEGHAM, NAJEH. "Voix du dire/Voies du lire." *Itinéraires et contacts de cultures* 14 (1991): 114–118.

Aida A. Bamia

Medical Technology in the Nineteenth Century

European medical advances brought to the Middle East have influenced health care in the region.

European medical advances of the seventeenth and eighteenth centuries were brought to the Middle East by European doctors attached to legations or trading companies, as well as by the young Greeks,

Armenians, and Jews who studied medicine in Europe, then returned to practice in the major cities. In the nineteenth century, the Ottoman, Persian, and Egyptian governments launched programs to upgrade medical facilities, especially for military units and seaport quarantine units (lazarettos), with the aid of European doctors working under government contracts.

At the beginning of the nineteenth century, ordinary people in the Middle East had access to two types of medical treatment: the *tibb ilahi* (sacred medicine) or the medicine derived from the teaching and practice of the Galenic and Arab medical traditions. The tibb ilahi consisted mainly of folk remedies, magic formulas, and quackery, whereas the Galeno–Arab medicine of Al-Razi, Ibn Sina, and Maimonides was the same tradition upon which European medical science had drawn before developing new systems and techniques in the seventeenth and eighteenth centuries. By the first decades of the nineteenth century, European medical systems were being fostered in the leading Middle East countries as governments were pressured by European powers to provide quarantine facilities to slow the spread of cholera and plague in their seaports.

Because large amounts of state funds were being invested in European military equipment and training, governments did not want their armed forces to be decimated by sickness and death. Moreover, with the establishment of permanent European diplomatic missions and trading companies in the Middle East, doctors came from the mother countries to administer to the health needs of their nationals. Finally, with the rise of the Christian missionary movement, supported in particular by Britain and the United States, medical missionaries were sent to the Middle East to care for their own people and also to bring modern medicine to Eastern Christian populations and some Muslims, with the long-term hope of winning converts to Christianity.

By the beginning of the eighteenth century, European governments were convinced that the plague and cholera epidemics originated in the eastern Mediterranean and its hinterlands. Austria and Prussia built quarantine stations on their eastern borders and channeled all traffic through them. Merchants also could meet at a border point, known as a *rastel*, where goods and money, after fumigation, could be exchanged without the merchants having physical contact. By the end of the eighteenth century, these measures had eliminated plague from Europe west of the Carpathian Mountains.

With Europe having prevented the spread of deadly diseases through quarantine and advances in medicine, Middle Eastern leaders in the early nine-

teenth century came under increasing pressure to establish quarantine systems and modern medicine. Muhammad Ali, Ottoman governor in Egypt (1805–1849), and Sultan Mahmud II in Ottoman Turkey (1808–1839), early took the lead in introducing the new services to their subjects. Naser al-Din Shah of Persia (1848–1896) followed shortly thereafter.

Egypt. When Dr. Antoine Clot arrived in Egypt in 1825, he found about fifty European-trained doctors whose main function was to take care of Muhammad Ali's army of about 150,000. Working closely with Egyptian doctors, he soon put in place a board of health and a hierarchy of doctors and their assistants, then turned to redesigning and repairing the military hospital at Khanka. In 1826 he presented Muhammad Ali with a plan to establish a medical school. French would be the language of instruction, but key scientific textbooks would be translated into Arabic. The board of health would oversee all examinations. Clot immediately received approval and had the school running by 1827.

A group of conservative *ulama* instructed Clot not to teach with cadavers or to conduct autopsies because such practices were unacceptable to Muslims. Because dissection of the human body was essential to teaching modern medicine, Clot took up his case with the Shaykh al-Islam. He emphasized that just as a watchmaker must examine a watch's works to repair it, so must the surgeon examine the human body. He won his point with the learned shaykh, but all dissections had to be conducted in the utmost privacy. Although plague epidemics took more than 500,000 lives in 1831 and 1834, and cholera struck in 1831, 1848, 1850, and 1855, the new doctors and students in the medical school saved many lives.

In 1837, the principal medical hospital in the region was moved to Qasr al-Ayni in Cairo, where it had a facility comparable with those in leading European centers. By 1850, 1,500 doctors had graduated from the medical school, many of whom received advanced training abroad. A school of pharmacy was established at Khanka in 1829, and a maternity hospital in 1832. Muhammad Ali's sons did not fully appreciate the need for advanced medical facilities. Prince Abbas (1849–1854) cut the medical budget, and his successor, Prince Sa'id (1854–1863), closed the school in 1855. Clot returned in 1866, under the regime of Khedive Isma'il (1863–1879), to reopen the medical college. The French medical system in Egypt flourished until the British occupation of 1882.

Ottoman Empire. Ottoman medical reform along Western lines was first contemplated under Sultan Selim III (1789–1807), but the rebellion of the janissaries and the murder of Selim set back plans to open a medical college in Constantinople (now Istanbul). After the destruction of the Janissary Corps in 1826, Sultan Mahmud II (1808–1839) authorized the founding of the Imperial Medical College and the Imperial School of Surgery, to be housed in the former janissary barracks. Medical students were taught in Italian and surgical students in Turkish. Medical students studied for five years, whereas surgeons were trained in three. In 1832 the school was transferred to the grounds of Topkapı Palace, where the staff consisted of both Ottoman and foreign instructors. When the school again needed more space in 1837, it was moved to Galatasaray, where palace aides had been trained. The curriculum was updated and the school was renamed the Celebrated Imperial Medical College. In the year prior to the college's grand opening in 1839, Sultan Mahmud had initiated, with the aid of Dr. Franz Minas, an Austrian specialist, a reform of quarantine procedures in the empire's key seaports. With the assistance of Prince Metternich, two physicians, Jacob Neuner and Charles Bernard, and a pharmacist, Antoine Hoffmann, arrived at the end of 1838. Neuner was appointed personal physician to the sultan and head of the empire's health and sanitary institutions, and Bernard was asked to head the new medical college. Neuner served the sultan until the latter's death in 1839.

Bernard set up a professional medical college along Austrian lines. His efforts were made possible by the chief Ottoman doctor, Abdullah Mollah. Following Bernard's death in 1844, another Austrian physician, Sigmund Spitzer, who had joined Bernard's staff to teach anatomy in 1839, took over the running of the school. Spitzer had early gained high praise because he was able to introduce autopsies into medical practice in Constantinople (1841). During the early years of the college, the language of instruction was French, but by 1860 Turkish was being used. After Sultan Abdülmecit was almost drowned in a suspicious sinking of the admiral's flagship in 1850, the favorable attitude toward the medical school began to change. Spitzer was warned that he might be poisoned and received a number of death threats; he returned to Vienna. A traveler to Constantinople in 1847 reported that the college was training 454 students and 23 midwives, and that all graduates were assured of positions in the Imperial Medical Service "without distinction of religion." Spitzer noted in his ten-year report that the queen mother had founded a private medical college in 1843.

Persia. Although Persia profited from the knowledge of largely Austrian-trained physicians, the real renaissance in European medical training did not get under way until 1851, when the Dar al-Fonun (House of Sciences) was established by the vizier, Amir Kabir, "the Great Prince," with the support of Naser al-Din Shah (1848–1896). Prior to the founding of the Dar al-Fonun, Persia had had its share of medical charlatans; high-quality missionary medical facilities, such as the American mission hospital founded at Urumia in 1835; and a host of European doctors serving diplomatic and economic missions since the sixteenth century.

The most prominent Austrian physician to serve as a catalyst for placing Persia on the path of modern medical science was Eduard Jacob Polak. Upon his arrival in 1851, he realized that his students had major deficiencies in the basic medical sciences. He labored to fill that gap in the hope that his best pupils might be able to study abroad. Besides theoretical training, Polak believed in hands-on experience; hence, he took students with him when he made hospital rounds or visited patients in their homes. In spite of strong opposition from the *ulama* and the general public, Polak performed an autopsy in 1854. Two years earlier, he had first used ether while removing kidney stones. These innovations were readily accepted by the students.

Perhaps most noteworthy were Polak's efforts to found a modern hospital in 1854. He drew up the plans so that the rooms would be bright and airy. He also planted grass and shrubs outside the hospital. Other contributors to Persia's medical modernization included one Dr. Schlimmer, a Dutchman, who arrived in Persia in 1851. He compiled a dictionary of medical terms in French and Persian. Polak had published the first modern medical book, *The Anatomy of the Human Body,* printed in Persian by the Dar al-Fonun Press. Toward the end of his ten-year stay, Polak became the personal physician to Naser al-Din Shah, replacing Ernest Cloquet, who had done much to promote scientific training in Persia. These men, together with the young Persian physicians who had graduated from the Dar al-Fonun and gone to Europe for further training, transmitted modern medicine and "scientific thinking" to Persia. Before his departure from Persia, however, Polak noted that conditions at his hospital had deteriorated greatly. No longer was there routine cleaning of the hospital, and the grass and shrubs had died.

Other Areas. Outside of the leading capitals in the Middle East, newly trained indigenous doctors were practicing medicine alongside Western-trained missionaries. In 1863 a medical school was founded along with the American University of Beirut, where, for the first twenty years, the American professors taught in Arabic. In Jerusalem the German

Temple colony was founded in the 1860s, followed somewhat later by the American colony. These salvation-seeking Christians brought modern medical ideas to the Holy Land. Scientific training was also fostered by the Alliance Israélite Universelle, a Paris-based Jewish organization that opened French-style lycées for young Jews in Middle Eastern cities. Jewish doctors, trained in Europe, Russia, or the Middle East, served in major Middle Eastern cities. An important medical mission was set up in the Persian Gulf by the Dutch Reformed Church in the last decade of the nineteenth century.

BIBLIOGRAPHY

DOLS, MICHAEL. *The Black Death and the Middle East.* Princeton, N.J., 1976.
GALLAGHER, NANCY. *Medicine and Power in Tunisia 1780–1900.* Cambridge, U.K., 1984.
PANZAC, DANIEL, *Quarantines et lazarets.* Aix-en-Provence, 1986.
SONBOL, AMIRA. *Creation of the Medical Profession in Egypt.* Syracuse, N.Y., 1991.

C. Max Kortepeter

Medicine and Public Health

An improving field based on a combination of traditional and modern practices.

The largest populations, comprising 52 percent of the Middle East, are in Egypt, Turkey, and Iran. About half of the Middle East population is urban. Because of public health advances, a Middle Eastern child born in 1990 can expect to live for seventy years, thirteen years longer than his or her parents. Death rates have fallen faster than birthrates, and at the current pace the

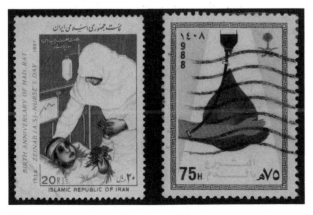

Postage stamps from Iran celebrating Nurse's Day (1987) and from Saudi Arabia honoring blood donors (1988). (Richard Bulliet)

Two 1988 Turkish stamps commemorating the health of children and the health of workers. (Richard Bulliet)

population will double in twenty-nine years. Cultural traditions, including Islam, shape some curative options, but socioeconomic factors prevail. Local beliefs in breast feeding and birth spacing enhance maternal and child health. Access to health services, quality of environment, and labor opportunities remain uneven. Israel's comprehensive, Western-style health-care system and developed economy exclude it from many generalizations here.

Typhoid fever, cholera (on the decrease because of better sanitation and improved water sources), typhus, leishmaniasis, trachoma, and gastroenteritis are characteristic of the area. Increased irrigation has raised the incidence of malaria and schistosomiasis. Smallpox was eliminated by the 1970s through systematic vaccination, but measles remains a problem in some countries. Tuberculosis, which replaced smallpox as the illness of crowded cities, decreased after a 1950s World Health Organization (WHO) and UNICEF immunization program but could resurge if AIDS expands. Ministries of health have combated AIDS, which is seen as the scourge of Western decadence, with frank public health campaigns.

Curative Options: Humoral, Prophetic, Local, and Cosmopolitan. Health care resonates with curative resources and one's life situation. Most people self-prescribe for mild symptoms, whether by taking vitamin C or consulting the local herbalist. Middle Easterners pick eclectically from a repertoire that includes humoral, prophetic, local-practice, and cosmopolitan (modern or western) cures. Western medicine was introduced in the nineteenth century in medical schools in Cairo, Tunis, and Istanbul, and by the 1920s most governments required practitioners to be licensed.

Humoral medicine, predicated on the balance of the four humors, as in the allopathic, Galenic tradition, is important for herbal pharmacists (*attarin*) who provide such household remedies as ginger for sore throats.

Prophetic medicine (*at-tibb an-nabawi*) is based on sayings of the Prophet Muhammad, such as the *Sahih* by al-Bukhari (d. 870). The *Sahih* contains eighty paragraphs (2.3 percent of the entire collection) concerned with medical issues, including the ever popular "God did not send down an illness without also sending down a cure."

In the twentieth century, prophetic medicine has assumed two forms: popular literature, which intermingles standard collections of prophetic sayings with local wisdom, including humoral principles of balanced, normal bodily functions; and formal medical practice, or Islamic medicine, advocated by such groups as the Islamic Medical Organization (IMO). Founded in Kuwait in the 1970s, the IMO administers a hospital that treats patients by the tenets of Islamic medicine and tests Prophetic cures under controlled, laboratory conditions. The experiments concentrate on symptoms ambiguous in etiology and cure, such as renal failure and eczema. The IMO ethical code critiques Western medicine's origin in a "spiritualess" civilization and adjures the Islamic physician to include the patient's therapy managers in the treatment. Other Middle Eastern physicians who consider themselves Islamic practice cosmopolitan medicine but within an Islamic-medicine moral context, such as Islamic benevolent association clinics.

Local and cosmopolitan medicine frequently overlap. Local practitioners, a trusted first recourse, cooperate with cosmopolitan practitioners. For instance, the traditional birth attendant may encourage the mother through delivery but call the licensed midwife to cut the umbilical cord and provide postnatal care. Training by the ministries of health targets socially accepted but technically inadequate midwives, herbalists, and self-made nurses.

Such local practices as amulets against the evil eye or shrine visitation to enhance fertility, which is forbidden by official Islam, are part of a complex curative strategy. Caretakers calibrate symptom severity: They make a vow for a sickly child but rush a fevered child to the hospital. Western, cosmopolitan medicine may be construed in local terms. Traditional Egyptian physiology speaks of circulation of microbes that bombard a patient, much as black magic does, and are neutralized by the injection of a powerful agent, or exorciser. Western medicine may be well understood but not used. For instance, agriculturalists will return to snail-infested irrigation canals to cultivate, though they know doing so means reinfection with schistosomiasis.

Public Health: Child Survival and Maternal Health. Major public health problems among infants and children are dehydration from diarrhea; malaria and immunizable diseases; acute respiratory infections; and injuries from war. Among women, maternal mortality and morbidity from inadequate prenatal, delivery, and postpartum care are often problems. Infant mortality rates (deaths per one thousand live births) dropped in the period 1960–1995 from 214 to 109 in Yemen, 139 to 62 in Iraq, and 89 to 12 in Kuwait.

With oral rehydration solution widely available to parents, mortality from dehydration is no longer a major threat to infants. Nevertheless, early childhood acute diarrhea—exacerbated by nonpotable water, poor sanitation, and malnutrition—may cause more than fifty deaths per one thousand per year in preschool children. Public health programs consider local perceptions of diarrhea and dehydration and teach mothers the warning signs of dehydration and home recipes for oral rehydration solutions in case mothers cannot obtain commercial packets. Given the synergy between malnutrition and diarrhea, these programs have promoted supplements based on such local dietary practices as Egypt's seven grains, which has been marketed as Supramin.

The percentage of children who are fully vaccinated ranges from 88 percent in Jordan and 85 percent in Morocco, to 45 percent in Yemen. Full-immunization rates have fallen in recent years, most notably in Iraq, after a decline in support from UN agencies previously leading this worldwide effort. While tuberculosis has subsided, acute respiratory infection remains a significant problem, in part because there is no vaccine to prevent it. In most Middle Eastern countries, it has replaced acute diarrhea as the number-one cause of infant mortality.

War exerts a heavy price on women and children, including death from military operations; starvation; orphaning; disruption of services that protect health, such as water, sewer, irrigation works, and health services; rape and sodomy; and separation of children from their families. For political reasons, there are no accurate data on children killed or maimed in Middle Eastern wars. Estimates are as high as two million killed and five million disabled.

The long conflict in Lebanon severely damaged the quantity and quality of drinking water. One 1990 study found that 66 percent of urban Lebanese water sources were contaminated and that one-third of urban communities were using cesspools for sewage disposal. It is more difficult to assess war's psychic trauma for children than its physical wounds. Civil strife in the Levant, West Bank, Gaza, and Israel has created a generation of children with dead parents and siblings, lost limbs, and nightmares of bombs and mines. Women and children pay much of the human price after several years of sanctions against Iraq. The food-rationing system provides less than 60 percent of the required daily calorie intake, and the water and sanitation systems are in a state of collapse. During the Gulf War, Iraq laid multitudes of mines; the allies also laid some one million land mines along the Iraq–Kuwait border. These pose serious threats to life and limb.

Countries are just beginning to recognize at the policy level the importance of maternal health to the health of a nation. Very few have as yet provided adequate resources. Reproductive morbidity—illness related to the reproductive process—remains relatively unstudied but critical. Over half of a sample of rural Egyptian women had such gynecological morbidities as reproductive-tract infections and anemia. Maternal mortality—fewer than 30 per 100,000 births in developed countries—remains high. Morocco averaged 332 in the late 1980s, an Egyptian province, 126 in the 1990s.

Poor maternal health and nutrition, too-short birth intervals, prematurity, and low birth weight underlie 40 to 60 percent of all infant and child deaths. In 1992, Egypt reported 26 percent of children from zero to thirty-five months with stunted growth, while Jordan and Tunisia reported 18 percent.

Public Health: The Politics of Population, Body, and Food. Women have always sought to control their fertility, first with folk remedies, such as aspirin vaginal suppositories, and now with largely safer, modern technology. Women obtain abortions in private clinics and also try such folk remedies as drinking boiled onion leaves. While birth-control pills, and more recently implants, have been widely used, IUDs (intrauterine device) have been popular in places such as Syria, Egypt, and Jordan. In 1994, 63 percent of Turkish, 47 percent of Egyptian, and 50 percent of Tunisian married women used contraceptives. Side effects or a pregnancy history with at least one infant death often prompt a woman to abandon the pill.

With population (as with all public health), local custom and socioeconomic context play a more critical role than what Islamic culture allows. For example, fertility rates have dropped in poor Islamic countries, such as Tunisia and Morocco, and remained higher in oil-rich Islamic countries where governments have until recently subsidized child rearing and de-emphasized female education, which is often associated with smaller families.

The Egyptian Shaykh al-Azhar has in the past given *fatwas* (religious pronouncements) in support of family planning. The Qur'an is silent on birth control, but jurisprudence texts record the use of *azl* (coitus interruptus). Muslim promotion of population control waxes and wanes for political and economic, more than religious, reasons. In Pahlavi Iran, the regime legalized abortion, but the Islamic revolution promptly condemned family planning as a Western imperialist plot. Population skyrocketed and threatened economic growth. In the mid-1980s, Friday sermons in Iran took a 180-degree turn and began to advocate family planning.

Child-survival and maternal-health programs are an integral part of family planning. While the population of the Middle East is growing at 2.7 percent a year, the labor force is growing at 3.3 percent. Jobs for forty-seven million new entrants to the labor force must be found by 2011. The Cairo conference on population in 1994 and the Beijing women's conference in 1995 hotly debated such issues as gender equity, employment and economic development, and a woman's right to control her body. Some Muslim *ulama* (theologians) united with Roman Catholics to oppose a platform seen as threatening family values.

Female excision—a non-Islamic custom practiced locally in Egypt, Sudan, and parts of Africa—is vehemently critiqued by Western feminists. In the Middle East, folk beliefs link excision and fertility; in traditional areas of Egypt, a recently excised girl who crosses before another woman is believed able to strike that woman with infertility. While Egypt outlawed female excision in the mid-1950s, the practice, referred to in the Western press as "female genital mutilation," continues in traditional areas. Middle Easterners criticize Western feminists for seeking to impose their standards cross-culturally.

The politics of medicine includes not only issues of population and cross-cultural judgments, but also such issues as access to food and health facilities. The Sudanese famine of the late 1980s was not a problem of food, because the harvests had been ample; rather, it was an issue of the logistics of food placement during civil strive. Finally a quick review of public health can not cover specialized treatment and scientific advances in Middle Eastern hospitals and research centers in such fields as oncology and cardiology.

BIBLIOGRAPHY

BURGEL, J. CHRISTOPH. "Secular and Religious Features of Medieval Arabic Medicine." In *Asian Medical Systems: A Comparative Study*, ed. by Charles Leslie. Berkeley, Calif., 1977.

EARLY, EVELYN A. "The Baladi Curative System of Cairo, Egypt." *Culture, Medicine, and Psychiatry* 12, no. 1 (1988): 65–85.

KUHNKE, LAVERNE. "Disease Ecologies of the Middle East and North Africa." In *The Cambridge World History of Human Diseases*, ed. by Kenneth F. Kiple. New York, 1993.

MIDDLE EAST REPORT. "Gender, Population, Environment: The Middle East beyond the Cairo Conference." Washington, D.C., 1994.

UNICEF. *The State of the World's Children.* 1996.

WORLD BANK. *Claiming the Future: Choosing Prosperity in the Middle East and North Africa.* 1995.

Evelyn A. Early

Medina

Derived from the root "to civilize," the Arabic word for city.

Medina is also the name of one of the holy cities of Islam, located in western Saudi Arabia. After fleeing Mecca in 622, Muhammad and his followers went north to Yathrib, which they renamed Medina. Today, Medina with its tomb of Muhammad is a site of pilgrimage, and non-Muslims are not allowed to enter.

Zachary Karabell

Mediterranean Sea

Sea between Europe, Africa, and Asia.

The Mediterranean Sea, about 2,400 miles (3,861 km) long, covers an area of about 965,000 square miles (2,500,000 sq. km) ringed by a winding coastline of peninsulas and mountains. The sea opens to the Atlantic Ocean through the Strait of Gibraltar, the Black Sea through the Dardanelles, and the Red Sea through the Suez Canal.

Since antiquity, the Mediterranean has been one of the world's most important waterways for trade, and so has fostered great civilizations on all of its shores. The sea's strategic significance declined after the sixteenth century as trade routes shifted to the Atlantic, but increased once again with the 1869 opening of the Suez Canal and its subsequent use for oil shipping.

BIBLIOGRAPHY

BRAUDEL, FERNAND. *The Mediterranean and the Mediterranean World in the Age of Philip II.* New York, 1972.

Elizabeth Thompson

Medjerda Valley

Valley in northern Tunisia through which flows the country's principal river, the Oued Medjerda.

Arab refugees from Spain in the fifteenth century developed extensive irrigated agriculture here. Later, it became a major center of colonization during the French protectorate (1881–1956). Today, the Medjerda is one of Tunisia's most important agricultural regions, producing wheat as well as citrus, wine, and other irrigated crops.

Will D. Swearingen

Meged, Aharon   [1920–   ]

Israeli writer.

Born in Poland, Meged emigrated to Palestine in 1926. Meged was a member of kibbutz Sedot Yom, which he left in 1950 for Tel Aviv. He was an editor of the journal *Ba-Sha'ar* and founded the literary biweekly *Massa*. From 1960 to 1971, he was Israel's cultural attaché to London.

Meged's works often have autobiographical content, and the anti-hero, as an outsider, is prominent in his writings. In his most notable opus, *Ha-Hai Al Ha-Met* (The Living on the Dead, 1965), he criticizes Israeli society for abandoning the Zionist ideals of the early *halutzim* (pioneers). Among his plays are *Hannah Szenes, Genesis,* and *I Like Mike,* a comedy. Meged's works have been translated into several languages, including English.

Ann Kahn

Mehiri, Taieb   [1924–1965]

Tunisian politician.

Holding a law degree from the Law Faculty in Paris, Taieb (also Tayyib) Mehiri joined the DESTOUR political party while a student; he played a prominent part in the struggle for Tunisia's independence against France (which held a protectorate since 1881). Following independence in 1956, Mehiri remained a leading member of the ruling party and served until his death as minister of the interior, under President Habib Bourguiba.

BIBLIOGRAPHY

HAHN, LORNA. *North Africa: Nationalism to Nationhood.* Washington, D.C., 1960.

ZARTMAN, I. WILLIAM, ed. *Man, State and Society in the Contemporary Maghrib.* New York, 1973.

Matthew S. Gordon

Mehmed Hilmi   [?–1900]

Ottoman artist.

Mehmed Hilmi was a well-known calligrapher and follower of Kazasker Mustafa Efendi, a prominent calligrapher at the court of Sultan Abdülhamit II. He produced a typographical style used in book printing of the period.

Elizabeth Thompson

Mehmed Rauf [1874–1932]

Ottoman Turkish writer.

Mehmed Rauf was born and died in Constantinople (now Istanbul). He graduated from the Naval Academy and became an officer. In the 1890s, he was a member of the group that published *Servet-i Fünün*. In 1901, he published his most famous novel, *Eylul* (September), which is considered the first Turkish example of the psychological novel. Among the ten novels Mehmed Rauf wrote are *Genç Kız Kalbı* (1914; A Young Girl's Heart), *Karanfil ve Yasemen* (1924), *Son Yıldız* (1927; The Last Star), and *Halas* (1929). In addition to his novels, he wrote poetry, some of which was collected in a volume entitled *Siyah İnciler* (1900; Black Pearls); plays, including *Cidal* (1922), *Sansar* (1920), and *Ceriha* (1923); and dozens of short stories. Mehmed Rauf also published two women's magazines, *Mehasin* (1909) and *Süs* (1923).

David Waldner

Mehmet Ali, Damat [1813–1868]

Ottoman military official and grand vizier.

Born in Hemsin province near Trabzon, Mehmet Ali was the son of Haci Ömer Ağa, head agha of Galata in Constantinople (now Istanbul). As a boy, Mehmet Ali worked as an apprentice box-maker. He entered government service in low-level positions. In 1839, he joined Hafız Paşa's army in Nizip and in the following years rose in military rank. In 1845, he married Sultan Mehmet II's daughter, Adile Sultan, and took the title *damat* (literally, son-in-law of the sultan).

Between 1845 and 1863, Mehmet Ali served several terms as grand admiral of the Ottoman navy and as *serasker*, or commander in chief of the military. Like his predecessor, Hüsrev Paşa, he sought to counterbalance the growing influence of the grand vizier by personally training a number of protégés for state service to compete with those trained by the Sublime Porte. Mehmet Ali himself attained the title of grand vizier for just six months in 1852 and 1853.

BIBLIOGRAPHY

SHAW, STANFORD J., and EZEL KURAL SHAW. *History of the Ottoman Empire and Modern Turkey*, vol. 2. New York, 1977.

Elizabeth Thompson

Mehmet Bey [1843–1874]

Radical opponent of the Ottoman regime.

The son of a high Ottoman bureaucrat and son-in-law of a grand vizier, Mehmet Bey was schooled in France and began work in the translation office in Constantinople (now Istanbul), where he founded a secret society linked to the YOUNG OTTOMANS. He later broke with this group and advocated more rapid and thorough political change in his opposition newspaper, *Ittihad* (Union). He then moved to Geneva, where he published the journal *Inkilab* (Revolution) with Hüseyin Vasfi Paşa. He fought with the Paris Commune in 1871 and returned to Turkey shortly before his death.

BIBLIOGRAPHY

LEWIS, BERNARD. *The Emergence of Modern Turkey*. New York, 1961.

Elizabeth Thompson

Mehmet Emin, Kibrisli [1813–1881]

Ottoman grand vizier.

Born in Cyprus and one of the last graduates of the old palace school, Kibrisli Mehmet Emin entered palace service at a young age with the support of his uncle, Mahmud II's chief treasurer. In the 1840s, Mehmet Emin advanced quickly in the military; he attained the rank of general and completed his studies in France. He was appointed grand vizier for three terms, each time when the Tanzimat reformers fell out of favor between 1854 and 1861. He held the post when the 1856 HATT-I HÜMAYUN was proclaimed and was known for his zeal in rooting out bureaucratic corruption.

BIBLIOGRAPHY

SHAW, STANFORD J., and EZEL KURAL SHAW. *History of the Ottoman Empire and Modern Turkey*, vol. 2. New York, 1977.

Elizabeth Thompson

Mehmet Emin Rauf [1780–1859]

Ottoman grand vizier.

Born in Constantinople (now Istanbul) the son of a government official, Mehmet Emin Rauf received a private education before joining the palace service as a clerk. He rose steadily in the bureaucracy and in 1815 became grand vizier, an office he would later hold almost continuously between 1833 and 1846. The archetypical high bureaucrat of the pre-Tanzimat era, Mehmet Emin Rauf was more known as a talented mediator able to check the influence of opponents than as an adept policymaker.

BIBLIOGRAPHY

SHAW, STANFORD J., and EZEL KURAL SHAW. *History of the Ottoman Empire and Modern Turkey,* vol. 2. New York, 1977.

Elizabeth Thompson

Mehmet Küçük Sait

See Sait, Küçük

Mehmet V Reşat [1844–1918]

Ottoman sultan, 1909–1918.

A brother of Sultan Abdülhamit II, Mehmet V, was sixty-five years old in April 1909 when he was chosen by the Young Turks parliament to succeed the deposed Abdülhamit as sultan of the Ottoman Empire. Mehmet V is usually seen as a weak ruler who functioned mostly as a figurehead for the Young Turks and the Committee of Union and Progress (CUP). His powers were severely circumscribed by the constitution, which had been restored in 1908. He could not even nominate his own ministers without the approval of parliament and the CUP. He remained sultan during World War I, but his influence on policy seems to have been negligible. The war was conducted by the Young Turk oligarchy headed by Enver Paşa, and Mehmet V did not command an independent base of support. He died of natural causes on June 28, 1918, before Istanbul was occupied by the Allies, and was succeeded by his younger brother Mehmet VI Vahidettin.

BIBLIOGRAPHY

LEWIS, BERNARD. *The Emergence of Modern Turkey.* New York, 1961.

SHAW, STANFORD J., and EZEL KURAL SHAW. *History of the Ottoman Empire and Modern Turkey,* vol. 2. New York, 1977.

Zachary Karabell

Mehmet VI Vahidettin [1861–1926]

Last Ottoman sultan.

Sultan Abdülmecit's eldest son and Abdülhamit's brother, Mehmet VI Vahidettin became sultan in the last months of World War I. He sided with the Allies occupying Istanbul against the forces of the emerging Kemalist national movement, which was centered in Ankara. On November 16, 1922, after the Ankara Grand National Assembly abolished the sultanate, Vahidettin fled Istanbul aboard a British destroyer and settled in San Remo.

BIBLIOGRAPHY

SHAW, STANFORD J., and EZEL KURAL SHAW. *History of the Ottoman Empire and Modern Turkey,* vol. 2. New York, 1977.

Elizabeth Thompson

Mehterhane

Ottoman military band.

The Mehterhane, and its attendant institutions, go back to the early years of the empire, when it consisted simply of drums and flags. Its drills and formations were inherited from the Seljuks. In later years, the Mehterhane became part of the Janissary Corps. In 1826, the old institution was destroyed when Sultan Mahmut II eliminated the janissaries. A new organization, also called Mehterhane, was a combination of the military band and the former Tent Corps, and was responsible for transporting military equipment to army camps in wartime. The formal Imperial Band was established in 1829. The Mehterhane was revived in 1911 by Ahmed Muhtar, and reorganized again in 1952. In the twentieth century its musical repertoire included traditional songs from the janissary period as well as European classical music, such as pieces by Mozart. The Mehterhane's traditions are said to have influenced European military music organizations through contacts with the German army in the early twentieth century.

BIBLIOGRAPHY

SHAW, STANFORD J., and EZEL KURAL SHAW. *History of the Ottoman Empire and Modern Turkey*, vol. 2. New York, 1977.

Elizabeth Thompson

Meir, Golda   [1898–1978]

Israeli politician; prime minister, 1969–1973.

Golda Meir was born Goldie Mabovitch in Kiev. Her family moved to Milwaukee, Wisconsin in 1906, where she spent her early years. She was active in the Milwaukee Labor Zionist Party, later becoming its leader. In 1921, she migrated to Palestine with her husband, Morris Myerson, and joined the KIBBUTZ MOVEMENT. She was a kibbutz movement representative to the Histadrut and served as secretary of the Women's Labor Council of Histadrut from 1928 to 1932; in 1934, she became a member of the

Israeli Prime Minister Golda Meir. (Israel Office of Information)

Executive Committee of the Histadrut. During the 1930s, she was also active in MAPAI.

In April 1947, Meir participated in discussions with Abdullah of Jordan about Arab League policy in Palestine, and she traveled to Jordan in disguise in May 1947 for further negotiations. In the last years before independence, she served as acting director of the JEWISH AGENCY's political department, where she developed her knowledge of Arab politics. On May 14, 1948, when the State of Israel was declared, she was one of the signers of the Declaration of Independence. She was appointed to serve as Israel's first minister to the Soviet Union in September 1948.

Elected to the first Knesset in 1949, Meir remained a member until she resigned from the prime ministership in 1974. She served as minister of labor from 1949 to 1956 and in that capacity was credited with initiating significant housing and road construction in the early years of statehood.

In 1956, Prime Minister David Ben-Gurion asked Foreign Minister Moshe Sharett for his resignation and replaced him with Golda Meir. (This was also the year she assumed the Hebraized name of Golda Meir.) Shortly thereafter, Meir traveled to Paris with Defense Minister Moshe Dayan to buy French arms and to negotiate future arms purchases. As foreign minister, one of Meir's primary goals was to develop ties with Africa. She traveled extensively in Africa and helped to establish a network of contacts that would benefit Israel in the future. In 1966, Meir became secretary-general of MAPAI, and in 1967, as one of the leaders of MAPAI, she participated in negotiations with the leadership of the AHDUT HA-AVODAH party to create a new political party, the Israel LABOR PARTY.

In February 1969, at the age of seventy-one, Meir became Israel's fourth prime minister, chosen as a compromise candidate following the death of Prime Minister Levi Eshkol. During her tenure, she endorsed what was known as the ALLON PLAN of maintaining a "security frontier" on the Jordan River. The plan encouraged the creation of Jewish settlements in the Jordan valley, in the Hebron area, in the Gaza Strip, in northern Sinai, and in the Golan area.

Meir served as prime minister until the Yom Kippur war in October 1973. Despite repeated appeals from her military advisers for preemptive strikes against Egypt and Syria, Meir was convinced by the United States that Israel could not risk the diplomatic fallout from another preemptive attack against the Arab powers. She decided that Israel would have to absorb the first blow and then respond. On October 6, 1973, Israel was attacked by a number of hostile Arab nations, and although Israel eventually won the

Yom Kippur War, it sustained substantial casualties. Because of criticism of her government for its lack of preparedness for that war, Meir resigned in April 1974. She died on December 8, 1978, in Jerusalem.

BIBLIOGRAPHY

MEIR, GOLDA. *My Life.* New York, 1975.
SACHAR, HOWARD M. *A History of Israel: From the Rise of Zionism to Our Time.* New York, 1981.

Gregory S. Mahler

Meknes

A city of northern Morocco.

Meknes is situated 40 miles (60 km) west of Fez and 90 miles (140 km) east of Rabat and is surrounded by Arab and Berber tribes. Its population was estimated in 1992 as 484,000 inhabitants. Close to the fertile plain of Sais, Meknes benefits from its rich agriculture.

Meknes (or Miknas al-Zaytun) is one of the oldest Moroccan cities. The gathering of one faction of the Miknasa tribes (tenth century) seems to be the beginning of the founding of the city, which flourished later under different dynasties that ruled the Maghrib. Meknes gained prestige in the seventeenth, eighteenth, and nineteenth centuries when it became a *makhzaniya* city. Sultan Mulay Ismail built palaces and made this city the capital of his kingdom.

Numerous religious groups—such as the Hamadish Brotherhood and the Isawiyya Brotherhood—consider Meknes to be sacred and hold celebrations there. The most important occurs in the month of Mulud and honors Shaykh al-Kamel.

Rahma Bourqia

Bab Mansur, the gate to the city of Meknes. (Richard Bulliet)

Meknes, Treaty of

The second treaty between Morocco and the United States, signed at Meknes on September 16, 1836.

With two exceptions (a final clause continuing the treaty beyond its fifty years validity until it was actually cancelled by one of the parties and an addendum concerning protection of U.S. ships in Moroccan ports against third-party enemies), the Meknes treaty precisely mirrored the first U.S.-Moroccan treaty, signed in Marrakech on June 28, 1786. Both treaties focused on two concerns: the protection of U.S. shipping against pirate attacks by Moroccan ships and the enhancement of commercial relations. The question of pirates, or COR-SAIRS, was indeed an important issue in 1786, but by 1836 it was no longer relevant: the Moroccan corsairing fleet existed only on paper. Moreover, U.S. commerce with Morocco was insubstantial, and U.S. interest in the country minimal. The consul who signed the treaty, James Leib, left the conduct of negotiations to the vice consul and his interpreter.

The importance of the treaty lay in its symbolic value: it deeply worried the British consul general, E. W. A. Drummond-Hay, and the authorities in London. They believed, quite unjustifiably, that it marked the beginnings of an attempt by the United States to occupy physically a position on the Mediterranean coast of Morocco that would be used to expand U.S. influence. At this time Britain was easily Morocco's largest trading partner, particularly through the garrison colony of Gibraltar, and dominated Morocco's foreign relations. Drummond-Hay tried to steer a path that would open Morocco to foreign—especially British—commerce, while ensuring that other powers—especially France—would not extend their influence too much. The supposed agreement about a U.S. base on the coast would undercut British predominance. In fact nothing of the sort happened; British predominance was sealed by the Moroccan–British treaty of 1856, which paved the way for the real opening of Morocco to international commerce.

BIBLIOGRAPHY

HALL, LUELLA J., *The United States and Morocco.* Metuchen, N.J., 1971.
The texts of the treaties are in CLIVE PARRY, ed., *The Consolidated Treaty Series* (Dobbs Ferry, N.Y., 1969–1981), vols. 50 (for the 1786 treaty) and 86 (1836 treaty).

C. R. Pennell

Mekorot

Israel's national water supply agency.

Israel's national water company was founded in British-mandated Palestine in 1936. After the State of Israel was established in 1948, it embarked on a major nationwide water-supply project. The main emphasis in the 1950s and 1960s was the NATIONAL WATER SYSTEM. Later, the focus was on utilizing flood runoff, sewage water, and DESALINIZATION.

BIBLIOGRAPHY

Mekorot Water Company Ltd. and Its Role in Israel's Development. Tel Aviv, 1963.

Sara Reguer

Mekteb-i Harbiye

Ottoman war academy.

Founded at Constantinople (now Istanbul) in 1834 to train military officers, the Mekteb-i Harbiye or Mekteb-i Ülüm-ü Harbiye (School for Military Science) enrolled 200 students by 1839. It was one of several higher technical schools founded before and during the TANZIMAT era. The academy continued to prosper in the late nineteenth century as the crown of an expanding system of provincial military high schools (RÜŞDIYES). It graduated 3,918 students between 1873 and 1897. After 1882, there were German military advisers and teachers, notably Colmar Freiherr von der Goltz. Curriculum included German, Russian, French, war history, weapons, strategy, tactics, and military literature.

In the latter years of the Ottoman Empire, the war academy became a site of military opposition by Turks and Arabs to the regime of Abdülhamit II.

Gate to the former Ottoman War College, now the entrance to Istanbul University. (Richard Bulliet)

Banned opposition tracts were circulated among students, and secret cells were formed. Mustafa Kemal Atatürk, the future nationalist leader, entered the academy in 1899. The academy was transferred to Ankara in the early years of the Turkish republic and has remained a principal training ground for the national elite.

BIBLIOGRAPHY

HUREWITZ, J. C. *Middle East Politics: The Military Dimension.* New York, 1969.
LEWIS, BERNARD. *The Emergence of Modern Turkey.* New York, 1961.

Elizabeth Thompson

Mekteb-i Mülkiye

See Civil Service School

Melkite

See Christians in the Middle East

Mellah

Jewish quarter of Morocco's cities and rural areas.

The mellah (Arabic, to salt) is associated with the 1438 ghettoization of the Jewish community of Fez, which was resettled on a nearby "saline area." Mellah then became a synonym for "Jewish quarter" in the rest of Morocco. Urban mellahs, near the sultan's palace, were surrounded by gated walls. Rural mellahs, Jewish villages separated from Muslim ones, were near the governor's fortress.

Rhimou Bernikho-Canin

Melliyun Party

One of two political parties created in Iran in 1957 by the shah, this one to support the government.

One of the two parties created by Mohammad Reza Shah Pahlavi in Iran in 1957, the Hezb-e Melliyun (Nationalist) party was a conservative royalist party, popularly known as the "yes" party because of its relentless support of the shah and his policies. Its leader was the prime minister, Manuchehr Eqbal. The MARDOM (People's) party was established as opposition to the Melliyun. Discredited by electoral fiascoes in early 1960s, the Melliyun party was dissolved in 1963 and replaced by the New Iran (or IRAN NOVIN) party.

BIBLIOGRAPHY

ABRAHAMIAN, E. *Iran between Two Revolutions.* Princeton, N.J., 1982.
KEDDI, N. *Roots of Revolution: An Interpretive History of Modern Iran.* New Haven, Conn., 1981.

Parvaneh Pourshariati

Memmi, Albert   [1920–   ]

Tunisian Jew; émigré French novelist and sociologist.

Memmi was raised in a poor Jewish quarter in Tunis; however, his evident abilities enabled him to be educated at an elite French-colonial secondary school. After university studies in Algiers and Paris, he returned to Tunis where he taught philosophy at a lycée and served as the director of a research institute. Following Tunisia's independence in 1956, he emigrated to France, where he had an illustrious academic career as a sociologist. The alienation he felt growing up—belonging to neither the Muslim nor European cultures and removed from his traditional Jewish background through French education, yet snubbed by his wealthier European classmates—was a powerful influence on the themes of his various works. Memmi is best known for two types of works: (1) his largely autobiographical novels of alienation; and (2) his essays exploring the social psychology of colonization and the exploitation of minority groups. These works include his first novel, *La Statue de Sel* (1953, published as *Pillar of Salt* in 1955), and the influential essay, *Portrait du Colonisé* (1957, published as the *Colonizer and the Colonized* in 1965).

BIBLIOGRAPHY

WAKEMAN, JOHN, ed. *World Authors, 1950–1970: A Companion Volume to Twentieth-Century Authors.* New York, 1975.

Will D. Swearingen

MENA

See Middle East News Agency

Menderes, Adnan   [1899–1961]

Turkish politician.

Menderes was born in İzmir and educated at the American College in İzmir and the Law Faculty of Ankara University. He was elected to the Turkish Grand National Assembly in 1930 and, in 1946, became a founder of the DEMOCRAT PARTY, which became the opposition to Turkey's single-party system. He was prime minister from 1950 to 1960, at which point his government was ousted by the armed forces, and charged with corruption and abuse of power. He was tried at Yassıada, convicted, and executed.

BIBLIOGRAPHY

WEIKER, WALTER F. *The Turkish Revolution 1960–1961.* Washington, D.C., 1963.

Walter F. Weiker

Menemencioğlu, Turgut   [1898–1958]

Turkish diplomat and politician.

Born in Baghdad, Menemencioğlu graduated from the University of Lausanne with a law degree. He began his career in 1914 as a junior secretary at the Turkish embassy in Bern, Switzerland. He subsequently held posts at the Turkish embassies in Paris, Athens, and Budapest. Menemencioğlu was promoted to the rank of ambassador in 1933 and became the general secretary of the Turkish foreign ministry. In 1935 he was elected to parliament. From 1942 to 1944 he was foreign minister. In the latter year he was named Turkey's ambassador to France, a post he held until his retirement in 1957. From then until his death a year later, in Ankara, he was a deputy in the legislature.

Niyazi Dalyanci

Menou, Jacques François   [1750–1810]

French military officer; governor of Egypt, 1800–1801.

The last leader of the French forces that occupied Egypt from 1798 to 1801, Menou succeeded General Kléber as Napoléon Bonaparte's governor of Egypt in July of 1800. He converted to Islam in order to marry an Egyptian and changed his name to Abdullah. Believing that French occupation of Egypt would continue for a long time, Menou drafted proposals to encourage Egyptian agriculture, commerce, and industry. When Menou began to survey landholdings in preparation for the assessment of new land taxes to pay for these reforms, Egyptians of all social classes, already alienated by Menou's declaration of Egypt as a colony of France, opposed him.

In March of 1801, a joint Anglo–Ottoman force occupied the Nile river delta. Leaving the defense of Cairo, the capital, to General Belliard, Menou led his troops to Alexandria. When Belliard surrendered, Menou, isolated in Alexandria, was forced to surrender. French forces left Egypt in October of 1801.

BIBLIOGRAPHY

GOLDSCHMIDT, ARTHUR, JR. *Modern Egypt: The Formation of a Nation-State.* Boulder, Colo., 1988.

WUCHER KING, JOAN. *Historical Dictionary of Egypt.* Metuchen, N.J., 1984.

David Waldner

Menzies Mission

Attempt of Sir Robert Gordon Menzies, prime minister of Australia, to confer with Egypt's president on international supervision of the Suez Canal.

Following the nationalization of the Suez Canal on July 26, 1956, Britain and France convened a conference in London, August 16–23, attended by twenty-two countries. Eighteen of them adopted a proposal to place the canal under the supervision of an international body that would recognize Egypt's sovereignty over the canal. Because Egypt's President Gamal Abdel Nasser had declined to attend the conference, Menzies was dispatched to Egypt on September 2, 1956, to negotiate with him. When Nasser refused to negotiate, Menzies implied that this refusal would lead to efforts by other countries to regain control over the canal.

According to some accounts, Nasser understood this as a threat and ended all discussion with Menzies. Another account, by a U.S. official, says that Nasser understood that it was not a threat—but that U.S. President Dwight D. Eisenhower's declaration of September 5 that the United States would not use force to regain the canal made Menzie's mission futile.

According to Selwyn Lloyd, in *Suez 1956, A Personal Account,* Menzies flew to Cairo on September 2; met Nasser on September 3 to plan talks; presented the case to Nasser on September 4; Eisenhower rejected force on September 5; Nasser rejected the Eighteen-Power Proposal on September 9 and asked for negotiations; U.S. Secretary of State John Foster Dulles rejected his request.

BIBLIOGRAPHY

HOPWOOD, DEREK. *Egypt: Politics and Society, 1945–1981.* London, 1983.

David Waldner

Meretz

Israeli left-wing political party formed for the 1992 election.

Comprising MAPAM, SHINUI, and the Citizens Rights Movement, Meretz won twelve seats in the Knesset and became the most important coalition partner in Israel's Labor party. Although its most widely publicized program is advocacy of more cooperative policies on negotiations with the Palestinians, many young Israelis are also attracted to its reformist views on education, economic, and environmental issues. Among its well-known leaders are Yair Tzaban, Amnon RUBINSTEIN, Shulamit Aloni, and Yossi SARID.

Walter F. Weiker

Meriç, Cemil   [1917–1987]

Turkish writer.

Meriç was born in Reyhanli to a distinguished family of the Hatay region of Turkey during the last year of the Ottoman Empire. He attended local schools and obtained a degree in literature at Istanbul University, where in 1946 he became a lecturer, a post he held until he retired in 1973. Meriç wrote numerous articles on culture, society, and philosophy and, in the 1970s, became a leading essayist. He represented the angry voice of a new generation seeking to reawaken Turkish culture and to reconcile the discordances of a rapidly changing society. He wrote in dense, choppy prose, which he claimed was necessary to articulate a new worldview that combined Eastern and Western philosophies.

BIBLIOGRAPHY

Günümüz Türkiyesinde Kim Kimdir 1987–1988. Istanbul, 1987.

Yeni Türk Ansiklopedisi. Istanbul, 1985.

Elizabeth Thompson

Mes'adi, Mahmoud al-   [1911–]

Tunisian essayist, playwright and politician.

Al-Mes'adi was born in Tazerka, Tunisia, obtained his *agrégation* in Arabic literature from the Sorbonne in 1947, and was a teacher and educational administrator until 1958. He subsequently held various posts in Tunisia's cabinet and was named the nation's representative to UNESCO. He was editor of the journal *al-Mabahith* from 1944 to 1947.

Although bilingual in Arabic and French, al-Mes'adi writes only in Arabic. He occupies a unique place in modern Tunisian literature. His writings are characterized by a hermetic style that is strongly reminiscent of the language of the Qur'an. He was deeply influenced by European existentialism and culture as well as by Arab Islamic culture. According to him, existentialism and commitment are strongly linked. His deeply philosophical writings are primarily concerned with a person's role in life and the significance of existence. His play *Al-Sudd* (1955; The Dam) is an expression of al-Mes'adi's philosophical outlook on man and his destiny, whereas his novel *Haddatha Abu Hurayra, Qala . . .* (1923; Abu Hurayra Said . . .) transposes this philosophical inclination into an Islamic frame. The collection of short stories titled *Mawlid al-Nisyan* (1974; The Birth of Forgetfulness) portrays the struggle between good and evil in the human being.

BIBLIOGRAPHY

BACCAR, TAOUFIC, and SALAH GARMADI. *Ecrivains de Tunisie*. Paris, 1981.

FONTAINE, JEAN. *La littérature tunisienne moderne*. Tunis, 1989.

Aida A. Bamia

Mesopotamia

See Iraq

Mesopotamia Campaign

World War I British military campaign in part of the Ottoman Empire.

In November 1914, within days of the British declaration of war on the Ottoman Empire (which was allied with Germany in World War I), the British landed an Indian Expeditionary Force (IEP) at Basra in Mesopotamia (present-day Iraq). Meeting scant resistance from the Ottoman Turks, the IEF moved north and, in April 1915, Sir John Nixon took command. Nixon ordered his lieutenant, Sir Charles Townshend, to advance north—up the river Tigris toward Baghdad. By November 1915, Townshend succeeded in advancing to Ctesiphon, just south of Baghdad, but his supply lines were stretched thin, and he was repulsed by the newly invigorated Ottoman armies under the command of German General Kolmar von der Goltz. Townshend retreated south to Kut al-Amara, where he was trapped by the Ottoman Turks.

The British failed to reinforce Townshend, and after a 146-day siege, he surrendered his entire force on April 29, 1916. Lacking men and matériel, the Turks were unable to take advantage of the victory. Under the command of Sir Frederick Maude, the British again advanced north, retook Kut on February 22, 1917, and entered Baghdad on March 11. By September, the British were in control of central Iraq, and by the war's end in 1918, they had occupied all of Mesopotamia south of the city of Mosul.

BIBLIOGRAPHY

BARKER, A. J. *The Bastard War*. New York, 1967.

FROMKIN, DAVID. *A Peace to End All Peace*. New York, 1989.

SHAW, STANFORD, and EZEL KURAL SHAW. *History of the Ottoman Empire and Modern Turkey*. Cambridge, U.K., 1977.

SLUGLETT, PETER. *Britain in Iraq 1914–1932*. London, 1976.

Zachary Karabell

Messaadia, Mohammad Cherif [1924–]

Algerian Front de Libération Nationale (FLN) leader.

Messaadia was a university student in Tunis before joining the Armée de Libération Nationale (ALN). After the Algerian War of Independence, 1954–1962, he was a deputy in Algeria's Constituent National Assembly and the National Assembly. He became a member of the Central Committee of the FRONT DE LIBÉRATION NATIONALE (FLN) (National Liberation Front) in 1964, subsequently serving in a number of functions. He served as minister of veterans (*mojahedin*) (1979/80) before he was chosen by President Chadli Benjedid to head the FLN Permanent Secretariat. This prestigious appointment was unpopular, given Messaadia's undistinguished career. He also became a member of the Political Bureau (1981). He was replaced on October 30 by Abdelhamid Mehri, in order to revitalize the FLN and restore the party's image after rioting earlier that month had destabilized the government. Messaadia then became associated with the anti-Benjedid faction within the FLN.

BIBLIOGRAPHY

ENTELIS, JOHN P. *Algeria: The Revolution Institutionalized*. Boulder, Colo., 1986.

Phillip C. Naylor

Messianism

The expectation that a prophet will arrive at the end of time to usher in the divine kingdom.

Messianism is common to all three Middle Eastern religions. The word *messiah* is derived from the Hebrew Old Testament, where it was used to refer to actual kings who were annointed (*mashiah*) with oil. In the intertestamental period, the term was applied to the future king who would restore the Kingdom of Israel and deliver the people from evil. In Christianity, Jewish ideas about the messiah were applied to Jesus. The word *messiah* was translated into Greek as *Christos,* or Christ, thereby identifying Jesus with Jewish messianic expectations. Though Christianity builds on Jewish messianic precedents, it adds the idea that Christ has already fulfilled messianic expectations in person and that he will return to bring these expectations to their final fulfillment. Comparable ideas are found in Islam in the person of the MAHDI (the rightly guided one), a person who will come at the end of time to defeat the enemies of Islam and thus create a just world. Islamic messianism does not, however, deal strictly or solely with the end of the world; it has played a role in various reformist and revivalist movements.

BIBLIOGRAPHY

ELIADE, MIRCEA, ed. *The Encyclopedia of Religion.* New York, 1987.

David Waldner

Mestiri, Ahmad [1928–]

Tunisian political opposition leader, formerly an important figure in the Neo-Destour (later the Socialist Destour) Party (PSD).

Mestiri, from an upper-middle-class family, was trained as a lawyer and achieved prominence within the Neo-Destour in the early 1950s. While the party was outlawed (1952–1954), he served on its clandestine Political Bureau, where he had responsibility for maintaining links with the armed resistance against France and providing funds for Neo-Destour groups overseas. Mestiri failed to win election to the legally constituted Political Bureau in 1955, but was rewarded for his party services with a ministerial appointment in the first independent government. He became minister of finance in 1959. In the meantime, Neo-Destour leader Habib Bourguiba had appointed Mestiri to the Political Bureau in 1957; he was elected to it in 1959. Mestiri also was elected a National Assembly deputy.

During the 1960s, Mestiri became disenchanted with the unrestrained power exercised by Bourguiba as both president and party leader. He and other opponents of the economic strategies of Planning Minister Ahmed Ben Salah were particularly critical of Bourguiba's resistance to demands for Ben Salah's removal, even when the weight of evidence indicated the failure of his policies. As a result, Mestiri broke with the PSD in the mid-1960s. Following Ben Salah's disgrace in 1969, Mestiri resumed his affiliation with the party. Although widely acknowledged as the leader of a liberal current within the PSD, he was appointed minister of the interior and, in 1971, was elected to the party's Central Committee. Mestiri initiated a campaign to open important party business to broader participation by advocating the direct election of Political Bureau members. He also called for the establishment of institutional constraints on the president. Bourguiba responded by dismissing Mestiri and, in 1972, ordering his expulsion from the party.

Mestiri continued to protest the unlimited power of the presidency, the exclusion from the PSD of any serious opposition element, and the government's refusal to legalize other parties. In 1977, he proposed the creation of a "national pact" that would permit significant reform. Prospects for the success of any such program, however, were damaged by widespread antigovernment rioting during a general strike in January 1978. Mestiri's request that his Mouvement des Démocrates Sociales (MDS) be accepted as a political party was denied, but he was recognized as the leader of a loyal opposition and was permitted to publish a newspaper, *al-Ra'i.*

The appointment of Mohammed Mzali as prime minister in 1980 inaugurated a more open political era. The PSD again rehabilitated Mestiri, even giving him a minor cabinet post. He accepted the government's invitation to opposition political groups to participate in the 1981 National Assembly elections, but the MDS list failed to gain the 5 percent of the total vote needed to be sanctioned as a political party; its official recognition was delayed for two years.

Prior to the 1986 elections, Mestiri was imprisoned for organizing a demonstration protesting America's bombing of Tripoli in April. The MDS therefore boycotted the elections. Relations with the government remained poor until the removal of Bourguiba from the presidency in 1987. Thereafter, Mestiri consulted with President Zayn al-Abidine Ben Ali about implementing an effective system of political pluralism.

BIBLIOGRAPHY

RUF, WERNER. "Tunisia: Contemporary Politics." In *North Africa: Contemporary Politics and Economic Develop-*

ment, ed. by Richard Lawless and Allan Findlay. London, 1984.

STONE, RUSSELL. "Tunisia: A Single Party System Holds Change in Abeyance." In *Political Elites in Arab North Africa,* ed. by I. William Zartman. New York, 1982.

Kenneth J. Perkins

Metni, Nassib   [?–1958]

Lebanese newspaperman of the opposition.

A Maronite Christian who published and owned the daily *al-Tallaghraf* (The Telegram), Metni was prosecuted twice in 1957 for publishing manifestos of the United National Front, a political group which opposed the reelection of President Camille Chamoun. His assassination on May 8, 1958, triggered the outbreak of the Lebanese Civil War. His last article, published on the morning of his death, called for the president's resignation.

BIBLIOGRAPHY

QUBAIN, FAHIM. *Crisis in Lebanon.* Washington, D.C., 1961.

Bassam Namani

Metternich, Klemens von   [1773–1859]

Austrian statesman and prince.

After various ambassadorial posts, Metternich became foreign minister of Austria in 1809 and continued in that position until forced to resign in 1848. Metternich was the architect of the Congress of Vienna (1814–1815). He was hostile to the Greek War of Independence, 1821–1830. Like most of his European counterparts, he walked a fine line between supporting the integrity of the Ottoman Empire and preventing the empire from resuscitating itself.

BIBLIOGRAPHY

ANDERSON, M. S. *The Eastern Question.* London, 1966.

Zachary Karabell

Meushi, Paul Peter   [1894–1975]

Maronite patriarch who worked to preserve peaceful Christian–Muslim relations in Lebanon.

Meushi was born April 1, 1894, in the town of Jezzine (southern Lebanon) to a Maronite Christian family. He completed his elementary and secondary education in Lebanon, then left for Rome to join the Gregorian University, where he completed a degree in philosophy and theology. In 1917, Meushi was ordained a priest in Rome and, at the end of World War I, he came back to Lebanon. From then until 1934, when he was nominated to be bishop for the city of Tyre, Meushi served as a priest for two Maronite parishes in the United States (New Bedford, Massachusetts, and Los Angeles, California). In May 1955, by papal decree, Meushi was appointed Maronite Patriarch of Antioch and all the East.

In 1958, Lebanon plunged into civil war, the partisans of then-President Camille Chamoun pitted against the opposition—led mostly by Muslims and Christians. Meushi opposed the Chamoun policy of aligning Lebanon with the West, thus alienating the country's Muslim population. Chamoun, however, suspected the patriarch of wanting to reassert religious authority in Lebanon's political affairs, but Meushi was concerned about the fate of Christianity in the Middle East and the preservation of Christian–Muslim coexistence in Lebanon. Cardinal Meushi died January 11, 1975.

BIBLIOGRAPHY

KERR, DAVID. "The Temporal Authority of the Maronite Patriarchate, 1920–1958: A Study in the Relationship of Religious and Secular Power." Ph.D. diss., Oxford University, 1973.

George E. Irani

Mevlevi Brotherhood

Sufi order.

Named after its founder, Mevlana Jalal al-Din al-Rumi (d. 1273), an Iranian mystic and poet, the Mevlevi Brotherhood developed the unique contemplative ceremony known as *sama'a*. Sama'a consists of four sessions in which musical instruments, mainly the flute, are played so as to evoke a dialogue with nature, while members methodically join in an individual but synchronized whirling dance that emulates the movement of planets on their journey of spiritual fulfillment. Highly tolerant of other religions, the Mevlevi order flourished during the Ottoman era in Asia Minor, the Balkans, and Syria and was closely associated with the sultanate, particularly after the mid-seventeenth century when Mevlevi masters presided over the imperial investiture ceremonies. In the 1925 secularist drive of Mustafa Kemal Atatürk, the order was suppressed, but the ban has since been lifted. Today, however, the "whirling dervishes" order thrives mainly in its historical center in Konya, Turkey, which houses the tomb of Rumi and attracts devotees and tourists alike.

BIBLIOGRAPHY

BALDICK, JULIAN. *Mystical Islam: An Introduction to Sufism.* New York, 1989.
SCHIMMEL, ANNEMARIE. *Mystical Dimensions of Islam.* Chapel Hill, N.C., 1975.

Tayeb El-Hibri

Mezzian, Muhammad   [1893–1975]

Moroccan military figure.

At his death, Mezzian was a field marshal, the highest rank in Morocco's army. He received his military training in Toledo, Spain, and later became the first non-Spaniard to attain the rank of general in the Spanish army. Mezzian served as governor-general of the Canary Islands from 1954 to 1956. He joined Morocco's military following that nation's independence in 1956 and held the post of inspector general of the armed forces. Mezzian served as minister of defense in 1964 and minister of state in 1970.

Bruce Maddy-Weitzman

Michael, Sami   [1926–   ]

Israeli author.

Sami Michael was born in Baghdad, Iraq. A leftist activist, he was forced to leave his homeland and arrived in Israel via Iran in 1948. He studied psychology and Arabic literature and published nine novels for young adults and adults. He is best known for his literary representation of Middle Eastern Jews and Arabs, their political and ethnic struggles and cultural systems.

His first novel, *Equal and More Equal* (1974), depicts the socioeconomic and cultural frustrations of Jewish immigrants from Arab countries as they arrive in Israel, which established Eastern European culture as its dominant code. In *Refuge* (1977), which has been translated into English, Michael exposes the personal and political strife of a group of young Jews and Arabs in an Israeli communist organization during the Yom Kippur War of 1973. His literary excellence, however, reached its height in his later books and eventually brought him both popular and literary acclaim with the best-selling *Victoria* (1993), a biographical novel in which he tells the life story of his mother. The novel relates the traditions and customs of the Jewish quarter of Baghdad with great detail and decorous language, focusing particularly on the male-dominated society, lack of privacy, and intensity of sexual motivation. It ends in Israel, where the men are disempowered by the cultural clash with a new reality and hierarchy. Victoria, as her name implies, is the ultimate winner, seasoned, as it were, by her experience of self-denial and accommodation.

Zvia Ginor

Middle East

Regional name with various usages and meanings.

The usage and meaning of "Middle East" have been a source of heated debate. As early as 1949, when other terms, particularly "Near East," were still used, Winston Churchill said: "I had always felt that the name 'Middle East' for Egypt, the Levant, Syria, and Turkey was ill-chosen. This was the Near East. Persia and Iraq were the Middle East. . . ." Despite the tacit acceptance of the term by most scholars, journalists, and politicians, few specialists would deny a lingering discomfort with the two words.

Regional geographic names based upon directions are always problematic. They necessarily imply a perspective—in this case, obviously that of "the West." "The East" brings to mind the "Eastern Question" that had plagued Europe since the eighteenth century. Earlier, Europeans had used "the Levant," from the French *lever* (to rise), meaning the place where the sun rises: the eastern coast of the Mediterranean (or of Spain). In the Middle Ages, the favored term was *outremer* (overseas).

"The East," and its adjectival form "oriental," connoted in the European mind more than just a geographic locale. It evoked a world of strange customs, religious fanaticism, exotic sexual practices, and sybaritic culture. As travels and colonial activity made India, and then China, familiar, the need arose to define "East" further. By the late nineteenth century the Ottoman realm was the "Near East" in contradistinction to China and Japan, the "Far East."

It is generally accepted that the earliest reference to "Middle East" occurs in Alfred Thayer Mahan's "The Persian Gulf and International Relations," in the September 1902 issue of the *National Review* (London). Popularization of the new usage is credited to Valentine Chirol, Tehran correspondent for *The Times* who, in the title of the first in a series of articles, "The Middle Eastern Question," dated 14 October 1902, retrieved the term from Mahan's text. An additional factor in its popularization was the shifting balance of power from mainland Europe to the American side of the Atlantic. From an American point of view, everything on the European side of the Atlantic is, geographically, east. Thus, the further reaches occupied by Arabs, Turks, and Persians plausibly seemed more "middle" than "near."

Since the 1950s "the Middle East" has been the favored American term for newly founded academic institutes, programs, and professional associations, though use of "Near East" has persisted in archaeological circles and academic departments founded before World War II. The U.S. Department of State compromised with a division for "Near and Middle East" affairs.

Today "the Middle East" encompasses the lands that stretch from Egypt to Turkey and Iraq, including the Arabian peninsula, usually Iran, and, somewhat less frequently, Morocco, Algeria, Tunisia, Libya, and Sudan.

The term is in no way coterminous with "the Muslim (or Islamic) world." The majority of the world's Muslims live outside "the Middle East," by any definition. It has been suggested that "the Middle East" is best considered a purely geographical term that encompasses roughly the area of the earliest wave of Muslim conquests, stretching from Morocco to Afghanistan and Pakistan, with the later inclusion of Anatolia (modern Turkey). Others disagree, saying that such a historical definition would also include parts of Europe (e.g., Spain and Sicily) and central Asia.

BIBLIOGRAPHY

DAVISON, RODERIC H. "Where Is the Middle East?" *Foreign Affairs* 38, no. 4 (July 1960): 665–675.
KEDDIE, NIKKI R. "Is There a Middle East?" *International Journal of Middle East Studies* 4 (1973): 255–271.

Karen Pinto

Middle East Command

See Baghdad Pact

Middle East Defense Organization (MEDO)

U.S.-proposed group for military security in the Middle East; never formed.

The beginning of 1952 saw riots in Egypt and a continuing erosion of Britain's position in the Middle East. The U.S. foreign policy establishment considered plans to replace Britain as the preeminent power in the Middle East. Paul Nitze, then head of the U.S. Policy Planning Staff, proposed the creation of a Middle East Defense Organization that would protect the Suez Canal and provide military security to the petroleum-producing regions and to the Northern Tier countries of Iran, Pakistan, and Turkey. Cosponsored by Turkey, MEDO was not endorsed by

Egypt's President Gamal Abdel Nasser, who viewed MEDO as a tool of American imperialism.

Although both U.S. President Harry Truman and Secretary of State Dean Acheson were committed to MEDO, Egypt's resistance and the generally lukewarm reaction of other Arab states made the realization of MEDO impossible. In 1953, Truman left the White House, and MEDO became defunct. The ideal of a NATO-like security arrangement for the Middle East remained alive, however, and aspects of MEDO were included in the BAGHDAD PACT.

BIBLIOGRAPHY

HUREWITZ, J. C., ed. *The Middle East and North Africa in World Politics*. New Haven, Conn., 1979.
LEFFLER, MELVIN. *A Preponderance of Power*. Stanford, Calif., 1992.
LENCZOWSKI, GEORGE. *The Middle East in World Affairs*, 4th ed. Ithaca, N.Y., 1980.

Zachary Karabell

Middle East News Agency

Egyptian news agency founded in 1956 to provide a national alternative to Western news agencies.

The Middle East News Agency (MENA) was nationalized in 1962. Under the jurisdiction of the ministry of information and with over twelve hundred employees, it is the main provider and controller of news—in Arabic, English, and French—in Egypt. MENA provides its reports free to the information services of other Arab countries, and the news agencies of Qatar, Oman, and Saudi Arabia funnel their foreign reports through it. As a service to foreigners, MENA publishes its English-language *Cairo Press Review* daily and *Party Press Review* (with translations from the opposition press). MENA runs numerous training programs for journalists, radio and TV personnel, administrators, accountants, and engineers. Its contracts with Reuters and Agence France-Presse, along with its photo exchange and television services, supply much of its budget.

BIBLIOGRAPHY

KAMALIPOUR, YAHYA R., and HAMID MOWLANA, eds. *Mass Media in the Middle East*. Westport, Conn., 1994.

Donald Malcolm Reid

Middle East Supply Center (MESC)

World War II agency in Cairo set up to coordinate supply and transport problems of the Middle East.

The economic strength of the Middle Eastern countries was necessary to the success of the Allied war effort. A multitude of agencies—British and American, military and civilian—had roles in ensuring that Middle Eastern economies remained viable and strong. In April 1941, the British established the Middle East Supply Center (MESC) as a clearinghouse for all matters of civilian supply in the Middle East; it reported directly to the ministry of war transport in London. The goal was to regulate and control shipping and commerce among the countries of the Middle East, to eliminate nonessential shipping and trade, and to avoid the political and military hazards posed by populations made hostile because of hunger, unemployment, and the other problems of disorganized economies.

The U.S. Lend-Lease Act of 1941 sent massive amounts of American-made matériel, and after May 1942, the United States joined the British in the MESC, using it to coordinate the American war effort in the Middle East.

BIBLIOGRAPHY

VAIL MOTTER, T. H. *United States Army in World War II. The Middle East Theater: The Persian Corridor and Aid to Russia.* Washington, D.C., 1952.

Daniel E. Spector

Middle East Technical University

Public university in Ankara known as METU.

Founded in 1959 as a joint project between the Turkish government and the United Nations, METU was the first English-language university in Turkey. It now comprises faculties of economics and administrative sciences, architecture, education, engineering, and arts and sciences; it also has the School of Foreign Languages and the Institute of Marine Sciences. In 1990 it had a teaching staff of 1,500 and 16,500 students, about one-third female. Its 1991 budget, state funded, amounted to 191 billion Turkish lire, of which about 60.5 billion Turkish lire was for capital investment.

This university is a prime example of the enormous U.S. influence on Turkey since World War II, especially during the economic liberalization era of the 1950s. It was envisaged as bringing American methods of education and organization as opposed to European influence, such as exists at the older universities—Istanbul, Ankara, and İzmir. Instruction in English was expected to provide excellent language training for local students and also to enable students from other countries of the region to attend the university. In its early development, it received considerable financial support from the U.S. Agency for International Development, the Ford Foundation, the Organization for Economic Cooperation and Development, and the Central Treaty Organization. Its governance, too, resembled that of an American state university, unlike the others where a board of trustees, appointed by the Turkish government, appointed the university president and the deans.

In view of this significant American influence, it may seem paradoxical that, in the 1960s liberal atmosphere of worldwide student movements, METU developed into the major anti-American campus in the country, a stronghold of the as yet unfractured Marxist left. After the 1971 military intervention and because of its administrative features, which made it especially responsive to political pressures, student activism on the campus abated, or at least was overshadowed by much more violent clashes at other major universities. Nevertheless, after the 1980 military takeover of the Turkish government and the establishment of the highly centralized and authoritarian Higher Education Council (YÜKSEK ÖĞRETIM KURULU, or YÖK), METU suffered proportionally worse than other universities in terms of faculty members fired without cause or forced to resign. In all, more than 300 faculty members were thus alienated. Once again, it may seem paradoxical that this university that caused such frustration to authoritarian governments and administrators served as the model for the centralizing 1981 law governing higher education. It is very likely that the METU board of trustees was the source of inspiration for YÖK itself. YÖK is analogous to a super board of trustees for all universities in the country; its relation to government, on one hand, and to university administration, on the other, is practically the same as that of the original METU board of trustees. In the 1990s, METU has recovered its academic prominence.

BIBLIOGRAPHY

Higher Education in Turkey. UNESCO, European Centre for Higher Education. December 1990.
World of Learning. 1990.

I. Metin Kunt

Mideast Force

Small U.S. naval force based at the former British naval base at al-Jufayr, near Manama in Bahrain, since 1949.

In 1971, the United States and Bahrain concluded an agreement for the U.S. Navy to use the al-Jufayr port facilities. From 1971 to the mid-1980s, a flagship and two small destroyers docked. Because of the sensitive nature of the agreement, U.S. government officials were always careful to refer to al-Jufayr as a "facility" rather than a "base." The Mideast Force (MIDEASTFOR) was always one of the U.S. Navy's smallest commands. On June 20, 1973, as a reaction to the ARAB–ISRAEL WAR of 1973, Bahrain gave the U.S. Navy one year to dismantle its presence at al-Jufayr, which took until 1977 for compliance.

MIDEASTFOR was commanded by a rear admiral, who made friendly visits to countries in the area to show the flag—establishing harmonious relations with the governments and peoples of the region.

The 1971 agreement was renegotiated in 1975; by 1977, a new agreement was concluded, somewhat altering the legal status of the U.S. Navy in Bahrain. Instead of the phrase "United States Force" that was used earlier, the 1977 agreement used "Administrative Support Unit." The agreement and the intended limited U.S. presence in Bahrain were overshadowed by the developments in the Gulf in the late 1970s and the formation of the Rapid Deployment Joint Task Force. The first Gulf war (1980–1987), the U.S. reflagging of Kuwaiti ships in the late 1980s, and the 1990/91 GULF CRISIS (when Iraq invaded Kuwait) dramatically expanded U.S. Navy presence in the Gulf.

BIBLIOGRAPHY

NAKHLEH, EMILE. *The Persian Gulf and American Policy.* New York, 1982.

Emile A. Nakhleh

Midfa'i, Jamil al-   [1890–?]

Iraqi soldier, politician, and businessman.

Jamil al-Midfa'i was born in Mosul in what is today northern Iraq. He fought in the Ottoman army in World War I but subsequently joined the ARAB REVOLT. He became minister of interior in the first cabinet of Nuri al-SA'ID in 1930, holding the post until November 1933. He was prime minister of Iraq seven times between 1933 and 1953.

Peter Sluglett

Midhat Paşa   [1822–1884]

Ottoman provincial governor, grand vizier, and father of the first written Ottoman constitution.

Midhat Paşa (also called Ahmed Şefik) was born into an Ottoman Turkish family in Istanbul. His father, a native of Rusçuk on the Danube, held judgeships in Muslim courts. In his youth, Midhat studied Arabic and Persian in mosque schools, while employed from the age of twelve in offices of the Ottoman Empire's central government at the Sublime Porte. He began to learn French when he was about thirty-five; in 1858, he spent six months on leave in Europe, improving his French.

Midhat was on the payroll of the Supreme Council of Judicial Ordinances from the 1840s to 1861, but was often sent out of Istanbul as inspector or trouble-shooter on short-term missions that took him to Damascus, Konya, Kastamonu, Edirne, Bursa, Silistre, and Vidin. In 1861 he achieved the rank of vizier when appointed governor of the *eyalet* (province) of Niş, where he proved successful as a provincial administrator. In 1864 he was brought back to Istanbul to help the grand vizier, Mehmed Fuad Paşa, draft a law recasting provincial government in larger units (the VILAYET). Midhat then became governor of the Tuna (Danube) *vilayet,* the first one created, a Bulgarian area with its capital at Rusçuk. Midhat's reputation as an effective provincial governor continued to grow as he built roads and bridges, curbed banditry, settled refugees, and started small factories. He established the first official provincial newspaper in the empire, and created agricultural credit cooperatives that evolved into modern Turkey's Agricultural Bank (Ziraat Bankasi). He tried to incorporate Bulgarians into the government councils, but he repressed Bulgarian nationalists.

In 1868 Midhat was appointed head of the new Council of State, created to draft laws, in Istanbul. But friction with Grand Vizier Mehmed Emin Ali Paşa led to his transfer in 1869 to the governorship of the Baghdad *vilayet,* together with command of the Sixth Army. Midhat used his civil and military powers with partial success to settle tribes, to collect taxes, and to institute conscription. Thereafter, Iraqi nomads declined in numbers, and cultivators increased. Midhat's application of the 1858 Ottoman land code furnished *tapu* (title) deeds to individual cultivators, but principally tribal shaykhs, city merchants, and former tax farmers took advantage of the law. In the city of Baghdad, Midhat introduced municipal improvements including street lighting and paving, a bridge over the Tigris, schools, and a horse-car tramway line to a suburb. Here also he established the first Iraqi newspaper, the *Zawra,* a semi-weekly in Turkish and Arabic. In the Baghdad *vilayet,* he established government schools—a technical school and two secondary schools, one preparing students for the military and one for the civil service, with free tuition. Disagreements with the grand vizier, Mahmud Nedim Paşa, caused Midhat's resignation in 1872.

Returning to Istanbul, Midhat persuaded Sultan Abdülaziz to appoint him grand vizier, on July 31, 1872. But political opponents, backed by the Khedive Isma'il of Egypt and the Russian ambassador, managed his dismissal on October 18. He had been impolitic, too outspoken. During this time, Midhat had begun to think about a constitution for the empire. Such thoughts occupied him during the next three years, when he had two brief terms as minister of justice, one as governor of Salonika, and periods out of office. By the spring of 1876, Midhat was a key member of a group that sought to bring change to an Ottoman government perceived as ineffectual in the face of financial bankruptcy and of revolts in Bosnia and Herzegovina.

Midhat and others used popular discontent to force the dismissal of Grand Vizier Mahmud Nedim, and then engineered the bloodless deposition of Sultan Abdülaziz on May 30. Sultan Murad V succeeded. Midhat became president of the Council of State again, and began pressing for a constitution. When Murad V suffered a nervous breakdown, following the deposed Abdülaziz's suicide, Midhat and the ministers deposed Murad in turn for his younger brother. Abdülhamit II succeeded on August 31, 1876, after promising Midhat that he would speedily promulgate a constitution.

Midhat chaired a commission in the fall of 1876 that drafted a constitution providing for an elected chamber of deputies. The sultan accepted it only after his own powers were augmented to include the power of exiling. On December 19, Abdülhamit appointed Midhat grand vizier, and on December 23 promulgated the constitution. At the same time, representatives of the European great powers were meeting in Istanbul to devise reformed administration for the Balkan provinces of the Ottoman Empire. Midhat's hopes that Europe would accept the constitution as the fundamental reform were deceived. An Ottoman consultative council, convened by Midhat, in turn rejected the powers' proposals. The stand-off eventually led to Russia's invasion in April 1877 and the RUSSO–OTTOMAN WARS of 1877/78.

Meanwhile, Midhat seemed to act less like a grand vizier responsible to the sultan, and more like a prime minister responsible to the nation. Abdülhamit, who feared Midhat also as a sultan-deposer, exiled him to Europe on February 5, 1877. In late 1878, Midhat was allowed to return, but not to Istanbul. He became governor of the Syrian *vilayet*. In Damascus he was almost as vigorous as in Rusçuk and Baghdad but was refused the broader military power he requested. Abdülhamit transferred Midhat in August 1880 to İzmir as governor, apparently to keep a closer eye on him. There Midhat was arrested on May 18,

1881, taken to Istanbul, tried on trumped-up charges of having participated in the murder of former Sultan Abdülaziz, and convicted. Abdülhamit converted his death sentence to life banishment. Midhat was transported to a prison in Ta'if in Arabia. On May 8, 1884, he was strangled by soldiers, presumably on Abdülhamit's order.

As administrator, especially as provincial governor, Midhat achieved much, although some of his innovations were superficial. He was known for his energy, his fairness, his honesty, his Ottoman patriotism, his secular-mindedness, and his zeal for borrowing Western techniques and institutions. Midhat was also known for his blunt speech and his haste to act, qualities that helped terminate his two short grand vizierates. But without him, there would have been no 1876 constitution.

BIBLIOGRAPHY

Two biographies of Midhat by his son, ALI HAYDAR MIDHAT, are basic sources, incorporating letters and parts of a memoir by Midhat himself: *The Life of Midhat Pasha* (London, 1903) and *Midhat-Pacha* (Paris, 1908). MIDHAT PASHA, "The Past, Present, and Future of Turkey," *Nineteenth Century* 3, no. 18 (June 1878): 981–993, includes some of his own ideas. RODERIC H. DAVISON, *Reform in the Ottoman Empire, 1856–1876* (Princeton, N.J., 1963), and ROBERT DEVEREUX, *The First Ottoman Constitutional Period* (Baltimore, 1963), add many details and bibliographical references.

Roderic H. Davison

Midhat, Ahmet   [1844–1912]

Ottoman writer and newspaperman.

In addition to newspaper and periodical articles, Midhat produced some 150 works that included translations and adaptations of French classics; plays; a European travelogue; historical, political, philosophical, religious, and scientific studies; literary criticism; and, especially, popular novels. Seeking to introduce Turks to modern European thought and to reveal social problems, he used simple language and an entertaining yet informative style reminiscent of traditional storytelling.

Born in Constantinople (now Istanbul), Midhat was orphaned in early childhood, worked as apprentice to a druggist, then lived with his stepbrother in Vidin and Niş. His formal education ended with middle school, but he continued to study privately. In 1864 the family moved to Rusçuk, under the patronage of the governor, Midhat Paşa; Ahmet worked in the provincial chancery and began writing for the provincial newspaper, of which he was soon appointed editor in chief. When Midhat Paşa was appointed governor of Baghdad (1869), Ahmet joined him, heading the official newspaper and press. When his stepbrother died, he assumed responsibility for the family and, returning to Constantinople (1871), established his own press.

Like many other intellectuals, Midhat experienced exile; however, he found favor with Abdülhamit II, who put him in charge of the Imperial Press, and Tekvim-i Vekayi, who helped finance Midhat's TERCÜMAN-I HAKIKAT, and appointed him later to the Quarantine Administration (1885) and the Public Health Commission (1895). Due to his connections with Abdülhamit, the Young Turks distrusted Midhat and forced him from government employment and publishing. He spent his last years teaching at the university and institutions in Istanbul.

BIBLIOGRAPHY

EVIN, AHMET Ö. *Origins and Development of the Turkish Novel.* Minneapolis, Minn., 1983.
FINN, ROBERT P. *The Early Turkish Novel, 1872–1900.* Istanbul, 1984.

Kathleen R. F. Burrill

Mihrab

An indicator of the direction toward which Muslims face in prayer.

While the etymology of the word is the subject of some debate, mihrab (pl. *maharib*) is the Arabic term used to refer to any object, marking, or architectural feature that indicates the direction Muslims must face (i.e., toward Mecca) in the performance of the five daily prayers. Since the mihrab commonly takes the form of a distinctive recess in the wall of a mosque, the word is often translated as "prayer niche." Traditionally crafted in stucco, marble, or tile and adorned with calligraphic scriptural inscriptions, the mihrab is usually the most elaborately decorated piece of architecture in a mosque and in some simpler settings may be the only ornamented part of a mosque's interior.

Scott Alexander

Miletus

Ancient city in western Anatolia.

Miletus (in Turkish, Milet) is one of the earliest archeological sites in Anatolia. It began as a Creto-

Mycenean settlement in the sixteenth century B.C.E. Greek Ionian colonists probably arrived in the area as early as the eleventh century B.C.E. Today Miletus is stranded in the middle of deserted scrub and marshland, but three thousand years ago, before the Büyük Menderes river silted up its port and isolated it from the coast, Miletus stood on a promontory at the head of the gulf of Latmus, jutting out into the Aegean. Its exceptional location for maritime activity brought Miletus prosperity and made it, from the seventh until the fifth century B.C.E., one of the wealthiest cities in the Aegean. This prosperity in turn fostered a climate for learning, which produced a number of well-known Greek philosophers and scientists of the seventh through the fifth centuries B.C.E., such as the mathematician Thales, the natural philosophers Anaximander and Anaximenes, and the famous courtesan-orator Aspasia, a friend of both Socrates and Plato. Its last famous native, long after it had declined, was Isidorus, the architect of the Aya Sofya cathedral in Constantinople (now Istanbul).

BIBLIOGRAPHY

Encyclopaedia of Islam, vol. 1.

Karen Pinto

Military and Politics

Due to the end of colonialism, the rise of radical nationalist movements, and the desire for economic and political development, the military has played a large role in the politics of the Middle East.

Military authoritarianism has been the way of life for most Arab Middle Eastern and North African states since 1949. Since 1951, Libya, Algeria, Syria, Iraq, Egypt (1952–1970), and North and South Yemen have been dominated by military regimes. Considered deviant occurrences before 1945, instances in which the military played an increasingly active role in politics became widespread with the end of British and French colonialism in the Middle East. Since then a new phenomenon, praetorianism, has become the rule of the day in Middle Eastern politics.

By the mid-1970s, with the exception of conservative oil shaykhdoms and states, radical nationalists had captured and taken control throughout the Middle East, and have since dominated the militaries of Syria, Iraq, and Libya. Before World War II, the status of professional military personnel in the Middle East, with the exception of Egypt, was low. They were also low in the hierarchy of the nationalist movement. Over time, they were influenced by the Soviet Union, creating a hybrid called Arab socialism. If their orientation was nationalist, they sought mass support. Most were middle-echelon officers, and they were perceived as instruments of radical nationalists and Islamic fundamentalists. The Arab military elite arose from the lower middle classes, highly nationalist and militant; in Egypt they were the children of village notables and chiefs and civil servants, Gamal Abdel Nasser being the quintessential model.

In order to establish an analytical model, one must distinguish between historical and modern praetorianism. An example of historical praetorianism would be the action of a small military contingent in Rome, moving to preserve the legitimacy of the empire by defending the Senate against rebellious military garrisons marching on the capital. Roman praetorianism was based on the monopoly of local military power, the absence of definitive rules of succession, and the absence of legitimacy.

> A modern praetorian state is one in which the military tends to intervene and *potentially* dominate the political system. The political processes of this state favor the development of the military as the core group and the growth of its expectations as a ruling class; its political leadership (as distinguished from bureaucratic, administrative, and managerial leadership) is chiefly recruited from the military, or from groups sympathetic, or at least not antagonistic, to the military. Constitutional changes are effected and sustained by the military, and the army frequently intervenes in the government. In a praetorian state, therefore, the military plays a dominant role in political structures and institutions. (Perlmutter, "The Praetorian Army and the Praetorian State," p. 383)

Max Weber points out that the ruler whose sole authority rests on threats and power ultimately cannot maintain rule. He calls this system "sultanism," which is the equivalent of praetorianism. It involves a bureaucracy that depends either on the state or on ethnic and social contracts, a situation neither reliable nor efficient, and that prefers to serve either the ruling classes or the ethnic groups. What is most significant is the absence of a large, organized, and cohesive middle class, the group from which complex organizations and political diversity emerge.

The praetorian army operates in a praetorian state. It becomes praetorian when a few key activists succeed in propelling the military into politics. It is never more than 5 percent of the total officer corps. In the most extreme form, which I call the ruler type, the military establishes an independent executive and a political organization to dominate society and politics. The less extreme type, which I call the

TABLE 1		
Types of Praetorian Armies, 1936–1995		
	Ruler Type	*Arbitrator Type*
Syria	1970–1995	coups in 1949, 1952–1954, 1958–1969
Iraq	1970–1995	1936–1941
Egypt	1953–1960	1952–1954 1961–1995 coalition
Algeria	1965–1970	1970–1995

arbitrator type, has no independent political organization and shows little interest in manufacturing a political ideology (see Table 1, Figures 1 and 2).

The arbitrator army has the following characteristics: (1) an acceptance of the existing social order; (2) a willingness to return to the barracks after disputes are settled; (3) a lack of independent political organization; (4) a time limit to army rule; (5) a tendency to operate behind the scenes as a pressure group; and (6) no fear of civilian retribution. The arbitrator type is tolerated by civilian institutions. There is a tacit mutuality and consent between the two. The arbitrator-type army has no intention of permanently replacing the political institutions of the country. There is no retaliation, no fear, no imprisonment, and no harassment of one another, in or out of office.

The ruler-type army, by contrast, (1) rejects the existing order and challenges its legitimacy; (2) lacks confidence in civilian rule; (3) has no expectation of returning to the barracks; (4) prefers to establish a political organization of its own—either security services or an army party; (5) is convinced army rule is the only alternative to political disorder; and (6) has little fear of civilian retribution. What distinguishes it from the arbitrator type is that it is more ruthless, vindictive, and intolerant of any competing political forces in society. Whereas the arbitrator type tries to correct executive and administrative rule, leaving society and politics to their own devices, the ruler type intervenes in all aspects of society.

When the army party (or the party dominated by the army) serves as the foundation for the military, the ruler type prevails—as is the case in Syria and Iraq since 1970. Thus, army party and military party coups are more durable and sustaining than the organizational coup (a coup by a small elite of the army).

FIGURE 1
The Arbitrator Regime

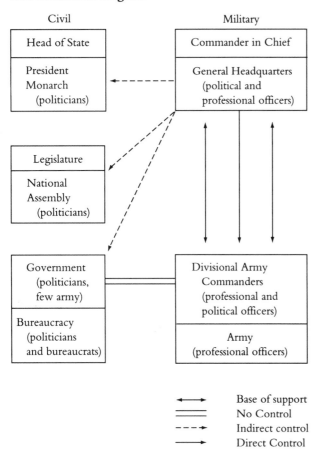

Source: Amos Perlmutter, *Egypt, the Praetorian State* (New Brunswick, N.J., 1974), p. 133.

The arbitrator type encourages a coalition with bureaucratic, professional, and technocratic civilian groups. It sees political organizations as corrupt, selfish, interest-oriented, and unpatriotic. The principle of arbitration is the Kemalist legacy in Turkey, where the army serves as the guardian of the constitution—but from the barracks. In Egypt examples of arbitrator regimes include that of General Muhammad Naguib (1952–1954) and those of presidents Anwar al-Sadat and Husni Mubarak since 1971. The arbitrator type is dedicated to the military's professionalism and autonomy, as well as to preserving the integrity of the military organization. In other words, there was a realization after Nasser's rule that the army's mission had not prepared it for political, economic, and social modernization and change, and that the greater involvement of officers in politics may threaten the arbitrator type.

But the arbitrator type is the exception to the rule in the Middle East. In Syria and Iraq, the ruler type has dominated politics since the late 1960s. In Iraq, it po-

liticizes the professionals and threatens their behavior. It operates clandestinely, but it has little fear of political retaliation. There are subtypes of the ruler type: the antitraditionalist reformer radical army and the conservative antiradical army. "Antitraditionalist" indicates opposition to *Shari'a*, Islamic canon law, and to patrimony. Examples of the antitraditionalist radical army are the regime of Abd al-Karim Kassem in Iraq (1958–1963) and the military regimes of Gamal Abdel Nasser (1952–1970) and of Algeria since 1965. This is especially true of Syria and Iraq since 1970. The conservative antiradical army is exemplified by the regime of Col. Muammar al-Qaddafi in Libya since 1969.

In Syria and Iraq, political systems were established by colonial powers, and the authority of one group was established over the others without legitimacy. In Iraq, three Ottoman *vilayet*s are each populated by different ethnic and religious groups: the Sunni, the Shi'ites, and the Kurds. Since its formation Iraq has been dominated by the military, first by the British Royal Air Force, and then by the first military regime in the Middle East (1936–1939), whose function was to suppress ethnic groups, especially the Kurds. Saddam Hussein is a late heir to this orientation. In Syria, the Druze, Alawi, Sunni, and Shi'a factions were governed by a French colonial

FIGURE 2
The Ruler Regime

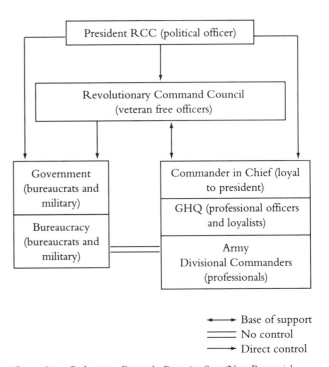

Source: Amos Perlmutter, *Egypt, the Praetorian State* (New Brunswick, N.J., 1974), p. 136.

regime that dominated it militarily, and the ethnic and tribal struggles were continuously quelled by military force. Thus the ruler type prevails here, because no accommodation exists among the competing ethnic groups and the modern nation-state tolerates no political and ethnic diversity. The ruler type, to quote Gamal Abdel Nasser, must "permanently patrol society."

The civilian politicians' distrust of competing ethnic nationalisms is a constant challenge to Sunni Arab domination in the Middle East. The military in Iraq is of Sunni origin or must represent—as does Hafiz al-Asad of Syria, who is an Alawi—a guardian of Sunni domination. The regimes of Iraq and Syria, both ruler types, are dominated by minorities. The Alawi population of Syria is about 12 percent, yet among the senior officers of the security service corps, they account for over 70 percent. Sunnis are 74 percent of the population, Christians are 10 percent, and Druze are 4 percent. In Iraq, the Sunni minority (32–37 percent) rules the state. Here the use of modern cohesive institutions is becoming the role of the military regime in a multiethnic society. The Shi'ites are 60 to 65 percent of the population.

The success of the regimes in Syria and Iraq in sustaining themselves in power since 1970 is directly connected with two developments: (1) the emergence of an army party political organization, such as the Ba'th party that dominates the state, and (2) the rise of a complex web of security and political police structures, all of them combined to make up for the absence of the regime's legitimacy and to secure the regime from rival military conspirators and their aspirations for coups. These highly institutionalized security services as well as the party, formerly a civilian radical nationalist organization that has been captured by the army, have served the regimes of Iraq and Syria by creating stability in the absence of legitimacy. The praetorian state has been dominated by the praetorian army.

Between 1936 and 1995, there were fifty-two military interventions in the Middle East (see Table 2); twenty-five were successful and twenty-seven were not. Of the fifty-two coup attempts, twenty-five were supported by organized civilian groups, six were supported by the masses, forty-four were nationalist, forty were by senior officers, and nine were ideological.

What are the explanations for the rise of the military and the future of civil–military relations in the Middle East? The military's emergence converges with three interconnected political, ideological, and economic factors: the end of colonialism, the rise of a radical nationalist movement, and the role this movement would play in economic modernization and po-

Table 2
Coups in the Middle East, 1936–1995

I.	Military Intervention	
	Initiated, organized, and executed by military	51
	Initiated, organized, and executed by nonmilitary	1
II.	Support of Organized Civilian and Political Groups	
	Support	25
	Opposition	27
III.	Mass Support	
	Support	6
	No opposition	38
	Opposition	8
IV.	Orientation of Coup	
	Nationalist	44
	Fascist	3
	Leftist	5
	Religious fundamentalist	0
V.	Rank of Intervening Officers	
	Senior	40
	Middle and junior	12
VI.	Types of Regime Legitimation	
	Personal	25
	Structural	18
	Ideological	9
VII.	Outcome of Coup	
	Successful	25
	Unsuccessful	27

Source: Amos Perlmutter, "The Arab Military Elite," *World Politics* 22, no. 2 (January 1970).

litical development. The rise of a political radical nationalist movement—which the armies of Egypt, Syria, and Iraq have captured—has led to its becoming the task force of radical nationalism, anticolonialism, and the force that has assigned itself the roles of economic and social modernizers. A lesser factor, but not insignificant, is the Arab defeat in a war with Israel (1948–1949) and the promise by these officers, in Egypt and Syria in particular, to avenge this defeat. The military, which was an unacceptable social elite group, has surged to the forefront as the savior of the country in the war against colonialism, Zionism, poverty, and economic misery.

By the 1980s, all these promises had come to naught, however, especially in Egypt, Syria, and Iraq, but also in Algeria. The military modernizers, having no political, economic, or social skills, utterly failed to catapult the countries from their economic backwardness into rising modern, developed societies. In economic development, where the great promise was not realized, there emerged a populist, popular radical nationalist force known as Islamic fundamentalism—a direct consequence of the military's great failure in economic development. In political development (i.e., the creation of stable parliamentary institutions, a free electoral system, a competitive political party system, interest groups), these regimes have not been improved much over what they were under colonial and traditional monarchical rules before 1949. The only area that has been improved, especially in Iraq, Syria, and Egypt, has been military modernization: from an army of less than 100,000 in the 1950s, Egypt's military has grown to over 1.2 million; Iraq's military under Saddam Hussein is close to 500,000, as is Syria's.

The arms race between Israel and the Arab states, as well as among the Arab states themselves, was frantic and costly. For instance, Egypt's military expenditure as a percentage of GNP was 12.8 percent in 1985, 11.7 percent in 1986, 11.2 percent in 1987, 8.6 percent in 1988, and 5.0 percent in 1989; for Syria, these percentages were 21.8 percent, 18.0 percent, 10.8 percent, 9.3 percent, and 11.6 percent, respectively. And yet, the military leaders' promise to destroy Israel did not materialize. In fact, these armies suffered monumental losses, in equipment and personnel, not only in conflicts with Israel but in conflicts among themselves. For instance, the Iran–Iraq War cost an average of $500 billion for each side, and for Iraq the cost of damage to infrastructure was estimated at $188 billion (excluding revenue losses). The number of casualties, according to John Keegan, a highly respected military analyst, was 1 million lives for both, but possibly as high as 2 million. In addition, Saddam Hussein attempted to eliminate the Kurds by exposing 49 Kurdish villages to chemical weapons, including an attack on Halabja, where 5,000 to 6,000 people were killed.

Even with great defeats, however, military regimes have continued to dominate the politics of their states. In Egypt and especially in Syria and Iraq, some fourteen to twenty security services have come under the single command of the military leader—Anwar al-Sadat and Husni Mubarak in Egypt, Hafez al-Asad in Syria, and the Tikriti family of Saddam Hussein in Iraq.

What is the explanation for the survival of military authoritarianism in the Arab Middle East? No alternative political or other institutional structures have emerged to challenge the military. Political autonomy of social groups has been curtailed. Elections in Egypt are totally dominated by the army party, the Arab Socialist Union, even if there is greater representation of opposition parties—the Wafd party of landowners and rich Copts gained considerably in

the 1988 election. There are two explanations for this in the literature. The first is the decline of authority. Almost every student of the military and politics in developing countries posits the decline of authority to explain the frequency of military coups. The other explanation is the historical legacy and failure of democracy, as well as the history of colonialism, which prohibited the growth of independent political parties and institutions. This is an insufficient explanation, however, in view of the fact that Egypt in the 1930s, the era of great political renaissance, established a successful political party system and a working parliament, as well as the most distinguished Arab free press in the Middle East. Nevertheless, an obscure lieutenant colonel of the Egyptian army succeeded in bringing an end to the decaying monarchy and in destroying party and parliamentary politics.

What, then, is the sufficient explanation? We must turn to the dynamics of military coups. According to the literature, military groups replace an existing regime (a) when the military is the most cohesive and politically the best-organized group at a given time in a given political system; (b) when, relatively, no more powerful military opposition exists (in fact, the Egyptian officers hesitated to intervene for a long time, in view of the fear of combined forces of the Egyptian court and its political allies); (c) when there is coup legitimization—as discussed earlier, the role of security and political police services as the foundation for sustaining military rule.

When we speak of military authoritarianism, we clearly must distinguish it from totalitarianism. Military rulers are authoritarian and secular. The one who most closely approximates the head of a totalitarian system is Saddam Hussein in Iraq. What distinguishes a totalitarian regime is its intervention in every aspect of political, economic, cultural, and social life. But this is not true in Arab military regimes (except, of course, in Iraq). There is no ideological party state (except in Iraq and Syria), in the Soviet style, because nationalism is not a sufficient force to enable the regime to penetrate and dominate every aspect of society. Nevertheless, the technological and institutional improvement of the political police and the security services has strengthened and enhanced military authoritarianism in both Syria and Iraq, and thus has brought about stability and an end to frequent military coups. However, not unlike communist totalitarianism, military authoritarianism is not guaranteed to survive forever in the Middle East. This of course means the growth of independent and autonomous political institutions and structures, and the rise of a modern, better-educated intellectual and political group—which is well represented, especially in the Arab press and the universities.

Yet the threat to military authoritarianism and military rule in general comes from a different source completely, more awesome and more ruthless. This is Islamic fundamentalism. It is quite clear, in Egypt and Algeria, that Islamic radicals have gained considerable influence among the middle classes as well as among the secular intelligentsia, and especially in the military. Sadat's assassins were members of a military cell in the Egyptian army indoctrinated by the radical fundamentalists. This group is totalitarian in orientation and poses a threat to the military, which has failed to mobilize the masses and to provide the peoples of Egypt and Algeria with economic and social improvement and care.

Thus, the argument that military regimes are on the way out—as some are certainly out in Latin America and off and on in sub-Saharan Africa—does not promise greater democracy and freedom, or more efficiency and modernization, in the Middle East. It may promise an Iranian Khomeni-like political system, which certainly would be less benevolent and more ruthless and efficient than the present military regimes, even that of Saddam Hussein. Military regimes that now lead by virtue of security services, terror, and assassination, will continue unless the radical Islamicists replace them. Once the radical Islamicists replace them, there will be civilian domination and ideological control of society and politics, which the military never succeeded in establishing.

BIBLIOGRAPHY

BEERI, ELIEZER. *Army Officers in Arab Politics and Society.* New York, 1970.

DEKMEJIAN, R. HRAIR. *Egypt under Nasser: A Study in Political Dynamics.* Albany, N.Y., 1971.

HELLER, MARK A., et al. *The Middle East Military Balance.* Westport, Conn., 1985

HUNTINGTON, SAMUEL. *The Soldier and the State: The Theory and Politics of Civil-Military Relations.* Cambridge, Mass., 1981.

KRAMER, MOFID. "After the Gulf War." *The World Today,* March 1986, p. 49.

PERLMUTTER, AMOS. "Egypt and the Myth of the New Middle Classes: A Comparative Analysis." *Comparative Studies in Society and History* (October 1967).

———. *Military and Politics in Israel: Nation-Building and Role Expansion.* London, 1969.

———. *Military and Politics in the Middle East.*

———. "The Praetorian Army and the Praetorian State: Toward a Taxonomy of Civil–Military Relations in Developing Polities." *Comparative Politics* (April 1969).

RABINOWITZ, ITAMAR. *Syrian Army and the Baath Party, 1963–1966.* Tel Aviv, 1973.

VATIKIOTIS, P. J. *The Egyptian Army in Politics.* Westport, Conn., 1961.

———. *Nasser and His Generation.* New York, 1978.

Amos Perlmutter

Military Command Council

The ruling group of the Yemen Arab Republic in 1974.

The small group of army officers, chaired by Lt. Colonel Ibrahim al-HAMDI, that assumed supreme power in the Yemen Arab Republic (YAR) in 1974 when the regime headed by President Abd al-Rahman al-Iryani was overthrown and the 1970 constitution was suspended. The term fell into disuse within a year when civilians were added to the group, and it ceased to be the center of power.

Robert D. Burrowes

Military in the Middle East

An important sector of each nation's economy.

The history of the modern Middle East has been one of almost constant conflict. Study of these conflicts must focus on three often interlocking levels: internal, regional, and international security. The history of each nation reflects a variety of religious, ethnic, tribal, ideological, social, and economic conflicts that often result in violence and a prominent role for the military in internal security. At the regional level, there have been wars among Middle Eastern states, as well as exploitation of the internal problems of rival

Israel Defense Forces on patrol in Jerusalem. (Mia Bloom)

Parade ground with Sudanese troops lined up for inspection. (D.W. Lockhard)

nations. Finally, the Middle East has been an important arena in the international rivalries of the great powers.

Military Organization. European nations and the United States have had a great impact on training, organizing, and equipping the military in the Middle East. This accelerated during the nineteenth century, largely due to rivalries among European countries. The result has been a tendency for Middle Eastern nations to organize their militaries along Western lines. More traditional tribal armies, such as that led by Emir Faisal and T. E. Lawrence in World War I, continued to play a role but decreasingly so as they were eclipsed by modern forces. For instance, the Ottoman army had significant successes, including the decisive defeat of 200,000 Allied troops at Gallipoli in 1915, the surrender of an entire British army in Mesopotamia in 1916, and continued occupation of Medina throughout the war. The legacy of the Ottomans continued long after the end of the empire in the contributions of trained officers, Arab as well as Turkish, to the emerging nations of the Middle East. Foremost among these was Atatürk, but many Arab leaders, such as Iraq's Nuri al-Sa'id, were graduates of Ottoman military colleges and learned from Ottoman officers.

This trend toward westernization of the military has continued to the point that most Middle East militaries are mirror images of one or more Western models. The model chosen is normally a function of which of the great powers has provided the most support to a nation. Turkey, as part of NATO, organizes its forces along American lines, with doctrine, training, and equipment closely paralleling that of the U.S. military. Iraq, since the 1958 revolution, has traditionally looked to the Soviet Union for sup-

port, and its military reflects this. It has often been said that the success of the United States and its European allies in Desert Storm stemmed from their fighting the enemy they had been training to fight for decades: the Soviet military organization. Political alliances with Cold War rivals have changed, often rapidly, while change in the military comes more slowly. The result is often a hybrid military. The end of the Cold War is likely to result in changes that will further complicate the picture.

Israel presents a unique case. At first glance, its military appears much like that of the NATO nations from which much of its equipment comes. There are, however, factors that make Israel different. Much of its equipment is captured, and imported equipment is often dramatically modified; how else could World War II–vintage Sherman tanks be successful in the Arab–Israel War of 1973? The successes of the Israeli military affect doctrine and organization, not only in Israel but in other nations whose military study those successes and, in turn, contribute to the Israeli military. Finally, the organization of the Israeli military is more reminiscent of the Swiss citizen army than the armies of other countries. While most militaries have a reserve system, few have one as extensive as Israel. Almost all males and many females of military age are in the reserves, on active duty at least thirty consecutive days annually and available for mobilization in seventy-two hours.

The table on active-force levels shows the impact of the military in the Middle East since the Suez crisis of 1956 (see Table 1). These figures reflect the many conflicts with which nations in the area have been involved. The figures for Israel are illustrative. In excess of 10 percent of the population was in the military through the 1960s because the military included citizen-armies. The figures after 1969 reflect only those reservists on active duty, but even here, Israel has maintained the highest percentage of the population in the military of any Middle Eastern nation. This is a heavy burden but reflects the price that Israel has had to pay for the protracted Arab–Israel conflict. A defeat for Israel would likely result in the end of the nation, while defeats for Arab nations do not cause even a change in government. Nevertheless, Arab nations around Israel have maintained large military establishments. Egypt, for example, had almost 1 percent of its population in the military at the end of the 1970s, and both Jordan and Syria had over 2 percent. As a benchmark, in 1990, the United States had 0.68 percent of its population on active military duty, with global-force-projection objectives far greater than any Middle Eastern nation.

Regardless of the current level of forces, any reduction would have a long-term benefit. Such a re-

TABLE 1

Active Force Levels

Country	1955 or 1956			1965			1969			1975			1979			1991		
	Population in millions	Force level in thousands	Force as percentage of population	Population in millions	Force level in thousands	Force as percentage of population	Population in millions	Force level in thousands	Force as percentage of population	Population in millions	Force level in thousands	Force as percentage of population	Population in millions	Force level in thousands	Force as percentage of population	Population in millions	Force level in thousands	Force as percentage of population
Afghanistan	—	—	—	12	90	0.75	15.8	110	0.70	19.1	88	0.46	21.3	90	0.42	20.8	45	0.22
Algeria	—	—	—	11.7	65	0.55	12.6	66.5	0.53	16.9	63	0.37	19.1	88.8	0.46	26.3	125.5	0.48
Bahrain	—	—	—	—	—	—	—	—	—	—	—	—	0.4	2.3	0.65	0.5	7.5	1.49
Egypt	22.9	80	0.35	29.6	180	0.61	31.5	216	0.68	37.5	322.5	0.86	40.5	395	0.98	56	420	0.75
Iran	18.5	135	0.73	23.4	185	0.79	26.3	236	0.90	33.1	250	0.75	39.3	415	1.05	53.8	528	0.98
Iraq	6	40	0.68	7.4	82	1.11	8.5	92	1.08	11.1	135	1.21	12.7	22.2	0.17	19.9	382.5	1.93
Israel	1.8	250	13.88	2.6	375	14.42	2.8	280	10.18	3.4	156	4.59	3.8	165.6	4.33	4.8	141	2.92
Jordan	1.4	23	1.64	2	45	2.25	2.1	55	2.62	2.7	80.3	2.97	3	67.2	2.20	4.3	101.3	2.36
Kuwait	—	—	—	0.4	7	1.50	0.6	7.5	1.37	1.2	10.2	0.84	1.2	11.1	0.92	2.1	8.2	0.39
Lebanon	1.7	6.2	0.35	2.4	13	0.54	2.6	15.5	0.60	3.2	15.3	0.47	2.7	8.8	0.33	2.7	17.5	0.65
Libya	—	—	—	1.6	18.2	1.13	1.8	7	0.40	2.3	32	1.39	2.9	42	1.46	4.8	55	1.15
Morocco	10.6	30	0.28	13	42	0.32	14.2	78.3	0.55	17.3	61	0.35	19.3	98	0.51	25.4	195.5	0.77
Oman	—	—	—	—	—	—	0.8	2.8	0.37	0.8	14.1	1.85	0.9	19.2	2.21	1.5	34.1	2.21
Qatar	—	—	—	—	—	—	—	—	—	—	—	—	0.2	4.7	2.23	0.4	7.5	1.71
Saudi Arabia	—	—	—	3.2	45	1.41	6	56	0.93	8.9	63	0.71	8	64.5	0.81	10.6	131.5	1.24
Sudan	10.2	5	0.05	13.5	18.5	1.37	14.4	30	0.21	17.9	48.6	0.27	20.9	62.9	0.30	26.1	71.5	0.27
Syria	5.8	40	0.69	5.6	60	1.07	5.7	67.9	1.20	7.4	177.5	2.40	8.4	227.5	2.72	12.8	404	3.16
Tunisia	3.8	1.3	0.03	4.6	17.5	0.38	4.7	23	0.49	5.8	24	0.42	6.4	22.3	0.35	8.2	35	0.43
Turkey	24.8	400	1.61	31.4	480	1.52	33	534	1.62	39.9	453	1.14	44.4	566	1.27	57	579.2	1.02
United Arab Emirates	—	—	—	—	—	—	0.4	6	1.50	—	—	—	0.9	25.1	2.78	1.7	44	2.57
Yemen, North	—	—	—	—	—	—	5	60	1.20	6.5	32	0.49	7.5	36.6	0.49	11.5	65	0.56
Yemen, South	—	—	—	—	—	—	1.3	10.5	0.84	1.7	18	0.23	1.9	20.8	1.11	—	—	—

Sources: J. C. Hurewitz, *Middle East Politics: The Military Dimension* (1969); T. N. Dupuy, *The Almanac of World Military Power* (1970); and publications of the International Institute for Strategic Studies.

duction would minimize the potential for conflict and the destruction of lives and property that results from conflict. It would also free manpower for more productive activities. The table on defense costs as a percentage of gross national product (GNP) or gross domestic product (GDP) illustrates the amount of fiscal resources that could be put to other uses (see Table 2). An example of this may be seen in the figures for Iran. As war with Iraq loomed, and as a carryover of the shah's perceived role as policeman of the Persian Gulf, Iran spent 13.24 percent of its GNP on defense in 1979. After the end of the war with Iraq and the subsequent weakening of Iraq after Desert Storm, that percentage went down to 6.34.

The high force levels in the Middle East reflect more than the conflict between Israel and its neighbors. Internal conflicts tend to drive up the levels.

The figures for Iraq illustrate this tendency. The Kurdish minority in the north was in a state of rebellion when the Ba'th came to power in 1968, forcing a growth in the force level from 0.68 percent of the population in 1955 to over 1 percent in 1965, 1969, and 1975. The temporary end of the revolt in 1975 may have contributed to the reduction in the force level in 1979. However, the relatively low force levels for strife-torn Lebanon may be deceptive. These do not reflect sectarian militias or the presence of Israeli and Syrian troops; if these were factored in, the Lebanese force levels would likely be much higher and more reflective of the level of civil unrest.

Military involvement in the internal affairs of other nations also requires an increase in the force level; Egypt's dispatching almost seventy thousand troops to Yemen by 1965 to support the military revolt there

TABLE 2

Defense Costs as Percentage of Gross National or Gross Domestic Product

Country	1965		1969		1975		1979		1991	
	GNP (billions of U.S. $)	Defense (% of GNP)	GNP (billions of U.S. $)	Defense (% of GNP)	GNP (billions of U.S. $)	Defense (% of GNP)	GNP (billions of U.S. $)	Defense (% of GNP)	GNP (billions of U.S. $)	Defense (% of GNP)
Afghanistan	1.25	1.8	1.50	1	1.6	2.81	2.30	2.65	3.70	7.74
Algeria	2.63	3.8	2.80	6.20	8.8	3.24	15.90	3.81	45.43	1.99
Bahrain	—	—	—	—	—	—	1.70	5.76	4.01	5.04
Egypt	5.06	9.1	5.10	13.50	17.9	34.10	18.10	11.99	39.45	3.98
Iran	5.83	5.4	7.60	6.44	35.6	29.20	75.10	13.24	59.49	6.34
Iraq	1.92	12.7	2.30	10.90	5.6	14.30	15.50	13.03	40.78	21.11
Israel	3.40	9.3	3.93	16	11.7	29.90	10.50	15.43	51.22	12.03
Jordan	0.50	12	0.50	16.20	1	15.50	1.85	20.59	3.87	14.76
Kuwait	1.71	4.2	1.87	2.94	5.4	3	11.90	2.82	25.31	5.94
Lebanon	0.89	3.3	1.20	3.70	3.7	3.90	3.40	6.91	3.37	4.15
Libya	1.20	5.1	1.73	1.62	5.9	3.44	19	2.36	24.38	6.19
Morocco	2.60	3.9	2.90	5.17	6	3.17	9.50	9.64	25.36	5.28
Oman	—	—	0.16	—	—	—	2.55	26.98	8.40	16.55
Qatar	—	—	—	—	—	—	1	6.10	7.05	13.25
Saudi Arabia	1.52	8.6	2.40	13.40	12	52.90	64.20	22.09	87.97	36.22
Sudan	1.35	4.4	1.63	3.30	2.8	3.46	6.15	3.97	11.03	4.18
Syria	1.08	8.8	1.35	10.20	2.9	23.03	7.10	28.73	17.41	9.30
Tunisia	0.88	1.6	0.94	1.50	3.6	1.56	5.83	2.49	12.42	3.23
Turkey	8.78	5	10.60	4.45	31.9	6.82	45.30	5.72	80.93	2.59
United Arab Emirates	—	—	0.49	—	—	—	12	6.25	33.67	7.69
Yemen, North	—	—	0.52	2.70	—	—	1.50	5.27	7.98	12.53
Yemen, South	—	—	0.23	14.60	0.5	5.20	0.50	11.20	—	—

Sources: J. C. Hurewitz, *Middle East Politics: The Military Dimension* (1969); T. N. Dupuy, *The Almanac of World Military Power* (1970); and publications of the International Institute for Strategic Studies.

partially accounts for the increase in Egypt's level from 0.35 percent in 1955 to 0.61 percent in 1965. Conflicts among nations in the Middle East also tend to drive up force levels. This can be seen not only in the figures for Israel and its immediate neighbors but also for Iran and Iraq. After the fall of the shah in 1979, and before the long war between Iraq and Iran and the Gulf War of 1990–1991, the force levels for Iraq increased dramatically. Finally, the potential for conflict outside the Middle East has an impact on force levels. Turkey, as part of NATO and with commitments to that alliance in the Cold War, has maintained relatively high force levels. The conflict with Greece over Cyprus also had an impact on the force levels of the Turkish military. The end of the Cold War, however, may allow Turkey to reduce the percentage of its population in the military.

The tables on force structure and defense equipment reflect modernization of the military in the Middle East, as well as its projected role (see Tables 3 and 4). With the exception of Turkey, naval forces are modest. Turkey's commitment to NATO has resulted in the largest navy in the area by far, not only in the number of ships but in their size. Egypt, Israel, and Libya have large numbers of naval vessels, but most of these are small and include patrol craft, which are more defensive than offensive. Most area nations rely on ground and air forces. For example, Israel in 1991 had 104,000 active army, 28,000 active air force, and only 9,000 active navy; Syria's figures were 300,000, 40,000, and 4,000, respectively. The equipment of the ground and air forces reflects modern force structures. Ground forces are heavily mechanized, as the figures for heavy and medium tanks show. Accompanying these tanks are large numbers of tracked armored personnel carriers for mechanized infantry, tracked artillery pieces, and modern rocket artillery. Most of this is imported, but an increasing amount is available from local industries. The Israelis have displayed ingenuity in weapons development with the Merkava main battle tank; reactive armor; small-arms weaponry, such as the Uzi submachine gun and Galil assault rifle; and a purported nuclear capability. Other nations have vigorous programs, as shown by the Iraqi attempt to develop an ultra-long-range artillery tube, the attempt to develop a nuclear capability aborted by the Israelis, development of chemical weapons for the war with Iran, and a biological-weapons program.

The Middle East has developed a modern and lethal military capability to wage war on the ground, including sophisticated air-defense forces. Matching this modern capability to wage war on the ground is an equally modern air capability. Many Middle Eastern air forces have fielded the latest American and Soviet aircraft and avionics, all of which are capable of destroying opposing aircraft and supporting ground forces.

Conflicts. The conflicts in which Middle Eastern military forces have been involved include internal security missions, revolutions, coups d'état, wars between area nations, and wars with forces from outside the area.

All Middle Eastern countries have police forces dedicated to internal security. Civil strife, however, has often overwhelmed the police forces of many nations. In such cases, the military has assisted in maintaining internal security. Success has been mixed. In Lebanon, the military has usually failed to achieve domestic peace. This has led to the creation of militias by sectarian rivals with the roles of maintaining order in their areas, fighting other groups, and ensuring that the central government remains too weak to impose order through police powers or military force. The Israel and Syrian militaries have also assumed a role in maintaining internal security in parts of Lebanon with mixed results.

The Kurds in Turkey, Iran, and Iraq have presented internal security problems, resulting in the use of the military to restore order. Turkey and Iran have usually been able to achieve a modicum of order through normal police powers and occasional use of the military. Iraq, by the mid-1970s, had also restored order through military force, but this broke down during the war with Iran and again after Desert Storm.

Israel has had to resort to military force for internal security, not within Israel proper, but in the occupied territories. Military force has been used against Arabs in the territories but may also have to be used to control Jewish militants who oppose giving up any territory to Arab authorities.

Other Middle Eastern states have had similar experiences with the use of the military for internal security. A strong central government, such as in Israel, Turkey, and Iraq, at times leads to a level of internal violence that can be handled through police powers, with the military called on for special problems, such as the Kurds or Arabs in occupied territories. A weak central government can lead to a total breakdown of civil order, such as in Lebanon, and a military so weakened that it cannot restore order. In the case of Iraq, a weakened central government like that after Desert Storm resulted in total reliance on the military for internal security with success dependent on the strength of dissident movements and any external assistance they obtain.

Participation in revolutions and coups d'état is one way in which the Middle Eastern military differs from those of Europe and North America, at least since World War II. Even in Israel, the state was-

TABLE 3

Force Structure: Active and Reserve Troops in Thousands

Country	1969 Army Active	1969 Army Reserves	1969 Air Force Active	1969 Air Force Reserves	1969 Navy Active	1969 Navy Reserves	1975 Army Active	1975 Army Reserves	1975 Air Force Active	1975 Air Force Reserves	1975 Navy Active	1975 Navy Reserves	1979 Army Active	1979 Army Reserves	1979 Air Force Active	1979 Air Force Reserves	1979 Navy Active	1979 Navy Reserves	1991 Army Active	1991 Army Reserves	1991 Air Force Active	1991 Air Force Reserves	1991 Navy Active	1991 Navy Reserves
Afghanistan	84	200	5	—	—	—	80	150	8	12	—	—	80	150	10	12	—	—	40	—	5	—	—	—
Algeria	55	100	2	—	1.5	—	55	50	4.5	—	3.5	—	7.8	100	7	—	3.8	—	107	150	12	—	6.5	—
Bahrain	—	—	—	—	—	—	—	—	—	—	—	—	2.3	—	—	—	0.2	—	6	—	0.45	—	1	14
Egypt	180	70	20	4	12	5	275	500	30	20	17.5	15	350	500	25	—	20	15	290	500	30	20	20	—
Iran	175	—	15	—	6	—	175	300	60	—	15	—	285	300	100	—	30	—	305	350	35	—	18	—
Iraq	70	—	10	—	2	—	120	250	12	—	3	—	190	250	28	—	4	—	350	—	30	—	2.5	—
Israel	60	200	8	6	3	3	135	240	16	4	4	2	138	237	21	6	6.6	3.4	104	494	28	9	9	—
Jordan	55	35	0.2	—	0.25	—	75	30	5	—	0.25	—	60	30	7	—	0.2	—	90	30	11	—	0.3	—
Kuwait	4.5	2.5	0.5	—	0.035	—	8	—	2	—	0.2	—	9	—	1.9	—	0.2	—	7	—	1	—	0.2	—
Lebanon	11	—	0.8	—	0.20	—	14	—	1	—	0.3	—	8	—	0.5	—	0.25	—	17.5	—	0.8	—	0.5	—
Libya	6	—	0.8	—	0.20	—	25	—	5	—	2	—	35	—	4	—	3	—	55	40	22	—	8	—
Morocco	50	—	3	—	1	—	55	—	4	—	2	—	90	—	6	—	2	—	175	100	13.5	—	7	—
Oman	2.8	—	—	—	—	—	12.9	—	1	—	0.2	—	16.2	3.3	2.1	—	0.9	—	20	4	3	—	3.4	—
Qatar	—	—	—	—	—	—	—	—	—	—	—	—	4	—	0.3	—	0.4	—	6	—	0.8	—	0.7	—
Saudi Arabia	30	20	5	—	1	—	40	16	5.5	—	1.5	—	35	20	8	—	1.5	—	45	55	18	—	9.5	—
Sudan	24	—	0.5	—	0.50	—	45	3.5	3	—	0.6	—	60	3.5	1.5	—	1.4	—	65	—	6	—	0.5	—
Syria	50	40	9	—	1.5	—	150	100	25	—	2.5	2.5	200	100	25	—	2.5	2.5	300	392	40	—	4	8
Tunisia	17	—	0.5	—	0.50	—	20	9	2	—	2	—	18	2.5	1.7	—	2.6	—	27	—	3.5	—	4.5	—
Turkey	425	500	5	—	39	70	365	750	48	—	40	25	470	400	51	—	45	25	—	—	—	—	—	—
United Arab Emirates	6	—	—	—	—	—	—	—	—	—	—	—	23.5	—	0.75	—	0.9	—	40	—	2.5	—	1.5	—
Yemen, North	10	20	—	—	—	—	30	20	1.7	—	0.3	—	35	20	1	—	0.6	—	60	40	2	—	3	—
Yemen, South	10	—	0.35	—	0.15	—	15.2	—	2.5	—	0.3	—	19	—	1.3	—	0.5	—	—	—	—	—	—	—

Sources: T. N. Dupuy, *The Almanac of World Miliary Power* (1970); and publications of the International Institute for Strategic Studies.

TABLE 4

Defense Equipment

Country	1969			1975			1979			1991		
	Medium and Heavy Tanks	Combat Aircraft	Naval Vessels	Medium and Heavy Tanks	Combat Aircraft	Naval Vessels	Medium and Heavy Tanks	Combat Aircraft	Naval Vessels	Medium and Heavy Tanks	Combat Aircraft	Naval Vessels
Afghanistan	200	130	0	150	160	0	800	169	0	800	253	0
Algeria	400	150	25	400	186	26	500	260	47	960	241	35
Bahrain	—	—	—	—	—	—	—	—	11	81	24	13
Egypt	630	450	159	1,945	500	96	1.600	563	109	3,190	495	94
Iran	—	186	28	1,160	238	52	1,735	447	47	700	213	63
Iraq	535	213	30	1,290	247	29	1,800	339	49	2,300	261	13
Israel	975	295	32	2,700	461	66	3,050	576	63	4,488	591	120
Jordan	230	36	5	440	42	12	500	73	9	1,131	113	1
Kuwait	—	16	2	100	32	29	280	50	31	36	34	2
Lebanon	40	37	6	85	24	6	—	16	5	175	3	17
Libya	—	10	7	345	92	17	2,000	201	21	2,150	409	109
Morocco	130	46	6	145	60	5	140	72	19	284	90	34
Oman	—	12	1	—	47	6	—	35	18	82	57	17
Qatar	—	—	—	—	—	—	12	4	35	24	18	10
Saudi Arabia	18	44	23	175	95	4	350	178	134	700	253	43
Sudan	—	35	4	130	43	15	160	36	18	230	51	4
Syria	400	150	30	2,100	400	16	3,600	389	26	4,350	651	42
Tunisia	0	14	8	30	24	18	30	14	22	84	53	21
Turkey	—	520	202	1,500	292	183	3,500	303	187	3,783	530	152
United Arab Emirates	—	—	3	—	—	—	0	52	9	131	100	21
Yemen, North	30	24	—	30	12	5	232	11	10	1,275	101	39
Yemen, South	—	18	3	50	27	9	260	109	16	—	—	—

Sources: T. N. Dupuy, *The Almanac of World Military Power* (1960); and publications of the International Institute for Strategic Studies.

established in 1948 through the use of military and paramilitary force. Iran has faced two changes of power since World War II—the temporary assumption of power by Mossadegh in the early 1950s and the overthrow of the shah in 1979—but the military did not play a major role in either. In Lebanon, the central government has never been strong enough to develop a powerful military, and no revolt by a government military has been feasible. Saudi Arabia, the Arab Gulf states, Jordan, and Morocco are all monarchies that have shown remarkable stability in a tumultuous area, and none has faced a serious political threat from its military. The use of tribal levies loyal to the monarch to form large parts of the military may explain this. Tunisia, also, has not faced a military revolt, though its president, Habib Bourguiba,

was deposed by a general serving as prime minister in 1987. Presumably, the military approved.

The experience of other Middle Eastern states has been different. Turkey, long viewed as a paragon of stability in the area, has had three military coups since World War II in 1960, 1971, and 1980. In all three cases, however, power was eventually returned to civilian politicians. Elsewhere, military coups have resulted in governments run by military leaders, some retaining their uniforms, some shedding them for civilian garb but still relying on the military for their power. King Farouk of Egypt was overthrown in 1952 by a group of military officers led by Gamal Abdel Nasser. Since that time, Egypt has been ruled by a succession of military officers: Nasser, Sadat, and Mubarak. Algeria achieved independence from

France through military revolt in 1962, and the Algerian military has played a primary role in governing the nation since that time. In 1965, led by Colonel Boumédienne, it overthrew the government of Ben Bella and in 1991 obtained the resignation of President Benjedid after elections appeared to presage a turn to Islamic fundamentalism. Syria, Iraq, and Libya have all had similar experiences with their militaries taking control of the government.

Violence between countries is not uncommon in the Middle East. The Israeli declaration of independence in May 1948 was quickly followed by the invasion of Palestine by armies from Egypt, Jordan, Syria, and Iraq, with volunteers from elsewhere. These were repulsed by an Israeli military that was at the time, and has been since, underrated in terms of numbers and equipment. Since 1948, there has been a succession of wars between Israel and its Arab neighbors. The first, in 1956, was fought in collusion with two aging empires—Britain and France—and resulted in a quasi-blitzkrieg campaign in the Sinai by Israel. The United States negated the gains of that war, harbinging the pattern that became common in conflict in the Middle East for decades. No local government or its military would be able to act without seriously considering how its actions would be viewed by the great powers. But this did not prevent continued conflict. The Six-Day War of 1967 followed the Sinai campaign of 1956 with dramatic gains by Israel. The use of the surprise attack and the tempo of the war may be partially explained by the Israeli assessment of the reaction of the great powers.

After 1967, Israeli military successes were not nearly so spectacular. Caught by surprise in the October War of 1973, the Israelis fell victim to their success in 1967. Ignoring some of the lessons of combined-arms warfare that led to a quick victory in the earlier war, particularly the need for infantry support of armor and the critical role artillery plays, Israel was eventually able to repulse the Egyptians and Syrians. The humbling of the Israeli military and the aura of Arab success led to a peace treaty between Israel and Egypt. The lesson might be that a military force does not have to win to achieve political success, but the problem is how to engineer a loss that leads to success. The experience of Israel in Lebanon in the 1982 Peace for Galilee campaign is also instructive. Israel had not faced a military coup since its establishment, but the role of Defense Minister Ariel Sharon in this operation came close to such a coup. Sharon directed operations far beyond those envisioned but was restrained by both international and national pressures. Given the potential power of the Israeli right, a Sharon of the 1990s might be a threat to the Israeli government, much like the majors and

colonels who have overthrown numerous Arab governments since World War II.

Arab–Israel wars captured headlines, but these were not the only wars between nations in the Middle East. There have been several mini-wars, mostly border skirmishes between Egypt and Libya, Syria and Jordan, Morocco and the former Spanish Sahara, and others. In the 1960s, Egypt became involved in a protracted campaign in Yemen in support of the revolutionary regime against the royal counterrevolution. This involved thousands of troops, the use of chemical weapons, and the weakening of the Egyptian military to the point that it could not cope with the Israeli surprise attack in June 1967.

The most protracted conflict was that between Iraq and Iran from 1980 to 1988. The causes of this war included disputes over the border between Iran and Iraq, exploitation of minority and sectarian unrest, particularly among the Kurds and Shi'ites, and the question of which nation would be the primary force in the Persian Gulf. The border dispute centered on the Shatt al-Arab and went back to Ottoman times. The Constantinople Agreement of 1915 gave Iran the right of navigation on the waterway but gave the Ottomans sovereignty over the entire waterway, including the east bank. A 1937 treaty revised this and set the border at the thalweg, or main channel, for most of the way, with Iran having control of the Shatt al-Arab for a few miles around Khorramshahr. By 1974, Iranian support for Iraqi Kurds had made them such a threat to the state that Iraq agreed to the 1975 Algiers Accord in return for cessation of Iranian aid to the rebels. This made the thalweg the border for the entire length of the Shatt al-Arab, essentially making the waterway international.

The fall of the shah in 1979 gave Iraq a window of opportunity to assert primacy in the Gulf. This, the threat of the expansion of Iran's Islamic revolution, and continued subversion of dissident groups in each country led to escalation of fighting along the border, and, on 17 September 1980, Iraq's declaration that the Shatt al-Arab was totally Iraqi. The eight-year war that followed was costly. The cost to Iran was about $206 billion, while Iraqi costs were around $147 billion. Firm casualty figures may never be established, but Iranian casualties are estimated at between one million and two million, Iraqi casualties between one-half million and one million. Of these, the number of dead ranges from 450,000 to 730,000 for Iran and 150,000 to 340,000 for Iraq. The failure of both sides to force a decision may have been as much political as ideological in nature. In both countries, loyalty to the regime is a valued commodity for the leadership, and promotion in the military is as much a factor of loyalty as of military skill. In Iran, the fall of the shah was followed by a decimation of the officer corps and a reliance on religious fanaticism that led to mass attacks by poorly trained soldiers and militia with horrendous casualties. Finally, the war was controlled from Baghdad and Tehran with relatively little freedom of action for the commanders on the scene. It may be that victory was associated with a higher level of discretion by local commanders and defeat with strategic and tactical decisions made by the political or ideological leadership in the capitals.

The high costs of the war, and the failure of either side to win a decisive victory in spite of the extensive use of chemical weapons, led to the cease-fire of 8 August 1988, brokered by the United Nations with heavy pressure from the United States, European nations, and Iraq's Arab neighbors. Both sides set about rebuilding their military establishments, embarking on ambitious programs to increase their chemical-warfare potential and develop nuclear weapons. There were also efforts to improve artillery and missile-delivery capabilities to provide a more accurate means of projecting munitions.

It was not long before one side felt strong enough to again challenge its neighbors. Less than two years after the cease-fire between Iran and Iraq, on 2 August 1990, Iraq invaded Kuwait. The conflict between these two nations has a long history. Although Kuwait has been governed by the Saba family since the eighteenth century and was a British protectorate after 1899, it was part of the Ottoman Empire. Iraq has on several occasions claimed Kuwait as a province based on governmental relationships during Ottoman times. That Iraq has such a short shoreline on the Persian Gulf provides a geostrategic motive for making this argument. Kuwait's oil reserves are also attractive, and Kuwait actually provided substantial financial aid to Iraq during the war with Iran. This was a major cause of the 1990 conflict, as Iraq was demanding relief from its debts to Kuwait. This, plus the claim that Kuwait was tapping into Iraqi oil fields, led to the invasion. Within hours, an Iraqi force that eventually numbered 140,000 with 1,800 tanks dispatched a Kuwaiti military of 16,000 troops and occupied the nation.

The world responded with the first of a series of actions that led to war in 1991. The day the invasion began, the UN Security Council passed Resolution 660 condemning the invasion and demanding withdrawal of Iraqi troops. Discounting the possibility of any military reaction to the invasion, Iraq refused to withdraw. This miscalculation proved disastrous.

Iraq began the invasion able to field an army of one million, seasoned by eight hard years of fighting with Iran. By the beginning of the ground war in February 1991, about 250,000 troops were in the Kuwaiti theater of operations. These were backed by 4,000 tanks, 3,000 pieces of artillery, and 3,000 armored personnel carriers. Iraq also had SCUD missiles capable of reaching Israel and chemical-warfare capability. The Iraqi navy, however, was negligible, and the air force, though sizable, was not a factor after substantial numbers of American aircraft arrived in the area.

Iraq's potential enemies were not well situated in August 1990. Kuwait's ability to fight had been destroyed. Iran continued to be exhausted from its earlier war, and Iraq quickly took diplomatic measures to ensure Tehran would not interfere. Saudi Arabia, viewed by many as Iraq's next target, had a force of only 70,000 troops, 550 tanks, and 850 artillery pieces, far smaller than the force Iraq had. The Saudis did have a credible air-defense capability and 155 F-15 and F-5 fighter aircraft. The other Arab Gulf states had some forces but not nearly enough to match those of Iraq. Syria was a potential problem but not in the immediate area. Without outside intervention, Iraq had every expectation of retaining Kuwait and possibly threatening Saudi Arabia and other Arab Gulf states.

Contrary to what Iraq expected, the building of that outside force began within hours of the invasion. Iraq was isolated under the umbrella of UN resolutions; most of the Arab world began discussions on how to oppose the Iraqi aggression; and the United States decided to implement Plan 1002-90, designed to defend Saudi Arabia. On the day of the invasion, orders went out to prepare for implementing the plan, and on 6 August, the first deployment was issued. Within a week, the United States deployed 122 F-15s and F-16s to augment the air cover available to the Saudis. By the middle of September, almost seven hundred aircraft were in place. Operation Desert Shield was under way.

As the weeks rolled by, the United States, operating under the authority of the United Nations, set about building a coalition force to defend Saudi Arabia and expel Iraq from Kuwait. By January 1991, the coalition force included contingents from the Arab Gulf states, Egypt, Syria, the United States, and several European countries, including some from the old Warsaw Pact bloc. The numbers deployed were impressive—almost 800,000. Still, Iraq refused to budge.

The transition from Operation Desert Shield to Operation Desert Storm began on 16 January at 7:00 P.M., Washington time (3:00 A.M., 17 January in Iraq). The war began with an intensive air campaign of four phases. The first aimed at achieving air superiority and crippling Iraq's command and control systems. Following this was a shift of targeting closer to

Kuwait to destroy Iraqi forces. The third phase suppressed air-defense systems in Kuwait. Finally, air power focused on strategic targets and the Iraqi military. The goal was to force Iraq to sue for peace or, if that failed, to so debilitate its ability to fight that an invasion by ground would not be costly.

The land war began on 24 February and lasted only one hundred hours. The success of the air campaign may be seen in the numbers of tanks, armored vehicles, and artillery pieces remaining on 24 February. Of an estimated 4,280 tanks, 1,772 were out of operation. Iraq had only 53 percent of its prewar artillery and just 67 percent of its armored vehicles. The ground campaign was even more brutal. Total Iraqi losses in January and February were 3,847 tanks, 1,450 armored vehicles, and 2,917 artillery pieces. Although there are no firm numbers on Iraqi casualties and the original estimates of 100,000 killed were exaggerated, a total of 35,000 is not unlikely. This compares to 240 deaths for coalition forces.

It is too early to assess the impact of Operations Desert Shield and Desert Storm on the military in the Middle East. Arab nations have been notably weak in coalition warfare, as shown by the wars with Israel. The successes in 1990 and 1991 under the tutelage of the United States may help overcome this weakness. The experience of war should enhance the readiness of the nations involved as their military now know that they can not only fight, but do so successfully. As with Egypt after 1973, this may instill a confidence that will allow for some risks in making peace. As a minimum, the Middle Eastern countries now have a noncommissioned-officer corps and an officer corps with extensive practical experience that can be transmitted to younger soldiers. Finally, the status of the military, especially the mechanized ground forces and the air forces, should be enhanced. As these are the most modern components of the forces, this may result in a more favorable view of modernization in Arab nations. If the prospects for peace in the area improve and the numbers in the military decrease, then more military personnel with this modern experience will return to civilian life.

In addition to internal conflicts and wars among area nations, the military in the Middle East have also been involved in conflicts with and among the great powers. In some cases, the local military has had to repulse the incursions of the great powers. This was generally not successful, but there are notable exceptions. The Afghans were formidable foes of the British in the nineteenth century and of the Soviets after 1979. Such success enhanced the status of those under arms and led to greater participation of the military in political decision making. The numerous conflicts in which the Ottoman Empire was involved

until the end of World War I led to the increasing power of the military in political life and effective control of the government by such military leaders as Enver Paşa. This pattern continued after World War I as political leadership in the Middle East often devolved on military heroes. During both world wars, the military in the Middle East gained a great deal of experience. Many Arabs remained loyal to the Ottoman Empire and fought in its armies, while others joined forces with Britain against the Turks. French North African divisions fought in the trenches of the western front in World War I. Other European nations had levies of colonial troops in both world wars, and Jews from Palestine served with the Jewish Mule Corps at Gallipoli in World War I and with the Jewish Brigade in Italy in World War II. The experiences of these veterans were critical to the revolutionary movements that ousted Europeans from the Middle East after World War II, and many assumed leadership roles in the new governments.

The Role of the Military. Because of the level of conflict in the Middle East, the role of the military looms large. This is because large portions of the population and much of the national wealth are devoted to military establishments. One way of understanding the Middle Eastern military is in terms of the homogeneity or heterogeneity of the state. In a homogeneous state, such as Egypt, the military serves as a mechanism of upward mobility for the lower-middle classes, as seen in the careers of Nasser and Sadat. In a heterogeneous state, such as Iraq or Syria, the military serves as the means for a minority, such as the Syrian Alawites or Iraqi Sunnis, to achieve power.

Much as been made of the notion of the military as the school of the nation. The military has been increasingly a modern segment of Middle Eastern society, and many believe that that modernization carries over into societies in general. This may be true, but it should not be exaggerated. As the military becomes more career oriented, fewer officers return to civilian life to influence society through their modern skills. Enlisted personnel may learn to operate sophisticated equipment, but if they do not have such devices when they return to their villages, that skill may be of little use. The experience of Israel as a diverse society is instructive. That state was created by peoples from all over the world, who spoke different languages. From 1948 on, their common experience was in the Israeli military where they learned a common language and shared a common experience in training and fighting for the continued existence of their nation. This model could be instructive for other Middle Eastern nations with diverse populations. Whether it is, however, will depend on internal developments within the societies of the Arab, Turkish, and Iranian nations of the area. Whether it will continue to be the pattern in Israel is also questionable. In recent years, Israel has incorporated a large number of graduates from religious Zionist military academies into its military establishment. Not sharing the common experience of other Israelis in the military, these recruits may cause the military to become less of a school of the nation than it traditionally has been.

The Future. What does the future hold for the role of the military in the Middle East? As long as there is internal and international strife in the area, the military will continue to play a large role. National resources will be devoted to military affairs, and a large number of the populations will serve. There will be economic and technological spin-offs, sometimes beneficial, but usually not. The experience of Desert Storm may result in a level of confidence in the Middle East that allows for more dependence on international guarantees for peace than has previously been the case. The end of the Cold War, however, may provide more hope for eventual stability in this volatile area. Without this irritant, there may be a chance for a decrease in the level of conflict. If this returns more people trained in modern and Western ways to the civilian sector, it may have a long-term benefit.

BIBLIOGRAPHY

The entry on the Middle East in *A Dictionary of Military History and the Art of War,* edited by ANDRÉ CORVISIER and JOHN CHILDS (1994), provides a brief introduction to the subject with references to related topics in the dictionary and a short reading list. For a much more detailed discussion, see *The Military in the Middle East,* edited by S. N. FISHER (1963), and J. C. HUREWITZ's *Middle East Politics: The Military Dimension* (1969). The latter contains a useful bibliographical note that critiques the sources available to 1969. E. BE'ERI has an excellent account of the role of the military in Arab society in his *Army Officers in Arab Politics and Society* (1970), which also has a short but good bibliography. *Security in the Middle East: Regional Change and Great Power Strategies,* edited by S. F. WELLS and M. BRUZONSKY, provides a more recent exploration of the topic. A heavily illustrated, popular account of military conflicts from 1948 through Desert Storm can be found in J. N. WESTWOOD's *The History of the Middle East Wars* (1991).

The Arab–Israeli conflict has spawned a mass of literature. The primary source for this is CHAIM HERZOG's *The Arab–Israeli Wars: War and Peace in the Middle East from the War of Independence through Lebanon* (1982). For general background see M. J. COHEN's *The Origins and Evolution of the Arab–Zionist Conflict* (1987), and R. OVENDALE's *The Origins of the Arab–Israeli Wars* (1984). The

Arab–Israeli Conflict: Two Decades of Change, edited by Y. LUKACS and A. M. BATTAH (1988), has a number of good articles on the conflict. *The Arab–Israeli Wars, the Chinese Civil War, and the Korean War,* edited by T. E. GRIESS (1987) provides a short account of the conflict, and his *Atlas for the Arab–Israeli Wars, the Chinese Civil War, and the Korean War* (1986) contains thirteen useful maps on this conflict; both books are part of the *West Point Military History Series.* MARTIN GILBERT has over one hundred maps in his *Atlas of the Arab–Israeli Conflict* (1974).

There are many books on the wars between Israel and its Arab neighbors. For the 1948 war, see journalist DAN KURZMAN's *Genesis 1948: The First Arab–Israeli War* (1970), a readable narrative with a good bibliography. M. LARKIN has a detailed account of one of the critical battles of that war in *The Six Days of Yad-Mordechai* (1963). For the 1956 Suez War, see MOSHE DAYAN's *Diary of the Sinai Campaign* (1965), S. L. A. MARSHALL's *Sinai Victory* (1958), T. ROBERTSON's *Crisis: The Inside Story of the Suez Conspiracy* (1964), H. THOMAS's *Suez* (1966), and S. I. TROEN and M. SHEMESH's *The Suez–Sinai Crisis, 1956: Retrospective and Reappraisal* (1990). For the Six Day War of 1967, see D. KIMCHE and D. BAWLY's *The Six-Day War: Prologue and Aftermath* (1968), and R. MACLEISH's *The Sun Stood Still: Israel and the Arabs at War* (1967). Y. B. SIMAN-TOV has a good account of the 1969–1970 War of Attrition along the Suez Canal in *The Israeli–Egyptian War of Attrition, 1969–1970* (1980). For the October 1973 War, see J. ASHER and E. HAMMEL's *Dual for the Golan: The 100-Hour Battle that Saved Israel* (1987) and E. O'BALLANCE's *No Victor, No Vanquished* (1978). Z. SCHIFF and E. YA'ARI have an excellent account of the Lebanon War of 1982 in *Israel's Lebanon War* (1984). Works on the Israeli military include N. LORCH's *Shield of Zion: The Israeli Defense Forces* (1991), a well-illustrated, popular account with an introduction by Yitzhak Rabin, and Z. SCHIFF's *A History of the Israeli Army: 1874 to the Present* (1985), a definitive work.

There have been many other conflicts in the Middle East since World War II that have led to war. D. A. SCHMIDT describes Egypt's involvement in Yemen in the 1960s in *Yemen: The Unknown War* (1968). S. KHALAF discusses Lebanon in *Lebanon's Predicament* (1987). A. H. CORDESMAN and W. R. WAGNER cover Soviet involvement in Afghanistan in *The Afghan and Falklands Conflicts,* vol. 3 of *The Lessons of Modern War* (1990). T. C. WIEGELE discusses Libya's attempt to build chemical-warfare capability in *The Clandestine Building of Libya's Chemical Weapons Factory: A Study in International Collusion* (1992). The Iran–Iraq War of 1980 to 1988 and the ongoing conflict between these two nations can be studied in J. M. ABDULGHANI's *Iraq and Iran: The Years of Crisis* (1984); A. H. CORDESMAN's *Iran & Iraq: The Threat from the Northern Gulf* (1994); A. H. CORDESMAN and A. R. WAGNER's *Iran–Iraq War,* vol. 2 of *The Lessons of Modern War* (1990); *The Iran–Iraq War: Impact and Implications,* edited by E. KARSH (1989); and S. T.

PELLETIERE et al., *Iraqi Power and U.S. Security in the Middle East* (1990). For the Persian Gulf War, see L. FREEDMAN and E. KARSH's *The Gulf Conflict, 1990–1991: Diplomacy and War in the New World Order* (1993), which contains a recent evaluation of casualty figures; N. FRIEDMAN's *Desert Victory: The War for Kuwait* (1991); R. H. SCALES, JR., et al., *Certain Victory: The U.S. Army in the Gulf War* (1993); H. N. SCHWARZ-KOPF's *It Doesn't Take a Hero* (1992); *The Gulf War Reader: History, Documents, Opinions,* edited by M. L. SIFRY and C. CERF (1991); and B. W. WATSON et al., *Military Lessons of the Gulf War* (1991).

In addition to the literature on the military in the Middle East, there are also works that address the peace process and its prospects. W. B. QUANDT has authored and edited volumes on peacemaking in the Arab–Israel conflict: *The Middle East: Ten Years after Camp David* (1988) and *Peace Process: American Diplomacy and the Arab–Israeli Conflict since 1967* (1993). Also of interest are S. D. BAILEY's *Four Arab–Israeli Wars and the Peace Process* (1990); *Arms Control and Confidence Building in the Middle East,* edited by A. PLATT (1992); and J. L. RASMUS-SEN and R. B. OAKLEY's *Conflict Resolution in the Middle East: Simulating a Diplomatic Negotiation between Israel and Syria* (1992).

Daniel E. Spector

Millet System

The term commonly used to describe the institutional framework governing relations between the Ottoman state and its large and varied non-Muslim population.

Although recent research has challenged both the systemic quality and the traditional origins of the arrangements under the millet system, the term, for want of a better one, remains in use. According to the traditional accounts, the Ottoman sultan, Mehmed II, upon his conquest of Constantinople (now Istanbul) in 1453, granted extensive autonomy to the Greek, Jewish, and Armenian millets—that is, religiously defined communities of the empire—through, respectively, Gennadios Scholarios, the then-reigning patriarch of the Greek Orthodox church in the capital; Moses Capsali, a leading rabbi; and Joachim, a bishop of the Armenian church. They and their successors thereby became titular heads of their coreligionists throughout the land. The traditional accounts, furthermore, claim that the state did not deal with Christians and Jews as individuals, but only as members of their respective communities. Correspondingly, non-Muslims dealt with the state only through the titular heads of their community. Lastly, in matters of taxation—specifically the JIZYA, the poll tax required of non-Muslim heads of household—once the state determined the amount, its ap-portionment between individuals was left to the community leader, who supervised its collection and was responsible for its payment. Subsequent research has challenged these claims by noting that they are in no way confirmed by contemporary Ottoman sources and that the non-Muslim chronicles on which they were based were compiled centuries after the events they claim to describe.

What the traditional story does accurately repre-sent, however, is the Ottomans' relative indifference to (and to that degree, tolerance of) much of the ac-tivities of their non-Muslim subjects before the nine-teenth century. They allowed them much autonomy, particularly in matters of religious observance, edu-cation, and personal status (birth, marriage, death and inheritance). The sphere of internal communal con-trol, however, was far more limited than that claimed by the traditional accounts, and the opportunities for direct contact between the individual non-Muslim and the Ottoman Muslim state and society were far greater, extending even into the realm of personal sta-tus. Thus recent research in Ottoman records has re-vealed that Christians and Jews regularly had recourse to Muslim courts, in addition to their own courts, even in questions of divorce, inheritance, and other supposedly internal communal matters. Furthermore, the claim by the traditional accounts of hierarchical centralization under the patriarch or chief rabbi in Constantinople is contradicted by the abundant evi-dence of local arrangements, often under lay control, and often independent of the capital, as well as by the differing structural traditions of each community. Jewish communal organization, unlike that of the Or-thodox church, was not pyramidal, and even the Or-thodox patriarch of Constantinople (unlike the bishop of Rome) was merely first among equals. As for the Armenian church, it had long been divided by competing centers of hierarchical authority. Certainly no empirewide fiscal administrative systems existed under the control of the so-called millets, and the term itself was not consistently used to designate the communities. Thus in the classical age of Ottoman rule, during the sixteenth and seventeenth centuries, there were neither millets nor a millet system, al-though there was a considerable, but by no means ab-solute, degree of local communal autonomy. In this age, from time to time the clerical leaders in Con-stantinople did assert claims of empirewide authority, but they were rarely successful.

This complex Ottoman practice was by no means an innovation but reflected ancient Near Eastern and Islamic administrative practices (DHIMMI), as well as contemporary reality and communal traditions. In the aftermath of war, conquest, and dynastic turmoil, religious institutions often were the only institutions to survive. Individuals were most comfortable identifying and organizing themselves according to religion, so the state, even a new one, had no interest in defying them.

The situation began to change, however, late in the seventeenth century. The Ottoman state's indifference to its non-Muslim subjects diminished when the great powers made their status a stick with which to beat the Turks. As the empire became weaker, European rivals started to vigorously push claims for the protection of the rights and privileges of their coreligionists and other non-Muslims. The Hapsburgs protected the Catholics, particularly those strategically located in what is now Slovenia and Croatia. More aggressive were the Romanovs, who laid claim to the huge Orthodox population conveniently concentrated in provinces adjacent to Russia's frontier. The French asserted an interest in the welfare of the Catholics of the Levant, particularly those in Syria and Lebanon. The British, who had few coreligionists in the region, opposed the claims of their rivals while they protected the few Protestants there and, at times, the Jews. The process of protection was often the first stage of invasion and territorial annexation. The Ottomans proved too weak on the battlefield to confront these challenges directly, and so they were forced to respond with diplomatic maneuverings, administrative accommodation, and, ultimately, commitments to reform. This program for reform in the nineteenth century (the TANZIMAT) formally defined and, to a large degree, created the millet system, as it has conventionally come to be understood. For the first time, an attempt was made to impose uniform administrative systems upon all non-Muslim communities throughout the empire. The attempt was consistent with a guiding element of the Tanzimat, the drive toward centralization of all spheres of governance.

The creation of the formal millet system and the consequent abandonment of local autonomy, noninterference, and flexibility, which were the hallmarks of the traditional nonsystem, forced the communities themselves and the Ottoman government to become increasingly embroiled in religious-diplomatic entanglements, which in turn were resolved by the creation of yet more millets. The religious imperialism of Catholic and Protestant missions, which sought to win souls from the indigenous Orthodox and Monophysite churches, as well as other, smaller, churches of the East, complicated the process further. Since these missions were fully supported by the Western powers (i.e., by France, the Hapsburgs, and Great Britain respectively), religious quarrels easily escalated into international crises. The pattern was repeated throughout the nineteenth century.

The Armenian community was the first to succumb to these difficulties. Catholic missions had been very successful in winning converts to Rome from among Monophysite Armenians. Accustomed to the formal hierarchical structure of the Roman church, Catholics repeatedly pressed to replace the traditional lack of system in the relations between Muslims and non-Muslims with a formalized set of institutions. During the late 1820s, they got their opportunity when the Ottomans, desperately in need of foreign support with which to resist the Greek revolt and a Russian invasion, acceded to French pressure to improve the conditions of these converts by establishing a Catholic millet, which was formally recognized in 1831. Since the Ottoman and Roman criteria and procedures for selecting the head of the millet were at odds, however, the millet itself became a source of tension. Furthermore, many important communities within the Ottoman Empire that supposedly came under the jurisdiction of this new institution—notably the wealthy Armenian Catholics of Aleppo, the influential Melkite Catholics (converts from Eastern Orthodoxy), and the numerous Maronites of Mount Lebanon—either resented or ignored it. In 1848 the Melkites obtained their own millet status. In 1850 Protestants followed suit. Other millets were formed: the Bulgarian Uniates in 1861 and the Bulgarian exarchate in 1870. Despite the proliferation of these communal-religious structures, many of the oldest and most deeply rooted Christian churches in the East—the Copts (the indigenous Monophysite church in Egypt), the Jacobites (the indigenous Monophysite church in Syria), and the Nestorians (based in Iraq and southeastern Anatolia) never sought millet status.

The major communities of the empire—Greek Orthodox, Armenian Gregorian, and Jewish—never sought formal millet status in the nineteenth century, since by accepted tradition (the complex historical reality notwithstanding), they had always had it. The reforms of this era nevertheless had a drastic effect upon them as well. The most far-reaching effect derived from the Reform Decree of 1856, which laid the foundation for formal constitutional arrangements reducing the power of the clergy and increasing lay influence. Although Ottoman leaders sponsored these changes in the hope that they might lead to a greater, supracommunal sense of Ottoman patriotic loyalty, the result was often the opposite. Lay leaders, stirred to political activity by the new opportunities that the constitutions now offered, devoted their energies to agitation on behalf of their communities, which increasingly defined themselves as nation-states in the making.

BIBLIOGRAPHY

BRAUDE, BENJAMIN, and BERNARD LEWIS, eds. *Christians and Jews in the Ottoman Empire: The Functioning of a Plural Society*, 2 vols. New York, 1982.

DAVISON, RODERIC H. *Reform in the Ottoman Empire, 1856–1876*. Princeton, N.J., 1963.

Benjamin Braude

Milli Gorus

A term used for the political ideology and program of pro-Islamic political organizations in Turkey.

Milli Gorus, meaning National Outlook, has been used by organizations ranging from the National Order party and National Salvation party to the present-day Welfare party. Motivated by the tradition of criticizing Turkish modernization, this ideology brings together elements of anti-Westernism and economic development. Put differently, National Outlook combines ideas, making a sharp distinction between "culture" and "civilization" identified with "technology." According to this distinction, culture makes up the essence of a "nation" to be preserved against the changes brought about by technological advancement. (The Turkish word "milli," in total contrast to the secular "nation," refers to a shared communal identity defined exclusively on religion—in this case Islam.) For the proponents of this ideology, Turkish modernization as practiced especially after the founding of the republic amounted to what they viewed as a total submission of Islamic culture to Western (Christian) civilization. In opposition to political parties and movements of the establishments regarded by the advocates of National Outlook as member organizations of the "Westernists Club," there is an endeavor to formulate a new program, incorporating advanced technology with Islamic culture. Thus, in economy, National Outlook favors "heavy industrialization," a synonym for "nationally independent" (as opposed to dependent industry). A very important component of National Outlook is the idea of an Islamic "just order," a statist, centrally planned economic model that provides principles of redistribution vaguely drawn from Islamic notions of solidarity and secular notions of corporatism. In fact, a closer examination of this economic program uncovers a hostility toward market economy associated with capitalism (i.e., individualist materialism of the Christian West) favoring a kind of state socialism characteristic of third-world nationalism. As for education, some of the most important elements—like compulsory religious education in primary and secondary schools and a "na-

tional" education that will nurture an awareness of a glorious past history and superiority of Islamic conscience—have been effectively put into practice by the military governments of the early 1980s, ironically with the purpose of minimizing the appeal of "foreign" ideologies like socialism and communism to younger generations. A very important component in National Outlook pertains to the legal system that will enable the implementation of various principles of this program. This is the point where it becomes more explicit how this program stands in sharp contrast to the secular principles of the Turkish republic. Besides a proposed adjustment of economic laws to the requirements of Islamic "just order," the program includes a project to restructure the Turkish legal system on Islamic principles. The secular principle of "equality before the law," as it has been practiced since the first years of the republic, came to mean for Islamic fundamentalists a sign of "tyranny." According to this idea, Muslims should be treated as Muslims before the law and should never be subject to non-Islamic laws, i.e., to secular laws of the Turkish state adopted from the Christian West, like the Civil Code. Thus, some Islamic writers suggest a renewal of the Turkish legal system, enabling a recognition of religious differences. Drawing examples of a plurality of legal systems from the golden age of "Muhammad at Medina" and the "millet system" (a system based on relative autonomy of religious communities in conducting their internal private affairs) of the Ottomans, they claimed that this is a system based on the Islamic principle of "tolerance" and it is "authentic," unlike the "pseudo-democracy" of the West, exercised within the potentially totalitarian modern state. At this conjunction of legal and political issues, it seems quite evident that National Outlook is pursuing a total transformation of Turkish economy, society, and politics in harmony with the principles of Islamic *Shari'a*. The extent to which such a transformation is possible seems to depend upon the role of the Welfare party as the main agent of National Outlook and the capacity of Turkish political processes for the accommodation of a now "political" Islam.

Nermin Abadan-Unat

Milli İstihbarat Teşkilatı

The Turkish government's intelligence bureau, referred to as MIT.

MIT was organized in 1965, as the reformulation of the older National Security Organization of Turkey. At the time, its 4,000 personnel, linked directly to the prime minister, were to track conspiracies within the armed forces and among radical leftist groups. In later years, officials of the Turkish National Security Council sat on MIT's board.

In the 1970s, MIT was criticized for inefficient intelligence on urban guerrilla groups and for subversive infiltration of leftist and Kurdish groups. It did not inform the government, intentionally or out of ignorance, of secret meetings among generals before the 1980 coup. Officials blamed MIT's inefficiency on understaffing—it had only 390 officers in 1979—and a small budget (equivalent to about $30 million in 1983).

BIBLIOGRAPHY

AHMAD, FEROZ. *The Turkish Experiment in Democracy 1950–1975.* Boulder, Colo., 1977.
BIRAND, MEHMET ALI. *The Generals' Coup in Turkey.* New York, 1987.

Elizabeth Thompson

Milliyet

Daily newspaper in Turkey.

Milliyet (Nationality) is a liberal paper that distinguishes itself as a vehicle for news analysis and commentary. It publishes twenty-five political columnists and devotes much space to investigative stories. In the 1980s, for example, *Milliyet* was taken to court by the government of Turkey over the then-restricted coverage of the Kurds and their separatist movement. The paper also has a large pool of international correspondents and is a leader in sports coverage. *Milliyet,* with a circulation of 500,000, targets readers who are professionals, with at least some university education.

The newspaper was founded in 1950 by Ali Naci KARACAN, a former reporter and press attaché in Turkish embassies, who dubbed *Milliyet* the "People's Paper." Upon his death in 1955, his U.S.-educated son, Ercument, became publisher. In 1979, the son sold the paper to Aydın Doğan, following the assassination of his editor, Abdi İpekci, by a rightist terrorist.

In 1980, the Doğan Group was established, building a widely diversified investment and service organization on a large media base that included *Milliyet, Hürriyet* and *Spor* newspapers; various women's, teen, health, economic and news magazines; and some forays into radio and television.

Stephanie Capparell

Millo, Josef [1916–]

Israeli theater producer, director, and actor.

Born in Prague, during the Austro-Hungarian Empire, Millo emigrated to Palestine in 1921. He studied theater in Vienna and Prague and began his career at the satirical Ha-Matate theater in Palestine. He played a dominant role in the establishment of the CAMERI theater in Tel Aviv, which he directed until 1958. He founded Haifa's municipal theater in 1961 and Beersheba's in the 1970s. Millo has directed about one hundred plays in Israel and Europe, acting many of the leading roles.

Ann Kahn

Millspaugh, Arthur [1883–1955]

American political scientist.

Arthur Chester Millspaugh was born in Augusta, Michigan, March 1, 1883. He received degrees from Albion College in 1908, the University of Illinois in 1910, and Johns Hopkins University in 1916. After teaching political science at Johns Hopkins in 1917 and 1918, Millspaugh joined the U.S. State Department in 1918, serving as a petroleum specialist from 1920 to 1922. In 1922, he was appointed financial adviser to the Persian government, then dominated by Reza Khan Pahlavi (Reza Shah after 1925) and just after that government had annulled the Anglo–Persian Agreement and canceled all debts due to Russia. Millspaugh set about increasing revenues and affecting economies, improving the credit of the Persian government, and balancing the budget by requiring that the Majles (legislature) increase taxes when increasing expenditures. His measures, although initially supported by Reza Khan, met some opposition toward the end of his tenure in 1927. As his contract neared its end, the Persian government tried to reduce his authority by insisting that any difference between Millspaugh and the minister of finance would be referred to the Council of Ministers or the Majles. Millspaugh argued that his contract left it to the Majles to resolve any problems, a position the government refused to honor. At this point, the government decided to employ German and Swiss financial advisers whose powers were more limited. Millspaugh then went on to work with the government of Haiti with its financial problems and with the Brookings Institute. During World War II, he returned to Iran in 1942 as an economic adviser, virtually the country's economic czar. Iran had matured and developed a technical bureaucracy that resented the more rigid Millspaugh and his assistants. This mission was not a success, and Millspaugh found himself at odds with both the Iranian government and press as well as the American embassy. In 1945 he returned to the United States to work with the Brookings Institute. He died September 24, 1955.

BIBLIOGRAPHY

MILLSPAUGH, ARTHUR C. *Americans in Persia,* New York, 1946.

Daniel E. Spector

Milner Mission

Official British Foreign Office commission sent to Egypt to ascertain Egypt's political aspirations "within the framework of the Protectorate" during the 1919 revolution.

Formation of the commission, headed by Colonial Secretary Alfred Milner, was announced eight months before its arrival in Egypt, weakening its effectiveness. The WAFD organized a nationwide boycott of the Milner Mission to show that the Egyptian people would oppose any extension of Britain's rule. Muslim *ulama* (religious scholars), Coptic priests, students, and women aided the boycott. The Mission was able to meet only King Fu'ad, the ministers, and a few notables. Milner's final report admitted that most Egyptians wanted independence and greatly influenced later British thinking on Egypt. Milner resigned his post in 1921, when the British Cabinet rejected his proposal for giving modified independence to Egypt.

BIBLIOGRAPHY

MARLOWE, JOHN. *Anglo–Egyptian Relations, 1800–1956.* London, 1956.
MCINTYRE, JOHN. *Boycott of the Milner Mission.* New York, 1985.

Arthur Goldschmidt, Jr.

Mimar Sinan University

Public university emphasizing the arts in Istanbul.

Its nucleus was founded in 1883 as the Academy of Fine Arts, but Mimar Sinan University gained its present name and structure in 1982. It now comprises the faculties of architecture, fine arts, and sciences and letters; it also administers the State School of Music and the State Museum of Painting and Sculpture. In 1990 it had a teaching staff of four hundred and thirty-five hundred students, slightly more than half female. Its 1991 budget, state-funded, amounted to 48 billion Turkish lire, of which 11.6 billion was for capital investment.

The earlier Academy of Fine Arts has a distinguished place in the cultural Westernization of the Ottoman Empire and the Republic of Turkey. From the mid-1800s, Ottoman painters had shown themselves to be exceptionally adept at European-style art. With the foundation of the academy, Ottoman and later Turkish painters strengthened their integration in the European art world; meanwhile, the academy also provided some training in traditional decorative arts. Almost all of Turkey's foremost artists have studied and/or taught art at the academy. Its School of Architecture, too, has maintained a higher reputation—with a greater flair for style and aesthetics, many believe—than its rival establishment, ISTANBUL TECHNICAL UNIVERSITY.

BIBLIOGRAPHY

Higher Education in Turkey. UNESCO, European Centre for Higher Education. December 1990.
World of Learning. 1990.

I. Metin Kunt

Mimouni, Rachid   [1945–   ]

Algerian writer.

Rachid (or Rashid) Mimouni was born to a peasant family and educated in his native village of Boudouaou with secondary and higher studies respectively at Rouiba and Algiers. He became a specialist in the economics of development. Like other writers of his generation, he criticized the myth and realities of contemporary Algeria. His novels include *Printemps N'en Sera Que Plus Beau* (1978); *Fleuve Détourné* (1982); *Tombéza* (1984); and the acclaimed *L'Honneur de la Tribu* (1989; recently translated as Honor of the Tribe).

Phillip C. Naylor

Mina al-Ahmadi

Kuwait's principal oil port.

Located about twenty miles south of Kuwait City, Mina al-Ahmadi is the site of Kuwait's largest oil refinery. The oil produced from Kuwait's enormous

Burgan Oil Field flows by gravity to the loading terminal at Mina al-Ahmadi.

BIBLIOGRAPHY

BONINE, MICHAEL E. "The Urbanization of the Persian Gulf Nations." In *The Persian Gulf States: A General Survey,* ed. by Alvin J. Cottrell. Baltimore, 1980.

HELD, COLBERT C. *Middle East Patterns: Places, Peoples, and Politics,* 2nd ed. Boulder, Colo., 1994.

Malcolm C. Peck

Minaret

Tower associated with a mosque.

The minaret has been used for centuries by muezzins (Arabic *mu'adhdhin,* Muslim criers) for the call to daily prayers, but its original use is unclear. The earliest mosques in Arabia had no minaret, and the first towers in seventh-century Cairo (Egypt) and Damascus (Syria) may not have been built expressly for the call.

Minarets have been designed in many styles over time and space. Early ones were often square or octagonal, some with winding exterior staircases, while the sixteenth-century Ottomans built needle-thin, cylindrical minarets with conical peaks. Today, the muezzin does not always climb the minaret to call for prayers; minarets are often outfitted with loudspeakers.

BIBLIOGRAPHY

GIBB, H. A. R., ed. "Masdjid." *The Shorter Encyclopedia of Islam.* Ithaca, N.Y., 1953.

Elizabeth Thompson

Mina Sulman

The major port facility in Bahrain.

Mina Sulman was named for Shaykh Sulman ibn Hamad al-Khalifa, former ruler of Bahrain, the father of the ruler Shaykh Isa. The port, both commercial and military, has also provided homeport facilities for the U.S. Navy, initially under the 1971 and 1977 Jufair agreements, and more recently since the Gulf crisis of 1990/91, when Iraq invaded Kuwait. The opening of the Bahraini–Saudi causeway in 1986 increased the shipping business at Mina Sulman, which in 1958 became a free-transit port. The port also offers numerous industrial facilities, including an engineering firm and internationally renowned ship-repair yard.

BIBLIOGRAPHY

NYROP, RICHARD, ed. *Persian Gulf States: Country Studies.* Washington, D.C., 1985.

Emile A. Nakhleh

Minorities

Subdominant or subordinate groups.

The term *minorities* is misleading and inappropriate when discussing subdominant or subordinate groups in Middle Eastern history and society. It is a term rooted in the naive assumption of Western social scientists that minor demographic groups can wield only minor political and economic power. In the states of the Middle East, demographic minorities have exercised considerable—even dominant—political and economic power. In the past, an ethnically distinctive minority, Muslims from the Caucasus, ruled the Arabic-speaking majority for centuries (the Mamluk dynasty of Syria [1250–1516] and Egypt [1250–1517]). During the twentieth century, in Iraq and Lebanon, the only two Arab states where SUNNI Muslim Arabs are a minority, the traditional dominance of Sunni Islam has given its adherents disproportionate—in Iraq, dominant—power. The internal disorders that have torn these polities apart are due in no small part to the contradiction between the majoritarian democratic principles to which all pay lip service and the very different realpolitik.

Furthermore, the bases—religious, ethnic, or linguistic—by which one defines such groups are inconsistent over time and place. In addition, the very existence of such groups and the markers that define them have become a controversial political and intellectual issue. A given group might be considered part of the majority by one criterion in one century; in the next, by very different criteria, it might be considered or—more significantly—might consider itself an oppressed minority. The process also may be reversed so that an oppressed minority may attempt to join the formerly oppressing majority.

Groups in the Islamic Middle East have been defined largely by religion. The traditional minorities—or, more accurately, subdominant groups—have been Christian and Jewish. Within these there have been further divisions by virtue of dogma, rite, and ethnic-linguistic identity. The Ottoman Empire, which dominated the Middle East and North Africa into the twentieth century, recognized most such groups as components of the so-called MILLET SYSTEM. The traditional states of Morocco and Iran followed practices that reflected their different social and religious needs. Because in Morocco, unlike the

Ottoman Empire, the Jews were the only significant indigenous non-Muslim group, the institutional arrangements governing them were less elaborate, and their status tended to vary with the reigning Alawite dynasty (1654–). The most significant Christian and Jewish groups in Iran under Qajar rule (1795–1925) were the Armenians, with small groups of Jews and NESTORIANS, as well as Zoroastrians. Because of the hostile attitude of Iranian Twelver SHI'ISM toward non-Muslims, the opportunities of such groups have been much more restricted than in the Sunni world. However, because of their larger number and economic importance, Armenians in Iran on the whole have fared better than other non-Muslims.

In addition to Christians and Jews, there was another religiously defined subdominant category, Muslim sectarians. For the Ottomans these were Shi'ites. In Iran, in addition to Sunni Muslims, there arose a messianic syncretistic offshoot of Shi'ism, the BAHA'I FAITH. Such groups, unlike Christians and Jews, presented a unique threat to Muslim states because they articulated claims to power based on a similar religious discourse. Unlike Christians and Jews, who had been conditioned by more than a millennium of Muslim rule to accept the principle of status quo, religiously dissenting Muslims had to be retaught that principle from time to time.

Shi'ism represented a significant challenge to Ottoman authority in the sixteenth and seventeenth centuries when the rival Safavid dynasty in Iran attempted to use its Shi'ite coreligionists in eastern Anatolia as a fifth column in the Persian-Turkish wars. As this conflict diminished, both Ottoman Sunni rulers and Shi'ite subjects pretended that their differences did not really exist. This process was hastened by the Shi'ite application of the Islamic principle of *taqiyya* (caution), a doctrine of dispensation that justifies concealing one's true beliefs lest they antagonize the authorities. In the mid-nineteenth century an offshoot of Shi'ism, the DRUZE of Syria and Lebanon, emerged as a short-lived irritant to Ottoman rule in the region when they helped precipitate a conflict with a rival sectarian group, the Christian MARONITES. However, it was only in the last quarter of the twentieth century, decades after the collapse of the Ottoman Empire, that Shi'ites became a force in the Arab world. In Lebanon, as a result of the urbanization of previously rural populations and emigration of the Christian elite brought on by years of civil war and foreign invasions, the poor and ignored Shi'ite community of southern Lebanon became a majority that could no longer be ignored. In Iraq, despite comparable upheaval, a Shi'ite community nearly as large, in relative terms, failed to gain comparable influence.

By the nineteenth century in Iran, as a result of the Safavids' successful campaign to convert the country to Twelver Shi'ism centuries earlier, Sunni Islam was reduced to the unaccustomed status of a statistically insignificant religion largely limited to the rural Kurdish community, and thus trebly marginalized. There was also a smaller Sevener Shi'ite community. A far more dangerous religious challenge arose from within Twelver Shi'ism. At first it manifested itself in the Bab movement, which arose in open rebellion to proclaim a new scripture superseding the Qur'an. Once defeated, it reemerged nonviolently as the Baha'i religion, whose tolerant outlook proved attractive in the twentieth century. However, Shi'ite religious authorities regard it as heresy.

In the twentieth century, recognized markers of group identity became newly significant in political terms, with extremely disruptive consequences. Ethno-linguistic-regional identity, as it was called, tried to superimpose itself on strong religious affiliations. The quality of being Aleppine, Arab, Azeri, Berber, Cairene, Damascene, Egyptian, Hijazi, Khorasani, Kurdish, Jerusalemite, Najdi, Persian, Syrian, Turkish, and so forth had always existed. Traditionally such identities had been sources of group feeling, of ethnic pride and humor, of poetry, of distinctive cuisine and speech; but they had not been the basis for political organization, power, and sovereignty. Muslims (whether Arabic-speaking or Turkish-speaking or whatever) ruled non-Muslims (whether Arabic-speaking or Turkish-speaking or whatever). Although the latter might on occasion have wealth and exercise political influence, it was always behind the scenes and under the table. Modeling themselves on the newly dominant European notions of national political sovereignty, in the wake of the collapse of the traditional Islamic polities during and after World War I, Middle Eastern peoples attempted to fit the round peg of their traditional religious communal identities into the square hole of ethno-linguistic politics. This seemed to change the basis for determining dominant versus subdominant roles. And it required a number of uneasily and inconsistently reached decisions, none of which were—or are—self-evident. What were the new identities to be? Egyptian, Syrian, or Arab? Turkish or Turanian? Azeri, Turcoman, or Persian? These are merely samples of the host of complex questions that had to be answered for new nations and states to emerge.

In the new nation-states of the Arab world all speakers of Arabic—Christian, Jew, and Muslim (both Sunni and Shi'a)—were to be equal; there no longer were to be religious minorities. But that theory hardly described the far more complex and tortured reality. Different Christian groups chose different responses to these opportunities. By and large the Orthodox of Syria and Lebanon identified themselves with their traditional allies, Sunni Muslims, and attempted to support the cause of Arab nationalism. The Maronites, by contrast, preferred the independence of Lebanese identity. Although individual Copts had played a notable role in the rise of Egyptian nationalism, they grew marginalized as it increasingly transformed into Arab nationalism. Even less than Christians, some individual Jews participated in the early stage of Egyptian and Syrian nationalism; but the rise of ZIONISM and the conflict over Palestine, along with strong religious discrimination, excluded them from any lasting role. There has, however, been one political success story in the politics of religious minorities: the Alawites who dominate Syria's ruling elite, a small Shi'ite sect so extreme that some Muslims deny they are part of Islam. Two factors explain their unique achievement. During the colonial period the French recruited them for military service, so that by the 1960s they were overrepresented in the Syrian officer corps, the country's only electorate. They also denied their sectarian traditions and flocked to the Ba'th party, a bastion of secular Arab nationalism.

The smaller ethnic groups of the Muslim world that lost in the game of national musical chairs—notably the Kurds of western Asia and the Berbers of North Africa, who previously had some claim to power and dominant status by virtue of their Sunni identity—are now ignored and suppressed minorities within new political boundaries. During the 1920s Mustafa Kemal Atatürk and his Turkish Republic, through war and diplomacy, rid Anatolia of most of its Armenians and Greeks—though a large proportion of them in fact spoke Turkish as their first language—and then tried to redefine the only non-Turkish group remaining, the Kurds, as Mountain Turks. Iran has been more successful than most states in the Middle East in welding its varied subdominant groups—Turkic-speaking Azeris, Turcomans, Qashqa'is, as well as the Arabs of Khuzistan and the Sunnis—into a relatively coherent polity. Although Persian speakers constitute a bare majority—if that—they have successfully used the appeal of Shi'ite Islam, to which 90 percent of the population adheres, to maintain the country's unity.

The redrawing of the map of the Middle East and North Africa after World War I created new subdominant groups without abolishing the old. In short, the region suffers from the worst of both worlds: it is riven both by the old confessional loyalties and by the new political demands of ethnic nationalism.

[See also Christians in the Middle East; Jews in the Middle East.]

BIBLIOGRAPHY

BRAUDE, BENJAMIN, and BERNARD LEWIS, eds. *Christians and Jews in the Ottoman Empire: The Functioning of a Plural Society.* New York, 1982.

ERHARD, FRANZ. *Minderheiten im Vordern Orient: Auswahlbibliographie.* Hamburg, 1978.

STEFANOS, YERASIMOS. *Questions d'Orient: Frontières et minorités dès Balkans au Caucase.* Paris, 1993.

Benjamin Braude

Minufiyya

An Egyptian delta province (governorate).

In Egypt's delta, Minufiyya has a land area of 591 square miles (1,532 sq km) and a 1986 population estimated at 2,227,100. Its capital, originally at Minuf, has been at Shibin al-Kom since 1826.

BIBLIOGRAPHY

Europa World Yearbook, 1994, vol. 1. London, 1994, p. 1024.

Arthur Goldschmidt, Jr.

Minya

A Middle Egyptian province (governorate).

Minya has a land area of 873 square miles (2,262 sq km) and a 1986 population estimated at 2,648,000. Its capital and principal city, also called Minya, El-Minya, or Menia, located on the west bank of the Nile, had about 203,000 inhabitants in 1986.

BIBLIOGRAPHY

Europa World Yearbook 1994, vol. 1. London, 1994, p. 1024.

Arthur Goldschmidt, Jr.

Minz, Benjamin   [1903–1961]

A leader and founder of the Po'alei Agudat Israel, a religious Zionist labor movement and political party in Israel.

Minz was born in Lodz, Poland, and immigrated to Palestine in 1925. Under his leadership, the political party was established in Tel Aviv in 1933, and in 1946 Minz became its head. He served as chairman of the World Union of Po'alei Agudat Yisrael. Unlike leaders of AGUDAT ISRAEL, he advocated close cooperation with the Zionist yishuv (Jewish community of Jerusalem) and its institutions. During World War II, he was active in rescuing Jews from the Holocaust. In 1948 Minz was a member of the Provisional State Council of Israel and served as deputy speaker of the second and third Knessets. In 1960/61, he served as postmaster general. He wrote numerous books on topics relating to the beliefs and practices of the Hasidim.

Ann Kahn

Mir, Ahmad al-   [1922–   ]

Syrian military officer.

Born in Masyaf during the French mandate over Syria, and of Isma'ili descent, Ahmad al-Mir served in the military command of the BA'TH party beginning in 1960. He unsuccessfully commanded Syrian troops on the Golan Heights during the Arab–Israel War of 1967.

As a supporter of General Salah Jadid, he was removed from the Ba'th party by Syria's new leader and then president, Hafiz al-Asad, who appointed him ambassador to Spain in 1968.

BIBLIOGRAPHY

SEALE, PATRICK. *Asad: The Struggle for the Middle East.* Los Angeles, 1988.

Charles U. Zenzie

Mir, Juliette al-

Syrian political figure.

Juliette al-Mir was the wife of Antun SA'ADA, the charismatic and influential founder of the Syrian Social Nationalist party (PPS), of which she became the nominal president upon his death on July 8, 1949. In this position, she was indicted for offenses linked to the murder of Colonel Adnan al-Malki, and was sentenced to twenty-two years in prison. She was awarded the honorary title *al-Amina al-Ula* (first trustee) on the occasion of the death of her husband, Antun Sa'ada.

BIBLIOGRAPHY

SEALE, PATRICK. *The Struggle for Syria: A Study of Post-War Arab Politics, 1945–1958.* London, 1958.

Charles U. Zenzie

Mirat

First illustrated journal in the Ottoman Empire.

Established in 1862, *Mirat* followed the example of *Mecmua-i Fünün,* publishing maps and illustrations related to science and industry. The editors of the magazine clashed with the prime minister, however, and it was ordered closed after only three issues.

David Waldner

Mir'at al-Sharq

Palestinian newspaper.

Mir'at al-Sharq was founded in Jerusalem in 1919 by Bulus Shihada, a Christian. From 1923 the paper, published twice weekly, became the official organ of the Nashashibi-led Palestine Arab National party. Ahmad Shuqayri, the future founder of the Palestine Liberation Organization (PLO), was the paper's editor from 1928 to 1930. Akram Zu'aytir was its editor through the 1930s.

Mir'at al-Sharq often followed a contradictory political line. In 1923, the paper criticized the failure of the Palestinian delegation to London to achieve revisions in Palestine's constitution, but it generally took a moderate stand toward British rule. Although it once sought funding from Zionist groups, the paper published regular attacks on the Arab Executive for its tolerance toward Zionism.

BIBLIOGRAPHY

LESCH, ANN MOSELY. *Arab Politics in Palestine, 1917–1939.* Ithaca, N.Y., 1979.
PORATH, Y. *The Emergence of the Palestinian-Arab National Movement 1918–1929.* London, 1974.

Elizabeth Thompson

Mir Sadeghi, Jamal   [1933–   ]

Iranian writer and editor.

Mir Sadeghi was born in Tehran and studied Persian literature at Tehran University. His novel *Derazna-ye Shab* (The Length of Night) depicts religious rituals in the holy month of Muharram while narrating the story of a young boy. Mir Sadeghi also has published several books on literary theory that discuss contemporary Iranian fiction, such as *Anasor-e Dastan* (The Elements of Story). Mir Sadeghi resides in Tehran.

BIBLIOGRAPHY

MOAYYAD, HESHMAT, ed. *Stories from Iran: A Chicago Anthology, 1921–1991*. Washington, D.C., 1991.

Pardis Minuchehr

Misa', al-

Daily evening newspaper of Cairo.

Al-Misa' was founded in October 1956 by Free Officer Khalid Muhyi al-Din, with Nasser's consent, as a legal and controlled platform for the Egyptian left. Until Muhyi al-Din's dismissal in March 1959 during a general purge of the left, *al-Misa'* furnished Marxists and other leftists with an important vehicle for their ideas.

BIBLIOGRAPHY

ABDEL-MALEK, ANOUAR. *Egypt: Military Society*. New York, 1968.

Donald Malcolm Reid

MI-6

Branch of the British government responsible for the collection and analysis of foreign intelligence.

The function of this government service is primarily espionage, the obtaining of accurate information from the enemy by means of spies or agents; double agents generally work for MI-5, the British internal security agency. Cooperation between both services was necessary when working with enemy spies who were uncovered in Great Britain and convinced to work for the British from then on, thus double-crossing their original masters. Other agencies included primarily the Admiralty, the Air Force, the Home Office, and the Foreign Office; in both World War I and World War II, university faculty members and special professions were inducted into the intelligence services. After the last war, MI-6 continued to work in the Middle East, as did the U.S. Central Intelligence Agency (CIA).

BIBLIOGRAPHY

MASTERMAN, J. C. *The Double-Cross System in the War of 1939 to 1945*. New Haven, Conn., 1972.
ROOSEVELT, KERMIT. *Countercoup*. New York, 1979.
STEVENSON, WILLIAM. *A Man Called Intrepid*. New York, 1976.
WEST, NIGEL. *MI-6*. New York, 1983.

Zachary Karabell

Misri, al-

Egyptian newspaper.

Established in 1938, *al-Misri* was the daily newspaper of the WAFD party. It was edited by Mahmud Abu al-Fateh and later by his brother Ahmad. It boasted a circulation of 150,000, the largest in the Arab world, at the time it was banned by the government in 1954.

Michael R. Fischbach

Misri, Aziz Ali al-   [1879–1965]

Egyptian officer and Arab nationalist politician.

Born in Cairo, of mixed Arab and Circassian parentage, Aziz Ali al-Misri (also Masri) was trained at the Istanbul Military Academy and was commissioned as an Ottoman army officer in 1901. He joined the COMMITTEE OF UNION AND PROGRESS (CUP) (Young Turks), but after the Young Turks seized power in 1908, he turned against the organization and became an Arab nationalist. It is often alleged that Misri's change of heart occurred because of a personal quarrel that erupted between him and CUP leader Enver while both were serving in the Ottoman army during the Libyan war. Misri formed secret Arab societies called al-Qahtaniyya in 1909 and al-AHD (Covenant) in 1913. He was arrested by the Ottoman government, tried for treason, and condemned to death, but the Turks let him go to Egypt instead. When the Arab Revolt broke out in 1916, he served briefly as Sharif Husayn's chief of staff. After World War I, he joined several Egyptian fringe groups committed to Arab nationalism. He directed the Cairo Police Academy from 1927 to 1936 and was inspector general of the Egyptian army in 1938. In 1939, Premier Ali Mahir named him chief of staff, but he was dismissed from that post in 1940 at Britain's insistence. He deserted the Egyptian army and tried to reach the Axis forces in the Libyan desert but was caught and court-martialed in 1941. After Aziz Ali had helped the Free Officers prepare for the revolution of 1952, they named him ambassador to Moscow in 1953 and considered making him president in place of Muhammad Naguib, but he retired in 1954. Fiercely nationalistic, Azi Ali was hampered in his career by his political idealism, which got the better of his discretion.

BIBLIOGRAPHY

KHADDURI, MAJID. *Arab Contemporaries*. Baltimore and London, 1973.

Arthur Goldschmidt, Jr.

Missionaries

See Protestantism and Protestant Missions; Roman Catholicism and Roman Catholic Missions

Missionary Schools

Primary and secondary schools, colleges, and universities established by Christians to do charitable work and promote conversion.

In the Middle East, Christian missionary schools were founded in the wake of the extension of Western power and influence in the Ottoman Empire during the seventeenth, eighteenth, and nineteenth centuries. With the demise of the empire, the European domination of the region, and then the European mandates over the post–World War I successor states, a variety of motives led both lay and religious organizations to aid in the educational enterprise of modernizing the peoples of the region.

Muhammad Ali in Egypt and his son Ibrahim Pasha in Syria facilitated the entry of such groups; the Ottoman millet system—which granted limited autonomy to the various Christian communities—allowed Christians to bring in missionaries to staff new schools and train teachers in the sciences, which were considered the secret of Western power and prestige. Practically all Western nations sent missionaries at some time, but the most sustained efforts were those of the American Board of Christian Missions (ABCM) and the Arabian Mission (both U.S. Protestant), the North African Mission (French Protestant), the Church Missionary Society (British Anglican), and a variety of Roman Catholic orders and congregations.

Until almost the end of the twentieth century, the desire of Westerners to bring education and enlightenment to the peoples of the Middle East coincided with the peoples' desire for learning and was considered a service rather than a cultural intrusion. Moreover, the schools registered a presence and an influence that were not considered religious per se. Christian missionary schools were, in fact, religiously motivated, but the sensitivity of the dominant Muslim population was respected, since Islam opposed any attempts at direct conversion or proselytization. Christian religious efforts remained within the faith—with Roman Catholics trying to attract Christians separated from Rome and with Protestants trying to convert Roman Catholics and Eastern Orthodox Christians. Many Roman Catholic educational efforts began as seminaries that trained local clergy for the Eastern churches.

Several missionary schools developed into notable institutions and have become landmarks in the history of the region: the AMERICAN UNIVERSITY OF BEIRUT, SAINT JOSEPH UNIVERSITY of Beirut, Aleppo College, Baghdad College (see BAGHDAD UNIVERSITY), Robert College of Istanbul (now BOĞAZIÇI UNIVERSITY), and the AMERICAN UNIVERSITY IN CAIRO. Undoubtedly, the widespread elementary schools in Lebanon and Syria had the broadest impact. In 1894, for example, the Jesuits (Society of Jesus) had 192 primary schools in the region with students numbering some 8,000 boys and 3,000 girls, and the American Protestant Mission had 130 primary schools with more than 7,000 students. Today, the teaching orders of men, of women, and of dedicated Christian lay teachers—all citizens of Middle Eastern countries—still direct primary and secondary schools that were formerly mission operations.

After the demise of the Ottoman Empire, during the European-dominated years of the first half of the twentieth century, only a limited opposition to these schools existed, mostly in Islamic religious circles. The national governments produced by the post–World War II revolutions of the 1950s and 1960s, however, tightened controls over all education—limiting not only missionary schools but all private education—as in Syria in 1967 and Iraq in 1969. In North Africa the new governments also limited private schools, and then in the 1970s, an Islamic religious dimension was added to the growing regional preoccupation with national cultural identities—culminating in a growing Islamist political movement and the successful Iranian Revolution of 1979, which set out to eliminate all non-Islamic cultural influences. Since that time, a new set of forces, both social and political, has been in the making throughout the region.

BIBLIOGRAPHY

BARRET, DAVID, ed. *World Christian Encyclopedia*. Oxford and New York, 1982.

John J. Donohue

Mission Civilisatrice

French term for "civilizing mission," describing the essence of French colonial policy.

As the primary rationalization for colonialism, the "civilizing mission" signified France's attempt to convert its colonial subjects into French people. Whereas the British tended to reject the notion that an Indian, for example, might become British, the French believed that if properly taught French values and the French language, Algerians and Vietnamese alike would slowly evolve and become French. Hence the term *evolué*, which was used to refer to those who had adapted to French culture. There was also a moral component to the civilizing mission, in that some French held that it was their duty as a more enlightened race to elevate the ignorant masses of the non-Western world.

BIBLIOGRAPHY

FIELDHOUSE, D. K. *Economics and Empire, 1830–1914.* London, 1984.
HOBSBAWM, E. J. *The Age of Empire, 1875–1914.* London, 1987.

Zachary Karabell

Misurata

City in Libya that is the site of an important military base.

An iron and steel manufacturing plant was built at Misurata in the 1980s. The city is located near the Libyan capital of Tripoli and forms the western point of Libya's territorial claim over the Gulf of Sidra.

Stuart J. Borsch

MİT

See Milli İstihbarat Teşkilatı

Mitla Pass

See Arab–Israel War (1956)

Mixed Armistice Commissions

Four tripartite committees established in accordance with the Israel–Egypt, Israel–Jordan, Israel–Lebanon, and Israel–Syria General Armistice Agreements (GAAs) of 1949.

Equal numbers of military delegates met periodically under the chairmanship of the chief of staff of the UNITED NATIONS TRUCE SUPERVISION ORGANIZATION (UNTSO) or his authorized representative. Informal civilian advisers often assisted the official military personnel. Their purpose was to provide for the implementation and supervision of the various articles of the GAAs. As hopes for political negotiations in other forums faded after 1949, the Mixed Armistice Commissions (MACs) also became, by default, one of the

last channels through which Arabs and Israelis could communicate directly with each other—although not always with the result of relieving tensions or contributing to a positive atmosphere.

In dealing with a growing number of complaints, the commissions took on quasi-judicial functions, quickly becoming (in the words of one critic) "courts and scoreboards." In the early 1950s, the MACs proved unable to meet their peacekeeping functions effectively when faced with an increase of infiltrations, expulsions, cross-border raids, and reprisals. As time went on, both Arab and Israeli authorities made the tasks of MAC observers and investigators increasingly difficult. Offering lip service rather than true cooperation, the parties—Israel, Egypt, Jordan, Lebanon, and Syria—became skilled at manipulating the MACs for the purpose of scoring political and propaganda points. The effectiveness of the MACs as organs for conflict management also suffered from periodic walkouts and boycotts, by one party or the other, and from recurring challenges to the impartiality and integrity of various UN officials who served as chairmen.

After the 1956 Arab–Israel War, the truce supervisory machinery was further weakened, with some MACs virtually inoperative. The MACs ceased to exist following the June 1967 Arab–Israel war. In 1974, Israel officially declared the four General Armistice Agreements, which had provided the legal basis for the MACs, to be null and void. During the 1970s and 1980s, the UNTSO (with a staff of 220 military observers and offices in Jerusalem, Amman, Beirut, and Gaza) continued to monitor Arab–Israeli frontier incidents.

BIBLIOGRAPHY

BERGER, EARL. *The Covenant and the Sword: Arab–Israeli Relations, 1948–1956.* Toronto, 1965.
BURNS, E. L. M. *Between Arab and Israeli.* New York, 1963.
MORRIS, BENNY. *Israel's Border Wars, 1949–1956: Arab Infiltration, Israeli Retaliation, and the Countdown to the Suez War.* Oxford, 1993.
PELCOVITZ, NATHAN A. *The Long Armistice: UN Peacekeeping and the Arab–Israeli Conflict, 1948–1960.* Boulder, Colo., 1993.

Neil Caplan

Mixed Courts

Egyptian courts that tried commercial and civil cases from 1875 to 1949.

Although they had analogues in the Ottoman Empire and elsewhere, mixed courts achieved their classic form in Egypt between 1875 and 1949. As premier of Egypt, Nubar Pasha negotiated European treaties that approved the courts for Egypt's Khedive Isma'il; he promptly fell victim to their decisions in favor of his foreign creditors and was forced to sell his Suez Canal shares to Britain in 1875.

Western and Egyptian mixed court judges heard the commercial and civil cases involving Westerners, but criminal cases remained under consular courts. The mixed courts used French law codes, and their working language was French. After 1882, British administrators often saw these courts as an impediment to their own plans for reform and political control. From the 1920s on, Egyptian nationalists campaigned for the abolition of any institution that infringed on Egyptian sovereignty. The Anglo–Egyptian Treaty of 1936 paved the way for the MONTREUX CONVENTION of 1937, which provided for ending the mixed courts and the capitulations by 1949. The example of the mixed courts' bar association, law codes, structure, and procedures had a significant influence on Egypt's other court systems—the National (*Ahliyya*) and SHARI'A (Islamic law) courts.

BIBLIOGRAPHY

BRINTON, JASPER YEATES. *The Mixed Courts of Egypt,* 2nd ed. New Haven, Conn., 1968.
CANNON, BYRON. *Politics of Law and the Courts in Nineteenth-century Egypt.* Salt Lake City, 1988.

Donald Malcolm Reid

Mizan

Young Turk newspaper.

Mizan (The Scale) was published weekly in Constantinople (now Istanbul) between August 21, 1886, and December 1, 1890, by Mehmet MURAT. In 1894, Murat went into exile in Cairo where, in 1896, with the encouragement of the Ottoman high commissioner, he resumed publication. In 1897, he moved to Europe, publishing the paper from Geneva and Paris, and distributing it in Constantinople through the English and French post offices. When Murat tried to return to Constantinople in 1909, the paper was ordered closed.

David Waldner

Mizrachi Movement

Orthodox Zionist organization, founded in Europe in early 1902.

Mizrachi was founded by Rabbi Isaac Jacob Reines as the religious Zionist organization within the World Zionist Organization (WZO), after the fifth Zionist Congress of 1901 resolved to enter the educational sphere. Since many members of the WZO believed secular nationalism to be antithetical to Judaism, they could not agree to a program of secular Zionist education.

They founded the Mizrachi organization, an acronym for *mercaz ruhani* (spiritual center), under the banner "The Land of Israel for the people of Israel according to the Torah of Israel." In 1904, a world conference of Mizrachi was convened in Bratislava, Czechoslavakia (then Pressburg, Hungary), and the Mizrachi World Organization was founded with the objective of educating and promoting religious Zionism. The first convention of the American Mizrachi organization was convened in 1914, under the influence of Rabbi Meir Bar-Ilan, then general secretary, who had recently toured the United States.

After World War I, Ha-Po'el Ha-Mizrachi (Mizrachi Labor) was founded, which established a group of religious kibbutz and moshav settlements in Palestine. Although Ha-Po'el Ha-Mizrachi worked very closely with Mizrachi, the two were separate and autonomous and remained so as new political parties in the Israeli Knesset (parliament), until they merged in 1956, becoming the National Religious party (NRP). From 1951 to 1977, they occupied 10 to 12 seats in the Knesset. Although the Mizrachi–Ha-Po'el Ha-Mizrachi movement played a major role in establishing the public religious character of Israel in its initial decades of nationhood, the party's power and prestige declined by the 1980s. Always they struggled to establish the Sabbath rest and kashrut (dietary laws) in all national institutions, settlements, and organizations, so that a state constitution should be based on Halakhah (Jewish religious law).

Since 1981, the number of NRP Knesset seats declined by more than 50 percent. This has been attributed to the perceived accommodative stance of the majority party, Likud, to religious tradition; to ideological confusion, stagnation, and an absence of NRP leadership development; and to a move by NRP to the religious right, which led many former Mizrachi loyalists into the more sectarian religious parties, such as Agudat Israel and SHAS.

BIBLIOGRAPHY

FRIEDMAN, MENACHEM. "The NRP in Transition—Behind the Party's Electoral Decline." In *Politics and Society in Israel* (Studies in Israeli Society 3), ed. by Ernest Krausz. New Brunswick, N.J., 1985.
LIEBMAN, CHARLES S., and ELIEZER DON-YEHIYA. *Civil Religion in Israel: Traditional Judaism and Political Culture in the Jewish State.* Berkeley, Calif., 1983.
LUZ, EHUD. *Parallels Meet: Religion and Nationalism in the Early Zionist Movement, 1882–1904.* Philadelphia, 1988.

SCHIFF, GARY S. *Tradition and Politics: The Religious Parties of Israel*. Detroit, 1977.

Chaim I. Waxman

Mobil Oil

One of the original "seven sister" oil companies that for a time controlled the entire oil production of the Middle East.

Formed after the break-up of Standard Oil in 1911, Mobil (known as Socony until after World War II) was given a 10 percent share of the Iraq Petroleum Company consortium at the 1920 San Remo Conference. In addition to Iraq, Mobil had concessions in Iran and in the Gulf states (Bahrain, Kuwait, Qatar, United Arab Emirates, and Oman), but its major interest has been in Saudi Arabia.

As one of the four parent companies of ARAMCO (the ARABIAN AMERICAN OIL COMPANY), Mobil shared monopolistic control of Saudi petroleum until the 1960s, when the Saudi government began to demand a greater stake. Although the Saudis obtained full ownership of ARAMCO in 1976, Mobil continues to be a major distributor and refiner of Saudi crude. Mobil also leases oil concessions from Egypt in the Gulf of Suez, and it pays Egypt for use of SUMED (the SUEZ–MEDITERRANEAN PIPELINE).

BIBLIOGRAPHY

LENCZOWSKI, GEORGE. *The Middle East in World Affairs*. Ithaca, N.Y., 1980.
SHIMONI, YAACOV, ed. *Political Dictionary of the Middle East in the Twentieth Century*. New York, 1974.
YERGIN, DANIEL. *The Prize*. New York, 1991.

Zachary Karabell

Moda'i, Yitzhak   [1926–   ]

Israeli military leader, politician, and diplomat; held various ministerial positions.

Born in Tel Aviv, Moda'i (orginally Madrovich) joined the Haganah in 1941 and the mandatory police force in 1943. He served in the Israel Defense Forces (IDF) after statehood, reaching the rank of lieutenant-colonel. After being posted as military attaché to London and, upon return, heading committees for cease-fire agreements with Syria and Lebanon, he received chemical engineering and law degrees at Haifa Technion (1957) and Hebrew University (1959) respectively. From 1961 to 1977 Moda'i was chief executive officer of Revlon (Israel). As a member of the party's directorate (1965–1968) he urged the Liberals to unite with Menachem Begin's Herut party. He was appointed military commander of Gaza after its possession by Israel in the Arab–Israel War (1967) and was elected to the Knesset in 1974. Moda'i became the minister of energy and infrastructure in the first Likud party government of 1977 and was additionally minister of communication and later minister without portfolio. In the National Unity government of 1984, Moda'i, as finance minister, worked closely with Prime Minister Shimon Peres on the relatively successful economic stabilization program. Tension between him and Peres soon forced Moda'i to switch to the Ministry of Justice and finally to leave the government (1986). When Yitzhak Shamir took over the premiership later in the same year, Moda'i returned as minister without portfolio and from 1988 was minister for economy and planning.

Zev Maghen

Modarres, Sayyed Hasan   [1861–1937]

Iranian cleric who participated in the constitutional revolution of 1905–1911, was a deputy to the majles, and opposed the coming to power of Reza Shah Pahlavi.

Sayyed Hasan Modarres was born into a family of religious scholars in Ardestan, Iran, and pursued his religious training in Isfahan. In 1891, he went to Iraq to pursue further his education and studied there with the famous Akhund Molla Mohammad Kazem Khorasani (d. 1911). He returned to Isfahan in 1898 and taught Islamic jurisprudence at a small school. In 1910, Modarres was appointed to the newly established national assembly of Persia as part of an overseeing committee of the Shi'a *ulama* in Najaf. The existence of such a body had been stipulated in the constitution. He helped in the drafting of Article 35 of the Supplementary Fundamental Law, which secured for the clergy an important role in legitimizing kingship in post-constitutionalist Iran. Sovereignty was said to be a divine gift, bestowed by the people upon the king. Modarres favored political reform but shunned cultural modernization, as manifested in his disapproval of secular education in Iran.

In 1915, he joined the government in exile of Mirza Hoseyn Qoli Khan Mafi Nezam al-Saltaneh, who opposed British involvement in Persian affairs and the premiership of Nosrat al-Dowleh Firuz. There Modarres was appointed minister of justice. After clashes with the government, the provisional government of Nezam al-Saltaneh in Kermanshah was defeated, and after some time in exile, the participants returned to Tehran. Modarres was repeatedly elected to the parliament as a representative from

Tehran. In the fourth national assembly, convened in 1922, Reza Pahlavi sought an alliance with the conservative Reformers' party, to which Modarres belonged. The alliance did not last long, however, for the cleric flatly rejected Reza Pahlavi's bill for compulsory military service. As far as Modarres was concerned, two years of training as a soldier in a secular institution by anti-religious officers was enough to corrupt the soul of Islam.

In 1924, Reza Pahlavi, who had acted as the last QAJAR dynasty's prime minister since the previous year, sought to abandon the monarchy and install a republican regime in Iran. Modarres, along with other conservatives in the *majles,* were highly opposed to this move and identified Reza Pahlavi as an agent of British interests. Furthermore, Modarres was aware of Reza Pahlavi's intention of emulating the Turkish model. The dissolution of the Ottoman Empire had brought an end to the caliphate, and Modarres foresaw a similar outcome for Iran. Thus, Modarres announced that an attack on the monarchy was an attack on Islam. Reza Pahlavi then proceeded to depose the Qajars and install himself as the new king of Iran. To this, neither the British nor the majority of the national assembly objected. Modarres was forced into retirement in 1927 and died under suspicious circumstances in 1937.

BIBLIOGRAPHY

ABRAHAMIAN, ERVAND. *Iran between Two Revolutions.* Princeton, N.J., 1982.
AKHAVI, SHAHROUGH. *Religion and Politics in Contemporary Iran.* Albany, N.Y., 1980.

Neguin Yavari

Modernization

Process of sociocultural change in the Middle East that began about 1800 with European colonial expansion into the area.

Modernization is the term commonly used to denote the process of social change that the Middle East (and other parts of the world) has been experiencing for the last two hundred years. It may be traced to the Industrial Revolution and the impact of European industrial expansion and colonialism that was continually promoted by European agents—merchants, bankers, consuls, administrators, and missionaries. This process was embraced by early modernizing monarchs such as Selim III and Mahmud II of the Ottoman Empire and Muhammad Ali of Egypt. Five aspects may be distinguished: economic, political, social, intellectual, and psychological.

Economic. The Middle East has long been integrated in the world market. The region has mainly exported primary products, agricultural goods such as cotton, tobacco, fruits, and coffee; recently, it became the prime producer and exporter of petroleum. To facilitate both export and the importation of manufactured goods, certain raw materials, and foodstuffs, a network for mechanized transport was developed (railroads, seaports, river traffic, roads [with bridges and tunnels], airports), along with a banking and finance system. This entailed vast investments of foreign and, more recently, national capital. A large manufacturing sector has been established, and the region encompasses the world's most abundant petroleum deposits—exploited by a large production and exporting industry.

Political. Modernization here constitutes the emergence of centralized nation-states. In addition to the ruling bodies, large, and usually cumbrous, civil services administer the various countries and provide social services. Taxation has risen steadily as a proportion of Gross National Product. Suffrage often excludes women, but elections are held for presidents and parliaments (although in practice many countries are under a one-party dictatorship). The prevailing political ideology is nationalism—utilizing certain elements of socialism—mainly as the outcome of working toward independence from European imperialism during the twentieth century.

Social. Many changes have occurred because of the great increase in population; the sharp fall in death rates has not been matched by a decline in birthrates, so the population has increased at about 3 percent per annum (including both immigration and emigration). Cities have grown to the point where more than 50 percent of the population is urban. Family structure has consequently shown some changes; most young middle-class couples live on their own and make their own decisions, instead of following the practices and decisions of their patriarch. Social services have been greatly expanded; those that were provided by religious or private philanthropy are now usually provided by the state. Education is available to almost all boys of school age (and to the majority of girls), and the literacy rate has risen from an average 5 percent in the early nineteenth century to an average of more than 50 percent today (in Israel, more than 90 percent).

Intellectual/Psychological. Intellectual modernization meant, originally, the absorption by a small elite of the bulk of Western science, scholarship, literature, and to a smaller extent, the arts. This was achieved primarily through the French language, but British and American sources have been increasingly used. Diffusion of Western-style culture has resulted in the establishment of a vast network of Western-style schools, which are secular and therefore distinct from the traditional Muslim/Christian/Hebrew schools. They include many universities and technical and research institutes.

Although printing was available in the eighteenth century, it became significant only during the nineteenth century, when books and pamphlets were followed by newspapers and periodicals that reached the general reading public. Concurrently, the traditional written languages—mainly, Persian, Turkish, Arabic, and Hebrew—which were highly elaborate, formal, and remote from everyday speech, have been both simplified and enriched. New and hitherto unknown literary genres have developed, notably novels and plays, based on Western models. It is perhaps in them that one sees most clearly the psychological modernization that has occurred—the growing individualism, the weakening of traditional ways, and the participation in what may be called a world culture. The expanding fundamentalist tendencies in both Islam and Judaism may be explained by sociopolitical problems that continue to need attention, *not* by a growing traditionalism.

BIBLIOGRAPHY

Berkes, Niyazi. *The Development of Secularism in Turkey.* Montreal, 1964.

Brown, L. Carl. *The Modernization of the Ottoman Empire.* Princeton, N.J., 1991.

Hourani, Albert. *Arabic Thought in the Liberal Age.* London, 1962.

———. *A History of the Arab Peoples.* Cambridge, Mass., 1991.

Issawi, Charles. *An Economic History of the Middle East and North Africa.* New York, 1982.

Lewis, Bernard. *The Emergence of Modern Turkey.* London, 1961.

Charles Issawi

Modir al-Molk, Mahmud Khan Jam
[1885–1969]

Iranian politician, prime minister.

Born in Tabriz, Mahmud Khan Jam Modir al-Molk studied medicine and was appointed physician to the Qajar crown prince. In 1909, he moved to Tehran, where he worked as a translator at the ministry of justice and then at the French embassy. At the time he entered government service, in 1919, the prime minister was Vozuq al-Dowleh, who granted him the title of Modir al-Molk. Mahmud Khan Jam subsequently became head treasurer, held several cabinet posts, was appointed prime minister in 1935, and, after the abdication of Reza Shah Pahlavi in 1941, was made ambassador to Egypt. He was elected to the senate in 1956 and died in Tehran in 1969.

Neguin Yavari

Mogador

See Essaouira

Mohammad Ali Qajar   [1872–1925]

The sixth ruler of the Qajar dynasty in Iran.

Mohammad Ali Qajar was the eldest son of MOZAFFAR AL-DIN Shah Qajar. His mother was the daughter of Mirza Mohammad Taqi Khan Amir Kabir, Iran's reformist prime minister executed by Mohammad Ali Shah's grandfather, Naser al-Din Shah, in 1852.

In 1892, Mohammad Ali became commander of the troops in Azerbaijan in northwestern Iran. In 1896, his father succeeded to the throne and Mohammad Ali was proclaimed crown prince. As was customary in the Qajar court, the crown prince also became governor of Azerbaijan, and Mohammad Ali took up residence in Tabriz. In 1907, he became shah following the passing away of his father.

While in Tabriz, Mohammad Ali had fallen under Russian influence, and this pro-Russian sentiment left its mark on Mohammad Ali's reign. In 1905, his father, Mozaffar al-Din Shah, had left him as regent in Tehran while he paid a visit to Europe. That year, the merchants of Tehran closed the bazaars and took refuge in the shrine of Shah Abd al-Azim in Rayy, protesting against Belgo–Russian economic influence. Mohammad Ali was able to disband the protestors with the aid of a prominent pro-constitutionalist cleric, Sayyed Abdallah Behbehani. This brought the young crown prince into contact with the reformist tide prevalent both at the Qajar court and throughout political groupings in Tehran.

From the outset, Mohammad Ali found himself at odds with reformist aspirations. The constitutionalists were aware of Mohammad Ali's anti-reformist stance, and on several occasions asked him to pledge his allegiance to the constitution. In 1907, Ali-Asghar Amin al-Soltan, the prime minister, was murdered. In 1908, after an attempt on his life, Mohammad Ali blamed the disorder and instability in the capital on the constitutionalists and abruptly banned their activities. He closed down political societies and shut down newspapers. He imposed military rule in Tehran and appointed the commander of the Russian-trained Cossack Brigade as the military governor.

During this period of Mohammad Ali's reign, Russian influence was gaining ground in Tehran. The Russians had opposed the constitutional revolution of 1905–1911. It mainly found support in the British camp in Tehran. In 1908, the Cossack Brigade bombarded the parliament, and four days later the Shah dissolved parliament and abrogated the constitution, accusing it of violating Islamic law and principles.

In April 1909, Russian troops occupied Tabriz anew, as anti-royalist sentiments were on the rise in the city. In July 1909, pro-constitutionalist forces attacked Tehran, and Mohammad Ali Shah sought refuge in the Russian legation in the capital. He then left Tehran for Russia in September 1909. While abroad, he gathered his forces and resources and returned to Iran on a chartered Russian steamer, capturing Astarabad in 1911. The constitutionalists assembled their forces and defeated Mohammad Ali Shah in September 1911. In 1912, the shah sailed for a second time to Russia. In the meantime, the Russians all but withdrew their support for the exiled shah, as they had negotiated an agreement with the British on the fate of the Persian government. Mohammad Ali Shah died in April 1925.

BIBLIOGRAPHY

ALGAR, HAMID. *Religion and State in Iran, 1785–1906.* Berkeley, Calif., 1980.

Neguin Yavari

Mohammadi, Maulawi Mohammad Nabi
[1921–   ]

Islamic resistance leader.

Born in Logar in a Pushtun family, Mohammadi was educated in *madrasas* (religious colleges) in Logar province. He became politically active within the religious establishment in Afghanistan and, as early as the 1950s, was particularly critical of the leftist and secular elements in the government. In 1964, he was elected to parliament during the period of constitutional reform. In 1978, after the Saur Revolution, he fled to Pakistan and organized a network of *maulawi* (graduates of madrasas) to fight against the Marxist government. In 1992, he returned to Kabul with the other Islamic leaders to participate in forming an Islamic government. His party, Islamic Revolutionary Movement, is considered one of the moderate political groups.

BIBLIOGRAPHY

ROY, OLIVIER. *Islam and Resistance in Afghanistan.* New York, 1986.

Grant Farr

Mohammad Ya'qub Barakzai   [1849–1923]

Afghan emir, 1879.

The son of Emir Sher Ali Khan, Ya'qub Barakzai was governor of Herat. In 1878, he went to Kabul as the British were invading Afghanistan and became regent when his father fled to northern Afghanistan. In 1879, Sher Ali died and Ya'qub declared himself emir. When, in late 1879, the British took control of the government, Ya'qub was forced to abdicate. He sought exile in India, where he lived until his death.

BIBLIOGRAPHY

ADAMEC, LUDWIG. *Historical Dictionary of Afghanistan.* Metuchen, N.J., 1991.

Grant Farr

Mohammadzai

See Barakzai Dynasty

Mohieddin

See under Muhyi al-Din

Mohilever, Samuel   [1824–1898]

Rabbi, early Zionist leader.

Born in Russia, Mohilever helped to organize Jewish emigration to Palestine in the 1880s and persuaded Baron Edmond de Rothschild to support Russian families settling there. In 1882, he founded the first Hoveve Tziyon group, in Warsaw. In 1890, he was a founder of Rehovot in Palestine. As head of Hoveve Tziyon in Bialystok, he helped Theodor Herzl plan the First Zionist Congress (Basel, 1897).

BIBLIOGRAPHY

HERTZBERG, ARTHUR. *The Zionist Idea.* New York, 1979.

Martin Malin

Mojahedin

Afghan Islamic resistance fighters.

The Afghan rebels who took up the resistance war against the Marxist government, beginning in 1978, called themselves *mojahedin* (fighters of the holy war), from the Arabic *jihad* (holy war). By using the appellation *mojahedin,* they invoked a number of Islamic beliefs associated with the concept of jihad, particularly that a person who dies in a jihad becomes a martyr (*shahid*) whose soul goes immediately to the side of God. In addition, all good Muslims should support a holy war.

The Afghan mojahedin are organized into groups that represent the sectarian and ethnic divisions of Afghanistan. Seven main parties represent SUNNI Afghans; three are led by traditional and moderate clergy, and four are led by Islamist and more radical leaders. The moderate-traditional parties are Harakat-e Inqilab-e Islami (the Islamic Revolutionary Movement), led by Mohammad Nabi MOHAMMADI; Jebhe-ye Nejat-e Milli (National Liberation Front), led by Sebghatullah Mojaddedi, a Sufi *pir*; and Mahaz-e Islami (Islamic Front), led by Pir Sayyed Ahmad GAILANI, head of the Qadiri Sufi order. The Islamist groups are HEZB-E ISLAMI (Islamic Party), led by Golbuddin HEKMATYAR; Hezb-e Islami, led by Mohammad Unis KHALIS; JAMI'AT-E ISLAMI (Islamic Society), led by Burhanuddin RABBANI; and Ittihad-e Islami (Islamic Union), led by Abd al-Rasul Sayyaf.

In addition there are a number of Shi'a parties (Shi'ite Muslims constitute between 15 and 20 percent of the Afghan population). They include Shura-ye Ittifagh-e Islami (Islamic Union), led by Sayyed Beheshti; Harakat-e Islami (Islamic Movement), led by Shaykh Mohseni; and Hezb-e Wahadat (Unity Party), an alliance of eight Shi'a groups.

Each mojahedin party depended on followers in Afghanistan and on other governments for support. During the resistance war, the parties with the largest following were the Jami'at-e Islami, the only Sunni party with non-Pakhtun leadership, and thus popular in the non-Pakhtun areas of Afghanistan (especially the North and West), and the Hezb-e Islami, led by Hekmatyar, which had the support of the Pakistani military (and therefore received a lion's share of the weapons and arms). The Shi'a groups generally received support from Iran.

When the Marxist government of Najibullah fell in 1992, the mojahedin parties returned to Kabul to form a government. Mojaddedi, the leader of Jebhe-ye Nejat-e Milli, became the first president. In 1993, in an orderly rotation of the presidency, Rabbani, leader of the Jami'at, became president. However, beginning in December 1993 and continuing into 1994, the coalition between the mojahedin groups broke down. Rival camps split the parties between those led by Hekmatyar and those led by Rabbani. Much of Kabul was destroyed in the fighting.

BIBLIOGRAPHY

ADAMEC, LUDWIG. *Historical Dictionary of Afghanistan.* Metuchen, N.J., 1991.
FARR, GRANT. "The Failure of the Mujahedin." *Middle East International* 476 (1994): 19–20.
ROY, OLIVIER. *Islam and Resistance in Afghanistan.* New York, 1986.

Grant Farr

Mojahedin-e Khalq

The Sazman-e Mojahedin-e Khalq-e Iran (Holy Warrior Organization of the Iranian People), better known as the Iranian Mojahedin, is the main armed force challenging the Islamic Republic of Iran.

The Mojahedin was formed in the mid-1960s by Tehran University students who tried to synthesize Islam with Marxism, interpreting the former to be the divine message of revolution and the latter to be the main analytical tool for analyzing society, history, and politics. While influenced by these features of Marxism, they rejected the philosophy of dialectical materialism. They also adopted the strategy of guerrilla warfare from Che Guevara, the Vietminh, and Algeria's Front de Libération Nationale (National Liberation Front, FLN). Some of their founding leaders received guerrilla training from the Palestine Liberation Organization (PLO).

From 1971 until 1979, the Mojahedin tried to destabilize the regime of Reza Pahlavi with a series of assassinations, bank robberies, and daring armed assaults. In the process, over eighty of their members lost their lives. Most of these were engineers, teachers, and university students. The group was further weakened by factional infighting. In 1975, one faction denounced Islam as a "conservative petty bourgeois ideology" and declared itself a pure Marxist-Leninist organization. This faction later became known as the Paykar (Combat) organization. By the time of the Iranian Revolution of 1979, little remained of the Mojahedin, and the remaining members had been imprisoned.

Despite this, the Mojahedin regrouped during the Islamic revolution and quickly grew to become a major threat to the Islamic Republic of Iran. Ma'sud RAJAVI, one of the few survivors from the 1960s, took over the leadership. The Mojahedin grew rapidly in part because of its mystique of revolutionary martyrdom; in part because of its adherence to Shi-'ism; in part because of its social radicalism; and in part because of its anticlericalism and opposition to the theocracy of the Ayatollah Ruhollah Khomeini. By 1981, its publication, *Mojahed,* was one of the country's most read newspapers; its parliamentary candidates were winning a substantial number of votes; and its rallies were drawing hundreds of thousands. The regime reacted by ordering a major crackdown. The Mojahedin, in turn, retaliated by launching an assassination campaign against the top figures of the Islamic republic.

Since 1981, the Mojahedin has created in exile an umbrella organization named the National Council of Resistance and has waged from Iraq an armed struggle against the Iranian regime. In the process, over 10,000 members of the organization have lost their lives—some before firing squads, others in guerrilla assaults and military ventures. Their martyrs continue to come from the ranks of the intelligentsia, but with one significant difference—increasing numbers are now high school students. In 1992, the Mojahedin had publicity offices in most Western capitals and a well-trained and well-equipped army of some 9,000 in Iraq. It also had a radio station operating from Iraq. But its structure within Iran had been devastated by arrests, executions, and heroic "deeds of propaganda" (suicidal armed assaults).

BIBLIOGRAPHY

ABRAHAMIAN, ERVAND. *The Iranian Mojahedin.* New Haven, Conn., 1989.
IRFANI, SUROOSH. *Revolutionary Islam in Iran.* London, 1983.

Ervand Abrahamian

Mojtahed

See Molla

Mokhber al-Saltaneh, Mirza Mehdi Qoli Khan Hedayat   [1863–1950]

Iranian politician.

After receiving his education in Germany, Mirza Mehdi Qoli Khan Hedayat Mokhber al-Saltaneh returned to Iran in 1880 to teach at the Dar al-Fonun school in Tehran. In 1893, he entered government service as special assistant to the Qajar NASER AL-DIN SHAH (see QAJAR DYNASTY). He was a member of the council that oversaw the elections after the CONSTITUTIONAL REVOLUTION of 1911; he also served as

governor of Fars and Azerbaijan and was a cabinet minister several times. He authored *Khaterat va Khatarat* (Memories and Perils), which provides insightful information on court politics and is an important source for late Qajar and early Pahlavi history. He died in 1950.

Neguin Yavari

Mokhtar Ould Daddah   [1924–]

First president of Mauritania, 1960–1978.

Ould Daddah was born December 25, 1924, in Boutilimit in the Trarza district, southwestern Mauritania. A member of a prestigious Marabout tribe, he became Mauritania's first university graduate, earning a law degree in Paris. During the late 1950s, he assumed a leadership role in organizing Mauritania's independence, with the approval of both the French administration and local, youthful elites. In 1961 Ould Daddah officially became head of state as well as head of government under a newly established presidential regime. Central to his efforts at nation building was the idea of a unique desert civilization, encompassing Spanish Sahara (now Western Sahara), southern Morocco, and Mauritania to the banks of the Senegal river. From the mid-1960s onward, he moved to centralize his authority and promote closer ties with the Arab world, which increased internal tensions between Maures and blacks.

In the early 1970s, he distanced himself from France, only to renew his dependence on it during the WESTERN SAHARA WAR. At the same time, he reestablished relations with Morocco's King Hassan II, leading to the partition of Western Sahara between their two countries. But the ensuing war there placed inordinate stress on Mauritania, and Ould Daddah lost the support of key sectors of the society. He was overthrown by a military committee in a bloodless coup on July 10, 1978.

BIBLIOGRAPHY

HODGES, TONY. *Western Sahara: Roots of a Desert War.* Westport, Conn., 1983.
VERNET, R., et al. *Introduction à la Mauritanie.* Paris, 1979.

Bruce Maddy-Weitzman

Molla

Iranian clergyman.

Molla, meaning a learned person in the religious sciences, is generally used to designate a member of the clergy in Iran. Although the term is applied universally to men in the profession of religion, it generally designates a lesser standing in the clerical hierarchy. Mojtahed is a higher rank.

BIBLIOGRAPHY

ALGAR, HAMID. *Religion and State in Iran, 1785–1906.* Berkeley, Calif., 1969.

Neguin Yavari

Mollet, Guy [1905–1975]

French socialist and statesman.

Head of the French Socialist party (1946–1969) and premier of France (February 1956–May 1957), Guy Alcide Mollet sought an end to the civil war in Algeria (the ALGERIAN WAR OF INDEPENDENCE, 1954–1962). In October 1956, he allowed the French military to hijack a plane carrying several Front de Libération Nationale (FLN) leaders, including Ahmad Ben Bella. Convinced that Egypt's President Nasser was aiding the FLN, Mollet authorized French participation in the Suez invasion of October–November 1956.

BIBLIOGRAPHY

HORNE, ALISTAIR. *A Savage War of Peace.* London, 1977.

Zachary Karabell

Moltke, Helmuth von [1800–1891]

Prussian officer.

As a young lieutenant, in the 1830s von Moltke was sent to Turkey to help train the army of the Ottoman Empire. At the battle of Nezib (1839), the Ottoman commander rejected his advice, and the Ottoman forces were then routed by the Egyptian army of Ibrahim Pasha. From 1858 to 1888, von Moltke was chief of the General Staff in Berlin.

BIBLIOGRAPHY

SHAW, STANFORD J., and EZEL KURAL SHAW. *History of the Ottoman Empire and Modern Turkey.* New York, 1977.

Zachary Karabell

Monastir

Seaport on the northeastern coast of Tunisia; center of the governorate of the same name.

Probably a Punic port before Islam, Monastir became the site of a well-known Arab Islamic *ribat* (fortified religious center), founded by the Muslim commander Harthamah ibn A'yan in 796. The fortress, enlarged over the centuries, is today an important tourist site. To bolster the tourist trade, a large hotel and commercial complex was begun in the late 1980s.

Never a political center, it was a religious hub for several centuries in the medieval Islamic period. Two mosques of architectural importance were built at the turn of the eleventh century. Monastir was the hometown of Tunisia's President Habib Bourguiba. Under his government, an international airport was built in Monastir, used primarily for the tourist trade. Its population for 1984 was 35,546.

BIBLIOGRAPHY

Encyclopaedia of Islam, 1st ed.
Tunisia: A Country Survey. Washington, D.C., 1988.

Matthew S. Gordon

Mond, Alfred Moritz [1868–1930]

British industrialist and politician.

Son of a prominent German–Jewish industrialist, the Baron Alfred Moritz Mond was a Liberal member of Parliament (1906–1928). In 1926, he was one of the founders of ICI (Imperial Chemical Industry). An ardent promoter of Zionism, he visited Palestine in 1921 and contributed an estimated 100,000 British pounds to the Jewish Colonization Corporation.

BIBLIOGRAPHY

Dictionary of National Biography, 1922–30. London, 1937.

Zachary Karabell

Moniteur Ottoman

Ottoman newspaper.

First appearing in 1831, *Moniteur Ottoman* was the French-language version of the official Ottoman newspaper, *Takvim-i Vekayi* (Calendar of Events). *Moniteur Ottoman* was read by high officials and foreign diplomats and had a circulation of about three hundred copies.

David Waldner

Monophysitism

See Christians in the Middle East

Montazeri, Hosayn Ali [1920–]

Iranian religious scholar and activist, close for many years to Ayatollah Ruhollah Khomeini.

Born to a peasant family in Najafabad, central Iran, Montazeri began his formal religious studies at Isfahan at the age of fifteen, moving in his early twenties to Qom (Qum) to benefit from the scholars teaching there. In 1944, he joined the circle of Ayatollah Hosayn BORUJERDI, principal religious leader of the time, and before long began assisting him in his classes on Shi'a jurisprudence. Also in Qom, he became a close associate of KHOMEINI, whose revolutionary vision he came swiftly to assimilate. Among the most active of Khomeini's associates in the uprising of June 1963, Montazeri was detained in its aftermath. He was to be rearrested several times in the following years, most notably in 1975 when he was sentenced to ten years' imprisonment (cut short in October 1978), as well as undergoing banishment to various remote parts of Iran.

In 1979, after the success of the IRANIAN REVOLUTION and the establishment of the Islamic republic, Montazeri acted as a member of the council for reviewing the draft constitution, consultant on the appointment of revolutionary judges, adviser on land reform, and leader of the Friday prayers, first in Tehran and then in Qom. His eminence among the associates of Khomeini was confirmed by his selection as successor to the leadership in December 1985. However, a letter addressed to Khomeini early in 1989, in which Montazeri criticized the shortcomings of the revolutionary order, led to his resignation from the successorship on March 28, 1989. Montazeri then taught Islamic jurisprudence in Qom.

BIBLIOGRAPHY

IZADI, MOSTAFA. *Faqih-e Aliqadr* (The Eminent Jurist). Tehran, 1983.

Hamid Algar

Montefiore, Moses [1784–1885]

Philanthropist and Zionist.

Born in Italy, Sir Moses Haim Montefiore made a fortune in stockbroking in London and retired in 1824. He devoted the remainder of his life to Jewish philanthropy and the cause of Zionism. Between 1827 and 1875, he made numerous trips to Palestine to aid the Jewish community there, and in 1839 he developed a program to improve Palestine's agricultural and industrial output and sought to obtain autonomy for the Jewish community. Among his many philanthropic activities, he endowed a hospital and a school for girls in Jerusalem in 1855 and purchased land outside of the walled city. Montefiore was also involved with the plight of the Moroccan Jews, whose situation seriously deteriorated after expeditions by France to Morocco in the 1840s. At the urging of the Rothschilds, Montefiore went to Morocco in 1864 and met with Sultan Mulay Sidi Muhammad, who issued an edict easing restrictions and forbidding hostile acts against the Moroccan Jews. Montefiore travelled throughout the Mediterranean Muslim world and was treated as an important dignitary wherever he went.

BIBLIOGRAPHY

HALPERN, BEN. *The Idea of the Jewish State.* New York, 1961.
PATAI, RAPHAEL. *The Seed of Abraham.* New York, 1986.

Zachary Karabell

Montgomery, Bernard Law [1887–1976]

British soldier.

A Sandhurst graduate, Montgomery (first viscount of Alamein) became commander of the Eighth Army in North Africa in August 1942, after General Sir Claude Auchinleck had checked German General Erwin Rommel at the first Battle of El Alamein. On Prime Minister Winston Churchill's urging, Montgomery attacked in late October and won a decisive victory at the second Battle of El Alamein, leading to a full-scale retreat of Rommel's forces. Montgomery was later commander in chief of the ground forces during the Normandy invasion.

BIBLIOGRAPHY

BARNETT, CORRELLI. *The Desert Generals.* Bloomington, Ind., 1982.
Dictionary of National Biography 1971–1980. New York, 1986.

Zachary Karabell

Montreux Convention

Agreement of 1936 giving Turkey sovereignty over the Turkish Straits.

Under the Treaty of Lausanne (1923), the Turkish Straits (the Dardanelles, the Sea of Marmara, and the Bosporus) were demilitarized and placed under international control. This settlement infringed on Turkish sovereignty, and after repeated demands by Turkey to reform the relevant clauses of the Lausanne agreement, the Montreux Convention was signed on July 20, 1936. Under the terms of the convention, sovereignty of the Straits reverted to Turkey, and the Turks were permitted to remilitarize the Straits as they saw fit. Furthermore, passage of the Straits in times of war was to be restricted to nonbelligerents. All of the Lausanne powers endorsed the convention, with the exception of Italy and the addition of the USSR. Britain was represented by Foreign Secretary Anthony Eden. Alarmed by the growing power of Nazi Germany, Eden and the other European signatories felt it expedient to mollify Turkey.

BIBLIOGRAPHY

LENCZOWSKI, GEORGE. *The Middle East in World Affairs,* 4th ed. Ithaca, N.Y., 1980.
SHIMONI, YAACOV, ed. *Political Dictionary of the Middle East in the Twentieth Century.* New York, 1974.

Zachary Karabell

Moors

See Spain and the Middle East

Mopsy Party

The forerunner of the anti-Zionist Communist party in Palestine.

Mopsy (derived from Mifleget Po'alim Sozialistim; Socialist Workers' Party) was established in 1919, when its members broke away from Poale Zion (Workers of Zion), after members of Poale Zion had joined with unaffiliated socialists to form AHDUT HA-AVODAH. Mopsy was one of the founding parties of the Histadrut (the General Federation of Workers in the Land of Israel). In December 1920, Mopsy elected 6 of the initial 87 delegates to the Histadrut. By 1921, Mopsy itself had splintered into the Communist Party of Palestine, the Palestine Communist Party, and Po'ale Zion Social Democrats.

BIBLIOGRAPHY

WOLFFSOHN, MICHAEL. *Israel: Polity, Society and Economy, 1882–1986.* Atlantic Highlands, N.J., 1987.

Shimon Avish

Moresby, Treaty of

1822 agreement regarding the Oman slave trade.

These engagements, concluded September 4 and 9, 1822, by Oman's ruler, Sa'id ibn Sultan, and British India's representative, Captain Fairfax Moresby of Britain's Royal Navy, forbade the SLAVE TRADE to Christians and allowed seizure of Arab vessels involved in such dealings. Although tolerating continued slave traffic among Muslims, the treaty signaled its eventual suppression.

BIBLIOGRAPHY

AITCHESON, C. U., compiler. *A Collection of Treaties, Engagements and Sanads Relating to India and to Neighbouring Countries.* Vol. 11, 5th ed. Delhi, 1933. Reprint, 1973.

Robert G. Landen

Moroccan–Algerian War

Conflict in October and early November 1963 along the northern frontier between the two countries.

The causes of the Moroccan–Algerian War were rooted in colonialism, decolonization, and nationalism. Morocco considered the border established by colonialists artificial. During the Algerian War of Independence (1954–1962), the Provisional Government of the Algerian republic (Gouvernement Provisional de la République Algérienne; GPRA) agreed in July 1961 to address the frontier question after the liberation struggle. Ahmed Ben Bella further put off this issue as he attempted to secure power in 1962–1963. A revolt in Kabylia in late September 1963 offered Morocco an opportunity to seize the contested land. This resulted in a brief conflict, with Algeria receiving the heavier blows (60 dead and 250 wounded according to the French newspaper *Le Monde*). Mediation by the Organization of African Unity (OAU) produced a cease-fire in early November. In 1972 Morocco and Algeria signed conventions that delineated the frontier and agreed to the common exploitation of natural resources. Algeria ratified the agreements, but Morocco did not and subsequently engaged in its Western Sahara expansion (beginning with the GREEN MARCH in 1975). The WESTERN SAHARA WAR included a brief engagement between Moroccan and Algerian troops in 1976. In the late 1980s, bilateral relations improved as demonstrated by Morocco's ratification of the 1972 conventions, the full restoration of diplomatic relations (1988), and the formation of the Arab Maghrib Union (1989).

BIBLIOGRAPHY

HEGGOY, ALF A. "Colonial Origins of the Algerian–Moroccan Border Conflict of October 1963." *African Studies Review* 13, no. 1 (April 1970): 17–21.

HODGES, TONY. *Western Sahara: The Roots of a Desert War.* Westport, Conn., 1983.

Phillip C. Naylor

Moroccan Question

Name given to the final phase of European imperialist rivalries over Morocco, 1900–1912.

Morocco owed its continued independence into the twentieth century to its rugged topography and combative rural populations, as well as the ability of Moroccan diplomats to play off the European powers against one another. In 1900 the diplomatic stalemate was broken when France annexed territories claimed by Morocco.

Each of the chief European rivals for Morocco—France, Britain, Spain, Germany, and Italy—cited reasons why its claims on Morocco should be recognized. Each cited historic and material interests, as well as nationalist ones, in justification. None took any cognizance of Moroccan wishes in the matter.

Between 1900 and 1904, French Foreign Minister Théophile Delcassé persuaded Spain, Italy, and Britain to renounce claims to Morocco by a series of bilateral agreements. Germany was not consulted and sought to compel France to grant it comparable territories elsewhere, which it did in 1911. By the 1912 Treaty of FES, an independent Morocco ceased to exist.

The Moroccan Question is generally portrayed as a chapter in the diplomatic history of Europe. But Moroccans also played a major role in both its unfolding and its ultimate resolution. Sultans Abd al-Aziz (1884–1908) and Abd al-Hafid (1908–1912) opposed French ambitions, but ended up acquiescing to the inevitable. Moroccan official pusillanimity and European troop landings between 1902 and 1912 were opposed by various popular rebellions, peasant revolts, and millenarian movements.

BIBLIOGRAPHY

ANDREW, CHRISTOPHER. "The Entente Cordiale from Its Origins to the First World War." In *Troubled Neighbors: Anglo-French Relations in the Twentieth Century,* ed. by Neville Waiter. London, 1970.

BURKE, EDMUND, III. *Prelude to Protectorate in Morocco: Precolonial Protest and Resistance, 1860–1912.* Chicago, 1976.

Edmund Burke III

Morocco

Arab kingdom in the extreme northwest corner of Africa.

Morocco is bounded on the west by the Atlantic Ocean, on the north by the Mediterranean Sea, on the east and southeast by Algeria, and on the south by Western Sahara (claimed by Morocco). Spain administers two urban enclaves in northern Morocco—CEUTA and Melilla—and the offshore islands of Alhucemas, Peñón de Vélez de la Gómera, and Chafarinas. Most of Morocco was a protectorate of France from 1912 until 1956; northern Morocco was administered by Spain during that period. An 1860 war between Spain and Morocco established Spain's claim to Ifni, on the Atlantic coast of southern Morocco. Tarfaya became Spanish with the 1912 Treaty of FES. A 1958 treaty ceded Tarfaya to Morocco, and in 1969 Spain returned Ifni. King HASSAN II has ruled Morocco since 1961.

Geography and Climate. Morocco has an area of 446,550 square kilometers (178,620 sq. mi.). It is dominated by the ATLAS MOUNTAINS, which run through the center of the country from southwest to northeast, and the Sahara desert, which dominates its eastern frontier with Algeria and its southern frontier with Western Sahara and Mauritania. The Atlas chain comprises the High, Middle, and Saharan ranges, as well as the RIF mountains, along Morocco's Mediterranean coast. The northern Atlantic coastal plains of the GHARB constitute the chief agricultural area. Others include the Tadla plain of the Oum al-Rbi'a (Mother of Spring) river south of CASABLANCA, the Haouz plain of the Tensift river near MARRAKECH, and the Sous river valley in southwestern Morocco. These rivers, navigable only in small boats, provide water for irrigation.

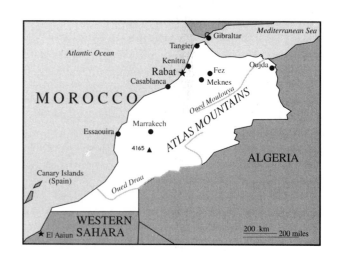

The Qarawiyyin mosque in Fez. (Richard Bulliet)

The Mediterranean and Atlantic coasts have relatively moist, mild winters and hot, dry summers. Eastern and southern Morocco have semiarid climates governed by the Sahara's heat and winds. Higher elevations of the Atlas mountains, particularly the High Atlas between Marrakech and Ouarzazate, can be bitterly cold, and remain snow-covered year round. Morocco's highest peak, Mount Tubkal, is easily accessible from Marrakech and is a popular skiing area.

People, Language, and Religion. Morocco has 26.2 million people (1992 est.). About 46 percent (12,052,000) of Moroccans live in urban areas, primarily in Casablanca (2,904,000), RABAT (1,287,000; the nation's capital), and Marrakech (1,425,000). Other major towns include FEZ (933,000), Oujda (895,000), Kenitra (833,000), TETUAN (800,000), Safi (793,000), MEKNES (704,000), Agadir (700,000), and TANGIER (509,000). Population density is about 149 per square mile. The population growth rate is 2.5 percent. Over 70 percent of the population is under twenty-nine. Life expectancy for males is sixty-two; for females, sixty-five. Morocco's literacy rate is about 71 percent, largely due to the emphasis on education since independence. Most Moroccans are engaged in agriculture, but an increasingly large number are in tourism, the liberal professions, commerce, industry, and government.

Morocco's ethnic groups are Arabs, mixed Arab-Berbers who identify as Arabs, and BERBERS. "Berber," primarily a linguistic term, applies to about 40 percent of the population; over 5.6 million Moroccans speak one of the three primary Berber dialects: Tarrifit, Tamazight, and Tachelhit.

Morocco's national language is Arabic. French serves as a second national language in commerce, education, diplomacy, and government. Newspapers, radio, and television use standard Arabic. Moroccan Arabic differs from the Arabic of Algeria. It is characterized by an intense clipping of vowels and a vocabulary that is not understood outside of Morocco. Many Moroccans have a rudimentary understanding of the Egyptian dialect because films and television soap operas produced in Egypt are widely popular.

Islam is the state religion. Most Moroccans profess Sunni (mainstream) Islam. A small Jewish community survives in Morocco. King Hassan II, as the symbol of Islam, maintains the caliphal title Amir al-Mu'minin (Prince of the Believers). His BARAKA is considered to be national in scope. During periods of drought, he offers prayers for rain. To demonstrate his strong faith, Hassan II had the world's largest mosque constructed in Casablanca. It opened for prayers in August 1993. To prevent challenges to the monarchy, political parties based on Islam are banned; they include the al-Jama'a group of Abdesalam Yacine and the Islamic Youth Society of Abdelkarim Mottai. Islamists are tightly controlled, their political leaders are periodically arrested and jailed, mosques are under surveillance, and pro-government imams are appointed to all mosques under the direction of the ministry of religion. On regional saints' birthdays (*moussems*) government ministers give speeches praising the local saints and extolling their followers as mojahedin (holy warriors). The most eminent saint's day is that celebrated in Mulay Idris, a small town near Meknes. Mulay Idris is the patron saint of Morocco. The Qarawiyin Mosque University of Fez and the Kutubiya (Booksellers) Mosque of Marrakech receive substantial endowments from the state.

Economy. Morocco's economy is still suffering from a drought that began in 1992 and that has ravaged the

Water wheel in Rabat. (Richard Bulliet)

A leather tannery in Fez. (© Yto Barrada)

agricultural industry. About 40 percent of the labor force is engaged in agriculture, which contributes 15 to 20 percent of gross domestic product. Service industries account for about 35 percent of Morocco's employment. Manufacturing is geared to phosphate production, but higher fuel costs have sparked inflation and phosphate price declines have reduced export earnings. Tourism experienced good growth in the 1980s and has become an important source of jobs and hard currency. Attempts by nations in Europe to limit the number of immigrants from Morocco concern politicians, who fret about this restriction on Morocco's safety valve for its unemployed population. About 500,000 to 1 million Moroccans reside in Europe as expatriate workers; their remittances are an important source of foreign exchange for Morocco.

Since independence, Morocco has utilized central planning for key economic sectors while supporting free-market practices in others. In the early 1970s, the government encouraged private investment by Moroccans; subsequently it adopted a policy of promoting foreign investment by reducing taxes and providing special investment codes for non-Moroccans.

History. Between 4000 and 2000 B.C.E., Berber peoples arrived from the Sahara and Southwest Asia. Most lowland Berber peoples eventually Arabized and Islamized. Beginning in the twelfth century B.C.E., Phoenicians began to explore the North African coastline. Their early coastal enclaves have been found in northern Morocco. By the late first century B.C.E., Rome's power had reached northern Morocco, and by the middle of the first century C.E., Morocco was the province of Mauretania Tingitana. The Vandals moved into North Africa in the 420s and ended Rome's presence. The Arabs' invasion of the late seventh–early eighth centuries transformed Morocco into an Islamic society with a powerful Arabic-speaking ruling class. Ruling dynasties were the Idrisids of Fez (early ninth century), the Almoravids and the Almohads of Marrakech (eleventh to thirteenth centuries), the Sa'adis (sixteenth century), and the ALAWITE DYNASTY (seventeenth century to the present).

After the death of Mulay Idris in 1728, a period of civil war brought the division of Morocco into *bilad al-makhzan* (area under government control) and *bilad al-siba* ("land of dissidence" outside government control). The government territory corresponded roughly to the lowland areas and key cities; the "dissidence" area was controlled by tribal groups in remote areas.

Europe began to focus on Morocco after 1878. After 1882 France began to look upon Morocco as its "sphere of interest," rounding out its North African empire. In 1900 economic interests based in France began construction of a new commercial port at the small fishing village of Casablanca. In 1912, a treaty divided Morocco into a protectorate under

Tasi palace in Tangiers. (Rhimou Bernikho)

Marshan mosque in Tangiers. (Rhimou Bernikho)

France over most of the country, and a protectorate under Spain over the north, including the Rif mountains. Once the protectorates were established, the military forces of Spain and France became preoccupied with suppressing rebellion primarily among the highland Berbers of the Rif and Atlas mountains. World War I interrupted the pacification process. After the war, the troops of France began a long and systematic campaign of subjugating Atlas Berber rebels that finally ended successfully in 1934. Those of Spain, with assistance from France, finally broke the Rif rebellion of ABD AL-KARIM in the late 1920s and consolidated Spain's rule from the capital of Spanish Morocco at Tetuan.

After the collapse of the armed rebellions, Morocco remained quiet until 1944, when the nationalist Allal al-FASI founded the ISTIQLAL (Independence) party in collaboration with Sultan (later King) MUHAMMED V (1927–1961). Istiqlal launched nationalist agitation immediately after the end of World War II. Muhammad V supported these efforts, and as a result was exiled from 1953 to 1955. Morocco gained its independence in 1956, and the following year Muhammad V changed the Sultanate of Morocco to the Kingdom of Morocco. In the nationalist

fervor that accompanied the first few years of independence, the king was able to push through a law making a one-party state illegal. This enabled the monarchy to break the power of Istiqlal by encouraging leftist elements to splinter off and create the National Union of Popular Forces (UNION NATIONALE DES FORCES POPULAIRES; UNFP). The monarchy supported the fractionalization of political parties and the emergence of new ones in order to split the opposition and to introduce royalist parties such as the National Rally of Independents (RASSEMBLEMENT NATIONAL DES INDÉPENDANTS; RNI) and the Constitutional Union (Union Constitutionnelle; UC). Often these royalist parties aimed to organize groups that did not have a representative party. Two parties emerged, for example, to cater to the interests of rural and urban Berbers. When Muhammad V died in 1961, Hassan II became king. His inexperience led to some early mistakes. Opposition to Hassan peaked in 1971–1972 with two failed coup attempts, one by army cadets and a second by air force personnel. These threats to Hassan's regime seemed to be linked to Berber elements within the military and led to the king's removal of disaffected Berber members, and to the consequent Arabization of the armed forces.

King Hassan's resolve to recover Western Sahara led to a crisis with Spain when he ordered a GREEN MARCH of 300,000 Moroccans in October 1975. His strategy bore almost immediate fruit, for in November, Spain negotiated a withdrawal of its forces and the reversion of the area to Morocco and Mauritania. In February 1976, Morocco received the northern two-thirds and Mauritania gained the southern third.

In the meantime, indigenous inhabitants of Western Sahara (who call themselves Sahrawi, "Saharans") had undertaken a war of national liberation

Northern coast of Morocco and the Strait of Gibraltar. The famous rock can be seen in the hazy distance at the upper right. (Rhimou Bernikho)

from Spain, establishing the Popular Front for the Liberation of Saqiya al-Hamra and Rio de Oro (Frente Popular para la Liberación de Sakiet el Hamra y Rio de Oro; POLISARIO), with a national government in exile (Saharan Arab Democratic Republic; SADR) in Algeria. As Morocco's forces replaced those of Spain in 1976, POLISARIO irregulars began a guerrilla war against Morocco that lasted until 1991.

Internally, King Hassan II has co-opted labor and the political parties to reinforce the monarchy while playing to international audiences in his determination to democratize and improve Morocco's human rights record; the Moroccan Human Rights League (Organisation Marocaine des Droits de l'Homme; OMDH) held its first congress in May 1991. Hassan has sought to prepare for his succession by naming Crown Prince Muhammad as heir apparent.

BIBLIOGRAPHY

BOWEN, DONNA LEE, and EVELYN A. EARLY, eds. *Everyday Life in the Muslim Middle East*. Bloomington, Ind., 1993.

BURGAT, FRANÇOIS, and WILLIAM DOWELL. *The Islamic Movement in North Africa*. Austin, Tex., 1993.

DAMIS, JOHN. *Conflict in Northwest Africa: The Western Sahara Dispute*. Stanford, Calif., 1983.

MERNISSI, FATIMA. *Beyond the Veil: Male-Female Dynamics in Modern Muslim Society*. Rev. ed. Bloomington, Ind., 1987.

NELSON, HAROLD D., ed. *Morocco: A Country Study*. 5th ed. Washington, D.C., 1988.

NORRIS, H. T. *The Arab Conquest of the Western Sahara*. Singapore, 1986.

OUSSAID, BRICK. *Mountains Forgotten by God: The Story of a Moroccan Berber Family*. Washington, D.C., 1989.

SPENCER, WILLIAM. *Historical Dictionary of Morocco*. Metuchen, N.J., 1980.

ZARTMAN, I. WILLIAM, and WILLIAM MARK HABEEB, eds. *Polity and Society in Contemporary North Africa*. Boulder, Colo., 1993.

Larry A. Barrie

Morocco, Political Parties in

Political parties have been an integral part of Morocco since the early 1930s.

The severe constraints under which the parties have had to operate, the parliament's lack of real power vis-à-vis the monarch, and the fragmented nature of Morocco's society have combined to prevent them from establishing a basis of support beyond particularist, sectoral interests, and personal ties and have rendered them vulnerable to both manipulation and repression. Overall, Morocco's political parties have served a significant, albeit adjunct, function in what has been essentially a monarchy-dominated, traditional, patrimonial system of rule.

The COMITÉ D'ACTION MAROCAINE was established during the early 1930s to promote nationalist demands. A later incarnation, the ISTIQLAL party, played a central role in the nationalist struggle during the decade before Morocco's independence in 1956. The Istiqlal and its offshoot, the UNION NATIONALE DES FORCES POPULAIRES (UNFP), led a vigorous challenge, during the first decade of independence, to the king's efforts to rule as well as reign. The result was an unmitigated triumph for the king. Opposition political parties were co-opted and repressed. Examples of repression included bannings, arrests, imprisonments, and, in the case of the UNFP's Mehdi Ben Barka, assassination. In addition, the monarchy supported the establishment of the MOUVEMENT POPULAIRE (MP), the short-lived FRONT POUR LA DÉFENSE DES INSTITUTIONS CONSTITUTIONELLES (FDIC), the RASSEMBLEMENT NATIONAL DES INDÉPENDANTS (RNI), and, in the 1980s, the Union Constitutionelle (UC), in order to counter the opposition.

Since the mid-1960s, the king has governed with the assistance of the pro-monarchy groupings and parties. From the mid-1970s, he has had considerable success in controlling the pace of political change, including the holding of three general elections at intervals suitable to his political requirements (1977, 1984, and 1993), pushing through cosmetic constitutional reforms, and mobilizing nearly the entire political spectrum on behalf of his Western Sahara policies. Although the direct election of two-thirds of the members of parliament has been conducted with considerable fairness, the indirect election for the rest of the seats has always been subject to manipulation.

Concurrently, the Istiqlal, the UNION SOCIALISTE DES FORCES POPULAIRES (which had split in the early 1970s from the UNFP), and the Parti du Progrès et du Socialisme (PPS) played the political game, to a large degree, according to the king's rules: between 1977 and 1984, Istiqlal even participated in the ruling coalition. At the end of the 1980s, Morocco's diplomatic and military successes in regard to the Western Sahara, sustained macroeconomic gains, and successful restructuring of the external debt strengthened the regime's confidence in its ability to loosen its grip a bit. On the other hand, widespread poverty, Western pressure regarding human rights issues, and the specter of increasing radical Islamic activism compelled the regime to seek to broaden political participation. (The organized Islamic movement is fragmented, and its various manifestations are barred

Political Parties Holding Seats in the Chamber of Deputies after the 1984 and 1993 Elections.		
Parties	*Year*	*Seats*
Centrist/Right-of-Center (traditionally loyal to monarchy)		
Union Constitutionelle (UC) head: Maati Bouabid	1984 1993	83 51
Rassemblement National des Indépendants (RNI) head: Ahmad Osman	1984 1993	61 41
Mouvement Populaire (MP) head: Mohand Laenser	1984 1993	47 51
Mouvement National Populaire (MNP) heads: Ahmad Fadil, Mahjoubi Ahardane	1993	25
Parti National Démocratique (PND)	1984 1993	24 24
Parti Démocratique Independent (PDI) head: Thami al-Wazzani	1984 1993	0 9
Left-of-Center (traditionally oppositionist)		
Istiqlal head: Muhammad Boucetta	1984 1993	41 52
Union Socialiste des Forces Populaires (USFP) head: Abderrahman Youssoufi	1984 1993	36 52
Confédération Démocratique du Travail (CDT) (allied with USFP)	1984 1993	3 4
Parti du Progrès et du Socialisme (PPS) (Communist) head: Ali Yata	1984 1993	2 10
Organisation pour l'Action Démocratique et Populaire (OADP) (Marxist-Leninist splinter) head: Muhammad Bensaid	1984 1993	1 2
Union Marocaine du Travail (UMT)	1984 1993	5 3
Others		
Parti de l'Action (PA)	1984 1993	0 2

from running in elections; its most prominent figure, Abdsalem Yasine, has been held in custody for much of the period since 1984.)

In May 1992, the Istiqlal, the USFP, the PPS, the rump UNFP, and the splinter Marxist–Leninist Organisation pour l'Action Démocratique et Populaire (OADP) formed the Democratic Bloc (*al-kutla*), a parliamentary group pressing for constitutional and electoral reform, and especially for enhancing the powers of parliament. Three of the center–right parties—the UC, the MP, and the PARTI NATIONAL DÉMOCRATIQUE (PND)—formed the Entente Nationale; like the kutla parties, the center–right ran individual candidates.

Both the Istiqlal and the USFP achieved gains in the 1993 parliamentary elections. Istiqlal won forty-three seats in the direct balloting and the USFP won forty-eight. Both suffered drops in the indirect balloting. Each now had fifty-two seats, making them roughly equal in size to the UC and MP as the largest parliamentary factions. King Hassan offered the kutla opposition a total of nineteen ministerial positions in his proposed new cabinet, but reserved the key posts of prime minister and the interior, foreign, finance, and justice portfolios for his close associates. Both the Istiqlal and the USFP refused the terms. Some secular intellectuals hope that Hassan's son and designated successor, Crown Prince Sidi Muhammad, will be more amenable to a substantive liberalization of political life, including a more genuine and effective multiparty parliamentary system.

Bruce Maddy-Weitzman

Morrison–Grady Plan

A 1946 Anglo–American report calling for the division of Palestine into semi-autonomous Arab and Jewish regions.

At the end of World War II, the British position in Palestine, its mandate, was becoming untenable. With thousands of European Jewish refugees needing to immigrate to Palestine, Britain and the United States dispatched a commission of inquiry to that territory in April 1946. In July, headed by Herbert Morrison, representing Britain's Labour government, and Henry Grady, representing the United States, the commission drew up its report in London.

Called the Morrison–Grady Plan, the report suggested a division of Palestine into semi-autonomous Arab and Jewish regions, while the British high commissioner would remain in control of defense, foreign relations, customs, and immigration. The plan also called for a one-year quota of 100,000 Jewish refugees to enter Palestine, after which time the immigration quotas would be set by the British. Morrison–Grady would have meant an increase of British control over Palestine and was rejected by both the Arabs and the Jews.

BIBLIOGRAPHY

SACHAR, HOWARD. *England Leaves the Middle East.* New York, 1972.
SHIMONI, YAACOV, ed. *Political Dictionary of the Middle East in the Twentieth Century.* New York, 1974.
SPIEGEL, STEVEN. *The Other Arab–Israeli Conflict.* Chicago, 1985.

Zachary Karabell

Morrison–Knudsen Company

Engineering and heavy construction firm.

Founded in Idaho in 1912, Morrison–Knudsen is an internationally recognized heavy construction and engineering firm that was engaged by the government of Iran in 1947 to prepare the preliminary studies that became the basis for Iran's first seven-year plan. The company completed several projects in Iran over the next three decades, including the 590-foot (180 m) high Karaj Dam near Tehran in 1961.

BIBLIOGRAPHY

The eMKayan (magazine of Morrison Knudsen Corporation, Boise, Idaho), 75th anniversary issue (March 1987).

Jack Bubon

Mosad le-Aliyah Bet

See Ma'pilim

Moshav

Collective village, based on agriculture, in Israel.

The moshav (plural, moshavim) is a collective village, of which there were 410 in 1991 with a combined population of 152,500. The collective provides agricultural inputs and marketing services to the families living there and the various moshav movements have national and regional organizations to provide these services. Land on the moshav is divided between the member families. In the early years, hired labor was banned and communal cultivation of some land prevailed. This changed in the 1960s and 1970s when Arab labor became an important part of the economy of many moshavim. The moshavim have their own bank, savings and pension schemes, insurance company, and regional purchasing organizations.

The foundations of the moshav go back to 1919, when Eliezer Yaffe published a pamphlet suggesting the creation of moshavim on nationally owned land, with mutual aid, cooperative purchasing and marketing, and the family as the basic unit. Like the kibbutz, the moshav was to be a pioneering institution, emphasizing national and social rejuvenation for the Jewish people and the Land of Israel. The first moshav was founded at Merhavia in the Galilee. Yaffe's ideas were influential in the founding of the second moshav, Nahalal, in 1921, the model for future settlements of this kind. Between 1949 and 1956, 250 moshavim were set up to house and provide employment for immigrants mainly from North Africa and Asia, who were not attracted to the communal life of the kibbutz, but for whom agriculture was the only possible basis for employment. By 1970 the moshavim had a population of 100,000. They had, in terms of numbers of settlements and total population, become more important than the kibbutzim.

During the 1980s, many of the moshav movement's economic organizations, responsible for marketing and purchasing inputs, went bankrupt as a result of overexpansion and high interest rates. Many moshavim were badly affected, and the mutual guarantee, by which each member or family supported other members, fell into disfavor. During the 1980s, an increasing number of urban families moved to moshavim; they commute to towns and are not involved in agriculture.

Members of each moshav elect a management committee that organizes the provision of economic services as well as education and health services to the community. The moshavim are also affiliated with different political parties, the largest moshav is affiliated with the Labor party. Others are affiliated to religious parties.

The *moshav shitufi* is a moshav with many of the characteristics of the kibbutz. In 1991 there were 46 moshav shitufi with a total population of 12,600. Production is organized communally and members' work is determined by an elected committee. Consumption is private, with families eating at home and providing their own domestic services, as on other moshavim and in contrast to the kibbutzim.

BIBLIOGRAPHY

EISENSTADT, S. N. *Israeli Society*. London, 1967.
VITELES, H. *A History of the Cooperative Movement*. Vol. 4, *The Moshav Movement*. London, 1968.

Paul Rivlin

Moshir al-Dowleh, Mirza Hasan Khan Pirnia [1870–1935]

Iranian statesman.

Mirza Hasan Khan Pirnia Moshir al-Dowleh (whose father, Mirza Nasrollah Khan Pirnia Moshir al-Dowleh, had been prime minister of Iran several times) was born in the province of Na'in, into a prominent family of the Qajar period (see QAJAR DYNASTY). He studied law in Moscow and attended military college. His first appointment was as military attaché to the Iranian embassy in St. Petersburg. He rose to prominence as a reform-minded bureaucrat of the Qajar era, among the few remembered favorably by historians. He founded the first military school of Iran, held numerous cabinet positions, and, from 1920 onward, served as prime minister four times. After the fall of the Qajar dynasty, in 1921, he limited his participation in the political affairs of the country to running for parliamentary seats. In 1923, he detached himself completely from public life and devoted himself to writing a three-volume history of ancient Iran, from the earliest period to the fall of the Parthian dynasty. This was one of the first works of the kind to be published in Iran. He died in Tehran.

Neguin Yavari

Moshir al-Saltaneh, Mirza Ahmad Khan [?–c. 1911]

Iranian politician.

The brother of Mirza Mahmud Khan Modir al-Dowleh, Mirza Ahmad Khan Moshir al-Saltaneh came from the northern province of Mazandaran and entered government service in 1854. In 1867, he became head scribe to MOZAFFAR AL-DIN QAJAR, the crown prince stationed in Tabriz. He was given the title Moshir al-Saltaneh in 1883, held several cabinet posts, and served as prime minister four times. The success of the revolutionaries in capturing Tehran in 1911 forced Moshir al-Saltaneh, who was opposed to the Constitutional Revolution on religious grounds, to seek refuge at the Ottoman embassy. He purchased his freedom from the revolutionaries and died in Tehran in 1911, only a few months after surviving an attempt made on his life.

Neguin Yavari

Moslem Philanthropic Benevolent Society

An educational charity established in 1878 by Sunni Muslim families of Beirut.

Founded partly as a reaction to Western missionary activities and partly owing to the influence of the reformist ideas of Muhammad ABDUH, the society expanded its philanthropic services to include hospitals, orphanages, boy scout organizations, and old people's homes in various areas of Lebanon and in Jerusalem. Although it was apolitical to a degree, the mufti and a number of community leaders of Beirut coveted the presidency of the society. The SALAM family retained control of the society for such long periods, however, that the name of the society became associated with the bestowal of their political patronage.

BIBLIOGRAPHY

JOHNSON, MICHAEL. *Class and Client in Beirut: The Sunni Community and the Lebanese State*. London and Atlantic Highlands, N.J., 1986.

Bassam Namani

Moslem Youth Organization

The organization that was to give rise to the Najjada party.

The organization began as the alternative to the Christian youth organization in both Syria and Lebanon. Although in the early years the Najjada party, founded in 1946, recruited members from the ranks of the Moslem Youth organization, the organization later severed all ties to the party.

As'ad AbuKhalil

Mosque

Islamic place of worship.

Mosque is an anglicized French cognate for the Arabic word *masjid,* which literally means "place of prostration." In the most abstract sense, any private or

Fatih mosque in Istanbul, Turkey. (D.W. Lockhard)

Lotf Allah mosque in Isfahan, Iran, seen across the royal square. (Richard Bulliet)

BIBLIOGRAPHY

CRESWELL, K. A. C. *Early Muslim Architecture.* 2 vols., rev. ed. Oxford, 1969.
HOAG, JOHN D. *Islamic Architecture.* New York, 1977.

Scott Alexander

Mosque of Umar

See Temple Mount and Haram al-Sharif

Mossad

One of the three main Israeli intelligence agencies.

Mossad (Mossad LeBiyyun U'Letafkidim Meyuhadim; Institute for Espionage and Special Duties) was founded as Mossad L'Aliyah Bet (Institute for Illegal Immigration). It was instrumental in the effort (begun in 1937) of the Jewish underground, Haganah (Defense), to mobilize and transfer, by sea and land, Zionist and non-Zionist Jews to Palestine. This clandestine organization was specially organized to defy British mandatory authority, which from 1939 restricted immigration to Palestine in an effort to appease Palestinian Arabs. Mossad was under the domination of the Jewish Agency, the official government of the Jewish community (*yishuv*) in Palestine.

David Ben-Gurion, the chairman of the Jewish Agency from the mid-1930s, and later prime minister of Israel (1948–1963, except for 1953–1954), was the founding father of Israel's intelligence services. He recruited members from kibbutzim and youth labor organizations for what would be known as Mossad. These individuals mainly were from Ahdut ha-Avodah, the militant arm of the labor movement.

public space properly prepared for the purposes of performing the five obligatory prayers of ISLAM (*salat*) constitutes a mosque. The term *mosque,* however, is most commonly used to refer to a space which has been permanently or semipermanently demarcated as a place of public Muslim worship.

While many mosques share such common features as a prayer niche (*mihrab*), pulpit (*minbar*), and area for performing ritual ablutions, the size, layout, and architecture of any given mosque is usually particular to its own specific historical, social, and cultural context. In many well-established Muslim communities, the largest and most centrally located mosque will often function as the *masjid al-jami,* or central mosque, where a large number of worshippers gather for the Friday noon congregational prayer (*salat al-jum'a*) and sermon (*khutba*). Not unlike their counterparts in other religious traditions, mosques and larger mosque complexes often serve as a primary locus for a variety of communal gatherings and activities, ranging from social-service programs and political rallies to QUR'AN study groups and scholarly lectures.

The function of Mossad, once the State of Israel was established in May 1948, was to reform and reorganize all security defense structures. The first task was turning Shai, the Haganah intelligence service, into a more elaborate system that would deal with both domestic and regional security.

In some ways, the Mossad can be compared with the U.S. Central Intelligence Agency (CIA) as the overall intelligence service. The reform and reorganization strengthened Ben-Gurion's domination of all security services. Independent of Mossad and SHIN BET, the Israel Defense Forces (IDF) established an intelligence department, Aman, in 1949 that was part of its general staff, dealing with field and military intelligence.

Mossad is involved in all of Israel's regional and international spying, as is Shin Bet, which deals with counterintelligence and disorder in Arab regimes. The first director of Shin Bet, Isser Harel, was appointed to head Mossad and to be the director general of all security services in 1952. Since his March 1963 resignation, Shin Bet and Mossad have been under the direction of the prime minister.

Harel, the most significant head of Israel's security and intelligence services, began his career in Shai, which mainly infiltrated the underground organizations of Etzl and LOHAMEI HERUT YISRAEL (Lehi). In this period, Israel's security services gained an international reputation. Harel was very close to Ben-Gurion; among his outstanding accomplishments was his command of the operation to capture the war criminal Adolf Eichmann. Also, in the area of internal security, he brought about the capture of three Soviet spies: Israel Baer, Kurt Cita, and Aaron Cohen.

The major purposes of Israeli intelligence were established by Ben-Gurion, who institutionalized the system: infiltrating and spying in the Arab world, and spying on and threatening political regimes that supported or sponsored individuals or institutions deemed detrimental to Israeli security, such as the Nazi scientists who worked for Egypt's military and scientific missile research system.

Mossad was involved in political deception, penetration, and infiltration into elements hostile to Israel (as defined by Ben-Gurion). It supported and shored up conservative Arab regimes such as Morocco in the late 1950s, backing the regime against its opposition; and in conjunction with French security services, it helped King Hassan of Morocco to stabilize his regime. Mossad also was involved in organizing the rescue of Jews from Egypt during the 1956 war. It had very important connections with Iran's SAVAK intelligence security organization, and agents of Mossad were political counselors to the shah's regime. Support of minority groups

opposed to Sunni-dominated Arab regimes, such as the Kurds in Iraq, was one of Mossad's most brilliant coups—highlighted by a planned defection of an Iraqi air force pilot and his MiG plane in August 1966, with Kurdish help. Mossad also had an important role in helping Emperor Haile Selassie of Ethiopia crush a coup attempt (December 1960) by giving him information about his opponents as he was returning from a trip abroad. Mossad worked closely with CIA counterintelligence when James Jesus Angleton was its director, furnishing the United States with the first information on the anti-Stalinist speech by Nikita Khrushchev, delivered in September 1963.

The bureaucratic struggles between Mossad and the IDF's Aman were notorious, especially during the French–Israeli alliance of the 1950s. Much to the annoyance of Mossad, IDF intelligence conducted its own foreign operations during this period, especially the preparations for French–Israeli collusion in war against Egypt in 1956. Mossad was extremely successful in its penetration of Arab regimes, the most notorious instance being the spy Elie Cohen, who in the late 1950s and early 1960s penetrated Syria's army intelligence and ministry of defense. In fact, he was an unofficial adviser to Amin al-Hafiz, the dictator of Syria. Through Cohen the IDF was given full information on Syria's strategic positions in the Golan Heights, and he played a key role in Israel's occupation of the Golan Heights in the 1967 war.

One of Mossad's great achievements was the destruction of the Black September group, which was responsible for the murder of Israeli athletes at the 1972 Munich Olympic games. This was not without a fiasco, however. In Lillehammer, Norway, an Arab waiter was mistakenly assassinated as a member of Black September, straining relations between Israel and Norway for some time.

The major achievements of Shabak, a counterintelligence, antiterrorist group, came after 1967, when it succeeded in curtailing Palestinian efforts to disrupt Israel's military authority in the occupied territories. Another successful Shabak effort was its war against Jewish extremists; it captured a clandestine group of revolutionary settlers who sought to sabotage Israel's occupation of the West Bank in order to achieve greater independence for the settlers.

If Mossad, Shabak, and Aman have had great achievements separately, they also have had great fiascos—not equal to the failures of the CIA but certainly very serious. The most notorious was Shabak's elimination of German scientists through air "accidents" and other terror activities, which seriously worsened Israeli–German relationships. Mossad's activities in London, fighting against hijacking, created friction with the British government. And, as mentioned earlier, the mistaken murder of the Arab waiter in Lillehammer hurt Israel's relations with Norway. One cannot speak of Israel's intelligence services without mentioning Aman's notorious failure in the Lavon Affair (1953–1954), in which a group of Israel's intelligence officers attempted to damage Egyptian–American relationships by implicating Egypt in the bombing of U.S. information services in Cairo. Aman's main failure involved its inability to predict Egypt and Syria's surprise attack on Israel in 1973, the Yom Kippur War. Aman's failure created the opportunity for Egypt to call for political victory, even if in retrospect its crossing of the Suez Canal was one of the reasons President Anwar al-Sadat decided to make peace with Israel.

Mossad's greatest failure was the Department of Dirty Tricks, which was responsible for collecting scientific and intelligence information, especially in the United States. It became infamous with the case of the American spy Jonathan Pollard, who secured top-secret naval intelligence dealing with Soviet–Arab connections. Mossad also infiltrated French military industries and played a key role in stealing heavy water from France.

BIBLIOGRAPHY

BAR-ZOHAR, MICHAEL. *Isser Harel and Israel's Security Services.* London, 1970.

BLACK, IAN, and BENNY MORRIS. *Israel's Secret Wars: The Untold History of Israeli Intelligence.* London, 1993.

EISENBERG, DENNIS, et al. *The Mossad: Israel's Secret Intelligence Service.* New York, 1979.

PERLMUTTER, AMOS. "Institutionalization of Civil–Military Relations in Israel: The Ben-Gurion Legacy and Its Challengers." *Middle East Journal* (Autumn 1968): 415–432.

———. *Military and Politics in Israel: Nation-Building and Role Expansion.* London, 1969.

Amos Perlmutter

Mossadegh, Mohammad   [1882–1967]

Iranian politician and leading speaker for the nationalist-democratic movement; prime minister, 1951–1953.

Mirza Mohammad Khan, later called Mossadegh (also Mosaddeq, Musaddiq) al-Saltaneh, was born in Tehran in 1882, into a wealthy family connected to the bureaucracy of the Qajar dynasty. His father, Mirza Hedayatollah Vazir Daftar, belonged to the Ashtiyani family, many of whom, such as Qavam and Vosuq, became important public figures in nineteenth- and twentieth-century Persia, now Iran. His mother Najm al-Saltaneh (known as Shahzadeh Khanom), was Prince Regent Abbas Mirza's granddaughter. Mossadegh married at age nineteen Khanom Zia al-Saltaneh, from an Islamic clerical family.

When Mossadegh's father died, he inherited his position as a chief *mostowfi* (representative of the state treasury) in the province of Khurasan. In support of the CONSTITUTIONAL REVOLUTION (1905–1911), Mossadegh joined, briefly, the Adamiyat and Insaniyat societies. In 1909, he went to Europe but returned because of an illness. On recovery, he returned to Europe in 1911, studied law at Neuchâtel University in Switzerland, and completed his doctoral dissertation on the jurisprudence of Islam. He returned home in 1914 and became known as Dr. Mohammad Khan Mossadegh al-Saltaneh. During World War I, from 1914 to 1918, he wrote essays on legal and political matters, was active in the Democratic party (Hizb-i I'tidal), taught at the Tehran School of Law and Political Science, and became the deputy (*mo'avin*) of the ministry of finance.

In 1920, Mossadegh was appointed governor of Fars, but he soon resigned when he refused to recognize the new government of Sayyed Zia Tabataba'i that was formed following his and Reza Khan's coup of February 1921. When Ahmad Qavam became prime minister, Mossadegh was appointed minister of finance. His attempts to reform the ministry were blocked by the *majles* (parliament) and the royal court, which led to the downfall of the cabinet. In 1922, Mossadegh was appointed governor of Azerbaijan and, in 1923, became foreign minister for about four months—his last office until he became prime minister in 1951.

Mossadegh's parliamentary activities began when he was elected Tehran representative to the fifth Majles. During his political career, Mossadegh increasingly personified Persia's nationalist and democratic aspirations. His first major move for nationalism was opposition to the ANGLO–PERSIAN AGREEMENT of 1919. His commitment to democracy was reflected in his vehement opposition to Reza Khan's move to dethrone the Qajar dynasty to found his own, the PAHLAVI.

After Reza Khan became Reza Shah Pahlavi, in 1925, Mossadegh remained a major critic of the regime, despite the shah's frequent efforts to co-opt him. With the rise of Pahlavi's despotism, many of Mossadegh's associates were exiled, jailed, or killed. Being very cautious, he withdrew from politics, shutting himself away at his rural estate in Ahmadabad, west of Tehran. (Meanwhile, in 1935, Persia was renamed Iran.) In 1940, he was arrested and imprisoned in Birjand. He was soon released, because Reza Shah was ousted by the Allies (Britain and the Soviet Union) in 1941 for being pro-Nazi; the shah was succeeded by his son, Mohammad Reza Pahlavi.

Mossadegh then returned to politics. In October 1949, he led a crowd of politicians, university students, and bazaaris into the shah's palace to protest voting fraud in Iran's fifteenth parliamentary elections. Once inside, the demonstrators elected a committee of twenty, headed by Mossadegh, which soon became the nucleus of the NATIONAL FRONT. Under his leadership, the front was instrumental in pressuring the parliament to nationalize the British-run petroleum industry. On April 30, 1951, Mossadegh was elected prime minister by a large margin. The shah had no option but to ratify the oil-nationalization bill and, on May 1, the law went into effect. Although the United States initially supported the oil nationalization movement, it soon joined Britain in engineering the coup that overthrew Mossadegh in August of 1953.

An aborted coup took place several days before the successful one. The shah fled the country after hearing that the coup had failed, but Mossadegh refused to have the shah arrested. Following the referendum that had given him the mandate in 1951, Mossadegh dissolved the parliament and had several military officers arrested for their roles in plotting against him. He continued to act constitutionally until he was removed by Fazlollah Zahedi, whom the shah named premier.

Pro-Pahlavi commentators have long accused Mossadegh's nationalism of being negative and destructive, and the current rulers of the Islamic Republic tend to belittle his policies, because of his secularism and liberalism. Many social historians and political scientists, however, portray Mossadegh as a man deeply committed to the ideals of a democratic nation. Considering the economic difficulties that he faced after nationalizing the oil industry, he might have compromised his ideals and struck a deal with Britain or the Soviet Union while protecting his democratic government. Mossadegh lived to be 85; he died on March 5, 1967.

BIBLIOGRAPHY

ABRAHAMIAN, ERVAND. *Iran between Two Revolutions.* Princeton, N.J., 1982.

KATOUZIAN, HOMA, ed. *Musaddiq's Memoirs.* Tr. by S. H. Amin and H. Katouzian. London, 1988.

Mansoor Moaddel

Mostowfi al-Mamalek, Mirza Hasan Khan

[1875–1932]

Iranian politician.

Mirza Hasan Khan Mostowfi al-Mamalek inherited the ministry of finance in 1882 at the age of seven. He then went to Europe and returned in 1907, having been appointed minister of war in the cabinet of Amin al-Soltan. After the CONSTITUTIONAL REVOLUTION, he held fifteen ministerial positions, was prime minister eleven times, and simultaneously served as one of Tehran's deputies to the *majles*. He also headed the first government of Reza Shah Pahlavi after the latter's ascension to the throne in 1921, but he resigned in 1922 because of quarrels with members of parliament and never returned to political life. During his premiership, the bill for the construction of a national railroad service was ratified. Mostowfi al-Mamalek was one of the few Iranian politicians of the Qajar period (see QAJAR DYNASTY) who served British as well as Russian interests in World War I.

Neguin Yavari

Mosul

City in northern Iraq (Mesopotamia).

Mosul (also spelled Mawsil) is located on the west bank of the Tigris river opposite the ancient city of Nineveh. It was a significant center during the early Islamic period with a sizable Christian population. Destroyed by the Mongols, Mosul regained importance under the Ottoman Turks. Some of the older mosques and churches survived.

Located on the trade routes that led to eastern Anatolia and thence to the Black Sea, Syria, Lebanon, Iraq, and Iran to the south, goods from Mosul were shipped by raft down the Tigris to Baghdad or overland to Aleppo and Damascus or points north. The city was a center for regional and international trade: Grain export, the manufacture of cotton thread and fabric (whence the term *muslin*), and trafficking in sheep hides and wool were important activities.

The government at Istanbul regained administrative control of the city from local rulers in 1834; in 1879 it became a separate Ottoman province that included Kirkuk, Arbil, and Sulaymaniya, but real power remained in the hands of local families—Mustafa Çelebi Sabunci was virtual dictator from 1895 to 1911. The population of the mud-brick-walled city in the later nineteenth century was estimated at forty thousand, including seven thousand Christians and fifteen hundred Jews. By World War I the population of Mosul had risen to seventy thousand, and the city became the economic and administrative capital of the Ottoman province of Mosul, one of three (Baghdad, Basra, Mosul) that would make up modern Iraq.

With the breakup of the Ottoman Empire after World War I and the consequent protracted negotiations between Britain and Turkey for sovereignty over the city, Mosul became part of Iraq rather than Turkey. Though its stature as a center of trade waned as Baghdad became Iraq's capital, the city continued to expand. During the 1940s and 1950s many of the traditional families came to own much of the land and were instrumental, together with local Arab nationalists, in fomenting a rebellion against Abd al-Karim KASSEM in 1959.

With the discovery of oil nearby and the construction of a refinery, Mosul has retained its importance. It has rail links to Baghdad, Syria, and Turkey, a university, an airport, and a religiously diverse population. The population (estimated at 571,000 in 1985) is mainly Kurdish with a significant Christian minority and a Yazidi population that lives in the Sinjar mountains to the west of Mosul.

BIBLIOGRAPHY

BATATU, HANNA. *The Old Social Classes and the Revolutionary Movements of Iraq*. Princeton, N.J., 1978.

Reeva S. Simon

Mosul, Anglo–Turkish Dispute over

Dispute over oil deposits in Iraq, c. 1920–1928.

Mosul, a province in northern Iraq, is rich in oil deposits and serves as a transit center for trade with Turkey and Syria. Its population consists of Arab Sunni Muslims, a sizable Kurdish minority, and various Christian sects. In 1916, the Sykes–Picot Agreement between England and France designated Mosul as a French zone. In 1920, the San Remo Conference transferred Mosul to the British, with the stipulation that France would have a share in the Turkish Petroleum Company.

Mosul became a point of contention between Turkey and Britain in the early 1920s. Turkey claimed that Mosul was part of its territory because the majority of inhabitants were Ottoman non-Arabs and because Mosul had not been in the hands of Britain when the Mudros armistice pact was signed in 1918. Britain wanted Mosul to be part of Iraq for myriad reasons. It believed Mosul had substantial oil deposits and could be used as a

bargaining chip with the newly established government of Iraq to extend Britain's mandated power over that country. Faisal I, the newly crowned king of Iraq, wanted Mosul to be part of his country in order to strengthen his authority and influence over nationalistic elements who opposed Britain's continued interference in Iraq's domestic affairs.

The dispute between Turkey and Britain continued for several years. The two countries failed to resolve their conflict when the Lausanne Peace Treaty of 1923 was signed by the Allies and Turkey, and again at the special conference convened at Istanbul in 1924. They finally agreed to settle the dispute through the League of Nations. The League appointed a fact-finding commission to visit Iraq, survey public opinion in Mosul, and meet with officials on both sides. On 16 July 1924, the commission's report to the League called for the inclusion of Mosul in Iraq, retaining the Brussels line as the border between the two countries. Additional conditions attached to the recommendation included (1) allowing Iraq to remain under the British mandate for twenty-five years; (2) recognizing the rights of the Kurds to use their language in educational institutions and administration of justice, and (3) encouraging the hiring of Kurds as administrators, judges, and teachers. Iraq welcomed the decision. Mosul was one of the few issues that united the full spectrum of public opinion.

Turkey rejected the recommendation of the League of Nations and vowed to use any means necessary, including military action, to stop the implementation of the resolution. On 5 June 1926, however, Turkey signed a tripartite agreement with Britain and Iraq confirming Mosul's inclusion in Iraq. Iraq agreed to give a 10 percent royalty on Mosul's oil deposits to Turkey for twenty-five years. On 19 January 1926, Iraq had signed a new treaty with Britain, despite opposition from nationalist elements, to extend the mandate period for twenty-five years, as stipulated by the League's resolution. This treaty was ratified in January 1928, on the condition that Britain would recommend Iraq for membership in the League of Nations at four-year intervals for the next twenty-five years. If admission was approved, the British mandate would end.

BIBLIOGRAPHY

LONGRIGG, STEPHEN HEMSLEY. *Iraq, 1900–1950: A Political, Social and Economic History*. London, 1953.
SHIKARA, AHMAD. *Iraq Politics, 1921–1941*. London, 1987.

Ayad al-Qazzaz

Motahhari, Mortaza [1920–1979]

Iranian religious scholar and writer; a close associate of Ayatollah Khomeini, he fostered the intellectual developments that contributed to the Islamic revolution of 1978/79.

Born to a religious scholar who was also his first teacher, Motahhari (also Mutahhari) began his formal schooling in Mashhad at the age of twelve, swiftly discovering his fascination with philosophy and mysticism, which remained with him throughout his life. In 1937, he moved to Qom where he studied law and philosophy under teachers that came to include Ayatollah Ruhollah KHOMEINI. In 1952 he left for Tehran where, in addition to teaching philosophy at a traditional seminary, he accepted a position at the Faculty of Theology of Tehran University. He also collaborated with religiously inclined laymen in popularizing a view of Islam as a comprehensive and socially applicable ideology.

Briefly imprisoned after the uprising of June 1963, Motahhari remained in contact with Khomeini throughout the years of his exile in Iraq and participated in a series of clandestine religio-political organizations. Named to the Revolutionary Council established by Khomeini in the early weeks of 1979, after the success of the IRANIAN REVOLUTION, he was assassinated on May 1 of the same year by members of Furqan, a group holding a radically modernist view of Shi'ism that saw Motahhari as its chief intellectual opponent.

Motahhari's literary legacy is important, including works that express his passionate devotion to mysticism and philosophy as the ultimate core of Islam, as well as other works designed to present Islam as a fully coherent ideology, superior to all its numerous competitors.

BIBLIOGRAPHY

MUTAHHARI. *Fundamentals of Islamic Thought.* Tr. by R. Campbell. Berkeley, Calif., 1985.

Hamid Algar

Motherland Party

Turkish political party.

Founded in 1983, this party, Anap in Turkish, was led by Turgut OZAL, the author of a major economic stabilization plan promulgated in January 1980 by the government of Süleyman DEMIREL and continued under the military junta headed by General Kenan EVREN, who kept Ozal as deputy prime minister. Policy differences led to Ozal's resignation in 1982, however. Despite the active opposition of the military regime, the Motherland party won the parliamentary election of 1983 with 45 percent of the votes and 211 of a total of 400 seats. The party assumed a center-right posture, promising economic development and greater scope for private entrepreneurship, shrinkage of the public sector, strengthening Turkey's economic ties with its Middle East neighbors, respect for traditional values, a nonideological approach to politics, and abandonment of the bitter partnership of the 1970s. It attracted the support of both former JUSTICE PARTY activists and backers of the anti-system parties of the 1970s (the NATIONAL SALVATION PARTY and the NATIONALIST ACTION PARTY).

Once in power, its fortunes began to decline, despite a heavy emphasis on service delivery. This was due to a number of factors, including high rates of inflation, the reactivation of pre-1980 political leaders, particularly Süleyman Demirel at the head of the TRUE PATH PARTY, a conciliatory stance toward the military, and allegations of personal power seeking and corruption on the part of Ozal and members of his family.

Tensions within the party between the liberal, nationalist, and religionist trends also contributed to the political decline of the party. In the 1987 election, the Motherland party won only 36 percent of the vote, although it retained control of the parliament with 292 of 450 seats. In 1989, Ozal was elected president of the republic, thus diluting his control of the party to some extent. The party continued to decline, garnering only 24 percent of the vote and 115 of 450 seats in the 1991 election. Under the leadership of the moderate liberal Mesut Yılmaz, the party faced the decade of the 1990s in continuing competition with Demirel's True Path party.

BIBLIOGRAPHY

ERGÜDER, U. "The Motherland Party." In *Political Parties and Democracy in Turkey,* ed. by M. Heper and J. M. Landau. London, 1991.

Frank Tachau

Moudjahid, al-

Algerian newspaper.

Al-*Moudjahid* was the organ of the revolutionary FRONT DE LIBÉRATION NATIONALE (FLN; National Liberation Front); its first edition appeared in June

1956. The title means "one who struggles" or "freedom fighter." During the Algerian war of independence (1954–1962), it appeared bimonthly. After the war, it was the official French-language newspaper and had the largest daily circulation in the country. With the precipitous decline of the FLN after the October 1988 riots and official toleration of a freer press, the newspaper—like the party it represented—confronted intense competition from new rivals.

BIBLIOGRAPHY

HORNE, ALISTAIR. *A Savage War of Peace: Algeria, 1954–1962,* 2nd ed. New York, 1987.

Phillip C. Naylor

Moulay

See Mulai

Mouvement de l'Unité Populaire (MUP)

Tunisian political party in exile.

Ahmed BEN SALAH formed the Popular Unity Movement in 1973. The party is ideologically socialist and personally hostile to former Tunisian president Habib BOURGUIBA. In the 1960s Ben Salah developed socialist planning as Tunisia's economic system. Disastrous attempts to collectivize agriculture led to his fall in 1969. Tried and imprisoned, he escaped from the country in 1973 and remains in exile. Little support exists for the party within Tunisia; most supporters are Tunisian expatriates living in Europe. The party still adheres to a staunchly socialist, state-managed economic program.

MUP attitudes toward the Bourguiba regime were highly personalized as a result of contest of wills between Bourguiba and Ben Salah. The latter's refusal to participate in Tunisia's elections (which became somewhat more liberal after 1980) disillusioned many of the party's members, who consequently condoned a split in the party in 1981. A more flexible MUP emerged and renamed itself the Popular Unity Party (PARTI DE L'UNITÉ POPULAIRE; PUP). Under Mohamed Belhaj Amor, the PUP retained its earlier socialist and nationalist orientation but ceased Ben Salah's personal vendetta against Bourguiba. The party adopted a more flexible approach to participation in the political process. Following the 1988 political liberalization under President Zayn al-Abdine Ben Ali, PUP became one of seven legal parties in Tunisia. As of 1993 its membership was limited (about 12,500).

BIBLIOGRAPHY

PERKINS, KENNETH J. *Historical Dictionary of Tunisia.* Metuchen, N.J., 1989.

Larry A. Barrie

Mouvement des Démocrates Socials (MDS)

See Tunisia, Political Parties in

Mouvement National Algérien

An Algerian nationalist organization that rivaled, and eventually lost to, the FLN.

The Mouvement National Algérien (MNA; Algerian National Movement) was founded in Paris in December 1954 by Messali al-HADJ in reaction to the launching of the FRONT DE LIBÉRATION NATIONALE (FLN; National Liberation Front) by his revolutionary rivals in Algeria. It was a continuation of his branch of the MOUVEMENT POUR LE TRIOMPHE DES LIBERTÉS DÉMOCRATIQUES (MTLD; Movement for the Triumph of Democratic Liberties) established at Hornu, Belgium, during the summer.

One element after another of the Algerian political spectrum rallied to the FLN during 1955 and 1956. Claiming that this demonstrated that the FLN contained too many moderates and reformists, Messali's MNA was, by June 1956, the only major party remaining outside the nationalist coalition. Polarization led to bloody fighting between MNA and FLN factions within Algeria. Also, the FLN waged a concerted effort to win over the loyalties of the Algerian community in France, long commanded by Messali, and to tap its financial resources. Intra-communal fighting in France took many lives. The MNA lost in both arenas and, from 1958 onward, was of little political consequence, going formally out of existence on June 19, 1962.

BIBLIOGRAPHY

STORA, BENJAMIN. *Messali Hadj, 1898–1974.* Paris, 1982.

John Ruedy

Mouvement Populaire (MP)

Pro-monarchy political party in Morocco.

The Mouvement Populaire was organized in 1956–1957 in the Rif. Its supporters were BERBER notables and tribesmen, some of whom belonged to the Army of Liberation, and small landholders. It was founded to oppose the political domination of newly independent Morocco by the Istiqlal party and to serve as a mechanism for Berber political participation in cooperation with the monarchy. At the same time, the MP sought to avoid being cast as a purely Berber party and took on the role of spokesman for the rural masses neglected by the Istiqlal. Its founders were Abdelkarim KHATIB, a former head of the Arab Liberation Army (and ethnically an Arab), and Mahjoub AHARDANE, the governor of Rabat province.

In the fall of 1957, the Istiqlal-led government banned the party, removed Ahardane from office, and briefly imprisoned the two party heads, resulting in the first Rif rebellion. The relationship between the monarchy and the MP was strengthened during the early 1960s, following the ascension to power of Hassan II and the split in the Istiqlal. In 1962-1963, the MP was the only organized group within the monarchist coalition; it thus was able to take advantage of the boycott of the 1963 elections by Istiqlal and the Union Nationale des Forces Populaires and fill many of the positions in provincial assemblies, chambers of commerce, and communal councils. Its base of economic and political power was strengthened by the regime's policy of Moroccanizing large tracts of land that had been controlled by the French administration and settlers.

The MP did not field candidates in 1963, instead operating within the framework of the FRONT POUR LA DÉFENSE DES INSTITUTIONS CONSTITUTIONELLES (FDIC), but reasserted itself in 1964. In 1965 the defection from the ruling coalition of a single MP member deprived the government of its majority, sparking a constitutional crisis that led to King Hassan's assumption of emergency powers. In 1967, the MP split over personality differences between Ahardane and Khatib; the latter's breakaway faction took the name Mouvement Populaire Démocratique et Constitutionelle. Ahardane was expelled from the MP in 1985 for "authoritarian practices"; in July 1991, he cofounded the rival Mouvement National Populaire. In the 1993 parliamentary elections, the MP won a total of fifty-one seats, a gain of four from the 1984 elections.

Bruce Maddy-Weitzman

Mouvement pour le Triomphe des Libertés Démocratiques

Algerian organization that sought to attain national rights through electoral participation.

The Mouvement pour le Triomphe des Libertés Démocratiques (MTLD; Movement for the Triumph of Democratic Liberties) was created in 1946 by Messali al-HADJ, leader of Algeria's clandestine Parti du Peuple Algérien (PPA; Party of the Algerian People), which colonial authorities had banned in 1939. Under French detention almost continuously since 1937, Messali urged his followers after World War II to boycott French elections. Released in 1946, he hastily organized the MTLD, however, to enter candidates in the elections to the first National Assembly of the Fourth Republic held in November. In spite of harassment by the authorities, the MTLD won five of the fifteen parliamentary seats reserved for Muslim Algerians. Major business of the National Assembly included drafting what became the 1947 Organic Law of Algeria. MTLD deputies regularly denied the competence of a French legislature to determine Algeria's status in any way. In the meantime, the MTLD became by far the most popular party in ALGERIA. But colonial authorities, fearful of a nationalist victory, openly rigged the Algerian legislative elections of 1948, and they tampered again with the elections of 1949, 1951, 1953, and 1954.

After years of urging Algerians to spurn the process, Messali's abrupt decision to present slates of candidates in 1946 confused many Algerians. They did not know whether the party was seeking national rights by direct action or through electoral participation. In fact, it was doing both. At a clandestine party congress in February 1947, delegates determined that the MTLD would pursue political strategies within the existing colonial framework, while a secret PPA would continue to press for independence by whatever means necessary. By the end of 1947, the PPA–MTLD leadership had, in fact, approved the creation of an Organisation Spéciale (OS), which conducted armed robberies and other acts of violence until broken up by the authorities in March 1950.

It appears that MTLD cohesiveness was constantly torn through these years by the partisans of direct action and those of political participation. The decision to pursue both strategies simultaneously reflected irreconcilable internal contradictions more than rationally chosen strategy. This fundamental conflict lay at the heart of a series of internal disputes that progressively sapped the party's effectiveness in the early 1950s. The weakening of the party was hastened by conflicts between the Central Committee and Messali Hadj, widely accused of authoritarianism and of attempting to establish a cult of personality. Banned from Algerian soil in 1952, Messali in 1954 called a party congress at Hornu, Belgium, that declared the Central Committee dissolved and elected him president for life. Since the Central Committee failed to recognize the authority of the Hornu Congress, the party was split down the middle.

In the spring of 1954, a group of militants—mainly veterans of or sympathizers with the OS—formed the COMITÉ RÉVOLUTIONNAIRE D'UNITÉ ET D'ACTION (CRUA; Revolutionary Committee of Unity and Action). Disillusioned with the ''politicals'' and their failure to produce, they determined to launch an insurrection. By 1956, most of the MTLD centralists had rallied to the Front de Libération Nationale (FLN; National Liberation Front), which the CRUA had created. Messali, in Europe surrounded by the émigré loyalists who were his original base, refused to join. His wing of the MTLD became the MOUVEMENT NATIONAL ALGÉRIEN (MNA; Algerian National Movement) entering into often violent conflict with the FLN both at home and in France.

BIBLIOGRAPHY

HORNE, ALISTAIRE. *A Savage War of Peace: Algeria 1954–1962.* London, 1977.
RUEDY, JOHN. *Modern Algeria: The Origins and Development of a Nation.* Bloomington, Ind., 1992.

John Ruedy

Mouvement pour l'Unité Populaire (MUP)

See Tunisia, Political Parties in

Movement of Renewal

Formerly the Tunisian Communist party.

Founded as an offshoot of the French Communist party in 1920, the Parti Communiste Tunisien (PCT) broke with the French party in 1934. It remained legal after TUNISIA gained its independence in 1956 but was banned by President Habib BOURGUIBA in 1963. In 1981, however, Bourguiba legalized the PCT in order to offset the growing influence of the Islamist movement in Tunisia. PCT influence remained marginal, however, and the party has never succeeded in capturing the imagination of Tunisia's young people.

Disintegration of the Soviet Union in 1991 dealt the PCT a heavy blow. General-Secretary Moham-med Harmel (head of the party since 1981) sought at the party's tenth national congress (1993) to capitalize on the BEN ALI ''regime of change'' by renaming the PCT the Movement of Renewal (Mouvement Ettajdid; ME; Harakat al-Tajdid, in Arabic) and emphasizing the party's reformist credentials. Until 1989, the party published a tabloid, *al-Tariq al-Jadid* (The New Path). Suspended during the April 1989 national elections, it reemerged as a monthly magazine with the same title in 1993.

BIBLIOGRAPHY

AMRI, LAROUSSI. ''La Gauche tunisienne: Le tournant.'' *Haqa'iq/Réalités* no. 396 (30 April–6 May 1993): 12.
PERKINS, KENNETH J. *Historical Dictionary of Tunisia.* Metuchen, N.J., 1989.

Larry A. Barrie

Moyne, Lord

See Guinness, Walter Edward

Mozaffar al-Din Qajar   [1853–1907]

Fifth monarch of Persia's Qajar dynasty.

Mozaffar al-Din became shah in 1897, after his father Naser al-Din Shah was slain by an assassin's bullet. Mozaffar had lived in Tabriz in Azerbaijan, the traditional seat of the heir to the throne. He was of a timid but kindly nature and had been overshadowed and humiliated by forceful *pishkars* (ministers of Azerbaijan), appointed by his father, so he had little experience of statecraft upon his accession. His father had radiated an aura of royalty, although he had become despotic and unpopular toward the end of his reign.

The courtiers who came with the new shah to Tehran were greedy for the spoils of office they had long awaited; politics and court intrigues undermined the shah's authority and prestige. Mozaffar al-Din Shah's reign began badly, since Anglo–Russian rivalry was at its worst, compromising Persia's independence both financially and politically. A deep dissatisfaction among all the classes gave rise to widespread nationalism. The shah allowed some freedom of political discussion and activity, which soon resulted in the formation of political societies (*anjomans*), where reforms were discussed and contacts between various leaders were established. The printing and distribution of political tracts caused politics to be discussed and the government criticized.

Mozaffar al-Din Shah dismissed his father's unpopular minister, Amin al-Soltan, and appointed the liberal-minded Amin al-Dowleh, whose efforts to negotiate a much-needed loan from a neutral country failed. The shah recalled him and negotiated instead two loans from Russia at onerous terms. The monies were soon spent on trivialities during the shah's European trips in 1900, 1902, and 1905. These journeys were criticized and made him unpopular with the merchants, who resented the concessions granted to non-Persians; with the *ulama* (body of mollas), who were afraid of Western cultural influence; and with the liberals who feared a threat to Persia's independence. All the while, growing inflation and lawlessness weakened the central government. The dismissal of Amin al-Soltan and the appointment of the more autocratic Ayn al-Dowleh only exacerbated the situation.

Another cause of great resentment was the employment of Belgian customs officials at the borders, the proceeds of which were pledged as a guarantee against the loans from Russia and Britain. Naus, the director, was particularly hated; it was no coincidence that a photo of him, wearing the habit of a religious man to a costume party, was distributed with other propaganda by the opponents of the regime, to show the disrespect that foreigners had for the religious class. This was the spark that triggered the revolution in 1904. The first demands were for law and a House of Justice (ADALAT-KHANEH), formulated by those merchants and *ulama* who took *bast* (sanctuary) in the Shrine of Shah Abd al-Azim in 1904. The shah agreed to their demands but took no real action; therefore a protest began that took the life of a religious student. As a result the *ulama* left Tehran in a body for Qom, and 14,000 merchants gathered at the British embassy. Their demands included the granting of a constitution and a national constituent assembly (a *majles-e shura-ye melli*). The shah reluctantly agreed, and the preparation of the constitutional laws and the promulgation of electoral laws were accomplished quickly. The elections were rushed since the shah was ill, and it was feared that his successor, Mohammad Ali Mirza, might not continue his father's new policies. The electoral law was so devised that Tehran was purposely to receive half the 120 seats. In fact, Mozaffar al-Din Shah died a few months after he made the October 1906 inaugural speech in the *majles*.

Since the events of the succeeding reign confirmed the fears of the people, Persia was to face a long period of political turmoil. Mozaffar al-Din is therefore remembered with reverence, and those who built the entrance to the *majles* adorned it with the motto: "*Adl-e Mozaffar*" (The Justice of Mozaffar), which was left untouched even after the change of dynasty in 1925.

BIBLIOGRAPHY

AVERY, P. *Modern Iran*. London, 1965.
BROWNE, E. G. *The Persian Revolution of 1905–1909*. Cambridge, U.K. 1910.
KASRAVI, A. *Tarikh-e Mashrutiyat dar Iran* (The History of the Constitutional Revolution in Iran). Tehran, 1966.
KAZEMZADEH, F. *Russia and Britain in Persia, 1864–1914*. New Haven, Conn., 1968.

Mansoureh Ettehadieh

M'Rabet, Fadela

Pseudonym of Fatma Abda, an Algerian journalist and essayist.

M'Rabet, born in Constantine, Algeria, is married to a French journalist. M'Rabet was a high school teacher after Algeria gained its independence in 1962. She then joined the staff of the newspaper *Alger-Républicain* and was in charge of a woman's program on the radio. She now lives in France.

M'Rabet's first book, *La femme algérienne* (Paris, 1964; The Algerian Woman) was inspired by the correspondence she received while working as a journalist and radio commentator. Its tone is defiant, meant to shake the apathy of the reader and focus attention on women's suppressed rights. M'Rabet was critical of Islamic law, which granted a Muslim man the right to marry a non-Muslim woman while denying a Muslim woman the right to marry a non-Muslim man. Her second book, *Les Algériennes* (Paris, 1967; Algerian Women) is optimistic in its view of the future as a result of women's greater access to education. M'Rabet echoed the concerns of a growing number of women to protect their rights, newly acquired as a result of their participation in the Algerian War of Independence.

BIBLIOGRAPHY

GORDON, DAVID. *Women of Algeria: An Essay on Change.* Cambridge, 1968.

Aida A. Bamia

Muallim Naci   [1850–1893]

Ottoman poet and writer.

Considered the last of the neo-classical writers, Muallim Naci was born under the name Ömer in the Fatih district of Constantinople (now Istanbul), the son of a leather worker. Following the death of his father, he was raised by an uncle in the Bulgarian port of Varna. In 1867, he began teaching at the RÜŞDIYE at Varna, earning the title *muallim* (teacher). Later, he took the name Naci from the hero of a popular story.

Naci worked as an official in the administration of the district governor Kürt Sait Paşa, later accompanying him to Constantinople where he briefly worked in the foreign ministry and subsequently, beginning in 1883, became the literary editor of the newspaper TERCÜMAN-I HAKIKAT, a newspaper published by Ahmet Midhat Efendi. During the period of Naci's editorship, *Tercüman-i Hakikat* became one of the most widely read literary digests in the empire.

Although his artistic works are not held in high esteem, Muallim Naci had a profound influence on Turkish literary and intellectual development. For example, he was a crucial figure in the development of modern Turkish prose, writing in a clear, simple style. More generally, his influence stemmed from his position as teacher, at the Law School and at the Galatasaray Lycée, and as a prolific writer and critic.

David Waldner

Mu'ata University

Jordanian university.

Mu'ata (also Mu'ta) University was established in 1981 to provide courses in the liberal arts, law, technology, and other fields primarily for officers in the Jordanian military and police. The campus, opened in 1985, is located ninety miles (150 km) south of the capital, Amman, at the site of the 632 C.E. battle of Mu'ata (Mu'ta). In the mid-1990s there were four thousand students.

BIBLIOGRAPHY

Jordan: A MEED Practical Guide. London, 1983.

Abla M. Amawi

Mu'ayyad, al-

Egyptian daily newspaper founded in 1889 with the backing of Mustafa al-Riyad, former prime minister.

Al-Mu'ayyad disappeared in the repressive climate of 1915, shortly after the death of its editor, Shaykh Ali Yusuf (1863–1913), and the exile of its patron, Khedive ABBAS HILMI II. During the 1890s, its vigorous attacks, rooted in Islam and nationalism, on the British occupation made it a popular Arabic-language opponent of the pro-British al-Muqattam. At the turn of the century and after, al-Liwa and other nationalist papers cut into al-Mu'ayyad's popularity, especially as the latter's uncritical subservience to Khedive Abbas became clear.

BIBLIOGRAPHY

AYALON, AMI. *The Press in the Arab Middle East: A History*. New York, 1995.

Donald Malcolm Reid

Mubarak, Husni [1928–]

Egyptian officer and politician; president of Egypt since the assassination of Anwar al-Sadat.

Born in Minufiyya province to a peasant family, Mubarak graduated from the Military Academy in 1949 and from the Air Force Academy the next year. After a brief stint as a fighter pilot, he served as an instructor at the Air Force Academy from 1954 to 1961. He spent the following academic year at the Soviet General Staff Academy. He was the commandant of the Air Force Academy from 1967 to 1969, air force chief of staff from 1969 to 1971, and then commander in chief from 1971 to 1974. He took charge of Egypt's aerial preparations for the Arab–Israel War, 1973. Because of his outstanding performance in the war, he was promoted to the rank of air marshal in 1974. Egypt's President Anwar al-Sadat appointed him vice president in 1975, and Mubarak served him loyally for the next six years.

After Sadat was assassinated in October 1981, Mubarak assumed the presidency, was officially nominated within a week by the National Democratic party, and confirmed without any opposition by a nationwide referendum. Upon taking over, he promised to address the country's economic and social problems, tried to curb the favoritism and corruption that had marred Sadat's final days, and released many of the political and religious leaders whom Sadat had sent to prison. Many of Sadat's henchmen were quietly removed from office.

On the other hand, Mubarak maintained Egypt's ties with the U.S. government, on whose economic aid it had become increasingly dependent. He did not break diplomatic relations with Israel (although he did recall Egypt's ambassador from Tel Aviv during Israel's invasion of Lebanon) and slowly restored good relations with the other Arab governments and even the Palestine Liberation Organization (PLO), which had withdrawn their ambassadors from Cairo upon Sadat's signing the Egyptian–Israeli peace accord (CAMP DAVID ACCORDS) in 1979. Although his government encouraged Western and Arab investment in Egypt's economy, he curbed the operation of foreign multinational corporations with the country. His efforts to mediate the 1990 dispute between Iraq and Kuwait failed and instead became a precipitating factor in Saddam Hussein's decision to invade and occupy Kuwait. Although Mubarak initially hoped for an Arab solution to the problem, his government soon rallied behind Operation DESERT SHIELD, sending 40,000 troops to join the allied coalition in Saudi Arabia. Egypt was later rewarded by the cancellation of some twelve billion U.S. dollars worth of accumulated foreign debt. The Mubarak government has not, however, curbed the resurgence of Islamist political movements in Egypt, and the gap between rich and poor remains wide—a potential threat to the stability and survival of his regime.

BIBLIOGRAPHY

BAKER, RAYMOND WILLIAM. *Sadat and After: Struggles for Egypt's Political Soul.* Cambridge, Mass., 1990.

OWEISS, IBRAHIM M., ed. *The Political Economy of Contemporary Egypt.* Washington, D.C., 1990.

REICH, BERNARD, ed. *Political Leaders of the Contemporary Middle East and North Africa: A Biographical Dictionary.*

SPRINGBORG, ROBERT. *Mubarak's Egypt: Fragmentation of the Political Order.* Boulder, Colo., 1989.

Arthur Goldschmidt, Jr.

Mubarak, Muhammad al-   [1912–?]

Syrian educator and politician.

Born in Damascus in 1912 to Abd al-Kader al-Mubarak, Muhammad al-Mubarak was educated at the University of Damascus and at the Sorbonne. Serving as deputy for Damascus in 1947, he became minister of public works in 1949 and minister of agriculture in 1951. A professor at the University of Damascus in 1956, al-Mubarak was a member of the Arab Science Academy and a leader in both the Muslim Brethren and in the Islamic Social Front. In these capacities he favored a political state and social order based upon Islamic law.

BIBLIOGRAPHY

Who's Who in the Middle East, 1967–1968.

Charles U. Zenzie

Mubarakiyya School, al-

Kuwaiti school, founded in 1912.

Some three decades before the introduction of public education, Kuwait's merchant community established the Mubarakiyya School to teach practical skills to students whose only other instruction had been obtained in Qur'anic schools. The curriculum included history, geography, and bookkeeping. Kuwait's current ruler, Shaykh Jabir Al Sabah, attended the school as a young boy.

BIBLIOGRAPHY

CRYSTAL, JILL. *Kuwait: The Transformation of an Oil State.* Boulder, Colo., 1992.

Malcolm C. Peck

Mudanya Armistice

An agreement between Mustafa Kemal (Atatürk) and the Allies of World War I.

The armistice restored Turkish rule in Istanbul and eastern Thrace, thereby marking the last phase of the Turkish War of Independence. The Greeks acceded to the armistice, negotiated by Britain on October 14, and moved their army west of the Maritsa river. Refet Pasha entered Istanbul on October 19 to cheering crowds.

The armistice was superseded by the Treaty of LAUSANNE, signed July 24, 1923, in which Turkey accepted international control of the Straits (the Bosporus and Dardanelles).

BIBLIOGRAPHY

LEWIS, BERNARD. *The Emergence of Modern Turkey.* New York, 1969.

Elizabeth Thompson

Mudros Armistice

Agreement that ended World War I in the Middle East with the Ottoman Empire surrendering.

On October 30, 1918, Britain signed an armistice with the Ottoman Empire aboard H.M.S. *Agamemnon,* off Mudros (also Moudhros)—a town on the southern end of the island of Lemnos in the Aegean Sea—ending World War I. It was not an unconditional surrender, but the Ottoman forces were to be demobilized and the Allies would control the Turkish Straits (Bosporus and Dardanelles) as well as other strategic points.

BIBLIOGRAPHY

HUREWITZ, J. C., ed. *The Middle East and North Africa in World Politics: A Documentary Record.* New Haven, Conn., 1979.

Sara Reguer

Mufide Kadri   [1889–1911]

One of the first modern Turkish women painters.

Although she had no formal art education, Müfide Kadri took lessons from Osman Hamdi Bey and Salvatore Velery, teachers at the Istanbul Fine Arts Academy, which for many years did not admit women. She was a prolific painter, and despite her death at an early age, forty of her works remain in existence today. Her oil paintings can be seen in the Istanbul Art Museum.

BIBLIOGRAPHY

BAŞKAN, SEYFI. *Ondokuzuncu Yüzyıldan Günümüze Türk Ressamları.* Ankara, 1991.

David Waldner

Müftüoğlu Ahmet Hikmet　[1870–1927]

Ottoman Turkish writer.

Müftüoğlu Ahmet Hikmet was born in Constantinople (now Istanbul), the son of a religious leader (*mufti*). After graduating from the prestigious Galatasaray Lycée, he entered the foreign ministry. He published his first poetry, short stories, articles, and translations in the journals *Hazine-i Fünün* and *Servet-i Fünün*. He was a member of the *Yeni Lisan* (New Language) and *Türkçülük* (Turkism) movements and helped establish the journal *Türk Yurdu* (The Turkish Homeland) in 1911. Ahmet Hikmet also wrote a novel, *Gönül Hanım*.

David Waldner

Muhammad　[570–632]

The Prophet of Islam.

Muhammad is referred to by Muslims as *rasul allah* (the messenger of God) or *al-nabi* (the Prophet), an appellation that they always follow with the invocation *salla allah alayhi wa sallam* (May God's peace and blessing be upon him). He was born in MECCA in 570, the year of the Elephant, a fortuitous year in tradition, since Mecca in that year survived an Abyssinian invasion directed through Yemen. Although one of various pagan centers in Arabia, Mecca was considered the most important one on account of the KA'BA, a cubical religious sanctuary revered since ancient times. A spiritual focal point for devotees, who came to it as pilgrims with sacrifices, Mecca provided a convenient meeting point for merchants who exchanged goods there and poets who displayed their literary talents and competed for the attention of its wealthy guests and residents. Authority over the city rested in a loose confederation of tribal groups largely dominated by the tribe of Quraysh. Muhammad was born to the clan of Banu Hashim (Hashimites), a branch within Quraysh that was less known for its wealth than for its religious prestige. The patriarch of the clan was traditionally entrusted with caring for

the Ka'ba and maintenance of the pilgrimage facilities, such as the renowned well of *zamzam,* where Islamic tradition states that in ancient times Isma'il, abandoned with his mother Hagar by Abraham (Ibrahim), struck water in the desert and thereby attracted settlement in that spot. Because Mecca is situated on the overland route between Yemen and Syria, its importance as a station, market, and religious center grew with the increasing caravan trade in the region.

Muhammad grew up as an orphan, having lost both of his parents by the age of six. He was then cared for briefly by his grandfather, Abd al-Muttalib, the patriarch of his clan, and afterward by his uncle Abu Talib. In his adolescent years, Muhammad joined his uncle on trade journeys, the most notable of which were to Syria, and he noticed the effects of this commercial boom on his city. The growth of excessive competition in Mecca was gradually undermining traditional Arab tribal values that emphasized principles of solidarity, mutual help, and magnanimity (*muru'a*), and leaving a pool of destitute and disenfranchised Meccans who were abandoned by a new, wealth-driven generation. In this troubled Arab milieu, Muhammad, who attracted attention in Mecca because of his fair dealing, honesty, and moral sensitivity, was commissioned by a wealthy widow, Khadija, to take charge of her caravan trade. Aged twenty-five, Muhammad married Khadija, fifteen years his senior; she bore him two sons (al-Qasim and Abdallah), who died in infancy, and four daughters (Zaynab, Ruqiyya, Umm Kulthum, and Fatima).

Beyond his distress about the social malaise in Mecca, Muhammad was dissatisfied with the pagan beliefs of the Meccans. The Ka'ba, surrounded by idols that catered to various pagan cults, had become a platform for profit making and opportunism. Seeking a full break with this society, Muhammad found solace in spiritual retreats that he undertook in a mountain cave, Hira, on the outskirts of Mecca. According to tradition, Muhammad spent long stretches of time alone in the cave, and it was on one of these occasions, in the year 610, that the angel Gabriel appeared to him and presented him with the words, ''Recite in the name of thy Lord, the Creator'' (Sura 96:1). Gabriel announced to Muhammad that he was to be the messenger of God and called on him to warn his people against polytheism and to lead them to the worship of the one God. The first words of the QUR'AN came to light in the month of RAMADAN—hence the religious importance of that month—and other verses followed in later years in various contexts over the course of Muhammad's life. Those closest to Muhammad—his wife, Khadija, his cousin Ali, his companion Abu Bakr, and his servant Zayd—were the first to hear the words of the Qur'an and to embrace the new message, Islam (meaning literally surrendering oneself to the will of God). After overcoming some initial hesitation, Muhammad grew confident in his sense of mission and took the message to the public arena of Mecca.

The earliest Qur'anic recitations of Muhammad emphasized the belief in absolute monotheism. Meccans were called on to cast aside all polytheism and to worship the one God, Allah, the creator of the universe. The Qur'an described the omniscience and omnipotence of God and invited the people (al-nas) to ponder the signs of creation. The Qur'an also admonished the Meccans for their exploitative business practices, involving usurious transactions and unfairness, and warned them of the existence of Judgment Day, when all would be rewarded or punished according to their deeds. This admonishment, together with Muhammad's public denigration of paganism, elicited the hostility of the leading Meccan merchants, who, in addition to feeling their pride offended, feared that the Islamic concept of one God would undermine the status of Mecca as a pagan center and an economic hub. Recognizing the significance of Hashimite solidarity, the Meccans at first attempted to make Muhammad abandon his attack on paganism by such methods as offering to make him king of Mecca, but when all failed, they declared a boycott against him and tried to extend it to all his clan.

In Mecca, Muhammad gained few Islamic converts (primarily young men, some from affluent families), and his attempt to preach in the neighboring town of Ta'if elicited even greater hostility than in Mecca. Finally, in 620, the prospects of the new religion began to change when Muhammad met six men from Medina who were visiting Mecca. This Medinese group, from the tribe of Khazraj, had long been familiar with messianic expectations that circulated in the discourse of Jews and Christians living in the region and proved receptive to the Islamic prophecy. The next year, this group held a larger meeting between Muhammad and seventy residents of Medina who pledged loyalty to the Prophet and invited him to their town. After years of rivalry in Medina between its two leading tribes, the Aws and the Khazraj, Muhammad's leadership offered the possibility of a neutral authority that could mediate disputes, administer the affairs of a diverse community, and contribute to its social recovery. As the hostility of the Meccans to the new religion and its adherents mounted, Muhammad finally decided to migrate, with Abu Bakr, to Medina in a secret journey that took place on September 17, 622. The trip, known in Arabic as *hijra* (migration), would later mark the beginning of the Islamic lunar calendar.

Once established in Medina, Muhammad set about organizing the nascent Islamic community and strengthening fraternalist ties between the Meccan emigrants (al-muhajirun) and the Medinese, known as the helpers (al-ansar). In a document referred to by scholars today as the Constitution of Medina, Muhammad declared the unity of the community (umma) of Medina under his leadership and stipulated that all matters of legal and political concern were to be referred to him. Medina's hosting of the new religion soon made it the target of Meccan hostility. In 624, mounting tension between the two cities finally led to the first military confrontation at the battle of Badr, where a small Muslim force succeeded in beating back a larger Meccan army. The significance of Badr was not so much military as political. Muhammad's victory strengthened his support in Medina, attracted the admiration of tribal leaders from around the Arabian peninsula, and undermined the prestige of the Meccan order. Between the years 624 and 628, Mecca engaged the Medinese in numerous military skirmishes and battles, the most famous of which was the battle of al-Khandaq (the Trench) in 626. In that year, Mecca assembled a massive confederation of neighboring tribes to invade Medina, but the campaign was forestalled by the Medinese strategy of digging a trench around Medina. The Meccan army, unprepared for a siege and composed of tribal groups that had united for a quick battle only, soon dispersed and retreated.

This last confrontation definitively turned Muhammad into the central leadership figure, and it was then only a matter of time before Mecca would itself become vulnerable to conquest. In 628, Muhammad set out to Mecca on pilgrimage with the new community, only to find his way blocked by the Meccans. At the peace of al-Hudaybiyya in that year, the Meccans called for a long-term truce, after which Muslims would be allowed access to Mecca for pilgrimage. Two years later, the treaty was violated by confederate tribesmen of Mecca, and this opened the way for the Islamic conquest of Mecca, which took place peacefully in 630. A year later, various Arab tribal chiefs from around the peninsula converged on Medina to pay homage or pledge allegiance to the Prophet. Whether nominal or effective, Muhammad's political authority had extended over the greater part of the peninsula, and texts of letters can be obtained from Islamic sources that Muhammad sent to neighboring kings of Persia and Byzantium, as well as various regional princes, inviting them to embrace Islam.

Medina continued its role as the capital of the Islamic state, although Mecca, after the destruction of the idols around the Ka'ba, became the spiritual center of Islam. In 632, soon after completing pilgrimage at Mecca and setting out again for Medina, Muhammad fell mortally ill from a fever. In his final days, he made no specific arrangements for succession. With illness preventing him from leading the prayers, the Prophet asked Abu Bakr to lead the community in prayers, and this gesture would later be interpreted in Sunni Islam as a recommendation for political succession. Shi'a Islam, in contrast, turns to other traditions describing Muhammad's praise for Ali as a reflection of the Prophet's general designation of Ali as his successor. Ali was also, through his marriage to Fatima, the father of Muhammad's two grandchildren, al-Hasan and al-Husayn.

The life of Muhammad has long captivated the attention of Muslims and non-Muslims alike. Muslims look on him not only as a spiritual guide but also as an exemplar in social, ethical, and political terms. Islamic law grew not only from Qur'anic edicts but also from the Islamic understanding of Muhammad's day-to-day manner of handling all sorts of temporal issues. Oral tradition (*hadith*) transmitted through Muhammad's companions recounts in detail his instructions and how he lived. Outside observers, on the other hand, continue to weigh Muhammad's achievements in comparison with those of other spiritual masters. In his confrontation with polytheism and his experience of migration, he is compared to Abraham, whereas as promulgator of the rudiments of Islamic law, he evokes a connection with Moses; in his political leadership of the community, he evokes a connection with David. In the vast desert on the fringes of the urban and sophisticated empires of the time—those of the Byzantines and the Sassanians, each with long traditions of structured governmental institutions—Muhammad united both the nomadic and sedentary Arabs into a coherent social unit that would later conquer these powers. Although this political expansion took place under his successors, Muhammad had laid the foundation for an Islamic universalist social vision that was rooted in a unifying monotheistic belief. The memory of the prophetic experience of hijra between cities henceforth inspired its emulation on a grander scale outside Arabia.

BIBLIOGRAPHY

BUHL, FRANTS. *Das Leben Mohammeds.* Berlin, 1930.
COOK, MICHAEL. *Muhammad.* Oxford, 1983.
GUILLAUME, ALFRED. *The Life of Muhammad: A Translation of Ibn Ishaq's "Sirat Rasul Allah."* London, 1955.
LINGS, MARTIN. *Muhammad.* Rochester, Vt., 1983.
MUIR, SIR WILLIAM. *The Life of Mohammad.* Edinburgh, 1923.
RODINSON, MAXIME. *Mohammed.* London, 1971.
WATT, W. MONTGOMERY. *Muhammad at Mecca.* Oxford, 1953.
———. *Muhammad at Medina.* Oxford, 1956.
———. *Muhammad: Prophet and Statesman.* Oxford, 1961.

Tayeb El-Hibri

Muhammad, Ali Nasir

See Ali Nasir Muhammad al-Hasani

Muhammad, Aziz [1933–]

First secretary of the Iraqi Communist party, 1963–1978.

A Kurd, born in Sulaymaniyya, Aziz Muhammad al-Haj joined the Communist party in 1948. He was arrested the same year and jailed until the end of the monarchy in 1958. Soon after his release, he entered the Central Committee of the Iraqi Communist party and was appointed head of the Central Organizational Committee. From February 1963 to August 1965, he resided in Moscow and in 1963 was elected first secretary of the Iraqi Communist party (in exile). Starting in 1978, following the rapprochement between the Soviet Union and the Ba'th regime in Iraq, Aziz Muhammad led the Iraqi Communist party to cooperation with the Ba'th. On July 17, 1978, Aziz Muhammad, the president of Iraq, and the secretary of the Ba'th party signed the National Action Charter, which became a basis for strategic alliance between the Iraqi Communist party and the Ba'th.

BIBLIOGRAPHY

BATATU, HANNA. *The Old Social Classes and Revolutionary Movements of Iraq.* Princeton, N.J., 1982.

Michael Eppel

Muhammad Ali [1770–1849]

Ruler (pasha) of Egypt, 1805–1849.

Muhammad (also Mehmet) Ali Pasha was born to a military family in the Macedonian port city of Kavalla (in what is today Greece). He was apprenticed to the tobacco trade by his father, Ibrahim Agha, and took over the family business upon Ibrahim's death in 1790. He also succeeded his father as commander of the local militia, in which post he came to the attention of the Ottoman authorities in Istanbul, who assigned him a warship to protect the surrounding waters against pirates. He married a well-to-do widow, Amina, who bore him three sons, Ibrahim, Ahmad Tusun, and Isma'il, and two daughters, Tevhide and Nazli.

In 1801, Muhammad Ali was appointed second in command of the 300 troops from Kavalla ordered to take part in the Ottoman Empire's expedition to drive Napoléon's army from Egypt. Muhammad Ali took over the regiment when its commander hastily returned to Macedonia; his skill on the battlefield prompted the Ottoman general to promote him to the rank of *binbashi* during the first weeks of the campaign. After the evacuation of the French, the Kavallan regiment stayed on to assist the Ottomans in subduing the Mamluk commanders. When the new governor let their pay slide into arrears, Muhammad Ali led these irregulars in a demonstration demanding it and then collaborated with the Mamluks to overthrow Egypt's Ottoman governor, taking control of Cairo in 1804 with the support of the religious notability and rich merchants. In June 1805, he was confirmed as governor-general (*wali*) of Egypt by the Ottoman Porte (government).

During the next six years, he suppressed the Mamluks and confiscated their lands, disarmed the urban population, and established a regular fiscal administration. These steps set the stage for military campaigns in the Sudan and the Hijaz (Arabia) in 1810/11, which were followed by expeditions to Crete and the Peloponnese (Greece) from 1820 to 1824 and an invasion of Palestine and Syria in 1831.

After reaching the gates of Istanbul at the end of 1832, his armies were gradually forced out of Anatolia through the intervention of the British and Russians. Repeated attempts to conciliate Britain failed, and in 1840 the LONDON CONVENTION was effected, with the Ottomans supported by Britain, Austria, Prussia, and Russia. British warships then bombarded Beirut and appeared off Alexandria (Egypt), forcing Muhammad Ali to agree to give up his empire in Syria, Arabia, and the Aegean in exchange for the hereditary right to rule Egypt. He traveled to the Ottoman capital in 1846 to confirm his family's succession, but he succumbed to dysentery and dementia on August 2, 1849. His descendants continued to rule Egypt, taking the titles of wali and khedive until 1952, when Farouk was ousted by a revolutionary government.

BIBLIOGRAPHY

DODWELL, HENRY. *The Founder of Modern Egypt.* Cambridge, U.K., 1931.

LAWSON, FRED H. *The Social Origins of Egyptian Expansionism during the Muhammad 'Ali Period.* New York, 1992.

MARSOT, AFAF LUTFI AL-SAYYID. *Egypt in the Reign of Muhammad Ali.* Cambridge, U.K., 1986.

Fred H. Lawson

Muhammad Ali Mosque

Mosque commissioned by Muhammad Ali for Cairo's Citadel.

By its size and hilltop location, the Muhammad Ali Mosque at the Citadel dominates the Cairo skyline. As early as 1820, MUHAMMAD ALI of Egypt asked French architect Pascal Coste to draw up plans for mosques in the Citadel and at Alexandria. Coste's plan was not used, however, when construction began in the early 1830s, just as Muhammad Ali was challenging his Ottoman overlord by invading Syria. Turning his back on local Mamluk-influenced architectural styles that had persisted through three centuries of rule by the Ottoman Empire, Muhammad Ali symbolized his ambitions by appropriating the style of great Ottoman mosques of Constantinople (now Istanbul). Sultan Ahmet's Blue Mosque, the Nuru Osmaniye, and the Yeni mosques have all been cited as influencing Yusuf Bushnaq, the Greek architect brought from Constantinople to construct the mosque. Its embellishments are in the baroque-rococo style in vogue in Constantinople in the eighteenth and early nineteenth centuries.

The mosque also symbolized Muhammad Ali's victory over the Mamluks, whom he had murdered in the Citadel in 1811. Dominating the citadel founded by Salah al-Din (known as Saladin [1137–1193]), it rose on the leveled ruins of the Qasr al-Ablaq (Striped Palace) of al-Nasir Muhammad, the Mamluk sultan whose mosque stands nearby.

The mosque is built of local Muqattam limestone, with columns and sheathing of alabaster—a stone softer than marble previously used mainly for vases and other small objects—from a quarry near Beni Suef. The mosque was completed in 1857 under Sa'id Pasha. Colonnades topped with small domes bound its open courtyard. The side opposite the great dome has a clock tower with an ornate timepiece presented by King Louis-Philippe of France; Muhammad Ali returned the favor with the obelisk now standing in the Place de la Concorde in Paris. Two slender Ottoman minarets rise 270 feet (82 m) on square bases only ten feet (3 m) on a side. The great Byzantine Ottoman dome rests on four arches with four massive piers. Four half-domes lead out of the arches, four smaller domes fill in the corners, and a lower half-dome tops the *mihrab* (the niche at the east end of the mosque pointing to Mecca). Above the alabaster sheathing, the interior walls and domes are ornately painted. Muhammad Ali is buried beneath a marble monument to the right of the entrance, behind a bronze grill. Hundreds of lights hang from the ceiling on great chandeliers. Muhammad Ali's Jawhara (Bijou) Palace stands nearby.

The Muhammad Ali Mosque lacked local successors as well as local antecedents. In the second half of the nineteenth century, either Western or eclectic Mamluk-revival styles were preferred for major Egyptian buildings.

BIBLIOGRAPHY

Egypt. Blue Guide. London, 1984.
WIET, GASTON. *Mohamed Ali et les beaux-arts.* Cairo, 1949.

Donald Malcolm Reid

Muhammad al-Sadiq   [1814–1882]

Ruler of Tunisia, 1859–1882.

Muhammad al-Sadiq Bey was the son of Husayn Bey (ruler of Tunisia, 1824–1835) and the third Husaynid *mushir* (marshal). His reign saw Tunisia's first experiment with constitutionalism, parliamentary rule, and restrictions on the bey's authority; the unbridled control of Prime Minister Mustafa KHAZNADAR; disastrous foreign loans; increased taxes; a bitter revolt; Europe's economic control; the reformist ministry of KHAYR AL-DIN (1873–1877); and the imposition of a protectorate by France (1881).

From all reports, Muhammad al-Sadiq was a weak ruler who was easily influenced by his political entourage of MAMLUKS, especially Khaznadar. Like his predecessor, Ahmad Bey, al-Sadiq evinced an early fascination with the military and showed some talent in that area. Soon after his accession, he sought to reconstitute the army and introduced a military code that provided for conscription of all able-bodied male adults for a period of eight years. An individual could send a proxy if he chose not to enter the army.

Upon assuming the throne in 1859, al-Sadiq declared that he would uphold the principles of the FUNDAMENTAL PACT of 1857. He proclaimed a new constitution in April 1861. It included the principle of ministerial responsibility, financial control vested in the Grand Council, a strict budget controlled by the Grand Council, and a secular court system. Also provided was a "bill of rights" that included provisions for religious freedom and conversion from Islam.

Although the document appeared to guarantee constitutionalism and individual rights, it actually provided for a system that perpetuated the Turkish-Mamluk political elite and increased their power at the bey's expense. It was not, therefore, a parliamentary democracy that emerged, but a traditional elitist oligarchy. The limitations placed on the bey's authority by the constitution increased Khaznadar's confidence and freedom of action. He used the constitution to eliminate his enemies on the Grand Council and install his close associates. He increased his financial exactions from the state treasury and more than doubled the national debt within one year. For this reason, he floated his first foreign loan in 1863. To pay for that loan, Khaznadar increased the unpopular personal *majba* tax twofold. This led to the revolt of 1864.

From 1865 to 1869, Khaznadar ran the state. In the latter year, after poor harvests, famines, and epidemics, al-Sadiq accepted the International Finance Commission, which aimed to ensure Tunisia's payment of its financial obligations. Khayr al-Din, Khaznadar's son-in-law, represented Tunisia on the commission. In 1873 he convinced the bey to remove Khaznadar and install himself as prime minister.

Under Khayr al-Din's prime ministry, a number of reforms were instituted: regulation of the education at Zaytuna University, the founding of Sadiqi College, elimination of abuses in the administration of *hubus* (religious trust) properties, reformation of the tax system, abolition of the MAHALLAS, improvements in administrative accountability, introduction of protective tariffs on imports, and numerous public works projects. Sharp curtailment of public spending by the bey and support for Ottoman claims to sovereignty over Tunisia forced Khayr al-Din to resign in July 1877. Constraints on the bey's powers were lifted, and the weak Mustafa ibn Isma'il became prime minister.

Using the excuse of Tunisia's violations of its border with Algeria, France invaded Tunisia in 1881. On May 12, 1881, Muhammad al-Sadiq Bey signed the treaty, known as the Treaty of Bardo, officially establishing France's protectorate, which lasted until 1956. It was later repudiated by the bey, an action that forced the signature of a second treaty in July. Although this second treaty was never ratified, the La Marsa Convention of June 1883 (signed by Ali Bey, ruler of Tunisia from 1882 to 1900) confirmed the provisions of the Bardo treaty and France's imposition of a protectorate.

BIBLIOGRAPHY

ANDERSON, LISA. *The State and Social Transformation in Tunisia and Libya, 1830–1980.* Princeton, N.J., 1987.
BARRIE, LARRY A. "Tunisia: The Era of Reformism, 1837–1877." Master's thesis, Harvard University, 1966.

NELSON, HAROLD D., ed. *Tunisia: A Country Study,* 3rd ed. Washington, D.C., 1988.

PERKINS, KENNETH J. *Historical Dictionary of Tunisia.* Metuchen, N.J., 1989.

Larry A. Barrie

Muhammad ibn Abd al-Wahhab

[1703–1792]

A great Muslim religious reformer from Najd.

Muhammad ibn Abd al-Wahhab was an implacable opponent of what he saw as impure outgrowths of Islam, such as Sufism, insisting instead on strict interpretation of Islamic law according to the HANBALI LAW SCHOOL. Driven from his hometown, he made a pact in 1744 with the Saudi ruler of Deraiyeh (or Dir'iyya), who promised to follow him in religion. The Wahhabi teachings (see MUWAHHIDUN) helped to create the first large Saudi state, and they remain official doctrine in Saudi Arabia today.

BIBLIOGRAPHY

Encyclopaedia of Islam, 2nd ed.

Khalid Y. Blankinship

Muhammad ibn Abd al-Wahhab

[c. 1901–1991]

An illustrious name in twentieth-century Arab music.

An Egyptian with acknowledged talent and a long artistic career extending roughly from the early 1920s to the late 1980s, Abd al-Wahhab emerged as a leading singer, film star, and composer who wrote hundreds of songs that he and others sang and recorded. Through his mastery of traditional Arab singing and exposure to Western music, he developed a multifaceted repertoire that combined local and European elements in ways that seemed to reflect both his own artistic outlooks and modern Egyptian taste. Growing up in a poor and conservative Cairo family, Abd al-Wahhab was exposed to Islamic religious music at an early age. After performing traditional vocal genres and taking roles in local musical plays, he composed distinctive works and acted and sang in seven feature films released between 1933 and 1946. Through his early association with the well-known poet Ahmad SHAWQI, he gained access to Egypt's distinguished social, literary, and political circles and to the musical culture of the West. Among Abd al-Wahhab's recognized innovations are: the gradual enlargement of the performing ensemble; the intro-duction of European instruments and instrumentations; the creation of irregular forms, often with sections in strikingly contrastive styles; the quoting of melodic themes from Romantic and post-Romantic European composers; the occasional use of Western ballroom dance meters; and the composition of numerous descriptive, or programmatic, instrumental works. Muhammad Abd al-Wahhab represented both the mainstream and the vanguard in Arab music. Although at times his music was criticized by artistic purists, his legacy is highly acclaimed by musicians, critics, and government officials throughout the Arab world.

BIBLIOGRAPHY

AZZAM, NABIL S. "Muhammad Abd al-Wahhab in Modern Egyptian Music." Ph.D. diss., University of California at Los Angeles, 1990.

RACY, ALI JIHAD. "Musical Aesthetics in Present-Day Cairo." *Ethnomusicology* 26 (1982): 391–406.

Ali Jihad Racy

Muhammad ibn Rashid   [?–1897]

Arabian emir of the nineteenth century.

Muhammad ibn Abd Allah ibn Ali ibn al-Rashid of the AL RASHID FAMILY, became emir of Ha'il in northern Najd (in what is today Saudi Arabia) in 1872. He was an effective ruler who soon put the Rashidi state on a stable basis, so that it eclipsed the Saudi emirate of Riyadh. In 1887, Muhammad placed the Saudis under his domination, and by crushing a revolt of Riyadh and Qasim in 1890/91, he united all Najd under his direct rule. However, his state had a personal basis and waned after his death in 1897.

BIBLIOGRAPHY

WINDER, R. BAYLY. *Saudi Arabia in the Nineteenth Century.* New York, 1965.

Khalid Y. Blankinship

Muhammad ibn Thani

Ruler of Qatar, 1868–1876 (also called Muhammad Al Thani).

Muhammad ibn Thani was a leading figure in Doha, Qatar's capital, when that state's overlords, the Al Khalifa rulers of Bahrain, sent a punitive military expedition against restive Qataris in 1867. Great Britain intervened against Bahrain for treaty violations and recognized Muhammad as representative of the Qatari people in 1868. This led to eventual Qatari independence under the rule of the Al Thani with Muhammad the founder of the dynasty.

BIBLIOGRAPHY

AL SABAH, SALEM AL-JABIR. *Les emirates du Golfe*. Paris, 1980.

ZAHLAN, ROSEMARIE SAID. *The Creation of Qatar*. New York, 1979.

Malcolm C. Peck

Muhammara

A Middle Eastern dip.

Made with walnuts and concentrated pomegranate juice, *muhammara* is seasoned with hot red pepper and cumin. It is a Syrian specialty commonly associated with the cuisine of Aleppo. It is served as an appetizer, as part of a MAZZA, or as a condiment with a meat dish.

Jenab Tutunji

Muhammara, Treaty of

The treaty that established the boundary between Iraq and the future Saudi Arabia.

Signed in 1922 between Abd al-Aziz ibn Sa'ud Al Saud and British officials representing Iraq, the Treaty of Muhammara was later incorporated into the UQAYR CONFERENCE, which established a 7,000 square mile (18,000 sq. km) diamond-shaped Iraq–Saudi Arabia NEUTRAL ZONE adjacent to the western tip of Kuwait. The purpose was to safeguard water rights for bedouin of both countries, and it was agreed that neither Iraq nor Saudi Arabia would build permanent dwellings or installations in the zone. In 1981, Saudi Arabia and Iraq signed an agreement that reaffirmed the boundary and provided for the division of the neutral zone between them. The agreement in effect dissolved the neutral zone.

Eleanor Abdella Doumato

Muhammed V   [1910–1961]

Sultan and king of Morocco from 1927 to 1961.

Sidi Muhammed Ben Yusuf was the third son of Mulay Yusuf, a colorless prince and brother of the sultan of Morocco, Mulay Hafid. Muhammed was born in Fez in 1910, at the beginning of the protectorate period; it seemed unlikely he would reign. Two years later, the French nominated his father to succeed the sultan, whom they had deposed because he refused to rule as they wanted. Muhammed V came to power after his father's death in 1927, because French authorities considered him to be more flexible and less ambitious than his brothers. However, he used his popularity and his skills in international diplomacy to involve himself in a struggle, at first unequal, with the protectorate's authorities.

After the Berber *dahir* in 1930, which relieved Berber tribes from submitting to *Shari'a* (Islamic law), Muhammed became more sensitive to Moroccan nationalism, which was just beginning to awaken. Without breaking off from the protectorate, he supported demonstrations by young traditional and modern intellectuals, such as Allal al-Fasi, Hassan El Ouezzani, and Ahmed Balafrej, which, in 1944, gave birth to the Istiqlal (Independence) party. World War II presented the opportunity to convince the protectorate to move toward a cooperative regime more faithful to the spirit of the original agreement between France and Morocco.

Muhammed opposed the French attempt to protect Moroccan Jews from persecution while he helped rebuild military forces to fight again with the Allies. The 1942 Casablanca meeting with U.S. President Franklin D. Roosevelt and Britain's Prime Minister Winston S. Churchill strengthened his resistance. From then on, he utilized a strategy of promoting gradual change to regain the sovereignty his country had lost in 1912. He approached French authorities directly to avoid the obstacles set up by both settlers and French civil servants, who opposed any change. But he did not succeed desite his good relationship with General Charles de Gaulle. At the local level, opposition to the French became more and more violent and led to the sultan's deposition and exile in Madagascar on August 20, 1953.

But France could not depose Muhammed in 1953 in the same way it deposed his uncle Mulay Hafid in 1912. The international environment was unfavorable to France, French public opinion accepted unwillingly the pro-consuls' plots, and, above all, Muhammed was the symbol of a very deep opposition movement, which mobilized Moroccan cities as well as the countryside. The nation could no longer be governed, and the French administration collapsed within two years in the face of the uprisings. Muhammed was called back to preserve the French economic and military presence, which, otherwise, could have been swept out by nationalistic currents far more radical than those represented by the king and the Moroccan bourgeoisie.

Once he regained his throne, in November 1955, Muhammed took on the role of spokesman for nationalism. He let the Istiqlal party exert power without, however, becoming a prisoner of the nationalist movement. He continued to defend the monarchy's privileges. Muhammed kept his country out of the confrontation between France and the Algerian Front de Libération Nationale (FLN), which he supported. But, profoundly hurt by the 1956 hijacking of a Moroccan plane with FLN leaders on board, he then attempted to play an intermediary role in the Algerian conflict, hoping, in vain, that de Gaulle's return to power in 1958 would facilitate his reconciliation with France. The king would die without witnessing success. But, he was careful not to jeopardize his country's position within a new Maghrib that, already, some perceived as dominated by a revolutionary Algeria, the main heiress of the former colonial power.

Having succeeded in reestablishing his country's independence on the international stage, Muhammed also consolidated the position of the monarchy within an institutional system, which was shaken by the 1953–1955 crisis. Some among the nationalists welcomed a king who reigned without governing. But Muhammed did not share that philosophy for himself or his son, Prince Mulay Hassan, his heir, whom he had gradually introduced to power since the end of World War II.

The support he gained by fighting with the Istiqlal against the protectorate helped him keep his authority over an important part of the nationalist movement. In that struggle, the monarchy recovered its powers that the Treaty of FES (1912) had alienated and, added to that, the administrative means set up by the protectorate. The military and police forces were placed under monarchical authority, but other administrative sectors depended upon a government dominated by the Istiqlal. Without the help of the monarchy, it was not possible to ensure either the control of the resistance movement or the settlement of rural uprisings. A pluralist text related to public freedom rights allowed, in April 1958, the legalization of new political parties and soon favored the split of the Istiqlal party, with a right wing remaining close to the king and a left wing following a moderate line. In May 1960, Muhammad took the reins of power by naming Mulay Hassan prime minister. The prince had been, at the beginning of independence, chief of staff in the Royal Armed Forces.

As Algeria's independence approached, the more anxious Muhammed became to grant his country a constitution and to organize its democratization under the monarchy's control. He died suddenly in March 1961 after surgery and left the country to the authority of his son, Hassan II.

During this thirty-two-year reign, Muhammed V listened to his country and took part in its evolution, which allowed it to recover its independence and to project itself into modernity. Chosen because of his apparent docility, he proved, in the long run, to be a cautious opponent, capable of appreciating the modernizing actions of such French resident generals as Gen. Auguste Nogues or Eric Labonne. They reciprocated by respecting his dignity. In extreme circumstances, he displayed firmness and intuitively anticipated the reactions of common Moroccan people. As far as the rivalry with the nationalist movement, which gradually replaced the common fight against the protectorate, is concerned, he knew how to take advantage of time, how to safeguard his best cards; he went on being attentive to the rural world and sometimes contributed to undermining the credit modern leaders were already losing. Thus, four years after his return, he regained all the power without having to share it. While favoring Algeria's independence, he feared Nasserist or Marxist influences, which could have come from that neighboring country and be exerted upon Morocco.

A man of tradition, Muhammed V was the symbol both of independence and modernity. That symbol continues today to stamp the monarchy's image and to give Morocco a strong identity highly differentiated from that of its neighbor countries.

Rémy Leveau

Muharram

First month of the Islamic lunar calendar, containing thirty days.

The events that took place on the tenth of Muharram in the year 680 changed forever the character of this month by making it a month of mourning, at least for Shi'ites. On that date, Husayn—the grandson of the Prophet Muhammad and the third Imam of Shi'a Islam—was brutally killed on the battlefield of Karbala. In this battle Husayn's sons, male relatives, and followers also perished. The women of his encampment were taken as captives to Caliph Yazid in Damascus. This tragic event overshadows any other event in that month. Husayn's ordeal started on the first of Muharram, when he and his party were intercepted by Yazid's troops, and continued even after his death, with the captivity of the Karbala survivors. Although the tenth of Muharram (known as *Ashura*), is the actual date of Husayn's death, the mourning has been extended to cover the whole month.

For Shi'ites, the Muharram tragedy of Husayn is the greatest act of suffering and redemption in history. It acquired a timeless quality, and, therefore, apart from the yearly Muharram observances, the Shi-'ites continually try to measure themselves against the principle of the paradigm of Husayn whenever they regard themselves as deprived, humiliated, or abused. In fact, one of the main slogans during the Islamic revolution in Iran (1978/79) chanted by the crowds or scribbled as graffiti on town and village walls was "Every day is Ashura; every place is Karbala; every month is Muharram." This same slogan was intoned on radio and television and was graphically depicted on posters and even postage stamps during Iran's eight-year (1980–1988) war against Iraq.

The Muharram commemoration of Husayn's passion and martyrdom is charged with unusual emotions throughout the world's Shi'a communities. Even the followers of Sunni Islam and the members of other religions who live among the Shi'ites are greatly affected by these commemorative rituals. That participation in the annual observance of Husayn's suffering and death is considered an aid to salvation on the day of judgment provides an additional incentive for Shi'ites to engage in the many mourning rituals. Elaborate Muharram observances were already carried out in the fourth Islamic century in Baghdad during the reign of Mu'izz al-Dawla of the Shi'a Buyid dynasty. Many Muharram rituals have developed since, and although they may differ in form from one locality to another, passionate participation in them is universal.

These rituals may be divided into two categories, the ambulatory and the stationary. They are primarily performed during the first ten days of Muharram, with the greatest discharge of emotions and the greatest number of rituals occurring on the day of Ashura. The most common ambulatory rite is a procession, and the participants are divided into different groups of self-mortifiers—those who beat their chests with the palms of their hands; those who beat their backs with chains; and those who wound their foreheads with swords or knives. Some mortify themselves with stones, and others carry the *alam*, which signify the standard of Husayn at Karbala. In Iran, in some processions, floats with live tableaux representing the scenes from the Karbala tragedy can be seen, as well as Husayn's symbolic bier, called *nakhl* (date palm). Nakhl is carried because, according to tradition, Husayn's beheaded corpse was carried on a stretcher made of date palm branches. Some nakhl are so large that they require more than 150 people to carry them. Processions are accompanied by bands of martial and mournful music. The most characteristic features of Muharram on the Indo-Pakistani subcon-

tinent are the huge artistic interpretations of Husayn's mausoleum carried or wheeled in the procession. At the end of Ashura day, these structures, called *ta'ziya,* are either cremated or buried at the local cemetery, called Karbala, or are immersed in water.

The Muharram observances were brought as far as the Caribbean basin in the years 1845 to 1917, when indentured laborers from India went there. Muharram is still, after carnival, the most important event in Trinidad. Although the Muharram rituals in Trinidad have more of a festive than a mourning character, the main features continue to be processions. In this case, the processions are parades of colorful cenotaphs for Husayn, called *tadja*. In India, the Sunni and even the Hindus actively participate in many Muharram rituals. In Trinidad as well, this is a true ecumenical event.

To the stationary rituals belong *majalis al-aza,* recitation and singing of the story of Husayn at the Battle of Karbala. In Iran, this ritual is called *rawda khwani*. The storyteller (called *rawda khwan*) of the Shi'a martyrology sits above the assembled crowd on a *minbar* (pulpit) in a black tent, under an awning, or in a special edifice (*Husayniyya* or *takiya* in Iran; *ashurkhanah* or *imambarah* in India) and brings the audience to a state of frenzy with recitation, chanting, crying, sobbing, and body language. The most unusual stationary ritual is the ta'ziya of Iran—the only serious drama and theater developed in the Islamic world depicting the martyrdom of Husayn and other Shi'a martyrs. Originally, it was performed in the month of Muharram, but now it is staged year round.

The Muharram processions actually served as prototypes for the massive demonstrations in Tehran and other Iranian cities during the 1978/79 revolutionary upheavals. The mixing of Muharram mourning slogans with political ones has been an old Muharram tradition. The Iranian Revolution utilized the Husayn Muharram paradigm and was carried out in accordance with the Islamic calendar. Ayatollah Khomeini's revolution started in Muharram on Ashura, June 3, 1963, when he delivered a speech at the Fayziya Madrasa in Qom, criticizing the internal and external policies of the shah, Mohammad Reza Pahlavi, and his government. In the article "Islamic Government," written while he taught in exile in Najaf, Khomeini states: "Make Islam known to the people, then . . . create something akin to Ashura and create out of it a wave of protest against the state of the government" (*Islam and Revolution,* p. 131). A few days before Muharram on November 23, 1978, in order to accelerate the revolution, Khomeini issued from Neauphle-le-Château, France, a declaration called "Muharram:

The triumph of blood over the sword," which was recorded in France and distributed in Iran through its network of mosques. The opening paragraph of the declaration reads as follows:

> With the approach of Muharram, we are about to begin the month of epic heroism and self sacrifice—the month in which blood triumphed over the sword, the month in which truth condemned falsehood for all eternity and branded the mark of disgrace upon the forehead of all oppressors and satanic governments; the month that has taught successive generations throughout history the path of victory over the bayonet. (*Islam and Revolution,* p. 242)

Less than two months later, the shah left Iran, enabling Khomeini to return from fourteen years of exile.

Muharram affects the entire Islamic community; however, it is primarily felt among Shi'ites. Muharram could be expressed both as a mourning depression and an exuberant agitation and will to act. These expressions of Muharram can be and have been converted into political actions.

BIBLIOGRAPHY

MAHMOUD AYOUB's *Redemptive Suffering in Islam* (The Hague, 1978) is subtitled *A Study of the Devotional Aspects of Ashura in Twelver Shi'ism;* this is the most important study of Ashura. ELIAS CANETTI's "The Muharram Festival of the Shi'ites," in his *Crowds and Power* (New York, 1978), is a masterpiece of psychological interpretation of Muharram crowds. Volume 12 of *Alserat* (Spring/Autumn, 1986) contains the proceedings of the Imam Husayn Conference conducted in July 1984 in London, with a wealth of information on Muharram. *Islam and Revolution* (Berkely, Calif., 1981) contains writings and declarations of Imam Khomeini, translated and annotated by HAMID ALGAR. As for Muharram on the Indo–Pakistani subcontinent, the *Roots of North India Shi'ism in Iran and Iraq* by J.R.I. COLE (Berkeley, Calif., 1988) is a must; SAIYID ATHAR ABBAS RIZVI's *A Socio-Intellectual History of the Isna Ashari Shi'is in India* (Canberra, 1986) is the most thorough research on the subject. The pioneering book by JOHN NORMAN HOLLISTER, *The Shi'a of India,* (London, 1953), deals at length with Muharram. A behavioral interpretation of Muharram was written by A. R. SAIYID, "Ideal and Reality in the Observance of Muharram," in *Ritual and Religion among Muslims of India* (New Delhi, 1981). The *Census of India, 1961* (New Delhi, 1965) contains a very important account, "Moharram in Two Cities, Lucknow and Delhi." See also PETER J. CHELKOWSKI, *Ta'ziyeh: Ritual and Drama in Iran* (New York, 1979), and G.E. VON GRUNEBAUM, *Muhammadan Festivals,* (London, 1958).

Peter Chelkowski

Street in the Old Market in Muharraq, Bahrain. (Richard Bulliet)

Muharraq

The second-largest city in the State of Bahrain and the second-largest island of the archipelago in the Persian/Arabian Gulf.

During the early nineteenth century, Muharraq (also Moharek, al-Muharraq) was ruled by leaders of the Abdullah branch of the al-KHALIFA (who rule Bahrain). They used it as a base for their long-standing rivalry with the Sulman branch, centered in Manama (the capital, on the main island of Bahrain, now across a short channel-bridge). More homogeneous in population than Manama, Muharraq has mainly Sunni Arabs and only two predominantly Shi'a residential districts. During the 1950s and 1960s, both radical and Arab nationalist movements appealed to the city's people in an effort to remove the British. Muharraq was the site of the British air force and army bases during the later years of the British protectorate (1880–1971), as well as the international airport. In 1981, the city's population was about 62,000.

BIBLIOGRAPHY

CLARKE, ANGELA. *The Islands of Bahrain.* Manama, Bahrain, 1981.

Fred H. Lawson

Muhbir

Ottoman newspaper.

Muhbir (the Reporter) was founded on August 31, 1867, by Ali Suavi, who wrote most of the articles.

An organ for Young Ottoman ideas, *Muhbir* was published in London, and included English and French translations. The paper ceased publication following its fiftieth issue on November 3, 1868.

David Waldner

Muhlis Sabahattin   [1889–1947]

Turkish composer.

Muhlis Sabahattin was born in Adana and died in Istanbul. His compositions, which include twenty-seven operas, synthesized Turkish classical traditions with western music.

David Waldner

Muhsin, Zuhayr   [1936–1979]

Palestinian politician and guerilla leader.

Born in Tulkarm in mandatory Palestine, Muhsin joined the BA'TH party at age seventeen and later became a teacher in Jordan. He was accused in 1957 of pro-Nasser subversion, and left to live briefly in Qatar and Kuwait, before finally settling in Damascus, Syria. In 1970, he became leader of Sa'iqa (Thunderbolt), the Syrian Ba'th party's Palestinian guerilla organization. The following year, he was appointed to the PALESTINE LIBERATION ORGANIZATION (PLO) executive committee as Sa'iqa's representative. Later, he became head of the PLO's military department.

Muhsin is believed to have led a battalion that attacked the Lebanese town of Damour in January 1976, where 582 people were killed. Sa'iqa also played a role in defending the Tal al-Za'ter Palestinian refugee camp in Lebanon under siege by the Phalange the following summer. At the 1977 Palestinian National Council meeting, Muhsin argued against partial, negotiated settlements on the Palestine question. He was assassinated by an unknown assailant July 15, 1979, on a street in Cannes, France.

BIBLIOGRAPHY

COBBAN, HELENA. *The Palestinian Liberation Organization.* New York, 1984.

SEALE, PATRICK. *Abu Nidal: A Gun for Hire.* London, 1992.

Elizabeth Thompson

Muhtar, Gazi Ahmet   [1839–1918]

Ottoman soldier and grand vizier.

One of the great Ottoman war heroes of the late nineteenth century, Ahmet Muhtar's first notable victory was his halt of Russian advances on the eastern front in the Turkish–Russian War (1877/78). In appreciation, Sultan Abdülhamit II awarded him the title of *gazi* and appointed him to head an imperial military inspection commission. From 1895 to 1906, Ahmet Muhtar served as the sultan's representative, or high commissioner, to Egypt.

During this time, Ahmet Muhtar became a prominent advocate of modernization and westernization and was loosely affiliated with the COMMITTEE OF UNION AND PROGRESS (CUP) and other groups. In July 1912, liberal officers opposed to the CUP's autocratic rule used military threats to bring down its grand vizier. They chose Ahmet Muhtar, then an elderly statesman considered above politics, to replace him. His government, known as "the great cabinet," consisted of several former grand viziers chosen to unite the empire in face of the Balkan crisis and Italian war. But Muhtar's government fell after only a few months, with the grave Ottoman losses at the outbreak of the Balkan War in October.

Elizabeth Thompson

Muhyi al-Din, Khalid   [1923–   ]

Egyptian military officer and politician.

From a well-to-do farming family near Mansura, Khalid Muhyi al-Din was an original member of the FREE OFFICERS and the REVOLUTIONARY COMMAND COUNCIL that overthrew King Farouk in 1952. One of only two Communists among the Free Officers, he sided with Gen. Muhammad Naguib in his struggle for supremacy with Gamal Abdel Nasser, leading to Muhyi al-Din's marginalization within the political elite when Nasser won out.

In June of 1977, Muhyi al-Din formed the NATIONAL PROGRESSIVE UNIONIST PARTY, which called for Arab unity, stronger ties with the Soviet Union, and the strengthening of the public sector.

BIBLIOGRAPHY

WATERBURY, JOHN. *The Egypt of Nasser and Sadat: The Political Economy of Two Regimes.* Princeton, N.J., 1983.

David Waldner

Muhyi al-Din, Zakariyya [1918–]

Egyptian military officer and politician.

Zakariyya Muhyi al-Din comes from a well-to-do landowning family outside Mansura, Egypt. He was educated at the Military College and the Staff Officers College in Cairo and was an original member of the FREE OFFICERS and the REVOLUTIONARY COMMAND COUNCIL that overthrew the monarchy of King Farouk in 1952.

He served as the minister of interior from 1953 to 1962 and in various executive posts until 1967, when President Gamal Abdel Nasser appointed him vice-president. After the Arab–Israel War of 1967, Nasser named him his successor, and Muhyi al-Din proposed promoting the private sector as the leading economic sector. In March 1968, however, he left public life.

BIBLIOGRAPHY

WATERBURY, JOHN. *The Egypt of Nasser and Sadat: The Political Economy of Two Regimes.* Princeton, N.J., 1983.

David Waldner

Mujaddara

A lentil and rice dish.

Mujaddara, which traces its origins to medieval times, is considered the food of the poor because the ingredients are cheap and plentiful, and it does not contain meat. It is nevertheless a great favorite and occurs in many variations throughout the Middle East.

Jenab Tutunji

Mujaddedi, Sebghatullah [1925–]

Afghan resistance leader; Sufi pir; Afghan president, 1992–1993.

Born in Kabul to a family of hereditary leaders of the Naqshbandi Sufi order, Mujaddedi was educated at al-Azhar University in Cairo and at Kabul University. He fled Kabul in the 1970s and headed the Islamic center in Denmark from 1974 to 1978. After the Saur Revolution (1978), he went to Peshawar, Pakistan, where he formed the National Liberation Front of Afghanistan and began an armed insurgency in Afghanistan against the Marxist government. He was elected president of the Afghan Interim Government in Pakistan in 1989, and after the Marxist government fell in 1992, he returned to Kabul to be the first post-Marxist president.

BIBLIOGRAPHY

ROY, OLIVIER. *Islam and Resistance in Afghanistan.* New York, 1986.

Grant Farr

Mukalla

An important port in south Yemen.

Located three hundred miles (485 km) to the west of Aden, Mukalla is a key element in Yemen's expanding fishing industry and a cosmopolitan city with important trading links with Oman, the Persian/Arabian Gulf, and points east. It historically served as the port of the HADRAMAWT and the seat of both the Quayti sultanate and British colonial administration in the Eastern Aden Protectorate.

Robert D. Burrowes

Mukhabarat

Arabic word for "intelligence service."

Each of the Middle Eastern countries has its own mukhabarat (a word derived from a root meaning "to know thoroughly"), but those of Syria and Iraq have particular reputations as instruments of governmental control.

BIBLIOGRAPHY

WEHR, HANS. *Arabic-English Dictionary.*

Zachary Karabell

Mukhtar

The village headman or leader of an urban quarter.

In the Tanzimat period of the Ottoman Empire, mukhtars were appointed to serve as local leaders and points of contact for government information and control. They have been associated with government efforts at centralization and the displacement of local religious leaders.

Stuart J. Borsch

Mukhtar, Umar al- [c. 1862–1931]

Preindependence Libyan guerilla leader.

Umar al-Mukhtar was born into the Minifa tribe, which lives along the eastern Cyrenaican coast, otherwise known as Marmarica. His family was part of the

Farhan lineage, itself part of the Braidan fraction. The Minifa were a client tribe of the al-Abaidat *sa'adi* tribe, to whom they paid dues as *marabtin al-sadqan* (clients for protection). Most of the tribe were seminomads, but some lineages were camel-herding nomads. The tribe had long been under Sanusi influence, with the closest *zawiya* (Islamic religious center) being located at Janzur, on the coast.

Umar al-Mukhtar's early education was provided at the Janzur *zawiya*. He then moved to the Sanusi order's headquarters at Jaghbub, one hundred miles (160 km) inland, near the modern border between Libya and Egypt. He proved an adept pupil and a committed member of the Sanusi *ikhwan* (brotherhood), with the result that he was nominated shaykh of the al-Qasur *zawiya,* in the Abid tribe, just to the south of al-Marj in the Jabal al-Akhdar.

At the turn of the century, after only two years at al-Qasur, Umar al-Mukhtar was sent southward to the new Sanusi headquarters at al-Kufra, which had been created in 1895. From there he was sent to Wadai, to participate in the Sanusi resistance to French penetration into what today is central Chad. He returned to al-Qasur in 1906 and took a prominent role in the first Italo–Sanusi War, which followed on the Italian invasion and occupation of Darna and Tripoli in September 1911.

The war was brought to an end by the Treaty of Akrama in January 1917. The treaty was, in effect, a truce, enforced on the Sanusi by British pressure, which left the Italians in charge of the coastal areas, while the Sanusi controlled the hinterland. Sanusi armed forces were gathered into a series of camps running eastward along the southern slopes of the Jabal al-Akhdar from Ajidabiya to Akrama. The *badu* (bedouin) forces in these camps were controlled by Sanusi ikhwan and shaykhs. Umar al-Mukhtar was responsible for the camps at al-Abyar, due east of Banghazi and south of al-Marj, and Taknis, just southeast of al-Marj.

In November 1921, in accordance with the terms of the Accord of Bu Mariyam, four of these camps were transformed into *campi misti* (mixed camps), in which Italian and Sanusi units, under their own independent commands, were garrisoned side by side. Both the camps controlled by Umar al-Mukhtar were included in this bizarre experiment, which was designed to promote joint policing and security arrangements. The fascist march on Rome at the end of 1922 also marked the beginning of the end of this experiment in joint policing and, on March 6, 1923, Italian forces attacked the campi misti, thus ushering in the second Italo–Sanusi War.

Although the Sanusi family did not take direct charge of the new war—most of its members fled to Egypt for British protection—Sanusi ikhwan played

a prominent role, alongside some of the younger members of the Sanusi family. Umar al-Mukhtar was to take charge of operations against the Italians. He took charge of all the guerilla bands (*adwar*) on the plateau formed along the southern slopes of the Jabal al-Akhdar in Cyrenaica, as the *al-Na'ib al-Amm* (general representative) of the Sanusi.

According to E. E. Evans-Pritchard, the adwar were usually between 100 and 300 men, and each was the nominal responsibility of a particular tribe. However, its membership was often heterogeneous, including members of other tribes, ikhwan, and sympathizers from the Sudan and Tripolitania. The overall numbers involved in the fighting were very small—around 600 to 700 toward the end of the war—simply because the terrain did not permit major movements of personnel. Umar al-Mukhtar's responsibilities were to determine strategy, to arrange logistics and to ensure discipline, particularly in terms of pillage and vendettas.

The guerilla war obeyed few of the rules to which the Italians were accustomed. In a telling passage, Teruzzi, when governor of Cyrenaica, pointed out to the authorities in Rome that superiority in men and arms was "a vain illusion, because the struggle was not against an organized enemy, but against an enemy who had no consistency of form." It was difficult, for example, for the Italians to distinguish between friend and foe, because those tribes that were apparently submitted to Italian rule still provided material support to the guerillas.

The strategy of al-Mukhtar was to hold the southern slopes of the plateau formed by the Jabal al-Akhdar to the south of the littoral escarpment. Although the Italian forces were able to establish themselves on the coast and to control the immediate hinterland of their major bases at Ajidabiya and al-Marj, they found it very difficult to ensure control of the land between. They were able to use air power to attack badu camps in the flatlands of the plateau, but could do little about the plateau itself. Even a line of permanent forts and outposts along the plateau of the Jabal did little to increase the effectiveness of Italian units, while an attempt to divert guerrilla activity by the capture of Jaghbub in 1926 proved to be irrelevant to the struggle.

Nonetheless, the constant military pressure severely depleted al-Mukhtar's forces; in 1928, both provinces of Libya were placed under a single administration. An offer of negotiations persuaded al-Mukhtar, his companion guerilla leader, Sidi Fadil Bu Umar, and a young scion of the Sanusi family, Sayyid al-Hasan al-Rida, to accept a five-month truce. The negotiations broke up in disorder, however, with al-Mukhtar and his supporters rejecting the arrangements agreed to by Sayyid al-Hasan al-Rida. By late January 1930, al-Mukhtar was forced to back into his last redoubt, after his forces were severely beaten at Wadi Mahajja; 800 men and 2,000 camels were lost during 1929, compared with Italian losses of only 114 men.

Command of the Italian campaign in Cyrenaica was then taken over by General Rodolfo Graziani, who applied a ruthless policy—providing Italian troops with great mobility, isolating the guerilla bands from their logistics support base by herding the nomadic population of Cyrenaica into concentration camps, and cutting the guerillas off from their Egyptian bases by a barbed-wire barricade.

On September 11, 1931, Sidi Umar al-Mukhtar was captured at Suluq and, five days later, was hanged before 20,000 Libyans in a demonstration of Italian power. The war was effectively over, even though 700 guerillas had remained on the plateau. The last engagement was fought on December 19, 1931. The death of al-Mukhtar had destroyed the spirit of the Libyan resistance.

BIBLIOGRAPHY

EVANS-PRITCHARD, E. E. *The Sanusi of Cyrenaica.* Oxford, 1947.

HAHN, LORNA. *Historical Dictionary of Libya.* Metuchen, N.J., 1981.

NYROP, R. F., et al., eds. *Libya: A Country Study.* Washington, D.C., 1979.

WRIGHT, JOHN. *Libya: A Modern History.* London, 1982.

George Joffe

Mukrani Family

Prominent family in preindependence Algeria.

During the late Ottoman period (c. 1800–1830), the Mukranis controlled a key section of the route between Algiers and Constantine. Under the French, Muhammad al-Mukrani was a regional commander until the military regime was weakened by Prussia's defeat of France in 1870. His revolt of 1871/72, supported by the Rahmaniyya brotherhood of Kabylia, was the largest and most harshly suppressed indigenous uprising prior to the War of Independence.

Peter von Sivers

Mulai

Arabic honorific used in addressing the caliph, king, or sultan, either directly or by reference.

The literal translation of *mulai* is "My Lord." It is rarely used today, having been replaced by translit-

erations of Western-style honorifics such as "Your Highness," "Your Majesty," and "My Lord."

Jenab Tutunji

Mulki, Fawzi al-   [1910–1962]

Prime minister of Jordan in 1953/54, heading the first cabinet after King Hussein's accession.

Known for espousing free political expression, Fawzi al-Mulki was imbued with modern ideas about democracy. A graduate of the American University of Beirut and Edinburgh University, he was the first prime minister in Jordan to have a postgraduate degree from a Western university. He served as ambassador to France and Britain before becoming prime minister in May 1953. In that capacity, he sought to develop what he saw as a liberal democratic trend launched by the adoption of the constitution of 1952. His declared policy was to govern according to the wishes and needs of the people; to this end, he allowed open political debate by licensing newspapers and supporting free expression. His policies were opposed and criticized by conservatives, who believed that communists and socialists would take advantage of liberalization and would undertake subversive activities against the state. Mulki was not a leftist himself and often accused the leftists in Jordan of being subversive. His government succumbed to conservative pressure in 1954, and he later took up ambassadorial posts.

BIBLIOGRAPHY

ABIDI, AZIL HYDER HASAN. *Jordan: A Political Study, 1948–1957.* New Delhi, 1965.

Jenab Tutunji

Mulla

See Molla

Mulukhiyya

Arabic name for the plant called jew's mallow, the main ingredient of a popular Arab dish by the same name.

Mulukhiyya is prepared in two ways: the Lebanese, where the leaves are left whole and are cooked with stew meat, garlic, and dried coriander; and the Egyptian style, in which the finely chopped leaves are cooked with chicken, rice, vinegar, and finely chopped onion. Eating mulukhiyya is prohibited within the Druze community.

Tayeb El-Hibri

Munassir, Qasim

Yemeni tribal leader instrumental in resolving the first civil war.

Munassir was an able and respected tribal leader and royalist military commander who defected with his forces to the republican side late in the YEMEN CIVIL WAR in the 1960s. He was assassinated in a private dispute shortly thereafter. To many, Munassir's defection marked the breaking of the republican-royalist stalemate in the long Yemen civil war, setting the stage for the reconciliation and the survival of the republic.

Robert D. Burrowes

Münchengratz, Convention of [1833]

Agreements to maintain and defend the Ottoman Empire by Austria and Russia.

In September 1833, Czar Nicholas I of Russia, Emperor Francis II of Austria and his foreign minister, Prince Metternich, signed a series of agreements at Münchengratz, Bohemia. Austria and Russia agreed to maintain the integrity of the Ottoman Empire and to defend it from external aggression (referring in separate secret articles to the problematical pasha of Egypt, Muhammad Ali, who had wrested Egypt away from the Ottoman state). In the event that the Ottoman Empire disintegrated from internal strains, Austria and Russia agreed to work together to find a solution that would not endanger their two states or the European balance of power.

BIBLIOGRAPHY

ANDERSON, M. S. *The Eastern Question.* London, 1966.
HUREWITZ, J. C., ed. *The Middle East and North Africa in World Politics.* New Haven, Conn., 1975.

Zachary Karabell

Munich Olympics

International competition of 1972, where Palestinians took Israeli athletes hostage.

On September 5, 1972, eleven Israeli Olympic athletes competing in Munich, Germany, were attacked by a group of Palestinians linked with the BLACK SEPTEMBER organization of the PLO (Palestine Liberation Organization). Two of the athletes were killed immediately, and nine were taken hostage. The guerrillas demanded an airplane and safe conduct, as well as the release of certain Palestinians imprisoned in Israel. At the airport, German security forces stormed the plane, and the remaining nine athletes, as well as five of the Palestinians, were killed.

BIBLIOGRAPHY

COBBAN, HELENA. *The Palestinian Liberation Organization.* New York, 1984.
Encyclopedia of the United Nations. Philadelphia, 1985.

Zachary Karabell

Munla, Saadi [1893–1973]

Lebanese prime minister, 1946; justice minister, 1945–1946.

A Sunni politician from Tripoli, Saadi Munla was a close associate of Abd al-Hamid KARAME under the French mandate. Following World War II, he belonged to a group of reform-minded Lebanese leaders who called for electoral reform, the adoption of measures to curb administrative corruption, and a stronger, more effective, autonomous state. In August 1945, he became minister of justice in a cabinet headed by Sami al-Sulh, and he retained that position until May 1946, when he was appointed prime minister. His cabinet collapsed only a few months afterward, however, in December 1946. In 1952, he was tapped to become President Camille Chamoun's first prime minister but failed to receive the appointment largely because of Kamal Jumblatt's opposition to his candidacy.

BIBLIOGRAPHY

HUDSON, MICHAEL C. *The Precarious Republic: Political Modernization in Lebanon.* Boulder, Colo., 1985.

Guilain P. Denoeux

Muntada al-Adabi, al-

A pro-Arab club founded in Istanbul in 1909; centered in Jerusalem after 1918.

Al-Muntada al-Adabi was originally founded in Istanbul in 1909 by Abd al-Karim al-Khalil of Tyre, Lebanon, to act as a meeting place for Arab visitors and residents in the capital of the Ottoman Empire.

The club played a role in the prewar reformist Arab movement in late Ottoman times. Membership of the club included politically conscious Lebanese, Palestinians, and Syrians. After the dissolution of the Ottoman state, the club reemerged in Jerusalem in November 1918 with new members and a new political program. It was largely dominated by prominent members of the NASHASHIBI FAMILY, most notably Is'af, a man of letters. Adopting a stance in favor of Arab nationalism, the club demanded complete Arab independence and Palestinian–Syrian unity. From its major center in Jerusalem, the club helped organize an anti-Zionist movement whose activities spread in Lebanon and Syria, where the club had branches. With the fall of the Syrian Arab government of Faisal I (1920), the club lost a major source of support and was eclipsed by the emergence of the ARAB EXECUTIVE in 1920.

BIBLIOGRAPHY

MUSLIH, MUHAMMAD. *The Origins of Palestinian Nationalism.* New York, 1988.

Muhammad Muslih

Muntafiq Tribe

A tribal confederation in southern Iraq.

Muntafiq designates a 300,000-member tribal confederation of settled, semi-nomadic, and nomadic tribes, including the Ajwad, Bani Malik, Bani Sa'id, Dhafir, and Jasha'am. They occupied the banks of the Euphrates from Chabaish to Darraji, and the Shatt al-Gharraf as far as Kut al-Hai. Led by the SA'DUN FAMILY, they were independent from the Ottomans who relied upon them to defend lower Iraq against the Wahhabis and the Persians. Before and during the MAMLUK period (1749–1831), they contested the court of Baghdad for power over Basra. After 1831, the policy of ILTIZAM, which required tribal shaykhs to collect government duties and revenues, eroded tribal relationships as the leaders demanded ever-increasing taxes on behalf of the government. When the Sa'dun became Ottoman landlords and government officials in 1870, reducing their tribes from landholders to tenants, the intense sense of betrayal further undermined their authority and weakened tribal power.

BIBLIOGRAPHY

LONGRIGG, STEPHEN HEMSLEY. *Four Centuries of Modern Iraq.* Oxford, 1925.

Albertine Jwaideh

Muntasir Family

Prominent Tripolitanian Arab family in Libya.

The Muntasir family resided in the coastal town of Misurata. It collaborated with the Turkish administrators of Libya during the second Ottoman occupation, after 1835, but fell out with the Young Turk revolution of 1908, since one of its leading members was murdered, allegedly, at Young Turk instigation.

The Muntasirs switched support to Italy during Italy's entry into Libya, before the military occupation of 1911, and cautious support continued during the first Italo–Sanusi War that ensued.

When the United Nations took charge of Libya's transition to independence in 1950, Mahmud Bey Muntasir was made premier of the provisional government, a position that was confirmed upon independence until his resignation in 1954. As an intimate of the royal family, he became premier and interior minister again in 1964, during pro-Arab nationalist agitation in Tripoli. Since the Great September Revolution (1969), members of the family have acted in a ministerial capacity and Umar Muntasir has been seen as the leading light of the technocrat faction within the Jamahiriya.

BIBLIOGRAPHY

WRIGHT, JOHN. *Libya.* London, 1969.

George Joffe

Muqattam, al-

Cairo daily newspaper.

Founded in 1889 with the covert encouragement of the British Agency, al-Muqattam served for many years as the political mouthpiece of pro-British Syrians in Egypt; it even printed Arabic translations of the annual reports issued by Cromer and his successors. Its founders were Ya'qub SARRUF, Faris NIMR, and Shahin Makarius, all Syrian writers who had come to Cairo to publish their scientific weekly, *al-Muqtataf,* unhindered by Ottoman censorship. After the revolution of 1919, *al-Muqattam* abandoned its pro-British policy. Edited later by Khalil Thabit, it remained a conservative evening newspaper and survived until 1952.

BIBLIOGRAPHY

BERQUE, JACQUES. *Egypt: Imperialism and Revolution.* Tr. by Jean Stewart. New York, 1972.

Arthur Goldschmidt, Jr.

Murabitun

Military arm of Harakah al-Nasiriyyun al-Mustaqillun (Independent Nasserite Movement); largest Sunni Muslim militia in west Beirut from the beginning of Lebanon's civil war of 1975 until the Arab–Israel War of 1982.

Founded by Ibrahim Qulaylat in early 1972, the Murabitun (Arabic for sentinels) of Lebanon maintained a close alliance with al-FATH (of the Palestine Liberation Organization, PLO) and continuously replenished its arms stockpiles through the largesse of Libya. Qulaylat was a veteran of the Lebanese Civil War of 1958 and had cultivated a personal relationship with his hero, Egypt's President Gamal Abdel Nasser.

During the early stages of the LEBANESE CIVIL WAR of 1975, the Murabitun expelled the Maronite (Christian) militias from the hotel district of downtown Beirut, and they maintained a sizable presence in the capital from then on. The dispersal of the PLO and the Murabitun's disarmament by Israel in 1982 greatly weakened the movement; in 1984, Syria's allies, the Shi'a Amal and the Druze militias of the PROGRESSIVE SOCIALIST PARTY conducted a series of multiple strikes against Qulaylat, who increasingly advanced himself as the protector of the Sunni community. Qulaylat now lives in exile in France.

BIBLIOGRAPHY

JOHNSON, MICHAEL. *Class and Client in Beirut: The Sunni Muslim Community and the Lebanese State, 1840–1985.* London, 1986.
SALIBI, KAMAL. *Crossroads to Civil War: Lebanon, 1958–1976.* Delmar, N.Y., 1976.

Bassam Namani

Murad V   [1840–1904]

Ottoman sultan.

As a young prince in the 1860s, Murad gained a reputation as an intelligent, reform-minded man among liberal intellectuals. After 1873, opponents of Sultan Abdülaziz, particularly Midhat Paşa, began talking of replacing the sultan with Murad. They achieved this in a coup on May 30, 1876. But Murad's mental health, already unstable, deteriorated rapidly after Abdülaziz was found dead on June 4. The cabinet deposed Murad on August 31, on grounds of insanity, and he was imprisoned in a palace for the remainder of his life.

BIBLIOGRAPHY

SHAW, STANFORD J. and EZEL KURAL SHAW. *History of the Ottoman Empire and Modern Turkey,* vol. 2. New York, 1977.

Elizabeth Thompson

Murat, Mehmet   [1853–1912]

Ottoman Turkish intellectual.

First named Mehmet Murat Efendi, Murat Bey was born in Daghistan near the Caspian Sea in the Russian Caucasus. After an education in Russia, he fled to Constantinople (now Istanbul), seat of the Ottoman Empire, in 1873. Working first as a civil servant and then as a teacher in the Mülkiye Civil Service School, he started to write history. He also became the editor of the political journal *Mizan.* Murat moved to Europe near the end of 1895 to avoid the inevitable constraints of the censors of Sultan Abdülhamit II. Murat (known as Mizanci Murat because of the fame of *Mizan*) soon was at the center of the YOUNG TURKS movement in Europe. Along with Abdullah CEVDET and AHMET RIZA, Murat criticized Abdülhamit's government and called for reform. In 1897, Abdülhamit invited the exiled Young Turk dissidents to return to Constantinople to help reform the flagging Ottoman Empire. Murat returned and sat on the Council of State. It was soon apparent that the sultan had made an empty offer. Murat was marginalized. With the Young Turk revolution in 1908, Murat became a proponent of pan-Islam, and he supported the ill-fated April 1909 Liberal coup whose failure resulted in the exile of Abdülhamit.

BIBLIOGRAPHY

LEWIS, BERNARD. *The Emergence of Modern Turkey.* New York, 1961.
RAMSAUR, E. E. *The Young Turks.* Princeton, N.J., 1957.
SHAW, STANFORD J., and EZEL KURAL SHAW. *History of the Ottoman Empire and Modern Turkey.* New York, 1977.

Zachary Karabell

Murrah, al-

A bedouin tribe of Saudi Arabia.

The al-Murrah inhabit the Empty Quarter (RUB AL-KHALI), southern Najd, south-central al-Hasa, and as far west as the Najran oasis. Considered to be a SHARIF tribe (one claiming noble descent), they are renowned both for their utilization of the Empty Quarter for grazing camels and for skills of desert tracking and have therefore been called the "nomads of the nomads." Although the majority still remain nomadic, in recent years al-Murrah households have begun to build permanent housing near traditional watering places, replacing camel herding with herding sheep and goats, and to derive part of their income from urban occupations and service in the Saudi National Guard.

Eleanor Abdella Doumato

Musa, Salama   [1887–1958]

Egyptian socialist essayist.

Salama Musa was born into a Coptic, well-to-do, landed family in Zaqaziq, a town in Egypt's Nile delta. While still in high school, Musa left Egypt for Europe, where he studied in France and England. In England, he met and was influenced by several prominent members of the Fabian Society, including H. G. Wells and George Bernard Shaw. Fabianism was a doctrine that combined economic socialism with an emphasis on social and moral regeneration through the cultivation of traditional moral values such as culture, decency, and order.

Returning to Egypt, Musa sought to spread this doctrine, urging his readers to leave behind Asian civilization and to embrace European—specifically, British—civilization. Other themes he dealt with were the scientific spirit, the theory of evolution, and social democracy. He founded Egypt's Socialist party in 1920 and established a journal, *al-Majalla al-Jadida* (the New Magazine), a forum for radical critiques. In several of his works, Musa also developed the theme that the Coptic period was the apex of Egyptian civilization and that the COPTS were the true present-day descendants of the ancient Egyptians.

BIBLIOGRAPHY

EGGER, VERNON. *A Fabian in Egypt: Salamah Musa and the Rise of the Professional Classes in Egypt, 1909–1939.* New York, 1986.

David Waldner

Musa Dagh

Mountain site of Armenian resistance to 1915 deportation orders in the Ottoman Empire.

Of the hundreds of villages, towns, and cities across the Ottoman Empire whose Armenian population was ordered removed to the Syrian desert, Musa Dagh was one of only four sites where Armenians organized a defense of their community against the deportation edicts issued by the Young Turk regime beginning in April 1915. By the time the Armenians of the six villages at the base of Musa Dagh were instructed to evict their homes, the inhabitants had grown suspicious of the government's ultimate intentions and chose instead to retreat up the mountain and to defy the evacuation order. Musa Dagh, or the Mountain of Moses, stood on the Mediterranean Sea south of the port city of Alexandretta and west of ancient Antioch.

With a few hundred rifles and the entire store of provisions from their villages, the Armenians on Musa Dagh put up a fierce resistance against a number of attempts by the regular Turkish army to flush them out. Outnumbered and outgunned, the Armenians had little expectations of surviving the siege of the mountain when food stocks were depleted after a month. Their only hope was a chance rescue by an Allied vessel that might be roaming the coast of the Mediterranean. When two large banners hoisted by the Armenians were sighted by a passing French warship, swimmers went out to meet it. Eventually five Allied ships moved in to transport the entire population, more than four thousand in all.

The Armenians of Musa Dagh had endured for fifty-three days: from July 21 to September 12, 1915. They were disembarked at Port Sa'id in Egypt and remained in Allied refugee camps until the end of World War I when they returned to their homes. As part of the district of Alexandretta, or Hatay, Musa Dagh remained under French mandate until 1939. The Musa Dagh Armenians abandoned their villages for a second, and final, time when the area was incorporated in the Republic of Turkey.

In the face of the complete decimation of the Armenian communities of the Ottoman Empire, Musa Dagh became a symbol of the Armenian will to survive in the postwar years. Of the three other sites where Armenians defied the deportation orders, Shabin Karahissar, Urfa, and Van, only the Armenians of Van were rescued when the siege of their city was lifted by an advancing Russian army. The Armenians of Urfa and Shabin Karahissar were either murdered or deported to face starvation in the Syrian desert much as the rest of the Armenians of the Turkish empire. In what became known as the Armenian genocide, Musa Dagh stood as the sole instance where the Allies averted the death of an Armenian community. That story inspired the Prague-born Austrian writer, Franz Werfel, to write a novelized version of the events as *The Forty Days of Musa Dagh*. Published in 1933, the book became an instant best-seller, but with the rise of Hitler, Werfel himself fled Vienna that same year. *Forty Days of Musa Dagh* was eventually translated into eighteen languages, and Metro-

Goldwyn-Mayer bought the rights to the book and announced plans for the production of a film version of the novel. The Turkish ambassador's protestations to the Department of State resulted in the intervention of the U.S. government in the matter. With a veiled threat to ban U.S.-made films from Turkey, MGM studios permanently shelved plans to produce the movie.

BIBLIOGRAPHY

MINASIAN, EDWARD. "The Forty Years of Musa Dagh: The Film that Was Denied." *Journal of Armenian Studies* 2, no. 2 (1985/6): 63–73.
WALKER, CHRISTOPHER J. *Armenia: The Survival of a Nation.* New York, 1980.

Rouben P. Adalian

Musahiban Brothers

Influential Afghan family.

Musahiban Brothers is a term used to describe the male family members descended from Mohammad Yahya (1879). They were called *musahiban* (Arabic for "companions"), because they all became very influential and were companions of HABIBOLLAH KHAN (1901–1919) and other Afghan kings. Members of the family included Mohammad NADIR, king of Afghanistan from 1929 to 1933, and his brothers or half brothers Mohammed Aziz, Mohammad Hashim, Shah Wali, and Shah Mahmud.

BIBLIOGRAPHY

DUPREE, LOUIS. *Afghanistan.* Princeton, N.J., 1980.

Grant Farr

Musahipzade Celal   [1870–1959]

Turkish dramatist.

Born in Constantinople (now Istanbul) the son of a government official, Musahipzade Celal studied in state secondary schools before entering the grand vizier's translation office as a clerk. He held a variety of government jobs until 1923, when he quit to work full time in the burgeoning theater scene of Constantinople. Musahipzade Celal's first play, *Köprüller,* was completed in 1912. From that time on, and through the early republican period, he wrote many historical and comedic plays full of social and political commentary.

Elizabeth Thompson

Musa Kazım   [1858–1919]

Ottoman Turkish religious leader.

Musa Kazım was the SHAYKH AL-ISLAM of the Ottoman Empire after the deposition of Sultan Abdülhamit II in 1909. He was also a member of Talat's cabinet in 1917. Musa Kazım Efendi called for a return to the foundations of Islam as the only way to restore the empire to its former glory. He believed in an orthodox Islam based on the Qur'an and the *Shari'a* (Islamic law) and not open to what he perceived to be the liberal interpretations of the educated elite. Though he urged the adoption of Western technology, he claimed that Western culture was incompatible with the *Shari'a,* and cultural Westernization was therefore forbidden to Muslims. He was a staunch defender of the institution of the caliphate, and he championed reforms in the teaching of religion. Musa Kazım was a Sufi (a Muslim mystic) though there is some dispute as to whether he was of the Naqshabandi or the Bektashi order.

BIBLIOGRAPHY

BERKES, NIYAZI. *The Development of Secularism in Turkey.* Montreal, 1964.
LEWIS, BERNARD. *The Emergence of Modern Turkey.* New York, 1961.
RAMSAUR, E. E. *The Young Turks.* Princeton, N.J., 1957.
SHAW, STANFORD J. and EZEL KURAL SHAW. *History of the Ottoman Empire and Modern Turkey.* New York, 1977.

Zachary Karabell

Musandam

Northernmost territories of the Sultanate of Oman.

Musandam (Arabic, Ra's Masandam) includes an island cape that forms the southern shore of the Strait of Hormuz, where the Arabian/Persian Gulf joins the Gulf of Oman and an adjacent mountainous peninsula separating the gulfs. Sparsely settled by Shihuh tribespeople, the chief town is Kumzar. Musandam is separated from Oman by some land of the United Arab Emirates.

BIBLIOGRAPHY

LORIMER, J. G. "Musandam." *Gazetteer of the Persian Gulf, Oman, and Central Arabia.* Vol. 2B, *Geographical and Statistical.* Calcutta, 1908–1915. Reprint, 1970.

Robert G. Landen

Musawwar, al-

Egyptian magazine.

Established in 1924, *al-Musawwar* is a weekly political magazine published by the Dar al-Hilal publishing company. It boasts a circulation of 130,000 and is one of the two most widely read periodicals in Egypt today. Dedicated to free speech and investigative journalism, *al-Musawwar* has provoked controversy. Religious zealots tried to assassinate its editor, Makram Muhammad Ahmad, on June 3, 1987.

Michael R. Fischbach

Music

Musicians in the Middle East have, over the centuries, produced a great classical tradition in a variety of regional forms.

Historically, Middle Eastern music has been predominantly melodic, drawing from a complicated system of modes called *maqam* in Arabic, *makam* in Turkish, and *mugam* in Azerbaijani. The melodic system of Iran is based on *dastgaha,* similar in principle if not in practice. These systems and their repertoires frequently have written histories—music theories that date back to the time of al-Farabi and earlier.

Sung poetry is fundamental to the musical art of the region. The elegant or clever text and the performance that highlights the affective phrase or the play on words often are highly valued by listeners.

Instrument types include long- and short-neck lutes, plucked and hammered dulcimers, end-blown reed flutes, hourglass drums, frame drums, and sev-

An assortment of musical instruments for sale in a Marrakech, Morocco, market. (© Yto Barrada)

Yemeni musician in the 1940s. (D.W. Lockhard)

eral sizes of double-reed wind instruments often played in concert with large field drums. These instruments have different names, shapes, and playing styles.

Overarching genres of performance occur throughout the region, often consisting of suites of instrumental and vocal music, both improvised and formally composed. They occur in devotional rituals, dance, neoclassical performance, and performances by folk musicians. Despite the disparate sounds, contexts, and audiences, these performances are often linked by listeners with their Arabic musical-poetic heritage (*turath*), which encompasses a broad range of religious, classical, and folk musics. Typologies common in the West that separate the religious and the secular, or the classical, the folk, and the popular, do not always apply to Middle Eastern repertoires. For instance, in Iran the classical *radif* stands in stark contrast to Kurdish folk songs but is colored by Iranian Sufi performance. By contrast, the Azerbaijani *mugam*, a classical genre, includes and arguably depends on Azeri folk music in its structure.

Nay-maker demonstrating his musical-instrument wares in downtown Alexandria, Egypt, 1992. (Virginia Danielson)

Regional Distinctions. Over the years these historic materials and aesthetics have yielded distinct styles, genres, and practices in different times and places. For example, the governments of Morocco and Tunisia and private agencies in Algeria have participated in the revitalization of local forms of *nawba,* a suitelike genre. It is believed to have originated in Andalusia and to have been carried from there to North Africa. What results, in the twentieth century, is "classical" music so emblematic of a particular region that it is really not possible to speak of "Algerian" classical music, let alone "Arab" classical music but rather the repertories of Tlemcen, Constantine, Algiers, Fez, Tunis, and so on. However in general, revitalization of these genes serves to mark cultures as "Arab" rather than Berber.

On the other hand, styles drawn from the peoples of southern Morocco, Algeria, Tunisia, and Libya have created distinctly North African popular genres exemplified by the Moroccan group Nas al-Ghiwan. Similiarly, Algerian *ra'i* offers an excellent example of a style rooted in local musical practice, transformed with imported electronic instruments and modern texts. These styles draw the historic aesthetic of the clever, sometimes stinging colloquial text and favorite local instruments into contact with the electronics, and sometimes the staging, of rock music. The result may or may not be considered "westernized" by local listeners.

Regional distinctions have long been part of *mashriq* performances. Microtonal intervals tend to be tuned slightly higher in Turkey and Syria than in Egypt and North Africa. The *buzuq* is an important part of Lebanese folk culture. The resurgence of "classical" repertoires has been discouraged in Turkey since the establishment of the republic (1923). The governments of Egypt, Iraq, and Lebanon have sponsored neoclassical ensembles that often give concerts in opera houses, with musicians in evening dress performing without the extemporization that is historically part of Middle Eastern traditions. In other words, Arab pieces of music are presented in the context of a Western concert.

Transformed classical and folk traditions have emerged in nongovernmental venues as well. Perhaps the best-known are the plays by Fayruz and the Rahbani brothers, articulating local pride and local concerns by using distinctly Lebanese styles and a combination of local and Western instruments. The Western models of the musical play and film, popular in the Arab world, serve local purposes well. The best-known recent exponent of music from the *turath* is the Syrian Sabah Fakhri, who travels internationally, performing *muwashshahat, taqasim,* classical instrumental pieces, and newer songs in suitelike arrangements. UMM KULTHUM and MUHAMMAD IBN ABD AL-WAHHAB are well-known performers of "new" or "popular" music that has attracted a large audience throughout the Arab world. Abd al-Wahhab's style is the more innovative, creating a pastiche of Western and Arab musical styles in a single composition and establishing the free-form instrumental piece (*al-qit'a al-musiqiyya*) as an important independent genre. Although both Umm Kulthum and Abd al-Wahhab sing complicated neoclassical works, Umm Kulthum has claimed this area as her own.

Instrumental improvisations (*taqasim*) and a historic suite-like genre, the Iraqi maqam, have persisted throughout the twentieth century, partly supported by the Arab diaspora. The performances of Munir Bashir, Nazim al-Ghazali, and Muhammad al-Qubbanji have been rereleased by firms in Paris and Baghdad. Iraq and the countries of the Arabian peninsula support rich traditions of singing and dancing that have been documented by local musicologists and by folklore institutes such as that established in Oman.

Teaching and performing classical Persian music have formed part of musical life in Tehran throughout the twentieth century, especially among elites. The musical culture of Iran encompasses a range of folk and religious musics as well. Cabaret music also has become popular. Following the Iranian Revolution, the new government moved to suppress musical performance, including music at weddings. In the long run, the primary target was cabaret music, often associated with consumption of alcohol and prostitution. In recent years, *radif* recordings have become readily available, and performance of traditional music persists.

Israel presents a unique musical culture, consisting of a patchwork of musics from Europe, the former Soviet Union, the Arab world, and Africa, brought together in a small space over a relatively short period of time. A few syncretic repertoires have emerged, but musics more often persist as individual emblems of the immigrant communities.

Musical Occasions. Weddings and special occasions, often religious in nature, have long offered venues for musical performance. Starting the pilgrimage to Mecca, celebrating the birthday of Muhammad, remembering the martyrdom of Husayn, and the ceremonies of Sufi *dhikr*s have all involved music. During the nineteenth and twentieth centuries, urban nightclubs and cabarets often featured musical entertainment and dancing, as did tourist hotels. Generally speaking, there is a long history of professionalism in Middle Eastern music. In some areas, notably Iran, professional musicians tend to belong to minority groups; musical performance in the majority culture tends to be amateur.

These tendencies have persisted in the twentieth century. Often they have been transformed through the mass media, which quickly took hold throughout the Middle East and became very popular. Many would argue that the mass media have become primary patrons of musicians.

Commercial recording took hold in the first decade of the twentieth century, mainly in Algiers, Cairo, Beirut, Constantinople (now Istanbul), and Tehran. Radio became more popular than the phonograph in the 1930s. Television, beginning in the 1960s, and videocassettes in the 1970s, proliferated, especially among the middle and upper classes. This development is significant particularly because cassettes, which are inexpensive and portable, gave control over production to local artists, or at least to agencies that were closer to the artists than a national radio company or a European-based recording company. Artists were able to produce their own recordings and market them locally, circumventing those

who select music for radio and television stations and the requirements of international production firms. In the 1990s, despite the opportunities for Middle Eastern artists to produce internationally marketed videos and compact disks, some of the most interesting performances are locally released cassettes.

Musical Processes and Issues. As a constituent of social life, musical performances in the Middle East have engaged local histories with the flow of new materials from other societies. Unsurprisingly, this engagement has fed debates on authenticity, music and sociocultural identity, modernity, and the proper nature of culture in the late twentieth century.

The development of mass media centered in urban areas has tended to promote the musics of those areas over others. Local musics from Morocco to Iraq have been dominated in the mass media by musics produced in Cairo and Beirut, for instance. Only in recent years, with the less expensive cassette and a recent interest in the musics of southern Morocco, Nubia, and the Gulf states, has this situation changed.

Contact with Europe and the United States has led some musicians to borrow, adapt, and integrate new sounds into local music. The accordion, cello, string bass, and electronic instruments have become widely popular and virtually consolidated with some local musics. Latin rhythms, disco, and nineteenth-century orchestral music (especially for film scores) have been borrowed outright. This vast array of sounds—ranging from religious chanting by a solo voice to improvisations on lutes, dueling songs, formally composed orchestral pieces, and special electronic effects—is being employed by musicians and their listeners to identify themselves and to suggest directions and affinities within their societies.

Boundaries are not always clear. The process of musical creation transforms past practices to contribute to the lively culture of Middle Eastern societies intent on maintaining an identity while responding to the challenges of the present.

BIBLIOGRAPHY

Browning, Robert, ed. *Maqam: Music of the Islamic World and Its Influences.* New York, 1984.

During, Jean, et al. *The Art of Persian Music.* Washington, D.C., 1991.

Farhat, Hormoz. *The Dastgah Concept in Persian Music.* Cambridge, U.K., 1990.

al-Faruqi, Lois. "Music, Musicians, and Muslim Law." *Asian Music* 17, no. 1 (1985): 3–36.

Jenkins, Jean, and Poul Rovsing Olsen. *Music and Musical Instruments in the World of Islam.* London, 1976.

Nettl, Bruno. *The Radif of Persian Music: Studies of Structure and Cultural Context in the Classical Music of Iran,* 2nd ed. Urbana, Ill., 1992.

SIGNELL, KARL. *Makam: Modal Practice in Turkish Art Music.* Seattle, 1977.

Virginia Danielson

Muslim Brotherhood

Egyptian Sunni revivalist group founded in 1929.

The Muslim Brotherhood (*al-Ikhwan al-Muslimin*), also known as the Society of Muslim Brothers, has been the ideological and institutional fountainhead of SUNNI revivalism in the Arab world. Founded in 1929 by Shaykh Hasan al-Banna in Isma'iliyya, Egypt, the Muslim Brotherhood has survived internal splits and recurrent repression by the state for over sixty years. The society came into being as a response to the prevailing conditions of crisis in Egyptian society and the resulting confluence of powerful social currents with Banna's charismatic personality.

The Muslim Brotherhood flourished during the years between the world wars, which were characterized by the struggle between the nationalist WAFD party, the monarchy, and the British and the failure of Egypt to develop an ideological synthesis to guide the process of nation building and socioeconomic development. Within this milieu, Banna proclaimed his *da'wa*—a call to return to the basics of Islam as a framework for personal and collective identity, a medium of spiritual salvation, and an ideology to guide social and political action.

As the Muslim Brotherhood's General Guide, Banna was destined to become the pioneer of twentieth-century Sunni revivalism. The embodiment of the Sufi spiritualist and Islamic scholar turned activist, Banna had the rare ability to evoke mass support by translating doctrinal complexities into social action. Indeed, the Brotherhood possessed certain characteristics that set it apart from other revivalist and secular movements. It had (1) an activist ideology, (2) organized cadres, (3) charismatic leadership, (4) a pragmatic orientation, and (5) a mass following. Unlike Muhammad Abduh's SALAFIYYA MOVEMENT, the Brotherhood was a mass movement built around its leader's salvationist message, which was translated into social action by the society's apparatus. Banna's ideology lacked the philosophical depth of the Salafiyya, but it succeeded in galvanizing a mass following through effective propaganda techniques; at the same time, Banna strove to implement his program of action in a pragmatic manner by setting up a plethora of social, educational, and philanthropic institutions and business enterprises. In addition, the Brotherhood was an urban movement, lacking the primitivism of its MU-

WAHHIDUN SANUSI, and MAHDIST predecessors; this feature contributed to its transnational appeal and support among recently urbanized masses.

Despite its traditionalist ideology, the movement founded by Banna was a modern one that in many ways resembled the totalitarian movements that had arisen in Europe and Russia. By the late 1930s, the Brotherhood had become a powerful organization with a million members and followers drawn from a cross section of Egyptian society. During the World War II period, Banna began coming into conflict with the British authorities and with the Egyptian government itself. The central problem was the ambiguous nature of the Brotherhood's challenge to the Egyptian state. Banna declared that his movement was not a political party but was rather "a new soul in the heart of this nation to give it life by means of the Qur'an"; its stated aim was to establish an Islamic order through proselytization and social activism. In the late 1940s, however, the Brotherhood engaged in repeated confrontations with the regime, going to the brink of revolutionary action but without an unequivocal ideological, pragmatic commitment to seizing power. This ambiguity stemmed from the relative weakness of the Brotherhood's secret military apparatus vis-à-vis the regime, as well as the incipient state of Banna's political thinking regarding the recourse to revolution. Indeed, it was difficult for Banna to break with the tradition of conformism to state authority that had characterized Sunni political theory and practice, particularly in Egypt. Except in rare instances, the Sunni *ulama* (clergy) had counseled obedience to the state and had limited recourse to JIHAD to fighting non-Muslim enemies. Given this heritage, Banna and most of his followers tended to shy away from outright revolutionary action, and though not excluding the utility of violence in self-defense, Banna remained an advocate of gradualism in the pursuit of his Islamic order. This stance caused a split in the Brotherhood's ranks between the advocates of militancy and those favoring gradualism. In December 1948, the government dissolved the society because of its role in street violence and the assassination of several prominent leaders. Banna's personal efforts to negotiate with Nuqrashi Pasha's government were unsuccessful, and the prime minister unleashed the full powers of the state against the society. On December 28, 1949, Nuqrashi was assassinated by a member of the Muslim Brotherhood; this act caused a reign of terror to be mounted against the society that led to Banna's assassination on February 12, 1949, by government agents.

The Brotherhood regained legal status when the Wafd government came to power in January 1950. In October 1951, as the society's guerrillas were fighting the British in the Suez Canal zone, a brotherhood member, Hasan al-Hudaybi, a judge, was elected General Guide. The Muslim Brotherhood was allegedly involved in the mass rioting that broke out in January 1952 and culminated in the burning and destruction of Western-owned establishments in Cairo. They did not participate directly in the overthrow, on July 26, 1952, of King Farouk by a military junta led by Gen. Muhammad Naguib and Lt. Col. Gamal Abdel Nasser.

Although the society's relations with the military regime were initially cordial, by mid-1953 it became clear that the Nasser-led Revolutionary Command Council intended to establish a secular, rather than an Islamic, polity. In the ensuing power struggle between Nasser and Naguib, the Muslim Brethren joined the outlawed parties in demonstrations that called for a civilian regime under Naguib. The confrontation intensified in July 1954 when the Brotherhood rejected as treasonable Nasser's conclusion of an agreement with Britain on the evacuation of the latter's forces from the canal zone. An assassination attempt against Nasser in October 1954, allegedly undertaken by the Brotherhood, resulted in massive repression and the arrest of thousands of the society's members. Six of its leaders were tried and executed, and Hudaybi was sentenced to life imprisonment. For the next decade, the Brotherhood's appeal was neutralized by Nasser's charismatic popularity, which centered around his secular pan-Arab ideology. In 1964 Nasser freed the imprisoned Muslim Brethren, presumably in the hope that they would act as a counterbalance to the Communists at a time when Nasser's regime was weakened by the Yemen war and by economic problems. In mid-1965, the Muslim Brethren once again became embroiled in a conspiracy, which led to many arrests and the hanging of three prominent members, including Sayyid QUTB, the society's theoretician.

The Arab defeat in the June 1967 Arab–Israel War discredited secular pan-Arabism and set the stage for the increased influence of the Muslim Brethren. Nasser's death in September 1970 brought to power Anwar al-Sadat, who sought allies and a new medium of legitimacy. Sadat began to use Islamic themes in his discourses, and he let the Muslim Brethren out of jail as a means of neutralizing his rivals, the former supporters of Nasser. In this nascent alliance with the Muslim Brethren, Sadat did not include the society's military offshoots, which arose to plague the regime in the 1970s and were implicated in his assassination in October 1981. The radical societies, the products of an ideological split that harked back to Banna's time, had reemerged in the 1960s under Sayyid Qutb's influence. A follower of Ibn Taymiyya and Mawdudi, Qutb had developed a theory of revolution, an unprecedented feature in Sunni political thinking. It involved a divinely sanctioned right to overthrow Islamically illegitimate rulers through jihad, to be fought by a vanguard of earnest believers, in order to establish Allah's authority on earth. Qutb's doctrine was a direct challenge to Hudaybi, the society's General Guide, who preached the primacy of proselytization as the means of establishing an Islamic order. To this day, the latter gradualist orientation has remained the basic policy of the Brotherhood's mainstream fundamentalism, and it is shared by the society's affiliates in several neighboring Arab countries.

Since the mid-1980s, the Muslim Brethren, spurred by the deteriorating socioeconomic conditions in Egypt, have gone beyond proselytization and have expanded their social service functions. Under the successive Guides Umar al-Tilmisani and Hamad Abu al-Nasr, they have also participated in elections, under the guise of forming alliances with legal political parties, and have won seats in the Egyptian People's Assembly. At the same time that they have rejected the kind of antiregime violence perpetrated by the militant Islamist groups, the Brotherhood has continued to call for the establishment of an Islamic polity based on the *Shariʿa* (Islamic law).

BIBLIOGRAPHY

BINDER, LEONARD. *The Ideological Revolution in the Middle East.* Binghamton, N.Y., 1964.
DEKMEJIAN, R. HRAIR. *Islam in Revolution.* Syracuse, N.Y., 1985.
HUSAINI, ISHAK MUSA. *The Moslem Brethren.* Beirut, 1956.
MITCHELL, RICHARD P. *The Society of the Muslim Brothers.* London, 1969.

Richard Dekmejian

Muslim–Christian Association

Group established to organize Palestinian opposition to Zionism.

The Muslim–Christian Association (MCA) first appeared in Jaffa early in November 1918, and in Jerusalem later the same month; subsequently it set up branches in various Palestinian towns. The purpose behind creating the MCA was to organize a Palestinian national struggle against the threat of ZIONISM. The top leadership of the MCA was drawn largely from the older generation of urban notables who had social standing in Ottoman times.

According to the intelligence reports of the ZIONIST COMMISSION, the establishment of the MCA was prompted by Captain C. D. Brunton, a British military intelligence officer posted in PALESTINE during the war and in the Jaffa area after the armistice. Brunton was assisted by a local notable named Ali al-Mustaqim. Years later, Sir Wyndham DEEDES, chief secretary of the Palestine government during the years 1920–1923, claimed in a conversation with Chaim M. KALVARYSKI, who headed the Arab Department of the Zionist Executive in Jerusalem in the early 1920s, that from the start the MCA received "support and financial aid" from the Palestine government.

Initially, the MCA did not have much political power, and its significance derived from the fact that it embodied the novel concept of political cooperation between Muslims and Christians in Palestine. Gradually, however, it became a group of leaders and activists who were able to mobilize important segments of Palestinian society around a program of independence and opposition to Zionism. The notables who led the MCAs were interested in maintaining friendly relations with the British. Their main instruments of political action were petitions submitted to the Palestine government, and the organizing of demonstrations and other campaigns on instructions from the Jerusalem secretariat, which was headed by Jamal al-HUSAYNI.

As part of its efforts to promote Palestinian national demands, the MCA was instrumental in convening a nationwide congress in early February 1919. Called the first PALESTINIAN ARAB CONGRESS, it was followed by six more, the last being held in 1928. The MCA also initiated the formation of the ARAB EXECUTIVE, a committee of politicians who tried to coordinate the national struggle in the 1920s and early 1930s. In the late 1920s, a younger generation of Palestinian political activists began to challenge the leaders of the MCA and to criticize their policies toward the British. By that time, many of the MCAs had disintegrated, partly as a result of internal Palestinian divisions and partly as a result of lack of funds to carry on day-to-day operations in the secretariat. The emergence of new political groups and the proliferation of political parties in the early 1930s spelled the end of the MCAs and the Arab Executive, thus setting the stage for the creation of a new umbrella organ, the ARAB HIGHER COMMITTEE.

BIBLIOGRAPHY

LESCH, ANN MOSELY. *Arab Politics in Palestine, 1917–1939: The Frustration of a Nationalist Movement.* Ithaca, N.Y., 1979.

MUSLIH, MUHAMMAD Y. *The Origins of Palestinian Nationalism.* New York, 1988.

PORATH, YEHOSHUA. *The Emergence of the Palestinian-Arab National Movement, 1918–1929.* London, 1974.

Muhammad Muslih

Muslim World League

International Muslim organization.

The Muslim World League (in Arabic, Rabitat al-Alam al-Islami), headquartered in Mecca and funded by the government of Saudi Arabia, was founded under the auspices of King Faisal in 1966. The league promotes the cause of Islam throughout the world by holding conferences, distributing classical Islamic texts and modern religious publications, and paying the salaries of mosque preachers and missionaries.

Khalid Y. Blankinship

Musqat

Capital of the Sultanate of Oman.

Between the fifteenth and mid-twentieth centuries, Musqat (also Muscat or Masqat) was OMAN's leading international seaport. Its fortune was founded on its harbor, its relative security from land attack, and its strategic Gulf of Oman location, where routes linking the Persian/Arabian Gulf, India, South Arabia, the Red Sea, and East Africa converge.

Musqat, an old town whose founding date is unknown, became an important Indian Ocean port during the fifteenth century while a Hormuzi dependency. Portugal seized Musqat in 1507, developed it as a base to support its Afro-Asian maritime empire, and built the massive forts that still guard the harbor. Portugal ruled until the Ya'ariba imamate

Modern residential neighborhood in Musqat. (Richard Bulliet)

restored Omani rule in 1649. Although not Oman's capital, Musqat thrived under Ya'ariba patronage as a leading Indian Ocean emporium, shipping center, and hub of an expanding maritime empire. After dynastic and tribal dissension sapped Ya'ariba power in the 1730s, Musqat suffered occupation by Iranians. Recovery followed after Ahmad ibn Sa'id (1749–1783), founder of Oman's present Al Bu Sa'id dynasty, ejected the Iranians, and restored Musqat's marine and commercial capabilities. By 1780, the port was the western Indian Ocean's main trading center. After Imam Ahmad's death, Oman split into several autonomous Al Bu Sa'id fiefdoms. Musqat became Sultan ibn Ahmad's (1792–1804) capital and the center of his secular, coastal-based, trade-oriented regime—the precursor of today's Sultanate of Oman. Musqat's late-eighteenth to early-nineteenth century affluence depended on control of the Yemen to Iraq coffee trade, the India to West Asia and East Africa rice and textile trade, and the East Africa to West Asia and India slave trade. Musqat's prosperity began to decline in the 1830s, as Omanis reacted to contracting political and economic opportunities in the Gulf by increasingly exploiting their Zanzibar and East Africa dominions. The slide continued after 1860, following the Al Bu Sa'id domain's partition into African and Arabian states, loss of Musqat's once-lucrative carrying trade to British steamships, Britain's suppression of slave trading, and tribal unrest that brought continuing security threats and even occasional attacks.

By the early twentieth century, despite some arms smuggling, Musqat had become a sleepy steamer port. Its faltering business was conducted mainly by British-protected Indian merchants. Economic depression reduced the population to 6,000 before a revival was instituted after the 1970 coup that installed Sultan Qabus ibn Sa'id AL BU SA'ID's modernizing regime. Subsequent improvements included a sumptuous royal palace, a road to Oman's interior, and restoration of historic structures. Nevertheless, construction of modern port facilities in neighboring Matrah doomed Musqat's traditional seaport function. Still the seat of Oman's ruler, Musqat is only part of the rapidly expanding thirty-mile (48-km)-long capital area, where most development occurs beyond its walls.

BIBLIOGRAPHY

HAWLEY, SIR DONALD. *Oman and Its Renaissance,* rev. ed. London, 1984.
LORIMER, J. G. "Masqat Bay and Town" and "Masqat District." In *Gazetteer of the Persian Gulf, Oman, and Central Arabia.* Vol. 2B, *Geographical and Statistical.* Calcutta, 1908–1915. Reprint, 1970.

Robert G. Landen

Mustafa IV [1781–1808]

Ottoman sultan.

Mustafa IV came to power in 1807 when the janissaries and their allies deposed the reformist Sultan Selim III. He remained a captive of the janissaries' politics of reaction. In 1808, Selim III's supporters deposed him and placed Mahmud II, who shared Selim's reformist ideas, on the throne. Mahmud II had Mustafa IV executed in order to prevent further challenges to his rule.

BIBLIOGRAPHY

SHAW, STANFORD J., and EZEL KURAL SHAW. *History of the Ottoman Empire and Modern Turkey.* Vol. 2. New York, 1977.

Elizabeth Thompson

Mustafa Fazıl [1829–1875]

Egyptian prince and supporter of Young Ottomans.

Prince Mustafa Fazıl was the son of Ibrahim Paşa and brother of the Egyptian Khedive Isma'il. In 1845, Mustafa Fazıl traveled from Egypt to Constantinople (now Istanbul), where he took up politics. He served on the Council of Tanzimat from 1857 to 1862, and as minister of education in 1862 and 1863. In 1866, Isma'il secured a change in succession from Sultan Abdülaziz, thereby excluding Mustafa Fazıl from the Egyptian throne. Mustafa Fazıl, apparently in revenge, bankrolled the movement of YOUNG OTTOMANS, first in Constantinople, and later from Paris. His 1867 open letter to the sultan was widely reproduced for forty years as a manifesto for political reform.

BIBLIOGRAPHY

DAVISON, RODERIC H. *Reform in the Ottoman Empire 1856–1876.* Princeton, N.J., 1963, pp. 197–218.

Elizabeth Thompson

Mustafa Reşid [1800–1858]

Ottoman foreign minister, grand vizier, and reformer.

Mustafa Reşid is considered one of the major forces promoting the TANZIMAT reforms that modernized the Ottoman Empire in the mid-nineteenth century. He was born in Constantinople (now Istanbul), the son of Mustafa Efendi, an administrator of religious foundations. Intending a career as a religious scholar, he studied at the *ilmiyye,* but at the age of ten his father died and he was forced to withdraw from school and live with his uncle, Ispartali Ali Paşa, a court chamberlain of Sultan Mahmud II. In 1816, Reşid accompanied Ali Paşa to the province of Morea, where the latter had been appointed governor. It was during Ali Paşa's second term as governor (1820–21), that Reşid witnessed the rout of Ottoman forces by the European-supported Greek rebels and by the modernized army of Muhammad Ali, governor of Egypt, in the Greek War of Independence. Reşid learned two lessons from this experience: first, that reform of the basic institutions of the Empire was needed, and second, that diplomacy aimed at acquiring European support for the empire was as crucial as modernization of the army.

In 1826, with the help of an influential family friend, Mustafa Reşid entered the civil service as a clerk in the scribes bureau of the foreign minister, where he quickly rose to become assistant to the minister in charge of foreign affairs. From this position, Mustafa Reşid participated in negotiations with Muhammad Ali in 1830; the latter was so impressed with his talents that he offered him a high position in the Egyptian administration. In 1832, Reşid was appointed *amedçi* in the foreign ministry. Between 1834 and 1836, he was ambassador to France, where he became acquainted with European statesmen, including the famous Austrian foreign minister, Prince Metternich. In 1836, he was transferred to Britain as ambassador to the Court of Saint James, where he discussed reforms with Lord Palmerston. In 1837, Sultan Mahmud II, seeking a counterweight to Mehmet Koja HUSREV, the leader of the conservative opposition to reform, appointed Mustafa Reşid, now a leading advocate of reform, foreign minister, giving him the title Paşa. For the next eighteen months, Reşid Paşa remained in London and Paris, while attempting to bolster Mahmud II's reform program and to convince the sultan to place his trust in the British. He returned to Constantinople only upon receiving news of the death of the sultan and of the ascension to the throne of his son, Abdülmecit I.

In 1839, Mustafa Reşid Paşa skillfully blended his mastery of domestic and foreign affairs to deter military disaster while advancing reform. As foreign minister and representative of the Sublime Porte in London, he had been unable to prevent his conservative rival Mehmet Koja Husrev Paşa from becoming grand vizier. But when Muhammad Ali, governor of Egypt, sent an army commanded by his son Ibrahim into Syria, Husrev Paşa responded by attempting to appease Muhammad Ali, offering to appoint him lifetime governor not only of Egypt, but of Syria and Adana. Recognizing that this would result in a virtual dismemberment of the empire that would guarantee

Russian domination, Mustafa Reşid Paşa negotiated with British foreign minister Lord Palmerston for the European support needed to counter the Egyptian advance. European, particularly British, military and diplomatic support, which was crucial in defusing the crisis, was linked to a commitment to support internal reform. Sultan Abdülmecit recognized the key role played by Reşid Paşa and rewarded him with a promise to advance the program of the reformers. On November 3, 1839, Sultan Abdülmecit initiated this reform program with the proclamation of the Imperial Rescript of Gülhane, a document which was composed by Mustafa Reşid and which is considered the opening salvo of the Tanzimat. Though the Tanzimat was initiated at a time of increased European involvement in the empire, it was promoted by Ottomans like Mustafa Reşid Paşa who recognized the need for continued reforms to remedy defects in the administration of the empire. Mustafa Reşid sought British support, but he was not acting under British pressure.

Mustafa Reşid Paşa's importance did not cease with the proclamation of the Tanzimat. He was one of the architects of a new commercial code, promulgated in 1841, that was based on French commercial law. When asked whether the new law was in comformity with Islamic law, he reportedly replied, ''the Holy Law has nothing to do with it.'' Vociferous reaction from Islamic scholars led to suspension of the law and Mustafa Reşid's Paşa's dismissal. He served as ambassador to France until 1845, when he began a second period as leader of the reform movement. Over the next fifteen years, he served six times as grand vizier (September 28, 1846 to April 28, 1848; August 12, 1848 to January 26, 1852; March 5 to August 5, 1852; November 23, 1854 to May 2, 1855; November 1, 1856 to August 6, 1857; and October 22, 1857 to January 7, 1858) and three times as foreign minister.

In addition, Reşid played a crucial role in recruiting and training a cadre of reform-minded bureaucrats who, under his leadership, became known as the ''men of the Tanzimat'' (*tanzimatcılar*). In order to learn more about Islamic law, he retained Ahmed CEVDET as a tutor, subsequently hiring him as his personal scribe, and then appointing him to educational positions in the administration. The most well-known of his protégés were Mehmet Emin Ali Paşa, who served as Mustafa Reşid's translator and scribe in the embassy in London and later served as foreign minister and as grand vizier, and Mehmet FUAD Paşa, who became Mustafa Reşid's protégé in 1837. Mehmet Ali and Mehmet Fuad led the reform program during the last two decades of the Tanzimat. Whereas Mustafa Reşid had always sought alliance with Britain, his two protégés sought to orient empire politics toward an alliance with France. Partially as a result of this difference, the two eclipsed Mustafa Reşid Paşa in the early 1850s, though at the time of his death in 1858, Mustafa Reşid was once again grand vizier. After his death, his sons carried on the tradition of service to the empire, serving as ministers and ambassadors.

BIBLIOGRAPHY

BAYSUN, CAVID. "Mustafa Reşid Paşa." In *Tanzimat.* Istanbul, 1940, pp. 723–746.
SHAW, STANFORD J., and EZEL KURAL SHAW. *History of the Ottoman Empire and Modern Turkey,* vol 2: *Reform, Revolution, and Republic: The Rise of Modern Turkey, 1808–1975.* New York, 1977, pp. 56–63.

David Waldner

Mustafa Suphi [1883–1921]

Turkish communist leader.

The son of a district governor, Mustafa Suphi was born in the Giresun district on the Black Sea. He studied law in Constantinople (now Istanbul) in the late 1890s and then continued his education in Paris and Rome. A leftist thinker, Mustafa Suphi fled Ottoman police shortly before World War I and took up residence in Russia where he organized a communist movement among Turkish prisoners. He began publishing communist propaganda in Turkish, which was distributed in Anatolia. After the war, Suphi supported the nationalist movement against the sultan, although the Kemalists coldly received his small group of about two hundred communists. Suphi was arrested in January 1921, shortly after returning to Turkey. While being transported by boat to Erzurum for trial, he and several friends were assassinated by pro-ENVER PAŞA supporters who believed Suphi would discredit the former COMMITTEE OF UNION AND PROGRESS (CUP) leader.

Elizabeth Thompson

Mutasarrif

In the Ottoman Empire, the government's recipient of the tax revenue from a sanjak.

Although this term was officially instituted in the mid-nineteenth century, it may have been in use earlier to distinguish the recipient of the revenue (the *mutasarrif*) from his agent who did the collecting (the *müsellim* or *mütesellim*). The term went out of use in 1921 with the transformation of *sanjak*s into *vilayet*s.

Stuart J. Borsch

Mutawakkil, Yahya Muhammad al-

Yemeni government official.

Mutawakkil is considered an able, ambitious leader of the Yemen Arab Republic. His political rise in the late 1970s and 1980s was blocked because, despite his republicanism, he came from a great clan of SAYYID aristocrats, one too close historically to the Yemeni imamate. He served as a member of the Command Council and as interior minister in the regime of Ibrahim al-Hamdi in the mid-1970s and then was "exiled" to Washington, D.C., as ambassador to the United States for about a decade. He held a top position in the ruling General People's Congress under Ali Abdallah Salih in the early 1990s and became interior minister in the new Republic of Yemen in 1993.

Robert D. Burrowes

Mutawwa

In Saudi Arabia, a policeman of public morality.

Employed by government through the Committee for the Promotion of Virtue and Prevention of Vice, the *mutawwa* (Arabic, pl. *mutawwa'in,* literally, "obedience causer") is charged with overseeing compliance with rules of behavior in such matters as alcohol consumption, modest dress for men and women, closing of shops at prayer time, the separation of unrelated men and women in public, and, formerly, mosque attendance by men and tobacco smoking. A morals police force has been supported by the state in Najd since the inception of Saudi rule in the eighteenth century, and its members have served as missionaries and as preachers in the Friday mosque services as well as enforcers of public morality. Upon conquering the Hijaz, King Ibn Sa'ud sent mutawwa'in to the Hijazi towns to propagate and enforce the MUWAHIDDUN vision of Islam.

In Oman, the mutawwi (pl. *mutawi'a*) is a religious leader of the IBADIYYA sect.

Eleanor Abdella Doumato

Mutayr Tribe

A tribe of northeastern Arabia.

The Mutayr cover an area that ranges from Kuwait in the north to al-Dahna, the sand belt in the south. The Mutayr were active in the IKHWAN movement in the first quarter of the twentieth century. Among the first to be induced to settle under the movement's influence, Mutayr tribespeople in 1912 built

al-Artawiya, an Ikhwan settlement that achieved fame for its zealotry in attempting to create a religious community living by God's laws and for trying to convert others to the same goal. Some of the Mutayr, such as Faisal al-Duwish, led the Ikhwan rebellion against King Ibn Saʿud in 1929/30.

Eleanor Abdella Doumato

Mutran, Khalil [1872?–1949]

Lebanese poet and journalist.

Mutran was born in Baʿalbak, Lebanon during the Ottoman Empire and fled to Paris in 1890 to avoid Ottoman persecution. In 1892, he joined the growing colony of Syrian and Lebanese emigrés in Cairo and eventually became known as *shaʿir al-qutrayn* (the poet of the two countries). Mutran worked for the Egyptian daily *al-Ahram* for more than ten years and briefly edited his own daily newspaper. His four-volume collection of poetry, *Diwan,* the first volume of which appeared in 1908, was completed in 1949. Mutran composed poetry in diverse styles, from traditional verse to narrative poetry, as well as lyrical poems stressing subjectivity and the predicaments of the individual.

BIBLIOGRAPHY

BECKA, JIRI. *Dictionary of Oriental Literatures,* vol. 3: *West Asia and North Africa.* New York, 1974.

David Waldner

Muwahhidun

Members of a reform movement that began in the eighteenth century to revive puritanical Islamic zeal.

The movement was started by a religious scholar from Najd (Saudi Arabia), Muhammad ibn Abd al-Wahhab (1703–1792). He was schooled by the *ulama* (Islamic clergy) in what is now Iraq, Iran, and the Hijaz (western Arabia). He then called for a return to the sources of Islam that stressed the absolute unity of God and strict obedience to the Qurʿan (the sacred book of Islam) and the *hadith* (sayings and traditions attributed to the Prophet Muhammad). His teachings displayed a preference for Ahmad ibn Hanbal's (780–855) school of law and its later interpretation by Ibn Taymiyya (1263–1328).

By 1736, Ibn Abd al-Wahhab, whose followers preferred to be called *muwahhidun* (unitarians) and who are often referred to as the Wahhabi sect, rejected condemnable innovations (*bida*) that promoted polytheism and unbelief, such as reverence given to saints as interceders with God and the special devotions of some of the extreme Sufi orders. In 1744, Ibn Abd al-Wahhab allied himself with the ruler of the small town of Dirʿiyya in Najd—Muhammad ibn Saʿud—where together they created the model of a state wherein the *Shariʿa* (Islamic law) reigned supreme instead of tribal customs. The movement spread rapidly, by conquest, among the tribes of central Arabia. After Ibn Abd al-Wahhab's death, the Wahhabi forces had by 1806 sacked the Shiʿite shrines of Karbala (in southwestern Iraq), occupied the holy cities of Mecca and Medina (in the Hijaz) where they destroyed the tombs of revered saints, and raided the Syrian interior.

This direct challenge to the power and legitimacy of the Ottoman Empire, led its sultan to dispatch his most efficient proconsul, Muhammad Ali Pasha of Egypt, to suppress the Wahhabi movement in the Arabian peninsula. The Egyptian governor and two of his sons, Tuman and Ibrahim, campaigned with mixed success until in 1822 they finally destroyed the core of Wahhabi power in the Najd.

Ottoman Turkish and Egyptian garrisons in the Hijaz were not able to prevent the restoration of the Wahhabi state in the twentieth century by the Al Saʿud family in their capital, Riyadh. It began when their relations with the Al Rashid family, a Wahhabi clan governing the Shammar region, became strained and, in 1884, the Saudi family was forced to seek sanctuary with the Mubarak rulers of Kuwait. In 1901, ABD AL-AZIZ IBN ABD AL-RAHMAN IBN SAʿUD, son of the last Saudi governor of Riyadh, led a daring raid that restored his family's power. He steadily enlarged his domains by relying on the devotion of the *ikhwan* (brotherhood)—members of militarized agricultural colonies he created in 1912 transcend tribal loyalties and adhere strictly to the puritanical tenets of the Wahhabi school.

During World War I, in 1915, Ibn Saʿud entered into an agreement with the British to receive subsidies and arms to use against the pro-Ottoman Rashids. In 1921, he finally entered Haʿil, the capital of Shammar, overthrowing the Rashid family in the process. In 1924, he occupied the Hijaz, the site of Islam's holiest cities and shrines, and overthrew Sharif Husayn ibn Ali, who had earlier claimed the title of caliph, based on descent from the Prophet Muhammad. In 1926, he took the Asir province, formerly under the protection of the Imam Yahya of Yemen, but he did not advance after Italy conducted naval maneuvers off the coast. The *ikhwan* wished to continue their advances into other areas under British protection, such as Iraq, only to be prohibited by Ibn

Sa'ud, who in 1926 had been proclaimed king of the Hijaz. The ikhwan revolted in 1927 but were crushed with difficulty in 1929, in their garrison town of Artawiyya.

In 1932, Hijaz and Najd became a single country, which was officially named the Kingdom of Saudi Arabia. Henceforth, the fortunes of the Wahhabis became inextricably linked to it. King Ibn Sa'ud attempted to exert some military pressure against Hashimite Transjordan in 1932 but desisted with Britain's recognition of his rule of the new kingdom. In 1934, Imam Yahya invaded and lost decisively in the valley of Najran at the Asir plateau. Thereafter, Ibn Sa'ud strove to consolidate his power in those areas of the Arabian peninsula where he ruled. In alliance with the *ulama,* he strictly imposed the *Shari'a* and paid careful attention to the services accorded to the *hajj* (pilgrimage to Mecca). He did placate Hijazi opinion by allowing the use of *ijtihad* (learned opinion) in the cases brought against the government before the *mazalim* courts. In dire financial straits, he signed a petroleum concession with a U.S. company in 1932, and oil was discovered in 1936. His 1944 meeting with U.S. President Franklin D. Roosevelt stressed the growing international importance of Saudi Arabia; by the end of World War II, oil production would begin in earnest.

The Wahhabi model appealed to other Islamic reform movements, such as the SALAFIYYA MOVEMENT in Egypt in the late nineteenth century and, more succinitly, the fundamentalist MUSLIM BROTHERHOOD (al-Ikhwan al-Muslimin) founded by Shaykh Hasan al-Banna in 1928. Like other Arab potentates, Ibn Sa'ud was greatly preoccupied with Palestine, and he sent a military contingent to participate in the Arab–Israel War of 1948, when Israel became a state. Wary of Western influence, Saudi Arabia joined Egypt and Syria in the 1950s in resisting a regional Middle East defense organization. The threat of a Nasser-type military coup (as occurred in Egypt), brought Saudi Arabia's defection from that alliance and placed it more in line with the Hashimites.

As oil wealth began to permeate Saudi society in the early 1960s, the Wahhabi movement retained a profound influence on the social and economic development of Saudi Arabia. The *mutawwa'in* (religious volunteers), a carryover from the ikhwan, oversaw strict observance—challenging the melodious recitation of the Qur'an, excessive veneration at the tombs, desegregation of the sexes, and the appearance of the full (unveiled) female form on television.

In 1953, Ibn Sa'ud died. Politically, by the 1960s, the call by King Faisal for an Islamic pact split the Arab world. It put him in hostile ideological conflict with the Egyptian Gamel Abdel Nasser's revolutionary, socialist, and by implication, secular, brand of nationalism. Egypt's swift defeat by Israel in the Arab–Israel War of 1967 seemed to vindicate Faisal's position. Conversely, he successfully coordinated with Egypt's new president, Anwar al-Sadat, to achieve more attention to Islamic symbolism in the Arab–Israel War of 1973, although a cease-fire was called within two weeks.

The 1973 Arab oil embargo and the rise in OPEC's (Organization of Petroleum Exporting Countries) oil prices brought riches to Saudi Arabia and enhanced the kingdom's position within the Arab-Islamic world. Somehow, this aided what may now be called the Islamic "revival" and led the Wahhabi kingdom to extend assistance to the building of mosques and the provision of aid to many Islamic movements—indirectly contributing to the strengthening of Islamist fundamentalist political groups and parties.

The Islamic revolution in Iran (1979) and Israel's pursuit of the PLO (Palestine Liberation Organization) into Lebanon (1982), however, ushered in a new radical wave of politically motivated Islamic fundamentalism that does not share either the Wahhabi doctrinal approach to Islam or Saudi Arabia's pro-American policy.

In 1988, Saudi Arabia broke relations with Islamist Iran because Iranian pilgrims to Mecca rioted and the Iranian navy fired on Saudi vessels in the Gulf. Saudi aid given to anticommunist MOJAHEDIN in Afghanistan may be seen as keeping in line with the martial spirit of the early Wahhabi movement. Saddam Hussein's invasion of Kuwait in 1990 and the ensuing Gulf Crisis caused Saudi Arabia and Kuwait to align themselves with the United Nations Coalition led by the United States.

If Islamic fundamentalism and Islamist political parties are perceived as anti-Western, it will be left to see how much the Wahhabiyya will influence the direction taken by the Islamic reformist movements.

BIBLIOGRAPHY

BOURNE, KENNETH, and D. CAMERON WATT, eds. *British Documents on Foreign Affairs: Reports and Papers from the Foreign Office Confidential Print;* Part 2: *From the First to the Second World War;* Series B: *Turkey, Iran, and the Middle East, 1918–1939;* Vol. 4: *The Expansion of Ibn Saud, 1922–1925.* Frederick, Md., 1986.
HOURANI, ALBERT. *A History of the Arab Peoples.* Cambridge, Mass., 1991.
MARGOLIOUTH, D. S. "Wahhabiya." *Encyclopaedia of Islam.* Leiden, 1913.

Bassam Namani

Mzab

Berber-speaking area in the arid pre-Saharan hamada 360 miles (600 km) south of Algiers.

The five original towns—al-Ateuf, Bou Noura, Ghardaïa, Melika, and Beni Isguen—were founded in the eleventh century along the bed of the Wadi Mzab. Berriane and Guerrara were added outside the wadi in the seventeenth century. The people are mainly Kharidjite Ibadites, a sect of Islam dating from the schism at the time of the fourth caliph, Ali, that adheres to a doctrine of puritanical and egalitarian religious and social obligations. The Mzab is noted for its highly developed, essentially theocratic organization and the economic maintenance of strong communities through the extraordinary commitment and success of its people as tradesmen throughout Algeria.

Thomas G. Penchoen

Mzali, Mohammed [1925–]

Prime minister of Tunisia from 1980 to 1986.

Born in Monastir, the home village of Tunisia's first president, Habib Bourguiba, Mohammed Mzali began his professional life as a university professor of Arabic and Islamic philosophy. In 1980 he was named by Bourguiba to succeed stroke-victim Hedi Nouira as Tunisia's prime minister and the president-for-life's designated successor. Mzali's accession was heralded at the time as marking a relaxation of the political authoritarianism associated with Nouira's tenure; he was younger, in closer contact with the country's young people, and associated with support for political liberalization. Under his aegis, in fact, the first contested elections for the national assembly were held and, although the results were widely believed to have been falsified in favor of the ruling party, several independents took seats, establishing that party membership was not necessary for assembly membership. Soon thereafter, some opposition political parties, including the Tunisian Communist party and several social democratic parties, were legalized, and the decades-long monopoly on Tunisian political life held by the ruling Neo-DESTOUR party was broken.

Despite his success at initiating political reform, Mzali proved unable to solve the country's pressing economic problems, nor could he control the increasingly virulent political infighting among the Tunisian political elite. Even though Mzali had been designated by Bourguiba as his official successor, the Tunisian ruling elite openly jockeyed for position as the aging president's health began to deteriorate. In 1984, government-dictated consumer price increases touched off widespread rioting, prompting rescission of the increases. Mzali accused his rivals of deliberately encouraging the rioters to embarrass him.

In July 1986, worried that Mzali had lost the confidence of the government and the people, Bourguiba dismissed him in favor of economist Rachid Sfar. A year and a half later, Bourguiba himself would be removed from the presidency by a Mzali appointment, the first military officer ever to sit in a Tunisian cabinet, General Zayn al-Abidine BEN ALI. Mzali himself was later accused of malfeasance and took exile in France, where he wrote a book, *Lettre ouverte à Habib Bourguiba* (1987), accusing many of his former political collaborators of corruption, mismanagement, and disloyalty.

Lisa Anderson

N

Nabahani, Taki al-Din

Founder of the Liberation party in Lebanon.

The LIBERATION PARTY is an Islamic organization founded in 1952 on the West Bank. Nabahani's writings called for relying on the centrality of Islam in social change and in the liberation of Palestine.

As'ad AbuKhalil

Nabi, Belkacem   [1929–   ]

Algerian minister.

A former *wali* (provincial governor) (1970–1974) and adviser to the presidency (1974–1979), Nabi distinguished himself as minister of energy (1979–1988) in Algeria. During this period, the trans-Mediterranean natural gas line was inaugurated (1983); Algeria also strove for contractual parity between gas and petroleum prices. Nabi reportedly underscored this policy with the statement that "a therm is a therm." Algeria succeeded in concluding several accords with clients (e.g., France in February 1982) that linked natural gas purchase prices to "baskets" of selected crudes. But plunging petroleum prices in the mid-1980s had a disastrous effect upon Algerian revenues, which had significant political ramifications, including the October 1988 riots.

BIBLIOGRAPHY

NAYLOR, PHILLIP, and ALF HEGGOY. *Historical Dictionary of Algeria,* 2nd ed. Metuchen, N.J., 1994.

Phillip C. Naylor

Nabih Salih, al-

Uninhabited island in the Bahrain archipelago of the Persian/Arabian Gulf.

Lying some two and one half miles (4 km) to the southeast of Bahrain's capital, Manama, al-Nabih Salih is situated midway between the island of al-Awal and the island of Sitra. Extensive date-palm gardens covered al-Nabih Salih in the eighteenth and nineteenth centuries. Sizable groves remain along the western and northern shores, watered by several natural springs. Bahraini Shi'ites revere the large pool at the center of the island, as well as the tomb of the local saint, Salih, from whom the island takes its name.

BIBLIOGRAPHY

COTTRELL, ALVIN J., ed. *The Persian Gulf States: A General Survey.* Baltimore, 1980.

Fred H. Lawson

Nabi Musa Celebrations

Annual spring pilgrimage to the mosque near Jericho, located, according to Muslim tradition, on the site of the tomb of Moses.

This spring festival falls at about the same time as both the Orthodox Christian Easter and the Jewish Passover. In 1920, a Muslim crowd, inflamed about what they saw as Zionist encroachment (with Britain's collaboration) in Palestine, erupted into violence against Jews in Jerusalem. Between April 4 and April 10, the violence claimed nine dead and over two hundred wounded, most of whom were Jews.

BIBLIOGRAPHY

KAYYALI, ABD AL-WAHHAB. *Palestine: A Modern History.* London, 1978.

Benjamin Joseph

Nabizade Nazım   [1862–1893]

Ottoman Turkish writer.

Nabizade Nazım was born in Istanbul, where he graduated from military school. He served as an army officer, attaining the rank of captain. In the 1880s, his poetry appeared in a number of journals, but his reputation as a writer dates to the stories he published in *Servet-i Fünün* beginning in 1891; the first issue of the journal included his story "Seyyire-i Tesamüh." With his novel *Zehra* and his story "Kara Bibik," he established himself in the vanguard of Turkish literary realism; his later work was focused largely on the depiction of life in the villages of rural Turkey. His 1886 story "Yadigarlarm" told the story of his alcoholic father.

David Waldner

Nablus

The largest West Bank city.

Nablus is thirty miles (48 km) north of Jerusalem in a valley between Mount Ebal and Mount Gerizim. Known in the Bible as Shechem, it was the home of Jacob, Jacob's well, and the tomb of Joseph; it was the place of Jeroboam's rebellion and, as chief city of Samaria, became his capital of the kingdom of Israel. It was rebuilt and renamed Neapolis by the Roman Emperor Vespasian, suffered damage in the Crusades, and became part of the Ottoman Empire.

After the defeat and dismemberment of the Ottoman Empire in World War I, it became part of the British mandate territory of Palestine. With Israel's statehood in 1948, it was occupied by Jordan during the first Arab–Israel War. Until the Arab–Israel War of 1967, when Israel occupied the West Bank area, it was a center of guerrilla warfare against Israelis. The 1986 population was estimated at about eighty thousand (mainly Muslim).

BIBLIOGRAPHY

MUSLIH, MUHAMMAD Y. *Origins of Palestinian Nationalism.* New York, 1988.
YAAKOV, SHIMONI, and EVYATAR LEVINE, eds. *Political Dictionary of the Middle East in the Twentieth Century.* New York, 1974.

Benjamin Joseph

Nabulsi, Sulayman al-   [c. 1908–1976]

Prime minister of Jordan, 1956–1957.

Sulayman al-Nabulsi was the only prime minister in Jordan's history to be invited to form a government by virtue of his support in parliament and despite major policy differences with the king. He was prime minister of Jordan from October 1956 to April 1957 when he was suspected of participation in a conspiracy led by the chief of staff, General Ali Abu Nuwwar, to overthrow King Hussein ibn Talal. Nabulsi was born in Salt in Jordan of a modest farming family, originally from the Nablus area in Palestine. He was an outspoken Arab nationalist, ideologically pro-Nasser, and a pan-Arabist. Active in politics since gaining a seat in parliament in 1948, he was constantly critical of the government. He published an article opposing Prime Minister Tawfiq Abu al-Huda's negotiations on the Anglo–Jordanian treaty, for which he was arrested and sent to prison for nine months. Nabulsi then established the National Front party but was unable to obtain a license for it. Ironically, he ended up leading another political party, the National Socialist party, whose chairman had been Hazza al-Majali, a political rival and ideological adversary. Despite its name, analysts describe the party as principally Arab nationalist, social reformist, and pro-democracy. As with most political parties at the time in Jordan, this one would be more correctly described as a parliamentary bloc. The party won eleven seats out of a total of forty in the October 1956 elections and was able to form a coalition government with Nabulsi as prime minister. It was comprised of seven National Socialists, one Ba'thist, one Communist, and two independents. This was the first "popular front" government of the Arab world and as such was dedicated to the struggle against domestic conservatism and Western influence.

Nabulsi negotiated with Britain to abrogate the Anglo–Jordanian treaty of 1948 and carried out negotiations with Saudi Arabia, Egypt, and Syria for financial aid to substitute for British subsidies. An agreement signed on January 19, 1957 included a promise from the three Arab states to pay Jordan 12.5 million Egyptian pounds over the next few years. An accord with Britain abrogating the Anglo–Jordanian treaty was signed on February 13, 1957. Both these moves had popular support, particularly as they came in the wake of the Suez Canal crisis and the anti-Western feelings it had created. In the meantime, King Hussein had negotiated with the United States for aid under the Eisenhower Doctrine (proclaimed in January 1957) to make up for the budgetary loss expected when Britain withdrew its subsidy. To ensure U.S. support, King Hussein played up his anticommunism position, while Nabulsi's government was purging government officials loyal to the monarch. King Hussein broadcast a message directed at Nabulsi on February 2, 1957, in which he claimed that communist doctrine had infiltrated the government. Nabulsi reacted indignantly, repudiating "alien creeds" and reasserting his Arab nationalism. On April 7, 1957, a coup attempt was mounted by a group of Ba'thist and pro-Nasser officers, but it was foiled by loyal army troops who rallied to the king. By April 13, it had become clear that the coup attempt had been led by Abu Nuwwar, and the simultaneous antiroyalist purges and discordant relations between Nabulsi and the king led many to believe that Nabulsi was implicated. The government was asked to resign, but Nabulsi was asked to be a minister in a new cabinet headed by a conservative premier. Despite Nabulsi's participation in the new cabinet, a wave of strikes and protests demanded the resignation of the government, the return of the "popular front" government, and the repudiation of the Eisenhower Doctrine. King Hussein responded by replacing the government with a cabinet made up entirely of ministers loyal to him, proclaiming martial law, abolishing political parties, suspending parliament, imposing a curfew, and placing security forces under army control. Nabulsi was placed under house arrest for the next four years. He never resumed political activity, although he was eventually pardoned by King Hussein and appointed to the Senate in 1971. Until his death, he remained virtually out of the public eye.

BIBLIOGRAPHY

DANN, URIEL. *King Hussein and the Challenge of Arab Radicalism: Jordan, 1955–1967.* New York, 1989.

GUBSER, PETER. *Jordan: Crossroads of Middle Eastern Events.* Boulder, Colo., 1983.

LENCZOWSKI, GEORGE. *The Middle East in World Affairs,* 4th ed. Ithaca, N.Y., 1980.

Jenab Tutunji

Naccash, Alfred

See Naqqash, Alfred

Nadi, Yunus   [1880–1945]

Turkish nationalist, journalist, and publisher.

Nadi was born in Istanbul to the Abalioğlu family, although he dropped the use of the family name in later life. He studied at the Medrese-i Süleymaniye and Galatasaray and attended law school before taking his first newspaper job at the age of twenty. He became editor in 1910 of the COMMITTEE OF UNION AND PROGRESS newspaper in Salonika, *Rumeli,* and in 1918 established the *Yeni Gün* paper in Istanbul. During Turkey's war of independence, he moved the paper to Ankara and there befriended Atatürk. Returning to Istanbul after the war, in 1924 Nadi founded CUMHURIYET, known today as the *New York Times* of Turkey.

Nadi was a fervent nationalist. During the war of independence, he printed the headline "Greece must be destroyed" in his paper daily. He joined the Green Army, the most famous of the private armies in that war, but it was disbanded in 1921 by Atatürk because of its radical politics. Nadi wrote four books about the independence war, which were published posthumously in 1955. Nadir Nadi became publisher of *Cumhuriyet* when his father died.

BIBLIOGRAPHY

SHAW, STANFORD, and EZEL KURAL SHAW. *History of the Ottoman Empire and Modern Turkey,* vol. 2. Cambridge, U.K., 1977.

Elizabeth Thompson

Nadi al-Arabi

See Arab Club

Nadir Barakzai, Mohammad   [1883–1933]

King of Afghanistan, 1923–1933; known as Nadir Shah.

Nadir Shah was born to Sardar Mohammad Yusuf Khan from the Yahya Khel lineage of the Mohammadzai clan of the Barakzai branch of the Durrani Pushtun tribe. He was active in the court of Habibollah Khan but was arrested as a murder suspect when Habibollah was assassinated in 1919. He was freed by Emir Amanollah (reigned 1919–1929) and served briefly in his court. He left Afghanistan and spent some time in Paris before returning to India. In 1923, he led a revolt against Habibollah Kalakani and became king in 1929 but was assassinated in 1933 by a Hazara student who was the adopted son of Kalakani.

BIBLIOGRAPHY

ADAMEC, LUDWIG. *Historical Dictionary of Afghanistan.* Metuchen, N.J., 1991.

Grant Farr

Naftali, Perez   [1888–1961]

Israeli economist, author, and politician.

Born in Berlin, Naftali gained renown in Germany as economic editor of the *Frankfurter Zeitung* (1920–26) and achieved fame in the labor movement through his pioneering studies in "economic democracy." He immigrated to Palestine in 1933, where he lectured at the Haifa Technion and Tel-Aviv University. From 1937 to 1949 he was director of Bank Hapoalim. Naftali served on the Tel Aviv municipal council, the Histadrut (federation of labor) executive committee as a member of the first and second Knessets, and successively from 1951 to 1959 as minister without portfolio, minister of agriculture, and minister of social welfare.

Zev Maghen

Nafud Desert

A desert in northern Saudi Arabia.

The Great Nafud desert of the Arabian peninsula extends over some twenty-five hundred square miles (6,500 sq. km) of sand dunes, with elevations rising to three thousand feet (915 m). Iron oxide in the sand gives the Nafud a unique reddish color. Winter rain produces grasses sufficient to support grazing in the winter and spring. The southeast portion of the Nafud is considered to be part of the tribal territory of the Shammar bedouin, who make use of its wells and pastures.

Eleanor Abdella Doumato

Nafuri, Amin al-   [1921–   ]

Syrian military officer and politician.

Of Sunni Islamic heritage, Amin al-Nifuri was made a company commander in 1949 and was a close ally of Adib SHISHAKLI. Serving as deputy chief of staff of the Syrian army, he led a loose coalition of indepen-

dent officers in the mid-1950s. They vacillated in their political allegiances but generally sided against the Ba'th party. Al-Nafuri actively promoted the United Arab Republic. He served as minister of communications in 1963.

BIBLIOGRAPHY

Who's Who in the Middle East, 1967–1968.

Charles U. Zenzie

Naga Hammadi Aluminium Complex

One of two centers of Egypt's metallurgical industry, located downstream from the Aswan Dam.

Construction of the plant on Egypt's Nile river began in 1969 with Soviet financing. The plant began operation in 1975, using surplus electricity from the ASWAN DAM, which is supplied at a low cost. The bauxite used in production is imported from Australia. Capacity in 1982 reached 166,000 tons (151,000 t), requiring well over half of the output of the Aswan Dam. Because of the low cost of energy, the aluminum produced by the plant has competed well on world markets.

BIBLIOGRAPHY

NYROP, RICHARD F., ed. *Egypt: A Country Study,* 4th ed. Washington, D.C., 1983.
WATERBURY, JOHN. *The Egypt of Nasser and Sadat: The Political Economy of Two Regimes.* Princeton, N.J., 1983.

David Waldner

Naguib, Muhammad   [1901–1984]

Egyptian military officer and politician.

Born in the Sudan to a professional family, Naguib (also spelled Najib) was a graduate of Egypt's military academy. He served on the general staff during World War II and won respect from junior officers for his distinguished service in Palestine during the ARAB–ISRAEL WAR of 1948.

The Free Officers who overthrew King Farouk in 1952 decided to present Naguib as the head of the REVOLUTIONARY COMMAND COUNCIL, to endow the revolution with his legitimacy. The monarchy was abolished in 1953 and Naguib took the posts of provisional president and premier, but he refused to be satisfied with a titular role. He favored a return to parliamentary government and, after a protracted struggle with Colonel Gamal Abdel Nasser, leader of the ruling military junta, Naguib was ousted in 1954.

In 1955, Naguib published *Egypt's Destiny*. In 1956, Nasser was confirmed as president of Egypt by referendum.

BIBLIOGRAPHY

WATERBURY, JOHN. *The Egypt of Nasser and Sadat: The Political Economy of Two Regimes*. Princeton, N.J., 1983.
WUCHER KING, JOAN. *Historical Dictionary of Egypt*. Metuchen, N.J., 1984.

David Waldner

Nahal

Acronym for Noar Halutzi Lohem (Fighting Pioneer Youth), a division of the Israel Defense Forces integrating military training with agricultural labor and settlement.

Nahal was founded in 1948 at the urging of a delegation of kibbutz and youth-group representatives to Prime Minister David Ben-Gurion. Zionism's ideological notions of national redemption through work on the land coupled with the nascent state of Israel's pressing need for massive cultivation led to the institution of these units of "warrior-farmers." Nahal recruits entered the army in groups, under the joint command of a youth-movement instructor and Israel Defense Forces (IDF) officer, and either reinforced existing kibbutzim and moshavim or, more significantly, established new "holding settlements" (*he-akhzuyot*) on the country's vulnerable borders. Nahal paratroopers have been heavily involved in Israeli military operations since the 1950s.

The perception of Nahal as a restructured continuation of the recently defunct PALMACH (dissolved in 1948), where informality, egalitarianism, and individual daring were the rule, led to persistent tension as military discipline was imposed on the rank and file. Nahal was opposed by much of the military establishment for attracting some of the most highly qualified recruits away from active combat duty. As the necessity for prolonged professional and specialized military training became more apparent to the IDF, increasing numbers of troops were diverted from Nahal, and agriculture figures less than previously in the unit's activities.

Zev Maghen

Nahalal

First moshav, founded in the Jezreel valley in 1920.

Nahalal was a unique form of agricultural settlement in Palestine; called a MOSHAV, it was based on coop-
eratively owned land, individual family farms, and homesteads with family labor—but mutual aid and a cooperative framework for purchasing and marketing. The majority of Nahalal's founders had been members of a kibbutz (an agricultural collective), who disagreed with the arrangements made for family life, child care, and education. They wished to preserve the integrity of the nuclear family within a cooperative community. The parents of Israeli soldier and statesman Moshe Dayan—who were among the founders of the first kibbutz, Degania—also helped establish Nahalal.

BIBLIOGRAPHY

WEINTRAUB, D. M. LISSAK, and Y. ASMON. *Moshava: Kibbutz and Moshav*. Ithaca, N.Y., 1969.

Donna Robinson Divine

Nahar, al-

Lebanese daily newspaper.

Al-Nahar is one of the most important daily newspapers in the Arab Middle East. *Al-Nahar* was founded as *al-Ahrar* by Jubran Twayni, a Lebanese Christian, in 1933. It soon became known as the most neutral and objective newspaper in the region. After Harvard-educated Ghassan Twayni took over the paper from his father, he introduced a format and style similar to those of respected American dailies. Although in his youth Twayni's sympathies were with the Syrian Social Nationalist Party, the paper was the only one in Lebanon that was not automatically identified with any of the local political parties or embassies. Ghassan Twayni's articles and those of his deputy, Michel Abu JAWDAH, were widely read throughout the Arab world and were quoted by local politicians and foreign news agencies.

The independent, generally centrist views of the paper brought it trouble with the law. After a series of critical articles appeared in the early 1970s, Presidenta Sulayman Franjiyya had Twayni jailed and ordered his security apparatus to force advertisers to boycott the paper. His tactics aroused popular sympathies, however, and Twayni was freed.

The outbreak of the Lebanese Civil War in 1975 damaged the reputation of *al-Nahar* because Twayni became identified with the moderate factions of the Maronite (Christian) establishment. His son Jubran was a leader of the right-wing forces in East Beirut. Twayni's plans to modernize the paper were frustrated by the civil war. He also encountered stiff competition from the openly partisan newspapers. Twayni transformed *al-Nahar* into a publishing house that continues to be considered one of the most prestigious in the Middle East.

As'ad AbuKhalil

Nahayyan, Khalifa ibn Zayid, al-

Crown prince of Abu Dhabi.

Khalifa is the oldest son of Shaykh Zayid, the ruler of Abu Dhabi and the founder and president of the United Arab Emirates. Crown Prince Khalifa has helped to build modern Abu Dhabi. He is also president of the executive council of the national petroleum company and the investment fund. Within the government of the United Arab Emirates, he has been the deputy supreme commander of the armed forces since 1976.

BIBLIOGRAPHY

ABDULLAH, M. MORSY. *Abu Dhabi Past and Present.* Abu Dhabi, 1969.

REICH, BERNARD, ed. *Political Leaders of the Contemporary Middle East and North Africa.* London and New York, 1990.

TAMMAM, HAMDI. *The Leader Zayed bin Sultan of Nihayan.* Abu Dhabi, 1984.

M. Morsy Abdullah

Nahayyan, Zayid ibn Sultan al-

[c. 1918–   ]

Founder and ruler of Abu Dhabi; president of the United Arab Emirates since 1971.

Shaykh Zayid was born in Abu Dhabi (a shaykhdom on the south coast of the Persian/Arabian Gulf); he was raised in the desert in the traditional bedouin way. This remained an influence throughout his more than forty-year political career as a leader in the Arab world. Zayid represented his brother, Shakhbut, in the al-Ayn oasis region from 1946 to 1966. In 1962, just after the discovery of oil but before oil revenues boosted the economy, and with very few funds allocated to him, he earned the title Reformer, because of his modernization of education, the economy, and security.

In August 1966, members of the al-Nahayyan family elected Zayid ruler of Abu Dhabi. He then established a modern city and emirate and extended financial aid to neighboring emirates. In January 1968, the British declared their intention to withdraw from the Gulf. On February 18, with Shaykh Rashid ibn Sa'id, ruler of Dubai, Shaykh Zayid formed a union and extended an invitation to other neighboring emirates to join them. After almost three years of

unsuccessful meetings, Qatar and Bahrain declared their independence from Britain and, on December 2, 1971, a federation of six emirates was established—Abu Dhabi, Dubai, Sharja, Ajman, Umm al-Qaywayn, and Fujayra—the United Arab Emirates.

Shaykh Zayid was elected president and Shaykh Rashid, vice president. The emirate of Ra's al-Khayma joined later, on February 22, 1972. The creation of the United Arab Emirates remains Shaykh Zayid's political legacy. Many critics believed this federation would not survive, because of internal rivalries and regional threats. Shaykh Zayid, however, pressed for rapid consolidation of the central government by unifying internal security forces in 1973 and military defense units in 1976. Aware of the problems that accompany rapid urbanization and social change in traditional societies, Zayid reconciled modernization with tradition. Shaykh Zayid was reelected president of the United Arab Emirates four times.

In this position, Shaykh Zayid has repeatedly proven himself a leader among Arabs. During the October 1973 Arab–Israel War, he was the first Arab leader to announce an oil embargo on the countries that backed Israel. He tried for years to stop the Iran–Iraq War. In May 1981, Abu Dhabi hosted the heads of the Gulf states when they declared their new council. His efforts to reconcile differences among Arab leaders and his backing of the Palestinians has also gained him wide respect in the Arab world. He reached a high point in his political career at the November 1987 Arab summit in Amman, Jordan, when he pressed for the return of Egypt to the Arab League. He was also the first Arab leader to visit Egypt after the Camp David Accords of 1979 in an effort to restore diplomatic relations.

BIBLIOGRAPHY

ABDULLAH, M. MORSY. *The United Arab Emirates.* London and New York, 1978.

HEARD BEY, FRAUKE. *From Trucial States to United Arab Emirates.* London and New York, 1982.

MANN, C. *Abu Dhabi: Birth of an Oil Shaikhdom.* Beirut, 1964.

REICH, BERNARD, ed. *Political Leaders of the Contemporary Middle East and North Africa.* New York, 1990.

TAMMAM, HAMDI. *The Leader Zayed bin Sultan of Nihayan.* Abu Dhabi, 1984.

M. Morsy Abdullah

Nahayyan Family, al-

Ruling family of the Banu Yas tribal federation in the Gulf emirate of Abu Dhabi.

Shakhbut ibn Dhiyab (1793–1816) transferred his capital from the Liwa oasis in the interior to ABU

DHABI island in the Gulf, where he built a fort. He was renowned for his bravery in defending his country against the Wahhabis of Arabia. His grandson Zayid ibn Khalifah (1855–1909) extended his authority to the al-Ayn oasis and established friendly relations with the al-Maktum family of Dubai, the Qawasim in Sharja, and the Al Bu Sa'id sultan of Musqat (Oman). The British established the Treaty of Protection in 1892 with him, which transformed the area into a British protectorate known as the TRUCIAL COAST. During his long reign, the island of Dalma witnessed its golden days of pearl fishing.

His sons ruled until 1928. His grandson Shakhbut ibn Sultan succeeded them, and, during his rule, oil was discovered in 1958. Shakhbut's brother Zayid ibn Sultan became the next ruler, in 1966; he founded the UNITED ARAB EMIRATES in 1971 and has been its president since the founding.

BIBLIOGRAPHY

ABDULLAH, M. MORSY. *The Emirates, Oman, and the First Saudi Dynasty.* Cairo, 1979.

REICH, BERNARD, ed. *Political Leaders of the Contemporary Middle East and North Africa.* London and New York, 1990.

M. Morsy Abdullah

Nahda, al-

An Arabic term meaning "revival" or "renaissance."

Al-Nahda refers to cultural and literary developments that took place in mid-nineteenth-century Syria and Egypt. Translating and adapting European scientific and literary works to Arabic affected the way the modern language developed, and rediscovering and printing Arabic medieval literature made it available for the first time to a larger audience.

BIBLIOGRAPHY

CACHIA, PIERRE. *An Overview of Modern Arabic Literature.* Edinburgh, 1990.

Mahmoud Haddad

Nahhas, Mustafa al-   [1879–1965]

Egyptian politician.

After graduating from the Khedivial law school in 1900, Nahhas worked as a lawyer and judge. He entered politics in 1919, joining the nationalist WAFD movement. British authorities exiled him to the Seychelles (1921–1923) in the wake of the 1919 revolution and anti-British nationalist agitation.

Nahhas became one of the most important and popular Egyptian politicians from the 1920s until the Free Officers' coup d'état in 1952. He was elected to the chamber of deputies in 1923 and assumed leadership of the Wafd following the death of Sa'd Zaghlul in 1927. As head of the most popular party in Egypt, Nahhas served as prime minister, interior minister, and foreign minister on numerous occasions. His acceptance of the prime minister's portfolio in February 1942 after an armed ultimatum delivered by the British to King Farouk, however, discredited the Wafd's nationalist credentials in the eyes of many Egyptians.

Nahhas exerted tremendous influence over Anglo–Egyptian relations. As prime minister, he represented Egypt in failed negotiations with the British in May 1930 over a proposed bilateral treaty. He headed the Egyptian delegation in talks that produced the 1936 Anglo–Egyptian treaty, though he abrogated the treaty in October 1951 after negotiations over the future of British military bases in Egypt failed. Nahhas was also instrumental in the West's decision to abandon the capitulations at the 1939 MONTREUX CONVENTION.

On the inter-Arab level, Nahhas brought together Arab leaders in October 1944 to sign the ALEXANDRIA PROTOCOL, which laid the basis for formation of the League of Arab States. He was prime minister when the Free Officers' coup deposed Egypt's civilian government in July 1952. He was attacked for corruption afterward, though not imprisoned.

Michael R. Fischbach

Nahlawi, Abd al-Karim

Syrian military officer.

With another Damascus officer, Haydar al-Kuzbari, Colonel Abd al-Karim Nahlawi led a 1961 coup against the recently established United Arab Republic (Egypt and Syria). Nahlawi was linked to the Muslim Brethren (who opposed Egypt's President Nasser and who feared Egypt's domination of the Syrian army). The coup found little support outside Damascus but did elicit some concessions. He was exiled in April 1962 but later returned and became counselor to the Syrian embassy in Rome.

BIBLIOGRAPHY

HINNEBUSCH, RAYMOND A. *Authoritarian Power and State Formation in Ba'thist Syria: Army, Party and Peasant.* Boulder, Colo., 1990.

Charles U. Zenzie

Nahum, Halfallah   [1880–1963]

President of the Jewish community in Tripoli, Libya; industrialist and philanthropist.

Nahum was born in Tripoli to a prominent, affluent Jewish family. He received his primary and advanced technical-business education in Italian schools in Tripoli and Manchester, England, where his uncle lived.

In 1917, after renouncing the Dutch citizenship held for generations by his family and becoming a naturalized Italian, he was elected the first president of the newly reconstituted Jewish community of Tripoli under the Italian occupation. Soon, his leadership was challenged by the young Zionists headed by E. Nhaisi. A power struggle ensued, but Nahum was reelected president from 1919 to 1924.

In 1943, after the Allies took Tripoli, Nahum was asked to head the Jewish community until 1945, when a British subject, Zachino Habib, took over. With the English branch of the family, Nahum built a commercial and industrial empire. He was known for his modesty and for aiding the needy. He was ambushed and killed one night by ten Arabs and one Maltese.

BIBLIOGRAPHY

ARBIB, LILLO. *Gli Ebrei in Libia fra Idris e Gheddafi, 1948–1970.* Rome, 1989.

DE FELICE, RENZO. *Ebrei in un paese arabo: Gli Ebrei nella Libia contemporanea tra colonialismo, nazionalismo arabo e sionismo (1835–1970).* Bologna, 1978.

Maurice M. Roumani

Nahum, Hayyim   [1873–1960]

Chief rabbi of Istanbul, 1901, and of Egypt, 1925–1960; Turkish representative to the post–World War I peace conferences and to Washington in the early 1920s; Egyptian senator, 1931.

Nahum (called Nahum Effendi) was born in Manisa, Turkey, and studied law in Istanbul and at the Rabbinical College of Paris, where he also learned Oriental languages. He had ties with the Young Turks and their Committee of Union and Progress, and when he returned to Turkey following the Young Turks revolution, he was made chief rabbi (*haham bashi*) of Istanbul. In 1918/19, he joined the Turkish delegation for the armistice negotiations at The Hague and also served, unofficially, as Turkey's representative in Washington, D.C., during

the early 1920s. In 1923, Nahum served as adviser to the Turkish delegation at the Lausanne Peace Conference.

When he moved to Egypt, King Fu'ad I made Nahum chief rabbi of Egypt in 1925, a position he held until his death in November 1960. Not only was he the most powerful figure of Egyptian Jewry vis-à-vis the Egyptian government, but in June 1931 the king appointed him a senator and in 1933 a member of the Egyptian Academy.

BIBLIOGRAPHY

BENBASSA, ESTHER. *Haim Nahum Effendi, dernier grand rabbin de l'empire ottomane (1908–1920), son rôle politique et diplomatique.* Paris, 1989.

KRÄMER, GUDRUN. *The Jews in Modern Egypt, 1914–1952.* Seattle, Wash., 1989.

LASKIER, MICHAEL M. *The Jews of Egypt, 1920–1970: In the Midst of Zionism, Anti-Semitism and the Middle East Conflict.* New York, 1991.

Michael M. Laskier

Na'imi Mirza Nasr Allah Khan al-Dowleh   [?–1907]

Iran's first prime minister, 1906–1907.

Na'imi was appointed minister of foreign affairs in 1899, and prime minister in 1906. As foreign minister, he was one of the signatories to the D'Arcy Concession (1901), granting the rights to all oil exploration and extraction in southern Iran to a Briton, Sir William D'Arcy.

Neguin Yavari

Najaf, al-

The capital of the governorate Najaf Muhafaza in central Iraq.

One of Iraq's two holy cities (the other is KARBALA), al-Najaf (1980 pop. 276,000) lies on a ridge just west of the Euphrates river. The caliph Harun al-Rashid is reputed to have founded the city, whose growth occurred mostly in the tenth century, in 791 C.E. In the center of al-Najaf is the mosque containing the tomb of Ali ibn Abi Talib (c. 600–661), cousin and son-in-law of Muhammad, fourth Muslim leader, the spiritual founder of the Shi'a sect; still encircled by most of its original walls, al-Najaf is therefore one of the sect's greatest shrines. With a reputation for providing higher education in Islamic theology, especially Shi'a jurisprudence, the city has schools and libraries that are valuable repositories of such knowledge. Al-Najaf has long been a hotbed of Shi'a resistance against the Sunni rulers in Baghdad, and in the twentieth century, this resistance has been a source of tension between the Sunni government of Iraq and the Shi'a government in Iran (see SHI'ISM and SUNNI ISLAM).

Al-Najaf Muhafaza is a flat region extending for 10,615 square miles (27,794 sq km) from the Euphrates river in the northeast to the Saudi Arabian border in the southeast. The governorate's population is concentrated near the river; the rest of the region is sparsely populated. Established in 1976, al-Najaf Muhafaza was formed from areas of the governorate of Qadisiyya in the east and the governorate of Karbala in the west.

Mamoon A. Zaki

Najd

The central plateau region of Saudi Arabia.

A geographically isolated region of the Arabian peninsula, Najd (the Arabic word for plateau or highland) is bounded in the south by the great sand desert, the Rub al-Khali, and on the east by a long, narrow strip of sand desert known as al-Dahna. To the north lies another sand desert, the Nafud, and to the west, Najd is separated from the Red Sea coast by the mountains of Hijaz and Asir. The plateau is divided into three regions: southern Najd, the home of the eighteenth-century Wahhabi movement and the original home of the ruling Al Sa'ud family (main city, Riyadh); Qasim, an agricultural district in the center of Najd (main city, Unayza); and Jabal Shammar in the north (main city, Ha'il). Because of its geographic isolation, Najd, unlike other areas of the Gulf and Arabian Sea, was not subject to European colonialism. Most of the great camel-herding bedouin ranged at least part of the year in Najd, but the bulk of its permanent population were town dwellers and seminomadic oasis gardeners. Najd is today the central administrative district and home to the capital city of Saudi Arabia, Riyadh.

Eleanor Abdella Doumato

Najib, Muhammad

See Naguib, Muhammad

Najibullah [1947–]

President of Afghanistan, 1986–1992.

Najibullah was born in Kabul, into a Ahmadzai family of the Gilzai Pakhtuns. He was educated at Habibia High School and studied medicine at Kabul University, graduating in 1975. He was active in politics at a young age and was a founding member of the PEOPLE'S DEMOCRATIC PARTY OF AFGHANISTAN (PDPA) in 1965. When the PDPA split in 1967, he became a leader of the PARCHAM faction along with Babrak Karmal. After the Saur Revolution in 1978, he was named ambassador to Iran in a move by the Khalq faction to send the Parchamis out of the country. He returned to Kabul in 1980, when Babrak Karmal was named president, and was made president of the Afghan Secret Police, Khad, a job that he pursued ruthlessly. In 1986 he became secretary general of the PDPA and president of Afghanistan.

Najibullah was a powerful and ruthless leader, the strongest and most capable of the four PDPA presidents. He made a number of attempts to reunite the country and to pacify the Islamic resistance by modifying the Marxist ideology of the PDPA, by moving the country away from socialism, and by restoring the role of religion. However, he was unable to overcome the PDPA's initial mistakes or to make himself acceptable to the MOJAHEDIN. In 1992, his government collapsed, and he fled to the UN compound in Kabul, where he sought sanctuary.

BIBLIOGRAPHY

ADAMEC, LUDWIG. *Historical Dictionary of Afghanistan.* Metuchen, N.J., 1991.

Grant Farr

Najjada, al-

Name of several Arab paramilitary youth organizations.

One group, called al-Najjada (Helpers), was formed in 1936 in Beirut by journalist Muhieddine Nsouli as a Sunni Muslim counterpart to the Christian PHALANGE party. In the 1950s, it emerged as a pro-Nasser party with about ten thousand members under the new leadership of Adnan al-HAKIM; it clashed with the Phalangists in the 1958 Lebanese Civil War. It has since adopted an Islamist ideology.

Another group of the same name was established at Jaffa, Palestine, in 1945 by a Muslim lawyer, Muhammad Nimr al-Hawari, as a counterpart to the Jewish Haganah. The Palestinian group quickly grew to an estimated six thousand members in at least ten cities. It played a prominent role in the 1947 Palestinian protests and the 1948 Arab–Israel war.

BIBLIOGRAPHY

HUDSON, MICHAEL C. *The Precarious Republic.* Boulder, 1985.

KHALAF, ISSA. *Politics in Palestine: Arab Factionalism and Social Disintegration, 1939–1948.* Albany, N.Y., 1991.

Elizabeth Thompson

Najran Oasis

A town in southwest Saudi Arabia.

Located on the border with Yemen, Najran is the center of an administrative district (emirate) of the same name. Citrus, grains, and vegetables are produced in the area. In 1930/31 Najran was a focus of contention between Yemen and Saudi Arabia, when a series of border incidents led to Yemeni occupation of Najran and a counterthrust by Saudi forces. The border was subsequently fixed by the treaty of al-TA'IF in 1934, by which Saudi Arabia annexed the Najran area. The town of Najran is ancient, with pre-Islamic ruins, and is noted as the site of a mass killing of Christians under a Jewish Himyarite king in the sixth century. After the Muslim conquest in the seventh century, at least a portion of the town's Christian population is believed to have resettled in the region of Basra in Iraq.

Eleanor Abdella Doumato

Namazi, Mehdi   [1901–?]

Iranian politician and businessman.

Born in Shiraz, Mehdi Namazi was the son of Haj Muhammad Hoseyn Namazi, himself a famous businessman. A major capitalist, Mehdi Namazi was a deputy to the *majles* from 1933 to 1954, after which he was appointed to the senate. He left politics after the Iranian Revolution of 1979.

Neguin Yavari

Namık Kemal   [1840–1888]

Turkish intellectual.

The son of an Ottoman aristocrat, Namık Kemal was born in Tekirdağ. He entered the civil service in Constantinople (now Istanbul) when he was seventeen and began working with İbrahim Şinasi on the Young

Ottoman journal *Tasvir-i Efkar,* which among other things championed constitutionalism and parliamentary democracy. Namık Kemal's essays were widely read, and he left for Europe in 1867 to avoid persecution by the Ottoman authorities. He returned to Constantinople in 1871, and in 1873 he wrote *Vatan,* a play that dealt with the issue of fatherland and Ottomanism. After the deposition of Sultan Abdülaziz in 1876, Kemal was one of the many framers of MIDHAT PAŞA's 1876 Constitution. After Sultan Abdülhamit II assumed power, Namık Kemal again went into exile and died on Chios in 1888. Kemal was one of the most important nineteenth-century Ottoman Turkish thinkers and reformers and a founder of the Young Ottoman movement. He wrote extensively about the meanings of *vatan* (fatherland), democracy, liberalism, and freedom in an Ottoman context. Though influenced by French philosophers, Kemal looked to Islam as the root of his ideas.

BIBLIOGRAPHY

HOURANI, ALBERT. *Arabic Thought in the Liberal Age, 1798–1939.* New York, 1983.

LEWIS, BERNARD. *The Emergence of Modern Turkey.* New York, 1961.

Zachary Karabell

Namir, Mordekhai   [1897–1969]

Israeli labor official, ambassador, member of Knesset, and mayor of Tel Aviv (1959–1969).

Born in the Ukraine, Namir (originally Nemirovsky) settled in Palestine in 1924 after graduating from the University of Odessa. Beginning his political career as secretary of the Akhdut Ha-Avodah party, he served in the administrations of the Histadrut (Federation of Workers), and the World Zionist Organization both before and after Israel's statehood. Namir joined the Haganah command from 1933 to 1948, and filled many foreign ministry positions in the Soviet Union and eastern Europe. He was elected to the Knesset (parliament) and appointed general secretary of the Histadrut in 1951, until becoming minister of labor and housing in 1956.

Zev Maghen

Nammur, Musa

Parliamentarian and member of the pre-independence (French mandate) Lebanese government.

Between 1926 and 1927, Nammur was elected deputy of the Biqa' valley to the first Lebanese parliament. He was reelected from 1929 to 1931 and from 1937 to 1939. In 1927, he was minister of the interior under the second president of Lebanon, Habib Pasha al-Saad. In 1929, Nammur was appointed minister of finance, and in 1930 he served as minister of health and interior.

BIBLIOGRAPHY

Arab Information Center, Beirut.

George E. Irani

Napoléon

See Bonaparte, Napoléon

Naqib, Talib al-   [1862–1929]

Iraqi politician.

Talib al-Naqib, from the southern city of Basra, belonged to an Arab family of *sadah* (claimants of descent from the Prophet Muhammad); thus he had the title of SAYYID. His authority in the province of Basra was well known to Sultan Abdülhamit II, who appointed him in 1901, in a co-optive move, as governor of al-Ahsa region in Najd.

When the YOUNG TURKS came to power in the Ottoman Empire in 1908, Sayyid Talib was elected as a deputy of Basra in the lower chamber of deputies. During the Young Turk period, he stirred up feelings for Arab autonomy in Iraq, in general, and in the Basra province, in particular. This was an expression of opposition to the centralization policies of the ruling COMMITTEE OF UNION AND PROGRESS and a reaction to the increasing political and economic influence that Britain was being allowed in Iraq.

He was exiled to India for two years after British troops occupied Basra during World War I. He then cooperated with the British after the war and in 1920 served as minister of interior in the first provisional Iraqi government. When he opposed nominating Faisal I ibn Husayn to be the future king of Iraq, the British again sent him into exile from 1921 to 1925. He died in Germany.

BIBLIOGRAPHY

HADDAD, MAHMOUD. "Iraq Before World War I: A Case of Anti-European Arab Ottomanism." In *The Origins of Arab Nationalism,* ed. by Rashid Khalidi et al. New York, 1991.
AL-ZIRIKLI, KHAYR AL-DIN. *Al-A'lam,* 3rd ed. Beirut, 1969.

Mahmoud Haddad

Naqqash, Alfred   [c. 1886–c. 1977]

President of Lebanon, 1941–1942.

Naqqash attended Jesuit schools in Lebanon before going to Paris to study law. He then went to Cairo, where he practiced law while editing the newspapers *La Bourse Egyptienne* and *Le Journal du Caire.* Articles he published in those papers demanded an end to control of Lebanon by the Ottoman Empire and the annexing of the port city of Juniye (Juniyah) to the Mount Lebanon district. The Ottoman government issued a death warrant for him in response to his articles. After World War I, Naqqash returned to Lebanon, where he served as a lawyer and a judge, and then as a member of the Consultative Council. In court, he had a reputation for moderation and fairness. He also was known as a client of the French government.

Naqqash became president in October 1941, not because of his popularity or his political shrewdness but because he was chosen by the French government following the controversial resignation of President Emile Eddé. The French were looking for an obedient person who would not challenge their authority or stir political controversy after the French dissolved the parliament and suspended the constitution. Naqqash's appointment was also intended to appease the Jesuits. Naqqash had the support of the influential thinker Michel Chiha.

When Naqqash's prime minister, Sami al-Sulh, became too independent and insisted that he would not resign unless Naqqash did, the French mandate authority dismissed both of them. Naqqash retired to private life until he was urged by supporters to run for a seat in parliament from Beirut. He was elected in 1943 and 1953 and appointed a minister in the administration of Camille Chamoun. After leaving office he gave lectures and wrote articles in French for the magazine *al-Shira.* In the government of Fu'ad Chehab, Naqqash was chair of the Social Welfare Department and represented President Chehab at national and international conferences. He was briefly considered as a successor to Chehab but withdrew from public life in the 1960s. He died in his nineties.

As'ad AbuKhalil

Naqshbandi

One of the major Sufi orders in the Islamic world.

The most distinctive characteristics of the Naqshbandi order are the tracing of the *silsila,* or initiatic chain, from the Prophet Muhammad to Abu Bakr al-Siddiq, a companion of the Prophet Muhammad;

use of the silent invocation of God (*dhikr*); and a strong adherence to the SHARI'A, or Islamic law.

The first figure of importance in the history of the Naqshbandiya is Yusuf Hamadani (born 1048). In addition to providing four successors, he set down eight principles, or "sacred words," that provided the doctrinal framework of the order.

Although it is not possible to conclude that all branches or members of the Naqshbandiya were politically active throughout the history of the order, the fervent belief in the adherence to the *Shari'a* and the SUNNA and a worldly attitude toward the role of Sufis in Islamic society contributed to the political participation of some Naqshbandi leaders. In the late medieval and premodern periods, it was not uncommon for Naqshbandi leaders to mediate in political disputes, pay taxes on behalf of a population, act in defense of popular sentiment, influence administrative policy, or control large tracts of land. In the regions of Khorasan and Transoxiana, in which Turko-Mongols ruled over predominantly Persian populations, Naqshbandi leaders at times played the role of defending Sunni Islam against Shi'ism and of thwarting the influence of Turko-Mongol nomadic customary law in favor of Islamic law. The Naqshbandi order gained adherents among both the Turkic and Persian populations of Central Asia and was prevalent in both urban and rural areas. However, at the height of its power in Khorasan, the Naqshbandiya was firmly entrenched in the intellectual and cultural milieu of the capital city of Herat, enjoying great renown under the leadership of Sa'd al-Din Kashgari (died 1462) and then Abd al-Rahman Jami (died 1492).

Several separate branches of the Naqshbandi order developed, the main ones being the Yasavi, begun by Ahmad Yasavi (died 1167); the Mujaddidi, established first in India by one of the four successors of Hamadani, Shaykh Ahmad Sirhindi (born 1563); and the Khalidi, established by Maulana Khalid Baghdadi (born 1776), the last branch of the Naqshbandi to achieve strong adherence throughout the Islamic world. There was an extraordinary diffusion of the different branches into regions as widespread as Ottoman Turkey, Kurdistan, Eastern Turkistan, Syria, Palestine, India, central Asia, and the Indonesian-Malaysian world.

A major renewal of the Naqshbandiya came through the leadership of Maulana Khalid Baghdadi (died 1827), who founded the Khalidi branch that became particularly strong in Turkey and spread as far as Malaysia. His concern with the preservation of the *Shari'a* was especially significant during a time when the Ottoman state was facing increasing challenges from the West. The Khalidi Sufi network spread throughout the Turkish, central Asian, and Arab world but was strongest in Anatolia and Kurdistan. The legacy of Naqshbandi activity is reflected today in the eminent position of established Naqshbandi families within Kurdish society, although over time most of those assumed political rather than spiritual leadership, one of the most well-known examples being that of the BARZANI FAMILY.

In the modern period, particularly the nineteenth and twentieth centuries, Naqshbandis played a role in reformist and anticolonial resistance movements. Among the numerous examples are Shaykh Shamil's resistance to Russian imperialism in Dagestan in the nineteenth century, the active role of the Naqshbandiya in the mojahedin in the Soviet–Afghan war, the role of Shah Abd al-Aziz (died 1826) in the legal reform movement in India under British rule, and the role of Naqshbandi-led rebellions in China. Although it is difficult to ascertain the true extent of Naqshbandi activity in the new central Asian states today, there is particularly strong adherence in the regions of Dagestan and the Fergana valley, and Naqshbandi shrines continue to be popular places of pilgrimage. In other regions of the Islamic world, the Naqshbandiya maintains a following, particularly in Turkey, but also in Afghanistan, the Kurdish regions of Syria and Turkey, India, Indonesia, and China.

[*See also:* Sufism and the Sufi Orders]

BIBLIOGRAPHY

ALGAR, HAMID. "A Brief History of the Naqshbandi Order." In *Naqshbandis: Cheminements et situation actuelle d'un ordre mystique musulman,* ed. by Marc Gaborieau, Alexandre Popovic, and Thierry Zarcone. Istanbul and Paris, 1990, pp. 4–43.
——. "The Naqshbandi Order: A Preliminary Survey of Its History and Significance." *Studia Islamica* 44 (1976): 123–152.

JoAnn Gross

Narcotics

See Drugs and Narcotics

Narghila

Arabic word denoting a water pipe.

In cafés throughout the Middle East, it is common to see the patrons, which are almost exclusively male, smoking a water pipe known as a narghila, or qalyan. A long, thin hose with a mouthpiece is attached to a standing glass pipe containing water, with a small bowl on which are placed embers and tobacco, occasionally mixed with honey.

Zachary Karabell

Naser al-Din Shah   [1831–1896]

The fourth ruler of the Qajar dynasty in Iran. Naser al-Din's reign was marked with the birth of modernism in Iran.

Naser al-Din's ascension to the throne was made possible by the then commander of the army in Azerbaijan, Mirza Taqi Khan Amir Kabir, who subsequently was appointed as the new shah's first prime minister. The Queen Mother (d. 1873) was also helpful. She orchestrated the removal from power of Hajji Mirza Khan Aqasi, the previous prime minister.

The first phase of Naser al-Din's reign, from 1848 to 1850, was marked by his struggle to assert control over Amir Kabir. He also needed to undermine the QAJAR nobility. In addition, the interim period following the death of Mohammad Shah, the previous monarch, and the coming to power of Naser al-Din Shah, had loosened state control over many of Iran's provinces. It was not until 1850 that the Qajar state succeeded in subduing most of its territories. In addition, Amir Kabir's efforts at fostering the institutions of a modern nation state clashed with the interests of the Qajar bureaucracy, nobility, and *ulama* (clergy). The bureaucracy scorned standardization (a strong state implied a weak nobility), and reforms would inevitably undermine the social standing of religious scholars. Thus the forces of establishmentarianism united with the shah, and Amir Kabir was doomed. Amir Kabir was subsequently dismissed in 1851 and executed in 1852. The fall of Amir Kabir resulted in an increase in the power of the *ulama,* who resumed control of the judiciary, the endowments, and education.

The second phase of Naser al-Din Shah's reign is marked with the premiership of his second prime minister, Mirza Aqa Khan Nuri E'temad al-Dowleh. In this period, clergy and state relations were improved, mainly because the shah was aware of increasing foreign encroachment, and that was a battle he could not wage without *ulama* support. In 1856, Naser al-Din launched a campaign to recapture Herat from the British, under the command of his uncle, Soltan Morad Mirza. The city was captured in the same year, and the shah not only awarded the *ulama* but also sent some money to repair Shi'a holy sites in Najaf. The British, in turn, responded with the landing of Anglo–Indian forces in Bushehr in December 1856. The British proceeded toward the interior,

and Naser al-Din was forced to withdraw from Herat and accept the terms of the Paris Peace Treaty of 1857. Blaming the defeat on his prime minister, the shah sent him into permanent exile.

From 1858 to 1871, the shah abolished the office of prime minister, assumed the duties himself, and manifested a slight interest in modernizing reforms. In his efforts to contain the rivalry of different factions at the court, the conservative faction headed by Mizra Hasan Khan Mostowfi al-Mamalek and the reformist faction of Farrokh Khan Amin al-Dowleh, Naser al-Din was forced to pursue an unstable, often chaotic and disorderly administrative policy.

In 1870, the shah visited Shi'a holy sites in Iraq and met with the Iranian ambassador to Istanbul, Mirza Hoseyn Khan Sepahsalar. Impressed with the Turks' achievements, Naser al-Din installed Mirza Hasan Khan Pirnia MOSHIR AL-DOWLEH as his prime minister. In addition, the shah's three European tours greatly increased his appreciation, at least for the physical beauty, of the West. In 1873, the Reuter concession, giving control of Persia's natural resources, finance, and communication, was agreed upon to finance the shah's trip to Europe. Upon his return, faced with widespread dissent, Naser al-Din was forced to repeal the concession and demote Moshir al-Dowleh to the ministry of war in 1881. After the fall of Moshir al-Dowleh, Naser al-Din installed Mostowfi al-Mamalek as prime minister.

Moshir al-Dowleh's reforms were patterned on the Ottoman TANZIMAT. The shah often resorted to the conservative factions in the court to resist the reformists. Naser al-Din also tried to balance Anglo–Russian rivalry, in order to preserve the territorial integrity and national sovereignty of Iran. In this he succeeded to a certain degree, although he was forced to relinquish Khivah, Marv, Sarakhs, Herat, eastern Sistan and Bahrain.

The shah also agreed to the use of the Karun river for navigation in 1888 and allowed for the operation of the British-owned Imperial Bank of Persia in 1889. In 1888, after the death of Mostowfi al-Mamalek, Naser al-Din installed Ali Asghar Amin al-Soltan as prime minister. This prime minister negotiated the terms of many concessions with foreigners on the shah's behalf. In 1889, the shah granted the Regie tobacco monopoly to a British subject. Widespread protests led by the cleric Mirza Hasan Shirazi led to its repeal. The agitations of other Islamic activists, such as Sayyed Jamal al-Din Asadabadi, also contributed to the general unrest. Naser al-Din Shah was assassinated in 1896, outside the Shah Abd al-Azim shrine in Rayy, by an Islamist acolyte and disciple of Sayyed Jamal al-Din Asadabadi, Mirza Reza Kermani.

Leaders such as Mirza Malkam Khan argued for westernization, and prominent clerics such as Sayyed Jamal al-Din Asadabadi favored the strengthening of the Islamic nation by borrowing from the West scientific and technical innovations, while discarding the cultural baggage that accompanies it. Naser al-Din oscillated between reform and traditionalism. On the one hand he promoted Amir Kabir, and on the other he was opposed to his reformist measures. While immensely enjoying his trips to Europe, the memoirs of which are extant and published, little in terms of enlightenment returned with the Shah to Tehran. Western innovations such as the railroad and the telegraph were coveted, yet the shah did not recognize the implications of enhanced communications for a despotic government. Amidst confusion and misapprehensions, the seeds of the constitutionalist revolution of 1904–1911 were sown. Yet constitutionalism in Iran was marked by a paradoxical, ill-defined, and poorly understood concoction of traditionalism and change. Both the reign of Naser al-Din and the constitutionalist revolution failed to structurally alter the socio-cultural composition of Iranian society. Naser al-Din succeeded in bringing to the forefront, however, the conflict between religion and the modern state in Iran.

Naser al-Din Shah was a deeply superstitious man. Histories tell us of his veneration for ritualized religion, ostentatious displays of religiosity, and eclectic observance of Islamic tenets.

BIBLIOGHRAPHY

ALGAR, HAMID. *Religion and State in Iran, 1785–1906.* Berkeley, Calif., 1969.

AMANAT, ABBAS. "Nasir al-Din Shah." In *Encyclopedia of Islam,* 2nd ed. Leiden, 1993.

YARSHATER, EHSAN. "Observations on Nasir al-Din Shah." In *Qajar Iran: Political, Social, and Cultural Change, 1800–1925,* ed. by E. Bosworth and C. Hillenbrand. Edinburgh, Scotland, 1983.

Neguin Yavari

Nashashibi, Fakhri al- [1899–1941]

Controversial Palestinian political figure who was a bitter foe of the mufti of Jerusalem.

Fakhri al-Nashashibi was born in Jerusalem, the nephew and right-hand man of Raghib al-Nashashibi. Early in his political career, he was secretary of al-Muntada al-Adabi (The Literary Club) and aide to Ronald Storrs. Nashashibi helped establish a number of anti-mufti organizations, including the Palestinian Arab National party (1923), the Con-gress of the Palestinian Muslim Nation (1931), the Defense party (1934), and the Peace Bands (1938/39) that were intended to serve as a counterforce to the pro-Husayni leaders of the rebellion of 1937–1939. In his relentless pursuit to undermine the Husayni camp (al-Majlisiyyun) and strengthen the Nashashibi-led opposition (al-Mu'aridun), Fakhri did not hesitate to use unorthodox methods, including seeking financial support from the Jewish Agency. His overambition and questionable tactics of expediency, together with his advocacy of a compromise settlement with the mandatory government and the Zionists, created many enemies for him and put him on the death list of the leaders of the rebellion in November 1938. Three years later, unknown assailants assassinated Fakhri in Iraq while he was riding a bicycle.

BIBLIOGRAPHY

PORATH, YEHOSHUA. The *Palestinian Arab National Movement.* London, 1977.

Muhammad Muslih

Nashashibi, Raghib Bey al- [1883–1951]

Prominent Palestinian politician who led the opposition against the Husayni camp (al-Majlisiyyun) during the British mandate.

Born in Jerusalem, Raghib al-Nashashibi was elected as a representative of the Jerusalem District in the Ottoman parliament in 1914. In 1920, the British dismissed the mayor of Jerusalem, Musa Kazim al-Husayni, for the role that he played in the nationwide demonstrations against Zionism of March 8 and appointed Raghib in his place, since he had taken no part in the demonstrations. Raghib held the post until 1934 when he lost the mayoral elections to Dr. Husayn Fakhri al-Khalidi. Raghib organized and led the National Defense party (1934–1946) and served as member on the Higher Arab Committee when it was initially formed in 1936 and when it was reconstituted nine years later. Raghib's advocacy of conciliation with the British and Zionists, and his attempts to secure Jewish support in his confrontation with the Husayni camp, cast doubts on his patriotism in the minds of many Palestinians. After 1948, Raghib held a ministerial post in the government of Jordan. He also served as governor of the West Bank and as a member of Jordan's upper house of parliament.

BIBLIOGRAPHY

PORATH, YEHOSHUA. The *Palestinian Arab National Movement.* London, 1977.

Muhammad Muslih

Nashashibi Family

Notable Muslim Palestinian family that established itself in Jerusalem in the fifteenth century.

The family is said to be of Circassian or Kurdish origin; it gained prominence in the late nineteenth century when some of its senior members served in the administration of the Ottoman Empire. Uthman al-Nashashibi was elected to the Ottoman parliament as deputy of the Jerusalem *sanjak* (province) in 1912. Raghib al-Nashashibi (1883–1951) was elected to the same post in 1914. During the British mandate, Raghib became the most influential figure in the family and head of the anti-Husayni (opposition) camp. Ronald Storrs, governor of the Jerusalem district, appointed Raghib mayor of Jerusalem in 1920 as a reward for not participating in the anti-British demonstrations during the al-Nabi Musa celebrations in Jerusalem on April 4, 1920. Since the post was occupied by Musa Kazim al-Husayni, who was dismissed for allegedly inciting the al-Nabi Musa celebrants, Raghib's acceptance of the mayoralty raised questions about his nationalism and exacerbated the Husayni–Nashashibi rivalry.

In 1934, after he had lost his position as mayor to Dr. Husayn Fakhri al-Khalidi, Raghib formed the National Defense party. Although the party's main source of support was from the mayors and elites of the larger towns in Palestine, it was also able to reach the peasantry through the network of prominent families that supported the Nashashibi camp. After Israel became a state in 1948, Raghib served as minister in the Jordanian government, governor of the West Bank, and member of the Jordanian senate.

Fakhri al-Nashashibi (1899–1949), a colorful and controversial political organizer, was, from late 1920 until his assassination, the family's strong-arm man. After holding a number of posts in the mandate government, including aide-de-camp to High Commissioner Sir Herbert Samuel, he became Raghib's chief aide. Fakhri was a principal organizer of opposition to al-Hajj Muhammad Amin al-HUSAYNI, and, at the peak of the PALESTINE ARAB REVOLT of 1936–1939, he organized the Peace Bands, with help from the British military and the Zionist movement, to protect the Nashashibi camp from the campaign of intimidation launched against it at al-Hajj Amin's bidding. Fakhri favored a compromise settlement with the British and the Zionists.

Is'af al-Nashashibi (1882–1948), son of Uthman and a writer known throughout the Arab world, was described by contemporaries as an "Arabic dictionary that walks on two feet." Ali al-Nashashibi cofounded in 1912 a decentralization party for the Arab provinces of the Ottoman Empire; in 1916, Cemal Paça executed him on charges of treasonable political activities. Nasir al-Din al-Nashashibi (1924), a journalist and political writer living mostly in Egypt, served for some time as League of Arab States representative in Europe. Muhammad Zuhdi al-Nashashibi, a politician, has occupied senior positions in the Palestine Liberation Organization (PLO), including membership on its Executive Committee.

Throughout the mandate years, the term *Nashashibi* denoted opposition to al-Hajj Muhammad Amin al-Husayni, a founder of Palestinian nationalism and the leader of the Palestine National Movement until 1948. The leadership of the Nashashibi family was also well known for its advocacy of a policy of compromise with the Jewish Agency and the British mandate authorities. This position did not receive the same degree of support enjoyed by the Husayni program, which was based on the total rejection of the British government's Balfour policy. After 1948, the political influence of the Nashashibi family sharply declined, as did the influence of some other notable Palestinian families.

BIBLIOGRAPHY

PORATH, YEHOSHUA. *Biographical Dictionary of the Middle East.* London, 1977.

Muhammad Muslih

Nasif, Malak Hifni   [1886–1918]

Egyptian poet, writer, and feminist, who wrote under the pseudonym Bahithat al-Badiya (Seeker in the Desert).

Nasif was born in Cairo. With the encouragement of her father, who had studied at al-Azhar with Muhammad ABDUH, Nasif received her secondary education at the Saniyya School in Cairo, the first teacher-training school for women in Egypt, and later taught there. Her marriage to a bedouin chief and exposure to the institution of polygamy led Nasif to become a strong advocate of women's rights. In her collection of essays *al-Nisa'iyyat,* published in two volumes in 1910 in Cario, Nasif advocated the amelioration of women's conditions in marriage and the advancement of women through education; she did not, however, argue for strict equality between the sexes. She emphasized that Islam permitted polygamy only under conditions of equality for each wife, an almost impossible condition to achieve. In 1962, her brother collected and published her writings in a volume entitled *Athar Bahithat al-Badiyya* (The Heritage of Bahithat al-Badiyya).

BIBLIOGRAPHY

BADRAN, MARGOT, and MIRIAM COOKE, eds. *Opening the Gates: A Century of Arab Feminist Writing.* Bloomington, Ind., 1990, p. 134.
VATIKIOTIS, P. J. *The History of Modern Egypt,* 4th ed. London, 1991.

David Waldner

Nasir, Ahmed Sayf al-   [c. 1880–1960]

Libyan tribal and political leader.

The Sayf al-Nasir family were hereditary shaykhs of the Awlad Slaiman tribe of the Sirtica and Fezzan regions of Libya. Ahmed Bey fought the Italian conquest of Libya from 1915, seeking exile in French Equatorial Africa (now Chad) toward its end in 1930. During World War II, he returned to Fezzan with Free French Forces advancing from Chad (1943) and became the chief instrument through which the French administered the territory. In February 1950, the French authorities set up a Fezzanese Representative Assembly that elected Ahmed Bey as *chef du territoire,* unopposed, and he headed a local administration under French supervision. Although associated with often unpopular French decisions, he promoted Fezzan's incorporation into a federal Libyan kingdom under Muhammad Idris al-Sanusi and thereby strengthened the hands of those who sought that form of independent Libyan state. After independence in 1951, Ahmed Bey became *wali* of Fezzan, the head of its provincial administration.

BIBLIOGRAPHY

WRIGHT, JOHN. *Libya.* London and New York, 1969.

John L. Wright

Nasir, Hanna   [1936–   ]

Founder and president of Bir Zeit University.

Nasir, born in Jaffa, Palestine, is a graduate of the American University of Beirut. He was expelled by Israel to Lebanon in November 1974, charged with supporting the Palestine Liberation Organization (PLO). He remained in exile until the summer of 1993.

While in exile, Nasir remained president of BIR ZEIT UNIVERSITY. He was also an elected member of the Executive Committee of the PLO from 1981 to 1984.

Jenab Tutunji

Nasir, Jamal Abd al-

See Nasser, Gamal Abdel

Nasir, Najib   [1865–1948]

Palestinian newspaper publisher and early anti-Zionist writer.

Born to a Greek Orthodox family in Tiberias, Najib al-Khuri Nasir converted to Protestantism while working for fifteen years in a hospital run by missionaries. He then worked briefly as a land sales agent for the JEWISH COLONIZATION ASSOCIATION before founding the daily newspaper *al-Karmil* in 1908 in Haifa. Nasir used his knowledge of land sales to Jews to write articles against Zionism and the first history of the Zionist movement in Arabic, *Zionism: Its History, Object and Importance.* Also, before World War I, he founded several activist organizations to limit Jewish immigration and land sales. *Al-Karmil* was closed permanently by court order in 1944. Nasir died in Nazareth.

BIBLIOGRAPHY

MANDEL, NEVILLE J. *The Arabs and Zionism before World War I.* Berkeley, Calif., 1976.
SHAFIR, GERSHON. *Land, Labor and the Origins of the Israeli-Palestinian Conflict.* New York, 1989.

Elizabeth Thompson

Nasiri, Ahmad ibn Khalid al-   [1835–1897]

Moroccan historian and essayist.

Educated in Sale, al-Nasiri held various mid-level administrative posts for the ALAWITE DYNASTY. His writings include a history of the Zawiya (Islamic compound often associated with Sufism) of Tamgrut; a study of the schisms in Islam; and his most significant work, a history of the Marinid dynasty that became a chronicle of the dynastic history of Morocco. *Kitab al-Istiqsa li-Akhbar Duwal al-Maghrib al-Aqsa* was published in Cairo in 1894, in four volumes, and is possibly most valuable for its detailing of the Alawi dynasty during the author's lifetime.

BIBLIOGRAPHY

Encyclopaedia of Islam, 2nd ed.

Matthew S. Gordon

Nasruddin Hoca

A well-loved character in Turkish oral prose tradition; protagonist of humorous anecdotes told from the Balkans to Central Asia.

Known as Nasr al-Din in Iran and as Juha in Arabia, Nasruddin Hoca in some stories appears as a wise folk philosopher or witty (if unconventional) preacher. In others, he is naive and uninformed, the butt of youngsters' pranks, a figure of gentle ridicule who shows great resilience. However foolish he may seem, he survives all disasters and, having the last word, often turns the tables on those wielding power over or making fun of him.

Although a village near Sivrihisar in central Anatolia is claimed as Nasruddin's birthplace, and a mausoleum in Aksehir is said to be his 1284 burial place, a connection between the stories and a historical person is questionable.

The earliest Ottoman manuscript collections (early sixteenth century) contain under 100 stories. The first printed edition appeared in 1837 and contained 125 stories; later publications present a body of several hundred items, and translations have appeared in many Western and Asian languages. Several good collections in Engish are out of print, but examples of stories related in Turkey in the 1960s are translated in *Tales Alive in Turkey* by Warren S. Walker and Ahmet E. Uysal (Lubbock, Texas, 1990), which also gives a bibliography.

BIBLIOGRAPHY

"Naṣr al-Din Khodja" and "Djuhā." In *The Encyclopaedia of Islam*. 1965.

Kathleen R. F. Burrill

Nasrullah, Maulawi

Resistance leader.

A deputy in the Harakat-e Inqalab-e Islami party of Mohammad Nabi MOHAMMADI, Maulawi Nasrullah was educated in the traditional Islamic madrasas. He is an important leader in the Afghan Maulawi network that was used by the Harakat party to fight the Marxist government in Kabul during the war of resistance (1978–1992).

BIBLIOGRAPHY

ROY, OLIVIER. *Islam and Resistance in Afghanistan*. New York, 1986.

Grant Farr

Nasser, Gamal Abdel   [1918–1970]

President of Egypt, 1956–1970.

Few Arab politicians rivaled the impact of Nasser (also known as Jamal Abd al-Nasir) on the Arab world in the twentieth century. His mid-century revolution and his rule of Egypt followed the corrupt monarchy of King Farouk and was fueled by nationalism. It held out the promise of socialism and Arab unity, stirring the imaginations of Arabic-speaking intellectuals and common people.

Born in Alexandria into the Muslim family of a modest postal clerk, Nasser received his primary education in the small Nile delta village of al-Khatatiba, to which his father had been assigned. After completing his secondary education in Cairo, where he lived with an uncle, Nasser attended law school for several months before gaining entry to the Royal Military Academy in 1936.

The military provided the vehicle for Nasser's rise to power. His historical role began as the leader of a military conspiracy, the FREE OFFICERS, who launched a coup d'état and seized power in July 1952, overthrowing King Farouk. A republic was proclaimed, June 18, 1953, under General Muhammed Naguib as both provisional president and premier; he gave up the premiership in 1954 to Nasser, then the leader of the ruling military junta. Naguib was deposed and Nasser was confirmed as president by referendum on June 23, 1956.

In the eyes of a trusted minister, "the Nasir revolution cohered around the ideas and principles of PAN-ARABISM, positive neutrality, and the social revolution." Nasser, as his ex-minister put it, "took the side of the poor, just as he took the side of development, democracy, Arab unity, and nonalignment." Such admirers believe that even with the changed conditions after Nasser's death, "these principles will undoubtedly take new forms; yet, the ideas are still alive and they still move people" (Baker, 1990, p. 80).

Nasser's critics have emphasized his authoritarianism and his bitter defeats. Anwar al-Sadat, his successor as president, charged that Nasser's vaunted social revolution degenerated into "a huge, dark, and terrible pit, inspiring fear and hatred" and that Nasser's relentless hostility toward Israel had given Egypt only "years of defeat and pain," undermining prospects of achieving peace and prosperity while accomplishing little to realize Arab goals (Sadat, 1977, p. 20; and *al-Ahram*, June 27, 1977).

Debate about the ultimate meaning of Nasser's rule does not preclude identification of key turning points that both supporters and detractors accept as decisive. A domestic power struggle and the neces-

sity of coming to terms with the former British colonial power, which retained its base at Suez, gave
early definition to the new regime. General Muhammad Naguib, the figurehead for the Free Officers'
movement, challenged Nasser's leadership from February to April 1954 by drawing support from the
small middle class, the movement of the MUSLIM
BROTHERHOOD, and the former political parties who
all opposed the authoritarian and plebeian thrust of
the military regime. Rallying urban mass support
through a newly created party called the LIBERATION
RALLY, Nasser relied on the military and police to
defeat the middle- and upper-class political forces
arrayed against him. The formula worked, and the
newly consolidated regime immediately launched an
agrarian reform program that added peasant support
and undermined the powerful landowning families
that had backed the monarchy.

Regime priorities of power consolidation and
domestic reform were reflected in moderation on
the three major foreign-policy issues confronting
Egypt—the Sudan, the British, and Israel. While an
activist foreign policy later became the hallmark of
Nasserism, as a new ruler Nasser established himself
as a moderate in foreign affairs. In 1954, Egypt signed
a conciliatory agreement for a transitional period of
self-government for the Sudan, which became an
independent republic in 1956. Negotiations also produced an Anglo–Egyptian agreement in 1954 that
provided for the gradual withdrawal of the British
from their remaining Suez Canal zone base. Opponents, including the Muslim Brotherhood, charged
that Nasser had compromised the national interest.
An assassination attempt against Nasser in October
1954 justified the crushing of the Muslim Brotherhood; in fact, throughout Nasser's rule, the brotherhood suffered severe repression.

Nasser emerged only reluctantly as the champion
of the Arab struggle against Israel. A few dangerous
paramilitary actions had drawn Egypt into the conflict
in the early to mid-1950s. Small bands of Palestinians, including some operating from the Egyptian-
controlled Gaza Strip, launched raids against Israel.
Israel immediately developed a policy of massive re-
prisal against the Arab states sheltering the raiders.

When the West failed to respond to Nasser's need
for arms, he announced an arms agreement with
Czechoslovakia (an intermediary for the Soviet
Union). A dispute with the United States and Britain
over their financing of a high dam project at Aswan
accelerated the radicalization of Egypt's foreign policy in 1955 and 1956. The Egyptians looked to the
electricity that the dam would provide to fulfill their
dreams of industrialization. The Western powers,

alarmed by Nasser's flirtation with the East, denied
funds previously promised. In defiance, Nasser nationalized the Suez Canal Company on July 26,
1956. The response came swiftly.

In 1956, Egypt was invaded by Israel in October
and by France and Great Britain in November.
Militarily, the invading armies triumphed, but the
Egyptians resisted fiercely under Nasser's inspiring
leadership. They fought just long and well enough
to give international opinion time to force the invaders to withdraw. Most dramatic were the Soviet
missile threats against Europe and Israel, but U.S.
diplomatic pressure actually proved effective in securing a cease-fire and the withdrawal of the invaders. Defeated militarily, Nasser triumphed politically;
he remained in power with the Suez Canal Company in Egyptian hands.

Buoyed by obtaining Suez, Nasser launched a bold
bid for Egyptian leadership of the Arab world and laid
the ground work for an ambitious program of domestic change. On February 1, 1958, Syria voluntarily
united with Egypt to form the United Arab Republic
(UAR), which was later joined by Yemen. Although
the union lasted only until 1961, it gave substance to
the rhetoric of pan-Arabism. Nasser blamed the
breakup of the UAR on reactionaries and responded
by intensifying the revolution at home. A Charter of
National Action then committed Egypt to socialism
and announced the formation of a new mass political
organization, the ARAB SOCIALIST UNION (ASU).

Before he was forced to retreat, Nasser tried to
realize a socialism for Egypt that had industrialization
and improvement of mass welfare at its heart. The
long-range goal was the creation of a heavy industrial
base. Aziz Sidqi, Nasser's minister of industry, presided over a remarkable expansion of the nationalized public sector. Unfortunately, advances in agriculture did not match the industrial gains registered
in the decade after Suez, which were diluted further
by a rapidly expanding population. Still, Nasser did
create the public sector and improvements in health
and education reached even the rural countryside in
limited ways. The issue of rural transformation was
put on the national agenda.

The collapse of the union with Syria dealt a blow
to Nasser's pan-Arab standing. He sought to regain
momentum in the Arab arena by intervening in the
YEMEN CIVIL WAR in 1962, hoping that a victory by
the republican side would give Egypt leverage on the
strategic Arabian peninsula. Instead, the intervention
merely provoked conflict with the Saudi regime that
supported the Yemeni royalists and with the Americans who stood behind the Saudis. Fearing Nasser's
pan-Arabism as a destabilizing force, the Americans

turned against the regime. Until this point, republican Egypt had earned impressive aid for its development effort from both the United States and the Soviet Union. After the intervention in Yemen, the United States cut off its aid to Egypt. The period of growth and expansion at home and abroad was over by the mid-1960s.

These reversals created a mood of desperation that culminated in Nasser's abandoning the heretofore cautious policy that he had pursued with Israel. In the Arab summit conferences of the 1960s, Nasser had consistently urged restraint. For ten years after Suez, Egypt lived in relative peace with Israel because the presence of a United Nations Emergency Force (UNEF) stationed on the Egyptian side of the border. Pressures mounted, however, as the Palestinians launched raids from Lebanon, Jordan, and especially Syria. Israel responded with deadly force. An outcry provoked by the response forced a weakened Nasser to act. Chided for hiding behind the United Nations, Nasser requested the withdrawal of UN forces from the Sinai peninsula in 1967. The UN commander interpreted the order to mean the removal of his forces at the head of the Gulf of Aqaba. Egyptian troop replacements there meant closing the gulf to Israeli ships.

Israel viewed the closing of the Gulf of Aqaba as a cause for war. On June 5, 1967, Israel launched an attack, destroying the entire Egyptian air force in a matter of hours. In the course of the 1967 ARAB–ISRAEL WAR, Israel seized Jerusalem and the West Bank from Jordan and the Golan Heights from Syria, sweeping across Sinai and the Gaza Strip and routing the Egyptian army to leave an estimated ten thousand dead. On June 9, Israel's forces reached the Suez Canal. On June 10, a cease-fire was called by the United Nations; Egypt had lost the war, and Nasser then resigned.

In Cairo, Egyptians took to the streets to urge Nasser to remain as leader. For three more years Nasser ruled, refusing to accept an Israeli-dictated peace. In April 1969, he launched the so-called War of Attrition (1969–1970) in the canal zone that prolonged the Egyptian struggle against the Jewish state. At home, he announced a program that promised to revitalize the revolution. But Nasser's revolution never regained momentum. The exhausted Egyptian leader died on September 28, 1970 and was replaced by Anwar al-Sadat.

BIBLIOGRAPHY

BAKER, RAYMOND WILLIAM. *Egypt's Uncertain Revolution under Nasser and Sadat.* Cambridge, Mass., 1978.

———. *Sadat and After: Struggles for Egypt's Political Soul.* Cambridge, Mass., 1990.

SADAT, ANWAR EL-. *In Search of Identity: An Autobiography.* New York.

STEPHENS, ROBERT. *Nasser: A Political Biography.* London, 1971.

WATERBURY, JOHN. *The Egypt of Nasser and Sadat: The Political Economy of Two Regimes.* Princeton, N.J., 1983.

Raymond William Baker

Nasser, Lake

A reservoir of the Nile located in southern Egypt and northern Sudan created by the Aswan High Dam after 1971.

Lake Nasser is about three hundred miles (480 km) long and has an optimum water capacity of 212 billion cubic yards (162 billion cu. m), of which 39.2 billion cubic yards (30 billion cu. m) serve as dead storage for sediment and 118 billion cubic yards (90 billion cu. m) as live storage capacity. The largest man-made lake in the world, it has a major role in Egypt's fishing industry, yielding from fifteen to twenty-five thousand tons per annum. Some of the Nubians displaced from the Upper Nile valley during the Aswan High Dam construction have tried to build villages on the lake's shores, but the original hopes that Lake Nasser would support agriculture in its vicinity have not been realized. About one quarter of all the Nile waters entering Lake Nasser are lost to evaporation or seepage.

In 1978 the Ministry of Irrigation authorized construction of an emergency canal at the Upper Tushka inlet to carry away surplus water to the New valley in the Western desert, in case a high flood upstream caused Lake Nasser's waters to pass over the spillway, leading to damage to dams and bridge abutments downstream. The lake is named for Egypt's president at the time of the building of the dam, Gamal Abdel Nasser. The lake has flooded sites of ancient Egyptian buildings such as Abu Simbel.

BIBLIOGRAPHY

WATERBURY, JOHN. *Hydropolitics of the Nile Valley.* Syracuse, N.Y., 1979.

WHITE, GILBERT F. "Environmental Effects of the High Dam at Aswan." *Environment* 30, no. 7 (September, 1988): 4–11, 34–41.

Arthur Goldschmidt, Jr.

National Banks

See under Banks

National Bloc

Lebanese political party headed by Emile and Raymond Eddé.

Established in 1934, the National Bloc became the political vehicle for Emile EDDÉ and his son Raymond. Originally from Jubayl (Byblos), the Eddé family played an important role in the history of Lebanon. Elected president of Lebanon in 1936, Emile Eddé was the first Maronite Catholic president to appoint a Muslim prime minister—thus establishing the tradition. In 1949, Emile Eddé died and was replaced as chairman of the National Bloc by his son Raymond.

As a member of the Lebanese parliament since 1953, Raymond EDDÉ, a firm believer in the free-enterprise system, introduced several important pieces of legislation—notably the 1956 law on bank secrecy, the law introducing the death penalty in 1959, and the joint banking-account law in 1961. Since the beginning of the Lebanese Civil War in 1975, Raymond Eddé has kept the National Bloc from becoming a party of warlords. He was the first Lebanese politician to warn of the dangers of Lebanon becoming a hostage to her two neighbors: Syria and Israel. In 1969, Raymond Eddé and the National Bloc were the only group to vote down the Cairo Agreement between Lebanon and the Palestine Liberation Organization (PLO). In 1976, as a result of seven assassination attempts, Raymond Eddé opted for the relative safety of exile in Paris.

BIBLIOGRAPHY

RONDOT, PHILIPPE. "Raymond Eddé." *Maghreb-Machrek* 80 (1978): 22–25.

George E. Irani

National Charter, Palestine

See Palestine National Charter

National Congress of Popular Forces

A congress, convened twice by the Nasserist regime in Egypt at moments of transition and crisis, first in 1961 and again in 1967.

The withdrawal of Syria from union with Egypt occasioned the first call for a national body to review "mistakes" and crystallize the revolutionary will.

Defeat at the hands of Israel prompted the second call for a national congress "of popular working forces" charged to provide it a sound constitutional basis for political action. Neither produced any practical results.

Raymond William Baker

National Congress Party

The principal opposition political party in Libya immediately after independence.

Government tampering in national assembly elections in 1952 deprived the National Congress party of its victory. Party stalwarts reacted violently, leading, first, to the expulsion of its founder, Libyan nationalist Bashir Bey SADAWI, from the country and then, soon thereafter, to the demise of party politics in Libya.

BIBLIOGRAPHY

ANDERSON, LISA S. *The State and Social Transformation in Tunisia and Libya, 1930–1980.* Princeton, N.J., 1986.
KHADDURI, MAJID. *Modern Libya: A Study in Political Development.* Baltimore, 1963.

Lisa Anderson

National Council, Palestine

See Palestine National Council

National Covenant

See National Pact, Lebanon

National Defense Party

Palestinian Arab political party that accepted the concept of territorial partition during the British mandate.

The National Defense party was formed in mandated Palestine on December 2, 1934 by the supporters of Raghib al-Nashashibi, the former mayor of Jerusalem. The leaders encompassed most Arab mayors;

important politicians from large landowning families, such as Hajj Nimr al-Nabulsi (treasurer) and Hasan Sidqi al-Dajani (secretary); influential middle-class Christians, notably Yaqub al-Farraj (Greek Orthodox) and Mughannam al-Mughannam (Protestant); and the Jaffa branch of the Palestine Arab Workers Society, headed by Fakhri al-Nashashibi.

The party denounced the sale of land to Zionist companies and sought limitations on Jewish immigration. Nonetheless, it tacitly accepted the Peel Commission concept of territorial partitioning, in the hope of linking the Arab portion of the mandate to Transjordan. The party was criticized by other Palestinian politicans for deviating from the consensus that opposed partition; then Fakhri al-Nashashibi was assassinated in Baghdad, in November 1941. By the 1940s, the party had become inactive, although Raghib al-Nashashibi continued to issue statements in its name.

BIBLIOGRAPHY

LESCH, ANN MOSELY. *Arab Politics in Palestine, 1917–1939.* Ithaca, N.Y., 1979.
PORATH, YEHOSHUA. *The Palestinian Arab National Movement, 1929–1939.* London, 1977.

Ann M. Lesch

National Democratic Front (NDF)

Leftist organization of the Yemen Arab Republic.

The NDF is the umbrella organization created in 1976 by six leftist opposition groups in the Yemen Arab Republic (YAR). The NDF first sought through political means to pressure the government to accept them and their goals. Then, in the late 1970s and early 1980s, an armed rebellion was carried out against the YAR regime with the support of Marxist South Yemen. When the NDF rebellion was put down in 1982, many NDF members accepted the regime's terms for reconciliation; almost all of the others reconciled on the occasion of Yemeni unification in 1990.

The roots of the NDF can be traced to the expulsion of the left from the YAR polity following the San'a mutiny in 1968. In addition to an increasingly radical program of socioeconomic reform along socialist lines, the NDF sought to unify the YAR with the revolutionary state of South Yemen, to loosen ties of political dependency with Saudi Arabia, to curb the influence of tribal leaders, and to open up the closed political system of the YAR to popular participation.

BIBLIOGRAPHY

BURROWES, R. D. *Yemen Arab Republic: The Politics of Development, 1962–1986.* Boulder, Colo., 1987.

Robert D. Burrowes

National Democratic Front for the Liberation of Oman and the Arab Gulf

Radical antigovernment organization (1970/71), known as NDFLOAG.

NDFLOAG was formed in June 1970 by the merger of several small groups of foreign-educated Omanis. The front's members, fewer than a hundred, were united by shared antipathy for the reactionary sultan, Sa'id bin Taymur Al Bu Sa'id. Their aim was to carry out attacks on the government in northern Oman paralleling those that had been launched by the POPULAR FRONT FOR THE LIBERATION OF THE OCCUPIED ARABIAN GULF (PFLOAG) in Dhufar in the south. Mortar assaults on garrisons at Nizwa and Izki failed, and most of the perpetrators were captured. The attacks, however, caused Omani supporters of the government, as well as its British protectors, to fear that rebellion could spread throughout the country. This fear led them to work with Sa'id's son, Qabus ibn Sa'id Al Bu Sa'id, to overthrow his father in July 1970. In December 1971 NDFLOAG, reduced to impotence, was absorbed by PFLOAG, which changed its name (but not its acronym) and became the Popular Front for the Liberation of Oman and the Arab Gulf.

BIBLIOGRAPHY

ALLEN, CALVIN H., JR. *Oman: The Modernization of the Sultanate.* Boulder, Colo., 1987.

Malcolm C. Peck

National Democratic Party, Egypt

Centrist faction of Egypt's multiparty experiment.

With the dissolution of the ARAB SOCIALIST UNION (ASU) in 1976 into right, left, and center factions, Egypt began its multiparty experiment. The three factions became parties. The centrist faction of the ASU represented government power and was later renamed the National Democratic Party (NDP). The NDP enjoys overwhelming political predominance, operating essentially as a bureaucratic extension of the regime.

Raymond William Baker

National Democratic Party, Iraq

*A political party in Iraq, known as the NDP
(Arabic, Hizb al-Watani al-Demoqrati); licensed in
1946 under the leadership of Kamil Chadirchi.*

An outgrowth of the old al-AHALI GROUP, (People's
Group) the party had semi-socialist views and attracted supporters from the wealthy, well-established
families as well as from Shi'ites and left-leaning
middle-class people who believed in gradual change.
In 1949 the party was banned along with the Iraqi
Communist party. Even so, its members were involved in the strikes and riots that occurred in the
early 1950s in opposition to the Anglo–Iraqi treaties.
When free elections were held in 1954, the NDP
won six seats but lost them when Prime Minister
Nuri al-Sa'id suspended parliament and banned opposition parties. In 1956 the NDP applied for permission to form a party with Istiqlal (Independence
party) the supported neutrality, an Arab federation,
the liberation of Palestine, and political freedom. Denied, the Istiqlal, NDP, the Communist party, and
the Ba'th party formed the United National Front,
or United Popular Front.

Supporting the opposition to the monarchy, Chadirchi initially backed Abd al-Karim Kassem in his
coup that overthrew the monarchy in June 1958. By
1961, Chadirchi opposed Kassem, even though Muhammad Hadid, second-in-command of the NDP,
accepted the post of minister of finance in Kassem's
government. As a protest to the anti-democratic nature of the regime, in October 1961 Chadirchi closed
the NDP and ceased publishing *al-Ahali*.

BIBLIOGRAPHY

MARR, PHEBE. *The Modern History of Iraq.* Boulder, Colo.,
1985.

Reeva S. Simon

National Dialogue Committee

*Representatives of all sides in the Lebanese Civil
War met to find an end to the conflict.*

Created a few months after the beginning of the
1975 Lebanese Civil War, the National Dialogue
Committee included prominent representatives from
the various communities and warring factions. The
purpose of the committee was to narrow the gap
between the conservative Christian political leadership and the Islamic–Leftist coalition. Pierre Jumayyil, head of the PHALANGE party, was opposed to
the military involvement and political meddling of
the Palestine Liberation Organization (PLO) in Leb-

anese politics. The Phalange and its allies had, in fact,
called for the cancellation of the Cairo Agreement
with the PLO and the relocation of Palestinian refugees from Lebanon to other Arab countries.

Kamal Jumblatt, head of the Lebanese National
Movement (Muslim and leftist), did not agree with
Jumayyil and the Christian leadership. For Jumblatt
and the Muslim community in Lebanon, the fundamental issue was that of political reforms. In light of
the demographic changes that had occurred in Lebanon since 1920, Muslims claimed that the distribution of power had been to their disadvantage.
Moreover, Jumblatt and his allies had expressed their
total support to the Palestinians and a better distribution of economic wealth. The National Dialogue
Committee was, in the course of its brief existence
(September–November 1975), mired in these two
opposing questions on the future of Lebanon: What
comes first, sovereignty or political reform?

BIBLIOGRAPHY

KHUWAYYRI, ANTOINE. *Hawadith Lubnan, 1975.* Beirut,
1976.

George E. Irani

National Front, Egypt

*An unrealized ideal that plays an active role in the
political imagination of Egyptians.*

The Nasserist regime evoked the notion of a national
front when it established the NATIONAL UNION as a
"united National Front of all political forces that
combat occupation and build an independent
Egypt." Later, in the seventies, eighties, and nineties,
opposition forces regularly called for a national front
to curb some abuses of the regime. Yet, in fact,
Egypt has never had a national front government nor
a unified national front opposition.

Raymond William Baker

National Front, Iran

*Organization for nationalist democratic ideology,
which became the dominant political discourse in Iran
following the overthrow of Reza Shah's despotic
regime by the Allies in 1941.*

Led by Mohammad Mossadegh, the National Front
(Persian, Jebhe-ye Melli) fought for a genuine
constitutional monarchy and for Iran's control of its
own natural resources. It was responsible for the
nationalization of the British-run Iranian oil indus-

try in 1951. Its political influence declined following the American-British–engineered coup of 1953 that overthrew Premier Mossadegh and reinstalled the shah.

The rise of the National Front was triggered by voting fraud during the fifteenth parliamentary elections. In October 1949, Mossadegh led a group of people into the palace of Mohammad Reza Shah Pahlavi to protest the lack of free elections. Once inside, the demonstrators elected a committee of twenty, headed by Mossadegh, to negotiate with Abdulhosseyn Hazer, the court minister. Hazer promised to end electoral problems. The committee, however, reconvened in Mossadegh's house and decided to form the National Front—which covered such diverse political tendencies as socialists, constitutional monarchists, and a group of the *ulama* (Islamic clergy). Its social basis consisted of the bazaar merchants and craft guilds, a small industrial bourgeoisie, and the new middle class. The National Front was also enhanced by the postwar growth of U.S. power and its competition with Britain for international leadership.

Eager to fight foreign domination, the National Front rigorously pursued the task of ending British control of the Iranian petroleum industry. It demanded that the principle of fifty-fifty division be applied to the total profit of the Anglo–Iranian Oil Company. This was initially rejected by Britain; when Britain was prepared to accept Iran's demand, it was too late. When Iran's parliament nationalized the oil industry, the shah refused to ratify the nationalization bill for some six weeks. On April 30, 1951, Mossadegh was elected prime minister, and the shah had no option but to ratify the nationalization bill. On May 1, therefore, the law went into effect.

The 1953 coup that removed Mossadegh debilitated the National Front. Many of its active members were repressed brutally by the shah's new government. In 1954, the National Resistance Movement (Nahzat-i Moqavemat-i Melli) was formed by the remaining leaders of the National Front but was unable to challenge effectively the shah's dictatorship. The National Resistance Movement gave way to the Second National Front in the early 1960s; it soon experienced internal disputes over tactical and organizational matters. The Third National Front was formed in 1965. Although it was unable to play a leading role in the opposition movement, its Muslim religious wing led by Mahdi Bazargan played an important role in the IRANIAN REVOLUTION of 1977–1979. After the overthrow of the shah in 1979, Bazargan became prime minister of the provisional government, and a good portion of his cabinet were members and sympathizers from the National Front. However, with the monopolization of power by the Ayatollah Ruhollah Khomeini and his followers and

the establishment of the Islamic Republic of Iran, the supporters of the National Front were expelled from the government. Many of its followers and sympathizers then began to engage in oppositional activities in the West.

BIBLIOGRAPHY

COTTAM, RICHARD W. *Nationalism in Iran*. Pittsburgh, 1979.

MOADDEL, MANSOOR. *Class, Politics, and Ideology in the Iranian Revolution*. New York, 1993.

Mansoor Moaddel

National Front, Lebanon

Coalition of left-wing Lebanese and Arab political parties and forces formed in 1984.

In 1984 in Lebanon, the leftist-nationalist coalition known as the Lebanese National Movement was dissolved as a result of internecine battles. In Israel, elections led to the victory of the Likud under Yitzhak Shamir. In the United States, Ronald Reagan was on the brink of being reelected for a second term.

The National Front was created as a result of these events. This coalition included representatives of the Progressive Socialist party, the Lebanese Communist party, the Ba'th party, the Syrian Socialist National party, the Arab Democratic party, and the Arab Socialist Union. The platform of the National Front contained six principles: (1) consolidate the resistance to the Israeli occupation in south Lebanon, (2) stress the unity and integrity of Lebanon in the struggle against partition plans, (3) emphasize the Arab identity of Lebanon, (4) adopt an independent foreign policy, (5) call for political reforms and the abolition of the confessional system, and (6) call for economic and social reform. The mainstream Shi'ite AMAL movement was later invited to join the coalition.

George E. Irani

National Front, People's Democratic Republic of Yemen

The ruling party in South Yemen after independence in 1967.

After the National Liberation Front (NLF) assumed power in Aden in late 1967, the name was changed to National Front (NF) to signify that the liberating at home had been done. However, English retained the name "National Liberation Front" and, even more so, "NLF." In any case, the NF was replaced in the early 1970s by the Unified Political Organization/ National Front (UPO/NF), a ruling coalition in which the NF nominally shared power with the Ba'th party and the Yemeni Communist party (the People's Democratic Union). In turn, in 1978, the UPO/NF was replaced by the fully merged Yemeni Socialist Party (YSP). The direct descendant of the NLF that fought for independence and came to power in 1967, the YSP ruled South Yemen for more than a decade, only to retreat from its doctrinaire Marxism in the late 1980s and to lead South Yemen into unification with nonsocialist North Yemen in 1990.

Robert D. Burrowes

National Front for the Liberation of South Yemen

An association opposed to Britain's role in South Yemen in the 1960s.

The National Front for the Liberation of South Yemen, an association of seven organizations, first met in San'a (capital of North Yemen) in 1963 to discuss strategies against the British position in South Yemen; three additional groupings joined later. Its intellectual and ideological origins lie primarily with the ARAB NATIONAL MOVEMENT. It differed from other groups in two respects: its members agreed on the necessity of military action; and its primary popular base lay in the protectorates rather than Aden. In 1967, the British turned over South Yemen to the NLF, which governed the country until the merger with North Yemen in 1990.

Manfred W. Wenner

National Front for the Salvation of Libya

The principal opposition to Qaddafi's regime in Libya.

The National Front for the Salvation of Libya (NFSL) was established in 1981. Illegal in Libya, it operates in exile under the leadership of its secretary-general, Muhammad Yusuf al-Magarief, a former Libyan ambassador to India. Encompasing opponents of Muammar al-Qaddafi of a variety of political persuasions, many of whom served in early Qaddafi governments, the NFSL has broadcast radio programming into Libya, published several newspapers and magazines abroad, and is credited with having organized a 1984 attack on the military barracks at Bab al-Aziziyya, where Qaddafi often stayed. During the mid-1980s, at the height of the American confrontation with

Libya, the NFSL denied widespread allegations that it received assistance from the United States. By the 1990s, leadership positions in the NFSL were being assumed by younger Libyans who had grown up in exile and lived most of their lives outside the country.

Lisa Anderson

National Guidance Committee, Palestinian

Organization of West Bank Palestinian leaders.

The National Guidance Committee was established in 1978 in response to the CAMP DAVID ACCORDS and to the Israeli Likud party's settlement policies in Gaza and the West Bank. The committee included eight West Bank mayors, three journalists, and representatives from Palestinian welfare societies, labor and professional unions, student organizations, and the Islamic Supreme Council.

The committee criticized the Camp David accords for ignoring the problems of settlements in the territories occupied by Israel in 1967 and of the status of East Jerusalem. It also sought to broaden the popularity of the Palestine Liberation Organization (PLO) and to extend West Bank leaders' constituencies beyond their home cities through rallies, strikes, and boycotts organized between 1978 and 1980. It countered the reassertion of Jordan's influence by distributing funds allocated by the Arab Summit Conference in Baghdad (the BAGHDAD SUMMIT of 1979).

After 1980, the committee's activities were curtailed by assassination attempts against three mayors and by the Israeli government's expulsion of two others. Two additional committee members were placed under house arrest. The Israeli government outlawed the committee in March 1982.

BIBLIOGRAPHY

BENVENISTI, MERON. *The West Bank Handbook: A Political Lexicon.* Jerusalem, 1986.
SAHLIYEH, EMILE. *In Search of Leadership.* Washington, D.C., 1988.

Elizabeth Thompson

Nationalism

A people's sense of its political identity or a movement to achieve such identity.

The word *nationalism* refers to the feeling of political unity or of identity and patriotic sympathy that a people usually focuses on its own language or culture or on a land that it regards as its own. It also refers to that component of various political ideologies according to which this feeling is held to be essential to the existence of a state or to a political movement's aspirations to statehood. Finally, it is used in the arguments advanced by historians, ideologues, and politicians to justify actual or proposed actions on behalf of the people they see as embodying the nation.

Evidence of nationalism, in any of these related senses, is difficult to discern in the Middle East prior to the nineteenth century. Individuals often felt affinity with their coreligionists, but it was assumed that whatever the religion of the ruler might be, the state was not exclusively defined by religion. Tolerance of religious plurality was the norm, even though the ruler's coreligionists usually enjoyed greater official favor than people of a different religion. Language similarly served as a bond between people and as a dividing line between groups, but no state was linguistically homogeneous or disposed to regard language as the defining quality of a ruler's subjects. As for territory, strong feelings of identity with places of origin, particularly cities and their environs, were much in evidence in such guises as folk sayings, humor, and local traditions, but they were seldom accorded a political valuation.

As in most other parts of the world, the appearance of elements of national feeling in the Middle East preceded formal nationalist statements or political manifestos. Historians have debated the degree of indebtedness (certainly heavy) that various Middle Eastern nationalist writers and political leaders owed to European models in seeking to express their nationalism, but it would be an oversimplification to consider these models the sole source of nationalism in the region.

The earliest nationalist movement manifested itself in the Greeks' war to obtain independence from the Ottoman Empire (between 1821 to 1832). The earlier revolt of the south Slavs (between 1804 and 1830) that culminated in the creation of an autonomous principality of Serbia had been a manifestation of widespread discontent with Ottoman maladministration and military disorder. Its leaders did not articulate nationalist positions, however, and the Slavs would presumably have been content with a return to competent Ottoman rule.

In Greece, however, despite a patchwork leadership ranging from bandit chiefs to Greek intellectuals educated in Western Europe, a distinctly nationalist ideology came in time to be accepted as the best expression of the people's will. However, this ideology was associated with a revolutionary organization called the Philike Hetairia that was based in

Greek communities outside Greece (the most important one was in Odessa). Nationalist ideology followed rather than preceded the Greek rebellion, and many Greeks fought to escape Ottoman rule without being aware of any ideology. Many of the ideologues were more familiar with conditions and ideas in Western Europe than in the Peloponnesus. Rhigas Pheraios, for example (who wrote in his immensely popular "War Hymn": "How long, my heroes, shall we live in bondage,/alone like lions on ridges, on peaks?/. . . Better an hour of life that is free/than forty years in slavery!"), had a personal history of involvement with numerous revolutionary groups in Western Europe dedicated to the ideals of the French Revolution.

Independent Greece not only fostered a revival of classical language and a glorification of ancient greatness—both common practices in later examples of Middle Eastern nationalism—but also developed the Megali Idea, an ideology that harked back to the Byzantine Empire and whose proponents visualized a broad Balkan realm extending to Istanbul (then Constantinople) in which people of various languages and ethnic groups would be led by Greeks. This approach to nationalism, manifesting a vision of the Greek people as a political entity rather than a geographical entity, reflects the thinking of Jean Jacques Rousseau and other French ideologues rather than the German vision of complete identity of people and land. The concept of one people dominating others within a specified territory later becomes commonplace in Middle Eastern nationalism.

Although other nationalist stirrings in the nineteenth century were not consciously patterned on the Greek example, they had some common features. Many advocates of Turkish and Arab political and linguistic distinctiveness, for example, were educated in Europe or were familiar with European ideas. Namık Kemal, whose Turkish drama *Vatan* (Fatherland) helped establish that word (*watan* in Arabic) as an element of nationalism, spent three years in exile in Europe; and the Lebanese Christian Butrus al-BUSTANI, one of the most industrious advocates of a revived Arabic literary language, worked closely with American Protestant missionaries. Like the Greeks, the Turks and Arabs encountered difficulty in harmonizing their particularist views with a history of pluralistic empire. Just as adherents to the Megali Idea could visualize, on the Byzantine model, an ethnically plural state dominated by Greeks, the Arabs and Turks mostly aspired to a revival or assertion of ethno-linguistic identity within the pluralistic Ottoman Empire.

One difference between Greeks and other nineteenth-century nationalists was the association of religion with a people's identity. All Greeks were orthodox Christians, even though not all orthodox Christians were Greek, nor all Greek clergy nationalist in sympathy. By contrast, Christian Arabs were prominent in the protonationalist Arab literary revival, and the Turkish protonationalists supported the religiously plural Ottoman system. Therefore, even though the great majority of Turks and Arabs were Muslims, Islam did not from the outset become an integral element of nationalist thought.

Written expressions of nationalist views among Turks and Arabs circulated during the last decades of the nineteenth century. Religion, however, remained a problem. The foremost Turkish ideologue, Ziya GÖKALP, concentrated his analysis of Turkish identity on language and folk customs and dismissed Islam as a transitory civilizational attribute that should not stand in the way of the adoption of European customs. The Arab Abd al-Rahman al-KAWAKIBI, on the other hand, called for a revival of the caliphate under an Arab of the Prophet Muhammad's tribe, the Quraysh, instead of under the despotic Ottoman sultan Abdülhamit II.

The Committee of Union and Progress, a group of military officers that took control of the Ottoman Empire through a coup d'état in 1908, espoused Turkish nationalism and mandated the use of the Turkish language in certain administrative offices that had previously used local languages. Resentment against such Turkizing measures contributed to the formation of small Arab nationalist groups in Syria and Istanbul (see PAN-TURKISM). Most of these Arab nationalists remained wedded to the concept of an Ottoman Empire, however, until the outbreak of World War I.

Ottoman defeat and the publicizing of Woodrow Wilson's advocacy of self-determination of peoples encouraged an outpouring of nationalist expressions throughout the Middle East. Kurds and Armenians, as well as Arabs whom Britain had encouraged in a nationalist revolt against the Ottomans during the war, tried to influence the peace negotiations in their favor. The most successful nationalist movement of the period, however, was that of an Ottoman army officer, Mustafa Kemal ATATÜRK, who established a Turkish republic that was ideologically rooted in the ideas of Ziya Gökalp. The new Turkish state expelled a Greek expeditionary force from western Anatolia; it also abolished the offices of sultan and caliph, and legislated the most strenuously secular form of nationalism known in the region.

Nationalism dominated Middle East politics from the end of World War II until the Iranian revolution of 1979. ARAB NATIONALISM flourished once the collapse of the Ottoman Empire resolved the question of whether or not to remain loyal to an ethnically plural state. Although some Muslims pushed for re-establishment of the caliphate, most nationalists were caught up in the tide of secularism, actually anticlericalism, that had engulfed Turkey. The Ba'th party was founded in 1947 on a platform of Arab national unity and separation of religion from public affairs. Some other groups, such as the Parti Populaire Syrien, espoused an Arab nationalism based on a single country. The Arabic term qawmiyya (from qawm, group of people) distinguishes this type of nationalism from wataniyya, which calls for political unity of all the Arab peoples. Gamal Abdel Nasser, considered by many the most popular and effective Arab nationalist leader, strove for Arab unity but also inspired Egyptians with the feeling that Egypt was the center of the Arab world.

Zionism, a Jewish nationalist movement that originated in Europe and embodied many European ideas, came into bitter conflict with Arab nationalism, whose leaders viewed the Zionist community in Palestine as a manifestation of European colonialism. The basic elements important to Zionism—language, religion, land, and identity as a people—differed little from those that are important to Arab nationalism.

Being farther removed geographically from European cultural influence, Iran did not manifest a strong nationalist identity until the post–World War I period. Earlier anti-imperialist actions, such as the Tobacco Revolt of 1891 to 1892, engaged religious feelings as much as they did patriotic feelings. When the military commander Reza Khan assumed the throne as Reza Shah in 1925, he took the surname PAHLAVI to indicate continuity with the pre-Islamic imperial past, since the word is normally used to designate the form of the Persian language spoken at that time. The Pahlavi dynasty promoted a nationalist ideology focused on the person of the ruler and the historical sequence of imperial Iranian dynasties. It emphasized the dominant role of Persians and of the Persian language in a multiethnic kingdom.

In 1950, Prime Minister Mohammad Mossadegh became the focus of a strong nonroyal nationalist movement. Suppression of this movement on the shah's behalf by U.S. and British intelligence agencies detoured nationalist feelings in an antiroyal revolutionary direction. Thus the revolution that overthrew the monarchy in 1979 had a strong nationalist coloring along with its dominant religious ideology.

Some modern Muslim theorists maintain that nationalism can have no place in Islam because of the seamless unity of the umma, the community of Muslims. Observers of Middle Eastern politics often use the term *religious nationalism* to describe politically active Islamic movements. Proponents of current theories of nationalism often speak of the "peoples" for whom nationalist movements speak and act as "imagined communities." Rather than accepting nationalist myths proclaiming the unity of a particular tribal, ethnic, linguistic, or territorial group of people from time immemorial, these theorists emphasize that each factor adduced to explain or describe a group's national character is partly an invention of ideologues, a deliberate emphasis upon one or another characteristic that had not previously been considered so important. A new nationalism can thus develop whenever a community imagines itself as a unified entity deserving of special recognition. From this perspective, nationalism appears less as an immutable division of the human population into natural units than it does as an instrument for shaping and reshaping community identities and politics along varying lines. Consequently, the frequently posed question as to whether the new Middle Eastern states created after World War I would ever become genuine national communities (a question often answered in the affirmative in light of the loyal participation of Iraqi Shi'ites in Iraq's war with Shi'ite Iran) may be of little relevance in an unsettled region where communities of people may well reimagine their identities in future decades.

BIBLIOGRAPHY

ANDERSON, BENEDICT. *Imagined Communities.* London, 1983.
COTTAM, RICHARD. *Nationalism in Iran.* Pittsburgh, 1979.
GÖKALP, ZIYA. *The Principles of Turkism.* Leiden, 1968.
HAIM, SYLVIA, ed. *Arab Nationalism: An Anthology.* Berkeley, Calif., 1962.
HOURANI, ALBERT. *Arabic Thought in the Liberal Age, 1798–1939.* New York, 1983.
KHALIDI, R., et al., ed., *The Origins of Arab Nationalism.* New York, 1991.
MARDIN, SERIF. *The Genesis of Young Ottoman Thought.* Princeton, N.J., 1962.

Richard W. Bulliet

Nationalist Action Party

Turkish political party of the 1970s.

This name was imposed on the REPUBLICAN PEASANTS' NATION PARTY in 1969 by its leader, Colonel Alparslan TÜRKEŞ. It reflected right-wing militancy, national chauvinism, pan-Turkism, and adamant anticommunism. The structure of the party was authoritarian, emphasizing indoctrination of youth,

including training in the use of firearms, and organizing Gray Wolf squads to fight leftist groups in the streets in the 1970s. Parliamentary arithmetic catapulted Türkeş into a powerful role in coalition governments of that time and enabled his supporters to infiltrate the civil service.

BIBLIOGRAPHY

LANDAU, J. M. *Radical Politics in Modern Turkey.* Leiden, 1974.
———. "Turkey." In *Political Parties of the Middle East and North Africa,* ed. by Frank Tachau. Westport, Conn., 1994.

Frank Tachau

Nationalist Democracy Party

Political party formed by the military after the 1980 coup in Turkey.

The NDP (or Milliyetçi Demokrasi Partisi, MDP) was formed by the military junta in Turkey after all previous parties were banned in the 1980 coup. Headed by retired General Turgut Sunalp, the party was a favorite to win the November 1983 elections but was unexpectedly trounced by the Motherland party of Turgut Ozal.

While the NDP also did poorly in the March 1984 municipal elections, it did attract many right-wing nationalists at its July 1985 convention. In the late 1980s, the new True Path and Social Democratic parties grew at the expense of the NDP.

BIBLIOGRAPHY

BIRAND, MEHMET ALI. *The Generals' Coup in Turkey.* New York, 1987.

Elizabeth Thompson

National Liberal Party

Lebanese political party established by and in support of the Chamoun family.

The National Liberal Party (NLP) was established by Camille CHAMOUN when he left the presidency of Lebanon in 1958. The NLP is a political vehicle used by the Chamoun family to reward its followers and partisans. While not having a defined political ideology, the NLP favored free enterprise and strong ties between Lebanon and the West, while at the same time it championed Maronite authority over Lebanon's politics. In the 1970s, the NLP claimed some

60,000 to 70,000 members, most of them from the Maronite Christian community, with some Shi'ite, Druze, and Greek Orthodox followers.

During the Lebanese Civil War of 1975, the NLP's militia, the Tigers (al-Numur), fought alongside the Phalange militias against the Islamic–Leftist coalition. In 1980, the Tigers were defeated, following an attack by the Lebanese Forces headed by Bashir Jumayyil. Following their defeat, the Tigers joined the Lebanese Forces and recognized Jumayyil as their leader. The NLP remains the party of Camille Chamoun, who used it to maintain his political power after leaving the presidency of Lebanon. Under his mandate, Lebanon was engulfed in a short civil war that ended with the 1982–1984 intervention of a multinational force composed of U.S. Marines and British, French, and Italian troops.

During the Cold War, Chamoun chose the anticommunist camp but created many enemies in Lebanon and the Arab world. In 1987, Camille Chamoun died and was replaced by his son Dany as the chair of the NLP. In 1990, Dany was assassinated and was replaced by his brother Dori.

BIBLIOGRAPHY

SULEIMAN, MICHAEL W. *Political Parties in Lebanon: The Challenge of a Fragmented Political Culture.* Ithaca, N.Y., 1967.

George E. Irani

National Liberation Front

See Front de Libération Nationale

National Liberation Front, Bahrain

Organization advocating political reform in Bahrain.

Following a general strike in Bahrain in the summer of 1954, liberal reformers from both the Shi'a and Sunni communities organized a Higher Executive Committee (HEC) to press demands for an elected popular assembly, an appellate court, and the right to form trade unions. Protracted negotiations between the ruler, Shaykh Sulman ibn Hamad al-Khalifa, and the HEC led to the formal recognition of a Committee of National Unity in return for the HEC's agreeing to end its calls for a parliament. Activists based in the industrial labor force responded by forming a National Liberation Front, Bahrain (NLFB) calling for more fundamental changes in Bahrain's political structure.

Bahrain had been under a British protectorate since 1880; anti-British demonstrations at the time of the Arab–Israel War of 1956 precipitated restrictions on all opposition forces and the declaration of a state of emergency that effectively suppressed the reform movements of the 1950s. In 1971, Bahrain's independence from Britain was declared, but NLFB leaders boycotted the parliamentary elections held in December 1972, on the grounds that they were sponsored by the regime. Police once more moved against the organization when the national assembly was dissolved in May 1975. The NLFB has, in recent years, been overshadowed by the activities of Bahrain's varied Islamist political movement, although it continues to find support among younger professionals and intellectuals unsympathetic to the Islamists.

BIBLIOGRAPHY

HALLIDAY, FRED. *Arabia without Sultans.* Harmondsworth, England, 1974.
LAWSON, FRED H. *Bahrain: The Modernization of Autocracy.* Boulder, Colo., 1989.

Fred H. Lawson

National Liberation Front, People's Democratic Republic of Yemen

South Yemeni nationalist group that led the rebellion against British rule.

Shortly after its formation in 1963 out of the Aden branch of the Arab Nationalist Movement and other minor groups, the National Liberation Front (NLF) launched the Radfan rebellion against both the British colonial power and the traditional up-country rulers. The NLF defeated the Front for the Liberation of South Yemen (FLOSY) in the fierce struggle to succeed the British in late 1967 and dominated the ruling coalition that it fashioned with the Ba'th party and the Yemeni Communist party (the People's Democratic Union) in the 1970s. Then it merged with these two lesser parties to create the ruling YEMENI SOCIALIST PARTY (YSP) in 1978. Over these years, the NLF moved relentlessly toward the Left and toward greater internal homogeneity and more effective and centralized control, with the result that by the mid-1980s the YSP bore some resemblance to the Marxist-Leninist party to which some of its leaders aspired. The NLF espoused what it called "scientific socialism," an ideology that amounted to a third-world Marxism.

Robert D. Burrowes

National Oil Corporation, Libya

The state oil holdings of Libya.

In 1970, the government of Libya enacted Law 24, reorganizing its oil holdings as the Libyan National Petroleum Corporation, now the National Oil Corporation (NOC). This law directed future foreign investment in Libyan oil to be organized as a partnership with NOC. It also transferred to NOC concessions relinquished by foreign oil companies and oil properties acquired by nationalization. By September 1973, NOC owned a minimum of 51 percent of every oil operation in Libya.

Since then, NOC has expanded its operations, negotiating directly with foreign oil companies to set up new joint ventures. In response to the imposition of economic sanctions by the United States in 1986, NOC devised model exploration and production-sharing agreements (EPSAs) featuring terms highly favorable to foreign partners. These model EPSA contracts have allowed NOC to continue to attract new partners based outside the United States, despite the additional risks to foreign investors that U.S. and UN economic sanctions against Libya impose. Today NOC operates refineries, a petrochemical complex, and a tanker fleet.

BIBLIOGRAPHY

Middle East Economic Survey. Nicosia, Cyprus.
ORGANIZATION OF PETROLEUM EXPORTING COUNTRIES. *OPEC Member Country Profiles.* Vienna, 1980.

Mary Ann Tétreault

National Order Party

Turkish political party, 1970–1971.

The National Order party (NOP) was formed by Necmeddin ERBAKAN on January 26, 1970, after he was elected to parliament. He adopted a shrill anti-Western tone, denouncing the Justice party as a tool of Freemasons and adamantly opposing prospective Turkish entry into the European Common Market. The NOP openly criticized the secular principles of the republic and advocated Islamist views. Consequently, although the press ridiculed the party, the government closed it in May 1971 (though its leaders were not punished); it reemerged as the NATIONAL SALVATION PARTY in October 1972.

BIBLIOGRAPHY

AHMAD, F. *The Turkish Experiment in Democracy, 1950–1975.* Boulder, Colo., 1977.

LANDAU, J. M. "The National Salvation Party in Turkey." *Asian and African Studies* 2, no. 1 (1976): 1–57.
———. "Turkey." In *Political Parties of the Middle East and North Africa,* ed. by Frank Tachau. Westport, Conn., 1994.

Frank Tachau

National Pact, Lebanon

Agreement between Christian and Muslim communities in Lebanon.

The National Pact (Al-Mithaq al-Watani), an unwritten agreement, came into being in the summer of 1943 as a result of numerous meetings between Bishara al-KHURI (a Maronite Christian), Lebanon's first president after independence, and the first prime minister, Riyad al-SULH (a Sunni Muslim). At the heart of the negotiations was the Christians' fear of being dominated by the Muslim communities in Lebanon and the region, and the Muslims' fear of Western hegemony. In return for the Christians' promise not to seek foreign (i.e., French) protection and to accept the "Arab face of Lebanon," the Muslims agreed to recognize the country's independence and to accept the legitimacy of the 1920 boundaries. Muslims also were expected to renounce demands for unity with Syria. The National Pact was intended to reinforce the sectarian system of government by formalizing the confessional distribution of high-level posts in the government based on the results of the 1932 census, with Christians outnumbering Muslims by a ratio of six to five. Although some historians dispute the point, the terms of the National Pact are believed to have been incorporated in the statement of the first cabinet after independence (October 1943).

Specifically, the National Pact decreed that the presidency shall be reserved for a Maronite Christian, the prime ministership for a Sunni Muslim, and the speakership of parliament for a Shi'a Muslim. Other top government posts—commander in chief of the army, head of military intelligence, head of internal security, and some important ambassadorships—were reserved for Maronites. It was agreed that the deputy prime minister should be a Greek Orthodox and that "minorities" (not one of the six major religious sects) should be occasionally represented in the cabinet and always in the parliament.

The confessional system outlined in the National Pact was a matter of expediency, an interim measure to overcome philosophical differences between Christian and Muslim leaders. It was hoped that once the business of governance got under way, and as national spirit grew, the importance of confessionalism in the political structure would diminish. Over the years, the frequent political disputes—the most notable of which were manifested in the Lebanese Civil Wars of 1958 and 1975, and the Palestinian controversies in the 1960s and 1970s have borne clear testimony to the failure of the National Pact to produce societal integration. Moreover, along with the system of *zuʿama* clientelism, it has guaranteed the maintenance of the status quo and the continuation of privilege for the sectarian elites.

The National Pact was affected by the TAʾIF ACCORD of 1989. Its weakness stems from the sectarian representation that was allowed to prevail in the 1940s. The Maronites were accepted as representatives of all Christians. Furthermore, nobody within either religious community assigned Khuri and al-Sulh the task of dividing the national government along sectarian lines. The Taʾif accord juridically legitimized the basic provisions of the National Pact but changed the representational formula. Muslims and Christians are now represented equally in parliament, although the top government posts will continue to be divided along the lines of the pact. The Taʾif accord constituted the first revision of the pact.

As ʿad AbuKhalil

National Party, Egypt

Egyptian nationalist movement and political party.

The National party (al-Hizb al-Watani) is the name of two successive movements of resistance in Egypt against foreign rule. The first emerged in November 1879, after Khedive Ismaʿil ibn Ibrahim's deposition. Although it purported to be an Egyptian protest movement against the privileges of Turks and Circassians and against the Anglo–French Dual Financial Control, its initial patron was probably Prince Halim, who claimed that Ismaʿil had deprived him of the khedivate. Former Premier Muhammad Sharif, a constitutionalist, also claimed to have formed the party. During the Urabi revolt (1881–1882), it became associated with the most radical elements in the national assembly and the officer corps, but it lacked a formal organization, and it is not easy to determine its role in the revolt. When British troops occupied Egypt in September 1882 to restore order, the party vanished.

The National party was revived in 1893 as a secret society, under the aegis of Khedive ABBAS HILMI II and with strong ties to the government of the Ot-

toman Empire. Its leaders were Mustafa KAMIL, Muhammad FARID, and several other professional men. In the 1890s, it disseminated propaganda in Europe against the British occupation of Egypt and among Egyptians to back the khedive against the British agent and consul general, Lord Cromer. In 1900, Mustafa Kamil founded a daily newspaper, *al-Liwa* (the Banner), which became the National party's organ. The Nationalists broke with Abbas in 1904, but they became reconciled after the 1906 DINSHAWAY INCIDENT. Mustafa Kamil publicized the party's existence in his long speech of October 22, 1907, convening the first Nationalist assembly in December. He died two months later, and the Nationalists chose Muhammad Farid to succeed him. Farid tried to widen the party's appeal by circulating petitions demanding a constitution and supporting the YOUNG TURK revolution in Constantinople. It split, however, over whether to cooperate with the khedive in spite of his reconciliation with the British, whether to espouse pan-Islam even if doing so would alienate the Copts (Egyptian Orthodox Christians), and whether to seek Egypt's liberation by legal or by revolutionary means. Cromer's successors, Sir Eldon Gorst and Lord Horatio Kitchener, encouraged the khedive and his ministers to muzzle the press and, after a Nationalist killed Premier Butros Ghali in February 1910, passed special laws, banned or suspended newspapers, and jailed editors—even Farid—to intimidate and weaken the party. Farid's departure from Egypt in 1912 left the party leaderless and divided. During World War I, its emigré leaders sided against the British—that is, with the Ottoman Empire and Germany—but British security measures prevented them from inspiring an Egyptian uprising. The Nationalists aided the WAFD in the 1919 revolution and, when parliamentary rule was established in 1923, ran candidates for election. Led by Hafiz Ramadan, the National party remained a small but vocal element in the fabric of Egyptian politics until the 1952 revolution, after which all political parties were abolished.

BIBLIOGRAPHY

DEEB, MARIUS. *Party Politics in Egypt: The Wafd and Its Rivals, 1919–1939.* London, 1979.
GERSHONI, ISRAEL, and JAMES JANKOWSKI. *Egypt, Islam, and the Arabs: The Search for Egyptian Nationhood, 1900–1930.* New York, 1976.
GOLDSCHMIDT, ARTHUR. "The Egyptian Nationalist Party, 1892–1919." In *Political and Social Change in Modern Egypt,* ed. by P. M. Holt. London, 1968.
SCHÖLCH, ALEXANDER. *Egypt for the Egyptians!* London, 1979.

Arthur Goldschmidt, Jr.

National Party, Syria

Alliance of Syrian urban upper-class notables and politicians, formed in 1947 with Damascus as its center.

During the French mandate period in Syria (1920–1946), this alliance of notables and politicians had formed the Damascus branch of the NATIONAL BLOC (al-Kutla al-Wataniyya), which had led Syria's nationalist political struggle against the French. The most prominent leaders of the National party (al-Hizb al-Watani) were Shukri al-QUWATLI, Jamil MARDAM, Faris al-Khuri, Lutfi al-HAFFAR, and Sabri al-ASALI.

The National party did not have a modern political party structure—rather, it depended on its leaders, their loosely organized followings, and their extended family relations. Socially, the party represented industrial and merchant interests, which favored independence from France, in contrast to the largely more conservative landowning milieu, which was lukewarm toward such a prospect. The position of the National party together with the position of its Aleppo-based rival, the PEOPLE'S PARTY (Hizb al-Sha'b), was undermined in the late 1940s and early 1950s. This took place through the rise of more radical political parties like the BA'TH party and by the increased role of the military in Syria's politics during that period.

BIBLIOGRAPHY

KHOURY, PHILIP. *Syria and the French Mandate.* Princeton, N.J., 1987.
SEALE, PATRICK. *The Struggle for Syria.* New Haven, Conn., 1965.

Mahmoud Haddad

National Progressive Front, Syria

Syrian political organization originated and controlled by Hafiz al-Asad..

The National Progressive Front was established in Syria on March 7, 1972, by presidential decree, to serve as a building block of the system of government of President Hafiz al-ASAD. Besides the BA'TH, which dominates the Front, the organization's other constituent members are the Arab Socialists Union (a relic of the Syrian–Egyptian union of 1948–1961), the Syrian Communist party, the Arab Socialists party (the last of Akram al-HAWRANI's party), and the Organization of Socialist Unionists (a group of ex-Ba'thist Nasserists).

With the exception of the Ba'th, the parties that comprise the Front are not allowed to canvass for supporters in the army or the student unions. Legally speaking, the Front is governed by a charter with twenty-nine articles. It has a central command headed by al-Asad, local leadership at the governorates' level, as well as various bureaus and offices.

BIBLIOGRAPHY

SEALE, PATRICK. *Asad of Syria: The Struggle for the Middle East.* Los Angeles, 1988.

Muhammad Muslih

National Progressive Unionist Party

Originated as the left faction of the official Arab Socialist Union (ASU).

When Anwar al-Sadat dissolved the ASU in 1976, the National Progressive Unionist Party (NPUP) emerged as the official left opposition party. A coalition of leftist forces, including Nasserists and Marxists, the NPUP under the leadership of Khalid Muhyi al-Din, formerly a member of the FREE OFFICERS, has played the role of active and vocal opposition in the PEOPLE'S ASSEMBLY.

Raymond William Baker

National Religious Party

Israeli political party, also known as Mafdal.

The National Religious party (NRP) was for many years the largest and most influential in the religious bloc and a member of every Israeli government up to 1992. It had the reputation of being less militant and more pragmatic than some of the others in the bloc. This image at times led to its being overshadowed by parties such as TAMI and SHAS, both of which also charged that the NRP failed to give adequate representation to Oriental Jews. During the 1950s, 1960s, and 1970s, the NRP always had ten to twelve seats in the Knesset. After 1981 it fell to a consistent level of four to six. The losses led it to move further to the right on domestic issues and to a somewhat more moderate position in regard to the territories occupied by Israel. Among the party's best-known leaders have been Yosef BURG, Zevulun HAMMER, and Yehuda ben-Meir.

Walter F. Weiker

National Salvation Front, Lebanon

Lebanese nationalist group.

After the signing of the agreement between Amin Jumayyil's government and Israel on May 17, 1983, opposition groups and politicians met to commit themselves to aborting the accord. The three founders of the National Salvation Front were Sulayman FRANJIYYA, Rashid KARAME, and Walid JUMBLATT. Minor members of the Front were the Lebanese Communist Party and the Syrian Social Nationalist Party. All of these groups were loyal to the Syrian regime and opposed Jumayyil's government, which was then, with U.S. support, launching a war against the opposition. The Front wanted to annul the agreement with Israel, which amounted to a peace treaty, and to oppose the Phalangist takeover of the Lebanese government and administration under Jumayyil. The Front cooperated with Nabi Berri of the AMAL movement, and as a result of direct Syrian military and political support was able to pressure Jumayyil to nullify the agreement.

As'ad AbuKhalil

National Salvation Party

Political party in Turkey whose aim is the restoration of Islamic theocracy; a fundamentalist party.

The political climate created by Turkey's 1961 constitution allowed for steady changes toward liberalism and democracy. It also permitted Islam to become an independent political force, because of the new growth of religious associations. The first initiative was undertaken by the predecessor of the National Salvation party (NSP)—the NATIONAL ORDER PARTY (NOP) (Milli Nizam Partisi)—founded January 26, 1970, by Necmeddin ERBAKAN (and seventeen others). He was a former university professor, industrialist, and then general secretary of the Turkish chamber of commerce. Its program contained more than one hundred articles, dealing mainly with the relationship between secularism and education. It demanded the widening of freedom of conscience in favor of Islam. The NOP was banned by the Constitutional Court on May 19, 1971, because it aimed for the "restoration of a theocratic order in Turkey."

On October 11, 1972, the National Salvation party (Milli Selâmet Partisi, NSP) was founded by S. Arif Emre and nineteen others, many of whom had been involved in the National Order party. Er-bakan, former president of that party, refrained from assuming any position in the new party, which was able to organize by April 1973, with local branches in sixty-seven provinces. In the election of 1973, the party received 11.8 percent of the vote and eighty seats, thus becoming the third party in the Turkish Grand National Assembly. Erbakan, who only joined the party officially on May 16, 1973, became its elected leader on October 21, 1973.

The National Salvation party ideology is reflected in the moral virtues and traditional values of Islam, Turkey's national religious heritage. Western values such as art and tourism are wholly rejected, and the party also opposes family planning, encouraging instead population increase. The party is neither socialist nor materialist; instead, it is idealist. It encourages rapid industrialization throughout the country and rejects all foreign investment, opposing Turkey's entry into the European Economic Community. It wants, rather, to establish close ties with the Arab states.

The NSP played an important role in the coalition politics of the 1970s. The first coalition government was formed on January 26, 1974, by Bülent Ecevit and the Republican People's party; the relationship was always tense. The first crisis occurred on the issue of determining the dimensions of a general amnesty, and the NSP opposed the inclusion of anyone charged with association to an illegal communist party. The second and more serious crisis occurred after the military intervention in Cyprus, when the NSP demanded large territorial annexations. This led to Ecevit's resignation as prime minister and the end of the coalition.

The NSP later participated in the Nationalist Front, forged under the leadership of Süleyman Demirel of the Justice party. In the 1977 elections, however, the NSP lost about 25 percent of its votes and 50 percent of its seats in the assembly. After the 1980 military coup, NSP leaders were accused of having conspired against the secular character of the state but were acquitted by the court.

The third pro-Islamic party that stepped into the succession of the dissolved NSP, the Welfare party (Refah Partisi), was founded on July 19, 1983, by A. Türkmen. After the September 1987 referendum that reestablished the right of former prominent politicians to pursue political activities, Erbakan was elected chairman of the Welfare party in November; the party received 7.1 percent of the vote, and because a party must have 10 percent of the vote for legislative representation, it did not qualify. In the local elections of 1989, however, Welfare received 9.8 percent of the vote and was able to win municipalities in five provincial centers—Konya, Sivas, Sanliurfa, Kahramanmara, and Van.

The electorate of the NSP and Welfare comes from the Anatolian and urban middle class. Religious sects, such as the NAQSHBANDI and the NURCU, substantially supported the NSP in the past and continue to support its successor, the Welfare party. The increasing fundamentalist tendency of Welfare and its plea for a return to the SHARI'A (Islamic law) is echoed by its newspaper, *Milli Gazete*. The party enjoys considerable support among Turkish workers in Europe, especially Germany. Outside Turkey, party sympathizers associate in an organization called Milli Gorus, the National View.

BIBLIOGRAPHY

LANDAU, JACOB M. "The National Salvation Party in Turkey." *Asian and African Studies* 11, no. 1 (1976).

Nermin Abadan-Unat

National Theater

See Theater

National Union, Egypt

Founded in 1956 to succeed the Liberation Rally.

The National Union was the second of Egypt's official mobilization bodies, to be followed in its turn by the ARAB SOCIALIST UNION. The National Union was an indirect outgrowth of the Tripartite Aggression of 1956, when Egypt was invaded by the colluding forces of the British, the French, and the Israelis. The FREE OFFICER's regime sought to consolidate the internal political front by creating a more effective mobilization vehicle for the solidification of patriotic sentiment behind the military regime.

The National Union structured a network of quasi-governmental intermediary organizations, such as a youth movement and women's organizations, that aimed to absorb and canalize popular energies in the service of regime goals. Though officially labeled a political party, the National Union, like its predecessors and successor, proved merely a bureaucratic extension of the authoritarian regime, failing to provide effective means of mass political participation.

Raymond William Baker

National Unity Committee, Turkey

A group of military officers, commonly referred to as the NUC, who seized control of Turkey's government on May 27, 1960.

The National Unity Committee (in Turkish, Milli Birlik Komitesi) was a group of military officers, led by General Cemal GÜRSEL, that staged the revolution of May 27, 1960 and subsequently ruled Turkey through November 20, 1961. Although the coup was prepared by officers of middle and junior rank, it was the senior officers who took control of the National Unity Committee and the government. Serious divisions separated the two groups: junior members favored radical reform requiring longer-term retention of power by the military. Senior members supported an early return of elected civilian government. One of the first acts of the NUC was to convene a constitutional commission to draft a new constitution. On June 12, 1960, a provisional constitution granted sovereignty to the NUC until new elections could be held. The NUC exercised legislative power directly and executive power indirectly through a civilian council of ministers appointed and controlled by the NUC. On November 13, 1960, in a move to rid the group of its more radical elements, thirteen of the original thirty-eight members of the committee were purged, including the ultranationalist Colonel Alparslan Türkes, paving the way for convocation of a civilian constituent assembly to draft a new constitution. The constitution was approved in a popular referendum on July 8, 1961, though a large negative vote was cast. On October 15, 1961, parliamentary elections produced indecisive results, leading to the election of the NUC leader, Cemal Gürsel, as president of the republic, and to the necessity of organizing coalition governments for the first time.

The NUC implemented some social and economic reforms designed to stabilize politics in Turkey. In addition, it abolished the Demokrat Parti and brought almost six hundred of its members to trial, three of whom were subsequently executed.

BIBLIOGRAPHY

AHMAD, FEROZ. *The Turkish Experiment in Democracy, 1950–1975.* Boulder, Colo., 1977.

ÖZBUDUN, E. *The Role of the Military in Recent Turkish Politics.* Cambridge, Mass., 1966.

SHAW, STANFORD, and EZEL KURAL SHAW. *History of the Ottoman Empire and Modern Turkey.* Vol. 2, *Reform, Revolution, and Republic: The Rise of Modern Turkey, 1808–1975.* New York, 1977, pp. 414–416.

Frank Tachau

National Unity Government, Israel

The name given to Israeli governments that, on two occasions, included both major political blocs, even though they were philosophically opposed.

The first National Unity Government was formed on the eve of the Arab–Israel War of 1967. It involved the MAPAI, Rafi, and Herut parties and included such major figures as Moshe Dayan and Menachem Begin. It lasted until the disagreement over the Rogers Plan in 1969. The second was in 1984 as a result of an election stalemate in which neither the Labor party nor Likud could form a coalition without the other and when there was a need to address the severe economic crisis. Under its terms, the leaders of each of the major blocs, Shimon Peres and Yitzhak Shamir, occupied the office of prime minister for two years, and other offices were parceled out according to the size of the Knesset membership of each bloc and of some smaller parties. The National Unity format proved to be indecisive and immobile, however, making decisions only through lowest common denominator programs. There were also objections that it undercut the essence of Israeli democracy by reducing the opposition to small numbers and to only extremist parties. It was disbanded before the 1988 election.

BIBLIOGRAPHY

ROLEF, SUSAN, ed. *Political Dictionary of the State of Israel.* New York, 1987.

Walter F. Weiker

National Water System, Israel

Agency that oversees the planning and development of Israel's water resources.

With the establishment of the State of Israel in 1948, much effort was expended on drawing up an inventory of national water resources, defining growth objectives for the country, and planning methods of development. The first comprehensive water-development plan was adopted in 1950, stressing the maximum conservation of water. In 1952, Tahal, the Israel Water Planning Corporation, was set up to plan the water, sewage, and drainage systems and to supervise development. In 1959, Israel's Knesset (parliament) passed the Water Law, vesting all water rights in the state and giving the water commissioner in the ministry of agriculture the sole authority to fix tariffs, allocate water, and issue licenses for exploiting water resources.

All water development schemes are closely integrated with plans for agriculture and the realities of the scarcity of both land and water. The development plans must also take into account shortages of capital. The price of water is therefore high and, until recently, farmers paid the least, since preference was given to irrigation installations that facilitated control of the amounts of water used, minimized conveyance losses, and were economical in the use of labor.

Israel's climate is typically Mediterranean, with rainfall occurring only in the winter and decreasing from north to south. Rainfall in the north averages thirty-nine inches (1,000 mm) yearly; in the central coastal plain nineteen inches (500 mm); in the extreme south only one inch (30 mm)—but there are yearly fluctuations. Its only major river running from north to south is the Jordan river. Its smaller rivers include the Yarkon, the Kishon, and the Soreq. They all empty into the Mediterranean Sea, along with more than a dozen major streams. National development projects aim at utilizing groundwater, springs, storm runoff, and reclaimed waste water. The largest project predated the JOHNSTON PLAN and was completed in the 1960s—the National Water Carrier—which conveys water from the northeast to the center and, at the same time, integrates all local and regional waterworks into one national water "grid," operated according to a national plan.

Israel claims that the integrated water sources available for the nation amount to about 370 million gallons (1,400 million cu m) per year. The majority of this water comes from the upper Jordan river and includes water from the springs around the Sea of Galilee (Lake Tiberias or Lake Kinneret), from the lake itself, and from coastal and foothill groundwater sources. A smaller amount of this water comes from the groundwater of the Galilee mountains, the Kishon river system, the Yarkon river system and the springs, storm runoff, and reclaimed waste of Israel's cities of Haifa and Tel Aviv.

Regulation is aided by the use of two main storage facilities: (1) the Sea of Galilee in the north, which is used for excess Jordan river waters during the rainy season, and (2) the aquifer under the central hills, which was integrated into the grid system after the 1967 Arab–Israel War.

A major priority in Israel's early decades was the expansion of irrigation, with domestic and industrial water supply taking second place. Priorities have now changed, and irrigation is being cut back as both population and industrialization have grown.

BIBLIOGRAPHY

BLASS, SIMCHA. *Water in Strife and Action.* Ramat Gan, Israel 1973.

WIENER, AARON. *The Role of Water in Development.* Tel Aviv, 1972.

Sara Reguer

NATO

See North Atlantic Treaty Organization

Natural Gas, Economic Exploitation of

A mixture of hydrocarbons that are vapors at normal temperature and above-normal pressure.

Methane (CH_4) is the primary component of natural gas; other components are ethane (C_2H_6), propane (C_3H_8), butane (C_4H_{10}) and pentane; nonhydrocarbons, such as nitrogen, hydrogen, and water vapor; and traces of rare gases, such as helium. The heavier-than-methane hydrocarbons are collectively termed natural gas liquids.

"Associated" gas is gas dissolved in petroleum; it sometimes also appears as a gas cap over an oil-bearing formation. Associated gas is the primary source of the pressure supporting oil production and is a by-product of this process. An estimated one-quarter of the world's natural gas reserves is associated gas.

The flammability of natural gas and the complexity and cost of the technology needed to recover and exploit it prompted oil companies at first to "flare," or burn, most of the natural gas they produced. During the 1920s, research into production of petrochemicals led to the development of a number of commercial processes utilizing natural gas as a feedstock, but the great mass of the natural gas produced continued to be flared. At that time, the American Petroleum Institute commissioned a major study of the role of natural gas in oil production. Published in 1929—when industry leaders and government officials were worried about imminent fossil fuel depletion—the study was the first empirical demonstration of the relationship between gas pressure and recovery of oil reserves. In response to the study, the large, vertically integrated oil firms took the lead in changing traditional methods of oil production and processing so as to conserve natural gas.

Other modern uses of natural gas date back to the nineteenth century, when it was substituted for coal and wood in boilers located near oil fields. During the mid-nineteenth century gas synthesized from coal became the chief illuminating fuel in urban areas until it was displaced by the invention of the incandescent light bulb. During the first half of the twentieth century, gas gained a share of the home-heating market and was used as a fuel in manufacturing. But the high cost of gas infrastructure, coupled with the large profits brought by petroleum, made natural gas the stepchild of the oil industry.

The economic exploitation of natural gas depends on its commercial value, which in turn is a function of the size, quality, and location of the gas deposit, the projected rate of production, the price of natural gas, and the price of alternative fuels. The dependence of gas collection, transmission, and distribution on expensive infrastructure has historically been the biggest factor limiting the use of natural gas as a fuel. Oil-exporting countries in the Middle East have long protested the "waste" of their natural gas by flaring, but it was not until they could assume at least some of the cost of providing infrastructure that other than limited local uses for their natural gas became common.

Internationally, however, gas exporters have encountered resistance from importers with respect to the sharing of costs, particularly for pipeline construction and the expensive cryogenic facilities needed to liquefy and transport liquid natural gas. Another difficulty adding to the cost is the load factor, the average rate of capacity usage. Because so much natural gas is used for heating, demand is highly cyclical. The development of strategies to reduce these inherent costs have increased the attractiveness of natural gas as a fuel.

The ORGANIZATION OF PETROLEUM EXPORTING COUNTRIES (OPEC)—including gas exporters such as Algeria, Iran, and Libya—has engaged in repeated pricing disputes with its customers. These disputes have led to interrupted deliveries, canceled contracts, and even the scrapping of entire projects. OPEC has tried repeatedly to achieve a unified organizational position on natural gas pricing by developing formulas linking gas prices to crude oil prices. However, its efforts have been stymied by consumer resistance to the substantial price increases demanded by producers, by competition from non-OPEC gas sources (such as Russia) and nongas fuels (such as petroleum), and by the sustained weakness in oil prices that has reduced producer incentives to link natural gas prices to crude oil prices.

At the same time, improvements in transmission and storage technology and the growing global market for natural gas are positive economic signs. Although demand for natural gas in key industrial markets weakened in the 1980s as a result of recession, warmer winters, and conservation, the market is expected to grow strongly into the twenty-first century.

Some OPEC countries see expanding internal consumption and manufacture of petrochemicals as superior alternatives to natural gas exports. However, neither the market for petrochemicals nor the domestic economies of most gas-rich members of OPEC are sufficient to absorb the quantities of natural gas available. At the same time, antipollution regulations in fuel-importing countries make natural gas more attractive to consumers and lower its total cost compared with that of alternative fuels. Recent financial and regulatory changes in national and international markets support the expansion of supplies by improving security guarantees for producers as well as consumers.

[See also: Petroleum, Oil, and Natural Gas.]

BIBLIOGRAPHY

DAVIS, J. D. Blue Gold: The Political Economy of Natural Gas. London, 1984.

INTERNATIONAL ENERGY AGENCY. Natural Gas: Prospects and Policies. Paris, 1991.

MOSSAVAR-RAHMANI, BIJAN, and SHARMIN MOSSAVAR-RAHMANI. The OPEC Natural Gas Dilemma. Boulder, Colo., 1986.

STERN, JONATHAN P. European Gas Markets: Challenge and Opportunity in the 1990s. Brookfield, Vt., 1990.

Mary Ann Tétreault

Natural Gas, Middle East Reserves of

The Middle East holds 25 percent of the world reserves of natural gas but generates only 4.62 percent of world production.

Natural gas must be transported by pipeline or liquefied by refrigeration in the form of liquid natural gas (LNG) and transported on specially built ships. The liquefaction process is substantially more expensive. But since the main demand for gas from the Gulf has come from users in the Far East, Europe, and the United States, liquefaction has been the only option and has made the production of the main Gulf gas fields less competitive. Gas from Algeria—because it can be piped under the Mediterranean—has been extensively used in Europe.

Natural gas has become the major feed stock for petrochemicals. The development of the petrochemical industry in the Gulf region has given impetus to the development of the fields. Saudi Arabia uses most of its produced natural gas for firing desalination plants, running power plants, and producing over seventeen million tons per year of petrochemicals and fertilizers, which are exported worldwide.

In the mid-1990s some major projects were undertaken to develop fields and liquefaction plants for exports, mainly in Qatar and Oman. Qatar planned

TABLE 1

1993 Gas Production and Reserves in the Middle East*

Country	Gas Production	Gas Reserves	Years in Production Remaining
Algeria	51	3,624	71
Bahrain	8	167	21
Iran	27	20,671	766
Iraq	3	3,101	1,034
Kuwait	4	1,498	375
Libya	6	1,296	316
Oman	3	566	189
Qatar	14	7,079	506
Saudia Arabia	36	5,262	146
Syria	4	198	50
United Arab Emirates	25	580	23
Total Middle East	181	44,042	
% of World Total	4.6	26	

*In billions of cubic meters
Sources: British Petroleum Review of World Gas; MEES; OPEC Facts and Figures 1993; computed and updated by The Lafayette Group, Inc.

to develop large liquefaction plants for export of gas to India and the Far East. Oman planned to build a pipeline across the Arabian Sea to deliver gas to India.

Jean-François Seznec

Na'um Pasha   [1846–?]

Ottoman administrator in Lebanon.

Na'um Pasha was born in Istanbul to a Latin Christian family originally from Aleppo. After completing his formal education, he was appointed to the Foreign Ministry of the Ottoman Empire. In August 1892 he was appointed *mutasarrif* for Lebanon for five years. Na'um Pasha dissolved the Administrative Council upon his arrival in Lebanon and renewed the mandate of its members by launching a purge of the adminstration to root out corruption. His rule is known for the construction of bridges and the opening of carriage roads. He was credited with improving Lebanon's finances and security, and his term was renewed for another five years. His second term ended in August 1902.

As'ad AbuKhalil

Navarino, Battle of

An 1827 naval battle during the Greek War of Independence in which British, French, and Russian vessels defeated an Ottoman Egyptian navy.

During the Greek revolution (Greek War of Independence, 1821–1830) against the Ottoman Empire, Sultan Mahmud II dispatched Muhammad Ali Pasha, the viceroy of Egypt, to suppress the rebellion. Muhammad Ali's son, Ibrahim Pasha, conducted a series of highly successful campaigns in the Morea (Peloponnesian) peninsula, and the Greeks seemed on the verge of defeat. The European powers, with the notable exception of Austria, were sympathetic to the Greek cause and agreed to arrange for a cease-fire between the rebels and the Ottomans. In September 1827 an Egyptian fleet arrived at Navarino on the western coast of the Morea. Shortly thereafter, a squadron from Britain commanded by Admiral Edward Codrington that included contingents from Russia and France was dispatched to neutralize the Ottoman fleet. On October 20, the European flotilla destroyed more than fifty ships of the Ottoman fleet in Navarino harbor in less than three hours of fighting. Rather than leading to negotiations, this action only intensified Mahmud's determination to fight, and within months the Ottoman Empire and Russia were at war. However, the Battle of Navarino forced Ibrahim to withdraw from the Morea and thereby guaranteed Greek independence.

BIBLIOGRAPHY

ANDERSON, M. S. *The Eastern Question*. London, 1966.
SHAW, STANFORD, and EZEL KURAL SHAW. *History of the Ottoman Empire and Modern Turkey*. New York, 1977.

Zachary Karabell

Navigation Treaties

See Commercial and Navigation Treaties

Navon, Yizhak [1921–]

Fifth president of Israel.

Yizhak Navon was born in Jerusalem to a Sephardic family of rabbinical lineage. Educated in religious schools and then at the Hebrew University of Jerusalem, Navon was a member of the Haganah. From 1949 to 1950, he was an Israeli diplomat in Argentina and Uruguay, and he served as political secretary to Foreign Minister Moshe Sharett from 1951 to 1952. He worked in the same capacity for Prime Minister David Ben-Gurion from 1952 to 1963. From 1963 to 1965, Navon served as the director of the Division of Culture and the Ministry of Education and Culture.

Navon was a member of the Knesset for the Labor party (originally part of the Rafi party before it united with the MAPAI party) and was the chairman of the Knesset Committee on Foreign Affairs and Defense. From 1978 to 1983, Navon was the fifth president of Israel, nominated by the opposition Labor party and chosen over the Likud candidate. In 1984 he was the Israeli vice president and the minister of education and culture. At present he is out of public life and living in Jerusalem.

Miriam Simon

Nayır, Yaşar Nabi [1908–1981]

Turkish publisher, poet, writer.

Born in Üsküp, in the Balkans, Nayır's family migrated to Istanbul, where he attended Galatasaray high school. As a youth he joined the national literary movement and began writing poetry and articles for arts magazines. He later published several anthologies of poetry and stories, which he translated from French, Roman, and Balkan literature.

Nayır was also among the most important arts publishers in mid-century, most known for his journal *Varlık* (Existence), which he founded in 1933 and published until his death. His publishing house has published thousands of books, particularly Turkish language and world classics, in translation. Nayır wrote several collections of short stories, novels, memoirs, and poetry. Later in life, particularly after the 1960 coup, he moved from his earlier Kemalist leanings toward leftist and socialist political attitudes.

BIBLIOGRAPHY

Yeni Türk Ansiklopedisi (New Turkish Encyclopedia). Istanbul, 1985.

Elizabeth Thompson

Nazareth

City in northern Israel.

Nazareth is about 18 miles (29 km) southeast of Haifa, at the junction of the highways from Haifa and Jerusalem northeast to Tiberias. It has a population estimated at about 45,000 (1983). It was the home of Joseph and Mary during the childhood of

Jesus. After the Muslim advance, it was taken several times by the Crusaders. Its Christians were murdered by Baybars in 1263.

It was taken by the Ottoman Turks in 1517 and incorporated into the Ottoman Empire. After World War I, with the dismemberment of the empire, it became part of the British mandate territory of Palestine. When Israel became a state in 1948, it was taken in the first Arab–Israel War by the Israeli Defense Forces, but unlike the people in most Palestinian cities and towns, its population stayed.

Nazareth is famous for its great Christian churches, among them the Roman Catholic Church of the Annunciation, completed in 1966 and now the largest in the Middle East; there is also the Synagogue-Church, Gabriel's Church, and the Mensa Christi Church. Each is associated with major events in the lives of Mary or Jesus.

Modern Nazareth is a regional center for trade in Galilee. A prosperous industrialized town, Natzrat Illit (Upper Nazareth) has been built since 1957 for Jewish immigrants, mostly on lands in the hills east of the city.

BIBLIOGRAPHY

Encyclopaedia of Zionism and Israel. New York, 1971.

Benjamin Joseph

Nazım, Hüseyin   [1854–1927]

Ottoman bureaucrat.

From 1890 to 1897, Nazım served as Abdülhamit II's minister of police. He later held various other posts, particularly that of provincial governor. He was appointed minister of war in 1912, just before the outbreak of the Balkan Wars. On January 23, 1913, he was shot dead by a group of officers, including future war minister Enver Bey, who feared the government was going to cede the city of Edirne to Bulgaria.

BIBLIOGRAPHY

LEWIS, BERNARD. *The Emergence of Modern Turkey.* New York, 1961, pp. 224–225.

Elizabeth Thompson

Nazir, Hisham   [1932–   ]

Government official of Saudi Arabia.

Nazir attended the University of California at Los Angeles. As one of Saudi Arabia's first technocrats,

he served as deputy to the first oil minister, Abdullah Tariki. He then went on to become minister of planning (1975–1986) and in 1986 was named minister of oil.

BIBLIOGRAPHY

YERGIN, DANIEL. *The Prize: The Epic Quest for Oil, Money and Power.* New York, 1991.

Les Ordeman

Nazmi, Ziya   [1881–1937]

Turkish painter.

The son of a financial official in the Ottoman Empire, Nazmi was born in the Aksaray quarter of Istanbul. Under the conservative influence of his father, he studied at the School of Political Science; but when his father died, he entered the Imperial Academy to study art and later went to France. While in France, Nazmi was influenced by Impressionism, and his landscapes depict people, buildings, and trees with pinks, greens, and yellows bathed in soft, diffuse light.

Upon his return to Istanbul, he taught art and held several exhibitions of his Impressionistic work. Nazmi and his generation of painters replaced the formal realism of nineteenth-century painters with informal and natural depictions of everyday life in cities and villages, including nude portraits. Nazmi was an enthusiastic follower of Mustafa Kemal Atatürk's cultural reforms, and he painted one of the best portraits of Atatürk, who was president of Turkey from 1923 to 1938.

BIBLIOGRAPHY

GÜVEMLI, ZAHIR. "Nazmi Ziya Güran." In *Çağdaş Türk Resimden Örnekler.* Istanbul, 1982.
RENDA, GÜNSEL. "Modern Trends in Turkish Painting." In *The Transformation of Turkish Culture: The Atatürk Legacy,* ed. by Günsel Renda and C. Max Kortepeter. Princeton, N.J., 1986.

David Waldner

Ne'eman, Yuval   [1925–   ]

Israeli military strategist and physicist.

From the War of Independence until the late 1950s, Ne'eman held various positions with the Israeli armed forces, and he is considered one of the most important developers of the basic strategy of the Israel Defense Forces. In the 1960s, he turned away from his earlier career and became one of Israel's leading physicists, doing pioneering work in elementary particle physics. From 1971 to 1975, he served as president of Tel Aviv University. In 1979, he became head of the Tehiyah party and entered the Knesset in 1981, serving as minister of science and development. A strong opponent of any Israeli withdrawal from the West Bank and Gaza, he supports expulsion of Palestinians from those territories.

Walter F. Weiker

Negev Desert

Desert region in the southern half of Israel; the northern extension of the Sinai desert.

The Negev is a triangular area, with a maximum elevation of 3,300 feet (1,000 m), consisting of more than half of Israel's land area. The Negev hills are a series of ranges with gentle northwesterly slopes and steep southeasterly slopes. Some craters were formed by the erosion of upward-folded strata, being 6 to 19 miles (10–30 km) long by up to 3 miles (1–5 km) wide, surrounded on all sides by precipitous slopes. On their eastern side is an opening, through which they drain into the ARAVAH VALLEY. The heat of August averages 79° F (26° C), but 90° F (32° C) in the southern area and Aravah. The cold of January averages 52° F (11° C), but 59° F (15° C) in the south and Eilat. The gateway from the north is the Negev's largest city, Beersheba, with a population of some 120,000. To the south it opens onto the Gulf of Aqaba at Eilat. The Negev has been irrigated in the northwest for agriculture; it contains some mineral resources, such as copper, phosphates, bromine, potash, natural gas, and petroleum.

Under the British mandate (1922–1948), the Negev was inhabited mainly by bedouin; a few Jewish settlements were established by 1946. Control of the desert was contested by both Arabs and Jews in the various PARTITION PLANS of Palestine. In 1947, the UN General Assembly assigned parts of the Negev to the Arabs, but the Arabs rejected the partition. The Negev was assigned to Israel in the 1948 partition of Palestine, and Egypt invaded in the opening days of the first ARAB–ISRAEL WAR. With the conclusion of that war by armistice agreement, the Negev remained part of Israel. A nuclear reactor was built in the 1950s near Dimona. The late 1940s and early 1950s brought hundreds of thousands of immigrants to Israel; with an aggressive settlement program, the Negev reached a population of more than 250,000 by the 1980s, mostly of Oriental Jews (Edot ha-Mizrah)—that is, those from the North African and other Muslim countries.

BIBLIOGRAPHY

BRAWER, MOSHE. *Atlas of the Middle East.* New York, 1988.
HUREWITZ, J. C. *The Struggle for Palestine.* New York, 1950, 1976.
SACHAR, HOWARD M. *A History of Israel.* New York, 1982.

Elizabeth Thompson

Neo-Destour Party

See Destour Party

Nerses   [1837–1884]

Patriarch of the Eastern Orthodox Church in Istanbul.

Nerses was born to an Armenian family, the Varzhabedians, in the Khaskugh (Hasköy) neighborhood of Istanbul during the time of the Ottoman Empire. After five years as a teacher at a local school, he was ordained a priest and was elected patriarch of Constantinople in 1873.

During negotiations ending the Russo–Ottoman War of 1877/78, Nerses went to San Stefano and asked Russia to support the establishment of an independent state of Armenia. He was instrumental in establishing a local network of schools that helped spread a common Armenian culture within the Ottoman Empire.

BIBLIOGRAPHY

WALTER, CHRISTOPHER J. *Armenia: The Survival of a Nation.* New York, 1980.

David Waldner

Nesin, Nüsret Aziz   [1915–]

Turkish playwright, novelist, short story writer, and journalist.

Nesin was born in Istanbul, where he attended military high school and college until 1939. He worked as a journalist in Turkey in the 1940s, joining the leftist daily *Tan* in 1945, just before it was closed down by an anticommunist mob. He began writing novels and plays in the 1950s and quickly became known for his satirical style. He is considered by many the best Turkish humorist of recent years. He cofounded *Karikatür,* a humor magazine, in 1958. Since then, this prolific author has written dozens of short stories, several novels, and volumes of poetry, memoirs, and travel accounts. In the late 1980s, he served as chairman of the Turkish Writers Syndicate.

Nesin was an innovative playwright and was among the few to experiment with the theater of the absurd in the 1950s; he went on to write the leading plays of the 1970s. These included the antiwar play *The War between the Whistlers; Brushers;* and *Yasar, Neither Dead nor Alive.*

BIBLIOGRAPHY

ŞENER, SEVDA. "Contemporary Turkish Drama." In *The Transformation of Turkish Culture,* ed. by Günsel Renda and C. Max Kortepeter. Princeton, N.J., 1986.

Elizabeth Thompson

Nesselrode, Karl Robert von   [1780–1862]

Diplomat and chancellor of the Russian Empire, 1844–1862.

Karl Robert von Nesselrode was born in Lisbon, where his father, Wilhelm, was Russia's ambassador to Portugal. It was not at all uncommon for a German Roman Catholic from Westphalia to accept service with a foreign power. Karl's mother, née Gontard, belonged to a bourgeois, Protestant family from Frankfurt am Main. Karl was baptized an Anglican and, throughout his life, even when chancellor of the Russian Empire, held to that faith.

In 1796, Karl graduated from a gymnasium in Berlin and, through his father's influence, obtained an appointment as a Russian naval midshipman. Transferring to the army, he attracted the attention and patronage of Czar Paul I. After the czar's assassination in 1801, Nesselrode entered the diplomatic corps, beginning sixty-one years of service to the czars Alexander I, Nicholas I, and Alexander II. In 1811, Alexander I appointed him secretary of state without portfolio. By 1816, he was first secretary of state for foreign affairs. He became vice-chancellor in 1829 and served as chancellor of the Russian Empire from 1844 until his retirement, just before his death in 1862.

Nesselrode has always incurred Russian nationalist criticism because of his sympathy for Great Britain and because he remained a Westerner. It is certainly true that he believed that Russia ought to cooperate closely with Britain, especially with regard to any potential partition of the Ottoman Empire.

When the Russo–Turkish War of 1828/29 led to freedom for Greece, the Nationalist party censured Nesselrode because in deference to Britain, the triumphant Russians desisted from seizing Constantinople and the Turkish Straits (Bosporus and Dardanelles). When Mohammed Ali of Egypt fought to break free of Turkish suzerainty from 1830 to 1833, many Russians feared that Egypt might become a French satellite. Nevertheless, from Nesselrode's viewpoint, the crisis ended satisfactorily when the Treaty of HUNKÂR-ISKELESI (1833) barred any nation hostile to Russia from passing through the Dardanelles into the Black Sea. When Muhammad Ali again threatened Turkey from 1839 to 1841 with French support, the London Straits Conventions of 1840/41 satisfied Nesselrode, since they closed the Straits to foreign warships while the Ottoman Empire was at peace.

In 1847, Nesselrode offered to transfer to British protection all expatriate Russian Jews in Palestine whose exit visas had expired. This made possible a great growth in British influence in Palestine by transferring an undetermined number of diplomatic "protégés" to British status.

In 1850, Czar Nicholas I revived old Russian claims as protector of all Greek Orthodox Christians in the Ottoman Empire. Nesselrode blundered when he assumed that Britain would tolerate threats to Ottoman sovereignty as long as Britain and Russia profited equally by the demise of "the sick man of Europe." As late as 1853, Nesselrode still opposed the use of force. The advent of the CRIMEAN WAR (1853–1856), however, represented the ruin of Nesselrode's policy. The Treaty of Paris (1856) neutralized the Black Sea, depriving Russia of its only warm-water naval bases in southeastern Europe.

After that debacle, Nesselrode lost his position at the foreign ministry to the Russian nationalist Aleksandr Mikhailovich, Prince Gorchakov. Nesselrode remained chancellor of the empire until his retirement.

BIBLIOGRAPHY

INGLE, HAROLD N. *Nesselrode and the Russian Rapprochement with Britain, 1836–1844.* Berkeley, Calif., 1976.
PURYEAR, VERNON JOHN. *England, Russia, and the Straits Question.* Berkeley, Calif., 1931.

Arnold Blumberg

Nestorians

The Nestorian, or Assyrian, Church, also known as the Church of the East; heir to the Antiochene tradition of Christianity.

The Nestorian Church was condemned at the Council of Ephesus in 431 C.E. Nestorius, Patriarch of Constantinople (428–431), was also condemned there for appearing to endorse the Antiochene position—which, as doctrinal controversy, preached that in Jesus Christ a divine person and a human person were joined in perfect harmony of action but not in the unity of a single individual. Accepted church doctrine was that Jesus was the perfectly united and undivided individual, both God and human; Mary had given birth to God's Son and was therefore *theotokos* (bearer of God). Nestorius laid greater emphasis on the distinction between Jesus Christ the Son of God and the human Jesus, preferring to call Mary *christotokos,* bearer of the man Jesus, the anointed one.

After the Council of Ephesus deposed Nestorius for heresy, most of the eastern regions of the Church of the East continued to follow the Antiochene position, especially as it spread into Persia, India, Mongolia, and China. The church is erroneously called Nestorian, since Nestorius holds no special status, and he in fact was banished to the Libyan desert in 436.

During the centuries, the fortunes of the church changed as Islam grew in the seventh century and began taking over territory that had been Byzantine (the eastern Roman Empire) and dedicated to the Church of the East. The early Arab caliphs, aided by having no official ties to Byzantium or the Byzantine state church, tolerated Nestorians, who had prominent positions as bankers, merchants, and government officials under the caliphate. Nestorians were also instrumental in transmitting classical culture to the new Arab ruling elites.

The Nestorian Church had spread into Persia and was the chief sponsor of missionary activities in the Turkic- and Mongol-speaking lands of central Asia and China; however, there were periods of persecution and internal conflict. Defections by entire communities to Roman Catholicism also occurred. By 1800, in the Ottoman Empire only small remnants survived, chiefly in Kurdistan. During the nineteenth century, the Nestorians attracted missionaries of various Western churches, such as the American Presbyterians and the Church of England. The nineteenth century was also a period of increased tension between the Nestorians and the Kurds, who organized numerous attacks on Nestorian communities.

During World War I, the Nestorians tried to overthrow Ottoman control. They revolted against the Ottomans in 1915, but the collapse of the Russian Empire and the ensuing Russian Revolution (1917–1921) led to mass flight toward the British lines in Iraq. Some hundred thousand central Asian refugees left their homes, only half of whom succeeded in reaching safety; the rest were ultimately resettled in northern Iraq. At the Versailles Peace Conference after World War I, a group of Nestorians petitioned for an independent Assyrian state in northern Iraq, and the newly established Iraqi kingdom under Faisal granted a degree of autonomy to them in 1921. Their leadership continued to agitate for complete independence, so the Iraqi government ordered them to desist or emigrate. After a series of incidents, their leader, MAR SHIM'UN, was deported and eventually became a citizen of the United States.

The total world population—variously estimated at 100,000 to 300,000—is concentrated in Iraq, Syria, Iran, and the United States (chiefly around Chicago, Illinois).

BIBLIOGRAPHY

BADGER, GEORGE. *The Nestorians and Their Rituals.* London, 1987.

Jon Jucovy

Netanyahu, Benjamin   [1949–   ]

Israeli politician; prime minister, 1996–

Born in Israel, Netanyahu was raised in both Israel and the United States, where his father worked in academia. Netanyahu served in the elite unit Sayeret Matkal in the Israel Defense Forces from 1967 to 1972, where he reached the rank of captain. After the army, he studied business administration at Massachusetts Institute of Technology, where he received his masters degree in 1976. That same year, Netanyahu's older brother, Yonatan, became an Israeli hero when he was killed while directing the rescue of a hijacked Air France airplane in Entebbe, Uganda. Netanyahu worked for several years for a furniture company in Jerusalem. In 1980, he founded an institute on terrorism, which he named after his brother.

From 1982 to 1984, Netanyahu served as consul general in Washington, D.C., and then as the Israeli ambassador to the United Nations until 1988. Netanyahu, who speaks perfect English, is very popular with the American Jewish community. In 1988, he was elected to the Knesset on the Likud list and served as deputy minister of foreign affairs under the Shamir government. In 1990, after the establishment of the right-wing coalition, Netanyahu was appointed deputy minister in the prime minister's office. Netanyahu has been a consistent supporter of reforming the electoral system in Israel, especially the law for direct election of the prime minster, which took place in the national elections in May 1996. In the aftermath of the Labor electoral victory in 1992, Yitzhak Shamir announced he would not seek another term as the Likud party leader, and Netanyahu became the top contender for the spot. In March 1993, he won the primary for the Likud leadership, a position he maintained into May 1996, at which time he was elected prime minister.

Julie Zuckerman

Neturei Karta

Group of ultra-Orthodox Jews who lived in Jerusalem and who, because they oppose Zionism prior to divine redemption, left the Orthodox political party, Agudat Israel, in 1935.

Neturei Karta is Aramaic for "Guardians of the City." They are so named because their ideology rejects not only secular Zionism but all forms of Jewish sovereignty in Palestine prior to divine redemption. They deny all forms of cooperation with political Zionism, which they view as the handmaiden of Satan. They opposed the establishment of the State of Israel in 1948 and Israeli jurisdiction over Jerusalem.

Centered in the Meah Shearim district of Jerusalem, they do not recognize the validity of Israel's existence or participate in its political process. They maintain their own autonomous communal, religious, and educational structures and view themselves as the protectors of the religious nature of the city. The much larger Satmar Hassidic sect is highly supportive of Neturei Karta and often serves as its voice in Jewish communities outside Israel. Both groups have undertaken numerous public demonstrations against Zionism and the State of Israel.

BIBLIOGRAPHY

DOMB, I. *The Transformation: The Case of the Neturei Karta.* London, 1958.
MARMORSTEIN, EMIL. *Heaven at Bay: The Jewish Kulturkampf in the Holy Land.* London, 1969.

Chaim I. Waxman

Neutral Zone

An area shared by Iraq, Saudi Arabia, and Kuwait.

The neutral zone was originally devised because the boundary between Kuwait and Saudi Arabia, de-

marcated by the Anglo–Turkish Convention of 1913, was not ratified due to the outbreak of World War I. When the British government recognized the sovereignty of Ibn Sa'ud in 1915, a compromise was reached on the disputed boundary that involved the establishment of a 2,000 square mile (5,180 sq. km) neutral zone. This was incorporated in the UQAYR CONFERENCE in 1922, which set up a similar neutral zone between Saudi Arabia and Iraq, which abuts the Kuwaiti–Saudi neutral zone. The convention allowed the parties to explore, on an equal basis, the natural resources (presumably petroleum—oil and gas) of the neutral zone but did not address the question of sovereignty ("sharing equal economic rights" in the neutral zone does not necessarily mean that the two parties are co-sovereign in the zone). In fact, each of the two countries administers its part of the zone as if it were a part of its state, but both states share in the oil exploration in the zone. For years political sovereignty was not an issue, because the zone remained isolated and uninhabited. With the expansion of oil and gas exploration, both onshore and offshore, divergent claims propelled the neutral zone to the forefront of regional politics.

Accepted practice has been that Kuwait or Saudi Arabia could grant separate oil concessions to foreign companies for exploration in the neutral zone without prior approval from the other. Neither Kuwait nor Saudi Arabia can sign any binding agreement, however, regarding the entire zone without the other's approval. In July 1965, Kuwait and Saudi Arabia agreed to partition the neutral zone equally, with each of the two states annexing its own part of the zone; however, the two states retained a shared sovereignty arrangement regarding the exploitation of natural resources. The status of the neutral zone did not change after the 1990 GULF CRISIS.

BIBLIOGRAPHY

BAHARNA, HUSAIN AL-. *The Arabian Gulf States.* Beirut, 1975.

Emile A. Nakhleh

Nevruz

Ottoman Turkish literary journal.

Established and edited by Halid Ziya Uşaklıgil, Tevfik Nevzad, and Bıçakçızade Hakkı in 1884, *Nevruz* (Persian New Year's Day) was originally published in Istanbul but soon became the first and most important literary magazine in İzmir. In addition to contributions from Turkish writers, *Nevruz* regularly featured translations from French, Arab, and Farsi-language literature.

David Waldner

New Order

See Nizam-i Cedit

News and Newspapers

Established in the mid-nineteenth century in the Middle East, the number of newspapers expanded rapidly in the twentieth century.

The Earliest Newspapers

Egypt. 1824. *Al-Waqa'i al-Misriya* (really a gazette, and partly in Turkish).

Turkey. 1831. *Takvim-i Vekayi* (the first within Turkey).

Iran. 1837. *Akhbar-i Vaqayi.*

Algeria. 1847. *Al-Mubashir.*

Lebanon. 1858. *Hadiqat al-Akhbar.*

Syria (Damascus). 1865. *Suriya.*

Iraq. 1869. *Al-Zawra.*

Tunis. 1860. Al-Ra'id al-Tunisi.

Arabia (Mecca). 1908. *Hijaz.*

Newspapers Current in 1994

Afghanistan. 16 principal daily papers. *Anis* (founded 1927), issued in Dari and Pashtu, has a circulation of 23,000.

Algeria. 6 dailies in French, or Arabic and French. *Al-Moudjahid* (circulation 390,000) was founded in 1965.

Bahrain. 5 principal dailies, some in English. *Akhbar al-Khalij* has a circulation of 22,000.

Egypt. 17 principal dailies. The government owns 51 percent of each major paper. *Al-Ahram,* founded in 1875 by Lebanese immigrants, has a circulation of 900,000 and is international in scope. *Al-Akhbar* (founded 1952) is second in size with a circulation of about 800,000.

Iran. 10 principal dailies. Under the Shah, strong censorship prevailed. During the Islamic Revolution many papers closed, but in 1994 a more liberal attitude prevails as long as nothing antithetical to Islam is printed. The Velayat-i Faqih controls the two principal newspapers, *Kayhan* and *Ettela'at.*

Iraq. 7 chief dailies. *Al-Thawra* (founded 1968), the principal paper, is the organ of the ruling Ba'th party and has a circulation of 250,000.

Israel. 11 Hebrew dailies. According to a Gallup poll, over 85 percent of adults read a paper every day. The largest are *Yediot Aharonot* (circulation 180,000) and *Ma'ariv* (circulation 150,000). The *Jerusalem Post* is the English-language daily. In Gaza and the West Bank the largest Arabic daily is *al-Quds* (circulation 50,000). *Al-Nihau* (circulation 2,500) is pro-Jordanian. The pro-Fath *al-Fajr* and the leftist *al-Sha'b* closed due to financial difficulties in 1993.

Jordan. 5 principal dailies, including one in English. *Al-Ra'y* (founded 1971) has the largest circulation at 80,000.

Kuwait. 7 major dailies. *Al-Qabas* (founded 1972) has a circulation of 110,000. The *Kuwait Times* (founded 1963) is an influential English-language paper.

Lebanon. Before the Civil War (1975–1976), Lebanon had the liveliest and freest press of the entire Middle East. In 1994, 40 dailies are issued. *Al-Nahar* (founded 1933) has the largest circulation at about 85,000, followed by *al-Anwar* (founded 1959) and *al-Liwa* (founded 1963), each with a circulation of about 75,000.

Libya. 1 daily, *al-Fajr al-Jadid* (founded 1969), with a circulation of 40,000.

Morocco. 11 dailies in Rabat and Casablanca. The Istiqlal party's *al-Alam* (founded 1946) is the largest and arguably the most influential (circulation 100,000). *Le Matin du Sahara,* issued in French and Arabic in Casablanca, has a circulation of 100,000.

Oman. 1 Arabic and 2 English daily newspapers. *Al-Watan* (founded 1971) has a circulation of over 23,000.

Qatar. 4 dailies. Chief are *al-Arab* (founded 1972), with a circulation of 25,000, and *al-Sharq* (founded 1985). The *Gulf Times* (founded 1978) is an important paper in English.

Saudi Arabia. 10 dailies. *Al-Riyadh* has the largest circulation, up to 140,000. *Arab News,* issued in Jidda, is the largest English-language paper of the Middle East, with a circulation of 110,000.

Sudan. 10 dailies prior to the 1989 coup. *Al-Ayyam* (founded 1953) was the most influential, circulation 60,000. In 1994, the main dailies, both under government control, were *al-Sudan al-Hadith* and *Inqadh al-Watan.*

Syria. 10 major dailies, all under government control. *Al-Ba'th,* the organ of the Ba'th Arab Socialist party, is the primary paper. Its circulation is 65,000.

Tunisia. 6 dailies. The largest in circulation, 90,000, is *al-Sabah* (founded 1951).

Turkey is fertile ground for journalism. About 40 principal dailies are issued. *Sabah,* published in Istanbul, is the most popular with a circulation of 600,000. *Milliyet* (founded 1950) and *Cumhuriyet* (founded 1924) are counted among the most influential of the Islamic world. In general the Turkish press flourishes and represents various shades of political opinion; nevertheless, severe censorship is sometimes applied to the owners of influential papers.

United Arab Emirates. Dailies *al-Ittihad* (founded 1972) of Abu Dhabi and the *Khaleej Times* (founded 1978) of Dubai have circulations of 58,000 and 55,000.

Yemen's chief paper, *al-Rabi Ashar min Uktubar,* is issued in Aden and has a circulation of about 20,000.

Newspapers require presses, a reading public, and (in the Middle East) government approval. These conditions have been met at varying times in different areas of the Middle East. Although printing was available in Constantinople (now Istanbul) and Syria early in the eighteenth century, it was not until the mid-nineteenth century that true newspapers were established. American missionaries and their educational efforts were important in preparing the way for the press. The first true Arabic newspaper, *Hadiqat al-Akhbar,* was established by Khalil al-Khuri, a Christian, in Lebanon in 1858. Other papers, founded by Muslims and Christians, soon followed. Restrictive Ottoman policies later in the nineteenth century led some publishers to emigrate, and newspapers were established wherever Syrian/Lebanese Arabs went. New York, Philadelphia, and Boston—as well as several smaller U.S. cities—and cities in South America had Arabic newspapers. At least ten Arabic newspapers were printed in New York City, including *al-Ayyam* (1898), *al-Dalil* (1910), and *al-Saih* (1912). *Fatat Bustun* was published in Boston. These papers provided a combination of news of Syria/Lebanon, local social events, and literary notices. Many promoted Arabic as a means of ordinary and literary expression. To varying degrees these *Mahjar* (emigrant) papers were a reflection of the political factions of the homeland.

Toward the end of the nineteenth century, the Ottoman government restricted the freedom of the press in its Arab dependencies; however, after constitutional reforms were enacted in 1908, the number of newspapers in the Arab world increased rapidly. This steady increase was also connected with a newly expanding literacy rate in the countries, as well as improvements in existing technology and expansion of the economic infrastructure.

The origin of the Hebrew-language press can be traced to the publication in 1750 of *Kehillat Musar,* which appeared irregularly and primarily published literary articles. The first paper to resemble a modern news publication was *Ha Maggid* (1856). The advent of the Zionist movement gave a boost to the creation and spread of Hebrew newspapers, especially through the efforts of Eliezer Ben-Yehuda to revive the Hebrew language. As Jewish immigration to Palestine increased, so did the number of newspapers, many reflecting the views of the various Zionist movements.

In Iran, the first newspaper appeared in Tehran in 1837; the press underwent major expansion after 1906. With the coming of the Islamic Revolution in 1979, there was a period of major growth in the range of views reflected and the number of papers published.

The first Turkish newspaper, *Takvin-i Vekaya,* was published in Istanbul in 1831. When the Republic of Turkey adopted the Turkish (i.e., modified Latin) alphabet as part of Mustafa Kemal Atatürk's efforts to modernize the nation, the Turkish press expanded considerably.

State control of the press varies; the freest Arab press is Lebanon's, because of its political history, and to a lesser degree, Morocco's. Israel's newspapers have been characterized by freedom and competitiveness; nevertheless, a form of censorship does exist through restrictions on national security issues. Among the Hebrew press the censorship has been voluntary but has been strained since Israel's invasion of Lebanon. The Arabic press has been used for national security and political purposes by Israel's government. In the areas under the control of the Palestine National Authority (PNA), the Palestinian press has been independent, but it has been pressured by the PNA to present coverage generally favorable to the PNA. In Turkey, meanwhile, the press enjoys constitutional guarantees. In single-party countries such as Iraq and Syria, the press represents the ruling party. The number of papers created in Iran after the overthrow of the Pahlavi regime remains the same; however, the freedom that existed just after the revolution has diminished.

Except for religiously oriented newspapers, the formats of these dailies are similar; they include coverage of international news, local news, social events, and sporting events. The major Turkish and Arabic newspapers devote much space to current Western technology and culture. Because of improvements in education and the value placed on Arabic poetry, some papers carry important literary sections in which poetry, novels, and criticism are presented.

BIBLIOGRAPHY

GEDDES, CHARLES L. *Guide to Reference Books for Islamic Studies.* Denver, Colo., 1985.

KAMALIPOUR, YAHYA R., and HAMID MOWLANA, eds. *Mass Media in the Middle East.* Westport, Conn., 1994.

RUGH, WILLIAM A. *The Arab Press: News Media and Political Process in the Arab World.* 2nd ed. Syracuse, N.Y., 1987.

Bryan Daves
David H. Partington

New Towns Development

See Satellite Cities Development

New Turkey Party

Turkish political party, 1961–1969.

The New Turkey party was established in 1961 after the military coup of 1960 to gain the votes of supporters of the defunct DEMOCRAT PARTY. It had the backing of the NATIONAL UNITY COMMITTEE (NUC) government but failed to gain popular support and was overshadowed by the JUSTICE PARTY. It gained 14 percent of the vote and 65 seats in the election of 1961 and participated in coalition governments over the next four years, but its electoral support eroded rapidly, and it did not compete in elections after 1969.

BIBLIOGRAPHY

LANDAU, J. M. "Turkey." In *Political Parties in the Middle East and North Africa,* ed. by F. Tachau. Westport, Conn., 1994.

Frank Tachau

New Valley Development Scheme

Egyptian land-reclamation project.

The New Valley Development Scheme is a project to reclaim for agriculture a large expanse of desert land in Egypt's New Valley governorate, which extends from Aswan to the Qattara Depression.

Michael R. Fischbach

New Wafd

Egyptian political party.

The legalization of the New Wafd under Sadat was the most important sign of the return to political life of the most important parties and movements of the pre-1952 era. Born out of the turmoil of the colonial confrontation with the British, the original WAFD was the symbol of liberal nationalism. The New Wafd asserted its continuity with this past in the person of its party leader, the venerable Wafdist Fu'ad Serrageddine.

Raymond William Baker

Nezam al-Saltaneh, Mirza Hoseyn Qoli Khan Mafi   [1832–1908]

Iranian politician.

Descended from the Mafi tribe, which originated in Luristan, Nezam al-Saltaneh entered government service at the provincial governor's office of Bushehr in 1852. In 1874, he was appointed governor of Yazd and awarded the title Sa'd al-Molk. After holding several consecutive governorships, he received the title Nezam al-Saltaneh and was appointed governor of Arabestan, Bakhtyari, and Chahar Mahal. In 1896, he was named minister of justice but resigned because of disagreements with Prime Minister Ayn al-Dowleh. When Amin al-Soltan was reinstated as premier in 1898, Nezam al-Saltaneh headed the Bureau of Taxation. After 1900, he took up residence in Tehran and wrote his memoirs. After holding several governorships, he was appointed prime minister in 1908, lost his son in the same year, resigned from his post, and died a few months later.

Neguin Yavari

Nezzar, Khaled   [1937–   ]

Algerian general and defense minister.

A veteran of the Algerian War of Independence (1954–1962), Nezzar continued his military career. He was stationed along the Moroccan border during the 1963 Moroccan–Algerian War and commanded a battalion sent to Egypt in solidarity after the Arab–Israel War (1967). Nezzar's military education included studies in the Soviet Union and France. He was appointed to the Central Committee of the Front de Libération Nationale (FLN; National Liberation Front) in 1979 and promoted to general and assistant chief of staff in 1984. Nezzar received particular publicity as Algeria's first minister of defense since 1965 (a portfolio usually held by presidents), continuing his pursuit of the military's modernization and quelling the destabilizing October 1988 riots. Faced with the prospect of an Islamic Salvation Front (FIS) government, Nezzar and others deposed President Chadli Benjedid in January 1992 and established the High Security Council (HSC). Given his command of the military, he is regarded as the chief power within the HSC.

BIBLIOGRAPHY

"Le haut conseil de sécurité." *Le Monde,* 14 January 1992.

Phillip C. Naylor

Nhaisi, Elia   [1890–1918]

Zionist pioneer who mobilized the Libyan Jews in Tripoli.

Nhaisi was born in Tripoli, Libya, to a poor Jewish family. He earned his living as a photographer, sold photographic postcards, and was the Tripolitanian correspondent for the Florentine Jewish weekly, *La Settimana Israelitica,* later known as *Israel.* In 1913, he established the Jewish Cultural Club and, in 1914, the Talmud Torah evening school for modern Hebrew. In 1916, he founded the Zionist Club, *Circolo Sion,* which by 1923 evolved into a Libyan Zionist organization. His movement was supported by the community rabbis but opposed by the "Italianized" president and community council members, who championed Italianized assimilation for the Jews. The Italian Jewish press was his staunch supporter, and his Zionist group prevailed. Nhaisi died after a short illness at the age of twenty-eight.

BIBLIOGRAPHY

DE FELICE, RENZO. *Ebrei in un paese arabo: Gli Ebrei nella Libia contemporanea tra colonialismo, nazionalismo arabo e sionismo (1835–1970).* Bologna, 1978.
ROUMANI, MAURICE M. "Zionism and Social Change in Libya at the Turn of the Century." *Studies in Zionism* 8, no. 1 (1987).

Maurice M. Roumani

Niavaran

Luxurious, elegant Iranian palace.

Situated on the slopes of north Tehran, Niavaran is a reminder of a 2,500-year-old tradition of Iranian monarchical rule. In 1965 the Pahlavi family took up residence in the palace, the first part of which was built under the Qajar kings and the second under the auspices of Mohammed Reza Shah Pahlavi and Queen Farah. It has been converted since the Iranian Revolution of 1979 into a museum.

Roshanak Malek

Nicholas I [1796–1855]

Russian czar, 1825–1855.

Born Nikolai Pavlovich, Nicholas succeeded his brother Alexander I in 1825. Nicholas immediately lent his support to the Greek revolt (Greek War of Independence, 1821–1830) and fought a brief but successful war against the Ottoman Empire from 1828 to 1829. In 1832, after the Ottomans had been defeated by Muhammad Ali Pasha, viceroy of

Egypt, at Konya, Nicholas responded to the sultan's request for aid and dispatched troops to Constantinople (now Istanbul), seat of the Ottoman Empire. Nicholas subsequently concluded the Treaty of HUNKÂR-ISKELESI in 1833, which immeasurably strengthened Russia's influence in the Ottoman Empire relative to the other European powers. In the 1840s, Nicholas took an interest in the Greek Orthodox community of the holy places in Palestine, and he began competing with France for influence there. In 1853, the Ottomans rejected Russian demands concerning the holy places, and the two countries went to war. Nicholas miscalculated the determination of the European states to protect the empire from Russian incursions, and France and Britain entered the war on the side of the Ottomans. Nicholas died in 1855 and did not live to see the Russian defeat in the Crimean War. He is credited with describing the Ottoman Empire as "the sick man of Europe."

BIBLIOGRAPHY

ANDERSON, M. S. *The Eastern Question.* London, 1966.
SHAW, STANFORD, and EZEL KURAL SHAW. *History of the Ottoman Empire and Modern Turkey,* vol. 2. New York, 1977.

Zachary Karabell

Nile River

The longest river in Africa and, probably, the world.

The Nile (in Arabic, al-Bahr or Bahr al-Nil) dominates the landscape of northeastern Africa as well as the lives and livelihood of its people. Measured from its remotest source in Tanzania to the mouths of its delta (120 miles/193 km wide) at the Mediterranean Sea, the Nile river is 4,187 miles (6,700

The Nile river delta, 1948. (D.W. Lockhard)

A felucca sailing on the Nile in Upper (southern) Egypt. (D.W. Lockhard)

km) long. It flows through Uganda, Sudan, and Egypt. Its waters drain a basin having an area exceeding one million square miles (2.6 million sq. km). About twelve miles (20 km) south of Cairo, the Nile enters the delta, which in ancient times had seven mouths but today has two (each about 146 miles/235 km long). For Egypt and Sudan, the river is almost the sole source of drinking water and irrigation, and their inhabitants have always been intensely concerned with the utilization of its waters. The delta region has the richest agriculture, including Egypt's cotton industry.

Some sixty-eight billion cubic yards (52 billion cu. m) of water flow through the Nile yearly. Most of the Nile's water comes from the Ethiopian highlands, via the Blue Nile and the Atbara—the flow varying widely over the course of each year. From the melting of winter snows in Ethiopia, the waters rise during the summer and reach a peak in September. The water entering Sudan and Egypt from Central Africa, via the White Nile, however, is relatively constant throughout the year. Swamps in Sudan and surface evaporation reduce the combined Nile flow considerably.

Ever since humans began raising crops to control their food supply (c. 10,000 B.C.E.), they have tried to harness and channel the Nile flood, using basin irrigation and water-raising devices and, more recently, the perennial irrigation of most land in Egypt and northern Sudan—made possible by such large-scale works as the DELTA BARRAGES and the ASWAN HIGH DAM. As the population grows along its banks (with modernization, industrialization, and urbanization), the quality of the Nile has become degraded by pollution and its discharge has declined markedly.

BIBLIOGRAPHY

HOWELL, P. P., and J. A. ALLAN. *The Nile: Resource Evaluation, Resource Management, Hydropolitics, and Legal Issues.* London, 1990.
HURST, H. E. *The Nile.* London, 1952.
WATERBURY, JOHN. *Hydropolitics of the Nile Valley.* Syracuse, N.Y., 1979.

Arthur Goldschmidt, Jr.

Nimr, Faris   [1856–1951]

Lebanese Christian intellectual, publisher, and journalist who played an important role in popularizing modern science and Western ideas in the Arab East in the late nineteenth century.

A Greek Orthodox from Hasbeya, Lebanon, Faris Nimr was among the first Lebanese to study at the Syrian Protestant College (later renamed the American University of Beirut). He graduated at eighteen and became a tutor in astronomy and mathematics at the college. In 1876, he and fellow Syrian Protestant College graduate Ya'qub SARRUF (1852–1927) began publishing in Beirut a scientific-literary journal called *al-Muqtataf* (The Selection). In 1882, the two editors became embroiled in a fierce controversy over Darwinism that shook the college, where they were still teaching. Their support of Darwinism, articulated in *al-Muqtataf,* put them at odds with the college authorities, and they were dismissed in 1884. They then moved to Egypt, taking their periodical with them. In Cairo, *al-Muqtataf* rapidly developed into a leading opinion maker. Spurred by their success, the two Lebanese expatriates decided in 1889 to found al-MUQATTAM, a pro-British newspaper that promoted free enterprise. Sarruf retained primary responsibility for *al-Muqtataf,* and Nimr concentrated on *al-Muqattam,* which soon became one of the most influential dailies in Egypt.

Faris Nimr is remembered as one of the most prominent members of the early wave of Western-educated Lebanese intellectuals who played a leading role in introducing modern scientific knowledge and positivist ideas into the Arab East. What distinguished Nimr from most of his peers was his wide range of interests (which cut across the scientific-literary divide), his dual career as an intellectual and a publisher, and the remarkable sense of initiative and entrepreneurship that he demonstrated throughout his life, from his creation of *al-Muqtataf* when he was only twenty to his decision to relocate his business to Egypt and create a newspaper there. His writings and activities as a publisher in Cairo ensured that the impact of his ideas was felt much beyond his country of origin. Through *al-Muqattam* in particular, he inspired an entire generation of Arab intellectuals attracted to Western notions of individualism and laissez-faire economic ideas.

BIBLIOGRAPHY

REID, DONALD M. "Syrian Christians, the Rags-to-Riches Story, and Free Enterprise." *International Journal of Middle East Studies* 1 (1970): 358–367.
SHARABI, HISHAM. *Arab Intellectuals and the West*. Baltimore and London, 1970.
TIBAWI, A. L. "The Genesis and Early History of the Syrian Protestant College (Part 2)." *The Middle East Journal* 21, no. 2 (Spring 1967): 199–212.

                                        Guilain P. Denoeux

Nir, Nahum   [1884–1968]

Labor politician and second speaker of the Knesset.

Born in Warsaw, Nahum Nir (originally Rafalkes Nir) practiced law in Saint Petersburg, joining the Po'alei Zion party in 1905 and continuing as secretary of the World Union of Left Po'alei Zion after the movement split in 1920. Arriving in Palestine in 1925, Nir represented his party in the Histadrut and pre-state National Assembly.

A member of the Knesset (Israel's parliament) from 1948 to 1965 representing Ahdut Ha-Avoda-Po'alei Zion, Nir was elected speaker in 1959, a position that he filled for one year. By then Nir was the oldest member of the Knesset.

                                        Zev Maghen

Nissim, Isaac   [1895–1981]

An unofficial leader of Iraqi Jewry in Israel.

Born in Baghdad, Isaac Nissim moved to Jerusalem in 1926. Nissim was elected Sephardic Chief Rabbi of Israel in 1955, a position he held until 1972, although not without controversy. In 1964, he overcame a challenge by those Sephardim who sought to elect Rabbi Ya'acov Moshe Toledano, the politically unaffiliated Chief Rabbi of Tel Aviv. At the time, Nissim was the candidate of the National Religious party.

                                        Chaim I. Waxman

Nixon, Richard Milhous   [1913–1994]

U.S. president, 1969–1974.

Born in Yorba Linda, California, Nixon attended Whittier College and Duke University Law School. After serving in World War II, he was elected to Congress (1946–1950), where he was a member of the House Un-American Activities Committee during the McCarthy era of anti-Communism, then to the U.S. Senate (1950–1952), where he continued his strongly anti-Communist stance. He was selected to run as vice president on the Republican ticket with Dwight D. Eisenhower in 1952 and again in 1956. During the Eisenhower administration, Nixon was given substantive foreign policy missions to fifty-six countries, including the USSR. In 1960, he ran for president but lost to John F. Kennedy. Nixon won the presidency in the 1968 election.

Nixon's Middle East policy was marked by crisis abroad and conflict at home. Abroad, the WAR OF ATTRITION and the ARAB–ISRAEL WAR of 1973 demanded the full attention of the State Department while the U.S. government was still trying to repel the Communists in Vietnam. Nixon's secretary of state, William Rogers, and his national security adviser, Henry Kissinger, pursued separate and often contradictory Middle East policies. With the collapse of the Rogers Plan for Arab–Israeli peace, Kissinger emerged as the dominant adviser, and this was consolidated when he was made secretary of state in 1973.

Under Nixon, the United States sold both Israel and Iran large amounts of miliary equipment, including Phantom jets to Israel. In May 1972, during a visit to Iran, Nixon promised that the United States would sell them an unlimited supply of nonnuclear weapons, and by the end of the Nixon administration, Israel and Iran emerged as the "two pillars" of U.S. policy in the Middle East.

The major crisis of Nixon's administration began with the 1973 Arab–Israel War and the resulting Arab oil embargo by OPEC (the Organization of Petroleum Exporting Countries). This began an escalating spiral of price gouging and inflation that continued into the 1980s in the United States. Nixon attempted to placate the Arab states, especially Saudi Arabia. Until August 1974—when Nixon resigned the presidency—he and Kissinger had to negotiate numerous cease-fires and armistice lines between Israel, Egypt, and Syria. They also visited both Communist China and the USSR, improving relations with both.

In his desire for another term in office, Nixon and his White House staff became involved in a cover-up of their actions involving a break-in at Democratic national headquarters at the Watergate complex. The escalating investigation over this impeachable set of offenses resulted in Nixon's resignation.

BIBLIOGRAPHY

AMBROSE, STEPHEN. *Nixon: The Education of a Politician, 1913–1962.* New York, 1987.
———. *Nixon: 1963–1972.* New York, 1990.
SPIEGEL, STEVEN. *The Other Arab-Israeli Conflict.* Chicago, 1985.

Zachary Karabell

Nizam al-Din, Abd al-Baqi

Syrian politician.

Born in Qamishli, Abd al-Baqi Nizam al-Din served as deputy for this northeastern border town in 1943, 1947, 1949, and 1954. A leader of the Republican Front, Nizam al-Din was appointed minister of agriculture in 1951; of public works and communications in 1955; and of health in 1956.

BIBLIOGRAPHY

Who's Who in the Middle East, 1967–1968.

Charles U. Zenzie

Nizam al-Din, Tawfiq   [1912–   ]

Syrian military officer.

Born to a wealthy Turkish family, Tawfiq Nizam al-Din became army chief of staff in July 1956 but was replaced within months for his campaign against leftist officers. To some observers, this event served to deepen U.S. fears that Syria was moving closer to the Soviet Union.

BIBLIOGRAPHY

SEALE, PATRICK. *The Struggle for Syria: A Study of Post-War Arab Politics, 1945–1958.* London, 1958.

Charles U. Zenzie

Nizam al-Jadid, al-

Regular Egyptian army of the early nineteenth century, established by Muhammad Ali Pasha, consisting of conscripted men trained in the European style.

In 1805, as soon as MUHAMMAD ALI Pasha gained some independence from the Ottoman Empire and consolidated his position as *wali* (provincial governor) in Cairo, he began conscripting skilled laborers to work on government projects. His model was the conscript armed force instituted by Ottoman Sultan Selim III. The existing Egyptian military force, to which the Mamluks (powerful landlords) sent their own retainers for use by the state, was then replaced by 1822 with a new, drafted, regular army called *al-nizam al-jadid.*

The first four thousand men called up came from Upper Egypt. Those from the region between Manfalut and Qina were assembled at a training camp near Farshut, and those from the region between Qina and Aswan were gathered in Aswan. Their initial tour of duty was set at three years. Their replacements were selected from lists of prospective draftees drawn up by the officers in charge of the training camps as part of a comprehensive system of village census taking. Conscripts were drilled according to European procedures and organized into defined regiments, with a centralized command structure to supervise the distribution of arms, clothing, and other equipment. State officials even orchestrated a propaganda campaign in support of the new army, urging prominent religious scholars to write treatises sanctioning these innovative practices.

Regular infantry and artillery units were complemented by a flotilla of warships built along European lines in government yards. Both the new army and navy played major roles in the Egyptian campaigns in the Aegean Sea and Syria after 1824. Both were also strictly limited by Britain after Muhammad Ali's capitulation to the European powers in 1838. Thus ended this army.

BIBLIOGRAPHY

LAWSON, FRED H. *The Social Origins of Egyptian Expansionism during the Muhammad Ali Period.* New York, 1992.
MARSOT, AFAF LUTFI AL-SAYYID. *Egypt in the Reign of Muhammad Ali.* Cambridge, U.K., 1986.

Fred H. Lawson

Nizam-i Cedit

Turkish for "new order"; Ottoman government reforms in the seventeenth and eighteenth centuries.

The term *nizam-i cedit* was used by Ottoman statesmen during the seventeenth and eighteenth centuries to designate various administrative and organizational reforms. The term, however, became identified in particular with the efforts of Selim III (ruled 1789–1807) to establish a new, regular, European-style infantry corps. This was a marked departure from the policies of previous eighteenth-century reforming rulers, who modernized only relatively small, technical branches of the Ottoman armed forces (artillery, bombardiers, and navy) but who, because of opposition by the janissaries, stopped short of modernizing the infantry, then the most important element in any army. Indeed, Selim's attempt was regarded by contemporaries as so revolutionary and daring that the term *nizam-i cedit* came to be identified with his entire reign and all his other policies.

The immediate impetus for the establishment of the Nizam-i Cedit Corps was the poor performance of the Ottoman armies, and above all the janissaries, in the most recent of the Russo–Ottoman Wars, this one with Russia and Austria (1787–1792). The beginnings of the new corps were modest and experimental. In March 1792, 100 men were recruited for the new unit, which was instructed, at first, by Russian and Austrian prisoners of war. Later, British, French, Swedish, and Italian instructors replaced the Russians and Austrians. Fear of janissary opposition forced Selim to quarter the new unit at Levent Çiftlik, a safe 10-mile (16-km) distance from the capital, Istanbul, and to recruit additional troops slowly and cautiously. By 1799, the Nizam-i Cedit consisted of a single regiment, numbering some 2,500 men, organized and trained on the French model. To provide for the expenses of the new corps, the New Treasury (İrad-i Cedit) was created.

In 1799, when the New Treasury had accumulated sufficient funds, and to counter the challenge of Napoléon Bonaparte's invasion of Egypt, the Nizam-i Cedit was greatly expanded. Provincial governors in Anatolia were ordered to recruit new regiments, and new barracks were established at Üsküdar and Kadiköy, the Asiatic suburbs of the capital. By 1807, the new corps had a total strength of some 30,000 men, largely consisting of Anatolian recruits. Selim's attempts to raise men in the Balkans were foiled by the local notables, who had strongly opposed the new corps. Most of the *ulama* (Islamic scholars) also criticized the new project as contradictory to the principles of Islam.

Due to the large influx of Anatolian recruits, the new regiments were poorly trained and disciplined. Their men often clashed with the population of Istanbul and with the janissaries, leading to the growing unpopularity of the new corps. The opposition of the janissaries was particularly constant and stubborn. They refused to take part in campaigns alongside the new troops. The Nizam regiments participated, therefore, only in some minor engagements against the French in Egypt and Palestine, and in pursuit of local bandits. In these operations, the new troops proved themselves to be far superior to the janissaries.

Rebellion in the Balkans and a new war with Russia, which erupted in 1806, created severe economic crises and extended periods of famine in the empire's principal towns. Popular unrest was skillfully directed by the janissaries and the conservative *ulama* against the reforms. The populace in Istanbul, for example, widely believed that the suppression of the Nizam and the New Treasury would ease the burden of taxation. Faced with mounting difficulties, Selim proved to lack courage and confidence in his abilities to maintain the reforms, and he exhibited a growing tendency of yielding to conservative demands.

On May 25, 1807, the janissary auxiliary (*yamak*) troops mutinied; they were soon joined by janissaries, *ulama,* religious students, and others who opposed the reforms. Fearing a wide-scale civil war, Selim ordered the dissolution of the new corps. On May 29, he was deposed and, a year later, assassinated. The conservative factions hunted down and killed many officers and men of the new corps, and political leaders associated with it. The new barracks, factories, and schools identified with the Nizam were burned down or damaged. Conservatism and reaction won a decisive victory. Still, the experience and hopes generated by Selim's experiment, and especially his tragic fall, made a great impact on Ottoman society, and their memory continued to live on. For some time thereafter, the very term *nizam-i cedit,* or simply *nizam,* was popularly applied to any European-style military reform effort, even when its official designation was entirely different.

BIBLIOGRAPHY

LEVY, AVIGDOR. "Military Reform and the Problem of Centralization in the Ottoman Empire in the Eighteenth Century." *Middle Eastern Studies* 18 (1982): 227–249.
SHAW, STANFORD J. *Between Old and New: The Ottoman Empire under Sultan Selim III, 1789–1807.* Cambridge, Mass., 1971.

Avigdor Levy

Nizamiye Courts

Secular Ottoman courts.

The Nizamiye (or Nizami, meaning regulation) courts were organized in 1869 by Minister of Justice Ahmed CEVDET to decide cases under new criminal and commercial law codes. The new court system extended from the lowest regional level, the *nahiye,* through the *kaza, sanjak,* and *vilayet* or provincial levels. It was capped by the Council of Judicial Regulations (Divan-i Ahkam-i Adliye) in Constantinople (now Istanbul), which was the final court of appeal. After 1876, the courts were administered by the Court of Cassation (Temyiz Mahkemesi) in the ministry of justice. Under Abdülhamit II, Minister of Justice Küçük Sait Paşa introduced the institution of public defender in the Nizamiye courts and revised the commercial and criminal codes. A law school founded in 1878 produced one hundred graduates a year who staffed the expanding Nizamiye system.

Despite underfunding and overcrowding, the court system was generally considered efficient. Because of this, and the fact that the new law codes were prepared with the counsel of religious legal scholars, the *ulama*'s opposition to the Nizamiye was diminished, even though the new courts challenged the jurisdiction of *Shari'a*, or religious, courts.

Elizabeth Thompson

Nizip, Battle of

Town, now in southern Turkey, where Egyptian forces defeated the Ottoman army on June 24, 1839, prompting the European powers to take steps to push Egypt out of Syria.

Throughout the spring of 1839, the Ottoman Empire encouraged unrest along the border between Anatolia and its former Syrian provinces, which had been captured in 1831 by the armies of Egypt's Muhammad Ali Pasha—who named his son Ibrahim Pasha to govern them. Ibrahim at first refrained from responding to Ottoman activities, but was forced to mobilize when the Ottomans struck south across the Euphrates river in June. The two armies clashed at the town of Nizip, resulting in a crushing defeat of the Ottomans. Ibrahim immediately advanced north toward Konya, halting only when his father, who was worried about the impact that this move might have on regional diplomacy, ordered him not to go beyond the Taurus mountains. Meanwhile, an Ottoman fleet that had been sent to attack Alexandria in Egypt voluntarily surrendered to Muhammad Ali.

At the height of the crisis, the Ottoman sultan died. His successor had little choice but to enter negotiations with the victorious Egyptians. Egypt demanded control of the southern Turkish districts of Diyarbakir and Urfa—which commanded the primary trade routes between Syria and northern Iraq. The British government interpreted these demands as a direct threat to British interests in the region. France, on the other hand, signaled that it supported Egypt. Britain eventually persuaded Russia, Austria, and Prussia to agree to cooperate in expelling the Egyptian army from Syria, a commitment which was codified in the LONDON CONVENTION of July 1840.

British warships then bombarded the Mediterranean ports of Beirut and Acre, forcing Ibrahim to withdraw his troops from all of Syria. Muhammad Ali returned the captured Ottoman fleet in exchange for recognition as the hereditary ruler of Egypt, which the Ottoman sultan granted on February 13, 1841. France returned to the European concert in July 1841, signing the STRAITS CONVENTION with the other great powers.

BIBLIOGRAPHY

MARSOT, AFAF LUTFI AL-SAYYID. *Egypt in the Reign of Muhammad Ali.* Cambridge, U.K., 1986.
RODKEY, FREDERICK S. *The Turco-Egyptian Question in the Relations of England, France, and Russia, 1832–1841.* New York, 1924.

Fred H. Lawson

Nizwa

A town in northern Oman, also called Nazwa.

Nizwa is the principal town in the relatively fertile area of northern Oman between the Hajar moun-

Guards at the citadel of Nizwa. (Richard Bulliet)

tains and the Rub al-Khali desert. In the mid-eighth century, it became the principal seat of the IBADIYYA imamate, established by a moderate branch of the Kharijites to which the majority of Oman's population still belongs. Nizwa is noted for its silversmiths.

BIBLIOGRAPHY

ALLEN, CALVIN, H., JR. *Oman: The Modernization of the Sultanate.* Boulder, Colo., 1987.

Malcolm C. Peck

Njeym, Jean   [1915–1971]

Lebanese army officer and commander.

Born to a Maronite family in the village of Kfertay (Kisrawan) in 1915, Njeym attended the Christian Brothers and Marists schools in Beirut and Sidon. In 1935 he began his military career by attending the military academy in Lebanon (al-Madrasa al-Harbiyya), where he was hired as a military trainer for graduating officers. In 1945, year of the creation of the Lebanese army, he was appointed director of the military academy. Between 1946 and 1962, Njeym joined army intelligence and in 1962 was appointed commander of the Biqaʿ region. In 1966, he was appointed commander for southern Lebanon and western sector until 1968. At that time, he was promoted to general and succeeded Colonel Emile al-Bustani as commander in chief of the Lebanese army. On July 24, 1971, Njeym died in a helicopter crash. He is the recipient of several Lebanese, Arab, and foreign medals.

BIBLIOGRAPHY

Arab Information Center, Beirut.

George E. Irani

NLF

See under National Liberation Front

Nokta

Turkish weekly news magazine.

Nokta first appeared in February of 1983. Its founder, Ercan Arıklı, had planned to begin publishing a weekly news magazine in Turkey in 1978, but did not feel the political environment was appropriate until five years later. Despite this circumspection,

Nokta was ordered by the government to stop publishing in August of 1983, although the order was rescinded soon afterward.

Nokta is explicitly modeled on Western news magazines. In addition to political and economic issues, the magazine covers social and cultural affairs. It attempts to cover subjects neglected by the daily press. Its circulation has increased from about 25,000 copies in 1983 to 60,000 in the early 1990s.

BIBLIOGRAPHY

The Middle East and North Africa 1992, 38th ed. London, 1992.

David Waldner

Nomadism

A pattern of mobility within a well-defined territory, usually seasonal, involving a society and its basic livelihood.

Nomads in the Middle East have attracted the attention of travelers and scholars for millennia, and in the 1990s they continue to be viewed as special, but threatened, people. Everywhere, nomadic societies find that their traditional patterns of movement are in jeopardy, and many are under pressure to settle permanently. Those who continue to be nomadic have found ingenious ways to sustain customary cherished patterns and to adopt new ones.

For many, the term *nomad* conjures up an image of a desert-dwelling bedouin who rides camels, raises herds of domesticated animals (usually sheep and goats), and lives in black goat-hair tents. "Nomad,"

Desert bedouins. (Richard Bulliet)

however, may refer to a person with no fixed permanent residence who moves from place to place in pursuit of a livelihood, and, according to this definition, individuals such as migrant workers, gypsies, and even some academics could be included. Here, "nomad" refers to a member of a pastoral society.

Nomads are found throughout the Middle East, but in no country do they comprise a large proportion of the total citizenry. They are often part of larger ethnic and national-minority groups, and their territories sometimes cross international borders. Almost all are Muslims. As pastoralists, they raise domesticated animals—usually sheep, goats, and/or camels but also horses, mules, and donkeys—for their livelihood. They usually occupy ecologically marginal territory that cannot sustain year-round or permanent grazing for their animals, hence the reliance on movement (nomadism) from place to place and on pack animals (camels, mules, donkeys, horses) or, increasingly after the 1960s, motorized vehicles for transport. Nomads move between warmer and cooler regions, lower and higher altitudes, or wetter and drier zones, or some combination of all these. Some nomads depend on seasonal and climatic changes and move accordingly, while others do not. Some nomads in unpredictable ecozones range widely, relying flexibly on movement to take them to locations where water and vegetation are reported. Parts of the deserts of Saudi Arabia go for years without rainfall, for example, and the bedouin there rely on wide networks of communication for news of rainfall and on camels or vehicles to move them long distances in relatively short periods of time. Other nomads have more predictable sources of water and vegetation and move between two or more territories on a seasonal basis, sometimes using the same territories for many years at a stretch. Some nomads rely on the same economic patterns all year, while others have more mixed economies, such as sheep-and-goat pastoralism for part of the year and agriculture (grains, fruits, especially dates), hired transport, or smuggling for the rest. In the latter part of the twentieth century, nomads often incorporate wage labor in agriculture or in towns and cities for part of the year. In Saudi Arabia, where the bedouin form a crucial part of the National Guard (in a country lacking a large standing army), many bedouin men are regularly away from their families for a month or more each year. By the 1990s, most Middle Eastern nomads had mixed economies based on animal husbandry, agriculture, wage labor, weaving, and other craft production. Changes in the size and composition of the local social groups of nomads reflect these differing demands and patterns.

Most nomadic pastoralists in the Middle East live in tents, often black in color, constructed of felt (pressed fibers) or woven goat hair, and supported by wooden poles. Some nomads construct reed or branch huts, especially where the heat of the sun is severe. Canvas tents, especially for the poor, are also in use. Possessions are limited in size, weight, and number by the peoples' and their animals' ability to transport them. Nomads produce many of these possessions themselves from the wool, hair, and skin of their animals and from resources they gather in their diverse environments.

Middle Eastern nomads rely on notions of kinship and descent and on political and economic ties to form their social groups. Almost all nomads are tribally organized; they are part of sociopolitical groups represented by leaders who mediate between their groups and the wider society (competing tribal groups, local economic elites, government agents, merchants, and religious leaders). In some cases (the Kurds of Iran, Iraq, and Turkey, for example), tribal organization includes millions of people. In other cases (such as the Komachi of central Iran), a tribe can be a small group of only several hundred people (see TRIBALISM). Most tribal people are part of a series of nested groups: a local kinship-based group, a (patri) lineage, a subtribe, a tribe, and, for some, a tribal confederacy.

Tribal organization owes its emergence to the needs of the nomads to interact with other societies (especially states) and to defend and protect their pastures and other resources and their rights of migration. Tribal organization has sometimes also been a military organization—and has been seen as a threat to states and as a means of forming new states.

A greater degree of equality between men and women is often found in nomadic societies than in the surrounding settled society—primarily because of economics—the necessary and full participation of both men and women in the diverse economic activities of the household. Boys and girls of all ages are active participants in subsistence activities and learn their roles from an early age.

By the 1990s, nomads in the Middle East fell under many kinds of pressures to settle and to join settled society, and it is only the minority who, under increasingly special conditions, are able to sustain full nomadism. Rulers of modernizing nation-states aim to control and administer their citizens, and the nomadic sectors of society have often been among the least amenable to such control. For many rulers, the settlement of nomads is the only solution to this problem. Those governments wanting to bring modern services, such as formal education and health care, to all their citizens find it difficult to implement for nomads. Ecological pressures on nomadic pastoralists also lead to their settlement. As grazing lands decrease (primarily by the expansion of agriculture) and the remaining lands are overgrazed and depleted, nomadic pastoralists who wish to retain their livelihood and mobility must often seek alternative grazing in the form of cultivated or purchased fodder.

The future of nomadism in the Middle East is not bright. Few nation-states permit nomads to continue their past adaptations or aid them in adapting to new conditions.

BIBLIOGRAPHY

BARFIELD, THOMAS. *The Nomadic Alternative.* Englewood Cliffs, New Jersey, 1993.
BECK, LOIS. *Nomad: A Year in the Life of a Qashqa'i Tribesman in Iran.* Berkeley, Calif., 1991.
JOHNSON, DOUGLAS. *The Nature of Nomadism: A Comparative Study of Pastoral Migrations in Southwestern Asia and Northern Africa.* University of Chicago Department of Geography Research Paper, no. 118. Chicago, 1969.
LANCASTER, WILLIAM. *The Rwala Bedouin Today.* Cambridge, Mass., 1981.
SPOONER, BRIAN. *The Cultural Ecology of Pastoral Nomads.* Reading, Mass., 1973.

Lois Beck

Noradungian, Gabriel   [1852–1936]

Armenian diplomat; Ottoman minister of foreign affairs, 1912–1913

Noradungian was born in Istanbul to one of the families of the old *amira* class representing the crust of Armenian society once associated with service to the Ottoman dynasty and the palace. After attending local Armenian and French schools, he went to Paris in 1870 to pursue a degree in international law. Returning to Istanbul in 1875, he entered the Foreign Ministry and served as legal counsel. In a four-volume collection published in Paris between 1897 and 1903, Noradungian issued his *Recueil d'Actes Internationaux de l'Empire Ottoman.* The collection offered the texts, translated into French, of the principal treaties and agreements reached by the Sublime Porte with neighboring states and European powers.

Noradungian filled his first cabinet post as minister of public works after the 1908 Young Turk revolution and the restoration of the Ottoman constitution. Whereas this appointment was in line with other Ottoman Armenians who had risen to positions of responsibility in the services sector of the government, Noradungian's second cabinet position under Prime Minister Gazi Ahmet Muhtar gave an Armenian Christian the exceptional distinction of

being tasked with policymaking as minister of foreign affairs of the Ottoman Empire in 1912. His tenure ended with the outbreak of the Balkan War in 1913.

Noradungian was active in Armenian affairs for all his adult life. He participated in the Armenian National Assembly in Istanbul and was elected its chairman in 1894 (see ARMENIAN MILLET). He represented the conservative elements of Armenian society and opposed programs to involve the Western powers in the Armenian question (see ARMENIAN REVOLUTIONARY MOVEMENT). After World War I Noradungian joined Boghos Nubar as part of the Armenian National Delegation organized to represent the interests of the Western Armenians at the Paris Peace Conference. Though the Armenians were not accorded official representation, Noradungian remained involved in the efforts to negotiate international recognition for the republic founded in Russian Armenia and for the establishment of a national home for the surviving Armenian population of the Ottoman Empire who had been deported during World War I by the order of the Young Turk regime. Ultimately his efforts came to naught as Turkey refused to accede to any Allied plan to resettle the Armenians in the former Armenian provinces. Noradungian spent the rest of his years in Paris where he served as the vice president of the Armenian General Benevolent Union. Before his death he dictated his autobiography of which only fragments survive.

Rouben P. Adalian

Nordau, Max   [1849–1923]

Author and Zionist leader.

One of Theodor Herzl's earliest supporters, it was Nordau who formulated the goal for the Zionist movement in Basle Program at the First Zionist Congress in 1897: "The creation for the Jewish people of a publicly recognized, legally secured Home in Palestine." Following Herzl's death, Nordau became a close adviser to David Wolffsohn, the second president of the World Zionist Organization. Nordau was a staunch advocate of Herzl's brand of political Zionism and was opposed to Ahad Ha-Am's cultural Zionism and Chaim Weizmann's practical Zionism.

BIBLIOGRAPHY

HERTZBERG, ARTHUR. *The Zionist Idea.* New York, 1979.

Martin Malin

North Atlantic Treaty Organization (NATO)

Post–World War II alliance for the defense of its members—including Turkey—against the Soviet Union.

On April 4, 1949, twelve countries including the United States, France, Great Britain, and Canada signed the North Atlantic Treaty—a defense agreement that established the basis for the North Atlantic Treaty Organization. NATO was designed as a security system for the countries of Western Europe in the face of a perceived threat from the Soviet Union and its Communist satellite states who formed the Warsaw Treaty Organization.

Middle Eastern Petroleum was vital to European security, and Turkey occupied the key strategic position between Europe and the rest of the Middle East. Concerned about Soviet Premier Josef Stalin's postwar intentions, Turkey pressured the United States to be included in NATO and, in August 1950, Turkey formally applied for membership. Since Turkish troops joined the United Nations (UN) forces against North Korea in the Korean War (1950–1953), NATO acquiesced. On February 18, 1952, Turkey was admitted and received the security guarantees it desired; in return, in addition to troop commitments to NATO forces, Turkey provided NATO with secure access to the Straits at Istanbul and to the Black Sea. Turkey remained in NATO throughout the Cold War.

BIBLIOGRAPHY

LEFFLER, MELVIN. *A Preponderance of Power.* Stanford, Calif., 1992.
LENCZOWSKI, GEORGE. *The Middle East in World Affairs,* 4th ed. Ithaca, N.Y., 1980.
SHAW, STANFORD, and EZEL KURAL SHAW. *History of the Ottoman Empire and Modern Turkey,* vol. 2. Cambridge, U.K., 1977.

Zachary Karabell

Northern Tier

The group of Middle Eastern states bordering on the Soviet Union.

American policymakers in the 1950s were concerned about securing the Northern Tier against Soviet and communist influence. They tried with only moderate success to weave Iran, Iraq, and Turkey into defense alliances. In fact, Turkey was a member of NATO (the North Atlantic Treaty Organization).

BIBLIOGRAPHY

LENCZOWSKI, GEORGE. *The Middle East in World Affairs,* 4th ed. Ithaca, N.Y., 1980.
SHIMONI, YAACOV, ed. *Political Dictionary of the Middle East in the Twentieth Century.* New York, 1974.

Zachary Karabell

Nouira, Hedi   [1911–   ]

Tunisian nationalist and politician.

Educated in Tunis and Paris, Hedi Nouira played an important role in shaping and publicizing the nationalism of Habib BOURGUIBA in the early days of the NEO-DESTOUR political party, largely through his work on the party's French-language newspaper. Following several periods of imprisonment by the French colonial administration (France held a protectorate over Tunisia from 1881), and participation in the negotiations toward independence in the 1950s, Nouira became a leading member of Bourguiba's inner circle.

With independence in 1955/56, he was appointed minister of finance (1955–1958), then head of the Central Bank of Tunisia (1958–1970). In November 1970, he was appointed to be the new prime minister by Bourguiba, a post he held for seven years; in 1974, during a party congress, he was named heir apparent by Bourguiba. As prime minister, Nouira initiated a period of economic liberalization—by placing new emphasis on the private sector, encouraging trade and foreign investment, and distributing large parts of state farms to small landholders. When these policies led to social and economic dislocation, Nouira (with Bourguiba's support) met the ensuing political turmoil with repression. In early 1980, shortly after the GAFSA INCIDENT (a clash between Libya and Tunisia), Nouira was reported to have fallen seriously ill and was replaced.

BIBLIOGRAPHY

PERKINS, KENNETH. *Tunisia: Crossroads of the Islamic and European Worlds.* Boulder, Colo., 1986.
Who's Who in the Arab World, 1990–1991.

Matthew S. Gordon

Nowruz

The Iranian New Year, corresponding to March 21, the first day of spring and the sun's vernal equinox.

The celebration of the arrival of the spring as the beginning of the new year is an old tradition in Iran, going back to pre-Islamic times. The prophet of Zoroastrianism, Zarathushtra (who lived sometime between 1500 to 500 B.C.E.), seems to have reestablished what used to be an ancient practice, possibly a spring cult, of paying tributes to the symbols of fertility. In the sculptured reliefs at Persepolis, a capital of the Achamenids who ruled Iran from 553 to 331 B.C.E., people from various parts of the empire are shown bringing tribute to the ruler. Art historians believe that the occasion depicted is the Nowruz (new day) celebrations.

In preparation for Nowruz, almost two weeks in advance, households in present-day Iran plant wheat or lentils in special plates, which by the new year become fresh shoots (called *sabzi,* green) several inches high and which symbolize spring. In addition they prepare a special table called HAFT SIN (seven items whoses name begins with the Persian letter *s.*) At the exact moment of the new year, families gather around the Haft Sin. Later, families visit their relatives in order of precedence, usually determined by age.

BIBLIOGRAPHY

BOYCE, M. *Zoroastrians.* New York, 1986.
WILBER, D. *Iran: Past and Present,* 4th ed. Princeton, N.J., 1958, pp. 185–187.

Parvaneh Pourshariati

NSP

See National Salvation Party

Nu'aymi, Rashid ibn Humayid, al-
[?–1981]

Ruler of the Emirate of Ajman, 1928–1981, in the United Arab Emirates.

Rashid ibn Humayid was the eighth Al Bu Khriban family ruler of the Nu'aymi tribe, which inhabited the lands that became the Emirate of Ajman. His rule was long and stable, and during a time of trouble in the 1930s, his people enjoyed security because of his bravery against bedouin raids. His lands included the mountainous areas of Masfut and Manamah, as well as the area around Ajman town. Beginning in 1952, Shaykh Rashid encouraged modern education for girls as well as boys, and Ajman was distinguished for its Islamic college. Shaykh Rashid was a member of the TRUCIAL STATES Council in 1952 and joined the United Arab Emirates when it was formed in 1971. His son Humayid succeeded him as ruler of Ajman after his death in September 1981.

BIBLIOGRAPHY

ABDULLAH, M. MORSY. *The United Arab Emirates.* London, 1978.
HEARD BEY, FRAUKE. *From Trucial States to United Arab Emirates.* London, 1982.
REICH, BERNARD, ed. *Political Leaders of the Contemporary Middle East and North Africa.* London, 1990.

M. Morsy Abdullah

Nubar, Boghos   [1825–1899]

Legal reformer, cabinet minister, and three-time prime minister of Egypt.

An Armenian born in İzmir, educated in France and Switzerland, Boghos Nubar was brought to Egypt by his uncle, who was a translator for Muhammad Ali. Nubar worked for his uncle and his successors. Having learned eleven languages and spent his youth in Europe, he knew how to charm Europeans and often mediated with them on Egypt's behalf, meanwhile making his own fortune. He successfully negotiated with the European powers to gain their consent to set up the MIXED COURTS to try cases between Egyptian and foreign nationals. He presided over the short-lived "European cabinet" set up by Khedive Isma'il in 1878.

Not involved in the Urabi revolution, Nubar returned to power in 1884, at a time when Britain obliged Egypt to give up the Sudan, and led a third cabinet in 1894/95. Clever and subtle as an intermediary between Egypt and Europe, he was both admired and resented by most Egyptians, who accused him (not unjustly) of enriching himself by exploiting his power.

BIBLIOGRAPHY

HUNTER, F. ROBERT. *Egypt under the Khedives.* Pittsburgh, Pa., 1984.
MOBERLY-BELL, C. F. *Khedives and Pashas.* London, 1884.
AL-SAYYID, AFAF LUTFI. *Egypt and Cromer.* London, 1968.
SCHÖLCH, ALEXANDER. *Egypt for the Egyptians!* London, 1981.

Arthur Goldschmidt, Jr.

Nubar, Boghos   [1851–1930]

Armenian political leader and philanthropist.

Boghos Nubar was born in Alexandria, Egypt. He was the son of Nubar Pasha, the late-nineteenth-century prime minister of Egypt, and nephew and protégé of Boghos Bey Yusufian, his son's namesake and the great minister of Muhammad Ali, the founder of modern Egypt. Boghos Nubar received his training as a civil engineer in France and served as a director of the state railways in Egypt.

In 1906 Boghos Nubar, heir to his father's title and family fortune, took the lead, along with a group of wealthy Armenians in Egypt, to found the Armenian General Benevolent Union (AGBU) in Cairo, Egypt. Growing out of the concern for the tens of thousands of Armenians made destitute by the massive loss of life at Hamidian (1894–96) (see Maghakia ORMANIAN), the AGBU hoped to support the recovery of the Armenians from the brutalization suffered at the hands of the Ottoman government. Within three years of its founding, the 1909 mass killing of Armenians at Adana precipitated the AGBU to focus its resources in building orphanages, hospitals, and shelters for widows and elderly survivors in the region of Cilicia. The 1915 deportations and killings of Armenians required the AGBU to recommit significant funds to attempt a measure of relief for the entire Ottoman Armenian community now made refugees. The AGBU set up orphanages and clinics all across the Middle East wherever the Armenian refugees concentrated.

Boghos Nubar in Paris headed the Armenian National Delegation to Paris in 1918 to represent the disenfranchised Armenians of the Ottoman Empire with the hope of establishing a national home for them. In France Boghos Nubar was also instrumental in getting the French army to approve the formation under its command of the *Legion d'Orient* manned mostly by Armenians who saw some fighting in the Allied campaign in Palestine. Though a person of conservative political leanings, with his pedigree Boghos Nubar emerged as the leading spokesman for the Armenians at the Paris Peace Conference (see Avetis AHARONIAN and Garbriel NORADUNGIAN).

While the independent Armenian republic was too short-lived to see the AGBU extend its philanthropy to Russian Armenia, in the 1920s the AGBU responded to a disastrous earthquake that struck the city of Leninakan (formerly Alexandropol, presently Gyumri) and stayed to build educational and medical facilities in Soviet Armenia during that decade. Shut out of Armenia after Stalin's rise to power, the AGBU returned to Armenia in December 1988 after another devastating earthquake shattered the same city and the surrounding countryside.

Boghos Nubar died in Paris. Before his death, he had already set the AGBU in a new direction. After the immediate minimum physical needs of the Armenian refugees had been met, he donated funds to the AGBU, and in so doing set an example emulated since by other well-to-do Armenians, for the establishment of educational programs and institutions to begin the moral and intellectual recovery of a generation of Armenians which had known nothing but exile, hunger, and privation. Over the decades the organization founded by Boghos Nubar Pasha grew to become the largest in the Armenian diaspora with chapters around the world supporting schools, orphanages, clinics, libraries, youth centers, theaters, publications, and a host of other activities designed to sustain Armenian culture and identity in diaspora communities.

BIBLIOGRAPHY

HOVANNISIAN, RICHARD G. *The Republic of Armenia: The First Year 1918–1919.* Berkeley, Calif., 1971.
———. *The Republic of Armenia: From Versailles to London 1919–1920.* Berkeley, Calif., 1982.
WALKER, CHRISTOPHER J. *Armenia: The Survival of a Nation.* New York, 1980.

Rouben P. Adalian

Nubians

Egyptians and Sudanese who speak the Nubian language.

Nubia may derive from a word in the Nubian language meaning "slaves" or from the ancient Egyptian word *nab* (gold); Egypt obtained gold from southern neighbors who were considered slaves. Or the origin may be *nebed,* used in an inscription of Thotmes I (c. 1450 B.C.E.) to designate curly-haired people whose land Thotmes had invaded. *Nubia* is now a linguistic and ethnic term applied to an area in Egypt and Sudan occupied primarily by resettled Nubians.

Estimates of the number of Nubian speakers range from two hundred thousand people, one-quarter of whom live in Egypt and the rest in Sudan, to one million.

Today Nubian is generally considered an Eastern Sudanic language, a branch of Nilo-Saharan. There are two groups of Nubians, each represented in both Egypt and Sudan: the Kenuz speak a dialect called Matoki in Egypt and Dongolawi in Sudan; the Fadicca, a dialect called Fadicca in Egypt and Mahasi in Sudan. Within each group, variations distinguish Egyptian and Sudanese Nubian speakers.

BIBLIOGRAPHY

ARKELL, A. J. *A History of the Sudan from the Earliest Times to 1821,* 2nd ed. London, 1961.
VOEGELIN, C. F., and F. M. VOEGELIN. *Classification and Index of the World's Languages.* New York, 1977.

Aleya Rouchdy

Nuclear Capability and Nuclear Energy

Nuclear proliferation in the greater Middle East is a central issue in international affairs.

This issue was underscored in the spring of 1995 by the contentious exchanges between Egypt and Israel over the latter's nuclear weapons program in the context of global negotiations regarding the extension of the Nuclear Non-Proliferation Treaty (NPT). The broader context of this question involved the looming threat of Iraq and Iran acquiring nuclear weapons; the recognition that India and Pakistan quite probably possessed operational nuclear weapons (raising the additional specter that the latter's nuclear program might produce an "Islamic bomb"); the beginnings of Algeria's nuclear program as that nation lurched toward fundamentalism; the possession of chemical and/or biological weapons by nonnuclear states such as Egypt, Libya, and Syria; and the proliferation of various delivery systems—ballistic and cruise missiles, long-range aircraft—by several states in the region that might be joined to nuclear weapons arsenals.

Israel was the first of the region's nations to cross the nuclear threshold. But despite a growing body of writings about the history of its nuclear program, there are vast gaps in the literature about some of the essential facts of its history, pertaining to the size of its arsenal, the dates of its initial deployments, and its current command and control structure. It appears that the initial decisions to move toward nuclear weapons status were made very early in the life of the Jewish state. Crucial was Franco–Israeli nuclear cooperation that grew out of the two nations' close relations at the time of the 1956 Suez War and throughout the subsequent period (until 1967/68). Israel's nuclear development was centered on the French-supplied Dimona reactor, which went into operation around 1961, and continued to produce plutonium despite remonstrances from the Kennedy administration and some limited U.S. inspections.

Israel probably began plutonium separation and the deployment of operational nuclear weapons between the 1967 and 1973 wars, with the Soviet Union's active involvement in the Suez "war of attrition" (1969/70) perhaps a final trigger. In 1973, Israel's implicit threats to use nuclear weapons after the initial military setbacks in Sinai and on the Golan Heights appear to have impelled the U.S. arms resupply airlift, after initial hesitation.

In 1979, U.S. satellites detected a flash over the southern Indian Ocean that was widely, though not definitively, attributed to an Israeli or joint Israeli–South African nuclear test. In 1986, Mordechai Vanunu, a disaffected Israeli who had worked at the Dimona reactor, leaked voluminous information and photographs that revealed the scope of the Israeli nuclear program. Those disclosures, now widely considered credible, indicated a program consisting of both fission and fusion weapons, involving up to or more than 200 weapons, mounted on delivery systems that could cover the entire Middle East.

Various rationales have been offered for the Israeli nuclear program. Central is its intended role to provide a credible deterrent against the threat of an overwhelming Arab conventional force, deemed inevitable by some. The large size of Israel's program appears to imply the prospective use of tactical nuclear weapons in such a scenario, backed by a threat against cities. Other rationales are increased assurance of American arms resupply during crises; the convincing of Arab nations of Israel's permanence, with the hope thereby of nudging them along in the "peace process"; and the deterrence of involvement in the Arab–Israeli conflict by powerful peripheral nations such as Iran, Pakistan, and Turkey.

Iraq's initial efforts to become the second Middle Eastern nuclear power were thwarted by Israel's bombing of the Osirak reactor in Baghdad in 1981. During the subsequent decade, Iraq built an elaborate clandestine nuclear infrastructure with the aid of numerous Western suppliers of relevant technologies, most notably that of gas centrifuges. That operation apparently was vastly underestimated by Western intelligence services, and the full scope of the program was revealed only in the wake of Iraq's defeat in the Gulf War of 1991 and its subsequent submission to UN inspections. Whether Iraq's nuclear program has been seriously curtailed or it has the wherewithal for rebuilding it after UN sanctions are lifted is widely speculated upon.

Since the end of the Iran–Iraq War in 1988 and subsequent to the Gulf War, Iran is widely believed to have embarked upon an energetic effort to acquire nuclear weapons. That effort is centered on its nuclear research complex at Isfahan, and there are reports of extensive outside assistance, particularly from Pakistan, and perhaps China and Russia. The United States has attempted to thwart a prospective sale by Russia of up to four large nuclear power reactors, despite Iran's adherence to the NPT. Israel in particular dreads the possible advent of an Iranian nuclear weapon program that would include long-range missiles capable of reaching Israel.

Algeria has acquired a small nuclear reactor, which has caused anxieties in western Europe because of the threat that Islamic fundamentalism and its possible ramifications will lead to conflict between it and Algeria. Libya reportedly has made efforts to acquire nuclear weapons and/or technology, to no avail. Kazakhstan, after breaking off from the Soviet Union, was left with hundreds of nuclear warheads and their delivery systems, but has pledged to give them up.

The vast oil and gas resources of the Middle East presumably render almost irrelevant the acquisition of nuclear power reactors for peaceful purposes. Statements about generating electricity presumably act only as a rhetorical cover for intended nuclear weapons programs. There are no nuclear power reactors in the Middle East. Iran embarked on a program to build four such reactors during the latter part of the shah's reign, which resulted in the near completion of one reactor by a West German firm. Iran has been negotiating with Russia over the building of four new reactors, plans that have been fiercely contested by the United States.

BIBLIOGRAPHY

ARONSON, SHLOMO. *The Politics and Strategy of Nuclear Weapons in the Middle East*. Albany, N.Y., 1992.

BERES, LOUIS RENE, ed. *Security or Armageddon: Israel's Nuclear Strategy*. Lexington, Mass., 1986.

BURROWS, WILLIAM E., and ROBERT WINDREN. *Critical Mass*. New York, 1994.

CORDESMAN, ANTHONY. *Weapons of Mass Destruction in the Middle East*. Washington, D.C., 1991.

FELDMAN, SHAI. *Israel's Nuclear Deterrence: A Strategy for the 1980s*. Boulder, Colo., 1988.

HARKAVY, ROBERT E. *Spectre of a Middle Eastern Holocaust: The Strategy and Diplomatic Implications of the Israeli Nuclear Weapons Program*. Denver, Colo., 1977.

SAGAN, SCOTT, and KENNETH WALTZ. *The Spread of Nuclear Weapons: A Debate*. New York, 1995.

Robert E. Harkavy

Nuer

People who live along the Nile in Sudan.

The Nuer, who call themselves Nath, number some 200,000. They live in the swamps and open savanna on both sides of the Nile south of Malakal in Sudan. Culturally they have a common origin with the DINKA, with whom their relationship over the generations has been both hostile and peaceful, with much intermarriage and cultural borrowing. Traditionally, their political and cultural life was governed by personal rather than territorial relationships, but under both the Anglo–Egyptian Condominium (1899–1956) and independent Sudan, authority devolved upon individuals who act as "chiefs." The Nuer were the last of the Sudanese people to submit to British rule—and then only after a substantial military campaign in 1930 known as the "Nuer Settlement." In more recent times the Nuer, some of whom have become well educated and politically active, have played an aggressive role in the southern Sudanese

insurgency movement and remain the dominant military force in Nuerland.

Robert O. Collins

Nu'man, Ahmad Muhammad

Father and prime minister of Yemen Arab Republic.

The revered head of the once powerful Nu'man family in North Yemen who, as a founder of the FREE YEMENIS, shares with only a few the title of father of modern Yemen and Yemeni nationalism. Nu'man served the Yemen Arab Republic in a number of capacities, twice as prime minister. Despite his role as a nationalist symbol, he never realized his political potential during the republican era, on at least two occasions leaving the political fray rather than fighting on. His withdrawal became complete in the mid-1970s and is attributed to sorrow over the assassination of his eldest son and close political colleague, Muhammad Ahmad Nu'man. From this time on, he lived abroad.

Robert D. Burrowes

Nu'man, Muhammad Ahmad   [1934–1974]

Government official of Yemen Arab Republic.

The highly regarded heir apparent to the powerful Nu'man family of North Yemen served the Yemen Arab Republic as roving ambassador on occasion and as deputy prime minister and foreign minister in 1973. He was assassinated at age forty on the streets of Beirut in 1974. Some blame his demise on certain politicians in Yemen who conspired to keep him out of Yemen for years out of fear of his skills as a leader and politician.

Robert D. Burrowes

Numeiri, Muhammad Ja'far

Military dictator of Sudan, 1971–1985.

Muhammad Ja'far Numeiri (also Numayri) was born at Wad Nubaw'i, a suburb of Omdurman, Sudan. After education at the local Qur'anic school, El Hijra Elementary School, then at the Medani Government School, and the Hantoub Secondary School, he entered the military college in 1949 and graduated as a second lieutenant in 1952.

Thereafter, Numeiri served with the Western Command and the armored corps at Shendi. He be-

President Muhammad Ja'far Numeiri of Sudan. (© Chris Kutschera)

came a great admirer of Gamal Abdel Nasser's revolution, a view reinforced by training in Egypt and by his arrest and suspension from duty (1957–1959) after supporting an abortive coup by Abd al-Rahman Kabedia. He later served in Juba, in southern Sudan, and in Khartoum, where he proved troublesome and consequently was sent on military training courses in Cyprus, Libya, West Germany, and Egypt. Numeiri returned to play an active role in the overthrow of the government of General Ibrahim ABBUD in October 1964, which resulted in his arrest and transfer to the American Command School at Fort Leavenworth, Kansas. Upon his return to Sudan, he was implicated in another abortive coup but survived to become the commanding officer of the military school in Khartoum.

From this prestigious position Numeiri successfully carried out a military coup on May 25, 1969, against the government of Isma'il Azhari, whom he replaced with the REVOLUTIONARY COMMAND COUNCIL (RCC). The first challenge to his new regime came from the Ansar (Mahdists) in March 1970; he defeated them at their sanctuary on Aba Island, south of Khartoum in the White Nile.

The second challenge came from the Communist party of Sudan, which originally had been included in the RCC but sought full control of government by a coup d'état on July 19, 1971. After a three-day struggle, Numeiri emerged triumphant, ending the Communist challenge. Having defeated his enemies on both the right and the left, he called for a plebiscite that elected him president of Sudan, after which he promptly dissolved the RCC and established the Sudanese Socialist Union (SSU) as the single ruling party.

Having consolidated his control in northern Sudan, Numeiri turned to the seventeen-year SUDANESE

CIVIL WAR, which he and the respected Southerner, Abel Alier, brought to an end by the Addis Ababa Peace Agreement on February 27, 1972. With Sudan at peace, he enjoyed ten years of complete authority despite several abortive attemps to overthrow him. These halcyon years were accompanied by an economic boom resulting from Numeiri's encouragement of foreign investment and his attempts to forge national unity with the Ansar. These initiatives were accompanied by a change in his lifestyle and ideology. Abandoning the habits of a tough soldier, Numeiri became engrossed in the more rigorous interpretations of Islam at a time when there were endless political disagreements with the southern Sudanese and a decline in the economic prosperity of the 1970s.

In October 1981, after a series of strikes and demonstrations, Numeiri dissolved the National Assembly and dismissed the leadership of the SSU. He next unilaterally repudiated the Addis Ababa Peace Agreement, thereby eliminating southern autonomy. The rapid deterioration of his popularity was accompanied by the introduction of the *Shari'a* (Islamic law) with its restrictions on individual behavior and its draconian penalties for violations. This led to criticism by Muslims and non-Muslims, dismay among the northern Sudanese, and the revival of the insurrection movement in southern Sudan led by John GARANG and his Sudan Liberation Army.

Numeiri declared a state of emergency. His religious policies were combined with stringent economic decrees, which produced serious riots. He left for the United States, seeking additional financial assistance. He never returned. On April 6, 1985, he was deposed in a bloodless coup led by his chief of staff, Lieutenant General Suwar al-Dhahab. He was granted asylum in Egypt.

Robert O. Collins

Numismatics

The study of coins and related objects.

Numismatics is an ancillary science to history that seeks to identify coins as to place, date, and government of issue so that the inscriptions, images, and other features of the coins can be used as evidence for political, economic, social, and cultural history. For archeologists, coins are the most consistently datable evidence. Islamic coins produced in Muslim countries and similar coins sometimes issued by non-Muslims are especially useful for historical research—nearly all were inscribed with their city and date of issue and usually (according to the tradition of Islam) did not have images. This left space for long inscriptions, including the names and titles of the rulers under whom they were issued and something of their religious beliefs.

As a field of study, numismatics began during the European Renaissance as part of the general rediscovery of the classical world. Muslim historians did not use coins as historical evidence, although occasionally an extraordinary issue might be mentioned or described. More often they noted changes in the monetary system of their countries, and some writers, notably al-Baladhuri in the ninth century and al-Maqrizi in the first half of the fifteenth century, wrote brief treatises on monetary history. A few descriptions of mint operation were written as well as a few disquisitions on monetary theory, of which the most interesting is by the great historian Ibn Khaldun of fifteenth-century Egypt.

Some Islamic coins were noted in passing in works on other subjects, but the first study of Islamic numismatics was a twenty-page article in 1759. The first catalog of an Italian Islamic collection was published by Adler in 1782, followed by Assemani's catalog of a collection in Padua in 1787 and Tychsen's catalog of the Göttingen collection in 1787/88. Catalogs of public and private collections continued to be published throughout the nineteenth century, culminating at the end of the century in the great catalogs of the national collections of England, France, Germany, and Russia. Stanley Lane-Poole's ten-volume set of the British Museum Islamic coins (1875–1890) continues to be a standard reference, partly because of his excellent scholarship and also because it was the only complete catalog of any collection (the British Museum has acquired many more coins since that time). His introductions to the volumes, describing the history and coinage of each Muslim dynasty, are still useful. Lavoix's three massive volumes on the collection of the Bibliothèque Nationale, in Paris, and Nützel's two volumes on the collection of the Königliche Museum, in Berlin, are also standard references. Markov's catalog of the Hermitage collection, in Saint Petersburg, is less used because the inscriptions are brief, the work is difficult to find in the West, and it is reproduced directly from his Russian manuscript.

A major impetus to European numismatic research on Islamic coins in the countries from Scandinavia through the Baltic states and into Russia has been the immense quantities of seventh-to-tenth-century Islamic silver coins brought to those countries and buried by the Vikings. Stockholm is one major center for this study, beginning with Tornberg's several catalogs and studies from 1846 to 1870, and culminating with the great *Corpus Nummorum Saeculorum IX–XI,* a collective project to publish (first volume 1975) all the Islamic (and English and German) silver coins of the

Viking age that were found in Sweden. The other major center for such study, founded by C. M. Fraehn, was Saint Petersburg. His works, beginning in 1808, were important not only for Russian numismatists but for scholars throughout Europe. In particular, he devised a scheme for the arrangement of the Islamic coin-issuing dynasties that was followed, with subsequent modifications, by most Islamic numismatists until recently. Russia's numismatic research was also impelled by Russian interest in the coinage of its newly conquered territories in the Caucasus and central Asia.

Toward the end of the nineteenth century, the leading Russian scholars were Markov, mentioned previously, and Tiesenhausen, who published the only general corpus of Abbasid coins produced to date (a corpus attempts to assemble all known coins of a historical period or place, whereas a catalog is limited to the coins of a single collection or several related collections). Perhaps the most brilliant scholar of the Russian school, Vasmer, was executed in 1938. Numismatic scholarship remained active in the Soviet Union, however, with major centers in Leningrad, Moscow, and the cities of Muslim central Asia.

Islamic numismatics has an early history in Spain, since the coinage of the Arabs there (the Moors) was part of that country's heritage from 711 to 1492. Vives's catalog of all Muslim Spanish issues remains a standard reference. George Miles founded Islamic numismatics at the American Numismatic Society in New York City, which remains one of the principal centers for the field. In 1989, Tübingen University, in Germany, acquired an extremely important collection of Islamic coins and has begun to develop a center for research and training.

The Turks of the Ottoman Empire were the first people of the Middle East to join in numismatic research, publishing in European journals as early as 1862. At the turn of the century, the Müzei Humayun (Imperial Museum) published a series of major catalogs in Ottoman Turkish that rank in importance with the productions of the large European museums. This promising beginning was halted by World War I and the series was never finished. Europeans living in Arab countries produced various works of significance during the first part of the twentieth century, but few Arabs contributed until the demise of the Ottoman Empire and the establishment of some Arab states.

Abd al-Rahman Fahmi produced several important catalogs and studies based on the collection of the Museum of Islamic Art, in Cairo, and Nasir al-Naqshbandi founded a school of numismatists in Baghdad, where the Iraq Museum is a major center for research with a journal devoted to Islamic coins called *al-Maskukat.* The Damascus Museum, in Syria, also has an active collection, and its late curator, Muhammad Abu al-Faraj al-Ush, produced several important works. Recently the Bank al-Maghrib of Rabat, Morocco, has created a numismatic center and published two major corpora of Moroccan coins by Daniel Eustache. Some public collections were built in Iran in the 1970s, but little has been published there. In Jordan, a center for numismatic research has been established at Yarmuk University with private support; a journal, *Yarmouk Numismatics,* was founded there.

The real explosion in Islamic numismatics began in the 1970s as a result of the new wealth brought by OPEC (Organization of Petroleum Exporting Countries) oil. Many private collectors in the Gulf countries began to bid up the price of Islamic coins, and the interest generated by rising prices led to great collector interest in Europe, the Americas, and Japan. This, as well as the expansion of Islamic studies in the West, has made the field extremely active.

BIBLIOGRAPHY

L. A., MAYER, *Bibliography of Moslem Numismatics, India Excepted* (2nd ed., London, 1954), lists virtually everything published on the subject to that time. For work since then, see the survey of the field by MICHAEL L. BATES, "Islamic Numismatics," *Middle East Studies Association Bulletin* 12, no. 2 (May 1978): 1–16; 12, no. 3 (December 1978): 2–18; 13, no. 1 (July 1979): 3–21; 13, no. 2 (December 1979): 1–9; the research surveys published approximately every six years in *Survey of Numismatics Research,* published by the International Numismatic Commission and the International Association of Professional Numismatists; and the bibliographical periodical *Numismatic Literature* (New York: semi-annual). Current research is chronicled in the *Newsletter of the Oriental Numismatic Society,* a membership organization open to all. General histories of Islamic coinage include STEPHEN ALBUM, *A Checklist of Popular Islamic Coins* (Santa Rosa, Calif., 1993); MICHAEL BROOME, *A Handbook of Islamic Coins* (London, 1985); MICHAEL MITCHINER, *Oriental Coins and Their Values: The World of Islam* (London, 1977); and MICHAEL L. BATES, *Islamic Coins* (ANS Handbook 2, New York, 1982). The coinage of the Middle East since 1800 is cataloged in CHESTER L. KRAUSE and CLIFFORD MISHLER, *Standard Catalog of World Coins* (Iola, Wisc., annual editions).

Michael L. Bates

Nuqrashi, Mahmud Fahmi al-   [1888–1948]

Egyptian educator and politician.

Mahmud was educated in Alexandria and at Nottingham University, England. When he returned to Egypt, he taught school, then was promoted in the administration until he became director of public instruction for Asyut. A WAFD supporter, he became vice-governor of Cairo, then deputy interior minister under Sa'd Zaghlul. Implicated in Sir Lee STACK's murder, he was briefly imprisoned and then cleared.

Nuqrashi held ministerial positions in the Wafdist cabinets of 1930 and 1936 but broke with Mustafa al-NAHHAS in 1937. With Ahmad MAHIR, he formed the Sa'dist party, which took part in several non-Wafdist coalition governments. After Ahmad Mahir was assassinated in 1945, Nuqrashi became the leader of the Sa'dist party and headed cabinets in 1945/46 and from 1946 to 1948. He led the 1947 Egyptian delegation to the UN Security Council to demand that Britain withdraw from Sudan and allow it to unite with Egypt, but he did not gain UN support. When the State of Israel was declared in May 1948 and the Arabs attacked Israel, Nuqrashi reportedly tried to delay committing Egyptian troops, but he was overridden by Egypt's King Farouk. As setbacks to the Arab forces led to rising discontent within Egypt, he tried to outlaw the Society of Muslim Brothers (the MUSLIM BROTHERHOOD). He was assassinated by a student member of that society on December 28, 1948.

BIBLIOGRAPHY

The Times (London), December 29, 1948, pp. 4d, 5c, 7d.
AL-ZIRIKLI, KHAYR AL-DIN. *Al-A'lam,* 4th ed. Beirut, 1980.

Arthur Goldschmidt, Jr.

Nur, Nur Ahmad   [1937–   ]

Afghan Marxist leader.

Nur Ahmad Nur was born in 1937 in Panjwa'i in Kandahar province, where his father was a prominent landlord. He attended school in Kabul at Habibia high school. An early member of the Marxist movement in Afghanistan, he was ambassador to Warsaw from 1988 to 1991 and was assigned to be ambassador to Havana in 1991.

BIBLIOGRAPHY

ARNOLD, ANTHONY. *Afghanistan's Two-Party Communism: Parcham and Khalq.* Stanford, Calif., 1983.

Grant Farr

Nurcu

A follower of the twentieth-century Nurculuk Islamic movement in Turkey.

The Nurcus, an Islamic community in contemporary Turkey, claim to have more than two million adherents. The movement's founder, Said Nursi

(1873–1960), was a Kurd who grew up in the eastern Anatolian province of Bitlis. Nursi was trained in religious schools, and as a young theologian, he engaged in relentless debates with the *ulama* of his region. In the first decades of the twentieth century he sought, unsuccessfully, to establish a new type of religious high school in which both modern sciences and traditional religious subjects would be taught, with Arabic, Turkish, and Kurdish as the languages of instruction. After the establishment of the Turkish republic, his opposition to westernization and secularization brought him into conflict with the Kemalist regime. From 1925 until his death in 1960, his life was stamped by trials, imprisonment, enforced residence, and strict surveillance by the authorities. Under those conditions, he wrote about 130 brochures, collectively called the Risale-i Nur (Epistle of Light), which his followers copied on printing presses and distributed. The production of these brochures marked a transformation of his life, which he later described as a transition from the old Said, who devoted his energies to religious polemics and political struggle, to the new Said, who devoted himself to worship and meditation.

The Risale-i Nur, which is available in eleven printed volumes, consists of lengthy meditations on a variety of moral and metaphysical issues that are dealt with in a rather arbitrary order. In the Risale, Nursi tries to defend Qur'anic truths against modern skepticism and materialism. A central theme is the beauty of nature, which proves the existence of a power that created and sustains the universe.

After Nursi's death, his disciples succeeded in expanding the Nurcu network, primarily in Turkey, but also in western Europe and the United States, where a Risale-i Nur Institute of America was established in Berkeley, California. In February 1970, a group of Nurcus started to publish the Turkish daily *Yeni Asya,* which became an important instrument not only to propagate Nursi's ideas, but also to influence the political opinions of the adherents. During the 1990s, the *Yeni Asya* group strongly supported the Justice party of Süleyman Demirel, while another group of Nurcus chose the side of the Islamist National Salvation party.

However, the main activity of the Nurcu movement continues to be the distribution and study of the Risale-i Nur. This study is done in small groups that gather in private homes, mosques, secondary schools, and universities. Although the participants are predominantly male, the number of women's Risale-i Nur study groups has grown since the 1970s. Other Muslim groups in Turkey have criticized the Nurcus for their exclusive loyalty to the Risale-i Nur and their neglect of the study of other religious literature, even the Qur'an. In recent years, however, the Nurculuk has become more accepted as a part of the larger Islamist movement.

BIBLIOGRAPHY

MARDIN, S. *Religion and Social Changes in Modern Turkey: The Case of Bediüzzaman Said Nursi.* New York, 1989.

Nico Landman

Nuri, Abd al-Malik

Iraqi author.

Nuri, one of the most gifted writers of fiction in modern Iraq, was born in Baghdad. He studied law, graduating in 1944. Concurrently he showed an interest in contemporary fiction, especially that of James Joyce. His first collection of short stories, *Rusul al-Insaniyya* (Baghdad, 1946; Messengers of Humanity) contains stories in a naturalist vein, expressing sympathy with the underdogs of Baghdad society. His second volume, *Nashid al-Ard* (1954; The Song of the Earth) inaugurated a new phase in the language and techniques of modern fiction in Iraq. Stream-of-consciousness is judiciously employed, and the exterior movement that characterizes earlier stories is replaced by an internal flow of thoughts and emotions.

In 1972, Nuri published a short allegorical play, *Khashab wa-Mukhmal* (Wood and Velvet); his third and last collection of short stories to date, *Dhuyul al-Kharif* (Autumn's Tails), appeared in 1980.

Like many other Iraqi intellectuals, Nuri was attracted to leftist ideas, especially in the 1940s. In subsequent years his political commitment seems to have declined markedly. Like several other Iraqi novelists of his generation (e.g., his close friend Fu'ad Takarli), Nuri wrote the dialogue of his stories in the vernacular of Baghdad rather than in *fusha*, the literary language of Arabic writing. This gave his stories a distinctive local color but made it difficult for readers outside Iraq to understand his works fully. In his drama, however, he used fusha.

[*See also:* Literature, Arabic]

BIBLIOGRAPHY

BADAWI, M. M, ed. *Modern Arabic Literature.* New York, 1992.

Sasson Somekh

Nuri, Ali Akbar Nateq-e   [1943–   ]

Iranian cleric; speaker of the majles.

Nuri was born in Nur Mazandaran. His political activities before the revolution are said to have begun in 1963, against the Pahlavi regime. He lived briefly in Lebanon and Syria, and after the revolution in 1979, became Ayatollah Khomeini's representative in the Construction Crusade (*Jihad-e Sazandegi*). Nuri served as minister of the interior between December 1981 and August 1985. He is currently (1996) the speaker of Iran's parliament (*majles*).

Farhad Arshad

Nuri, Fazlollah [c. 1842–1909]

Iranian religious scholar, important for his objections to Western-style constitutionalism during the revolution of 1906–1909.

After completing his preliminary religious studies in Iran, Nuri traveled to Iraq to study with the great authorities of Shi'ite Islam, such as Mirza Hasan Shirazi. Returning to Iran in 1883, he soon established himself as the most influential religious leader of Tehran, controlling several theological colleges. When the CONSTITUTIONAL REVOLUTION began in 1907, Nuri initially collaborated with his colleagues who favored the cause. He soon began to turn his weight against the movement, however, claiming that its original aim—the implementation of *Shari'a* (Islamic law)—had been subverted by the emergence of unbelievers among the constitutionalists. In protest, in July 1907, Nuri withdrew from Tehran to a nearby shrine where he began publishing broadsheets that denounced constitutionalism as a European import, incompatible with Islam, and he called for a form of constitutional government more in accord with Islam. He objected in particular to concepts such as parliament possessing the right to legislate, the legal equality of Muslims and non-Muslims, and the unqualified freedom of the press. When in June 1908 the parliament was closed down by a royalist coup, Nuri effectively sided with the shah, although he continued to advocate his own concept of an Islamic-style constitution. In July 1909, the parliamentary regime was restored, and Nuri was executed at the end of the month. His violent end caused revulsion even among the constitutionalist religious scholars and contributed heavily to a disillusion with political involvement that was to last several decades.

BIBLIOGRAPHY

ARJOMAND, S. A. "The Ulama's Traditionalist Opposition to Parliamentarianism: 1907–1909." *Middle Eastern Studies* (1981).

Hamid Algar

Nuri Pasha

See Sa'id, Nuri al-

Nuristan

Region of Afghanistan.

The mountainous region of Nuristan is located in northeastern Afghanistan in Logar and Laghman provinces. The Nuristanis, who number about 100,000, are primarily Sunni Muslems who were converted to Islam during the reign of Abd al-Rahman (1880–1901); before their conversion, the area was called Kafiristan (Land of the Unbelievers). The Nuristanis' belief that they are descended from Alexander the Great's army has no historical basis. The Nuristanis speak several languages that contain elements of both Indian and Iranian languages. In some valleys, Nuristanis with blond hair and blue or green eyes can be seen.

BIBLIOGRAPHY

DUPREE, LOUIS. *Afghanistan*. Princeton, N.J., 1980.

Grant Farr

Nursi, Said [1873–1960]

Founder of the Nurculuk movement in Turkey.

Said Nursi wrote *Risale-i Nur* (Epistle of Light), a collection of 130 brochures in which Islamic values are defended against modern skepticism. With these brochures he attracted thousands of disciples and created the Nurculuk movement (see NURCU).

BIBLIOGRAPHY

MARDIN, S. *Religion and Social Change in Modern Turkey: The Case of Bediüzzaman Said Nursi*. New York, 1989.

Nico Landman

Nusayba, Anwar [1913–]

Palestinian diplomat and politician in Palestine and Jordan.

Born in Palestine, Nusayba graduated from Queen's College, Cambridge (M.A.), and trained as a lawyer. His political career began as a member of the ALL-PALESTINE GOVERNMENT. He was the chief Arab delegate on the Jordan and Israel Mixed Armistice Commission in 1951, and held ministerial posts in

Jordan: defense in 1953, education in 1954–1955, and reconstruction and development in 1954 and 1955. He was made governor of Jerusalem in 1961 but was demoted in 1963 by Prime Minister Wasfi al-Tal.

Jenab Tutunji

Nusayba, Sari [1949–]

Palestinian leader on the West Bank.

Sari, the son of Anwar NUSAYBA, was born in Jerusalem. After studying at Oxford and at Harvard, where he earned a Ph.D. in Islamic philosophy in 1978, Nusayba taught at Hebrew and Bir Zeit universities until the latter was shut down by Israel in 1988. Since then he has directed his own research center, Maqdes, in Ramallah. Nusayba has helped to establish political and technical committees to prepare the way for replacing Israel's civil administration of the territories it occupied in 1967.

Jenab Tutunji

Nusayba Family

Prominent Palestinian family from Jerusalem that traces its roots in the Old City to ancient times.

According to tradition, the family took its name from a woman named Nusayba, who went to the Prophet Muhammad with a delegation of women and complained to him about the unfair treatment they received. Since the Muslim conquest of Jerusalem in the seventh century, the Nusayba family has held the keys of the Church of the Holy Sepulchre. This arrangement emerged during the days of the second Muslim caliph, Umar, who hoped to avoid clashes among rival Christian dominations for control over the church. Although symbolic, the arrangement has provided the Nusayba family a visible role in Christian activities in Jerusalem, which include pilgrimages and visits by Western Christians.

Notable members of the family have included Anwar Nusayba, who was governor of Jerusalem in the early 1960s, and Hazem Nusayba, who was a member of various Jordanian governments. Today, Sari Nusayba, a Harvard-educated professor and peace advocate, is active in Palestinian politics.

BIBLIOGRAPHY

MUSLIH, MUHAMMAD Y. *The Origins of Palestinian Nationalism.* New York, 1988.

Lawrence Tal

Nusayri

See Alawi

OAPEC

See Organization of Arab Petroleum Exporting Countries

OAS

See Secret Army Organization

Oasis

A fertile area, in a desert or arid region, that is usually spring-fed from artesian wells.

An oasis may be very small, serving only as a way station for travelers, or a vast territory that includes several thousand acres of cultivated land dotted with towns and urban centers. Smaller oases can disappear after prolonged periods of drought. The survival of oases, regardless of size, depends on maintaining a balance between water consumption and its replenishment.

Jenab Tutunji

Oasis Group

Consortium of three U.S. oil companies in Libya.

The Oasis Group (originally the Conorada Group) is a consortium composed of three U.S. "inde-pendent" oil companies: Amerada (now Amerada-Hess), Continental (now Conoco), and Marathon. Bidding independently, the companies won conces-sions throughout LIBYA during the first auction of oil rights in 1955. Their properties included "compro-mise parcels" constructed by reorganizing the most desirable shorefront blocks into narrow strips extend-ing deep into central Libya. Following the conces-sion awards, the Oasis companies pooled their acquisitions so as to achieve the best position of all the successful bidders, thereby provoking protests from their competitors. By 1965, when Libya opened a second round of concession building, Oasis was the number-two producer of oil in Libya, bring-ing in more than 300,000 barrels per day.

The division of Libya into multiple concessions operated by different companies allowed the govern-ment to apply selective pressure to force oil prices upward while maintaining a high level of oil income. Beginning in mid-1970, the government threatened to limit or halt production unless target companies agreed to higher prices. Two weeks after OCCIDEN-TAL PETROLEUM capitulated to this pressure, the Oasis Group followed suit. Soon most of Libya's other concession holders were forced to go along. The government nationalized part of Oasis, amounting to 51 percent by 1973.

U.S. relations with Libya deteriorated steadily, reaching a nadir in 1986, when the United States imposed economic sanctions on Libya in retaliation for what it asserted had been terrorist attacks spon-sored by the government of Libya. Many U.S. companies left Libya. The Oasis partners were three of only five U.S. oil companies to retain properties in Libya, by that time amounting to only 40.8 percent of Oasis. The sanctions required them to halt operations. Under an agreement with the government, the NATIONAL OIL CORPORATION has been operating the Oasis fields and selling the oil on its own account. In 1992, the addition of UN sanctions further dimmed prospects for Oasis and the other U.S. oil companies hoping to resume their operations in Libya.

BIBLIOGRAPHY

RAND, CHRISTOPHER T. *Making Democracy Safe for Oil: Oilmen and the Islamic East.* Boston, 1975.
SAMPSON, ANTHONY. *The Seven Sisters: The Great Oil Companies and the World They Shaped.* New York, 1975.
TÉTREAULT, MARY ANN. *Revolution in the World Petroleum Market.* Westport, Conn., 1985.

Mary Ann Tétreault

Occidental Petroleum

American firm active in Libya.

Occidental Petroleum was a small, nearly bankrupt independent oil company when it was purchased in 1956 by Armand Hammer, an American entrepreneur. It won oil concessions in Libya during the 1965 bidding round and struck oil shortly afterward. Within two years, Occidental had become a major shipper of oil to Europe as a result of its rate of production, the high quality of Libya's oil, and the closure of the SUEZ CANAL during the ARAB-ISRAEL WAR of 1967 that made the tanker transport of crude from the Persian/Arabian Gulf more costly.

Occidental's dependence on Libya's oil made it a prime target for "the Libyan squeeze." The government of Muammar al-QADDAFI, which took over Libya in a bloodless coup in 1969, threatened concession holders with production cuts if they did not agree to raise oil prices. Occidental and Exxon were the first to be squeezed. Getting no response, Qaddafi ordered Occidental to cut back production in May and June. Hammer appealed to the Exxon chairman, J. Kenneth Jamieson, to sell him crude at close to cost so he could continue supplying his customers. Jamieson refused, though he did agree to sell Hammer what he needed at third-party prices, an offer that was refused. In August, Hammer agreed to pay the government of Libya 30 cents more per barrel as well as a higher rate of taxes. Other companies followed his lead, touching off the "oil price revolution" of the early 1970s.

Although Occidental discovered and produced oil in other regions, it continued to hold its operations in Libya despite the nationalization in 1973 of 51 percent of the company. In 1985, Occidental sold 21 percent of its equity in its operations in Libya to the Austrian firm OMV. In 1986, U.S. economic sanctions against Libya required all American firms operating there—including Occidental and four other oil companies—to halt operations. These sanctions were augmented in 1992 by UN sanctions, imposed in retaliation for Libya's refusal to extradite two suspects in the December 1988 bombing of a Pan American flight over Lockerbie, Scotland. Both sets of sanctions persisted into 1994, continuing the suspension of Occidental's operations in Libya.

BIBLIOGRAPHY

RAND, CHRISTOPHER T. *Making Democracy Safe for Oil: Oilmen and the Islamic East.* Boston, 1975.
SAMPSON, ANTHONY. *The Seven Sisters: The Great Oil Companies and the World They Shaped.* New York, 1975.
TÉTREAULT, MARY ANN. *Revolution in the World Petroleum Market.* Westport, Conn., 1985.

Mary Ann Tétreault

October

Weekly Egyptian magazine devoted to culture and news.

October is a public-sector publication and its title commemorates the Arab–Israel War of 1973. Estimates of *October*'s circulation range from twenty to seventy thousand per issue. It aims at a wide audience and has always been closely associated with the ruling National party. As a relatively recent creation of the regime, *October* tends to be used more often than other public-sector magazines as a vehicle for disseminating the views of the political establishment. The first seventeen issues, for example, featured a series of articles titled "From the Pages of President al-Sadat"—the personal reminiscences of the late president. Although the magazine is government-owned, it was launched just as Sadat began to loosen restrictions on the opposition press. Its editors include Anis Mansur (until February 3, 1985), Salah Muntasir (until January 9, 1994), and Rajab al-Banna (January 16, 1994 to the present).

BIBLIOGRAPHY

OCHS, MARTIN. *The African Press.* Cairo, 1986.

Walter Armbrust

October War

See Arab–Israel War (1973)

Oǧlu

In Turkish, oǧlu means "son of" and when used as a suffix in a patronym, serves the same purpose as "-son" or "-sen" in European names.

In 1935, as part of the reformist moves during Mustafa Kemal ATATÜRK's rule, a law was passed requiring all Turks to adopt a family name. Appending *oǧlu* to a name was one of several devices used to create a family name out of an ancestral name.

Jenab Tutunji

Oil Embargo

Arab nations reduced oil production in response to the Arab–Israel War of 1973.

Members of the Organization of Arab Petroleum Exporting Countries (OAPEC) decided in late October 1973 to cut oil production by 25 percent until Israel withdrew to the 1949 armistice lines. OAPEC also decided to cut off oil to the United States and the Netherlands to protest U.S. military and Dutch political support for Israel. Exempted from the boycott were France, Spain, Muslim countries, and Great Britain (conditionally). The remaining countries divided whatever oil was left between them. The result was a fourfold increase in the price of oil. The embargo was lifted in March 1974.

BIBLIOGRAPHY

YERGIN, DANIEL. *The Prize: The Epic Quest for Oil, Money, and Power.* New York, 1993.

Bryan Daves

Oil Fields

[This entry includes the following articles: Burqan Oil Field, al-; Dukhan Oil Fields; Qamar Onshore Oil Field; Qarah Shuk Oil Fields; Rumayla Oil Fields; Suwaydiya Oil Fields.]

Burqan Oil Field, al-

The major oil and natural gas field of Kuwait.

Discovered in 1938, the Burqan oil field, about 30 miles (48 km) south of Kuwait City is one of the world's largest and most productive oil fields. Since in the Burqan field petroleum rises under its own pressure, production costs are among the lowest in the world. Its development was delayed during World War II, but was resumed beginning in 1948. By 1956, Kuwait's oil production, principally from Burqan, was the largest in the Middle East (more than fifty-five million tons [50 million metric tons] per year). The British protectorate ended in 1961.

In the early 1970s, the State of Kuwait constructed a large oil tanker port at al-Ahmadi, near the Burqan field. By the early 1980s, it controlled all phases of its oil industry by the establishment of the Kuwait Petroleum Corporation (KPC) for coordinating the activities of the four existing companies: the Kuwait Oil Company, the Kuwait National Petroleum Company, the Petroleum Industries Company, and the Kuwait Oil Tanker Company. Kuwait's oil production was interrupted for more than a year during the 1990/91 Gulf Crisis, when Iraq invaded and tried to annex Kuwait; it was resumed in the fall of 1991.

BIBLIOGRAPHY

The Middle East and North Africa, 1991, 37th ed. London, 1991.

Emile A. Nakhleh

Dukhan Oil Fields

Largest onshore oil field in Qatar.

Discovered in 1939, production did not begin until after World War II. By 1949, a pipeline was constructed to carry petroleum from the Dukhan oil fields on the west coast of Qatar to the terminal facilities at Umm Sa'id on Qatar's east coast. About 50 percent of Qatar's proven oil and gas reserves are in the Dukhan oil fields; however, the oil reserves are rapidly diminishing.

BIBLIOGRAPHY

NYROP, RICHARD, ed. *Persian Gulf States: Country Studies.* Washington, D.C., 1985.

Emile A. Nakhleh

Qamar Onshore Oil Field

Saudi-held oil field in Yemen.

Located in the interior of the Hadramawt in the Republic of Yemen, the Qamar oil field is currently held under concession by the private, Saudi-owned Nimr Petroleum Company. Nimr had a considerable presence in Yemen by the mid-1990s, having also taken over production and further exploration in the troubled, Russian-developed Iyad concession in Shabwa. Nimr also expressed interest in a variety of other large-scale economic ventures.

Robert D. Burrowes

Qarah Shuk Oil Fields

Syrian oil fields.

In May 1955, Syria granted a 5,625 square mile (14,570 sq. km) exploration permit to the U.S.-based James W. Menhall Drilling Company, and petroleum was discovered at Qarah Shuk (also Karatchok), in northeastern Syria near Iraq, by the U.S. team in October 1956. The Qarah Shuk concession was taken over by the Syrian branch of the General Petroleum Authority in 1960, and a pipeline to the Homs refinery was completed under Soviet supervision in 1968. When the oil fields went into production in 1969, an output of thirty thousand barrels per day was achieved, which was lower than expected. The oil at Qarah Shuk is high in sulfur (4.5%) and has a density of 19 API. In the early 1980s, some nine million tons of crude were produced annually; however, poor quality necessitated blending with higher-grade oil. Syria therefore imported oil for refining from the Gulf.

BIBLIOGRAPHY

BRAWER, M., ed. *Atlas of the Middle East.* New York, 1988.
COLELLO, THOMAS. *Syria: A Country Study.* Washington, D.C., 1988.

Charles U. Zenzie

Rumayla Oil Fields

Petroleum deposits located at the Iraq–Kuwait border.

First identified by the British-owned IRAQ PETROLEUM COMPANY in the 1950s, the North Rumayla oil fields in Iraq were at the center of the Iraqi-British oil nationalization disputes during the 1960s. After a 1967 agreement, the fields were finally developed by the Iraq National Oil Company with Russian financing and opened in 1972. The North Rumayla fields produced 400,000 barrels of oil per day by 1975. The Rumayla fields on the Iraqi side of the border are much larger than those in Kuwait. Jurisdiction over the fields was one of many issues leading to the Iraqi invasion of Kuwait in August 1990.

In a July 18, 1990, letter to the Arab League, Iraqi's foreign minister Tariq AZIZ accused Kuwait of pumping $2.4 billion worth of oil from Iraq's share of the Rumayla fields. Two weeks later, Iraq invaded and occupied Kuwait. The following October, a Soviet report stated that Iraq would withdraw from Kuwait if it received control of the entire Rumayla fields and nearby Warba and BUBIYAN islands. That ultimatum was nullified by the Gulf Crisis in early 1991.

BIBLIOGRAPHY

METZ, HELEN CHAPIN, ed. *Iraq: A Country Study.* Washington, D.C., 1988.
STORK, JOE. *Middle East Oil and the Energy Crisis.* New York, 1975.

Elizabeth Thompson

Suwaydiya Oil Fields

Largest oil field in Syria, with a yearly output of one million tons (907,000 t)

The first Suwaydiya oil well was discovered towards the end of 1960 by the German company Concordia at a depth of 5617 feet (1712 m). This well is located southeast of Qarah Shuk in al-Jazira plateau in northeastern SYRIA. It was the second oil field to be discovered in Syria after the Qarah Shuk field, which was discovered in 1958 and contained nine wells. Between 1960 and 1962, the Concordia Company's field showed minimal progress. Three more wells were drilled in the Suwaydiya field, capable of production from the upper Cretaceous rock layer, with average depths of 5,000 feet (1525 m). But the heaviness of the crude oil produced was discouraging, unless it was blended with lighter crudes from Iraq, in which case the HOMS refinery could handle it. At that time, the Suwaydiya reserves were assessed at about 35 million tons (31.7 million t). The Suwaydiya fields were then thought capable of producing 12,000 barrels per day. In 1964, Concordia, which had begun a deep test-well a year earlier, had its license suspended when the Syrian government nationalized the oil industry. The Syrian Petroleum Authority, which was attached to the Ministry of Industry, undertook drilling with assistance from USSR geophysicists and drillers. In 1965, the Suwaydiya oil fields were considered commercial. Towards the end of 1974, a ministry for oil and mineral resources was established in Syria. It became responsible for concerting efforts with foreign oil companies for oil drilling, which has intensified since then. Compared with the Qarah Shuk, the Rumayla, and the Tayyim oil fields, the Suwaydiya fields are the largest, with an established reserve of 410 million tons (372 million t) and a yearly output of 1 million tons (907,000 t).

BIBLIOGRAPHY

LONGRIGG, STEPHEN H. *Syria and Lebanon under French Mandate.* London, 1958.

Al-Mu'jam al-Jughrafi li'l-Qutr al-Arabi al-Suri. (The Geographical Dictionary of Syria). Vol. 1. Damascus, 1990.

Abdul-Karim Rafeq

Olam Ha-Zeh, ha-

See Avneri, Uri

Olayan Family

One of the largest and most important Arabian business families.

Salih Olayan was a modest merchant in Medina early in the twentieth century. His son, Sulayman, who has close ties with Saudi Arabia's defense minister Prince Sultan ibn Abd al-Aziz Al Sa'ud, launched his career by working for the California–Arabian Standard Oil Company (later ARAMCO, the Arabian American Oil Company). His brother Abdullah and several of their sons are also involved in the business.

BIBLIOGRAPHY

FIELD, MICHAEL. *The Merchants: The Big Business Families of Arabia.* London, 1984.

Malcolm C. Peck

Olives

A staple of Middle Eastern cuisine.

Olives have been cultivated since ancient times, and both olives and olive oil constitute an important part of the diet in the Middle East. Olive trees grow in nonirrigated, rain-fed areas and bear fruit for generations. Green olives are cured in brine to extract the bitter taste, whereas black olives are cured by packing them in sea salt. Olive oil, pressed from green olives, is a staple in the Mediterranean area. In Arab cuisines, it is favored for frying vegetables and fish.

Jenab Tutunji

Olives, Mount of

Multisummited limestone ridge in East Jerusalem with biblical associations.

The 2,652-foot (809 m) Mount of Olives is the ridge's southernmost peak. Mount Scopus, the northernmost peak on the ridge, is the site of Hebrew University. The ridge was part of the Jordanian-ruled WEST BANK between 1948 and the 1967 Arab-Israel War, when the Israelis incorporated it into the municipality of Jerusalem.

The Mount of Olives is associated with Zechariah and King David in the Old Testament and with Jesus's last night and ascension in the New Testament. It is also the site of an old burial ground built by Jews in the belief that the messianic era would begin on its slopes.

BIBLIOGRAPHY

SACHAR, HOWARD M. *A History of Israel.* New York, 1982.
SHLAIM, AVI. *The Politics of Partition.* New York, 1990.

Elizabeth Thompson

Oman

Gulf sultanate formerly known as Musqat and Oman

Oman, which officially became the Sultanate of Oman in 1970, is located on the southeast coast of the Arabian peninsula, on the Arabian Sea and the Gulf of Oman. Approximately 82,000 square miles (213,200 sq km), it has a population of some 1,377,000 (UN 1988 estimate; no Omani census exists). Separated from the rest of Arabia by deserts, yet open to the sea, insularity is Oman's most important geographic characteristic. The western border is im

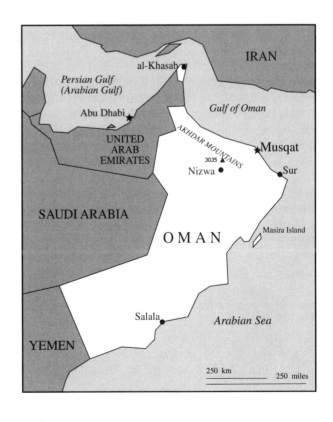

A fish market in Matrah. (Richard Bulliet)

precisely delineated with Yemen, Saudi Arabia, and the United Arab Emirates, as well as a Strait of Hormuz maritime border with Iran.

Physically, Oman has a narrow coastal plain about 1,000 miles long (1600 km), a parallel mountain chain with peaks exceeding 10,000 feet (3000 m), and along its western limits a dry gravel plain that blends into the Rub al-Khali desert. The major urban center, where about 300,000 people live, is the Musqat capital area, an amalgam of several formerly separate coastal towns adjacent to Musqat, the capital city; other cities are Salalah, Nizwa, and Sohar.

Politically, the country incorporates North Oman, where 90 percent of the people live, and South Oman, or Dhufar, including its Masira and Kuria Muria island dependencies; separated from North Oman by a fifty-mile (90-km) corridor of United Arab Emirates territory is the mountainous Musandam peninsula—the Rus al-Jibal exclave—that forms the Strait of Hormuz's south shore. Oman is divided into forty-one political districts, each administered by a *wali* (governor). The climate is hot, with summer temperatures reaching 120° F (49° C); dry inland, the coast is extremely humid.

From about 1870 to 1970, Oman subsisted upon a depressed agricultural and fishing economy. These activities now benefit from modernized irrigation, livestock, and fishery practices and still support most Omanis. Much larger revenues are today produced by the country's newly developed mineral resources—notably oil and gas—and, since the mid-1980s, copper and chromite. The government directs mineral development but leaves virtually everything else in private hands. Oman's trade balance is favorable; 90 percent of its exports are oil products, while it imports machinery, transport, and consumer goods

mainly from Japan, Britain, the United Arab Emirates, the United States, and South Asia. Oman's population is 80 percent local Arab, plus a significant South Asian minority. Arabic is the predominant language, but English is used widely too. Oman is unique because Ibadi Islam is the majority faith and its values form its cultural bedrock. Other Muslims include large Sunni and small Shi'a minorities. A substantial Hindu community exists as well. Since 1970, Omani education boasts a rapidly developing system, enrolling over 300,000 youth in 700 elementary, secondary, and vocational schools; Sultan Qabus University, a comprehensive, 3,000-student-capacity institution, opened in the late 1980s.

Oman has no formal constitution or political parties. Its sultan is an absolute monarch ruling by decree and assisted by his ministers. However, a protolegislature, the appointed Consultative Assembly, meets regularly. This governmental structure is rooted in past practice. Indeed, Oman's history in general reflects the interplay of two continuing traditions. One,

A frankincense tree in the Dhufar district of Oman. (Richard Bulliet)

Residences in Musqat. (Richard Bulliet)

identified with Oman's interior, sought to preserve both tribal autonomy and an ideal Ibadi Islamic society, preferably ordered by an elected imam. The other, associated with seaports, particularly Musqat, promoted maritime commerce, cosmopolitanism, and even a dynastically ruled overseas empire.

Oman's modern history began in 1749, when Ahmad ibn Sa'id (1749–1783), founder of its present Al Bu Sa'id dynasty, restored Omani independence, became imam, and merged the two traditions. Courting tribal and religious support, he also encouraged maritime and commercial expansion. Despite several attempts, his successors could not perpetuate Ahmad's accomplishment. Consequently, until 1970, Oman seldom was united. Under Sultan ibn Ahmad (1792–1804), and Sa'id ibn Sultan (1804–1856), a coastal-based, maritime-oriented, essentially dynastic government—the antecedent of today's sultanate—was consolidated at Musqat. In the early nineteenth century this regime was the western Indian Ocean's leading maritime state. Its position rested on its control of large commercial and naval fleets, strategic Arabian, Iranian, and East African ports, and the commodity and slave trade that linked India, western Asia, and eastern Africa. Initially, Oman's 1798 alliance with Britain buttressed its ascendancy. But this protosultanate was considered illegitimate by Omanis committed to the imamate ideal, and even at its height, its writ was contested. This underlying internal instability was aggravated by foreign intervention, first by the Sa'udis and then by Oman's British allies who were called in to protect the country against Sa'udi subversion. With his options in Arabia steadily shrinking, Sa'id virtually transferred his government to Zanzibar in the 1830s and Oman's troubles accelerated. By the 1860s, the country entered a century-long depression following the Al Bu Sa'id realm's

division into African and Arabian states, loss of Oman's carrying trade to British steamships, and suppression of the slave trade. As the bankrupt sultanate disintegrated, Azzan ibn Qays (1868–1871), leader of an Al Bu Sa'id cadet branch, became imam and briefly reunited the country. The British government, however, supported restoration of a weak, subservient sultanate and soon turned it into a thinly veiled protectorate that did not regain genuine independence until the 1960s.

In the early twentieth century, the imamate again reappeared in Oman's interior but, following its failure to destroy the British-defended sultanate, in 1920 the rival Omani governments regularized the conditions whereby they coexisted for thirty-five years. Sa'id ibn Taymur AL BU SA'ID (1932–1970) signaled Oman's revival by taking control of his government back from Britain, suppressing the imamate and reuniting Oman, and initiating exploitation of its oil resources. But his opposition to socioeconomic development led to widespread disaffection, rebellion, and eventual deposition by his son, Qabus ibn Sa'id, in 1970. After ending Oman's long diplomatic isolation and quelling South Yemeni–supported guerrillas in Dhufar, Qabus's prestige in Oman and abroad soared. Currently, wholesale modernization,

Sultan Qabus. (Omani Embassy)

Musqat's Ruwi district, the new downtown. (Richard Bulliet)

largely financed by substantial oil revenues and coupled with other development and defense initiatives undertaken cooperatively with neighboring Gulf states, is transforming Oman rapidly.

[*See also:* Sib, Treaty of]

BIBLIOGRAPHY

ALLEN, CALVIN H., JR. *Oman: The Modernization of the Sultanate.* Boulder, Colo., 1987.
LANDEN, ROBERT G. *Oman Since 1856: Disruptive Modernization in a Traditional Arab Society.* Princeton, N.J., 1967.
LORIMER, J. G. *Gazetteer of the Persian Gulf, Oman, and Central Arabia.* Calcutta, 1908–1915. Reprint, 1970.
WILKINSON, JOHN C. *The Imamate Tradition of Oman.* Cambridge, U.K., 1987.

Robert G. Landen

Oman Oil Company

Company that manages oil and gas development and trade.

The Oman Oil Company (OOC) supervises foreign investments and overseas petroleum activities of the Omani Ministry of Oil. The company is registered in Bermuda. It manages oil and gas trading.

From 1993 to 1994 it actively pursued investments in oil field development in Kazakhstan and Azerbaijan. It is a leading party to the plan to build a 1.5 million barrels per day pipeline from Kazakhstan to the Black Sea in partnership with the Kazakh and Russian governments. It is also considering building a pipeline across the Gulf of Oman to India. OOC controls 60 percent of a partnership with Caltex to own and operate a refinery in Thailand and one in India.

BIBLIOGRAPHY

Middle East Economic Survey. Nicosia, Cyprus.

Jean-François Seznec

Omar Mukhtar Club

Cyrenaican (Libyan) political organization.

The club was founded in 1943 by younger men advocating an independent and unitary Libya. It became increasingly critical of the British military administration and older leaders cooperating with it. By 1949, it had accepted that a federation of the provinces of Cyrenaica, Tripolitania, and Fezzan was an essential feature of Libyan independence.

John L. Wright

OMDH

See Organisation Marocaine des Droits de l'Homme

Omdurman

Largest city in the Republic of Sudan.

Omdurman has an estimated population of well over one million inhabitants that fluctuates according to drought and civil disorder in the rural regions. Originally an insignificant fishing village on the west bank at the confluence of the Blue Nile and the Bahr al-Abyad, it became a major city at the end of the nineteenth century when Khalifa Abd Allahi selected it as the site of the capital of the MAHDIST STATE (1885–1898). After the reconquest of the Sudan by forces from Egypt and Britain led by General Horatio Herbert Kitchener, the capital returned to Khartoum, across the Bahr al-Abyad. In the markets (SUQ) of Omdurman, livestock and agricultural produce are exchanged, and shops provide the necessities of life. All of the major political groups have their headquarters in the city, as do the television and radio networks and the air force. Although the official headquarters of the army are in Khartoum, the principal military installations are in Omdurman.

Robert O. Collins

OPEC

See Organization of Petroleum Exporting Countries

Open Bridges

The Allenby and Damiya bridges over the Jordan river were opened by Israel in 1967.

In the 1967 Arab–Israel War, Israel occupied the West Bank of the Jordan river, and when Moshe Dayan was Israel's defense minister, the bridges became links in a network that included Israel, the West Bank, and Jordan. The bridges had been closed by Jordan since the first Arab–Israel War of 1948.

Israel consented to the movement of people and agricultural products over the bridges, albeit with restrictions, which grew in number over time. Without the open bridges policy, the Palestinians in the West Bank and Gaza would have been cut off from Jordan and the other Arab countries.

In 1982 almost 400,000 people crossed the bridges, not counting the more than 100,000 visitors who cross annually. The Allenby Bridge is a short distance north of the Dead Sea, on the highway from Amman to Jerusalem. The Damiya Bridge is farther north, on the road from al-Salt, Jordan, to Nablus.

BIBLIOGRAPHY

Rolef, S. H., ed. *Political Dictionary of the State of Israel.* New York, 1987.

Benjamin Joseph

Open-Door Policy

See Infitah

Operation Jonathan

See Entebbe Operation

Operation Moses

See Ethiopian Jews

Operation Peace for Galilee

See Arab–Israel War (1982)

Opium

Papaver somniferum, the air-dried, milky juice obtained from incisions to the unripe seed pods of the poppy plant.

Opium is a powerful analgesic of mixed blessings. It is one of the richest sources of many useful medicinal alkaloids, such as codeine, morphine, and papaverine. But repeated and extensive use of it and its derivatives—most notoriously heroin—are known to cause severe addiction.

The poppy plant grows wild just about everywhere in the plains of Asia and the Mediterranean, and by the late medieval period there are references to opium use in various parts of the Middle East, as both a medicine and a narcotic. No place, however, is more famous in the Middle East for the cultivation and use of opium than Iran. Indeed, it is said that the highest quality opium, made exclusively from the white-flowered poppy, comes from there. The primary opium producing centers were the cities of Isfahan and Tehran and the Khorasan region.

The escalation of opium production and trade seems to have been closely linked to burgeoning European colonial and commercial interests in Asia, and official international controls of opium trafficking, cultivation, and consumption are a twentieth-century phenomenon. The United States spearheaded this effort with an international conference convened by President Theodore Roosevelt in Singapore in 1909. This was followed by a series of conventions held in the Hague, culminating in the convention of 1912.

Since then much has changed, but despite all the superpower interventions of the mid-twentieth century, Turkey, Iran, India, and China still produce a substantial portion of the world's opium supply.

BIBLIOGRAPHY

Encyclopaedia Iranica, vol. 1.
Encyclopaedia of Islam, 2nd ed., vol. 1.

Karen Pinto

Oran

Largest urban center in western Algeria (pop. 650,000, 1993).

On a bay of the Mediterranean Sea, Oran is the administrative, commercial, and educational hub of the petrochemical complex of Arzew–Bethioua (50 km [30 mi.] to the east).

Oran was founded in 903 C.E. by Muslim merchants from Andalusia searching for an alternative port to Ceuta on the West African gold route. The waters of the Ra's al-Ayn river supported the foundation of a sizable walled city with a citadel (qasaba, or CASBAH). Muslim CORSAIRS succeeded the merchants at the end of the fourteenth century, then were ousted in 1509 by Christian Spaniards. The Ottomans fiercely opposed Spain's expansion and incorporated ALGERIA into their empire, but it was only in 1791 that Turkish troops wrested Oran from the Spanish.

The French entered western Algeria in 1831 and occupied Oran, which had some 3,000 Muslim and Jewish inhabitants. European settlers far outnumbered Muslim rural migrants prior to World War I; it was only after World War II that the indigenous population rose to about 40 percent of a total of 413,000 inhabitants.

In the 1840s a canal system and a safe port with breakwaters were constructed. Administrative, commercial, and cultural functions shifted from the Muslim city to the east, along an east–west axis. The Muslim population was forcibly removed in 1845 to its own quarter in the south, resulting in de facto segregation of European settlers and Muslims well into the twentieth century. An urban streetcar system and a main train depot were in place around the turn of the century, an airport was constructed in the 1920s, and paved streets appeared by the 1930s.

During the colonial period Oran was the leading exporter of agricultural goods (red wine, olive oil, soft wheat, citrus, artichokes, tobacco, esparto, wool, and leather). There was little interest in industrialization; apart from mostly small construction and food-processing enterprises, two steelworks were financed by foreign capital. Trade disruptions during World War II encouraged the establishment of import-substitution industries (bottles, containers, cement, and hardware), but these struggled to survive after the war. The Plan of Constantinople (1958), with which France sought to jump-start industrialization in response to the ALGERIAN WAR OF INDEPENDENCE (1954–1962), created jobs in public works projects but did not enlarge the industrial sector.

After independence Algeria's government embarked on a gigantic program of state industrialization. In 1967 the Oran region was selected to become the main center for the exportation of hydrocarbons and the production of industrial chemicals. These basic industries were supplemented with factories for agricultural machinery and consumer goods. Private investment went primarily into the textile, plastic, food-processing, metalworking and footwear sectors. By the early 1980s the industrial base had grown to 112 state and 284 private businesses with 10 or more employees and total workforces of 32,000 (state) and 10,000 (private).

When the European settlers left Algeria in 1962, they abandoned close to two-thirds of the housing stock of Oran. By 1970 housing was scarce, however, and during the 1970s and 1980s some 12,000 new apartments (about a quarter of what was needed) were constructed. In spite of the periodic razing of shantytowns and the forced return of the inhabitants to their villages of origin, by the mid-1980s about one-third of the rural population had permanently settled in Oran and the other cities of the industrial region. The rural migrants who flooded the city found jobs primarily in construction, low levels of administration, retail, private industry, and the informal sector. Jobs in state industries typically were open only to qualified older workers.

Given the lack of convenient housing, the commute between residence and workplace often is as far as fifty kilometers (30 mi.), mostly by public bus or company van. Nearly half of Oran's industrial workforce works outside the city. The new suburbs require additional trips for shopping and entertainment, given the continued concentration of retail shops, services, and entertainment in the city center. On the other hand, many local and regional administrative offices, a new technical university, and vocational colleges have been moved to the suburbs, evening out the distribution of traffic.

In the center of Oran there has been a proliferation of bars, most of which sell coffee and tea. During the interwar period, they were the birthplace of rai, a music of bedouin immigrants that has become Algeria's rock 'n' roll. Also, the mixture of apartment buildings and small commercial and crafts establishments, typical of European inner cities prior to World War II, is still largely intact. Traditional food, clothing, and kitchenware shops are clustered in downtown Oran, and Medina Jadida (a kilometer to the south).

In downtown Oran, upscale residences, professional practices, airline offices, banks, restaurants, and furniture, jewelry, perfume, leather, and record shops coexist with less expensive apartment buildings, retail businesses, and bars as well as mechanical and electrical repair shops (the latter mostly on the periphery). The inner city is no longer the place where established families and rural migrants are neighbors, as was the case in the 1960s, but they still share the same neighborhoods.

The cancellation of the first national elections in 1992 and the return to de facto military rule has slowed the process of devolution. Although Oran has experienced less violence in the ruinous struggle between the military and the Islamists than Algiers, the paralysis is severe. How it will be overcome is difficult to discern.

BIBLIOGRAPHY

THOMPSON, IAN B. *The Commercial Centre of Oran.* Glasgow, 1982.

Peter von Sivers

Orbay, Hüseyin Rauf [1881–1964]

Ottoman naval officer and Turkish prime minister.

A naval hero in World War I, Minister of the Navy Orbay signed the Mudros Armistice (1918) ending Ottoman involvement in the war. Although he allied with Mustafa Kemal Atatürk in the Turkish war of independence, he later led a group in the Grand National Assembly that opposed Atatürk's modernism and secularism. He was prime minister for a year until Atatürk was elected president (August 1923). Orbay resigned from the Assembly after the caliphate was abolished in 1924, formed the opposition Progressive Republican party, and later was exiled by President Atatürk.

BIBLIOGRAPHY

LEWIS, BERNARD. *The Emergence of Modern Turkey.* New York, 1961.

SHAW, STANFORD J., and EZEL KURAL SHAW. *History of the Ottoman Empire and Modern Turkey.* Vol. 2. New York, 1977.

Elizabeth Thompson

Ordu Yardimlasma Kurumu

See OYAK

Organisation Marocaine des Droits de l'Homme

Moroccan human rights organization, also known as OMDH.

Prior to the establishment of the OMDH, the IS-TIQLAL party had founded the Moroccan League for the Defense of Human Rights (Ligue Marocaine de Défense des Droits de l'Homme; LMDDH) in 1972, and the Socialist Union of Popular Forces (UNION SOCIALISTE DES FORCES POPULAIRES; USFP) had established the Moroccan Association of Human Rights (Association Marocaine des Droits de l'Homme; AMDH) in 1979. During the 1980s, human rights abuses in Morocco skyrocketed. As a result, a group of Moroccan professionals created a nonpartisan movement to address a wide range of human rights issues and investigate cases of human rights abuses. The organization, the Moroccan Human Rights Organization (Organisation Marocaine des Droits de l'Homme), planned its first congress for May 1988. The government initially banned it because of its "extremist" membership, but in December 1988, it permitted the OMDH to hold its inaugural assembly at Agdal. Omar Azziman was elected head of the executive committee, and Medhi El Mandjra became the organization's first president.

The OMDH's focus on abuses of prisoners' rights led the government to release over one thousand prisoners by the end of 1989. In response to published OMDH reports, King Hassan II founded the Consultative Council of Human Rights (Conseil Consultatif des Droits de l'Homme; CCDH). But by mid-October 1989 political infighting among the executive committee members had caused the departure of the seven political independents and the resignation of President El Mandjra. Political parties now dominated OMDH.

Disturbances in late 1990 sparked renewed activism on the part of OMDH in 1991, and it continued into 1992 and 1993. Under the leadership of President Abdelaziz Benani (who replaced Ali Oumlil in January 1993), OMDH has become more proactive. A lawyer from Rabat, Benani is a former USFP activist who is more aggressive than his predecessor. To its earlier agenda of torture, the "disappeared," and prison conditions, OMDH added passport denials, violations of travel freedom, an independent judiciary, and press controls as points of contention with the government.

Morocco's three human rights organizations have their main offices in Rabat and are organized in sections around the country. AMDH, smallest of the three, boasts twenty-five sections with around three thousand members. Abderrahmane Benameur is its president. AMDH publishes an Arabic-language newspaper, *Tadamun* (Cooperation), that details human rights cases, AMDH activities, and related matters. OMDH has regional offices in Casablanca, Fez, and Tetuan and plans to open one in Tangier. LMDDH is headed by Mohamed Abdelhadi Qabbab, who also edits its newspaper, *al-Asabah* (The League). OMDH materials often appear in publications of the National Rally of Independents (RASSEMBLEMENT NATIONALE DES INDÉPENDANTS; RNI), the former Communist paper *al-Bayan* (The Clarion), and USFP newspapers.

In February 1993, CCDH Secretary-General Mohamed Mikou recommended that the government cooperate with human rights organizations and that King Hassan ratify the UN Convention on Torture. The government agreed on 14 June 1993 to ratify the UN Convention on Torture; the United Nations acknowledged the Moroccan ratification on 21 July. Amnesty International's April 1993 report on Morocco stated that five hundred persons had "disappeared" in Morocco since 1963. It named secret detention centers and provided a list of forty-eight Sahrawi prisoners who had "died" in detention between 1976 and 1990.

King Hassan II periodically releases political prisoners in reaction to unfavorable reports on human rights in Morocco. Prominent prisoners often are then deported. A case in point is Abraham Serfaty, released in September 1991 and immediately deported to France as a "veritable impostor." Morocco claimed he was really a Brazilian citizen who had no right to be in Morocco. Although the king has co-opted the efforts of human rights groups to a certain extent, they continue to play an effective if sometimes marginal role in Moroccan politics.

BIBLIOGRAPHY

AMNESTY INTERNATIONAL. "Morocco: Breaking the Wall of Silence: The 'Disappeared' in Morocco." New York, 1993.

DWYER, KEVIN. *Arab Voices: The Human Rights Debate in the Middle East.* Berkeley, Calif., 1991.

EUROPA PUBLICATIONS. *Europa World Year Book 1992.* New York, 1992.

SERFATY, ABRAHAM. "For Another Kind of Morocco." *Middle East Report* 2, no. 6 (November/December 1992): 24–27.

Larry A. Barrie

Organization for the Liberation of the Occupied South

Yemeni independence group, founded 1965.

Created through a merger of organizations and leading personalities in North and South Yemen (including Muhammad Ahmad NU'MAN, Abdullah Ali ASNAJ, and Muhammad Ali JIFRI) OLOS was originally a rival of the National Liberation Front (NLF) but later joined elements of the NLF to create the Front for the Liberation of South Yemen (FLOSY). Not long thereafter, the NLF insisted on its independence, and the two organizations were again rivals.

Manfred W. Wenner

Organization of African Unity

An alliance of African states (known as OAU) formed for mutual support in economics, self-government, and security.

In May of 1963, the OAU was founded at Addis Ababa, Ethiopia, by thirty-two African states, including Algeria, Tunisia, Morocco, Egypt, Libya, Djibouti, Mauritania, Somalia, and Sudan. Devoted to issues such as colonialism, economic development, and mutual security, the OAU, like most multistate coalitions, has had limited success in transforming its ideals into reality. Although the OAU was an active supporter of liberation movements in Mozambique, Angola, and Zimbabwe, it had difficulty providing more than moral and diplomatic encouragement; in intra-African conflicts, such as that over the Western Sahara, the OAU has found itself in a quandary. The Arab states of the Maghrib (North Africa) have been and continue to be its ardent members.

Egypt's President Gamal Abdel Nasser pressured the OAU to his side in his stand against ISRAEL, so through the 1960s, the OAU moved gradually toward the Arab camp. In 1971, the OAU issued a strong resolution criticizing Israel's handling of the Palestinian issue. By the end of 1973, all but four (Lesotho, Malawi, Swaziland, and Mauritius) of the OAU member states had broken relations with Israel. The Camp David Accords between Egypt and Israel (1979) caused a slow process of renewal of diplomatic relations with Israel—Zaire was first in 1982.

BIBLIOGRAPHY

AMATE, C. O. C. *Inside the OAU.* London, 1986.

MANSFIELD, PETER. *The Arabs.* New York, 1985.

Zachary Karabell

Organization of Arab Petroleum Exporting Countries

Organization (known as OAPEC) formed to protect and promote cooperation among Arab oil states.

Established in 1968, OAPEC aims at safeguarding the interests of the Arab petroleum-producing and exporting states, including cooperation in the oil industry (e.g., production, pricing, and marketing) and other related economic activity. OAPEC, which produces approximately 25 percent of the total world oil production, includes ten Arab states: Algeria, Bahrain, Egypt, Iraq, Kuwait, Libya, Qatar, Saudi Arabia, Syria, and the United Arab Emirates. Egypt's membership was suspended in 1979, in the aftermath of the Camp David Accords (when a peace agreement was signed with Israel) but was restored in 1987. One of OAPEC's first political activities was the decision to impose an oil embargo on selected Western countries following the Arab–Israel War of October 1973, allegedly for their pro-Israel posture during and after that war. The embargo was rescinded by OAPEC in

March 1974. OAPEC's decision-making bodies include a Ministerial Council, consisting of the oil ministers of the member states; an Executive Bureau, consisting of a high-level official from each of the ten member states; and a Secretariat.

The secretary-general, Abd al-Aziz al-Turki (1992), supervises four departments within OAPEC: Finance and Administrative Affairs; Information and Library; Technical Affairs; and Economics. OAPEC participates in joint undertakings in various activities of the oil business. Among these are the Arab Maritime Petroleum Transport Company, the Arab Petroleum Investments Corporation, and the Arab Petroleum Services Company. OAPEC also organizes seminars and conferences in energy, mineral resources, geology, and petrochemicals; it also provides technical training in documentation, storage, and retrieval of data.

BIBLIOGRAPHY

The Middle East and North Africa, 1992, 38th ed. London, 1992.

Emile A. Nakhleh

Organization of Petroleum Exporting Countries

Group formed to protect economic interests of oil-exporting countries, 1960.

In the early 1950s, international oil companies developed the posted price system to help host governments estimate oil revenues in advance. Posted prices were accounting devices that host governments used to calculate the amount of taxes the companies would pay under industrywide 50–50 profit-sharing agreements. Despite normal fluctuations in the real prices at which crude oil was traded, posted prices were not adjusted, and fixed posted prices became an industry norm. When competitive pressures forced oil companies to reduce posted prices unilaterally in February 1959, an immediate outcry arose from the affected host governments.

The first Arab Oil Congress met later in 1959. Delegates from oil-exporting countries came to plan concerted action against the oil companies. Structural differences among national oil industries made coordination among these countries difficult technically. Conflicts of interest over investment and production shares made it difficult politically. Competition between Venezuela and Middle Eastern oil exporters was heightened by the 1959 posted price cuts. British Petroleum reduced prices more in parts of the Middle East than in Venezuela, in an attempt to break the AS-IS AGREEMENT, a mediated connection between world oil prices and the U.S. market. Venezuelan oil thereby became even less competitive, requiring further downward price adjustments and convincing oil exporters that their responses to the companies had to be closely coordinated.

Political conflicts ended the first institutional attempt at coordination, the Oil Consultation Commission. But when the oil companies imposed yet another round of price cuts in August 1960, five oil-exporting countries set aside political differences to salvage their economic interests. Venezuela, Saudi Arabia, Iran, Iraq, and Kuwait formed the Organization of Petroleum Exporting Countries (OPEC) in September 1960. OPEC's first resolutions included calls to restore posted prices to their pre-February 1959 levels and to stablize oil prices by regulating production.

The U.S. government refused to recognize OPEC, forbade U.S. oil companies to negotiate with it, and imposed trade sanctions on OPEC members to discourage other countries from joining. This suited companies that saw an advantage in continuing their accustomed practice of dealing with host governments one at a time. OPEC responded creatively, developing joint negotiating positions with the understanding that any member able to gain an additional advantage on its own should do so, thus establishing a new floor for bargaining in the next round. During its first ten years, such leapfrogging earned OPEC members incremental gains in oil revenues. These in turn increased OPEC's international stature and attracted new members to the organization.

Perhaps OPEC's most significant contribution to the oil revolution was its support and implementation of "participation," a plan for the gradual nationalization of foreign oil properties. Even though members did not follow the participation strategy to the letter, the years of discussion and planning provided the opportunity to prepare for the responsibilities that would come when they became full owners of their oil industries. This accomplishment was overshadowed by OPEC's successful utilization of leapfrogging to achieve rapid oil price increases, within Libya in 1970 and afterward between groups of oil-exporting countries in the Mediterranean and the Persian Gulf. This set the stage for OPEC's complete takeover of crude oil pricing when the Arab–Israel war of 1973, with its well-designed Arab OIL EMBARGO, provided the opportunity.

OPEC's success in taking over oil pricing created new problems for the group. Oil-importing countries, led by the United States, demonized OPEC as the primary cause of worldwide economic decline. Inside OPEC, structural differences among its members led to disagreements over pricing strategies. "High price preference" members such as Saudi Arabia, with huge oil reserves and small populations, favored moderation in oil prices to discourage consumers from switching to alternative fuels. "Low price preference" members like Algeria, with smaller reserves and larger populations, wanted high prices to pay for economic development programs. Some members with large reserves, like Iran and Libya, also favored high prices. Iran had a large population and an ambitious development program, whereas Libya was politically motivated.

In 1978, when the threat of revolution pushed Mohammad Reza Shah Pahlavi of Iran to seek external allies, the low price preference countries succeeded in gaining agreement for a moderate pricing strategy to replace what had, until then, been an ad hoc method of setting oil prices. However, customer panic during the Iranian Revolution made this instantly obsolete. Oil prices doubled in one year. The resulting drop in demand for oil heightened the effects of the growth in oil exports by non-OPEC producers. OPEC became the marginal supplier of crude oil to the world market.

The market weakness of the early 1980s led OPEC to try again to reach consensus on an oil production-sharing plan that would allow the group to control oil prices by regulating the supply of crude. A voluntary production-sharing plan went into effect in 1982, but, as in the case of the voluntary oil import quota in the United States, it was ignored. A mandatory system was introduced in March 1983. At the same time, OPEC hoped to stimulate demand by lowering prices, the first time they had been reduced since 1960. An Austrian accounting firm was hired to monitor member production in order to discourage cheating.

The quota system had another flaw in addition to enforcement problems. Saudi Arabia, OPEC's largest producer, refused to agree to a formal quota on the grounds that this would be an unacceptable limit on its sovereignty. As a result, Saudi Arabia was marginalized within OPEC. As crude from many sources flooded the market, demand for OPEC oil declined. Its role as "swing producer" ensured that Saudi Arabia would absorb more than a proportional share of demand reduction, and dependence on associated gas presented difficulties when oil production in Saudia Arabia fell to below 3 million barrels per day in mid-1985. Later that year, Saudi Arabia decided to produce oil with only its own needs in mind. Supplies burgeoned and oil prices plummeted, dipping below ten U.S. dollars per barrel in June 1986. Al-

though oil prices recovered, they have yet to return to pre-1985 levels.

Political conflicts continue to divide OPEC members. The Iran–Iraq War (1980–1988) so split the organization that OPEC could not agree on a new secretary-general when it was Iran's turn to nominate one of its nationals. An assistant secretary-general, Fadhil al-Chalabi of Iraq, served as acting secretary-general from 1983 to 1988. Hostility among members made meetings acrimonious and reduced the usefulness of OPEC as a forum for hammering out nonprice-related strategies. The end of the Iran–Iraq War provided an opportunity to mend intra-OPEC relations, but Iraq's invasion of Kuwait in 1990 brought new turmoil. Iraq's justification for the invasion as a response to Kuwait's overproduction masked the behavior of virtually every OPEC member with excess production capacity: to counter low crude oil prices and domestic unrest by boosting production in order to increase revenues.

UN sanctions against Iraq, imposed in retaliation for the invasion and maintained into 1994, limit Iraq's oil exports to whatever can be smuggled out. But overproduction by other OPEC members continues to affect prices, and conflicts among them continue. Many members are expanding production capacity, thereby contributing to the existing conflict over production ceilings and quota allocations. Ecuador left OPEC in 1993 to escape the organization's efforts at market discipline.

OPEC's internal conflicts moved one prominent industry observer to call it "the Organization of Political Enemy Countries." The almost exclusive concentration of governments, press, and public on oil pricing has reduced the group's ability to devote resources to other aspects of industry development and coordination. An unexpected firming of oil prices in mid-1994 improved the immediate financial situations of all OPEC members. However, it is likely that politics and markets will continue to drive OPEC rather than the other way around.

BIBLIOGRAPHY

AHRARI, MOHAMMED E. OPEC: The Failing Giant. Lexington, Mass., 1986.

MIKDASHI, ZUHAYR. The Community of Oil Exporting Countries: A Study in Government Cooperation. Ithaca, N.Y., 1972.

SKEET, IAN. OPEC: Twenty-five Years of Prices and Politics. Cambridge, U.K., 1989.

TÉTREAULT, MARY ANN. Revolution in the World Petroleum Market. Westport, Conn., 1985.

WEISBERG, RICHARD C. The Politics of Crude Oil Pricing in the Middle East, 1970–1975. Berkeley, Calif., 1977.

Mary Ann Tétreault

Organization of the Islamic Conference

Organization founded in 1972 by Muslim states to promote their cooperation in achieving shared goals.

As a response to the August 1969 burning of the Aqsa mosque in Jerusalem, the first Islamic Conference of Kings and Heads of State was convened in Rabat, in September of the same year. This summit resolved that Muslim nation states should foster "close cooperation and mutual assistance in the economic, scientific, cultural, and spiritual fields." As a first step toward facilitating such cooperation, the summit also established the Islamic Conference of Foreign Ministers, which eventually ratified the charter of the Organization of the Islamic Conference (OIC) at its third meeting in March 1972. According to the charter, membership in the OIC is based on a commitment to the United Nations and its declarations on human rights, as well as an affirmation of the fundamental principles of mutual equality, respect for sovereignty, and the peaceful settlement of disputes among member states. The charter also enumerates the following principal objectives: the promotion of global "Islamic solidarity," the eradiction of racial discrimination and colonialism, the liberation of Palestine, support for the struggles of oppressed Muslim peoples everywhere, and a dedication to international peace, security, and justice. In accordance with these objectives, the OIC has, for example, issued condemnations both of the 1990 Iraqi invasion of Kuwait and the Serbian aggression against the Muslims of Bosnia-Herzegovina. The general secretariat of the OIC has permanent observer status at the United Nations and maintains its headquarters in Jidda, Saudi Arabia, until such time as Jerusalem will have attained political status that is independent of the State of Israel. The following states were members of the OIC as of August 1993: Afghanistan, Albania, Algeria, Azerbaijan, Bahrain, Bangladesh, Benin, Brunei Dar es Salaam, Burkina Faso, Cameroon, Chad, Comoros, Djibouti, Egypt, Gabon, Gambia, Guinea, Guinea-Bissau, Indonesia, Iran, Iraq, Jordan, Kuwait, Kyrgyzstan, Lebanon, Libya, Malaysia, Maldives, Mali, Mauritania, Morocco, Niger, Nigeria, Oman, Pakistan, Palestine, Qatar, Saudi Arabia, Senegal, Sierra Leone, Somalia, Sudan, Syria, Tajikistan, Tunisia, Turkey, Turkmenistan, Uganda, United Arab Emirates, Yemen, and Zanzibar, with Mozambique and the Turkish Muslim community of Cyprus as observers.

BIBLIOGRAPHY

MOINUDDIN, HASAN. *The Charter of the Islamic Conference.* Oxford, 1987.

Scott Alexander

Orientalism

See Historiography

Orientalists, International Congress of

A group whose meetings were devoted to the spread of learning in Oriental subjects.

Initiated in Paris in 1873, these periodic meetings of scholars—dedicated, as one scholar put it, to "the propagation of the knowledge of the History, Languages and Civilizations of Oriental people among Western Nations"—represented the academic profession of Orientalism as it was recognized in nineteenth-century Europe. Few non-Europeans attended the early meetings, and no meetings were held outside Europe until the fourteenth congress in Algiers in 1905. Papers on Asian and African topics of all sorts, but primarily focusing on philology and archaeology, were presented in sessions organized by geographical region or language family. The small size of the academic community concerned with Asia and Africa is indicated by the fact that the number of members, on all topics combined, remained in the hundreds throughout the nineteenth century. Some members, however, attended as representatives of national Oriental societies. Congress proceedings were normally published. (The latest published proceedings were those for the twenty-ninth congress, held in Paris in 1973.)

Richard W. Bulliet

Oriental Jews

See Edot ha-Mizrah

Orlov, Aleksey Feodorovich   [1786–1861]

Russian diplomat.

Count Orlov represented Russia at the London Conference of 1832. In 1833, as ambassador to the Ottoman Empire, he negotiated the Treaty of HUNKÂR-ISKELESI, whereby Russia agreed to protect the Ottoman sultan from Muhammad Ali Pasha of Egypt. After the Crimean War, in 1856, Orlov was a member of the Russian delegation to negotiate the Peace of Paris. He was domestic and foreign adviser to Nicholas I and Alexander II.

BIBLIOGRAPHY

ANDERSON, M. S. *The Eastern Question*. London, 1966.
Chambers Biographical Dictionary. New York, 1990.

                                    Zachary Karabell

Ormanian, Maghakia   [1841–1918]

Armenian clergyman and scholar; Armenian patriarch of Constantinople, 1896–1908.

Born in Istanbul, Ormanian was sent to seminary in Rome (1851) and was subsequently ordained a Roman Catholic priest. In 1877 he left the Roman Catholic Church to join the Armenian Apostolic Church. He was ordained a celibate priest in 1879 by Nerses Vazhapetian, Armenian patriarch of Constantinople, who employed his linguistic skills to prepare appeals to embassies and foreign governments concerning the situation of Armenians in the Ottoman Empire. In 1880 Ormanian was elected primate of Erzurum, and in 1887 he became a teacher of theology at Echmiadzin in Russian Armenia. Banished by the czarist government for his political views, in 1889 Ormanian became the dean of the seminary of Armash, near İzmir.

Ormanian was appointed Armenian patriarch of Constantinople in 1896, just after a series of mass killings attributed to the policies of Sultan Abdülhamit II had been unleashed against the Armenians of the Ottoman Empire. As religious leader of the Armenians, Ormanian steered a cautious course during an era of repression. This brought him much animosity from radical elements in the Armenian community who opposed policies of the sultan. In 1908, during the Young Turk revolution, he was removed from office.

Thereafter, Ormanian devoted his time to writing one of the great works of Armenian historical scholarship. His three-volume *Azgapatum* (National history; 1912 to 1927) is an exhaustive Armenian ecclesiastical history. In 1914 Ormanian entered the Armenian monastery of St. James in Jerusalem. He was exiled to Damascus in 1917 by the Young Turk regime and died a year later in Istanbul.

                                    Rouben P. Adalian

Ormsby-Gore, William George Arthur
[1885–1964]

British colonial official, also known as Lord Harlech.

In 1918 Ormsby-Gore went to Palestine as assistant political officer for the ZIONIST COMMISSION. In April of that year he defended the Balfour Declaration, but urged restrictions on Jewish immigration and land purchases because of growing indigenous impoverishment. However, in a speech in London in August 1918, Ormsby-Gore asserted that the indigenous population west of the Jordan river was not Arab and that the real Arab national movement lay outside of Palestine with Prince Faisal of the Hijaz (now part of Saudi Arabia), who was soon to be named king of Syria.

Ormsby-Gore became the British member of the PERMANENT MANDATE COMMISSION (1921–1922). As Britain's colonial secretary from 1936 to 1938, he rebuffed advocates of the partition of Palestine, and retired from office amidst the controversy.

BIBLIOGRAPHY

ABBOUSHI, W. F. *The Unmaking of Palestine*. Brattleboro, Vt., 1990.
INGRAMS, DOREEN, ed. *Palestine Papers 1917–1922: Seeds of Conflict*. London, 1972.

                                    Elizabeth Thompson

Orontes River

River in Lebanon, Turkey, and Syria.

From its source in the Lebanon valley (Biqaʿ, or Bekaa) in north-central Lebanon, the Orontes river (al-Asi) drains a large part of the northern Levant into the Mediterranean Sea. Flowing north, between the Lebanon and Anti-Lebanon mountains into Syria, the river has been dammed to form Homs lake. It then flows into Turkey before reaching the Mediterranean. Most of its 250-mile (400-km) length is unnavigable, but the river is an important source of irrigation.

                                    Mark Mechler

Orta Doğu Teknik Üniversitesi

See Middle East Technical University

Ortaoyunu

The Ottoman popular theater-in-the-round.

Sometimes described as "karagöz come to life," Ortaoyunu has frequently been compared to the commedia dell'arte because of its improvisational character. An urban entertainment, it was traditionally an open-air presentation performed by an all-male cast in a space encircled by the audience (women separated from men). Performances also were presented in taverns, palaces, and eventually theaters. Scenery was minimal: a chair or table to indicate a shop or booth, and one or two folding screens painted to represent a building, a forest, and so on.

A small group of folk musicians supplied music for dancers who appeared before the main presentation. This was followed by a burlesque dialogue between the two main characters, Pişekâr and Kavuklu, who correspond closely to the shadow play figures Hacivat and Karagöz, respectively. The play might be chosen from the special ortaoyunu repertory or, like karagöz, retell the plot of a well-known romance (Leyla and Mecnun, Ferhat and Şirin, etc.). The presentation was always open in form, however, and rather than a plot, might offer various scenes that entertained while imparting a human or political message.

At the beginning of the twentieth century, the improvisational aspect of ortaoyunu inspired the tuluât theater, but attempts (including the staging of Western plays) failed to preserve the Turkish theater-in-the-round as a viable form of entertainment.

BIBLIOGRAPHY

Encyclopaedia of Islam, new ed., vol. 8. Leiden, 1993, pp. 178–179.

HALMAN, TALÂT SAIT. *Modern Turkish Drama.* Minneapolis, Minn., 1976, pp. 13–28.

Kathleen R. F. Burrill

Osirak

A French-produced nuclear reactor sold to Iraq.

Osirak was originally developed in 1964 as a material-testing reactor. The purchase contract was signed on 17 November 1975; on 13 January 1976, Iraq signed a contract with Italy to purchase "hot cells" used to separate plutonium, which would make the reactor capable of producing fissionable material for an atomic bomb. Construction began in the late 1970s on the outskirts of Baghdad and was supposed to be completed by late 1981. Osirak was destroyed by Israel's air force on 7 June 1981; part of a smaller reactor survived.

BIBLIOGRAPHY

TIMMERMAN, KENNETH R. *The Death Lobby.* New York, 1991.

Ronen Zeidel

Oslo Agreement

Agreement between Israel and the PLO negotiated in Oslo, Norway, 1993.

Israel and the Palestine Liberation Organization (PLO) agreed in September 1993 to recognize each other and signed a Declaration of Principles (DOP) covering Palestinian self-government in the West Bank and Gaza Strip for five years.

The agreement resulted from the convergence of events and trends to create an optimal opportunity for peace. The *intifada* (uprising) by the Palestinian population of the West Bank and Gaza against Israel's occupation, starting in December 1987, empowered the PLO, as their representative, to seek a diplomatic settlement with Israel. In 1988, PLO chairman Yasir Arafat recognized Israel, accepted Security Council resolution 242, and renounced terrorism. The PLO could not capitalize on these concessions, however, because Israel did not reciprocate. Its position deteriorated because of the collapse of the Soviet Union, which left the PLO without superpower support. Furthermore, the government of Yitzhak Shamir adamantly refused to deal with the PLO or to make territorial concessions for peace. Believing that Iraq could help diplomatically, Arafat sided with Saddam Hussein during the Gulf Crisis (1990–1991), and thereby lost the financial support of the Gulf states.

The collapse of the Soviet Union, mass Jewish immigration, and the destruction of Iraq's army in 1991 enhanced Israel's security. Yet, Iraqi Scud missile attacks during the Gulf War made many Israelis realize their vulnerability. The Intifada convinced them that Israel could not continue to suppress two million Palestinians without diplomatic, financial, and moral costs. Labor party leaders were concerned that nonresolution of the Palestine problem was likely to increase Palestinian despair and violence, and Israeli repression. For the Labor and left-of-center parties, annexation of the West Bank and Gaza, mass expulsion, and continued occupation and repression were deemed costly in terms of international isolation and domestic discord, whereas granting self-government was increasingly viewed as least objectionable.

Both peoples and their leaders increasingly concluded that mutual recognition and sharing historic Palestine was the only viable option. The PLO had galvanized Palestinians and gained international recognition, but its armed struggle against Israel failed to liberate an inch of Palestine, and even though Israel was considered the fourth strongest military power in the world, it could not destroy the PLO or subdue a civilian population of occupied territory.

President George Bush and Secretary of State James Baker III thus had an unprecedented opportunity to broker peace in the Middle East by arranging the Madrid peace conference (1991) between Israel and the Arabs, including the Palestinians. When Prime Minister Shamir appeared to be stalling, Bush and Baker withheld a guarantee for a $10 billion loan for Israel. In the next elections in Israel, the public brought to power a moderate coalition, headed by Yitzhak Rabin, with a "territory for peace" policy. But eleven sessions and twenty-two months after Madrid, the negotiations still proved unproductive. The PLO regarded the framework for talks as unfair, and did not consider the United States nor its middle-range officials as "honest brokers." Israel realized that Palestinian negotiators from the occupied territories were unwilling or unable to negotiate independently from the PLO. Norway's Foreign Ministry arranged for a private, secret channel in Oslo for two Israeli scholars, Yaer Herschfeld and Ron Pundik, who were in touch with Yossi Beilin, Israel's dovish deputy foreign minister, and a PLO economist and aide to Chairman Arafat, Ahmad Sulayman Karia (Abu Ala). The negotiations took place in the winter and spring of 1993. When they progressed, Israel's foreign minister, Shimon Peres, took charge, and convinced security-conscious Prime Minister Rabin to support the agreement. Israel and the PLO initialed two sets of documents in Oslo in late August: an exchange of letters of mutual recognition and the DOP.

On 9 September, Arafat signed the PLO letter recognizing Israel's right to exist, accepted Security Council Resolution 242, renounced the use of terror and violence, and pledged to remove clauses in the Palestinian Covenant calling for the elimination of Israel. By recognizing Israel, the PLO renounced the Palestinian people's claim to 77 percent of historic Palestine, which they had occupied for centuries. The next day Rabin signed Israel's letter, recognizing the PLO as the representative of the Palestinian people and Israel's intention to negotiate with the PLO. Implicit was Israel's recognition of Palestinian demands for self-determination, possibly leading to independence in the West Bank and Gaza.

The second document, the DOP, which was signed at the White House on 13 September, outlines a five-year plan for Palestinian self-government, starting with Israel's withdrawal of troops from the Gaza Strip and the West Bank town of Jericho, and the transfer of authority over economic development, education and culture, taxes, social welfare, and tourism. This was followed by elections of an interim self-government council. After the second year, negotiations will begin on Jerusalem, refugees of 1948, Jewish settlements, and borders.

Majority reactions in Israel and among the Palestinians were initially favorable. Most Palestinians were disappointed that the most fundamental issues were deferred but supported the agreement because there was no credible alternative. There were, however, vocal rejectionists in both camps. In Israel, leading figures in the Likud party, such as Ariel Sharon and Benjamin Netanyahu, stated that should they come to power, they would not honor the agreement, and Jewish settlers warned of violent resistance. Palestinian radicals initiated deadly violence against settlers and soldiers. Negotiation over implementation of the interim agreement dragged on until another was signed in Cairo in May 1994. Then Israel's troops withdrew and Palestinian police took over in Jericho and the Gaza Strip. Violence by both sides and postponements diminished support for the Oslo agreement, yet the parties managed to reach a number of agreements, including Oslo II, signed at the White House on 28 September 1995. Oslo II set the stage for Israel's further withdrawal from the West Bank and for Palestinian elections. With each new agreement, the opponents of a peaceful settlement increased their violence. Hamas and Islamic Jihad conducted a number of deadly terrorist acts against Israelis. In Israel, the Likud party increased its violent rhetoric against Rabin, providing Jewish extremists with the climate that resulted in the assassination of the prime minister. Nevertheless, the new prime minister, Shimon Peres, moved forward with the peace process.

BIBLIOGRAPHY

ASHRAWI, HANAN. *This Side of Peace: A Personal Account.* New York, 1995.

BAKER, JAMES A., III., with Thomas M. DeFrank. *The Politics of Diplomacy: Revolution, War and Peace, 1989–1992.* New York, 1995.

PERES, SHIMON. *Battling for Peace.* New York, 1995.

SAID, EDWARD. *Peace and Its Discontents.* New York, 1996.

SHLAIM, AVI. "The Oslo Accord." *Journal of Palestine Studies* 23, no. 3 (Spring 1994).

Philip Mattar

Osman, Gazi [1832–1897]

Ottoman military hero and politician.

A heroic general in the 1877–1878 Russian–Turkish war, Osman held off the Russians at Plevna, Bulgaria, until forced to surrender in January 1878. He was rewarded with influential posts in the sultan's palace staff, where he engineered Abdülhamit's Islamist revival through funds for Muslim schools and *ulama* and public celebrations of Islamic holidays.

BIBLIOGRAPHY

SHAW, STANFORD J., and EZEL KURAL SHAW. *History of the Ottoman Empire and Modern Turkey.* Vol. 2. New York, 1977.

Elizabeth Thompson

Osman, House of

The longest ruling dynasty in Islamic history, 1300–1922.

The Osmanlı dynasty was named for Osman I, the Turkish leader in whose time (ruled c. 1299–1324) the foundations were laid of a state that later became the Ottoman Empire. The name was corrupted to Othoman, which became Ottoman in European usage. Succession went to the most successful son, often as a result of civil war or at least the threat of it. To prevent further strife, the new sultan was obliged to kill all his brothers and their sons. From the early 1600s, lateral succession became possible; and by the end of the 1600s, seniority had become the rule.

During the reign of the thirty-sixth sultan Mehmet VI Vahidettin, the Ankara government abolished the sultanate (November 1, 1922) and, on March 3, 1924, also the caliphate—the office of the head of Islam—which had been assumed by Ottoman sultans. Abdülmecit II, the last caliph and thirty-seventh ruler, and all members of the dynasty were immediately sent into exile, from which they were to be allowed back into the Republic of Turkey fifty years later—thirty years for female members of the family.

BIBLIOGRAPHY

ALDERSON, A. D. *The Structure of the Ottoman Dynasty.* Oxford, 1956.

I. Metin Kunt

Osseyran, Adel   [1905–   ]

Lebanese government official.

Born in Sidon in southern Lebanon of a prominent Shiʻa family, Osseyran obtained his degree in political science at the American University of Beirut. In 1943, he was elected to the Lebanese Chamber of Deputies (parliament) and joined the first Lebanese government after independence from France. In 1947 he was reelected to parliament and joined the Lebanese delegation at the United Nations (1947–1948). As a Shiʻite, Osseyran was reelected three times as speaker of the Chamber of Deputies (1953,

1957, and 1958). In 1969, Osseyran was appointed minister of the interior and minister of justice in the government headed by Prime Minister Rashid Karame, and between 1984 and 1989 he was minister of defense.

Osseyran is the holder of several awards, among them the Grand Cordon of the National Order of Cedar, the highest honorific award, granted by Lebanon. During the 1992 elections Osseyran's son, Ali, was elected as a parliamentarian from southern Lebanon and served as minister without portfolio in the government of Rafiq al-Hariri.

BIBLIOGRAPHY

Who's Who in Lebanon 1970–1971. Beirut, 1971.
Who's Who in Lebanon 1990–1991. Beirut, 1990.

George E. Irani

Othman, Othman Ahmad

See Uthman, Uthman Ahmad

Ottoman Empire

Multiethnic, multireligious, monarchical Muslim empire founded by the Ottoman (or Osmanlı) Turks in the late thirteenth century; it survived until after World War I, when, as one of the losing Central powers, it was formally dissolved by the peace treaties of 1918–1922. Mustafa Kemal (Atatürk) overthrew the last sultan in 1922.

In the thirteenth century, as the power of the Seljuk Turks declined, the Ottoman Turks began to absorb their small states. In the fourteenth century, the Ottomans took over some of the Byzantine Empire's territories and, late in that century, several Balkan states. Under Selim I and Süleyman I (the Magnificent), the Ottomans brought Hungary and much of the Balkan peninsula, parts of Persia (now Iran), and the Arab lands under their rule. In 1453, they conquered Constantinople (now Istanbul) and made it their capital. During the sixteenth and seventeenth centuries, the Ottoman Empire was at its peak and controlled much of southeastern Europe, the Middle East, and North Africa, comprising some 1.2 million square miles (1.9 million sq. km) with some sixteen million people. That area would today include parts or all of the following: southeast Hungary, Albania, the six republics that were pre-1991 Yugoslavia (Serbia, Montenegro, Croatia, Macedonia, Slovenia, and Bosnia and Herzegovina), Greece, Bulgaria, Romania, southern and Caucasian Russia, Turkey, Syria, Iraq, Lebanon, Is-

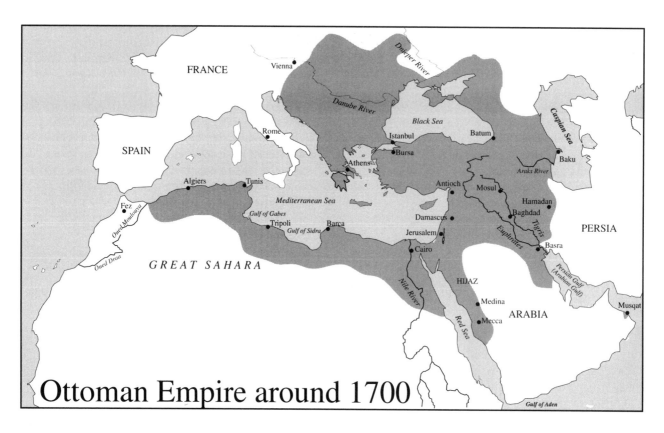

Ottoman Empire around 1700

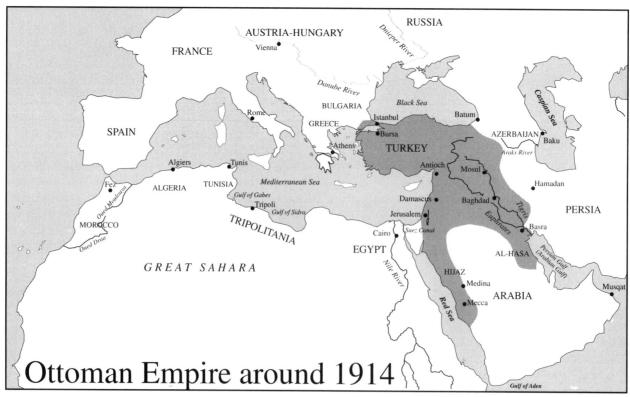

Ottoman Empire around 1914

rael, Jordan, Egypt, Saudi Arabia, Kuwait, the United Arab Emirates, Libya, Tunisia, and Algeria.

By 1914, only about 11,000 square miles (17,700 sq. km) remained of the Ottoman Empire in Europe of the 232,000 square miles (373,000 sq. km) controlled during the sixteenth century, with 613,000 square miles (986,000 sq. km) remaining overall— about half the territory of the sixteenth century. That greatly reduced territory included only what is now Turkey, the Arab states, and Israel until the empire's official dissolution (1918–1922).

The empire's early capitals included Bursa and Edirne (formerly Adrianople), but Constantinople (Turkish, Konstantiniye) served as its capital from its capture in 1453 until 1923, when the Republic of Turkey declared its new capital at Ankara. Constantinople was by far the largest Ottoman city, with about 400,000 population in 1520 and some 1 million in 1914. Other major Ottoman cities included Belgrade, Aleppo, Cairo, and Damascus. After 1800, cities such as Izmir (Smyrna), Beirut, and Alexandria rose to prominence—products of increasing nineteenth-century economic ties with Europe.

The empire's administrative divisions changed with time. By the nineteenth century, most provinces (vilayets) were divided into districts (sanjaks) and subdistricts (kazas), each of which had a number of village areas (nahiyes).

Geography and climate varied greatly, since the empire ranged over three continents, including much of what is today's Middle East. Mountains of modest height cut by corridor valleys and heavy forests characterized part of the European provinces, while in Anatolia, narrow coastal plains and high interior plateaus with little vegetation rose to rugged snowcapped mountains in the eastern part of the peninsula. In the Syrian province, similarly narrow coastal plains bordering the Mediterranean rose to the mountains of Lebanon. To the east, highlands yielded to desert and, beyond, to the alluvial lowlands of Mesopotamia (now Iraq). A spine of mountains branches south from the Syrian province, just inland—with one range heading into the Sinai peninsula and the other emerging along the western edge of the Arabian peninsula, reaching the greatest height in Yemen. The great rivers of the empire included the Danube, Tigris, Euphrates, and Nile—but navigable rivers were comparatively rare in both the European and Middle Eastern areas of the empire.

Climatic conditions ranged from the cold heights of eastern Anatolia to the heat of the Egyptian, Arabian, and North African deserts, including the sweltering heat and humidity of the coast of the Persian / Arabian Gulf. Almost everywhere rainfall was sparse—a fact of Ottoman life.

The empire had a wide base of natural resources; and much of its expansion can be understood as an effort to seize and control areas rich in various resources. For example, the Ottoman conquest of Serbia derived, in part, from an interest in its silver mines. As the empire lost territory in the nineteenth and twentieth centuries, it also lost the rich diversity of its resource base. The Ottoman state bent the economy to meet its imperial needs before any others. Edicts directed mineral, agricultural, and industrial products to satisfy both the imperial military and the bureaucracy.

Agriculture was the basic economic activity, providing a livelihood for the majority of Ottoman subjects through the centuries—although the produce varied according to time and place. Some areas were not cultivated during periods of political disorder but were tilled again with the guarantee of political security. During the sixteenth century, the areas under cultivation were so extensive that they remained at peak production until the post-1830 period of increasing governmental recentralization. The fertility of the soil was legendary in some areas, such as the Nile delta or the Aydin river valley in western Anatolia. More commonly, however, the soil was not rich or, when fertile, lacked sufficient rainfall. In many areas, agriculture was a precarious enterprise; crop failures and famines were normal in the cycle of life. Consequently, to survive, many families mixed animal raising and handicraft production with farming. Landholdings were usually small, a pattern preferred by the state, which sought direct relations with the farming families (and fiscal and political control over them). Large estates became more common after 1750, as agriculture became increasingly commercial—particularly on new land being brought into cultivation. Hence, great estates were most common in the eastern Syrian and Iraqi regions that were settled or resettled in the later nineteenth century. Such large holdings grew cereal grains; generally, overall grain output increased because of rising market opportunities. Vineyards and olive orchards flourished in the Mediterranean provinces of the empire, and cotton grew in the Macedonian, Anatolian, Syrian, and Egyptian regions—but their yields fluctuated greatly over time. Forest products were common to the Balkan regions and along sections of the Anatolian Black Sea coast, while dates were harvested in the Iraqi areas.

Industrial production first served both international and domestic markets but, after about 1800, internal demand predominated. Textiles, leather making, and food processing were of great importance; urban-based enterprises were highly visible, but rural manufactories were extensive and important. Until the nineteenth century, guildlike bodies (*esnaf*) in the cities and towns played important roles in organizing and controlling production. They worked in an uneasy cooperation with the state, helping it to obtain goods in exchange for government support of esnaf privileges.

Significant economic changes in the Ottoman Empire resulted from the rising economic, political, and military power of Europe in the late eighteenth and nineteenth centuries. Until about 1750, the Ottoman economy was autarkic—that is, relatively self-sufficient—by government design. It imported comparatively little and exported a variety of textiles and other manufactured goods, both to the East and the West. Thereafter, the export of many finished products decreased, but the export of agricultural products and raw materials, such as cereal grains and raw cotton, increased—almost exclusively to Western markets. Ottoman industry received a rude shock from the competition of European manufactured goods. Ottoman textile manufacturers then restructured their enterprises along nonguild lines with unregulated production and lower wages, so most of the craft guilds lost power and ceased functioning. Using machine-made thread and other low-technology imports, many nineteenth-century local textile makers survived and even increased production for the expanding domestic market. In addition, several new international export industries emerged that employed tens of thousands of poorly paid workers, notably in raw-silk reeling and carpet making.

The ethnic and religious makeup of the Ottoman Empire was diverse and intermingled. As if to lead by example, the Ottoman ruling family was truly international, counting dozens of ethnic groups among its ancestors. The relative size of the empire's ethnic groups is very difficult to determine, since the pertinent statistics were manipulated for use as weapons by nineteenth-century nationalism. Various ethnic groups sought their own states or attempted to deny the claims of competitors. In the era before territorial shrinkage, speakers of Turkish and of the Slavic languages formed the two largest groups in the empire. The largest ethnic groups were the Turks, Arabs, Greeks, Slovenians, Serbs, Albanians, Ruthenians, Wallachians, Moldavians, Croatians, Armenians, Laz, and Kurds. The official language of the empire was Ottoman Turkish, an administrative language consisting largely of Turkish grammar, with Turkish, Arabic, and some Persian vocabulary. The elite classes spoke and wrote in Ottoman Turkish, exchanging official correspondence and sharing a high culture, which gave the empire a unity that was superimposed over its diversity. The religious makeup was equally diverse. Until the nineteenth century,

when districts with large Christian populations broke away, most Ottoman subjects were Christians of various denominations, usually of the Orthodox church, the descendant of the Byzantine state church. There also were Armenian and Greek Orthodox Catholics, Maronites, and those belonging to smaller Christian denominations; there was as well a diverse but small population of Jews. Within the Ottoman Islamic community, adherents of Sunni Islam slightly outnumbered adherents of Shi'ism. During the nineteenth century, Islam became the predominant religion in the empire, just as Turks became the dominant ethnic group. By 1914, about 83 percent of the population practiced Islam.

During the four centuries before 1850, the Ottoman state had sought to organize the various ethnic and religious communities into a smaller number of religious nations, called millets. Under the leadership of its own religious authority, each millet organized, funded, and administered its own religious and educational institutions. The Greek Orthodox millet, for example, ran schools and churches for the lay population, as well as seminaries to train its clergy.

The sultan, who had descended from Osman, the fourteenth-century founder of the dynasty, ruled the empire throughout its history. Until 1453, the sultans shared power with other important families, as the first among equals. Thereafter, they theoretically were without peer, although power passed from the sultan to members of his government after about 1640. Until the end of the seventeenth century, power rested with the central state in the capital; during the eighteenth century, power became dispersed among provincial notables. A centralized state emerged during the early 1800s—based on internal evolutionary developments, as well as borrowings from Western models. Struggles for control of the state between the reforming sultans and the reforming bureaucrats swung in favor of the bureaucracy between 1839 and 1878 and then back to the sultan until 1908. After the revolution of the YOUNG TURKS in July of 1908, the last sultans reigned rather than ruled.

During the nineteenth century, the Ottoman Empire lost its Balkan territories to rising European nationalism and imperialism—especially pan-Slavism as instigated by Russia. Various Balkan ethnic groups—the Serbs, Greeks, and Bulgarians—abandoned, with great-power sponsorship, the Ottoman multicultural formula and opted for nation-statehood, which aspired to ethnic homogeneity but did not achieve it. Government efforts to create a competing Ottoman nationality foundered in the face of exclusivist nation-state identity. Efforts to eradicate differences among its remaining subjects were similarly unsuccessful. Take for example the state program to abolish the millets; fearing a loss of influence, various religious authorities—both Christian and Muslim—as well as many European statesmen opposed the move.

At the same time, ongoing domestic-reform efforts produced a revitalized, powerful Ottoman state that reasserted its presence in an unprecedented fashion. A series of reform decrees—the HATT-I ŞERIF OF GÜLHANE (1839) and the HATT-I HÜMAYUN (1856)—presented the path that Ottoman leaders intended to follow. Ottoman military forces successfully adopted Western weapons, strategy, and tactics and crushed local notables, nomadic tribes, and other domestic challenges to the central regime. The state apparatus became marked by increasing centralization, specialization of function, and ever greater size. Knowledge of Western languages, administrative practices, and culture became critical to advancement in the political and, finally, social spheres. The government, for example, founded a vast network of secular, nonsectarian, Westernizing schools to inculcate the new values. In the realm of popular culture, entertainment forms of Western origin—the theater and novels—became increasingly popular, as did European-style clothing and manners. Nineteenth-century Ottoman experiences foreshadowed those of third-world states of the twentieth century in yet other ways. After increasing taxation to finance the expensive civil and military changes, the Ottoman Empire ultimately resorted to borrowing vast sums from abroad, which eventually resulted in virtual bankruptcy and a partial foreign takeover of the Ottoman economy. Toward the end, despite centuries of success, the empire could not compete with the explosion of twentieth-century European economic, military, and political power; after participating as a member of the losing Central powers in World War I, it was partitioned.

BIBLIOGRAPHY

DAVISON, RODERIC. *Turkey*. London, 1968.
FARUQHI, SURAIYA. "Agriculture and Rural Life in the Ottoman Empire, ca. 1500–1878." *New Perspectives on Turkey* 1 (1987): 3–34.
GERBER, HAIM. *The Social Origins of the Modern Middle East*. Boulder, Colo., 1987.
EL-HAJ, RIF'AT ALI ABOU. *Formation of the Ottoman State: The Ottoman Empire, Sixteenth to Eighteenth Centuries*. Albany, N.Y., 1991.
INALCIK, HALIL. "Application of the Tanzimat and Its Social Effects." *Archivum Ottomanicum* (1973): 97–128.
KARPAT, KEMAL. *Ottoman Population 1830–1914: Demographic and Social Characteristics*. Madison, Wis., 1985.
LEWIS, BERNARD. *The Emergence of Modern Turkey*, 2nd ed. London, 1968.
MURPHEY, RHOADS. "Ma'din." *Encyclopaedia of Islam*, 2nd ed. Leiden, Neth., 1986.
OWEN, ROGER. *The Middle East in the World Economy, 1800–1914*. London, 1981.
PAMUK, ŞEVKET. *The Ottoman Empire and European Capitalism, 1820–1913*. Cambridge, U.K., 1987.
PITCHER, DONALD EDGAR. *An Historical Geography of the Ottoman Empire*. Leiden, Neth., 1968.
QUATAERT, DONALD. *Social Disintegration and Popular Resistance in the Ottoman Empire, 1881–1908*. New York, 1983.

Donald Quataert

Ottoman Empire, Civil Service

Government administrative service exclusive of the military.

In the sense of an administrative system that recruits and promotes officials on merit and operates by impartially applied rules, civil service is an anachronistic concept almost anywhere (except China) before the mid-nineteenth century. Even after that time, to apply the concept to the Ottoman Empire is questionable, in that the regulatory apparatus, although created, was used to thwart its impartiality.

For centuries, however, the Ottoman Turks had had a branch of the ruling elite whose functions were civil—in the sense of being neither military nor religious. Until the end of the eighteenth century, this group is best understood as scribes. Ottomans referred to them with terms like *kalem efendileri* ("men of the pen" or "of the offices"), or the corresponding abstract noun *kalemiye*. The scribes conducted the government's correspondence and kept its financial accounts and records on land tenure. Nineteenth-century reforms expanded and changed this branch of service into something like the civil services then emerging in Europe. From the late 1830s on, it also was referred to with a different term, *mülkiye*, having implications associated with land tenure and sovereignty. Particularly relevant to local administration, this term came to refer generally to civil officials, *memurin-i mülkiye*.

The state of the late eighteenth-century scribal service shows where this change began. It had a core of fifteen hundred men, serving in Istanbul in the Land Registry (*Defterhane-i Amire*), the grand-vizierial headquarters that Europeans called the Sublime Porte (*Bab-i Ali*), and the Treasury (*Bab-i Defteri*). Considering that scribes also served in military organizations or on provincial governors' staffs, an outside total can be estimated at two thousand. While it may seem odd that so few could suffice for a large empire, the Ottomans did not historically use scribes as administrators. In the years of conquest and through the sixteenth century, for example, local administration had been largely in cavalry officers' hands. By the eighteenth century, an able man might rise through scribal ranks to provincial governor, a kind of proto-foreign minister (*reis ül-küttab*), or grand vizier. Such careers were exceptional, and an ordinary scribe's role remained that of secretary (*kâtib*).

Many traits of the scribal service indicated its obscurity within the ruling elites. It had as yet no recruitment system beyond familial and patronage networks. It lacked its own form of training, other than apprenticeship. Except for those raised to heights that exposed them to elite factional politics, career patterns bore imprints of the guild tradition and the Sufi ethos that permeated it. To serve as a scribe was the chief practical application of the *adab*-tradition—the worldly, literary aspect of the learned Islamic culture. Building on an ancient Middle Eastern cultural elitism, Ottoman scribes had elaborated their craft to a high point in which mastery of stylistic conventions became more important than clear communication.

The shift from scribal to civil service began under sultans Selim III (1789–1807) and Mahmud II (1808–1839). In response to defeat by Russia during the last quarter of the eighteenth century, Selim's "New Order" (NIZAM-I CEDIT), the first attempt at comprehensive governmental overhaul, included both reform of existing agencies and the first Ottoman attempt to create European-style systems of permanent consular and diplomatic representation. In 1821, Mahmud II created the Translation Office (*Tercüme Odası*) at the Sublime Porte, which trained young Muslims as translators. Following his abolition of the janissary infantry (1826), administrative reform accelerated. In the 1830s, Mahmud II revived the diplomatic corps and reorganized government departments as ministries. To support his efforts at centralization, he also laid the bases of civil personnel policy by reforming conditions of service. He created a new table of civil ranks, abandoned the practice of annual reappointment (*tevcihat*) to high office, replaced old forms of compensation (such as fee collecting) with salaries, founded the first secular civil schools, and enacted laws eliminating some insecurities inherent in officials' historical status as the sultan's slaves. These reforms climaxed with the Gülhane Decree, which proclaimed "security for life, honor, and property" and equality for all—civil officials included.

Several weak sultans followed Mahmud II. This enabled top civil officials—their position in relation to the ruler now much secured, and their importance increased by their role in negotiating with the Eu-

ropean powers on whom the empire was becoming dependent—to run the government until another strong sultan emerged. The period so opened became known as the TANZIMAT (the Reforms, 1839–c. 1871). The center of power shifted from the palace to the Sublime Porte. As civil officialdom's Westernizing diplomatic vanguard grew in power, a new line of promotion appeared, running from the Translation Office through the embassies to the post of Foreign Minister and the grand vizierate. Westernizing policy changes followed en masse, as the Ottoman government grew in size and in its impact on people's lives. Civil officials now did take responsibility for local administration. Westernizing legal reform and the creation of secular courts gave them judicial roles. Modern census and population registration systems required Ottomans to face civil officials to get identity papers and passports. The teachers in the new secular schools were civil officials. Out of the Westernist official elite a literary vanguard emerged, too; from it the region's first Western-style political protest movement, the YOUNG OTTOMANS (Yeni Osmanlılar), in turn arose to exploit the tensions created by rapid change.

Between the death of Grand Vizier Âli Paşa (1871) and Sultan Abdülhamit II's accession (1876), the Tanzimat political configuration broke up. Abdülhamit shifted power back to the palace, making it the hub of a police state. Administrative reform continued along the lines charted during the Tanzimat, however. For example, Abdülhamit's reign became a growth period for education, publishing, and public works, especially railroads. In addition, his reign became the most important since Mahmud II's for the development of personnel policy for civil officials. The process began with creation of the personnel records system (*sicill-i ahval*, 1877). A decree on promotion and retirement followed, in 1880, introducing the idea of a retirement fund (*tekaüd sandığı*) financed by salary deductions. Commissions were set up to supervise the appointing of civil officials. With these, the civil personnel system assumed the general outlines of a modern, merit-based civil service, except that Abdülhamit manipulated the system, using it rather as a tool by which to control his officials. Under him, the growth of civil officialdom continued, as he pressured the politically conscious to accept office, in which they would become dependent on him. Ultimately, he had about 35,000 career officials and an equal number of hangers-on in civil service.

With the revolution of the YOUNG TURKS (Jön Türkler) in 1908 came a bold start in purging civil officialdom and streamlining administrative agencies. Despite gains like the 1913 provincial administration law, World War I and the dismemberment of the empire overcame these efforts. Still, in terms of elites, legislation, and organization, the Republic of Turkey inherited enough so that the early development of its administrative system has been described as evolutionary, rather than revolutionary.

BIBLIOGRAPHY

ÇADIRCI, MUSA. *Tanzimat Döneminde Anadolu Kentleri'nin Sosyal ve Ekonomik Yapıları*. Ankara, 1991.
FINDLEY, CARTER VAUGHN. *Bureaucratic Reform in the Ottoman Empire: The Sublime Porte, 1789–1922*. Princeton, N.J., 1980.
———. *Ottoman Civil Officialdom: A Social History*. Princeton, N.J., 1989.

Carter V. Findley

Ottoman Empire, Debt

Borrowing in the Ottoman Empire by the government and within the private sector.

Throughout most of its history, from 1300 to 1922, the government of the Ottoman Empire relied on short-term loans from individual lenders as well as currency debasement and short-term notes to resolve fiscal shortfalls. On occasion, the Ottoman government just confiscated the monies needed, either from the lenders or from state officials. In the private sector, individuals, who only sometimes were professional moneylenders, lent their surplus to others. Both public and private borrowers commonly paid interest for the privilege.

Both public and private borrowing persisted until the end of the empire—although confiscation became rare after about 1825. Very important changes occurred in the forms of borrowing, within and outside the government, beginning about 1850, when foreign capital became available and assumed an unprecedented role.

In many ways, the international borrowing experiences of the Ottoman Empire during the nineteenth century anticipated those of today's third-world nations. The Ottoman economy was competing in a world dominated by the industrialized nations of the West, which possessed superior military technologies and political and economic power. Ottoman survival strategy required large, modern military forces and state structures. As both were exceedingly expensive, government expenditures mounted accordingly. Unlike the economies of many of the countries with which it was competing—notably Britain and France—the Ottoman economy remained essentially agrarian and incapable of generating the funds needed

for increasingly complex and costly military and civilian structures. Thus, the government borrowed to modernize and survive.

Acutely aware of the dangers, Ottoman statesmen resisted international borrowing until the crisis provoked by Ottoman participation in the Crimean War, 1854–1856. International loans then quickly succeeded one another, on decreasingly favorable terms. These loans were private, the creditors being European bankers and financiers who were usually given diplomatic assistance by their own governments. By the early 1870s, Ottoman state borrowing too easily substituted for financial planning; between 1869 and 1875, the government borrowed more than its tax collectors took in. The Ottoman state suspended payments on its accumulated debt in 1875, after crop failures cut revenues between 1873 and 1875 and the global depression of 1873 dried up capital imports.

Perhaps fearing occupation by the European governments of its creditors, the Ottoman government eventually honored its obligations. Prolonged negotiations resulted in a reduction and consolidation of the total Ottoman debt and the formation, in 1881, of the Ottoman Public Debt Administration; this body took control of portions of the economy. The Ottoman Public Debt Administration supervised the collections of various tax revenues, turning the proceeds over to the European creditors—an international consortium representing bondholders of Ottoman obligations. Residents of France, Great Britain, and Germany held most of the bonds. The ceded revenues came from the richest and most lucrative in the empire—taxes imposed on tobacco, salt, silk, timber, alcohol, and postage stamps.

Although nominally a branch of the Ottoman government, the Debt Administration actually was independent and answerable only to the bondholders. Many scholars consider its founding as the beginning of Ottoman semicolonial status—when the state lost control over parts of its economy. Still worse, perhaps, the state's legitimacy and relevancy also declined in the eyes of subjects who had to pay their taxes to a foreign group rather than their own state. The Debt Administration represented a true loss of Ottoman sovereignty, but, as the government may have hoped, the consortium reassured foreign investors, who provided still more loans to the state, which needed still more cash to finance modernization.

Foreign capital invested in the Ottoman private sector became significant only after 1890. A part of the more general diffusion of European capital into the global economy, these investments also derived from the comforting presence of the Debt Administration, which was involved in many of them. Industrial or agricultural investment was nearly completely absent. Railroads, port facilities, and municipal services absorbed most of these monies, more firmly linking the Ottoman and international economies by facilitating the outward flow of raw materials and the import of finished goods. French financiers were the most important single source of funds, while the British and Germans also were significant providers. Almost all these new loans were administered by the Debt Administration.

By 1914, Ottoman public and private debts to foreign financiers consumed, in roughly equal shares, more than 30 percent of total tax revenues. In one way or another, the Debt Administration administered virtually the entire amount. This pattern of indebtedness makes clear the ongoing subordination of the late Ottoman economy to the European until the demise of the empire after World War I.

BIBLIOGRAPHY

BLAISDELL, DONALD. *European Financial Control in the Ottoman Empire.* New York, 1929.
ISSAWI, CHARLES. *An Economic History of the Middle East and North Africa.* New York, 1982.

Donald Quataert

Ottoman Empire, Imperial Council

The Imperial Council (Turkish, Divan-ı Humayun) was composed of state officials appointed by the sultan.

The council assembled four times a week in Topkapı palace, presided over by the grand vizier. In 1654, the office of the grand vizier, which had gradually gained independence from the sultan, acquired an official office and residence outside the palace, known as the *Bab-i Ali* (the Sublime Porte). From this time on, the Imperial Council was mainly relegated to ceremonial functions.

BIBLIOGRAPHY

LEWIS, BERNARD. *The Emergence of Modern Turkey,* 2nd ed. London, 1968.
SHAW, STANFORD, and EZEL KURAL SHAW. *History of the Ottoman Empire and Modern Turkey.* Cambridge, U.K., 1977.

David Waldner

Ottomanism

A supranational and protonationalist political principle that stressed patriotism and the group feeling of all Ottoman citizens.

Political elites used Ottomanism to achieve consensus among different ethnic and religious communities and foster political and social unanimity in allegiance to the sultan. It originated as a response to foreign encroachments and separatist movements during the TANZIMAT period and was sustained by enhanced social and political mobilization. While Ottomanism was sufficiently vague and malleable to serve different political platforms, the territorial indivisibility of Ottoman domains was its constant concern. The administrative principle of centralization was integral to Ottomanist policies.

Ottomanism germinated from the Tanzimat recognition of the notion of citizenship. The YOUNG OTTOMANS infused Ottomanism with constitutionalist ideas, which Sultan Abdülhamit II supplanted with Islamic symbols and solidarity. The YOUNG TURKS subscribed to secular and constitutionalist Ottomanism but were divided about the nature of the underlying administrative framework. The centralist position prevailed after the revolution of 1908. The piecemeal dismemberment and secession of non-Muslim parts of the empire compromised the secularist thrust of Ottomanism. Ottomanism was not a coherent ideology but blunted the growth of particular nationalisms, particularly among the Muslim groups.

BIBLIOGRAPHY

BERKES, NIYAZI. *The Development of Secularism in Turkey.* Montreal, 1964.

Hasan Kayali

Ottoman Land Code of 1858

See Land Reform

Ottoman Liberal Union Party

Political party opposed to the Committee of Union and Progress, also known as Osmanlı Ahrar Fırkası.

The Liberal Union party was established in 1908 by Riza Nur, as the major opposition party after the 1908 revolution. Rooted in Prince Sabahettin's wing of the Young Turk movement, it espoused a platform that sympathized with the ethnic aspirations of Albanians and Armenians, and thus opposed the Committee of Union and Progress's (CUP) strongly centralist and Turkish leanings. The Liberal Union won only one seat, as against the CUP's 288 seats, in the November 1908 parliamentary elections. In 1909 the party was repressed under the martial law that followed the April counterrevolution.

The Liberal Union was revived in November 1911 as an umbrella opposition group called the Freedom and Accord party (Hürriyet ve Itilaf Fırkası). It won a Constantinople (now Istanbul) by-election in late 1911, but it lost the national elections in April 1912. It then allied with the Group of Liberating Officers who dislodged the CUP from power that summer. The coalition ruled only until January 1913, when the CUP forced Grand Vizier Mustafa Kamil Pasha to resign at gunpoint after losses in the Balkan War. The CUP government dissolved the Liberal Union in June 1913, executing and exiling its leadership after Grand Vizier Mahmut Şevket was assassinated. Damat Mehmet Ferit briefly revived the party in 1919 to replace the CUP, but the party split and its liberal wing joined the Kemalists.

BIBLIOGRAPHY

SHAW, STANFORD J., and EZEL KURAL SHAW. *History of the Ottoman Empire and Modern Turkey.* Vol. 2. New York, 1977.

Elizabeth Thompson

Ottoman Military

[This entry includes the following articles: Ottoman Army; Ottoman Navy.]

Ottoman Army

Military organization that defended the Ottoman Empire and helped establish the Turkish republic.

The origins of the modern Ottoman army date to the destruction of the janissaries by Sultan Mahmud II (June 1826). Mahmud then laid the foundation for a new military organization based on Western models. Its centerpiece was a European-style infantry corps, the Trained Victorious Troops of Muhammad (Muallem Asakir-i Mansure-yi Muhammadiye, Mansure for short). Other military services—cavalry, artillery, and transport—were established mainly by reforming existing military units. Mahmud also created a modern corps of imperial guards out of the Bostanci corps, which had guarded imperial palaces.

There also were attempts to centralize the command structure. The authority of the commander in chief (*ser asker*) of the Mansure was gradually extended over the other services and branches. Thus his headquarters (Bab-i Ser Asker) gradually came to combine the roles of a ministry of war and general staff, and eventually was in charge of all land forces.

Under Mahmud II the military engineering schools were rejuvenated and reformed. He also established a military medical school (1827) and an officer school

(1834). Russia and Britain sent military instructors. Most useful services were rendered by a Prussian military mission that grew from one officer (Helmuth von Moltke) in 1835 to twelve in 1837.

In the 1830s Mahmud sought to strengthen the army. Large permanent units with regular commanding officers and staffs were formed. In 1834 a provincial militia (*redif*) was established to provide reserve forces. However, the commissary system could not support the rapid increase of the military. Epidemics were rife, and over a quarter of all recruits succumbed to disease. Desertion was very common. Although the army had been successfully employed as an instrument of coercion and centralization, as a military force it remained relatively small and poorly organized, trained, and equipped. By the end of Mahmud's reign there were only some 90,000 men in all the services. The wars with Russia (1828–1829) and with Muhammad Ali's Egypt (1831–1833, 1839) resulted in heavy losses and the disruption of the army's development.

During the Tanzimat period (1839–1876) the army consolidated and built on the shaky foundations laid in the previous era. The Bab-i Ser Asker continued to acquire new departments. The army steadily grew, and recruitment and training improved. In 1843 the army, renamed the Regular Imperial Troops (Asakir-i Nizamiye-yi Şahane, Nizamiye for short), was organized in permanent territorial commands, each consisting of an army corps (*ordu*) under a field marshal (*müşir*). The field marshals, directly responsible to the *ser asker,* had wide jurisdiction in all military matters. This limited the provincial governors' ability to intervene in military affairs, and was intended to centralize further the military organization and strengthen the authority of the *ser asker.* Five territorial army corps were established, with headquarters in Istanbul, Üsküdar, Monastir, Sivas, and Damascus. In 1848 a sixth corps was established with headquarters in Baghdad. In 1849 the Nizamiye had some 120,000 men and the *redif,* 50,000. With local and semiregular organizations, the empire's land forces numbered some 250,000 men.

The reign of Abdülaziz (1861–1876) witnessed considerable increases in military appropriations and improvements in the army's equipment and training. Modern weapons were purchased abroad, mainly from Germany, and with them came German military instructors. Since the majority of the officers were poorly educated, in 1855 the army initiated its own network of schools to prepare youths to become soldiers and officers. In 1867 over 8,000 students were enrolled in these schools.

In 1869 the army was reorganized into seven territorial corps, with headquarters in Istanbul, Shumla,

Monastir, Erzurum, Damascus, Baghdad, and San'a in Yemen. Each corps was required to have some 26,500 men. During the Russian war of 1877–1878 the Ottoman army had some 500,000 men, of whom some 220,000 took the field. During this period the Ottoman Empire reemerged as an important military power in southeastern Europe and the Middle East. Its army performed well during the Crimean War (1853–1856) and in the early stages of the Russian war of 1877–1878. In the latter conflict, however, the Ottomans were outclassed by the superior Russian army.

Under Abdülhamit II (1876–1909) the army benefited from ever increasing allocations, improved recruitment and training, and modern weaponry (mostly from Germany). It received assistance from a German military mission led by Kolmar von der Goltz (1883–1896). At the same time, however, Abdülhamit weakened the authority of the *ser asker* and placed military affairs under the supervision of permanent commissions staffed by his confidants. He personally approved the appointment and promotion of officers, and established networks of informers throughout the army.

By the 1890s the officer corps had become rife with discontent and sedition. The great expansion of the military had brought growing numbers of young officers from classes whose loyalty to the regime was not unconditional. Furthermore, the officers were better educated, and many espoused liberal ideals. In addition, officers and men were poorly paid, with salaries usually months in arrears. Finally, throughout most of Abdülhamit's reign the army was employed, with little success, in suppressing national and ethnic uprisings as well as lawlessness, especially in Macedonia and eastern Anatolia. Many officers, frustrated by the growing numbers of casualties, believed that the government was either unwilling or unable to provide the necessary means to restore order and protect the empire's territorial integrity. This led many officers, especially in the junior and intermediate ranks, to join the Young Turk movement, which called for the overthrow of Abdülhamit. The Young Turk Revolution (July 1908), which restored constitutional government and led, a year later, to Abdülhamid's deposition, began as a mutiny in the Third Army Corps, based in Macedonia.

In the following years, the Young Turk regime provided the army with increased allocations, modern weapons, and another German military mission, led by Gen. Otto Liman von Sanders (November 1913). At the beginning of World War I, the Ottoman army had some 640,000 men. During the war the Ottomans mobilized an estimated total of some 4 million men. Although the army was plagued by problems of logistics and command, it generally fought well and was successful, especially in Gallipoli (1915–1916) and in Iraq (1915–1916), and in defending Anatolia from foreign invasion following the war. In the end, however, the army could not save the empire from final collapse. Nevertheless, as the institution that had benefited more than any other from reform and modernization, it played a crucial role in the rise of the Turkish republic.

BIBLIOGRAPHY

LEVY, AVIGDOR. "The Officer Corps of Sultan Mahmud II's New Ottoman Army, 1826–1839." *International Journal of Middle East Studies* 2 (1971): 21–39.

RALSTON, DAVID B. *Importing the European Army.* Chicago, 1990.

SHAW, STANFORD J., and EZEL KURAL SHAW. *History of the Ottoman Empire and Modern Turkey.* Vol. 2. Cambridge, U.K., 1977.

Avigdor Levy

Ottoman Navy

Military vessels and fleets of the Ottoman Turks.

In the fifteenth and sixteenth centuries, sea power played a central role in the expansion of the Ottoman Empire, and Ottoman fleets operated on the high seas in the Atlantic, the Mediterranean, and east into the Indian Ocean. In the seventeenth and eighteenth centuries, the Ottoman navy was generally neglected and its effectiveness declined, but it was revived at times during the nineteenth and early twentieth centuries. The decline of the navy in the seventeenth and eighteenth centuries was largely due to the new geostrategic realities, whereby the main challenges to the empire no longer came from the naval powers of Spain, Portugal, and Venice, but from the land powers of Austria, Poland, Russia, and Persia (now Iran).

The origins of the modern Ottoman navy can be traced to the RUSSO-OTTOMAN WARS of 1768–1774. A Russian fleet based in the Baltic circled the European continent and destroyed the Ottoman fleet at Cheshme (July 1770). This led to a massive effort to rejuvenate the navy. During the reigns of Abdülhamit I (1774–1789) and Selim III (1789–1807), scores of modern warships were constructed under the supervision of European shipwrights. The Naval Engineering School (Tersane Mühendishanesi) was founded (1776), and the navy's command structure was modernized and placed under the supervision of the newly established Ministry of the Navy (1805). At the beginning of the nineteenth century, the navy was once again a formidable, though largely untested, force. In 1806, it listed 27 ships of the line and 27 frigates, as well as smaller vessels, armed with 2,156 guns and manned by some 40,000 sailors and marines.

After the fall of Selim III (1807), the navy was again neglected, and its strength declined. During the GREEK WAR OF INDEPENDENCE (1821–1830), it suffered many losses at the hands of the Greeks. The heaviest single blow, however, came on October 20, 1827, when a combined British-French-Russian fleet destroyed the Ottoman-Egyptian fleet inside the harbor of Navarino (now in Greece). The Ottomans alone lost thirty-seven vessels and thousands of sailors. It took the navy more than a decade to recover from the disaster at Navarino. By 1838, it had fifteen ships of the line and an equal number of frigates, as well as smaller vessels.

As of 1838, there was growing cooperation between the Ottoman and British navies: Ottoman and British squadrons conducted joint maneuvers; the navy was reorganized on British lines; Ottoman officers were sent to Britain for training; and British naval officers and engineers arrived in Constantinople (now Istanbul), the Ottoman capital, to serve as advisers from time to time.

In July 1839, the Ottoman grand admiral, Ahmet Fevzi Pasha, suddenly sailed the entire fleet to Alexandria and surrendered it to Egypt's ruler, Muhammad Ali, who was trying to become independent from the empire. This extraordinary act was the result of a power struggle within the Ottoman government following the death of Mahmud II. The fleet was returned in the following year as part of a general settlement of Ottoman–Egyptian relations, giving Egypt its autonomy.

During the TANZIMAT (reform) era (1839–1876) in the empire, considerable resources were directed toward the further development and modernization of the navy, and sailing vessels were replaced with steamships. On the eve of the CRIMEAN WAR (1853–1856), the Ottoman navy had 10 ships of the line and 14 frigates, as well as smaller vessels, with a total of 2,080 guns and a staff of more than 20,000 men. On November 30, 1853, Russia's Black Sea squadron, using new shell-firing guns, destroyed an Ottoman wooden fleet at Sinop. This had important political consequences, since it enraged British public opinion against Russia, leading to the Crimean War. It also marked an important milestone in naval history, resulting everywhere in the construction of iron-clad warships. The Ottoman navy also replaced most of its main wooden warships with iron-clads. By 1877, it had thirteen iron-clad frigates in addition to three wooden frigates, four corvettes, and various smaller craft.

During the reign of Abdülhamit II (1876–1909), priority was given to the development of the army, while the navy, because of financial constraints, was neglected, leading to its decline. In 1912, the navy listed four battleships, two cruisers, eight destroyers, three corvettes, and smaller craft. During the BALKAN WARS (1912/13), it was outclassed by the Greek navy, which dominated the Aegean Sea.

Following the Balkan Wars, the Ottoman government, led by the Young Turks, placed great emphasis on modernizing and strengthening the navy. A British naval mission led by the Admiral Arthur H. Limpus helped reorganize the navy and its various departments. The navy was to be greatly strengthened by two modern battleships ordered from Britain whose delivery was expected in August 1914. On August 3, however, the British government announced that with the impending European crisis (that very soon became World War I), the ships would not be delivered. On August 11, the Ottoman government permitted two powerful German cruisers, *Goeben* and *Breslau,* to enter the Dardanelles; they subsequently announced their purchase by the Ottoman navy as replacement for the British-built warships. The cruisers were given Turkish names, but they remained under the command of their German crews. On October 29, Ottoman warships, including the two former German cruisers, suddenly attacked Russian ports in the Black Sea, marking the entry of the Ottoman Empire into the war.

BIBLIOGRAPHY

MARMONT, DUC DE RAGUSE, MARSHAL. *The Present State of the Ottoman Empire.* Tr. and annotated by Frederic Smith. London, 1839.

OSCANYAN, C. *The Sultan and His People.* New York, 1857.

SHAW, STANFORD J., and EZEL KURAL SHAW. *History of the Ottoman Empire and Modern Turkey.* Cambridge, U.K., 1977.

UZUNÇARŞILI, İSMAIL HAKKI. *Osmanlı devletinin merkez ve bahriye teşkilâtı* (The central administration and naval organization of the Ottoman state). Ankara, 1948.

Avigdor Levy

Ottoman Parliament

Attempt at representative government in the empire between 1877 and 1920.

The Ottoman parliament met in 1877/78 and between 1908 and 1920. The constitution of 1876 stipulated a bicameral parliament: a lower Chamber of Deputies elected popularly and a Chamber of Notables nominated by the sultan. The parliament of the First Constitutional period (1876–1878) had two terms that convened March to June, 1877, and December 1877 to February 14, 1878, when Sultan Abdülhamit II abolished parliament. The Young Turk Revolution of 1908 forced Abdülhamit to re-institute it. The three parliaments of the Young Turk period met December 1908 to January 1912, May to

August 1912, and May 1914 to December 1918. The last Ottoman parliament that convened in January 1920 dissolved itself after the Allied occupation of Istanbul in March 1920.

For the 1877–1878 parliament, previously elected provincial administrative councils selected the deputies according to quotas based on population and proportionate allocations of Muslims and non-Muslims (seventy-one Muslims and forty-eight non-Muslims in the first session; sixty-four Muslims and forty-nine non-Muslims in the second). Due to inaccurate population figures in remoter Asian and African provinces and the political exigency of catering to separatist Christian elements and their European protectors, non-Muslim communities and European provinces received higher quotas.

Abdülhamit intended to legitimate his rule by giving his consent to parliament but stripped it of the authority to legislate independently and to limit the executive. Nevertheless, the deputies, who on the whole represented the provincial elites, were vocal in their criticism of the government. Abdülhamit closed parliament indefinitely on the pretext of the national emergency engendered by the ongoing war with Russia.

Thirty years later, the Young Turk Revolution of 1908 reintroduced the constitution and parliament. Constitutional amendments enhanced parliament's legislative prerogatives vis-à-vis the sultan, provided for ministerial accountability to parliament, and eliminated religious quotas. In the two-tier elections, males above the age of twenty-five voted for secondary electors, who then elected the deputies. Candidates had to be literate males who knew Turkish and were above the age of thirty. The election of one deputy for every 50,000 males produced chambers of around 250 deputies. The COMMITTEE OF UNION AND PROGRESS (CUP) managed to dominate the elections due to its revolutionary élan and moral authority in 1908, through electoral manipulation in 1912, and by suppressing opposition and effectively instituting a single-party regime in 1914. Electoral victory did not guarantee CUP's domination of parliament, which was the breeding ground of opposition.

From the dissolution of the body in August 1912, which followed a government crisis and anti-CUP rebellions, to May 1914, parliament remained in suspension. New elections were delayed until the winter of 1913/14 due to the extraordinary circumstances of the BALKAN WARS, the forcible CUP takeover in January 1913, and the assassination of Grand Vizier Mahmut Şevket Paşa in June 1913. As World War I began, emergency powers were ceded to the cabinet, and parliament's significance diminished even though it continued to meet with interruptions.

The two-tier election system favored the election of representatives of privileged social groups: Ulama, officials, landowners, and professionals. However, party politics produced a more diverse Chamber of Deputies in the Second Constitutional period compared with 1877/78. Parliament always served as a forum where both local and national issues were voiced. Newspapers reported its proceedings on a daily basis. Despite the executive's attempts to control parliament, the Chamber of Deputies served as a check on the sultan, the cabinet, and occasionally on the CUP's extralegal interventions.

BIBLIOGRAPHY

DEVEREUX, ROBERT. *The First Ottoman Constitutional Period: A Study of the Midhat Constitution and Parliament.* Baltimore, 1963.

FEROZ, AHMAD. *The Young Turks: The Committee of Union and Progress in Turkish Politics, 1908–1914.* London, 1969.

Hasan Kayali

Ouary, Malek   [1916–   ]

Algerian novelist and poet.

A Christian born in Ighil Ali, Ouary was educated in his village and became a radio journalist in Algeria; he then worked at the ORTF in Paris. Ouary was devoted to Kabyle oral traditions. His works include *Par les Chemins d'Emigration* (investigative report); *Cahier d'Epreuves* (1955); *Poèmes et Chants de Kabyle* (1972); also the novels *Le Grain dans la Meule* (1956) and *La Montagne aux Chacals* (1981).

Phillip C. Naylor

Ouchy, Treaty of

Italian–Ottoman agreement that ended the Tripolitanian War.

Signed on October 15, 1912, the treaty formally ended the Tripolitanian War between Italy and the Ottoman Empire. Italy was confirmed in possession of Tripoli and Cyrenaica, and it agreed to respect Islam and the rights of Muslims in these territories. Italy also remained in de facto possession of the Dodecanese Islands seized during that war.

BIBLIOGRAPHY

ANDERSON, M. S. *The Eastern Question.* London, 1966.

HUREWITZ, J. C., ed. *The Middle East and North Africa in World Politics.* New Haven, Conn., 1975.

Zachary Karabell

Oufkir, Muhammad   [1918–1972]

Moroccan general and politician.

Oufkir was from Middle Atlas Berber stock, from central Morocco. He served with distinction in the French army in Italy and Indochina during World War II and thereafter. When Morocco became independent of French colonialism in 1956, he was promoted to general and, in 1964, was appointed by King Hassan II as minister of the interior. In 1965, he was at the center of the BEN BARKA affair and sentenced by a French court to life imprisonment (in absentia). In 1971, Oufkir led the suppression of an army coup attempt against King Hassan and was made minister of defense. In the next year, however, he helped organize a second coup attempt; following its collapse, he committed suicide.

BIBLIOGRAPHY

Morocco: A Country Survey. Washington, D.C., 1986.
Who's Who in the Arab World, 1971–1972.

Matthew S. Gordon

Oujda

Moroccan city on the northeastern border with Algeria.

Because of its location on the border, Oujda (also Ujda, Wujda) has repeatedly been the scene of occupation by armies crossing into or from Morocco. In March 1907, Oujda was seized by the French at the start of their push into Morocco. Under French colonialism, it was, along with other cities, the site of nationalist demonstrations against the French. Today it has an international airport, a large cement plant, a central prison, and a population of some 261,000 (1982).

BIBLIOGRAPHY

Morocco: A Country Survey. Washington, D.C., 1986.

Matthew S. Gordon

Oujda Group

Algerian nationalists instrumental in winning independence and in governing the new nation.

The term *Oujda group* refers to Houari BOUMÉDIENNE and a circle of colleagues that emerged in Oujda, Morocco, during the later years of the ALGERIAN WAR OF INDEPENDENCE. The best-known members of that circle included Ahmed KAID, Ahmed Medeghri, Cherif Belkacem, Abdelaziz BOUTEFLIKA, Mohamed Tayebi, and Ali Mendjli.

As French repression of Algerian guerrillas intensified during 1957 and 1958, more and more of them were forced across the borders into Tunisia and Morocco. Boumédienne, who had begun his revolutionary career fighting in Wilaya Five, the western Algeria military district, ended up in Oujda, about seven miles (12 km) from the Algerian border. There he helped to organize the Moroccan branch of the external ARMÉE DE LIBÉRATION NATIONALE (ALN; National Liberation Army), which he eventually rose to command. When the separate commands of the ALN were unified in December 1959, Boumédienne became chief of its general staff, bringing members of the Oujda group with him.

In 1960 and 1961, factional divisions within the political leadership of the FRONT DE LIBÉRATION NATIONALE (FLN; National Liberation Front) began to lessen the effectiveness of the Provisional Government of the Algerian Republic (Gouvernement Provisoir de la République Algérienne; GPRA). The ALN general staff, dominated by the Oujda group, emerged as the most cohesive of the revolutionary institutions. It was frequently in conflict with the civilian leadership. Within days of independence in 1962, Ben Youssef BEN KHEDDA, president of the GPRA, fired Colonel Boumédienne, and Majors Ahmed Kaid and Ali Mendjli. The officers refused to recognize the GPRA's authority to take such action and instead entered Algeria to begin building internal support.

At Tlemcen, near the Moroccan border, there coalesced a group hostile to Ben Khedda and the GPRA that was headed by Ahmed BEN BELLA. Support for Ben Bella, who had spent most of the war years in French prisons, came from disillusioned liberal politicians, some radical socialists, and especially from Boumédienne and the Oujda group. The latter provided the military support that enabled Ben Bella to take over Algiers and manage his election as Algeria's first president in September 1962.

Ben Bella was to remain in power until June 1965, devoting much of his time to attempts to eliminate political competitors inside the government and the party. By October 1963 he had managed to eliminate many opponents. By then, power was about equally divided between his own followers and those of Boumédienne. Thereafter, he moved gradually to eliminate the latter, until, by early 1965, only Boumédienne in the War Ministry and Abdelaziz Bouteflika in the Foreign Ministry survived. During May and June, Ben Bella moved to undercut the authority of Bouteflika, threatening to dismiss both him and Boumédienne, but the latter intervened.

On July 19, 1965, the military overthrew Ben Bella in a bloodless coup engineered in the name of a body called Council of the Revolution. The heart of this council was the Oujda group, which also took over key posts in the cabinet (defense, interior, foreign affairs, finance). Houari Boumédienne headed both the Council of the Revolution and the government. These allies helped him, through the remainder of the decade, to consolidate his own power. But, between 1972 and 1976, as cleavages developed in the inner circle over difficult political choices, Boumédienne eliminated one after another the members of the Oujda group from his government.

BIBLIOGRAPHY

BOURGÈS, HERVÉ. *L'Algérie à l'épreuve du pouvoir (1961–1967)*. Paris, 1967.
QUANDT, WILLIAM B. *Revolution and Political Leadership*. Cambridge, Mass., 1969.
RUEDY, JOHN. *Modern Algeria: The Origins and Development of a Nation*. Bloomington, Ind., 1992.

John Ruedy

Ouled Sidi Cheikh

A nineteenth-century tribal confederation/brotherhood of western Algeria.

Because of their location in western Algeria, this powerful group of tribes was often influenced by the sultan of neighboring Morroco. The Ouled (also Awlad Sidi Shaykh) had capricious relations with the authorities of French colonialism. They cooperated with Governor-General Thomas-Robert Bugeaud de la Piconnerie against the renowned Emir Abd al-Qadir. One of the chief collaborators, however, Mohammed ben Abdallah, later turned against the French. This led to conflicts at Laghaout (1852) and Touggourt (1854). Then, during this campaign, Si Hamza, of the Ouled (Cheraga), joined the French.

A basic lack of French sensibilities toward the confederation's traditions produced a major insurrection in 1864/65. During the Great KABYLIA Revolt of 1871, the Ouled were generally restive rather than rebellious—then passive thereafter in relations with the French.

BIBLIOGRAPHY

JULIEN, CHARLES-ANDRÉ. *Histoire de l'Algérie contemporaine: La conquête et les débuts de la colonisation (1827–1871)*. Paris, 1979.

Phillip C. Naylor

Ouziel, Ben Zion Meir Hai   [1880–1953]

Sephardic chief rabbi.

Ben Zion Meir Hai Ouziel was born in Jerusalem and studied in various yeshivot there. He became chief rabbi of Jaffa in 1914. After serving as rabbi of Salonika from 1921 to 1923, he was selected as Sephardic chief rabbi of Tel Aviv, and in 1939 he became the Sephardic chief rabbi of Palestine, a position he occupied until his death. Ouziel was active in the MIZRACHI MOVEMENT, served as a delegate to several Zionist congresses, and held several committee positions in the JEWISH AGENCY. He testified before the Anglo–American Committee of Inquiry and the United Nations Special Committee on Palestine. In addition to being active in the political sphere, Ouziel published extensively on practical Jewish religious law (HALAKHAH) and on Jewish thought.

BIBLIOGRAPHY

Ohr Hameir: Essays in Honor of the Rabbi's Seventieth Birthday. Jerusalem, 1950. In Hebrew.

Chaim I. Waxman

Oveisi, Gholam Ali   [1918–   ]

Iranian general.

Born in 1918 in Tehran, Gholam Ali Oveisi attended military school and graduated from the War College in 1938. A special adjutant to Mohammad Reza Shah Pahlavi, in 1969 he was promoted to four-star general and commander of the army. He was appointed military governor of Tehran when martial law was declared in autumn 1978, mainly because of his reputation as a military hawk who was determined to suppress the uprisings, regardless of the human toll. In December 1978, all efforts at salvaging the shah's government having failed, Oveisi left Iran for Europe.

Neguin Yavari

Oxus River

See Amu Darya

OYAK (Ordu Yardimlasma Kurumu)

Turkish military pension program that became a public conglomerate with political power.

Ordu Yardimlasma Kurumu Army Mutual Assistance Association was founded in Turkey in 1961 as a pension program to protect career military officers from inflation, but it soon became Turkey's largest and most diversified public conglomerate. By 1984, OYAK's assets totaled more than 300 million U.S. dollars, with heavy investments in the automotive, electronics, construction, and food-processing industries, among others.

Since the late 1960s, OYAK's economic clout has enhanced its political influence. It is an example of the Turkish state's use of professional associations and social-insurance programs to implement economic policy. OYAK is nominally attached to the ministry of defense but is run autonomously by civilians and technocrats.

BIBLIOGRAPHY

BIANCHI, ROBERT. *Interest Groups and Political Development in Turkey.* Princeton, N.J., 1984.

Elizabeth Thompson

Oz, Amos   [1939–   ]

Israeli author.

Oz was born Amos Klausner, in Jerusalem. He studied in a religious elementary school and in a secular high school. His mother died when he was thirteen, and he went to live in kibbutz Hulda, of which he later became a member. His first short story was published in 1961. Thereafter he studied literature and philosophy at the Hebrew University of Jerusalem and taught at the kibbutz high school. His first collection of short stories was *Where the Jackals Howl* (1965). Oz left the kibbutz in the 1980s. In 1996 he resided in Arad and taught literature at Ben-Gurion University of the Negev. He has published twelve novels, novellas, and books of short stories; three books of essays; and one volume of literary criticism.

Oz has received the French Prix Femina, the 1992 Frankfurt Peace Prize, the Brenner Prize, and the Israel Prize. He was a visiting fellow at Oxford University and author in residence at the Hebrew University. A member of the "Peace Now" movement, he voices his opinions in the daily newspapers and in frequent appearances in the mass media and at political rallies.

The kibbutz is the locus of several stories and novels in which Oz examines the relationship between the individual and the collective in modern Israel. The closed society of the commune may be viewed as a human laboratory where national ideals are measured against personal needs and desires. The enemy, often depicted as lurking outside the geographical enclave, proves to be internal, harbored and suppressed within the protagonist.

Closely associated with that time is Oz's study of the family unit, love and loyalty within the family, obsessions, separations, and dissatisfaction. The tension between fathers and sons as representatives of two generations of Israelis, the founders and the followers, is not resolved by oedipal revolt and independence but, rather, by compromise and surrender. This is in line with Oz's political view, which calls for dialogue and harnessing of violence.

In *Black Box* (1987), an epistolary novel, a divorced couple is entangled in a passionate concern with their straying teenage son, who is perceived as a possible symbol of Israel's future: the broken family serves as a metaphor for political allegory. In *To Know a Woman* (1989), the hero is a former intelligence officer who withdraws from public service in order to come to terms with private emotions, a crumbling family, and a need for confronting his femininity, translated as the need for nurturing the self and the need for human compassion.

BIBLIOGRAPHY

BALABAN, ABRAHAM. *Between God and Beast: On Amos Oz.* University Park, Pa., 1991.
FUCHS, ESTHER. "Amos Oz: The Lack of Conscience." In *Israeli Mythogynies: Women in Contemporary Hebrew Fiction.* Albany, N.Y., 1987.

Zvia Ginor

Ozal, Turgut   [1927–1993]

Turkish prime minister, later president.

Turgut Ozal was born in Malatya, a provincial city in southeast Turkey. His father, trained as a religious teacher, taught in the secular schools of the Turkish republic and later worked as a civil servant; his mother was also a teacher. Ozal attended Istanbul's Technical University, graduating in 1950 with a degree in electrical engineering. After studying economics and engineering in the United States, he worked under Süleyman Demirel at the Electric Power Survey Administration, which was responsible for several hydraulic and electrical projects. In 1961, Ozal participated in the establishment of the STATE PLANNING ORGANIZATION, which issued five-year development plans, and throughout the 1960s, he was an important economic adviser to Prime Minister Demirel. He was one of the architects of the 1970 stabilization program, but following the 1971 military intervention, he left the State Planning Office to work for the World Bank in Washington,

D.C. Returning to Turkey two years later, he served as managing director of two large private sector companies and, in 1977, entered politics as a candidate for the religiously oriented NATIONAL SALVATION PARTY from Izmir. Ozal failed in this campaign, but in 1979, Demirel made him responsible for developing a solution to Turkey's growing economic crisis. As undersecretary of the State Planning Organization, Ozal proposed a series of measures to stabilize and reform the Turkish economy known as the January 24 Measures. Following the September 1980 coup, which removed Demirel from power, the military officers that ruled Turkey asked Ozal to remain as deputy prime minster in charge of the economy, a position he held until July 1982, when a banking scandal led to his removal from government. In response, Ozal and several close associates established, in May 1983, the MOTHERLAND PARTY (Anavatan Partisi; ANAP), which contested the elections of 1983. Despite opposition from the military leadership that supported the Nationalist Democracy party, Ozal's Motherland party won an overwhelming victory.

During his years as prime minister, Ozal focused on two major goals: reforming the Turkish economy and enhancing Turkey's position in world affairs. In the economy, he sought to tame triple-digit inflation, modernize industry, increase Turkey's exports in order to put an end to persistent shortages of foreign exchange, and privatize Turkey's large public industrial sector. Under his supervision, the economy grew at a rapid rate, and exports expanded dramatically. In addition, many of his reforms have created an environment more conducive to foreign and domestic private investment. He was less successful, however, in selling off the inefficient state sector and in reducing inflation; these failures and subsequent macroeconomic instability have dampened investment.

In foreign affairs, Ozal worked to integrate Turkey into the world economy, a strategy leading to his formal request for admission into the European Community in 1987. In the late 1980s, he initiated a new era in Greek–Turkish relations that would be more conducive to a settlement of their conflict. At the same time, he worked to further links with many Middle Eastern countries that were becoming important markets for Turkish exports. His desire for Turkey to play a leading role in regional affairs led him to strongly support the allied coalition against Saddam Hussein, a policy that sparked domestic opposition.

In the late 1980s, Ozal faced a number of political challenges. First, Turkey's persistent economic problems, coupled with rampant rumors about his personal corruption and that of his family, led to a precipitous decline in his personal popularity as well as that of the ANAP. Second, the conservative Islamic wing of the Motherland party, which dominated the party's organization, began to challenge the policies of Ozal and the more liberal wing of the party. Finally, the party faced challenges from its competitors, the True Path party on the right and the Social Democratic party on the left. In 1989, seeing the declining political fortunes of the ANAP, he engineered his election to the presidency. In doing this, Ozal faced a great deal of opposition, both from his own party and from the opposition parties, and was elected only on the third ballot. As president, Ozal sought to transform his office from its traditionally above-politics status to the preeminent political position in the country. As a result, he was accused, even by members of the Motherland party, of interfering in politics and forcing his will on the government. In addition, many of his policies were extremely controversial, particularly his enthusiastic support for the American-led coalition against Saddam Hussein and his calls for a conciliatory position toward the Kurdish issue. When Süleyman Demirel became prime minister in 1991, he vowed to remove his former protégé from the presidency.

One of Ozal's final projects was to project Turkish influence into the newly independent Turkic countries of central Asia. Following an exhaustive tour of the republics in the spring of 1993, he died of a heart attack in Istanbul.

BIBLIOGRAPHY

AHMAD, FEROZ. *The Making of Modern Turkey*. London, 1993.

HEPER, METIN. "Consolidating Turkish Democracy." April 1992.

SAYARI, SABRI. "Turgut Ozal." In *Political Leaders of the Contemporary Middle East and North Africa: A Biographical Dictionary,* ed. by Bernard Reich. New York, 1990.

David Waldner

Oz Ve Shalom

Israeli ideological forum, founded in 1971.

Oz Ve Shalom (Strength and Peace) was initially affiliated with the National Religious party, but became independent in 1975. It advocated moderation, tolerance and pluralism in matters involving religion and the state. Oz Ve Shalom also advocated settling of the Arab–Israeli dispute through territorial compromise.

Walter F. Weiker

P

Pachachi, Muzahem al- [?–1987]

Iraqi statesman.

Born in the small town of Bujaila (now al-Nu'maniya), Muzahem al-Pachachi graduated from the college of Saur in 1913. He began his active public life in 1924 as a member of the Constituent Assembly. From 1924 to 1925, he was minister of labor and communication and, from 1925 to 1927, the deputy of Hilla province. In 1931, he was appointed permanent representative of Iraq in London, minister of labor and communication, and also minister of the interior. He served as permanent representative of Iraq to the League of Nations from 1934 to 1935, minister plenipotentiary in Rome from 1935 to 1939, and minister plenipotentiary in Paris and Vichy from 1939 to 1942. He was prime minister from June 26, 1948, to January 19, 1949, and deputy prime minister and minister of the interior from 1949 to 1950. He died in Geneva on September 23, 1987.

Mamoon A. Zaki

Pact of Alliance

See Sened-i İttifak

Pagis, Dan [1930–1986]

Israeli poet, professor.

Born in Bukovina, Pagis, spent three years in a Ukrainian concentration camp, from which he escaped in 1944. Arriving in Palestine after the war, he learned Hebrew and taught on a kibbutz. He obtained his doctorate in medieval Hebrew literature and taught at Hebrew University, the Jewish Theological Seminary of America, and Harvard University. Among Pagis's books of poems are *The Shadow Dial* (1959), *Late Leisure* (1964), and *Twelve Faces* (1981). Scholarly works include *Change and Tradition: Hebrew Poetry in Spain and Italy* (1976) and *The Riddle* (1986).

BIBLIOGRAPHY

PAGIS, DAN. *Variable Directions: The Selected Poetry of Dan Pagis.* San Francisco, 1989.

Julie Zuckerman

Pahlavi, Ashraf [1919–]

Twin sister of the late shah of Iran, Mohammad Reza Pahlavi.

Princess Ashraf played a crucial role in the overthrow of Premier Mohammad Mossadegh (1953) and was partially responsible for the return of her brother to the throne. A decade earlier, she negotiated the departure of the Russian troops from Iranian soil during a meeting with Josef Stalin, the first of many official meetings she had with some of the leading political figures of the world. Treated and respected as an equal by her male counterparts, the princess was a strong advocate for the advancement of women's rights, chaired the United Nations Human Rights Commission and the Commission on the Status of

Women, and led the Iranian delegation. She was active in the United Nations for a total of sixteen years. Married three times—first to Ali Qavam, then to the Egyptian businessman Ahmad Shafiq, and finally to Mehdi Bushehri—she had two sons, Shahram and the late Shahriar, and one daughter, Azadeh. Known throughout the world as the Black Panther, she was widely believed to be an important adviser to the shah.

Roshanak Malek

Pahlavi, Mohammad Reza   [1919–1980]

Shah of Iran, 1941–1979.

Mohammad Reza was born in Tehran on October 26, 1919, to Brigadier Reza Khan (later Reza Shah PAHLAVI). He was designated crown prince in April 1926 and graduated from a special primary military school in Tehran in 1931, from Le Rosey secondary school in Switzerland in 1936, and from Tehran Military College in 1938. In 1939, he married Princess FAWZIA, the sister of King Farouk of Egypt; they had a daughter, Shahnaz, in 1940 and were divorced in 1948. In 1950, he married Soraya Esfandiari Bakhtiari; this marriage, too, ended in divorce in 1958 because she was not able to produce a male heir. In 1959, he married Farah Diba, who gave birth to Crown Prince Reza in 1961, and three other children thereafter.

Mohammad Reza Shah's thirty-seven-year reign can be divided into five distinct phases: from the 1941 occupation of Iran by the Allied forces to the 1953 coup d'état; the postcoup period (1953–1959); the period of political strife (1960–1963); the period of the shah's increasingly autocratic rule (1963–1976); and the period of revolutionary crisis that ultimately led to the collapse of the Pahlavi dynasty (1977–1979).

Mohammad Reza acceded to the throne on September 17, 1941, after Russian and British troops invaded IRAN on August 25, forcing Reza Shah to abdicate. A major crisis in the early years of his reign came in 1945 when the Soviet Union refused to withdraw its forces from northern Iran. Through a combination of international pressures and internal maneuverings by Prime Minister Ahmad Qavam, the Russian force finally left Iran in late 1946, and the pro-Soviet republics of Azerbaijan and Kurdistan collapsed. For much of this period, the shah was forced to conform to the will of the *majles* (parliament), which as a political institution dominated both the young monarch and the cabinet. Following an assassination attempt on February 4, 1949, a Constitutional Assembly was convened on April 21; it granted

him the right to dissolve the *majles*. In March 1951, the British-dominated Anglo–Iranian Oil Company was nationalized by an act of the *majles* under the initiative of Mohammad Mossadegh, the leader of the National Front, who subsequently became prime minister. Although 1951 to 1953 were "the worst years" of the shah's reign, he did not take any initiative to dismiss Mossadegh until he was urged to do so by Prime Minister Winston Churchill and President Dwight Eisenhower, who also urged him to appoint Gen. Fazlollah Zahedi as prime minister. When Mossadegh refused to accept the shah's dismissal order on August 16, the shah fled the country and went to Rome. On August 19, 1953, he was reinstated to power in a coup conceived by MI-6 (British Military Intelligence) and carried out by the Central Intelligence Agency. The leading *ulama*, the old-guard politicians, the propertied classes, and a core of army generals supported the shah and the coup.

The period 1953 to 1959 began with the repression of members of the intelligentsia who had supported either the National Front or the pro-Soviet Tudeh party, and saw a gradual increase of the shah's power vis-à-vis the old-guard politicians, the propertied classes, and the *ulama*. In this period, the government signed an agreement with a consortium of major Western oil companies in August 1954, joined the BAGHDAD PACT (later the Central Treaty Organization, CENTO) in October 1955, established an effective intelligence agency (SAVAK) in 1957, and launched the 1954–1962 development plan.

The period from 1960 to 1963 began with a reactivation of opposition groups and increasing pressures from the administration of John F. Kennedy for reforms. In May 1961, the shah appointed Dr. Ali AMINI as prime minister and Hasan Arsanjani as minister of agriculture; the latter became the architect of land reform. The shah, who could not tolerate an independent-minded prime minister, dismissed Amini in July 1962 and asked Amir Asadollah Alam, his closest confidant, to form a new cabinet and continue the reform. The land reform program, which was the centerpiece of the shah's WHITE REVOLUTION, and women's suffrage met with strong resistance from the *ulama*, who joined the opposition forces and instigated urban riots on June 5, 1963, to protest Ayatollah Ruhollah Khomeini's imprisonment. The shah was indecisive in responding to the situation, but Alam took command and gave the shoot-to-kill order to the security forces; over one hundred were killed, and resistance of religious groups was crushed. This event marked the suppression of all opposition forces and the beginning of increasingly autocratic rule by the shah.

In the period 1973 to 1976, the shah emerged as the sole policymaker; he allocated oil revenues among various agencies and projects and directly supervised the armed forces and security organizations, foreign policy and oil negotiations, nuclear power plants, and huge development projects. In this period, Iran's gross domestic product grew in real terms by an average annual rate of around 10 percent. Meantime, public services substantially expanded and modernized, and the enrollment at all educational levels increased rapidly. The shah also dramatically expanded the military and security forces and equipped them with advanced weapon systems. In the early 1970s he played a key leadership role in the Organization of Petroleum Exporting Countries (OPEC) and helped the organization to raise the price of oil sharply. Meanwhile, he emerged as the leading figure in the Persian Gulf after the withdrawal of British forces in 1971. Furthermore, he signed an agreement with the Iraqi leader Saddam Hussein in 1975, ending the two countries' border disputes. By the mid-1970s, the shah managed to establish close ties not only with the United States, Western Europe, and Muslim countries but also with the Communist bloc countries, South Africa, and Israel.

The many diplomatic and economic achievements of the shah led to ostentatious displays of royal hubris. For example, in October 1971 he celebrated the 2,500th anniversary of the foundation of the Persian Empire by Cyrus the Great and formed, in March 1975, a one-party system. Both acts were resented by the intelligentsia and middle classes. He also replaced powerful, independent-minded politicians with more accommodating and submissive aides, a strategy that cost him dearly at times of international and domestic crisis. Concurrently, the shah's White Revolution had undermined the traditional foundation of his authority—the *ulama,* the bazaar merchants, and the landowning classes. They were replaced by the entrepreneurs, the young Western-educated bureaucratic elites, and new middle classes who had developed uneasy relations with the shah. The intelligentsia resented the lack of political freedom and violations of human rights, the rigged elections, corruption, and close ties with the United States. The old religious groups and the bazaar merchants and artisans resented the un-Islamic Western lifestyle promoted by the shah's modernization policies. The entrepreneurial and political elites were discontented with the shah's autocratic rule, and with the lack of their own political power and autonomous organizational base. Under these circumstances the nucleus of an anti-shah revolutionary coalition was formed by a large group of liberal and radical intelligentsia, and a small group of militant *ulama* and their important followers in the bazaar.

The opportunity for the opposition to challenge the shah came after the victory of Jimmy Carter in

Shah Mohammad Reza Pahlavi on an Iranian postage stamp. (Richard Bulliet)

the U.S. presidential race of November 1976 and the ensuing active support given by his administration to the cause of human rights. When the political upheavals began (1977), the shah's weak and indecisive character contributed to the collapse of the Pahlavi regime and the rise of the Islamic Republic under the leadership of Ayatollah Khomeini, a charismatic figure with a strong will to power. Despite the mass-based nature of the IRANIAN REVOLUTION, however, not all sectors of the population opposed the shah. The peasantry, for example, constituting over half of the population at the time, continued to support him, though passively. Even labor and the majority of public-sector employees and the middle and lower-middle classes did not join the uprising until the last phases of the revolution, when the shah's regime was on the verge of collapse. After a series of mass demonstrations, mass strikes, and clashes between the shah's security forces and opposition groups in the latter half of 1978, the shah left the country in January 1979; he died of cancer in Cairo on July 27, 1980.

For the shah the ideal model of the imperial persona was the Persian image of the "benevolent autocrat," as exemplified by great Persian monarchs, including his father, Reza Shah. Although this model implied that he should be determined, self-confident, and brave, in reality he was gentle, timid, and indecisive. The shah's inherently fragile character became evident particularly during periods of instability and crisis, whereas his "benevolent autocrat" tendencies came up during periods of stability and success. Furthermore, he was not immune to conspiracy theories. He therefore often saw the secret hands of foreign powers, specifically those of the British, behind virtually every international and domestic incident. He believed, for example, that the Anglophobic Mohammad Mossadegh and the xenophobic Ayatollah Khomeini were British agents. Referring to an Anglo–Russian conspiracy, the shah attributed the Islamic revolution to the "unholy alliance of Red and Black." Belief in conspiracy theories further intensified his inherent vulnerability during periods of crisis. As a result, in the critical periods of 1941 to 1953 and 1960 to 1963, Mohammad Reza showed considerable indecisiveness. On the other hand, in the postcoup period (1953–1959) he began to show more determination, and in the stable period of 1963–1976, he emerged as a "benevolent autocrat," who devoted himself, in his own way, to the welfare of his people. Finally, during the period of revolutionary crisis (1977–1979), the shah, for the third time during his reign, turned indecisive, once again embraced conspiracy theories, and displayed a mood of withdrawal—traits and reactions that may have contributed significantly to his downfall.

BIBLIOGRAPHY

The shah's autobiography and assessment of major events of his life are presented in MOHAMMAD REZA PAHLAVI, *Mission for My Country* (London, 1961) and *Answer to History* (New York, 1980). A review of the period 1941 to 1953 may be found in FAKHREDDIN AZIMI, *Iran: The Crisis of Democracy* (London, 1989). For the story of the 1953 coup d'état, see KERMIT ROOSEVELT, *Countercoup: The Struggle for the Control of Iran* (New York, 1979). For the postcoup period, see DENIS WRIGHT, "Ten Years in Iran," *Asian Affairs* 12 (1991): 259–271. For Iran's achievements under the shah in the 1960s and 1970s, see JANE JACQZ, ed., *Iran: Past, Present, and Future* (New York, 1976); see also ALI BANUAZIZI, "Iran: The Making of a Regional Power," in *The Middle East: Oil, Conflict, and Hope*, ed. by A. L. Udovitch (Lexington, Mass., 1976). For an analysis of causes, processes, and consequences of the shah's White Revolution, see AHMAD ASHRAF, "From the White Revolution to the Islamic Revolution," in *The Crisis of an Islamic State: Iran After the Revolution*, ed. by Sohrab Behda and Said Rahnema (London, 1995). For an eyewitness report of the shah in his last years, see ASADOLLAH ALAM, *The Shah and I: The Confidential Diary of Iran's Royal Court, 1969–1977*, ed. by Alinaghi Alikhani (London, 1991). For the shah's reactions during the 1977–1979 revolutionary upheaval, see AHMAD ASHRAF and ALI BANUAZIZI, "The State, Classes, and Modes of Mobilization in the Iranian Revolution," *State, Culture and Society* 1, no. 3 (1985): 3–40. For a psychological account of the shah's character, see MARVIN ZONIS, *Majestic Failure: The Fall of the Shah* (Chicago, 1991).

Ahmad Ashraf

Pahlavi, Reza [1878–1944]

Founding shah of the Pahlavi dynasty in Persia (now Iran), 1925–1941.

Reza Shah was born in Alasht, a small village in Savadkuh, some seventy miles (110 km) northeast of Tehran, into a military family. His father, Abbas Ali Khan, a colonel in the Seventh Savadkuh regiment, had a reputation as a brave officer and loyal servant of the Qajar shah. He had several wives, the last of whom was Nushafarin Khanom, Reza's mother. Abbas Ali fathered some thirty-two children, of whom four daughters and eight sons survived. Reza was about eight months old when his father died, on November 26, 1878. Nushafarin Khanom, being Tehrani and not at ease in Alasht, set out for Tehran in about mid-spring 1879.

For some years Reza and his mother lived with one of her maternal uncles, Abol Qasem Khan, who was an officer in the Cossack Brigade at Tehran. Very fond of his nephew and desiring to give him a better life, the uncle took the boy to the home of Amir Tuman Kazim Khan, a general in the regular Iranian army; there the boy was called Reza Khan. At about the age of fifteen, his uncle enrolled him in the Cossack Brigade, and Reza Khan steadily rose from the ranks to officer level. In 1915, Reza Khan was a major of the machine gun detachment at Tehran. In this same year, he married a sixteen-year-old daughter of Timur Khan Mir Panj, a commander of the regular army. (She was to become queen under the title of Taj Malik and was the mother of the second Pahlavi shah and three other children.) In 1916, Reza Khan was *sarhang do* (lieutenant colonel) at Kirmanshah. He took part in a number of military campaigns against rebellious tribes in the mountain areas of Mazandaran, Gilan, and Azerbaijan. In 1917, Reza Khan was put in charge of training the volunteers for the newly established regular army unit at Hamadan.

The Russian Revolution of 1917 brought disorganization within the Cossack division in Iran, a factor that worked to Reza Khan's favor. Reza Khan assisted pro-White Russian Colonel Starosselsky in replacing pro-Bolshevik General Clergé as commander of the Cossack division in Iran. As a result, Reza Khan was named *sarhang* (full colonel) almost at once. Enjoying the patronage of Colonel Starosselsky, Reza Khan was quickly promoted to brigadier general and placed in command of the Tehran battalion. In 1919, he was promoted to second general.

And in 1920, Reza Khan was promoted to *mir panj* (equivalent to full general) and was placed in command of all the Cossack troops reassembled at Qazvin, after they were defeated by the Russian troops.

At this time, Iran was suffering an acute political crisis that was produced by reformist and separatist movements in Gilan and Azerbaijan, continuous war between tribes, the presence of the Red army in the north and British army in the south, disorganization of the armed forces, and the inability of government to convene a parliament to ratify the unpopular ANGLO–PERSIAN AGREEMENT of 1919.

This situation prompted Reza Khan, with the support of the British, to march his troops, some three thousand men, into Tehran on February 21, 1921. Supported by junior officers from the gendarmerie and a young pro-British journalist, Sayyed Ziya Tabataba'i, he arrested some sixty prominent politicians, assured Ahmad Shah Qajar that the coup was designed to save the monarchy from revolution, and requested the appointment of Tabataba'i as prime minister. The shah complied and also created for Reza Khan the post of *sardar sepah* (army commander). Soon Reza Khan ousted Tabataba'i, and through successful maneuvering, he was first appointed minister of war and then the prime minister. In 1925, Reza Khan deposed Ahmad Shah and placed himself on the throne, establishing the Pahlavi dynasty. In 1935, he renamed the country Iran.

Reza Shah's political miscalculations led to his downfall. Although he came to power with the assistance of the British, Reza Shah began to approach Nazi Germany. In the late 1930s, Germany became Iran's major trade partner. Therefore, Reza Shah was ousted by the Allies (British and Soviet) in 1941. He was exiled to Mauritius island, where he died on July 26, 1944, and was succeeded by his son Mohammad Reza Shah PAHLAVI.

The interpretation of Reza Shah's rule varies from one extreme to another. Leftists treat him as an absolutist monarch who represented the interests of the landlord-bourgeois class and the British. Promonarchist historians and commentators portray Reza Shah as a self-made man who saved Iran from disintegration—who led a traditional and backward country into the modern era. Elements of truth may be found in both interpretations: Reza Shah was a ruthless despot. He violated virtually all the constitutional provisions concerning the separation of government power, parliamentary procedures, and fundamental freedoms. He used the state police to strengthen his personal rule and accumulate substantial wealth. His handpicked members of the parliament functioned only to rubber-stamp royal policies. His dictatorship rested on a combination of a bourgeoisie (including important merchants) and a landed aristocracy. Reza Shah, however, was a modernizer. Under his rule, modern educational institutions were founded and expanded and much of the country's basic infrastructure, such as roads, railways, and airports, was established. He also unleashed cultural reform; in 1935, he emancipated women—daringly outlawing the veil, which covered them from head to toe, as well as traditional ethnic clothes. He obliged people to wear Western-style dress, expelled the *ulama* (Islamic clergy) from the state bureaucracy, and also initiated many other secular reforms. Reza Shah was supported in these measures by leading Persian intellectuals—who, otherwise, were ambivalent about his rule in general.

BIBLIOGRAPHY

ABRAHAMIAN, ERVAND. *Iran between Two Revolutions.* Princeton, N.J., 1982.
ELWELL-SUTTON, L. P. "Reza Shah the Great: Founder of the Pahlavi Dynasty." In *Iran under the Pahlavis,* ed. by George Lenczowski. Stamford, Conn., 1978.
ESSAD-BEY, MOHAMMAD. *Reza Shah.* London, 1938.
WILBER, DONALD N. *Riza Shah Pahlavi: The Resurrection and Reconstruction of Iran.* New York, 1975.

Mansoor Moaddel

Pahlavi Dynasty

Ruling family established in Iran by Reza Khan, an officer in the Cossack Brigade.

Reza Khan overthrew the Qajar dynasty in 1921 and was proclaimed Shah by an act of the *majles* in 1925. His son Mohammad Reza Pahlavi succeeded him to the throne in 1941 and ruled until 1979, when he was deposed by a popular Islamic revolution.

Cyrus Moshaver

Pahlavi University

See Shiraz University

PAIForce

PAIForce, or Persia and Iraq Force, was a British military command created in 1941 for World War II operations in the Middle East.

Headquartered in Baghdad, Iraq, and under the command of General Henry Maitland Wilson, PAIForce had the responsibility of ensuring the security of rails, roads, and harbors against sabotage and Axis air, ground, and sea operations. A major responsibility was coordination with the U.S. Persian Gulf Service Command, responsible for Lend-Lease aid to the Soviet Union through Iran. PAIForce also provided support for petroleum products for the Persian Gulf Service Command and the Soviet Union. Although sometimes subject to criticism for lack of security for U.S. facilities in the area, PAIForce was never the subject of a formal complaint either to the U.S. Joint Chiefs of Staff or to the Allied Combined Chiefs of Staff.

Daniel E. Spector

Pa'il, Me'ir   [1926–   ]

Israeli colonel and a member of the Knesset.

Born in Jerusalem, Pa'il (originally Pilavsky) served in the Palmach, then in the Israel Defense Forces (IDF) where he held various command posts, including chief of tactics and operational doctrine on the general staff, and commander-in-chief of the Central School for Officers. He founded MOKED (Movement for Peace and Socialist Change in Israel) and was elected its lone Knesset member (1974), after which he sat as Sheli party member from 1974 to 1980. Pa'il lectures at Tel-Aviv University, where he obtained his Ph.D. in 1974 and is academic director of the IDF Center for Historical Research. He writes primarily on military history and strategy and has won two literary prizes.

Zev Maghen

Pakhtun, People and Language

Term by which the speakers of Pakhtu (Pashto) inhabiting the present territory of Afghanistan and the northwest frontier province of Pakistan have preferred to be known. Outsiders, however, have more frequently referred to them as Pathans or Afghans.

The Pakhtu language seems to be derived from Saka, a language spoken by central Asian nomads who conquered the present habitat of the Pakhtuns in the second millennium B.C.E. Little historical evidence or agreement exist for the ethnogenesis of the Pakhtuns. Stressing their monotheism, the Pakhtuns in their folklore equate their origin with the origin of Islam: Qais, their putative ancestor, is said to have led his followers from Ghur, in central Afghanistan, to Muhammad, the messenger of Islam, in Medina;

there he was converted by the messenger in person and renamed Abd al-Rashid.

The Pakhtuns represent their social relations in an organizational chart of hierarchical patrilineal segments, starting with Qais and his three or four sons and reaching those living in the present. In principle, every Pakhtun should know every chain of segmentation; in practice, however, a male Pakhtun is to know the names of his seven male ascendants and how their living descendants are linked to him. Beyond this minimal unit, he is required to know only the major segments, rather than the precise line of individuals through whom his minimal unit is linked to the higher-named segments.

There are no words in Pakhtu that refer exclusively to a "lineage," in which descent is demonstrated, or a "clan," in which descent is merely assumed; the suffixes -*zai* and -*khel,* added to names of males to imply descent from them, can mean either "lineage" or "clan." The ambiguity is very useful in practice. Instead of allowing their genealogy to dictate their behavior, the Pakhtuns can manipulate their tables of organization so as to change the significance of levels of segmentation, to the extent of incorporating totally alien groups within their genealogical fold. The critical variable in determining whether a group belongs is the exchange of women in marriage.

Durrani, Ghilzai, and Karlanri have been for the last two hundred years the names of the major groups of Pakhtun clans. Symbolically, the unity of the Pakhtuns is expressed through their adherence to *Pakhtunwali,* the ideal code of behavior, stressing honor, hospitality, and revenge; it is also a customary system of mediation that includes provisions for settling disputes ranging from theft to homicide.

Lacking established rules of succession, Pakhtuns have competed for positions of status and power and have seldom acted as a united group. The few leaders who have succeeded in unifying them are fondly remembered by all. The best known of these Pakhtun heroes are Khushal Khattak (1613–1689), the poet-warrior who led the politician resistance against the Moghuls; Mir Wais Hotak (died 1715), who freed Kandahar from the Safavid yoke and founded the Hotak state; and Ahmad Shah (ruled 1747–1772), who founded the Durrani dynasty and empire.

BIBLIOGRAPHY

CAROE, OLAF. *The Pathans, 550 B.C.–1957 A.D.* London, 1958.
DUPREE, LOUIS. *Afghanistan.* Princeton, N.J., 1980.

Ashraf Ghani

Pakhtu Tolana

Afghan research organization.

The purpose of the Pakhtu Tolana (Afghan Academy)—an umbrella organization that opened in 1937 combining the Afghan Literary Society and the Pashto Society—is to encourage the study of the Pashto (or Pakhtu) language and culture. The Pakhtu Tolana was founded because even though Pashto speakers constitute nearly half of the Afghan population, including much of the ruling class, most literary and scientific work in Afghanistan is written in Persian. The academy has published a number of dictionaries, a Pashto grammar and reader, several journals, and other works on and in Pashto.

Grant Farr

Pakistan and the Middle East

Pakistan's ties to the Middle East are based on history, religion, security, and economics.

Pakistan's historical links with the Middle East go back to the Arab invasion of Sindh in 712 A.D. The Arab–Islamic and Iranian cultures have deeply influenced the civilization of the areas that now comprise Pakistan. Contemporary geopolitical considerations have reinforced Pakistan's interest in the Arab region. For security as well as religous regions, Pakistan has attached great significance to its relations with the Arab Islamic states.

The perception of a security threat from India and their dispute over Kashmir have impelled Pakistan to look toward the Islamic countries as "natural allies." However, Pakistan's use of common Islamic symbols and shared religious identity did not satisfy the countries of the Middle East. Instead, Pakistan's decision to join the U.S.-sponsored security pacts in the 1950s provoked Arab hostility, particularly from Egypt, Syria, and Iraq. Arch-rival India found the political climate in the radical Arab states more congenial for its diplomacy. Pakistan's relationship with the West brought her closer to Iran, Turkey, and pro-West moderate Arab states.

In response to declining U.S. interest in military alliances, Pakistan's Middle East policy underwent a fundamental transformation in the early 1970s. As an alternative to dwindling Western support, Pakistan began to look toward the Arab oil-producing countries for economic assistance. Under Mohammad Reza Pahlavi, Iran became an important regional ally and also a source of much-needed foreign aid. Saudi Arabia and the Gulf states showed tremendous interest in Pakistan's security and economic development.

With the manifold increase in oil revenues, the Gulf region became more attractive for Pakistan as a market for its surplus manpower. Millions of Pakistanis have worked on developmental projects in the Gulf countries. The Pakistani workers abroad not only have lessened the pressure on unemployment at home but also have earned the country tens of billions of dollars. In the peak years (1980–1988), Pakistani workers remitted about three billion U.S. dollars a year that offset the huge gap in the balance of trade.

While Pakistan has unilaterally and unconditionally supported the Arab states in their disputes with Israel, including a Palestinian homeland, it has not received unanimous political backing of all the Middle Eastern countries in its disputes with India. In pursuit of bilateralism, Pakistan has carefully avoided taking sides in conflicts between the Muslim states. In the Iran–Iraq War in the 1980s, Pakistan remained strictly neutral. Pakistan's participation in Operation Desert Storm against Iraq in 1991 was a different matter. It was launched under the United Nations banner, and the coalition of Western and Arab states enjoyed broader legitimacy in forcing Iraqi invaders from Kuwait.

Over the years, Pakistan has emerged as an important regional actor in the Middle East, although it maintains a low profile. It has security protocols with a large number of Middle Eastern states. Pakistan provides training facilities to the armed forces of Saudi Arabia, Oman, Jordan, United Arab Emirates, Kuwait, and Bahrain. Also, Libya had access to these facilities in the 1970s. Pakistani military personnel serve in various capacities as trainers and advisers for Arab armies. In the 1980s, Pakistan stationed about 10,000 of her troops in Saudi Arabia. As a quid pro quo, Saudi Arabia financed the modernization of Pakistan's air force. In the last decade, among Third World countries, Pakistan had the second largest military presence overseas (after Cuba)—all of it was in the Middle East.

BIBLIOGRAPHY

BURKE, S. M., and LAWRENCE ZIRING. *Pakistan's Foreign Policy: An Historical Analysis*, 2nd ed. Karachi, 1990.
RIZVI, HASAN-ASKARI. *Pakistan and the Geostrategic Environment: A Study of Foreign Policy.* New York, 1993.

Rasul Bakhsh Rais

Paktia

Eastern Afghan province.

A province in eastern Afghanistan on the Pakistani border, Paktia has a population of approximately

500,000, most of whom are Gilzai Pushtun. The capital of Paktia is Gardez. The area is mountainous, but with sufficient water to permit the local farmers to raise wheat and barley. As a consequence of its proximity to the Pakistani border, the province is known for smuggled contraband and illegally harvested timber.

Paktia saw heavy fighting during the war of resistance (1978–1992), when over half of the population fled to Pakistan, but by 1994 most of these refugees had returned.

BIBLIOGRAPHY

DUPREE, LOUIS. *Afghanistan*. Princeton, N.J., 1980.

Grant Farr

Palestine

Area located on the eastern shore of the Mediterranean south of Lebanon and northeast of Egypt.

Palestine has since ancient times been a crossroad between Asia, Europe, and Africa. Its climate is arid. The southern half, the Negev, is desert, but in the north there are several fertile areas. The principal water source is the Jordan river, which flows south through Lake Tiberias into the Dead Sea. The river forms the border between the Kingdom of Jordan (formerly eastern Palestine) and what was mandatory (western) Palestine.

Palestine as a modern political entity came into existence as a result of the collapse of the Ottoman Empire in World War I. Before the war the area that became Palestine was part of the vaguely defined geographic region generally known as southern Syria. The name Palestine replaced the name Judea after the Romans suppressed the last Jewish rebellion from 132 to 135. Arab geographers in the tenth century referred to "Filastin" as one of the provinces of Syria, but by the twelfth and thirteenth centuries the term was no longer used. From the fifteenth century until the end of World War I, the region was part of the Ottoman Empire. Changing provincial boundaries within the empire blurred Palestine's separate existence. During the nineteenth century in Europe, Palestine was synonymous with the HOLY LAND on both sides of the Jordan river.

In an attempt to centralize government administration, the Ottoman Empire was divided into new administrative regions under the Vilayet Law of 1864. Under this arrangement the central and largest part of Palestine, as well as Transjordan, became part of the *vilayet* (province) of Damascus. The northern part of the country, including Acre, Haifa, Tiberias,

An artist's depiction of Abu Ghosh, the largest Arab village on the mountain route from Jaffa to Jerusalem. (Arnold Blumberg, Towson State University Media Services. From Count L.N.P. Auguste de Forbin, Voyage dans le Levant en 1817 et 1818. Paris, circa 1818.)

Safad, Nablus, Jenin, and Tulkarm, was part of the *vilayet* of Beirut. Jerusalem, Gaza, Hebron, and Beersheba became the *sanjak* (district) of Jerusalem, which, because of the city's special religious status and because of European interest, was established as an independent unit governed directly from Constantinople (now Istanbul).

By the mid-nineteenth century the population of Palestine was about 500,000, more than 80 percent Muslim Arab, 10 percent Christian, 4 percent Jewish, and about 1 percent Druze. The southern half of the country, later called the Negev, was mostly desert, sparsely inhabited by bedouin tribes. Overall, only about a third of Palestine was suitable for cultivation.

An integral part of the Ottoman reform effort (TANZIMAT) from 1839 to 1876 was the 1858 Land Law, by which Istanbul sought to establish control over state lands and large private holdings with a view to more efficient collection of taxes. However, most *fellahin* (peasant farmers) evaded the land registration required by the law, fearing that it would lead to their conscription into the Ottoman army and to higher taxes. As a result, much of the cultivated area was registered in the name of wealthy urban notables, and the fellahin became sharecroppers or hired workers. Under the Vilayet Law, the notables took over tax collection from rural shaykhs, thereby further increasing their hold on the economy. The 1858 Land Law established local administrative councils to help govern the cities and implement the *tanzimat* reforms. However, membership in the councils was restricted to those who could pay a tax that most villagers could

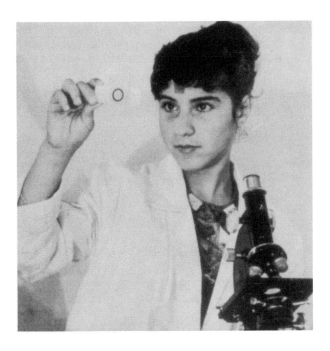

Palestinian woman in training in a medical laboratory. (UNRWA)

not afford. As a result of these "reforms," the urban notables soon dominated the country's economic and social life. By the end of the nineteenth century, some 250 Arab families owned about half the cultivated area, an amount equal to the land owned by the country's fellahin.

At various times quarrels would erupt among the notable families for any of a number of reasons—control of affairs or influence with the Ottoman rulers or the like. One division that cut across urban, rural, and bedouin lines was between the Qaysi and Yamani camps. The origins of this division can be traced back to the early days of Islam in Arabia. By the end of the nineteenth century, however, the Qaysi–Yamani rift was less significant than differences over other issues.

Jerusalem was the cultural, intellectual, religious, social, and economic center for the Muslim, Christian, and Jewish communities. The most influential notable families lived there, and it was the focus of the interest of European powers that used the city's importance to Christianity as an excuse to intervene in Ottoman affairs.

By the last third of the nineteenth century, a commercial bourgeoisie comprised of Palestinian Arabs, Christians, Jews, and Europeans played an important role in the incorporation of Palestine's economy into the world economic system. There was a major increase in cultivation of export commodities that included wheat, barley, sesame, olive oil, and oranges.

Small-scale industries produced textiles, soap, oil, and religious items.

Although the Arabs considered themselves a distinctive group, there was no serious conflict between them and the Ottoman Turkish establishment until the twentieth century. The Palestine elite approved of and benefited from the nineteenth-century Ottoman reforms, and many of them held influential posts in the ruling establishment in Constantinople. Several served in the Parliament; Nablus was reputed to be especially favored by Sultan Abdülhamit II.

The first politically significant Jewish immigration was in 1882. At the time the Jewish population was some 24,000, mostly Orthodox Jews unaffiliated with political Zionism. They were settled mostly in Jerusalem, Hebron, Safed, and Tiberias. There was little friction between these Jews, the "Old YISHUV," and the indigenous Arab population. However, as the number of Zionist settlements increased, quarrels arose between them and neighboring Arab villages over grazing, crops, and land issues. Between 1886 and World War I, there were several armed clashes resulting from Jewish settlers purchasing land from absentee Arab owners and subsequently dispossessing the peasant cultivators.

Growing opposition to Zionism and emergence of a new pan-Turkish ideology following the Young Turk Revolution in 1908 led to the beginnings of a distinctive Palestinian patriotism. Although most of the Palestinian Arab elite remained loyal to the Ottoman sultan during World War I, a few intellectuals identified with the nascent Arab nationalist movement. During the war, opposition to Ottoman authority increased because of economic disasters caused by a locust plague, drought, and famine with which the Ottoman authorities failed to cope, and due to the repressive measures imposed by the Turkish governor, Cemal Paça.

Palestine was occupied by British forces under General Sir Edmund Allenby in 1917 and placed under a military government administration identified as Occupied Enemy Territory South (OETS) until July 1920, when the military regime was replaced by a British civil administration.

With establishment of OETS, Palestine acquired fixed boundaries, its own government, and a political identity separate from the surrounding countries carved from the Ottoman Empire by Great Britain and France. Its separate identity was given international recognition when Great Britain assumed the mandate for Palestine and Transjordan under the League of Nations in July 1922. In 1923 the British unilaterally divided the area of the mandate into Transjordan, east of the Jordan River, and western Palestine. The area east of the river became the Emirate of Transjordan (later the Hashimite Kingdom of Jordan) under Prince Abdullah, son of the Sharif of Mecca.

According to the mandate for Palestine, Great Britain was ultimately responsible to the League of Nations for governing the country. However, Palestine was ruled much like a colony, under a high commissioner appointed by the British government; he was responsible to the Colonial Office in London rather than to the local population and had authority to make all government appointments, laws, rules, and regulations. The high commissioner was backed by British military forces and police. Most high commissioners were former British colonial officials or army generals. The government of Palestine had its own postal service, police force, customs, railroad and transportation network, and currency backed by the British pound sterling. Inhabitants of the country, both Arabs and Jews, were called Palestinians and considered British subjects.

Attempts to introduce some measure of self-government through establishment of advisory and legislative councils during the 1920s and 1930s failed because of disagreement over representation. Jews objected to elections based on proportional representation because they would be relegated to a minority position, unable to achieve their objective of establishing in Palestine a Jewish national home. Arab leaders objected to their underrepresentation; some refused participation because it implied recognition of the mandate.

The mandate included provisions of the BALFOUR DECLARATION calling for "establishment in Palestine of a national home for the Jewish people"; it also provided for support of Zionist objectives and gave preference to Jewish attainment of Palestinian citizenship, land acquisition, and settlement. Although the mandate made no specific reference to the Arab population, referring to them as the "non-Jewish communities," it prohibited "discrimination of any kind . . . between the inhabitants of Palestine."

As a result of the dual obligation to foster establishment of the Jewish national home and to ensure "that the rights and position of other sectors of the population are not prejudiced," British policy was ambivalent. Initial support for Zionist objectives was indicated in the appointment of the first high commissioner, Herbert Samuel, a British Jewish leader who was sympathetic to Zionism. However, opposition by the country's Arab majority to the establishment of a Jewish homeland, to the development of Arab nationalism, and to larger imperial interests were major obstacles to full cooperation with the Zionist leaders, who wanted to proceed full speed toward their objectives.

All attempts to bridge the gap between the Arab and Jewish communities were unsuccessful; each community proceeded to develop itself with little, if any, contact with the other. Various British royal or investigative commissions were unable to provide a solution to the conflict, and by 1939 Great Britain had retreated from its position on implementing the mandate.

Each community developed its own educational, health, welfare, cultural, political, and labor organizations. The Yishuv had its own schools, where the language was Hebrew, and its own Hebrew university. Arab schools supported by the mandatory Education Department were conducted in Arabic with their own curriculum. The two communities lived largely separated; contact was only at the peripheries, in government offices, or in a few business enter-

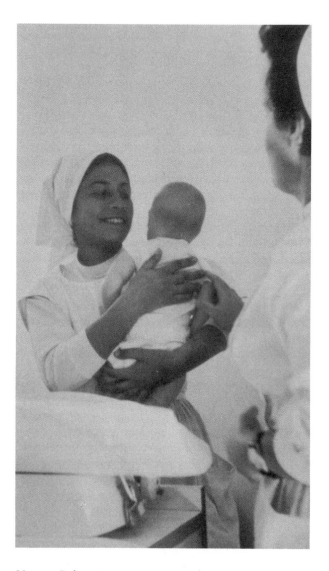

Young Palestinian woman in a preparatory nursing program. (UNRWA)

prises. The Yishuv was mainly urban, concentrated in the coastal region and in the city of Jerusalem, whereas the Arab sector was largely rural, in central Palestine.

From 1918 until the end of the mandate in 1948, the population of the Yishuv increased, largely through immigration, from about 60,000 to over 600,000. During this period the Arab population doubled, mostly through natural increase, from some 650,000 to 1.3 million. The increase in the Jewish population from about a tenth to a third of the population was accompanied by extensive physical expansion of the Yishuv. The number of rural collectives (kibbutzim), cooperatives (moshavim), and private farms increased several times; the all-Jewish city of Tel Aviv grew from an adjunct of Jaffa to the second largest municipality in the country. Jewish-owned industry dominated the economy. Despite the growth of its rural sector, the Yishuv was still 85 percent urban by the end of the mandate, and Jewish-owned land comprised less than 7 percent of the total although more than a quarter of the cultivated area was Jewish.

The Yishuv developed its own political parties and self-governing institutions that took responsibility for functions, such as education and social welfare, not under jurisdiction of the mandatory government. The British recognized the WORLD ZIONIST ORGANIZATION as the official agency to implement establishment of the Jewish national home. Within Palestine the Yishuv elected the Knesset, whose National Council (VA'AD LE'UMI) ran the day-to-day affairs of the Jewish community. Over a dozen political parties were divided into four principal categories: labor, general Zionist, Orthodox religious, and Sephardic or Oriental. The strongest political bloc was labor by virtue of its control of the Histadrut, the large labor federation that controlled much of the Yishuv's economy, and of the largest paramilitary group, the Haganah.

The Arab community was much less centralized and more loosely organized. The older politicians, representing the traditional elite and notable families who had been closely associated with the Ottoman establishment, formed the MUSLIM–CHRISTIAN ASSOCIATION (MCA) in 1918 at Jaffa. Branches of the MCA were later established in several Palestinian towns and cities. Although cooperating with the British rulers, the MCA was adamantly opposed to the Jewish national home and to provisions of the mandate supporting it.

The principal organizations representing the younger politicians, many of them also from notable families, were the Literary Club (LC) and the ARAB CLUB (AC). The LC was dominated by members of the NASHASHIBI FAMILY; the HUSAYNI FAMILY was more prominent in the AC. Both organizations were ardently Arab nationalist, initially supporting Palestine's unification with Faisal I's Kingdom of Syria in Damascus. The younger politicians were far less willing to accept British rule and demanded immediate independence. Both older and younger leaders were represented at the first Palestine Arab Congress, convened at Jaffa in 1919, which sought to make Palestine part of Syria.

With defeat of Faisal's Arab kingdom by the French in 1920, Palestine Arab leaders focused on local problems, primarily the struggle against the British mandate and the Jewish national home. A second congress was to be held in 1920, but it was banned by the Palestine government. Instead, a congress convened in Haifa focused on the struggle in Palestine. It established the ARAB EXECUTIVE and sent a delegation to plead the Palestinian Arab cause at the peace conference in Geneva. Neither the congresses nor the Executive was successful in attaining their objective, and both gradually lost credibility. When the Executive chairman, Musa Kazem al-Husayni, died in 1934, the Executive ceased to exist.

The most influential Palestine Arab leader was Al-Hajj Muhammad Amin al-Husayni, appointed by the British as mufti of Jerusalem and president of the Supreme Muslim Council. By virtue of these positions he commanded extensive financial resources and influence throughout the Arab community. Supporters of the mufti, called Councilites or "the Husaynis," were opposed by "the Opposition," led by the Nashashibi family. Both groups were supported by extensive clan (hamula) networks and client relationships. The Husaynis, the larger network, were considered more militant than the Nashashibis, who were willing to compromise with the British. Both factions rejected the Jewish national home.

Following demise of the Arab Executive in 1934, several Arab political parties were established. The two principal parties were the NATIONAL DEFENSE PARTY, headed by the Nashashibis, and the PALESTINE ARAB PARTY, organized by the Husaynis.

In 1936, Palestine Arab nationalist opposition to the mandate was galvanized in a general strike against the British authorities and the Yishuv. The strike soon became a rebellion enlisting support from the whole Arab community. The ARAB HIGHER COMMITTEE (AHC), chaired by the mufti and representing the spectrum of Arab political organizations, was formed to lead the uprising. Unity was short lived; when the rebellion entered its second phase in 1937, the Nashashibi member of the AHC resigned, leaving leadership in the hands of the mufti and his allies. In 1937 the British outlawed the AHC and arrested and deported several of its members. The mufti and several of his associates fled to Syria, Iraq, and Lebanon, from which they attempted to keep the rebellion alive.

In 1937 and 1938 there was a struggle between followers of the Nashashibis and Husaynis in which many Arabs were killed. Many more were killed in altercations with Zionist, British, and trans-Jordanian forces. These conflicts led to a political vacuum in the Palestine Arab community. By 1939 the rebellion petered out as a result of the conflict within the Arab community and the massive use of force by the British.

During World War II, political activity in Palestine was quiescent. Attempts to revive the AHC after the war were marred by the continuing rift between the Husaynis and Nashashibis, and by the absence of many exiled leaders whom the British prevented from returning to the country. A Husayni-dominated AHC was organized in 1945, but it was countered by an opposition Arab Higher Front. In 1946 the Arab League intervened, and another AHC was set up. In the struggle following World War II, the AHC rejected various British compromise proposals and the 1947 UN partition proposal. Para-military organizations formed to oppose partition were split between the Husayni FUTUWWA and the opposition al-NAJJADA. In the civil war from December 1947 to May 1948, between the Palestine Jewish and Arab communities, the Arab forces were defeated, leading to the departure of approximately half the Arab population of Palestine. Most fled or were driven by Jewish forces to the neighboring Arab countries.

With establishment of the Jewish State of Israel in May 1948 and occupation of the Gaza Strip by Egypt and of the West Bank by Jordan, Palestine ceased to exist as a separate political entity. Between 1964 and 1994 the Palestinian people were represented by the PALESTINE LIBERATION ORGANIZATION (PLO), which sought to reestablish a Palestinian Arab state in those parts of the country outside the borders of Israel.

[See also: Mandate System]

BIBLIOGRAPHY

CAPLAN, NEIL. Futile Diplomacy, 2 vols. London, 1983.
———. Palestine Jewry and the Arab Question, 1917–1925. London, 1978.
HUREWITZ, J. C. The Struggle for Palestine. New York, 1950.
KHALAF, ISSA. Politics in Palestine: Arab Factionalism and Social Disintegration, 1939–1948. Albany, N.Y., 1991.
KHALIDI, WALID, ed. From Haven to Conquest. Beirut, 1971.
LESCH, ANN M. Arab Politics in Palestine, 1917–1939: The Frustration of a Nationalist Movement. Ithaca, N.Y., 1979.
MUSLIH, MUHAMMAD Y. The Origins of Palestinian Nationalism. New York, 1988.
PORATH, Y. The Emergence of the Palestinian Arab Nationalist Movement, 1918–1929. London, 1974.
———. The Palestinian Arab Nationalist Movement, 1929–1939. London, 1977.
SHAFIR, GERSHON. Land, Labor and the Origins of the Israeli–Palestinian Conflict. Cambridge, Mass., 1969.

Don Peretz

Palestine, Agricultural Parties in

Political organizations formed in several Palestinian Arab towns and villages in 1924 with financial assistance and organizational advice from the Zionist Organization.

Based principally near Nazareth, Baysan, Jenin, and Hebron, the agricultural parties initially attracted Arab village leaders who resented the proponderant influence of the urban and landowning elite and hoped to receive agricultural loans and other material favors from the Zionist movement. Public awareness of their funding made most Arab farmers shy away from them. Moreover, Zionist officials failed to underwrite any loans and could not provide members with administrative posts or persuade the British government to reduce taxes and open village schools. When the Zionist officials curtailed their cash payments, the parties quickly disintegrated; none continued beyond 1926.

BIBLIOGRAPHY

LESCH, ANN MOSELY. Arab Politics in Palestine, 1917–1939. Ithaca, N.Y., 1979.
PORATH, YEHOSHUA. The Emergence of the Palestinian-Arab National Movement, 1918–1929. London, 1974.

Ann M. Lesch

Palestine Arab Party

Arab political party in Palestine during the British mandate, which advocated an unpartitioned independent state under Arab control.

The Palestine Arab party was founded in mandated Palestine in March 1935 by Jamal al-Husayni, a relative of al-Hajj Amin al-Husayni, mufti of Jerusalem and head of the Supreme Muslim Council. Many political activists who had previously supported the Arab Executive (1920–1934) joined its ranks. Its leaders maintained close contact with the Roman Catholic community through its officers, Alfred Rock and Emile al-Ghuri, and with the activist scouts' movement and workers' societies in Jerusalem and Haifa. Moreover, party leaders formed an underground paramilitary branch, which became active in the sustained Palestinian revolt of 1936 to 1939.

The party endorsed the basic national demands: repudiation of the Balfour Declaration, full stoppage of Jewish immigration and land purchases, and the immediate establishment of Palestine as an independent state under Arab control. When the party denounced the partition plan of 1937, the British exiled its leaders and curtailed its activities; however, enough leaders returned to Palestine during World War II to enable it to reopen its offices in April 1944 and use its connections with the Arab Bank and the local press to regain substantial influence. When Jamal al-Husayni returned in February 1946, he gained control over the Arab Higher Committee as well as the party and reestablished the paramilitary force, which subsequently formed an important component of the village forces that tried to resist dispossession of the Palestinian Arabs in the wake of the United Nations partition plan of November 1947.

BIBLIOGRAPHY

HUREWITZ, J. C. *The Struggle for Palestine.* New York, 1950. Reprint, 1976.
PORATH, YEHOSHUA. *The Palestinian Arab National Movement, 1929–1939.* London, 1977.

Ann M. Lesch

Palestine Arab Revolt

Arab revolt in Palestine to resist British support for a Jewish national home.

The revolt in Palestine (1936–1939) was in many ways the decisive episode in the efforts of the Palestinian Arabs to resist the British mandate's support for a Jewish national home in Palestine. Although it helped force a British policy reassessment, which led to the 1939 white paper curtailing Jewish immigration to Palestine, ultimately the revolt must be judged a failure. At its conclusion in 1939, the Palestinian Arabs were exhausted by more than three years of British repression. Perhaps 5,000 had been killed and 15,000 to 20,000 wounded; 5,600 of their leaders and fighters were in British detention; and most of the rest were scattered outside the country or dead. Such losses, in a population of about 1 million Palestinian Arabs in 1939, meant that more than 10 percent of the adult males were killed, wounded, or detained by the end of the revolt.

Equally important, the Palestinians failed to benefit politically. Their already divided leadership was

fragmented further by the events of 1936 to 1939; and with many of its leaders in exile from 1937 on, it was paralyzed by a division between those outside of Palestine and those inside it that persisted for decades thereafter. These divisions contributed to the failure of the Palestinians to capitalize on the potential advantages offered them in the 1939 white paper, which with its limits on immigration and promise of self-government within ten years, held out for the first time the prospect of Arab majority rule in Palestine. In any case, the government of Winston Churchill, which came into office soon after, was resolutely opposed to its implementation. After the war, the impact of the revelation of the Holocaust, the growing strength of the YISHUV in Palestine, and the rising power of the United States in the Middle East combined to render it moot. The Palestinians came out of this ordeal politically weaker than they had gone into it, and unprepared for the struggle for Palestine (1945–1948) that, attendant on the establishment of Israel, resulted in the dispossession of about half the Arab population of the country.

Economically, the revolt was a disaster for the Arabs. It had begun in April 1936 as a spontaneous strike and boycott of the British and of the Jewish economy of Palestine. Effective though it was at the outset, the result was measurably to weaken the Arab sector of the economy, which did not have the resources or the resilience to support the hardships of the revolt, and to strengthen the economy of the Yishuv, which did. The Arab labor boycott, moreover, had the paradoxical effect of furthering the Zionist policy of giving jobs only to Jews—cheaper Arab labor had heretofore been favored by many Jewish businesses—and spurred the economy of the Yishuv to greater self-reliance.

On the military level, the Palestinians lost several thousand of their best fighters and military commanders in combat or to British firing squads, which executed 112 Arabs. Many thousands of others were wounded, detained, or forced into exile. In addition, the British seized over 13,000 weapons and 350,000 rounds of ammunition from Arabs (about 500 guns were seized from Jewish groups in this period), at a time when the British were arming units like the Jewish Settlement Police and cooperating with the Haganah to repulse Arab attacks. All of these losses, particularly in combatants, military leaders, and weapons, were sorely felt when the Palestinians confronted the well-armed and organized forces of the Yishuv during the fighting that started immediately after the partition resolution was passed by the UN General Assembly in November 1947. This fighting grew in intensity until May 1948, by which time the Palestinians had been routed in many crucial areas, losing the cities of JAFFA, HAIFA, and TIBERIAS, and scores of villages, towns, and strategic roads and junctions to the advancing forces of the Haganah and its allies. In some sense, the outcome of these decisive battles (1947–1948) was determined by the disastrous political, economic, and military results of the 1936–1939 revolt for the Palestinians.

The revolt was notable for its spontaneous inception, with local committees springing up in April 1936 to organize a general strike and boycott that lasted until October of that year. Among the motives for the revolt was the rapid growth in Jewish immigration to Palestine: from 1932 to 1936 there were 174,000 immigrants, more than the total Jewish population of the country in 1931. The ARAB HIGHER COMMITTEE was formed by Palestinian notable leaders soon after the strike began, largely in response to this pressure from below, but never really gained control of events. In the sporadic fighting of 1936 and in the intense battles of the second phase of the revolt, which began in September 1937, local organization was paramount, with minimal coordination between the mainly peasant military bands, which bore the brunt of the fighting. In spite of this lack of coordination, the Palestinians initially had the British on the defensive for much of 1937 and 1938 and took control of most Arab cities, towns, and villages, and much of the countryside. Only the arrival of massive British reinforcements—which brought troop strength to over 20,000 by 1938—and the intensive use of air power were able to break the back of the revolt.

In much Palestinian historiography, the revolt has been glorified as the forerunner of the modern Palestinian "armed struggle" that was launched in 1965. It is commonly linked to the attempts of Shaykh Izz al-Din al-QASSAM to organize an armed rebellion against the British, which were aborted when he and some of his comrades were hunted down and killed by British forces in 1935. Qassam's example was very influential, however: many thousands marched in his funeral cortege, and hundreds of his followers, whom he had organized in clandestine cells in the northern part of the country, played crucial roles during the revolt; they included some of the most senior commanders. Qassam's legacy is a disputed one, however, claimed by al-Fath and other Palestinian nationalist groups, and more recently by the radical Islamic HAMAS movement, which has named its armed wing for him.

BIBLIOGRAPHY

KAYYALI, ABDUL-WAHHAB. *Palestine: A Modern History.* London, 1978.
PORATH, YEHOSHUA. *The Palestinian Arab National Movement, 1929–1939: From Riots to Rebellion.* London, 1977.

SWEDENBURG, THEODORE. "Memories of Revolt: The 1936–39 Rebellion and the Struggle for a Palestinian National Past." Ph.D. diss., University of Texas, Austin, 1988.
———. "The Role of the Palestinian Peasantry in the Great Revolt (1936–1939)." In *Islam: Politics and Social Movements,* ed. by Edmund Burke III and Ira M. Lapidus. Berkeley, Calif., 1988.

Rashid Khalidi

Palestine Colonization Association

See Rothschild, Edmond de

Palestine Economic Corporation

American-funded economic aid program to Jews in Palestine.

Founded in 1926 by a group of prominent American Jews, including Supreme Court Justice Louis D. Brandeis, the Palestine Economic Corporation provided material aid and technical assistance to Jewish business enterprises in Palestine. Funding was usually in the form of loans or equity investments. Subsidiaries to the corporation included the Palestine Mortgage and Savings Bank and the Central Bank of Cooperative Institutions, which provided funds for low-cost housing and credits to kibbutzim, among other social programs.

Through 1946, the corporation had funded more than ninety enterprises and played a key role in establishing basic industries like chemicals, citrus products, paper, plastics, and tires. The corporation later changed its name to PEC Israel Economic Corporation. By 1967 it had eleven thousand stockholders, mostly in the United States, with assets of more than $28 million in Israel's industrial, construction, and citrus sectors.

BIBLIOGRAPHY

LAQUEUR, WALTER. *A History of Zionism.* New York, 1972.
PATAI, RAPHAEL, ed. *The Encyclopedia of Zionism and Israel.* New York, 1971.

Elizabeth Thompson

Palestine Exploration Fund

British research group founded under the patronage of Queen Victoria for scientific study of the Holy Land.

Established in 1865 to study biblical sites, the Palestine Exploration Fund began work in Jerusalem in

1867, especially the work of Charles Warren on the Walls of Jerusalem. The fund expanded its scope in the 1870s to conduct a complete survey of the HOLY LAND. The fund's team of geographers, archaeologists, anthropologists, and orientalists published numerous articles that influenced British public opinion. Its maps, drawn between 1871 and 1877, were used by Sir Edmund Allenby in his victorious cavalry campaign in Palestine in World War I and are invaluable today to historians. The maps designated the historical boundaries of Palestine as extending a few miles east of the Jordan river. Some members of the fund, particularly its director, Claude Reignier Conder, advocated British colonization of Palestine and the restoration of its Jewish population. The group funded the work of archaeologists W.M.F. Petrie and Kathleen Kenyon.

BIBLIOGRAPHY

ELON, AMOS. *The Israelis*. New York, 1971.
SANDERS, RONALD. *The High Walls of Jerusalem*. New York, 1983.
SHAFIR, GERSHON. *Land, Labor and the Origins of the Israeli–Palestinian Conflict, 1882–1914*. New York, 1989.

Elizabeth Thompson

Palestine Foundation Fund

See Keren Hayesod

Palestine Land Development Company

Land-purchasing company of the World Zionist Organization.

Established in 1908 by Arthur Ruppin, a German Jew, as part of the WORLD ZIONIST ORGANIZATION, the Palestine Land Development Company (PLDC) used Jewish National Fund and private monies to purchase and populate tracts of land with Jewish immigrants. It acquired extensive holdings in northern Palestine (Galilee), particularly in the 1920s and 1930s.

The PLDC bought nearly 90 percent of its land from large landowners, rather than individual peasants. Many of the transactions created controversy, like the PLDC's purchase of 240,000 dunums (144,000 acres, 60,000 ha) of fertile land in the Jezreel valley between 1921 and 1925, its purchase of 30,000 dunums (18,000 acres, 7,500 ha) at Wadi Hawarith in 1929, and its assumption of the Lake Huleh concession in 1934.

BIBLIOGRAPHY

SHAFIR, GERSHON. *Land, Labor and the Origins of the Israeli–Palestinian Conflict*. New York, 1989.

Elizabeth Thompson

Palestine Liberation Organization

The institutional structure of the Palestinian national movement and the political representative of the six million Palestinian people.

The Palestine Liberation Organization (PLO; Arabic, Munadhdhamat al-Tahrir al-Filastiniyya) was created at the Arab summit in January 1964 to contain and channel Palestinian nationalism and prevent Palestinian guerrilla groups from taking independent and potentially destabilizing actions to liberate Palestine, a territory from which Palestinians fled or were expelled by the Israel Defense Forces (IDF) in 1948. The Palestine National Council (PNC), the PLO's parliament, convened with 422 members in Jerusalem in May 1964 and elected a 15-member Executive Committee, which chose as its chairman a lawyer, Ahmad Shuqayri. The PNC adopted a national charter (*al-mithaq al-watani*), calling for the elimination of Israel and the restoration of Palestine to the Palestinians, and established the Palestine Liberation Army (PLA), which was attached to the armies of Egypt, Syria, and Jordan.

When Israel defeated these countries in 1967 and occupied the West Bank and the Gaza Strip, both Arab and Palestinian leaders were discredited. Shuqayri was replaced by another lawyer, Yahya Hammuda. The guerrilla groups, the most significant of which was al-Fath, expeditiously moved to fill the political vacuum by increasing their attacks on Israel. On 21 March 1968, Israel massively retaliated at Karama, Jordan. The guerrillas' stiff resistance resulted in the deaths of at least 21 Israelis, about 100 Palestinians, and 40 Jordanian soldiers who aided the Palestinians. The guerrillas embellished their own accomplishment, inflated Israel's casualties, and gave little credit to the Jordanians. Karama became a symbol of struggle against Israel, which many had considered invincible. Al-Fath gained thousands of recruits, Arab admiration, and financial support, primarily from the Gulf Arab states. More important, the guerrilla groups won control over the PLO. They amended the national charter in July 1968 to underscore the rejection of Arab interference in Palestinian affairs, the total liberation of Palestine by Palestinians through armed struggle, and establishment of a democratic secular state of Arabs and Jews.

The "victory" at Karama propelled Yasir Arafat, head of al-Fath, into the leadership position. An engineer educated at Cairo University, he was elected at the fourth PNC (February 1969) to replace Hammuda as chair of the Executive Committee. The PLO was transformed from an Arab-controlled organization to an umbrella of disparate military and political groups. Although these groups had a common goal, the liberation of Palestine, they differed considerably on ideology and tactics. The dominant group was al-Fath, established in Kuwait by Salah Khalaf (Abu Iyad), Khalil al-Wazir (Abu Jihad), and Arafat (Abu Ammar), who became its spokesperson. It owed its broad appeal to Arafat's charismatic personality and to its pragmatic politics, which eschewed ideology for action toward a simple national goal: the liberation of Palestine. Al-Fath's chief rival in the PLO was the Popular Front for the Liberation of Palestine (PFLP), headed by George Habash, a Christian physician educated at the American University of Beirut. The PFLP is a Marxist group dedicated to the overthrow of conservative Arab governments. Its contempt for the government of Jordan led it to challenge Jordan's sovereignty, triggering the 1970–1971 civil war that resulted in the PLO's defeat and its relocation to Lebanon. An off-shoot to the left of the PFLP that espouses Marxism–Leninism is the Democratic Front for the Liberation of Palestine (DFLP), led by a Jordanian Christian, Nayif Hawatma. Another offshoot is the Popular Front for the Liberation of Palestine—General Command (PFLP-GC), led by Ahmad Jibril. Others include Sa'iqa, controlled by Syria, and the Arab Liberation Front (ALF), controlled by Iraq.

The influence of these groups has been disproportional to their numbers, but some see them as a necessary alternative to the centrist al-Fath. They have stimulated political debates. They have charged that the lack of a coherent ideology within al-Fath has led to an absence of vision regarding politics and society in the diaspora and the future state of Palestine; that many of its functionaries are inept and corrupt bureaucrats tolerated by Arafat; that the PLO drifts from crisis to crisis; that Arafat manipulates Palestinian institutions such as the PNC and the Executive Council and has autocratic powers that undermine Palestinian democracy; and that Arafat flirts with almost any nation—Jordan, Egypt, the United States—without a clear policy.

PLO diversity resulted in the groups working at cross-purposes or in costly blunders. For example, the Arab-controlled Sa'iqa and ALF emphasized Arab unity while others insisted on Palestinian self-reliance. Al-Fath denounced airplane hijackings in 1969 and 1970 by PFLP and PFLP-GC as counterproductive to the Palestinian cause. While al-Fath sought Arab support and generally avoided Arab problems, the leftist groups involved the PLO in the civil war in Jordan and contributed to PLO involvement in Lebanon's civil war and in the Gulf crisis. Disagreements have led groups to secede from the PLO or to leave it temporarily. These could have brought violent conflict and disunity had it not been for the dominance of al-Fath and Arafat's mass appeal and political skills. He often appeased or reflected diverse currents and articulated vague and, at times, contradictory positions—which, while damaging his credibility abroad and creating diplomatic immobility, enabled him to maintain the coalition. His leadership allowed the PLO to develop political, military, and socioeconomic institutions in Lebanon until 1982.

Foremost among these was the PNC, the PLO parliament, whose membership varied. It represented virtually all ideological tendencies and groups, including the commando organizations and their political branches, ten unions—those, for example, of workers, women, teachers, students, writers, and engineers—and Palestinian communities. It developed a large and complex infrastructure for the estimated 360,000 Palestinians in Lebanon. Its well-trained armed forces numbered about 16,000. Its social and economic institutions served almost half a million Palestinians and poor Lebanese. The Palestine Martyrs Works Society (SAMED) operated businesses and light industry grossing $40 million annually. The Red Crescent Society supervised sixty clinics and eleven hospitals, and the Department of Social Welfare provided financial assistance for the blind, day-care centers, the wounded, and families of "martyrs." By the early 1980s the PLO had gone from an umbrella of guerrilla groups to the institutional embodiment of Palestinian nationalism and a state within a state.

The political and economic institutions enhanced the PLO's prestige and legitimacy. The Arab League recognized the PLO as the sole legitimate representative of the Palestinian people at the Rabat conference (October 1974). A month later, the United Nations invited Arafat to address the General Assembly and awarded the PLO observer status. In 1976 West Bank and Gaza Palestinians voted out pro-Jordan mayors, replacing them with supporters of the PLO. By 1982, over 100 countries had recognized the PLO.

Despite such success, however, the PLO suffered major setbacks. After its expulsion from Jordan, it estalished a state within a state in Lebanon, thereby undermining Lebanon's sovereignty, incurring Israel's retaliation, and embroiling it in Lebanon's civil war (1976). In March 1979, at Camp David, Egyptian President Anwar al-Sadat signed a separate peace agreement with Israel that excluded PLO participation and provided for a limited Palestinian autonomy instead of full self-determination. With Egypt neutralized, Israel invaded Lebanon in June 1982 to destroy the PLO but succeeded only in forcing the PLO to move to Tunis; stripped of PLO protection, between 800 and 1,500 Palestinians in the Sabra and Shatila refugee camps were murdered in September by the Israel-allied Phalange. The 1982 Reagan peace plan, based on the Camp David autonomy proposal, once again excluded PLO participation. The following year, dissension within al-Fath caused a revolt by Abu Musa, with the help of Syria, which had long sought to control the PLO. When Arafat attempted to reestablish PLO power in Lebanon in 1983, Syria unleashed the forces of Abu Musa, who drove him out of Lebanon again. Israel attempted to undermine the PLO leadership by bombing its headquarters in Tunis in October 1985 but failed.

Unable to strike at Israel, the PLO relied primarily on diplomacy to achieve a compromise settlement. At the twelfth PNC in 1974 and the thirteenth in 1977, the PLO had moderated its goal of liberating all of Palestine to one of establishing a state in the West Bank and Gaza; it supported the 1982 Fahd Plan that implied a two-state solution. Empowered by the *intifada*, the Palestinian uprising that began against Israel's occupation in December 1987, Arafat in November 1988 led an enlarged PLO that included the DFLP to endorse the establishment of an independent Palestine state. It also endorsed the 1947 UN General Assembly Resolution 181. In December 1988, Arafat declared the PLO's acceptance of Israel's right to exist, recognition of Security Council Resolution 242, and the renunciation of terrorism. The United States promptly opened a dialogue with the PLO. Israel and its supporters, however, refused to acknowledge the change.

Israel's failure to reciprocate largely convinced Arafat to support Saddam Hussein in the 1990–1991 Gulf Crisis. This was a blunder that resulted in loss of financial support from the Gulf states. Without the support of the Soviet Union, short on funds, and fearing irrelevance, the PLO accepted the U.S. peace initiative that led to the 1991 Madrid peace conference between Israel and the Arab states and the Palestinians. However, twenty-two months and ten rounds of negotiations proved fruitless. The PLO regarded the framework for the talks as unfair and did not consider middle-level U.S. officials, especially those associated with pro-Israel lobbies, as "honest brokers." Norway established a secret channel in Oslo through which the PLO and Israel agreed to recognize each other. On 13 September 1993, at the White House, they signed a Declaration of Principles for a five-year Palestinian limited autonomy in the West Bank and Gaza, starting with the Gaza Strip and the town of Jericho, followed by elections for an interim council, Israel's withdrawal from other parts of the West Bank, and transfer of power. Unresolved final status issues—Jerusalem, Jewish settlements, refugees of 1948, and borders—were deferred.

In May 1994, the IDF withdrew from Jericho and most of the Gaza Strip, and Palestinian police and a civil administration took over. Despite a decline in support for the peace process due to the violence and the slow pace of the negotiations, the PLO and Israel reached a number of agreements regarding the interim period, especially Oslo II, signed on 28 September 1995, which set the stage for Israel's further withdrawal from less than 30 percent of the West Bank and the establishment of Palestine National Authority (PNA) control over this area. The PLO is to negotiate the final status issues that will arise between 1996 and the end of 1999. Other than as negotiator, its primary functions are being replaced by the PNA and by al-Fath. If elections take place and a state is established, the PLO is likely to decline further or even disappear, because its primary goal of establishing a state in the West Bank and Gaza will have been fulfilled.

BIBLIOGRAPHY

COBBAN, HELENA. *The Palestinian Liberation Organization.* New York, 1985.

GRESH, ALAIN. *The PLO, the Struggle Within: Towards an Independent Palestinian State.* London, 1986.

LESCH, ANN M. "Palestine Liberation Organization." In *Oxford Companion of Politics of the World,* ed. by Joel Krieger. New York, 1993.

MILLER, AARON DAVID. *The PLO and the Politics of Survival.* Washington, D.C., 1983.

NASSAR, JAMAL R. *The Palestine Liberation Organization: From Armed Struggle to the Declaration of Independence.* New York, 1991.

RUBIN, BARRY. *Revolution until Victory? The Politics and History of the PLO.* Cambridge, Mass., 1994.

Philip Mattar

Palestine National Charter

Amended version of the Palestine National Covenant with greater emphasis on armed struggle against Israel.

The fourth PALESTINE NATIONAL COUNCIL meeting (Cairo, July 1968) amended the 1964 PALESTINE NATIONAL COVENANT to produce this charter. Following the Arab defeat of June 1967, the leadership of the Palestine Liberation Organization (PLO) passed to the more action-oriented leaders of al-Fath, the Popular Front for the Liberation of Palestine (PFLP), the Palestine Liberation Front (PLF), and other commando groups. While these groups continued to strive in principle for the ideals of Arab nationalism, in practice their character and development became increasingly Palestinian. Their focus was on Palestinian nationalism and on armed struggle against Israel.

The 1968 charter incorporated new principles that were supposed to guide Palestinian political action after the 1967 defeat. The charter has thirty-three articles. Article 1 explicitly defines Palestine as the "homeland of the Palestinian Arab people," while Articles 3 and 9 in particular stress the principles of self-determination and Palestinian national sovereignty over Palestine. Reference to these principles is made eight times. Moreover, the concepts of self-determination and sovereignty are defined in explicit Palestinian terms. Although the ethno-cultural links of the Palestinians to the larger Arab homeland are emphasized, they do not predominate over the territorial connection between the Palestinians and their homeland Palestine.

The 1968 charter radicalized the instruments of political action to be employed for the liberation of Palestine. Armed struggle is posited as the "sole road" to liberation (Article 9), and the concept recurs thirteen times in an emphatic, declaratory tone. Armed struggle, however, does not exclude conventional warfare as Article 10 suggests, since the Arab countries are considered partners in the battle for liberation. In this formula, the role of commando action was given primacy and regarded as the "nucleus of the Palestinian popular liberation war" (Article 10).

The principles of the charter were superseded by subsequent Palestine National Council decisions. Above all, they were superseded by the Declaration of Principles concluded between Israel and the PLO in September 1993. The PNC voted in April 1996 to cancel the portions of the charter calling for the destruction of the State of Israel and to draft a new charter within six months.

BIBLIOGRAPHY

Brand, Laurie A. *Palestinians in the Arab World: Institution Building and the Search for State.* New York, 1988.
Gresh, Alain. *The PLO, the Struggle Within: Towards an Independent Palestinian State.* London, 1986.

Muhammad Muslih

Palestine National Council

The equivalent of a constituent assembly or parliament for the Palestinian people.

The Palestine National Council (PNC) is the highest decision-making body within the Palestine Liberation Organization (PLO) and the supreme representative institution of the Palestinian people.

The PNC, like the PLO itself, grew out of the first Arab Summit held in Cairo in January 1964. The summit resolved to create a Palestinian organization that would enable the Palestinian people "to play their role in the liberation of their country" and empowered the Palestine delegate to the League of Arab States, Ahmad shuqayri, to hold consultations on the implementation of this decision. Pursuant to a draft constitution Shuqayri prepared shortly thereafter, a "Palestinian General Congress," convening as "The National Conference of the Palestine Liberation Organization," was to meet in East Jerusalem in May 1964 to consider the ratification of this and other documents formally establishing the PLO and its institutions. The deliberations of the 397 invited delegates, representing a broad spectrum of Palestinian life, were later termed the first session of the Palestine National Council.

Among the proposed institutions the meeting approved was a National Assembly, which during the 1970s came to be known as the Palestine National Council. Its structure, powers, and procedural rules are set forth in the Fundamental Law appended to the palestine national covenant, which survives in amended form.

According to the Fundamental Law, the PNC is the supreme authority for formulating the policies and programs of the PLO and its institutions, and all who operate under the PLO umbrella are accountable to its decisions. It does not sit in permanent session, has no permanent committees, and by force of circumstance has no permanent location. It must convene in regular session once every year (changed from every two years in 1971) and in extraordinary session whenever so requested by the PLO Executive Committee (the executive branch of the PLO) or PNC membership. It elects its own presidential office, consisting of a chairman, two vice chairmen, and a secretary. The attendance of two-thirds of its delegates is required for a quorum, and its initial practice of "collective decision-making" was in 1981 defined as meaning majority voting. The PNC met in closed session until 1981, when foreign dignitaries and Palestinian observers were first invited. With few exceptions it publishes its resolutions and other documents, and the media may today observe and record most of its proceedings.

The PNC is neither an elected nor appointed body, and individual delegates have no fixed term. Formally speaking, candidates must be nominated by a committee (which since 1971 consists of the PLO Executive Committee, the PNC chairman, and the commander in chief of the Palestine Liberation Army [PLA]), and then elected by a majority of the entire membership at its subsequent session. The nominating committee must in turn ensure that the composition of the PNC is representative of the Palestinian people as a whole.

Although these rules remain in force, they have not been practiced since the Palestinian guerrilla organizations entered and took control of the PLO in 1968–1969. Rather, the PLO's constituent organizations and PLO mass unions and syndicates are each assigned a quota of seats (arrived at by negotiation and reflecting their respective size and importance), and then select their delegates according to their own procedures. Palestinian exile communities and other categories of unorganized Palestinians are also each assigned a quota of delegates, but these are directly selected by the PNC nominating committee. A quota has additionally been set aside for delegates resident in Israel and the occupied Palestinian territories, but for security reasons these have not attended PNC deliberations, and it is unclear if a secret list of such delegates, purportedly compiled by the nominating committee, in fact exists. Although the PNC is an integral PLO institution, PNC delegates are not necessarily serving officials in the PLO or members of its constituent factions.

The size of the PNC has varied over time. In 1968 its membership was reduced from 466 to 100 and limited to representatives of guerrilla factions (68) and political independents (32) to ensure more effective deliberations and increased guerilla control over the PLO. Representatives of PLO mass unions were admitted in 1971, as a result of which the membership was expanded to 150. And in 1977 the PNC again opened its doors to representatives of Palestinian exile communities and additional unorganized groups (e.g., deportees), increasing its membership to 293. The active membership of the PNC has since swollen to pre-1968 levels and would be half as large again if nonparticipant delegates from the occupied territories, first admitted in 1977, are taken into account. Delegates representing guerrilla organizations currently comprise less than 25 percent of the active membership, but at least as many of those representing other constitutencies are also members of PLO factions.

The PNC exercises major powers. At the beginning of each session, the PLO Executive Committee must submit a report on its activities and the status of the PLO since the previous session and submit its resignation. A new Executive Committee, whose size and membership is determined by the PNC and may be identical to the previous one, is elected at the end of each session. (Until 1966, the Executive Committee, known as the Executive Command, was ap-

pointed and presided over by the PNC chairman and, until 1968, appointed by its separately elected chairman.) The new Executive Committee's policy guidelines and other instructions, as well as other PLO proclamations, are set forth in resolutions adopted by the PNC, which are typically drafted in committee.

In 1970 the PNC also established the PLO Central Committee (since 1973 known as the Central Council) as an intermediate body between itself and the Executive Committee. It possesses combined legislative-executive powers and must meet at least once every three months to review the work of the Executive Committee, approve any commitments made by the latter, clarify PNC guidelines where necessary, and issue supplementary resolutions where relevant. For reasons related to its origins as a mechanism for improving coordination between guerrilla factions represented on the Executive Committee and those that were not, the Central Council is unlike the Executive Committee—neither elected by the PNC nor entirely composed of PNC members. In its current form it comprises the Executive Committee, the PNC chairman, the PLA commander in chief, representatives of PLO constituent organizations and institutions, and PNC members selected by the Executive Committee. It elects a General Secretariat from among its own members.

Among its other major powers, the PNC hears the report of the Palestine National Fund (the PLO treasury), approves its budget, (re-)elects its Board of Directors (which like the Executive Committee then elects its own officers), and considers the reports and structures of other PLO institutions. It does not, however, have the right to interfere in the internal affairs of the movements that operate under the PLO umbrella.

The PNC is the forum in which the official policies of the PLO are debated and formulated, and its resolutions and declarations represent the evolving consensus within the Palestinian national movement on major internal, regional, and international questions. At the same time, consensus has often come at the cost of clarity, and the meaning of PNC resolutions is often the subject of fierce debate both within and outside the PLO. For this reason PNC resolutions are often best understood by comparison to previous resolutions and in relation to their wider political context. Similarly, their interpretation by the PLO leadership is best judged by its subsequent actions.

The more important PNC sessions have included that of 1964, which established the PLO; 1968, which witnessed the entry of the guerrilla movement (a gradual process) and amended the Palestine National Covenant to insist on the total liberation of Palestine through armed struggle; 1969, at which Yasir ARAFAT was elected chairman of the Executive

Committee; 1971, which endorsed the concept of a secular democratic state; 1974, which took the first steps toward endorsing a two-state solution; 1979, which categorically rejected the Camp David Accords; 1983, which supported a confederal relationship between Jordan and an independent Palestinian state; 1988, which proclaimed an independent Palestinian state; and 1991, which authorized Palestinian participation in negotiations with Israel. A number of sessions have been boycotted by one or more PLO factions, and the 1984 PNC in fact witnessed bitter controversy over the subject of a quorum. In some years the PNC has not convened due to conflict (e.g., during the 1975–1976 Lebanese civil war), but in others this failure has been the subject of fierce criticism, most recently when the PNC was not called into session to debate the 1993 Israeli-Palestinian Declaration of Principles.

Given that regular general elections would be difficult and probably impossible to conduct under the fragmented conditions of Palestinian existence, the PNC is a genuine attempt at creating a representative body, which has met with significant success. The PLO leadership's lack of physical control over its constituency, and its consequent reliance upon consensus politics and popular support for legitimacy for authority, have also encouraged a significant degree of pluralism within the PNC. At the same time, the PNC exhibits some clearly undemocratic tendencies. Aside from the lack of elections, critics point out that the quota system (which is practiced in all PLO institutions) places powers of decision-making and accountability in PLO factions rather than constituencies or institutions and encourages perpetual hegemony by a dominant group. And the importance attached to consensus politics, aided by pressure from Arab states to include delegates who enjoy their sponsorship, has ensured representation for groups and individuals with no significant popular support. The increasing appropriation of power by the PLO leadership has also led to a lack of regard for PNC resolutions and procedures as well as its marginalization as the locus of Palestinian decision making.

Palestinian self-government in the West Bank and Gaza Strip poses difficult challenges for the PNC. It must overcome its marginalization during this process, which has led to the resignation of numerous delegates and undermined its legitimacy. Of equal importance, it must absorb any legislative authority established in the occupied territories without neglecting constituencies elsewhere, so as to remain the supreme political institution of the Palestinian people as a whole. And it must replace the quota system with democratic selection mechanisms while becoming a permanent body with all this entails if it is ever to become the genuine Palestinian parliament it already claims to be.

BIBLIOGRAPHY

"The PNC: Historical Background," published in al-Fajr (April 12, 1987) and reprinted in Journal of Palestine Studies 64 (1987): 149–152, provides summary descriptions of the first eighteen PNC sessions. Detailed treatment of most sessions is to be found in ALAIN GRESH's The PLO: The Struggle Within: Towards an Independent Palestinian State, rev. ed., translated by A. M. Berrett (London, 1988). CHERYL RUBENBERG, The Palestine Liberation Organization: Its Institutional Infrastructure (Belmont, MA., 1983), examines the PNC, Central Council, and Executive Committee as institutions, and these are critically examined from a democratic perspective in JAMIL HILAL, "PLO Institutions: The Challenge Ahead," Journal of Palestine Studies 89 (1993): 46–60. PNC resolutions and other relevant documents are regularly published in the "Documents and Source Material" section of the Journal of Palestine Studies, and the most important of these are collected in The Israeli-Palestinian Conflict: A Documentary Record, 1967–1990, edited by YEHUDA LUKACS (Cambridge, U.K., 1992).

Mouin Rabbani

Palestine National Council Meetings

Meetings of the highest policy-making body within the Palestine Liberation Organization.

As the PALESTINE LIBERATION ORGANIZATION'S (PLO) quasi parliament, the Palestine National Council (PNC) defines the organization's policies and programs. Indeed, the PNC in effect created the PLO when it adopted, at its first meeting, May to June 1964, the Fundamental Law setting forth the distribution of power among the various bodies of the PLO.

The places and dates of the PNC sessions are as follows:

1. Jerusalem, 28 May–2 June 1964;
2. Cairo, 31 May–4 June 1965;
3. Gaza, 20–24 May 1966;
4. Cairo, 10–17 July 1968;
5. Cairo, 1–4 February 1969;
6. Cairo, 1–6 September 1969;
7. Cairo, 30 May–4 June 1970;
8. Amman, 27–28 August 1970;
9. Cairo, 28 February–5 March 1971;
10. Cairo, 7–13 July 1971;
11. Cairo, 6–12 April 1972 (Palestine People's Congress);
12. Cairo, 6–12 January 1973;

13. Cairo, 1–8 June 1974;
14. Cairo, 12–20 March 1977;
15. Damascus, 15–23 January 1979;
16. Damascus, 11–19 April 1981;
17. Algiers, 14–22 February 1983;
18. Amman, 22 November 1984;
19. Algiers, 20–25 April 1987;
20. Algiers, 12–15 November 1988;
21. Algiers, 23–28 September 1991;
22. Gaza, 23–25 April 1996.

The main focus of the PNC meetings was the conflict between Israelis and Palestinians. Each meeting produced a set of resolutions that addressed this conflict. Examination of the PNC resolutions reveals three phases in the evolution of Palestinian thinking about the conflict with Israel. Each transition from one phase to the next involved a reformulation of Palestinian objectives and an increasing reliance on diplomatic means for achieving them.

In the first, or "total liberation," phase (1964–1968) the PLO was committed to regaining the sovereignty of Palestinians over their entire original homeland and believed that armed struggle was the only way to do so. It envisioned a liberated PALESTINE as an Arab state in which all Jewish residents who had lived there prior to 1947 (the year in which the UN General Assembly recommended the partition of Palestine) would have citizenship.

In the second, or "secular democratic state," phase (1969–1973), the PLO continued to stress the importance of armed struggle and to reject the partition of Palestine. However, as the program of the fourth PNC meeting demonstrated, the organization placed new emphasis on the specifically Palestinian (rather than Arab) character of the country and held out the hope that Palestine could be inhabited by all citizens—Jewish, Christian, and Muslim—on the basis of nonsectarian principles (democracy, equality, and mutual respect). Although Zionist institutions would be dismantled, Jewish Palestinians would have the same rights as other citizens, regardless of the date of their arrival in Palestine. A growing tendency to employ diplomatic as well as military means to achieve these goals appeared.

The "two-state solution" phase began in 1974 with the adoption of the twelfth PNC program and culminated in the acceptance of a Palestinian state alongside Israel, not as a transitional stage but as a final point. The strategy during much of this phase has been to concentrate on diplomatic efforts at the expense of military efforts, to contact moderate groups and individuals in Israel directly, to insist on PLO participation in a Middle East peace conference, and to affirm the PLO's readiness to open a direct dialogue with Israel's government. Starting with the seventeenth PNC program (1983), the PLO adopted the principle that Palestinian relations with Jordan should be along confederal lines between two independent states: the State of Palestine and the State of Jordan.

The political programs adopted by these PNC meetings have been superseded by the Israel-PLO Declaration of Principles (September 1993), and by subsequent agreements between the two parties.

In April 1996 the PNC met in Gaza to consider removing all references to the destruction of the State of Israel from its charter. As part of the Oslo Accords, Yasir Arafat agreed to rewrite the Palestine National Charter within two months of the February 1996 seating of the Palestinian Legislative Council. For its part, Israel allowed some of those it has declared its state enemies to enter Gaza in order to attend the meeting.

Following two days of often lively debate, the Palestine National Council voted by more than the necessary two-thirds majority to amend the PALESTINE NATIONAL CHARTER by canceling those clauses that contradicted the contents of the letters exchanged between the PLO and the Israeli government and to draft a new charter within six months.

BIBLIOGRAPHY

MUSLIH, MUHAMMAD. "The Political Programs of the Palestine National Council." Unpublished manuscript.
———. *Toward Coexistence: An Analysis of the Resolutions of the Palestine National Council.* Washington, D.C., 1990.

Muhammad Muslih

Palestine National Covenant

A 1964 document adopted by the Palestine Liberation Organization.

The Palestine National Covenant was adopted by the PALESTINE NATIONAL COUNCIL at its first meeting (May–June 1964) after being drafted by a special charter committee. The covenant reflected the Arab political mood of the time and the political mentality of its framers, who were, on the whole, notables selected from among Palestinian public officials, professionals, and businessmen. Five interrelated ideas constitute the thrust of the covenant. First, it emphasized the total liberation of Palestine, which in effect meant the dismantling of Israel. The concept of liberation recurs sixteen times in the twenty-nine articles of the covenant; all other concepts are subordinate to it. This concept encompasses Arab nationalism, Islam, and culture.

Second, and connected with liberation, came the concept of self-determination. However, it is not clearly articulated whether, after liberation, the Palestinians would exercise self-determination within the context of an independent Palestinian state or a Palestine that is united with one or more Arab states (Articles 4 and 10). The word "state" is absent from the covenant, but the tone of the articles and the political persuasion of the majority of the members of the charter committee suggest that preference was given to a liberated Palestine that would be united to a projected unitary Arab nation.

Third, the covenant offered a definition of who was a Palestinian and whether this definition applied to Jews. In an attempt to emphasize the indissoluble link between Palestinians and their homeland, Palestinians are defined as the Arab nationals who "resided normally in Palestine until 1947," that is until the start of the Palestinian exodus following the United Nations partition resolution of November 1947. In a supplementary article the covenant stipulated that the "Jews who are of Palestinian origin will be considered Palestinians if they are willing to live loyally and peacefully in Palestine" (Article 7).

Fourth, the covenant sanctioned the status quo that existed in the West Bank (under Jordanian control) and Gaza Strip (under Egyptian control) by stipulating that the PALESTINE LIBERATION ORGANIZATION (PLO) would not exercise any sovereignty over those areas (Article 24). At the time, the PLO leadership adopted this position because it lacked the desire and the ability to challenge the system of those Arab states whose political prescriptions rested more on perpetuating the status quo than on disrupting it. Moreover, the principle of territorial sovereignty was overshadowed by the dream of Arab unity, which gripped the imagination of the Palestinian and Arab masses. This explains why Article 16 vaguely linked "national sovereignty" to the abstract idea of "national freedom."

Fifth, the charter did not clearly articulate the means by which the goal of liberation should be achieved. Armed struggle and revolution, both being principles that occupied a central position in the ideology of most national liberation movements, had no place in the covenant. Given the mood of the time, it is not surprising that the framers of the covenant prescribed Arab unity as the principle instrument for liberation.

This 1964 covenant was amended in July 1968 as the PALESTINE NATIONAL CHARTER, and the amended version itself was superseded by subsequent Palestine National Council decisions.

BIBLIOGRAPHY

HARKABI, Y. *Palestinians and Israel.* Jerusalem, 1974.

Muhammad Muslih

Palestine Post

See Jerusalem Post

Palestine Research Center

Research and publication center of the Palestine Liberation Organization.

In 1965 the Palestine Research Center was founded in Beirut by the Palestine Liberation Organization, to study all aspects of Palestinian life in Israel and the Arab countries, Zionism, and contemporary politics and society in Israel. Among its many publications is the Arabic-language journal SHU'UN FILASTINIYYA (Palestine Affairs).

Jenab Tutunji

Palestine Supreme Court

High court and court of appeal during the British mandate, 1920–1948.

During Britain's civil administration in Palestine, the Supreme Court, sitting as a Court of Appeal, had jurisdiction to hear appeals to all judgments given in lower courts, such as district courts and land courts. Sitting as High Court of Justice, it heard and determined petitions over which none of the other courts had jurisdiction.

BIBLIOGRAPHY

ROLEF, S. H., ed. *Political Dictionary of the State of Israel.* New York, 1987.

Benjamin Joseph

Palestinian Arab Congresses

Seven congresses convened by Palestinian Arab politicians between 1919 and 1928 to oppose pro-Zionist British policies and gain independence.

The first of the Palestinian Arab congresses met in Jerusalem from January 27 to February 9, 1919. Organized by local Muslim and Christian associations, its thirty participants framed a national charter that demanded independence for Palestine, denounced the BALFOUR DECLARATION (and its promise of a Jewish national home), and rejected British rule over Palestine. A majority sought the incorporation of Palestine into an independent Syrian state, and the delegates strongly denounced French claims to a mandate over Syria. The congress expressed its request for independence in the language of U.S. President Woodrow Wilson's principles supporting the right of self-determination of subject peoples.

Scholars disagree about the second congress. Muslih argues that the British prevented it from being held, but other scholars view the Arab congress held in Damascus in March 1920 as the second congress. It proclaimed Syrian independence under Emir Faisal, son of Sharif Husayn of Mecca.

The third congress was held in Haifa in December 1920. The forty-eight delegates elected an executive committee (the ARAB EXECUTIVE), with a permanent secretariat based in Jerusalem; Musa Kazim al-HUSAYNI headed it. Scion of a leading Jerusalem family, he had been removed by the British as mayor after riots in the spring of 1920. The congress and executive committee were dominated by middle-aged men from ranking Muslim and Christian landowning and merchant families; but younger, more radical politicians also participated—those who had returned home from Damascus in July 1920, after the French overthrew Emir Faisal and established their mandate over Syria. In Palestine, a civil administration was established under Herbert Samuel, a British Zionist. The congress's resolutions omitted references to unity with Syria, but maintained firm opposition to Zionism, insisting that Palestine gain its independence as an Arab state. The resolutions appealed to the British sense of justice and fair play, in the hope that the pro-Zionist policies could be modified.

The fourth congress met in May 1921, in the wake of widespread riots in Jaffa. It resolved to send a delegation to London, headed by Musa Kazim al-Husayni, to alter British policy. The delegation remained in London through July 1922 and had some impact on British thinking: The Churchill memorandum of June 1922 indicated that the government might place some limits on Jewish immigration and promote a degree of Arab self-rule.

At the same time, a special assembly was convened in June 1922. More militant than the previous congress, the participants voted to hold a peaceful two-day demonstration in mid-July against the establishment of the British mandate. That militancy was enhanced in the fifth congress, held in Nablus in August 1922, with more than seventy-five delegates attending. It rejected the Churchill memorandum

and launched a boycott of elections for the legislative council. Soon afterward, a second delegation went to Istanbul, Lausanne, and London in a futile effort to persuade the Turkish government not to sign a peace agreement without taking into account the interests of its former Arab provinces, which were being ruled by British and French forces.

The sixth congress met in June 1923 at the insistence of local Muslim and Christian societies who feared that Sharif Husayn of Mecca would sign a treaty with London that would recognize the British mandate over Palestine, rather than demand independence for Palestine. The 115 delegates resolved to send a third delegation to London to monitor the negotiations. Moreover, the resolutions stiffened the Arabs' rejection of representative institutions that did not grant policymaking authority to the Arab community and even proposed such steps toward noncooperation as withholding taxes. However, the large landowners objected to that step, fearing that the British would seize their property in retaliation, and so action on those proposals was shelved.

The British mandate became effective in 1923, and the seventh congress convened June 20–22, 1928, ending five years of tension and division among the Arab politicians. In the intervening years, the NASHASHIBI FAMILY of Jerusalem withheld its participation in the institutions associated with the Arab congress, founded the National party (1923), and contested with the Husaynis and their adherents in elections for the Supreme Muslim Council (1926) and local municipal councils (1927). New groups also emerged among young educated Muslims and pan-Arab activists. The seventh congress sought to unite such factions behind the demand for a representative council and parliamentary government, which would help them attain their national goals. Since Jewish immigration had dipped in 1926 and 1927, the delegates had become less fearful of the Zionist movement than they had been in the past and hoped that a gradualist approach to self-government would attain their ends. Their resolutions also emphasized socioeconomic needs, such as reopening the Ottoman-period agricultural banks so that farmers could obtain loans, increasing the allotment to education in the government's budget, and reducing the authority of the Greek priests in the Orthodox Christian community. The congress elected an enlarged Arab Executive whose forty-eight members included twelve Christians. The various factions were balanced: Musa Kazim al-Husayni retained the presidency but both vice presidents (including a Greek Orthodox) favored the Nashashibi camp. The three secretaries were the young radical Jamal al-Husayni, the pro-Nashashibi Protestant lawyer Mughannam Ilyas al-Mughannam, and the pan-Arab, independent-minded lawyer Awni Abd al-Hadi.

The new Arab Executive immediately pressed the British to grant representative institutions, but its efforts coincided with renewed Arab–Jewish tension, centered on conflicting claims to the Western Wall in Jerusalem. The riots of August 1929 undermined the cautious negotiating efforts of the Arab Executive; its members were swept up in the growing militancy of the Arab community. The fourth delegation to London in the spring of 1930 presented maximalist demands: Immediate formation of a national government in which the Arabs would have the majority. The Arab Executive also supported the demonstrations and protests launched by youthful activists in the fall of 1933, as Jewish immigration and land purchases again escalated.

Following the death of Musa Kazim al-Husayni in March 1934, the Arab Executive held its final meeting in August. That meeting permitted the formation of political parties, but resolved to convene an eighth general congress in 1935. The congress never met. By then, politicians were preoccupied with forming their own parties and contesting municipal council elections. When the Arab general strike began in Palestine, in April 1936, a new coordinating body—the Arab Higher Committee—was constituted from the heads of the political parties. The Arab Executive then faded away. Although the Arab Executive had limited effectiveness, it had served as an informal spokesman for the Arab community for more than a decade. The congresses had provided an essential forum for Palestinian Arab politicians to debate fundamental policies and articulate their demands.

BIBLIOGRAPHY

INGRAMS, DOREEN. *Palestine Papers, 1917–1922.* New York, 1973.

LESCH, ANN MOSELY. *Arab Politics in Palestine, 1917–1939.* Ithaca, N.Y., 1979.

MCTAGUE, JOHN J. *British Policy in Palestine, 1917–1922.* Lanham, Md., 1983.

MUSLIH, MUHAMMAD Y. *The Origins of Palestinian Nationalism.* New York, 1988.

Ann M. Lesch

Palestinian Refugee Camps

Temporary living sites for the Arabs of Palestine who left the State of Israel around the time of its independence in 1948 and for those who left during the ensuing Arab–Israel wars.

The refugee camps for Palestinians were established during the 1948 Arab–Israel War by three international relief agencies—the American Friends Service Committee, the International Red Cross, and the League of Red Cross Societies—under the auspices of the UN Relief for Palestine Refugees (UNRPR). The camps were to provide temporary assistance for those who left Israel and went to surrounding Arab countries—Jordan, Syria, Lebanon, and Egypt—all of which were fighting Israel.

In 1949, the UN Relief and Works Agency (UNRWA) replaced UNRPR and the three private agencies. As the years went by and the Arab–Israel wars continued (1956, 1967, 1973, and 1982), the shelters continued to house refugees and their offspring—for several generations.

In the early 1990s, the number of UN-sponsored camps numbered sixty-one, located in five field-areas: the West Bank, 20; Gaza Strip, 8; Jordan, 10; Lebanon, 13; and Syria, 10. About 35 percent of the 2.6 million UN-registered refugees in 1992 lived in UNRWA camps, ranging from about 24 percent in Jordan to more than 50 percent in Lebanon. The largest camp, with more than 65,000 inhabitants, was Bakaa, near Amman, Jordan.

Facilities and services in the camps include elementary education, basic food rations, health care, and special programs for infants and pregnant women. Initially, UNRWA used most of its funds to supply food and housing, but in recent years more than half the budget has been used for education. UNRWA also provides services to refugees who live outside the camps, according to need; camp residents are entitled to use all UNRWA facilities and services.

Since international assistance to the Palestinian refugees was originally intended to be temporary, the first shelters were tents. When it became obvious that refugees would not soon return to their original homes, more permanent housing was provided. At first refugees resisted moving into new cement-block structures because they symbolized permanent resettlement. But UNRWA persuaded them that accepting more solid housing did not mean surrender of the right to return to their original homes.

Since the 1950s, most camps have become semipermanent, with many characteristics of the adjoining urban areas. Refugees have added rooms and facilities to the original UNRWA shelters. Markets and shopping areas have developed, and regular transportation service has been established both within the camps and to the surrounding cities or towns. Most refugee families have one or more members working in nearby areas, so that UNRWA services now supplement rather than provide sustenance. Although the camp populations have increased by about 3 percent each year, they have been unable to expand beyond their original boundaries—thus living conditions have become extremely overcrowded and very uncomfortable. UNRWA's budget has not increased rapidly enough to maintain high levels of education or health and other facilities—therefore services also are seriously strained.

UNRWA is not responsible for security or governmental affairs within the camps; the host countries are responsible. In each host country, local authorities maintain order, such as it is, and rule the camps with varying degrees of strictness. From the late 1960s until 1982, the Palestine Liberation Organization (PLO) assumed these responsibilities for many camps in Lebanon, since the government was unable to assert its authority.

For a short period, the PLO seized control of the Palestinian refugee camps in Jordan, but the organization was driven from the country by the Jordanian army after a Palestinian uprising in 1970. Most PLO functionaries then fled to Lebanon, where they took control of several camps in various parts of the country; however, political differences within the Palestinian community erupted into violence in the camps by the mid-1980s. After the PLO was driven from Beirut by Israeli forces in 1982, a major uprising against al-Fath leader Yasir Arafat began in the northern camps, where the anti-Arafat factions were supported by Syria. The restoration of PLO influence in the south Lebanon camps led to open warfare between Palestinians there and AMAL, a Shiʿa militia supported by Syria. This three-year struggle, from 1985 to 1988, called the "Battle of the Camps," had a devastating impact on the Palestinian community and was related to Syrian attempts to gain control of the Palestinian national movement.

The "Gaza–Jericho First" peace accord signed between Israel and the PLO in September 1993 was the source of divisiveness in the camps between those who supported and those who opposed the agreement.

BIBLIOGRAPHY

UNITED NATIONS. *Report of the Commissioner-General of the United Nations Relief and Works Agency for Palestine Refugees in the Near East.* Annual Reports 1950–1992. New York, 1992.

VIORST, MILTON. *Reaching for the Olive Branch: UNRWA and Peace in the Middle East.* Washington, D.C., 1989.

Don Peretz

Palestinians

Descendants of the Canaanites and other peoples who have lived in Palestine since ancient times.

The name "Palestinian" applies in contemporary times to Muslim and Christian Arabs who inhabited Palestine as a consolidated community until the creation of ISRAEL in May 1948, an event that shattered the community and dispersed about 725,000 Palestinians throughout the Middle East, primarily to Gaza, the West Bank, Jordan, Syria, and Lebanon.

In the mid-1990s, the total number of Palestinians was estimated at 6 million to 6.5 million. Approximately 85 percent are Muslims, and the other 15 percent are Christians. Until the initiation of the Palestine Authority in the summer of 1994, the largest concentration of Palestinians lived under Israeli occupation, approximately 1,225,000 in the West Bank, including East Jerusalem, and 725,000 in Gaza. Approximately 800,000 lived in pre-1967 Israel as Arab citizens of the Jewish state. Other Palestinians lived in different Arab countries, especially Jordan, which had approximately 2,170,000.

The politics and culture of the Palestinians from the latter part of the nineteenth century until after the signing of the Declaration of Principles between Israel and the PALESTINE LIBERATION ORGANIZATION (PLO) on September 13, 1993 can be divided into four stages. In the first stage, from 1876 to 1917, the Palestinians shared a common cultural heritage shaped primarily by the values of the Arab and Muslim empires that ruled the country with few interruptions from 638 C.E. to 1917. Palestinian society in this stage consisted of three major classes: peasants (*fellaheen*), commercial bourgeoisie, and urban notables or patricians. The patricians were the ruling class, and their influence ran deep in both the countryside and Palestinian cities and towns.

In 1897, the Basel program of the first Zionist Congress strongly affected the Palestinians. The program fixed the Zionist goal: "To create for the Jewish people a home in Palestine, secured by public law." This ushered in the first phase of a protracted struggle between indigenous Palestinians and Jewish immigrants. Opposition to Zionism was the focus of Palestinian political activities, as well as of Palestinian historiography and other forms of writing.

The second stage, from 1917 to 1948, was inaugurated with the collapse of the Ottoman Empire at the end of World War I. By the autumn of 1918, Palestine, Transjordan, and Iraq were under British control. This development made Palestine increasingly vulnerable to Zionist colonization, first, by isolating the country from its wider Arab environment and, second, by giving the British a free hand in implementing the BALFOUR DECLARATION of 2 November 1917. With the Balfour Declaration, the stage was set for a long struggle between the Palestinians and the Zionist immigrants. The Palestinians, who constituted approximately 90 percent of Palestine's population by the end of World War I, saw in the Zionists a potential threat to their national existence.

In strategic terms, the Palestinian–Zionist struggle was over the status quo. The Palestinians wanted to preserve the status quo, through political and diplomatic efforts beween 1917 and 1936 and through armed rebellion during the Great Revolt of 1936 to 1939 (see PALESTINE ARAB REVOLT). In contrast, the Zionists sought to revolutionize the status quo through mass immigration and land acquisition. The Jewish population in Palestine rose from 9.7 percent in 1919 to 35.1 percent in 1946, while Jewish-owned land increased from 2.04 percent of the total area of Palestine in 1919 to 7 percent in 1946. Meanwhile, British policy in the military sphere was aimed at disarming the Palestinians and arming the Jews. Thus, by 1947 the overall power equation was decisively in favor of the Zionists.

Palestinian society was also affected by three other factors: Zionist settlement activity, British colonial policies, and the expansion of Palestine's economy. While dominant members of urban notable families continued to control the politics of the country, other social forces were at play. The expansion of trade and the growth of coastal cities and towns enhanced the position of the middle class. Artisans and craftsmen, as well as people engaged in the finance, construction, and service sectors, also benefited from the expansion of trade. However, the peasants, who constituted almost two-thirds of Palestinian society, did not benefit from these economic developments. Their condition worsened in great part because of Zionist settlement and the lack of capital. While Jewish agricultural settlers had adequate land, the indigenous Palestinian peasantry lacked the space necessary for its growing population. The October 1930 report of Sir John Hope-Simpson acknowledged this problem, noting that there was not room for a substantial number of Jewish settlers on the land.

The depressed state of the peasantry, together with other developments, produced a revolutionary situation within Palestinian society by the mid-1930s. The most notable development was the escalating rate of Jewish immigration. The influx of Jewish immigrants had two major consequences: It produced panic and desperation among the Palestinians, reinforcing their fears of Jewish domination in the future; and it radicalized the Palestinians and convinced them that the British were unwilling or incapable of following an evenhanded policy. Against this background, a revolt erupted in May 1936 and continued unabated until the summer of 1939, with only a short lull between November 1936 and January 1937 while the Peel Commission toured Palestine to ascertain the causes of the revolt.

With the publication of the PEEL COMMISSION REPORT in July 1937, the rebellion exploded again in opposition to the commission's recommendation calling for a tripartite partition: a Jewish state; a Palestinian state to be incorporated by Transjordan; and a British mandate over other areas. There was a Palestinian consensus against partition because the proposed Jewish state would cover about 33 percent of the total area of the country at a time when Jewish ownership of land was roughly 5.6 percent and because a large portion of Palestinian villages, and a high percentage of Palestinians, would fall inside the Jewish state. The British responded to the Palestinian revolt with the full force of their military power. In terms of the cost in human lives, the revolt was a national calamity for the Palestinians: More than 3,075 were killed, 110 hanged, and 6,000 jailed in 1939 alone. At the same time, the British organized, trained, and armed special Jewish forces, creating in the process a Jewish military infrastructure that gave a decisive edge to the Jewish forces ten years later during the ARAB–ISRAEL WAR of 1948.

When the British realized that partition was not practicable, as indicated by the WOODHEAD COMMISSION report of November 1938, they convened the unsuccessful London Conference in February and March 1939 to resolve the issue of the future status of Palestine. To break the deadlock, Malcolm MacDonald, colonial secretary of state, issued a white paper on 17 May 1939. Although the white paper fell short of meeting long-standing Palestinian demands, it introduced a number of important modifications concerning immigration and the application of the Balfour Declaration.

The implementation of the white paper proved difficult, as a result partly of Palestinian and Zionist opposition and partly of the burdens of World War II. In these circumstances, the British, by the 1940s, were unable to handle the effects of the Balfour Declaration. The military and political structures of a Jewish national home were already in place in Palestine, in great part because of Britain's generosity. In almost every respect these structures were superior to those of the Palestinians.

Against this background, the United Nations divided Palestine into Jewish and Arab states in November 1947. The Palestinians rejected partition primarily because the United Nations proposed to give the Jews 55 percent of Palestine when Jewish ownership in November 1947 did not exceed 7 percent of the country's land. By contrast, the Jews found it in their interest to accept partition. Thus, the door for armed conflict in Palestine was wide open. A civil war between Jews and Palestinians followed the partition resolution. After the British departed Palestine in May 1948, war, interspersed with cease-fires, continued until July 1949.

Units of the Arab armies and volunteers from neighboring Arab countries came to the aid of the Palestinians who were losing the civil war and fleeing in large numbers. However, the Arab intervention was to no avail. The Jewish immigrant population was militarily superior to all the Arab soldiers combined. The Jews were also superior in terms of leadership, organization, and institutional links to the Western powers. In the end, the Zionists prevailed. Israel seized 77 percent of Palestine; about 725,000 Palestinians became refugees, many of them forcefully expelled by the Jewish forces while others fled out of fear. The Palestinians call this event *al-Nakba*, or the catastrophe.

The politics of the national struggle left a deep imprint on the intellectual life of the Palestinians, as is clearly illustrated in Palestinian historiography, art, and literature. There were literary and artistic works, for example, written in the Romantic tradition, such as those by Khalil Baydas, Khalil al-SAKAKINI, and Muhammad In'af al-Nashashibi. These works are marked by a focus on the social responsibility of men of letters and the relationship between culture and civilization. Other works were written in the realist tradition and reflected the philosophies of Ibn Khaldoun, Hegel, Marx, and Darwin.

The third stage, which lasted from 1948 to 1967, was characterized by formal armistice agreements between a number of Arab states—Egypt, Syria, Lebanon, and Jordan—and Israel; the disarray among Arab states unsuccessfully attempting to achieve Arab unity; the impact of Cold War politics on the Middle East; the eclipsing of Palestinian nationalism by Arab nationalism; and Israel's refusal to accept any responsibility for what had befallen the Palestinians in 1948. Uprooted, dispersed, and with no state of their own, diaspora Palestinians (60 percent of the Palestinian population in 1948) came under the guardianship of the host Arab countries in which they lived. Another 30 percent lived in the West Bank and Gaza, while the remaining 10 percent lived in Israel. As a whole, the life of Palestinians during this stage was marked by national dispersion, occupation, job insecurity, uncertain residency, discrimination, and political repression.

The post-1948 situation had many consequences. First, it made the Palestinians totally dependent on the Arab states. Second, geographical dispersal made it difficult for the Palestinians to work together within one organizational framework. Thus, some Palestinians identified with the Arab National Movement, others with the Arab Ba'th Socialist party or the Muslim Brotherhood; others acquired senior positions in the bureaucracies of Arab governments, particularly the Jordanian government, or formed independent Palestinian movements that advocated armed struggle against Israel. Life in the diaspora radicalized certain Palestinian groups that embarked on armed struggle against Israel in the mid-1960s in the hope of triggering an Arab–Israel war.

Against a background of inter-Arab rivalries and escalating Arab–Israel tensions, the Arab League created the PLO in 1964. The PLO's leadership was entrusted to Ahmad SHUQAYRI, a diaspora Palestinian of upper-class origin. In theory, the PLO was to work for the liberation of Palestine, but in practice it provided cover for Arab inaction toward Israel. The PLO charter of 1964 called for the total liberation of Palestine. Arab unity, rather than armed struggle or revolution, was posited as the instrument of liberation. Palestinian authors such as Abd al-Latif Tibawi, Fadwa TUQAN, and Fawaz TURKI gave expression to this goal. Many of them romanticized this goal by infusing it with the sentiment of the Palestinian concept of return. History books, novels, and collections of poems and pictures on Palestine poured forth during this period to express the pain of exile and the overpowering desire to return.

Literary and political themes were expressed by poets such as Mahmud DARWISH, Samih al-Qasim, and Tawfiq Zayyad and literary critics such as Salem Jubran, Ihsan Abbas, and Afif Salem. Palestinian and Islamic historiography was represented by Arif al-ARIF, Muhammad Izzat DARWAZA, and Akram Zuaytir. Stories of great Arab travelers were written by Iskandar al-Khuri al-Baytjali and Nicola Ziyada.

The fourth stage of contemporary Palestinian history, from 1967 to the present, began with the Israeli conquest of the West Bank and Gaza in June 1967, a development that resulted in the displacement of over 300,000 Palestinian refugees who fled the West Bank and the Golan area. Approximately 120,000 of these were second-time refugees who had lived in refugee camps under Jordanian or Syrian jurisdiction. The Arab–Israel War of 1967 also resulted in the placement of the West Bank and Gaza under the jurisdiction of the Israeli military government. During its occupation of these territories, Israel undertook settlement and other activities that had a devastating impact on the Palestinians, including the formal annexation of East Jerusalem and the doubling of its surface area; the settlement of over 120,000 Israelis in the Palestinian sector of the city; the confiscation of more than 55 percent of the West Bank and more than 40 percent of the Gaza Strip; and the deportation of a large number of Palestinians from both areas. Against the backdrop of these events, the story of the Palestinians has unfolded in the post-1967 era.

Soon after the 1967 War, the Palestinians arose as an independent political force. They asserted the primacy of Palestinian nationalism and expressed themselves in the idiom of revolution and armed struggle. The PLO charter, revised in 1968 to give expression to this new trend, called for the liberation of all of Palestine, emphasizing that armed struggle was the only way. Aware at the time that the problem of Israeli Jews must be addressed, the PLO articulated the idea of a secular democratic state anchored on nonsectarian principles of coexistence among the Jewish, Christian, and Muslim citizens of a liberated Palestine. In terms of political organizing, the Palestinians used Jordan as their early base of operations against Israel. In an attempt to attract international attention, radical Palestinian groups resorted to acts of violence, including the hijacking of civilian airliners and the murder of members of the Israeli Olympic team in Munich in September 1972. The unprecedented coincidence between the radicalization of the Palestinians and the emergence of pragmatism and a preference for a diplomatic settlement with Israel on the part of key Arab states led to tensions between revolutionary Palestinians and the new Arab political order. The JORDANIAN CIVIL WAR (1970–1971) epitomized the incongruence between the romanticism of revolutionary Palestinians and the pragmatism of the leaders of Arab states. The Palestinian guerillas were defeated in Jordan, but they moved to Lebanon where they reemerged as a strong political force in a country deeply divided by sectarian as well as socioeconomic differences. Their presence in Lebanon served as a catalyst for the civil war that was triggered in April 1975. After the Arab-Israel War of October 1973, a new Palestinian consensus emerged with respect to a diplomatic settlement with Israel. This consensus was reflected in the PLO's political programs of June 1974 and March 1977. Both programs implicitly called for peace with Israel and the establishment of a Palestinian state in the West Bank and Gaza.

Momentous events affected the Palestinians between 1982 and 1990. In June 1982, Israel invaded Lebanon. Thousands of Palestinians were killed, maimed, or taken prisoner by the Israeli invading force. After nearly three months of fighting, the PLO evacuated Lebanon under the protection of a multinational force and set up its new headquarters in Tunisia. While the PLO was trying to recover from the devastating impact of the Israeli invasion of Lebanon, the situation of the Palestinians in the West Bank and Gaza continued to deteriorate under the impact of massive Jewish settlements and the policies of the Likud government, which took power in Israel in 1977. The Palestinian response to this situation was the INTIFADA (uprising), which erupted in December 1987. The Intifada put the West Bank and Gaza Palestinians in the limelight after several years of neglect by Arab governments whose energies were focused on the Iran–Iraq War. The Intifada also catapulted the priorities of West Bank and Gaza Palestinians to the top of the PLO agenda. Before that, the PLO catered primarily to the preferences of diaspora Palestinians. This led to the further crystallization of the pragmatic trend that had begun to emerge in the previous phase. The Intifada forced the PLO to move definitively toward the peaceful pursuit of a state in the West Bank and Gaza, where the overriding priority of the Palestinians living in those territories was to end Israeli occupation. This was the crux of the PLO's political program of November 1988. Politically and intellectually, this phase witnessed the greater salience of religious activism with the emergence of the ISLAMIC JIHAD in 1986 and the Islamic Resistance Movement (HAMAS) in January 1988.

Despite their political difficulties, the Palestinians participated in the Arab national debate over cultural and sociopolitical issues. Hisham Sharabi wrote on Arab intellectuals and their interaction with Western culture. Using anthropological and sociological concepts, he also analyzed patterns of authority in contemporary Arab society. Edward Said, a scholar-critic, wrote on Western literature and authored books and articles on the Palestine question and other Middle Eastern topics. Walid KHALIDI wrote on the Palestinians in Palestine before their diaspora. Palestinian women, such as Fadwa Tuqan, Sahar Khalifa, and Salma al-Khadra al-Jayyusi, used poetry and other forms of literature to express the cause of women's rights in the Arab world. Other women, including Hanan Ashrawi, participated in politics and wrote on social and cultural topics.

Iraq's invasion and occupation of Kuwait in August 1990 set in motion a chain of political developments that led to the mutual recognition of Israel and the PLO and the signing of the historic Declaration of Principles in September 1993. The PLO's support for Saddam Hussein was to a significant degree responsible for the shattering of the Palestinian community that lived in Kuwait, a community that totaled approximately 350,000 people working as teachers, civil servants, and industrialists. However, the tragic results of the Gulf Crisis provided a propitious occasion for resolving the cause of the Palestinians. The launching of the Madrid peace process opened the way for the Israel–PLO accord of September 1993. This accord was followed by other agreements to implement Palestinian self-rule, including the Taba agreement of September 1995. The agreements resulted in the withdrawal of Israeli troops from Gaza and major West Bank towns and the establishment of the Palestinian Legislative Council. With the Palestinians exercising control over these areas, the realization of Palestinian self-determination seemed possible.

BIBLIOGRAPHY

BRAND, LAURIE A. *Palestinians in the Arab World: Institution Building and the Search for State*. New York, 1988.

HUREWITZ, J. C. *The Struggle for Palestine*. New York, 1976.

KHALIDI, WALID. *Before Their Diaspora*. Washington, D.C., 1984.

LESCH, ANN MOSELY. "Closed Borders, Divided Lives: Palestinian Writings." Universities Field Staff International Reports, Asia, no. 28 (1985).

LUKACS, YEHUDA, and ABDALLA M. BATTAH, eds. *The Arab–Israeli Conflict: Two Decades of Change*. Boulder, Colo., 1988.

MA'OZ, MOSHE. *Palestinian Leadership in the West Bank*. London, 1984.

MATTAR, PHILIP. *The Mufti of Jerusalem: Al-Hajj Amin al-Husayni and the Palestine National Movement*. New York, 1988.

MILLER, AARON DAVID. *The PLO: The Politics of Survival*. New York, 1983.

MUSLIH, MUHAMMAD. *The Origins of Palestinian Nationalism*. New York, 1988.

———. *Toward Coexistence: An Analysis of the Resolutions of the Palestine National Council*. Washington, D.C., 1990.

PERETZ, DON. *Palestinians, Refugees, and the Middle East Peace Process*. Washington, D.C., 1993.

SAID, EDWARD. *The Question of Palestine*. New York, 1979.

SCHIFF, ZE'EV, and EHUD YA'ARI. *Intifada: The Palestinian Uprising—Israel's Third Front*. New York, 1990.

SMITH, CHARLES D. *Palestine and the Arab–Israeli Conflict*. New York, 1992.

TESSLER, MARK. *A History of the Israeli–Palestinian Conflict*. Bloomington, Ind., 1994.

Muhammad Muslih

Palgrave, William Gifford   [1826–1888]

English traveler and writer.

Born in London to a barrister father and educated at Oxford, Palgrave was an army officer in the East India Company, a Jesuit missionary in Lebanon, a spy for Napoléon III, and a diplomat for the British Foreign Office. His *Narrative of a Year's Journey through Central and Eastern Arabia* (London, 1865) was the most widely read book about the Arabs before World War I.

BIBLIOGRAPHY

BRAUDE, BENJAMIN. "The Heine-Disraeli Syndrome among the Palgraves of Victorian England." In *Jewish Apostasy in the Modern World: Missionaries and Converts in Historical Perspective*, ed. by Todd Endelman. New York, 1987.

Benjamin Braude

Palin Commission Report

British Foreign Office report on the causes of the Arab violence in Palestine, April 1920.

The Palin Commission (formally the Palin Court of Inquiry) was set up in Palestine in May 1920, in the wake of violent protests by Arab residents of Jerusalem against the growing presence and political demands of the Jewish community. In early 1920, Arab protests had been mounted against the Balfour Declaration, against privileges accorded the Zionist Commission, and against the denial of Arab independence. They culminated in violent attacks on Jews in Jerusalem during the celebration of the Muslim holiday of Nabi Musa in early April, which coincided with Passover. Five Jews and four Muslim Arabs died. At that time, Palestine was ruled by a British military administration, headed by General Louis J. Bols, who sought to reassure the Palestinian Arabs that Britain would observe the status quo in that territory.

The British Foreign Office appointed a commission composed of three military officers and headed by Major General P. C. Palin, which filed its report on July 1, 1920. The report, which was never made public, argued that the disturbances were caused by the Arabs' disappointment over unfulfilled promises of independence, which the British had made during World War I to Sharif HUSAYN IBN ALI of Mecca; their belief that the Balfour Declaration implied the denial of their own right of self-determination; and their fear that the establishment of a Jewish National Home would lead to such substantial Jewish immigration that the Arabs would be subject to the Jewish community. The report argued that those feelings were aggravated by the proclamation of Sharif Husayn's son Emir Faisal as king of Syria, in March 1920, with a potential claim to Palestine, too. Feelings were also aggravated by the actions of the Zionist Commission, which sought a privileged status vis-à-vis the British military administration and asserted the right of the Jewish community to statehood. The report called the Zionist Commission "arrogant, insolent and provocative" and said that its members could "easily precipitate a catastrophe" (quoted in McTague, 1983, p. 102). Nonetheless, the report concluded that the British must rule with a firm hand, proving that the policy of the Balfour

Declaration would not be reversed but also that the Arabs would be treated fairly.

The report's substantive findings paralleled the views of General Bols, who wanted to reduce the authority of the Zionist Commission and reassure the Arabs. Instead, the British government decided that the Arabs would acquiesce once British pro-Zionist policy was implemented firmly. Therefore, London replaced the military administration with a civilian administration on the day before the Palin Report was submitted; that administration would be guided in its policy by the Balfour Declaration and presided over by a Jewish High Commissioner. The Palin Report's predictions proved accurate concerning mounting Arab–Jewish tension and the difficulty of reconciling their contradictory aims if Zionist aspirations were not moderated. But the report was never published or publicized and, therefore, failed to influence the public debate in London and Jerusalem at a time when British policy and the Arab–Jewish relationship might still have been modified.

BIBLIOGRAPHY

GOVERNMENT OF PALESTINE. *A Survey of Palestine*, vol. 1. Jerusalem, 1946. Reprint, Washington, D.C., 1991.
McTAGUE, JOHN J. *British Policy in Palestine, 1917–1922.* Lanham, Md., 1983.

Ann M. Lesch

Palmach

Jewish professional military elite from 1941 to 1948.

The Palmach was a Haganah elite group established in 1941 to create a permanent and independent Jewish professional military corps, around which the future of an independent army could be built (see ISRAELI MILITARY AND POLITICS). The Palmach essentially became the professional army of the Haganah, whose emphasis would be on the lowest ranking officers and upon an egalitarian concept of military organization. Except for a general staff, it was composed of part-time volunteers. Although it was not a sectarian military structure, it drew a great number of its members from the kibbutzim, mainly from the United Kibbutz Movement, a leftist, radical nationalist group. The purpose of the Palmach was ideological, intellectual, and cultural. Not merely a professional unit, it represented the first Israeli-born generation's esprit de corps.

In the years 1941–1943, it was supported by the British authorities. But after 1945 it participated in the struggle against the British mandatory authorities. In the underground years (1941–1947), Pal-

mach members, both male and female, were trained half a month and worked half a month in the various kibbutzim, which acted as an excellent cover for the organization. It created a naval air unit and what was called the German unit, i.e., Jews of German origin were trained to become the saboteurs of a future Nazi–Palestinian state if German Field Marshal Erwin Rommel succeeded in ousting the British from Egypt. It also created an Arab unit, composed of Jews from Arab countries who could act as infiltrators in what might become a Palestinian pro-Nazi administration. It is from the Palmach that various Jewish paratroopers were dropped in the Nazi-occupied Balkans, with the hope of organizing Jewish resistance against the Nazis. The Palmach especially emphasized the training of the individual and the commander. It was involved in large-scale pamphleteering publication. By 1947, there were already several Palmach battalions. During the underground years, Palmach was also used in the struggle against the renegade Irgun–LEHI Zionist revisionist underground. In fact, in the midst of the war of independence, the Palmach was used to capture the Irgun weapon ship ALTALENA.

The Palmach produced a number of senior officers in the 1948 War of Independence. In fact, since 1948, five Palmach officers served as commander in chief of the Israel Defense Forces (IDF): major generals Moshe Dayan (1953–1957), Yitzhak Rabin (1963–1967), Haim Bar-Lev (1968–1972), David Elazar (1972–1975), and Mordechai Gur (1975–1978). The founder and commander of Palmach, Yitzhak Sadeh, was a left-wing United Kibbutz Movement member and one of the most senior members of the Haganah. He was appointed as general staff officer for Palmach at Haganah headquarters in 1940. Three of the senior officers of the IDF's first high command (1948–1949) were Palmach commanders: Yigal Allon, Ratner, and Sadeh.

The military doctrines of Palmach were based on commander and guerilla activities and imbued with Zionist values of pride of country, the solidarity of fighters, devotion to the principle of socialism and the kibbutz movement, leadership training, intellectual pursuit and culture, and the integrity of the use of weapons. The cadre program of the Palmach was designed to produce not only professional, but institutional leaders, men trained to disseminate the ideas of socialist Zionism and its ideology. Over two-thirds of its membership came from the kibbutzim; one-third came from private agricultural settlements and the big cities.

During the War of Independence, Palmach, headed by seven battalions, was fighting on all the fronts (Galilee, central, and south). Especially important was the southern command, which was identical to the Palmach general staff, whose commander was Yigal Allon, a Palmach commander. The Palmach played a key role in the Israeli victory during the War of Independence. The Palmach, in fact, was responsible for Israel's conquest of the Negev desert during the dispute over this territory with UN special commissioner Count Folke Bernadotte, who recommended that the Negev not become part of the Jewish state. This suggestion was rejected by the Palmach victory against the Egyptian army in the Negev. Out of 4,470 casualties in the war, close to 1,000 were of the Palmach. This was about one-fifth of Palmach membership.

The Palmach was the first to train and create armored divisions and other services in the IDF. The Palmach also engaged in cultural activities and established what would become a tradition in the IDF: the formation of choirs, whose songs have been a tradition since 1948.

David Ben-Gurion, Israel's first prime minister and defense minister, was not very friendly to the Palmach, since most of its members were from rival organizations on the left. However, the reason he dissolved the Palmach on November 7, 1948, was part of the process of the institutionalization of the IDF. Ben-Gurion brought an end to the independent renegade Irgun–LEHI groups and dissolved the Palmach while keeping General Allon the commander of the southern front. Not that the Palmach had any idea of challenging the IDF. In the spirit of David Ben-Gurion, the IDF must be the one and united army of Israel, without any political or ideological divisions. The dissolution of the Palmach created a very serious debate within the Israeli labor movement. Many of Palmach's members resigned from the IDF. In fact, Ben-Gurion never forgave the young general Yitzhak Rabin for participating in a Palmach demonstration in Tel Aviv. Ben-Gurion recommended firing several Palmach officers, including Rabin and the future chiefs of staff, but was prevented from doing this by the 1948 acting chief of staff Yigal Yadin and General Chaim Laskov, who argued that the IDF would suffer from the absence of these experienced professional military men. In time, many of those who had resigned returned to active service and played a significant role in the Israeli wars of 1956 and 1973 and as reservists in 1967 and 1982.

BIBLIOGRAPHY

GELBER, YOAV. *The Emergence of a Jewish Army.* Jerusalem, 1986.
———. *Why Was the Palmach Dissolved?* Tel Aviv, 1986.
PERLMUTTER, AMOS. *Military and Politics in Israel.* London, 1969.
RABIN, YITZHAK. *Service Diary.* N.p., n.d.
SHAPIRA, ANITA. *The Army Controversy in 1948: The Ben-Gurion Struggle for Control.* Jerusalem, 1985.

Amos Perlmutter

Palmerston, Lord

See Temple, Henry John

Palmyra

Ancient city in an oasis of the northern Syrian desert at the site of present-day Tadmur.

The first mention of Tadmur (or Tamar, city of dates), Palmyra's ancient and modern name, goes back to the nineteenth century B.C.E. It was probably a Caananite town that later came under Aramaic influence. In the third century B.C.E., the city achieved international prominence when the Seleucids made it a transfer point of east–west trade. Through trade contacts, the city absorbed Hellenic culture and the Greek language, which was spoken alongside Aramaic, Arabic, Syriac, and other languages. From the time of the reign of Emperor Tiberius (14–37 C.E.), the city came under Roman control and was renamed Palmyra (city of palms). During the Pax Romana and with the benefit of paved Roman roads, the city's commercial fortunes expanded.

Palmyra's golden age was the third century C.E. Emperor Caracalla (211–217 C.E.) granted Palmyra the status of a Roman colony, exempting it from taxes. The city became the chief way station between Damascus and the Euphrates river. Goods came on caravans of camels from Rome, Egypt, India, the Persian Gulf, and from China along the silk route.

Aerial view of the ruins of Palmyra in the 1940s. (D.W. Lockhard)

Temple ruins at Palmyra. (Mia Bloom)

Ancient theater at Palmyra. (David Rewcastle)

Some Palmyran merchants owned ships that sailed the Indian Ocean. Palmyra's busy bazaars and ruling institutions were housed in fine Roman and Mesopotamian stone buildings with Corinthian colonnades, whose ruins remain in good condition today. Palmyra became the seat of the personal empire of Septimius Odaenathus, a member of a local Arab tribe, who gained the title Emperor of the East after saving the Roman Emperor Valerian in 260 from capture by the Sassanian king, Shahpur I.

From 267 to 272 C.E., the city was ruled by Queen Zenobia. Under her vigorous rule, Palmyra in 270 conquered Syria, Egypt, and Anatolia. Zenobia then declared the empire of Palmyra independent of Rome, but two years later, Roman Emperor Aurelian reconquered all the territory and plundered the city of Palmyra. Zenobia tried to flee by camel toward the Euphrates, but was captured and taken to Rome, where she lived the rest of her days. Palmyra was reduced from a capital to a small frontier city after the destruction caused by Aurelian's reconquest in 273.

Ancient Palmyrenes worshiped the deity Bol (also Baal or Bel) who presided over the movements of the stars. Bol's chief sanctuary, shared with the sun and moon gods Yarhibol and Algibol, still stands. Greek and Roman deities were incorporated into the local belief system. In the second century, the worship of a single unnamed god became important, and by 325, a Palmyra bishop attended the Nicaean Council.

In 634, Khalid ibn al-Walid conquered Palmyra and assimilated it into the expanding Muslim caliphate. The city was destroyed by an earthquake in 1089 and reportedly had a mere two thousand inhabitants in the twelfth century. After the city was sacked by Tamerlane at the end of the fourteenth century, it fell into ruins. In the seventeenth century, Fakhr al-Din of Lebanon used Palmyra as a military training ground and erected a castle on a hill nearby.

The city was first excavated in 1929, and restorations have continued since then. Today, Tadmur is a city of thirty thousand inhabitants, the site of tourist facilities and a prison.

BIBLIOGRAPHY

BULLIET, RICHARD W. *The Camel and the Wheel.* New York, 1990.

FEVRIER, J. G. *Essai sur l'histoire politique et économique de Palmyre.* Paris, 1931.

"Palmyra." In *Encyclopaedia Britannica.* Chicago, 1974.

STARCKY, J., and M. GAWLIKOWSKI. *Palmyre.* Paris, 1985.

Elizabeth Thompson

Pamir Mountains

Afghan mountain range.

The Pamir mountains run north to south from Tajikistan to northern Pakistan, separating the Oxus drainage from the plains of Kashgar in China. In Afghanistan, the Pamirs extend through the Wakhan corridor, an area inhabited by Kirghiz nomads until the nomads were relocated to Turkey during the war of resistance (1978–1992).

BIBLIOGRAPHY

DUPREE, LOUIS. *Afghanistan.* Princeton, N.J., 1980.

Grant Farr

Pan-Arabism

Movement for a set of beliefs that would unite the Arab world.

Despite political divisions that exist today, pan-Arabists see the Middle East as one indivisible community, sharing the same language (Arabic), the same cultural heritage, and the same religion (Islam), for the most part. Contemporary pan-Arabists propose an end to the present political divisions as unnecessary and undesirable. The rulers and ruling parties are not ready to yield their power, however, not to pan-Arabism or to pan-Islam.

Much of the Arab world was included in the Ottoman Empire before World War I. Arab nationalism became a political movement that was an issue during the postwar peace talks, although much of the empire was awarded to British and French mandates by the League of Nations. In 1937, the pan-Arab movement made itself known at a congress that met in Bluden (Syria), on September 8, to deal with the problem of Palestine; Syria had become a center of Palestine-insurgent activity during the Arab revolts that began in 1936, protesting Zionism and Jewish settlement in Palestine. Some four hundred nonofficial representatives of all the Arab countries met and attempted to create an Arab state allied with Great Britain. After World War II, the mandates were revoked and more Arab nations became independent throughout the Middle East and North Africa, often not without a battle. By the 1990s, the Islamist political movement became strong in many Arab nations, such as Egypt, Libya, and Sudan, based on the successful Iranian Revolution of 1979.

BIBLIOGRAPHY

LANGER, W. L., ed. *An Encyclopedia of World History*. Boston, 1948.
MANSFIELD, PETER. *The Arabs*. New York, 1985.
SHIMONI, YAACOV, ed. *Political Dictionary of the Middle East in the Twentieth Century*. New York, 1974.

Zachary Karabell

Pan–Islam

See Islamic Congresses

Pan-Turkism

A movement advocating the union of Turkish peoples.

In the second half of the nineteenth century, Turkish-speaking Ottoman intellectuals became familiar with European cultural nationalism. The result was increased awareness of the origins of Turkish peoples, an enhanced consciousness of a distinct Turkish identity, and interest in Turks living outside the Ottoman Empire. Aided by the political interest the Ottoman sultans took in the Muslim Turks of central Asia under the onslaught of Russian imperialism, Turkish con-

sciousness gradually became politicized and led to formulations for political unity of Turkish peoples.

Meanwhile, Eastern European scholars and nationalists fighting Russian expansionism stressed the Asian roots of their peoples and forged the notion of pan-Turanism. "Turan" refers to the Turkish-populated regions east of Iran and extending into the Ural and Altai mountains, also ancient homeland of Finns, Hungarians, and Mongolians. In strict terms "pan-Turanism" refers to a vague union of Ural-Altaic peoples. "Pan-Turkism," often used interchangeably with "pan-Turanism," refers to a political union of Turkish peoples who in the nineteenth century lived within and beyond Turan.

Pan-Turkish ideas influenced Young Ottoman leaders (particularly ALI SUAVI) and found systematic expression in a linguistic movement to simplify literary Turkish. From the 1880s on, Turks in Russia clung to pan-Turkish ideas to resist Russian cultural subjugation. The best-known propagandist was Ismail Gasprinski, a Tatar who published a journal called *Interpreter*. Emigrés from Russia propagated pan-Turkish ideas in the Ottoman realm. In 1904, Yusuf Akçura, a Kazan Turk educated in Constantinople (now Istanbul), wrote his influential *Three Kinds of Policy*, making a case for pan-Turkism against OTTOMANISM and Islamism. He also contributed to the foundation of cultural and literary Turkish societies, best known among them the Turkish Society and Turkish Hearth Association. Writers such as Halide Edip, Ömer Seyfettin, and Mehmet Emin Yurdakul joined Russian Turks (including Akçura, Ahmed Ağaoğlu, and Ali Hüseyinzade) in Turkish cultural activity.

In the Ottoman period, contrary to later nationalist contentions in the empire's successor states, pan-Turkism did not become the predominant ideology. Even in the thought of Turkists, such as Ziya Gökalp, Turkism could not be separated from Islamism or Ottomanism. As a political program pan-Turkism remained vague and marginal. Tekin Alp (Moise Cohen), a Jewish journalist, was an ardent propagandist. Pan-Turkish thought did promote nationalist consciousness among certain educated segments of Turks and, with the collapse of the Ottoman Empire, contributed to the crystallization of a Turkish nationalism limited in scope and restricted to Anatolia.

Pan-Turkism flourished at the end of World War I and until the consolidation of the Bolshevik state and the Turkish republic. The simultaneous collapse of the Russian and Ottoman empires stimulated fantastic, ill-conceived, and unrealistic schemes of unifying the Turks of Asia. ENVER PAŞA and CEMAL PAÇA, who fled Istanbul at war's end, spent their lives in uncoordinated attempts to establish the great Turkish state.

The Soviet governments discouraged and systematically undermined pan-Turkism in Central Asia.

Pan-Turkish sentiments briefly surged in Turkey during World War II with the aid of German propaganda and with the expectation that the Soviet Union would crumble. In the Republic of Turkey, pan-Turkish racialist ideas have inspired the ultranationalist right. A pan-Turkish political framework has not emerged as a realistic or popular scheme among the Turkish republics of central Asia since the breakup of the Soviet Union, while cultural and economic interchange among them and with Turkey has intensified.

BIBLIOGRAPHY

BERKES, NIYAZI. *The Development of Secularism in Turkey.* Montreal, 1964.
KUSHNER, DAVID. *The Rise of Turkish Nationalism, 1876–1908.* London, 1977.
LANDAU, JACOB M. *Pan-Turkism in Turkey.* London, 1981.

Hasan Kayali

Papen, Franz von [1879–1962]

German diplomat and politician; chancellor of Germany, June–December 1932; vice-chancellor under Hitler, 1933–1934.

Franz von Papen was born in Werl, Germany, to wealthy Roman Catholic landowners. He served as chief of staff to the Fourth Turkish Army in Palestine during World War I; he later joined German Catholic center party politics, serving as party deputy in the Reichstag and becoming chancellor in 1932. He helped bring Adolf Hitler to power in 1933 and stayed on as vice-chancellor until 1934. He then became ambassador to Austria from 1934 to 1938 and ambassador to Turkey from 1939 to 1944. His mission was to convince Germany's old ally from World War I to join the Axis or to stay neutral until the end of the war. During this period, the Mufti of Jerusalem, Hajj Amin al-Husayni, contacted him with an offer of Arab support against the British. In 1946, von Papen was acquitted of major war crimes by the Nuremberg tribunal, but a German denazification court in 1949 found him to be a major Nazi and sentenced him to prison. Since he had already served some prison time after the war, he was released and published his memoirs in 1952.

BIBLIOGRAPHY

SHIRER, WILLIAM L. *The Rise and Fall of the Third Reich: A History of Nazi Germany.* New York, 1960.

Daniel E. Spector

Parcham

Afghan Marxist political faction; also its newspaper.

Parcham (Banner), a faction of the PEOPLE'S DEMOCRATIC PARTY OF AFGHANISTAN (PDPA), was founded in 1965 as a worker's revolutionary party dedicated to a Marxist revolution in Afghanistan. In 1967, the PDPA split into the Khalq (People's) faction and the Parcham faction. The split was in part the result of rivalries between the two leading personalities of the PDPA. Babrak KARMAL was the leader of the Parcham faction, which attracted followers from the Persian-speaking Kabul intelligentsia; the Khalq faction had a predominantly rural and Pakhtun base.

In 1968, the Parcham faction published a newspaper also called *Parcham*. Published by Sulaiman Layeq and edited by him and Mir Akbar Khaiber, it was closed by the parliament after only six editions for being "anti-Islamic."

In April 1978 the two factions of the PDPA united to stage a successful revolution and took over the government. The Parcham faction was soon purged, however, and its leaders were jailed or sent abroad as diplomats by late 1978. On December 25, 1979, a large Soviet airlift began; two days later a Parcham faction staged a coup with the help of the Soviet Union. Babrak Karmal returned to Kabul, and the Parchamis took over the government. The government of Karmal attempted to move the party toward an ideological center and denounced many of the reforms and actions of the Khalq faction. Karmal and President Najibullah, who succeeded him in 1986, attempted to undo most of the radical reforms of the Khalqis and announced a plan of national reconciliation. They even changed the name of the PDPA to the Hezb-e Watan (Homeland party) in 1989. These changes, however, were unsuccessful in convincing the Afghan mojahedin leaders to put a halt to the war of resistance. The Parcham government collapsed in 1992.

BIBLIOGRAPHY

ADAMEC, LUDWIG. *Historical Dictionary of Afghanistan.* Metuchen, N.J., 1991.
ARNOLD, ANTHONY. *Afghanistan's Two Party Communism: Parcham and Khalq.* Stanford, Calif., 1983.

Grant Farr

Paris, Peace of

See Crimean War

Paris, Treaty of

Anglo–Iranian treaty that forced Iran out of Afghanistan and Musqat, 1857.

After Iran had tried to annex the Afghan city of Herat, British troops occupied Iran's Kharg Island and part of her mainland. Iran then signed this treaty, agreeing to withdraw from Afghanistan and relinquish Iranian claims to Herat, Afghanistan, and parts of Musqat in return for British withdrawal from Iran.

Farhad Shirzad

Paris Peace Settlements

Post–World War I treaties and agreements that reconfigured the Middle East, 1918–1923.

The defeat of the Ottoman Empire in 1918 signalled the end of the old era and the beginning of a new one. In the long term the victorious Allies' partition of the Ottoman territories was less important than their introduction of a new system of political organization based on the European model of the nation-state. The modern Middle East was physically and politically shaped during the peace settlements, which lasted from 1918 until 1923. The peace settlements, however, had their origins in the secret wartime agreements made by Great Britain, France, Russia, and Italy to carve up the Ottoman Empire among themselves. It is, therefore crucial to discuss not only the peace settlements but also the secret wartime arrangements.

The CONSTANTINOPLE AGREEMENT—one of the first secret arrangements between Great Britain, France, and Russia during March and April 1915—offered Russia Istanbul and the Straits, which were described later as "the richest prize of the whole war." In the 1915 secret treaty of London, Italy was induced to join the war by recognizing its territorial claims in the Mediterranean, the Dodecanese Islands, Libya, and a sphere of influence in Adalia in western Asia Minor.

Britain and France's concessions to Russia on the Straits reversed their traditional policy on this important strategic waterway as well as opening up the whole question of postwar settlement in the Ottoman Empire. British and French officials felt the need to agree on how to distribute the spoils of the Ottoman lands between themselves. In particular, French diplomats were anxious to conclude an agreement with Britain because they knew that the latter was negotiating with Arab nationalist leaders regarding the future of Ottoman Arab lands. The result was the January 1916 SYKES–PICOT AGREEMENT, which

became the key to the future settlement of Ottoman Arab lands. France received Cilicia, coastal Syria and Lebanon. Britain was given Basra and Baghdad, and Haifa and Acre in Palestine, with the rest of the country to be placed under an international administration.

Britain not only concluded secret agreements with its wartime allies but also gave conflicting commitments to the Arab nationalists and Zionists. First, in October 1915 Britain promised Sharif Husayn, a ruler of Mecca, in what came to be known as the HUSAYN–MCMAHON CORRESPONDENCE, "to recognize and support the independence of the Arabs within the territories included in the limits and boundaries proposed by the sharif of Mecca." Second, in direct disregard of the Husayn–McMahon correspondence, Britain, in an effort to appeal and win worldwide Jewish support for the war effort, promised to "view with favor the establishment in Palestine of a national home for the Jewish people." This pledge—the Balfour Declaration—was contained in a public letter addressed by the foreign secretary, Lord Balfour, to a prominent British Zionist, Lord Rothschild, in November 1917.

Far from being "compatible" as some historians claim, the various wartime secret agreements and commitments contradicted and conflicted with each other. As Winston Churchill lucidly and brutally put it, the truth is the first casualty of war. Tragically, some of these secret agreements became the basis for the postwar settlement. At the Paris Peace Conference in 1919 Britain and France, the victorious allies, were more concerned about adjusting their differences and harmonizing their territorial appetites than about a just and durable final settlement.

Hence Britain and France agreed to divide the former Arab provinces of the Ottoman Empire at the Conference of San Remo in April 1920 along the lines of the Sykes-Picot Agreement, with some minor modifications. France received the mandates of Syria and Lebanon, which the League of Nations confirmed in 1922. France waved its claims to Mosul in exchange for shares in the Turkish Petroleum Company (later the Iraq Petroleum Company). Britain got the mandates of Iraq, Transjordan (which it created in 1922), and the whole of Palestine. The Zionists succeeded at the Paris conference in convincing Britain to incorporate the Balfour Declaration into the preamble of the Palestine mandate. To the Arab nationalists, the Paris conference was a political disaster; it sowed the seeds of bloody future conflicts in the region.

Likewise, the victorious allies initially tried to enforce a similar settlement on the defeated Ottoman government in the 1920 Treaty of SÈVRES. In a nutshell, Sèvres was designed to partition Turkey into very small, unviable segments. But unlike their Arab counterparts, the Turkish nationalists, led by Mustafa Kemal (ATATÜRK), successfully challenged the clauses of the Sèvres settlement related to Anatolia and Thrace, forcing the Allies, after a long, debilitating military campaign, to renegotiate a new settlement at Lausanne in July 1923. The Treaty of Lausanne confirmed Turkish sovereignty over the whole of Anatolia; independence movements in Armenia and Kurdistan were overlooked. Atatürk's effective resistance against the humiliating terms of Sèvres represented the first birth pangs of the modern Turkish nation-state.

BIBLIOGRAPHY

HUREWITZ, J. C. ed. *The Middle East and North Africa in World Politics—a Documentary Record: British-French Supremacy, 1914–1945,* vol. 2. New Haven, Conn., 1979.
PERETZ, DON. *The Middle East Today.* New York, 1983.
SACHAR, HOWARD M. *The Emergence of the Modern Middle East, 1914–1924.* New York, 1969.
YAPP, M. E. *The Making of the Modern Middle East, 1792–1923.* London and New York, 1987.

Fawaz A. Gerges

Parliamentary Democratic Front

The members of Kamal Jumblatt's parliamentary bloc in Lebanon.

The Parliamentary Democratic Front was a powerful political group in the 1972 election although it did not have a clear political agenda beyond loyalty to the political leadership of Kamal JUMBLATT. It included members from various sects but was predominantly Druze-oriented, given the Druze basis of Jumblatt's leadership.

As'ad AbuKhalil

Parsipur, Shahnush [1946–]

Iranian author.

Born and raised in Tehran, Shahnush Parsipur graduated from Tehran University. Her first short stories (she writes in Persian) were published in the early 1970s. Her first book was the novel *Dog and the Long Winter* (1976). Riots, demonstrations, and the Iranian Revolution in 1978/79 caused the shah and his

family to leave. In 1979, the Islamic Republic of Iran was proclaimed, under the leadership of the Ayatollah Ruhollah Khomeini.

After two volumes of short stories, a second novel came out, *Tuba and the Meaning of Night* (1988), which Parsipur wrote after spending four years in prison for political reasons. In 1990, a slim volume of interconnected stories was published, *Women without Men,* which was banned by the Islamic republic, and her novel *Blue Reason* remained unavailable there as of the mid-1990s.

Parsipur, whose writings exhibit a woman-centered Iranian universe, stands as the leading figure in a fourth generation of Iranian women literary artists (see PERSIAN LITERATURE). The chief figure in the first generation was the traditionalist poet Parvin E'tesami (1907–1941); in the second, the prominent short-story writer and novelist Simin Daneshvar (born 1921); the third generation saw Iran's most famous woman writer, the poet Forugh Farrokhzad (c. 1934–1967).

Translations of Parsipur's stories appear in *Stories by Iranian Women since the Revolution* (1991) and *Stories from Iran: A Chicago Anthology* (1991). Her career and *Women with Men* receive treatment in M. Hillman's *From Durham to Tehran* (1991). English translations of Parsipur's major writings were in print by 1992, when the author toured the United States and participated in the International Writer's Program at the University of Iowa.

Michael C. Hillman

Parti de l'Avant-Garde Socialiste (PAGS)

Ideological successor to the Algerian Communist party.

PAGS (Socialist Avant-Garde party) was established in Algeria in 1966, after the suppression of the Algerian Communist party (Parti des Communistes Algériens, PCA) in 1962. It was critical of policies, such as an agrarian revolution, put forth by the Front de Libération Nationale (National Liberation Front, FLN), although it had no official standing as a legalized opposition party until the political liberalization following the October 1988 riots. The renowned PCA leader Sadek Hadjerès then became secretary-general of PAGS.

BIBLIOGRAPHY

ENTELIS, JOHN P. *Algeria: The Revolution Institutionalized.* Boulder, Colo., 1986.

Phillip C. Naylor

Parti Démocratique Constitutionel (PDC)

Moroccan political party founded in 1937.

The PDC was founded by Muhammad Hassan al-WAZZANI (Ouezzani) as the result of a split with the Bloc d'Action National owing to personal differences between Allal al-Fasi and Wazzani, as well as disagreements over negotiating strategies with the French authorities. The PDC remained a small group, more of a political club than a party, centered on Wazzani's followers and friends. After World War II, it cooperated periodically with the Istiqlal party and in 1953/54 joined the National Front, which opposed the continuation of the French protectorate. In 1958, it merged with the Parti Démocratique de l'Indépendance (PDI); in 1963 it operated within the FRONT POUR LA DÉFENSE DES INSTITUTIONS CONSTITUTIONELLES (FDIC).

Bruce Maddy-Weitzman

Parti Démocratique de l'Indépendance (PDI)

Political party in Morocco.

Formed after World War II by a splinter group originating in the Istiqlal party and led by Thami al-Wazzani, the PDI received five portfolios in the first representative Moroccan government, established in December 1955 after the sultan had returned from exile. Its only clear idea was uniting around the person of the king. In 1958, it joined for a time with Muhammad al-Wazzani's Parti Démocratique Constitutionel. In recent decades, the PDI has competed in local and national elections with little success, winning no seats in the 1977 and 1984 parliamentary elections. In the 1993 parliamentary elections, still headed by Thami al-Wazzani, it experienced a revival of sorts, winning nine seats.

Bruce Maddy-Weitzman

Parti d'Unité Populaire (PUP)

An opposition political party in Tunisia.

The Parti d'Unité Populaire (Party of Popular Unity), one of three opposition parties in Tunisia sanctioned by President Habib Bourguiba in the 1980s, was an offshoot of the Mouvement pour l'Unité Populaire (MUP) founded in Paris in 1973 by Ahmed Ben Salah and others opposed to the Bourguiba regime. In 1981, a rift between the Paris-based group and its Tunisian branch was formalized with the creation of a second Movement of Popular Unity (often called MUP-II). More moderate than the French wing, the new organization won authorization to establish an official party. In 1985, it was renamed the Parti d'Unité Populaire (PUP).

BIBLIOGRAPHY

Tunisia: A Country Survey. Washington, D.C., 1988.

Matthew S. Gordon

Parti du Peuple Algérien (PPA)

Algerian nationalist organization that used direct, often violent, action that led to the war of independence.

The Parti du Peuple Algérien (PPA; Party of the Algerian People) was founded early in 1937 by Messali al-HADJ, widely viewed as the father of the Algerian nationalist movement. An extension onto Algerian soil of the Etoile Nord-Africaine (ENA; STAR OF NORTH AFRICA), whose constituency was principally among the émigré community in Paris, it was remarkably successful in mobilizing urban working classes, lower middle-class Algerians, as well as the sons of some of the more affluent Algerians behind the nationalist cause. Messali al-Hadj and five of the PPA's directors were imprisoned in August 1937, and the party itself was banned in September 1939. During World War II, it functioned underground at reduced levels both in Algeria and France.

In 1943, leaders of the party approved the drafting of the MANIFESTO OF THE ALGERIAN MUSLIM PEOPLE and the more radical *additif* that followed it. When, in March 1944, the moderate Ferhat Abbas decided to organize a coalition of forces called the Amis du Manifeste et de la Liberté (Friends of the Manifesto and of Liberty), members of the underground PPA flocked to it in such numbers that they eventually came to dominate it in all but name. It was PPA elements that helped turn the V–E Day celebrations of May 8, 1945, into a series of bloody confrontations between nationalists and the colonial authorities that are considered a direct precursor of the Algerian revolution.

When he was released from prison in 1946, Messali al-Hadj made an abrupt decision to reenter the political process by creating the MOUVEMENT POUR LE TRIOMPHE DES LIBERTÉS DÉMOCRATIQUES (MTLD; Movement for the Triumph of Democratic Liberties) as a front for the outlawed PPA. From then on, until the war of independence, the MTLD ran candidates in most elections. But the PPA continued at a secret level in order to retain within the fold the growing group of militants who favored direct action. The party's detractors considered this dual approach one of its major weaknesses.

BIBLIOGRAPHY

RUEDY, JOHN. *Modern Algeria: The Origins and Development of a Nation.* Bloomington, Ind., 1992.

John Ruedy

Parti National

Moroccan political party.

Established in April 1937 by the bulk of Morocco's nationalist leadership (except Muhammad al-Wazzani and his followers) after the French authorities dissolved the COMITÉ D'ACTION MAROCAINE (CAM), the Parti National, to show continuity with the CAM, located its headquarters in the same premises, in Fez. Organizationally, it was similar as well, consisting of an executive committee, a national council, local branches, and party cells. Its program was the implementation of a new French protectorate as a step toward full independence. It also campaigned against the power of rural chieftains, especially Glawi Pasha.

The French authorities cracked down on the party in the fall of 1937, arresting many of its leaders, most of whom were exiled. Nevertheless, clandestine party cells continued to function. Following his release in 1938, Ahmad Muhammad LYAZIDI assumed leadership of the movement. In 1941, a reorganized supreme council was formed by Ahmad Maqwar and Lyazidi; the establishment of party branches followed the landing of Allied forces in 1942. Ahmad Balfarej was allowed to return from Paris in January 1943, and at the end of the year, together with the exiled Allal al-FASI, reconstituted the party as the ISTIQLAL.

Bruce Maddy-Weitzman

Parti National Démocratique (PND)

Political party in Morocco.

Originally known as the Parti des Indépendants Démocrates, the PND was founded in 1981 by a breakaway faction of the RASSEMBLEMENT NATIONAL DES INDÉPENDANTS (RNI). Led by Abdel Hamid Kacemi, it included fifty-seven members of parliament and three cabinet ministers. The group represented large landowning interests, who opposed International Monetary Fund recommendations to reduce credit to the agricultural sector, particularly the large commercial farms. Notwithstanding the split, the PND continued to constitute one of the pro-monarchy groups in Morocco's political spectrum. Its numbers in parliament declined by more than half in the 1984 parliamentary elections, to twenty-four; it maintained this figure in the 1993 elections.

Bruce Maddy-Weitzman

Parti Populaire Syrien (PPS)

Political party in Lebanon.

The Parti Populaire Syrien, now known as the Syrian Social Nationalist party (SSNP), has been one of the most influential multisectarian parties in Lebanon. Its main objective has been the "reestablishment" of historic Greater Syria, an area that approximately encompasses modern Syria, Lebanon, Jordan, and Israel. The PPS and SSNP have not refrained from the practice of violence to achieve their goals.

The PPS was founded as a secret organization in 1932 by Antun Sa'ada, a Greek Orthodox Lebanese man raised in Brazil. The party, greatly influenced by Fascist ideology and organization, grew considerably in the years after independence. Until 1935, when the French authorities arrested Sa'ada, the PPS operated in secret. Sa'ada left the country in 1938, reportedly traveling to Italy, Germany, and Brazil. He returned to the recently independent Lebanon in 1947 and resumed his agitation for a Greater Syria.

The PPS changed its name to the SYRIAN SOCIAL NATIONALIST PARTY in 1947/48. The party had 25,000 members, according to a 1948 survey by the French newspaper *L'Orient.* This made it Lebanon's second largest party—only the Phalange was larger.

Concerned by its strength, the government cracked down on the party in 1948, arresting many of its members. In response SSNP militias attempted a coup in 1949 that resulted in the execution of Sa'ada (1951).

The SSNP supported President Chamoun in the 1958 civil war and was legalized. Banned again in the 1960s, the SSNP's ideology made a leftward turn, and the party splintered into several factions, many former members joining the Lebanese National Movement.

BIBLIOGRAPHY

SHIMONI, YAACOV. *Political Dictionary of the Arab World.* New York, 1987.
SULEIMAN, MICHAEL W. *Political Parties in Lebanon.* Ithaca, N.Y., 1967.

As'ad AbuKhalil

Parti Socialiste Destourien (PSD)

See Destour Party

Partition Plans, Palestine

Plans for the territorial division of Palestine that attempted to reconcile the rival claims of the Jewish and Arab communities; first suggested in 1937 by Britain's Peel Commission.

Following the outbreak of the Arab rebellion in 1936, the British government, which had been granted the Palestinian mandate by the League of Nations, appointed Earl Peel to chair a Royal Commission. The commission learned that Jewish nationalism was as intense and self-centered as Arab nationalism, that both were growing forces, and that the gulf between them was widening. Partition was seen as the only method for dealing with the problem. In its final report (July 1937), the Peel Commission recommended that Palestine be partitioned into a small Jewish state; an Arab state to be united with Transjordan; and an area, including Jerusalem, to remain under a permanent British mandate. The Zionist leadership accepted the principle of partition and prepared to bargain over the details. But the Arab leadership refused to consider partition and reasserted its claims to the whole of Palestine. Although the Peel plan was not acted upon, the principle of partition guided all subsequent exercises in peacemaking (1937–1947).

On November 29, 1947, the UN General Assembly voted in favor of a resolution (no. 181) for replacing the British mandate with two independent states, thereby suggesting that the logic of partition had become inescapable. The UN partition resolution laid down a timetable for the termination of the British mandate and for the establishment of a Jewish state and an Arab state linked by economic union, along with an international regime for Jerusalem. An exceptionally long and winding border separated the Jewish state from the Arab one, with vulnerable crossing points to link three Jewish enclaves—one in eastern Galilee, one on the coastal plain, and one in the Negev. The Jewish state would also contain a substantial Arab minority within its borders.

Despite doubts about the viability of the state as proposed, the Zionist leadership accepted the UN partition plan. Local Arab leaders and the Arab states rejected it vehemently as illegal, immoral, and unworkable. To frustrate this partition, the Palestinian Arabs resorted to arms. The UN partition plan thus provided both an international charter of legitimacy for a Jewish state as well as the signal for the outbreak of war between Arabs and Jews in Palestine.

BIBLIOGRAPHY

KHALIDI, WALID, ed. *From Haven to Conquest: Readings in Zionism and the Palestine Problem until 1948.* Beirut, 1971.
SHLAIM, AVI. *The Politics of Partition.* New York, 1990.

Avi Shlaim

Paşabahçe Company

Turkish public sector company.

Founded in 1934 in the new Republic of Turkey, the Paşabahçe Glass Manufacturing Company also produces asbestos and wood products, asphalt coatings, and primary nonferrous metals. Production is primarily for domestic consumption, and glassware is sold to the public through Paşabahçe stores. The company employs 3,480 people, and 1991 sales were about 66 billion Turkish lira.

BIBLIOGRAPHY

Dunn's Principal International Business Directory, 1991.

David Waldner

Pasargadae

Site of the first Achaemenid capital; a ruined city of ancient Persia.

Northeast of Shiraz, in southern Iran, is the site of the palace of Cyrus the Great (c. 585–529 B.C.E.)—with a garden irrigated by stone-paved canals, a platform terrace, a gatehouse, a tower, a sacred precinct with a pair of stepped altars, and his tomb (a gabled chamber on a six-tiered platform, which Islam reinterpreted as the tomb of King Solomon's mother, incorporating it into a mosque). The city was said to have been founded in 550 B.C.E., on the site of Cyrus's great victory over Astyages.

BIBLIOGRAPHY

GHIRSHMAN, R. *The Arts of Ancient Iran.* New York, 1964.
STRONACH, D. *Pasargadae.* Oxford, 1978.

A. Shahpur Shahbazi

Pasdaran

See Revolutionary Guards

Pasdermajian, Garegin [1873–1924]

Armenian revolutionary leader.

Pasdermajian, born in Erzurum, attended the Sanasarian Academy, then continued his education in France. He joined the Armenian Revolutionary Federation (ARF) in 1895, assuming the alias Armen Garo. In 1896 Pasdermajian was among the Dashnaks who seized the Ottoman Bank in Istanbul on August 26. The bank was European-owned, and the takeover was staged to draw Europe's attention to the mass killings of Armenians since 1894 during the reign of Sultan Abdülhamit II. European representatives negotiated a pardon for the revolutionaries and removed them from the bank the following day. That night, however, some five thousand Armenians were killed in Istanbul.

Pasdermajian fled Istanbul and remained abroad until 1908. Between 1903 and 1905 he was in the Caucasus, where the Armenians of Russia were engaging in revolutionary activity. Pasdermajian returned to Erzurum with the restoration of the Ottoman Constitution and the legalization of the ARF, and he was elected to the Ottoman parliament. Anxious over the Young Turk government's war policy and its designs against the Armenians, he joined Russian Armenian volunteers in the campaign against the Ottomans when war broke out in 1914.

With the founding of the Armenian republic on former Russian territory after World War I, Pasdermajian was sent to Washington, D.C., as Armenia's unofficial envoy. He also was a member of the Armenian delegation to the Paris Peace Conference and worked to obtain U.S. support for an independent Armenia. Pasdermajian is reported to have been an organizer of Nemesis, the group formed by the Dashnaks to hunt down the Young Turk conspirators who had organized the killing of Armenians during World War I.

BIBLIOGRAPHY

WALKER, CHRISTOPHER J. *Armenia: The Survival of a Nation.* New York, 1980.

Rouben P. Adalian

Pasha

A title introduced by the Ottomans in the fourteenth century that was applied to persons of high military or civilian rank.

Originally the title (also paşa) was bestowed on the governor of a *sanjak* (a provincial division). Later, it was bestowed on men who had achieved prominence in military or civilian life. Turkey abolished the title, as well as all ranks and privileges that went with it, in 1934, during the reformist movement. Currently, *pasha* is used only honorifically and does not carry special privilege or rank.

Jenab Tutunji

Pashtun

See Pakhtun, People and Language

Passfield White Paper

See Webb, Sidney; White Papers on Palestine

Pathan

See Pakhtun, People and Language

Patriarch

A leader in an Eastern Christian church.

By the fourth century C.E., the Christian church was divided into five administrative districts: Jerusalem, Antioch, Alexandria, Constantinople (now Istanbul), and Rome. Each of these was headed by a bishop called a patriarch.

Today, "patriarch" is the title for the head of an Eastern Christian church, such as the Armenian patriarch or the Greek Orthodox patriarch (who still resides in Istanbul).

BIBLIOGRAPHY

DEANESLY, MARGARET. *A History of the Medieval Church.* New York, 1969.

SHAW, STANFORD, and EZEL KURAL SHAW. *The History of the Ottoman Empire and Modern Turkey,* vol. 2. New York, 1977.

Zachary Karabell

Patriarchs, Tomb of the

Ancient biblical shrine.

Located in Hebron in the West Bank, the Tomb of the Patriarchs is one of the most ancient biblical shrines. Among the most authentic sites, it is purported to be the burial place of Abraham and Sarah, Isaac and Rebecca, Jacob and Leah, and according to

The Tomb of the Patriarchs in Hebron, also known as the Tomb of Abraham. (Bryan McBurney)

Jewish folklore, Adam and Eve as well. Viewed as one of the holiest shrines by both Jews and Muslims, it has been the focal point of persistent struggles between Palestinian and Jewish nationalists.

Chaim I. Waxman

Patriotic Union of Kurdistan (PUK)

Kurdish political party.

Established in 1977, the Patriotic Union of Kurdistan (PUK) advocated the self-determination of Iraqi Kurds through armed struggle. Led by Jalal TALA-BANI, the PUK claims to be more leftist than the rival Kurdistan Democratic Party (KDP). In 1987, PUK put an end to ten years of internecine fighting and joined the Kurdistan Front of Iraq with KDP and six other smaller organizations.

BIBLIOGRAPHY

KUTSCHERA, CHRIS. "Les Kurdes d'Irak: Des révisions déchirantes." *Les cahiers de l'Orient* 12 (1988): 63–81.

Chris Kutschera

Paul-Boncour, Joseph

French jurist who advised on the Lebanese constitution of 1926.

In 1925 Paul-Boncour was appointed by the French mandate government to "advise" on the preparation of a constitution for Lebanon. He completed his mission in 1926, and the constitution became law that year. Lebanese deputies could not deviate from the terms of Paul-Boncour's draft.

As'ad AbuKhalil

PDRY

See People's Democratic Republic of Yemen

Peace and Amity, Treaty of

Treaty concluded in 1805 between the United States and Tripoli.

This treaty ended the conflict that began in 1801 when Yusuf Karamanli, pasha of Tripoli (in present-day Libya), closed the U.S. consulate, expelled the consul, and declared war on the United States. This conflict ended an uneasy peace in which the U.S. government paid an annual tribute of $18,000 in return for Tripoli's nonbelligerence vis-à-vis U.S. shipping in the Mediterranean. U.S.–Tripoli relations deteriorated in 1801 because Karamanli demanded $250,000 and the Americans refused to pay.

The treaty was concluded on 4 June 1805 and was ratified by the U.S. Senate on 12 April 1806. It was negotiated by Karamanli and Colonel Tobias Lear. The United States agreed to a one-time payment of $60,000 to secure the treaty and to ransom American prisoners of war. It also consented to abandon Derna (a provincial capital in eastern Libya occupied during the war) and not to supply its mercenary allies, who supported the pasha's brother, Ahmad Karamanli, in his claim to be the legitimate ruler of Tripoli. In return, Yusuf Karamanli agreed to release Ahmad's wife and children, whom he was holding hostage. A secret article (dated 5 June 1805), not revealed until 1807, granted Yusuf four years to release Ahmad's family, in return for the Americans' assurance that Ahmad not challenge Yusuf's legitimacy to rule Tripoli. In 1809, Yusuf permitted Ahmad to return to Tripoli as governor of Derna. But in 1811, he again felt threatened by Ahmad, who fled to Egypt.

Under terms of the treaty, prisoners were exchanged. On the American side, they consisted primarily of the 297-man crew of the U.S.S. *Philadelphia.* Five Americans had died in captivity, and five chose to remain in Tripoli. One week after the Americans were freed, eighty-nine Tripolitan captives were returned, along with the $60,000.

The political and economic effects of the war undermined Yusuf's government. Disorder broke out in the early 1830s, encouraging the Ottoman Empire to reestablish its presence in Tripoli in 1835, thus bringing the Karamanli dynasty to an end.

BIBLIOGRAPHY

ALLEN, GARDNER W. *Our Navy and the Barbary Corsairs.* Hamden, Conn., 1965.

DEARDEN, SETON. *A Nest of Corsairs: The Fighting Karamanlis of Tripoli.* London, 1976.

IRWIN, RAY W. *The Diplomatic Relations of the United States with the Barbary Powers, 1776–1816.* Chapel Hill, N.C., 1931.

KITZEN, MICHAEL L. S. *Tripoli and the United States at War.* Jefferson, N.C., 1993.

Larry A. Barrie

Peace Corps

U.S. volunteer agency for less-developed nations to share American expertise and enhance mutual understanding.

The Peace Corps was established by U.S. President John F. Kennedy on March 1, 1961, "to promote world peace and friendship" by providing developing nations with volunteer American personnel. It was hoped that, through daily contact with working Americans, developing nations would better understand the people of the United States and that in turn Americans would better understand other peoples and their situations.

The first director of the Peace Corps was Sargent Shriver. In its first twenty-five years, the Peace Corps sent some 120,000 American volunteers to almost 100 developing countries, including the Middle East: Iran, Morocco, Tunisia, Turkey, and the Yemen Arab Republic were part of the NANEAP region (North Africa, Near East, Asia, and Pacific). In all of these countries, Peace Corps volunteers were teachers, engineers, designers, and administrators of special programs.

In Iran, Peace Corps volunteers from 1962 until the 1979 Iranian Revolution founded kindergartens, taught English, built libraries, designed a new mosque in a Khorasan village after the old one was destroyed in a 1968 earthquake, and planned a college of dentistry in Mashhad. In Morocco, volunteers faced the challenge of learning both Arabic and French, and they were employed in activities ranging from irrigation projects to teaching physical education in secondary schools. In addition to teaching, the Peace Corps in Tunisia supplied the Habib Thameur Hospital in Tunis with nurses. In Turkey, some of the over two hundred volunteers founded a home for street boys in Istanbul, while others worked at the Middle East Technical University in Ankara. And in the Yemen Arab Republic (now Yemen) the Peace Corps helped construct a water-pumping station in Hodeida.

Though Peace Corps volunteers are sent only at the invitation of the host country, the program has not been without its critics. In Turkey, for example, the corps has been attacked as a vehicle for American influence and an unnecessary infringement on Turkish autonomy. Echoes of these criticisms have been heard in numerous other countries. In addition, the volunteers themselves often reacted negatively to their hosts. In Morocco, several volunteers complained of the bureaucratic corruption and inefficiency that they encountered. Still, although the Peace Corps has been something less than a vehicle for American altruism and although it has not always succeeded in encouraging mutual understanding, its record has been more benign and its effects more beneficial than most U.S. aid programs that developed during the height of the Cold War.

BIBLIOGRAPHY

COATES, REDMON. *Come As You Are: The Peace Corps Story.* San Diego, Calif., 1986.

RIDINGER, ROBERT MARKS. *The Peace Corps.* Boston, 1989.

RUPPE, L. M. "The Peace Corps." In *World Encyclopedia of Peace.* New York, 1986.

Zachary Karabell

Peace Now

Israeli political movement.

Peace Now was founded in 1978 by army reserve officers who wanted the Begin government to be much more vigorous in pursuing peace negotiations with the Palestinians. In particular, Peace Now insisted that the continued occupation of the West Bank and Gaza was an obstacle to peace. Peace Now was among the leaders in protesting the Arab–Israel War of 1982 and afterward regularly demonstrated against the Likud government's policies of a GREATER ISRAEL. On these grounds, it has often been the target of charges that it was betraying the Israeli state and was the object of periodic violent attacks. Peace Now has not run candidates for the Knesset.

Walter F. Weiker

Peake, Frederick Gerard

British military officer in Transjordan.

In September 1920, Capt. Frederick G. Peake was sent to Transjordan to investigate the condition of the police and gendarmerie. He subsequently received permission to raise two small forces to maintain law and order. The first, the 100-man Mobile Force, guarded the Amman–Palestine road. The other, of fifty men, helped the British official posted in Kerak. In April 1921, Peake was appointed one of Emir Abdullah ibn Husayn's advisers. During the summers of 1921 and 1923, he organized the 150-man Reserve Mobile Force, which became the nucleus of the ARAB LEGION.

As a result of regional skirmishes, the Reserve Mobile Force was reorganized with 750 officers and men and given additional financing. The reorganized force thwarted Wahhabi raids in 1922 and the Adwan rebellion in 1923.

In September 1923, all forces in Transjordan were merged with the Reserve Mobile Force, put under Peake's command, and renamed the Arab Legion. During the first three years of his command, Peake developed the Arab Legion into a highly effective force that accepted able-bodied volunteers from any Arab country, preferably men from villages and towns. John Bagot Glubb, who arrived in 1930 as Peake's second in command, created the DESERT MOBILE FORCE, composed mainly of bedouins, to shore up the Arab Legion, which had been weakened by the creation of the TRANSJORDAN FRONTIER FORCE in 1926. Peake retired in 1939 and was succeeded by Glubb.

Jenab Tutunji

Pearl Diving, Bahrain

Before the 1930s, pearling was the major industry in the island nation of Bahrain.

Boats from Manama, Muharraq, al-Hidd, and other towns on the Bahrain coast set out for the main oyster banks in the Persian/Arabian Gulf, to the east of the islands, during a season that lasted from June through September. Representatives of the merchants who financed the operation often accompanied the pearl fishing fleet, purchasing the day's catch on the spot. Profits were distributed among the owners, pilots, divers, and crew at the end of the season according to shares drawn up in advance. Delays in payment and the vagaries of diving usually left divers and crew in perpetual debt to the merchants and captains. Since Bahrain was a British protectorate from 1880 to 1971, British officials attempted to remedy this state of affairs by promulgating a formal code for the industry in 1923, but the risks and hardships of pearling led most divers and crew to take up jobs in the new petroleum and construction sectors that opened in the early 1930s. Respectable fleets continued to set out from Bahrain as late as the mid-

1940s, but by the end of World War II, the numbers dwindled so that only a handful of boats took part in the annual pearl harvest.

BIBLIOGRAPHY

AL-RUMAIHI, MOHAMMED GHANIM. *Bahrain: A Study on Social and Political Changes since the First World War.* Kuwait, 1975.

Fred H. Lawson

Peel Commission Report

Royal Commission Report that listed the causes of unrest between Arabs and Jews in mandated Palestine and recommended territorial partition, 1937.

As a result of the Arab general strike, which began April 1936, the British decided to send to Palestine a high-level fact-finding commission. In May, the colonial secretary stated that a Royal Commission would be appointed to "investigate the causes of unrest" after order was successfully restored, but the commission would not have the authority to "question the terms of the mandate" (Hurewitz 1976, p. 68). Soon after the strike ended in October 1936, the commission sailed to Palestine. The commission was headed by, and took its name from, William Robert Wellesley, the first Earl Peel, former secretary of state for India.

The report was issued by the British government as Command Paper 5479 on July 7, 1937, six months after lengthy commission hearings. It concluded that "the Arab grievances about Jewish immigration, Jewish land acquisition, and the mandatory's failure to develop self-governing institutions 'cannot be regarded as legitimate under the terms of the Mandate'" (Hurewitz, p. 73) but that the only way to continue observing those terms would be by repressing the Arab population. Since no mutual understanding had been reached between Arabs and Jews and both parties demanded political independence, the mandate had proved unworkable. Establishing an Arab state would violate the rights of the Jewish minority; but forming a Jewish state in the entire territory would violate those of the Arab majority and arouse international Arab and Muslim opposition. The commission concluded that the only feasible solution was partition: two sovereign states—Arab and Jewish—with a British zone encompassing Jerusalem, Bethlehem, and a narrow corridor to the Mediterranean near Jaffa. Britain would also temporarily control the strategic ports of Haifa and Aqaba. The Jewish state would cover about 20 percent of the country, from the Mediterranean coast from Tel Aviv north and all of Galilee. The Arab state would lie in the central mountains and the Negev, include Jaffa port, and probably be linked to the Hashimite state in Transjordan. The simultaneous government statement of policy agreed with those findings: the "irreconcilable conflict between the aspirations of Arabs and Jews in Palestine . . . cannot be satisfied under the terms of the present Mandate, and . . . a scheme of partition . . . represents the best and most hopeful solution to the deadlock" (Hurewitz, p. 76).

The Jewish Agency accepted the principle of partition but criticized the suggested boundaries and insisted that all of the Arab residents of the Jewish state be deported, at British expense (300,000 Arabs, a number equal to the Jewish residents in that area at that time, would be affected). The Palestinians' Arab Higher Committee denounced the partition plan and insisted that Palestine remain a unitary state, since 70 percent of the population was Arab and 90 percent of the land remained under Arab control. Arab residents of Galilee, who would have lost their homes under the partition plan, played leading roles in the rebellion that erupted in October 1937 and continued until early 1939.

Moreover, the Woodhead Partition Commission, appointed to recommend the precise borders for the partitioned states, concluded in Command Paper 5854 (November 8, 1938) that partition was not feasible. That commission could not find boundaries that would give reasonable prospect for self-supporting Arab and Jewish states and proposed much more limited zones of sovereignty within an economic federation. The government then reversed its earlier position in Command Paper 5893, stating "that the political, administrative and financial difficulties involved in the proposal to create independent Arab and Jewish states inside Palestine are so great that this solution of the problem is impracticable" (Government of Palestine, vol. 1, p. 47). A conference in London was called to review the problem; it concluded in another policy statement in May 1939 that Palestine should remain a unitary state. Nonetheless, the concept of partition had been legitimized by the Peel Commission report. That concept would form the basis of the decision by the United Nations in November 1947 to establish two states in Palestine—Israel and Jordan.

BIBLIOGRAPHY

GOVERNMENT OF PALESTINE. *A Survey of Palestine*, vol. 1. Jerusalem, 1946. Reprint, Washington, D.C., 1991.

HUREWITZ, J. C. *The Struggle for Palestine*. New York, 1976. Reprint of 1950 ed.

JOHN, ROBERT, and SAMI HADAWI. *The Palestine Diary: Volume One, 1914–1945*. New York, 1970.

Ann M. Lesch

Peled, Mattityahu   [1923–   ]

Israeli politician.

Born in Haifa, Mattityahu Peled served in the Haganah in the Palmach and, after the State of Israel was proclaimed (1948), in a number of command positions in the Israel Defense Forces. From 1984 to 1988, he served as a member of Knesset representing the Progressive Movement for Peace faction. He is the chair of the Coalition for Israeli–Palestinian Peace, which advocates a two-state solution to the Israeli–Palestinian conflict.

Bryan Daves

Pelly, Lewis   [1825–1892]

British official in the Middle East.

Pelly was born into a family long active in the East India Company, which he also served. The first British official to visit Riyadh, which later became the capital of Saudi Arabia, Pelly also helped establish the first telegraph links throughout the Persian Gulf area.

BIBLIOGRAPHY

KELLY, J. B. *Britain and the Persian Gulf, 1795–1880.* Oxford, 1968.

Benjamin Braude

Pelt, Adrian   [1892–?]

United Nations Assistant Secretary-General.

Pelt was appointed UN commissioner in Libya, December 1949, to implement the newly adopted General Assembly resolution on Libyan independence, which was achieved December 1951. His mission in Libya is very fully described in his book *Libyan Independence and the United Nations* (New Haven, Conn., 1970).

John L. Wright

People's Assembly

Egyptian political body.

The dominance of the executive branch of Egypt's goverment is tempered slightly by a strong tradition of judicial independence. In contrast, the People's Assembly is constitutionally weak. Moreover, rigged elections regularly give the National Democratic party, an extension of the government, overwhelming parliamentary majorities.

Raymond William Baker

People's Council

Syrian political body.

The al-BA'TH party of Syria inaugurated the Majles al-Sha'b—the People's Council—a legislative body representing all political parties, on February 17, 1971. Its first 173 members were appointed to two-year terms; later councils were to be popularly elected to four-year terms. The council grew to 195 members, has three regular sessions annually, and can enact laws, nominate the president, and express no-confidence votes to the Council of Ministers. The People's Council can be dissolved by the president and serves mainly to enact presidential decisions.

BIBLIOGRAPHY

COLELLO, THOMAS. *Syria: A Country Study.* Washington, D.C., 1988.

Charles U. Zenzie

People's Democratic Party of Afghanistan

Afghan Marxist political party; also called Democratic Party of the People of Afghanistan.

The People's Democratic Party of Afghanistan (PDPA) was formed in the period of constitutional reform in Afghanistan (1963–1973) during which parliamentary elections were held and political parties were allowed to organize. It officially came into being on New Year's Day, 1965, at the home of Nur Mohammad Taraki. Taraki was the first secretary-general of the party's central committee, and Babrak KARMAL was its first deputy secretary-general. Although its ideology, judging by the early literature, could be characterized as national democratic and progressive, later, after 1978, the PDPA became openly Marxist, with strong Leninist tendencies.

By 1965, the PDPA had split into two factions, each associated with the name of its newspaper: the Khalq (People) faction, led by Nur Mohammad Taraki and Hafizullah AMIN, and the PARCHAM (Flag) faction, led by Babrak Karmal. The Khalq faction was dominated by Pashto-speaking Afghans from outside of Kabul and had strong ties to the military, whereas the Parcham faction was dominated by Persian-speaking Afghans from Kabul.

On April 27, 1978, the two factions of the PDPA united to stage a coup and take control of Afghanistan. In 1978 and 1979, the PDPA began to institute a series of radical social reforms dealing with land tenure, education, and women's rights. These reforms, coupled with the PDPA's strong antireligious and anticlerical position, proved too progressive for

Afghans accustomed to the traditional social system, and by 1979 the Islamic opposition had begun to mount an aggressive guerilla war against the government. On December 23 and December 24, 1979, a large contingent of Soviet military forces entered Afghanistan and did not leave until 1989.

Calling itself a party of national socialism and having changed its name to Fatherland Party, the PDPA had by 1990 largely abandoned Marxism. It ruled Afghanistan until 1992, when its last president, Najibullah, resigned and Kabul was taken over by Islamic rebels.

BIBLIOGRAPHY

HAMMOND, THOMAS. *Red Flags over Afghanistan.* Boulder, Colo., 1984.

Grant Farr

People's Democratic Republic of Yemen

The name of South Yemen from late 1970 to May 1990, the first two decades of independence from Britain.

The People's Democratic Republic of Yemen (PDRY) spanned the twenty years between the constitution that ended the People's Democratic Republic of South Yemen and the unification of the two Yemens in May 1990. South Yemen had been created politically on November 30, 1967, when the victorious National Liberation Front (NLF) assumed power upon Britain's departure from Aden Colony and the Aden Protectorates. Britain had first occupied Aden in 1839. For the next century, Britain was preoccupied with the port of Aden, while neglecting the dozens or so states in the interior with which it signed treaties of protection only in the last quarter of the nineteenth century. As a consequence, no single political entity in modern times except the stillborn South Arabian Federation of the mid-1960s embraced even most of what was to become an independent South Yemen in late 1967. Instead, what existed was the seventy-five-square-mile (194 sq km) Aden Colony—a city-state, a partly modern urban enclave, and, by some measures, the world's second or third busiest port in the late 1950s—and the vast, mostly distant, politically fragmented interior states, which were, for the most part, based on subsistence agriculture and traditional sociocultural institutions. Neither the British administration nor the nationalists who first stirred in Aden in the 1940s had much knowledge of, interest in, or impact on these states, despite Britain's adoption of a new "forward policy" during the last decades of imperial rule. As a result, the people of Aden were closer, in more ways than just geographically, to the city of Ta'iz in North Yemen than to the Hadramawt, which lay far to the east of Aden and had its strongest business and familial ties with people in the Persian Gulf, India, Indonesia, and East Africa.

The infrastucture barely holding together the major settlement areas of South Yemen at independence in 1967 consisted of dirt tracks, unpaved roads, a number of airstrips, and the telegraph. The country consisted of many microeconomies, most of them agriculturally based and largely self-sufficient; isolated Wadi Hadramawt was an odd case, dependent as it was upon emigration to and remittances from the Gulf and Southeast Asia. What little market economy existed during the British period mostly centered on the port of Aden and its environs, and this in turn was plugged less into the surrounding states than into the international economic system via its sea-lanes. This fragile modern sector was dealt devastating blows near the time of independence when the blockage of the Suez Canal during the Arab–Israel War, 1967 (Six-Day War) nearly brought port activities to a halt, and Britain's rapid withdrawal ended both subsidies from London and the significant economic activity tied to the large British presence.

The history of South Yemen since independence is distinguished by five major periods: (1) During the period of political takeover and consolidation (1967–1969), the NLF established control in Aden and over the interior at the same time that the party's balance of power passed from the nationalists led by Qahtan al-Sha'bi to the party's left wing. (2) The long period of uneasy leftist coleadership of Salim Rabiyya Ali and Abd al-Fattah Isma'il (1969–1978) was distinguished by the efforts of these two rivals both to organize the country in terms of their versions of Marxist-Leninist "scientific socialism" and to align the country with the socialist camp and national liberation movements around the world. (3) The Isma'il interlude (1978–1980) began with the violent elimination of Salim Rubiyya Ali by Isma'il and was notable for the firm establishment of the YEMENI SOCIALIST PARTY (YSP) and bitter conflict between a militant PDRY and the YEMEN ARAB REPUBLIC (YAR), the other Yemen. (4) During the era of ALI NASIR MUHAMMAD (1980–1985), the consolidation of power in this single leader was paralleled by increasing moderation in both domestic affairs and external relations, especially with the YAR. (5) The final period of collective leadership and political weakness (1985–1990) began with the intraparty bloodbath that ousted Ali Nasir and otherwise decapitated the YSP. It ended with the merger with the YAR to form the Republic of Yemen. During the transition period that followed formal unification in May 1990, the YSP shared power with the ruling party of the YAR, the General People's Congress, under their respective leaders, Ali Salim al-Baydh and Ali Abdallah Salih.

Despite this pattern of bitter and sometimes lethal intraparty conflict, between 1967 and 1990 the PDRY regime did maintain rule and order throughout the country, made progress in bridging the gap between Aden and the rest of the country, pursued social goals with some success, and made good use of limited resources in efforts to develop a very poor country. Despite pressures toward fragmentation, especially urgings from Saudi Arabia that the Hadramawt go its separate way, South Yemen held together during difficult political and economic times. This was largely the result of political will, agitation, and organization. The gap between city and countryside remained a constant concern of the leadership, and progress was made in extending education, medical care, and other social services beyond Aden and the other urban centers. In addition, a campaign was waged to extend women's rights and other progressive ideas and institutions to the countryside. Great differences in wealth and property were eliminated, and the economy was organized along socialist lines, most notably in terms of a variety of agricultural and fishing collectives and cooperatives. In the end, however, the socialist experiment, short of time as well as money, failed; the discovery of oil, in 1986, simply came several years too late. Moreover, there was neither time nor resources to push the modern ideas and institutions into the countryside where entrenched tradition prevailed. Nevertheless, the regime remained relatively committed, egalitarian, and free of corruption.

In many ways, the PDRY of the 1970s and 1980s, like Cuba, became both heavily dependent and a great burden upon the Soviet Union. The sudden collapse of the latter and its socialist bloc in the late 1980s left the PDRY weak and in isolation, shorn of fraternal and material support. This as much as the bloodbath that decapitated the YSP in early 1986 left South Yemen unable to resist North Yemen's call for unification in late 1989.

Robert D. Burrowes

People's Democratic Union, People's Democratic Republic of Yemen

The first Communist party in Yemen.

The People's Democratic Union was formed in 1961 in Aden by Abdullah Abd al-Razzak Badhib. This small but influential party, Yemen's first Communist party, became in 1976 one of the constituent groups in the opposition NATIONAL DEMOCRATIC FRONT in North Yemen. Meanwhile, in South Yemen, it had joined with the National Liberation Front and the BAʿTH party in the mid-1970s to form the ruling coalition and in 1978, merged with these two parties to create the ruling YEMENI SOCIALIST PARTY (YSP).

Robert D. Burrowes

People's Houses

Institution founded on Atatürk's ideas, designed to strengthen Turkish culture among Turkey's people.

In Turkey, the Republican People's party (RPP) established the People's Houses (*Halk Evleri*) in 1932, during the single-party era. Party leader's conceptualized the People's Houses as a multipurpose institution designed to strengthen Turkish national identity, promote Western scientific thought, and educate the masses in KEMALISM—the six principles of republicanism, nationalism, populism, statism, secularism, and reformism—put forth by the first president of the Republic of Turkey, Mustafa Kemal Atatürk.

The People's Houses succeeded the Turkish Hearth Association (*Türk Ocağı*), having acquired the use of its property and its role as an institution of political indoctrination. But unlike the Turkish Hearth, which often promoted pan-Turkism and Islam, the People's Houses advanced secularism and confined their nationalist ideology to Turkey.

The RPP not only controlled the houses, but provided funds for their operation from the state budget. The RPP also held title in its own name to house property. The party central committee had authority to open houses in localities throughout the country. RPP by-laws required deputies to support the houses, and provincial RPP committees managed local house finances. The ministry of education strongly encouraged school administrators and teachers to join the houses and play an active role in their activities. The party provincial chairman appointed the house head; local party officials and teachers usually comprised each house's administrative board. Through direct supervision and frequent reporting requirements, national and local RPP leaders made certain that each house advanced party doctrine.

A house could have as many as nine activity sections: (1) language and literature, (2) fine arts, (3) library and publications, (4) history and museum, (5) drama, (6) sports, (7) social assistance, (8) educational classes, and (9) village development. House leaders encouraged teachers to research local Turkish history and culture and to write up their studies for the house's publication series. They also encouraged students to attend house functions and to use the house library. Hoping to make each house a focus of community activity, leaders invited local residents to utilize house facilities for their weddings, circumcision celebrations, and other special occasions. Despite these efforts, however, few houses became the friendly gathering places of the general public.

The RPP quickly established People's Houses in all of Turkey's provincial capitals and in many of its towns. In 1939, the party decided to extend the house's influence—by establishing People's Rooms (*Halk Odaları*) in small towns and villages. Each room was administratively attached to a local house. By 1950, there were 478 houses and 4,322 rooms spread over much of Turkey. Although house and room membership was open to all citizens, regardless of gender or class, most members were middle- and upper-class males. Of about 100,000 members in 1940, only 18,000 were women and some 27,000 were (male) farmers and workers. The remainder of the men and more than 17,000 of the women were government and party officials, teachers, and professionals. A majority of the workers were employed by state enterprises that encouraged their membership. Many, if not most, of the common people probably viewed the houses as alien institutions associated with the often oppressive RPP, dominated by the urban elite, and allied with antireligious forces. Some critics claimed, without solid foundation, that the People's House–concept had been inspired by the Soviet Union's *Narordi Dom* (People's House).

In the late 1940s, when the RPP allowed multiparty politics in Turkey, the opposition (Democrat party, DP) openly resented the RPP's attempts at promoting their agendas through the People's Houses at public expense. Shortly after the Democrat party came to power in the 1950 election, the RPP proposed to preserve the People's Houses as Atatürk's heritage, but to reorganize them in the light of Turkey's new multiparty political structure. The Democrats, who criticized the houses for closely identifying with the RPP—and for failing to serve all the people as originally intended—rejected the RPP proposal. The DP put an end to the houses in 1951 by confiscating the property they occupied, claiming it belonged to the state treasury.

Despite this ignoble end, many members of the RPP continued to regard the People's Houses as an admirable attempt by the political and intellectual elite to advance the Turkish nation along the path set by Atatürk.

BIBLIOGRAPHY

KARPAT, KEMAL H. "The People's Houses in Turkey: Establishment and Growth." *Middle East Journal* 17 (1963): 55–67.

Paul J. Magnarella

People's Party

An alliance of urban upper-class notables and politicians formed in 1948; it was based in northern Syria, mainly in the city of Aleppo.

During the French mandate period in Syria (1920–1946), a group of politicians formed the Aleppo branch of the NATIONAL BLOC (al-Kutla al-Wataniyya), which led Syria's political nationalist struggle against the French presence in the country.

The most prominent leaders of the People's party (Hizb al-Sha'b) were Rushdi al Kikhya, Nazim al-Qudsi, and Mustafa Barmada. The party was, on the whole, more liberal than its Damascus-based rival, the NATIONAL PARTY. It had forged a short-lived political alliance with the BA'TH party in 1947, but this position was quickly undermined by the increased role of the military in Syria's politics in the late 1940s and early 1950s. Since the People's party represented the entrepreneurial interests of northern Syria, which were oriented toward its natural markets in Anatolia (Asian part of Turkey) and Iraq, the party usually called for closer economic ties with those countries. This position was carried further politically in the case of Iraq, because the People's party usually favored a union between the two countries.

BIBLIOGRAPHY

KHOURY, PHILIP. *Syria and the French Mandate.* Princeton, N.J., 1987.
SEALE, PATRICK. *The Struggle For Syria.* London, 1965.

Mahmoud Haddad

People's Socialist Party

Yemeni political party.

Founded in 1962 by the Aden Trades Union Congress, the People's Socialist party (PSP) was led by Abdullah al-Asnaj (later an important participant in the politics of North Yemen as well). Modeling itself on the Labour party, it supported political means to accomplish its goals of British withdrawal, independence, and union with North Yemen. Its unwillingness to use political violence to accomplish these objectives resulted in a loss of influence to the rival National Front.

Manfred W. Wenner

Pera

The most Europeanized district of Istanbul during the last century of Ottoman rule.

Pera (Beyoğlu) comprised the long ridge stretching north above Galata, and its slopes to east and west. Galata, the Genoese and Venetian port concession on the northern shore of the Golden Horn in Byzantine Constantinople, remained such in the Ottoman city but was subject to greater government control. Especially after the arrival of large numbers of western and northern European traders in the seventeenth century, Pera became the site of embassies and merchants' mansions. Its great age of prosperity, power, and prestige came in the second half of the nineteenth century, after trade liberalization and social Europeanization. With tremendous expansion of European trade, the Grande Rue de Pera flourished with shops, restaurants, hotels, banks, and office buildings in the latest European styles; it was populated by foreigners, local non-Muslims, and Muslims in the vanguard of Europeanization. In republican times, though Turkified and much less cosmopolitan, the area managed to maintain, somewhat diminished, its social, cultural, and commercial importance.

BIBLIOGRAPHY

ÇELIK, ZEYNEP. *The Remaking of Istanbul: Portrait of an Ottoman City in the Nineteenth Century.* Berkeley, Calif., 1986.

I. Metin Kunt

Pera Palace

Turkish hotel built in the nineteenth century.

Named after the district in Constantinople (now Istanbul) in which it was located, the Pera Palace Hotel stands on a hilltop overlooking the Golden Horn. It is an eclectic building adorned externally by Ionic columns and pilasters, voluted balcony consoles, and intricate iron railings. Inside there are 150 spacious guest rooms on 5 levels above the public spaces of the ground floor. Among the public spaces, the tall reception room is especially noteworthy, with walls finished in horizontal, alternating stripes of ocher and black marble and an ornate ceiling composed of small decorative domes perforated with tiny round light holes.

Built by the architect Alexandre Vallaury for the Compagnie Internationale des Wagons-lits et des Grands Express Européens and completed in 1876, the year the Orient Express made its first trip to Istanbul, the ownership of the Pera Palace Hotel has passed on to a Turkish company. Having been extensively restored and renovated in the 1970s, the hotel is now in good condition and enjoys wide popularity as a symbol of a vanished era—the late Ottoman Empire.

BIBLIOGRAPHY

SUMNER-BOYD, HILARY, and JOHN FREELY. *Strolling through Istanbul*. Istanbul, 1972.

Aptullah Kuran

Peres, Shimon   [1923–   ]

Israeli politician, military leader, and cabinet member; prime minister, 1984–1986, 1995–1996.

Born in Poland under the name Shimon Perski, Peres migrated to Palestine in 1934. In 1947, he joined the Haganah, which was then led by David BEN-GURION, who became Peres's political mentor. In 1948, when the State of Israel was proclaimed, Ben-Gurion appointed Peres, then twenty-five, to head Israel's navy. Peres subsequently studied politics and economics in the United States. In 1952, he was appointed deputy director general of the Israeli Defense Ministry and served in that capacity until 1959. As a Defense Ministry leader, he participated in secret armament negotiations with the French prior to the Sinai campaign of 1956 (see ARAB–ISRAEL WAR of 1956).

Peres strongly advocated that Israel provide military aid to new states of Africa (in addition to other types of aid and to exchange programs that might be developed) because he thought this would be a good way for Israel to develop influence in that part of the world. In 1959, he was elected for the first time to the Knesset, where, along with his political ally Moshe Dayan, he argued forcefully for a change in government policy that would shift the emphasis from pioneering to enhancing the state's efficiency. From 1959 to 1965, he served as deputy defense minister.

Although being a protégé of David Ben-Gurion was advantageous in that it caused Peres's early career to develop quickly, it was disadvantageous later on, when Ben-Gurion's political capital decreased (and virtually disappeared); at that point, the political power of his protégés also declined. In 1964 Peres, Moshe Dayan, Abba Eban, and many other supporters of Ben-Gurion left MAPAI and went over to the AHDUT HA-AVODAH party because as followers of Ben-Gurion they perceived that once he had given up his leadership of MAPAI, they were being shut out of the party. Peres left the Defense Ministry in 1965 to help Ben-Gurion establish RAFI, a new political party, and in 1967 he helped negotiate a reconciliation between Rafi, MAPAI, and Ahdut Ha-

Avodah, which resulted in the creation of the new Israeli LABOR PARTY.

In 1972, Peres became transport minister in the government of Golda Meir. Although he was one of the chief contenders to succeed Meir when she resigned in 1974, he lost the leadership race in the Labor party to Yitzhak Rabin and, later the same year, was named defense minister, an office he held until the 1977 election. (The competition between Peres and Rabin for leadership of the Labor party continued until Rabin's assassination in 1995.) After Peres gained command of the Labor party in 1977, he led it twice in electoral defeats to Menachem Begin and the Likud party (1977, 1981). According to many observers, his losses could be ascribed to the public's inability to trust him, that is, to their skepticism about his rapid change from defense hawk to dove in relation to negotiations with the Palestinians.

In 1984, both major parties failed to win a majority of seats in the Knesset and a coalition government involving both the Labor and the Likud parties was formed. Shimon Peres served as prime minister and Yitzhak Shamir as foreign minister until 1986, whereupon Shamir became prime minister and Peres foreign minister for the remainder of the term of the Knesset. Following the Knesset election of 1989, the Labor party recaptured power and Peres was appointed foreign minister in the cabinet of Prime Minister Rabin. As foreign minister he negotiated the later stages of the OSLO AGREEMENT and convinced Rabin to support them. He shared a Nobel Peace Prize with Rabin and Yasir Arafat of the Palestine Liberation Organization in October 1994, in recognition of his efforts to achieve peace in the region.

Upon Rabin's assassination in November 1995, Peres again became prime minister.

BIBLIOGRAPHY

PERES, SHIMON. *David's Sling*. London, 1970.
SACHAR, HOWARD M. *A History of Israel: From the Rise of Zionism to Our Time*. New York, 1981.

Gregory S. Mahler

Pérez de Cuéllar, Javier   [1920–   ]

Peruvian diplomat; UN secretary-general, 1982–1992.

Pérez de Cuéllar received a law degree from the Catholic University in Lima in 1943. He subsequently entered the Peruvian foreign service, and in 1946 was a member of the Peruvian delegation to the opening session of the UN General Assembly. Pérez de Cuéllar was later ambassador to Switzerland, the Soviet Union, Poland, and Venezuela, and permanent representative to the United Nations.

In 1974, while president of the UN Security Council, Pérez de Cuéllar represented Secretary-General Kurt Waldheim in settling the Cyprus crisis and was able to avert further military confrontation. As undersecretary for political affairs, he dealt with the aftermath of the Soviet invasion of Afghanistan.

During his term as secretary-general, Pérez de Cuéllar led the United Nations in its confrontation with Iraq after the latter had invaded Kuwait. In 1995 he made an unsuccessful bid for the presidency of Peru.

Bryan Daves

Pergamon

A town in western Anatolia.

Pergamon, also known as Bergama, is a town of approximately forty-three thousand inhabitants located inland from the Anatolian coast of the northern Aegean. Used as a base by one of Alexander the Great's generals, Lysimachus, and ruled subsequently by his successors, it became, as a result, a central gathering place for a whole host of people—Jews, Phoenicians, and others from Asia Minor. With prosperity came an emphasis on learning; the arts, sciences, and literature, in particular, flourished, rivaling even legendary Alexandria. Pergamon was especially famed for its library. So serious a rival was it considered by the Egyptians that at one point they banned the export of papyrus. In an effort to find a suitable alternative to papyrus, the citizens of Pergamon revived the practice of writing on parchment (treated animal skin), which they referred to as "pergamena." Pergamena was produced in large quantities, and it is thought to have led eventually to the development of the *codex*, or paged book.

Eventually Pergamon came under Ottoman control. During the Turkish War of Independence, it was occupied by Greek forces (1919–1923). In the subsequent population exchange that took place between Greece and Turkey, Pergamon lost a substantial portion of its native Greek population and gained instead a completely new, retransplanted Turkish Greek community.

BIBLIOGRAPHY

Encyclopaedia of Islam, 2nd ed., vol. 1.

Karen Pinto

Perim

Yemeni island.

This small, barren volcanic island has a well-protected harbor in the Bab al-Mandab straits between Yemen and Djibouti in Africa. Seized by the British in Aden in 1857, Perim island became a part of South Yemen upon independence in 1967. It was used as a coaling station by the British until the 1930s but has had no real strategic or economic significance in the late twentieth century. A poor fishing village exists side-by-side with the rusting, collapsing remains of its more glorious days as a coaling station.

Robert D. Burrowes

Permanent Mandate Commission

Oversight body of the League of Nations.

The Geneva-based commission was established in 1919 under Article 22 of the Covenant of the League of Nations to supervise the administration under the mandate system of fifteen mandated territories including four in the Middle East—France's Lebanon and Syria and Britain's Palestine and Iraq. It required annual reports from mandatory governments and advised the Council of the League of Nations on policy regarding the mandates. The Commission, however, exercised little supervisory authority, and three of the mandates in the Middle East—Lebanon, Syria, and Palestine—were generally run autonomously, much like colonies.

Most members of the commission were representatives of colonial powers: Great Britain, France, Italy, Portugal, Spain, Belgium, the Netherlands, Germany, and Japan. Only two members were noncolonial states: Switzerland and Norway. Citizens of the mandates could appeal to the commission but only through their mandatory high commissioner. The commission repeatedly rejected Palestinian Arabs' appeals for the right to self-determination and tolerated France's delays in granting autonomy to Syria and Lebanon. However, the commission granted independence to Iraq in 1932. The commission existed until 1946, when the United Nations replaced it with its Trusteeship Council as the MANDATE SYSTEM became the trusteeship system.

BIBLIOGRAPHY

HENKIN, LOUIS, et al. *International Law.* St. Paul, Minn., 1987.
HUREWITZ, J. C. *The Struggle for Palestine.* New York, 1976.
LESCH, ANN MOSELY. *Arab Politics in Palestine, 1917–1939.* Ithaca, N.Y., 1979.

MOORE, JOHN NORTON, ed. *The Arab-Israeli Conflict,* vol. 3. Princeton, N.J., 1974.

Elizabeth Thompson

Perpetual Maritime Truce

An agreement between Britain and Oman.

A British-brokered agreement signed May 4, 1853, by five northern Oman coastal rulers who mutually renounced maritime warfare in perpetuity. Superseding several temporary truces initiated in 1835, and observed de facto throughout the Gulf, it was a keystone of Britain's pre-1971 regional hegemony. Signatory principalities were styled Trucial States.

BIBLIOGRAPHY

AITCHESON, C. U., compiler. *A Collection of Treaties, Engagements, and Sanads Relating to India and Neighbouring Countries,* vol. 11, 5th ed. Delhi, 1933. Reprint, 1973.

Robert G. Landen

Persepolis

Ancient capital of Persia (also known as Takht-e Jamshid), succeeding Pasargadae; dynastic center of the Achaemenid Empire.

The ruins are to the northeast of Shiraz, in southern Iran, covering an extensive area. Under the ancient city are villages that date back to about 4000 B.C.E.

Ruins at Persepolis. (D.W. Lockhard)

Royal rock carving at Persepolis. (D.W. Lockhard)

The site contains the terraced platform of Darius the Great (550–486 B.C.E.) on a foothill, with his private palace, treasury, and audience palace (completed by his son Xerxes, who added a grand staircase, a private palace, and the hundred-columned hall). Alexander the Great burned Persepolis to end the Persian Empire in 330 B.C.E.

BIBLIOGRAPHY

SCHMIDT, E. F. *Persepolis.* Chicago, 1953. Reprint, 1957, 1970.
SHAHBAZI, A. S. *Persepolis Illustrated.* Tehran, 1976.

A. Shahpur Shahbazi

Persia

See Iran

Persian

An Indo-European language related to English, Sanskrit, Kurdish, and Pashto.

Modern Persian arose about the ninth century C.E. It is the national language of Iran, Afghanistan, and Tajikistan. It is known generally and in Iran as Farsi; in Afghanistan, as Dari; and in Tajikistan, as Tajiki. It has exerted great influence on the Indian subcontinent and in Ottoman Turkey.

Persian has twenty-three consonants and six vowels. It has two consonants lacking in English: *gh* (similar to the French *r*) and *kh* (similar to the *ch* in the German *Buch*). It lacks the *th* sounds (as in *thin* and *this*); the consonant *w*; the vowels in *bit*, *but*, and *put*; and syllable-initial consonant clusters (as in *strip*). It has neither gender, articles, nor number agreement.

Persian uses a slightly modified Arabic script, written from right to left (except for the numerals). There are seven diacriticals (three seldom used). Seven letters cannot join each other or any following letter. Under Soviet rule, Tajiki briefly used the Latin script, then switched to the Cyrillic. Since the dissolution of the Soviet Union, there has been a movement for the return to the Arabic script. The Persian script's main features are inconsistent representation of certain vowels and alternative spellings of some consonants and vowels. These and other features, causing problems in reading and writing, have since the nineteenth century led some Iranians to advocate the adoption of Latin or some other script.

Persian has changed little in the last thousand years or so: a person who knows Persian can understand tenth-century Persian (except for a few words and phrases). Persian includes an extensive Arabic element, the language of Islam, and was for a time the language of science and scholarship for all Muslims. There are also a number of Turkish and Mongolian loanwords, reflecting Turkish and Mongol rule in Iran. Growing contacts with Europe since the nineteenth century have led to extensive borrowings from French and, since World War II, from English. Greek, Aramaic, and Indian languages also account for a few words. In its turn, Persian is the source of some words in Arabic, large numbers in Turkish and Urdu, and smaller numbers in Western and other languages. Most of these words have found their way into Western languages through classical Greek, Latin, Arabic, and Spanish (e.g., the English *tulip*, *narcissus*, *khaki*, *orange*, *sugar*, *julep*, *jasmine*, *pajamas*, *magic*, *arsenic*, and *cushy*, and the names Cyrus and Roxanne).

BIBLIOGRAPHY

JAZAYERY, MOHAMMAD ALI. "Western Loanwords in Persian, with Reference to Westernization." *Islamic Culture* 40 (1966):207–220 and 41 (1967):1–19.

SERJEANTSON, MARY S. *A History of Foreign Words in English.* London, 1935.

WINDFUHR, GERNOT L. "Persian." In *The World's Major Languages,* ed. by Bernard Comrie. New York, 1987.

M. A. Jazayery

Persian Gulf

See Gulf

Pertev, Mehmet Sait   [1786–1837]

Ottoman Turkish poet.

He was born in Darica in the Ottoman Empire and entered the civil service in 1805, traveling in this position outside the empire. In 1835, he was promoted to first minister and given the title *paşa* (pasha), but following a dispute with another bureaucrat, Sultan Mahmud II had him strangled. His poetry was composed in the traditional divan style, and it was collected and published in 1840.

David Waldner

Pesh Merga

Kurdish guerilla fighter.

Literally, the term *pesh merga* means "the one who faces death," in Kurdish. A fairly recent word, it appeared after the beginning of the 1962 war in Iraq against the Kurds. Recruited from the more traditional tribes of Kurdistan, extremely fit and brave fighters, the *pesh mergas* have been able to resist the Iraqi and Iranian armies since that time and continue to do so.

BIBLIOGRAPHY

KUTSCHERA, CHRIS. "Les Kurdes d'Irak: Des révisions déchirantes." *Les Cahiers de l'Orient* 12 (1988): 63–81.

Chris Kutschera

Petah Tiqvah

Farming community founded in Palestine by scholarly Jews of Jerusalem, 1878.

Petah Tiqvah was founded by a group of pious Jewish scholars from Jerusalem who sought an independent livelihood on the land. In its first decade, the community was beset with problems: malaria, insecurity, complicated disputes with Arabs living on adjacent lands, and financial shortages. Some of the settlers received financial aid from the Hibbat Zion movement and, eventually, substantial support from Baron Edmond de Rothschild.

BIBLIOGRAPHY

GVATI, CHAIM. *A Hundred Years of Settlement.* Jerusalem, 1985.

Donna Robinson Divine

Peter VII

109th Coptic patriarch of Egypt (1809–1852).

Originally chosen by MARK VIII (1796–1809) as *abuna* (archbishop) of the Ethiopian Orthodox Church, Peter instead became an important bishop close to the patriarch and eventually succeeded him. Peter was a thrifty and judicious administrator whose wise handling of accounts created a fortune that made possible the reforms of his successor, CYRIL IV (1854–1861). Peter assembled part of the patriarchal library in Cairo and had new copies of important treatises made from old versions, sometimes participating in the task. He wrote theological treatises clarifying the Coptic Church's position on Communion and Christ's nature. Peter's good relations with the viceroy of Egypt became legendary. In particular, Peter won great favor with Muhammad Ali when he refused an offer from the Russian czar to put the Coptic Orthodox Church under his protection.

[*See also*: Copts]

BIBLIOGRAPHY

SHOUERI, MOUNIR. "Peter VII." In *The Coptic Encyclopedia,* ed. by Aziz S. Atiya. Vol. 6. New York, 1991.

Donald Spanel

Petra

Ancient city carved from the cliffs in today's Jordan.

In about 500 B.C.E., the Nabatean Arabs established a presence in the region east of the great Jordan–Dead Sea rift. They built their capital and trading center at Petra, in southern Jordan, close to the Wadi al-Araba

Monastery at Petra. (Mia Bloom)

and adjacent to the contemporary village of Wadi Musa. In its location and appearance, Petra is a unique city. The only easy access is through a half-mile-long (1 km) narrow passage called the *siq*. At its terminus is the treasury, a large edifice carved into the rock of the rose-colored cliffs. This vista is repeated with additional buildings as well as with simple houses hewed within the stone precipices of the ancient city. They include a huge monastery, a palace, tombs, and an amphitheater, most of which were crafted in a modified Greco-Roman style. For tourism, Petra is one of Jordan's most important archeological sites and attractions.

BIBLIOGRAPHY

HARDING, G. LANKESTER. *The Antiquities of Jordan,* rev. ed. New York, 1967.

Peter Gubser

Petrochemicals

Chemicals isolated or derived from petroleum or natural gas.

Petrochemicals include industrial and agricultural chemicals synthesized from refinery still, gases and natural gas. Research into manufacturing processes was stimulated by the availability of raw materials (most of which would otherwise be waste products), and foreign demand. The global petrochemicals industry remained relatively small until World War II, when the United States concentrated government investment in petrochemicals in a few large, privately owned plants and in newly constructed state-owned facilities operated by experienced firms. This huge investment in petrochemicals during the war left the U.S. industry in a dominant position for many years, making it very difficult for the national oil companies (NOCs) of Middle Eastern countries to compete. Before the nationalization of their oil industries, the NOCs were hindered by the reluctance of the operating companies to supply enough raw materials and process technology to make the NOCs' local ventures competitive internationally. Exports were necessary because Middle East domestic markets for petrochemicals were very small. Another disadvantage grew out of the inability of the NOCs to conduct state-of-the-art research into process technology or to fabricate locally the equipment needed to establish and retain a position on the cutting edge of the industry.

These drawbacks decreased in importance after oil prices rose in the early 1970s. Increased costs of drill-

Petrochemical Plants in Production in the Gulf Region, by Country and Product

Country and Product	Major Owners	Plant Name	Capacity (tons/year)	Planned Capacity
SAUDI ARABIA				
Ammonia	SABIC 49%; Saudi Public 41% Employees	SAFCO	225,735	—
Benzene	SABIC 100%	PetroKemya	75,000	—
Butadiene	SABIC 100%	PetroKemya	100,000	—
Butene-1	SABIC 100%	PetroKemya	50,000	—
Caustic Soda	SABIC 50%; Pecten-Arabia (Shell) 50%	SADAF	450,000	—
Direct Reduction Steel	SABIC 100%	HADEED	2,200,000	—
D.T.B.C	SABIC 70%; Neste Oy 10%; Ecofuel 10%	Ibn Zahar	1,200,000	—
Ethanol	SABIC 50%; Pecten-Arabia (Shell) 50%	SADAF	300,000	—
Ethylene	SABIC 50%; Mobil 50%	YANPET	560,000	—
	SABIC 100%	PetroKemya	650,000	—
Ethylene Dichloride	SABIC 50%; Pecten-Arabia (Shell) 50%	SADAF	760,000	—
Ethylene Dichloride	SABIC 50%; Pecten-Arabia (Shell) 50%	SADAF	560,000	—
	SABIC 50%; Mitsubishi & other Japanese cos.	SHARQ	660,000	—
Ethylene Glycol	SABIC 50%; Mobil 50%	YANPET	250,000	—
Formaldehyde	Private: Al Lahiq, Al-Zamil, Y. Kanoo	SFCC	25,000	—
M.T.B.E.	ARAMCO, Mobil	PEMREF	120,000	—
M.T.B.E.	SABIC 50%; Hoescht 25%; Texas Eastern	Ibn Sinna	500,000	—
Melamin	SABIC 49%; Saudi Public 41% Employees	SAFCO	20,240	—
Methanol	SABIC 50%; Hoescht 25%; Texas Eastern	Ibn Sinna	900,000	—
	SABIC 50%; Mitsubishi Gas 50%	AL RAZI	1,200,000	—
Mono-, Di- & Triethylene	SABIC 50%; Mitsubishi & other Japanese cos. 50%	SHARQ	452,000	—
Nitrogen	SABIC 100%	GAS	460,000	—
Oxygen	SABIC 100%	GAS	960,000	—
Polyvinyl Chloride	SABIC 71%; Lucky Goldstar 15%; NIC 10%	Ibn Hayyan	300,000	—
Polyethylene	SABIC 50%; Mitsubishi & other Japanese cos.	SHARQ	188,000	—
	SABIC 50%; Mobil 50%	YANPET	430,000	—
Polypropylene	SABIC 70%; Neste Oy 10%; Ecofuel 10%	Ibn Zahar	200,000	—
Prilled Sulphur (solid)	ARAMCO	—	1,500,000	—
Propylene	SABIC 100%	PetroKemya	300,000	—
Steel Rebar	HADEED	SULB	250,000	—
Styrene	SABIC 50%; Pecten-Arabia (Shell) 50%	SADAF	360,000	—
Sulfuric Acid	SABIC 49%; Saudi Public 41% Employees	SAFCO	98,535	—
Urea	SABIC 50%; Taiwan Fertilizer 50%	SAMAD	600,000	—
	SABIC 49%; Saudi Public 41% Employees	SAFCO	353,774	—
IRAN				
2-ethyl hexanol & normal & iso-butanols	—	Arak Complex	45,000	—
Ammonia	—	Razi Complex	660,000	—
		Shiraz Complex	432,000	—
Ammonium Nitrate	—	Shiraz Complex	254,000	—

Country and Product	Major Owners	Plant Name	Capacity (tons/year)	Planned Capacity
Benzene	—	Kharg Island Complex	289,221	—
Butane	—	Kharg Island Complex	72,200	—
Carbon Black	—	Iran Carbon Complex	20,000	—
Caustic Soda	—	Abadan Complex	30,000	—
	—	Pazargad Complex	5,500	—
	—	Shiraz Complex	22,000	—
Chemical Fertilizers	—	Shiraz Complex	500,000	—
Chlorine	—	Pazargad Complex	4,600	—
	—	Shiraz Complex	20,000	—
DDB	—	Abadan Petrochem. Complex	10,000	—
Diammonium Phosphate	—	Razi Complex	240,000	—
	—	Shiraz Complex	20,000	—
Dioctyl Phthalate	—	Farabi Complex	40,000	
Ethylene Dichloride	—	Bandar Khomeini Complex	350,000	—
Heavy Sodium Carbonate	—	Shiraz Complex	51,000	—
Hydrochloric Acid	—	Pazargad Complex	5,900	—
	—	Shiraz Complex	66,000	—
Light Sodium Carbonate	—	Shiraz Complex	60,000	—
LPG	—	Bandar Imam Complex	1,900,000	—
	—	Bandar Khomeini Complex	1,300,000	—
Methanol	—	Shiraz Complex	84,000	—
Methanol: Acetic Acid	—	Kharg Island Complex	660,000	—
Monoammonium Phosphate	—	Razi Chemical Complex	240,000	—
Nitric Acid	—	Shiraz Complex	386,000	—
Pentane	—	Kharg Island Complex	182,002	—
Phosphoric Acid	—	Razi Complex	240,000	—
Phthalic Anhydride	—	Farabi Complex	5,500	—
Propane	—	Kharg Island Complex	145,710	—
PVC	—	Abadan Complex	60,000	—
PVC Fittings	—	Polika Factory	200	—
PVC Pellets	—	Polika Factory	3,000	—
PVC Rigid Pipes	—	Polika Factory	6,800	—
Sodium Bicarbonate	—	Shiraz Complex	30,000	—
Sodium Hypochloride	—	Shiraz Complex	13,000	—
Sodium Tripolyphosphate	—	Shiraz Complex	20,000	—
Sulfur	—	Kharg Island Complex	216,000	—
	—	Razi Complex	675,000	—
Sulfuric Acid	—	Razi Complex	966,000	—
Urea	—	Razi Complex	720,000	—
BAHRAIN				
Alkylation	—	Bahrain Refinery	—	4,600*
Atmospheric Crude Oil	—	—	—	180,000*
CCR	—	—	—	18,000
LPG	—	—	—	7,500*
M.T.B.E	—	—	—	750*

Country and Product	Major Owners	Plant Name	Capacity (tons/year)	Planned Capacity
BAHRAIN (*cont.*)				
Ammonia & Methanol	Bahrain National Oil	Gulf Petrochemical Industries	825,852	—
Urea				
Polypropylene & Methyl	Bahrain National Gas	—	—	—
KUWAIT				
Ethylene	Equate; Kuwait Petrochemical & Union Carbide	Bubayan Petrochemicals	—	650,000
Ethylene Glycol	—	—	—	350,000
Polypropylene HDPE	—	—	—	450,000
Butene-1	—	—	—	20,000
Ethylene	—	—	—	650,000
Polyethylene	—	—	—	450,000
Polyethylene Glycol	—	—	—	350,000
OMAN				
Liquid Natural Gas	51% government		—	5,000,000
QATAR				
Methanol	Qatar Methanol Company	—	—	720,000
Ammonia	Qatar Fertilizer Company	Umm Said Industrial	710,000	540,000
Urea	—	—	770,000	720,000
Ethylene	Qatar Petrochemical	—	300,000	170,000
LDPE	—	—	175,000	360,000
M.T.B.E.	50/50 QGPC; Penspen	—	—	550,000
Methanol	—	—	—	660,000
M.T.B.E.	QGPC 50%	—	—	500,000
UNITED ARAB EMIRATES				
M.T.B.E.	—	—	—	500,000– 700,000
Polymer-modified	Dubai Aluminum	—	—	30,000
Ammonia	Dubai Bitumen Company	—	330,000	—
Urea	Government of Abu	—	550,000	—
	Shiraz Complex	—	543,000	—
Vinyl Chloride Monomer (VCM)	Bandar Khomeini Pet. Comp.	—	180,000	—

* Barrels per day.

Source: Jean-François Seznec (© The Lafayette Group, Inc., Greenwich, Conn.).

ing for raw material in oil fields gave the NOCs a comparative advantage. Also helpful was the rise in importance of a third class of firms involved in petrochemicals: international contracting firms such as Fluor, Foster Wheeler, and Chiyoda that were able to design and construct state-of-the-art turnkey facilities and associated infrastructure. During the 1970s and after, Middle Eastern oil-exporting countries found it relatively easy to acquire petrochemicals facilities tailor-made for their needs.

A gas plant in Saudi Arabia. (SABIC)

Other trends in the late 1970s and the 1980s improved the relative position of oil-exporting countries in the global petrochemical industry. One was the obsolescence of older facilities owned by giant chemical and oil companies, which opened space in the market for new producers. Even more important was the trend toward joint ventures between the NOCs and chemical and oil companies based in industrialized countries. The NOCs brought capital and low-cost raw materials to these ventures; their partners brought expertise and market access along with capital. These trends are an important component of the late twentieth-century worldwide restructuring of manufacturing, and demonstrate a growing role for oil-exporting developing countries in global production of petrochemicals.

BIBLIOGRAPHY

CHAPMAN, KEITH. *The International Petrochemical Industry: Evolution and Location.* Oxford, 1991.

A petrochemical plant in Saudi Arabia. (SABIC)

TÉTREAULT, MARY ANN. *The Kuwait Petroleum Corporation and the Economics of the New World Order.* Westport, Conn., 1995.

Mary Ann Tétreault

Petroleum, Oil, and Natural Gas

Naturally occurring hydrocarbon compounds.

The petroleum industry in the Middle East dates to 3000 B.C.E., when Mesopotamians exploited asphaltic bitumen obtained from seepages and rock asphalt mining to produce construction mortar, mosaic cement, road surfacing, and waterproofing materials. This form of petroleum, called pitch, is the residue left after natural gas and volatile liquid fractions have evaporated from crude oil. Noah in the Bible used pitch to caulk the ark, and the ancient Bahrainis used pitch-coated pottery and baskets. An industry based on the distillation of crude oil began in Alexandria about the second century C.E. to produce fuel for lamps. About 500 years later, Byzantine armies began to use "Greek fire," a napalmlike substance distilled from crude oil that was poured or sprayed on enemy troops and ships, then set afire.

The modern oil industry can be thought of as a continuous process that pivots on the extraction or production of petroleum and natural gas from the earth. Upstream from production are exploration, the search for oil-bearing lands; and development, the construction of production infrastructure like oil wells and natural gas separators in oil fields. Downstream from production are transportation, including pipelines, tankers, trucks, and railroads; refining, which turns crude oil into usable products; and marketing, gasoline stations, and other outlets. Petroleum and natural gas not only are used to produce fuels but are also the raw materials from which petrochemicals, such as fertilizers and the building blocks of plastics, are manufactured.

Considering the oil industry in this way allows one to identify its "choke points" or stages where a powerful firm or government can exert political and economic leverage. One potential choke point concerns PETROLEUM RESERVES AND PRODUCTION. In the nations of the Middle East, as in most others, mineral rights belong to the state. Oil companies must negotiate with governments to get concessions (rights to extract oil on their territories). In exchange, they offer lump-sum payments, rents, taxes, and/or royalties (payments per unit of oil produced).

Before World War II, Middle Eastern countries had to compete for oil company investment. Many

The College of Petroleum and Minerals in Dhahran, Saudi Arabia. (Richard Bulliet)

oil companies were more fearful of a glut of oil that would depress prices than of oil shortages that would inconvenience consumers. Under the RED LINE AGREEMENT of 1928, the partners in the IRAQ PETROLEUM COMPANY agreed that none of them would explore for or develop new oil in the former Ottoman Empire unless every partner consented to each new project. Countries inside the Red Line had difficulty getting these companies to find and then develop the oil that could have increased their national incomes because the largest—and richest—Red Line companies were reluctant to add to already excessive oil production capacity.

Oil partnerships and concession patterns also limited the leverage of governments in the Middle East. Instead of one government dealing with several oil companies operating on various parts of its territory, the initial pattern of oil industry development in this region was to have a single operating company, often a joint venture or partnership, as the only oil producer in each country. Joint ventures are common in the oil industry because of its capital intensity and riskiness. Individual parent companies like Gulf (now part of Chevron) and the Anglo-Persian Oil Company (later ANGLO IRANIAN OIL COMPANY, now British Petroleum), set up jointly owned operating companies such as the KUWAIT OIL COMPANY (KOC) to enlarge their financial resources and reduce their risk. Thus, even though two separate parents invested in and profited from Kuwait's oil, their business in Kuwait was conducted by a single company, KOC. Such partnerships allowed the major companies to exercise some control over total world oil supplies by sharing production information. They also discouraged competition among the partners and provided a protected environment in which they could coordinate their global operations.

Kuwait's ability to choose which company would get its concession was limited by treaties between its ruler and the British government that gave Britain the final authority to approve concession agreements. Britain would not permit Kuwait to contract with a non-British company, although Kuwait successfully attracted a non-British firm to become a partner in KOC. The concession further limited Kuwait's autonomy, giving KOC exclusive rights to find and produce oil over the entire land area of Kuwait for ninety years. Had Kuwait tried to get better terms from another company during that time, that company would have faced legal challenges from the Anglo-Persian Oil Company and Gulf, preventing it from selling Kuwaiti oil in the international market.

Another threat was the possibility of intervention by one of the home governments of KOC's parents, Britain and the United States. Such an eventuality was realized in the early 1950s in Iran. The Iranian government, under Prime Minister Mohammad Mossadegh, nationalized the operations of Iran's oil company in 1951 following a conflict with its managers. The owner of the oldest oil production facilities in the Middle East, Iran's operating company had only one parent, the Anglo-Iranian Oil Company (AIOC), which obtained court orders enjoining other companies from buying Iranian oil.

Afraid of the example that a successful nationalization might provide to other Middle Eastern governments, the British and American governments worked to destabilize and eventually to overthrow the Mossadegh regime. The restoration of the Shah, Mohammad Reza Pahlavi, in 1953, following a brief period of ouster, also reinstated foreign oil companies as managers of the nationalized Iranian oil company. But instead of restoring AIOC to its former position as sole owner, the Iranian government sought a "Kuwait solution" and invited non-British

Drilling for oil in Turkey in 1952. (D.W. Lockhard)

Petroleum plant in Saudi Arabia. (Richard Bulliet)

participation in the National Iranian Oil Company (NIOC). When NIOC was reorganized, American companies and the French national oil company were given 60 percent of the shares, leaving AIOC with only 40 percent.

The one company/one country pattern of concessions throughout much of the Middle East contributed to making this region the marginal supplier of oil to the international market despite the cost advantages of Middle Eastern oil over that obtained from most other sources. This balancing act was made possible by the participation of all the major companies, whose production holdings stretched across the Middle East. The solution of the Iranian crisis in the 1950s made supply management even easier because the reorganized NIOC was the first operating consortium in the Middle East to include each of the major oil companies, the SEVEN SISTERS that dominated the industry from the end of World War II until the oil revolution. Once they had estimated the amount of oil needed to balance market demand, the major companies could regulate production by increasing or decreasing offtake in countries whose governments could not retaliate easily.

The one company/one country pattern in the Middle East changed in the 1950s. Following the reorganization of the Iranian concession, which included several independent companies, independents began to compete more vigorously against the majors to win new concessions. When the government of Libya opened bidding for concessions in 1955, it first divided its territory into independent parcels, eventually awarding rights covering 55 percent of its land area to fifteen operating companies whose owners included independents from France, Germany, and the United States. At about the same time, older producers with unallocated offshore properties began to auction them off. The independents were inno-

vative bidders for all these properties, offering terms that included higher-than-average lump-sum payments and royalties as well as equity shares for host governments. Better terms for new concessions moved host governments to demand that prior concession holders relinquish unexploited territories. The new concessions signed for these properties included provisions for automatic relinquishment according to a predetermined timetable, in order to discourage oil companies from failing to develop promising properties. As more and more independents won concessions and succeeded in finding oil, markets became glutted and prices weakened.

In what was perhaps the last straw for the international oil companies, the U.S. government imposed a quota on U.S. oil imports in 1959. The U.S. market, the largest in the world, was doubly lucrative because the high cost of domestically produced oil gave sellers of lower-cost foreign oil the potential to reap high profits. U.S. multinational oil companies had long been encouraged by their government to find oil overseas, and access to the protected U.S. market reinforced other incentives to invest abroad. When profits from international operations were squeezed by higher concession costs and competition from independents, multinationals with marketing outlets in the United States looked toward U.S. oil sales as a source of deliverance. However, cheap imports threatened the domestic price structure, and firms that owned only U.S. production sources fought the importation of oil, especially from the low-cost Middle East.

The U.S. government asked oil companies to limit imports voluntarily, but hard-pressed firms were unwilling to forgo profits from crude sales in the United States. Domestic producers, citing national security and the risk of becoming dependent on foreign imports, soon demanded real protection. In 1959, the voluntary quotas became mandatory. Meanwhile, the major companies had begun to consider reducing per-barrel prices paid to host governments as a way to improve their deteriorating finances. In February 1959, after consulting one another (but not their hosts), the companies unilaterally reduced the posted prices of crude oil used to calculate operating company tax obligations to host countries. Despite the outcry that followed, the companies lowered posted prices again in August 1960. In September, Iran, Iraq, Kuwait, Saudi Arabia, and Venezuela formed the ORGANIZATION OF PETROLEUM EXPORTING COUNTRIES (OPEC).

Through OPEC, the major oil exporters had the same opportunities to coordinate their oil policies that the major companies had long enjoyed. They used the companies' refusal to engage in joint negotiations with an OPEC representative to ratchet oil prices up in successive negotiations, each taking the best terms then available to any OPEC member as its floor for the next round, a pattern called leapfrogging. Following a failed Arab OIL EMBARGO imposed after the Arab–Israel War (1967), OPEC members became more militant in their efforts to improve their positions vis-à-vis the oil companies. In 1970, the Libyan government used its superior structural position to induce leapfrogging among its own concessionaires, enforcing production cuts on the most vulnerable to induce them to agree to oil price increases.

In 1971, OPEC moved to implement participation, a concept originating with Saudi Arabia's oil minister, Ahmad Zaki YAMANI, that would permit OPEC governments to nationalize their oil industries in gradual steps. Most of those that reached participation agreements with their operating companies in the early 1970s later accelerated the timetable to achieve full nationalization within a short time. However, the process itself provided an opportunity for every member of OPEC to develop a strategic plan to guide its assumption of control of its oil industry.

Although the parent companies of oil firms operating in OPEC countries and their home governments predicted that OPEC members would be unable to operate their own petroleum industries, most managed very well, some with the assistance of former concession owners. Following the example of the majors and largest independents, OPEC governments also acquired or expanded facilities to complement their production capacity. A few, such as Kuwait, Saudi Arabia, Libya, and Venezuela, also acquired overseas operations, re-creating to varying degrees the multinational vertical integration that had underpinned the old oil regime.

Ownership of downstream operations enabled OPEC members to guarantee a minimum level of production and sales through their own refining and marketing networks, thus also helping to stabilize oil profits because of the inverse relationship between movements in prices of crude and products—when one falls, the other generally rises. However, despite the transfer of control over the oil industries of Middle Eastern countries from multinational oil companies to national governments, the impact of market structure on the autonomy of oil producers did not change. The connection between OPEC and higher oil prices, coupled with perceptions of political instability in the Middle East, sent oil investors to other countries, eventually increasing the amount of production capacity outside the region. OPEC's Middle Eastern members became marginal suppliers to the

world market once again. This eroded OPEC cohesion and led the endemic overproduction, which in turn diminished the incomes of all owners of production properties, inside and outside of OPEC. Meanwhile, the acute economic and political dependence of Middle East nations on a wasting asset threatens the security of populations and regimes throughout the region.

BIBLIOGRAPHY

AHRARI, MOHAMMED E. *OPEC: The Failing Giant.* Lexington, Mass., 1986.

SAMPSON, ANTHONY. *The Seven Sisters: The Great Oil Companies and the World They Shaped.* New York, 1975.

SKEET, IAN. *OPEC: Twenty-five Years of Prices and Politics.* Cambridge, U.K., 1988.

TÉTREAULT, MARY ANN. *The Kuwait Petroleum Corporation and the Economics of the New World Order.* Westport, Conn., 1995.

Mary Ann Tétreault

Petroleum Reserves and Production

An industry based on the distillation of crude oil for the creation of fuel in local and world markets.

In 1993, the Middle East produced 36 percent of all the oil produced worldwide (21.6 million barrels/day out of a total of 59.6 mb/d), and held 67 percent of the total world proven crude oil reserves of 1,029 billion barrels. At this rate of production, the Middle East will exhaust its oil reserves by 2030 unless significant new reserves are found. The inflow of cash to the region from oil and related products can be estimated at $110 billion.

Within the Middle East, five countries (Iran, Iraq, Saudi Arabia, Kuwait, and the United Arab Emirates [U.A.E.] control 93 percent of all reserves and 73 percent of production. Should Iraq be in a position to resume its pre-war production, this group of five countries would produce 77 percent of the regional production and 29 percent of the world's demand. At present, the United States imports approximately 23 percent of its oil from the Middle East.

Production and Pricing. The cost of oil production in the Gulf is the lowest in the world. Marginal increases in production cost between $0.5/b and $2.0/b. The lower end of this range is most common in Saudi Arabia, the higher in the U.A.E. with higher costs of offshore drilling. (For comparison, incremental costs are $12 to $15/b in the North Sea fields, $3 to $5/b in Mexico, and $18/b to $20/b in U.S. offshore wells.)

TABLE 1

Crude Oil in the Middle East, 1993

Country	Production (barrel/day)	Reserves (in millions of barrels)	Value of Petroleum Exports (Million US $)	Years of Production
Algeria	751,400	9,200	7,980	33.54
Egypt	880,000	4,200	—	13.08
Iran	3,600,800	92,900	14,241	70.68
Iraq	481,200	100,000	364	569.35
Kuwait	2,000,000	96,500	9,986	132.19
Oman	860,000	4,300	—	13.7
Libya	1,400,000	22,800	7,607	44.62
Qatar	420,000	2,600	2,594	16.96
Saudi Arabia	8,000,000	261,200	41,353	89.45
Syria	610,000	1,700	—	7.64
United Arab Emirates	2,200,000	98,100	13,546	122.17
Yemen	380,000	—	—	—
Total	21,583,400	693,500	—	—

Sources: 1993 OPEC Annual Report, MEES, and Arab Finance and Banking.

Most of the oil produced in the Middle East is sold via long-term contracts between national oil companies and direct users, such as Exxon, Mobil, Total, and AGIP. The oil producers also sell to large trading companies, such as Mark Rich in Switzerland or Phibro in the United States, which in turn resell to ultimate users. The contracts between the users and producers generally specify that prices be set (often quarterly) by the producer based on a standard benchmark, such as prices of Brent or Dubai light, and adapted conditions such as distance, sweetness (level of sulfur), and gravity. Some producers also sell contracts to deliver oil through the main oil exchanges, primarily London and New York, but the exchanges are mostly used by the traders. Although the volume of oil traded on the exchanges represent only a small percentage of the total oil sold worldwide, the market price is indicative of world supply and demand and is the main source of information used by major producers in setting their prices. Likewise, the markets influence the price guidelines set by the ORGANIZATION OF PETROLEUM EXPORTING COUNTRIES (OPEC).

The most common benchmarks used in long-term contracts for shipments to the Far East are Dubai Light and Brent (North Sea) for shipments to Europe, and West Texas Intermediate (WTI) grade for shipments to the United States. Prices of a given crude are modified by adding or subtracting a certain amount per barrel reflecting the grade, the distance to the market served, and timing of the purchase relative to the benchmark quote.

When a producer is ready to effect a shipment under a given contract, it contacts the user, who in turn arranges to have a tanker of the right size ready at the point of sale for loading within forty-eight hours. Shippers and users, who have quite precise expectations on when to expect loading orders, often have tankers waiting nearby the loading facilities. In the case of Gulf shipments, tankers wait near Khor Fakkan on the Gulf of Oman.

API Gravity and Pricing. Crude oil are graded according to gravity, measured by the American Petroleum Institute degree of gravity (API)—the higher the number, the lighter the grade. Heavier grades require more energy to refine than the lighter grades, and are used to produce heavier and cheaper products. The region produces a large range of crudes from the Saudi newly developed ultra-light crude at API 50.4 to the Syrian Souediah Heavy at API 24. Standard light crudes in the Gulf have an average API of 34; Algerian crude is very light at API 44.

Many refineries are unable to use a wide range of API crudes. When refineries are overstocked with light crude, the discount on heavy crudes may decline and sometimes turn into a premium. In general, crudes of different API degrees from the same point of sale will be priced differently. For crude shipped out of Ra's Tanura in 1991, the average discount on

TABLE 2

FOB (Free on Board) Crude Oil Prices for Major Grades, 1991*

Type of Oil	Origin	API Grade	Average Price from Northwest Europe	Average Price from U.S. Gulf	Average Price from Singapore
Arab Light	Saudi Arabia	34	19.8	19.42	19.33
Arab Heavy	Saudi Arabia	27	17.68	17.12	16.69
Iran Light	Iran	34	19.35	—	19.39
Minban	U.A.E	39	20.92	—	21.58
Kirkuk	Iraq	36	20.46	—	—
Kuwait	Kuwait	31	17.89	—	17.99
Sahara Blend	Algeria	44	22.01	23.06	—
Zueitina	Libya	41	22.43	—	—
Oman	Oman	34	20.33	—	—

* In dollars per barrel.

Source: International Crude Oil Prices, Major Time Series from the 1860s to 1991. Middle East Petroleum & Economic Publications.

heavier grades amounted to 10.7 percent for an API difference of 7 degrees.

Prices, relative to the benchmark oils, are modified according to the sweetness of the relative crudes, the less sulfur the sweeter. In the Middle East, the light Gulf crudes tend to be relatively sweet, while the Syrian crudes are very sour. Sweet crudes are preferred by refiners because they are cheaper to process and less corrosive on equipment. Gulf countries now have large supplies of sulfur, which is either exported or used to make sulfuric acid, a major product in the chemical industry.

Pricing, Distance, and Timing of Sale. The distance and cost of transport between the point of sale and the place of delivery is reflected in prices. At similar API grade, Arabian Light 34 has sold on an average of seven years (1988 to 1994) at a discount of about $1.73 from North Sea Brent for shipments to Europe. Arabian Light 34 for the same period sold at a discount of $3.01 from WTI for shipments to the United States. (This last difference also reflects a difference in lightness in favor of WTI.)

Within the Gulf, prices also are adjusted for distance. In 1991, similar grade oil shipped to Europe, Oman Light 34 (shipped from Oman) sold at a premium of 2.7 percent over the Saudi Light 34 shipped from Ra's Tanura approximately 900 kms north, and at a premium of 5.1 percent over Iranian Light 34 shipped from Kharg island, 1,100 kms north.

Changes in market conditions between shipment announcement and loading is included in the com-

putation of price. For example, Saudi Light 34 was adjusted by $1.90/b on shipment to Europe ordered in December 1993 but effected only in January 1994.

Numerous other factors also affect the prices and the above-mentioned adjustments. The availability of tankers at any one time influences the cost of shipping; supply and demand for ships is arranged by numerous ship brokers worldwide. Price terms are quoted in reference to an index of total daily costs

TABLE 3

Main Middle Eastern Suppliers of Crude Oil to the United States, 1990–1994*

Imports from	1994	1993	1992	1991	1990
Saudi Arabia	1,299	1,268	1,587	1,660	1,179
Kuwait	307	342	39	4	79
Iraq	0	0	0	0	511
Algeria	21	22	24	44	66
Total	1,627	1,632	1,650	1,708	1,835
Total U.S. Imports	7,050	6,662	5,972	5,712	5,935
Percentage from the Middle East	23%	24%	28%	30%	31%

* In thousands of barrels per day.

Source: MEES.

called the "Worldscale." Insurance rates also influence prices. At times of turmoil in the Gulf, insurance rates rose significantly and forced the producers to absorb most of the increase to entice buyers to continue lifting crude from within the Gulf. During the Iran-Iraq war, Iran started a shuttle service to transport the crude from Kharg island, near the Iraq border, to Busheir island near the Strait of Hormuz, thus limiting the insurance cost to its buyers.

Purchases of Saudi and most other crudes in the region by the oil companies and major traders are usually done using 30-day sight letters of credits, confirmed by a local bank. However, the original ARAMCO partners are not required to issue such letters of credits and instead buy on open-book basis from ARAMCO. Upon loading of oil, the shipmaster signs the bill of lading. The seller then presents the bill of lading, the insurance documents, and a signed draft to the local bank for payment. Payment is then effected by the local bank within 30 days of the date of the bill of lading.

Pipelines. Pipelines allow producers to bring oil closer to the main users and thereby cut the cost of transport. The main pipelines in the regions have been laid to facilitate access to the European markets. Pipelines from the Gulf fields to the Mediterranean, which provide the most efficient transport, are subject to political problems. The tapline opened in 1975 from Saudi Arabia to Lebanon was closed by Syria; the Iraq–Syria pipeline was closed by Syria in 1982. The pipelines from Iraq to Turkey and from Iraq to Saudi Arabia were closed in 1990 due to the United Nations oil embargo on Iraq.

The major pipeline presently used in the Gulf is the East West Arabian pipeline (Petroline), which is 1,200 kilometers long and has a capacity of 4.8 million b/d. The other major pipeline is the Sumed pipeline in Egypt, which allows oil shipments to bypass the Suez Canal and has a capacity of 2.4 million b/d. Algeria exports gas by pipeline through Tunisia to Italy and the rest of Europe, and is building a gas pipeline through Morocco to Spain.

BIBLIOGRAPHY

HARTHSHORN, J. E. *Oil Trade: Politics and Prospects.* Cambridge, U.K., 1993.
Middle East Economic Survey. Nicosia, Cyprus.
MIDDLE EAST PETROLEUM & ECONOMIC PUBLICATIONS. *International Crude Oil Prices, Major Time Series from the 1860s to 1991.* Nicosia, Cyprus, 1993.
STAUFFER, THOMAS R. *Indicators of Crude-Oil Production Costs: The Gulf versus Non-OPEC Sources.* Occasional Paper #19. Boulder, Colo., 1993.

Jean-François Seznec

PETROMIN

Catalyst for the Saudi acquisition of ARAMCO.

The General Petroleum and Mineral Organization (PETROMIN) was established by Saudi Arabia in 1962. In 1963, PETROMIN began marketing petroleum products in the kingdom. By 1980 PETROMIN was marketing all the oil produced in the kingdom that was not lifted by the ARAMCO (ARABIAN AMERICAN OIL COMPANY) partners, about 20 percent of total production. Under its president, Dr. Abdal Hadi Taher, a U.S.-trained petroleum engineer, PETROMIN developed as a fully integrated oil company. It established a vast number of subsidiaries in refining, transport, and distribution. By the mid-1970s, PETROMIN was able to show the American owners of ARAMCO that the Saudi government, in the long run, could potentially control their oil operations independently from ARAMCO. It is not known if PETROMIN was actually an important factor in the negotiations for the friendly acquisition of the U.S. oil companies' interest in ARAMCO. However, after ARAMCO was turned over to the Saudis, the role of PETROMIN started to decline. In 1994, PETROMIN and its successor company SAMAREC were merged into ARAMCO.

Jean-François Seznec

Peyrouton, Marcel

French colonial administrator.

As resident general in Tunis in 1934, Peyrouton imprisoned Habib Bourguiba and the leaders of the neo-Destour party. As resident general in Morocco in 1936, his hostility to the demands of Moroccan nationalism led to his unpopularity and recall. He represented the Vichy government as governor-general in Algiers (1943) and was presented with the "Manifesto of the Algerian Muslim People" authored by Ferhat Abbas. Peyrouton was replaced by General Georges Catroux before he could formulate a response.

BIBLIOGRAPHY

ASHFORD, DOUGLAS. *Political Change in Morocco.* Princeton, N.J., 1961.
BRACE, RICHARD. *Ordeal in Algeria.* New York, 1960.

Zachary Karabell

PFLP

See Popular Front for the Liberation of Palestine

Phalange

Political party in Lebanon.

The Phalange (Kata'ib) party was founded in 1936 as a Maronite (Christian) paramilitary youth organization by Pierre JUMAYYIL (who modeled it on the fascist organizations he had observed while in Berlin as an Olympic athlete). It was authoritarian and centralized in organization, and its leader was all-powerful. It became a major political force in Mount Lebanon. After allying itself with the French mandate authorities, the Phalange later—just before independence—sided with those calling for independence; as a result, the party was dissolved in 1942 by the French high commissioner (it was restored after the French left Lebanon). Despite this dispute, over the years the Phalange has been closely associated with France in particular and the West in general. For many years, the party newspaper, *al-*AMAL, was printed in Arabic and French.

Consistent with its authoritarian beginnings, Phalangist ideology has been on the right of the political spectrum. Although it has embraced the need to modernize, it has always favored the preservation of the status quo. The Phalange party motto is "God, the Fatherland, and the Family," and its doctrine emphasizes a free economy and private initiative. It focuses on the primacy of preserving the Lebanese nation, but with a "Phoenician" identity distinct from its Arab, Islamic neighbors. Party policies have been uniformly anticommunist and anti-Palestinian, with no place for pan-Arab ideals.

The 1958 Lebanese Civil War and the intensification of sectarian conflict benefited the party; its membership increased from 300 in 1936 to 40,000 in 1958. The power of the party was reflected in parliament; from 1959 through 1968, 61 percent of its candidates were elected. In the 1972 parliament, the Phalange had seven deputies, including Pierre Jumayyil and his son Amin Jumayyil. By the start of the Lebanese Civil War in 1975, the party's membership had increased to 65,000, including a militia of nearly 10,000.

Throughout the civil war, the Phalange party was the most formidable Christian force, and its militia bore the brunt of the fighting on the Christian side. Because the party was part of the LEBANESE FRONT, the mostly Christian, right-wing coalition, the power of the Jumayyil family increased considerably. Ironically, as Pierre Jumayyil's son was consolidating his power through the integration of all right-wing militias into his Lebanese Forces, the role of the Phalange party diminished. Bashir Jumayyil, a member of the party, marginalized its traditional leadership, which he felt was too moderate.

During the 1980s, the Phalange lost much of its credibility and political stature. In 1982, under military pressure from Israel, which occupied a good deal of Lebanon, Bashir Jumayyil was elected president. He was assassinated before assuming office, and his brother Amin took his place. The corrupt and partisan rule of Amin further harmed the image of the party, and the death of Pierre Jumayyil in 1984 inaugurated a struggle for power within the party that has not ended. George Sa'ada, elected president of the party in 1987, tried to rejuvenate the organization, but the changing political sentiment in the country in favor of Syria did not help his cause. The party boycotted the 1992 election and remains factionalized, many of its prominent members having left.

As'ad AbuKhalil

Phanariot

The name given to the wealthy Greeks who lived in the Phanari district, the Greek section of Constantinople (now Istanbul) beginning in the sixteenth century.

From the fall of Constantinople in 1453 through the nineteenth century, the Phanariots were generally considered the aristocratic class of Greek society. They were well educated and, through their commercial and financial activities, maintained ties to Europe. The Ottoman Porte sought to exploit the skills of the Phanariots and their loyal support of the status quo by appointing a number of them interpreters, dragomans of the fleet, and (from the seventeenth century onward) regents of the Danubian principalities Moldavia and Walachia. Phanariot Greeks thus represented the Porte in major diplomatic agreements, as did, for example, Alexander Mavrocordatos with the signing of the Treaty of Karlowitz between Turkey and the Hapsburg Empire. The Greek Revolution of 1821 and the subsequent establishment of the modern Greek state weakened the position of the Phanariots considerably. Phanariots served as the Porte's diplomatic representatives through the late nineteenth century, but no more Phanariot dragomans of the fleet were appointed, and the line of Greek regencies in the Danubian principalities ended.

Alexander Kitroeff

Pharaon, Rashad [1912–]

Diplomat and physician in Saudi Arabia.

Pharaon, born in Syria, is a member of the faculty of Medicine at the University of Damascus. His most noteworthy accomplishments occurred while in the service of the Kingdom of Saudi Arabia. He was private physician to King Khalid ibn Abd al-Aziz Al Sa'ud (1936–1945). As a diplomat, he was ambassador to France and Spain (1960–1966); during the same period he was also minister of health in Saudi Arabia. He was Saudi Arabia's senior delegate to the United Nations (1963–1964) and also was a special adviser to King Faisal.

BIBLIOGRAPHY

Who's Who in the Arab World. Beirut, 1994.

Les Ordeman

Pharaonicism

An intellectual outlook found particularly in early twentieth-century Egypt.

Intellectuals of a Pharaonicist orientation assumed the existence of a unique Egyptian national character shared by ancient and modern Egypt; their writings attempted to demonstrate the ancient Pharaonic origins of many of the characteristics and traits of contemporary Egyptians. Expounded particularly by those Egyptians who were educated in Europe or who were Westernized intellectuals, Pharaonicism faded as Arab-Muslim nationalist sentiment grew in Egypt.

James Jankowski

Philae

Ancient Egyptian temple complex.

The island of Philae, in the Nile river south of the Aswan Dam, is now totally submerged. It was the site of numerous ancient temples, most of them built by the Ptolemies—fifteen kings of Egypt, 323–30 B.C.E.—and by the Romans in the first three centuries C.E. When the Aswan Dam project threatened to submerge the island permanently, an operation to save the temples was mounted by the United Nations Educational, Scientific, and Cultural Organization (UNESCO) between 1972 and 1980. The temples were cut into sections and then reassembled on the neighboring island of Agilka.

BIBLIOGRAPHY

Baedeker's Egypt. New York, 1987.

David Waldner

Philby, Harry St. John Bridger   [1885–1960]

The leading European explorer of Saudi Arabia.

Philby was born in Ceylon to a family of the Raj (British administration in India) and educated at Cambridge. He joined the Indian Civil Service after graduation in 1908, but when his temperament stalled his career, he transferred in 1915 to the Indian Expeditionary Force in Mesopotamia (now Iraq). Again he ran afoul of his superiors, who sent him off to central Arabia in 1917 to negotiate with an unreliable ally. In the course of this mission, which had only limited success, Philby discovered his life's passion—exploration of Arabia—and a patron, the unreliable ally himself, Abd al-Aziz ibn Abd al-Rahman, known in the West as Ibn Sa'ud, then ruler of Najd and, subsequently, founder of Saudi Arabia.

Although Philby eventually tied his fortunes to Ibn Sa'ud, immediately after World War I he was posted to Iraq and Transjordan (now Jordan) where he irritated superiors with his hostility to the Hashimites, the Hijazi family to whom the British entrusted the rule of these states newly carved from the Ottoman Empire. Since the Hashimites were rivals of the Saudis, they became his enemies too. In 1925, he finally quit colonial administration to become a merchant in Jidda. However, it was not until after his conversion to Islam in 1930 that his fortunes began to improve. In 1932, his long-planned voyage through Rub al-Khali (the Empty Quarter), a feat that had long eluded Europeans, finally gained Ibn Sa'ud's approval. To Philby's immense chagrin, a rival Briton, Bertram Thomas, had just preceded him, but Philby did complete a more ambitious course and his explorations of the peninsula continued throughout his life. These constitute the most enduring of his achievements, for he was a meticulous observer of the land, its flora and fauna, and archeological remains. His precise observations drew the map of Arabia.

In 1933, Philby helped negotiate the agreement that opened Saudi Arabia to American oil exploration, the first stage in the creation of the Arabian American Oil Company (ARAMCO). He had other business successes, including the Ford Motor Company concession.

His political instincts were less fortunate. Through much of his life, he waged a constant campaign against what he considered the stupidity and immorality of the policies of the British government. When World War II broke out and Philby's harangues included praise for Hitler and disparagement of the British war effort, the Foreign Office concluded that he was a dangerous crackpot. In 1940, during a stopover in India on his way from Arabia to the United States, he was arrested, shipped to England, and imprisoned for nearly a year. After the war, he was able to return to Arabia, but the death of Ibn Sa'ud in 1953 and Philby's criticism of his successors brought him banishment to Beirut in 1955. He resettled in Riyadh only after abandoning politics.

The charge that Philby was a secret agent is unfounded. However, he enjoyed the company of Western diplomats to whom he provided much gossip. And his son, Kim Philby, was a high-ranking official in British counterintelligence before being exposed as a Soviet mole.

BIBLIOGRAPHY

MONROE, ELIZABETH. *Philby of Arabia.* London, 1973.

Benjamin Braude

Philby, Kim   [1911–1988]

British reporter and intelligence officer.

"Kim" (Harold) Philby achieved notoriety when, as head of British counterintelligence, he defected to the Soviet Union in 1963. He was the son of Harry St. John Philby, whose friendship with Saudi Arabia's King Ibn Sa'ud provided the funds to support Kim's studies at Cambridge. Kim worked for MI-6 during World War II and was later the Beirut columnist for *The Observer* and *The Economist*.

BIBLIOGRAPHY

Chambers Biographical Dictionary. 1990.
YERGIN, DANIEL. *The Prize.* New York, 1991.

Zachary Karabell

Philistines

Biblical name for the people of Aegean origin who settled in the area between modern Gaza and Tel Aviv during the late Bronze Age.

The Philistines became the major foes of the ancient Israelites. The name Palestine is derived from the word *Philistine.* After the Jewish revolt against Rome in the second century (132–135), the Roman Emperor Hadrian expunged the name Judea (*Provincia Judea*) and officially designated the entire region as Provincia Syria Palaestina, or Palaestina, in order to suppress Jewish nationalist aspirations.

BIBLIOGRAPHY

DIO CASSIUS COCCEIANUS. *Dio's Roman History.* Loeb Classical Library. Cambridge, Mass., 1980–1990.

Reeva S. Simon

Phoenicianism

A Lebanese nationalist ideology.

Phoenicianism is based on the idea that Lebanon is unique in the Middle East for its location, people, and mission, and therefore should not be bound in any arrangement to neighboring countries, which are seen as inferior. The ideology of Phoenicianism flourished early in the twentieth century, when decentralization parties proliferated in the Arab region of the Ottoman Empire. Many Christians were dedicated Arab nationalists, although some Lebanese Christians believed that their nation should not be associated with the Arab region.

Phoenicianism is based on the belief that the Lebanese political entity is, contrary to historical realities, not the product of the twentieth century. Lebanese nationalists—a term that has come to describe the views of the right-wing Maronite (Christian) establishment and its allies in other sects—believe that Lebanon, both as a political entity and as a people, has been in continuous existence since Phoenician times. The Phoenicians are seen as ancient Lebanese, and Phoenician achievements are exaggerated to the point that the Greek and Roman civilizations are perceived as inferior to the "Lebanese Phoenician civilization." Lebanese nationalists argue that the Phoenician identity defines the Lebanese political identity. Other identities, such as those based on Islam or Arabism, are regarded as alien to the Lebanese historical experience.

The dispute over Phoenicianism is at the root of the Lebanese political problem. There is no consensus on the identity of Lebanon. Although the Maronite establishment has insisted that the Lebanese identity should be defined in purely historical terms (i.e., Phoenician), Lebanese Muslims and others who support their views argue that the Lebanese identity has been shaped by the Islamic Arab legacy. Arab nationalists dismiss the Phoenician claims and compare then to Zionist claims over Palestine. The political arrangement of Lebanon since 1943 has failed to settle this thorny political issue. The National Pact of 1943, for example, tried to please both sides by declaring that Lebanon has "an Arab face," leaving the determination of the identity of the "body" unspecified. For advocates of Phoenicianism, the only linkage between Lebanon and the Arab world rests in Lebanon's membership in the League of Arab States.

Phoenicianism has developed from an ideology into a full-fledged myth. Nobody has contributed to the nourishment of the myth more than Lebanese poet and ultranationalist Sa'id Aql, who traces most of the great discoveries of civilization to the Phoenician people. Even the discovery of America is attributed by Aql—among others in Lebanon—to

Phoenician travelers who preceded Columbus. The great Greek thinkers are called Phoenicians. The school curricula in Lebanon reinforce the myths about the Phoenician people among all who accept a version of history promulgated by ideologues who have dominated the Ministry of Education since independence.

As'ad AbuKhalil

Phosphates

Export of these compounds is vital to the economies of Israel, Jordan, and Morocco.

Phosphate reserves can be found in a large number of countries; Israel, Jordan, and Morocco are the main Middle East producers. These countries are situated on the Mediterranean, marine sediment, phosphorus belt that runs from Jordan to Morocco.

Israel mines phosphoric rock at Oron in the Negev desert and in the Arava north of Eilat. Approximately 2.4 million tons (2.2 million t) were mined in 1991, compared with a recent peak of 3.1 million tons (2.8 million t) in 1989.

Jordan is the fifth largest producer in the world, after the United States, countries in the former USSR, Morocco, and China. In 1989, it mined 7.3 million tons (6.6 million t) of phosphate rock. Phosphates accounted for 25 percent of Jordan's exports in 1987. It has an estimated 2.2 billion tons (2.0 billion t) of reserves.

Jordan's main deposit until 1985 was at Rusaifa, north of Amman, but this was closed because of a lack of international demand for low-grade phosphates. Mines currently in use are at Wadi Hasa, south of Amman; at Wadi al-Abyad; and at Shidiya, near Ma'an in the south of the country. This is by far the most important mine, with proved reserves of 1.3 billion tons (1.2 billion t). It is estimated that 7.7 million tons (7 million t) will be mined at Shidiya in the year 2000 and that this will be Jordan's only mine. In 1982, a phosphate fertilizer plant costing 400 million U.S. dollars was opened at Aqaba on the Red Sea coast.

Morocco is the world's largest phosphate exporter, accounting for one-third of international phosphate trade. In 1988, it produced about 27.5 million tons (25 million t) and exported 15.8 million tons (14.3 million t). Production capacity is 42 million tons (38 million t). Morocco has about two-thirds of estimated world reserves. Its proven reserves equal 11.7 billion tons (10.6 billion t) and probably reserves come to 63 billion tons (57.2 billion t). The main reserves are at Khouribga, Youssoufia, Ben Gueir, Bou Craa, and Sidi Hajjaj.

High phosphate prices in the early 1980s resulted in falling demand and a consequent fall in prices. This prompted Morocco as well as other producers to invest in downstream derivatives. By 1987, exports of derivatives exceeded those of phosphate rock.

Paul Rivlin

Piastre

See Qirsh

PICA

See Rothschild, Edmond de

Pieds Noirs

See Colons

Pilaf

A seasoned rice preparation.

Pilaf is a Persian and Turkish word denoting a rice dish boiled with meat and vegetables, seasoned with spices. But pilaf also means a way of cooking rice—knowing exactly the water-absorption capacity of the rice. In Turkish cuisine, pilaf is usually a side dish. In Persian cuisine, pilaf (*pilow*) is a main dish with other ingredients added to it. Pilaf is also made with bulgur in Turkey.

Clifford A. Wright

Pinsker, Leo [1821–1891]

Early Zionist leader.

Born in Russia, Pinsker was active in the Odessa branch of the Society for the Promotion of Enlightenment, which advocated assimilation as the solution to the problem of European Jewry. Following the pogroms of 1881, Pinsker changed his view and began calling for the resettlement of Jews in a country where they would constitute a majority and attain political independence. He proposed the establishment of a national fund based on contributions for the settlement of immigrants with financial needs. He expressed hope that those who oppressed the Jews might aid in their resettlement. He did not advocate any particular location for the Jewish center but suggested the convening of a congress to make such a decision. Pinsker published his ideas in German, in a pamphlet entitled *Autoemancipation: A Warning of a Russian Jew to his Brethren* (1882). The pamphlet made a profound impression on the Hovive Tziyon movement, which adopted it as its manifesto. In 1884, he was made chair of the Central Committee of Hovive Tziyon, serving as its head until 1889.

BIBLIOGRAPHY

HERTZBERG, ARTHUR. *The Zionist Idea*. New York, 1979.

Martin Malin

Pirate Coast

See Trucial Coast

Plague

Epidemic disease spread by fleas that infest rats.

Plague is caused by the bacillus *Pasteurella pestis*. Bubonic plague, which affects the lymph nodes, is most commonly identified with major epidemics since the fourteenth century; it can decrease infected populations by as much as one-third. Numerous outbreaks were recorded in the Middle East in the nineteenth century. The most severe bubonic plague epidemic in the twentieth century was in Egypt, some 520 miles south of Cairo, in 1912. Some 237 deaths out of a total of 357 cases were recorded.

Pneumonic plague, which affects the lungs, occurs more commonly during the winter; it is highly infectious, with a mortality rate of almost 100 percent. It is spread through the air from person to person. Septicemic plague, which affects the bloodstream, is the rarest form. It is 100 percent fatal, because death occurs within a few hours of infection.

Jenab Tutunji

Plevna, Battle of

Russian–Ottoman battle in Bulgaria.

During the 1877–1878 RUSSO-OTTOMAN WAR in the Balkans, the Russians advanced to the Bulgarian fortress of Plevna in July of 1877. Encountering unexpected resistence from the Ottoman commander, Osman Paşa, the Russians did not capture the fortress until December 11. The fierce resistance of the Ottomans at Plevna made a deep impression on European public opinion, leading to a settlement that favored the Ottoman Empire more than the one proposed by the 1878 Treaty of SAN STEFANO.

BIBLIOGRAPHY

ANDERSON, M. S. *The Eastern Question*. London, 1966.
SHAW, STANFORD, and EZEL KURAL SHAW. *History of the Ottoman Empire and Modern Turkey*. New York, 1977.

Zachary Karabell

PLO

See Palestine Liberation Organization

Plumer, Herbert Charles Onslow
[1857–1932]

British career officer who was High Commissioner for Palestine from 1925 to 1928.

Lord Plumer was born in Yorkshire, England, on March 13, 1857, and entered the British army in 1876. He served in the Sudan in 1884 and in South Africa during the Boer War (1899–1902), which led to his promotion to major general. He was a senior general on the European front during World War I and became a field marshal in 1919. Lord Plumer served as governor and commander in chief of Malta from 1919 to 1924, but he is best known for his three years as British high commissioner for Palestine from 1925 through 1928.

As a career officer in the British armed forces, Lord Plumer stressed the importance of maintaining security and stability in the volatile mandated territory. During his three years' rule, Jewish immigration stagnated, and therefore the Arabs became less fearful of eventual Jewish political domination. Lord Plumer, however, resisted requests by Palestinian Arab politicans to hold elections for a legislative council; he preferred to hold elections for municipal councils that would test the feasibility of self-government and provide combined representation for Arabs and Jews. The relative quiet of his years in office persuaded him that he could reduce the number of British troops in Palestine. In reality, tension was simmering below the surface, which led to major riots at the Western (Wailing) Wall in Jerusalem, August 1929.

BIBLIOGRAPHY

PORATH, YEHOSHUA. *The Emergency of the Palestinian-Arab National Movement, 1918–1929*. London, 1974.

Ann M. Lesch

Po'alei Agudat Yisrael

See Agudat Israel

Po'alei Zion

See Labor Zionism

Podgorny Mission

Soviet offer of aid to Iraq.

After the Arab defeat in the Arab–Israel War of June 1967, Soviet Premier Nikolai Podgorny visited Iraq. There he met with Iraq's President Abd al-Salam Arif and extended a comprehensive Soviet aid package, which included both military and economic assistance.

BIBLIOGRAPHY

LENCZOWSKI, GEORGE. *The Middle East in World Affairs,* 4th ed. Ithaca, N.Y., 1980.

Zachary Karabell

Po'el Ha-Mizrahi, ha-

See Mizrachi Movement

Pogrom

An armed riot by one ethnic, tribal, or religious group against another, incited by the government; usually accompanied by looting, mass property destruction, rape, and murder.

The term *pogrom* derives from the Russian *pogromit* (to destroy); Russia was the scene of the first modern pogroms, against its minority Jewish population, beginning in 1881. During the Russian Civil War (1918–1923), armed forces of all sides perpetrated atrocities against the Jews, though Lenin's government went on record as opposing anti-Semitic violence.

BIBLIOGRAPHY

LAQUEUR, WALTER. *A History of Zionism.* New York, 1972.

Jon Jucovy

Point Four

U.S. aid program to the Middle East under the Truman Doctrine.

The name refers to the fourth point made in U.S. President Harry Truman's 1949 inaugural speech, wherein he cited the need to support democracy and economic stability where small nations are threatened by outside (i.e., Soviet) influence.

Point Four led to unprecedented U.S. military and economic aid to the Middle East, allocated under various programs, expanding aid given to Turkey and Greece under the MARSHALL Plan since 1947. Of the $2.94 billion in military equipment sent to the region during the 1950s, Turkey received $1.87 billion, with Iran, Iraq, Jordan, Lebanon, Libya, Pakistan, and Saudi Arabia receiving lesser amounts. Aid also went to agricultural projects and to Palestinian refugees.

BIBLIOGRAPHY

BYRON, THOMAS A. *American Diplomatic Relations with the Middle East, 1784–1975.* Metuchen, N.J., 1977.

Elizabeth Thompson

POLISARIO

Acronym of Frente Popular para la Liberacion de Saguia el-Hamra y Rio de Oro, the movement struggling to establish the independent state of Western Sahara in Spain's former Spanish Sahara colony.

POLISARIO was founded on May 10, 1973, by a combined group of Moroccan students of Sahrawi background studying at Muhammad V University in Rabat, Morocco, a small number of veterans of anticolonialism during the late 1950s residing in Mauritania, and youth from within Spanish Sahara. The group evolved out of the earlier, more informal embryonic Movement for the Liberation of the Sahara. Its first head was the charismatic Mustapha Sayed al-Ouali. POLISARIO's founding manifesto spoke of the strategy of "revolutionary violence" and "armed struggle" against Spanish colonial rule, but it was not until the second congress, more than a year later, that independence was explicitly declared as POLISARIO's goal.

The notion of a "Sahrawi nation" was a new one, the combined product of the process of sedentarization among the formerly nomadic Saharan tribes, socioeconomic changes in Spanish Sahara, and new ideological currents linked to decolonization in Africa and the Third World. POLISARIO was a reflection of these changes, as it sought to transcend traditional tribal cleavages and fashion a supratribal Sahrawi national identity, although the majority of the POLISARIO leadership was Reguibat in origin, the largest of the Sahrawi tribal confederations.

Libya's Muammar al-Qaddafi was the first to provide support and until the early 1980s was an important supplier of arms. Algeria was hesitant at first, but by mid-1975 had become POLISARIO's main benefactor in its struggle against Morocco and Mauritania, and POLISARIO was rendered almost completely dependent on Algiers for all its needs. The Spanish departure in early 1976 and the entrance of Moroccan and Mauritanian troops inaugurated the WESTERN SAHARA WAR. One immediate outcome was a large-scale exodus (estimates range from one-third to two-thirds) of the Sahrawi population of what is now Western Sahara to the Algerian side of the border, around Tindouf. POLISARIO was granted a great degree of autonomy to run the refugee camps, which served as POLISARIO's military, political, and social base. Estimates of the number of men in POLISARIO's military wing, the Sahrawi Popular Liberation Army, also vary: between ten thousand and fifteen thousand during the early 1980s, and eight thousand to nine thousand in 1991. Politically, the POLISARIO leadership established a formal government-in-exile, SADR, which stands for the SAHARAN ARAB DEMOCRATIC REPUBLIC.

Al-Ouali was killed in June 1976 while returning from a daring attack of POLISARIO units on Mauritania's capital, Nouakchott. His replacement, Muhammad Abd al-Aziz, was chosen at the third POLISARIO congress, and was still head of POLISARIO and president of SADR in 1994.

Morocco's gradual attainment of military superiority and consolidation of control over Western Sahara during the 1980s and Algeria's increasing disengagement and decreased aid since 1988 neutralized much of POLISARIO's diplomatic gain (recognition of SADR by more than 70 countries and full membership in the Organization for African Unity, OAU). Some internal strains became evident in the late 1980s among the leadership and in the camps, perhaps marking a reassertion of tribal cleavages.

The UN effort between 1986 and 1992 to organize a referendum to determine the territory's status was POLISARIO's best hope, but also risky. Its winner-take-all formula stipulated that defeat would necessitate POLISARIO's disbandment. As of 1994, Morocco's superiority on the ground and the UN Security Council's preoccupation with other issues has placed the referendum process in limbo and POLISARIO on the brink of marginalization.

BIBLIOGRAPHY

DAMIS, JOHN. *Conflict in Northwest Africa: The Western Sahara Dispute.* Palo Alto, Calif., 1983.
HODGES, TONY. *Historical Dictionary of Western Sahara.* Metuchen, N.J., 1982.
————. *Western Sahara: The Roots of a Desert War.* Westport, Conn., 1983.

Bruce Maddy-Weitzman

Politi, Elie   [1895–?]

Jewish Egyptian journalist, publisher, and banker.

Politi was born in Cairo to a family of modest income. He obtained a rudimentary French education but was largely self-educated and turned to journalism during the 1920s. He founded and directed the daily *L'Informateur Financier Commercial* in the late 1920s and helped establish *al-Misri* in Cairo as one of the most acclaimed daily newspapers in the Middle East during the 1940s and 1950s.

From 1914, Politi was one of the leading businessmen and land developers in Egypt. He helped develop the new city of Muqattam, on the eastern hills overlooking Cairo, as well as the beach and urban area of the Ma'amura, east of Alexandria. Politi also directed and managed the Commercial Bank of Egypt, transforming it into a major and respected financial institution.

BIBLIOGRAPHY

MIZRAHI, MAURICE. *L'Egypte et ses Juifs.* Lausanne, 1977.
————. "The Role of the Jews in Economic Development." In *The Jews of Egypt: A Mediterranean Society in Modern Times,* ed. by Shimon Shamir. London, 1987.

Michael M. Laskier

Political Violence

Violent actions with a political goal.

The twentieth-century Middle East is a region that has been characterized by violence. It would be wrong to assume that it is uniquely violent, however, either in comparison to other Third World regions or to previous historical periods in the West. Intrastate and international political violence has been as prevalent in other parts of the Third World as it has been in the Middle East. No intrastate political upheaval in the twentieth-century Middle East has been as bloody as the European religious wars of the seventeenth century, the U.S. Civil War, or the Russian Revolution and ensuing consolidation of Soviet power. No international conflict in the twentieth-century Middle East has taken as many lives as either of the great European world wars of the same period. The Middle East region has no monopoly on violence, regardless of recent popular misconceptions in the West.

Nevertheless, it is also true that the level of violence in the Middle East is higher now than it has been at almost any time in history. It is useful to consider why this is so from three conceptual levels (specific acts of violence may have connections to any or all three levels): 1) the intrastate level—violence within existing state boundaries; 2) the regional level—violence between the states of the Middle East; and 3) the international level—violence between extraregional actors (like the great powers) and regional actors. At each level, factors specific to the Middle East interact with general political processes characteristic of state building and international relations and contributory to political violence in the region.

Much of the violence in the Middle East is within the confines of the existing states. The second half of the twentieth century has seen three full-fledged Middle Eastern civil wars (North Yemen, Jordan, and Lebanon), a violent anticolonial war (Algeria), one successful revolution (Iran), numerous insurrections suppressed by force, and countless military coups. Intrastate violence is related in part to the general process of state building. The assertion of central authority by the state over its society and economy has been, historically and worldwide, a very violent process. New states face challenges to their authority from geographically, economically, and ideologically based groups that are accustomed to autonomy if not independence from central control. The great majority of Middle Eastern states are in two respects still new.

First, the Middle Eastern states have recently emerged from direct or indirect European colonial control. Building bureaucracies and armies, the sinews of the modern state, helped create new social groups that contended with the old elites for power. The frequency of coups and attempted coups in the Arab world from the 1940s to the 1970s stems, in part, from the tensions created by state formation. The extension of central control into previously autonomous social realms, such as land ownership, industry, trade, and the religious establishment, has called forth opposition to the growing power of these new states. Islamic opposition movements throughout the region can be understood as responses to increasing intervention into all facets of society by secular nationalist governments. The lack of institutionalized avenues for popular participation in the politics of most Middle Eastern states has encouraged and continues to encourage opposition to be expressed in violent and illegal ways.

The second aspect of the newness of Middle Eastern states is that, with few exceptions (Morocco, Egypt, Iran), they have very short histories within their current boundaries. Most were drawn by the League of Nations for colonial powers—Britain and France—for their own strategic and economic convenience. As a result, governments face challenges both from ethnic and religious groups seeking autonomy, if not independence, at a subnational level and from supranational ideological movements that assert the illegitimacy of the current states and advocate much larger, unified political entities. Examples of subnational challenges to state authority include the following: the KURDS of Iraq, Turkey, and Iran; the various religious sects within Lebanon; PALESTINIANS resisting state authority in Israel, the occupied territories, Lebanon, and Jordan; and Shi'a (Islamic) majorities ruled by Sunni (Islamic) minorities in Iraq and Bahrain. Two salient types of supranational challenge to state authority include ARAB NATIONALISM and the revolutionary ideology of Islam. During the 1950s and 1960s Egyptian president Gamal Abdel Nasser used Arab nationalist appeals to mobilize domestic opposition to governments in Syria, Iraq, Lebanon, Jordan, Yemen, and Saudi Arabia. During the 1980s, the revolutionary and fundamentalist Islamic regime in Iran encouraged Islamic opposition groups in Iraq, Saudi Arabia, Kuwait, Bahrain, and Lebanon to rebel against their governments.

It is important to note that at the domestic level the state itself is the major and most successful perpetrator of violence. Only rarely, such as in the 1979 IRANIAN REVOLUTION, do opponents of state authority succeed in changing the political order. Coups, in effect, are attacks by one part of the state apparatus (the military or some faction of it) against another (the executive). Serious challenges to the state have been violently suppressed in many Middle Eastern countries: the Jordanian Civil War of 1970/71; the uprisings in Hama, Syria, in 1982; the Dhufar rebellion in Oman of 1967–1975; the POLISARIO opposition to Morocco in the former Western Sahara from 1976–1991; the Palestinian uprising (the INTIFADA) in the occupied territories in 1987–1992; various Kurdish uprisings in Iran, Iraq, and Turkey; the Shi'a uprising in Iraq in 1991. Ruthless and efficient internal security forces in most Middle Eastern states regularly use intimidation and violence against those whose loyalty is questioned.

On the regional level, the Middle East has witnessed a number of armed conflicts between and among its states during the second half of the twentieth century: six Arab–Israel Wars (1948/49, 1956, 1967, 1969–70, 1973, and 1982), the Iran–Iraq War (1980–1988), the Iraqi invasion of Kuwait (1990/91), and numerous border skirmishes. Hardly a border has not at some time seen confrontational military preparations. Moreover, Middle Eastern states have regularly interfered in the domestic affairs of their neighbors, increasing tensions and occasionally leading to direct armed conflict.

To some extent, the prevalence of regional conflict in the Middle East is built into the regional political structure. Numerous states with vastly different levels of military capability are contending for security and for power. None of them has the potential to dominate and impose order on the entire area. Rivalry is inherent in such situations.

Strong supranational challenges to the Middle East state system also contribute to the prevalence of regional conflict. By asserting that the states of the region are illegitimate colonial impositions, pan-Arabism and pan-Islamism provide rationales for armed interventions against neighbors and illicit involvement in their domestic politics. For example, both Iraq and Iran expected their "natural" allies in the other country (ethnic Arabs in southern Iran and Iraqi Shi'a Muslims, respectively) to support their military moves across the border, which encouraged Baghdad to attack southern Iran in 1980 and Tehran to carry the war into Iraqi territory in 1982. Iraq asserted both nationalist and religious justifications for its annexation of Kuwait in 1990. The strength of these ideologies permits leaders to develop constituencies in other states, which on occasion have invited their ally's troops into their territory. Syrian groups requested unity with Egypt in 1958. North Yemeni revolutionaries called for Egyptian troops to be sent to their country in 1962. Jordanian and Iranian troops helped the Omani government to put down the Dhufar rebellion in 1975. Various Lebanese groups supported both Syrian and Israeli interventions in their country. Palestinian organizations requested Syrian intervention in the Jordanian Civil War of 1970. Saudi Arabia requested Egyptian, Syrian, and Moroccan troops to be sent to help defend the kingdom and eventually retake Kuwait in 1990/91.

The ARAB–ISRAEL CONFLICT is another unique element in Middle Eastern regional conflict. Two peoples make nationalist claims to the same small area of land, making compromise extremely difficult, and encourage efforts to impose military solutions. Pan-Arab and Islamic sympathies with the Palestinian cause make it impossible for other regional powers to stand aloof from the conflict; the Palestinian cause is genuinely popular in the rest of the Arab and Islamic world. Even Egypt, the one Arab state that has formally recognized Israel and signed a peace treaty with it, continues to support Palestinian demands for self-determination as expressed by the Palestine Liberation Organization.

At the international level, extraregional (particularly European) powers have a long history of mili-tary intervention and the maintenance of military bases in the Middle East. While most formal basing rights have been withdrawn since the 1950s, many great powers maintain strong military relationships with local states, including the supply of sophisticated weaponry, the stationing of military advisers, and access to local military facilities. The end of colonialism in the region has not brought an end to outside military intervention. Since World War II, Soviet troops occupied Iranian Azerbaijan (1946) and Afghanistan (1979–1988), British and French troops attacked Egypt (1956), American and British troops were sent to bolster shaky governments in Lebanon and Jordan (1958), American and French troops became involved in the Lebanese Civil War (1982/83); Western naval forces, led by the United States, protected shipping in the Persian/Arabian Gulf (1987–88); U.S. military aircraft bombed Libya (1986); and a massive international force (United Nations coalition) organized by the United States drove Iraqi forces out of Kuwait (1990/91).

The involvement of outside powers in the Middle East is, in part, the result of great-power strategic rivalries. For example, during the Cold War both the United States and the Soviet Union sought to maximize their influence in the region. This was part of a global political and economic conflict that similarly affected other Third World regions; however, the Middle East is also intrinsically important to outside powers. The strategic location of the Middle East, connecting Europe, Asia, and Africa, has made it a military prize for centuries. The oil reserves of the region are today (and have been since World War I) of enormous importance to outside powers. The largest recent U.S. military intervention was aimed, not against the Soviets, but against a Middle Eastern state seeking dominance of the oil-rich Persian/Arabian Gulf region.

Terrorism as a genre of political violence cuts across these three levels of analysis. A terrorist act might have a domestic (intrastate) political goal, be supported by a regional power, and be targeted at the symbols or citizens of other states with whom they are in conflict. The term *terrorism* has become an epithet of fear that is also used to discredit one's enemies; it thus lacks definitional clarity. The labeling of the same act as an effort to overthrow repressive regimes, as a national liberation struggle, or as terrorism usually has more to do with political sympathies than with analytical standards. Although states perpetrate the great majority of violence in the region, both inside and outside borders, state violence is rarely called state terrorism. As a term, *terrorism* has usually been reserved for nonstate opponents of existing states, who rely on spectacular and unexpected attacks to gain publicity, encouraging an atmosphere of fear aimed at delegitimizing their opponents. It has also been applied to Middle Eastern states that support such nonstate groups.

The salience of terrorism in popular and official conceptions of the Middle East is the result of a number of factors. The intentionally public nature of terrorist acts, like hijacking or hostage taking, attracts media attention. The drama inherent in such acts makes them riveting journalism, guaranteeing coverage. That victims of terrorism are frequently innocent civilians causes public outrage and demands for government responses. The high profile of recent Middle East terrorism obscures the fact that it has thus far been ineffective in achieving the stated goals of its perpetrators.

BIBLIOGRAPHY

BEN-DOR, GABRIEL. *State and Conflict in the Middle East.* New York, 1983.

BILL, JAMES A., and ROBERT SPRINGBORG. *Politics in the Middle East,* 3rd ed. Glenview, Ill., 1990.

BROWN, L. CARL. *International Politics and the Middle East.* Princeton, N.J., 1984.

KERR, MALCOLM. *The Arab Cold War,* 3rd ed. New York, 1971.

LENCZOWSKI, GEORGE. *The Middle East in World Affairs,* 4th ed. Ithaca, N.Y., 1980.

RAMAZANI, R. K. *Revolutionary Iran: Challenge and Response in the Middle East.* Baltimore, 1988.

F. Gregory Gause, III

Politics

See Military and Politics

Polo

Team sport played on horseback.

In polo, players wielding long-handled mallets ride up and down a field, seeking to drive a ball between two goal posts (a set at each end of the field). The game originated in central Asia, then spread to India. In the Middle East, it was introduced by the British and played by members of the upper classes who could afford to keep or ride specially trained ponies at exclusive sports clubs. As a result, polo never developed mass appeal and is played mainly on a recreational basis.

Jenab Tutunji

Polygamy

Marriage in which a spouse of either sex may have more than one mate at a time.

Polygamy for men (polygyny) is sanctioned in Islam by direct reference in the Qur'an and is practiced to some extent in all countries with Muslim populations except where prohibited by law. Muslim men may have as many as four wives at a time but are admonished to treat all equally. The SHARI'A warns against the likelihood that the wives in a polygamous marriage can, in fact, be treated equally. Therefore, monogamy is the preferred condition.

Polygamy is statistically minimal in Middle Eastern countries that uphold the *Shari'a* in family law. This is partly due to legislation that makes polygamy difficult to enter into or to maintain. Economic considerations also make polygamy virtually impossible, since there must be a separate household for each wife. Consequently, those who practice polygamy are often relatively wealthy or influential. Community and political leaders are more likely to practice polygamy as a sign of respect and as a matter of prestige.

In bedouin and tribal cultures, tribal leaders practice polygamy both to enhance their own prestige and to form or strengthen alliances with other tribes.

Jenab Tutunji

Ponsot, Henri

French high commissioner in Lebanon.

Ponsot was appointed French high commisioner in Lebanon in August 1926, as successor to de Jouvenel. At the time of his appointment, he was a professional diplomat who had served as deputy director of the African and Levant Section at the Quai d'Orsay. He served in Beirut until 1933.

As'ad AbuKhalil

Popular Front

The 1930s French government that was supportive of Arab nationalism.

The Popular Front government came to power in France in June 1936, under the premiership of the socialist Léon Blum, author of the Blum-Viollette Plan. Tension between the French government and Arab nationalism was alleviated by the new government's vision of its commitment in the Middle East, particularly of the French mandate over the Levant. Stalled independence negotiations with nationalists of Syria were rejuvenated, and a Franco-Syrian treaty was signed in September 1936, in which France maintained some major supervisory powers. The treaty was never ratified by France, which by June 1937 had a new government with a more conservative colonial outlook.

BIBLIOGRAPHY

KHOURY, PHILIP S. *Syria and the French Mandate: The Politics of Arab Nationalism, 1920–1945.* Princeton, N.J., 1987.

Charles U. Zenzie

Popular Front for the Liberation of Oman

An offshoot of the Arab Nationalist Movement.

The Popular Front is supported by the South Yemeni National Liberation Front and related organizations: the Popular Front for the Liberation of Oman and the Arab Gulf, and the Popular Front for the Liberation of the Arab Gulf. The latter split off from the former and moved its operations to Bahrain in the 1970s.

Manfred W. Wenner

Popular Front for the Liberation of Palestine

Radical, left-wing Palestinian guerilla organization.

The Popular Front for the Liberation of Palestine (PFLP), after the Palestine National Liberation Movement (al-FATH) the most important constituent faction of the Palestine Liberation Organization (PLO), was formally established on December 11, 1967, as the result of a merger between the National Front for the Liberation of Palestine (NFLP) led by Dr. George HABASH and Dr. Wadi HADDAD; the Palestine Liberation Front (PLF) led by Ahmad JIBRIL; and the smaller Organization of the Heroes of the Return.

Historically, the PFLP emerged as the Palestinian branch of the pan-Arabist Movement of Arab Nationalists (MAN), which dissolved itself that same year. Habash, the PFLP's first and thus far only general secretary, had been the leading figure in MAN, and the NFLP had been established within MAN in 1964.

The PFLP has produced several offshoots. In October 1968, the former PLF reconstituted itself as a separate organization under the name of Popular Front for the Liberation of Palestine—General Command (PFLP-GC). In February 1969, a group of second-generation MAN activists led by politburo member Nayif HAWATMA seceded to form the (initially Popular) Democratic Front for the Liberation of Palestine ([P]DFLP) on account of the PFLP leadership's perceived "rightist" ideology and practices. In March 1972, a much smaller group left to form the Popular Revolutionary Front for the Liberation of Palestine, which disappeared soon thereafter. That same year PFLP politburo member Wadi Haddad, Habash's intimate associate since MAN days and the brain behind the PFLP's self-proclaimed campaign of international terrorism, left to form PFLP—External Operations (which persisted until his death in 1978) in protest of the PFLP's decision to terminate such actions at its 1972 National Congress.

The PFLP was explicitly founded as a revolutionary Marxist-Leninist guerilla organization to give the Palestinian national movement a radical social, political, and military character. It views the PLO as the framework for a united front of Palestinian organizations, and as such has endorsed critical alliances with al-Fath and other Palestinian factions as a means of strengthening Palestinian national unity. Where it has considered Fath to be deviating from the Palestinian national consensus or otherwise undermining the Palestinian struggle, however, it has not hesitated to suspend its membership in PLO institutions and establish parallel coalitions whose objective has been to change the policies of the PLO rather than replace the PLO itself. The most prominent examples in this regard are the Front of the Palestinian Forces Rejecting Surrenderist Solutions (the Rejection Front, 1974–1978) and the Palestine National Salvation Front (PNSF, 1985–1987). But most severely, it resigned its membership in all PLO bodies in protest of the September 13, 1993, Israeli–Palestinian Declaration of Principles on Interim Self-Government Arrangements (DOP) and has since pursued various alliances with the secular and Islamic opposition to dissolve this accord and evict its Palestinian signatories. While the PFLP's relations with Fath have been determined on the basis of concrete issues, they have also reflected the tensions between the PFLP's traditional role as the leader of the internal PLO opposition and its historical ambition to itself lead the PLO in accordance with its more militant agenda.

The PFLP's distinctive perspective was that it viewed Zionism, imperialism, and Arab reaction as the three organically linked foes of the Palestinian people. As such, it stressed the importance of revolutionary upheaval in the Arab world and beyond (which it actively sought to assist and exploit) to the struggle against Israel. Most prominently in this respect, the PFLP's declared intention of transforming the Jordanian capital Amman into an "Arab Hanoi," and in particular its hijacking of three civilian airliners to a Jordanian airfield in September 1970 and their subsequent destruction as a direct challenge to the authority of King Hussein, precipitated a violent confrontation between the PLO and the Hashimite monarchy, which led to the PLO's expulsion from Jordan. While the PFLP remains committed to its perspective, a combination of changed regional and international circumstances and the loss of its independent base of operations in first Jordan and then Lebanon (1982) have severely constrained its ability to translate theory into practice. Furthermore, its perspective has not prevented it from accepting the patronage of various Arab states, particularly Iraq during the mid-1970s and thereafter Libya and Syria, where it has been headquartered since 1982. But such alliances have been of a tactical rather than strategic nature, and its Palestinian credentials have survived intact.

Regarding the Israeli–Palestinian conflict, the PFLP has always been formally committed to the total liberation of Palestine through a popular war of liberation. To this end it fielded several thousand guerillas in Jordan and later Lebanon, and established numerous armed cells in the occupied Palestinian territories, where it led the armed campaign to oust Israel from the Gaza Strip between 1968 and 1972. It has also complemented its guerilla campaign with political mobilization, particularly in the occupied territories. Since 1981, it has been increasingly prepared to accept a political settlement negotiated by the PLO that guarantees the implementation of internationally recognized Palestinian national rights, although only as an interim solution. Its belief that the DOP surrenders rather than achieves these rights has led it to categorically reject this agreement as an act of high treason.

The PFLP is typically Marxist-Leninist in structure and internal discipline. Its basic unit is the cell, which are grouped into leagues governed by regional committees, and its main decision-making body the central committee, which elects a politburo, which appoints a general secretary. Its National Congress, which sets the organization's strategic framework, has met only five times (1967, 1969, 1972, 1981, and 1992). After Habash, its most important leaders are Deputy General Secretary Abu Ali Mustafa, politbureau member Abu Mahir al-Yamani, and the head of its military department, Abu Ahmad Fu'ad. Its influential spokesman, Ghassan KANAFANI, was assassinated by Israel's Mossad in Beirut in 1972.

Internal conflict has not been unknown and surfaced most prominently when its official spokesman,

Bassam Abu-Sharif, defected to Fath in 1986. More recently, a faction based inside the occupied Palestinian territories has emerged to argue that the PFLP must insert itself into the process created by the DOP despite its rejection of this agreement in order to remain credible.

The PFLP has played a major role in the development of the contemporary Palestinian nationalist movement and the debates that surrounded it and, at several critical moments, appeared poised to wrest control of the PLO from Fath. Although it still retains several thousand members, in recent years its position as the main rival to Fath has been effectively claimed by the Islamist Resistance Movement (HAMAS). With a program and ideology widely considered anachronistic, its main struggle today is to remain relevant, and it appears doubtful its ambition to serve as the ruling communist party in an independent Palestinian state will ever be fulfilled.

The PFLP has issued numerous publications, the most important of which is its official weekly *al-Hadaf* (the Target). It also publishes an English-language periodical entitled *Democratic Palestine* (previously *PFLP Bulletin*).

BIBLIOGRAPHY

ABUKHALIL, AS'AD. "Internal Contradictions in the PFLP: Decision Making and Policy Orientation." *Middle East Journal* 41 (1987): 361–378.

COBBAN, HELENA. *The Palestinian Liberation Organization: People, Power and Politics.* Cambridge, U.K., 1984.

KAZZIHA, WALID W. *Revolutionary Transformation in the Arab World: Habash and His Comrades from Nationalism to Marxism.* London, 1975.

MSEIS, NADIM. "The Ideology and Role of the Palestinian Left in the Resistance Movement." Ph.D. diss., Oxford University, 1991.

QUANDT, WILLIAM B., et al. *The Politics of Palestinian Nationalism.* Berkeley, Calif., 1973.

Mouin Rabbani

Popular Front for the Liberation of Palestine—General Command

Radical Palestinian group.

The Popular Front for the Liberation of Palestine—General Command (PFLP-GC) is a radical Palestinian guerilla organization that emphasizes military action to advance its rejectionist ideological agenda. Originating with a group of Palestinian refugees who served in the Syrian military during the 1950s, it was initially formed as the Palestine Liberation Front (PLF) in 1965, and under this name entered a brief merger with al-FATH that year before disbanding in

October 1967 to become one of the founding members of the POPULAR FRONT FOR THE LIBERATION OF PALESTINE (PFLP). In October 1968, however, differences with other PFLP elements led it to secede and reemerge as a PFLP splinter organization under the new name of PFLP-GC. According to the PFLP-GC, it left the PFLP on account of the latter's ostensible preoccupation with ideological debate and neglect of revolutionary warfare; other observers believe the split resulted from the inability of the former PLF leadership to dominate the PFLP. In either case, the PFLP-GC was admitted to the PALESTINE LIBERATION ORGANIZATION (PLO) in late 1969 and acquired a seat on the PLO Executive Committee in June 1974. Based first in Amman and then Beirut, its headquarters have since 1982 been located in Damascus.

In 1977, the PFLP-GC also underwent an internal split, when a faction led by Muhammad Abbas (nom de guerre Abu Abbas) and Tal'at Ya'qub seceded under the resurrected name of the Palestine Liberation Front, which later itself split into two factions. For some time during the late 1960s, moreover, another, unrelated PFLP splinter group, eventually known as the Organization of Arab Palestine (OAP) and led by Ahmad Za'rur, also used the name PFLP-GC, but was usually distinguished as PFLP-GC (B). During this period the PFLP-GC was therefore often known as PFLP-GC (A) and furthermore occasionally operated as the al-Aqsa Fida'iyin Front.

At several hundred members, the PFLP-GC is one of the smaller Palestinian organizations; its main recruiting grounds are the Palestinian refugee camps of Lebanon and Syria. It has since its PLF days been led by Ahmad JIBRIL, a former Palestinian officer in the Syrian army whose name has become synonymous with the organization and whose main deputy is Talal Naji. Its regular publications are *Ila al-Amam* (Forward), an Arabic weekly first issued in 1963, and *al-Jabha* (The Front), an internal bulletin that first appeared in 1969. It publishes occasional pamphlets as well.

Nominally Marxist-Leninist in ideology and structure, it is more accurate to describe the PFLP-GC as cultivating a stridently militant and rejectionist Palestinian nationalist image. In October 1974, it was a founding member of the Front of Palestinian Forces Rejecting Surrenderist Solutions (the REJECTION FRONT), which opposed a negotiated settlement of the Israeli–Palestinian conflict. The following year, it was one of the first Palestinian factions to become embroiled in the Lebanese Civil War. In 1983, it was one of only two PLO factions to actively join the Fath rebellion against PLO Chairman Yasir Arafat, and it has since, despite attempts at reconcilia-

tion, boycotted all PLO institutions. It was a founding member of the Syrian-sponsored anti-Arafat National Alliance in 1984, and in 1985 it joined the Palestinian National Salvation Front headquartered in Damascus. The PFLP-GC currently belongs to the Group of Ten, an association of Palestinian factions opposed to PLO strategy and/or Palestinian participation in the negotiations with Israel sponsored by the United States and Soviet Union (later Russia). The Group of Ten also reject the process inaugurated by the September 1993 Israeli–Palestinian Declaration of Principles.

Militarily, the PFLP-GC, which is regarded as competent, innovative, and indiscriminate, specializes in the use of small, highly trained units for high-profile operations. It is best known for its April 1974 suicide raid on an apartment building in the northern Israeli town of Qiryat Shmona in which eighteen Israeli civilians were killed, and for the November 1987 hang glider attack on an army camp in northeast Israel that left six soldiers dead (both attacks were launched from southern Lebanon). It is also presumed responsible for the February 1970 midair explosion of a Swiss airliner en route to Israel in which over forty-five people were killed.

More recently, the PFLP-GC's suspected involvement in the December 1988 midair explosion of an American airliner over the Scottish village of Lockerbie, resulting in the deaths of all passengers aboard and a number of villagers, has strengthened suspicions that the organization puts its services at the disposal of its patrons. Jibril is also believed to have ordered the 1978 bombing of a Beirut building housing PLO personnel, which resulted in over two hundred fatalities; if true, this constitutes the worst single act of internecine Palestinian violence. The purposes of its operations are to inflict maximum casualties on its enemies and undermine an Israeli–Palestinian settlement that deviates from its maximalist agenda. It has over the years also consistently participated in the more conventional military activities of the Palestinian movement, and its positions in Lebanon remain subject to regular Israeli attack.

The PFLP-GC has since its inception maintained extremely close links with Syria that have over the years progressively reduced its autonomy, and it has been the Palestinian organization most consistently supported by Libya, its main financier. More recently, it has been linked with Iran. Such alliances, particularly at times when these regimes have been in open conflict with the PLO, have severely undermined the PFLP-GC's credibility among Palestinians. (For example, in 1984 Jibril was expelled from the PLO for his collusion with Syria during Syria's 1983 confrontation with the PLO.) The PFLP-GC's presence in the West Bank and Gaza Strip is therefore negligible. At the same time, its 1985 prisoner exchange with Israel, under which hundreds of released Palestinians were permitted to remain in the West Bank and Gaza Strip rather than exiled, infused valuable (if primarily non-PFLP-GC) cadres into these territories, and its 1987 hang glider operation perceptibly emboldened the population of the occupied territories on the eve of the popular uprising, or Intifada. Its clandestine, Syrian-based radio station, Idha'at al-Quds (Radio Jerusalem), established to encourage the rebellious West Bank and Gaza Strip population, was despite its sectarian tone both popular and influential, with the result that the Israeli authorities repeatedly jammed it.

As a primarily military outfit that devotes few resources to political mobilization and is furthermore considered beholden to its sponsors, the PFLP-GC does not appear destined to play an important role in the Palestinian national movement. It is expected to face extreme difficulties in the event of a political settlement between Israel and Syria.

BIBLIOGRAPHY

COBBAN, HELENA. The Palestinian Liberation Organization: People, Power and Politics. Cambridge, U.K., 1984.
GRESH, ALAIN. The PLO—The Struggle Within: Towards an Independent Palestinian State, rev. ed. Tr. by A. M. Berrett. London, 1988.
QUANDT, WILLIAM B., et al. The Politics of Palestinian Nationalism. Berkeley, Calif., 1973.

Mouin Rabbani

Popular Front for the Liberation of the Occupied Arabian Gulf

Marxist, antigovernment organization of southern Oman (1968 to 1971); known as PFLOAG.

PFLOAG was organized in 1968 as the successor to the Dhufar Liberation Front, a largely tribal group attempting to overthrow the rule of Sa'id ibn Taymur Al Bu Sa'id's dynasty in Oman's southernmost province. PFLOAG not only aimed to enlarge the scope of the rebellion but gave it a radical, Marxist orientation and tried to impose a collectivist regime where its forces were in control. With financial support and weaponry from Iraq, the People's Republic of China, and the Soviet Union as well as a secure base in neighboring Marxist South Yemen (People's Democratic Republic of Yemen), the front took most of Dhufar from the shaky regime of Sultan Sa'id. The accession of his son, Qabus ibn Sa'id Al Bu Sa'id, by coup in July 1970, turned the situation

around, with the considerable foreign military assistance from Great Britain and Iran playing a key role. Well-funded civil action programs helped secure the loyalty of a population little drawn to PFLOAG's anti-Islamic ideology. In December 1971 it absorbed the NATIONAL DEMOCRATIC FRONT FOR THE LIBERATION OF OMAN AND THE ARAB GULF (NDFLOAG) and assumed its second identity as Popular Front for the Liberation of Oman and the Arab Gulf with acronym unchanged. In May 1974, after serious reverses, those favoring continued military action formed the POPULAR FRONT FOR THE LIBERATION OF OMAN (PFLO). By 1976 Dhufar was completely and securely in government hands.

BIBLIOGRAPHY

ALLEN, CALVIN H., JR. Oman: The Modernization of the Sultanate. Boulder, Colo., 1987.
PETERSON, J. E. Defending Arabia. New York, 1986.

Malcolm C. Peck

Popular Organization of Revolutionary Forces (PORF)

Elite military forces of the Front for the Liberation of South Yemen.

One of the many organizations competing for control of South Yemen in the mid-1960s, PORF was organized, trained, and controlled by Egypt, which attempted to use it as a counterweight to the National Front during the civil war.

Manfred W. Wenner

Population

Demographics are crucial to an understanding of social and political life in the Middle East.

Until the nineteenth century, the Middle East experienced a typical Malthusian demographic system: Normally, high fertility outpaced high mortality, but there was occasional extraordinary mortality from warfare, famine, or epidemic disease, particularly bubonic plague. The population grew slowly until one of these demographic crises occurred, dipped sharply, then began to grow slowly once again. This pattern ended in much of the Middle East in the nineteenth century. Despite minor outbreaks, truly catastrophic epidemics ended with the cholera epidemic of 1865. The increase in central government control facilitated security, trade, and delivery of food to famine regions. Egypt's numbers began to grow early in the

Residential crowding in a working-class neighborhood of Cairo. (D.W. Lockhard)

TABLE 2

Life Expectancy at Birth*

	1950	1990		1950	1990
Bahrain	51	72	N. Yemen	32	53
Egypt	42	62	Oman	36	68
Iran	46	67	Qatar	48	70
Iraq	44	66	Saudi Arabia	40	66
Israel	65	76	S. Yemen	33	53
Jordan	43	68	Syria	46	67
Kuwait	56	74	Turkey	44	66
Lebanon	56	67	U.A.E.	48	71

* "1950" is actually for the years 1950–1955, and "1990" is an estimate for the years 1990–1995.

Source: United Nations' *World Population Prospects, 1990.*

century, perhaps in the 1820s, as did numbers in Anatolia and the coastal provinces of Ottoman Syria in the 1870s. Iraq, Arabia, and Iran took little part in either the improvement in civil conditions or population growth.

The period of World War I and the wars in Anatolia that followed it was a demographic watershed in the Middle East, a period of great mortality and forced migration unequalled in the past millennium. After the war, the states of the Middle East began a new period of population growth, erasing the wartime population losses in the next decade. Turkey's population began to expand fairly rapidly, from 14.6 million in 1927 to 18 million in 1940. Egypt grew from 13 million inhabitants in 1917 to 16 million in

1937. Other countries grew less quickly, but population increased markedly all over the region. Nevertheless, the Middle East can be described as underpopulated before World War II. Large areas of potentially fertile lands were uncultivated. Population density was low, due to high mortality and lack of developed resources. By modern standards, mortality had declined only slowly. In late Ottoman times,

TABLE 1

Population of the Middle East, 1800 to 2025, in Millions*

1800	32.8	1925	54.7
1825	33.4	1950	79.2
1850	33.8	1975	154.3
1875	36.0	2000	304.2
1900	44.1	2025	491.0

* Including the areas of today's Bahrain, Egypt, Gaza, Iran, Iraq, Israel, Jordan, Kuwait, Lebanon, Oman, Qatar, Saudi Arabia, Syria, Turkey, United Arab Emirates, West Bank, and Yemen.

Source: Projections to 2000 and 2025 from the United Nations' *World Population Prospects, 1990.*

TABLE 3

Middle Eastern Censuses after World War II

Bahrain	1941, 1950, 1959, 1965, 1971, 1981
Egypt	1947, 1960, 1966, 1976, 1986
Iran	1956, 1966, 1976, 1986
Iraq	1947, 1957, 1965, 1977, 1987
Israel	1948, 1961, 1972, 1983
Jordan	1952, 1961, 1979
Kuwait	1957, 1961, 1965, 1970, 1975, 1980, 1985
Lebanon	(none)
N. Yemen	1975, 1986
Oman	1977, 1981
Qatar	1970, 1986
Saudi Arabia	1962/63, 1974
S. Yemen	1946, 1955, 1973, 1988
Syria	1947, 1960, 1970, 1981
Turkey	1927, 1935, 1940, 1945, 1950, 1955, 1960, 1965, 1970, 1975, 1980, 1985, 1990
U.A.E.	1968, 1971, 1975, 1980

mortality had averaged more than 3.5 percent per year. This condition only gradually improved between the two world wars. However, Egypt, Palestine, and Turkey managed to lower mortality through irrigation, public sanitation, and by ending conditions of civil unrest that had diminished the distribution of crops and goods. Medical improvement was a minor factor.

As in much of the world, after World War II the Middle Eastern population began to rise rapidly. Fertility, always high, remained so, while introduction of modern medicine greatly lowered mortality. Modern agricultural techniques and the new crops of the Green Revolution increased the ability of Middle Eastern economies to feed larger populations. The result was a population boom. From 1950 to 1990 the population of the Middle East increased

threefold. By the 1960s the rate of population increase meant that, if the high rates continued, future populations would double every twenty-five years. These rates of increase have put great strain on the economies of Middle Eastern nations. Results include rapid and unplanned urbanization and unemployment, as well as overuse of fertilizers and poor agricultural techniques that yield large crops temporarily but eventually exhaust the soil. Unless there is a rapid and unexpected decline in fertility, many Middle Eastern countries would seem to be threatened with eventual demographic disaster.

Fertility. The average fertility of Middle Eastern women changed little for centuries. Women who lived through their child-bearing years (many did not) could expect to have six to seven children (the

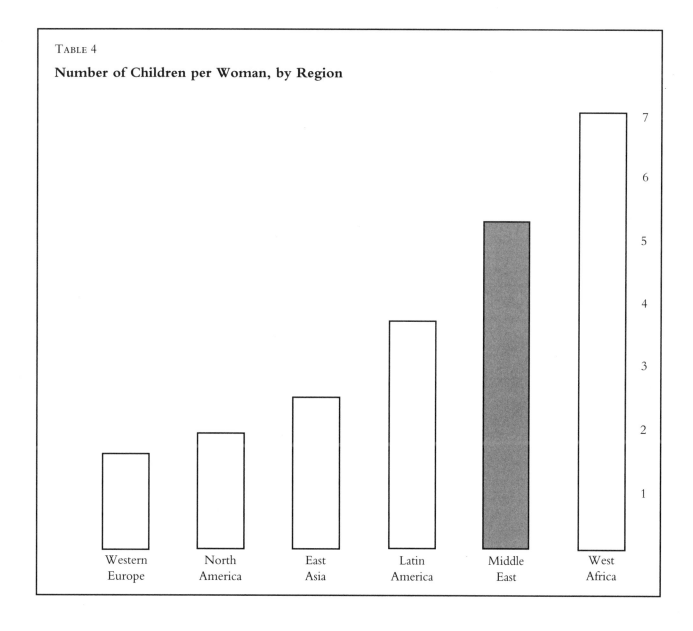

TABLE 4

Number of Children per Woman, by Region

TABLE 5

Population of the Middle East, 1800 to 2025

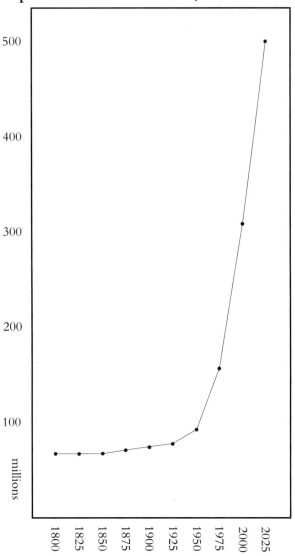

A history of high fertility has strained the carrying capacity of the Middle Eastern economies. Nearly one-half of the populations of countries such as Syria, Iraq, and Yemen are children under age fifteen. Even Middle Eastern countries with lower fertility, such as Turkey, have populations in which one-third are under fifteen. (Compare to 21 percent in the United States, 18–20 percent in Western Europe.)

If present fertility trends continue, future Middle Eastern populations will divide into two very different patterns. Israel is already nearing a European pattern of low fertility. Kuwait, Lebanon, Qatar, the Emirates, and Turkey are approaching that standard. Yemen, Syria, Iraq, Saudi Arabia, and others still retain high fertility. The populations of the latter countries will in fifty years look very different than the former, with very large numbers of children and a fast-growing population. For example, today Syria, Iraq, Jordan, and Saudi Arabia taken together have slightly less population than Turkey. If trends continue, in fifty years they will together have twice as many people as Turkey.

Mortality. In the absence of extraordinary causes, fertility would have always outstripped mortality in the traditional Middle East. The population would have risen at approximately 1 percent per year. In fact, epidemics, wars, and famines increased mortality to a rough equilibrium with fertility. The most common normal causes of death were gastroenteric diseases. Infant mortality was particularly high, with more than 40 percent of children dying before their first birthday, more than half before age five.

Epidemics of plague and cholera caused temporary high mortality. In Egypt, for example, cholera took more than 100,000 lives in each of the epidemics of 1855 and 1865 and almost 200,000 in 1831. Bubonic plague took 500,000 lives in 1835 alone.

Although often difficult to quantify, it is known that warfare also caused great mortality in the nineteenth century. The Ottoman wars with Russia were particularly deadly for both military and civilian populations. From the beginning of the Balkan Wars in 1912 to the end of fighting in the Turkish War of Independence in 1922, the region suffered some of the worst wartime mortality in history. The highest death rates were found in Eastern Anatolia—the result of war between the Ottomans and Russians and intercommunal conflict between Muslims and Armenians, in western Anatolia after the Greek invasion, and in Palestine. In Anatolia, 3.8 million died (22 percent), and in Palestine 50,000 (6 percent). In all those conflicts, starvation and disease took a higher toll than did actual battle. Lebanon also suffered mass starvation during the war.

Total Fertility Rate). Recently, however, fertility has begun to decrease in some countries. The average woman in Turkey today has 3.3 children, in Egypt 4, in Iran 4.7. However, in Syria, Jordan, and Saudi Arabia, the average remains very high, 6 or more per woman. Women in Yemen and Oman can expect 7 children on average. Contraceptive usage varies greatly, from more than 60 percent of Turkish women using some form of contraception at some time in their lives, to 27 percent in Jordan, to almost no use in many countries.

Despite recent reductions, the Middle East remains one of the world regions with the highest fertility. Only East, West, and Central Africa have higher fertility. All other regions of the world have lower.

After World War II, the rapid introduction of modern medicine, public sanitation techniques, and agricultural improvements greatly decreased mortality. The Middle East still had a high crude death rate (deaths divided by total population) of more than 2.3 percent a year in 1950, but a crude death rate of less than 0.8 percent a year by 1990. Some countries, such as Egypt (1.1 percent in 1990) and Yemen (1.6 percent in 1990) lagged behind. A major part of the postwar improvement came in infant mortality. In 1950, one in five Middle Eastern children died before age five; in 1990, only one in seventeen died before age five. (Compare to northern and western Europe, where one in 140 died before five.)

Migration. Refugee migrations have been a major demographic factor in the past two centuries. Only the most prominent population transfers can be mentioned here: In the nineteenth and early twentieth centuries, great population movements took place as direct results of Russian imperial expansion in the Crimea and Caucasus and of nationalistic movements among the Christian peoples of the Ottoman Empire. Russia expelled or caused the migration of approximately 1.2 million Circassian, Abhazian, and Laz Muslims from the lands of the Eastern Black Sea. Of these, 800,000 survived and most eventually settled in what today is Turkey, as did the 300,000 Crimean Tatars forced to emigrate in the 1850s and 1860s. A sizable group of the Circassians were settled in the Arab world. Russian expansion also fostered a century-long population exchange, with much attendant mortality, between the Turks and Kurds of Russian Transcaucasia and the Armenians of Ottoman Anatolia and Iran. Between the 1820s and 1920s, 500,000 Armenians and 400,000 Muslims (not including the Circassians and Abhazians) crossed the borders. During World War I, an estimated 1 million Muslims were internal refugees in Eastern Anatolia; an estimated 275,000 Armenians were deported to or were refugees in the Arab world, and 135,000 were refugees in Europe and the Americas.

Nearly 600,000 Turks (40 percent of the Turkish population) were surviving refugees from the new state of Bulgaria after the Russo–Turkish war of 1877/78. Greece, Bulgaria, Serbia, and Montenegro expelled to Anatolia and Eastern Thrace 414,000 Turks during and immediately after the Balkan Wars of 1912/13. In World War I, the Turkish War of Independence, and the Greek–Turkish population exchange that followed, more than 1 million Greeks from Anatolia and eastern Thrace went to Greece and 360,000 Turks from Greece to Turkey. Up to 1.5 million Turks were internal refugees within Anatolia and eastern Thrace during the Greek–Turkish war.

Before World War II a major immigration of primarily European Jews swelled the Jewish population of Palestine from 60,000 in 1918 to 600,000 in 1946. Nearly 700,000 Palestinian Arabs were refugees in the Arab–Israel War of 1948. Between 1948 and 1975, 1.6 million Jews came to Israel. Half of these were from the Middle East and North Africa, another third from Eastern Europe, especially the Balkans. Immigration to Israel has continued recently with Jews from Russia and successor states.

The only Middle Eastern country to be heavily affected by refugees from the Afghan War was Iran, which accepted more than 2 million Afghan refugees. Turkey took in 300,000 ethnic Turkish refugees from Bulgaria, as well as Iranian refugees after the Iranian revolution and Kurdish refugees after the Gulf War. Many of the refugees to Iran and Turkey have been repatriated or have moved to other countries. A significant number of the refugees from Afghanistan, Iraq, and Bulgaria have returned home at least once, only to leave once again when economic and political conditions changed.

The quest for employment has been a major cause of migration into and from the Middle East. In Ottoman times, 175,000 Turkish emigrants went to the United States from 1869 to 1914. More recently, the International Labor Organization estimated that 1.8 million Turks were working in Germany, the Netherlands, and Belgium in 1988. In the same year, 20,000 Koreans, 50,000 Indonesians, and 90,000 from the Philippines worked in the Gulf states. Before the Gulf War, up to 2 million foreign workers, mainly Egyptians, worked in Iraq.

Urbanization has been the most significant factor in internal migration in the modern Middle East. Driven by population pressure in rural areas, the urban population increased from 21 million (27 percent urban) in 1950 to 138 million (58 percent urban) in 1990. There is considerable variance between countries: in 1990, Syria's population was only half urban, Egypt's less than half urban, while the populations of Iraq and Turkey were over 60 percent urban. Istanbul was one of the twenty largest cities in the world. Smaller countries such as Israel and Lebanon were as urbanized as Europe or North America.

Censuses and Population Data. A census registers the entire population at one time. Prior to 1882 no real census was taken in the Middle East. In the place of censuses, the Ottoman and Egyptian governments made compilations of registration data. The registers were lists of inhabitants by household in each village, taken by government officials. These often produced surprisingly accurate counts of the population, especially in areas that were under close governmental control. On occasion, the central governments of Egypt and the Ottoman Empire ordered general updatings and compilations of the registers. In the 1860s the Ottoman government began to publish population numbers in the SALNAMES (yearbooks) of its provinces. The Ottoman compilations usually listed data by sex and religion only, even though age-specific figures were kept and are available in archives. The *1313 İstatistik-i Umumi* ("1895 General Statistics") was the only Ottoman publication to include data by age group. Population data was collected sporadically in Iran, but was not published officially.

The first real census in the Middle East was taken by the khedival government in Egypt just prior to the British occupation in 1882. Under British statistical influence, Egypt published censuses in 1897, 1907, 1917, 1927, and 1937. The British also undertook a limited form of census in Aden colony (later People's Democratic Republic of Yemen) in 1881, then published other counts of Aden, as part of the censuses of India, in 1891, 1901, 1911, 1921, and 1931. The Turkish republic began a modern census program with censuses in 1927 and 1935, followed by censuses every five years. The British mandate government in Palestine took fairly accurate and very detailed censuses in 1922 and 1931, and with limited success updated the census data through birth and death records and published the data in the *Palestine Blue Books*. The French collected data in Syria and Lebanon, but only published brief summaries that indicate poor recording. An incomplete census was taken in Lebanon in 1942/43.

Modern Middle Eastern censuses have routinely been supplemented by publications of detailed information on marriage, divorce, birth, and death, although these often have been accurate only for urban areas. Sample surveys of the population, often supported by the United Nations or other international bodies, have also been taken. These have yielded excellent data, particularly on fertility.

BIBLIOGRAPHY

Data on historical population are included in KEMAL KARPAT's *Ottoman Population, 1830–1914: Demographic and Social Characteristics* (Madison, Wis., 1985) and JUSTIN MCCARTHY's *The Arab World, Turkey, and the Balkans* (Boston, 1982). Data on modern population may be found in various publications of the United Nations, including the yearly *Demographic Yearbook* and the semiannual *Sex and Age Distribution of Population, World Population Prospects,* and *World Population Monitoring.* Bibliographies of primary and secondary materials include *Population Index* (available in machine-readable form) and "Demography" in the *Encyclopaedia of Islam,* 2nd edition.

Justin McCarthy

Populist Party

Turkish political party, 1983–1985.

The Populist party was one of only three political parties permitted to compete in the 1983 parliamentary elections, the first in the wake of the military coup of 1980. Led by the retired civil servant Necdet Calp, it was clearly intended (by the military junta) to fulfill the role of loyal opposition to the officially preferred NATIONALIST DEMOCRACY PARTY. In fact, it placed second in that election, polling some 30.5 percent of the vote and winning 117 of the 400 seats at stake. Popular support declined precipitously, however, leading the party to decide to merge with the more successful Social Democratic party in 1985.

BIBLIOGRAPHY

LANDAU, J. M. "Turkey." In *Political Parties in the Middle East and North Africa,* ed. by F. Tachau. Westport, Conn., 1994.

Frank Tachau

Port Sa'id

Egyptian city at the intersection of the Suez Canal and the Mediterranean.

Port Sa'id was founded in 1859. It was named after Sa'id Pasha, viceroy of Egypt from 1854 to 1863, who granted a concession to the French company organized by Ferdinand de Lesseps to build the Suez Canal, and was formerly the world's most important coaling station. During the Arab–Israel War of 1956, troops of Britain and France invaded Port Sa'id, transforming the city into a symbol of popular resistance to Western imperialism. During the War of Attrition, Port Sa'id was frequently shelled and bombed by Israeli forces, leading to mass evacuations of the city. Reconstruction of the city began in 1974. Its population was 382,000 in 1986.

BIBLIOGRAPHY

GOLDSCHMIDT, ARTHUR, JR. *Modern Egypt: The Formation of a Nation-State.* Boulder, Colo., 1988.

David Waldner

Portsmouth, Treaty of

See Anglo–Iraqi Treaties

Port Tawfiq

Egyptian port at the southern end of the Suez Canal.

Port Tawfiq is an island located at the head of the Gulf of Suez, near the city of Suez, Egypt. The island is composed of the soil that was accumulated when a channel two miles (3.2 km) long was cut to lead the Suez Canal into the deeper waters of the Gulf of Suez. The island is connected to the city of Suez by a stone causeway. On the southwest side of the island, the port installations of Port Ibrahim are located.

BIBLIOGRAPHY

Baedeker's Egypt. New York, 1987.

David Waldner

Positive Neutrality

Key element of the ideology behind Egypt's 1952 revolution.

Positive neutrality was one of the three key elements, along with socialism and Arab nationalism, of the eclectic ideology of Egypt's 1952 revolution from above. Nasser, leader of the military coup, embraced neutrality as a strategy for asserting Egypt's identity as a leading progressive Third World regime, thereby enhancing the country's international bargaining position.

Raymond William Baker

Positivism

Philosophical doctrine.

Positivist ideas began to gain acceptance in the Ottoman Empire during the Young Turk period of the early twentieth century. The term *positivism* was first used by the French Comte Henri de Saint-Simon to designate the scientific method and its extension to philosophy. Positivism states that science is the only valid source of knowledge and that the method used in philosophy is not different from the scientific method. Because it claims that observable facts are the only possible object of knowledge, positivism denies the intelligibility of metaphysics. Positivist philosophers seek these principles to use them in guiding human conduct and social organization.

BIBLIOGRAPHY

Encyclopedia of Philosophy. New York, 1967.
LEWIS, BERNARD. *The Emergence of Modern Turkey.* London, 1991.

David Waldner

Postage Stamps

Government-issued stamps encapsulate the history and culture of the region.

Although the early Islamic states of the Middle East had elaborate postal messenger systems, in 1840 England issued the world's first postage stamp—showing Queen Victoria. The Ottoman Empire put out its first stamp in 1863, Egypt in 1866, Persia in 1868, Afghanistan in 1871, the Hijaz (now in Saudi Arabia) in 1916, and Yemen in 1926. Elsewhere British, French, and Italian colonial officials in the Middle East designed the first stamps for their jurisdictions.

Early Middle Eastern stamps, like Islamic coins before them, rarely portrayed human figures—in keeping with a conservative interpretation of Islam. Arabesque designs, calligraphy, or a crescent and star served as symbols instead (Plate 1: 1). In 1876, Persia broke with tradition by showing its ruler on a stamp; the Ottomans did the same in 1913. Egypt, Iraq, and Transjordan followed in the 1920s; then Afghanistan, Syria, and Lebanon in the 1940s. Saudi Arabia, more isolated and conservative, waited until the 1960s.

Rulers were shown in traditional dress, in Western coat and tie, or in military uniform (Plate 1: 2, 3, 4). Turkey's Mustafa Kemal Atatürk, who secularized Turkey after the dissolution of the Ottoman Empire by, among other things, outlawing Muslim headwear, insisted on civilian dress on his stamps from 1926 on (as in Plate 1: 3), but many soldiers-turned-presidents preferred military uniforms. Since 1979, Iraq's President Saddam Hussein has appeared in coat and tie, army uniform, and Arab *kaffiyya*.

Some rulers promoted a cult of the leader on their stamps, with the hero towering above the masses he claimed to embody (Plate 1: 4). Syria's Hafiz al-Asad, Egypt's Anwar al-Sadat, and Iraq's Saddam Hussein saturated their stamps with various images. Egypt's President Gamal Abdel Nasser, surprisingly, did not—and Egypt's Husni Mubarak has followed his example, not Sadat's, in this regard.

The first stamps of the Ottoman Empire, Egypt, Persia, Afghanistan, Saudi Arabia, and Yemen bore

Plate 1: Postage stamps. (Donald Malcolm Reid)

only Arabic-script inscriptions (see Plate 1: 1). Although they were not French colonies, they soon added French, long the main language of world diplomacy (Plate 1: 7). All later switched to English as their second language on stamps—except Afghanistan, which kept French, and Turkey, whose adoption of the Latin alphabet made its Turkish-only stamps partly accessible to Westerners (Plate 1: 3). French colonial possessions used French, and British possessions English. French Algeria and Italian Libya used no Arabic on their stamps until independence, 1962 and 1951, respectively. Hebrew has been used as the main language on Israel's stamps since independence in 1948, with English and Arabic as secondary languages.

The European colonial stamps presented romantic and orientalist "colonial picturesque" themes—pre-Islamic ruins, old mosques, colorful landscapes, and folk scenes (Plate 1: 5, 6, 7). European officials first selected the pyramids and Sphinx as symbols for Egyptian stamps (Plate 1: 7); only later did Middle Easterners take up and revalue these and other symbols. Egypt often commemorates ancient pharaonic treasures on stamps; folk costumes are also shown as part of a proud national heritage. Even so, stamps with such themes are often issued with tourists and collectors in mind.

Revolutions drastically changed stamp designs. "The people"—symbolic soldiers, peasants, workers, professionals, and women in both traditional and Western dress—celebrate liberation, modernization, and the drive for economic development (Plate 1: 8, 9). Stamps advertise such things as petroleum pipelines, factories, and broadcasting stations (Plate 1: 10). Socialist countries commemorate land reform, the spread of health care, and five-year plans. In addition to such symbols of material and social progress, Israel also depicts themes from biblical history, Jewish history, and Zionism.

The stamps of Israel and the Arab states also reflect their respective versions of the Arab–Israeli conflict. Stamps commemorate the war dead, advertise the latest aircraft, and boast of specific victories. Most Arab countries have issued stamps deploring the Dayr Yasin massacre (as they describe the event), mourning the plight of Palestinian refugees, and celebrating Palestinian resistance to Israel. Since Israel's occupation of East Jerusalem in 1967, the Dome of the Rock (Haram al-Sharif) has often appeared on stamps as a symbol of Arab and Islamic claims to Jerusalem. The stamps of Arab countries that depict maps omit the name Israel, showing only the borders and sometimes the name of pre-1948 Palestine. Israel's stamp designers make it a practice to avoid showing national maps.

In the 1950s and 1960s, pan-Arab themes often overshadowed symbols of local territorial patriotism (Plate 1: 11). From the 1970s on, Islamic themes became popular—mosques, Qur'ans, hegira dates, and crescents—on stamps honoring the Prophet Muhammad's birthday, the Islamic New Year, and the Hajj. Islamic themes stand out above all on the stamps of the Islamic Republic of Iran since the 1979 revolution. They depict deceased Shi'a holy men, martyrs killed in the jihad (holy struggle) against Iraq, as well as anti-American symbols (Plate 1: 12).

BIBLIOGRAPHY

HAZARD, HARRY W. "Islamic Philately as an Ancillary Discipline." In *The World of Islam,* ed. by James Kritzeck and R. B. Winder. London, 1960.

REID, DONALD M. "The Symbolism of Postage Stamps: A Source for the Historian." *Journal of Contemporary History* 19 (1984): 223–249.

Scott 1993 Standard Postage Stamp Catalogue, 4 vols. Sidney, Ohio, 1992.

Donald Malcolm Reid

Potash Industry

With international assistance, Jordan developed this technologically sophisticated industry in the 1980s.

Potash, an important component of agricultural fertilizer, is extracted from the briny waters of the Dead Sea in extensive facilities on the lake's southeast shore. Because Jordan shares riparian rights to the Dead Sea with Israel, the two countries at a technical level coordinate their activities in the area.

Israel has been extracting potash from the Dead Sea since 1955. An earlier concession (during the British mandate of Palestine) exploited the Dead Sea's potash from 1930 until the facility was destroyed in the Arab–Israel War in 1948/49.

Peter Gubser

Potsdam Convention

Russo–German agreement concerning their involvement in the Middle East.

From its inception, the German-dominated BERLIN–BAGHDAD RAILWAY project aroused the suspicion of the other European powers. On August 6–9, 1911, Germany and Russia concluded an agreement at Potsdam, Germany, whereby Russia acquiesced to continued German involvement in the railway in return for a German affirmation of Russia's position in Persia (now Iran).

BIBLIOGRAPHY

ANDERSON, M. S. *The Eastern Question*. London, 1966.
HUREWITZ, J. C., ed. *The Middle East and North Africa in World Politics*. New Haven, Conn., 1975.

Zachary Karabell

PPS

See Parti Populaire Syrien

Progressive Republican Party

Turkish political party, 1924–1925.

Formed in November 1924, the Progressive Republican party involved no more than thirty members of parliament and established branches in only a handful of provinces. It was a thorn in the side of the government, however, for it was led by former military colleagues of Mustafa Kemal (Atatürk), specifically Ali Fuat Pasha CEBESOY and Kazım KARABEKIR. Also, it drew support from a variety of elements across the political spectrum who opposed and/or were threatened by the secularizing reforms and increasingly dictatorial tendencies of the Kemal regime. The party was dissolved by government decree after a few months because of alleged involvement in the Kurdish uprising of 1925. Its suppression inaugurated a lengthy period of one-party authoritarian rule.

BIBLIOGRAPHY

FREY, F. W. *The Turkish Political Elite*. Cambridge, Mass., 1965.

Frank Tachau

Progressive Socialist Party

Lebanese political party founded in Beirut in 1949 that played an important role in Lebanon after independence.

The Progressive Socialist party (PSP) can be considered a major vehicle for the political ambitions of its founder, Kamal JUMBLATT. Born in Mukhtara in 1917, Jumblatt belonged to one of the major Druze families in Lebanon.

The party is organized around its president, the management council, the general committee, dis-

tricts, and branches. Major policy decisions are undertaken by the president, who is the center of authority. Despite claims to the contrary, the PSP operates for the benefit of the Druze community.

The tenets of the party are made up of a mixture of social democratic practices and Hindu philosophy. Jumblatt believed that industrialization was inevitable but that it had to be reined in because of ecological concerns. The PSP has advocated the abolition of the political confessional system, the creation of civil courts for civil marriages, a unified educational system, the nationalization of important services, and a progressive inheritance taxation system. In foreign policy, the PSP has emphasized Lebanon's Arab identity and role, solidarity with the Palestinian cause, and support for major Third World issues and concerns. The PSP had a membership of around 10,000.

During the civil war (1975–1976), the PSP under Jumblatt became the linchpin for the LEBANESE NATIONAL MOVEMENT and fielded 2,000 fighters. Following the assassination of his father, Walid Jumblatt became the president of the PSP in 1977.

BIBLIOGRAPHY

SULEIMAN, MICHAEL W. *Political Parties in Lebanon*. Ithaca, N.Y., 1967.
ZHUBIAN, SAMI. *The Lebanese National Movement*. Beirut, 1977.

George E. Irani

Protectorate

Term in international law.

Protectorate has two meanings in international law. The first, and most prevalent in the Middle East, is the imposition of a colonial relationship by a stronger power upon a weaker power (e.g., France over Morocco). The other refers to a compromise over a piece of disputed territory.

Bryan Daves

Protectorate States

Traditional southern Arabian political entities protected by British treaty from 1839 to 1967 when they united to form South Yemen.

The dozen or so protectorate states to the north and east of the Aden colony occupied a huge area relative to that of the colony. They were viewed primarily as a political-military buffer for that highly valued port and military base. Over the 125 years of British occupation of Aden since 1839, the protectorates were defined and redefined geographically as well as administratively in a largely ad hoc way. Political-military pressure first from the Ottoman Turks and then from the imamate of North Yemen caused the British to become increasingly involved in the governance of the states in Aden's immediate environs during the first six decades of the twentieth century; local political turmoil in the decades after World War I drew the British more directly into the governance of the vast Hadramawt region far to the east of Aden. Out of these "independent," amorphous protectorates, eventually in combination with Aden itself, the British in the 1960s sought to build the South Arabia Federation, the ship of state they hoped would succeed them when they withdrew in 1967. They failed, but Aden and the protectorate states went on to comprise South Yemen, the People's Democratic Republic of Yemen (PDRY).

Robert D. Burrowes

Protestantism and Protestant Missions

Mission groups have gone to the Middle East to convert people to the various Protestant denominations since the nineteenth century.

Protestantism, one of the three major branches of Christianity, encompasses a large number of denominations with widely differing liturgical and theological structures. What they have in common is that they do not recognize the moral and doctrinal authority of the Roman pontiff, they stress the centrality of the Bible and each individual's interpretation of it, and they share the belief that in the matter of salvation, the relationship between the individual and God is unmediated.

Protestant missions have been active in most countries of the Middle East because of the worldwide missionary movement that emerged in Europe and the United States in the nineteenth century. Scores of missionary societies representing various Protestant denominations have sponsored missions to the region since that time.

In the United States, the most prominent sponsoring organizations were the American Board of Commissioners for Foreign Missions (ABCFM), supported by the Congregational Church, and the Board of Foreign Missions of the Presbyterian Church, which took over the activities of the ABCFM in 1870. The earliest permanent stations of the ABCFM were established in Lebanon in 1823, in Constantinople in 1831, and in Urmia (Iran) in 1834.

The Arabian Mission was founded as a nondenominational mission under the auspices of the Dutch Reformed Church in America in 1889, with its main stations located in Basra, Musqat, Bahrain, and Kuwait. In Great Britain, the leading missionary organization was the Church Missionary Society (CMS), which began work in Smyrna (Izmir) in 1815, in Egypt in 1825, in Julfa (Isfahan) in 1875, and in Damascus in 1860. Minor organizations included the short-lived Boston Female Society for Promoting Christianity amongst the Jews, founded in 1816, and the London Society for Promoting Christianity amongst the Jews.

The successful establishment of mission stations in the Middle East depended largely on British hegemony in the region. British shipping provided the means of securing essential supplies, mail, and transportation, and British consular protection was crucial in the face of opposition to the missionary enterprise from local religious leaders and Ottoman authorities. Missionary activity was encouraged in 1850 when the Ottoman sultan, under pressure from Stratford Canning, the British ambassador to the Sublime Porte, recognized a Protestant *millet* (legally recognized religious community), giving juridical status to Protestant converts.

The original purposes of the missionary movement were to evangelize the non-Christian world for Christ and to better humanity through benevolent action. Among Muslims, successful evangelism proved virtually impossible for theological, social, and political reasons, although the veneration of Jesus as a prophet of God was compatible with Islamic theology. However, deification of Christ in the Trinity contravened the essential Oneness of God in Islamic belief, conversion in religious communities meant separation from one's family and immediate society, the punishment for apostasy from Islam could have been death, and missionaries were forbidden under the Ottomans to preach among Muslims.

The attitude of missionaries toward the indigenous Christian communities determined the missionary agenda. In the opinion of the missionaries, the Nestorian, Armenian, Coptic, and Greek and Syrian Orthodox churches were bankrupt of Christian virtues and therefore could not set a positive example of true Christianity for their Muslim neighbors. If these so-called nominal Christian churches could be reformed from within, the missionaries thought, then they would serve as an inspiration and ultimately could become the instrument of evangelizing the Muslims, who were inaccessible to direct proselytism. It was, therefore, to the indigenous Christians of the Middle East that the Protestant missionaries turned their attention.

Missionary efforts were directed into three types of work—evangelical, medical, and educational. Evangelical work consisted of translating, printing, and distributing Christian literature, preaching, and systematic home visiting, especially by women missionaries. Medical work consisted of operating hospitals and clinics, often at great expense and under difficult physical conditions. Educational work was initially directed toward teaching at the primary and secondary level but eventually expanded to the college level.

Some combination of these efforts has been carried out in most of the major urban centers of the Middle East and in outlying areas, such as Bitlis, Kharput, Mardin, and Adana in eastern Turkey, and in Dohuk, Kirkuk, and the villages of Kurdistan. In Iran, the American Presbyterians set up stations in Tehran, Hamadan, and Tabriz, while the CMS worked in Isfahan, Kerman, Yazd, and Shiraz. Some idea of the extent of the missionary presence can be gauged by the size of the American mission to the Armenians in Turkey, which in 1895 held 14 main stations and 268 outstations, with a total of 152 missionaries and a staff of 800 Armenians.

Evangelical work often aroused the animosity of indigenous church leaders, so that reforming the churches from within became impossible. Instead, Protestant sympathizers gradually became converts, and numerous separate Protestant evangelical churches came into being. There were, for example, 111 Protestant churches in Turkey in 1895. In 1920, the first church in Iran formed entirely of converts was established in Mashhad; and in Egypt, by 1926 there were 150 congregations of evangelized Coptic Christians with 155 Egyptian clergy.

Most of the Protestant congregations in Lebanon and Syria are Presbyterian, while those in Jordan and mandate-era Palestine are Anglican. In Iraq, Egypt, and Turkey, there are both Anglicans and Presbyterians, as well as tiny congregations of other Protestant sects. In the mid-1970s, there were altogether about 250,000 indigenous Protestants in the Middle East. Since that time, however, the Christian population, including the Protestants, has drastically declined because of the Lebanese Civil War, the Iran–Iraq War, the Israeli occupation of the West Bank, the Intifada, and especially the Gulf War of 1991.

In measuring the success of the missionary enterprise from the viewpoint of evangelism, in no area were the missionaries ever successful in attracting significant numbers of Muslim or Jewish converts. By creating separate Protestant churches, the missionary movement only succeeded in creating more sectarianism in the already sectarian societies of the Middle East. At the same time, however, the schools affiliated with Protestant churches offered a type of education that was usually otherwise unavailable.

The missionary hospitals, like the schools, were exploited as opportunities for evangelism, but they provided to all the best medical care available at the time. Hospitals were set up by the Arabian Mission in Bahrain and Kuwait, by the CMS and American missions in Egypt, and by the Edinburgh Medical Mission in Damascus. The CMS also set up medical missions in Baghdad and Mosul, and by 1940, twelve missionary hospitals had been established in Iran.

The lasting achievement of Protestant missionaries lies in higher education, especially girls' education. The three premier universities in the Middle East were founded by missionaries: the American University of Beirut, established in 1864 as the Syrian Protestant College; Robert College in Constantinople (1863); and the American University of Cairo (1920). The Presbyterian Mission's American Junior College for Women in Beirut, the American College for Girls in Cairo, and Constantinople College for Girls were the first institutions of higher education for women in the Middle East. Around the Persian/Arabian Gulf and in many rural areas across the region, missionary schools were the only schools offering secular subjects for girls until well after World War I. The British Syrian Mission alone opened fifty-six schools for girls, starting in 1860.

By the end of World War I, missionary work in the Middle East began to decline along with Western enthusiasm for the missionary enterprise. In the 1930s and 1940s, governments of the newly independent states in the Middle East placed increasing limitations on missionary activities, so that many missionary societies consolidated their efforts or ceased operations. In 1991, the humanitarian and educational work of Protestant missions continues in Iran, Jordan, Lebanon, the occupied West Bank, Israel, and Turkey, under the umbrella of the United Church Board for World Ministries, and in the Gulf region, under the Arabian Mission.

BIBLIOGRAPHY

ADDISON, JAMES THAYER. *The Christian Approach to the Moslem: An Historical Study*. New York, 1942.
BETTS, ROBERT BRENTON. *Christians in the Arab East*. London, 1978.
GODDARD, BURTON L., ed. *The Encyclopedia of Modern Christian Missions*. Camden, N.J., 1967.
TIBAWI, A. L. *American Interests in Syria, 1800–1901*. Oxford, 1966.

Eleanor Abdella Doumato

Protocols of the Elders of Zion

Anti-Semitic forgery of a document purporting to detail a Jewish world conspiracy.

This anti-Semitic myth accuses the Jews of plotting an international government to control the press, finances, governments, and banks. In medieval times, it was suggested that Jews had a secret government in Muslim Spain.

The conspiracy myth of Jewish domination was employed by the extreme right in Germany to discredit the liberal revolution of 1848 and the emancipation of the Jews in 1871. It was embellished in Russia in the 1870s to include a fictive meeting of representatives of the twelve tribes of Israel with the devil. In 1903 the myth provided a pretext for the violent pogroms in Kishinev, Russia.

Various texts purporting to be minutes of the conspirators' meetings circulated in Europe. French and German anti-Jewish propaganda texts received official sponsorship in czarist circles. The Russian forgery that came to be known as the *Protocols,* consisting of lectures and notes for lectures expounding a plot to achieve world domination, appeared in the Saint Petersburg newspaper *Znamya* from 26 August to 7 September 1903. An edition of the *Protocols* by Sergei Nilus (1905) profoundly influenced Czar Nicholas II. This Russian text was a favorite propaganda piece of Adolf Hitler. In the United States, the *Protocols* gained a wide readership through Henry Ford's sponsorship of their publication. Although they were proven to be a forgery in 1934, the *Protocols* continue to elicit credence and support.

Arabic editions of the *Protocols* have been bestsellers in all parts of the Muslim world and are frequently cited as the cornerstone of Zionism at the highest levels of government.

BIBLIOGRAPHY

COHN, NORMAN. *Warrant for Genocide: The Myth of the Jewish World Conspiracy and the Protocols of the Elders of Zion.* New York, 1969.
YADLIN, RIVKA. *An Arrogant Oppressive Spirit: Anti-Zionism as Anti-Judaism in Egypt.* Oxford, 1989.

Jane Gerber

Public Health

See Medicine and Public Health

Pushtu

See Pakhtun, People and Language

Pyramids

Burial monuments for ancient Egyptian kings.

The pyramids of GIZA (Fourth dynasty, c. 2620–2480 B.C.E.) are the most famous and are easily visible from Cairo. They are objects of archeological research and tourism. First appearing on postage stamps in 1867 and giving their name to *al-Ahram* (now Egypt's leading newspaper) in 1876, they have become national symbols of Egypt.

BIBLIOGRAPHY

EDWARDS, I. E. S. *Pyramids of Egypt.* New York, 1986.

Donald Malcolm Reid

Q

Qabbani, Nizar   [1923–]

Syrian poet.

Born in Damascus on March 21, 1923, Qabbani completed his study of law at the Syrian University in 1945. He later joined the foreign ministry and served in Cairo, Ankara, London, Madrid, and Beijing, resigning in 1966 to establish in Beirut a publishing house carrying his name and devoted to printing poetry. He began writing at the age of sixteen and has so far published thirty-four of his own volumes. His major themes revolved around love, intermeshed with a sensuous, idealized, yet controversial evocation of woman's physical beauty. One poem, *Bread, Hashish, and a Moon* (1954), brought on him the wrath of the conservatives of the Syrian parliament who called for his resignation.

After the Arab defeat in the Arab–Israel War of 1967, Qabbani wrote a scathing attack on Arab mores and leadership in his poem *Marginal Notes on the Book of the Relapse* (1967), which won him wide popular acclaim. Henceforth, his writings addressed the political and social malaise of Arab society in a poetic diction that was intentionally simplified by the occasional use of Arabic vernacular. Large crowds attended his readings, attesting to his popularity in the Arab world. His works went into several editions and sold in exceptionally large numbers. He resides in London.

Qabbani's published works include *The Brunette Said to Me* (1944), *Childhood of a Breast* (1948), *Samba* (1949), *You Are Mine* (1950), *Poems* (1956), *My Beloved* (1961), *Poetry Is a Green Lamp* (1963), *Drawing in Words* (1966), *The Diary of a Blasé Woman* (1968), *The Book of Love* (1970), *A Hundred Love Letters* (1972), *Outlawed Poems* (1972), *Love Will Remain My Master* (1989), *I Have Married You Freedom* (1989), *The Match Is in My Hand, and Your States Are of Paper* (1989), *No Winner but Love* (1990), and *The Secret Papers of a Qarmati Lover* (1990).

BIBLIOGRAPHY

BOULLATA, ISSA J. *Modern Arab Poets, 1950–1975.* Washington, D.C., 1976.
JAYYUSI, SALMA KHADRA. *Trends and Movements in Modern Arabic Poetry,* 2 vols. Leiden, 1977.

Bassam Namani

Qaddafi, Muammar al-   [c. 1942–]

Ruler of Libya since 1969.

Muammar al-Qaddafi (also spelled Qadhdhafi) was born during World War II, probably in the spring of 1942, to a bedouin family near Sirte in northern Libya. The only surviving son of a poor family, he did not attend school until he was nearly ten, when he was sent to a local mosque school. He was evidently very intelligent, for he went on to secondary school in Sabha (or Sebha), in the southern province of Fezzan between 1956 and 1961. Like many young people in the Arab world at the time, he was an admirer of Gamal Abdel Nasser, the ruler of Egypt,

Colonel Muammar al-Qaddafi. (Embassy of Libya)

whose anti-imperialist and Arab nationalist foreign policies and egalitarian domestic reforms were then widely popular.

By 1961, when he was expelled from school in Sabha, Qaddafi's political inclinations were well known. His dismissal is variously attributed to an altercation with the son of the powerful governor of the Fezzan or to demonstrations he organized against the breakup of the union of Syria and Egypt (the United Arab Republic, UAR) that year. Qaddafi finished secondary school in coastal Misurata, where he renewed contact with some of his childhood friends, several of whom joined him in entering the Libyan Military Academy upon graduation. These friends subsequently became members of the group that plotted the successful overthrow of the pro-Western Libyan monarchy in 1969. This fact lends credence to Qaddafi's claim that he determined very early that only through a military coup could someone with his humble family background and ambitious political goals exercise power in Libya.

A six-month signals course in Britain followed graduation from the military academy in 1965, and Qaddafi was then posted near Benghazi. From there he readied his secret network of conspirators for September 1, 1969, when they took advantage of a vacation trip by aging King Muhammad Idris al-Sanusi

to Turkey to topple the monarchy in a bloodless coup. The Free Unionist Officers, as they called themselves, initially constituted themselves as a collective REVOLUTIONARY COMMAND COUNCIL (RCC) and appointed a number of more senior military and civilian figures to government positions. By December, however, when a countercoup was said to have been foiled, the RCC was given full authority, and Qaddafi was revealed as the regime's leading figure. Although he serves as head of state, to this day Qaddafi holds no formal position of authority.

The new regime's initial posture reflected Qaddafi's admiration of Nasser's Arab nationalism as well as his own admiration of Islam. (Indeed, although Qaddafi's politics were often controversial, his reputation for personal integrity has remained virtually untarnished through his tenure in office.) Soon alcohol was outlawed, churches and nightclubs closed, the British and American military bases evacuated, foreign-owned banks seized, the remaining Italian residents expelled (Libya was a colony of Italy before World War II), and only the Arabic language permitted in all official and public communications.

By the mid-1970s, Qaddafi was not only disenchanted with Nasser's successor in Egypt, Anwar al-Sadat, but he had come into his own as a political visionary. Between 1976 and 1979, he published the three slim volumes of the GREEN BOOK, in which he expounded the THIRD INTERNATIONAL THEORY. Disenchanted with both competitive and single-party politics, Qaddafi instituted instead a system of popular congresses and committees—composed of elected members—to run the country, including local administration, management of state-owned enterprises (and the universities), and national-policy review and implementation.

Contributing to the upheaval precipitated by these political innovations were Qaddafi's parallel economic reforms, which were based on his radically egalitarian precapitalist vision of economic relations. In his view, the exploitation entailed in wage labor, rent, and commerce must be replaced by equal partnerships and by nonprofit state-run distribution of goods and services. Workers were encouraged to take over the enterprises in which they were employed, landlords lost their property to their tenants, and retail trade disappeared. This immediately produced shortages and hoarding of basic commodities, halted housing construction, and increased already widespread economic inefficiency. That the country survived these disruptions was entirely a function of its very large petroleum revenues during the 1970s and the substantial expatriate workforce they subsidized.

By the late 1970s, Qaddafi had grown dissatisfied, however, with the performance of the committees and congresses—their lackluster record resulted partly from inexperience, partly from bad faith, and partly from unrealistic expectations on the part of their founder. To rectify the problems, he introduced watchdog "revolutionary committees." Domestically, these oversight groups did little more than further obscure lines of authority, but they earned considerable notoriety abroad. Because Qaddafi attributed the failures of his revolution to foreign and domestic subversion, he assigned the revolutionary committees responsibility for "liquidating the enemies of the revolution"—that is, assassinating government opponents at home and abroad.

Qaddafi was soon branded one of the world's principal sponsors of terrorism by many Western nations, notably the United States, which initially viewed his coup with tolerance. By the late 1970s, his vitriolic condemnation of the Camp David Accords capped a decade of increasingly hostile relations with the "imperialist" West. Libya's large arms purchases, his support of national liberation movements—from various Palestinian factions to the Irish Republican Army—and his campaign to assassinate Libyan opponents of the regime outside the country provided justification for the U.S. campaign that culminated in their bombing of Tripoli and Benghazi in April 1986. Qaddafi appeared to have been targeted personally—several of his family were wounded and an adopted daughter was killed in the raid—and his high-profile involvement diminished for some time thereafter.

Also contributing to his quieter demeanor, however, were his severe economic problems and, by the end of the 1980s, the collapse of the Eastern bloc and the 1991 demise of his superpower patron, the Soviet Union. As a result of the fall in oil prices during the 1980s (Libya ran negative growth rates for much of the latter half of the decade) and the imposition of economic sanctions by the United States and other Western powers, Qaddafi was required to reverse some of his domestic reforms. Small-scale retail trade was permitted to resume, and some political prisoners were released. Despite evidence that time and experience may have tempered Qaddafi's methods, however, there is no indication that his commitment to his utopian vision of unity, justice, and freedom for the Libyan people and their Arab compatriots has diminished.

BIBLIOGRAPHY

BEARMAN, JONATHAN. *Qadhafi's Libya*. London, 1986.
BIANCO, MIRELLA. *Gadhafi: Voice from the Desert*. 1975.

Lisa Anderson

Qaddumi, Faruq   [1930–   ]

Palestinian political activist.

Born in Nablus, Qaddumi studied economics and political science at Cairo University. In the late 1950s, he helped found al-FATH, the most significant organization in what became the Palestinian national liberation movement.

Known as Abu Lutf, Qaddumi has long been a member of al-Fath's Central Committee. He helped to secure funding from Arab Gulf states and represented the group's aims to Syria, Iraq, and Egypt in the 1960s.

Qaddumi has held important positions within the Palestine Liberation Organization (PLO). He was elected to its Executive Committee in February 1969 and has headed the Political Department since July 1974.

Qaddumi's 1967 proposal for establishing a Palestinian state in the West Bank and Gaza was an early step in what became official PLO policy in 1977. Qaddumi often clashed with PLO Chairman Yasir Arafat, questioning the wisdom of Arafat's embrace of various diplomatic solutions to the Arab–Israeli conflict. He opposed the Israeli–PLO accords and increased his attacks on Arafat and his policies.

BIBLIOGRAPHY

IYAD, ABOU, and ERIC ROULEAU. *My Home, My Land: A Narrative of the Palestinian Struggle*. Tr. by Linda Butler Koseoglu. New York, 1980.

Michael R. Fischbach

Qadi

Islamic judge.

According to Muslim legal doctrine, the *qadi* or "judge" is a public official whose primary responsibilities entail the administration of justice on the basis of the divinely revealed law of Islam, known in Arabic as the SHARIʿA. Eligibility for this office has been traditionally restricted to male jurists of majority age who have a reasonably comprehensive knowledge of the doctrine of their particular school of law. Because Islamic law construes the qadi as an agent of the legitimate governing authority, the government usually reserves the right to appoint qadis for the towns, cities, or regions under its control. In many historical and cultural contexts, judicial hierarchies have been established with the creation of one or more "chief judges" whose responsibility is to appoint and oversee the conduct of subordinate judges.

While in theory, the qadi is empowered to adjudicate cases involving every legal issue—both civil and criminal—addressed by the *Shari'a,* in practice the qadi's authority extends only as far as the *Shari'a* is actually applied as the law of a given Muslim society. In many medieval and modern contexts, government institution and application of far-reaching secular legal codes have limited the jurisdiction of the qadi to areas of personal status (i.e., marriage, divorce, child custody, and inheritance) and the supervision of religious endowments (*waqf*).

Scott Alexander

Qadiriyya Order

Sufi brotherhood.

The Qadiriyya Order was named for Abd al-Qadir al-Jilani (c. 1077–1166), Sufi teacher and founder of a HANBALI *madrasa* and religious hostel. Biographies of Abd al-Qadir date from more than a century after his death, so not much is known for certain about his life. Many apocryphal stories exist, attributing miracles, sayings, and poems to him.

Adb al-Qadir was born in the Jilan district of modern-day Iran, south of the Caspian Sea. He went to Baghdad at a young age to study philosophy and law and began preaching at about age fifty. The institutions that he founded in Baghdad were perpetuated, in large part by his forty-nine sons and other associates, until Baghdad fell to the Mongols in 1258. Abd al-Qadir is buried in Baghdad, and his tomb is a pilgrimage site.

Surviving works of Abd al-Qadir include *The Resource for Seekers of the Path of Wisdom* (a guidebook to Hanbali belief and practice, with a concluding section on SUFISM), *The Divine Beginning* (a collection of sixty-two sermons), and *The Revelation of the Hidden* (a collection of seventy-eight sermons). The main theme of his work is the integration of Hanbali and Sufi thought in Islam.

Some claim that the Qadiriyya was widespread during Abd al-Qadir's lifetime. Although he was unquestionably a charismatic figure with many followers, the founding and spread of a brotherhood with fully developed institutions probably date from well after his death. In any case, the Qadiriyya was one of the earliest and became the most widespread of Sufi brotherhoods, playing a significant role in the spread of Islam.

From Iraq, the Qadiriyya spread first to Syria in the late fourteenth and early fifteenth centuries, with centers in Damascus and Hama. Refugees introduced the Qadiriyya into Morocco after they were expelled from Spain in 1492. The Qadiriyya spread to other parts of the Fertile Crescent and the Maghrib (North Africa), then to central Asia, the Arabian peninsula, India, and Eastern Europe. In the nineteenth century, the Qadiriyya reached sub-Saharan Africa and the Malay peninsula.

Through his sermons, Abd al-Qadir taught asceticism, peacefulness, generosity, humanitarianism, and submission to the will of Allah. The emphases of the Qadiriyya have varied by time and place. Some brotherhoods venerate the personage of Abd al-Qadir and suggest that he performed miracles; others stress his teachings. Many brotherhoods are also derivative of the Qadiriyya but are named for followers of Abd al-Qadir.

BIBLIOGRAPHY

SCHIMMEL, ANNMARIE. *Mystical Dimensions of Islam.* Chapel Hill, N.C., 1975.
TRIMINGHAM, J. SPENCER. *The Sufi Orders in Islam.* Oxford, 1971.

Laurence Michalak

Qafih, Yihye ben Solomon   [1850–1932]

Yemenite Jewish scholar.

Qafih was born in San'a, capital of Yemen, orphaned as a child, and raised by his grandfather. His areas of scholarly expertise included the *Halakhah* (the body of Jewish law supplementing scriptural law and forming the legal part of the Talmud) and the works of both medieval and Enlightenment Jewish thinkers. Unlike other Yemenite scholars, he established communication with foreign contemporaries, among them the rabbis Abraham Isaac Kook and Hillel Zeitlin, with whom he communicated regarding the essence of Kabbalah (a system of Jewish theosophy and mysticism).

Qafih's most important enterprise was the Darda'im movement (named for Darda, one of the four ancient Jewish sages), founded on the eve of World War I, and emulating *Haskalah* (the Enlightenment) as it appeared among European Jewry during the eighteenth century. Although leading to partial Jewish intellectual revival in San'a, it provoked considerable controversy among local rabbis. Nevertheless, Qafih is considered the most important Jewish reformer of modern-day Yemen.

BIBLIOGRAPHY

RATZHABI, YEHUDA. *Yahadut Teiman* (Yemenite Jewry). Tel Aviv, 1958.

YESHA'YAHU, I., and A. ZADOQ, eds. *Shevut Teiman* (The Repatriation of Yemen). Tel Aviv, 1945.

Michael M. Laskier

Qahtan al-Sha'bi

First president and prime minister of independent South Yemen.

Arab nationalist and early member of the National Liberation Front (NLF), al-Sha'bi was supported by the nationalist, nonsocialist right wing of the NLF. He became its secretary-general and the first president and prime minister of independent South Yemen in late 1967. He was forced from office and jailed in 1969 in the June 22 Corrective Move led by the NLF's ascendant left wing.

Robert D. Burrowes

Qa'id

In Arabic, chief or leader.

In the administration of the traditional state of Morocco (Makhzen) *qa'id* means the chief. For each state function there was a qa'id: qa'id *djaysh* (chief of the army), qa'id *rha* (chief of 500 men in the army), qa'id *miya* (chief of 100 men in the army), qa'id *meshwar* (chief of palace affairs). All qa'id were appointed by *dahir* (decree). It was also the title given to a tribal chief in precolonial Morocco. The *amghar* (leader of a tribal council) becomes a qa'id when he receives a *dahir,* recognizing his authority over a tribe. The phenomenon of qa'id became an institution (*qa'idalism*) in the nineteenth century with the appearance of big chiefdoms in the High Atlas mountains with qa'ids such as Mtougui, Goundafi, and Glawi.

Today, the qa'id is a civil servant and a local authority appointed by the state in each region.

Rahma Bourqia

Qa'immaqam

Lower official in the Ottoman Empire.

Derived from a word meaning substitute, *qa'immaqam* was a title for deputies or lieutenants at various levels of the government and military. In the sixteenth and seventeenth centuries, the qa'immaqam was the deputy of the grand vizier in Con-

stantinople (now Istanbul) and deputy of a Mamluk bey in Cairo. The title also came to be used for a lieutenant in the Ottoman military and for an official appointed by a governor to run a SANJAK. In the 1840s, qa'immaqams were replaced in many districts by the new office of *muhassil,* but they were reinstated as governors of kazas, below the sanjak level, in the 1864 vilayet law. The qa'immaqam has continued in this function in the Turkish republic, Syria, and Iraq. While now obsolete in most military organizations, the term is still used in Tunisia's military for lieutenant colonel.

BIBLIOGRAPHY

SHAW, STANFORD J., and EZEL KURAL SHAW. *History of the Ottoman Empire and Modern Turkey,* vol. 2, Cambridge, U.K., 1977.

Elizabeth Thompson

Qairawan

City in north central Tunisia.

Qairawan (also Kairouan, al-Qayrawan) is located some 100 miles (156 km) south of Tunis. Its population in 1984 was calculated at almost 73,000. Its economy is based on agriculture, arboriculture, carpets, and leatherwork. Like many North African cities, it has a walled older section and a modern quarter established during colonialism. It was initially a military camp set up by the Arab Muslim invaders spreading Islam during the late seventh century. Gradually a town emerged with the building of mosques, shops, and fortresses; its founding is often associated with Okba (Uqba ibn Nafi), a Muslim general (to whom a mosque is dedicated); others also played a role, however.

Following upheaval brought on by Khariji revolts, the town came under Aghlabid rule in the ninth century, and under their patronage it was transformed into an important regional intellectual and religious center, known for its schools and pilgrimage stops. Decline followed, however, as did the pillaging of the city by nomadic groups in the mid-eleventh century. In the early thirteenth century, the capital was moved to Tunis, which became the hub of political and intellectual life in Tunisia. Today, Qairawan is considered a Holy City of Islam, and it is the center of the governorate of the same name.

BIBLIOGRAPHY

Encyclopedia of Islam, 2nd ed.
Tunisia: A Country Survey. Washington, D.C., 1988.

Matthew S. Gordon

Qajar, Abd Allah Mirza   [1849–1908]

Pioneering Persian photographer.

Abd Allah was the son of Jahangir Mirza, a member of the Qajar family—the rulers of Persia. Photography had been introduced to Persia in the 1860s, and the shah, Naser al-Din, was a keen photographer. Abd Allah studied photography in Paris and Vienna and was the official photographer at the Dar al-Fonun, the modern school founded by Mirza Taqi Khan Amir Kabir, the reform-minded minister of the shah.

Abd Allah Qajar was appointed chief of the imperial printing press during the reign of the succeeding shah, Mozaffar al-Din, and in 1900, accompanied him to Europe. He photographed public personalities, common people, urban and rural scenes, and buildings, and he signed them *Special photographer to His Imperial Majesty, and His humble servant, Abd Allah Qajar.* In 1896, he wrote a short account of the methods he had studied in Europe and about his career.

BIBLIOGRAPHY

AFSHAR, I. "Some Remarks on the Early History of Photography." In *Qajar Iran: Political, Social, and Cultural Change, 1800–1925,* ed. by C. E. Bosworth and C. Hillenbrand. Edinburgh, 1983.

Mansoureh Ettehadieh

Qajar, Agha Mohammad   [1742–1797]

Founder and first monarch of Persia's Qajar dynasty; Shah in 1796.

Qajar (also Aqa Mohammad Ghadjar) was born the son of Mohammad Hoseyn Khan of the Qovanlu branch of the Qajar family, a Turkic tribe that had settled in and near Astarabad, now in northeastern Iran. The chief of the tribe, Fath Ali Khan, was killed by Nader Shah Afshar, so his son Mohammad Hoseyn Khan took refuge with other Turkomans. After Nader was killed in 1747, his successor Adel Shah took Mohammad Hoseyn Khan's six-year-old son Agha Mohammad Khan and emasculated him. When Adel Shah died, Agha Mohammad joined Karim Khan Zand, who ruled in southern and central Persia, with a capital at Shiraz. Mohammad Hoseyn was killed in battle by Karim Khan Zand in 1758; Zand then took Agha Mohammad and his family as hostages to his capital.

Agha Mohammad was treated well and was trusted by Karim Khan, but when Karim died in 1779, Agha Mohammad escaped and raised the standard of revolt against the descendants of the Zands (Persian dynasty 1750–1794). Gradually, he succeeded in conquering, pacifying, and uniting Persia. Still, he had to contend with Lotf Ali Khan Zand, Karim Khan's successor. After being defeated by Agha Mohammad in Shiraz, Lotf Ali escaped to Kerman in southeast Persia. There he was finally captured by Agha Mohammad in 1794, who proceeded to sack the city and treat the citizens with great cruelty for sheltering Lotf Ali.

In 1796, Agha Mohammad had himself crowned king (becoming Agha Mohammad Shah Qajar), in Tehran, which he chose for his capital. At the time, Tehran was a small and insignificant township selected for its proximity to the seat of Qajar power in the north. Agha Mohammad set about reconquering Georgia, once a tribute state to Persia, but transferred by its ruler, Heracleus, to Russia. During his second expedition to Georgia in 1797, the shah was assassinated outside Shusha, Georgia's capital.

Though Agha Mohammad Shah was harsh and cruel, by his courage, astuteness, and endeavor he reunited his country and founded the dynasty that ruled Persia until 1925.

BIBLIOGRAPHY

CURZON, G. N. *Persia and the Persian Question.* 1892. Reprint, London, 1966.
LAMBTON, A. K. S. "Persian Society under the Qajars." *Journal of the Royal Central Asian Society* 48 (1961): 123–138.
MALCOLM, J. *History of Persia.* London, 1829.
PAKRAVAN, A. *Agha Mohammad Ghadjar.* Paris, 1963.
WATSON, R. G. *A History of Persia from the Beginning of the Nineteenth Century to the Year 1858.* London, 1866.

Mansoureh Ettehadieh

Qajar Dynasty

Turkoman tribe that consolidated power and united Persia, 1796–1925.

The Qajars were a Turkoman tribe that rose to prominence in Persia's Safavid period (1500–1722), serving that dynasty as governors and generals. In the turbulent tribal and civil wars that broke out after the Safavids fell, they gradually consolidated power in northern Persia by 1785, making Tehran their capital. Under Agha Mohammad Shah QAJAR, they defeated the Zand dynasty in the south by 1794, controlling all but Khorasan in the northeast. In the spring of 1796, Agha Mohammad crowned himself shah at Tehran, beginning the reign of the Qajar dynasty. He was killed a year later in his camp by two slaves, while campaigning in Georgia, and his nephew succeeded him as FATH ALI SHAH.

Fath Ali Shah ruled from 1797 to 1834, a period that encompassed the gradual extension of both Russian and English influence. Russia defeated Persia in two wars (1804–1813, 1824–1828), acquiring territory in the north, while England blocked Persian aspirations in Afghanistan. Both countries secured favorable treaty rights in Persia, acquiring a say in the succession, which went in 1834 to Fath Ali's grandson MOHAMMAD ALI, who ruled the country uneventfully until his death in 1848.

During the long reign of NASER AL-DIN SHAH, from 1848 to 1896, he had to confront an increasingly powerful European presence. British trade rose from 1.7 million pounds sterling in 1875 to 4.5 million by 1914; Russia's went from 1 million to 12 million—the two accounting for 83 percent of the total. Trade and budget deficits forced the shah to grant lucrative concessions in the north to Russia for the operation of the Caspian fisheries and, in the south, to the British, for telegraphs, tobacco exports, and river navigation. Realizing the need to reform his administration, Naser al-Din set up European-style educational institutions, brought in Russian advisers to drill his Cossack Brigade, created government printing offices, and tried to establish factories to supply the army. The financial and administrative side of the reforms were neglected, however, undermining all other efforts.

The Babis, a millenarian heterodox offshoot of the official Shi'a branch of Islam, caused armed uprisings in several provinces and an attempt on the shah's life between 1848 and 1852. Appealing to the needs of the middle and lower classes for social justice, Babism was violently suppressed and driven underground. A second serious challenge arose from 1890 to 1892, when the shah was forced to repeal a monopoly concession for tobacco that he granted to an English company. The entire nation, including the shah's wives, boycotted tobacco in the first mass social movement of the modern period; it was directed against European economic encroachment and the shah's acquiescence in this.

The aftermath of the TOBACCO REVOLT saw further popular unrest, which culminated in the assassination of Naser al-Din Shah on May 1, 1896, by Mirza Mohammad Reza Kermani, a pan-Islamic activist. Naser's son, MOZAFFAR AL-DIN, then became shah. Conditions continued to worsen during the early twentieth century. Inflation hurt the urban classes. The peasants and especially the artisans felt the negative effects of a growing commercialization because of the European presence. The *ulama* (Islamic religious leaders) came increasingly to see the country's

problems in terms of the shah's helplessness in the face of infidel pressures. The less numerous Western-trained intelligentsia began to criticize European economic control and Qajar absolutism.

In 1905, the beating of four sugar merchants (because of high prices) touched off a series of protests that soon engulfed Tehran. In the summer of 1906, the bazaaris went on strike, the *ulama* withdrew their religious services, and Mozaffar al-Din Shah, unable to rely on Russian support owing to the revolution there, was forced to agree to the formation of a national assembly (the *majles*), made up of Qajar princes, merchants, *ulama,* artisans, landlords, and urban notables. This body wrote a constitution in the fall of 1906 that the shah signed on his deathbed, December 30, 1906. He died nine days later.

The CONSTITUTIONAL REVOLUTION threw Persia into political turmoil between 1905 and 1911. The new shah, Mohammad Ali, proved to be autocratic—and, with Russian support, mobilized conservative *ulama* and the urban poor to close down the *majles* in June 1908. Constitutionalist resistance shifted from Tehran to Persia's second-largest city, Tabriz, which was run by social democratic radicals. The shah used tribal forces to occupy the city in April 1909, but the movement had bought valuable time to regroup. In July 1909, two constitutionalist armies, one of northern radicals and the other under Bakhtiyari tribal leadership from the south, converged on Tehran and deposed Mohammad Ali, who sought refuge in the Russian embassy. His eleven-year-old son, AHMAD QAJAR, was crowned, ruling under a regent and the watchful eye of the reconstituted second *majles*. This body was relatively conservative in social orientation—led by large merchants, landlords, and *ulama*—and had a smaller radical social democratic opposition. The hiring of a financial adviser from the United States, Morgan Shuster, in 1911, alienated both the Persian elite, who resisted paying taxes, and the Russians in the north. The former shah, Mohammad Ali, unsuccessfully attempted a comeback, with tribal support, in the summer of 1911. In the fall, the Russians demanded Shuster's dismissal and, when the *majles* refused, Russian troops entered the country with Qajar and other elite support, closing down the *majles* and bringing the Constitutional Revolution to an end.

England and Russia dominated Persian politics from 1911 to 1921; Russia controlled the cabinet until 1914 and increased its trade in the more populated north, while England controlled the Gulf area and the southern petroleum fields, discovered in 1908. The central government under the figurehead Ahmad Shah looked on helplessly as Turkish, Russian, and British troops fought during World War I, and local movements arose in several provinces, especially in northern Gilan, under radical Islamic and socialist leadership. The Russian Revolution removed that country's strong grip on Persia after 1917, leaving Persia open to the British, whose representatives lent some support to the coup of Reza Khan Pahlavi, in February 1921. As war minister, Reza repressed the provincial opposition movements, rising to prime minister in October 1923. In late 1923, Ahmad Shah left Persia for Europe on a trip of indefinite duration (he would, in fact, never return). Reza used his power base in the army, among the majority parties in the fifth *majles,* and with the British—who ultimately accepted him as the strongman needed to guarantee their oil and other interests—to bring about the deposition of Ahmad Shah on October 31, 1925. Two months later the *majles* vested the monarchy in the Pahlavi family, ending the rule of the Qajar dynasty, with the crowning of Reza Shah PAHLAVI. He officially renamed the country Iran in 1935.

BIBLIOGRAPHY

ABRAHAMIAN, ERVAND. *Iran between Two Revolutions.* Princeton, N.J., 1982.
ALGAR, HAMID. *Religion and State in Iran, 1785–1906: The Role of the Ulama in the Qajar Period.* Berkeley, Calif., 1969.
FORAN, JOHN. "The Concept of Dependent Development as a Key to the Political Economy of Qajar Iran (1800–1925)." *Iranian Studies* 22, nos. 2–3 (1989): 5–56.
———. *Fragile Resistance: Social Transformation in Iran from 1500 to the Revolution.* Boulder, Colo., 1993.
LAMBTON, ANN K. S. "The Qajar Dynasty." In *Qajar Persia: Eleven Studies.* London, 1987.

John Foran

Qal'at al-Bahrayn

The oldest existing fort in Bahrain.

The Portuguese Fort, as it is commonly known, was built by the Arabs and adapted by the Portuguese when they came to the island of Bahrain in the sixteenth century. The ruins of the fort are located approximately five miles (8 km) west of Bahrain's capital, Manama. In the 1950s, Danish archeologists discovered beneath the ruins of Qal'at al-Bahrayn an Islamic fort that dates to the eleventh century C.E., an Assyrian palace that dates to 900 B.C.E., a Greek fort that dates from the time of Alexander the Great, and the remains of a city that dates to the third millennium B.C.E.

BIBLIOGRAPHY

BIBBY, GEOFFREY. *Looking for Dilmun.* London, 1970.

Emile A. Nakhleh

Qalyan

See Narghila

Qalyubiyya

Egyptian province.

Located in Egypt's Nile delta, Qalyubiyya (also spelled Kalyubia) is one of twenty-five Egyptian governorates (provinces). Qalyubiyya covers 325 square miles (842 sq. km); its capital city is Benha. The 1986 census population of Qalyubiyya was 2,514,200.

David Waldner

Qanat

A subterranean channel supplying water to towns and irrigating fields.

A *qanat* is a subterranean canal or water channel usually built at the foot of mountains or hills. It collects the ground water in alluvial fans, or underground water tables and, following the descent of the terrain, carries the water to where it is needed, usually in the vicinity of a village or an irrigated field. At the desired location, the water of the qanat is led above ground and conducted through surface channels to fields for irrigation or to villages for consumption.

Gravity propels the flow of the water from its elevated source to its destination. The length of a qanat can be as great as 9.3 miles (15 km). The slope is between 1 and 3 feet per 1,000 feet (.2–.6 m per 305 m). For qanat construction, as well as maintenance, both high labor and cost are involved. Holes are dug into the ground at 50- to 150-yard (45.7 m to 137.1 m) intervals. These are then connected together underground. This ingenious and ancient system of irrigation is said to have originated in the first half of the first millennium B.C.E. in the Iranian and Armenian highlands. A substantial proportion of cities in Iran, including Tehran, owe their existence to the qanats. Because of the cost involved in their construction and maintenance, qanats have had a great influence on the social structure of the settlements they help maintain. Usually the rich built them and dwelled near their outlet, where the water is cleanest and freshest. The poor usually lived farther down, using already used, warm, or contaminated water. The owner of the qanat usually came to be considered the owner of the land it irrigated.

BIBLIOGRAPHY

GAUBE, H. *Iranian Cities.* New York, 1979.
STEVENS, R. *The Land of the Great Sophie.* New York, 1979.

Parvaneh Pourshariati

Qannut, Abd al-Ghani   [1923–   ]

Syrian military officer.

Abd al-Ghani Qannut, an officer from Hama and a Ba'th party sympathizer, became head of the Deuxième Bureau in 1950. He was named by the dying air force colonel, Muhammad Nasir, as one of two assailants in his assassination (1950). Qannut was acquitted for lack of evidence. In 1958, he was a member of the military delegation sent to pledge Ba'th support to President Gamal Abdel Nasser of Egypt and was elected to the Syrian regional cabinet in 1961.

BIBLIOGRAPHY

SEALE, PATRICK. *The Struggle for Syria: A Study of Post-War Arab Politics, 1945–1958.* London, 1958.

Charles U. Zenzie

Qansu, Assem   [1937–   ]

Lebanese Shi'a politician.

Born in Ba'albak, Lebanon, Qansu completed a degree in geology in the former Czechoslovakia, and in the 1960s he joined al-Ba'th, the Arab socialist party. In 1974, he was elected secretary-general of the party in Lebanon and kept his position until 1989. He is a member of the Shi'a Supreme Council, and in 1980 he was elected vice president of the LEBANESE NATIONAL MOVEMENT politburo.

BIBLIOGRAPHY

Arab Information Center, Beirut.

George E. Irani

Qanun

Secular law promulgated by ruler's decree.

Rooted in the legal tradition of *yasa* (a royal edict) in the Turkish and Mongol empires of central Asia, qanun was most fully developed by the sultans of the Ottoman Empire. Qanun (also Kanun) was theoretically restricted to those areas of public life not covered by *Shari'a* (Islamic law).

In the fifteenth century, Sultan Mehmed II was the first leader of the Ottoman Empire to codify his decrees into a *kanunname* (book of laws) on the rights of subjects, the organization of the state, taxes, landholding, and economic organization. Later sultans progressively extended the scope of secular law, thereby infringing on what had once been the monopoly of religious law. Qanun underwent extensive reform in the nineteenth century, when French law codes were incorporated into the Ottoman Empire's legal system.

BIBLIOGRAPHY

SHAW, STANFORD J. *History of the Ottoman Empire and Modern Turkey.* New York, 1976.

Elizabeth Thompson

Qaramanli Dynasty

Dynasty of Turkish origin that attained autonomous rule of Tripolitania under Ottoman suzerainty, 1711–1835.

The Qaramanli (also Karamanli) dynasty—Ahmed (1711–1745), Mehmed (1745–1754), Ali (1754–1793, 1795/96), Yusuf (1796–1835)—directed autonomous Tripolitanian domestic and foreign policies, including the signing of international treaties. Their economy was based on international trade and sea piracy; their pirates were the scourge of the Barbary Coast, known as the Barbary pirates. During Ali's reign the region suffered from epidemics, plague, and famine, as well as from power struggles among Ali's sons. Algerian strongman Ali Burghul (Bulghur) took advantage of the situation and with Ottoman approval ruled Tripoli between 1793 and 1795, causing the population severe hardship.

Under Yusuf, the European powers and the newly independent United States went to war against the Barbary pirates, ending the taking of ships, cargoes, and men (who were often sold into slavery). This forced Yusuf to impose high taxes, which caused a popular revolt. On May 27, 1835, an Ottoman naval force landed in Tripoli following a local request for Ottoman intervention. Its commander was proclaimed governor, and members of the Qaramanli family were arrested or exiled.

BIBLIOGRAPHY

DEARDEN, SETON. *A Nest of Corsairs: The Fighting Karamanlis of Tripoli.* London, 1976.

FOLAYAN, KOLA. *Tripoli during the Reign of Yusuf Pasha Qaramanli.* Ife, Nigeria, 1979.

Rachel Simon

Qarawiyyin, al-

First university in the Islamic world.

Al-Qarawiyyin was built as a mosque in Fez in 859. The building was enlarged in the tenth century and later under the respective rules of Almoravids, Almohads, Marinids, Sa'dis, and Alawi dynasties. Its architecture expresses the Arab-Hispanic art that makes Qarawiyyin one of the most prestigious monuments in Fez and in North Africa.

Since the twelfth century, most of the Moroccan *ulama* (Islamic clergy) received their religious teaching at Qarawiyyin. Students came from all regions of Morocco and from the Arab world.

Under the Alawite dynasty, Qarawiyyin was subject to a series of reforms regulating its organization and programs of teaching. The sultan Abd al-Rahman (1822–1859) reorganized the teaching there by DAHIR. This reorganization was oriented toward communicating to students religious disciplines guided by conformism to Islam. Among topics taught were Qur'anic exegesis, astronomy, dialectics, mysticism, lexicography, philology, geography, medicine, and divination.

The teaching was free of charge, and the student could join the university at any time of the year. However, each student had to spend five years in the university to receive an *ijaza* given by his teacher if the student showed regularity and attended courses successfully.

In the nineteenth century, the teachers constituted a body of *ulama* that gave allegiance to the sultan and

Courtyard of the Qarawiyyin mosque. (Richard Bulliet)

were consulted by him on different matters. They enjoyed high status in Fez, and *qadis* (judges) were recruited from among them. After the French takeover, the Sultan Mulay YUSUF signed a dahir (on May 19, 1914) creating a council charged with the task of improving the university's methods of teaching, its administration, and the status of its teachers. In 1918, the university became affiliated with the Ministry of Justice and was led by le Conseil de Direction.

The most important change occurred after two dahirs were promulgated by Muhammed V on April 1, 1931, and May 10, 1933. The teaching became organized in cycles: elementary, secondary, and higher. Higher education in Qarawiyyin had two sections: one specialized in religious law, hadith (legends and traditions surrounding the Prophet), and interpretation of the Qur'an; the second specialized in literature, Arabic language, history, and geography. Exams, hours of teaching, holidays, and the status of teachers were also regulated. In 1947, the Qarawiyyin became a state university.

After independence, Qarawiyyin became affiliated to the Ministry of National Education, having as objectives to teach religious knowledge and to promote scientific research in this field. Three other institutions became linked to Qarawiyyin: the Faculty of Arabic Language in Marrakech, Faculty of Theology in Tetuan, and Dar al-Hadith al-Hasaniyya in Rabat.

Rahma Bourqia

Qasemlu, Abd al-Rahman [?–1989]

Leader of the leftist Kurdish Democratic party of Iran (KDPI).

This political party of the KURDS was illegal in Iran from its inception during the post–World War II era of the shah, Mohammad Reza Pahlavi (ruled 1941–1979). Qasemlu (also Abdorrahman Qassemlou) led the KDPI in its support of the IRANIAN REVOLUTION in 1978 and the party was legalized by the Islamic Republic in the spring of 1979.

The KDPI rejected government proposals that would have resulted in something less than local autonomy for the Kurds and was banned that summer. Throughout the 1980s, KDPI and other Kurdish insurgents maintained control of areas of their native territory (Kurdistan) in western Iran. Iranian assassins killed Qasemlu and several other Kurdish leaders in Vienna in July 1989 and, fleeing Austria, were never brought to justice. In September 1992, while attending an international socialist congress, Qasemlu's successor as KDPI secretary-general was assassinated in Berlin, along with three other KDPI officials.

Michael C. Hillmann

Qashqa'i

Turkic-speaking (western Oghuz Turkic) tribal people of the southern Zagros mountains of southwestern Iran, in the vicinity of the city of Shiraz.

The Qashqa'i form a historically important tribal confederacy that originated in the late eighteenth century. Until the 1960s, the majority of Qashqa'i were nomadic pastoralists. In the 1990s, many Qashqa'i continue to rely on nomadism (increasingly by motorized vehicles) for a livelihood. Many have settled in villages, some for part of the year, and agriculture plays an increasingly important economic role.

Qashqa'i territory is ecologically rich and diverse. Low-altitude winter pastures near the Persian Gulf and high-altitude summer pastures to the north and northeast are separated by hundreds of miles, and the migrations of spring and autumn each last from two to three months. The people follow Shi'ism and numbered approximately 600,000 in 1990. The Qashqa'i have a strong sense of ethnic and national-minority identity, especially because of periodic repression of them by Iranian state rulers.

BIBLIOGRAPHY

BECK, LOIS. *Nomad: A Year in the Life of a Qashqa'i Tribesman in Iran.* Berkeley, Calif., 1991.

———. *The Qashqa'i of Iran.* New Haven, Conn., 1986.

Lois Beck

Qasim, Abd al-Karim

See Kassem, Abd al-Karim

Qasimi, Ibn Muhammad al-

Ruler of Ra's al-Khayma.

The shaykh was proclaimed ruler of RA'S AL-KHAYMA in 1948. He belongs to the family of Shaykh Salim ibn Sultan (ruled 1908–1917), founder of the Ra's al-Khayma branch of the Qasimi family. In 1952, he became a member of the Trucial States Council (of the Trucial Coast of the Arabian peninsula). Ra's al-Khayma joined the United Arab Emirates (UAE)

on February 11, 1972, and al-Qasimi became a member of the Supreme Federal Council.

His eldest son, Khalid, was appointed crown prince of Ra's al-Khayma in 1958. His second son, General Sultan, trained in a military college in England and is in command of the Badr regiment of the federal forces. Another son, Shaykh Saud, a graduate of the University of Michigan, is head of the Emiri Court.

Observing the traditions of Islam, al-Qasimi established the High Religious College. His emirate has provided many graduates as ministers for the federal cabinet. Since Ra's al-Khayma has a wide fertile cultivated plain, it can supply the other emirates with vegetables and fruits.

BIBLIOGRAPHY

ABDULLAH, M. MORSY. *The United Arab Emirates.* London, 1978.

Persian Gulf Gazette and Supplements 1953–1972. London, 1987.

Persian Gulf Historical Summaries 1907–1953. London, 1987.

M. Morsy Abdullah

Qasimi, Sultan ibn Muhammad al-

Ruler of Sharja.

Sultan ibn Muhammad is a descendant of Shaykh Khalid ibn Sultan (1866–1868), founder of the Qasimi family of the SHARJA emirate. He graduated from the Faculty of Agriculture at Cairo University in 1971 and was appointed Minister of Education on December 9, 1971, in the first federal cabinet of the United Arab Emirates (U.A.E.). After the death of his brother Khalid, Shaykh Sultan was proclaimed ruler of the Sharja emirate and member of the U.A.E. Supreme Federal Council on January 25, 1972. He showed his loyalty to the union when he joined Sharja's military units with the federal forces and raised the U.A.E. flag in November 1975.

Sultan was granted a Ph.D. in 1985 from Exeter University in England on the history of the Qawasim people of the Arabian peninsula. Since Sharja inaugurated modern education, it has become an important cultural, literary, and sports center in the United Arab Emirates. Sharja prides itself on providing some graduates as ministers in the federal cabinet.

BIBLIOGRAPHY

ABDULLAH, M. MORSY. *The United Arab Emirates.* London, 1978.

Persian Gulf Gazette and Supplements 1953–1972. London, 1987.

Persian Gulf Historical Summaries 1907–1953. London, 1987.

M. Morsy Abdullah

Qasimi Family, al-

Rulers of Sharja and Ra's al-Khayma, of the United Arab Emirates.

Their name was first mentioned by the Portuguese in the 1648 siege of Musqat and Oman and later during the 1747 Arab sailors' revolt in the Persian navy. Shaykh Rahma ibn Matar, who built RA'S AL-KHAYMA on the ruins of old Julfa around 1750, established a tribal federation on both sides of the Gulf. When the Al Bu Sa'id established their dynasty in Oman in 1741, the Qasimi family became independent. In 1800, the Qasimi federation adopted the MUWAHHIDUN reform doctrines of Islam and attacked British ships. The British called them pirates, bombarded their forts, and burned their ships in 1819. During the long reign of Shaykh Sultan ibn Saqr (1804–1866), the Qasimi federation began to disintegrate. Umm al-Qaywayn and Ajman became independent after 1820, Lingeh around 1860 (but occupied by the Persians in 1899), SHARJA in 1866, and Ra's al-Khayma in 1900.

BIBLIOGRAPHY

ABDULLAH, M. MORSY. *The United Arab Emirates.* London, 1978.

KELLY, J. B. *Britain and the Persian Gulf.* London, 1968.

M. Morsy Abdullah

Qasimi Imams

Important Yemeni family.

The Qasimi are among the important families from which ZAYDI imams have been drawn (along with the Sharaf al-Din, the Hamid al-Din, and the al-Wazir). In 1598, Ibn Muhammad al-QASIMI proclaimed himself imam and immediately began a revolt against the Ottoman Empire's presence in Yemen, as well as a program of administrative reforms. His son, al-Mu'ayyad Muhammad, continued the revolt, and by 1635 succeeded in driving the empire's forces out of Yemen, creating an independent Zaydi-ruled Yemen. Multiple disputes among members of the following generations seriously weakened the Qasimi line, but it managed to provide imams of varying abilities until 1852.

Manfred W. Wenner

Qassam, Izz al-Din al-   [c. 1880–1935]

Islamic militant who fought the French in Syria and the British in Palestine.

Qassam was born in Jabla, near Latakia, Syria. He studied in Cairo at al-Azhar University and reportedly came in contact with Rashid Rida, the precursor of Arab nationalism. Following the French occupation of Syria, he participated in guerilla activities (1919–1920) in the Alawiya region of Jabal Sahyun, for which he was sentenced to death by a French court-martial. After the French suppressed Syrian resistance, he escaped to Palestine. Qassam was hired to teach at an Islamic school in 1921, and a year later was appointed by the Supreme Muslim Council as a preacher at the new Istiqlal mosque in Haifa. He preached a puritanical way of life that alarmed some people enough to seek his dismissal. He was appointed marriage registrar in the *Shari'a* court at Haifa in 1929, which enabled him to travel throughout Palestine.

Qassam became convinced that Britain was facilitating Jewish immigration and land purchases, which ultimately would lead to a Jewish state. He therefore began to advocate a popular uprising against the British once the Palestinians were united and organized. In 1928 he was a founder of the Young Men's Muslim association, which with the Boy Scouts organized military drills and the stockpiling of arms, and initiated violent attacks on Jewish settlements (1931–1933). According to Subhi Yasin, his contemporary (and the source of most of our information about Qassam), Qassam sent a follower to the Mufti of Jerusalem Hajj Amin al-Husayni, requesting him to start a revolt in the south while he (Qassam) started one in the north. The mufti reportedly declined, stating that he was seeking a political solution. Qassam believed that a revolt should take place. However, with only 200 recruits and insufficient arms and training, he felt the Palestinians were not yet ready. Two factors made him change his mind: the discovery, on 18 October 1935, of an arms shipment destined for Jewish forces and the immigration that year of the largest number of Jews (almost 62,000) to Palestine. On 21 November he left Haifa with ten of his followers to attack a police arsenal to acquire its arms, but an unplanned clash, in which a police sergeant was killed, alerted the police. Hundreds of police chased and caught up with the group; rather than escape or surrender, Qassam and his men fought it out. He and two of his men were killed.

Qassam became a symbol of martyrdom for Palestinian youth groups such as Ikhwan al-Qassam (Qassamite Brotherhood), which formed resistance cells to take up the mantle of Qassam. The Qassamite attack in which two Jews were killed on 15 April 1936 was a catalyst for the most violent uprising against the British, the PALESTINE ARAB REVOLT (1936–1939).

Half a century later, the legacy of Qassam inspired another generation of Palestinians. Shortly after the INTIFADA began in 1987, an Islamic fundamentalist group, HAMAS (Islamic Resistance Movement), was established to resist Israeli occupation through its military wing, Kata'ib Izz al-Din al-Qassam. HAMAS played a major role in the Intifada and, opposing the 1993 Oslo agreement, conducted violent attacks against Israelis.

BIBLIOGRAPHY

MATTAR, PHILIP. *The Mufti of Jerusalem: Al-Hajj Amin al-Husayni and the Palestinian National Movement,* rev. ed. New York, 1991.

PORATH, Y. *The Palestinian Arab National Movement: From Riots to Rebellion, 1929–1939.* Vol. 2. London, 1977.

Philip Mattar

Qat

Plant whose leaves are chewed for a mild stimulant effect; part of Yemen's social and business life.

Qat (also khat; *Catha edulis*) is a small woody shrub that grows to a height of about six feet (2 m) and is primarily cultivated in the mountains of southwestern Arabia and East Africa. Scholars do not agree on which of these is its original home.

In Yemen, the consumption of qat—the young leaves of the plant are chewed—has become an integral part of the social fabric of society. At "qat chews," much of the social, economic, political, and business life of the country is transacted or discussed.

Qat market in Yemen. (© Mark Dennis)

Qat is often considered a narcotic, but it is instead a stimulant; the active ingredient is an alkaloid that acts like caffeine. Steady consumers cite the three most problematical effects as being insomnia, constipation, and impotence.

No reliable evidence exists for its use prior to the thirteenth century; however, by the fifteenth century, both qat and coffee—the other common alkaloid (caffeine) for which Yemen is famous—had become a regular part of Yemeni social and economic life.

Manfred W. Wenner

Qatar

Nation on the western shore of the Persian Gulf.

Land and People. Dawlat Qatar (the State of Qatar) occupies a mitten-shaped peninsula that extends about 105 miles (170 km) into the Arab/Persian Gulf roughly midway along its western coast. About 50 miles (80 km) across at its widest point, it has an area of 4,400 square miles (11,400 sq. km). Qatar shares a land border with Saudi Arabia and is separated from Bahrain to the west by about 30 miles (48 km) of water. It consists largely of desert sand and gravel with occasional limestone outcrops and *sabkhas* (salt flats). The absence of oases has made the establishment of permanent settlements in Qatar's interior impossible. Summer weather is severe, with temperatures as high as 122°F (50°C) and high humidity along the coasts; winters are pleasant, with temperatures generally around 60°F (17°C), with a continuous north wind. Scant rainfall sustains meager vegetation. Qatar's oil reserves of about 4 billion barrels will be exhausted by about 2015, but it possesses natural gas reserves of 163 trillion cubic feet (4.56 trillion cu. m), most of it in the North Dome field, the world's largest deposit of nonassociated gas.

Qatar's population is close to 500,000, having grown rapidly since oil income started to flow after World War II. Even earlier, the population included significant numbers of immigrant Iranians and East Africans originally brought as slaves and freed in the first half of the twentieth century. Oil wealth and the rapid economic development it has generated have brought large numbers of expatriates to Qatar, reducing the indigenous population to about one-fifth of the total. Iranians account for about a sixth, other Arabs for a quarter, and South Asians for a third. The great majority of the population is Sunni Muslim, with Qataris subscribing to the same strict Wahhabi interpretation of Islam as the Saudis (see MUWAHHI-DUN); an estimated one-sixth is Shi'a. About three-

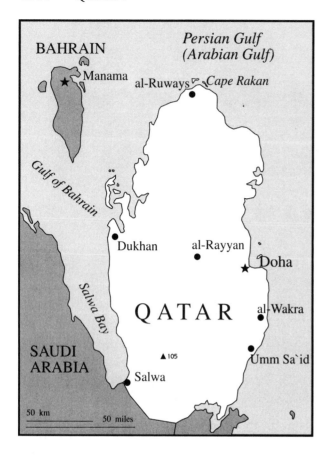

fifths of Qatar's population lives in DOHA, the capital and principal port, located on the east coast. Other major urban areas include KHAWR, located north of Doha, and the industrial complex of UMM SA'ID to its south.

History. In the 1760s the al-Khalifa, one of the Utayba clans from central Arabia that had earlier settled in Kuwait, migrated to Qatar and established its base at Zubara, on the west coast. After they seized the islands of Bahrain from the Persians in 1783, their hold on Qatar weakened and the Al Thani, a family from central Arabia, established a leading position on the east coast. An 1867 attack by the al-Khalifa and the ruling BANU YAS TRIBE of Abu Dhabi against Doha and other settlements led to British intervention that established MUHAMMAD IBN THANI as de facto ruler of Qatar. In 1893 his son, Qasim ibn Muhammad AL THANI, defeated superior forces of the occupying Ottoman Turks, who had extended their suzerainty over Qatar in 1871. In 1916 Abdullah ibn Qasim signed a treaty with Great Britain that conferred British protection over the emirate, forbade Qatar to have relations with or cede territory to other states without British agreement, and gave special rights to Great Britain and its subjects in Qatar.

Like the other Gulf Arab states, Qatar's pearling industry, virtually its sole source of income before oil, was devastated in the 1930s by the introduction of cultured pearls. In 1935 a concession was granted to a subsidiary of the Anglo–Iranian Oil Company (later British Petroleum). The modest concession payments enabled Abdullah ibn Qasim to solidify his position and that of the Al Thani clan, a process completed when the ruling family began to earn oil export income after 1949. Political independence was thrust upon Qatar in 1968, when the United Kingdom decided to end its protective relationships with the lower Gulf states by the end of 1971. It declared its independence on 3 September 1971, after the failure of efforts to join Bahrain and the seven Trucial Emirates in a federation.

Economy. Oil earnings have given Qataris one of the world's highest per capita incomes, nearly 16,000 dollars in 1990, and have made dramatic economic development possible. In 1991 Qatar began production of gas from its vast North Dome. Soon after the year 2000 gas production will have entirely replaced that of oil. The country's modern physical infrastructure includes excellent roads linking Qatar with the other Gulf states, an international airport, and a large, modern port at Doha. Attempts have been made to diversify the economy by building cement plants and flour mills, and expanding the shrimping industry. Modern techniques in agriculture have made possible vegetable and chicken production sufficient to meet an increasingly larger part of local demand.

Government and Politics. In 1970, a year before independence, Qatar became the first of the lower Gulf states to adopt a written constitution. It provided for a council of ministers or a cabinet to be appointed by the ruler, and an elected advisory council. Members of the ruling family dominate the cabinet, and the advisory council has, as of the mid-1990s, consisted only of members appointed by the ruler. With perhaps as many as 20,000 members, the Al Thani family is the largest ruling family in the region and has dominated most important areas of government. In June 1995, Shaykh Hamad ibn Khalifa overthrew his father, Shaykh Khalifa ibn Hamad AL THANI. He appears to have effectively managed the challenge of maintaining the balance in a family with many factions and potential rivalries while initiating moves toward a more open political system. In January 1993 fifty leading citizens petitioned the ruler to create an assembly with legislative powers. Although this has not occurred, there has been some broadening of the

A clock tower and mosque at Dahzi. (D.W. Lockhard)

advisory council's membership to make it more representative.

Foreign Relations. Apart from its wider oil interests, Qatar has focused its foreign policy largely on Gulf affairs. It has sought to maintain close and friendly relations with the other traditional, dynastic Gulf Arab states. However, a dispute with Bahrain over ownership of the Hawar Islands, adjacent to Qatar's west coast, and several reefs has long soured relations with that neighbor, and in September 1992 a border clash created tension with Saudi Arabia, hitherto Qatar's closest partner. Shayk Hamad has pursued a more active and independent foreign policy than his departed father. Qatar agreed to the deployment on its soil of American and other non-Arab military forces during the 1990–1991 Gulf Crisis, and its troops participated in the fighting to liberate Kuwait. It has signed a security treaty with the United States that provides for close cooperation in deployment of U.S. air power in the Gulf. Qatar has been somewhat ahead of its Gulf Arab neighbors in seeking normal relations with Iran, signing an economic accord with the Rafsanjani government in 1993.

BIBLIOGRAPHY

CARTER, LARAINE NEWHOUSE, and P. S. KLUCK. "Qatar." In *Persian Gulf States: Country Studies,* ed. by Richard F. Nyrop, Washington, D.C., 1984.
CRYSTAL, JILL. *Oil and Politics in the Gulf: Rulers and Merchants in Kuwait and Qatar.* Cambridge, U.K. 1990.

PETERSON, J. E. *The Arab Gulf States: Steps Toward Political Participation.* New York, 1988.
ZAHLAN, ROSEMARIE SAID. *The Creation of Qatar.* New York, 1979.

Malcolm C. Peck

Qatar General Petroleum Company

Replaced Qatar National Petroleum Company, 1974.

Qatar was a principal in the participation agreements worked out between Gulf oil exporters and their concession holders. However, the establishment of the Qatar General Petroleum Company (QGPC) signaled the government's decision to complete nationalization immediately. In December 1974, an emiri resolution provided for the transfer of ownership of the remaining shares in the Qatar National Petroleum Company and the properties of ROYAL DUTCH SHELL in Qatar to QGPC.

Like other ORGANIZATION OF PETROLEUM EXPORTING COUNTRIES (OPEC) national oil companies, QGPC moved downstream into refining and petrochemicals, and upstream into exploration and development. It purchased 40 percent of a petrochemicals complex located in Dunkerque, France, a joint venture between Qatar and France. QGPC also directs the development of Qatar's vast reserves of both nonassociated and associated natural gas. In 1992 it embarked on a strategy to enable it to compete in the world natural gas market, having completed the first phase of development of its huge North Field. It has contracts to deliver liquefied natural gas to Japan and Italy. The QGPC also embarked on an ambitious gas-based industrialization program. Many of QGPC's operations have been joint ventures with foreign firms.

BIBLIOGRAPHY

SKEET, IAN. *OPEC: Twenty-five Years of Prices and Politics.* New York, 1988.

Mary Ann Tétreault

Qatar University

The major institution of higher education in Qatar.

Qatar University is a coeducational institution that offers free education. For years the university was primarily staffed by Egyptian academics and has followed the Egyptian curriculum. Recently, more Qataris have joined the faculty, and the administration has adopted the American educational system, based on credits rather than the traditional yearlong courses. Courses are offered in education, psychology, *Shari'a* (Islamic Law), sciences, humanities, and engineering. A majority of its students, more than 50 percent of whom are women, major in education and teacher training.

BIBLIOGRAPHY

NYROP, RICHARD, ed. *Persian Gulf States: Country Studies.* Washington, D.C., 1985.

Emile A. Nakhleh

Qatif, al-

Saudi Arabian oasis on the Persian/Arabian Gulf.

Al-Qatif is an extensive oasis in al-HASA, the Eastern Province of Saudi Arabia. Its seaport, Qatif, is located on the Persian/Arabian Gulf coast north of Bahrain. A Christian center in the pre-Islamic period, it served as the capital of the Qarmatis, a Muslim sect, in the ninth century. Today, al-Qatif contains one of the two sizable Ja'fari Shi'a communities in Saudi Arabia.

John E. Peterson

Qattan, Abd al-Muhsin   [1929–   ]

Palestinian businessman.

Born in Jaffa, Abd al-Muhsin is the son of Muhsin al-Qattan, one of the earliest Palestinian refugees in Kuwait; he was a close associate of the ruling al-Sabah family. In 1959, Abd al-Muhsin founded the huge al-Hani Contracting Company, which has built major hotels and public works projects in Kuwait, Saudi Arabia, Jordan, and Lebanon. A supporter of the al-Fath faction of the Palestine Liberation Organization (PLO) since the 1950s, Abd al-Muhsin was elected president of the Palestine National Council in 1968, but he resigned in 1990 because of the PLO's support for Iraq after it invaded Kuwait (in what became known as the Gulf Crisis). As a philanthropist, he is a major supporter of social, cultural, and economic development among Palestinians.

BIBLIOGRAPHY

BRAND, LAURIE A. *Palestinians in the Arab World.* New York, 1988.
SMITH, PAMELA ANN. *Palestine and the Palestinians, 1876–1983.* London, 1984.

Elizabeth Thompson

Qattara Depression Scheme

Development project for one of seven large depressions in the Western desert of Egypt.

The Qattara is an uninhabited depression. It drops down to four hundred feet (122 m) below sea level and is the size of the state of New Jersey. It is the only depression that is not an oasis; it contains only salt water. In the 1980s, the feasibility of a project to construct a canal from the Mediterranean Sea to the Qattara depression was discussed by the government of Egypt. This project would generate electricity by using the 400-foot gradient in the depression.

BIBLIOGRAPHY

NYROP, RICHARD F., ed. *Egypt: A Country Study,* 4th ed. Washington, D.C., 1983.

David Waldner

Qattawi Family

See Cattaoui Family

Qavam al-Saltaneh   [1872–1954]

Iranian politician credited with the creation of the gendarmerie in Iran.

Best known by his titles of Dabir Hozur, Vazir Hozur, and Qavam al-Saltaneh, Qavam al-Saltaneh's rise to political prominence occurred during the reign of the Qajar and Pahlavi dynasties, during which he was appointed minister and prime minister in successive cabinets. He was accused of conspiracy twice, was jailed as many times, and succeeded repeatedly in restoring himself to power and wealth.

Cyrus Moshaver

Qawasim Emirate

See Qasimi Family, al-

Qawuqji, Fawzi al-   [c. 1887–?]

Military officer who led Arab nationalist forces against the imperial powers in Palestine.

Born in the late 1880s in Tripoli, Syria (later within Lebanon), Fawzi al-Din al-Qawuqji graduated from

the Ottoman military academy in Istanbul and served in the early part of World War I as a captain in the Ottoman cavalry. He switched sides to join the Arab revolt in 1916 and fought the French invasion of Emir Faisal's independent Syria in July 1920. Qawuqji commanded a cavalry company of the Syrian legion after the war and used that position to lead a revolt in October 1925, in Hama (Syria), against the French mandate forces. He coordinated with other nationalist forces in the landowning and merchant classes as well as with rural rebels. Qawuqji continued to lead a rebel band in the countryside during 1926/27 but fled to Iraq in April 1927 (where Faisal was king). Qawuqji then served in the Iraqi army, from where he hoped to launch an attack on Syria to free it from French rule. His 200-man guerilla force was, however, diverted to Palestine from August to November 1936 to assist the Palestinian general strike against British rule and Zionism. Qawuqji's forces were better prepared militarily than the Palestinian guerilla bands but did not cooperate effectively with the Palestinians. Qawuqji called himself Commander in Chief of the Arab Revolution in Southern Syria and failed to coordinate with Abd al-Qadir al-Husayni, leader of the Palestinian guerillas in the Hebron area.

Qawuqji spent World War II in Iraq and Axis-controlled Europe. Despite his tensions with Palestinian politicians, the League of Arab States requested Qawuqji to return to Palestine in January 1948 to head the Arab Liberation Army, which sought to prevent the partition of Palestine. Once again, Qawuqji failed to cooperate with Abd al-Qadir al-Husayni and other Palestinian guerilla leaders. He was severely defeated in his few encounters with the Haganah (the prestate armed forces of the Zionist movement). After Israel was established in May 1948 and the Arabs attacked, the Arab Liberation Army was forced out of central Galilee in July 1948 by Israeli forces—and from the rest of northern Galilee in October 1948. Qawuqji had taken a strong stand against the flight of Palestinian Arabs from their homes; he threatened to punish villagers who fled, and his forces even blocked roads to prevent them leaving. Nonetheless, his six-thousand-man force was too small to keep northern Palestine from being seized by Israel and many of its Arab residents being expelled by Israel's forces.

BIBLIOGRAPHY

KHOURY, PHILIP S. *Syria and the French Mandate: The Politics of Arab Nationalism, 1920–1945.* Princeton, N.J., 1987.
MORRIS, BENNY. *The Birth of the Palestinian Refugee Problem, 1947–1949.* New York, 1987.
PORATH, YEHOSHUA. *The Palestinian Arab National Movement, 1929–1939.* London, 1977.
EL-QAWUQJI, FAUZI. "Memoirs, 1948." *Journal of Palestine Studies* 4, 5 (1972): 27–58, 3–33.

Ann M. Lesch

Qena

An Upper Egyptian province (governorate).

Mainly agricultural, Qena has a land area of some 715 square miles (1,851 sq km) and a 1986 population estimated at 2,252,300. Its capital city, also Qina or Kena, had about 141,700 inhabitants in 1986 and is especially noted for the manufacture of a type of porous clay jar called a *ballas* or *qulla*. It was historically linked to the Red Sea port of al-Quseir by a well-used trade route. Originally called Coptos, it has been the seat of a bishopric of the Copts since the fifth century.

BIBLIOGRAPHY

Encyclopaedia of Islam, 2nd ed.
Europa World Yearbook 1994, vol. 1. London, 1994, p. 1024.

Arthur Goldschmidt, Jr.

Qirsh

One-hundredth of an Egyptian or Turkish lira.

The *qirsh* (plural, *qurush* or *kurush*), also known as the piastre, acquired its name from the Turkish *ghurush* (piastre). The piastre, the Italian name for the medieval *peso duro* (dollar), was introduced into the Levant in the early seventeenth century. The qirsh also serves as a monetary unit in Lebanon, Syria, and Sudan.

[*See also:* Lira]

Marilyn Higbee

Qiryat Arba

Jewish settlement outside of Hebron (Khalil).

One of the oldest and largest Jewish settlements in the occupied West Bank, Qiryat Arba was established in 1968 after Rabbi Moshe LEVINGER and followers checked into a HEBRON hotel and refused to leave. The planned residential/industrial center has grown steadily since then, reaching 350 families in 1977 and more than 800 families in the late 1980s.

While many settlers came to Qiryat Arba for purely economic reasons, the community is particularly known for its militant leadership committed to an ideology of extending Jewish sovereignty over the territories occupied by Israel in 1967 and provoking Arabs to emigrate. In 1974 Levinger helped found an extremist movement of Zionism, GUSH EMUNIM. In 1985 Qiryat Arba elected a member of Kach, the militant movement led by Meir Kahane, to its municipal council. Violent encounters with Palestinians in Hebron have continued through the years, turning particularly lethal from 1980 to 1982, when six Jews and three Arabs were killed.

BIBLIOGRAPHY

BENVENISTI, MERON. *The West Bank Data Project.* Washington, D.C., 1984.

―――. *The West Bank Handbook: A Political Lexicon.* Jerusalem, 1986.

HIRST, DAVID. *The Gun and the Olive Branch.* London, 1984.

LUSTICK, IAN S. *For the Land and the Lord: Jewish Fundamentalism in Israel.* New York, 1988.

Elizabeth Thompson

Qiryat Sefer

A Hebrew quarterly (in English, City of a Book) published in Jerusalem.

Founded in 1924, *Qiryat Sefer* (also spelled *Kirjath Sefer*) is published by the National and University Library. It is devoted to Jewish bibliographies of Hebrew and Jewish publications both in and outside Israel. A section of the journal is made up of book reviews by faculty members and other scholars at Hebrew University of Jerusalem on current Jewish literature.

Ann Kahn

Qiyomijian, Ohannes

Early twentieth-century Ottoman official in Lebanon.

Qiyomijian was born in Istanbul to an Armenian Catholic family. After completing his formal education, he was appointed to the Foreign Ministry. He served as a counselor for the embassy of the Ottoman Empire in Rome. He was twice asked to become a MUTASARRIF in Lebanon before he accepted the assignment in January 1912. Among his responsibilities

was adding a member from Dayr al-Qamar to the Administrative Council and revising the election laws. Qiyomijian established commercial courts and opened ports in Juniye (Juniyah) and Nabi Yunus. He enlarged the army to 1,200 and raised the salaries of the soldiers after their sit-in strike in Ba'abda. In 1913, he imported salt and tobacco directly into Lebanon in return for fees paid to the treasury of Mount Lebanon. Turkish mass killings of Armenians led Cemal Paça to insist on his dismissal and he tendered his resignation in June 1915.

As'ad AbuKhalil

Qom

Shrine town in Iran.

The city of Qom, 92 miles (147 km) south of Tehran, is, after Mashhad (the burial place of the eighth Shi'a *imam,* Ali Reza), the second most important shrine town in Iran. The sister of Imam Reza, Hazrat-e Fatima, is buried in Qom. The city was a winter capital as well as a royal mausoleum town during medieval times and was strongly patronized when the Shi'a Safavids came to power in the sixteenth century. In 1920 a religious center of learning (or *hauzeh-ye ilmiyeh*) was established in the city by Shaykh Abd al-Karim Ha'eri Yazdi. Through its *madrasa*s (or religious schools) Qom is one of the main centers of Islamic studies in Iran today. With the accession of Reza Shah Pahlavi to power in 1925, and the modernization reforms undertaken, the town soon became the scene of a struggle between the monarchy and the religious establishment. The first major episode of violence precipitating the IRANIAN REVOLUTION of 1978/79 occurred there. When Ayatollah Khomeini returned to Iran in 1979 as the leader of the revolution, he established his headquarters in the Madrasa-y Faiziyeh in Qom.

Parvaneh Pourshariati

Qotbzadeh, Sadeq   (1937–1982)

Iranian politician.

Charged with treason and plotting to kill Ayatollah Khomeini, Sadeq Qotbzadeh was executed in 1982 by partisans of the Islamic Republic of Iran, after having spent his entire life bringing about the downfall of the Pahlavi regime. He was born in Tehran in 1937 (1938 according to some accounts) to a conservative, religious merchant family. In 1958, fearful of being arrested by the government of Mohammad

Reza Shah Pahlavi because of his association with the more religious branch of the National Front, he left Iran to attend Georgetown University in Washington, D.C. While in America, he worked in the Islamic Student Association with Ibrahim Yazdi and Mostafa Chamran. His anti-shah activities in the United States led to the cancellation of his visa. He moved to Europe in 1963, where he joined an opposition movement led by Abolhasan BANI SADR. In 1979, he returned to Iran (on the same plane that was carrying Ayatollah Khomeini back to Iran) and became a member of the Revolutionary Council. In 1980, President Bani Sadr chose him to be foreign minister, but by February 1981, Bani Sadr had fled the country and Qotbzadeh was arrested on charges of conspiracy against the state and plotting to kill Ayatollah Khomeini. Qotbzadeh was not a radical and not a cleric, and as post-1979 Iran moved in both those directions, prodigal sons of the revolutionary movement were no longer favored. Qotbzadeh was, however, by some accounts, one of the key people involved in the disappearance of Imam Musa Sadr, Lebanese Shi'a leader, in Tripoli in 1979.

BIBLIOGRAPHY

JEROME, CAROLE. *The Man in the Mirror*. Toronto, 1987.

Neguin Yavari

Qsar Sa'id, Treaty of

See Bardo, Treaty of

Quarta Sponda

See Fourth Shore, The

Qudsi, Nazim al-

See Kudsi, Nazim al-

Qumran

See Dead Sea Scrolls

Qur'an

Holy book of Islam.

The Qur'an contains the written record of the Prophet MUHAMMAD's revelations, which he received between 610 and 632 C.E. Indeed, the word *qur'an* means "reading" or "recitation." Muslims believe that the Qur'an is the eternal and uncreated word of Allah. It is also considered the earliest and finest work of classical Arabic prose. The holy book is the foundation and primary source of Islamic law, SHARI'A.

The Qur'an's 114 chapters, called suras, are arranged in order of declining length, with the shortest, oldest chapters at the end. Muslims try to memorize as much of the holy book as they can, beginning in childhood.

BIBLIOGRAPHY

GIBB, H. A. R., ed. *The Shorter Encyclopedia of Islam*. Ithaca, N.Y., 1953.
GLASSÉ, CYRIL. *The Concise Encyclopedia of Islam*. London, 1989.
RAHMAN, FAZLUR. *Islam*, 2nd ed. Chicago, 1979.

Elizabeth Thompson

Qurai, Ahmad Sulaiman   [c. 1945–   ]

Palestinian economist; delegate to negotiations with Israel.

Ahmad Sulaiman Qurai (also called Abu Ala) was born in the village of Abu Dis near Jerusalem during the British mandate. He served as the chief Palestinian delegate to the secret Israeli–Palestinian negotiations in Oslo, Norway, which produced the September 1993 Israeli–Palestinian Declaration of Principles on Interim Self-Government Arrangements (DOP). In 1968, shortly after the West Bank came under Israeli occupation, he left for Jordan and subsequently Saudi Arabia, where he found employment in the banking sector. During this time he also joined the Palestine National Liberation Movement (al-FATH) and, after moving to Lebanon in the 1970s, was appointed director of Samid, the economic institution of the Palestine Liberation Organization (PLO). Relocating to Tunis after the PLO's 1982 evacuation from Beirut, he was appointed deputy director of the PLO's Department of Economic Affairs and was in 1989 elected to the Fath Central Committee. In 1994, Qurai was appointed director of the Department of Economic Affairs of the Palestinian Authority established in the autonomous regions of the occupied territories.

BIBLIOGRAPHY

CORBIN, JANE. *Gaza First: The Secret Norway Channel to Peace between Israel and the PLO*. London, 1994.

Mouin Rabbani

Qurayn, al-

Former local name of Kuwait.

Al-Qurayn is the name sometimes used during part of the eighteenth century and early in the nineteenth for the settlement since known exclusively as Kuwait. The spelling "Grane," found on European maps, reflected local pronunciation. The word is an Arabic diminutive that can mean either "little horn" or "hillock," with both representing appropriate translations since the town was established on a horn-shaped projection of land with a small rise.

BIBLIOGRAPHY

HOPWOOD, DEREK, ed. *The Arabian Peninsula: Society and Politics.* Totowa, N.J., 1972.

Malcolm C. Peck

Quraysh Tribe

The tribe of the Prophet Muhammad and the leading tribe of Mecca in the Prophet's time.

Before being converted to Islam, the Quraysh provided the strongest opposition to Muhammad, because the monotheism preached by the Prophet appeared to undermine tribal wealth derived from the pilgrimage to the KA'BA, then a house of idol-worship. In classical theory it was held that the leadership of the Muslim *umma* (community) should be held only by a descendant of the Quraysh tribe, and this idea has been used by political opposition groups in contemporary Saudi Arabia to challenge the legitimacy of the Al Sa'ud family, who are of the Anaza tribe. It has also been used to strengthen the legitimacy of the Sharifian dynasty of Morocco, which claims descent from the Quraysh.

Eleanor Abdella Doumato

Quseir, al-

Historic Egyptian port on the Red Sea.

This town in Egypt on the Red Sea is located slightly north of the twenty-sixth parallel, and linked to the Nile by a trade route to Qena. The site has been in use since pharaonic times and served as a port of embarkation for Muslim pilgrims to Mecca. It was a major commercial center in Mamluk and early Ottoman Empire times and experienced a revival under Muhammad Ali, but the pilgrimage traffic was diverted to Suez after the canal was built (1859–1869), eclipsing its importance.

BIBLIOGRAPHY

Encyclopaedia of Islam, 2nd ed.

Arthur Goldschmidt, Jr.

Qutayni, Rashad   [1923–?]

Syrian military officer.

Born to a Sunni family at Ma'arrat al-Nu'man, Qutayni was expelled from the army in April 1959 during a purge of Kurds, Druze, and Communists. He became chief of military intelligence in 1963, a position he used to help plan the March 1963 coup. Qutayni was deputy commander in chief after the coup until 27 April 1963, when he was dismissed for pro-Nasser activities. He escaped to Lebanon after an unsuccessful coup in July 1963 and was sentenced, in absentia, to life in prison for his participation.

Charles U. Zenzie

Qutb, Sayyid   [1906–1966]

Noted ideologue of the Muslim Brethren.

Born in Asyut, south of Cairo, to a family of impoverished rural notables, Qutb was trained as a teacher. Until 1942 he was an inspector in the Ministry of Public Instruction; he also wrote Wafdist political opinions in the popular press and published poetry, short stories, and literary criticism. From 1945 to 1948, he authored a series of articles critical of Egyptian politics. This earned him a de facto exile to the U.S. where he was sent by the Ministry to study the education system. It is during his three-year stay in the U.S. that Qutb, disturbed by what he considered to be American permissiveness and promiscuity, rediscovered his deep Muslim piety. Upon his return to Egypt in 1951 he was recruited by the Society of the Muslim Brethren (see MUSLIM BROTHERHOOD). In 1954, he was appointed editor-in-chief of the Society's newspaper *al-Ikhwan al-Muslimun* (the Muslim Brethren).

In the months before and after the July 1952 Revolution, Qutb and Gamal Abdel Nasser met regularly. Nonetheless, in the wake of a 1954 assassination attempt on Nasser's life by a Muslim Brother, Qutb spent ten years in prison. He was released in 1964 but reimprisoned in 1965. After being tortured and tried by a military court for conspiracy against Nasser, Sayyid Qutb, his brother, and a protégé were hanged on August 29, 1966.

During his incarceration from 1954 to 1964 Qutb wrote, and circulated outside prison, the most influential of his prolific Islamicist writings, *Ma'alim fi'l-Tariq* (Signposts). An account and interpretation of events in Nasser's concentration camps, it is a seminal work which served as the basis of the reconstituted Islamist movement in the early 1960s. *Ma'alim* preaches both the words and the actions ultimately necessary for the destruction of the secular regime and the creation of a Muslim state.

Qutb's theoretical writings, addressing the political, economic, and social organization of the Islamic state, vividly expressed the unity of *din* (religion) and *dawla* (civil society) in distinct contrast to the post-Enlightenment separation of Church and State prevalent in the West. Focusing on the intersection of *Shari'a* (Islamic law) and modern society, he maintained that the former was imbued with an inherent sense of *tajdid* (renewal). As such, it offered the principles necessary for progress through action. Moreover, Qutb held that laws and statutes were only one of Islam's two pillars; the other was education which alone could provide Muslims with an Islamic theory of life.

Through his writings, Sayyid Qutb established the theoretical foundations for Islamist organizations thriving in Egypt at the end of the twentieth century.

BIBLIOGRAPHY

KEPEL, GILLES. *Muslim Extremism in Egypt: The Prophet and Pharaoh.* Tr. by Jon Rothschild. Berkeley, Calif., 1985.
MITCHELL, RICHARD P. *The Society of the Muslim Brothers.* Oxford, 1969.

Jean-Marc R. Oppenheim

Quwatli, Shukri al- (1891–1967)

Three-time Syrian president; Arab nationalist.

Shukri al-Quwatli was born in Damascus to a Sunni Muslim family of prosperous landowners and bureaucrats who made their fortune through agriculture and trade with Abd al-Aziz ibn Abd al-Rahman Al Sa'ud in the Arabian peninsula. He was one of the most important figures in the political life of modern Syria. He received his education in the elite schools of Damascus and his public administration training in Constantinople (now Istanbul). Having no stake in the Ottoman Empire, he joined the secret Arab nationalist society al-FATAT and then the Hashimite-led ARAB REVOLT in 1916. His underground activities on behalf of the cause of Arab independence during World War I enabled him to emerge as a nationalist hero.

Although al-Quwatli served in the local administration of the Hashimite Prince Faisal ibn Husayn's Arab government, which was set up in Damascus after the defeat of the Ottoman state, he belonged to a group of avowed anti-Hashimite pan-Arabists who devoted most of their time to the ISTIQLAL PARTY (Arab Independence party). Forced to flee Syria after the French invasion of July 1920, al-Quwatli spent the next ten years in exile first in Cairo, which he used as a base for his activities on behalf of the Hashimite-leaning Syrian–Palestine Congress, and then in Europe, primarily Berlin, where he collaborated with other exiled Syrians in anti-French propaganda campaigns. He was active in supporting the Great Syrian Revolt of 1925–1927.

With the French amnesty of 1930, al-Quwatli returned to Damascus. Initially he maintained a low political profile devoting much of his time and energy to business ventures, primarily the processing and exporting of fruits and vegetables. The Syrian Conserves Company, which he founded in 1932, vaulted him into the limelight as an industrialist who promoted Syria's economic interests during a critical phase of its fight for independence.

Following the election of a Syrian parliament in 1932, al-Quwatli joined the NATIONAL BLOC, Syria's principal nationalist organization from 1927 until the end of the French mandate era. An uncompromising pan-Arabist devoted to the cause of Arab independence, al-Quwatli was soon disenchanted with the bloc's ineffectiveness and its policy of "honorable cooperation" with the French, and he became a leading instigator of the general strike that erupted in Syria on January 27, 1936, and brought commercial and educational life to a standstill for thirty-six days. When the all-bloc government was formed in Damascus in 1936, al-Quwatli served as minister of defense and of finance only to resign two years later. Although he was the leading nationalist politician in Syria during World War II, his anti-French activities forced him to go into exile in Iraq. However, his connections with Ibn Sa'ud made the British apply pressure on the French to accept his return. In the Syrian elections of 1943, he was elected to the presidency of a "formally" independent Syria. His nationalist sentiment, which was beyond reproach, enabled him to remain in office despite the factionalism and scandals that plagued his administration.

In March 1949, al-Quwatli was deposed as president by Col. Husni al-Za'im's successful coup and once again he went into exile, but this time in Egypt, a country on which he came to depend during the rest of his political life. Thanks to Egyptian and Saudi support, he returned to Syria in 1954 after the overthrow of the military regime of Col. Adib Shishakli. In August 1955, he was elected president of Syria for a third time. By that time, the political landscape in Syria had changed. The class of urban notables from which he hailed and which controlled Syrian politics from the latter part of the nineteenth century through the early years of independence was under attack by new political forces, including al-Ba'th and the communists. Syria's domestic politics was also weak and unstable, and the country itself was at the heart of a struggle for dominance between Hashimite Iraq and republican Egypt on the one hand, and the big powers on the other hand.

Al-Quwatli strongly supported the ideas of an Egyptian–Syrian union in 1957/58. With the consummation of the union and emergence of the United Arab Republic (UAR) in 1958, al-Quwatli's active participation in Syrian politics came to an end. He resigned his post as president to allow Gamal Abdel Nasser, Egypt's charismatic president, to take over the presidency of the UAR. Before his death in 1967, al-Quwatli witnessed the collapse of the UAR in 1961 and the coming to power of a factionalized group of Ba'thi military officers who came in the main from rural Alawi, Druze, and Isma'ili backgrounds significantly different from the landowning, scholarly, and mercantile Sunni families from which his generation of leaders hailed. The advent of these new groups to power brought with it the reorientation of Syrian politics, both domestically as well as in the area of foreign relations.

Muhammad Muslih

R

Raab, Esther [1894–1981]

The first Palestinian-born woman poet in the modern era to write and publish in Hebrew.

Raab's childhood in the early years of the first Jewish settlement of Petah Tiqvah shaped an intimate connection between her and the wild and primary landscape of Eretz Yisrael. This emotional relationship is expressed throughout her poems. In 1923 Raab's first poem, "I am Underneath the Bramble Bush" (*Ani Tachat Ha'atad*), was published in the new Hebrew literary periodical *Hedim,* but it was only in 1930 that her first book, *Thistles, (Kimshonim)*—containing thirty-two poems written between 1920 and 1930—was published.

Raab was a pioneer in her poetics. As early as the 1920s, Esther Raab's poems differed markedly from those of her mainstream male contemporaries and from those of other women poets of the time. Her early poetry is striking in its sensuous descriptions of the landscape of Eretz Yisrael and in its rebellious female voice. Moreover, this early work is notable for its rejection of the stanza and meter in favor of free verse and idiosyncratic syntax and word order. These elements of form and content, which set Esther Raab's poetry apart from the poetic and thematic conventions of her time, may have contributed to her fate as a poet. After the cool and sometimes openly hostile reception of her book, Raab fell into a two-decade-long silence. She started to publish again in the late 1950s.

Esther Raab died in Tiveon and was buried in the city of her birth, Petah Tiqvah. She requested that a few lines from her poem be engraved on her tombstone: "Your earth-clods were sweet to me/Homeland—just as the clouds of your sky/Were sweet to me."

Among Esther Raab's books of poetry are *The Poetry of Esther Raab* (1963), *As Last Prayer,* (1976), *Root's Sound* (an anthology; 1976), and *Esther Raab, Collected Poems* (1988). A second, enlarged edition of her collected poems was published in 1994, the one-hundredth anniversary of her birth.

BIBLIOGRAPHY

MIRON, DAN. *Founding Mothers, Stepsisters.* Tel Aviv, 1991.
SHAMIR, ZIVA. "The Buds of Poetry in an Unseeded Land—An Interview with Esther Raab." *Chadarim* 1: 101–118.
SHOHAM, REUVEN. *A Voice and an Image.* Haifa, 1988.

Shibolet Zait

Raad, In'am [1929–]

Lebanese politician.

Raad was born to a Greek Orthodox family in Ayn Zhalta. His father Tawfiq, a graduate of the American University of Beirut (AUB), was a pharmacist who emigrated for a few years to Australia. In 1949, Raad obtained his degree in political science at AUB. Until 1957, he taught Arabic, English, geography, and history at Broummana High School and other schools in Lebanon. In 1944, he joined the PARTI POPULAIRE SYRIEN (PPS, later the SYRIAN SOCIAL NATIONALIST

PARTY) and was elected several times to its politburo. Between 1958 and 1961, he was chief editor of the party's publications, *al-Bina* and *Sabah al-Khayr*. In 1961, following an attempted coup mounted by the PPS against the Lebanese government, Raad and his followers were condemned to death; then his sentence was commuted to a life sentence. In 1969, President Charles Hilu announced an amnesty for the civilian party members implicated in the coup. In 1992, Raad was elected president of the party.

BIBLIOGRAPHY

Arab Information Center, Beirut.
ZHUBIAN, SAMI. *The Lebanese Movement*. Beirut, 1977. In Arabic.

George E. Irani

Rabat

One of the four imperial cities of Morocco; national capital since 1912.

Since being named capital by the French in 1912, Rabat (also Ribat al-Fath) has grown in size and prestige as the new administrative, educational, and cultural center of Morocco. It is bordered by the Atlantic Ocean and the Bou Regreg river, which separates it from its rival sister city to the north, Salé.

Rabat takes its name from a small tenth-century *ribat* (monastery-citadel) manned by Muslim holy warriors (*murabit*s). The Almohad Sultan Ya'qub al-Mansur constructed a city on the site and named it Ribat al-Fath (Monastery of Conquest), in honor of a victory over Spain in 1195. Rabat's historical significance, along with its neighboring rival, Salé, stemmed from commercial trade and piracy in the seventeenth and eighteenth centuries. Spanish Muslims expelled from Spain in 1610 formed the core of Rabat's population.

At the beginning of the French protectorate in 1912, the French decision to relocate Morocco's capital to Rabat opened it to extensive development outside the original Arab city (*madina*) to the south and west. French colonial administrator General Louis-Herbert-Gonzalve Lyautey, in laying out the plan for Rabat, saw it as an opportunity to design an exemplary modern city. The major national university, Muhammed V, is located in Rabat, as are various national research institutes. Rabat and Salé together form an administrative prefecture that has grown at a rate of more than 5 percent annually since the late 1960s. The population of Rabat-Salé and environs numbers 1,287,000 (1987 figures).

The king's palace in Rabat. (Rhimou Berniko)

The Tower of Hasan, a minaret that is all that remains of a former royal mosque. (Rhimou Berniko)

BIBLIOGRAPHY

LEVI-PROVENCAL, E. "Rabat." In *Encyclopaedia of Islam*, 1st ed. Leiden, 1938. Reprint, 1978.
LUGHOD, JANET ABU. *Rabat: Urban Apartheid in Morocco*. Princeton, N.J., 1980
"Morocco." In *The Middle East and North Africa*. London, 1991.

Donna Lee Bowen

Rabat Arab Summit

Arab League conference in 1974 that recognized the PLO as leader of the Palestinians.

On October 25, 1974, the foreign ministers of nineteen of the League of Arab States (Arab League) convened in Rabat, Morocco, to coordinate an Arab strategy toward Israel and the West—to decide whether Jordan's King Hussein ibn Talal or the Palestine Liberation Organization (PLO) would represent the people of the West Bank in negotiations with Israel. The foreign ministers voted to recommend to their heads of state, who met the following day, to support the PLO's claim to any territory vacated by Israel, where Palestinians would have the right to establish a state of their own.

It was the seventh summit conference of the Arab League; a PLO delegation headed by Yasir Arafat participated. Only Muammar al-Qaddafi of Libya declined to attend. The final resolution of the conference affirmed the national rights of the Palestinians and their right to determine their own future. More importantly, it recognized the exclusive leadership of the PLO, choosing it to negotiate with Israel, and called for the return of any liberated Palestinian territory to the Palestinians themselves. Only Jordan voted against it. The Arab leaders also agreed on a multibillion dollar package of financial aid to Egypt, Syria, and Jordan, which border on Israel, and to the PLO.

The Rabat summit resolution is seen by many observers as an endorsement of a Middle East political settlement with a Palestinian state in the West Bank and Gaza alongside Israel. The following month, for the first time, Arafat spoke before the UN General Assembly as the acknowledged leader of the Palestinians.

BIBLIOGRAPHY

ROLEF, S. H., ed. *Political Dictionary of the State of Israel*. New York, 1987.

Benjamin Joseph

Rabbani, Burhanuddin   [1940–   ]

President of Afghanistan, 1993–   .

Born in Faizabad, Badakhshan province, in northern Afghanistan to a Tajik family, Rabbani was educated in Islamic studies at Kabul University and al-Azhar University in Cairo, where he received a master of arts degree (1968). He returned to Kabul to teach in the Faculty of Islamic law at Kabul University (1970) and was a leader of the Islamist movement in Afghanistan. In 1971, he joined the JAMI'AT-E ISLAMI and became its leader. In 1974, he fled Afghanistan for Pakistan, where he gained the help of the Pakistanis in the armed struggle against the Marxist government in Kabul. Because Rabbani is a Tajik, his political party drew most of its followers from the non-Pushtun Afghans, especially in the northern and western regions of Afghanistan.

With the collapse of the People's Democratic Party of Afghanistan (PDPA) government in 1992, Rabbani returned to Kabul, and he became president of the country in 1993.

BIBLIOGRAPHY

ROY, OLIVIER. *Islam and Resistance in Afghanistan*. New York, 1986.

Grant Farr

Rabbinate

Title derived from "rabbi," or "rav," which in Hebrew denotes a master.

In its talmudic origins, the mastery to which *rabbi* referred was a knowledge of both scripture and Jewish oral tradition, including competence in interpreting law and recalling legends. Although at first the title was honorific, it evolved into something more formal. Always connected with a level of superior scholarship and familiarity with sacred Jewish texts, it has in contemporary times also come to signify general religious leadership.

Although the requirements for acquiring the title are not stipulated in Jewish law, *semikha* or ordination—in which another rabbi attests to the scholarship and learning of the initiate—has become an assumed prerequisite of being called rabbi. Throughout much of Jewish history, this process occurred in the context of yeshivas; currently, it also takes place in theological seminaries.

Generally, civil authorities have recognized the right of the Jews to decide for themselves who may be called rabbi. This became more complicated after

Jews ceased to speak with a single communal voice in the modern period, with the consequence that different groups of Jews set various criteria for deciding who would be entitled to be called rabbi. Thus in the modern period in the United States, for example, there are four types of rabbis being ordained, to represent the four different denominations: Reformed, Reconstructionist, Conservative, and Orthodox. The Orthodox denomination, although it represents a minority of world Jewry, produces the most rabbis. Throughout Jewish history, the title has been granted only to men, but in the late twentieth century, non-Orthodox Jews began to ordain women as well. In Israel, only Orthodox rabbis are officially recognized, even though Reformed and Conservative rabbis are also there.

Two general categories of rabbis evolved in modern times: those who were primarily teachers, scholars, or legal decisors and remained in the academy of Jewish learning or sometimes served on a religious court, and those who ministered in the community and the synagogue. Rabbis have also become ratifiers of changes in personal status by officiating at weddings, funerals, and other rites of passage.

The rabbinate in modern Israel is unique in several important respects. Because there is no strict separation of religion and state in Israel, HALAKHAH is the governing law in all matters of personal status. Accordingly, the Orthodox rabbinical interpretation of Jewish law is dominant. In Israel, many rabbis exert their authority as officials of the state Ministry of Religion and the office of the Chief Rabbinate. Headed by two national chief rabbis elected by a board of fellow rabbis for a term of ten years, the Chief Rabbinate is divided into Ashkenazic and Sephardic wings. Ostensibly empowered to make all ultimate religious decisions, it also provides parish rabbis and chief rabbis for major municipal regions.

There are other rabbis in Israel, particularly within Hasidic and yeshiva circles. Unlike the state rabbis whose authority is official, these rabbis dominate by virtue of their charisma or perceived scholarship. The relatively few non-Orthodox rabbis in Israel have a limited following. During the last few decades, the chief rabbis and their subordinates have steadily lost moral authority. Today the majority of secular Israelis consider them irrelevant, and the minority of ultra-Orthodox Jews guide themselves by their own sages whom they endow with greater rabbinic authority. This leaves only a narrow band of Orthodox Jews—primarily religious Zionists—who recognize the moral preeminence of the Chief Rabbinate. Nevertheless, the Chief Rabbinate is assured of influence as long as it continues to control matters of personal status and religious certification in the state.

BIBLIOGRAPHY

SAMUEL C. HEILMAN, "Jewish Unity and Diversity: A Survey of American Rabbis and Rabbinical Students." In *Encyclopedia Judaica*, vol. 13.

Samuel C. Heilman

Rabi, Ali Salim

See Salim Rabiyya Ali

Rabil, Mubarak   [1935–   ]

Moroccan novelist and short story writer.

Rabil was born in Benma'ashu, near Casablanca, Morocco. He received a degree in philosophy from the Faculty of Arts in Rabat, and has a master's degree in psychology. He is at present associate professor at the Mohammad V University in Rabat. Rabil is a member of the Union of Arab Writers and writes in Arabic. After unsuccessful efforts at poetry, he has concentrated solely on fiction. He received the Maghribi Prize for the novel and the short story in 1971.

Rabil is primarily concerned with Moroccan life and the role of magic and traditional beliefs in people's lives. This is best illustrated in his collection of short stories, *Sayyidna Qadr* (1969; Saint Destiny). His books reveal a clear interest in human nature and a desire to discover the factors that shape it, producing good and bad. He is preoccupied with the loss of values in modern times and the ensuing conflicts among people. His fiction remains detached from the political turmoil in Morocco.

Rabil is deeply interested in the education of children, as is obvious from his most recent novel, *Badr Zamanihi* (1983; The Full Moon of His Time) and his collection of essays, *Awatif al-Tifl* (1984; The Child's Emotions).

[*See also:* Literature, Arabic, North African]

Aida A. Bamia

Rabin, Yitzhak   [1922–1995]

Israeli military leader and politician; member of the Knesset; prime minister, 1974–1977; 1989–1995.

Born in Jerusalem, Yitzhak Rabin received part of his early education at an agricultural school; later, he became active in the AHDUT HA-AVODAH (socialist labor) movement in the Galilee. In 1941, he joined

Prime Minister Yitzhak Rabin. (Israel Office for Information)

the PALMACH, the Jewish Defense Forces' commando unit. His early military experience included fighting against Vichy French forces in Syria and Lebanon. In the Israel War of Independence (1948), he fought against the Egyptians in the Negev campaign and also in Jerusalem. He subsequently studied in Britain at the army staff college, from which he graduated in 1953.

Rabin, whose first career was a military one, was appointed chief of staff of Israel's armed forces in 1964; at the time of the June, 1967 Six Day War he was Israel's commander in chief. In 1968, he retired from the army and became Israel's ambassador to the United States. He was very successful in that capacity, and this experience combined with his military career gave him the leverage to start a second career, in politics, at the age of fifty-one.

Rabin returned to Israel from Washington in March 1973; in the same year, he was elected to the Knesset for the first time and also served as minister of labor in the government of Prime Minister Golda

MEIR. In April 1974 when Meir resigned because of intense criticism of her handling of the 1973 Yom Kippur War, the LABOR PARTY's Central Committee could choose her successor from among a field of candidates that included Shimon Peres, Moshe Dayan, Yigal Allon, Pinhas Sapir, and Abba Eban, as well as Rabin. Rabin was selected (June 1974) because of his reputation as a war hero and because he was not associated with unpreparedness for the war.

In creating his majority coalition, Rabin, who was Israel's first sabra prime minister, refused to give in to demands of members of the National Religious party. He consequently achieved only a bare majority, with the help of the new and small Citizen's Rights movement, and this left his government vulnerable to periodic attacks in the Knesset. From 1974 to 1975, Rabin worked closely with Henry Kissinger when the latter was involved in the shuttle diplomacy for which he became internationally renowned.

Rabin's first term as prime minister was characterized by intraparty bickering, primarily because of his Defense Minister Shimon Peres's efforts to take over leadership of the party and become the prime minister. Domestic economic problems, chiefly in regard to inflation, continuing criticism of the Labor party's performance in the Yom Kippur War, and increased ethnic tensions between Ashkenazic and Sephardic Jews in Israeli society (see ASHKENAZIM and SEPHARDIM) all contributed to a gradual decline in the Labor party's popularity and the rise of the LIKUD party under Menachem Begin. Rabin resigned from the party leadership and from his post as prime minister in May 1977 because of a financial scandal involving his own and his wife's bank accounts in the United States. Shimon Peres then replaced him as party leader.

After twelve years, during which the Labor party, led by Shimon Peres, was the opposition party in a shared-power arrangement with the Likud, Rabin again became the party leader and the prime minister (1989). Over intense opposition from conservative forces in Israel, he pressed hard for a peace treaty with the Palestinians and Israel's Arab neighbors. In September 1993, he signed an Agreement on Principles on Interim Self-Government with Yasir Arafat of the Palestine Liberation Organization, and an Accord to Implement Self-Rule for the Palestinians was signed in May 1994. In October 1994, he signed a full peace treaty with King Hussein of Jordan. In the same year, he shared a Nobel Peace Prize with Foreign Affairs Minister Peres and Chairman Arafat.

On November 4, 1995, while he was speaking at a peace rally, Rabin was assassinated.

BIBLIOGRAPHY

RABIN, YITZHAK. *The Rabin Memoirs.* Boston, 1979.
SACHAR, HOWARD M. *A History of Israel: From the Rise of Zionism to Our Time.* New York, 1981.

                                        Gregory S. Mahler

Radio and Television

Radio and, later, television have played important roles in the social and political life of the Middle East.

The first radio station in the United States commenced broadcasting in Pittsburgh in 1920. Egypt did not lag far behind. The Egyptian State Broadcasting Corporation was authorized in 1932 and began broadcasting two years later under contract with the Marconi Company. However, this government station was preceded by six private stations in Cairo (e.g., Faruq, Fu'ad, Wadi al-Muluk) and two in Alexandria (Farid, Majestic). By 1932, these stations were already broadcasting Qur'an reading, news, and Eastern, Western, and Turkish music. Four years later, the first radio station was established in Jidda for broadcasting in the western part of Saudi Arabia (King Abd al-Aziz ibn Sa'ud had used a private wireless broadcasting system in 1932) and the British Colonial Office, with BBC assistance, established the Palestine Broadcasting Service in Jerusalem. The next year the Lebanese Broadcasting Station was founded. In 1940, Mohammad Reza Shah Pahlavi inaugurated Radio Tehran, which succeeded the small station, Bisim-e Pahlavi, established by his father Reza Shah at the time of his coronation in 1926.

Aside from early efforts at private broadcasting, radio and television have generally, but not entirely, been dominated by government authority and viewed as a means of communicating with the citizenry. King Ghazi of Iraq (1933–1939), for example, had his own station on which he attacked the government of Kuwait. Mustafa Kemal Atatürk ordered a radio installed in each of the PEOPLE'S HOUSES (*Halk Evleri*) to ensure universal dissemination of the reforms advocated by the government station. Between 1945 and 1951 the number of radios in Turkish villages almost quadrupled.

Stations outside the Middle East have beamed programs to the area in Arabic, Persian, and Turkish. Italy began broadcasting shortwave Arabic-language programs from Bari in 1934. These broadcasts, designed to enhance Italian influence, turned sharply anti-British the following year during the Abyssinian war. This, in turn, set off a governmental debate in Britain that culminated in the BBC beginning its shortwave Arabic Service in 1938. (This did not conflict with BBC's preexisting shortwave Empire Service that broadcast exclusively in English.)

During World War II, other countries competed for the Middle Eastern audience. The Palestinian leader Hajj Amin al-Husaini, having fled Iraq after the abortive Rashid Ali coup against Britain, broadcast anti-British messages from Berlin. Britain established al-Sharq al-Adna (Near East) station in Jaffa, which was on the air with news and light entertainment for more hours than the BBC Arabic Service and was more openly a propaganda arm of the British government than the quasi-independent BBC. It also broadcast in Turkish and Persian. The Voice of America began in 1942 and developed broadcasting in Arabic, Persian, and Turkish.

Gamal Abdel Nasser greatly expanded the use of radio as an instrument of propaganda and foreign policy. Al-SAWT AL-ARAB (The Voice of the Arabs) went on the air in 1953. By the early 1960s it was broadcasting in 24 languages for a total of 755 hours a week, a rate exceeded only by the United States, the USSR, the Federal Republic of Germany, and the United Kingdom. Rival stations, such as Kol Israel, could not match the influence of the Cairo transmitters. Political broadcasting was occasionally done by private stations, as was the case, beginning in the 1970s, with Abie Nathan's pleas for accommodation between Israelis and Arabs broadcast in Hebrew from a ship in international waters.

In the 1960s, with the spread of cheap transistor radios, broadcasting became more widespread and diverse. Riyadh's first station was inaugurated in 1965, and one in Dammam began two years later. In 1964, a commercial station called Middle East Radio was established in Egypt. Radio Monte Carlo, a French supported offshore broadcaster, also became

Communications tower in Kuwait City. (Richard Bulliet)

popular. A 1989 survey reported the most frequently mentioned stations received by its sample of Egyptian radio listeners were, in order, the BBC Arabic Service, Emirates radio, Kuwait radio, Radio Monte Carlo, various Saudi stations, Qatar radio, Middle East Radio, and Cairo radio. In Cairo, Riyadh, Kuwait, and elsewhere, immense broadcasting towers are urban landmarks.

Television has generally had less impact on international politics than radio because of the shorter broadcasting range, but its heavy use of programming imported from the West has made it, in some countries, a powerful instrument of westernization. Iraq inaugurated the television age in 1958. In that same year, permission was granted in Iran for a private commercial station, Televizion-e Iran. The Compagnie Libanaise de Télévision was founded in 1959 and Télé Orient, also in Beirut, in the following year. Saudi Arabia began broadcasting in 1965 despite strong religious objections. In 1967 National Iranian Television went on the air, increasing the number of viewers in that country from 2.1 million to 4.8 million, a number that more than tripled by 1974. By that time, Iran claimed the second largest broadcasting system in Asia, after Japan.

Satellite communications serve to transmit television as well as telephone, fax, and and other electronic signals. By this means, television from many parts of the world has become available in different parts of the Middle East. Arabsat IA and IB satellites were launched into orbit in 1985 to provide communications among the member states of the Arab League. Via satellite, Middle Eastern television stations can receive the broadcsts of CNN and other international services for rebroadcast. However, owners of home satellite antennas can receive these transmissions directly, thus jeopardizing the control governments have over what their citizens are viewing. Iran and Saudi Arabia are among the countries that have tried to limit the use of such private satellite antennas.

Videotape is also seen by many governments as a dangerous source of uncontrolled information and entertainment flow. A number of countries, e.g. Oman and Saudi Arabia, try to limit the influx of videotapes for both moral and political reasons. Nevertheless, pirating and smuggling of videotapes is widespread, though these are less often used for subversive political purposes than audiocassettes.

BIBLIOGRAPHY

KATZ, E., and D. SHINAR. *The Role of Broadcasting in National Development.* Jerusalem, 1974.
LERNER, DANIEL. *The Passing of Traditional Society: Modernizing the Middle East.* New York, 1958.

MOSTYN, TREVOR. "The Media of Communication." In *The Cambridge Encyclopedia of the Middle East and North Africa,* ed. by Trevor Mostyn. Cambridge, U.K. 1988, pp. 149–154.
PARTNER, PETER. *Arab Voices: The BBC Arabic Service 1938–1988.* London, 1988.
al-SHAL, INSHIRAH. *Al-Sawt al-Arab baina al-ams wa al-yawm.* Cairo, 1989.
SREBERNY-MOHAMMADI, ANNABELLE, and ALI MOHAMMADI. "Communications in Persia." In *Encyclopaedia Iranica,* vol. 6, pp. 89–95.

Richard W. Bulliet

Rafa Salient

Israeli town situated near the coast of the Mediterranean Sea.

Situated twenty-two miles south of Gaza, near the present day border between Egypt and Israel, Rafa is mentioned in Egyptian texts as early as 1300 B.C.E., and was the site of military conflicts between Egypt and such neighboring powers as the Assyrians and the Romans.

There was a Jewish community in Rafa from the ninth through the twelfth centuries. In the early years of the twentieth century, Zionists from Central and Eastern Europe made several unsuccessful attempts to settle there. After the Arab–Israel War (1948) Palestinian refugees settled in evacuated British Army camps. In 1956, Israeli forces briefly gained control of the area, and the Egyptians evacuated the Arab population in March 1957. During the Arab–Israel War (1967) Israel again gained control of Rafa.

BIBLIOGRAPHY

ORNI, EFRAIM, and ELISHA EFRAT. *Geography of Israel.* 1971.

Bryan Daves

Raffi   [1835–1888]

Armenian writer; major novelist of the nineteenth century.

Raffi was born Hakob Melik-Hakobian in the village of Payajuk, in northwest Iran. He received his elementary education locally and attended high school in Tbilisi. He returned to Payajuk, but his family's poverty led him to seek employment as a teacher in Tabriz and Agulis between 1875 and 1879. He then became a contributor to the liberal Armenian paper *Mshak* (Laborer), published in Tbilisi, where he spent the rest of his life.

Influenced by the European romantic novel, Raffi became the greatest epic novelist in the Armenian language, treating emancipation, social injustice, political inequality, and national identity. He was a student of Armenian traditional society, whose virtues and limitations he transcribed into fine literature.

The Russo–Turkish War of 1877/78 turned Raffi's attention to political emancipation and national liberation, themes he developed in his best works. *Khente* (The Fool; 1881) and *Kaydser* (Sparks; 1883–1887) explored the subject in a contemporary setting. *Davit Bek* (1882), named after the renowned Armenian leader, revived the Armenian liberation struggle of the early eighteenth century, and *Samuel* (1886) relocated the struggle for Armenian freedom and identity in the fourth-century contest between Byzantium and Persia over Armenia.

Raffi is regarded as a major figure in the Armenian cultural renaissance of the nineteenth century and in the creation of modern Armenian literature. Raffi's immense output recorded and analyzed the social and political issues of his era. His skill in crafting Armenian popular literature was matched by his influence in drawing the attention of an increasingly literate audience to the range of broader issues facing the Armenians as a people. In the companion volume to *Davit Bek, Khamsayi Melikutiunnere* (The Five Melikdoms [of Karabagh]; 1882), he published the historical evidence on which he had based his novel.

[*See also:* Literature, Armenian; Bek, Davit]

Rouben P. Adalian

Rafi Party

Israeli political party founded in 1965 by several dissidents from the MAPAI party.

Founders of the Rafi party expressed their dissatisfaction with the formation of the Alignment by the MAPAI party, their resentment over alleged inflexibility of MAPAI and its failure to give opportunities to young leaders, and their displeasure with the handling of the LAVON AFFAIR (a bitter dispute over government handling of a spying operation gone awry). The leading dissident was David Ben-Gurion, who was joined by others including Moshe Dayan, Shimon Peres, and Yizhak Navon. Among the programs that Rafi advocated were regional elections, personal election of mayors, gov-

ernment financing of elections, overhaul of much of the systems of health and unemployment insurance, and free compulsory education between the ages of three and sixteen. Rafi won ten seats in the Knesset in 1965. In 1958, Dayan and most other Rafi leaders, with the exception of Ben-Gurion, rejoined MAPAI and were among those who founded the Israeli LABOR PARTY.

BIBLIOGRAPHY

ARONOFF, MYRON J. *Power and Ritual in the Israeli Labor Party.* Wolfeboro, N.H., 1977.

Walter F. Weiker

Rafsanjani, Hashemi [1935–]

President of the Islamic Republic of Iran.

Born in the southeast Iranian city of Rafsanjan, Rafsanjani began his religious education at the early age of fourteen in Qom (Qum), where from 1958 onward he was a leading figure among the younger disciples of Ayatollah Ruhollah Khomeini. His first arrest for political activities against the regime of Mohammad Reza Shah Pahlavi came in 1964 when he was taken to the Bagh-e Shah garrison in Tehran; he succeeded in escaping after undergoing two months of torture. He thereupon joined the ranks of the Allied Islamic Associations, and in January 1965, after the assassination of Prime Minister Hasan Ali Mansur by four members of this organization, he was jailed at the Qezel Qal'eh prison in Tehran, this time for four and a half months.

Resuming his clandestine organizational work in Qom, Rafsanjani was next jailed in 1967 for publicly opposing the shah's extravagant coronation ceremonies. In 1973, he was sentenced to eight years in prison on charges of collaboration with the MOJAHEDIN-E KHALQ guerilla organization; in the end, Rafsanjani only served four years of this sentence.

After the triumph of the Iranian Revolution in February 1979, Rafsanjani was appointed to the council of Islamic Revolution, and when the government of Mehdi Bazargan resigned in November of that year, he was also appointed acting minister of the interior. A founding member of the Islamic Republican party (IRP), he was elected chairman of Iran's legislature, the *majles*—which was dominated by that party and its allies—on July 20, 1980. Through the skillful use of this office, he swiftly became one of the most visible and influential politicians in the country, a process that was accelerated when his senior colleagues in the IRP began falling victim to assassination. Important, too, for the growth of his popular appeal were the nationally televised sermons he frequently delivered at the Friday prayers in Tehran University. After the death of Ayatollah Khomeini on June 3, 1989, President Ali Khamene'i was elevated to the position of leader (*rahbar*) of the Islamic Republic, and Rafsanjani was elected the next president in August 1989. On June 11, 1993, he was elected to a second term with 63.2 percent of a turnout that represented 57.6 percent of the electorate. Once reputed to favor radical socio-economic reform, Rafsanjani now enjoys the reputation of a pragmatist concerned above all with the reconstruction of the Iranian economy.

BIBLIOGRAPHY

Hiro, Dilip. *Iran under the Ayatollahs*. London, 1985.

Hamid Algar

Ra'i, al-

Jordanian newspaper.

Founded in 1971, *al-Ra'i* (The Opinion) is an Arabic-language morning daily published by the Jordan Press Foundation. In August 1988, the government dismissed the paper's board of directors, following a general crackdown on the press, and exercised editorial control over it until December 1989, when it relinquished its control. With a circulation of 80,000, it is one of Jordan's three major daily newspapers in Arabic.

BIBLIOGRAPHY

The Middle East and North Africa 1991, 37th ed. London, 1991.

Abla M. Amawi

Railroads

See Berlin–Baghdad Railway; Hijaz Railroad; Trans-Iranian Railway; Transport

Raisuli

See Ahmad ibn Muhammad al-Raysuni

Raja'i, Mohammad Ali   [1933–1981]

Iran's second prime minister and second president after the Islamic Revolution of 1979.

Raja'i, born in Qazvin to a lower-class family, rose from being a street peddler to a high school mathematics teacher. He was active in the Liberation Movement of Iran from the 1960s until 1979. He then joined the more radical Islamic Republican party and subsequently served as prime minister and president of the country. Raja'i died in a bomb explosion.

BIBLIOGRAPHY

Bakhash, Shaul. *The Reign of the Ayatollahs*. New York, 1986.

Neguin Yavari

Rajavi, Masud   [1947–   ]

Leader of the Iranian Mojahedin-e Khalq since 1979.

Masud Rajavi was born in Tabas in central Khorasan. He completed secondary school in Mashhad and studied political science at Tehran University. Because of his activities with the MOJAHEDIN-E KHALQ, he was arrested in 1971 and condemned to death, but this sentence was commuted to life imprisonment. He remained in jail until the Iranian Revolution of 1979. Following the revolution, Rajavi rebuilt the mojahedin, attracting hundreds of thousands of supporters. Since a 1981 government crackdown, Rajavi has led the mojahedin in exile from Iraq.

BIBLIOGRAPHY

Abrahamian, Ervand. *The Iranian Mojahedin*. New Haven, Conn., 1989.

Ervand Abrahamian

Rakah

See Communist Party, Israel

Ramadan

The ninth month of the Islamic lunar calendar; a month of obligatory fasting for Muslims.

According to Islamic law, Ramadan is the sacred month during which Muslims of majority age are obliged to fast, to abstain from all food, drink, smoking, rumination, and sexual activity from dawn until sunset each day. One of the five principal duties, or "pillars," of Islam, the Ramadan fast is viewed by Muslims as a unique opportunity to alter the character and pace of their daily lives and renew their commitment both to the original "God" (Allah) and their fellow Muslims.

In addition to the central rite of fasting, Ramadan is marked by a number of supplementary activities designed to deepen personal religious devotion, while at the same time sustain and nourish communal solidarity among the faithful. Increased charitable giving and other forms of social service, spiritual retreats (i'tikaf) to the local mosque, reduced work hours, daily communal Qur'an recitation, evening gatherings of families and friends for fast-breaking (iftar), and other supererogatory worship practices are among the many special features of Ramadan observance in Muslim societies worldwide. Out of the entire sacred month, the final ten nights of Ramadan are considered particularly auspicious because, according to Muslim lore, one of the odd-numbered of these nights is the famed "Night of Power" (laylat al-qadr)—the night in which the Qur'an was first revealed to the Prophet Muhammad and the night which the Qur'an itself praises as "better than a thousand months" (97:3–5).

While every night of Ramadan is a celebration of another day spent in fasting and fellowship, the joyful mood of the month reaches its climax in the grand Festival of the Fast-Breaking (id al-fitr), which occurs on the evening of the new moon marking the end of Ramadan and the beginning of the month of Shawwal. Since the Muslim lunar year is eleven days shorter than the Western solar year, and has no intercalary month to keep, the month of Ramadan and the Festival of the Fast-Breaking recede through the Western calendar, occurring in different Western solar months and, therefore, different seasons every few solar years.

BIBLIOGRAPHY

GUILLAUME, ALFRED. Islam. Baltimore, 1962.

Scott Alexander

Ramadan Revolution

Ba'th coup that overthrew Abd al-Karim Kassem.

On the morning of February 8, 1963 (14 Ramadan, 1382), BA'TH party members and other pan-Arab army officers led a tank force and a few jet fighters against the regime in Iraq of General Abd al-Karim KASSEM. He was defended by a few army units and the Iraq Communist party, but on the next day he and his chief officers surrendered and were summarily executed. Street battles died out only a day or so later.

Following the coup, General Abd al-Salam Arif was made a figurehead president. Real power was shared between the Iraqi Regional Command of the Ba'th party and the National Council of Revolutionary Command (NCRC), in which the Ba'th had a majority. Accordingly, the government was placed under the Ba'thi generals Ahmad Hasan al-Bakr (prime minister), Salih Mahdi Ammash (minister of defense), Tahir Yahya (chief of staff), Hardan Abd al-Ghaffar al-Tikriti (commander of the air force), and a few non-Ba'thi officers.

The new regime failed in practically everything it tried, save for a horrendous slaughter of communists that went unabated throughout their nine-month-long rule. Lack of experience and conflicting views over nationalizations led to economic chaos. An attempt to forge a trilateral unity with Ba'thi Syria and Nasserite Egypt collapsed amid vitriolic recriminations. Relations with the Soviet Union reached bottom with the anti-communist campaign. Worst of all was the intense infighting. The civilian party leadership was torn between a so-called leftist group—led by Secretary-General Ali Salih al-Sa'di (a Sunni Arab)—and a rightist one—under Talib Shabib and Hazim Jawad (Shi'ites). The unruly party militia, the National Guard, was controlled by Sa'di, through its radical commander, Flight Major Mundhir al-Wandawi, but Jawad held the powerful position of minister of interior with its own internal security force. A group of Ba'thi senior army officers (with a few civilians, notably Tariq Aziz and Saddam Hussein) under Bakr formed a centrist faction, which tried in vain to mediate. Finally, the party lost control of the national guard, whose barbaric conduct antagonized the public and even the army. At the same time, however, many nonpartisan army officers that the party could not control held key posts.

From November 11 to 18, Baghdad became the scene of a chaotic struggle among all three Ba'th factions. The Damascus-based pan-Arab leadership of the party—headed by Secretary-General Michel Aflaq, Syria's president Amin al-Hafiz, and the Syrian Colonel Salah Jadid—flew in, but their arbitration attempt failed. When the confusion reached its peak, the army, under President Arif, crushed the national guard and took over. Even some of the party's centrist army officers supported Arif's coup. A few Ba'thi centrists were rewarded with government positions, but a few months later they were dismissed, to start clandestine activity all over again. A by-product of the Ba'th failure was the near-disappearance of Shi'ites from the upper echelon of party activists.

From this traumatic experience, Saddam Hussein drew a few drastic lessons—to purge the army and distance it from politics; to concentrate all power in one hand; and to never allow a split in the party, even if this meant the death of his colleagues.

BIBLIOGRAPHY

DEVLIN, JOHN F. *The Ba'th Party: A History from Its Origins to 1966.* Stamford, Conn., 1976.
AL-FUKAYKI, HANI. *Awkar al-Hazima.* London, 1993.

Amatzia Baram

Ramadan War

See Arab–Israel War (1973)

Ramallah

Palestinian city on the West Bank.

Located about sixteen kilometers (6.5 mi.) north of Jerusalem on the western side of the Nablus–Jerusalem road, Ramallah was an important urban center under the British mandate. After Jordan annexed the West Bank in 1950, it became part of the Jerusalem governorate. In the Arab–Israel War of 1967, Ramallah was occupied by Israel. It has been the site of many clashes between Israel's military authorities and Palestinians since then.

[*See also:* Mandate System]

Lawrence Tal

Ramgavar Azadagan Party

Armenian political party of Lebanon.

The ultimate goal of the Ramgavar Azadagan party, founded in 1921, was the liberation of Armenia. It has oriented its activities toward preserving Armenian culture among Armenian communities throughout the world. After a period of dormancy, the party was revived in the 1950s, in the wake of the increasing conflicts between the Dashnak party and the HUNCHAK PARTY. The Ramgavar party presented itself as an alternative that avoided issues divisive to the Armenian community. During the Lebanese civil war of 1975, the Ramgavar party opposed what it

considered to be the right-wing policies of the Dashnak party.

As'ad AbuKhalil

Ramla

Also called Er Ramle, a town in Israel located twelve miles (19 km) southeast of Tel Aviv.

Ramla was founded in 717 to replace nearby Lydda as the region's capital under the Arab caliphate. It soon outstripped its neighbor in size and prosperity, thriving on trade and industry, particularly soap and olive oil. More than three-quarters of Ramla's 1946 population of 16,380 was Palestinian. In the 1948 Arab–Israel War, Israeli troops occupied the area and forced the evacuation of thousands of the town's Palestinian residents. The town's population grew again after the war with the arrival of new Jewish immigrants. By 1968, its population of 38,500 included fewer than 5,000 Arabs.

BIBLIOGRAPHY

KHALAF, ISSA. *Politics in Palestine: Arab Factionalism and Social Disintegration 1939–1948.* Albany, N.Y. 1991.
SACHAR, HOWARD M. *A History of Israel.* New York, 1979.

Elizabeth Thompson

Rapid Deployment Force

See Central Command

Rasafi, Ma'ruf al-   [1875–1945]

Most prominent poet in Iraq between the world wars.

Rasafi was born in Baghdad into a family of Kurdish origin, and studied at the Rashidiyya school there. His knowledge of classical Arabic sources enabled him to teach Arabic language and literature in higher institutes of learning in Baghdad, Jerusalem, and Constantinople (now Istanbul). He represented Baghdad in the Chamber of Deputies in Constantinople, and after the establishment of the kingdom of Iraq, he was elected to parliament.

Although his poetry was composed in a classical language, Rasafi was regarded as a voice of the people who fearlessly attacked Iraq's social and political maladies.

A first edition of Rasafi's *Diwan* was published in Beirut in 1910. Subsequent editions in his lifetime appeared in 1925 in Cairo and in 1931 in Beirut. A five-volume annotated edition was published in Baghdad in 1986.

Rasafi published works on Arabic language and literature, including an important study on the modern dialect of Baghdad (serialized in al-Karmali's *Lughat al-Arab* in 1926–1928).

[*See also:* Literature, Arabic]

BIBLIOGRAPHY

BADAWI, M. M. *A Critical Introduction to Modern Arabic Poetry.* Cambridge, U.K., 1975.
———, ed. *Modern Arabic Literature.* Cambridge, U.K. 1992.
AL-JAYYUSI, S. K. *Trends and Movements in Modern Arabic Poetry.* Leiden, 1977.

Sasson Somekh

Ra's al-Khayma

Northernmost of the United Arab Emirates.

Ra's al-Khayma's two separate territories cover some 650 square miles (1,684 sq. km) and have coastlines on both the Persian/Arabian Gulf and the Gulf of Oman. It has greater topographical diversity than the other emirates, and its slightly greater rainfall makes significant agriculture possible. Fishing and the production of construction materials, such as stone aggregate and cement, are the other major economic activities. Most of its fewer than 100,000 people live in the capital city of the same name. Nearly 90 percent of the population is indigenous.

In the eighteenth and early nineteenth centuries Ra's al-Khayma's QASIMI rulers held sway along the shores of the lower Persian/Arabian Gulf and the northern Indian Ocean until attacks on its shipping to India brought a military reaction by Britain and, in 1820, the imposition of a maritime truce. These developments circumscribed the power of the Qawasim. The 1869 split of their domains into the separate emirates of Ra's al-Khayma and SHARJA (the British did not formally recognize Ra's al-Khayma as an independent emirate until 1921) further weakened their position and opened the way to the primacy of ABU DHABI among the Trucial States.

Abu Dhabi's oil wealth and dominance of the United Arab Emirates (U.A.E.) are sources of resentment in Ra's al-Khayma, though the U.A.E.'s largess has sustained economic development. At independence in 1971, Ra's al-Khayma's ruler, Shaykh Saqr ibn Muhammad, angered by his state's limited political role in the new federation and expecting imminent discovery of oil in his territory, remained out of the U.A.E. for six weeks after its formation on 2 December 1971. (Modest oil deposits were not discovered until 1983). On the eve of independence, Iran seized the Tunb islands from Ra's al-Khayma and continues to occupy them, a circumstance that contributes to current Iran–Gulf Arab strains.

BIBLIOGRAPHY

ANTHONY, JOHN DUKE. *Arab States of the Lower Gulf: People, Politics, Petroleum.* Washington, D.C., 1975.
HEARD-BEY, FRAUKE. *From Trucial States to Emirates.* New York, 1982.
PECK, MALCOLM C. *The United Arab Emirates: A Venture in Unity.* Boulder, Colo., 1986.

Malcolm C. Peck

Raslan, Abd al-Hasib al-   [1901–?]

Syrian banker and politician.

Born in Homs to Shafiq al-Raslan, Abd al-Hasib al-Raslan received his licentiate in pharmaceutical sciences from Damascus University. He served as president of the Homs chamber of commerce in 1932 and as a member of the finance higher council from 1945 to 1950. Elected deputy of Homs in 1949, 1950, and 1954, he went on to serve as minister of interior as a member of the Independents in 1954. As a member of the Constitutional Bloc, al-Raslan became minister of defense in 1956.

BIBLIOGRAPHY

Who's Who in the Middle East, 1967–1968.

Charles U. Zenzie

Rassemblement Constitutionel Démocrate

See Destour Party

Rassemblement National des Indépendants (RNI)

Parliamentary grouping of independent supporters of Morocco's monarchy, representing landowners, senior civil servants, technocrats, industrialists, and businessmen, many from old established families.

The RNI, founded in October 1978, projects a centrist liberal image and holds 141 seats in parliament, making it the largest single group there. It was led by King Hassan's cousin, Ahmed Alawi, and the king's brother-in-law, Prime Minister Ahmed Osman, who became the RNI's first president. In 1981, agricultural-based interests led by Abdel Hamid Kacemi broke away to form the Parti des Indépendants Démocrates, later renamed the PARTI NATIONAL DÉMOCRATIQUE (PND). Following the 1981 government reshuffle, the RNI was left out of the government, so as to create a "loyal opposition." In the 1984 parliamentary elections, the RNI lost 80 parliamentary seats and was replaced by the newly formed Union Constitutionelle (UC) as the single largest party in parliament, although it subsequently was part of the governing coalition. It suffered a further loss of 20 seats in the 1993 parliamentary elections and was left out of the newly formed government of technocrats.

Bruce Maddy-Weitzman

Rastakhiz Party

Created in 1975 as only legal political party in Iran.

The Rastakhiz (or Resurgence) party of Iran was created in 1975 when the shah, Mohammad Reza Pahlavi, abruptly decided to abandon the two-party system for a single-party one. The shah invited all Iranians to join the new party, inviting those who refused to leave the country. This decision ironically betrayed the shah's sentiments of more than a decade earlier when, at the foundation of the New Iran party in December 1963, he proclaimed that if he were "a dictator rather than a constitutional monarch . . . [he] might be tempted to sponsor a single dominant party." The Rastakhiz party declared that it would adhere to the principles of "democratic centralism," the choice aspects of socialism and capitalism, a dialectical relationship between the government and the people, and, finally, help rebuild Iran into a great civilization. The party created a central committee with Amir Abbas Hoveyda, the prime minister, as its secretary-general; set up a women's organization; convened a labor congress for syndicates controlled by the state; and enrolled some 5 million members. The party papers included the daily *Rastakhiz,* the *Workers' Rastakhiz* (or *Rastakhiz-e Kargaran*), the *Farmers' Rastakhiz* (or *Rastakhiz-e Keshavarzan*), the *Youth Rastakhiz* (or *Rastakhiz-e Javan*), and finally the theoretical *Andisheh-ye Rastakhiz.* The party also took over some very important ministries, such as Labor, Industry, Housing, Health, Information and Tourism, Culture, Science and Higher Education, as well as the National Iranian Radio and Television. The party headquarters were among the first places to be destroyed in the riots of 1978–1979 that preceded the Iranian Revolution.

BIBLIOGRAPHY

ABRAHAMIAN, E. *Iran between Two Revolutions.* Princeton, N.J., 1982.

Parvaneh Pourshariati

Ra's Tanura

A narrow headland on the Persian/Arabian Gulf coast of Saudi Arabia almost halfway between Bahrain and Jubail.

Close to Dammam, Ra's Tanura was the location of the first crude oil discoveries made in Saudi Arabia and became the site of the first port exporting oil from that country in 1939. Plans to construct a tank farm and refinery and to expand marine terminal facilities at Ra's Tanura were made during World War II; by the end of 1945, more than six hundred Americans, as well as nationals from Iraq, India, and Eritrea, were constructing these facilities. Artificial structures called sea islands were built offshore to enlarge the offloading capacity of the port, and liquefied petroleum gas processing, storing, and shipping facilities were added. Both crude oil and products are shipped from Ra's Tanura. It is also one terminus of a submarine pipeline carrying crude oil to the Bahrain Petroleum Company refinery on Bahrain.

BIBLIOGRAPHY

NAWWAB, ISMAIL I., PETER C. SPEERS, and PAUL F. HOYE, eds. *Aramco and Its World: Arabia and the Middle East.* Dhahram, Saudi Arabia, 1980.

Mary Ann Tétreault

Rasulids

See Yemen Dynasties

Ratebzad, Anahita   [1930–]

First Afghan female physician; Marxist politican.

Born in Guldara in Kabul province, Anahita Ratebzad attended the Malalai Lycée in Kabul. She received a degree in nursing from the Chicago School of Nursing and an M.D. degree from Kabul University. She became involved in leftist politics and was elected to parliament in 1965. A founder of the PEO-PLE'S DEMOCRATIC PARTY OF AFGHANISTAN, she was active in the Parcham wing of that party. She served as ambassador to Belgrade (1978–1980) and as minister of education. Popular among women in Afghanistan, she was the first woman to take an active role in Afghan politics.

BIBLIOGRAPHY

ARNOLD, ANTHONY. *Afghanistan's Two-Party Communism: Parcham and Khalq.* Stanford, Calif., 1983.

Grant Farr

Ratosh, Yonatan [1908–]

Hebrew-language poet and journalist.

Born in Russia as Uriel Halperin, Ratosh was raised in a completely Hebrew-speaking environment. In 1921, he moved to Palestine, where he worked as a journalist for *Haaretz* and *Ha Yarden* and where he also wrote many books of poetry.

Ratosh is known for his belief in the existence of a Hebrew people who are distinguishable from the people living in Israel and from the people of many different cultures who follow the Jewish religion. According to his belief, the distinctive Hebrew people, who are the descendants of the Canaanite nation, developed a new national identity based on Hebrew culture.

BIBLIOGRAPHY

SHAVIT, YAAKOV. *New Hebrew Nation: A Study in Israeli Heresy and Fantasy.* Lanham, Md., 1987.

Bryan Daves

Rauf Yekta [1871–1937]

Turkish composer and musicologist.

Rauf was born in the Aksaray section of Istanbul. His father was a clerk in the Ottoman Empire's ministry of war. Rauf studied French, Arabic, and Persian at the Language School and, at the age of thirteen, began to work as a clerk's assistant in the Imperial Council. At the age of sixteen, he began to study music theory with Salih Zeki Bey. In 1922, when he retired from the civil service, he began to teach history and musical theory at the newly established Istanbul Conservatory.

Although Rauf wrote more than fifty musical compositions in the classical style, he is remembered

more for his research; he founded Turkish musicology, in the modern sense, by devising an accurate system of notation for traditional Turkish MUSIC. In addition, he translated many works on music from Arabic and Persian into the Turkish language and published hundreds of classical scores.

BIBLIOGRAPHY

ORANSAY, GÜLTEKIN. "Music in the Republican Era." In *The Transformation of Turkish Culture: The Atatürk Legacy,* ed. by Günsel Renda and C. Max Kortepeter. Princeton, N.J., 1986.
Yeni Türk Ansiklopedisi. Istanbul, 1985.

David Waldner

Ravanipour, Moniro [1954–]

Iranian novelist and short-story writer.

Ravanipour was born in Jofreh, Bushehr province. After primary and secondary education in Bushehr, she majored in psychology at Pahlavi University in Shiraz. To gather material for her writings on villagers and their folk traditions, Ravanipour travels to remote villages in Iran. Her writing combines magic and reality. As one of the most popular Iranian women writers, Ravanipour has toured the U.S. and Europe. She lives in Tehran.

BIBLIOGRAPHY

MOAYYAD, HESHMAT, ed. *Stories from Iran: A Chicago Anthology, 1921–1991.* Washington, D.C., 1991.

Pardis Minuchehr

Ravikovitch, Dahlia [1936–]

Israeli poet.

Ravikovitch was born near Tel Aviv. Her father died when she was six, a trauma that is described in her autobiographical collection of stories, *Death in the Family,* and reappears in various guises throughout her work. Raised on a kibbutz and in Haifa, she studied at the Hebrew University of Jerusalem and in England, then worked as teacher but primarily as journalist. The author of several volumes of poetry and recipient of the Bialik Prize, Ravikovitch also has published short stories, and children's books, and Hebrew translations of English poetry.

Ravikovitch's poems, predominantly personal, are written in high diction, pedantic form, and idiosyncratic vocabulary—at times mythological or archaic.

These properties merge, in her highly charged poems, with simple, almost childlike syntax, tone, and point of view, creating a unique simultaneity of dreamlike beauty and lurking danger, a perfect aesthetic expression of struggle. This on-the-edge tension is dominant in *A Love of an Orange*, Ravikovitch's first collection (1959), and is recognizable in works such as *The Third Book* (1969). Later volumes manifest a tendency to simpler expression.

In the 1980s the war in Lebanon sparked a poetic-political protest in which Ravikovitch took part. The voice of her poetry identifies with the vulnerable poetic "I" that also speaks of the feminine condition. Her retrospective collection *All the Poems. Up to Now* (1995) confirms her status as one of Israel's leading poets and its foremost woman poet.

Nili Gold

Rawalpindi, Treaty of

Britain's affirmation of Afghanistan's independence.

In early 1919, AMANOLLAH KHAN (Barakzai) assumed power in Afghanistan, after the assassination of his father. Unsatisfied with the political situation—with Britain asserting power in Afghan affairs—he attacked a British outpost in the Northwest Frontier near the Khyber Pass. With some difficulty, the British repulsed Amanollah. They met with the Afghans from June to August before signing the Rawalpindi Treaty. Afghan independence was thus affirmed as Britain renounced its say in Afghan foreign relations.

BIBLIOGRAPHY

FROMKIN, DAVID. *A Peace to End All Peace.* New York, 1989.
HUREWITZ, J. C., ed. *The Middle East and North Africa in World Politics.* New Haven, Conn., 1979.

Zachary Karabell

Raysuli, al-

See Ahmad ibn Muhammad al-Raysuni

Razmara, Ali   [1903–1951]

Iranian military man; prime minister, 1950–1951.

Born in Tehran, Ali Razmara, a geographer by training, studied cartography in France, and attended the War College in Tehran. He was a professor at the War College and the Military Academy in Tehran, the chief officer of the Royal Guard. He was also the editor of the journals *Pahlavi* and *Artesh*. As one of the few educated military men of his time, Razmara advanced rapidly through the ranks and was appointed Chief of Staff at the age of forty-three. He was named prime minister in 1950, but, although a disciplined and efficient administrator, he failed to grasp the depth of nationalist sentiments in the country and opposed parliament's bid to nationalize Iranian oil. Upon his appointment as prime minister, he assembled a cabinet none of whose members had ever held a ministerial position; most of the members of parliament, however, were experienced politicians and National Front candidates. One of Razmara's first initiatives entailed the introduction of Iran's first seven-year development plan, which U.S. President Harry Truman had promised to help implement through the Four Point Program. Razmara was assassinated in 1951 by Khalil Tahmasebi, from the Feda'iyan-e Islam. News of his murder was greeted jubilantly by the nationalists, the religious factions, and the press, for it led to the immediate nationalization of Iranian oil. Some observers believe that Mohammad Reza Shah Pahlavi and Ayatollah Abu al-Qasem Kashani were involved in the assassination.

BIBLIOGRAPHY

KATOUZIAN, HOMA. *The Political Economy of Modern Iran.* New York, 1981.

Neguin Yavari

Reagan, Ronald   [1911–   ]

President of the United States, 1981–1989.

Reagan announced a plan for Arab–Israeli peace on 1 September 1982, following Israel's invasion of Lebanon and the evacuation of Palestine Liberation Organization (PLO) forces from Beirut. The Reagan Plan called for establishment of Palestinian self-government in the West Bank and Gaza, in association with Jordan, on the basis of the Camp David Accords. The self-government would function for five years, during which final status negotiations would take place, and would coincide with a freeze on Israel's settlement construction.

The plan also stated that the withdrawal by Israel mentioned in UN Security Council Resolution 242 applied to all fronts in the Arab–Israeli conflict, not just the Israel–Egypt front. It thus rejected Israel's claim that it had complied with 242 by withdrawing from Sinai. The plan refused to accept both Israel's annexation of the West Bank and Gaza and Palestinian statehood as permanent options.

Israel rejected the Reagan Plan, and the Arab States announced their own proposal, the Fez Plan, several days later.

Michael R. Fischbach

Re'aya

Ottoman society was divided into two classes: the rulers and the ruled (re'aya).

The ruling authority included the sultan, the bureaucracy, the military, and religious institutions. They were exempt from taxation. The re'aya, Muslims and non-Muslims alike, were the economic foundation of the empire. To ensure productivity, the ruler was obligated to protect the re'aya from oppression.

Cyrus Moshaver

Recaizade Mahmud Ekrem
[c. 1846–c. 1913]

Ottoman Turkish poet and literary reformer.

Recaizade was born in Istanbul during the Ottoman Empire and enrolled in the military academy. He later transferred to the Civil Service School where he met and became a disciple of NAMIK KEMAL. He worked for many years as Kemal's assistant on the newspaper *Tasvir-i Efkar*; in 1867, after Kemal's flight to Paris, Recaizade became chief editor of the newspaper.

Recaizade was a member of the second generation of Tanzimat writers who created the New Literature school, which sought literary inspiration in everyday life. Recaizade also contributed to the *Servet-i Fünun* (Wealth of Sciences) movement, which focused on the problems of the individual under the oppressive regime of Sultan Abdülhamit II. He is considered a transitional figure between the romanticism of Namık Kemal and the realism of Ömer SAYFETTIN. In addition to his poetry, his novels, and his plays, he published theoretical studies of literature that criticized traditional forms of artistic expression and created an environment for greater artistic experimentation.

BIBLIOGRAPHY

ERTOP, KONUR. "Trends and Characteristics of Modern Turkish Literature." In *The Transformation of Turkish Culture: The Atatürk Legacy,* ed. by Günsel Renda and C. Max Kortepeter. Princeton, N.J., 1986.

LEWIS, BERNARD. *The Emergence of Modern Turkey,* 2nd ed. London, 1968.

MITLER, LOUIS. *Ottoman Turkish Writers: A Bibliographical Dictionary of Significant Figures in Pre-Republican Turkish Literature.* New York, 1988.

David Waldner

Red Crescent Society

Name of the International Red Cross in Muslim countries.

The name was adopted at the urging of Ottoman Empire officials. A humanitarian organization, the International Red Cross was established in 1864 at the behest of Jean-Henri Dunant, a Swiss citizen who organized emergency medical aid for French and Austrian victims at the Battle of Solferino in 1859.

The mission of the Red Cross and its affiliates around the world has evolved since its founding. As delineated in the Geneva Convention of 1864, its primary mission was to care for the wounded. In subsequent years, provisions were added, such as those for the protection of victims of warfare at sea, prisoners of war, and civilians during war.

Shimon Avish

Red Line Agreement

Part of the post–World War I reorganization of the Turkish Petroleum Company (TPC) as the Iraq Petroleum Company (IPC).

TPC was formed in 1914, shortly before the outbreak of World War I. Fifty percent of TPC was owned by the Anglo-Persian Oil Company (later British Petroleum). A 5 percent beneficial interest was owned by the Armenian entrepreneur Calouste GÜLBENKIAN, who had put together the TPC consortium. The remainder was split between the Deutsche Bank and a subsidiary of ROYAL DUTCH SHELL. The original TPC agreement included a clause pledging the principals to refrain from seeking additional concessions in the Ottoman Empire except through TPC.

At the San Remo Conference in 1919, the German share of TPC was transferred to France. The Americans, also victors in the war, demanded a share as part of their spoils and accepted 20 percent in 1922 (later enlarged to 23.7 percent). However, this did not end the disputes impeding the company's reorganization. Gülbenkian insisted that the "self-denying clause" be retained in any new agreement. The French, with their 23.7 percent share, supported Gülbenkian; the other participants did not.

The final agreement establishing IPC was signed in July 1928 at Ostend, Belgium. It included the self-denying clause. However, the principals declared themselves unsure of the actual boundaries of the Ottoman Empire. Legend has it that Gülbenkian, then and there, took a red pencil and drew a line around what he meant by "Ottoman Empire"—the Red Line. With the exception of Kuwait and Iran, the Red Line encompassed most of what would become the great oil-producing areas of the region.

The Red Line, along with the AS-IS AGREEMENT, shaped the structure of foreign ownership and the tempo of development of Middle Eastern oil. For example, Gulf Oil (now owned by Chevron), an original party to the IPC agreement (it later dropped out), became an active contender for a share of the Kuwait concession, in part because its participation in IPC prevented it from seeking promising concessions elsewhere in the Gulf. Gulf's success in winning a share thwarted expectations that Anglo-Persian (APOC) would be able to monopolize Kuwait, then a British protectorate. The Red Line prevented APOC and the U.S. partners in IPC, chiefly Standard Oil of New Jersey (now Exxon) and Standard Oil of New York (now Mobil), from seeking concessions in Saudi Arabia. The rich fields in the eastern part of Saudi Arabia were discovered by Casoc, a subsidiary of Standard Oil of California (now Chevron). Texaco purchased half of Casoc in 1936. Neither was a Red Line company.

The need for additional capital to develop the Oil fields of Saudi Arabia led to the end of the Red Line. Once again, a world war provided the opportunity to reorganize oil concessions in the Middle East. After the Germans occupied France in 1940, the IPC holdings of Gülbenkian and the French were sequestered under British law. The IPC board in London was notified that the IPC agreement might have been invalidated by having become a contract with an enemy power. The IPC principals chose not to pursue this possibility during the war, but afterward, Standard of New Jersey's legal counsel brought the issue before U.S. officials, who joined the corporation in pressing for a revision of the IPC agreement to eliminate the self-denying clause. The successful conclusion of these maneuvers in 1947 ended the Red Line and allowed Standard of New Jersey and of New York to take shares in Aramco while retaining their shares in IPC.

BIBLIOGRAPHY

ANDERSON, IRVINE H. *Aramco, the United States, and Saudi Arabia: A Study of the Dynamics of Foreign Oil Policy, 1933–1950.* Princeton, N.J., 1981.

SAMPSON, ANTHONY. *The Seven Sisters: The Great Oil Companies and the World They Shaped.* New York, 1975.

Mary Ann Tétreault

Red Lion and Sun Society

Social welfare organization in Iran, equivalent to the Red Cross.

The Red Lion and Sun society (or *Jami'at-e Shir va Khorshid-e Iran*) was established in 1923, under the reign of Reza Shah Pahlavi, as a social welfare organization, equivalent to the Red Cross. The society is a member of the International Red Cross. As of 1971 it had 135 branches in the provinces providing relief for natural disasters such as flood, earthquake, and fire. Altogether the society engages in some 350 charity operations, including counseling centers for mothers and infants, blood banks, orphanages, clinics, and hospitals. The society's relief activities also extend to war victims.

BIBLIOGRAPHY

LENCZOWSKI, G., ed. *Iran under the Pahlavis.* Stanford, Calif., 1978.

Parvaneh Pourshariati

Red Sea

Narrow sea between the Arabian peninsula and northeast Africa.

The Red Sea extends over a distance of some 1,300 miles (2,000 km) in a northwest to southeast direction, from latitude 30°N to 13°N, between Africa

Red Sea underwater flora and fauna. (Mia Bloom)

The port of Eilat on the Gulf of Aqaba at the northern end of the Red Sea. (Mia Bloom)

and the Arabian peninsula. Its general shape is guided by the massive parallel faults of the Great Rift valley system, which continues north to the Jordan valley and south across the Horn of Africa. As a result, the sea is very deep, exceeding 3,000 feet (1,000 m) over much of its length, with a maximum depth of 8,645 feet (2,635 m), but shallowing to less than 650 feet (200 m) at its outlet to the Gulf of Aden and the Indian Ocean. Bounded on the west by Egypt, Sudan, and Eritrea and on the east mainly by Saudi Arabia and Yemen, the Red Sea has a width of 100 to 180 miles (160–290 km) over most of its length but narrows at either end to maritime choke points. These have considerable strategic significance in relation both to the various states that share its coastline and its function as a major international waterway.

At its northern end, the Red Sea bifurcates to form the narrow gulfs of Suez and Aqaba, which lie on either side of the Sinai peninsula. The Gulf of Suez forms the southern approach to the Suez Canal; at the northern end of the Gulf of Aqaba, some eight miles (13 km) of coastline belong to Israel, lying immediately adjacent to approximately fifteen miles (24 km) of shoreline that is Jordanian territory, Jordan's only outlet to the sea. The Gulf of Aqaba narrows at its southern end to the five-mile-wide (8-km) Tiran Strait, which is entirely within the territorial waters of Saudi Arabia and Egypt. The southern outlet of the Red Sea lies through the strait called Bab al-Mandab, which is about sixteen miles (26 km) across; this strait is divided into two channels by Perim island (Yemen's territory); the main shipping routes lie between Perim and the African shore, which are only ten miles (16 km) apart. These straits are located in the territorial waters of Yemen, Ethiopia, and Djibouti.

All the states bordering the Red Sea have ports along its shores, of which the most important are Suez and Port Safaqa in Egypt, Port Sudan, Mesewa in Eritrea, Eilat in Israel, Aqaba in Jordan, Yenbo and Jidda in Saudi Arabia, and Hodeida in Yemen. These are significant to those countries' maritime trade, but the importance of the Red Sea as an international trade route stems mainly from its link with the Suez Canal. Opened in 1869, the Suez–Red Sea route formed a shortcut from Europe to Asia, avoiding the long trip around the Cape of Good Hope. Of special interest to Europeans during the expansion of their empires, its importance increased with the boom in Middle Eastern oil production that followed World War II. With the construction of pipelines and the increased size of oil tankers, oil traffic in the Red Sea has diminished, but an estimated twenty thousand vessels still sail the sea each year.

BIBLIOGRAPHY

BLAKE, G. H., J. C. DEWDNEY, and J. MITCHELL. *The Cambridge Atlas of the Middle East and North Africa.* Cambridge, U.K., 1987.

John C. Dewdney

Refah Partisi

Politically, the most important organization of Islamic movements in Turkey.

Founded July 19, 1983, Refah Partisi, the Welfare party, garnered 19 percent of total votes in the local general elections of March 27, 1994. Party leader Necmeddin ERBAKAN, a mechanical engineer by education, former university professor, and former president of Turkish Chambers Union, has been an important figure in Turkish politics since the late 1960s. He was elected first chairman of the National Order party (NOP; Milli Nezam Partisi), set up in January 1970 by a group of dissident parliamentarians in the Justice party who first launched the "Movement of Independents," a term then used for the founders of this new pro-Islamic organization. Erbakan's leadership continued when the NATIONAL SALVATION PARTY (NSP; Milli Selâmler Partisi) was established in October 1972, almost a year after the Constitutional Court declared the NOP unconstitutional. The NSP had become a significant political organization, which culled 12 percent of total votes in 1973 and 1977 general elections. Accordingly, the NSP participated in virtually all coalition governments formed either by social democrats or liberal conservatives, Erbakan serving as deputy prime minister three times before the military intervention September 12, 1980. The Welfare party, still under Erbakan's leadership, made considerable progress increasing its electoral basis from 12 to 19 percent; its candidates in metropolitan areas including Istanbul and Ankara won the elections in 1994. Many observers of current Turkish politics regard Erbakan's new party as the first Islamic organization capable of winning a majority in the Turkish Grand National Assembly after the general elections of 1996.

Among the factors that contributed to this development, three different groups can be discerned in the present-day Welfare party, which correspond to the bases of electoral support. In large cities, the party receives support from the so-called new urban dwellers living in shantytowns, the margins of exuberant middle-class life. Istanbul is a good illustration of how the younger generation of the party assembled support from these groups of new urban dwellers, who voted for social democrats before the 1980s. This achievement in the cities is by and large a result of grassroots organizations, well-known in Turkey as the method of "prayer beads," which means an emphasis on face-to-face contact with the ordinary people in ways unprecented in Turkish political history. In central and eastern Anatolia, the party includes peripheral forces of local merchants and manufacturers; a majority of which are practicing Muslims and Turkish nationalists. This second stratum inside the party is the traditional basis for the religious movements connected with various Islamic brotherhoods, most notably the NAQSHBANDI order, loyal to the status quo of the Turkish state. Last but by no means least, the party made use of Islamic motifs to garner support from Kurdish groups, who seem to be searching for a political organization that is not part of the political establishment. The Welfare party conveys to the public political, economic, and cultural ideas described by the term "national outlook" (MILLI GORUS), now famous for its call to establish "just order" on Islamic principles. Within the framework of this ideology, the party stresses its discord with the establishment, but in reality it is still a matter of controversy whether the Welfare party represents a radical Islamic political movement or a political organization using Islam merely as a frame of political language so as to compromise with the secular state.

Nermin Abadan-Unat

Refik Fersan   [1893–?]

Turkish composer.

He was born in Istanbul and after graduating from Robert College (now part of Bosporus University),

studied chemistry in Switzerland. Refik studied music from the age of eleven with Tamburi Cemil Bey. In 1918, he became a music instructor in the sultan's palace, and after the establishment of the Republic of Turkey, he was a music instructor in the state orchestra. From 1928 to 1938 he worked for Istanbul Radio; in the 1940s he worked for Ankara Radio. In 1947, he established a music conservatory in Damascus, Syria. Refik has written several Turkish musical compositions.

BIBLIOGRAPHY

NEBIOĞLU, OSMAN. *Who's Who in Turkey.* Washington, D.C., 1963.

David Waldner

Reformed Church in America

See Arabian Mission

Refugees, Afghan

Between 1978 and 1992, nearly eight million Afghans fled their homes because of internal strife and the invasion by the Soviet Union.

Large-scale flight from Afghanistan began with the seizure of power on April 27, 1978, by the Marxist–Leninist People's Democratic Party of Afghanistan (PDPA). The PDPA's policies provoked spontaneous resistance. The December 1979 invasion of Afghanistan by troops of the Soviet Union plunged the country into open war. Islamic leaders declared that resistance to the Soviets and the Kabul regime was a jihad (holy war) and the fighters were termed mojahedin. Correspondingly, fleeing from areas controlled by Soviet or Kabul forces became *hijra* (emigration from non-Islamic territory). Refugees (*muhajirun,* those who engage in hijra) poured into neighboring Pakistan and Iran. Most of them fled not out of obedience to a doctrine but out of compulsion after their villages were bombed. The destruction of rural areas sheltering the mojahedin and the creation of refugees appeared to be part of the Soviet counterinsurgency strategy.

By 1980, there were about two million Afghans living in tented camps and squatter settlements outside the country. By the mid-1980s, over three million Afghans had spread across the border areas of Pakistan. About 80 percent of these were ethnic Pashtuns from southern and eastern Afghanistan. Another two million Afghans were in Iran, many of them Shi'ites belonging to the Hazara ethnic group and

Persian-speakers from the Herat area. The Afghans in these two countries, nearly one-third of the country's population, constituted the largest refugee group in the world. Another two to three million were displaced within the country.

The refugee settlements provided both a haven from the war and a base of support and logistics for the mojahedin. The Iranian government accepted aid from international agencies but provided all services and relief to Afghans directly. In Pakistan, the UN High Commissioner for Refugees (UNHCR) and other UN agencies assumed responsibility for those refugees living in over 500 camps administered by the Pakistani government. Over 160 international volunteer agencies assisted as well.

Refugee settlement patterns largely replicated those in Afghanistan, with groups tending to settle together where possible. Perhaps two-thirds of the refugees in the camps were women and children, as the men were either dead, at war, or away working in the Persian/Arabian Gulf or Pakistani or Iranian cities. In Iran, the refugees lived mainly in cities, where they provided much of the country's labor supply during the Iran–Iraq War. In Pakistan, the refugees lived mainly in camps.

The Geneva accords signed in April 1988 provided for the withdrawal of Soviet troops and the voluntary repatriation of Afghan refugees under the supervision of UNHCR. The PDPA government had declared a policy of national reconciliation offering generous terms to those who returned. Until the fall of that government in April 1992, however, only a trickle came back. After the declaration of the Islamic state of Afghanistan on May 6, 1992, by a coalition of mojahedin leaders, the flow of refugees back to Afghanistan increased.

Barnett R. Rubin
Steven Holtzman

Refugees, Balkan Muslim

Migratory peoples from Bulgaria, Montenegro, Serbia, and other countries.

Military invasion of the Ottoman Empire and the nationalist revolution caused mass migrations of Balkan Muslims. Although numbers are not precisely known, all of the Muslims of Southern Greece and of Serbia proper either died or became refugees as part of those countries' independence wars. As a result of the Russo–Ottoman War of 1877–1878, Muslims were forced from conquered areas in Bulgaria, Montenegro, and Serbia. Counting only those refugees who survived the 1877–1878 war, 515,000 Muslim refugees came from Bulgaria alone. The Bal-

kan allies either exiled or caused the deaths of a majority of the Muslims from territories they conquered during the Balkan Wars of 1912–1913. About 414,000 refugees survived the Balkan Wars. Other Balkan Muslims became refugees in regions taken by Greece after World War I.

Each of the migrations of Balkan Muslim refugees was accompanied by great mortality. For example, 27 percent of the Muslims of Ottoman Europe died in the Balkan Wars, 17 percent of the Muslims of Bulgaria died in the 1877–1878 war. Most of these died as refugees, from disease, starvation, exposure, and enemy attacks.

Some 400,000 refugees came to Turkey during the Greco–Turkish Population Exchange of the 1920s. After World War II, the Communist government of Bulgaria forced Muslims from the country in the 1950s and 1980s. In the 1990s, Muslim refugees have fled from Bosnia-Herzegovina and, in smaller numbers, from Kosovo and Western Thrace.

Justin McCarthy

Refugees, Jewish

Jews who fled to the State of Israel from the Muslim countries beginning in 1948.

After the State of Israel declared its independence in May of 1948, and in the wake of the 1948 Palestine War, the American Jewish Joint Distribution Committee (AJDC), the Jewish Agency for Palestine, and the Mossad Le-Aliya Bet (Special Organization for Immigration) created Operation Magic Carpet, to rescue Jews from Yemen and Aden and settle them in Israel. In 1949 and 1950, about 48,800 Yemeni Jews were brought to Israel on 430 flights (airplane travel was justified by the biblical passage "on the wings of eagles"). Joining them were 2,200 Jews from Aden, then a British crown colony. The operation was financed by AJDC, and the refugees arrived by chartered American planes.

Iraqi Jews, faced with pogroms, abuses, and persecution, also sought to leave for Israel. In 1950, Iraq's government allowed Jews to leave only if they renounced Iraqi nationality and promised never to return; they were required to leave most of their possessions and had difficulty selling any property or businesses. Iraqi authorities insisted that the evacuation be discreet and the official destination not be Israel; so Cyprus permitted the use of their airfields for transshipment to Israel. Between May 1950 and December 1951, Operation Ali Baba, as it was called, brought 113,545 Jews out of Iraq—and by 1959, about 123,425 of Iraq's 128,000 Jews had settled in Israel.

Egypt's Jews left for Israel in three phases: during and following the 1948 Palestine War; in the wake of the Sinai campaign of 1956; and as a result of the 1967 Arab–Israel War. They included Egyptian citizens, foreign nationals, and the stateless. Between 1948 and 1950, about 20,000 Jews left Egypt; more than 14,000 settled in Israel. Of the 45,000 that remained, at least 36,000 left Egypt between 1956 and 1964. After the 1967 War, another 2,500 became refugees in Europe before resettling there, in Latin America, or in Israel.

From North Africa came the Jewish refugees of the French colonial empire—Morocco, Tunisia, and Algeria. Difficulties were put in their path for emigration from Morocco to Israel and many were impoverished. Eventually, ways were found to evacuate them, as well as those who were permitted to sell their assets. Once settled in Israel their adjustment was relatively smooth. Those who wished to settle in France, however, faced problems that began when, in the 1950s and 1960s, some 40,000 from Morocco and 50,000 from Tunisia left to escape the growing economic and political uncertainties—as their countries became independent from France in 1956. Most did not possess French citizenship and were not entitled to French government assistance. Algeria's Jews were, however, considered "repatriates" after Algerian independence in 1962, as were all Algerians of French origin returning to France. They had become French citizens *en bloc* in 1870 by virtue of the CRÉMIEUX DECREE. The North African Jews more than doubled France's Jewish population between the mid-1950s and 1970, to almost 600,000; French Jewry thus became the second-largest Jewish community in Western Europe.

BIBLIOGRAPHY

HILLEL, SHLOMO. *Operation Babylon.* Tel Aviv, 1985.
LASKIER, MICHAEL M. *The Jews of Egypt, 1920–1970: In the Midst of Zionism, Anti-Semitism and the Middle East Conflict.* New York, 1991.
———. *North African Jewry in the Twentieth Century: A Social and Political History.* New York, 1995.
SACHAR, HOWARD M. *Diaspora.* New York, 1985.
SCHECHTMAN, JOSEPH B. *On Wings of Eagles.* New York, 1961.

Michael M. Laskier

Refugees, Kurdish

People of Kurdistan, a territory inhabited mainly by the Kurds of five countries, who fled to escape repression and possible death.

In September 1925, more than 20,000 Assyrian Christians (Nestorians) and Kurds arrived in north-ern Iraq, fleeing the repression that came after the end of the Kurdish revolt in Turkey of 1922–1924. This was the first time the international media mentioned the problem of Kurdish refugees.

More recently, thousands of Kurds sought asylum in Iran after the collapse of General (Mullah Mustafa) Barzani's independence movement in 1975. Kurds also fled to Iran and Turkey after the Iraqi Kurdish resistance in the aftermath of the Iran–Iraq War (1988). These were small flights compared to the huge refugee crisis that was caused in April 1991 by Saddam Hussein's attacks toward the end of the Gulf War (January–April 1991). Fearing for their safety after the failure of their uprising in March 1991, about two million Iraqi Kurds fled toward the Turkish and Iranian borders. The arrival of such huge numbers, thousands of whom died of hunger and cold, internationalized the Kurdish problem and forced unwilling Western governments to extend their protection to the Kurds. By the mid-1990s, many Kurds still live in hiding—some in the marshlands of river estuaries, successfully surviving Iraqi military squads. Others live in refugee camps protected by United Nations troops.

BIBLIOGRAPHY

KUTSCHERA, CHRIS. *Le mouvement national kurde.* Paris, 1979.
VAN BRUINESSEN, MARTIN. *Aghas, Shaikhs, and States.* London, 1992.

Chris Kutschera

Refugees, Palestinian

People of Palestine who fled or were driven out in 1948 and 1967; their repatriation remains a controversial issue.

A major consequence of the Arab–Israel War (1948/49) was the flight of approximately half the indigenous Arab population from their homes in those parts of mandatory Palestine that became the new state of Israel, a third of which included territory beyond the borders of the UN partition plan. Since 1948 the Palestine refugee problem has been one of the most important and controversial issues in the continuing conflict. It has appeared on the agenda of every UN session since 1948 and been the subject of numerous UN resolutions calling for repatriation and/or compensation to the refugees.

While the Palestinians, the Arab states, and their supporters assert that the refugees were forced by Israeli military or paramilitary units to leave their homes and property, the government of Israel has disclaimed responsibility, placing blame for the flight on Palestinian leaders and the surrounding Arab countries, which, Israel states, urged the refugees to leave. In recent years several Israeli revisionist accounts have produced evidence that in many instances the Israeli military did force Palestinians to depart. Another cause of the flight was the breakdown of Palestinian Arab society during the war in Palestine followed by chaos and the total disruption of civil society.

The total number of original Palestinian refugees is based on estimates rather than an accurate census. The UN estimated in 1949 that more than 700,000 of Palestine's 1948 Arab population could be classified as refugees. A second major exodus occurred following the June 1967 war when over 300,000 Palestinians left the West Bank and the Golan area in Syria, many of them second-time refugees who had lived in camps since 1948. Since then those classified by the UN Relief and Works Agency for Palestine Refugees in the Middle East (UNRWA) has increased to more than 2.7 million. UNRWA considers refugees those who lived in Palestine a minimum of two years preceding the 1948 conflict, who lost homes and means of livelihood, and who reside in areas where UNRWA services are available, and their direct descendants. According to this definition, about half the total number of Palestinians in the world were refugees in the 1990s.

The largest concentration is under Israeli jurisdiction, over 1 million in the occupied West Bank and Gaza. There are more than 1 million in Jordan, over 300,000 in Lebanon, and 300,000 in Syria. Initially most refugees lived in camps established by the UN. However by the 1990s, 1.7 million lived in other places but received education, health care, and other social services from UNRWA. More than half of UNRWA expenditures are for education. While education and social services received from UNRWA are of relatively high standards, the area of refugee camps has not been greatly extended despite the rapid population increase. Thus the camps have become extremely overcrowded; housing and other public facilities have become greatly overburdened.

In most areas the internal affairs of the camps are run by the Palestinians themselves. Refugee frustration with low wages, poor living conditions, and inability to return to their original homes has caused social and political unrest with the result that some camps in Lebanon have become bases for Palestinian guerilla activity. Political life in the camps is intense, and refugees are active in nearly every Palestinian political faction and paramilitary organization. On some occasions the camps have become targets of non-Palestinian military forces—of the Israeli army and various local militias in Lebanon and of the royal army in Jordan, resulting in thousands of Palestinian casualties.

The refugee question has been a focus of attempts to resolve the Arab–Israel conflict beginning in December 1948 with UN General Assembly Resolution 194(III) stating "that the refugees wishing to return to their homes and live at peace with their neighbours should be permitted to do so at the earliest practicable date, and that compensation should be paid for the property of those choosing not to return . . ."

The refugees themselves and the Arab states have emphasized the "right to return" as fundamental in a peace settlement. However Israel has opposed any large-scale repatriation, instead emphasizing resettlement in the surrounding Arab countries. Attempts at refugee resettlement have not been successful, largely because of refugee insistence on the "right of return." By the 1990s, the "right of return" was interpreted by many refugees and some Arab states as "return" to a Palestinian state in the West Bank and Gaza rather than within the borders of Israel. Following the 1991 Madrid Middle East peace conference, one of the five multilateral groups established to deal with functional problems dealt with the refugee issue.

BIBLIOGRAPHY

PERETZ, DON. *Palestinians, Refugees, and the Middle East Peace Process.* Washington, D.C., 1993.
VIORST, MILTON. *Reaching for the Olive Branch: UNRWA and Peace in the Middle East.* Bloomington, Ind., 1989.

Don Peretz

Rejection Front

Collective term for Arab countries and Palestinian organizations that oppose diplomatic negotiations with Israel.

The first Rejection Front formed in 1974 in Baghdad to oppose Yasir Arafat's plan to attend the Geneva peace conference after the 1973 Arab–Israel war. Backed by Iraq, Algeria, and South Yemen, the front was an umbrella organization for several Palestinian factions like the POPULAR FRONT FOR THE LIBERATION OF PALESTINE—GENERAL COMMAND (PFLP-GC), and the ARAB LIBERATION FRONT.

The movement waned in 1978 with the Camp David Accords and Iraq's reconciliation with Arafat's al-Fath faction. It was revived in the Israeli-occupied territories in 1982 as the Democratic Alliance, and was allied with the PFLP and the Communist party. By the mid-1980s it had gleaned support from about

20 percent of Palestinians in Gaza and on the West Bank, particularly university students. It opposed Arafat's alliance with moderate Arab countries and moderate Palestinian mayors who cooperated with Israel.

BIBLIOGRAPHY

SCHIFF, ZE'EV, and EHUD YA'ARI. *Intifada.* New York, 1989.
SEALE, PATRICK. *Abu Nidal: A Gun for Hire.* London, 1992.

Elizabeth Thompson

Religious Zionism

See Mizrachi Movement

Remez, Moshe David   [1886–1951]

Israeli labor leader.

Born in Russia and emigrated to Palestine in 1913, Remez was a key player in the establishment of the Histadrut and served as its secretary-general for many years. From 1944 to 1948, he was chairman of the VA'AD LE'UMI and actively participated in the anti-British struggle for Israel's independence. He was a member of MAPAI serving in the first two Knessets, first as minister of communications, 1948–1950, and then as minister of education, from 1950 until his death.

Ann Kahn

Renaissance Party

Outlawed Tunisian religious party.

In the 1970s Tunisia's Islamists led by Rashid Ghannushi and Abdelfattah Mourou organized a group called the Mouvement de Tendance Islamique (Islamic Tendency Movement; MTI). From their center at al-Zaytuna Mosque, they publicized their ideas in the journal *al-Ma'rifa* (Knowledge). Initially they emphasized religious issues, but by 1978 they were criticizing the government and society for being too Western, materialistic, and irreligious.

In 1976, the Islamists had begun to organize populist cells and to penetrate mosques not under government control; by 1981, they controlled 300 mosques. Islamist students seized control of the General Tunisian Union of Students (Union Générale des Etudiants Tunisiens; UGTE). To counter this growing threat, President Habib BOURGUIBA agreed to establish a multiparty system in June 1981. Islamists responded by declaring the MTI a political party.

Government inability to destroy the Islamist movement and deteriorating economic conditions provoked the crises that led to Bourguiba's removal (1986/87). In August 1987, bombings at tourist hotels led to the arrests of MTI leaders. By early November, Bourguiba decided that many Islamists should be executed, including Ghannushi. This decision and Bourguiba's mental instability led Prime Minister Zayn al-Abdine BEN ALI to remove the aging president for medical reasons on 7 November.

Many Islamists were pardoned and released from prison, but Ben Ali's regime still refused to legalize the MTI. In late 1987, Ben Ali promised economic and political liberalization and a multiparty system. An electoral code stipulated that parties could not have a religious or other sectarian base. In 1989, MTI therefore changed its name to Renaissance party (Hizb al-Nahda), but the government still refused to legalize it. Instead, Islamists could run as independent candidates in the April 1988 elections. They did so, and in some areas received as much as 30 percent of the vote. As a result of the electoral code's official "winner take all" policy, the CONSTITUTIONAL DEMOCRATIC RALLY (RCD) took all the seats in the National Assembly. Following the government's overwhelming victory, Ghannushi left the country. His attacks on Ben Ali became more vitriolic. In retaliation, Tunisia's press began to attack the Islamist movement.

During the Gulf Crisis (1990/91), MTI leaders attempted to seize control of pro-Iraq street demonstrations. In February 1991, Islamists attacked the RCD's offices in Tunis.

Later in 1991, Islamist military figures allegedly plotted to stage a coup, and other Islamists sought to assassinate President Ben Ali. Hundreds, probably thousands, of Islamists were arrested during 1991. In 1992, the regime turned the Islamists over to special military tribunals for trial. Since the conclusion of the trials, the Ben Ali regime has continued to label all Islamists as terrorists.

BIBLIOGRAPHY

AMERICAN MUSLIM COUNCIL. *The Renaissance Party in Tunisia.* Washington, D.C., 1991.
BOULBY, MARION. "The Islamic Challenge: Tunisia since Independence." *Third World Quarterly* 10, no. 2 (April 1988): 590–614.
BURGAT, FRANÇOIS, and WILLIAM DOWELL. *The Islamic Movement in North Africa.* Austin, Tex., 1993.
SALEM, NORMA. "Tunisia." In *Politics of Islamic Revolution,* ed. by Shireen T. Hunter. Bloomington, Ind., 1988.

Larry A. Barrie

Rendel, George William   [1889–1979]

British diplomat and explorer.

Rendell entered the diplomatic service in 1913 and was the head of the British Foreign Office, Eastern Department, during the 1930s. He represented Great Britain at the 1936 MONTREUX CONVENTION. In 1937, at the invitation of Saudi Arabia's King Ibn Sa'ud, he traveled across Arabia from the Gulf to the Red Sea. He later worked for the Foreign Office on Anglo–Egyptian financial relations.

BIBLIOGRAPHY

LACY, ROBERT. *The Kingdom.* New York, 1981.
Who Was Who, 1971–1980. New York, 1981.

Zachary Karabell

Republican Peasants' Nation Party

Turkish political party, 1958–1962.

Formed by a merger of the Republican Nation and Peasants' parties in 1958 and chaired by Osman Bölükbaşı, this moderately conservative party gained 14 percent of the vote and 54 of 450 seats in the 1961 elections and participated in coalition governments in the 1960s. It suffered a split when Bölükbaşı left it in 1962. Subsequently, the party leadership was assumed by former Col. Alparslan Türkeş, under whom it adopted a militant rightist stance and changed its name to NATIONALIST ACTION PARTY.

BIBLIOGRAPHY

LANDAU, J. M. "Turkey." In *Political Parties in the Middle East and North Africa,* ed. by F. Tachau. Westport, Conn., 1994.

Frank Tachau

Republican People's Party

The Republic of Turkey's first political party (RPP), founded September 11, 1923.

Until 1924, it was named the People's party (Halk Fırkası), and it represented the founding populist principles of its members, who came from the Ottoman Union and Progress party as well as from the various associations for the defence of rights in Anatolia. The word *Republican* was added on November 19, 1924, when it became Cumhüriyet Halk Partisi, the Republican People's party (RPP). Its first president was Mustafa Kemal (Atatürk); the vice president was İsmet İnönü; the general secretary was R. Peker. During the first years, the modernizing leadership focused on westernization. Denying social cleavages, the party refused to identify with any particular class.

KEMALISM, as an ideology, was first proclaimed at the second party congress of October 15, 1927, where Mustafa Kemal delivered a five-day speech on the goals of the revolution. His goals were adopted: republicanism, meaning rejection of monarchy and dictatorship; nationalism, rejection of any dynastic, religious, or racial basis for statehood; secularism, separation of religion from the state; and populism. Following the great economic crisis of 1929, the party gave up its liberal economic bent and opted for etatism (state economic enterprise)—an extensive role for government as a major tool of economic policy. At the third party congress of May 10, 1931, they adopted the first detailed program of etatism plus revolutionarism—nonviolent radical, social, and cultural changes. These goals became symbolized as the six arrows of Atatürk, the six principles of Kemalism.

In 1935, the party decided to merge with the administration. The minister of the interior became, ex officio, the general secretary of the party. In 1937, the six principles of Kemalism were incorporated in the constitution. After his death, in 1938, his successor, İnönü, became the National Chief.

Six elections followed the consolidation of Kemalist power—1923, 1927, 1931, 1935, 1939, and 1943—under the one-party regime. Although there were two brief incidences with competing parties (Republican Progress in 1925 and the Free party in 1930), both were quickly ended, and no legislative election occurred. Beginning in 1941, some democratic processes began, including elections of independent candidates, more candidates than available seats, and an independent group within the party. Party doctrine was not based on authoritarianism; it carefully maintained a democratic facade; institutionalized elections were held. The end of one-party rule came in 1945—on the initiative of President İnönü.

At the first competitive election, July 1946, the newly founded DEMOCRAT PARTY won all seats where its candidates were placed on the ballot. Challenging the existing electoral system, the Democrat party demanded radical reform: The new law of 1949 introduced the secret ballot, open counting of votes, and judicial supervision. On May 14, 1950, the Democrats received 53.3 percent of the popular vote but 83.8 percent of the assembly seats—since the majority system helped win all seats in one electoral district. Power was peacefully transferred, and the Republicans assumed the role of the opposition party. From 1950 to 1960, the two-party format continued but was considered distorted because of the seating distribution. In 1950, the Republicans received 40 percent of the vote but only 14.2 percent of the seats.

After 1953, the relations between government and opposition deteriorated. While the Republicans had a tutelary concept of development, the Democrat elites emphasized local initiatives. After the 1957 elections, the Democrat party became authoritarian. In April 1960, they set up a committee to investigate the subversive activities of the opposition and some of the press. The ensuing unrest led to the military coup of May 27, 1960, and the dissolution of the Democrat party. In the constituent assembly the Republicans played a determining role in the shaping of the new constitution, with a contingent of forty-nine members. The Republicans did not obtain a majority in the 1961 elections, and their participation in coalition governments lasted only until 1963.

The turning point in the history of the Republican People's party occurred in 1965, when President İnönü declared its orientation "left from the center." The ideological debate generated a confrontation between the more center-oriented wing led by T. Feyzioğlu and the left-oriented wing led by Bülent Ecevit. Following Ecevit's election as party general secretary in 1967, dissidents founded the Republican Reliance party. The next serious crisis occurred at the second military intervention, March 1971, when Ecevit refused to cooperate with the army, but the party participated with N. Erim in the formation of a nonpartisan government. This conflict was resolved in 1972, when Ecevit defeated İnönü and became the third leader of the party.

Redefining itself as a "democratic left" party, it started to support the process of civilianization—with the development of a liberal pluralist social order, a mixed economy, land reform, and a strong cooperative movement. The new image of the party appealed to the lower-income classes, which was reflected in the outcome of the 1973 elections. It signified a realignment in Turkey's party system as the old center–periphery cleavage began to be replaced by a new functional cleavage. The coalition governments headed by Ecevit did not last. Civil strife, violence, and the militarization of political conflicts led first to martial law and later to the third military intervention, on September 12, 1980. The Republican People's party was disbanded on October 16, 1981, by Turkey's National Security Council. The new constitution of 1982 brought a ten-year ban on all former politicians (lifted by referendum on September 6, 1987).

After 1983, the heritage of the party was claimed by three new parties. The POPULIST PARTY (Halkçı Parti, HP) founded by N. Calp lasted only one legislative period; it merged in 1985 with the Social Democrat party (Sosyal Demokrat Parti), becoming the SOCIAL DEMOCRATIC POPULIST PARTY (Sosyal Demokrat Halkçı Parti, SHP), which entered the assembly in 1987 with İnönü's son Erdal İnönü, a professor of physics, as its president. The third party claiming the votes of the dissolved party is the Democratic Left party (Demokratik Sol Partisi, DSP) headed by Bülent Ecevit.

BIBLIOGRAPHY

HEPER, METIN, and JACOB M. LANDAU, eds. *Political Parties and Democracy in Turkey*. New York, 1991.

Nermin Abadan-Unat

Republican Reliance Party

Turkish political party in the 1960s and 1970s.

The Republican Reliance party (RRP) was formed by a series of defections from the Republican People's party (RPP) in the late 1960s and early 1970s. The first break occurred in May of 1967 when the RPP adopted the slogan "left of center." This prompted a group of important figures, led by Turhan Feyzioğlu, to resign and form the Reliance party. In 1973, another group, led by Kemal Satir, left the RPP when Bülent Ecevit replaced İsmet İnönü as party chairman. This group formed the Republican party, which soon merged with the Reliance party to form the RRP. The RRP did not fare well in the elections of the 1970s and has not reappeared since the resumption of political party life in 1983.

BIBLIOGRAPHY

AHMAD, F. *The Turkish Experiment in Democracy, 1950–1975*. Boulder, Colo., 1977.

Frank Tachau

Reuter Concession

Concession proposed by the shah of Persia to grant Baron Reuter of Britain the right to create businesses in his country.

On July 25, 1872, Naser al-Din Shah Qajar granted to Baron Paul Julius de Reuter, a British citizen, the exclusive right for a period of seventy years to construct and operate a railroad between the Caspian Sea and the Persian/Arabian Gulf, to build streetcar lines throughout Persia (now Iran), to work all mines (except gold, silver, and precious stones), to undertake irrigation projects, and to lumber in state forests. For the building of the lines, government lands would be provided to the concessionaire free of charge, and private land would be appropriated at current prices. Also the management of customs revenues was to be entrusted to the concessionaire(s) for a period of twenty-five years, beginning March 1, 1874. Reuter was to have the first refusal in preference to any other parties for any further concession for public utilities, roads, postal service, manufacturing plants, or banks. In return, the Persian government was to receive twenty thousand pounds sterling annually for giving the privilege of operating customs for the first five years, then 60 percent of the customs' revenues for the remaining period, 20 percent of the profits from railroads, and 15 percent of the profits from forest, mines, and water.

When the concession was announced, Lord Curzon said, it "literally took away the breath of Europe" (p. 614); and the company that Reuter proposed to establish "might well have been called Persia Incorporated" (Frechtling, p. 518) for it would have brought the entire resources of Persia under its control for seventy years. The concession, however, was the result of the efforts of the Persian minister in London, Mohsen Khan Mo'in al-Molk, who actively solicited British businessmen with the objective of conferring an exclusive concession. While his approaches to several prominent London financiers were unsuccessful, Mohsen Khan found Reuter, the owner of a well-known news agency, quite receptive to proposals regarding the concession. The main promoter of the concession was Mirza Hoseyn Khan, the shah's grand vizier, who is considered one of Persia's early reformers.

The concession was bitterly opposed by the Russians as well as by a group of anti-British officials, the *ulama* (Islamic clergy), and Anis al-Dowleh, Naser al-Din Shah's favorite wife, who had a personal vendetta against the grand vizier. The British government was also ambivalent about the practicality of the concession. Consequently, it was withdrawn in November 1873. After several years of negotiations, Reuter managed to retain mining and banking privileges, which led to the establishment of the Imperial Bank of Persia.

BIBLIOGRAPHY

CURZON, GEORGE N. *Persia and the Persian Question.* London, 1892.

FRECHTLING, L. E. "The Reuter Concession in Persia." *Asiatic Review* 34, no. 119 (July 1938): 518–533.

KAZEMZADEH, FIRUZ. *Russia and Britain in Persia, 1864–1914.* New Haven, Conn., 1968.

RAWLINSON, HENRY. *England and Russia in the East.* London, 1875.

Mansoor Moaddel

Revisionist Movement

The political party that represented the revisionist oppositional trend in Zionism; led by Ze'ev Jabotinsky from the 1920s through the 1940s.

The Revisionist Movement sometimes referred only to the political party (Ha-Zohar; Union of Zionist-Revisionists) and sometimes to various subsidiary bodies and institutions that expressed the revisionist ideology and accepted the leadership of Ze'ev JABOTINSKY, in particular the Betar youth movement, an avant-garde mass movement of youth and incipient army founded in 1923. Hence, a distinction must be made between, on the one hand, any discussion of the political history of the union and, on the other hand, the history of Betar, the National Labor Federation, and *Brit ha-Hayyal* (a union of Polish army veterans)—all of which were part of the Revisionist Movement (although they preferred to regard themselves as belonging to the "national movement" or to the "Jabotinsky movement").

The union itself was founded in 1925 in Paris by a group of veteran Zionists, most of them Russians, to propose a "revision" in the aims of ZIONISM, which basically meant a return to the principles of political Zionism espoused by Theodor HERZL. It found its greatest support among the Jewish communities of Eastern Europe (Poland and the Baltic states), but it had branches worldwide. It grew rapidly; in the elections for the 1927 Zionist Congress, it drew 8,446 votes and in the 1933 elections, 99,729 votes. Consequently, its representation grew at the Zionist Congress and in the Asefat ha-Nivharim (the parliament of the Jewish YISHUV in Palestine), and it became the major opposition party, taking on the image of the Zionist Right or even Zionist fascism, from the end of the 1920s. This electoral growth and development of revisionist institutions led to a number of controversies between the revisionists and the labor movement and the "official" Zionism. This division was often expressed in acts of violence, leaving a deep imprint on the political history and political culture of Zionism and the Yishuv. An internal conflict also existed between moderate elements that wanted to remain within the Zionist Federation and those that demanded that the union break away. It was resolved in 1933 when the moderates seceded from the union and founded a small independent party called the Jewish State party.

A specific point of controversy with official Zionism was the union's "independent diplomacy." This was expressed in various activities, primarily in attempts to obtain the support of European countries, in particular of Poland, to pressure Britain in the Mandate Council of the League of Nations in Geneva. In 1934 the union organized a mass petition denouncing British policy, and after the rise of the Nazis to power, it organized a boycott against German goods. From the mid-1930s, it began disseminating propaganda (and engaging in clandestine activity) to encourage a mass emigration of 700,000 to 1.5 million Jews from Europe to Palestine within a ten-year period (the Evacuation Plan and the Ten-Year Plan). It also was active in organizing illegal immigration to Palestine.

In 1935, the union broke away from the Zionist Federation and set up the New Zionist Federation (NZO) that met with wide popular support. In 1945, it rejoined the Zionist Federation. The union maintained an extensive organizational system with centers in Paris, London, and Warsaw. In Palestine, the Ha-Zohar was the second largest political party. After establishment of the state, the IRGUN ZVA'I LE'UMI (IZL) founded an independent party while veteran members of the union had their own Revisionist party, which never attained any representation, so most of its members finally joined the new party.

The movement's platform reflected Jabotinsky's program and ideology: the future establishment of a Jewish state on both sides of the Jordan river under Jewish sovereignty. As an interim measure, a colonization regime would be set up to create the conditions necessary to achieve a demographic Jewish majority—a prerequisite for a state. For this purpose, it called on the mandatory government to adopt an economic and settlement policy that would foster Jewish immigration and settlement. It also demanded that the JEWISH LEGION be reinstated, i.e., that Jewish military units be activated as an integral part of the British garrison in Palestine.

The official program relating to socioeconomic matters was a combination of etatism (state socialism) and liberalism: on the one hand, support for the private sector and on the other a demand for involvement by the mandatory government and the JEWISH AGENCY in the creation of infrastructure, in providing assistance to the private sector, and in setting up legal arrangements to prevent strikes. The union viewed Palestinian Arabs as citizens with equal rights, on condition that they do nothing to impair the national character of the Jewish state. The revisionists believed that cooperation with the mandatory government and with Britain was essential. But to prevent Britain from reneging on its commitments, they thought it necessary to bring political and propaganda pressure to bear on Britain. In their view, the strategic cooperation in Palestine and Britain's readiness to help Europe's Jews in their distress were the basis for such cooperation. The party was not monolithic, and various views came to the fore. In the 1930s, its dominant mood was that of the "radical nationalists," who called for a more activist policy toward the British, beginning in 1930 but in particular after the events of 1936 (the revisionists opposed the partition plan recommended by the PEEL COMMISSION REPORT in July 1937).

As a result of the internal disputes, there was a great deal of tension in the movement, particularly between the union and Betar and various maximalist groups. This internal strife led to the creation of new organizations, weakly linked organizationally to the union (in particular, the IZL).

BIBLIOGRAPHY

SCHECHTEMAN, J., and Y. BEN ARI. *History of the Revisionist Movement,* vol. 1. Tel Aviv, 1970.
SHAVIT, YAAKOV. *Jabotinsky and the Revisionist Movement, 1925–1948.* London, 1988.

Yaakov Shavit

Revolutionary Command Council, Egypt

Egyptian political body formed in the summer of 1952.

The FREE OFFICERS movement formed the RCC following its overthrow of King Farouk (July 1952) and establishment of a military junta. Led by Colonel Gamal Abdel Nasser, the members of the RCC included Colonel Anwar al-Sadat, Major Abd al-Hakim Amir, Major Salah Salam, Major Khalid Muhyi al-Din, and other high-ranking officers. General Muhammad Naguib, an older and widely respected officer, was brought in as prime minister and, in June 1953, president of the newly declared Republic of Egypt. The RCC faced a series of challenges in consolidating power, that from the MUSLIM BROTHERHOOD probably the most significant. A power struggle between Nasser and Naguib led to Naguib's ouster in November 1955 and was an important step in Nasser's rise to power. The RCC was officially dissolved in 1956.

BIBLIOGRAPHY

HARRIS, CHRISTINA. *Nationalism and Revolution in Egypt.* The Hague, 1964.
VATIKIOTIS, P.J. *The History of Egypt from Muhammad Ali to Sadat.* Baltimore, 1980.

Matthew S. Gordon

Revolutionary Command Council, Libya

Leaders of Libya's 1970 revolution and subsequent government until 1977.

Emulating the Egyptian government of Gamal Abdel Nasser, the nearly dozen Free Officers who, led by Muammar al-Qaddafi, successfully overthrew the Libyan monarchy on September 1, 1969, constituted themselves as a ruling Revolutionary Command Council (RCC) when they came to power. The RCC members served as members of the Libyan government cabinet from January 1970, when it was formed, until 1977, when it was abolished in favor of the institutions of the JAMAHIRIYA. Over the course of the years, the membership of the original RCC shrunk, as several of its number died or joined the opposition, but those who remained in power, including Abd al-Salam Jallud, Mustafa al-Kharrubi, Khawayldi al-Hamaydi, and Abu Bakr Yunis Jabir—all of whom were childhood friends of Qaddafi—retained his confidence and held sensitive military and security positions.

Lisa Anderson

Revolutionary Guards

Iranian military corps entrusted with protecting and spreading the Islamic revolution.

The Islamic Revolutionary Guards corps, also called Sepah-e Pasdaran-e Enqelab-e Eslami, was formed by an official decree from Ayatollah Khomeini (May 5, 1979) as an ideologically committed force, fiercely loyal to the Iranian revolution and entrusted with protecting it equally from external and internal enemies. It evolved into one of the most effective political as well as military pillars of governmental power in Iran.

A significant portion of the population had acquired arms during the chaotic days of the revolution, and several military cells were formed throughout Tehran. The provisional government consequently charged Mostafa Chamran and Ibrahim Yazdi with organizing the various groupings into a centralized force, which became the Revolutionary Guards. One of the determining factors in the early consolidation of the revolution, the Revolutionary Guards suppressed not just political dissidence but also social defiance of Islamic decrees and norms. According to the *Echo of Iran,* the hierarchy of decision makers in the corps followed this order (starting from the top): the representative of the Spiritual Leader of the Revolution, a position occupied first by Ayatollah Khomeini and subsequently by his successor, Ayatollah Khamene'i;

the supreme council of the corps; the commander in chief of the corps; the acting commander; the area commander; and the base commander. The Revolutionary Guards were instrumental in crushing the Kurdish rebellions in 1980. They also assumed importance in a wider military sphere, by defending Iran in its war with Iraq, which lasted from 1980 to 1988. One of the many problems Iran confronted in the early days of the war was the lack of cooperation between the Revolutionary Guards and the regular army (in fact, rivalry between President Abolhasan Bani Sadr and the Islamic Republican party over control of the Supreme Defense Council was one of the major reasons for Bani Sadr's resignation). During the war with Iraq, the Revolutionary Guards were given the assignment of training the notorious people's militia, or Basij; these were the units composed of idealistic adolescents who were sent to the front as volunteers, mostly to clear minefields or to participate in human-wave attacks. The Revolutionary Guards have boasted their own ministry since 1983, charged with the provision of armaments as well as nonmilitary needs. (According to some reports, the Revolutionary Guards contain an intelligence branch.) The Guards today wield substantial power in Iran. In 1986, they consisted of 350,000 personnel, organized in battalion-size units that operated either independently or with units of the regular armed forces. They also had a demarcated area of the Persian Gulf under their control, and after 1986 they created an air force and a navy. Under the command of Mohsen Reza'i, the Revolutionary Guards eliminated armed insurgent groups such as the Mojahedin-e Khalq and the Feda'iyan-e Khalq.

The guards have also been effective in exporting the Islamic revolution—for example, in Lebanon, Afghanistan, Bosnia and Herzegovina, and the Sudan. After the 1982 Israeli invasion of Lebanon, the Guards had nearly 1,000 fighters in the Shi'a area of the Biqa' valley. They are allied with the HEZBOLLAHI, a militant Shi'a group.

BIBLIOGRAPHY

DEPARTMENT OF THE ARMY. *Iran: A Country Study.* Washington, D.C. 1987.
ECHO OF IRAN. *Iran Almanac, 1987.* Tehran, 1987.

Neguin Yavari

Revue du Liban

French-language Lebanese journal.

Founded in 1928, the *Revue du Liban* is the leading French-language journal dealing with political, social, and cultural issues in Lebanon. In 1992 its circulation was estimated at 22,000.

Guilain P. Denoeux

Rhabani Brothers

Lebanese music composers.

In 1955, Assi ar-Rhabani (b. 1923) married Nihad Haddad, Lebanon's most famous female singer, better known as FAYRUZ. Assi and his brother Mansour (b. 1925) wrote over three hundred of Fayruz's songs and also several musical comedies.

Guilain P. Denoeux

Rhodes Talks

Negotiations to settle the Arab–Israel War of 1948.

In the aftermath of the first ARAB–ISRAEL WAR, Dr. Ralph J. Bunche was sent as UN negotiator to discuss armistice terms. The negotiations were conducted on the Greek island of Rhodes between January and July of 1949; the Rhodes talks resulted in a set of armistice agreements between Israel and the Arab states of Jordan, Egypt, Syria, and Lebanon.

BIBLIOGRAPHY

LENCZOWSKI, GEORGE. *The Middle East in World Affairs*, 4th ed. Ithaca, N.Y., 1980.

SHIMONI, YAACOV, ed. *Political Dictionary of the Middle East in the Twentieth Century*. New York, 1974.

Zachary Karabell

Richmond, Ernest T.   [1874–1974]

Archeologist and architect in Egypt during World War I.

Richmond served the Mission to Palestine as consulting architect for the Dome of the Rock Mosque in Jerusalem (1918–1919). As assistant to Chief Secretary Wyndham Deedes and then to Gilbert Clayton (1920–1924), he was given control of the Political Department of the Secretariat as a result of High Commissioner Herbert Samuel's desire to protect Arab interests and to restrain Zionist excesses. Members of the Arab Executive saw Richmond as virtually their only friend in the British administration of Palestine. He was strongly disliked by the Zionists for his sympathies with the Arabs of Palestine and his opposition to Zionism.

Richmond helped secure the appointment of al-Hajj Amin al-Husayni as mufti of Jerusalem and president of the Supreme Muslim Council (SMC). He sought to expand the powers of the mufti and the jurisdiction of the SMC and to promote the latter as a partial counterweight to the Jewish Agency. Richmond became chief adviser to the high commissioner on Muslim affairs. When he resigned, he was appointed to the nonpolitical position of director of antiquities, in which capacity he served until 1937.

Jenab Tutunji

Rida, Rashid   [1865–1935]

Disciple and biographer of Egyptian religious reformer Muhammad Abduh; editor of the Islamic modernist magazine al-Manar.

Born in the Ottoman Empire, in the village of Qalamun, near Tripoli, in what is now Lebanon, Rida came from a family of local prominence and piety. He attended the local Qur'an school and continued his education in Tripoli at an Ottoman state school and an Islamic school run by Shaykh Husayn al-Jisr. Although exposed to the Turkish and French languages, as well as to mathematics and Western science, Rida considered languages other than Arabic unnecessary for a scholar of Islam like himself. Inspired by the classic *Revival of the Religious Sciences* by Ahmad Abd Allah al-Ghazali, Rida joined the Naqshbandi Sufi order. An encounter with the dance of Mevlevi dervishes, however, shocked him into publicly denouncing what he took to be the excesses of Sufism.

Al-Urwa al-Wuthqa (The Indissoluble Bond), the magazine that Jamal al-Din al-AFGHANI and his disciple Muhammad ABDUH issued from Parisian exile in the 1880s, awakened Rida to his life mission of reviving Islam. He hoped to join al-Afghani, who was then residing in Istanbul under Sultan Abdülhamit II's surveillance and never received Rida's letter. Afghani died in 1897; Rida went instead to Cairo to join Afghani's erstwhile disciple Muhammad Abduh—whom he had met twice before. Rida became Abduh's inseparable disciple, founding the magazine *al-Manar* in 1898 to spread Abduh's reformist Islamic, or Salafiyya, message.

For thirty-seven years, until his death, Rida wrote much of *al-Manar* himself and published other religious works on the *al-Manar* press. His books in Arabic, usually serialized in *al-Manar* first, include the *Biography of the Master Imam Shaykh Muhammad Abduh* (3 vols.), *The Caliphate or Supreme Imamate, The Muhammadan Revelation*, biographies of the Prophet Muhammad and the caliphs Umar and Ali; with Abduh, an unfinished twelve-volume *Commentary on the Qur'an*.

Like Afghani and Abduh, Rida made the Islamic *umma* (community) his central concern, asking why it had declined relative to the modern West and blaming the decline on medieval additions to Islam—such as the reverence for Sufi saints—which had obscured the pure religion of the ancestors (*salaf,* from which comes the name for the Salafiyya movement). He urged reformist *ulama* (Islamic leaders) to follow Abduh and himself in returning to the Qur'an and the *sunna* (body of customs) and interpreting them afresh for the modern age. At first *al-Manar* concentrated its fire on the conservative *ulama* entrenched in the mosque-university of al-Azhar in Cairo. Rida blamed them for succumbing to the blandishments of the state, tolerating folk superstitions, and failing to mount a vigorous defense of Islam; by the 1920s, however, Rida had grown more conservative and came to see Western-inspired secularism and liberal nationalism as greater dangers. He drew nearer to the strict literalism of the Hanbali Law School, its fourteenth-century juridical theologian Ibn Taymiyah, and their Muwahhidun proponents in Arabia. King Ibn Sa'ud of Arabia responded with financial support for Rida's activities.

After his early years with Afghani, Abduh had retreated from overt politics, but Rida made frequent forays into Ottoman, Syrian, Arab, and caliphal politics. He saw Sultan Abdülhamit II's rule in Syria as repressive, and *al-Manar* published the attack of Abd al-Rahman al-Kawakibi on Abdülhamit II and his call for restoring the caliphate (held by the Ottoman Turks) to the Arabs. Hoping that changed circumstances after the Young Turk Revolution of 1908 would allow him to open a school for Islamic propaganda and guidance, Rida spent a year in Istanbul. The authorities changed their minds, however, and Rida opened his school in Cairo in 1912, only to have it fall victim to World War I. Meanwhile, as a member of the Ottoman Decentralization Society, he protested the Young Turks' tightening grip on the Arab provinces. After the war, when Mustafa Kemal (Atatürk) abolished first the Ottoman sultanate and then the caliphate, *al-Manar* published a series of studies on the caliphate and the possibility of its revival by an Arab ruler. Rida had a hand in the rival caliphal congresses in Mecca and Cairo in 1926, which unsuccessfully advanced the claims of King Ibn Sa'ud of Arabia and King Fu'ad of Egypt for the office. In the mid-1920s, when Ali Abd al-Raziq denied the caliphate's Islamic legitimacy and Taha Husayn declared pre-Islamic Arabic poetry a later forgery, Rida found himself agreeing with the Azhari *ulama* in defending revered traditions. Rida had a final try at congress politics as a participant in the 1931 Islamic Congress in Jerusalem.

As a Syrian, Rida felt the tug of emerging Arab nationalism more than Iranian-born Afghani or Abduh, an Egyptian. *Al-Manar*'s publication of Kawakibi and Rida's Decentralization Society activities had Arabist implications, and he was even chosen president of the Syrian Congress, which in 1920 declared the independence of the short-lived Syrian Arab kingdom under Faisal ibn Husayn. After the French mandate over Syria was effected in 1921, Rida went to Geneva as vice president of a delegation to the League of Nations protesting the mandates granted to Britain and France in the Middle East as part of the peace settlements of World War I.

Rida's influence waned in the later years, and his death in 1935 attracted little notice. His most direct heir was Hasan al-Banna, who founded the Muslim Brotherhood in Egypt in 1928/29 and admired Rida's Islamic activism and his strict interpretation of the *Shari'a* (Islamic law). Banna put out a few issues of *al-Manar* after Rida's death, but it disappeared in 1940.

Rida displayed an unusual blend of timidity and combativeness. He lacked the charisma of Afghani and Abduh before him and Hasan al-Banna after him. Rida's works are not widely read today; nevertheless, he was an essential link in the chain of Islamic activism running from Afghani and Abduh to Banna and Sayyid Qutb—and the present-day Muslim Brethren and their more radical Islamist offshoots.

BIBLIOGRAPHY

ADAMS, C. C. *Islam and Modernism in Egypt.* London, 1933.
HAIM, SYLVIA, ed. *Arab Nationalism: An Anthology.* Berkeley, Calif., 1976.
HOURANI, ALBERT. *Arabic Thought in the Liberal Age, 1798–1939.* London, 1962.
JOMIER, J. *Le commentaire coranique du Manar.* Paris, 1954.
KERR, MALCOLM H. *Islamic Reform: The Political and Legal Theories of Muhammad Abduh and Rashid Rida.* Berkeley, Calif., 1966.
KRAMER, MARTIN. *Islam Assembled: The Advent of the Muslim Congresses.* New York, 1986.
SAFRAN, NADAV. *Egypt in Search of Political Community.* Cambridge, Mass., 1961.

Donald Malcolm Reid

Rif

Moroccan mountain chain.

Contiguous with the Jibala massif at the western end, the Rif mountains run along the Mediterranean coast of Morocco for a distance of nearly 200 miles (300 km) but are nowhere more than 50 miles (80 km) wide. Some peaks rise to a height of 6,600 feet (2,000 m). Heavily wooded until clearance began in the seventeenth century, the region now suffers from environmental degradation and drought, and its largely Berber-speaking inhabitants have a history of labor migration.

BIBLIOGRAPHY

McNeill, J. R. *The Mountains of the Mediterranean World: An Environmental History.* New York, 1992.

Mikesell, Marvin. *Northern Morocco: A Cultural Geography.* Berkeley, Calif., 1961.

C. R. Pennell

Rifa al-Gharbi, al-

Town located in the center of Bahrain.

Al-Rifa al-Gharbi (West Rifa) is situated next to al-Rifa al-Sharqi (East Rifa) and south of Isa Town, Bahrain's first new development town. The ruler of Bahrain and many members of the al-Khalifa family reside in al-Rifa al-Gharbi, where the ruler conducts his daily *majles* (assembly).

BIBLIOGRAPHY

The Gulf Handbook, 1978. London, 1978.

Emile A. Nakhleh

Rifa'i, Abd al-Mun'im al-   [1917–   ]

Prime minister of Jordan from August 1969 to June 1970 at a critical juncture of Jordanian–Palestinian and Jordanian–PLO relations.

Abd al-Mun'im al-Rifa'i wrote poetry and was considered an intellectual. He had served Jordan as delegate and ambassador to the United States and the United Nations in 1949, 1953 to 1957, and 1959 to 1965; ambassador to Lebanon in 1957 to 1958, the U.K. in 1958 to 1959, Egypt in 1966 to 1967; and minister of foreign affairs in 1967 to 1970. At the time he was asked to form a government, the Palestine Liberation Organization (PLO) was at the height of its military activities in Jordan and had gained considerable political power because of the strong support of the Palestinian refugee camp population. The PLO took advantage of this support and frequently undermined Jordanian government authority. Rifa'i was chosen to manage and help defuse tensions that had arisen because he had good relations with the PLO

and was considered pro-Palestinian. He also had good relations with Syria. Despite this, he was unable to halt the deterioration in relations with the PLO that led eventually to the violent showdown between the Jordanian armed forces and the PLO in September 1970. In retrospect, he was considered to be a weak prime minister, though he retains respect for his record as a diplomat.

BIBLIOGRAPHY

Bill, James, and Carl Leiden. *Politics in the Middle East.* Boston, 1979.

Gubser, Peter. *Jordan: Crossroads of Middle Eastern Events.* Boulder, Colo., 1983.

Jenab Tutunji

Rifa'i, Nur al-Din al-   [1899–1978]

Former Lebanese prime minister, 1975.

A Beirut-born Sunni, Nur al-Din al-Rifa'i studied at the military school in Constantinople (now Istanbul). He began his military career in 1918 as a *Sous-Lieutenant* (sublieutenant) and rose to become, successively, a commander of the Lebanese police force, an administrator of north Lebanon, and the director general of Lebanon's internal security forces. He was appointed to the rank of *Colonel-Général* (general) in 1950 and retired two years later. During his distinguished career, he earned a reputation for integrity and fair-mindedness. A horseback rider and horseracing enthusiast, he became assistant secretary-general of Beirut's racetrack in January 1966.

On May 23, 1975 (approximately five weeks after the shooting in the east Beirut suburb of Ain al-Rummaneh, which effectively started the 1975 Lebanese Civil War), Rifa'i was President Sulayman Franjiyya's surprise choice to head a cabinet composed of seven army officers and only one civilian. In what the press immediately called the Military Cabinet, Rifa'i held, concomitantly, the premiership and the ministries of health, justice, industry, and oil.

The Military Cabinet represented an attempt on the part of President Franjiyya and Maronite hardliners to apply a military solution to the civil conflict. It was a direct challenge to prominent Muslims who opposed the formation of an army-dominated government and favored the appointment of Rashid Karame to the premiership. The selection of Rifa'i as prime minister thus dangerously widened the gap between the Christian and Muslim sides of the Lebanese political establishment. Muslim leaders responded to Franjiyya's challenge by temporarily overcoming their differences to denounce the new cabinet. The occasion even produced an unexpected rapprochement between two eminent rival Muslim politicians, Sunni leader Sa'ib Salam and Druze warlord Kamal Jumblatt. On May 24, 1975, the day following the formation of the Military Cabinet, Beirut was racked by intense gunfire and artillery battles. When it became clear that he could not even muster support from within his own Sunni community, Rifa'i resigned. His cabinet had lasted a mere three days (May 23–May 26).

BIBLIOGRAPHY

COBBAN, HELENA. *The Making of Modern Lebanon.* Boulder, Colo., 1985.
SALIBI, KAMAL. *Crossroads to Civil War.* New York, 1976.
Who's Who in Lebanon, 4th ed. Beirut, 1970.

Guilain P. Denoeux

Rifa'i, Samir [1899–1965]

Prime minister of Jordan during the period 1944 to 1963.

Born in Safed, Palestine, Rifa'i was noted for his resourcefulness, subtlety, and intelligence. As prime minister in 1944 and 1945, he participated in negotiations to establish the League of Arab States and signed the charter on behalf of Jordan. As prime minister when King Abdullah ibn Husayn was assassinated, he handed power over to the veteran Tawfiq Abd al-Huda in July 1951.

Rifa'i was asked to form a government on January 9, 1956, in the aftermath of anti–BAGHDAD PACT protests. He proclaimed martial law and decisively rejected the Baghdad Pact, refusing to sign "any new pacts." This allowed him to reject the Convenant of Arab Union at the same time. To prevent a rupture in ties with the United Kingdom and subsequent loss of British subsidies, Rifa'i favored renegotiating rather than abrogating the 1948 Anglo–Jordanian treaty. But this stand was very controversial. He remained in office this time until October 1956, when Sulayman al-Nabulsi, who opposed the relationship with Britain, was asked to form a government.

Following the "royal coup" of April 25, 1957, which ousted Nabulsi's cabinet, Rifa'i served as deputy premier and effective leader of the government in the cabinet of Ibrahim Hashim. He guided negotiations for Jordan's federation with Iraq, headed the regional cabinet in Amman during the federation, then continued as prime minister of Jordan after its breakup in 1958. Rifa'i steered King Hussein ibn Talal through that difficult period and helped him survive plots by Colonel Abd al-Hammid Sarraj,

the interior minister of Syria, when it was the "northern region" of the United Arab Republic (UAR). Rifa'i also helped engineer Jordan's friendly ties with the United States and secured American subsidies, although Jordan never officially accepted the Eisenhower Doctrine. Unfortunately, Rifa'i became too closely identified with Jordan's quarrels with President Gamal Abdel Nasser of the UAR. A break in ties with the UAR followed, and Rifa'i resigned on May 5, 1959.

Rifa'i formed his sixth and last cabinet on March 27, 1963, with a mandate to improve relations with Syria, Egypt, and Iraq. However, when the three countries agreed to form an expanded United Arab Republic, public demonstrations favoring Jordan's participation in the union led to clashes with the army, notably in the West Bank. Rifa'i was on the verge of being denied a vote of confidence when he tendered his resignation. He went on to serve as president of the upper house of parliament, or Senate.

BIBLIOGRAPHY

ABIDI, AQIL HYDER HASAN. *Jordan: A Political Study, 1948–1957.* New Delhi, 1965.
DANN, URIEL. *King Hussein and the Challenge of Arab Radicalism: Jordan, 1955–1967.* New York, 1989.
MADI, MUNIB, and SULAYMAN MUSA. *Tarikh al-Urdun fi al-qarn al-ishrin* (The History of Jordan in the Twentieth Century). Amman, 1988.

Jenab Tutunji

Rifa'i, Zaid al- [1936–]

Jordanian politician.

Son of the prominent Jordanian politician of Palestinian origin Samir Rifa'i, Zaid al-Rifa'i is known as a boyhood friend and loyal confidant of King Hussein ibn Talal. He held numerous positions in the Foreign Ministry before beginning service to the king in 1964, where he eventually rose to chief of the royal court (1969), political adviser to the king (1972–1973), prime minister/defense minister/ foreign minister (1973–1976), and prime minister/ foreign minister (1985–1989).

Jordan suffered a series of setbacks in the early 1980s as the effects of petroleum pricing in the Gulf states battered its once-booming economy. Jordan became more dependent on loans and struggled with high inflation. The al-Rifa'i government introduced a series of austerity measures in November 1986 and March 1989, the latter in consultation with the International Monetary Fund. New taxes and sharp increases in consumer prices led to rioting in traditionally pro-regime districts, such as Ma'an and al-Karak, along with denunciations of corruption in the al-Rifa'i government and calls for his resignation. After al-Rifa'i quickly resigned, King Hussein announced that general parliamentary elections would be held in November 1989, for the first time since 1967.

BIBLIOGRAPHY

ABU GHAYDA, RASHID. *Man Huwa?* (Who's Who?). Amman, 1988.

The Middle East and North Africa, 1991, 37th ed. London, 1991.

Michael R. Fischbach

Rif War

One of the most successful Moroccan attempts to resist an initial European invasion, 1921–1926.

The Treaty of Fes (1912), imposing a French protectorate over Morocco, assigned northern and southern zones to Spain. Until the end of World War I, the Spanish army and economy were not strong enough to take advantage of this. But, in 1919, the Spanish army began to push westward from Melilla into the Rif mountains, and a loosely organized coalition was formed to oppose it. In 1920 Muhammad ibn Abd al-Karim al-KHATTABI took over leadership of the coalition and set about creating unity based on the strict imposition of the SHARI'A, allied with European military techniques.

By June 1921 Spanish military intelligence was warning that Abd al-Karim's supporters could resist further Spanish advances, despite the 25,000 troops in the eastern zone. The warnings were ignored, new advanced garrisons set up, and on June 2 the Rifis attacked a post at Dahar Abarran. The garrison was withdrawn, but other posts came under attack. On July 22, the main Spanish forward base at Anwal withdrew with heavy casualties. The retreat became a rout, and by August 9 all Spanish positions outside Melilla were lost and over 13,000 soldiers killed. Melilla was not occupied because Abd al-Karim, concerned that he might lose control, wanted to avoid the slaughter of civilians.

In little more than a year, Spanish forces had almost regained their old lines, but Abd al-Karim used the supplies they had abandoned to equip a regular army. He capitalized on the prestige of his victory to institutionalize a bureaucratic government in the central Rif, staffed largely by members of his own family. He emphasized the *Shari'a,* both for ideological reasons and to ensure order. An infrastructure—roads and a telegraph system—was built to maintain control and

better fight the Spanish. In February 1923 he received formal *bay'as* (declarations of allegiance) from the central Rif tribes and established a Rifi state.

Abd al-Karim overcame such local opponents as Ahmad ibn Muhammad al-Raysuni, a sharif of the Jibala mountains, and Abd al-Rahman al-Darqawi, head of the Darqawiyya *tariqa* whose headquarters at Amjutt were just over the figurative border of the French zone. Both of the local chiefs resented Abd al-Karim's growing authority, but in doing so came into conflict with the French and Spanish. The attack on isolated Spanish outposts in the Jibala began in August 1925, and in November Spanish forces withdrew from the town of Shawin. The Spanish army lost around 10,000 men.

Abd al-Karim was reluctant to attack the French zone. He did not want to have to fight two European armies. He agreed because he needed to secure food supplies and deal with the Darqawiyya and because of pressure from some of his commanders. The attack on Amjutt in April 1925 succeeded, and Rifi forces moved on Fez, overrunning many French positions. The French army held the Rifi attack, and in June 1925 a conference in Madrid agreed on a joint Franco–Spanish campaign to crush the Rifis.

In September 1925 Spanish landings at Alhucemas and French advances from the south were coordinated. By the winter, the Rif was surrounded and running out of food. The following April, brief peace negotiations at Oujda, in eastern Morocco, failed and Rifi resistance collapsed. On May 15, 1926, Abd al-Karim surrendered to the French.

BIBLIOGRAPHY

There are many book-length accounts of the Rif War. The military campaign is covered in CARLOS MARTÍNEZ DE CAMPOS *España bélica, el siglo veinte: Marruecos* (Madrid, 1969), and in DAVID WOOLMAN's *Rebels in the Rif, Abd el-Krim and the Rif Rebellion* (London and Stanford, 1969). Both rely on European published sources and consequently underplay the Rifi experience. C. R. PENNELL's *A Country with a Government and a Flag: The Rif War in Morocco, 1921–1926* (Wisbech, U.K., 1986) is based on Moroccan as well as European archival material and focuses on the politics and organization of the Rifi side.

C. R. Pennell

Rimawi, Qasim al-

Jordanian politician.

Of Palestinian origin, Rimawi has served Jordan in several governmental posts, including minister of state for municipal and rural affairs (1965–1967), parliamentarian representing the West Bank city of Ramalla (1967), and president of the chamber of deputies.

BIBLIOGRAPHY

Who's Who in the Arab World, 9th ed. Beirut, 1988. Reprint, 1989.

Michael R. Fischbach

Rishon le-Zion

City in central Israel.

Situated seven miles (11 km) southeast of Tel Aviv, Rishon le-Zion was founded in 1882 by Russian settlers under the leadership of Zalman LEVONTIN; it was the first town to be established by Zionist settlers. The settlers, who experienced severe difficulties in the early years (e.g., lack of funds and water resources), obtained the financial support of Baron Edmond de Rothschild. Rothschild helped build vineyards in Rishon le-Zion, and by 1889, the Carmel wine cellars were established there.

The first Hebrew kindergarten and elementary school opened in Rishon le-Zion in the 1880s as well as the first agricultural workers' association, which was founded there in 1887.

BIBLIOGRAPHY

SCHAMA, SIMON. *The Two Rothschilds and the Land of Israel.* New York, 1978.

Bryan Daves

Riyad, Mahmoud   [1917–1992]

Egyptian diplomat and former secretary-general of the League of Arab States.

In 1939, Riyad enrolled in the Egyptian Military Academy and obtained a master's degree in military sciences. In 1948, he headed the Egyptian delegation to the armistice talks with the Israelis in Rhodes. In 1955, he was appointed ambassador to Syria, and two years later he participated in the Syria–Egyptian unity talks. On June 1, 1972, he was elected secretary-general of the League of Arab States. As secretary-general he played an important role in mediating the conflict between the two Yemens (1972), the border conflict between Iraq and Kuwait (1973), and the Palestine Liberation Organization–Lebanese government clashes in 1973.

BIBLIOGRAPHY

Arab Information Center, Beirut.

George E. Irani

Riyad, Mustafa al-   [1834–1911]

Egyptian official, cabinet minister, and three-time premier.

Usually known as Riaz Pasha during his lifetime, Riyad's origin is obscure; he may have been Jewish. In Egypt, he began his career as a clerk in the foreign ministry and then in the army. Aide-de-camp for Abbas I, he then held a succession of provincial governorships. Khedive Isma'il entrusted various ministerial portfolios to him. He contributed to Egypt's intellectual life by inviting Jamal al-Din al-Afghani and the editors of *al-Muqtataf* to settle there and also provided an endowment for the newly founded National Library. He backed Egypt's foreign creditors against Khedive Isma'il and helped write the 1880 liquidation law, which reduced Egyptian government indebtedness by strictly limiting expenditures.

Riyad underestimated the strength of the Egyptian officers in his first term as head of Egypt's government. Having acceded to their demand to dismiss his war minister in February 1881, he had to resign after their Abdin demonstration in September of that year. He stayed in Europe as long as the followers of Ahmad URABI held sway. He served again as head of Egypt's government from 1888 to 1891 and from 1894 to 1895. He was widely thought to oppose the British occupation and to support the establishment of Cairo's first Muslim-owned daily, *al-Mu'ayyad.* He favored bringing in Western technology but resisted the growing power of Europeans over Egyptian finances, justice, and government.

BIBLIOGRAPHY

HUNTER, F. ROBERT. *Egypt under the Khedives.* Pittsburgh, 1984.
MOBERLY-BELL, C. F. *Khedives and Pashas.* London, 1884.
AL-SAYYID, AFAF LUTFI. *Egypt and Cromer.* London, 1968.
SCHÖLCH, ALEXANDER. *Egypt for the Egyptians!* London, 1981.

Arthur Goldschmidt, Jr.

Riyadh

Saudi Arabia's capital and largest city.

More correctly transliterated as al-Riyad (the gardens), the city, which is located in the southern Najd

A Riyadh street scene before the oil boom of the 1960s. (D.W. Lockhard)

A Saudi Defense Ministry building in Riyadh. (Richard Bulliet)

region, is also the capital of a large province of the same name. Nearby are the ruins of al-Dir'iyya, the original seat of the Al Sa'ud family until an invading Egyptian army destroyed the village in 1818 and put an end to the first Saudi state. The Al Sa'ud thereupon relocated at Riyadh, which became the capital of the second Saudi state of the mid-nineteenth century. A second decline in Saudi fortunes caused Riyadh to fall to the rival Al Rashid dynasty of Ha'il in 1891, but in 1902 Abd

al-Aziz ibn Abd al-Rahman (also known as IBN SA'UD) infiltrated the town with a small band of followers. Launching a surprise attack on al-Musmak fortress, Abd al-Aziz succeeded in capturing the Al Rashid governor and restoring Saudi control over Riyadh. Over the next two decades, the Al Sa'ud used Riyadh as their base from which to extend their authority again over all of Najd. From the late 1920s, Saudi Arabia had two capitals, with the king residing in Riyadh, the capital of Najd, but most of the ministries and embassies located in Hijaz. By 1955, most government ministries and head offices had moved to Riyadh; the foreign ministry and foreign embassies remained in JIDDA until 1985, when they too were required to move to the capital. Although Riyadh's population was estimated at only 169,000 in 1962, the oil boom (beginning in 1974) dramatically transformed the city and caused its population to increase to over 1.5 million. Very little of the old city remains intact, but the old mud-brick fort of al-Musmak fortunately has been saved. Many buildings in the new diplomatic quarter, known as al-Dir'iyah because of its proximity to the old village, have been built in the style of the traditional mud-brick architecture. The new King's Office Complex (al-Yamama Palace) and the headquarters of the Gulf Cooperation Council are located near the diplomatic quarter. Also nearby is the King Sa'ud University, which was founded in 1957 and is the country's oldest university. Imam Muhammad ibn Sa'ud University, one of the kingdom's three Islamic universities, is also located in Riyadh. The city is the inland terminus of a railroad coming out of Dammam on the Gulf coast; it also has a major air force base, which had previously served as an international airport.

A Riyadh thoroughfare in the 1990s. (Richard Bulliet)

BIBLIOGRAPHY

NYROP, R. F. *Saudi Arabia: A Country Study*. Washington, D.C., 1984.

John E. Peterson

Riyadh Arab Summit

Conference of Arab leaders that imposed a cease-fire to end the Lebanese Civil War.

The summit was convened by Saudi Prince Fahd on October 16, 1976, following Syria's entry the previous summer into the eighteen-month old LEBANESE CIVIL WAR. The summit called for a cease-fire to be imposed by a newly created Arab Deterrent Force. The new force legitimized the Syrian presence in Lebanon. While in theory the Arab Deterrent Force was to be international and under the command of Lebanese President Ilyas Sarkis, it actually consisted almost entirely of Syrian troops (twenty-five thousand of a total of thirty thousand) under Syrian command.

The Riyadh summit halted full-scale war but did not stop the fighting in Lebanon. Another resolution of the summit, the withdrawal of armed men and the confiscation of weapons, was not implemented. The summit also rebuffed the attempts of Yasir Arafat, head of the Palestine Liberation Organization (PLO), to address the Israeli presence in South Lebanon, where conflict flared soon after the meeting, leading to the LITANI OPERATION. The conference is often referred to as a mini-summit, because Fahd limited attendance to representatives of the PLO, Egypt, Syria, Lebanon, Kuwait, and Saudi Arabia. The summit's resolutions were ratified October 25, at a full Arab League meeting in Cairo, Egypt.

BIBLIOGRAPHY

JOHNSON, MICHAEL. *Class and Client in Beirut*. Lowell, Mass., 1986.
POGANY, ISTVAN. *The Arab League and Peacekeeping in the Lebanon*. London, 1987.

Elizabeth Thompson

Riyal

The monetary unit of Iran, Oman, Yemen, Qatar, and Saudi Arabia.

The riyal (a word of Spanish and French origin) was introduced into Iran in 1930 as part of the Gold Standard Act. It is popularly known as the *kran*. It was introduced into Saudi Arabia in the nineteenth century after the U.S. dollar was banned in the Ottoman Empire.

Marilyn Higbee

Robert College

See Boğaziçi (Bosporus) University

Rockefeller Museum

Name popularly given to the Palestine Archaeological Museum in Jerusalem.

The museum, which opened in 1938, was funded by $2 million pledged by John D. Rockefeller, Jr., to match an endowment fund. The building, designed by Austen St. B. Harrison, stands on ten acres facing the Old City walls. In addition to exhibition space, there are study galleries, record offices, a library, an auditorium, and offices of the Department of Antiquities. An ancient cemetery, dating from the sixth and fifth centuries B.C.E., was discovered on the site and excavated. Before the termination of the mandate in 1948, the building was turned over to an international board. In November 1966, Jordan nationalized the museum and took possession of the building and its contents. After the 1967 war, Israel's government entrusted the museum to the Department of Antiquities, which invited the Israel Museum to operate the exhibition galleries.

BIBLIOGRAPHY

REED, STEPHEN A. *The Dead Sea Scrolls Catalogue: Documents, Photographs and Museum Inventory Numbers*. Atlanta, 1994.

Mia Bloom

Rogers, William Pierce   [1913–   ]

American author of the Rogers Plan.

Rogers was U.S. secretary of state for President Richard M. Nixon from 1969 to 1973. In 1969, a series of peace proposals for the Middle East, known as the Rogers Plan, were promoted by the United States. Included were dual proposals for Israeli–Egyptian and Israeli–Jordanian treaties based on UN Resolution 242 and Israel's withdrawal from the occupied territories won in the ARAB–ISRAEL WAR of 1967. Owing to the intransigence of all parties concerned, including Henry Kissinger, the Rogers Plan was not effected.

BIBLIOGRAPHY

FINDLING, JOHN, ed. *Dictionary of American Diplomatic History*. New York, 1989.

SPIEGEL, STEVEN. *The Other Arab–Israeli Conflict*. Chicago, 1985.

Zachary Karabell

Rolo Family

Sephardic Jewish family of businessmen who had settled in Alexandria by the mid-nineteenth century.

The Rolo family produced a number of well-known and influential businessmen, among them Ruben (b. 1820), his sons Simon, Giacomo (1847–1917), Robert S. (b. 1869), and Robert J. (b. 1876).

Robert S. Rolo gained the strongest influence in Egypt's economy among the family's members, since he served as a legal advisor to Crown Prince Fu'ad and was later regarded as a close confidant of the king, serving as an indispensable intermediary between the royal court and the British residency. He also served as director of the Egypt National Bank for many years. Ruben, Simon, and Giacomo Rolo joined forces with other Sephardic families, notably the Suarès and Cattaoui, in promoting such economic enterprises as the Helwan Railway and in creating Kum Ombo, Egypt's well-known agricultural company. Robert J. Rolo served as the president of Alexandria's Jewish community between 1934 and 1948.

BIBLIOGRAPHY

KRÄMER, GUDRUN. *The Jews in Modern Egypt: 1914–1952*. Seattle, 1989.

LANDAU, JACOB M. *Jews in Nineteenth Century Egypt*. New York, 1969.

MAKARIYUS, SHAHIN. *Ta'rikh al-Isra'iliyyin* (History of the Jews). Cairo, 1904.

MIZRAHI, MAURICE. "The Role of the Jews in Economic Development." In *The Jews of Egypt: A Mediterranean Society in Modern Times,* ed. by Shimon Shamir. Boulder, Colo., 1987.

Michael M. Laskier

Roman Catholicism and Roman Catholic Missions

Native Middle Eastern groups or individuals or those who established religious institutions there to convert people to Roman Catholicism.

The term *Catholic* is ambiguous in the Middle East. In Arabic, it refers to the Melkites; in English, it refers to Christians of the Latin rite, usually called Roman Catholics in the United States.

Since the Christian Church evolved in the Middle East, differences in theology and ritual that had existed for centuries between the eastern and western parts of the Roman Empire led to a schism in 1054. In the West (Europe) the Latin rite became basic to the Roman Catholic church. In the East (Byzantium) the Byzantine state church prevailed until the rise of Islam in the seventh century C.E. The expansion of Islam was rapid, with Muslims conquering North Africa and the Iberian peninsula by the eighth century and ruling until the fifteenth century. In 1009 Muslims destroyed the Holy Sepulchre in Jerusalem; in 1095 Pope Urban II called for a holy war to "rescue the Holy Land from the Muslim infidels." To do this, the First Crusade was organized in 1096. The Crusaders, under Godfrey of Bouillon, succeeded in conquering Jersalem in 1099. Seven more Crusades followed, with successes and failures, until the Mamluks of Egypt conquered Acre in 1291, evicting the Crusaders.

The Roman Catholic Church was reestablished in the Middle East in 1099, when a hierarchy under a Latin partriarchate at Jerusalem was established. By the end of the thirteenth century, however, after the Crusaders were evicted from the region, only the Franciscan Brothers stayed on as custodians of the shrines. As the Crusader venture collapsed, the pope's contacts with the Mongols in central Asia inspired the Franciscan and Dominican orders to work among them, in the Ilkhanate of Persia, during the thirteenth and fourteenth centuries. Then after the fall of Constantinople (now Istanbul) to the Ottoman Turks in 1453—which ended the Byzantine Empire—Franciscan, Capuchin, Dominican, Carmelite, and later, Jesuit missionaries went to the provinces of the Ottoman Empire under the protection of European powers to try to convert Eastern Christians to Roman Catholicism.

In the nineteenth century the Latin-rite presence in North Africa increased because of the French occupation of Algeria. The ancient see of Carthage was restored in 1876. Cardinal Lavigerie was named primate of Africa, with more than one million Catholics in Morocco, Algeria, and Tunisia—where he founded the White Fathers and White Sisters to work in the region.

In 1847 the Latin patriarchate of Jerusalem had been reestablished and numerous missionaries, engaged in education and nursing, had been sent to Ottoman Palestine. During the twentieth century, however, with the dismantling of the Ottoman Empire by the Allies after World War I and the post–World War II independence of Israel, Tunisia,

Algeria, and Morocco, the Roman Catholic presence dwindled both in North Africa and in Palestine.

In 1990 the number of Latin-rite Roman Catholics throughout the Middle East was estimated to be 1.3 million (about 35 percent are migrant workers from Sri Lanka, India, and the Philippines). Some 566,000 Roman Catholics are indigenous to Sudan and more than 60,000 live in the West Bank and Jordan. These discrete communities are unusual for the region; most of the other Catholics form small communities or are family groups who left other local Christian churches, especially one of the Eastern Orthodox (which include the Nestorian and the Monophysite churches—the Coptic, Ethiopian, Armenian, and the Mar Thoma of India) or Uniate churches.

Arabia and the Gulf. The jurisdiction of the apostolic vicar for Arabia extends to the countries of the Arabian peninsula and the Gulf, excluding Kuwait, which has its own vicar. There are few local Catholics, but there are large numbers of Palestinian, Indian, Sri Lankan, and Filipino workers in the region. The *Annuario Pontificio* counts 470,000 for 1990. There are parishes in the United Arab Emirates (U.A.E.) and Bahrain and Catholic schools in the U.A.E. and in Kuwait. In Saudi Arabia chaplains for foreign workers are allowed to operate "clandestinely," although this provokes occasional troubles. In North Yemen the government has called in nursing sisters to staff hospitals, and there are a few priests to care for expatriate Catholics.

Egypt. The three vicariates in Egypt had been reduced to one at Alexandria. While the official count of Latin Catholics is only 8,000, there are some 200 men and 1,000 women members of Latin orders and congregations, mostly engaged in education.

Syria. Syria, with a vicariate at Aleppo, lists 12,000 Latin Catholics, with about 250 men and women engaged in social and apostolic work since Catholic schools were closed in 1967.

Iraq. Baghdad is an episcopal see with an archbishop, but Latins number only a few thousand, and since Catholic schools were closed in Iraq, only a few Latin-rite religious orders remain, staffing a seminary, a parish, and a hospital.

Lebanon. Lebanon has a large number of Latin-rite religious orders and congregations, with about 250 men and over a thousand women working in 150 Catholic schools, a university, several hospitals, and numerous social ministries. The community numbers about 20,000.

West Bank and Jordan. In the West Bank and Jordan a substantial Palestinian community of 60,000 Roman Catholics has its own patriarch and diocesan clergy (about 60) who celebrate the Latin rite in Arabic. There is a Catholic University at Bethlehem and over 270 educational establishments. As this region is the Holy Land, it is a center for several Catholic religious orders.

Sudan. The largest Middle Eastern indigenous Roman Catholic community is found in Sudan. Some 217,000 Roman Catholics are in Juba and some 348,000 are in Khartoum. Each city has its local ordinary with a growing diocesan clergy aided by a few hundred men and women in non-Sudanese orders. The famine in the south has caused the displacement of many Sudanese Catholics.

North Africa. Morocco has two residential sees, one in Tangiers and one in Rabat, caring for some 40,000 Catholics, including over 200 men and women in religious orders engaged in a variety of social and educational works.

Algeria has a metropolitan see at Algiers with suffragan bishops in Oran and Constantine ministering to over 40,000 Catholics. Men and women in religious orders number about 350, many engaged in secular roles. In both Morocco and Algeria the diocesan clergy is substantial (about 50 in each) but of European origin.

There has been a prelature in Tunis since 1964, when a Vatican accord with the government suppressed the see of Carthage and closed all but 7 of its 100 churches. Catholics number over 15,000, cared for by 15 priests. Over 200 men and women in religious orders work in a variety of apostolates, including the research institute and library of the White Fathers.

Libya has a vicar apostolic and about 30 women in religious orders working in hospitals. Four religious men and one diocesan priest care for the spiritual needs of the 30,000 or so expatriate Catholics.

Iran and Turkey. Iran has a bishopric at Isfahan and a few priests and nuns caring for the Latin-rite community of 2,000. Turkey has an episcopal see in İzmir and a vicariate in Istanbul for some 7,000 Catholics. The number of Roman Catholic expatriates fluctuates with economic conditions; still, their presence in the Middle East, which had been relatively stable, is now in decline. Missionary vocations are sparse, and the need for educational and social help from expatriates is narrowing. At the same time, the Vatican is concerned about the increased emigration from indigenous Latin communities that has been provoked by political constraint and the resurgence of pan-Islamic sentiment.

BIBLIOGRAPHY

ATIYA, A. S. *A History of Eastern Christianity*. 1968. Reprint, Millwood, N.Y., 1980.
BETTS, ROBERT BRENTON. *Christians in the Arab East*. Atlanta, 1978.

John J. Donohue

Romanization

Writing the Turkish language in the Latin alphabet.

Turkic peoples have used a variety of scripts in the course of their history, the earliest being the Orkhon script known through eighth-century inscriptions found in Mongolia. With conversion to Islam, the Turks adopted the ARABIC SCRIPT and used it over the centuries. On August 9, 1928, Mustafa Kemal (Atatürk), president of the new Republic of Turkey, announced its replacement by a Latin alphabet—essentially phonetic, omitting q, w, and x; adding ç (=*ch*), ğ ("soft" g), and ş (=*sh*); and including eight vowels: a, e, ı, i, o, ö, u, and ü.

Dissatisfaction with the Arabic script was not new. Discussion of and experimentation in modifying it date from the Tanzimat. The script, ill-suited to the Turkish phonetic system and hard to read and write (or print), was thus a prime cause of illiteracy. It symbolized adherence to Islam and Arab–Persian culture, and at a time when he was leading Turkey toward a new, Western-oriented way of life, Atatürk considered it a major obstacle to progress.

As for the Latin script, Namık Kemal was among the first to mention it as a suitable alternative (1879). Articles favoring it appeared in the early twentieth century, and Atatürk himself demonstrated its possibilities in Turkish sections of letters (otherwise in French) sent to a friend after becoming military attaché in Sofia (1913). During World War I, however, Enver Paşa devised a modified Arabic script for the military, but this had little effect.

Discussion continued under the republic, but a proposal for Latin letters was rejected at the 1923 İZMIR ECONOMIC CONGRESS. Interest increased, however, with the announcement of a romanization policy for the USSR's Turkic languages (a policy later reversed in favor of Cyrillic). On May 24, 1928, the Grand National Assembly legislated the introduction of international numerals, and Atatürk determined to proceed with the alphabet. A commission studying the plan submitted its proposed alphabet on August 1, 1928. Eight days later Atatürk an-

nounced its adoption, admonishing everyone to learn it as a patriotic duty.

Atatürk also demanded a speedy transition, and on November 3, 1928, the Grand National Assembly approved the new script. Turks were required to prove ability to use it in place of the Arabic by the beginning of 1929, passing an examination or attending "national schools" set up across the country. The assembly also decreed that printing in the old script was illegal, and by the middle of 1929 all publications were being printed in the new script.

Romanization coupled with language reform affected many aspects of Turkish life. By breaking with traditions of the Ottoman–Islamic past, it stimulated Turkish nationalism and secularization. It facilitated dissemination of information, improved education and the literacy level, speeded modernization and technology through increased interaction with the West, and helped lead Turks to ever greater social and political awareness.

[*See also:* Turkish Language]

BIBLIOGRAPHY

FEYZIOĞLU, TURHAN. "Secularism: Cornerstone of the Turkish Revolution." In *Atatürk's Way*. Istanbul, 1982.
LEVONIAN, LUTFI. *The Turkish Press: Selections from the Turkish Press Showing Events and Opinions, 1925–1932*. Athens, 1932.
LEWIS, BERNARD. *Emergence of Modern Turkey*. London, 1968.
SPERCO, WILLY. *Atatürk, 1882–1938*. Paris, 1958.

Kathleen R. F. Burrill

Rome, Treaty of

French–Italian pact in which some Middle Eastern territory changed hands.

In an effort to obtain Italy's support against Nazi Germany, France's foreign minister Pierre Laval signed the Treaty of Rome with Italy's dictator Benito Mussolini on January 7, 1935. France conceded small amounts of land in North and East Africa to Italy and, according to some accounts, the negotiations involved an unwritten pledge by Laval to support Italian claims in Ethiopia. When World War II began in 1939, Italy was allied with Germany, and Germany occupied France, so prewar agreements were negated or renegotiated.

BIBLIOGRAPHY

HUREWITZ, J. C., ed. *The Middle East and North Africa in World Politics*. New Haven, Conn., 1979.

TAYLOR, A. J. P. *The Origins of the Second World War*. New York, 1961.

Zachary Karabell

Rommel, Erwin   [1891–1944]

German general (field marshal) in World War II.

Rommel, the Desert Fox, is best known as the commander of the Afrika Korps, which took North Africa during the early years of World War II. Assuming command in February 1941, Rommel reversed Italian setbacks and crossed North Africa from west to east, driving the British into Egypt by May 1942. Hitler ordered a drive on Cairo and the Suez Canal, which led to the defeat of the Afrika Korps at al-Alamayn in November 1942, while Rommel was on sick leave in Germany. With his troops in retreat from the British Eighth Army, Rommel retired to Germany in March 1943, disenchanted with war and Hitler's politics. Implicated in a plot on Hitler's life, he committed suicide by poison in October 1944.

BIBLIOGRAPHY

YOUNG, DESMOND. *Rommel: The Desert Fox*. New York, 1950.

Daniel E. Spector

Roosevelt, Franklin Delano   [1882–1945]

Thirty-second president of the United States.

Franklin Delano Roosevelt was born at Hyde Park, New York; he died of a cerebral hemorrhage at Warm Springs, Georgia. Born into a wealthy family (a distant cousin of President Theodore Roosevelt), he attended Groton, Harvard, and Columbia Law. In 1905, he married Anna Eleanor Roosevelt (another distant cousin), and in 1907 began a law practice in New York City.

His political career began in 1910, with his election to the New York State Senate. An opponent of the Democratic party's machine in New York City called Tammany Hall, he soon gained a reputation for independence and progressivism within the Democratic party. He worked for Woodrow Wilson's presidential campaign and was made assistant secretary of the Navy in Wilson's administration from 1913 to 1920, becoming the Democratic nominee for vice president in 1920. When the Cox/Roosevelt ticket lost to the Republican Harding/Coolidge ticket, he returned to his law practice. In

August 1921, infantile paralysis left his legs and lower abdomen paralyzed.

Through exercise and treatment, Roosevelt recovered some movement of his lower limbs and was able to continue his law practice and civic affairs. He supported the popular New York City Democrat Alfred E. Smith in the presidential races of 1924 and 1928, then reentered elective politics himself to win the governorship of New York State in 1928 and 1930. In 1932, during the worst of the Great Depression, he won the first of his four presidential elections. His New Deal helped him remain in office throughout the Depression and World War II—one of the most pivotal periods of the nation's history.

During the 1930s, Roosevelt's foreign policy reflected the isolationist mood of the nation. Relations with Germany, Italy, and Japan cooled; neutrality prevailed after Italy's attacks in North Africa and Germany's on Poland (1939); and the Lend-Lease Program of March 1941 provided matériel to Britain and other nations at war before the United States formally entered World War II in December 1941, after Japan's attack on Pearl Harbor.

During World War II, Roosevelt cooperated closely with the Allies, including the Soviet Union. He traveled to hold a series of conferences with the heads of state of the major Allied powers, in which he agreed that Europe would be the first priority, with a second front opened against Germany and Italy (the Axis) at the earliest time. This began with the invasion of North Africa by U.S. and British forces in November 1942 (against German and Italian troops), followed by landings on Sicily (a German-occupied Italian island in the Mediterranean) in July 1943, and culminating with the invasion of German-held Normandy (northern France) in June 1944. Crucial to the European theater was the support of Middle Eastern countries. During the December 1943 Tehran Conference, Roosevelt sponsored a communiqué recognizing Iran's contributions to the war effort and expressing support for Iran's independence and territorial integrity. Shortly thereafter, Roosevelt and Britain's Prime Minister Winston Churchill met in Cairo and requested that Turkey enter the war, a goal that had been pursued by the British since late 1942. Turkey agreed in principal, in exchange for arms support, but a British mission in early 1944 was unable to achieve much; Turkey finally declared war on Germany in February 1945.

Japan's forces were being steadily conquered in the Pacific islands and nations under their occupation and control; and Roosevelt insisted on a policy of unconditional surrender, with the formation of a United Nations to guide world peace in the postwar years. Although he did not live to see either, his vice president, Harry S. Truman, became president on his death, April 12, 1945; Truman had two atomic bombs (developed during the Roosevelt Administration) dropped on Japan in August 1945 and received Japan's unconditional surrender August 14, 1945; Germany had already surrendered in May 1945. Truman also appointed Roosevelt's widow, Eleanor, to join the U.S. delegation at the United Nations; there she headed the UN Commission on Human Rights and was influential in helping to settle the Palestine partition in 1947/48 that resulted in the formation of the State of Israel (1948), which Truman was the first to recognize and back with diplomatic relations.

During the war years, victory had been Roosevelt's primary objective. By 1942, although it was clear that Hitler's program aimed at territorial conquest, it was also clear that total destruction of Europe's Jews was part of the Nazi plan. Advised by members of his administration that any increase in U.S. immigration would meet strong opposition and might affect a successful war effort, Roosevelt did not pursue that route of relief. He also declined to overcome the objections of the U.S. Department of State to ransoming Jews from Nazi-occupied Romania, Bulgaria, and France. He was told that using war matériel to move Jews to Palestine and/or North Africa might incite the Arabs or even cause vindictive action by the Nazis. As the war progressed, the role of petroleum-rich Saudi Arabia increased in importance to the United States.

Before 1940, the United States had no diplomatic representation in Saudi Arabia. The primary U.S. presence was the Arabian American Oil Company (ARAMCO), which had been operating a sixty-year oil concession since 1933. With the beginning of war, ARAMCO activities were curtailed and Muslim pilgrims ceased their pilgrimages to Mecca and Medina—both of which caused an economic crisis for Saudi Arabia. Although Germany and Japan would have welcomed the chance to provide assistance and gain an influential oil-rich ally, Saudi King Ibn Sa'ud preferred to continue his alliance with the United States; in early 1941, he requested a loan of thirty million U.S. dollars from ARAMCO to cover lost royalties and, when ARAMCO could not do this, applied to the U.S. government for assistance. Roosevelt was reluctant at first—he had no legislative authority to do this—but he soon managed to have loan monies that had gone to Britain partially diverted to Saudi Arabia, thereby averting that country's bankruptcy. By 1945, Britain had in this way provided some 2.5 million pounds sterling to Saudi Arabia (although after 1943 Lend-Lease was extended and included Saudi Arabia).

Roosevelt's policy on victims of Nazi oppression reflected the general mood of the United States. Fearing that immigration would bring foreign agents (who would cause trouble from within the U.S.) as well as an increase of unemployment (during what was still the Depression before war work increased necessary jobs nationwide), his administration strictly enforced the very limited quotas of the National Origins Act of 1924. In 1939, he allowed some 27,000 German and Austrian refugees into the United States; this was after the *Anschluss* (German annexation of Austria), when 190,000 Jews were being expelled from Austria, most into countries that were soon to be occupied by Nazi troops. In 1939, Roosevelt also sponsored a conference of thirty-two nations to discuss the refugee problem—the conference was not able to achieve anything of substance, and Britain refused to discuss the possibility of immigration to Palestine. U.S. immigration actually decreased in 1939 to below the level allowed by the quotas, but this decline was attributed to the transfer of the U.S. Immigration and Naturalization Service from the Department of Labor to the Department of Justice.

With regard to Jewish immigration to Palestine, Roosevelt was balancing an inclination to support Zionism with the realities of World War II and the consequent pressures from both his Arab and British allies. In 1943, he assured Abdullah Ibn Husayn, emir of Transjordan, that the United States would not make decisions about Jewish immigration to Palestine that would be hostile to the Arabs. Meeting with King Ibn Sa'ud after the Yalta Conference in February 1945, Roosevelt gave him similar assurances, recapping them in a letter on April 5th. At the same time, Roosevelt had also been expressing support for Zionism; in February 1944 a joint resolution was put before Congress (1) to support unrestricted Jewish immigration to Palestine and (2) for the development of Palestine as a Jewish commonwealth. The vote on this was postponed after General George C. Marshall expressed concern over the impact it might have in the Arab world. Instead Roosevelt made a public statement in favor of Zionism.

A month earlier, in January of 1944, Roosevelt had agreed to a proactive policy toward refugees from Nazi Europe, including the Jews. This had been the result of a report by Secretary of the Treasury Henry Morgenthau, Jr., "On Acquiescence of This Government to the Murder of the Jews." Roosevelt established the War Refugee Board, with its charter to rescue those singled out for destruction. The board avoided the problem of U.S. immigration quotas by establishing emergency rescue shelters to house the refugees temporarily. The change in policy was too late for most of Europe's Jews, and it was not accompanied by a change in bombing policies—which might have been aimed at disrupting the rail lines and ancillary activities that led to the concentration camps.

Roosevelt's strength began to fail during the last year of the war, although his charisma and charm continued to be felt by his people, who championed his efforts with his allies and against his enemies. His personal leadership during the war was recorded on news film and broadcast on radio. Only many years after his death was his administration criticized with respect to its handling of the Middle East situation.

BIBLIOGRAPHY

DALLEK, ROBERT. *Franklin D. Roosevelt and American Foreign Policy, 1932–1945*. New York, 1979.
LENCZOWSKI, GEORGE. *The Middle East in World Affairs*. Ithaca, N.Y., 1962.
SCHLESINGER, ARTHUR M., JR. *The Coming of the New Deal*. Boston, 1959.
———. *The Crisis of the Old Order, 1919–1933*. Boston, 1957.
———. *The Politics of Upheaval*. Boston, 1960.

Daniel E. Spector

Roosevelt, Kermit   [1916–   ]

Theodore Roosevelt's grandson, who, as a CIA agent, became involved in Middle Eastern affairs.

Born in Argentina, Kermit Roosevelt graduated from Harvard University and, after a short teaching career, joined the Office of Strategic Services and, following World War II, its successor, the Central Intelligence Agency (CIA). Roosevelt confirmed rumors that the 1953 coup in Iran leading to the downfall of the nationalist government of Dr. Mohammad Mossadegh and the restoration of the Pahlavi dynasty was staged by the CIA and, in his account of the events, was supported by the U.S. government. Roosevelt was also deeply involved in the Suez Crisis of 1956, and some sources hold him responsible for the failure of the American secretary of state, John Foster Dulles, to convince Egyptian president Gamal Abdel Nasser to cancel an arms deal with the Soviet Union. They moreover accuse Roosevelt, and the CIA, of undermining the State Department by counseling Nasser to ignore Dulles. Roosevelt resigned from the CIA during Eisenhower's administration and, after working in the oil business, founded his own corporation in 1964. In 1975, the Senate Foreign Relations subcommittee reported

that Roosevelt had used his CIA contacts in Iran and Saudi Arabia to win government contracts for Northrop Corporation, a major American aircraft manufacturer.

BIBLIOGRAPHY

ROOSEVELT, KERMIT. *Countercoup: The Struggle for the Control of Iran*. New York, 1979.
SCHOENEBAUM, ELEANORA W., ed. *Political Profiles: The Eisenhower Years*, vol. 2. New York, 1980.

Neguin Yavari

Rosen, Pinhas   [1882–?]

Israeli political leader.

Born in Berlin, Pinhas Rosen was educated in Freiburg and in Berlin. Later, he became a judge and had a private law practice in Berlin. As a youth, he was a leader of the Zionist student organization Kartell Judischer Verbindungen and helped found the Blau Weiss youth group in 1911. After serving in the German army in World War I, he continued his Zionist activities in Palestine and London as a member of the Zionist Executive. In 1931, he settled in Palestine, where he was one of the founders of the Aliyah Hadashah, the Progressive party, and the LIBERAL PARTY, and where he served as minister of justice from 1948 through 1961. He was a member of the Knesset as a representative of the Progressive faction and, later, of the Liberal faction. He resigned from the Knesset in 1968.

Bryan Daves

Rosetta Stone

Ancient Egyptian carved stone used to decipher hieroglyphics.

One of the French expedition's soldiers uncovered this key to hieroglyphics in 1799 while digging fortifications at Rosetta, near Alexandria. Seized by the British, it rests in the British Museum. Its Greek and Egyptian texts, written in Greek, hieroglyphics, and demotic (a simplified form of ancient Egyptian cursive writing), assisted Jean-François CHAMPOLLION in deciphering hieroglyphics.

BIBLIOGRAPHY

BUDGE, E. A. WALLIS. *The Rosetta Stone in the British Museum*. London, 1929. Reprint, New York, 1976.

Donald Malcolm Reid

Roshanfekr

Persian term for intellectuals.

Literally "enlightened thinker," *roshanfekr* is the Persian rendering of the term "intellectual." The Iranian intellectuals were regarded as a class and attacked by the contentious writer Jalal AL-E AHMAD in *On the Service and Treachery of the Intellectuals* (1978).

Farhad Shirzad

Rothschild, Edmond de   [1845–1935]

Jewish philanthropist active in Palestine.

Known as the Benefactor (*ha-Nadiv*), Edmond James de Rothschild, scion of the Rothschild banking family, was born in Paris. His concern in 1882 to give sanctuary to eastern European pogrom victims was translated into a commitment for the development of a self-supporting Jewish homeland and finally a state. His assistance to the Jewish settlements of Rishon le-Zion and Zikhron Ya'akov in Palestine (1883/84) rescued them from financial collapse. Rothschild purchased land and equipped the colonies he established. He also supported the development of cash crops and industry. For example, after establishing a winepress at Rishon le-Zion in the early 1890s, he formed a company that began to market its wines in 1896.

Insisting that his support not be purely charitable, Rothschild was determined that the colonies be self-supporting. When the Jewish immigrants could not make them succeed, he appointed his own managers and staff, hired workers, and underwrote agricultural experimentation, to the chagrin of the Zionist socialists who, after the turn of the century, began to dominate the Zionist enterprise.

Acceding to the wishes of the leadership of Hovevei Zion, Rothschild transferred the administration of his settlements to the JEWISH COLONIZATION ASSOCIATION, which had been established to administer philanthropic monies to Jews in need of economic support. In 1924, under the auspices of his son, James Armand de Rothschild, who had arrived in Palestine as a British soldier with Gen. Edmund Allenby, the Palestine Jewish Colonization Association (PICA) was established. It supported kibbutzim, moshavim, and Jewish settlements; swamp drainage; stabilization of sand dunes; agricultural research; and educational and cultural institutions. PICA encouraged the development of industrial enterprises, and after 1948 bought and modernized flour mills, saltworks, and chemical enterprises, many of which were turned over to the State of Israel after the death of James de Rothschild and the termination of PICA (both in 1957).

Rothschild visited Palestine often, touring his settlements and assessing their progress. In 1929, he was made honorary president of the Jewish Agency. Rothschild is buried in Israel overlooking the colonies Zikhron Ya'akov (named after his father) and Binyamina (named after himself; his Hebrew name was Avraham Binyamin), and the area near Caesarea where he had funded clearing of malarial swamps.

BIBLIOGRAPHY

SCHAMA, SIMON. *Two Rothschilds and the Land of Israel.* New York, 1978.

Reeva S. Simon

Round Table Conference

See London Conference

Royal Dutch Shell

An Anglo–Dutch petroleum conglomerate.

The Royal Dutch Shell group of companies was created in 1907 from the merger of the Royal Dutch and Shell oil companies. More commonly known as Shell, the group is one of the largest oil companies in the world and is one of the Seven Sisters. Though headquartered in London, the company's main interests were in Iraq, Iran, Kuwait, and Turkey until nationalization of oil resources by the Gulf countries. It had no sizable role in the oil industry of Saudi Arabia. In 1993, the company had 117,000 employees worldwide, sales of $54 billion, and assets of $61 billion.

Jean-François Seznec

Royal Geographic Society

See Egyptian Geographical Society

Rub al-Khali

A 200,000-square-mile (518,000-sq.-km) area of sand desert in southeastern Saudi Arabia; the largest desert in Arabia.

Rub al-Khali (the Empty Quarter) has no permanent settlements and is separated from populated areas by wide gravel plains devoid of vegetation. The northern part is watered by occasional winter rains, while the southern part is sometimes watered by spillover from monsoon rains from the Indian Ocean. Al-MURRAH bedouins inhabit parts of the Empty Quarter, where their camels feed on bushes and grasses that grow in the sand. In the eastern part of the Empty Quarter, the al-Murrah have a series of about twenty wells. The borders between Saudi Arabia, Abu Dhabi, the Sultanate of Oman, and parts of Yemen are undemarcated where their territories meld into the Empty Quarter. The potential for finding oil deposits beneath the sands has led to dissension and an interest on the part of leaders of these states to establish boundaries.

Eleanor Abdella Doumato

Rubinstein, Amnon   [1931–   ]

Israeli political leader and government minister.

Born in Tel Aviv, Amnon Rubinstein studied at the Hebrew University and became a member of the bar in 1963. He earned a Ph.D. in law from the London School of Economics in 1966 and has served as a professor and dean of the law faculty at Tel Aviv University. In 1974, he founded the centrist SHINUI party and became its chair in 1978. Rubinstein has served on a number of committees in the Knesset. For the 1992 elections, Shinui joined Ratz (Citizens' Rights Movement) and MAPAM (the United Workers party) to form MERETZ (Vigor), which won twelve seats in the Knesset. From 1984 to 1988, Rubinstein was communications minister in a national unity government; in 1993, he was appointed minister of education and culture.

Bryan Daves

Ruhi Arel   [1880–1931]

Ottoman Turkish painter.

Ruhi Arel was one of a generation of Turkish painters born in the Ottoman Empire of the 1880s who represent a transition from military to civilian painters. He belonged to the Ottoman Painters Society (founded in 1808) and published articles on art in its journal. Early in his career he painted landscapes of Istanbul; later, he turned to depicting women engaged in their daily work.

BIBLIOGRAPHY

BAŞKAN, SEYFI. *Ondokuzuncu Yüzyıldan Günümüze Türk Ressamları.* Ankara, 1991.

Tanzimat'tan Cumhuriyet'e Türkiye Ansiklopedisi. Istanbul, 1985.

David Waldner

Rumaytha Rebellion, al-

Tribal uprising in Iraq in 1935.

In May 1935, Shaykh Khawwam, a minor tribal leader in the Middle Euphrates, rose up in revolt against the Iraqi government of Yasin al-Hashimi (March 1935–October 1936), which had itself come to power by encouraging tribal risings. Khawwam's revolt was put down with great severity (including bombardment from the air) and great speed by Bakr Sidqi. Several of the rebels were sentenced to death, and others were given long prison terms.

Peter Sluglett

Rumelia

The European part of the Ottoman Empire, in particular the Balkan peninsula.

Formerly written as Rum-ili, the word *Rumelia* has its origins in the medieval Muslim practice of referring to the Byzantine as Rum and their territory as Bilad al-Rum. With the arrival of the Turks in Anatolia and, in particular, with the advancement of the Ottoman Empire, the use of Rum to designate Western Anatolia survived and evolved eventually into Rumelia or Rumeli.

During the reign of the Ottoman sultan Murad I (1362–1389), Rumelia emerged as a name to designate Ottoman territories in Europe, governed as a separate military-administrative region under the rule of a *beylerbeyi,* the first such governorate of its kind in the Ottoman Empire. It was around this time, too, that the empire was officially divided into two large administrative regions straddling the Sea of Marmara: Rumelia and Anadolu (Anatolia). At first, each successive territorial conquest in Europe, up to the Danube, was added to the beylerbeyi of Rumelia. After 1541, with the establishment of the governorate of Budin and Bosnia, the number of beylerbeyis began to proliferate. In the nineteenth century, during the Tanzimat, the administrative divisions of Rumelia underwent further changes. Finally, in 1894, Rumelia was officially subdivided into the *vilayet*s (provinces) of Edirne, Selanik, Qoskova, Yanya, Ishqodra, and Manastır.

Currently the word is generally understood to refer to the triangular region between Istanbul and

Edirne and the peninsula of Gallipoli—all that remains of Turkish Europe. The word is, however, no longer used in official documents or atlases; rather *Trakya*, a Turkish variant of Thrace, is used instead. The last official recorded use of Rumelia was during the Turkish War of Independence in 1919.

Today it is used most commonly by the residents of Istanbul to distinguish the European side of the city from the Anatolian. It forms an integral part of many a place name on the European side, such as Rumelihisari and Rumelifenerai.

BIBLIOGRAPHY

BIRNBAUM, H., and S. VRYONIS, eds. *Aspects of the Balkans: Continuity and Change.* The Hague, 1972.
Büyük Larousse, vol. 16.
Encyclopaedia of Islam, 2nd ed., vol. 8.
Yeni Türk Ansiklopedisi, vol. 27.
ZACOUR, P., and H. HAZARD, eds. *The Middle East and the Balkans under the Ottoman Empire.* Bloomington, Ind., 1993.

Karen Pinto

Ruppin, Arthur   [1876–1943]

Sociologist; Zionist leader and statesman in Palestine.

Born in the Prussian province of Posen (now Poznan in western Poland), he became head of the Palestine office of the World Zionist Organization in 1908. Ruppin's leadership opened a new epoch of Zionist settlement in Ottoman Palestine. The restoration of constitutionalism in the Ottoman Empire after the YOUNG TURK Revolution of 1908 created some opportunities for Jewish settlers. Ruppin, a technician and social theorist, negotiated the purchase of large tracts of land in the Jezreel valley and mobilized funds to add to Jewish neighborhoods in Haifa, Tel Aviv, and Jerusalem. Through his official position and personal influence, he provided financial support for young Jewish pioneers, who developed the kibbutz and moshav as new types of collective agricultural communities.

Ruppin grew up in Europe during a period of rapid economic change that brought ruin to his family, forcing him to leave school at fifteen. Apprenticed to a grain merchant, Ruppin was quickly promoted to office manager. After completing secondary school, he studied law and economics at the universities of Berlin and Halle. A scholar and a man of action, Ruppin's *The Jews in the Modern World* (1904) laid the foundation for the study of the sociology of Jewry. He lectured in Palestine, in sociology at the Hebrew University, and directed Palestine's Institute for Economic Research. On behalf of the Jewish Agency (the liaison between Palestinian Jews and the British mandate authorities), he promoted policies to develop Jewish industry and agriculture. During World War I, he saved Palestine's Jews from starvation by supervising the distribution of American funds, even after he was exiled in 1916 to Istanbul. In the last decade of his life, he aided the absorption of German Jews fleeing the Nazis. A founder of Brit Shalom (see BINATIONALISM) in 1925, Ruppin advocated, for a short time, the establishment of Palestine as a binational state. While he modified this view, he stressed the importance of Palestinian Jews reaching an agreement with Palestinian Arabs that would not compromise Zionist goals. He died in Jerusalem in 1943.

BIBLIOGRAPHY

BEIN, ALEX. "Arthur Ruppin: The Man and His Work." *Leo Baeck Institute Year Book* 17 (1972): 71–89.

Donna Robinson Divine

Ruşdiye Schools

Ottoman secular primary schools.

The first *ruşdiye* primary schools were established in 1838 at the Süleymaniye and Sultan Ahmet mosques in Istanbul by Sultan Mahmud II, to prepare young men to attend his new technical schools. These schools slowly became an alternative to the religious education system, numbering sixty by 1853. Their graduates staffed the Ottoman Empire's expanding administration and military during the TANZIMAT era and beyond. In the early years, students aged ten to fifteen years (and later even younger) studied languages, mathematics, science, history, and religion for four years. By the late nineteenth century, nearly every provincial town had a ruşdiye school. In 1895, more than thirty-five thousand students, about four thousand of them non-Muslim, attended the state-run ruşdiye schools. The first ruşdiye for girls was founded in 1858.

The military built its own system of schools beginning in 1855, and its ruşdiye schools enrolled eight thousand boys in 1895. IDADI (middle) SCHOOLS were added in the late nineteenth century. In addition, in 1895 a separate system of millet ruşdiye schools, run by various religious groups, enrolled seventy-six thousand non-Muslim students.

BIBLIOGRAPHY

KAZAMIAS, ANDREAS M. *Education and the Quest for Modernity in Turkey.* Chicago, 1966.

SHAW, STANFORD, JR., and EZEL KURAL SHAW. *History of the Ottoman Empire and Modern Turkey.* Vol. 2. New York, 1977.

Elizabeth Thompson

Rushdi, Husayn   [1864–1928]

Egyptian politician; prime minister during World War I.

Rushdi was born in Cairo to a Turkish–Albanian family, a member of the aristocracy. He studied law in Paris, served as a judge in Egypt's Mixed Courts, and became Egypt's minister of justice. He helped formulate the terms of the 1914 British protectorate over Egypt and was appointed prime minister that year. In 1918, he headed a failed delegation formed by Sa'd Zaghlul and the Wafd movement to demand autonomy for Egypt, which was not granted until 1922. He then headed the commission that formulated the constitution promulgated in 1923.

BIBLIOGRAPHY

HERAVI, MEHDI. *Concise Encyclopedia of the Middle East.* Washington, D.C., 1973.
WUCHER KING, JOAN. *Historical Dictionary of Egypt.* Metuchen, N.J., 1984.

Janice J. Terry

Russell, John   [1792–1878]

British politician; Whig prime minister, 1846–1852 and 1865–1866; first Earl Russell of Kingston Russell.

As an advocate of parliamentary reform, Russell helped frame the Reform Act of 1832. As colonial secretary in 1839, he opposed Lord Palmerston's policy of recognizing Muhammad Ali as pasha of Egypt, preferring to side with the Ottoman Empire. In 1851, he dismissed Palmerston as foreign secretary for recognizing Louis Napoléon's coup in France, but in 1852 Russell was defeated at the polls, and Palmerston became prime minister.

Russell was foreign secretary from 1852 to 1853, under Prime Minister Lord George Aberdeen, but his continuing support of the Ottomans against Russia and his mismanagement of events that resulted in the Crimean War (1854–1856) lost him that position. During the Crimean War, Britain and France attempted to block Russia's move toward the Mediterranean, but the results were strained relations between the two allies for many years. Russell became foreign secretary under Palmerston from 1859 to 1865; when Palmerston died in 1865, Russell succeeded him as prime minister. He resigned in 1866 after losing a compromise measure concerning British electoral reform.

BIBLIOGRAPHY

ANDERSON, M. S. *The Eastern Question.* London, 1966.
LANGER, WILLIAM L., ed. *An Encyclopedia of World History.* Boston, 1948.

Zachary Karabell

Russia and the Middle East

From Catherine the Great's 1774 victory against the Ottoman Empire until the late twentieth century, Russian/Soviet policy was to rule the Black Sea and the lands around it.

In the late eighteenth and early nineteenth centuries, Russia increased pressure on the Ottoman and Persian empires in an attempt to capture parts of the Black and Caspian seacoasts, as well as of the Caucasian interior. Persia's refusal to recognize Russia's 1801 annexation of Georgia led to a war (1804–1813) and a Russian victory. According to the Treaty of Golestan (1813), Persia lost a large part of the Caucasus, including Georgia, as well as parts of the western Caspian coast. Persia also recognized Russian naval preeminence in the Caspian Sea.

The next round for the control of the central Caucasus was fought between 1826 and 1828. It, too, ended in a Russian victory. Under the terms of the Treaty of TURKMANCHAI (1828), Persia relinquished to Russia part of Armenia and recognized the Aras river as the Transcaucasian boundary between the two states. In addition, Persia granted Russia important commercial concessions and extraterritorial privileges, enabling Saint Petersburg to establish a strong political and economic position in the Persian Empire. In the late 1850s, Russia turned its attention to Transcaspian Muslim central Asia, conquering the Khanate of Khiva in 1873 and Kokand and Bokhara in 1876. The process was completed in the mid-1880s with the annexation of Merv and Panjdeh, situated near the Afghan border. In 1881, Persia agreed to the Atrek river as the Transcaspian boundary with Russia.

Russia's southward expansion alarmed Great Britain, for Russian control of the Turkish Straits would threaten part of the maritime lifeline of the British Empire. London was also alarmed at the steady Russian encroachment into Persia and, later, Afghanistan. If unchecked, these advances would ultimately bring the Russians to the border of India, the crown jewel of the British Empire. Hence, throughout the nineteenth century, London attempted to prevent Russia from overrunning the Ottoman and Persian empires and from making major inroads into Afghanistan. In the early twentieth century, however, fear of imperial Germany prompted Britain and Russia to reconcile their differences in Asia. According to their 1907 treaty, Afghanistan became a British sphere of influence while Persia was split into three zones: Russia was to dominate the northern and Great Britain the southern parts of the country; separating them was a third, or neutral, zone. After the outbreak of World War I, the two allies concluded the CONSTANTINOPLE AGREEMENT (1915), stipulating that after the war Russia would occupy the Turkish Straits. This dramatic reversal of long-standing British policy was dictated by the necessity of keeping Russia in the allied coalition.

Czarist Russia did not survive to enjoy the fruits of victory over the Central powers. The communist regime, in power after November 1917, renounced the concessions secured by its predecessor, proclaimed itself an ally of the exploited masses, and, in 1921, concluded treaties of friendship and neutrality with Turkey, Persia, and Afghanistan. Nonaggression treaties with Turkey and Afghanistan were signed in 1925 and 1926, respectively.

During World War II, after Germany invaded the USSR in 1941, Soviet and British troops occupied Iran to secure a safe supply route for the flow of Allied war matériel to the Soviet Union. The treaty of alliance concluded between Iran, Great Britain, and the USSR in 1942 provided for the withdrawal of foreign forces not later than six months after the end of the war. By early 1946, the British had pulled out, but the Soviets remained. They left later in the year, after Tehran had signed an agreement permitting Soviet oil exploration in northern Iran (it was never implemented). More significantly, Washington exerted pressure on Moscow to abide by the 1942 agreement.

Stalin's refusal to leave Iran was but one of the perceived indications of his aggressiveness. As seen in the West, his ambitions in the Middle East complemented Soviet expansion in Eastern Europe and the Far East. In 1945, Stalin renounced the Soviet–Turkish nonaggression treaty and renewed czarist claims to Turkish territory, including the Straits. He was also held responsible for efforts by Greek communists to topple that country's pro-Western government. Washington responded by promulgating the Truman Doctrine (1947), which assumed responsibility for the defense of Greece and Turkey. The U.S. Sixth Fleet was deployed in the Mediterranean in 1946 and its presence was later augmented by strategic air command bombers, based in Morocco, Libya, Turkey, and Saudi Arabia. Jupiter missiles followed in the 1950s and the Polaris submarines in the 1960s. By means of the Eisenhower Doctrine (1955), Washington pledged to defend the Middle East against Soviet aggression, and the BAGHDAD PACT, consisting of Turkey, Iran, Iraq, Pakistan, and Great Britain, was formed during the same year.

The vast accumulation of American power in and near the Mediterranean was seen in Moscow as a threat to its security. Hence, for much of the post-Stalin period, the USSR worked hard to neutralize the U.S. military presence in the vicinity of its southern border. As part of the general superpower competition, the Soviets made a major effort to establish a viable naval and air presence in the Middle East. A naval squadron was permanently deployed in the Mediterranean in 1964, but naval and air bases became available in Egypt only in 1970. Cairo withdrew these privileges later in the decade; however, by then the Middle East had ceased to represent a major strategic threat to the USSR. Ironically, this was due not to Soviet countermeasures but to technological advances: Washington came to rely on land-based and submarine-launched intercontinental ballistic missiles. Until 1991, the USSR, mainly for political reasons, maintained its Mediterranean squadron and had access to facilities in Syria, Algeria, Libya, and Yemen. The most dramatic projection of Soviet power in the post-1945 Middle East occurred in Afghanistan. To preserve a faltering communist regime, Soviet troops entered the country in 1979. They were withdrawn in 1989, leaving Afghanistan stalemated militarily and politically.

An early Soviet political objective was to undermine Western positions in the Middle East. The trend was set by Stalin's support of the partition of Palestine and of the State of Israel (1947–1948), and it lasted into the Gorbachev period. Although Western influence has declined from the peak reached in 1945, this process was initiated by local actors, pursuing their own (not Soviet) interests. The USSR played a part, by lending moral and material support to regional leaders who were refused Western assistance or arms, but its role was facilitative and, therefore, secondary.

In addition, especially during the Khrushchev and Brezhnev periods, the USSR attempted to strengthen its own position and to gain U.S. recognition as a political equal in the Middle East. Efforts to improve Moscow's standing were crowned with some short-term successes. In the 1950s, the Soviet Union established working relations with Iraq, Syria, Egypt, and Algeria. Later, treaties of friendship and cooperation were signed with Egypt (1971), Iraq (1974), and

Syria (1980). However, these apparent gains did not net the USSR any permanent, long-term benefits.

Egypt abrogated its treaty in 1976. In 1980, Iraq attacked Iran without consulting the Kremlin. Moscow's ensuing attempts to maintain even-handed relations with the combatants during their eight-year war led ultimately to a deterioration of both sets of relationships. Gorbachev's realization of the cost-ineffectiveness of the Kremlin's political involvement in the Middle East was partly responsible for his decision to disengage from the Soviet commitment to the Arabs in their conflict with Israel, an obligation that Moscow maintained through the Khrushchev and Brezhnev periods. Lastly, efforts to gain U.S. recognition of Moscow's political parity in the Middle East had also been unsuccessful.

One of the regional problems that the USSR had used to advance its political interests in the Middle East was the Arab–Israel conflict. In 1955, in a major about-face, the Soviets abandoned Stalin's policy of support for the Zionist cause and sided with the Arabs. In the ensuing years, Moscow extended Egypt and Syria large-scale military and economic assistance and adopted a strong pro-Arab and anti-Israeli position. With some modifications, this attitude was maintained well into the 1980s. Among other things, the USSR recognized the Palestine Liberation Organization as the official representative of the Palestinian Arabs and backed the Arab states in the wars of 1956, 1967, and 1973. In 1967, Moscow broke diplomatic relations with Israel. As noted, a major change in the Soviet position occurred in the late 1980s, when "new thinking" in Gorbachev's foreign policy led the Kremlin to improve relations with Israel. Large-scale Jewish emigration from the USSR to Israel was accompanied by the restoration of diplomatic relations between the two states in 1991. As Moscow's policy became "even-handed," to the chagrin of the Arabs, the USSR ceased to play an important role in the Arab–Israel conflict.

Before 1970, the USSR had no important economic interests in the Middle East. In the 1970s and 1980s, the Soviets became heavily involved in selling arms to Iraq, Syria, Libya, Egypt, and Iran. These transactions, worth tens of billions of dollars, ranked second to petroleum as the USSR's main earner of foreign currency. (The stunning superiority of Western arms over the Soviet weapons in the hands of the Iraqi military during Operation Desert Storm has seriously eroded the market value of such Russian-made armaments for the foreseeable future.) In addition, the USSR bartered various types of goods and services for Iraqi, Libyan, and Algerian oil and Iranian gas. Until its dissolution, the USSR looked at the oil-rich Arab Gulf states as sources of capital in restructuring the Soviet economy.

On balance, between 1945 and 1991, the USSR can be said to have improved its military position vis-à-vis the Middle East in the sense that no strategic threat to Soviet security emanated from that region. But the USSR also suffered disappointments and setbacks, and its military and political gains usually proved temporary. In the 1990s, the USSR's position was further weakened by the collapse of the Soviet economy and Gorbachev's frantic efforts to revive it by normalizing relations with the Western powers, especially the United States. Given these priorities, the continuation of superpower competition in the Middle East made little sense from the new Soviet perspective. As contiguous states with a large Muslim population, however, Russia and the various independent republics that were formed from the Soviet Union (1992) will inevitably remain interested parties in the regional affairs of the Middle East.

BIBLIOGRAPHY

FREEDMAN, ROBERT O. *Moscow and the Middle East: Soviet Policy since the Invasion of Afghanistan.* Cambridge, Mass., 1991.

KUNIHOLM, BRUCE R. *The Origins of the Cold War in the Near East: Great Power Conflict.* Princeton, N.J., 1980.

LENCZOWSKI, GEORGE. *The Middle East in World Affairs,* 4th ed. Ithaca, N.Y., 1980.

RO'I, YAACOV. *From Encroachment to Involvement: A Documentary Study of Soviet Policy in the Middle East.* Jerusalem, 1974.

RUBINSTEIN, ALVIN Z. *Red Star on the Nile: The Soviet–Egyptian Influence Relationship.* Princeton, N.J., 1977.

SMOLANSKY, OLES M. *The USSR and Iraq: The Soviet Quest for Influence.* Durham, N.C., 1991.

Oles M. Smolansky

Russi Khan

One of Iran's first and most famous photographers.

Russi Khan was a student of Abd Allah Mirzal Qajar, one of the first Iranians to study photography abroad. He opened a photography shop in Tehran in 1906. He is most famous for his pictures of politicians and activists in Iran's constitutional movement (1906–1911). When Agha Mohammad Qajar was forced to abdicate in 1911, Russi Khan accompanied him to Russia. He never returned to Iran.

BIBLIOGRAPHY

AFSHAR, IRAJ. "Some Remarks on the Early History of Photography in Iran." In *Qajar Iran: Political, Social, and Cultural Change, 1800–1925,* ed. by E. Bosworth and C. Hillenbrand. Edinburgh, 1983.

Neguin Yavari

Russo–Ottoman Wars

Sixteenth- to nineteenth-century wars between the Russian and Ottoman empires over opposing expansionist policies.

In the sixteenth and seventeenth centuries, the expanding Russian and Ottoman empires faced each other in the regions situated north of the Black Sea. Both proceeded on the assumption that protection of their respective borders required acquisition of additional buffer zones. This premise led them to frequent encroachments on each other's territory. In the eighteenth century, as the Ottoman Empire continued to weaken, the initiative passed to Russia.

A major effort to dislodge the Ottoman Turks from the northern shore of the Black Sea was undertaken by Peter the Great (1694–1725). His initial success in capturing the fortress of Azov (1696) was followed by capitulation to a large Turkish force fifteen years later. The Treaty of Pruth (1711) restored to the Ottomans the territory lost in 1696. Azov and the section of the Ukrainian steppe situated between the Donets and Bug rivers were regained by Russia under the terms of the Treaty of Belgrade (1739), but the same treaty forbade it to have a navy in the Black Sea.

The decisive breakthrough was achieved by Catherine the Great (1762–1796). Her first war against the Ottoman Empire (1768–1774), fought during the reign of the sultans Mustafa III (1757–1773) and Abdülhamit I (1773–1789), ended in an Ottoman defeat. Under the terms of the 1774 Treaty of KUÇUK KAYNARJA, Russia occupied much of the northern Black Sea coast. The Crimea was annexed in 1783. Catherine's victory in her second Ottoman war (1787–1792) was sealed by the Treaty of JASSY (1792), which extended Russia's southwestern border to the river Dniester. This treaty concluded a century of turbulent interaction between the two empires. In the process, Russia inflicted decisive defeats on its declining adversary, established itself on the northern shore of the Black Sea, and generally emerged as the leading regional power.

During the nineteenth century, Russia's approach to the Ottoman Empire was governed by several distinct but interrelated considerations. In terms of military strategy, the Black Sea provided access to the rich Ukrainian plain, which became regarded as Russia's "soft underbelly." In turn, entry into the Black Sea was possible only through the Turkish Straits, the gateway to and from the Mediterranean. Hence, control of the Straits became an important Russian objective. As the European powers awakened to Russian ambitions, Russia modified its quest for annexation of Ottoman territory and attempted to establish protectorates in such regions as the princi-palities (Wallachia and Moldavia) and Bulgaria. Other Slavic nationalities struggling against Ottoman control also represented a political interest. Economically, trade in and beyond the Black Sea became an important concern, especially after the fertile lands along the northern shore were opened to cultivation. Lastly, reinforcing the above interests, Russia's posture as protector of Greek Orthodoxy in the Ottoman Empire added yet another dimension to the quest for dominance in the Black Sea region.

Europe's preoccupation with Napoleon early in the century enabled Russia to consolidate its position in the Black Sea area. The Treaty of BUCHAREST (1812), which ended a six-year war, ceded Bessarabia to Russia as well as territory in the western Caucasus and extended privileges in the principalities. The 1820s were dominated by the Greek war of liberation. In 1829, Czar Nicholas I (1825–1855) used the conflict to declare a war against the Ottoman Empire. The latter lost and the Treaty of Adrianople (1829) handed over to Russia the mouth of the Danube and additional territory in the Caucasus. It also conferred autonomy upon the principalities, placed them under Russian protection and, for the first time, guaranteed Russian merchant ships free passage through the Straits.

In 1833, Russia and the Ottoman Empire signed the Treaty of HUNKÂR-ISKELESI, one of only two treaties of mutual assistance entered into by the two states. (The first had been signed in 1805 and had been directed against Napoleon.) This unusual treaty resulted not from a war but from Russian assistance to Sultan Mahmud II (1808–1839), whose reign was being threatened by Muhammed Ali, the rebellious pasha of Egypt. Once the Russian troops arrived, at the Sultan's invitation, they were, for the first and only time, in control of the Straits area and Istanbul. They left later in the year after Mahmud II signed the Treaty of Hunkâr-Iskelesi, which closed the Straits to warships of all foreign nations. The establishment of a Russian protectorate over the Ottoman Empire proved unacceptable to Great Britain and Austria. The ensuing Treaty of London (1840), which sent Muhammad Ali back to Egypt, and the STRAITS CONVENTION (1841) made the independence and territorial integrity of the Ottoman Empire a common concern of Europe's great powers acting in "concert."

As an outgrowh of Czar Nicholas I's inability to resolve the Eastern (i.e., Ottoman) question to his satisfaction, the Crimean War (1854–1855) pitted Russia against the Ottoman Empire, which was allied with Great Britain, France, and the Kingdom of Sardinia. Russia capitulated after the allied troops had landed in the Crimea and Czar Nicholas had died. Under the terms of the Treaty of Paris (1856), the Ottoman Empire regained the mouth of the Danube and southern Bessarabia and agreed to the demilitarization of the Black Sea; the principalities became a protectorate of the victorious European allies; and an international commission was established to assure free navigation on the Danube. Russia also abandoned its claim to the protectorate of the Greek Orthodox church in the Ottoman Empire. Saint Petersburg regarded the restrictions imposed in 1856 as intolerable. In 1871, using the diplomatic upheaval caused by the Franco–Prussian War, Russia unilaterally renounced the Treaty of Paris.

The war of 1877–1878 grew out of the local disturbances in the Balkans. Their brutal suppression by the Turks, followed by the declaration of war on the Ottoman Empire by Serbia and Montenegro (1876), provided Russia with a pretext to intervene on their behalf. The defeat of the forces of Sultan Abdülhamit II (1876–1909) was reflected in the harsh terms of the 1878 Treaty of SAN STEFANO. The last armed confrontation between the two empires occurred during World War I. The Russians had made some headway in the Transcaucasus, but the Communists, who had seized power in 1917, took Russia out of the war and renounced all imperial claims to Ottoman territory.

BIBLIOGRAPHY

ANDERSON, M. S. *The Eastern Question, 1774–1923: A Study in International Relations.* New York, 1966.

JELAVICH, BARBARA. *A Century of Russian Foreign Policy, 1814–1914.* Philadelphia, 1964.

RIASANOVSKY, NICHOLAS V. *A History of Russia,* 2nd ed. New York, 1969.

SHAW, STANFORD. *History of the Ottoman Empire and Modern Turkey,* vol. 1. Cambridge, U.K., 1977.

Oles M. Smolansky

Russo–Persian Treaties

Russia's military assistance for Persian provinces.

In 1723, Czar Peter I responded to a request from Shah Tahmasp II of Persia for help against Afghanistan. This aid resulted in a treaty between Russia and Persia that provided for Russia's military assistance in return for Persia's cession of Shirvan, Dagestan, Gilan, Mazandaran, and Asterabad (now Gorgan). Persian military successes under the last Safavid shahs, and particularly under Nader Kuli, who succeeded the Safavids as Nader Shah (1736), preserved Persian independence. While still in the service of the Safavids, Nader Kuli imposed the Treaty of Rasht on Russia (1732), which provided for the restoration of Mazan-

daran and Asterabad. In 1735, Nader regained Baku and Derbent.

In October 1813, war between Russia and Persia led to the Treaty of Golestan, under which Persia ceded Derbent, Baku, Shirvan, Shaki, Karabakh, and part of Talish to Russia. Persia also gave up claims to Georgia, Dagestan, Mingrelia, Imeritia, and Abkhazia. In return, Russia agreed to support the succession of Abbas Mirza to the Persian throne. Another conflict in the 1820s led to the Treaty of Turkmanchai (February 1828), in which Persia ceded the provinces of Erevan and Nakhichevan and agreed to pay 30 million rubles. The treaty also defined the Russo–Persian border in the Caucasus, set a tariff of 5 percent on the import of Russian goods, established extraterritoriality for Russians, and enabled them to protect their Persian employees from government actions. Russia formally recognized Abbas Mirza as the successor to the throne of Persia.

Russia secured banking concessions in January 1900 and a more favorable tariff in December 1902. This was accomplished in vigorous competition with Britain, but Japan's defeat of Russia in 1905 and internal unrest the same year led Russia to an agreement with Britain regarding their interests in Persia. The Anglo–Russian Entente of September 1907 divided Persia into three spheres of influence. Russia would take the northern one and Britain would have the southern one, bordering the Persian Gulf. In between would be a neutral sphere in which both would compete equally. They agreed to the continued existence of Persia and its territorial integrity. Subsequently, Russia supported Shah Muhammad Ali in his struggle against revolutionaries occupying territory in northern Persia (1909, 1911).

In 1920 the Soviets, responding to counterrevolutionary moves by anti-Soviet forces backed by the British, seized Enzeli and Rasht, and established the Soviet Republic of Gilan. After leading a coup and his appointment as minister of war in 1921, Reza Khan supported a treaty with the Soviet Union providing for its withdrawal from Persia, abrogation of the capitulations, cancellation of debts and concessions, and the turning over of Russian property in Persia without compensation. Reza Khan became the first Pahlavi shah in 1925.

In late August 1941, British and Soviet forces entered Iran and pressured Reza Shah to abdicate, which he did, on 16 September. His son, Muhammad Reza Shah, cooperated with Britain and the Soviet Union by providing an overland supply link to the Soviet Union. In return, on 29 January 1942, Britain and the Soviet Union acknowledged the territorial integrity, sovereignty, and independence of Iran. Iran later joined the Allies in the war against

Germany, and when it was over in May 1945, formally requested withdrawal of Allied forces from its territory. Assurances were given that this would be done by 2 March 1946. The Soviet Union failed to do so because of its support for revolutionary activity in Azerbaijan. After Iran's protest to the UN Security Council on 19 March 1946, the Soviet Union finally withdrew its troops on 9 May. Iran soon sided with the United States in the Cold War, and joined the Baghdad Pact on 11 October 1955.

In spite of close ties with the West, Iran continued to seek an accommodation with the Soviet Union. Talks on boundaries throughout 1954 led to an agreement on 2 December that established procedures to delineate the border. The Soviet Union retained the village of Firuzeh and Iran gained about 120 square kilometers (48 sq. mi.) in the Moghan Steppe, the Sarakhs district, and the Dayman area, as well as the Yedi Evlar area near the Astara River. On 14 May 1957, Iran and the Soviet Union signed another treaty that settled issues regarding the frontier and set up a commission to arbitrate disputes. In 1958 and 1959, the two nations held discussions about a treaty of friendship and nonaggression to replace the 1921 treaty. The talks broke down, and on 5 March 1959, Iran signed an agreement with the United States that guaranteed U.S. aid in the event of aggression against Iran.

On 15 September 1962, Iran notified the Soviet Union that it would not allow any nation to establish missile bases in Iran and formally stated that Iran would not participate in any aggressive action aimed at the Soviet Union. Iran also signed trade treaties with the Soviet Union. These included a transit agreement (27 November 1962) and an agreement to increase Iran's exports from $20 million to $70 million annually for five years (2 March 1967). Before the expiration of the 1967 agreement, the two nations signed another (30 July 1970) increasing the value of trade between them significantly over the next five years. This was accompanied by an agreement to establish a joint transport company. A pact of 13 January 1966 provided for construction of a steel mill, a gas pipeline, and a mechanical engineering plant. A comprehensive, fifteen-year treaty on economic and technological cooperation was signed 12 October 1972.

The Islamic revolution that brought Ayatollah Ruhollah Khomeini to power in 1979 dramatically changed Iran's orientation toward the West. Because of its support of the shah, the United States became the "Great Satan," and Iran's ties to the West were severely curtailed. Some trade with the Soviet Union continued, and in 1986 the two nations agreed to electrify the rail line between Tabriz in Iran and Jolfa in the Soviet Union. This was followed in August 1987 by an agreement for oil pipelines and a rail line to the Persian Gulf.

BIBLIOGRAPHY

RAMAZANI, R. K. *The Foreign Policy of Iran, 1500–1941.* Charlottesville, Va., 1966.
———. *Iran's Foreign Policy, 1941–1973: A Study of Foreign Policy of Modernizing Nations.* Charlottesville, Va., 1975.
———. *Revolutionary Iran: Challenge and Response in the Middle East.* Baltimore, 1986.
SYKES, PERCY. *A History of Persia,* vol. 2, 3rd ed. New York, 1969.

Daniel E. Spector

Russo–Persian Wars

Territorial disputes (1800–1946) that led to war.

Russia had military forces in Gilan after 1723, a presence sanctioned by Shah Tahmasp II; they were withdrawn in 1732. From 1741 to 1742, Nader Shah faced rebellion by the Lesgians in Dagestan. A punitive expedition was repulsed, and when Russia sent forces to support the Lesgians, Nader Shah withdrew.

In 1796, the year Agha Mohammad Khan Qajar became shah, one of his opponents fled to Russia, seeking aid from Czarina Catherine. Hoping to acquire Georgia, she dispatched 40,000 troops. They promptly took Derbent and Baku, then camped for the winter on the plain of Moghan. The shah prepared for an offensive in the spring of 1797, but in the meantime Catherine died and was succeeded by Paul I, who withdrew Russia's forces.

Russia annexed Georgia in 1800. Believing that Georgia was historically part of the Persian Empire, the new shah, Fath Ali Shah, disputed the annexation. War came in 1804, when General Sisianoff led his forces toward Yerevan. Abbas Mirza, the heir apparent, met him at Echmiadzin in an indecisive engagement. After the Russians surprised his camp, Abbas Mirza retreated, and Sisianoff besieged Yerevan. Fath Ali Shah took personal command, and although he could not defeat the Russians, he prevented adequate supplies from getting through. Hostilities continued until the Battle of Aslanduz in 1812. A Russian column of 2,300 surprised Abbas Mirza and his army. Although the Persians held, Abbas Mirza ordered a retreat. Russia next seized Lenkoran, and Persia sued for peace in 1813.

The Treaty of Golestan (1813) was vague about the area between Yerevan and Lake Gökcha (now Sevan). The two countries negotiated but could come to no agreement. This led to Russia's seizure of Gökcha. Abbas Mirza was eager to recoup his reputation, and the forces he led were successful in their first battles. They captured Lenkoran, raided to the gates of Tbilisi, and within a month had secured Shirvan, Shaki, Talish, and Ganja. The first battle of Russia's counteroffensive was at Shamkar, near Ganja. Its force of 2,000 routed a larger Persian force, largely due to effective artillery fire that demoralized the Persian cavalry. In September 1826, Abbas Mirza led a force of about 30,000 against some 15,000 Russians under General Paskievich at Ganja. Again the Persians began well, and Abbas Mirza again ordered a retreat. Paskievich then besieged Yerevan, which again resisted. Russia took Nakhichevan and nearby Abbasbad, leading Persia to sue for peace. Russia refused and, in spite of a victory by Abbas Mirza near Echmiadzin, continued the siege of Yerevan into 1827 and occupied Tabriz the same year. The conflict was ended by the Treaty of Turkmanchai in early 1828.

The next Russian military action against Persia was in April 1909, as part of the unrest surrounding the Constitutional Movement in Persia and the 1908 coup by Mohammad Ali Shah. Tabriz held out against the shah, and in April 1909, Russia decided to send troops to protect foreign citizens, landing 3,000 men at Enzeli in July. The nationalists forced the shah to abdicate before the Russians could reach Tehran. By 1911, Russia was supporting the shah's restoration but did not use military force, and he was forced to return to Europe. In November 1911, Russia demanded the dismissal of W. Morgan Shuster, an American employed by Persia's government to help put its financial affairs in order. This led Persian nationalists to attack Russian troops in Tabriz and Rasht; Russia proceeded to march troops on Tehran. Persia gave in and dismissed Shuster.

During World War I, Russia in effect occupied northern Persia, conducted operations against the Ottoman Empire from Persian territory, and put down with military force attempts by Persians sympathetic to Germany and the empire to harass Russian troops. Russia's withdrawal from the war in March 1918 ended its effort in Persia for a time. However, fighting between White Russians and Bolsheviks spilled over into Persia in 1920. A White Russian fleet fled Baku and arrived at Enzeli in April, followed in May by a Bolshevik fleet that bombarded the port. The Bolsheviks then occupied Rasht and established the short-lived Soviet Republic of Gilan. This coincided with the rise to power of Reza Khan (later Reza Shah). Commanding the Cossack Brigade, he defeated the Persian rebels in Gilan, the Soviet Union withdrew its forces, and the republic

collapsed. A treaty between the Soviet Union and Persia in 1921 initiated a period of cooperation that lasted about a decade.

In the early 1930s Reza Shah, suspecting communist intrigue, promulgated the Anti-Communist Act (1931). The rise of the Nazis after 1933 led to friendlier relations with Germany. Therefore, in August 1941, Soviet and British forces entered Iran. After Reza Shah abdicated in September, Iran continued to be occupied by foreign troops.

At the end of the war, foreign troops were supposed to leave Iran. The British and Americans did so, but the Soviets stayed because they supported a separatist movement in Azerbaijan led by Ja'far Pishevari, an Iranian. When Iran's troops advanced on Azerbaijan to quell the movement, Soviet forces stopped them at the provincial border. This, and a similar situation in Iranian Kurdistan, led to an appeal by Iran to the UN Security Council and to negotiations with the Soviet Union over economic concessions. The Soviets withdrew in May 1946 and decided to not force the issue when the concessions were disapproved and the pro-communist regimes of Azerbaijan and Kurdistan were suppressed.

BIBLIOGRAPHY

ARMAJANI, YAHYA. *Iran.* Englewood Cliffs, N.J., 1972.
SYKES, PERCY. *A History of Persia.* Vol. 2. 3rd ed. New York, 1969.

Daniel E. Spector

Rustum Pasha   [1810–1894]

Ottoman official in Lebanon.

An Italian count, he was born at Florence and was educated in Italy, France, and England. After financial difficulties, his father died and his mother moved with her son to Rome, where she befriended the Ottoman ambassador. After serving as a special counselor to the ambassador, Rustum Pasha was transferred to Istanbul, where he joined the foreign service after becoming a citizen of the Ottoman Empire. Among the posts he held were interpreter for the foreign minister, secretary-general of the Foreign Ministry, and ambassador to Russia. Initially, he was reluctant to accept the post of MUTASARRIF in Lebanon (March 1873) because he felt it was inferior to the ambassadorship.

As *mutasarrif,* Rustum Pasha faced a budget deficit that forced him to cut the salaries of government officials. He increased taxes, which led to a strong protest by the clerical establishment. In response, he exiled Archbishop Butrus al-Bustani to Jerusalem.

This conflict with the clerical establishment, which Rustum Pasha feared was capable of instigating sectarian conflict between Druzes (Muslims) and Maronites (Christians), marred his term of office. Popular protests led to the intervention of European powers. He was replaced in May 1883 and was appointed ambassador to London, where he died.

As'ad AbuKhalil

Rutenberg, Pinchas [1879–1942]

Engineer, revolutionary, Zionist leader, and pioneer of hydroelectricity in Palestine.

Born in Romny, in the Ukraine, Rutenberg graduated from the Saint Petersburg Technological Institute. There he became active in the Russian revolutionary movement and participated in the "Bloody Sunday" march—the start of the 1905 Revolution. From 1907 to 1915 he worked as an engineer in Italy. During this period he became interested in Jewish affairs and wrote a pamphlet entitled "The National Revival of the Jewish People."

During World War I, Rutenberg went to London to try to influence the Zionist leadership to establish Jewish military units to liberate Palestine from the Ottoman Empire (and from potential British rule as well). When he discovered that Vladimir JABOTINSKY had similar interests, he contacted him to coordinate their efforts and went to the United States to spread the idea. While there, Rutenberg was caught up in the creation of the AMERICAN JEWISH CONGRESS, which would formulate proposals concerning Zionism in Palestine to be brought to the peace conference after the war.

After Kerensky's March Revolution of 1917 overthrew the czarist government of Russia, Rutenberg returned there to be appointed deputy governor of Saint Petersburg, in charge of civilian affairs. In November 1917, with the Bolshevik takeover, Rutenberg was arrested, spent six months in prison, and escaped to rejoin anti-Bolshevik groups. By 1919, perceiving anti-Semitism in the revolutionary movement, Rutenberg saw no future for himself in the new Soviet state and left for Palestine where he joined the British team in surveying Palestine's water resources, particularly the Jordan River.

Britain was to become the mandatory power for Palestine in 1923 but in 1919 was already in physical control of that area. Rutenberg drew up a far-reaching plan for creating a hydroelectric scheme to supply both sides of the Jordan with power and water for irrigation. From 1920 to 1923, Rutenberg worked at influencing the British mandate authori-

ties to grant him a preliminary concession for his Palestine Electric Corporation Limited and then, in 1926, the full concession over the use of the Jordan and Yarmuk rivers for supplying hydroelectricity to Palestine. He raised the money for the company mainly from Jews in the United States and Great Britain. In 1932, the first Jordan power station was opened in Naharayim, at the confluence of the Jordan and the Yarmuk; because of British political decisions, not one of the other power stations was built. The station at Naharayim functioned until it was destroyed during the 1948 Arab–Israel War.

Rutenberg was an active Zionist and headed the Va'ad Le'umi (National Council) in the crisis year of 1929. He joined Jewish leaders who sought a plan of Arab–Jewish coexistence. His water-development plans had already brought him into friendly contact with Abdullah ibn Husayn, the emir of Transjordan, but nothing came of these efforts. Rutenberg also attempted to bring about internal Zionist cooperation, since David Ben-Gurion's Histadrut party was constantly at odds with Jabotinsky's Revisionists, but nothing came of this either. In 1939, Rutenberg again became the head of the Va'ad Le'umi and served until he died in 1942.

BIBLIOGRAPHY

LIPSKY, LOUIS. *Gallery of Zionist Profiles.* New York, 1956.
SACHAR, HOWARD. *Zionist Portraits and Other Essays.* London, 1959.
SHALTIEL, ELI. *Pinchas Rutenberg, 1879–1942: Life and Times.* Tel Aviv, 1990. In Hebrew.

Sara Reguer

Ruz al-Yusuf

Weekly Egyptian magazine devoted to culture and politics.

With estimates of its circulation ranging from 20,000 to 70,000 per issue, this magazine was initially the personal venture of actress Fatima al-Yusuf, who bore the nickname Rose (transliterated *Ruz;* hence, the magazine's title). From 1922 to 1925, al-Yusuf had been the leading lady in the Ramsis theatrical troupe founded by Yusuf Wahbi. In 1925, citing artistic differences with Wahbi, al-Yusuf left the acting profession and founded her magazine ostensibly to create a forum for serious art criticism. Al-Yusuf's partners were Ibrahim Khalil, who worked for the newspaper *al-Balagh,* and Muhammad al-Tabi'i, a journalist who wrote theater criticism for *al-Ahram.* Due to the backgrounds of al-Yusuf and al-Tabi'i, early issues of *Ruz al-Yusuf* were indeed heavily oriented toward the theater. However, the magazine's founders also had sympathies for the Wafd political party—the nationalist and initially populist party founded by Sa'd Zaghlul in 1918, and brought to prominence by Zaghlul's insistence that Egypt be included in the Versailles negotiations following World War I. From the 1919 rebellion against British rule until the 1952 revolution, the Wafd was in and out of power. *Ruz al-Yusuf* was not an official organ of the Wafd, but when the paper began to express pro-Wafd sympathies, its publisher quickly found herself caught in the intrigues of interwar party politics.

Ruz al-Yusuf has never been an exclusively political magazine. It blends a concern for culture—particularly the performing arts—with a satirical and often combative stance on political and social issues. The combination proved popular and made the magazine one of the country's best sellers by the late 1920s—a status it has retained ever since. The magazine has always been known for its cartoons and caricatures, and to this day features few photographs. In 1960 the *Ruz al-Yusuf* publishing house, along with all other large Egyptian publishing companies, was nationalized. The *Ruz al-Yusuf* company is also a sizable publisher of books as well as a sister magazine entitled *Sabah al-Khayr*.

BIBLIOGRAPHY

AYALON, AMI. *The Press in the Arab Middle East: A History.* Oxford, 1995.
OCHS, MARTIN. *The African Press.* Cairo, 1986.
YUSUF, FATIMA. *Dhikriyat* (Memoirs). Cairo, 1967.

Walter Armbrust

Ruzname

Ottoman treasury offices and their registers.

Derived from the Persian words for "day" and "book," *ruzname* in Turkish meant "diary," "calendar," or "journal." In Ottoman government, *ruzname* was both the imperial treasury offices and the registers in which accounts were recorded. It also formed part of the name of several early Ottoman newspapers, such as *Ruzname-i Ceride-i Havadis* (1860) and *Ruzname-i Ayine-i Vatan* (1867).

BIBLIOGRAPHY

SHAW, STANFORD, J., and EZEL KURAL SHAW. *History of the Ottoman Empire and Modern Turkey.* Vol. 2. New York, 1976.

Elizabeth Thompson

S

Saad, Habib al- [1866–1946]

Second president of pre-independent Lebanon.

Born in Ayn Traz to a Maronite family, Saad completed his schooling at the patriarchal school and the Collège de la Sagesse. He obtained a law degree from the Jesuit-administered Saint Joseph University and was fluent in Arabic, French, and Turkish. In 1918, he was appointed governor of Lebanon under the al-Sharif government. He was elected deputy in 1922 and 1929. In August 1928, he was appointed prime minister. In January 1934, Saad was appointed president of Lebanon and prime minister by the French high commissioner.

BIBLIOGRAPHY

JIHA, ABDULLAH. *Lebanon under the Microscope.* Lebanon, 1984. In Arabic.

George E. Irani

Saad, Ma'ruf [1910–1975]

Lebanese politician and founder of the Popular Nasserite Organization.

Saad was born in Sidon to a Sunni father, Mustafa Saad, and a Christian mother, Jamila Ata Atiyya. He completed his education in Lebanon and taught for a while in Saudi Arabia (1928), Damascus (1931), and Beirut, where he taught English and physics. In 1935 and 1937, Saad joined the resistance to the Zionist movement in Palestine. In 1939, while in Syria, Saad requested military support from Husni al-Za'im to fight the British in southern Lebanon. The British authorities arrested and exiled him to the village of Rashayya al-Wadi. In 1957, 1960, 1964, and 1968, he was elected the deputy of Sidon in the Lebanese parliament. In February 1975, Saad organized a demonstration of fishermen protesting the establishment of a plant owned by former Lebanese president Camille Chamoun. Saad was wounded in a clash with the Lebanese army and died in March 1975.

BIBLIOGRAPHY

Arab Information Center, Beirut.

George E. Irani

Sa'ada, Antun [c. 1902–1949]

Syrian politician.

Antun Sa'ada was born in Brazil into the Christian family of Dr. Khalil Sa'ada of Shuwayr, Lebanon. Teaching German at the American University of Beirut, he was strongly influenced by German fascism. He founded the Syrian National party (PARTI POPULAIRE SYRIEN, PPS) in 1932, when Syria was under the French mandate granted by the League of Nations after World War I. A very charismatic leader and influential revolutionary thinker, Sa'ada (and the PPS) recognized a "natural" national identity and geographical area for Syria and was opposed to the

Pan-Arabism of the rival National Bloc. The PPS was a secret organization from its founding until 1935, when it went public and was increasingly suppressed by the French mandate authorities, who arrested Sa'ada on November 16.

In 1947, "Social" was added to the name of his party upon his return from self-imposed exile in South America. In a July 1949 meeting with Sa'ada, President Husni al-Za'im pledged sympathy with the SYRIAN SOCIAL NATIONALIST PARTY, then betrayed Sa'ada, sending him to Beirut, where he was sentenced to death and executed by the Lebanese government on July 8, 1949. Sa'ada writings include *The Rise of Nations*.

BIBLIOGRAPHY

SHIMONI, YAACOV. *Political Dictionary of the Arab World*. New York, 1987.

Charles U. Zenzie

Saade, George   [1930–]

Lebanese politician and president of the Phalange party (Hizb al-Kata'ib).

Born to a Maronite family, Saade completed his schooling in Lebanon. In 1955 he left for Spain where he enrolled as a student at Madrid's Central University completing degrees in literature and philosophy and Semitic languages. Elected to the Lebanese parliament in 1968, Saade was also appointed as minister in several governments. In 1945, while a student, he joined the PHALANGE party where he played important roles. He was adviser for educational matters to the party founder, Pierre Jumayyil. In 1969, following clashes between the Lebanese army and the Palestine Liberation Organization (PLO), Saade was appointed to a joint dialogue group with the Palestinians. In the 1970s, he played a key role in the Phalange party's relationships with the Arab countries. In 1986 he was elected president of al-Kata'ib. In 1991 and 1992, Saade was a member of the Lebanese government until his resignation in September 1992.

BIBLIOGRAPHY

Arab Information Center, Beirut.

George E. Irani

Saadet

Ottoman daily newspaper.

Established in Istanbul in 1885, *Saadet* was published until shortly before World War I. Its founding pub-lisher, Mehmed Nuri, made the paper a vehicle for political ideas despite Sultan Abdülhamit II's heavy censorship. Censors were avoided by veiling political columns as literary works.

Elizabeth Thompson

Saadettin Kaynak   [1895–1961]

Turkish composer.

Saadettin, born in Istanbul, studied theology at Istanbul University. While imam at the Mosque of Sultan Selim, he made religious and nonreligious musical recordings, and in 1926, he became a professional composer. He wrote the score for over eighty-five films, as well as for musicals and revues. Most of his more than 138 compositions were written in the *şarki* form.

David Waldner

Saba

See Sheba

Sabaeans

Ancient religious sect with no known descendants.

This religious sect of Mesopotamia was described in the Qur'an as monotheistic—thus acquiring protected status under Islam along with monotheistic Jews and Christians.

It is often assumed that Sabaean is the same as Sabian, a group that exists today; however, the ancient Sabaeans (of Queen of Sheba fame) have no known descendants. Today's Sabians have been identified with the Mandeans, an ancient sect of Gnostics, known as the Christians of St. John. They believe in the ascent of the soul, by way of an inner illumination, to reunion with the supreme being. They combine Judaism, Islam, and Christianity with ancient Babylonian worship. Baptism, for example—a process of purification—forms an important part of their ritual.

Jenab Tutunji

Saba Family

Prominent Palestinian/Lebanese business family.

The Sabas, Christians originally from Shefr Amr in Palestine, achieved prominence in the twentieth century through the extraordinary business and political career of Fu'ad Saba. In the 1920s, Fu'ad founded the now-huge accounting firm of Saba & Co. In the 1930s, he helped establish the Palestinian National Fund and acted as secretary to the Arab Higher Committee. He was briefly exiled by the British in the late 1930s for his political activities.

Fu'ad relocated Saba & Co. to Beirut before the 1948 Arab–Israel War and started other enterprises there, including the al-Mashriq Financial Investment Company (1963), the Arabia Insurance Company, and the Middle East Society of Associated Accountants. His business boomed after signing contracts with the American oil firm of J. Paul Getty and a top American accounting firm, Arthur Andersen and Company. He lived in Beirut until his death in the late 1980s.

Fu'ad's son Fawzi, born in 1931 in Jerusalem, attended the American University of Beirut, as his father did. He became a partner in Saba & Co. and has been living in Saudi Arabia and Dubai. (The family is of no known relation to Elias Saba, the 1970s Lebanese finance minister from northern Lebanon.)

BIBLIOGRAPHY

KHALAF, ISSA. *Politics in Palestine.* Albany, N.Y., 1991.
SMITH, PAMELA ANN. *Palestine and the Palestinians, 1876–1983.* London, 1984.
Who's Who in Lebanon, 1986–1987. Beirut, 1987.
Who's Who in the Arab World, 1990–1991. Beirut, 1991.

Elizabeth Thompson

Sabah

Popular entertainer in the Arab world.

Sabah, whose real name is Janet Farghali, is a seemingly ageless singer and entertainer. She began singing at an early age and later adopted the name Sabah ("morning," in Arabic). She started her career in Egypt and settled in Lebanon in the 1960s, when she emerged as one of the top stars of the Arab world. Known for a series of failed marriages, Sabah was active in the social life of Beirut before the Lebanese Civil War of 1975. She continued to work in Lebanon during the war and often performs for Lebanese communities throughout the world.

As'ad AbuKhalil

Sabah

Ottoman newspaper, 1876–1922.

Sabah (Morning), a daily Istanbul newspaper, was founded by a Greek merchant named Papadopoulis

and by Şemsettin Sami. In 1883, Mihran Efendi bought the paper and became its publisher. It was one of the most important papers of the period. (Shortly after World War I, *Sabah* merged with *Peyam*, becoming *Peyamı Sabah*). Dedicated to enlightening the masses, *Sabah* was written in simple language and sold inexpensively. By 1891, it had a daily circulation of 12,000.

BIBLIOGRAPHY

EMIN, AHMED. *The Development of Modern Turkey as Measured by Its Press.* New York, 1968.
SHAW, STANFORD, and EZEL KURAL SHAW. *History of the Ottoman Empire and Modern Turkey.* Vol. 2. Cambridge, U.K., 1977.

David Waldner

Sabahettin   [1877–1948]

Ottoman prince.

Sabahettin (Sabah al-Din) was a key figure in the early days of the YOUNG TURKS movement. A member of the "royal rebels," he, his brother Lutfullah, and their father, Damad Mahmud Celaleddin Paşa, fled the Ottoman Empire in 1899 and gave important political support to the exiled Young Turks in Paris. More important, Sabahettin championed the liberal wing of the Young Turks, which favored a decentralized and noninterventionist state. This view was influenced by Edmond Demolins, who argued that England's success as a political and economic power derived from education and decentralization.

In 1902, Sabahettin established the League for Decentralization and Private Initiative. Ultimately the liberal wing's position was rejectd by Young Turk leaders in favor of the centralist and inteventionist approach of the Committee of Union and Progress. Sabahettin was not active politically in the second constitutional period. Because he was a member of the royal family, he was deported from Turkey in 1924 and lived in Switzerland until his death.

BIBLIOGRAPHY

LEWIS, BERNARD. *The Emergence of Modern Turkey,* 2nd ed. London, 1968.

Stuart J. Borsch

Sabah Family

See under Al Sabah *for specific members of the dynasty.*

Sabanci, Sakıp   [1933–   ]

Turkish businessman.

Sabanci was born in Akçakaya-Kayseri, the son of a cotton merchant and textile manufacturer who founded the Turkish Bank Akbank in 1947 and owned a large construction business in Ankara. In the 1950s, Sabanci worked as an administrator in the agriculture ministry and took over the family business in the 1960s. Like VEHBI KOÇ, Sabanci profited from Turkey's state policies favoring large-scale monopoly capitalism beginning under Süleyman Demirel's administration in the late 1960s. By the 1980s, the family owned one of the largest textile enterprises in the world. It controlled ninety firms, rivalling the Koç empire in overall size and in several markets, such as tire manufacturing. Sabanci's company, like other holding companies, benefited from privatization in the early 1980s, with its capital turnover increasing from 185 billion to 308 billion Turkish lire between 1980 and 1983. Sabanci Holdings employed 32,000 workers in 1991.

The extent of political power accompanying such economic clout is disputed. Sabanci joined the Turkish Industrialists' and Businessmen's Association (TÜSIAD) along with ninety other businessmen after it was founded following the 1971 coup. Some historians note rumors of connections to the military—that in the 1970s the group became a major negotiator in the formulation of Turkey's economic policy. In 1977, Sabanci actively promoted Bülent Ecevit (and his austerity policies that favored exports) against Demirel.

BIBLIOGRAPHY

BIANCHI, ROBERT. *Interest Groups and Political Development in Turkey.* Princeton, N.J., 1984.

Elizabeth Thompson

Sab'awi, Yunis al-   [1910–1942]

Arab nationalist active in Iraqi anti-British politics.

Born in Mosul to a Sunni Arab family, he was one of fifteen children of an illiterate greengrocer. He attended a religious traditional school for two years, a government elementary school in Mosul, and high school in Baghdad. A graduate of the Baghdad Law College, al-Sab'awi became a lawyer in 1933.

Favoring Arab nationalism, in 1930 al-Sab'awi participated in the general strike in Baghdad and became a close associate of the colonels of the GOLDEN SQUARE. An active member of Yasin al-Hashimi's IKHA AL-WATANI (National Brotherhood) PARTY, he was also a member of the Arab nationalist al-Muthanna Club and the Palestine Defense Society. Active in politics in Mosul in 1939, al-Sab'awi supported Rashid Ali al-Kaylani in 1940 and, in January 1941 with Rashid Ali as prime minister, became minister of economics, albeit for only three days. At the end of the 1941 Iraqi war with Britain, he declared himself military governor of Baghdad in order to defend the city as the British advanced but was arrested and sent to Iran, only to be captured by the British and returned to Iraq, where he was executed in 1942.

BIBLIOGRAPHY

AL-HUSRY, KHALDUN S. "The Political Ideas of Yunis al-Sab'awi." In *Intellectual Life in the Arab East, 1890–1939,* ed. by Marwan R. Buheiry. Beirut, 1981.
AL-UMARI, KHAIRI. *Yunis al-Sab'awi sirat siyasi usami* (Yunis al-Sab'awi: The Biography of a Self-Made Politician). Baghdad, 1978.

Reeva S. Simon

Sabbagh, Hasib   [1920–   ]

Palestinian entrepreneur and philanthropist.

Hasib Sabbagh hails from the northern Palestinian town of Safed although he was born in nearby Tiberias. He matriculated from the Arab College of Jerusalem in 1938, and graduated from the American University of Beirut with a B.A. in civil engineering in 1941.

In 1943, Sabbagh and four other contractors established the Consolidated Contractors Company (CCC) in Haifa. Forced to abandon Palestine in April 1948, he and eight other Arab businessmen reestablished CCC in Beirut in 1950.

From modest beginnings, CCC grew over the next several decades into the region's largest multinational corporation and is among the largest contractors worldwide. It boasts four specialized subsidiary companies and has been involved in virtually every branch of construction throughout the Arab world. Active in other regions as well, its most important non-Arab market is the United States, where it is ranked the eighth largest contractor. Sabbagh, who is chairman of CCC, has since 1979 shared exclusive ownership of it with Riad Khoury.

Sabbagh has for many years also been active in Palestinian national affairs and is a member of both the Palestine National Council (PNC) and its Central Council.

In 1978, he founded the Dina Sabbagh Foundation in memory of his deceased wife. One of the largest Arab charitable foundations, it receives 5 percent of his income and has disbursed in excess of 30 million U.S. dollars, primarily to educational institutions. In 1982 Sabbagh co-founded the Welfare Association, a Geneva-based Palestinian charity and development fund, and serves as its deputy chairman. He is chairman of the Palestinian Students Fund and member of the boards of the Arab Bank, Massachusetts General Hospital, Georgetown University, and the Institute for Palestine Studies, among others.

BIBLIOGRAPHY

HINDLEY, ANGUS. "Profile—CCC: Arab Giant Achieves Global Reach." *Middle East Economic Digest* 38 (July 29, 1994): 30.

Mouin Rabbani

Sabbagh, Salah al-Din al-   [1889–1945]

Arab nationalist; Iraqi army officer who headed the Golden Square group that opposed the government and influenced politics from 1939–1941.

Born in Mosul of a Lebanese father and an Iraqi mother, Sabbagh was educated in Mosul and the Ottoman Military College in Istanbul, graduating as an officer in 1915. During World War I, he served in Palestine and Macedonia and was taken prisoner, ultimately joining Emir Faisal I ibn Husayn, who became King of Iraq, to return to Iraq in 1921 to a position in the Iraqi army. His military education also included courses in Belgium and in Britain. Sabbagh became an instructor at the Baghdad Military College in 1924 and later taught at the Staff College. By 1940 he was assistant chief of staff of the Iraqi army.

Sabbagh was an Arab nationalist and the head of the GOLDEN SQUARE, the group of army officers that from 1939 to 1941 influenced Iraqi politics from behind the scenes. An admirer of the Jerusalem Mufti (chief Muslim jurist) Hajj Muhammad Amin al-Husayni, Sabbagh worked with him and with Rashid Ali al-Kaylani in their negotiations with the Axis powers for support of their pan-Arab goals. Sabbagh backed Rashid Ali as prime minister in 1941 and was a major advocate of war with Britain in April and May. After the Iraqi defeat in the Anglo–Iraqi War of 1941, Sabbagh fled to Iran and then to Turkey, where he was extradited to Iraq and executed in 1945. His book *Fursan al-Uruba fi al-Iraq* (The Knights of Arabism in Iraq), an autobiographical account of his pan-Arabism, was published posthumously in Baghdad in 1956.

BIBLIOGRAPHY

SIMON, REEVA S. *Iraq between the Two World Wars*. New York, 1986.

Reeva S. Simon

Sabbath

The seventh day of the week; the day of religiously mandated rest.

In Judaism, the Sabbath (Hebrew, *shabbat* [rest]) was and is the holiest day of the week and, except for Yom Kippur, the holiest day of the year—since all ritual and holy-day observance is modified if it takes place on the Sabbath. Historically, no work of any kind could be done; hence, fire could not be made and, by extension, nothing that runs electrically or mechanically can be started up by observers. Food is prepared in advance and special customs followed to ensure rest, reflection on the week, and thereby restoration of the soul for the coming week.

The Jewish Sabbath begins at sundown Friday night and lasts twenty-five hours, until nightfall Saturday; the Christian Sabbath is usually celebrated on Sunday. In Israel, on the Sabbath, public facilities are closed; except in Haifa, buses of the state cooperatives do not run; no El Al state airliners take off or land; and no Hebrew newspapers are published.

BIBLIOGRAPHY

HESCHEL, ABRAHAM. *The Sabbath*. New York, 1966.

Samuel C. Heilman

Sabeti, Habib   [1920–   ]

Iranian businessman.

After obtaining his high school diploma, Sabeti began working in a bicycle-manufacturing factory. He subsequently was a cabdriver, opened an auto-repair shop, and rose to be one of the chief capitalists of Iran under the Pahlavi dynasty. A prominent Baha'i (and one of the major financial supporters of the Baha'i faith), Habib Sabeti owned several companies, including Pepsico Iran. He was a sales representative for Volkswagen in Iran and a major shareholder of The Iran and Middle East Bank. Sabeti also founded Iran Television, which he turned over to the government in 1968. He left Iran after the Iranian Revolution of 1979 and resides in Europe. Although Sabeti was influential, his direct participation in the political life of Iran was hampered by his religious affiliation.

BIBLIOGRAPHY

ECHO OF IRAN. *Iran Who's Who*. Tehran, 1972.

Neguin Yavari

SABIC

See Saudi Arabian Basic Industries Company

Sabra

Word ultimately derived from the Arabic for a variety of prickly pear found in Israel; also the name for a native-born Israeli.

Native-born Israelis are described as Sabras because their personality is often thought to be similar to the fruit of the plant: tough and prickly on the outside, sweet on the inside.

Bryan Daves

Sabra and Shatila Refugee Camps

Site of the killing of hundreds of Palestinians, September 16–18, 1982.

Shortly after Israel invaded Lebanon on June 6, 1982, the Israel Defense Forces (IDF) laid siege to Beirut. A cease-fire accord reached in August allowed the entry into West Beirut of a multilateral force, including a contingent of U.S. Marines. Following a U.S. pledge to protect Palestinian civilians, Palestine Liberation Organization (PLO) fighters and officials departed the city, as did the multinational force. The day after the president of Lebanon, Bashir JUMAYYIL, was assassinated (September 14), Israel sent troops into West Beirut, where they surrounded two Palestinian refugee camps in violation of the cease-fire agreement. Defense Minister Ariel Sharon and Chief of Staff Rafael Eitan arranged for the Israel-supported PHALANGE militia to enter the camps to clear out what Sharon described as "2,000–3,000 terrorists who remained behind. We even have their names." The Phalange murdered hundreds of Palestinians, mostly women, children, and older men. Israel put the figure at 800; others, at 1,500.

The international community condemned Israel's role in the mass killing, and up to 400,000 Israelis (8 percent of the population) demonstrated against the government of Menachem Begin and demanded a judicial inquiry. A three-man Israeli commission, headed by the president of the Supreme Court, Yitzhak Kahan, found that Israeli officials were "indirectly responsible" because they arranged for the Phalange, mortal enemies of the Palestinians, to enter the camps and, even though Israeli officers and government officials received reports about the atrocities, they ignored them and allowed the Phalange to extend their stay in the camps. The International Commission, chaired by Sean MacBride, former assistant secretary-general of the United Nations, charged that under international law, Israel was directly responsible because the camps were under its jurisdiction as an occupying power and because the IDF planned and facilitated its ally's entry into and activities in the camps, prevented survivors from leaving the camps, and did not stop the mass killing after hearing about it. Despite the findings of both commissions, no one was prosecuted.

BIBLIOGRAPHY

GOVERNMENT OF ISRAEL. *The Kahan Commission Report.* Jerusalem, 1982.
SMITH, CHARLES D. *Palestine and the Arab–Israeli Conflict.* New York, 1988.
TESSLER, MARK. *A History of the Israeli–Palestinian Conflict.* Bloomington, Ind., 1994.

Philip Mattar

Sabri, Ali [1920–1991]

Egyptian military officer and politician.

Sabri was educated at the Military Academy, taught at the Air Force Academy in 1949, and served as an air force officer. Though not a member of the FREE OFFICERS, he supported their movement and acted as liason to the U.S. embassy prior to the 1952 revolution in which the Free Officers overthrew King Farouk I. Between 1957 and 1962, Sabri was minister of presidential affairs, giving him access to President Gamal Abdel Nasser, who appointed him to the Supreme Executive of the ARAB SOCIALIST UNION (ASU) in 1962, a position he held through 1965, at which time he was appointed secretary-general of the union.

Sabri is well known in Egyptian politics as perhaps the most influential leftist. His tenure in the ASU is closely associated with Nasser's shift to the left in the early 1960s. As head of the ASU, Sabri sought to make it the leading political body in

Egypt by subordinating the public sector, the bureaucracy, labor unions, and professional syndicates to its control. On the death of Nasser, Sabri was one of the most powerful men in Egypt. He was responsible for naming Anwar al-Sadat president, under the mistaken assumption that he could control Sadat. In May of 1971, Sabri and his supporters publicly broke with Sadat. Sadat responded by arresting Sabri for plotting a coup. Sabri was sentenced to death, but this was commuted to twenty-five years in prison. Sabri was released from prison in 1981.

BIBLIOGRAPHY

HINNEBUSCH, RAYMOND. *Egyptian Politics under Sadat: The Post-Populist Development of an Authoritarian-Modernizing State.* New York, 1985.

WATERBURY, JOHN. *The Egypt of Nasser and Sadat: The Political Economy of Two Regimes.* Princeton, N.J., 1983.

WUCHER KING, JOAN. *Historical Dictionary of Egypt.* Metuchen, N.J., 1984.

David Waldner

Sa'd, Habib al-

See Saad, Habib al-

Sa'da

The northernmost province and large town of North Yemen.

A rather parochial town, the antithesis of Ta'iz far to the south, Sa'da is located about 150 miles (245 km) north of San'a and 50 miles (80 km) from the border with Saudi Arabia. The town is known for its strong identification with ZAYDISM, since it is the birthplace of the sect and the Zaydi imamate in Yemen, and for its multistoried buildings and serpentine outer walls, both made of mud. The graves of the first imam, al-Hadi, and other early imams are located just outside the walls. During most of the civil war, the town and its immediate environs were an island of republicanism, kept largely by force of arms in a status about which it was ambivalent. Rumors and talk since the 1960s of tribal revolt, Zaydi separatism, and revival of the imamate have often focused on Sa'da. The area's renegade status and suspicions of its loyalties are reinforced, at least symbolically, by the huge, sprawling, and famous smugglers' bazaar not many miles from the city—a major, open-air market

where goods brought into Yemen illegally from Saudi Arabia are exchanged.

Robert D. Burrowes

Sa'dabad Pact

A mutual security agreement between Iran, Iraq, Turkey, and Afghanistan.

The Sa'dabad Pact was signed July 8, 1937, at Reza Shah Pahlavi's Sa'dabad palace in Tehran, Iran. The signatories declared their adherence to the principles of the League of Nations and agreed to meet annually to discuss matters of common concern.

BIBLIOGRAPHY

HUREWITZ, J. C., ed. *The Middle East and North Africa in World Politics.* New Haven, Conn., 1979.

Zachary Karabell

Sa'd al-Dowleh, Mirza Javan Khan

[c.1840–c.1915]

Iranian politician.

One of the prominent constitutionalists of the Qajar period (see CONSTITUTIONAL REVOLUTION and QAJAR DYNASTY), Sa'd al-Dowleh was born in the 1840s into the milieu of the provincial aristocracy of Azerbaijan. His father was consul general in Baghdad. Sa'd al-Dowleh studied telegraphy in Russia, after which he returned to Iran to work in a communications center in Tabriz and became its director in 1874. Six years later, he became minister of post and telegraph and, in 1892, the Iranian ambassador to Belgium. He returned to Iran shortly before the Constitutional Revolution after having been appointed minister of commerce, but his pro-Constitutionalist sentiments led to his dismissal. With the triumph of the revolution, he returned to government and was appointed to several ministerships, but his difficult personality prevented him from achieving professional success. After the bombardment of the *majles* and the return to power of Mohammad Ali Shah Qajar, Sa'd al-Dowleh was made prime minister. In 1909, when the Constitutionalists conquered Tehran, he was forced to resign because he had accepted the premiership from Mohammad Ali Shah Qajar, who at first claimed to be supporting the Constitutional Revolution. He sought refuge in the Russian embassy and left Iran with Mohammad

Ali Shah. He returned to Iran in 1912, and three years later Ahmad Shah Qajar wanted to name him prime minister, but the British opposed the appointment. He died shortly thereafter in Tehran.

BIBLIOGRAPHY

BAMDAD, MEHDI. *Biographies of Iranian Notables in the Twelfth, Thirteenth, and Fourteenth Centuries,* vol. 1. Tehran, 1979.

Neguin Yavari

Sadat, Anwar al- [1918–1981]

President of Egypt from 1970 until his assassination in 1981.

Anwar al-Sadat was born December 25, 1918, in the village of Mit Abu al-Kum in the Lower Egyptian province of Minufiyya. His father, a mid-level government official, arranged for him to enroll in primary and secondary school in Cairo, from which he graduated in 1936. That same year, admission in the national military academy was opened to young men from nonaristocratic families, and Sadat seized the opportunity to pursue a career as a military officer. He graduated in 1938 and was posted to Manqabad

President Anwar al-Sadat. (Egyptian State Information Service)

in Upper Egypt, where he became friends with another ambitious young officer, Gamal Abdel Nasser. Transferred to the outskirts of Cairo in 1939, he immediately made contact with a range of underground political organizations working against the monarchy of King Farouk. They included the MUSLIM BROTHERHOOD (al-Ikhwan al-Muslimin) and a cell based in the signal corps sympathetic to Nazi Germany. Since World War II was raging in North Africa, his association with this cell led to his arrest in 1942 for conspiring against the British war effort (Britain maintained a protectorate over the Suez Canal and Egypt). Upon his escape from prison in 1945, he revived his contacts with the Muslim Brotherhood, taking part in a January 1946 plot to assassinate a prominent pro-British politician. He was arrested again in connection with this incident and spent two more years in prison awaiting trial. His longstanding connections with high-ranking but anti-British members of the armed forces won him reinstatement in the officers' corps in 1950.

Toward the end of 1951, Sadat was asked by Nasser to join the inner circle of the clandestine Free Officers movement. He played little direct part in the coup d'état headed by General Muhammad Naguib that overthrew the monarchy and brought the movement to power in July 1952, but he was chosen to broadcast the first announcement of the coup on the morning it occurred. He was thereafter editor of the newspaper *al-Jumhuriyyah,* a member of the ruling revolutionary command council, and a minister of state.

As secretary-general of the ruling political party, the Arab Socialist Union (ASU), Sadat assumed the role of faithful subordinate to Nasser, assisting him in moving first against the Muslim Brotherhood and then against his rivals within the Free Officers. When Nasser overcame Naguib to lead the ruling junta, he repaid Sadat's loyalty by appointing him first speaker of the reconfigured national assembly in 1962, one of four vice presidents in 1964, and then, in December 1969, vice president of the republic.

Nasser's unexpected death by heart attack in September 1970 precipitated eight months of intense jockeying for power at the highest echelons of the Egyptian regime. Proponents of continuing the government's socialist economic policies—led by the secretary-general of the ASU, Ali Sabri—faced firm opposition from advocates of a more liberal order, such as the editor of the semi-official *al-Ahram* newspaper, Muhammad Hasanayn Haykal. Sadat, who had been appointed provisional president by the cabinet shortly after Nasser's death, took advantage of his relatively insulated position in the national assembly to play these factions against one another, emerging as the regime's key figure when the cabinet of ministers tendered its resignation to the assembly in May 1971. He immediately charged the powerful minister of the interior with plotting to set up a police state and replaced him with a trusted ally, Mamduh Salim. He then moved to cultivate public approval by commissioning the national assembly to formulate a permanent constitution, pardoning most of the country's political prisoners and returning properties sequestered during the socialist era of the early 1960s to their original owners. At the same time, he attempted to undermine leftist influence by catering to those sympathetic to the Muslim Brotherhood through carefully choreographed displays of his own religiosity in the mass media and by tolerating the spread of Islamist political groups on university campuses.

These moves precipitated a wave of unrest among university students in January 1972 that convinced Sadat to initiate major shifts in Egypt's foreign policy as a way of consolidating his position at home. That July he ordered all Soviet military advisers out of the country and began planning for a campaign to recapture the Sinai peninsula, which Israel had occupied during the Arab–Israel War of 1967. While preparing to attack Israel's forces in the Sinai, Sadat effected a rapprochement with Saudi Arabia and created a working alliance with Syria as well, which enabled the Egyptian armed forces to strike across the Suez Canal on October 6, 1973. Although the attack was, in the end, repelled and Israeli units drove deep into the Egyptian delta before a cease-fire was arranged on October 23, the comparatively good showing made by Egyptian troops led Sadat to claim the honorific "the hero of the crossing" and invite U.S. Secretary of State Henry Kissinger to mediate an interim settlement with Israel. Two disengagement agreements negotiated under U.S. auspices in January 1974 and September 1975 laid the foundation for Sadat's November 9, 1977, surprise announcement that he intended to travel to Jerusalem to initiate peace talks with Israel's government. Ten days later he addressed the Israeli parliament, smashing what he called "the psychological barrier" to peace between the two states. He then took part in a series of face-to-face negotiations with Israeli Prime Minister Menachem Begin that culminated in the September 1978 CAMP DAVID ACCORDS, which in turn led to the signing of an Egyptian–Israeli peace treaty in March of 1979. This document resulted in the withdrawal of Israeli forces from the Sinai in April 1982.

Sadat's unprecedented trip to Jerusalem was prompted by internal as well as external developments. In June 1974, the regime implemented an economic program designed to attract greater amounts of foreign investment into the country and provide new opportunities for local entrepreneurs, which came to be known as the policy of *infitah* (opening up). At the same time, competing factions within the ASU were encouraged to organize into separate political groupings (*manabir*), which by 1976 had become established as autonomous parties; the largest of these, the centrist National Democratic party, continued to dominate the national assembly, while smaller rightist and leftist parties, the Social Democratic party and the National Progressive Unionist party, played the role of loyal opposition to the government. It was in these circumstances at the beginning of 1977 that the regime agreed to implement austerity measures demanded by the International Monetary Fund and cut state subsidies on a wide range of basic foodstuffs and other necessities. This decision sparked large-scale riots in Cairo, Alexandria, and other Egyptian cities, forcing the government to restore the subsidies. President Sadat immediately castigated the rioters as "thieves" and ordered wholesale revisions to the Parties Law of 1977 that substantially limited the activities in which political associations were permitted to engage. The subsequent electoral successes of the main prerevolutionary party, the Wafd, added to Sadat's displeasure with the new political order he had helped to create. In June 1978, he ordered the arrest of the Wafd's leadership; he supervised the de facto rigging of parliamentary elections a year later; and in September 1981, he issued new regulations that led to the imprisonment of virtually all opposition activists.

These measures added fuel to the smoldering popular discontent generated by Egypt's persistent economic difficulties and Sadat's unilateral peace treaty with Israel. The Camp David Accords failed to bring appreciably greater levels of U.S. assistance into the country, even as the policies associated with infitah steadily increased the gap between rich and poor. They did little better in persuading Israel to proceed with the direct talks concerning the future of the occupied territories that were envisaged as the second stage of the agreement. Furthermore, the very image affected by Sadat to win popular support in the United States—that of a benevolent patriarch, complete with sweater and pipe—grated on dissidents at home. Militant Islamist cells proliferated in poor neighborhoods, in the provinces of Upper Egypt and, most notably, within the armed forces. Members of one of these cells, al-Jihad, assassinated Sadat on October 6, 1981, as he reviewed a military parade commemorating the eighth anniversary of the attack across the Suez Canal. He was succeeded by his vice president, Hosni Mubarak.

BIBLIOGRAPHY

BAKER, RAYMOND W. *Sadat and After.* Cambridge, Mass., 1990.

COOPER, MARK N. *The Transformation of Egypt.* Baltimore, 1982.

HIRST, DAVID, and IRENE BEESON. *Sadat.* London, 1981.

WATERBURY, JOHN. *The Egypt of Nasser and Sadat.* Princeton, N.J., 1983.

Fred H. Lawson

Sadat, Jihan   [1933–   ]

Egyptian feminist and political activist.

Jihan Sadat was born on Roda Island in Cairo. Her father was Muslim and a civil servant in the Ministry of Health, and her mother was British. Sadat was raised a Christian and educated in a Christian missionary school. In 1949, she married Anwar al-Sadat, the future president of Egypt. Known as the First Lady of Egypt during her husband's presidency, she was an outspoken supporter of women's rights and peace with Israel. Along with other prominent feminists, she helped to draft what became known as "Jihan's laws," which gave a woman the right of divorce and custody of children and the family home if her husband took a second wife. Following the assassination of President Sadat in 1981, Jihan Sadat took up residence in the United States, where she gives lectures on women in developing countries and on the culture of Islam.

BIBLIOGRAPHY

SADAT, JIHAN. *A Woman of Egypt.* New York, 1987.

David Waldner

Sadawi, Bashir   [c. 1882–1957]

Libyan (Tripolitanian) politician.

Associated with the Tripolitanian republic after World War I, Sadawi was in exile for many years, during which he acted as adviser to the Saudi Arabian monarchy of Ibn Sa'ud. In 1947, with Arab League support, he founded the National Council for the Liberation of Libya in Cairo to promote the unity of the regions of Tripolitania and Cyrenaica. In 1949, popular protests against Anglo–Italian trusteeship proposals for Libya prompted several political groups to form the Tripolitanian National Congress party under Sadawi's leadership. During the many years of international debate on Libya's future (1945–1949) and the subsequent preparations for independence under UN supervision (1949–1951), Sadawi emerged as Tripolitania's leading politician, consistently supporting a unitary Libyan state and Emir IDRIS AL-SAYYID MUHAMMAD AL-SANUSI as the sole leader capable of uniting the country.

Sadawi's political hopes were dashed, first by the decision that independent Libya was to be a federal kingdom under Idris, then with the failure of his National Congress party to win as many seats as expected in the first postindependence elections in February 1952. The government used postelection riots as an excuse to deport Sadawi, who returned to Saudi royal service.

BIBLIOGRAPHY

PELT, ADRIAN. *Libyan Independence and the United Nations.* New Haven, Conn., 1970.

John L. Wright

Sa'dawi, Nawal al-   [1931–   ]

Egyptian doctor, writer, and feminist.

Al-Sa'dawi was born in the village of Kfar Tahla in Egypt's Nile delta. She graduated from the Faculty of Medicine at Cairo University in 1955, and her experiences as a general practitioner in the city and in the countryside inform much of her writing. While general director of health education in Egypt, al-Sa'dawi wrote about the sexual exploitation of women—prostitution, clitoridectomy, incest, and sexually transmitted diseases—leading to her dismissal from the Egyptian Ministry of Health.

Continuing to write against exploitation and oppression, she was imprisoned by Egypt's President Anwar al-Sadat in 1981. Al-Sa'dawi has published twenty-four books, which have been translated into ten languages. Among her books translated into English are *The Hidden Face of Eve* (1980), *Two Women in One* (1985), and *Memoirs from the Women's Prison* (1987). Al-Sa'dawi is president of the Arab Women's Solidarity Association.

BIBLIOGRAPHY

BADRAN, MARGOT, and MIRIAM COOKE, eds. *Opening the Gates: A Century of Arab Feminist Writing.* Bloomington and Indianapolis, Ind., 1990.

David Waldner

Sa'di, Ali Salih   [1928–   ]

Iraqi political leader.

An Arabized Shi'a (Fayli) Kurd, Sa'di joined the Ba'th party in 1952. He fled to Syria following the failed attempt by Ba'thists to assassinate Abd al-Karim Kassem. Upon returning to Iraq in 1960, he organized and expanded the Ba'th party. Sa'di was secretary of the Ba'th in Iraq from 1961 to 1963, and member of the Ba'th National Command from 1962 to 1964. He helped form the alliance between the Ba'th and the Nationalists, mainly Nasserite army officers, and Abd al-Salam Arif, who led the coup that overthrew Kassem on February 8, 1963. Following that coup, Sa'di's power reached its zenith. During the premiership of Hasan al-Bakr (1963), Sa'di was deputy prime minister, minister of the interior, and minister of guidance.

In 1963, Sa'di's left wing launched a struggle against the right wing, headed by Prime Minister Hasan al-Bakr, and against the Nasserites. Sa'di's attempt to expel his rivals in October 1963 led to military intervention, which crushed Sa'di's faction and removed the Ba'th from power. Sa'di and his aides were exiled. In 1963 and 1964, Sa'di was involved in the struggles in Syria and within the National Command of the Ba'th, supporting the left wing of the Syrian Ba'th. He returned to Iraq in March 1964.

BIBLIOGRAPHY

BATATU, HANNA. *The Old Social Classes and Revolutionary Movements of Iraq.* Princeton, N.J., 1982.
FAROUK-SLUGLETT, MARION, and PETER SLUGLETT. *Iraq Since 1958: From Revolution to Dictatorship.* London, 1987.
KHADDURI, MAJID. *Republican Iraq.* London, 1969.

Michael Eppel

Sadik Rifat   [1807–1856]

Ottoman reformer.

Born in Istanbul, Sadik entered government service at a young age. He became an associate of TANZIMAT reformer Reşit Paşa and was sent to Vienna (1837), where he studied Metternich's reforms. He later served on the Meclis-i Vala (Supreme Council), which formulated Tanzimat policies. Sadik wrote several books and tracts promoting modernism and positivism.

Elizabeth Thompson

Sadiq, Yusuf   [1910–1975]

Egyptian military officer and politician.

The son of an army officer, Sadiq graduated from the War College in 1933, and later, as commander of an infantry unit, participated in the 1952 revolution in Egypt, which overthrew King Farouk. Sadiq was a member of the Democratic Movement for National Liberation, a Marxist-inspired organization, and one of two Marxists on the Revolutionary Command Council. In January 1953, Sadiq left the junta following a crackdown on political leftists. After a brief exile in France, he returned to Egypt and publicly attacked the imposition of martial law.

BIBLIOGRAPHY

GORDON, JOEL. *Nasser's Blessed Movement: Egypt's Free Officers and the July Revolution.* New York, 1992.

David Waldner

Sadiqi College

Secondary school in Tunis.

Sadiqi was founded in 1875/76 by Khayr al-Din. Its curriculum, which included modern sciences and languages, was taught in Arabic and French. In an effort to modernize Sadiqi College, subjects such as translation, administrative law, and Islamic jurisprudence were added to the curriculum. During the French protectorate, French replaced Arabic as the language of teaching for most subjects. In 1892 the school acquired a French director.

Sadiqi attracted few students at first, but its enrollment increased steadily. As its popularity grew, it became very selective in the choice of its students, in contrast to Zaytuna University. Sadiqi graduated seventy-eight students in 1954.

The graduates of Sadiqi usually went to France for their higher education. As a result, they were criticized by those who considered the college an institution for bourgeois children and were accused of maintaining strong links with France and its culture.

Although Sadiqi was a model for many of the Franco-Arabic schools that arose in Tunisia during the French protectorate, it was only in 1911 that its diploma was officially recognized.

BIBLIOGRAPHY

ABUN-NASR, M. JAMIL. *A History of the Maghrib.* London, 1971.
GORDON, DAVID. *North Africa's French Legacy.* Cambridge, U.K., 1962.

HOURANI, ALBERT. *A History of the Arab Peoples*. New York, 1992.

Aida A. Bamia

SADR

See Saharan Arab Democratic Republic

Sadr, Muhammad Baqir al-   [1931–1980]

Iraqi Shi'a religious leader whose writings inspired and influenced the Islamic movement in Iraq.

Born in the Shi'a district of Kazimiyya, Baghdad, to an Arab family from Lebanon, Sadr studied in Baghdad and al-Najaf. Among his teachers was Muhsin al-Hakim, the highest Shi'a *Marja* of the time (see MARJA' AL-TAQLID). Sadr rose in the Shi'a clerical hierarchy to the rank of ayatollah, becoming the only Arab of eight living *marja*. He was placed under house arrest in June 1979, following the Shi'a riots in al-Najaf and Karbala. On April 8, 1980, he was hanged, following assassination attempts on several officials earlier that month. He was accused of being the leader of the outlawed al-Da'wa party, being the mastermind behind the assassinations, and plotting with Iran against Iraq's government. A prolific writer, Sadr published more than twenty books dealing with various subjects, including Islamic government and economy.

BIBLIOGRAPHY

WILEY, JOYCE N. *The Islamic Movement of Iraqi Shias*. Boulder, Colo., 1992.

Ayad al-Qazzaz

Sadr, Muhsin   [1871–1963]

Iranian politician.

Born to a clerical family from Mahallat, Muhsin Sadr entered the bureaucracy in 1907 as a clerk at the Ministry of Justice during the reign of Naser al-Din Shah Qajar. During the CONSTITUTIONAL REVOLUTION, he sided with Mohammad Ali Shah and became chief interrogator after the bombardment of the *majles*. An opportunist, Sadr exploited his links to the Iranian aristocracy after the restoration of the Constitutionalists and resumed his service at the Ministry of Justice. He was appointed minister of justice five times, speaker of the senate twice, governor of Khorasan once, and prime minister once.

Reza Shah Pahlavi removed him from the Ministry of Justice in 1936.

BIBLIOGRAPHY

BAMDAD, MEHDI. *Biographies of Iranian Notables in the Twelfth, Thirteenth, and Fourteenth Centuries*, vol. 3. Tehran, 1979.

Neguin Yavari

Sadr, Musa   [1928–c. 1978]

Iranian Shi'a cleric active in Lebanon.

Sadr was born in Qom, Iran, to a clerical family who traced their ancestry back to Musa ibn Ja'far, the seventh Shi'a imam. He enrolled at Tehran University's School of Law, and soon after his graduation began teaching *fiqh* (Islamic law) and logic at the seminary at Qom. In 1954, he moved to Iraq to continue his religious education. In late 1959, at the insistence of his mentor, Ayatollah Muhsin al-Hakim, Sadr agreed to go to Lebanon to assume the leadership of the Shi'a community at Tyre.

This community was at the bottom of Lebanon's socioeconomic scale. With modest government assistance and contributions from the community, Sadr established orphanages, clinics, schools, and vocational institutions. He launched the Institute for Islamic Studies and taught at the Amiliyya School in Beirut. To nationalize the cause of his community, Sadr joined the executive council of al-Haraka al-Ijtima'iyya, a multiconfessional movement in Beirut.

The political establishment, Christian and Muslim alike, began a campaign to discredit Sadr. He counterattacked at a press conference on 15 August 1966. He spoke of the discrimination that Shi'a Islam had long faced in Lebanon, and outlined a program of action that three years later culminated in the creation of the Supreme Islamic Shi'a Council (SISC). Sadr was elected its first chairman.

With a strong popular mandate and a clearly articulated determination to transform the status quo, Sadr fought against further Shi'a disenfranchisement. He sought to counter the pull that radical ideologies exerted on Shi'ite youth by invoking the Shi'a mythos and proposing it as an appropriate vehicle for change. On 26 May 1970, Sadr organized Lebanon's first nationwide strike in two decades to protest the government's indecisiveness in the face of Israel's devastating attacks on the frontier villages of South Lebanon.

In the early 1970s, Lebanon's capitalism was in disarray, and its territory was increasingly vulnerable to attacks by Israel. Sadr decided to increase pressure on the government. On 22 June 1973, under the aegis of the SISC and its chairman, thirteen of the nineteen Shi'a deputies in parliament signed a pact vowing not to participate in any government that did not work toward the satisfaction of the Shi'a demands. On 2 December 1974, the SISC presented the country with a set of demands ranging from full participation in the process of government to involvement in the implementation of development plans. On 19 December, 200 members of various denominations issued a statement of support for Sadr and his movement, which became known as Harakat al-Mahrumin (Movement of the Disinherited). Sadr galvanized his campaign by scheduling a "season of Shi'a rallies," which coincided with important dates on the Shi'a religious calendar, between February and May 1974.

On 13 April 1975, Lebanon's civil war began, ending Sadr's campaign for reform. Harakat al-Mahrumin gave way to Afwaj al-Muqawama al-Lubnaniyya (AMAL), which Sadr had founded in 1974 as a Shi'a militia to defend South Lebanon against Israel's incursions. After an initial flirtation with the Lebanese National Movement–Palestinian alliance, Sadr supported Syria's policy in the country, a move motivated by practical interest rather than ideology. Sadr also established a dialogue among the combatants and sought to disentangle Lebanon from the web of regional politics. Toward this end, he made a journey to Libya, where he was last seen on 31 August 1978.

Majed Halawi

Sadullah Paşa   [1838–1891]

Ottoman Turkish poet and author.

Born in Erzurum, Sadullah Paşa was educated privately. In 1853, he entered the civil service; subsequently he was appointed ambassador to Germany (1877) and to Austria (1883), where he committed suicide in Vienna. His best-known writings are a collection of poetry, *Ondokuzuncu Asır* (The Nineteenth Century), and a collection of writings, *Berlin Mektupları* (Letters from Berlin).

David Waldner

Sa'dun, Abd al-Muhsin al-   [1879–1929]

Leader of the Muntafiq tribe and Iraqi politician.

Son of Fahd Pasha al-Sa'dun, Abd al-Muhsin was head of one of the two major branches of the ruling house of the MUNTAFIQ TRIBE. He graduated from the Ottoman Military College in 1905, became aide-de-

camp to the sultan, but resigned his commission in 1909 and returned to Iraq. In 1910 and 1912 he was elected to represent the Muntafiq district in the Ottoman parliament. During the British mandate in Iraq, he headed al-Taqaddum (Progressive) party, which advocated termination of the mandate and independence through conciliation. President of the Constituent Assembly and twice president of parliament, Abd al-Muhsin held numerous cabinet portfolios and was four times prime minister. As principal Iraqi negotiator of the 1926 ANGLO–IRAQI TREATY, he obtained important amendments regarding oil, military, and finance and shepherded its ratification. He was knighted in 1926.

BIBLIOGRAPHY

IRELAND, PHILIP WILLARD. *Iraq: A Study in Political Development.* London, 1937.

Albertine Jwaideh

Sa'dun Family, al-

Ruling family of the Muntafiq in southern Iraq.

These are descendants of Mani, a sharif of Mecca who fled to the Euphrates around 1600 to escape a feud; won influence over the MUNTAFIQ TRIBES by adjudicating their disputes; and was finally acknowledged as their ruler. The family name derives from Sa'dun, a great leader who led numerous raids against the Turks before being captured and beheaded in 1741. As rulers of the powerful Muntafiq, the Sa'dun were almost independent of Turkish rule until 1870 when the Ottomans made an attempt at regular land settlement. At the behest of their shaykh, Nasir Pasha, who founded the town of Nasiriya and accepted high government office, the Sa'dun converted from tribute-receiving chiefs into regular landlords under Ottoman auspices. As a result of this "betrayal" to the Turks, the Sa'dun chiefs rapidly lost power over their tribes, whom they had reduced from landowners to tenants.

BIBLIOGRAPHY

LONGRIGG, STEPHEN HEMSLEY. *Four Centuries of Modern Iraq.* Oxford, 1925.

Albertine Jwaideh

Sa'ed, Mohammad   [1881–?]

Iranian diplomat and foreign minister.

Born in Maragheh, Mohammad Sa'ed was the son of a merchant who traded with Russia. Sa'ed spent his childhood in Russia, studied in Switzerland, returned to Iran in 1903, and began his career in the foreign service at the Iranian embassy in Turkey. He later became ambassador to the Soviet Union and Italy. In 1941 he was appointed foreign minister. After several cabinet shufflings, the prime minister could not form a majority and was forced to resign; in March 1944 the parliament gave the position to Sa'ed. Sa'ed's generally conciliatory attitude toward the Soviet Union allowed the Soviet-backed Tudeh party to hold its first congress in Iran during his tenure and many Communist representatives thus found their way into parliament. Tudeh instigated strikes in Isfahan, and Soviet intervention in government affairs led to Sa'ed's resignation in November 1944.

BIBLIOGRAPHY

AQELI, BAQER. *Iran's Prime Ministers from Moshir al-Dowleh to Bakhtiyar.* Tehran, 1991.

Neguin Yavari

Sa'edi, Gholamhossein   [1935–1985]

Iranian novelist, playwright, short-story writer, and scriptwriter.

Sa'edi, who used the pen name Gowhar Morad, was born in Tabriz and graduated from the medical school at Tehran University with a specialty in psychiatry. He was the first Iranian who seriously engaged in writing "village literature," representing a village and its population not as a romantic entity but showing its deprived and actual face. One of the most popular Iranian writers of the 1960s and 1970s in Iran, he produced several plays and collections of short stories. Sa'edi left Iran in the late 1970s for Paris, where he died. Much of his work is available in English.

BIBLIOGRAPHY

MOAYYAD, HESHMAT, ed. *Stories from Iran: A Chicago Anthology, 1921–1991.* Washington D.C, 1991.

Pardis Minuchehr

Safa, Muhammad

Syrian military officer.

Safa, a native of Aleppo, served in the Arab–Israel War of 1948 as a battalion commander under Fawzi al-Qawuqji. He was military attaché in France and in the United States (1952). He was relieved of his post after the December 1952 coup against Adib

Shishakli, and fled to Baghdad to head a "Free Syrian government." He returned, was made a colonel in 1954, and was arrested for suspected treason. He later became a chief conspirator with Iraq to install a pro-Iraq government in Syria (1956), for which he was indicted on 22 December 1956.

Charles U. Zenzie

Safed

City located in the upper Galilee region of Israel.

Situated atop a mountain at an elevation of 2,780 feet (848 m), Safed is 25 miles (40 km) north of Tiberias and 30 miles (48 km) east of Acre. Safed is not mentioned in the Bible but was cited by the Roman historian Flavius Josephus as one of the cities he fortified. The Crusaders built a fortress in Safed, and the Mamluks made it an administrative center. Safed was one of the hills from which fires were built to signal the beginning of the lunar cycle and festivals. In the sixteenth century Joseph Karo, the author of the legal rabbinical work *Shulhan Aruh* (The Set Table), and Isaac Luria, founder of practical cabala, turned Safed into a center for Jewish mysticism. In the late eighteenth century two large groups of Jews emigrated to Safed: Hasidim and their detractors, the followers of Rabbi Elijah, the Gaon of Vilnius. In 1837 an earthquake struck the area, killing 5,000.

In 1929, at a time when riots were breaking out throughout Palestine, Arabs attacked and destroyed the Jewish quarter of Safed; it was rebuilt in the 1930s. At the outbreak of the Arab-Israel War of 1948, the Jewish population in the city only numbered 2,000 out of a total of 12,000 inhabitants. When the British evacuated their position in Safed in April 1948, Arab forces attacked. Divisions of the Palmach counterattacked on May 10, 1948, putting to rout the Arab military units and the Arab population. Today the city is a center for artists and mystics.

BIBLIOGRAPHY

ROSSOFF, DAVID. *Safed: The Mystical City.* Spring Valley, N.Y. 1991.

Bryan Daves

Saffet, Mehmet Esat   [1814–1883]

Ottoman bureaucrat.

For many years Sultan Abdülaziz's scribe, Saffet was minister of trade in the mid-1860s, minister of education for three terms between 1868 and 1876, foreign minister for most of the period from 1873 to 1882 and grand vizier in 1878. His French-inspired educational reforms established structure of the state secular school system.

BIBLIOGRAPHY

SHAW, STANFORD J., and EZEL KURAL SHAW. *History of the Ottoman Empire and Modern Turkey.* Vol. 2. New York, 1977.

Elizabeth Thompson

Safir, al-

Lebanese daily newspaper established in 1974.

Al-Safir adopted a progressive, Arab nationalist policy. During the Lebanese Civil War, the newspaper opposed the confessional system in Lebanon and came out in support of reforms. Because of its opposition to the status quo, *al-Safir* journalists were threatened by the various militias operating in Lebanon. Its owner and founder Talal Salmaan escaped an assassination attempt in 1984. In May 1993, the Lebanese government ordered the newspaper to stop publication for one week.

BIBLIOGRAPHY

Arab Information Center, Beirut.

George E. Irani

Safveti Ziya   [1875–1929]

Ottoman Turkish writer.

Born in Istanbul, Safveti Ziya attended the Galatasaray Lycée. He held various government posts, and in the early years of the republic, he became chief of protocol in the Foreign Ministry. In 1896 he joined the French-influenced Servet-i Fünün literary movement. Safveti Ziya is best known for his novel *Salon Köşelerinde* (1910), a portrait of the cosmopolitan social life of Istanbul.

Elizabeth Thompson

Sagues, Albert   [1883–c. 1950]

Educator employed by Alliance Israélite Universelle.

Sagues, born in IZMIR, Turkey, was one of the most effective architects of the ALLIANCE ISRAÉLITE UNI-

VERSELLE (AIU) schools, bolstering French cultural influence in Morocco and Tunisia. His efforts proved crucial for the spread of French language and culture among urban Jews. Sagues was a school principal for the AIU in Casablanca (1909–1912), Tunis (1912–1924), and Tangier (ca. 1925–post 1945). A firm advocate of the preservation of French colonial influence in the Maghrib, Sagues opposed political Zionism while favoring a modern Hebrew cultural renaissance.

BIBLIOGRAPHY

LASKIER, MICHAEL M. *The Alliance Israélite Universelle and the Jewish Communities of Morocco: 1862–1962.* Albany, N.Y., 1983.

Michael M. Laskier

Sahara

World's largest desert.

The Sahara (in Arabic, desert) encompasses an area of 3.320 million square miles (8.6 million sq. km), stretching across eleven countries and Western Sahara, and covering nearly the entire northern region of Africa from the Atlantic Ocean to the Red Sea hills. Parts of the Sahara reach all the way north to the Mediterranean; to the south, it extends nearly fifteen hundred miles (2,400 km). The two countries with the highest percentage of desert are Libya (99 percent) and Egypt (98 percent). Fifteen percent of the Sahara consists of sand "seas"; the rest is a mixture of *hammada* (barren rocky plateaus), coarse gravel, two mountain chains in the central regions—with the highest point being 11,204 feet (3,417 m) at

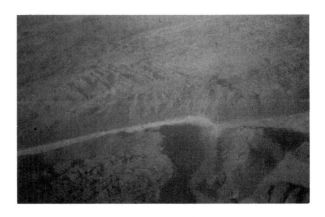

A dry riverbed in the Tassili mountains of the southern Sahara. (Richard Bulliet)

Mountains in the Erg Admer sand sea. (Richard Bulliet)

the peak of Emi Koussi in Chad—low lands, depressions—the lowest point being 436 feet (133 m) below sea level at the Qattara depression in western Egypt—oases, and transition zones.

The Nile and Niger are its only two permanent rivers. Transition zones receive between five and ten inches (12.7 and 25.4 cm) of rain per year; most of the rest receives less than five inches (12.7 cm). Large portions of the area receive no rainfall for years at a time. Its climate is among the most inhospitable—the highest evaporation rates, highest temperatures, and lowest humidity (a life-threatening 2.5 percent) have all been registered there. Extreme wind velocities and massive drops in nighttime temperatures, sometimes to sub-freezing level, are also a regular feature of the Sahara.

Desertification has slowly encroached upon previous transition zones, such as the *sahel* belt of vegetation covering fossil sand dunes that separate the

The Serpentine Dunes of the Erg Issaouane. (Richard Bulliet)

Sahara from Equatorial Africa; some also occurs in Arab North African countries. The reasons for the Sahara's continuing expansion range from climatic changes to some direct human influence, such as overgrazing by sheep herds and wood gathering for fuel. The most important minerals found in the Sahara include petroleum and natural gas fields, uranium, phosphates, iron ore, and a long list of other metals.

The four main ethnic groups of the Sahara are all predominantly Berber in origin: the Arabo-Berbers in the north; the Moors (Maures), a mixture of Arab, Berber, and black African groups in the southwestern regions (encompassing parts of present-day Mauritania, Mali, and Western Sahara); the distinctive Twaregs, the most numerous of the four, of the south-central area; and the Tibu of the Tibesti area of Chad, who are also of Berber and black African mixture. Apart from livestock grazing, the old traditional economy included a profitable trade in gold and slaves from West Africa, salt from the desert, and cloth and other products from the Mediterranean coast. The camel, probably introduced in the second century B.C.E., was the backbone of trans-Saharan trade.

Before the prolonged droughts of the 1970s and 1980s, best estimates of the Sahara's population were approximately two million persons; about two-thirds were concentrated in oases; the rest engaged in seasonal movements and some were purely nomadic. In Arab North Africa, sedentarization had become almost complete, owing to the erosion of the pastoral economic base. Both "push" and "pull" factors were at work: desertification, which reduced livestock herds; displacement stemming from anticolonial struggles; the exploitation of oil and gas fields, which provided employment; and the extension of governmental authority, resulting in increased enclosure of land for farming, as well as expanded health and education services.

Historically, the Sahara was a large barrier to aspiring conquerors—Egyptians, Romans, Carthaginians, and Arabs. Islam spread steadily, however, in part from the activities of Muslim traders and scholars. Explorers from Britain and France began to penetrate the Sahara in the early part of the nineteenth century. French conquests began in 1830. Political boundaries in the Sahara were defined only in the late nineteenth and the twentieth centuries. Much was left imprecise by the French, who ruled over most of the region, resulting in a number of border disputes after decolonization, including those between Morocco and Algeria over the Tindouf area, and Libya and Chad with regard to the Aozou strip.

Bruce Maddy-Weitzman

Saharan Arab Democratic Republic

The official government-in-exile of POLISARIO, known as SADR.

The founding of SADR was proclaimed at Bir Lehlou, a town in northwestern Western Sahara, on February 27, 1976, one day after the departure of Spain's authorities from the territory, by a previously established Provisional Sahrawi National Council. Its constitution, adopted at the third POLISARIO Congress in August 1976, proclaimed SADR to be a "democratic Arab republic," with a "republican political system." SADR was declared part of the Arab nation and Islam the state religion. Fundamental objectives included socialism, social justice, and the attainment of Maghrib unity as a step toward Arab and African unity. Polisario's executive committee was charged with presiding over SADR's executive organ until independence and sovereignty were attained. POLISARIO's August 1991 congress adopted a new draft constitution for the future Saharan state, including provisions for a multiparty system, a free enterprise economy (with strategic resources controlled by the state), universal suffrage, a free press, and cooperative relations with Morocco.

SADR's main value for POLISARIO has been in the diplomatic sphere: it attained recognition from more than seventy countries, and, after years of struggle, assumed its seat in 1984 as a full member of the Organization of African Unity (OAU), triggering a Moroccan walkout. In contrast to the OAU, the League of Arab States (Arab League) kept SADR and POLISARIO at arm's length.

BIBLIOGRAPHY

DAMIS, JOHN. *Conflict in Northwest Africa: The Western Sahara Dispute.* Palo Alto, Calif., 1983.
HODGES, TONY. *Historical Dictionary of Western Sahara.* Metuchen, N.J., 1982.
———. *Western Sahara: The Roots of a Desert War.* Westport, Conn., 1983.

Bruce Maddy-Weitzman

Sahib ibn Isa

Paramount shaykh of Oman's powerful Hirth tribe, 1947–1955.

Sahib ibn Isa was a major leader of the conservative Ibadi imamate that dominated Oman's interior. With the imamate's suppression he fled and labored ineffectually into the 1970s in Saudi Arabia, Iraq, and Egypt to reestablish the independent status of interior Oman.

BIBLIOGRAPHY

WILKINSON, JOHN C. *The Imamate Tradition of Oman.* Cambridge, U.K., 1987.

Robert G. Landen

Sahil

The eastward-facing coastal region of Tunisia.

The Sahil is a fertile plain connecting the steppes of the interior of Tunisia to the Mediterranean seacoast. In its narrow use, the term refers to the area approximately from Hergla in the north to Mahdia in the south, although broader definitions of the Sahil include Sfax and go as far south as Gabes. The core of the Sahil is the old fortified towns of Sousse, Monastir, and Mahdia, which protected Kairouan—the first major Arab-Islamic capital of the Maghrib (North Africa)—from the sea. The Sahil has many villages, each with its distinct identity and separate market day. Gradually, the Sahil has turned to agriculture, and in the nineteenth and twentieth centuries, grazing land on the plain has given way to olive orchards and truck farms. Since Tunisian independence in 1956, the coast has been lined with many tourist hotels. The Sahil is also the birthplace of many of Tunisia's government officials and Tunisia's first two presidents (Habib Bourguiba, from Monastir; Zayn al-Abidine Ben Ali, from Hammam-Sousse).

BIBLIOGRAPHY

DESPOIS, JEAN. *La Tunisie orientale, Sahel et basse steppe: Etude géographique,* 2nd ed. Paris, 1955.

Laurence Michalak

Sa'id [1822–1863]

Son of Muhammad Ali and governor of the semiautonomous province of Ottoman Egypt, 1854–1863.

Sa'id's childhood friendship with the French consul, Ferdinand de Lesseps, paved the way for the latter's concession to build the Suez Canal. Increasing European penetration of the country under the pro-French Sa'id hastened Egypt down the road to British occupation in 1882.

BIBLIOGRAPHY

HUNTER, F. ROBERT. *Egypt under the Khedives, 1805–1879.* Pittsburgh, 1984.

Donald Malcolm Reid

Sa'id, Ali Ahmad

See Adonis

Sa'id, Nuri al-   [1888–1958]

Frequent minister or prime minister of Iraq and one of Iraq's leading statesmen from 1921 to 1958.

Nuri al-Sa'id was born in Baghdad during the Ottoman Empire into a middle-class Sunni Islamic family of Arab Turkish stock. At an early age he was enrolled in primary religious school before going to the Ottoman military secondary school. Later he attended the military college in Istanbul and was graduated an officer in 1906. He returned to Baghdad where he worked in an army unit responsible for collecting taxes from tribesmen, a position that enabled him to travel, to gain intimate knowledge of the country, and to establish contacts with shaykhs (tribal leaders), which he later used to his political advantage. In 1910, Nuri returned to Istanbul to attend the Ottoman staff college. In 1912, the year he graduated, he saw action against Bulgaria in the Balkan Wars.

In his youth, Nuri believed in Arab nationalism and the modernization of the Ottoman Empire (along the lines of the principles of the Young Turks, who seized power in Istanbul in 1909). He was, however, disillusioned by their anti-Arab policy and in 1913 joined al-Ahd (the Covenant), a secret society supporting self-determination for Arabs. When the Turks became suspicious of his activities, Nuri, fearing arrest, fled to Cairo, Egypt, in the spring of 1914. From there he went to Basra (Iraq), where he aligned himself with Sayyid Talib Pasha al-Naqib, a well-known leader of the Arab cause and the head of a local important family.

Nuri was in a Basra hospital, recovering from an illness, when the British seized the city at the beginning of World War I. They arrested him as an Ottoman officer and sent him to India, where he was put under loose house arrest.

Nuri was released in 1915 and left India for Cairo where, encouraged by the British, he joined the movement of Sharif Husayn ibn Ali of Mecca, who had called for Arab independence from the Turks. Nuri played a major military role in the revolt (which Sharif Husayn finally proclaimed) against the Turks on June 5, 1916.

With the collapse of the Ottoman Empire at the end of World War I, Nuri became chief of staff for Prince Faisal I ibn Husayn, one of the sons of Sharif Husayn. He went with Faisal to Paris and London as an adviser during the peace talks.

In 1920, the British were awarded a mandate over Iraq by the League of Nations and established an indigenous Iraqi government. Ja'far al-Askari, Nuri's brother-in-law, became minister of defense and called Nuri to Iraq, where he was nominated chief of staff of the army. The following year, Faisal became king of Iraq, an objective at which Nuri had worked hard. In the years that followed, Nuri was active in building the Iraqi army and police.

In 1929, Nuri assumed the first of his many prime ministeries. It was he who negotiated the Anglo–Iraqi treaty of 1930, which officially ended the British mandate over Iraq, but which allowed Britain military bases and an assured influence in Iraq until 1955. His ability to secure its passage through parliament led the British to appreciate Nuri's skills and personality. This act inaugurated his long career as Iraq's dominant politician and demonstrated his strong belief in collaboration with the British. These British leanings met with strong opposition from nationalists, however, who wanted complete independence. In dealing with the opposition, Nuri used tactics for which he later became famous—censorship of the press, proroguing parliament, and manipulating elections.

In 1936, Ja'far al-Askari was killed in a military coup, and a number of the pro-British politicians were removed. Nuri left Baghdad for Cairo in self-imposed exile and did not return until October 1937.

King Ghazi ibn Faisal of Iraq, who inherited the throne in 1933, died in a 1939 automobile accident. His infant son Faisal II ibn Ghazi was declared king, and his uncle Abd al-Ilah ibn Ali became regent, with Nuri's blessing.

After his return to Iraq, Nuri began to associate with a group of rising Arab nationalist military officers, who became prominent after the 1936 coup. They frequently intervened in politics, with Nuri's connivance. The harmony between Nuri and these officers slowly dissipated, however, after the beginning of World War II. While Nuri advocated a pro-British stand during the war, the officers slowly shifted to a pro-Axis one. The tension between the two camps rose when the British, fearing direct intervention from Nazi Germany, landed troops in southern Iraq. The nationalist officers staged a coup in May 1941, and the regent and Nuri fled the country. After encountering some resistance, the British were able to quell the nationalist movement and gain control of Baghdad.

The regent then returned to Baghdad, and a pro-British government headed by Jamil al-Midfa'i, was formed. Nuri chose to stay in Cairo as ambassador but was called back in October 1941 to head a new cabinet as prime minister, a post he held until 1944. During that period Nuri worked closely with the British in prosecuting both nationalist officers and civilians; they were arrested, tried, and in some cases executed. These measures left a deep wound among Iraqis, who had considerable sympathy toward the nationalists. Soon, most of the Iraqis lost faith in Nuri and became critical of both his policies and his leadership.

Nuri kept Iraq quiet for the remainder of the war, but the war left its imprint on Iraq. A high inflation rate and the widening gap between poor and rich allowed the leftists, a small but aggressive group, to gain strength. They became a target of suppression by Nuri and his successors.

Nuri was the first to advocate a council or League of Arab States, even before the end of the war. He was successful in launching his idea when a protocol for the foundation of the Arab League (as it is also called) was signed in Alexandria, in 1944.

In the postwar period, Nuri's influence over Iraq was unchallenged; even when he did not hold office he was able to steer the body politic in the direction he desired. A pro-Nuri majority was assured in parliament—especially among rich landlords and shaykhs. Nuri used this position to gain support among the Shi'ites and the Kurds. When the Kurdish leader Mulla Mustapha al-Barzani revolted in 1945, Nuri—with the backing of the British—crushed the revolt and compelled him to take refuge outside Iraq.

With the rise of petroleum prices and Iraq's increased oil income, Nuri turned part of his attention to the establishment of an economic development program. In 1950, Nuri engineered the passage of a law establishing a development board, composed of Iraqi and foreign experts, to lay down a five-year development plan. Between 1950 and 1958, four such plans were passed, and some 70 percent of oil revenue was devoted to Iraq's long-term development.

In 1952, Nuri negotiated a 50–50 split of oil revenues with the Iraq Petroleum Company (IPC). Between 1951 and 1958, Iraq's oil revenues rose dramatically from 32 million to 237 million U.S. dollars. Iraq's dependence on oil revenues rose, too. By 1958, oil revenues accounted for 28 percent of Gross National Product and 60 percent of the budget. Increased oil revenues were not accompanied by a change in social structure; rich landlords and tribal shaykhs gained title to much of the arable land, while urban merchants grew increasingly wealthy on government contracts.

The development of Iraq's human resources also lagged behind its needs. Between 1950 and 1958, although higher-education institutions expanded, by 1958 they still graduated only a few thousand students a year, and secondary education remained concentrated in urban areas. Opposition to the regime

increasingly erupted in street violence. In 1952, when a riot broke out at the College of Pharmacy in Baghdad, it quickly spread throughout Iraq, so a military government was appointed to maintain order.

Between 1952 and 1958, regional Arab issues played a dominant role in internal politics. In 1952 a coup d'état in Egypt brought to power a group of Arab nationalist military officers, led by Gamal Abdel Nasser. The fall of King Farouk's monarchy in Egypt and the anti-Western tone taken by the new Egyptian regime had broad effects in the Arab world—particularly in Iraq, where the regime was pro-West. These events helped to destabilize Iraq's regime and eventually led to its fall.

The 1930 Anglo–Iraqi treaty was due to expire in 1955, and Nuri was searching for a vehicle to replace it. Britain proposed what became known as the Baghdad Pact, which would include the northern tier of the Middle East—Iran, Turkey, and Pakistan—as a new shield against Communism. Nuri wanted to include Kuwait and even Egypt, but Nasser would have nothing to do with any instrument tied to the West. Nuri's most significant impact on Iraq was in foreign policy, since he tied Iraq to the Western alliance and the Baghdad Pact. This provided for a shield against encroachment from the Soviet Union but seriously isolated Iraq from its Arab neighbors. The group of agreements that constituted the Baghdad Pact was signed in 1955—between Iraq, Turkey, Britain, Iran, and Pakistan.

The Iraqi people virtually rejected the pact. Eventually, Nuri dissolved parliament and fostered the election of a majority that favored his policies. Thus was the pact effected. In 1956, Egypt's President Nasser nationalized the Suez Canal, and England, France, and Israel attacked Egypt, taking the canal. Iraqi popular opposition to Nuri's regime then intensified and, faced with uprisings, Nuri imposed martial law to bring about control.

In February 1958, Egypt and Syria announced the formation of the United Arab Republic. Popular support for this union was strong in Iraq and Jordan, but the governments of these two countries saw it as a serious threat to their regimes; a federation between Iraq and Jordan was then announced. Nuri's last post was that of the federation's prime minister—and one of his last political acts was an attempt to bring Kuwait into the federation.

In 1957, while Nuri was involved in foreign policy, four opposition parties—the Istiqlal (Independence), National Democratic, Ba'th, and Communist parties—joined together as a national front against the Iraqi government. Far more serious opposition to the regime came from the army, where junior officers were busy organizing military cells to topple the monarchy. Nuri downplayed as insignificant warnings of trouble in the army.

In May 1958, civil war broke out in Lebanon. The Jordanian government, fearing the war might spill over, asked its federation partner, Iraq, to send troops to Jordan. On July 14, 1958, they complied. Nevertheless, under the command of the Free Officers, Iraqi troops also occupied strategic points in Baghdad—the ministry of defense, the radio station, and the king's palace. The monarchy was abolished, and the Republic of Iraq was declared. The king and the regent were killed, and Nuri escaped from his residence—but the following day, fleeing in the streets disguised as a woman, he was shot dead. His only son, Sabah, was also killed during the coup.

The new Iraqi government under Prime Minister Abd al-Karim al-Kassem dismantled much of Nuri's work, dissolved the federation with Jordan, and allowed Iraq's membership in the Baghdad Pact to lapse. Political ties with the Soviet Union, severed in 1954, were reestablished, and Iraq turned to the Soviet bloc for arms. Rapprochement with Egypt's Nasser was brief, and the revolution failed to eliminate the most lasting contributions of Nuri and the British—the Iraqi state and its two foundations, the army and the bureaucracy.

BIBLIOGRAPHY

BATATU, HANNA. *The Old Social Classes and the Revolutionary Movements of Iraq*. Princeton, N.J., 1978.
BIRDWOOD, LORD. *Nuri as-Said*. London, 1959.
GALLMAN, WALDEMAR J. *Iraq under General Nuri*. Baltimore, 1964.
KHADDURI, MAJID. *Independent Iraq, 1932–1958: A Study of Iraqi Politics*. London, 1960.
LONGRIGG, STEPHEN. *Iraq, 1900–1950*. London, 1953.
MARR, PHEBE. *A Modern History of Iraq*. Boulder, Colo., 1985.

Louay Bahry

Sa'id al-Mufti   [1896–   ]

Prime minister of Jordan four times between 1950 and 1956.

A member of the ethnic Circassian minority in Jordan, Sa'id al-Mufti was considered to be loyal to the monarchy and pro-establishment and was noted for his integrity. As interior minister, he supervised the elections of August 29, 1951. He was prime minister from May to December 1955 during the period when Britain was conducting serious negotiations with Jordan to join the alliance with Turkey and Iraq, known popularly as the Baghdad Pact. But he

was replaced by Hazza' al-Majali on December 15 because King Hussein ibn Talal thought Majali had a better chance of pushing the alliance through parliament. Mufti's cabinet was divided on the issue, with several members threatening to resign if Jordan joined the alliance, particularly since Egypt, Syria, and Saudi Arabia had declined to join. Cabinet members who supported the alliance had hopes of winning greater military and economic support for Jordan from the West, though there were reservations about the impact of the alliance on the Arab–Israeli issue and inter-Arab relations. The divisions in the cabinet reflected a larger rift along Palestinian–Jordanian lines, with the former largely opposing the Baghdad Pact and the latter supporting it. Mufti favored the alliance as long as it was clearly in the interests of Jordan and did not jeopardize Arab claims to Palestine. Mufti became prime minister again (May–July 1956), briefly taking over the position from Samir Rifa'i.

BIBLIOGRAPHY

MADI, MUNIB, and SALAYMAN MUSA. *Tarikh al-Urdun fi al-qarn al-ishrin, 1900–1959*. Amman, 1988.

Jenab Tutunji

Sa'id Aql   [1912–   ]

One of Lebanon's most prominent poets and intellectuals, whose career spans the 1930s to the 1990s.

Born in Zahle, Lebanon, Sa'id Aql is the foremost representative of the symbolist movement in Arabic poetry. He once noted that poetry's power derives from its ability to hint at and allude to something. His poems indeed are rarely explicit; instead they are characterized by images and a gifted use of words to convey emotions. A prolific writer, he is the author of some thirty books, plays, and anthologies, several written in French. Early in his career, he became the leading proponent of "Lebanonism," according to which modern-day Lebanese are viewed as the descendants of the ancient Phoenicians and thus as having a separate Lebanese identity that has little to do with Islam or Arabism. Aql has argued that the distinctiveness of the Lebanese people is also reflected in a separate language, Lebanese, which he regards as being more than merely a dialect of Arabic. He even developed a version of the Latin alphabet that he thought was better suited to the Lebanese language, and he has repeatedly contended that Lebanon's children should be taught this language instead of standard classical or modern Arabic.

In the 1930s, his ideas found a favorable reception among Maronites who were trying to build a Lebanese Christian brand of nationalism that emphasized distinguishing Lebanon from its Arab Muslim environment. Although the appeal of Lebanonism declined after Lebanon became independent in 1943, Aql's ideas were revived in the 1970s, when they served to inspire the Guardians of the Cedars, a quasi-fascistic, violently anti-Palestinian Maronite militia whose proclaimed mission it was to fight for the survival of a Christian Lebanon. Sa'id Aql also founded The World's Most Beautiful Books publishing house in 1968 and the weekly *Lebnaan* in 1975.

BIBLIOGRAPHY

ALLEN, ROGER, ed. *Modern Arabic Literature*. New York, 1987.
NASR, NAGI. *Said Aql Philosopher*. Beirut, 1980.
RABINOVICH, ITAMAR. *The War for Lebanon, 1970–1985*. Ithaca, N.Y., 1985.

Guilain P. Denoeux

Saimi, Shams al-Din [1850–1904]

Tanzimat writer, lexicographer, and encyclopedist.

Shams al-Din Saimi, also known as Şemsettin Sami, was born at Frasheri in the province of Janina (Ioannina), Albania, and educated at a Greek school. In 1872 he moved to Constantinople (now Istanbul), where he began a career that included government service and writing for or publishing newspapers and journals including *İbret*, *Sabah*, *Tercüman-i Şark*, and *Muharrir*. He was a pioneer in the development of a Western-style Ottoman literature, publishing translations and writing what is generally considered to be the first Turkish novel, *Taaşşuk-i Talat ve Fitnat* (The Romance of Talat and Finat), a work drawing attention to the evils of arranged marriages (1872). The first of his three plays, *Besa yahut Ahde Vefa* (The Pledge, or Keeping to One's Oath), reflecting the unrest in Albania, was performed in 1874; as a result, Shams al-Din spent a period of exile in Tripoli, where he assumed editorship of the newspaper *Trablusgarb* (1874–1875).

Although he later gained the support of Abdülhamit II and worked in government service, Shams al-Din always remained suspect and under surveillance because of his Albanian interests, which included a proposal for a Latin script for Albanian and the development of an Albanian literature separate from the Ottoman. He is best remembered

for his study of early Turkic inscriptions; the compilation of Turkish–French and French–Turkish dictionaries; a Turkish dictionary (*Kamus-i Türki*); a general encyclopedia (The Dictionary of Proper Names) that included biographies of major political and literary figures; and a series of studies known as Cep Kütüphanesi (Pocket Library), an encyclopedia in serial form that included classics of Islamic and Ottoman literature as well as general modern knowledge. Shams al-Din also promoted the simplification of Ottoman Turkish and wrote in support of *Türkçe Şiirler* (Poems in Turkish) by Mehmet Emin YURDAKUL.

BIBLIOGRAPHY

EVIN, AHMET Ö. *Origins and Development of the Turkish Novel*. Minneapolis, Minn., 1983.
FINN, ROBERT P. *The Early Turkish Novel, 1872–1900*. Istanbul, 1984.
SHAW, STANFORD J., and EZEL KURAL SHAW. *History of the Ottoman Empire and Modern Turkey*, vol. 2. Cambridge, U.K., 1977.

Kathleen R. F. Burrill

Saint Catherine's Monastery

A Christian monastery in Egypt's Sinai peninsula.

Saint Catherine's Monastery is located approximately four miles (6 km) from Mount Sinai in the Sinai peninsula, Egypt. In 337, the first chapel on the site was built by order of the Empress Helena of Byzantium. The valley was sacred because it was believed that Moses had talked to God in the burning bush near where the monastery now stands. In the sixth century, Emperor Justinian constructed the Church of the Transfiguration and walls to fortify the monastery; the architect was Saint Stephanos. The church and monastery were given their present name of Saint Catherine in the ninth century after monks found what they thought was the body of Catherine the martyr, who had perished centuries before in Alexandria. Between the fourteenth and seventeenth centuries, the monastery was often abandoned, and though there was a brief resurgence since then, it presently houses fewer than twenty monks. Visitors to Mount Sinai pass by the monastery on their way to the summit, and the monks allow visitors for a limited number of hours each week.

BIBLIOGRAPHY

Blue Guide: Egypt.

Zachary Karabell

Saint Helena

British island in South Atlantic Ocean.

This volcanic island is situated in the middle of the South Atlantic Ocean, some 1,200 miles (1,900 km) west of Africa and 680 miles (1,100 km) southeast of Ascension island. About 4,800 people (1987) live on the 47 square miles (122 sq. km). Saint Helena has no industry and produces only staple foodstuffs for local consumption.

From 1659, when the British captured the island from the Dutch, to the opening of the Suez Canal in 1869, the harbor at Jamestown served as an important port of call for British vessels sailing between India and Europe by way of the Cape of Good Hope. The French emperor Napoléon Bonaparte was exiled here in 1815, and in 1834 the territory was proclaimed a British crown colony.

Political prisoners continued to be transported to the island well into the twentieth century: In December 1956, for example, the ruler of Bahrain requested that three of the leaders of that country's nationalist movement, who had just been sentenced to fourteen years' imprisonment by a local court, be exiled to Saint Helena to serve out their sentences. This arrangement caused a stir in the British House of Commons but was upheld on appeal.

BIBLIOGRAPHY

DRYSDALE, A., and G. H. BLAKE. *The Middle East and North Africa: A Political Geography.* Oxford, 1985.
AL-RUMAIHI, MOHAMMED GHANIM. *Bahrain: A Study on Social and Political Changes since the First World War.* Kuwait, 1975.

Fred H. Lawson

Saint James Conference

See London Conference

Saint-Jean-de-Maurienne, Treaty of

Secret World War I agreement concerning the postwar division of the Ottoman Empire.

The Treaty of Saint-Jean-de-Maurienne was signed April 17, 1917, on the French–Italian border by representatives of the European allies: Great Britain, France, and Italy. This agreement, dealing specifically with Anatolia, was the last of a series of secret wartime pacts dividing up the territorial spoils of the Central powers (Germany, Austria-Hungary, and the Ottoman Empire) among the allies in case the Central powers were defeated in the ongoing conflict.

The meeting at Saint-Jean-de-Maurienne was convened to reconcile conflicting French and Italian claims to southwestern Anatolia. The treaty secured Italian acquiescence to the terms of the SYKES–PICOT AGREEMENT of 1916. If the allies were victorious, France was to receive the Adana region, and Italy would take control of the rest of southwestern Anatolia, an area which included Konya and İzmir.

The allies signed the treaty subject to Russian approval. Representatives of czarist Russia did not attend the conference as their government had just fallen to the Bolsheviks.

At the postwar Paris Peace Conference, Greek Prime Minister Eleuthérios Venizélos requested that his country be given control of İzmir. Thus, the Italian provision of the Saint-Jean-de-Maurienne treaty was overridden in 1919.

BIBLIOGRAPHY

FROMKIN, DAVID. *A Peace to End All Peace.* New York, 1989.
SHAW, STANFORD, and EZEL KURAL SHAW. *History of the Ottoman Empire and Modern Turkey.* New York, 1977.

Zachary Karabell

Saint Joseph University

Jesuit university in Lebanon.

Saint Joseph University, established in 1875, was administered by the Society of Jesus and had strong ties to the University of Lyons in France. It had branches in Tripoli, Sidon, and Zahla. French is the primary language of instruction, although some courses are offered in English and in Arabic. The Department of Arabic and Oriental Studies is considered very strong. Faculties in 1994 included theology, medicine, pharmacy, dentistry, engineering, law and political science, economics and business administration, and letters and humanities.

As'ad AbuKhalil

Saint Mark's Cathedral

Seat of the Coptic patriarchate.

Built in the 1970s, Saint Mark's Cathedral provided a new seat of the Coptic patriarchate and a cultural and religious focal point for Egypt's COPTS, one of the largest and most important Christian minorities in the Middle East. On 2 June 1968, the relics of Saint Mark were returned to the Coptic church by Pope Paul VI with great fanfare. They are now interred beneath the main altar of Saint Mark's and lend the cathedral an enhanced importance and venerability. Located in the once-fashionable Abbassiya district of greater Cairo, the cathedral offers Coptic rite services in Arabic, English, and French.

Raymond William Baker

Sa'iqa

Palestinian guerilla organization.

Officially known as the Organization of the Vanguards of the Popular Liberation War—Forces of the Thunderbolt, this Palestinian organization represents the pro-Syrian wing of the BA'TH party within the Palestinian national movement. Sa'iqa was founded by Palestinian Ba'thists in 1968, following a 1966 resolution by the party's pan-Arab leadership to create a Palestinian chapter. (The rival, pro-Iraqi wing of the party later established the Arab Liberation Front.) The militant environment of post-1967 Palestinian politics, and Syria's desire for influence within the emergent Palestinian guerilla movement, dictated the group's military character.

Sa'iqa joined the PALESTINE LIBERATION ORGANIZATION (PLO) in February 1969. Until Syria's 1976 intervention in Lebanon, which brought Damascus into direct conflict with the PLO but was openly supported by Sa'iqa, the latter was generally (though not consistently) associated with the PLO mainstream and al-FATH in particular. Relations thereafter deteriorated, however, to the point where Sa'iqa was one of only two PLO factions to join the 1983 al-Fath rebellion against PLO Chairman Yasir Arafat, and it has since boycotted all PLO institutions. It was a founding member of the Syrian-sponsored anti-Arafat National Alliance in 1984, and in 1985 it joined the Palestinian National Salvation Front headquartered in Damascus. Sa'iqa currently belongs to the Group of Ten, an association of Palestinian factions opposed to PLO strategy and/or Palestinian participation in the U.S.- and USSR-sponsored negotiations with Israel. The Group of Ten also reject the process inaugurated by the September 1993 Israeli–Palestinian Declaration of Principles.

A number of Sa'iqa's founders, including its first secretary-general, Dafi Jumani, were ousted in 1970 by the new Syrian regime of Hafiz al-Asad in con-

nection with internal Syrian power struggles in which Sa'iqa had become involved on the losing side. At Syrian insistence, Jumani was replaced by Mahmud al-Ma'ita and, in 1971, by Zuhayr Muhsin. Assassinated in Cannes, France, in July 1979 under circumstances that remain unclear, Muhsin was succeeded by Issam al-Qadi. The organization's publications include *al-Tala'i* (The Vanguards), an Arabic weekly, that first appeared in 1969, and its internal bulletin, *al-Sa'iqa*. It publishes occasional pamphlets as well.

Throughout its existence, Sa'iqa has received its political, military, and financial support from Syria, whose Palestinian refugee camps and whose own military also provide most of the group's recruits. Sa'iqa's policies on Palestinian, regional, and international questions have traditionally been either indistinguishable from those of Damascus or calculated to serve a specific Syrian interest within the Palestinian national movement. On the strength of Syrian patronage, Sa'iqa was for many years the second largest constituent member of the PLO and acquired a generous quota of seats in the Palestine National Council and the PLO Executive Committee. However, its negligible presence in the occupied Palestinian territories and other arenas beyond Syrian control attests to its significantly weaker political standing and to widespread resentment of its role as an instrument of Syrian policy.

Militarily undistinguished, Sa'iqa has since 1976 become an increasingly marginalized organization. Its support that year of Syria's intervention in Lebanon led to mass defections from its ranks and its total elimination from areas under the control of the PLO and the Lebanese National movement. In the process, the original ambition to establish an autonomous movement for all Palestinian Ba'thists (of which only a pretence had survived) and the modicum of autonomy the group had enjoyed in Amman and then Beirut were lost as it became completely dependent upon Damascus.

Sa'iqa's absence during the 1982 siege of Beirut and its open collusion with Syria in the latter's efforts to impose its hegemony over the PLO and Lebanon during the 1980s (including the presence of regular Syrian soldiers among its ranks) have strained its credibility to the limit. As the Palestinian faction most closely associated with Syrian interests, and one that remains firmly outside the PLO framework, its fortunes will continue to reflect the state of Syrian–Palestinian relations and its lack of independence. Similarly, an Israeli–Syrian political settlement, and even more so the removal of the Ba'th party from power in Damascus, would entail dire prospects for Sa'iqa.

BIBLIOGRAPHY

COBBAN, HELENA. *The Palestinian Liberation Organisation: People, Power and Politics.* Cambridge, U.K., 1984.

GRESH, ALAIN. *The PLO—the Struggle Within: Towards an Independent Palestinian State,* rev. ed. Tr. by A. M. Berrett. London, 1988.

QUANDT, WILLIAM B., et al. *The Politics of Palestinian Nationalism.* Berkeley, Calif., 1973.

Mouin Rabbani

Saison

Retaliation operation authorized by one Zionist group against another in British-mandated Palestine.

Saison, meaning "the hunting season," was an operation authorized by David Ben-Gurion from November 1944 to March 1945, using the Haganah (which became the Israel Defense Forces) against the militant IRGUN ZVA'I LE'UMI (IZL).

The murder of Lord Moyne, the resident British minister in the Middle East, by the LEHI (Lohamei Herut Yisrael; a splinter group of IZL) led Ben-Gurion to cooperate with the British. Lists of names were given to the British police and, in some cases, Haganah members gave IZL members directly to the British. The IZL did not retaliate, and the Saison caused no further actions by IZL until the end of World War II.

BIBLIOGRAPHY

BAR-ZOHAR, MICHAEL. *Ben-Gurion: A Biography.* New York, 1977.

Miriam Simon

Sait, Küçük   [1838–1914]

Ottoman grand vizier.

Born in Erzurum, Sait entered government service and rose to become Abdülhamit II's chief scribe. As grand vizier (1879–1885, 1895, 1900), he was the architect of many of Abdülhamit's reforms. An elder statesman respected by liberals, he was grand vizier three times after the constitutional revolution.

BIBLIOGRAPHY

LEWIS, BERNARD. *The Emergence of Modern Turkey.* New York, 1961.

SHAW, STANFORD J., and EZEL KURAL SHAW. *History of the Ottoman Empire and Modern Turkey,* vol. 2. New York, 1977.

Elizabeth Thompson

Sait Halim   [1863–1921]

Ottoman grand vizier.

An Egyptian prince and grandson of Muhammad Ali, Sait Halim entered Ottoman politics in the early twentieth century and wrote several works advocating an Islamic revival. While a member of Parliament, he allied with the COMMITTEE OF UNION AND PROGRESS (CUP).

In 1913, Sait Halim was chosen by CUP leaders to replace Grand Vizier Mahmut Şevket, assassinated by CUP opponents. He served from June 12, 1913, to February 3, 1917. He was in essence a puppet of the CUP, whose triumvirate of leaders—Enver, Talat, and Cemal—held true authority in the empire during World War I. Although he was directly involved in the negotiations that led to alliance with Germany, Sait Halim grew increasingly disillusioned with the triumvirate's conduct of war policy. He resigned in protest and was replaced by Talat. In 1918 Sait Halim, along with Young Turk and other intellectual leaders, was arrested after the Allies occupied Constantinople.

BIBLIOGRAPHY

LEWIS, BERNARD. *The Emergence of Modern Turkey.* New York, 1961.

SHAW, STANFORD J., and EZEL KURAL SHAW. *History of the Ottoman Empire and Modern Turkey,* vol. 2. New York, 1977.

Elizabeth Thompson

Sakakini, Khalil al-   [1878–1953]

Palestinian writer and educator.

Born in Jerusalem to a Greek Orthodox family, Sakakini's early life was devoted to Arab letters. In 1909, he founded the Dusturiyya school in Jerusalem, which developed an influential model for a secular, Arab curriculum. Also before World War I, he played a leading role in the Nahda Urthuduksiyya (Orthodox Revival) movement. During the mandate period in Palestine, Sakakini continued his advocacy of public education and became principal of the Dar al-Mu'allimin (Teacher's College) in Jerusalem. He is perhaps best remembered for his books on teaching Arabic to beginners, some of which are still used in the Arab world.

Sakakini also participated in the early Palestinian national movement, and his diaries are an important source for scholars of the period. He argued that Jewish immigration threatened to disrupt the unity of Arabic culture. An ardent pan-Arabist, he admired

Faisal I, who led the Arab revolt of 1916 and, from 1921 to 1933, was King of Iraq. In 1923, Sakakini became secretary for the ARAB EXECUTIVE Committee in Jerusalem. He and his family fled to Cairo in early 1948, during the Arab–Israel War.

BIBLIOGRAPHY

KEDOURIE, ELIE. "Religion and Politics: The Diaries of Khalil Sakakini." *St. Anthony's Papers* 4: 77–94 (1970s).

MANDEL, NEVILLE J. *The Arabs and Zionism Before World War I.* Berkeley, 1976.

SAKAKINI, KHALIL. *Kadha Ana Ya Dunya: Yawmiyyat Khalil Sakakini* (Such Am I, O World). Jerusalem, 1955.

ZIADEH, FARHAT J. *A Reader in Modern Literary Arabic.* Seattle, 1981.

Elizabeth Thompson

Şakir Ağa [1779–1840]

Ottoman Turkish composer.

Born in Vezirköprü, the son of a wealthy merchant from the Crimea, Şakir Ağa, also known as Haci İzzet, studied at the Enderun-i Hümayun (Royal Academy), training in singing, violin, and tambour. Subsequently he entered the sultan's household. Of his seventy-one extant works, sixty-six are in the *şarki* genre.

David Waldner

Salafiyya Movement

Modernist Islamic intellectual movement of the nineteenth and twentieth centuries, which had some following among Sunni elites living in the Ottoman Empire.

The Salafiyya movement sought to engineer a religious revival and reform that would incorporate Western conceptions of modernity and assert the religious and cultural identity of Islam at the same time. The most prominent spokesmen of the movement were Jamal al-Din al-Afghani (1838–1897), Muhammad Abduh (1849–1905) and Rashid Rida (1865–1935). The members of the movement (*salafis*) took the line that the values of early Islam were compatible with those of modern Europe. In so doing, they attributed to Islam mainly secular virtues such as rationalism, the encouragement of sciences, political power, and democracy. In this way they were able to place blame for the relative decline of Islamic societies and power vis-à-vis the West on Muslims who over time had diverged from Islam's original teachings. For this trend, the *salaf* or "forefathers," had in fact two complementary meanings. One was the early companions of the Prophet Muhammad, who were perceived to have abided by the Qur'an and the *sunna* (deed and/or utterance of the Prophet) as closely as possible. Using this conception of the *salaf*, the Salafiyya emphasized the return to the scriptures. The second meaning of the *salaf* denoted reverence for the founders of the Islamic schools of law and for particular medieval jurists, such as al-Ghazali, who influenced the Salafiyya in one way or another.

The central part of the Salafiyya program consisted of legal reform through reinterpreting Islamic law (the SHARI'A) to make it compatible with Western and modern values. In fact, the Salafiyya became caught between two opposing trends: (1) a Westernizing trend, which wanted to adopt Western secular codes and legislate completely outside Islamic law, and (2) a traditional trend, which was perceived as adhering to rigid and premodern interpretations of the four jurisprudence schools of Sunni Islam. Striving to pursue a third alternative, the Salafiyya renounced the widespread nineteenth- and twentieth-century belief in Sunni circles that the gate of reinterpretation of Islamic law (*ijtihad*) had been closed at some point between the tenth and twelfth centuries. For the Salafiyya, *ijtihad* should be permissible in all aspects of transactions (*mu'amalat*), except where there is an explicit text (*noss*) in the Qur'an or in an authentic sunna. The Salafiyya also called for unifying the interpretation of the *Shari'a* by employing two general principles. The first was the principle of public interest (*maslaha*), which was treated as one of the sources of Islamic law. The second principle was a combination (*talfiq*), whereby, for the interpretation of a religious precept in the field of transactions, the judge would not be confined to the opinion of one Islamic school of law but could make use of the interpretations of any school.

The Salafiyya movement may also be regarded as a forerunner of Arab nationalism, since it emphasized Arab-based Islam and the Arabic language, albeit concurrent with modern sciences.

Politically, the Salafiyya produced two trends. One was the trend of Jamal al-Din al-Afghani, which emphasized fighting the advance of Western imperialism into the East, in general, and in Muslim lands, in particular. This made al-Afghani validate several lines of political approach to mobilize various Muslim and non-Muslim groups against the West. He thus spoke in terms of both religious and secular nationalism. He called for healing the divisions between the Sunnis and Shi'ites by concentrating on the common religious basics among these two largest of Muslim sects.

The second trend was that of Muhammad Abduh. After working closely with al-Afghani for a short period, Abduh dissociated himself from his friend's politics, shunned political activism, and concentrated on the issues of Islamic religious reform through education and jurisprudence.

As for Rashid Rida, generally speaking, he followed Abduh's political line during the period preceding World War I; however, he shifted his position and adopted an anti-Western activist political line, akin to that of al-Afghani, after the war—as a reaction to the establishment of direct European rule in most of the core Arab-Islamic areas, namely Syria and Iraq.

In Morocco, as in the Arab East, the Salafiyya movement condemned the doctrines and practices of popular Sufi orders, which it regarded as having no textual basis in Islamic thought. Politically, the Moroccan Salafiyya championed the nationalist liberal anticolonial cause and gained popularity thereby, especially because the rival Sufi orders cooperated with the French, in one way or another, after France proclaimed Morocco a protectorate in 1912. As an intellectual reformist movement, however, the Salafiyya of Morocco, and especially one of its leaders, Allal al-Fasi, emphasized the need for internal reform in Muslim society and to that end pursued a social line of self-help.

BIBLIOGRAPHY

ABUN-NASR, JAMIL. "The Salafiyya Movement in Morocco: The Religious Basis of the Moroccan Nationalist Movement." *Middle Eastern Affairs*, no. 3, *St. Antony's Papers*, no. 16, ed. by Albert Hourani (1963).

COMMINS, DAVID DEAN. *Islamic Reform: Politics and Social Change in the Late Ottoman Period*. New York, 1990.

GIBB, H. A. R. *Modern Trends in Islam*. Chicago, 1947.

LAOUST, HENRI. "Le reformisme orthodoxe des 'Salafiya' et les caracteres generaux de son orientation actuelle." *Revue des Etudes Islamiques* 6 (1932): 175–224.

Mahmoud Haddad

Salam, Malik

Lebanese Sunni politician, brother of Sa'ib Salam.

Malik, an engineer, was on bad terms with his brother Sa'ib SALAM for much of the latter's career and chose to align himself with his brother-in-law Rashid KARAME. He assumed ministerial responsibility once.

As'ad AbuKhalil

Salam, Sa'ib   [1905–?]

Major Sunni politician in Lebanon.

Salam was born in Beirut to a wealthy family headed by his father, Abu Ali Salam. He attended the American University of Beirut and the University of London but received a degree from neither. He came to political prominence during the Lebanese Civil War of 1958, when he championed the cause of those who opposed the government of Camille CHAMOUN. Salam articulated the sentiments of "the Beiruti street" by emphasizing Sunni political support for Gamal Abdel Nasser. He was identified with the Wasat (center) political bloc during the 1960s and criticized the government of Fu'ad Chehab. In 1970, after the election of Wasat member Sulayman Franjiyya as president, he was appointed prime minister. He resigned in 1973 to protest the refusal of Franjiyya to dismiss the Maronite commander in chief of the Lebanese army, whom Salam held responsible for Israel's raid on Beirut that resulted in the assassination of three top Palestine Liberation Organization (PLO) leaders. Salam's views became consistently pro-Saudi, and his educational enterprises (al-Maqasid) received funding from the Saudi government. Salam opposed the right-wing militias during the war but was more opposed to the leftist coalition. He has lived in Geneva, Switzerland, since 1984, and his son Tammam has assumed the political leadership of the family.

As'ad AbuKhalil

Salang Pass

Afghan mountain pass.

The Salang Pass crosses the Hindu Kush mountain range in central Afghanistan and provides a major north–south route between Kabul and northern Afghanistan. In spite of the high altitude of the pass, 13,350 feet (4,071 m), the Soviet Union helped Afghanistan build a tunnel (the Salang Tunnel) 1.7 miles (2.7 km) long at an altitude of 11,100 feet (3,386 m). During the Soviet intervention in Afghanistan (1979–1989), the pass became a major battleground, since it represented the main route for transporting supplies and weapons from the Soviet Union to Kabul. More than once the mojahedin were successful in blocking the tunnel, trapping Soviet soldiers inside.

BIBLIOGRAPHY

DUPREE, LOUIS. *Afghanistan*. Princeton, N.J., 1980.

Grant Farr

Salant, Samuel   [1816–1909]

Renowned scholar of traditional Jewish law and chief rabbi of Jerusalem.

Salant was born in Bialystok and studied in a number of yeshivas (Jewish religious schools) in Eastern Europe. He arrived in Jerusalem in 1841 and was soon appointed rabbi of the Ashkenazic community; he became Jerusalem's chief rabbi in 1878. In Palestine, Salant led the development of a vast network of Ashkenazic educational, medical, and social institutions. With Sir Moses Montefiore, he advocated the growth of the Jewish community in Jerusalem's Old City and in new areas beyond its walls.

BIBLIOGRAPHY

GELLIS, YA'AKOV. *Shiv'im shanah be-Yerushalayim* (Seventy Years in Jerusalem: The Biography of Rabbi Samuel Salant). Jerusalem, 1959.

Chaim I. Waxman

Salih, Ali Abdallah   [c. 1945–]

President of Yemen Arab Republic, then of Yemen, since 1978.

Salih became a public figure in the mid-1970s as the military commander of Ta'iz province of North Yemen and supporter of the reform policies of Ibrahim al-HAMDI (assassinated in 1977). Hamdi's successor, Ahmad Husayn Ghashmi (who had been responsible for Salih's appointment), made no major policy changes but moved to consolidate his position. This produced opposition from some army leaders, the most important of whom was Maj. Abdullah Abd al-Alim (a member of Hamdi's Command Council), who moved to the area south of Ta'iz with forces loyal to him. Troops loyal to Gashmi, under Salih's command, moved against Alim, who fled into South Yemen. Shortly thereafter, Gashmi was assassinated (1978). Thereupon a four-man Presidential Council was formed, one of whose members was Salih. After intense political maneuvering, he was elected president by the People's Constituent Assembly (originally created by Gashmi).

Salih's origins did not augur well for his success: he is a member of the Sanhan tribe, a minor element of the HASHID TRIBAL CONFEDERATION. Though this made him a part of one of the major political forces in the country, he was not able to draw immediately upon the support of any of its major constituent elements, and it was widely assumed that his tenure would be brief. He undertook no radical policy shifts and moved to develop his own basis of support

within the military and in civilian society. By shrewdly exploiting North Yemen's very limited room to maneuver in the international arena (in view of Saudi Arabia's strong interests and more developed international associations), and promoting significant economic development programs, Salih grew in stature and popularity.

In the 1980s, Salih moved to develop a broader basis of support and legitimacy for his government. This required dealing with a number of foreign and domestic policy issues; in foreign policy, the two important issues were relations with South Yemen and with Saudi Arabia. In domestic policy, he moved away from complete reliance upon the military through the National Pact, the National Dialogue Committee, and eventually the General People's Congress—the framework for an eventual popularly elected national legislature.

Relations with South Yemen produced two wars in less than a decade (1972, 1979); at the same time, Saudi Arabia's fears concerning the ideologies and policies of the two Yemens led it to follow policies designed to destabilize both. The discovery of oil in the border areas between the two Yemens and the dissolution of the Soviet Union led to the union agreement of 1990. Under its terms, Salih became president of the unified state.

Most observers regard Salih's role in these developments as crucial, and though many criticize certain aspects of the regime (including its personalism, favoritism, and occasional corruption), few would suggest that his innate political shrewdness is not in considerable measure responsible for the economic and political development that has characterized his years in power.

Manfred W. Wenner

Salim, Ali   [1936–]

Egyptian dramatist.

After a successful career as a comic actor, Salim turned to writing and became one of the major comic dramatists in Egypt. His early plays are full of farcical situations and telling criticism of the idiocies of bureaucracy and the phobias of the common man; notable among these are *Il Nas Ill fi s-Sama' il-Tamina* (People in Eighth Heaven, 1966) and *Bir al-Qamh* (The Wheat Well, 1967). Salim has written several more serious works, of which *Al-Buffeh* (The Buffet, 1968) and *Kumidiya Udib: Int Illi Atalt al-Wahsh* (The Comedy of Oedipus: You're the One Who Killed the Beast, 1970) have had considerable success on stage. The latter, which transports the Oedipus legend to Egyptian Thebes, provides Egyptian audiences contemplating the consequences of the Arab–Israel War of 1967 with a telling view of a nation ruled by an idealistic leader whose bold plans divert his attention from the fact that his security forces are terrorizing the nation.

BIBLIOGRAPHY

BADAWI, M. M. *Modern Arabic Drama in Egypt.* Cambridge, U.K., 1987.

Roger Allen

Salim, Jawad   [1919–1962]

Iraqi sculptor and painter.

Salim, one of the two best-known sculptors in modern Iraq (the other is Khalid al-Rahhal), was born in Baghdad into a middle-class family. His father, his two brothers (Sa'ud and Nizar), and his sister (Naziha) were avid painters. Salim's talents became apparent early in his life, and in 1938 he was sent by the government to study art in Paris. He moved to Rome in 1939, and toward the end of that year he returned to Baghdad, where he was appointed instructor of sculpture at the newly established School of Fine Arts. He was also employed by the Iraqi Museum in the restoration of Mesopotamian artifacts.

During World War II, Salim met a group of Polish artists who had fled to Iraq. Paris-trained post-Expressionists, they encouraged him to pursue an "Iraqi path" in his painting and sculpture but also awakened his enthusiasm for such artists as Cézanne, Renoir, and Goya. Around 1944, Salim befriended a British artist, Kenneth Wood, who was a diplomat in Baghdad. According to Salim's diary, Wood exerted significant influence on his development. During that period, Salim produced such sculptures as *al-Usta* (The Master Builder), which portrayed modern Iraqi masons but drew inspiration from Ibsen's play of the same title.

In 1946, Salim went to London to study at the Slade School of Art; he returned to Iraq some five years later. He was much impressed by such modern British artists as Henry Moore. In Baghdad, he both painted and sculpted, and established the Baghdad Group for Modern Art. After the fall of the monarchy in 1958, he was commissioned by the regime of Abd al-Karim Kassem to design and execute a massive monument entitled *al-Hurriyya* (Freedom), consisting of fourteen bronze units. This work, placed in one of the main squares of Baghdad, consumed the

last two years of his life. He died of a heart attack while working on the monument.

[*See also:* Art: Arab Art]

BIBLIOGRAPHY

JABRA, JABRA IBRAHIM. *Al-Rihla al-Thamina.* Sidon and Beirut, 1967.

Sasson Somekh

Salim Hasan   [1888–1961]

Egyptian Egyptologist.

The second Egyptian Egyptologist of note after Ahmad Kamal, Salim Hasan was educated in Cairo and Paris. He taught at Cairo University and reached the second highest post in the Egyptian Antiquities department, under its French director. Salim Hasan excavated extensively at Giza, site of the Sphinx and the great pyramids, worked at Saqqara, and published voluminously in Arabic, English, and French.

Donald Malcolm Reid

Salim Rabiyya Ali

Yemeni politician and government leader.

Salim Rabiyya Ali (or Ali Salim Rabi) came from South Yemen's interior northeast of Aden and made his name fighting up-country in Radfan in the mid-1960s. He and his rival Abd al-Fattah ISMA'IL were founders of the National Liberation Front (NLF), early leaders of its left wing, and allied with one another to rout decisively its right wing in 1969. Rabiyya Ali served as co-ruler with Isma'il of the PEOPLE'S DEMOCRATIC REPUBLIC OF YEMEN (PDRY). Rabiyya Ali came to be identified with state institutions as well as popular organizations in contrast to the ruling party and its cadres, which were Isma'il's territory. He was executed after losing to Isma'il in an increasingly bitter intraparty struggle.

Robert D. Burrowes

Sallal, Abdullah al-   [1919–1994]

The Yemen Arab Republic's first president.

Soldier and dissident, al-Sallal served as president of the Yemen Arab Republic from 1962 until 1967. At that time, he was ousted by a combination of factions that opposed both the long civil war between the republicans and the royalists and the increasing dependence of republican Yemen on Egypt as led by Gamal Abdel Nasser. In 1982, the regime invited al-Sallal to return from his exile. He died in Yemen in 1994 at the age of seventy-four.

Robert D. Burrowes

Salman, Muhammad

Lebanese film director.

Salman began his career in the 1950s as an actor in Egypt, after teaching Arabic in Beirut for a few years. He wrote and directed many movies with comedic themes. Arab critics consider his movies mindless entertainment; Salman believes that popularity is all that counts. He was married for years to the Lebanese singer Najah Salam. A gifted poet, he has received large sums of money from wealthy oil princes whom he has praised. In 1973 he wrote an anthem praising Syrian participation in the Arab–Israeli War (1973).

As'ad AbuKhalil

Salname

Ottoman statistical yearbook, published 1847–1922.

*Salname*s were yearly almanacs filled with historical, institutional, biographical, and geographical information. First published by the central government, after 1865 they also were produced by provincial Ottoman officials. The salnames were the first attempt by the Ottoman government to provide public information on its activities. They contained statistics on state expenditures and revenues, population, and education, as well as the names of all officials serving in particular provinces and ministries. By World War I, elaborate salnames were issued by virtually every government department and province. They became popular among the public but were intended primarily to help bureaucrats perform their duties.

BIBLIOGRAPHY

DAVISON, RODERIC H. *Reform in the Ottoman Empire, 1856–1876.* Princeton, N.J., 1963.
MCCARTHY, JUSTIN. *The Arab World, Turkey and the Balkans (1878–1914): A Handbook of Historical Statistics.* Boston, 1982.

Elizabeth Thompson

Salonika

Second largest city in modern Greece and a principal city in the Ottoman Empire.

Located at the head of the Gulf of Salonika, Salonika (also known as Salonica or Thessalonika) was captured by the Ottoman Sultan Murad I in the late fourteenth century. Its Jewish population increased greatly in the fifteenth and sixteenth centuries with the arrival of refugees from Spain. The city flourished as a trade and cultural center through the seventeenth century and revived in the nineteenth century, becoming an industrial center and the seat of political and cultural wings of the Young Turk movement. In 1901, the modern port was opened, and in 1908 the Committee of Union and Progress launched its revolution there.

The Greeks captured Salonika from the Ottomans on November 8, 1912, during the First Balkan War. Five years later, a fire destroyed much of the city. Its Jewish community was wiped out under German occupation (1941–1944). Today, Salonika, with a population of more than 700,000, is the site of a NATO base, a university, and industries emphasizing textiles, chemicals, metal products, and tobacco.

BIBLIOGRAPHY

SHAW, STANFORD J., and EZEL KURAL SHAW. *History of the Ottoman Empire and Modern Turkey,* vol. 2. New York, 1977.

Elizabeth Thompson

Salt, al-

A small, picturesque town in Jordan.

Al-Salt is located about 20 miles (29 km) northwest of Jordan's capital, Amman, in the hills overlooking the Jordan valley to the west. It contains some beautiful examples of Islamic residential architecture. The archaeological evidence shows that Salt has been inhabited since about 3000 B.C.E. It was the principal town in Transjordan in the 1920s and one of the gateways from Palestine to Transjordan and countries further east and south. Salt suffered a steady decline, as other population centers flourished in Jordan and routes to Palestine moved south or north. It has never fully recovered from this decline, although it is a regional capital (Balqa district) and boasts several "firsts": the first hospital and the first secondary school in Jordan. The latter lays claim to having educated many of Jordan's prime ministers, most of its ministers, and a large number of prominent members of Jordanian society. Salt also has a substantial

Christian minority that enjoys cordial relations with the Muslim community.

BIBLIOGRAPHY

GUBSER, PETER. *Jordan: Crossroads of Middle Eastern Events.* Boulder, Colo., 1983.

Jenab Tutunji

SAMA

See Saudi Arabian Monetary Agency

Samarec

Interim management entity between American and Saudi ownership of Saudi Arabian oil industry.

Until ARAMCO (Arabian American Oil Company) became totally Saudi owned in the mid- to late 1980s, Saudi Arabia encouraged the development of an independent oil company to compete with the "majors," which controlled ARAMCO. The Saudi oil company, called PETROMIN, developed crude-oil trading and investment structures, which were parallel and often overlapping with ARAMCO's. After ARAMCO became Saudi ARAMCO, the overlapping structures became obsolete. The government thus created the Saudi Arabian Marketing and Refining Company (Samarec) to replace PETROMIN and placed it under the control of the minister of petroleum. Between 1990 and 1993, Samarec was responsible for the marketing of 677,000 barrels/day of crude and managed the local refineries, which processed 400,000 barrels/day as well as all the other PETROMIN ventures, such as the tanker company. In June 1993, this new entity was merged fully into ARAMCO. This streamlined the technical and commercial management of petroleum products. Saudi ARAMCO as successor to ARAMCO could also provide a more established base of technical and commercial competence to the Saudi oil industry.

BIBLIOGRAPHY

Middle East Economic Survey. Nicosia, Cyprus.

Jean-François Seznec

Samaritans

Those who claim descent from the original inhabitants of biblical Samaria; remnant of the northern tribes of ancient Israel.

Only a few hundred Samaritans remain, mainly in and around Nablus (Shechem), near their sacred Mount Gerizim. They are known for their Passover reenactment of paschal sacrifices. Although they practice circumcision and other Jewish customs, they are not considered Jews by either the State of Israel or the rabbinate.

BIBLIOGRAPHY

PURVIS, J. D. *The Samaritan Pentateuch and the Origin of the Samaritan Sect.* Cambridge, U.K., 1968.

Samuel C. Heilman

Samarra

One of the oldest cities in Iraq, sixty-five miles (104 km) north of Baghdad.

Samarra was founded on the east side of the Tigris river by the caliph Abbasid al-Mu'tasim in 835 C.E. It was a capital of eight Abbasid caliphs from 836 to 892, when Caliph al-Mu'tamad moved again to Baghdad. During the Abbasid period, the caliphs were eager to make Samarra a beautiful city, with new palaces, lakes, and wide squares. They brought in many types of plants from all over the Islamic world. The founder divided the city into quarters, based on types of business and professions.

With its rich Islamic history, Samarra has many archeological sites. The most important is the al-Malwiyya mosque and its spiral minaret, 171 feet (52 m) in height, with a round room summit 19.6 feet (6 m) high, begun in 1443 by al-Mutawakkil. Also of interest are the House of the Caliph, which contains three divans and several basements and rooms; the mosque of Abu Dulaf and its spiral minaret; al-Mankur palace; and many walls, especially al-Quadissiyya, Isa, Ashnas, and Shaykh Wali. A museum was established in Samarra for the artifacts found during excavations in the area.

Two apostolic imams, Ali al-Hadi and his son Hasan al-Askari, were buried in Samarra; therefore it is a holy city of Shi'ism. The imams' shrine is visited by Shi'ites from all over the Islamic world. Part of the mosque marks the spot where, according to the Shi'ites, the twelfth and last apostolic imam, al-Mahdi, disappeared.

The majority of the population today is composed of members of tribes of the surrounding countryside who follow Sunni Islam. Linked to Baghdad, Iraq's capital, by highways and railroads, Samarra is governed by the *qa'immaqam,* chief of the administrative unit, who reports to the *muhafidh,* the representative of the central government in Baghdad.

Samarra has a desert climate, with great temperature differences between day and night, summer and winter. The high reaches 110°F (50°C), and the low is just above freezing. Annual relative humidity is 18 to 30 percent; annual rainfall ranges from four to sixteen inches (10–40 cm). Besides cereal crops, citrus fruits, apples, and many types of vegetables are part of the area's agriculture. A pharmaceutical plant and an electrical power plant are the major industries there.

One vital project is the al-Tharthar Dam, opened in 1956, which prevents the flooding of Baghdad by shifting the flow of the Tigris during its rise to the al-Tharthar valley, a depression between Samarra on the Tigris and Hit on the nearby Euphrates.

BIBLIOGRAPHY

HARRIS, GEORGE L. *Iraq: Its Society, Its Culture.* New Haven, Conn., 1958.

AL-HASSANI, ABDUL RAZZAK. *The History of Modern Iraq.* Baghdad, 1980.

LONGRIGG, S. H. *Iraq, 1900 to 1950: A Political, Social, and Economic History.* London, 1956.

Nazar al-Khalaf

Samud

Principle adopted by the Palestinian national movement of clinging to the soil of the homeland.

The Samud (Steadfastness) Fund was established at the Baghdad Arab Summit in 1978 to discourage Palestinian emigration from the territories occupied by Israel in 1967. The annual budget of $150 million was to be administered by the Joint Committee, composed of members from the Palestine Liberation Organization (PLO) and the government of Jordan. Funds were distributed to Palestinian leaders, trade unions, universities, newspapers, and cooperatives. Samud paid unemployment benefits and pensions for retirees and granted interest-free housing loans. In the early 1980s, about $87 million per year was transferred to the occupied territories. Funds dried up in the mid-1980s as oil-rich Arab countries defaulted on their contributions.

In the late 1980s, the principle of samud was revived in an altered form by Palestinian residents of the Gaza Strip, Golan Heights, and West Bank who resented their passive role as welfare recipients. Under the leadership of Dr. Hisham Awartani, an economist at al-Najah University in Nablus, samud was transformed into a call for Palestinian residents to think and act for themselves.

BIBLIOGRAPHY

BENVENISTI, MERON. *The West Bank Handbook: A Political Lexicon.* Jerusalem, 1986.

COBBAN, HELENA. *The Palestinian Liberation Organization.* New York, 1984.

SCHIFF, ZE'EV, and EHUD YA'ARI. *Intifada.* New York, 1989.

Elizabeth Thompson

Samuel, Herbert Louis [1870–1963]

First British civil high commissioner of mandated Palestine, 1920–1925.

Viscount Samuel's tenure established the pattern for British control of Palestine, including Transjordan. It was his idea to set an "economic absorptive capacity" for Palestine, thus putting limits on Jewish immigration; this became British policy in the Churchill WHITE PAPER of 1922.

BIBLIOGRAPHY

Encyclopedia Judaica. Jerusalem, 1972.

Sara Reguer

San'a

Political capital of the Republic of Yemen.

One of the world's oldest continuously inhabited sites, San'a became the capital of united Yemen in 1990. It had been the capital and chief city of a succession of political systems over the centuries: the Yemen Arab Republic; the Hamid al-Din dynasty of imams; the occupation by the Ottoman Empire; successions of earlier Zaydi imams; and numerous other regimes, major and minor, indigenous and foreign. Regardless of the ruler of the day, San'a was for centuries the great Zaydi urban center in the highlands of North Yemen, surrounded by tribes, great and small, which accepted and defended ZAYDISM. The city has been Islamic since the early days of Islam, and its major mosque is said to be built on the ruins of a mosque built before the death of the Prophet Muhammad. In recent decades, the city has been the stage for much of Yemen's highest political drama: the sacking of San'a by the northern tribes as punishment for its alleged role in the aborted 1948 revolution and the heroics of its citizens and republican defenders during the seventy-day siege of San'a in early 1968.

San'a is located at about 7,500 feet (2,300 m) in the geographical center of modern North Yemen, northeast of Hodeida (al-Hudayda) on the coast and north of Ta'iz in the southern uplands. Its barren setting conveys an austere, almost monastic aura, but it is blessed with a dry temperate climate, seasonally marred by lip-cracking dryness and dust-filled winds. Wells and erratic rains in the spring and late summer allow for both irrigated and dry farming as well as extensive animal husbandry in the region around the city. San'a is not a green place; people and factories have won out decisively over trees, grass, and flowers in the competition for water in recent decades.

Guarded by Jabal Nuqum, San'a stretches across a wide, flat plain from that small, bald mountain's western flank. Before the 1962 revolution, San'a had a figure-eight or hourglass configuration: the Jewish quarter (Qa al-Yahud) to the east separated by a half mile of gardens and the usually dry watercourse from the much larger, walled Islamic city at the foot of the mountain. This configuration was largely erased by the unplanned growth of the 1960s and 1970s and, even more so, by the urban sprawl of the 1980s. Still, the old Islamic city remains one of the urban treasures of the world, the object of a major UNESCO preservation campaign since the mid-1980s. In addition to its main gate, restored portions of thick wall, and dozens of slender minarets, the city is distinguished by the dense concentration of houses of cut stone and baked and sun-dried bricks, many of them at least several stories tall. The domestic architecture of San'a, dating back at least two millennia, is a triumph of art and engineering.

San'a has ancient, still living, thriving suqs or marketplaces, the most famous at the core of the old city. In addition to the shops selling goods from all over the world, this suq is also home to artisans and traditional manufacturers. In recent years, the new city and the outskirts have become the locale for modern stores, distribution centers, showrooms, and light industry. San'a has also become a city of schools, most notably the University of San'a.

While Ta'iz claimed to be the commercial and business center of Yemen, the more modern city, more open to the ideas and practices of the outside world, San'a boasted handsome stone government offices and other public buildings, old and new, as well as many mosques, schools, and fine homes. By the 1980s, however, with a population of more than 500,000 and growing, San'a had emerged as the undisputed center of political, cultural, and even economic life in North Yemen. With Yemeni unification in 1990, and the flood of government officials and supplicants from Aden to San'a, the political capital, the preeminence of San'a became even more apparent. It remains to be seen what ranking and division of labor prevails between San'a and Aden, the designated economic capital of unified Yemen. The cities, while similar in size, are wildly different in appearance and lifestyle, making them a very complementary pairing. As they grow, both must cope with traffic congestion, water shortages, limited sewerage facilities, housing shortages, and the inadequacies of other urban services.

Robert D. Burrowes

San'a University

One of two universities in the Republic of Yemen.

The national university—the sole university—of the former Yemen Arab Republic has grown dramatically in size of student body and faculty and has improved its quality of education since its founding in 1970. The university began on a modest ad hoc basis with a teachers' college and a law school; the first external aid for the university, a grant from Kuwait, was secured in its first year. Its arts and science faculties underwent rapid growth during its first decade, and among the departments created in the 1980s are those of engineering, agriculture, and medicine. It now spreads over two large urban campuses, filled with modern buildings. San'a University was funded over the years almost totally by Kuwait, modeled on and guided by Kuwait University, and staffed until recent years mostly by Egyptians. As a consequence, it has struggled to escape being a carbon copy of Kuwait University's carbon copy of Cairo University by attempting to create a Yemeni identity in terms of its program, faculty, and administration. From the outset, classes have been coeducational, making it a battleground between secular modernists and Islamic conservatives. With the Gulf Crisis in 1990/91 and the loss of Kuwaiti funding, the university entered a difficult period, one that it shared with its sister university in the newly created Republic of Yemen, Aden University.

Robert D. Burrowes

Sancak

See Sanjak

Sanjabi, Karim   [1904–1995]

Iranian politician.

Born in Kermanshah, Karim Sanjabi studied in France and returned to Iran to join the Faculty of Law at Tehran University. In 1946, he was a member of the nationalist Iran party, which formed a coalition with the Communist Tudeh party to oppose the rule of Mohammad Reza Shah Pahlavi. Sanjabi was also one of the founding members in 1949 of the National Front (see NATIONAL FRONT,

IRAN). Active in the National Resistance Movement of the 1950s, he was a leader of the Second National Front (formed in the early 1960s) and was signatory to the famous open letter of 1977 that publicly criticized the shah. He refused the prime ministership offered him by Mohammad Reza Shah in 1978 and instead traveled to Paris to negotiate a working arrangement between the National Front and Ayatollah Khomeini. He was appointed the first foreign minister of the Islamic Republic of Iran in 1979 but resigned the same year in protest against the chaos that characterized the regime. He left Iran and published his memoirs in 1989.

BIBLIOGRAPHY

IRAN RESEARCH GROUP. *Who's Who in Iran.* Berlin, 1990.

Neguin Yavari

Sanjak

Meaning "banner" in Turkish, a sanjak was an administrative district in the Ottoman Empire.

Traditionally, the Ottoman Empire was divided into provinces (*vilayet*s), which in turn were divided into *sanjak*s. The sanjaks themselves were divided into counties (*kaza*s), and the sanjak was governed by a sanjak bey appointed in Istanbul. The sanjak bey was responsible for local administration, and he was answerable to the provincial governor.

During the empire's TANZIMAT period (mid-nineteenth century), the sanjak underwent considerable change. The districts were redrawn, and the sanjak was granted semi-representative councils and a degree of local autonomy. Certain sanjaks, such as those that formed the core of modern Lebanon, were the objects of particular attention during the Tanzimat. The sanjak was abolished as an administrative unit after the demise of the empire and the establishment of the new Republic of Turkey.

BIBLIOGRAPHY

SHAW, STANFORD, and EZEL KURAL SHAW. *History of the Ottoman Empire and Modern Turkey,* vol. 2. New York, 1977.

Zachary Karabell

Sanjari, Heshmat   [1918–1995]

Iranian conductor, musician, and composer.

Sanjari was born in Tehran. He graduated from the music school in Tehran, then studied conducting in Vienna. He also studied the violin under Serg Khutsiev. In 1954, Sanjari became conductor of Tehran's symphony orchestra, and in 1955 he made a six-month tour of the United States, conducting orchestras in New York, Boston, Chicago, and Washington, D.C. In 1956 he went to Vienna, returning to Iran in 1960 as the permanent conductor of Tehran's symphony orchestra, a position he held until 1990. Sanjari composed several pieces, including "Persian Suites" and "Niyayesh" (The Prayer), that are adaptations of Persian folk themes and motifs.

Pardis Minuchehr

San Remo Conference

Post–World War I talks at which Great Britain and France were awarded mandates over Middle East countries.

In April 1920, the victorious World War I allies, with the exception of the United States, met in San Remo, Italy. At the conference, Britain was awarded mandates over Palestine and Iraq, and France was awarded mandates over Syria and Lebanon. Technically, a mandate held the territories in trusteeship for the League of Nations until the political systems of these territories were developed enough to warrant independence and admission to the League of Nations.

The San Remo Conference also discussed petroleum in Mesopotamia (now Iraq). France agreed to renounce its claims to the province of Mosul in return for a 25 percent share in the Turkish Petroleum Company. Italy was also promised access to this oil; but the issue of Mosul—whether it was to be an autonomous region of Kurds or a province of Iraq—was not decided until 1926, when it was officially incorporated into Faisal's new kingdom of Iraq.

BIBLIOGRAPHY

SHIMONI, YAACOV, ed. *Political Dictionary of the Middle East in the Twentieth Century.* New York, 1974.
YERGIN, DANIEL. *The Prize.* New York, 1991.

Zachary Karabell

San Stefano, Treaty of

Signed on March 3, 1878, this treaty concluded one of the major wars fought between Russia and the Ottoman Empire (1877–1878).

Among the provisions of the Treaty of San Stefano were the following:

(1) Serbia and Montenegro received their independence from the Ottoman Empire and were granted additional territory.

(2) Independence was also gained by Romania, which lost southern Bessarabia to Russia but was compensated by the acquisition of the Black Sea province of Dobrudja.

(3) Bosnia and Herzegovina were granted autonomy and were promised reforms, to be supervised jointly by Russia and Austria.

(4) In addition to southern Bessarabia, Russia also acquired a substantial part of northeastern Anatolia, including the provinces of Batum, Kars, and Ardahan.

(5) Unexpectedly, the treaty also called for the creation of Greater Bulgaria. Its territory extended from the Danube and the Black Sea to the Aegean Sea in the south and included much of Macedonia. Nominally a part of the Ottoman Empire, Greater Bulgaria was to be ruled by a Christian government and to possess a national militia. For the next two years, it was also to remain under Russian occupation—a clear indication of the direction in which Russia was moving: Bulgaria guards the northern access to the Turkish Straits.

It soon became obvious that the Treaty of San Stefano—a major gain in Russia's contest with the Ottoman Empire for supremacy in the Balkan–Black Sea region—would not be allowed to stand. Among the great powers, early concern was expressed by Great Britain and Austria-Hungary. Britain had long opposed Russia's aggrandizement at the expense of the Ottoman Empire and particularly the Russian drive toward the Turkish Straits. Austria-Hungary shared British apprehensions and was also perturbed by the creation of the Russian puppet state of Greater Bulgaria. Bowing to the British, Austro-Hungarian, and later German pressure, Russia agreed to submit the terms of the treaty of San Stefano to a great power congress—the Congress of Berlin.

The resulting Treaty of Berlin (1878) endorsed many of the provisions negotiated at San Stefano. Russia and Romania kept their territorial gains. Romania, Serbia, and Montenegro retained their independence, and the latter two retained much of the territory allocated to them. Bosnia and Herzegovina were, however, placed under Austrian control, and England was permitted to occupy Cyprus. Finally, despite Russian objections, the Congress of Berlin dismantled Greater Bulgaria. The latter was split into three parts: Bulgaria proper, located north of the Balkan mountains; East Rumelia, situated south of them; and Macedonia. All remained under Ottoman suzerainty but were granted autonomy and were promised reforms.

Great Britain was the main beneficiary of the Congress of Berlin. Supported by Austria-Hungary, Britain denied Russia the opportunity to become the sole arbiter of the affairs of the Ottoman Empire. The congress also prevented Russia from becoming the patron of Greater Bulgaria. Great Britain also acquired Cyprus; strategically located in the eastern Mediterranean, the island was used four years later to effect the British occupation of Egypt.

BIBLIOGRAPHY

LANGER, WILLIAM L. *European Alliances and Alignments, 1871–1890,* 2nd ed. New York, 1950.
SUMNER, BENEDICT H. *Russia and the Balkans, 1870–1880.* Oxford, 1937.

Oles M. Smolansky

Santa Sophia

See Aya Sofya

Sanu, Ya'qub   [1839–1912]

Egyptian nationalist playwright and satirical journalist.

Born into a Jewish family in Alexandria, Sanu, also known as James Sanu, is considered the father of modern Arabic satire. He organized the first popular theater in Egypt, which presented plays in colloquial Arabic. Influenced by the Muslim reformer Jamal al-Din al-Afghani, Sanu established a political newspaper, *Abu Nazzare Zarqa* (The Man with the Blue Glasses). In 1877 or 1878, the royal court deemed his writings offensive and expelled him from Egypt. Settling in Paris, Sanu continued his campaign of attacking the members of Egypt's political establishment for collaborating with the colonial powers and betraying Egypt.

BIBLIOGRAPHY

GENDZIER, IRENE. *The Practical Visions of Ya'qub Sanu'.* Cambridge, Mass, 1966.
GOLDSCHMIDT, ARTHUR, JR. *Modern Egypt: The Formation of a Nation-State.* Boulder, Colo., 1988.

David Waldner

Sanusi, Ahmad al-Sharif al-   [1873–1932]

Third leader of the Islamic Sanusi order, 1902–1917.

A leader in the Cyrenaican resistance to Italian rule, from 1911 to 1918, he participated in the German–Ottoman-initiated invasion of Egypt (November 1915–early 1916), following which the leadership of the Sanusi order passed to Idris al-Sanusi. He then left for Turkey in 1918 and went to the Hijaz (western Arabia) in 1924.

BIBLIOGRAPHY

EVANS-PRITCHARD, E. E. *The Sanusi of Cyrenaica.* Oxford, 1949.

SIMON, RACHEL. *Libya between Ottomanism and Nationalism.* Berlin, 1987.

ZIADEH, NICOLA. *Sanusiya.* Leiden, Neth., 1958.

Rachel Simon

Sanusi, Muhammad ibn Ali al-

[1787–1859]

Muslim scholar and founder of the Sanusi order, 1837.

Sanusi studied Arabic and Islam in Algeria, Morocco, Egypt, and the Hijaz of western Arabia. He quarreled with leading *ulama* (Muslim scholars), became active in Sufi circles, and was successful among Muslim nomads. A follower of Sidi Ahmad al-Fasi, he moved to Cyrenaica, Libya, in 1838, which became the base for the spread of the Sanusi order.

BIBLIOGRAPHY

EVANS-PRITCHARD, E. E. *The Sanusi of Cyrenaica.* Oxford, 1949.

SIMON, RACHEL. *Libya between Ottomanism and Nationalism.* Berlin, 1987.

ZIADEH, NICOLA. *Sanusiyah.* Leiden, Neth., 1958.

Rachel Simon

Sanusi, Muhammad Idris ibn Muhammad al-

See Idris al-Sayyid Muhammad al-Sanusi

Sanusi Order

Islamic order founded in 1837 by Muhammad ibn Ali al-Sanusi (died 1859); followed by Muhammad al-Mahdi (1859–1902), Ahmad al-Sharif (1902–1917), and Idris al-Sanusi.

Combining orthodoxy and SUFISM, the Sanusi Order aimed to unite all religious orders by returning to the sources. It called for closeness to the Prophet Muhammad through study, training, and intention, but rejected ecstacy. It advocated a modest life-style and refraining from daily pleasures. Its main support was tribal (in Cyrenaica and central Africa). The Sanusi organization was based on a network of *zawiya*s (religious compounds), which were strategically located and served as centers of study and trade, to which neighboring affiliates contributed their *ushr* (tithe) and manpower. The Sanusi political power was recognized by the Ottoman Empire and by central African kingdoms. The order was a key factor in the resistance to Italian rule (1911–1933), which caused the death and exile of many Sanusi leaders and followers, the confiscation of *zawiya*s, and the de facto collapse of the order.

BIBLIOGRAPHY

CORDELL, D. D. "Eastern Libya, Wadai and the Sanusiya: A Tariqa and a Trade Route." *Journal of African History* 18(1977): 21–36.

AL-DAJJANI, AHMAD SIDQI. *Al-Harakah al-Sanusiya.* Beirut, 1968.

EVANS-PRITCHARD, E. E. *The Sanusi of Cyrenaica.* Oxford, 1949.

ZIADEH, NICOLA. *Sanusiyah.* Leiden, Neth., 1958.

Rachel Simon

Sapir, Joseph   [1869–1935]

Zionist leader.

Joseph Sapir was an active member of Hoveve Zion in Vienna, and following the appearance of Theodor HERZL, he became an advocate of political Zionism. He published a book on the topic in 1903 that was translated into numerous languages. In 1925, he immigrated to Palestine, practiced medicine, and remained active in the general Zionist movement.

Martin Malin

Sapir, Pinhas   [1907–1975]

Israeli Labor party leader, minister of finance.

Pinhas Sapir, born in Poland as Koslovsky, received a religious education as a child and later became a leader in the He-Halutz movement.

In 1929 he immigrated to Palestine. From 1937 to 1947 Pinhas Sapir was Levy Eshkol's deputy at Mekorot Water Company. Later Pinhas Sapir served in a number of high government and cabinet positions including director general of the Ministry of

Defense (1948–1953) and director general of the Ministry of Finance (1953–1955). He was minister of commerce and industry from 1955 to 1964 and again from 1970 to 1972. He also served as minister of finance from 1963 to 1968 and again from 1969 to 1974.

He was known to be a power broker within the Labor party and played an active role in uncovering the details of the Lavon affair (1960–1961). As finance minister after the Arab–Israel War of 1967 (Six-Day War), he expressed reservations about Moshe Dayan's proposals for integrating the occupied territories with Israel. He was suggested as a successor to Golda Meir, after her resignation as prime minister in 1974, but he refused the offer. He left the government in 1974 to become chairman of the Jewish Agency executive.

Martin Malin

Sarid, Yossi   [1940–   ]

Israeli political leader and government minister.

Israeli-born Yossi Sarid was appointed minister of the environment in 1993. A columnist for the newspaper *Haaretz*, Sarid has been a member of the Knesset since 1974. He served on the Knesset's Education and Culture Committee, House Committee, and Foreign Affairs and Security Committee as well as leading the leftist Meretz faction.

Bryan Daves

Sarkis, Ilyas   [1924–1985]

President of Lebanon, 1976 to 1982.

Sarkis studied law at the Université Saint Joseph, then joined the audit office as a magistrate in Lebanon. His integrity and discipline brought him to the attention of Lebanon's President Fu'ad Chehab, who appointed him legal adviser in 1959 and director general of his cabinet in 1962. Chehab's successor, Charles Hilu, appointed him chairman of the Banking Control Commission and, in June 1968, governor of the Central Bank.

As the major Chehabist contender in the presidential election of 1970, Sarkis lost by one vote to Sulayman Franjiyya, whose tenure developed into one of the contentious issues in the Lebanese Civil War (1975). The legislature then specifically amended the constitution to allow early presidential elections to permit the accession of Sarkis in May 1976. Considering him Syria's candidate, Kamal Jumblatt, the leader of the leftist forces and ally of the Palestine Liberation Organization (PLO), tried unsuccessfully to disrupt the parliamentary session in favor of the candidacy of Raymond Eddé.

As prescribed by the Arab summit conferences at Riyadh and Cairo, Sarkis attempted, using a neo-Chehabist team, to disarm all the Lebanese militias with the help of the Syrian-dominated Arab Deterrent Forces (ADF). He was blocked in doing so by the Phalange and the National Liberal party (NLP), who insisted that the PLO disarm first. Since Israel would not allow Syrian troops to descend south of the Litani river, PLO guerillas remained in southern Lebanon, where raids and counterraids across the border finally led to Israel's invasion of the area in March 1978. Although UN peacekeeping troops were deployed in the wake of Israel's withdrawal, Israel would not allow Sarkis to send Lebanese army units to the southern border area, propping up instead the local Christian militias under Major Sa'd Haddad. In September 1978, tensions between the Maronite Christian militias and the Syrian troops of the ADF culminated in the bombardment of the Ashrafiyya quarter in east Beirut, bringing the president close to resignation.

Henceforth, all that Sarkis could do was maintain the status quo among the disparate armed groups and try to manage the crisis. In 1980, the rise of Bashir Jumayyil as the charismatic militia leader of the Maronite community forced Sarkis to mend fences. He ultimately convinced the young Jumayyil to steer his course more toward the United States instead of relying exclusively on Israel. Toward the end of his term, Sarkis increasingly believed in the desirability of electing the strong Bashir to office. Sarkis refused suggestions that he remain for two more years as an extraordinary measure—even in the wake of Israel's 1982 invasion and after Bashir Jumayyil's assassination while president-elect.

Although accused by critics in the Maronite and leftist camps of being weak and vacillating, Sarkis was an honest and moderate president. He insisted that he had transferred power to his successor, Amin Jumayyil (Bashir's brother), with the government's apparatus still united and the economy strong despite the intermittent civil war. In retrospect, these were by no means negligible accomplishments.

BIBLIOGRAPHY

BAKRADOUNI, KARIM. *La paix manquée: Le mandat d'Elias Sarkis, 1976–1982.* Beirut, 1984.
COBBAN, HELENA. *The Making of Modern Lebanon.* Boulder, Colo., 1985.

Bassam Namani

Sarraj, Abd al-Hammid

Syrian army officer who, until 1967, played an active role in the public and political affairs of his country.

Sarraj had close connections with the Ba'thists but was not a formal member of the Ba'th party. He played an important part in creating the Egyptian–Syrian union in 1958. He served as minister of the interior in the Syrian *qutr* (region) of what came to be known as the United Arab Republic (UAR) (1958–1961). During the union years, he was by all accounts the most influential man in Syria acting on behalf of the UAR's president, the late Gamal Abdel Nasser. His power was as much a function of his control of the security services as it was of Nasser's support for him. In 1962, almost one year after the dissolution of the Egyptian–Syrian union, Colonel Sarraj fled to Egypt and from there he tried in vain to bring Syria back into Egypt's fold. After 1967, Sarraj quietly withdrew from politics.

Muhammad Muslih

Sarruf, Ya'qub   [1852–1927]

Lebanese publisher, writer, and educator of the Arab renaissance movement.

Born in Lebanon to a Christian family, Sarruf was a teacher at the Syrian Protestant College when he and Faris Nimr founded their highly regarded literary and scientific journal *al-Muqtataf.* The journal advocated a simpler style of Arabic and the advancement of science in the Arab world.

In 1884, Sarruf and Nimr moved to Cairo in order to escape Ottoman censors. There they continued to publish *al-Muqtataf* and started an influential daily newspaper, *al-Muqattam.* They also introduced adult education in Egypt. Sarruf, an elegant essayist, wrote some of the earliest novels in Arabic in 1905 and 1907.

BIBLIOGRAPHY

BADAWI, M. M. *Modern Arabic Literature and the West.* Ithaca, N.Y., 1985.
HAYWOOD, JOHN A. *Modern Arabic Literature 1800–1970.* New York, 1971.

Elizabeth Thompson

Sartawi, Issam   [1935–1983]

Palestinian doctor and political activist.

Issam Sartawi was born in 1935 in Acre during the British mandate over Palestine, received his university and medical education in Iraq, and then went to Ohio University in the early 1960s to specialize in heart surgery. In 1968, he returned to the Middle East and joined his family in Amman, Jordan. That year he formed the Organization of Action for the Liberation of Palestine, which carried out clandestine attacks against Israel from Jordan. In 1970, after King Hussein's forces fought to keep the armed Palestinian guerrilla groups in Jordan from overthrowing the government that had given them sanctuary, Sartawi disbanded his small force and joined al-Fath, the armed Palestinian group led by Yasir Arafat.

Later, he became an advocate of recognizing Israel and seeking Israeli–Palestinian peace on the basis of a directly negotiated two-state solution. He frequently advised Arafat, who was by then Palestine Liberation Organization (PLO) chairman, and was roving representative for the PLO, although not a member of the PLO Executive Committee. In addition, Sartawi served as informal liaison between Arafat and the Israeli doves and Western leaders. Sartawi had to contend with mounting criticism within the PLO. This led to his resignation from the Palestine National Council in 1981, though Arafat refused to accept it.

In April 1983, against a background of failed negotiations between Arafat and King Hussein on whether the latter would take part in U.S.-sponsored negotiations representing the Palestinians, Sartawi attended a meeting of the Socialist International in Portugal. On April 10, he was assassinated there by a gunman. Abu Nidal's Revolutionary Council, which had broken away from the PLO nine years earlier, took responsibility for the shooting.

BIBLIOGRAPHY

SARTAWI, ISSAM. "Dr. Sartawi Speaks His Mind." *New Outlook* (March 1982).
TESSLER, MARK. *A History of the Israeli–Palestinian Conflict.* Bloomington, Ind., 1994.

Benjamin Joseph

Sasna Tsrrer

Armenian national folk epic, Wild Men of Sasun.

First transcribed in 1874 by Bishop Garegin Srvandztyants, the historical core of the narrative is reminiscent of the Armenian uprising in Khoyt of 851 C.E. against the Arab caliphate, represented here by the character Msra Melik, the king of Egypt. Khoyt, later Sasun, is an isolated, mountainous district west of Lake Van, in western Armenia, whose ferocious people managed to maintain their independence from the domination of Islam until recent times. The epic describes the brave deeds of the descendants of Queen Tsovinar, who may originally have been an aquatic goddess—her name contains the Armenian word *tsov,* "sea." Briefly escaping Arab captivity, she drank of a milky fountain in the sea and gave birth to the heroes Sanasar and Baghdasar, who fled home to Armenia. The biblical flight of Sennacherib's sons is interwoven with a motif of virgin birth found also in Zoroastrianism in the legend that describes how Zoroaster's seed, preserved in Lake Hamun-e Sistan, will enter a maiden bathing there and she will then give birth to the saviors of the world.

The brothers are succeeded by Arriuts (Lionslayer) Mher (Mithra) and Davit (David), who perform deeds of valor that are often also naive or madcap, with the help of the Victorious Cross (Armenian, *khach patrazin,* the latter word possibly from Persian *piruzin,* "victorious," though some versions have what is apparently a *lectio facilior, paterazmin,* "of war"). Here, as in medieval talismanic texts, Armenian popular culture has rendered magical the various holy crosses of the official church. Davit wields also the Lightning Sword (Armenian, *t'ur ketsaki*) and rides the intrepid, intelligent stallion Jelali, whose own history seems to be derived from the legend of Rustam's steed, Rakhsh, in the Iranian *Shah-nameh* (as, indeed, does the wonderful horse Bor, in the Kurdish romance *Mam u Zin*). Although most places mentioned are real—many are situated in the Van area or in Mesopotamia (now in Iraq) to the south—some mythical localities appear, such as the Bronze City (a popular episode of the *Thousand and One Nights,* which was translated into Armenian as early as the eleventh century).

Davit has a son, P'ok'r (Little) Mher, leaves for Georgia, meets the boy years later and fights with him (as neither recognizes the other), on the banks of a stream, over a pretty girl. There are echoes here, both of the tragedy of Rustam and Sohrab (though Mher is not killed) and of the Armenian epic of King Artashes (Artaxias I, second century B.C.E.), who kidnapped the Alan (Ossete) princess Sat'enik on the banks of the Kura river. But the heroes devote most of their energy to fighting the Muslim enemy, especially the White Dev ("demon," again, a character out of the *Shah-nameh*), who is emir of Akhlat, north of Lake Van. This enclave persisted in fact, a thorn in the side of the Armenian Bagratid dynasty.

P'ok'r Mher is the last of the heroes. Abandoned by parents and loved ones—each one of whom in a set speech dismisses him—to his fate (the end of the Byzantine epic hero Digenes Akrites probably echoes the Armenian tale here), he and his horse are led by a talking raven to a rock at Van. A gate—identified locally as an Urartian blind ritual portal of the eighth century B.C.E.—opens to receive him, and he remains there until Judgment Day, holding the wheel of destiny. The cave opens once a year, on Ascension Eve. Though *Sasna Tsrrer* abounds in mythological material of great antiquity, as well as folkloric and epic material drawn from or similar to the literatures of the Iranians (both Persians and Kurds), the Byzantine Greeks, and the Turks, Little Mher's is the longest connected episode. Many elements of his story may help explain aspects of ancient Roman Mithraism and, indeed, to localize the origins of that religion in Armenia.

BIBLIOGRAPHY

ABEGHYAN, MANUKA, ed. *Sasma tserrer.* Yerevan, Armenia, 1939.
ORBELI, ISOIF, ed. *Sasunts'i Davit.* Yerevan, Armenia, 1961.
RUSSELL, JAMES R. "On the Armeno-Iranian Roots of Mithraism." In *Studies on Mithraism,* ed. by J. R. Hinnells. Rome, 1992.
SHALIAN, ARTIN K. *David of Sassoun.* Athens, Ohio, 1964.
SURMELIAN, LEON. *Daredevils of Sassoun.* Chicago, 1964.

James R. Russell

Sasson, Eliyahu   [1902–1978]

Israeli diplomat and expert on Arab affairs.

Born in Damascus and educated at Beirut's St. Joseph College, Sasson edited an Arabic-language Jewish newspaper to build a bridge between Arab and Jewish nations. In 1920 he went to Palestine and in 1930 he worked in the Jewish Agency's political department as head of the Arab section. During World War II, he led the British anti-Nazi campaign in the Middle East. Sasson was a member of the Zionist delegation that went to the United Nations in 1947 and 1948. He then became head of the Middle East department of Israel's newly formed Foreign Ministry.

He was a member of most Zionist and Israel delegations that negotiated the political future of Israel–Arab relations. In 1949 he participated in the armistice talks at Lausanne. From 1950 to 1952, he was Israel's minister to Turkey and until 1960, to Italy. In 1961 he was ambassador to Switzerland. He was recalled to Israel and was the minister of police from 1966 to 1969.

BIBLIOGRAPHY

NACHMANI, AMIKAM. *Israel, Turkey and Greece: Uneasy Relations in the Eastern Mediterranean.* London, 1987.

Miriam Simon

Sassoon Family

Family of international renown, which originated in the Jewish community of Baghdad.

Sassoon ben Salih (1750–1830) was a banker to the *vali* (provincial governor) of Baghdad. His son David (1792–1864) fled from a new and unfriendly vali, going first to the Gulf port of Bushehr in 1828 and then to Bombay, India, in 1832, with his large family. In Bombay, he built the international business called David S. Sassoon, with the policy of staffing it with people brought from Baghdad. They filled the functions of the various branches of his business in India, Burma, Malay, and east Asia. In each branch, he maintained a rabbi. His wealth and munificence were proverbial, and his business extended to China and then to England.

His eight sons also branched out into many directions. Elias David (1820–1880), his son by his first wife, left the firm to establish E. D. Sassoon. Three of his other sons became prominent in England and were great friends of the Prince of Wales, later Edward VII. Of those who settled in England, Sir Edward Albert Sassoon (1856–1912) was a Conservative member of Parliament from 1899 until his death, and the seat was inherited by his son Sir Philip Sassoon (1888–1939) from 1912 until his death. Sir Philip served in World War I as military secretary to Field Marshal Sir Douglas Haig and, during the 1920s and 1930s, as Britain's undersecretary of state for air. The English poet Siegfried Sassoon (1886–1967) is David's great-grandson. Intermarriage in England has caused the general loss of Judaism within this branch.

The branch that carried on the ancestral tradition has been represented by Rabbi Solomon David Sassoon (1915–1985), who moved from Letchworth to London and then to Jerusalem in 1970. He was the son of the David Sassoon who collected Jewish books and manuscripts and who catalogued them in *Ohel David,* in two volumes. This David was the son of Flora Abraham, who had moved from India to England in 1901 and established a famous salon in her London home.

BIBLIOGRAPHY

For a detailed entry and family tree, see the *Encyclopedia Judaica.*

Sylvia G. Haim

Satellite Cities Development

A new Egyptian industrial town.

Satellite Cities Development, known as Tenth of Ramadan, was built in the desert thirty-five miles (56 km) from the center of Cairo toward Isma'ilia. The construction of this new community began in 1978 as a result of a new urban policy, adopted by Egypt's government on April 5, 1974. Its objective was to redirect urban growth toward the desert and away from the limited arable land.

According to the master plan, Tenth of Ramadan is to be built in four stages, each taking eight to ten years to complete. The first stage of development was finished in 1988, and the second stage progresses. When completed the new community is expected to accommodate 500,000 people with an optimum population of one million.

The physical plan for the new community reflects a concern for human habitability. Of the 155 square miles (398 sq. km) slated for development, 26 square miles (68 sq. km) are designated as open green space. Traffic routes are separated from pedestrian routes, and shopping facilities are located within walking distance of all parts of the city. To minimize workers' dependence on cars and public transportation for commuting to work, industrial parks have also been situated within walking distance of residential zones.

According to the master plan, the new community is being constructed to be a self-sufficient industrial town. As of July 1992, 467 industrial factories were operational and 234 other industrial projects were under construction. It was estimated that 40,000 people were employed in industry. The majority of these workers did not live in Tenth of Ramadan but commuted to work from neighboring governorates (provinces).

As of December 31, 1991, 20,837 dwelling units had been constructed and 6,250 were under construction. However, community officials estimated that 10,000 people were living in Tenth of Ramadan as of July 1992. This is below the master plan's projection for this stage of development.

BIBLIOGRAPHY

"Tenth of Ramadan: New Industrial City." Egyptian Ministry of Housing and Reconstruction, January 1976.
"Tenth of Ramadan: New Industrial City." Egyptian Ministry of Housing and Reconstruction, December 31, 1991.

Hani Fakhouri

Sati, Shawkat al-

Personal physician to King Abdullah of Jordan.

Although never a politician, al-Sati was entrusted by King Abdullah ibn Husayn to carry out some sensitive missions regarding negotiations with Jewish officials over the partition of Palestine (1947–1948). In this capacity he carried messages back and forth between Amman and Jerusalem. The Jewish officials considered him trustworthy because he did not impose his personal views. In 1949, al-Sati participated in armistice talks to end the Arab–Israel War.

Jenab Tutunji

Sattar Khan   [?–1914]

A hero of the Constitutional Revolution in Iran, 1905–1911.

Sattar Khan headed the pro-constitutionalist forces of Tabriz against the armies of Mohammad Ali Shah Qajar, which had besieged the city. In 1909, Russia invaded Tabriz, on the pretext of providing food for its foreigners, and Sattar Khan sought refuge in the Ottoman consulate. In 1910, he left Tabriz for Tehran. Owing to his background as a Luti (chivalrous brotherhood) member, Sattar Khan's group became an embarrassment for the now victorious constitutionalist government; they were consequently disarmed in that year (1910).

BIBLIOGRAPHY

BROWNE, E. G. *The Persian Revolution of 1905–1909.* Cambridge, U.K., 1910.

Neguin Yavari

Sa'ud Family

See under Al Sa'ud *for specific members of the dynasty. See also* Abd al-Aziz ibn Sa'ud Al Sa'ud; Fahd ibn Abd al-Aziz Al Sa'ud; Faysal ibn Turki Al Sa'ud.

Saudi Arabia

A country whose influence is grounded in an old ruling family and new oil wealth, Saudi Arabia faces the twenty-first century adhering to conservative, traditional Islam while making use of technology and education to create better lives for its people.

The Kingdom of Saudi Arabia occupies the greater part of the Arabian peninsula, with a size of approximately 830,000 square miles (2.150 million sq. km) and a population of 17 million (1992 census). The country is bounded on the west by the Red Sea; on the north by Jordan and Iraq; on the east

by the Persian/Arabian Gulf and the small states of Kuwait, Qatar, the United Arab Emirates, and the island state of Bahrain just off the Saudi shore; and on the south by Oman and Yemen. The country forms a rough triangle, tilting from west to east. The HIJAZ, the westernmost of the three principal regions, rises from a low, barren coastal plain to a craggy, mountainous spine before leveling out into a gravel plateau. As the birthplace of Islam, Hijaz contains Islam's holiest cities, Makka (MECCA) and al-Madina (MEDINA). It also boasts Saudi Arabia's second largest city, JIDDA, with the country's biggest port. The center of the country is occupied by the NAJD, the historic center of modern Saudi Arabia and the location of its capital, RIYADH. The Eastern Province (al-HASA), lying between Riyadh and the Gulf, contains nearly all of the kingdom's massive oil deposits. Besides the cities of al-Zahran (Dhahran), al-DAMMAM, and al-Khubar (al-KHOBAR), the province also embraces the extensive and ancient oases of al-Ahsa and al-Qatif. Along the southeastern border, Saudi Arabia shares with Oman and Yemen the world's largest sand desert, RUB AL-KHALI, or the Empty Quarter. In the southwest, the mountains of Hijaz grow higher as they proceed south across Asir into Yemen. The country is divided into thirteen provinces.

As nearly all the country is desert, the climate is generally very hot in the summer and humid along the seashores. While the coastal plains are mild in winter, the interior desert can be cold. Small juniper forests exist only at several spots in the western mountains. There are no rivers or permanent bodies of water. Rainfall is sparse.

Traditionally, the majority of the people were engaged in pastoral nomadism, herding camels, goats, and sheep. Subsistence agriculture was practiced in the extensive oases of al-Ahsa and al-Hufuf in the Eastern Province as well as in other smaller oases across the country. Cultivation was also intense in the southwest highlands, and fishing was a feature along both the Red Sea and Gulf coasts. The west, particularly Mecca, Jidda, and Medina relied on the hajj (the annual Muslim pilgrimage) for income. Trade was important throughout the country, but especially for the small ports along the coastlines and for intermediary stops such as Buraida and Unayza in the Najd.

Oil exploration began in the Eastern Province in the 1930s, and commercially exploitable reserves were discovered in 1938. The advent of World War II delayed large-scale production until the late 1940s. Production levels reached 1 million barrels per day (b/d) in 1949, doubling by 1955, and rising to 3

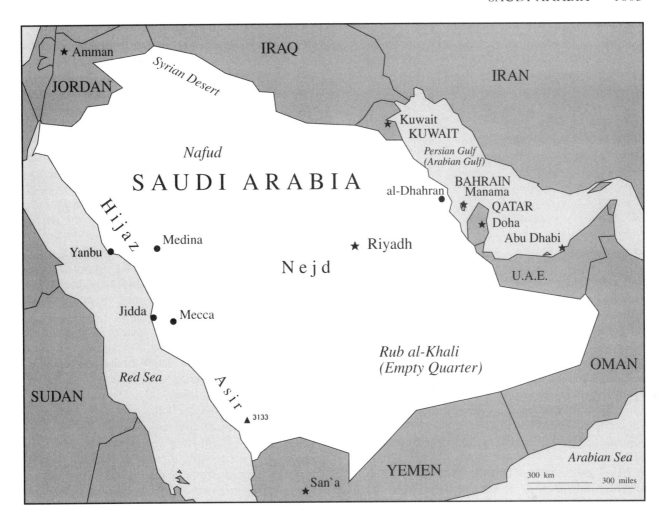

million b/d by 1968. By the beginning of the 1980s, Saudi Arabia was producing about 10 million b/d. This declined to less than 4 million b/d as a result of the subsequent decline in world demand for oil, but at the beginning of the 1990s, the kingdom was again producing over 8 million b/d and had become the world's largest crude oil exporter. Total reserves were estimated at 258 billion barrels in 1992, giving Saudi Arabia about 25 percent of the world's total. Other natural resources are negligible, although several small gold mines were put into operation in the early 1990s.

Oil completely transformed the Saudi economy. Prior to oil, the nascent Saudi kingdom was a poor state, highly dependent on hajj revenues for the government's income. Since then, Saudi Arabia has become a highly developed social welfare state. In the 1980s, it also embarked on a large-scale program of industrialization with emphasis placed on petrochemical industries and other energy-intensive industrial programs that could make effective use of locally refined oil or gas for fuel. The small ports of al-JUBAYL on the Gulf and YANBU on the Red Sea were selected as complementary sites for new industrial cities. Other industrial efforts have gone into import substitution, and a highly subsidized agricultural program has created enormous wheat surpluses in the central Najd.

Nearly all Saudi citizens are Arab, although there has been considerable ethnic mixing in the Hijaz as a result of centuries of emigration connected with the hajj. Arabic is the sole indigenous language, although English is widely spoken. All Saudis are Muslims, and most are Sunni. The HANBALI school of Islamic jurisprudence predominates because of the Wahhabi movement within Sunni Islam, founded in eighteenth-century Najd by Muhammad ibn Abd al-Wahhab, emphasizing the ascetic values of early Islam and widely followed within the kingdom (its adherents prefer to be known as MUWAHHIDUN, or Unitarians). Saudi Arabia also accepts special responsibility for the protection of the Islamic holy places. As many as 500,000 inhabitants of al-Qatif and al-Ahsa oases are (Ja'fari) Shi'a, and small Shi'a commu-

A Saudi officer's home in Jidda. (Richard Bulliet)

nities are to be found in and around Medina and the Najran oasis.

Great strides have been made in education over the past fifty years—about 62 percent of the citizens are literate. The country boasts seven universities, with the oldest dating from 1957: three universities specialize in Islamic disciplines, while the other four offer broader curricula. In addition, several hundred thousand Saudis have received university education abroad, notably in the United States and the United Kingdom.

Saudi Arabia is a monarchy, headed by a king drawn from the royal AL SA'UD FAMILY. The country's four monarchs since 1953 have all been sons of King Abd al-Aziz ibn Abd al-Rahman (ruled 1902–1953): Sa'ud ibn Abd al-Aziz (r. 1953–1964), Faisal ibn Abd al-Aziz (r. 1964–1975), Khalid ibn Abd al-Aziz (r. 1975–1982), and Fahd ibn Abd al-Aziz (r. since 1982). King Fahd also holds the title of prime minister. His half-brother Abdullah is heir apparent and first deputy prime minister. Fahd's full brother Sultan ibn Abd al-Aziz Al Sa'ud is next in line of succession and serves as second deputy prime minister in addition to minister of defense and aviation. Although the king holds enormous power, he is not an absolute monarch, being required to rule according to Islamic precepts and tribal tradition. Important decisions are made only after gaining the consensus of an inner circle of male members of the royal family. Generally, the process of consensus building also broadens to include the rest of the family, other key families (such as the AL SHAYKH FAMILY, descendants of Muhammad ibn Abd al-Wahhab, and collateral branches of the Al Sa'ud), the religious establishment, tribal shaykhs, senior government officials, and prominent merchant families.

The first Council of Ministers was established in 1953, and its ranks have since expanded to include a majority of commoners along with members of the Al Sa'ud. The family continues to hold the key portfolios of defense, interior, and foreign affairs. The armed forces are divided into four services: army, air force, air defense, and navy. There is also a large national guard, which serves as a counterbalance to the regular armed forces and is said to be particularly loyal to the Al Sa'ud. Saudi Arabia's orientation in foreign policy traditionally has been first to the Arab states and then to the Islamic world. Since the 1940s, the United States has been a key partner in oil exploitation, socioeconomic development, trade, and military and security matters. Staunchly anticommunist, the Saudi kingdom established diplomatic relations with the former Soviet Union only in 1990 (earlier relations in the 1920s and 1930s had been allowed to lapse).

The present kingdom is the third Saudi state established since an alliance was struck in 1744 between Islamic reformer Muhammad ibn Abd al-Wahhab and Muhammad ibn Sa'ud Al Sa'ud, then the head of the small town of al-Dir'iya (Deraiyeh) in Najd. Imbued by the religious fervor of Wahhabism, Muhammad ibn Sa'ud and his successors were able to extend their authority over much of Arabia, thus creating the first Saudi state. However, their success, and especially the occupation of Mecca, aroused the anxiety of the Ottoman Empire, which instructed its viceroy in Egypt, Muhammad Ali, to send an army to Arabia to recover Ottoman territory and to extinguish the Wahhabi/Saudi flame. An Egyptian army sacked al-Dir'iya in 1818, and the Al Sa'ud family's seat was subsequently moved to Riyadh, where it has remained ever since. Saudi fortunes revived in the mid-nineteenth century under Turki

Interior of an Arab bedouin tent. (Richard Bulliet)

A street in the Old Market of Ta'if. (Richard Bulliet)

ibn Abdullah, who founded the second Saudi state, and his son FAYSAL IBN TURKI, who regained many of the territories won by his predecessors and added new ones. However, another disastrous period in the late nineteenth century saw the Al Sa'ud forced to surrender Najd to a rival family, the AL RASHID FAMILY of Ha'il, and flee to Kuwait.

The origins of the third Saudi state lie in a surprise attack by young Abd al-Aziz ibn Abd al-Rahman on Riyadh in 1902. With Riyadh restored to Al Sa'ud control, Abd al-Aziz (commonly known in the West as Ibn Sa'ud) was able to conquer the rest of southern Najd and most of the Eastern Province before World War I. A British subsidy enabled him to harry the Al Rashid but precluded him from attacking King Husayn al-Hashimi of Hijaz, who had declared independence from the Ottomans in 1916. After the war, the Saudi leader first absorbed the Al Rashid state and then conquered Hijaz. At the beginning of 1926, Abd al-Aziz was able to proclaim himself king of Hijaz and sultan of Najd. Over the next decade, he gradually extended his boundaries to their present limits, being prevented from further expansion on all sides by British-protected states (apart from Yemen with whom a border war was fought in 1934). In 1936 the name of the country was changed to the Kingdom of Saudi Arabia.

The later years of King Abd al-Aziz's reign witnessed the infusion of oil income into a traditional society and the waste of much of it on consumer goods and palaces of the Al Sa'ud. Breaking with tradition, which held that succession should go to the strongest, King Abd al-Aziz appointed his weak son Sa'ud as his heir, instead of the more capable son Faisal. The early years of Sa'ud's reign brought the kingdom to the brink of financial disaster, and Sa'ud's flirtation with Egypt's socialist leader Gamel Abdel

Nasser did not prevent Egyptian intervention in Yemen in 1962. In 1964, an Al Sa'ud family council, with the backing of the powerful religious establishment, deposed King Sa'ud and named Faisal king. Faisal was able to continue the reforms he had already instituted as prime minister and to lay the foundations of a modern government and social welfare system. While he resisted Arab demands for a Saudi oil boycott of the West during the 1956 Arab–Israel War, he was unable to refrain during the Arab–Israel War of 1973 (the October War). The resultant shortage sent the price of oil soaring and put the kingdom on the world's center stage.

In 1975, King Faisal was assassinated by a cousin, and his half-brother Khalid succeeded him, but Khalid left much of the day-to-day governing to his half-brother Fahd. When Khalid died in 1982, King Fahd inherited a country faced with much reduced oil revenues and increasingly severe external challenges. The Iranian Revolution (1979) and the Iran–Iraq War (1980–1988) had refocused Saudi and

A modern mosque in Riyadh. (Richard Bulliet)

Western assessment of the principal threat to the kingdom away from the Soviet Union to a resurgent Iran. The threat acquired particular urgency with the shooting down of an invading Iranian combat plane in 1984, the attacks on Saudi-bound shipping during the tanker war of 1987/88, and the eruption of violence by Iranian pilgrims during the 1987 hajj, which resulted in more than four hundred deaths. However, an even more serious threat emerged in August 1990, when Iraq invaded Kuwait and thereby raised fears that it had designs on Saudi oil fields as well. Riyadh invited Arab and Western governments to participate in a coalition to drive the invading forces out of Kuwait. Operation Desert Storm was launched from Saudi territory in early 1991 and accomplished the liberation of Kuwait and the destruction of a substantial part of Iraq's military and industrial capability.

BIBLIOGRAPHY

HELMS, CHRISTINE MOSS. *The Cohesion of Saudi Arabia: Evolution of Political Identity*. London and Baltimore, 1981.

HOLDEN, DAVID, and RICHARD JOHNS, with James Buchan. *The House of Saud: The Rise and Rule of the Most Powerful Dynasty in the Arab World*. New York, 1982.

HOPWOOD, DEREK, ed. *The Arabian Peninsula: Society and Politics*. Studies of Modern Asia and Africa, no. 8. London, 1972.

NIBLOCK, TIM, ed. *State, Society and Economy in Saudi Arabia*. London, 1982.

WINDER, R. BAYLY. *Saudi Arabia in the Nineteenth Century*. London, 1965.

AL-YASSINI, AYMAN. *Religion and State in the Kingdom of Saudi Arabia*. Boulder, Colo., 1985.

John E. Peterson

Saudi Arabian Basic Industries Company

Ownership conglomerate for the Saudi oil industry.

SABIC was founded in 1976 to centralize and organize the development of oil resources in Saudi Arabia. SABIC is owned 70 percent by the Saudi government through the Public Investment Fund and 30 percent by the public at large through shares traded on the stock markets in the kingdom. As of the mid-1990s share ownership was restricted to Saudi citizens and Gulf Cooperation Council citizens.

SABIC operates through sixteen subsidiaries, either in joint venture with a foreign partner in nine cases or as 100 percent owner. SABIC earned a profit of 1.01 billion U.S. dollars and produced 20 million tons of products from all its affiliates. The table on page 1607 presents SABIC's affiliates, ownership, and products.

Jean-François Seznec

Saudi Arabian Monetary Agency

Saudi Arabia's central bank.

The Saudi Arabian Monetary Agency (SAMA) was founded in 1951. SAMA issues the kingdom's currency—58.7 billion Saudi riyals in 1991. It invests the kingdom's reserves and regulates the commercial banks and money changers. It also implements monetary policy and issues development bonds and treasury bills. SAMA is a signer of the Basle Concordat, which harmonized the regulatory processes of the main central banks in the world. SAMA is considered to be a very conservative regulator and ensures that the banking system in the kingdom remains liquid and maintains a low leverage of assets to capital (14 to 1 in 1991).

BIBLIOGRAPHY

SAUDI ARABIAN MONETARY AGENCY. Annual Reports.

Jean-François Seznec

SAVAK

The acronym for the Iranian State Security and Intelligence Organization.

SAVAK was formed in 1957 with the aid of the American and Israeli intelligence organizations. Its first director, General Timur Bakhtiar, was murdered in 1970 by order of Mohammad Reza Shah Pahlavi. Originally conceived to contain communist infiltration after the turbulent period of Mohammad Mossadegh and the nationalization of Iranian oil (during which the Soviet-backed Tudeh party played a major role), SAVAK quickly turned into a domestic secret police. Also in charge of censorship, SAVAK monitored all potential and actual dissident activity, whether it was armed or civilian and inside or outside the country. The Evin Prison, completed in the late 1970s, housed the political prisoners apprehended by SAVAK. Officially a civilian institution, SAVAK was attached to the office of the prime minister, and its director held the office of deputy prime minister for national security affairs. The activities of SAVAK were monitored by the Special Intelligence Bureau, which reported directly to the

SABIC Affiliates

Company	Ownership	Product Capacity (metric tons/year)
Saudi Petrochemicals Company (Saddaf)	50:50 SABIC/Shell Oil	Caustic Soda (450,000) Ethanol (300,000) MTBE (700,000) Styrene (360,000) Ethylene Dichloride (760,000)
Arabian Petrochemical Company (Petrokemya)	100% SABIC	Butene-1 (50,000) Ethylene (650,000) Butadiene (100,000) Benzene (75,000)
Eastern Petrochemical Company (Sharq)	50:50 SABIC/Mitsubishi and other Japanese companies	Linear Low Density Polyethylene (LLDPE) (188,000) Ethylene Glycol (660,000)
Saudi Yanbu Petrochemical Company (Yanpet)	50:50 SABIC/Mobil	Ethylene (560,000) Ethylene Glycol (250,000) Polyethylene (430,000)
Al-Jubail Petrochemical Company (Kemya)	50:50 SABIC/Exxon	LLDPE, HDPE, HOA (340,000)
National Plastic Company (Ibn Hayyan)	100% SABIC	Polyvinyl Chloride (PVC) Vinyl Chloride Monomer (VCM) (200,000)
Saudi Methanol Company (Ar-Razi)	50:50 SABIC/Mitsubishi Gas Chemical Company	Chemical Grade Methanol (1,200,000)
National Methanol Company (Ibn Sina)	50% SABIC; 25% Hoescht; 25% Texas Eastern	Chemical Grade Methanol (900,000) MTBE (700,000)
Saudi European Petrochemical Company (Ibn Zahr)	70% SABIC; 10% Apicorp; 10% Neste Oy; 10% Ecofuel	MTBE (120,000) Polypropylene (200,000)
Saudi Arabian Fertiliser Company (Saffco)	49% SABIC; 41% Saudi Public; 10% Employees	Sulfuric Acid (98,535) Melamin (20,240) Urea (353,774) Ammonia (225,735)
Ibn al-Baytar (National Chemical Fertiliser Company)	50:50 SABIC/SAFCO	Granular Urea (800,000)
Al-Jubail Fertiliser Company (Samad)	50:50 SABIC/Taiwan Fertiliser Company	Diethyl Hexanol (150,000) Ammonia Urea (600,000)
Saudi Iron & Steel Company (Hadeed)	100% SABIC	Steel Billets, Rebars (2.2 million)
Steel Rolling Company (Sulb)	100% SABIC	Steel Rebar (250,000)
Arabian Industrial Fibers Company (Ibn Rushd)	48% SABIC + 8 companies	Purified Terephtalic Acid (PTA) (start-up 1995)
National Industrial Gases Company (Gas)	100% SABIC	Liquid and Gas Oxygen (960,000) Liquid and Gas Nitrogen (460,000)

Sources: MEES; APS Review; OPEC Bulletin; OPEC Annual Report; SAMA Annual Report.

king and was headed by his childhood friend, General Hoseyn Fardust. Having failed to control the riots and disturbances during the parliamentary elections of 1960, Bakhtiar was removed as head of SAVAK in 1962. After the clerical riots of 1963, which were led by Ayatollah Khomeini, the new chief, General Naser Pakravan, was replaced by General Ne'matollah Nasiri, who had arrested Mossadegh in 1953 and hence proven his loyalty. Nasiri retained the position of chief until 1978, when he was replaced by General Naser Moqaddam as part of the shah's strategy of appeasement. Late in 1978, the shah even offered to dissolve SAVAK to placate the leaders of a revolution that the organization had failed to predict. A highly effective institution, SAVAK was perceived by the Iranian public to be omnipresent, omniscient, and omnipotent. Universal disdain for the institution made it a primary target of postrevolutionary violence; of the 248 military personnel executed between February and September 1979, 61 were SAVAK officials. General Nasiri himself was killed by a frenzied mob, and SAVAK was accused of murdering such revolutionaries as Ali Shari'ati. Upon its disbandment by Ayatollah Khomeini in 1979, SAVAK was superseded by SAVAMA, its Islamic counterpart. General Fardust, who died in prison in 1987, was reportedly the first director of the SAVAMA. SAVAMA itself was rendered obsolete by the creation of the Ministry of Intelligence and State Security, led by Ayatollah Muhammad Reyshahri. It is believed that low-ranking SAVAK agents were recalled by leaders of the Islamic Republic who made use of their experience in combating the Iranian left.

BIBLIOGRAPHY

COTTAM, RICHARD W. *Iran and the United States: A Cold War Case Study.* Pittsburgh, 1988.
SIMPSON, JOHN. *Behind Iranian Lines.* London, 1988.

Neguin Yavari

Sawt al-Arab

Egyptian radio station.

Launched in July 1953, one month after Egypt's republic was proclaimed, Sawt al-Arab (Voice of the Arabs) broadcast pan-Arab propaganda and soon became the most influential station in the Arab East. It was the creation of Gamal Abdel Nasser, who was deputy prime minister and interior minister at the time.

With Nasser's rise to the presidency, Sawt al-Arab became a powerful instrument of Egyptian foreign policy, particularly in the 1950s and 1960s. Until the Arab–Israel War of 1956, the station carried a forceful campaign against imperialism, particularly the Baghdad Pact. (Sawt al-Arab's powerful transmitters were, ironically, a gift from the U.S. government.) The station's anti-Zionist message contributed to Nasser's rise as a popular hero among Palestinians. During the 1958 crisis in Lebanon, it transmitted denunciations of President Camille Chamoun and espoused the Lebanese Muslim cause. It also played a significant role in mobilizing the revolutions in North and South Yemen in the 1960s. Although closely identified with Nasser, Sawt al-Arab continued to broadcast after his death in 1970.

BIBLIOGRAPHY

GOLDSCHMIDT, ARTHUR, Jr. *Modern Egypt.* Boulder, Colo., 1988.
HOPWOOD, DEREK. *Egypt: Politics and Society, 1945–1981.* Winchester, Mass., 1982.
HUDSON, M. *Arab Politics.* New Haven, Conn., 1977.
RUGH, WILLIAM A. *The Arab Press.* 2nd ed. Syracuse, N.Y., 1987.

Elizabeth Thompson

Sawt al-Sha'b

Jordanian newspaper.

Founded in 1983, *Sawt al-Sha'b* (Voice of the People) is an Arabic-language evening daily published by the Dar al-Sha'b Company. In August 1988, the government dismissed the paper's board of directors, following a general crackdown on the press, and exercised editorial control over it until December 1989, when it relinquished its control. The government maintains the majority share of the company's stock, however. With a circulation of thirty thousand, it is one of Jordan's three major daily newspapers in Arabic.

BIBLIOGRAPHY

The Middle East and North Africa 1991, 37th ed. London, 1991.

Abla M. Amawi

Sayfettin, Ömer   [1884–1920]

Turkish novelist and nationalist.

Sayfettin was born in Gönen to an immigrant family from the Caucasus and by age nineteen earned a veterinary degree from the Istanbul Military Academy. Fighting in the Balkan War, he was taken prisoner by the Greeks for ten months in 1913. He sympathized with the Turkish nationalist movements of the Committee of Union and Progress and of Ziya Gökalp, and he joined many other writers in producing patriotic propaganda during World War I. Sayfettin died of a sudden illness at age thirty-six.

Sayfettin was known for his elegant, simple style in writing Turkish. With Gökalp he led the GENÇ KALEMLER (Young Pens) literary movement in reaction to the turgid prose of the Servet-i Fünun (Wealth of Knowledge) circle. His highly esteemed novels and short stories treated nationalist themes, like the atrocities of the enemy during war, and social themes, like corruption, hypocrisy, and superstition. He made use of Turkish folklore in his works and often wrote with humor and irony.

BIBLIOGRAPHY

MITLER, LOUIS. *Ottoman Turkish Writers.* New York, 1988.

Elizabeth Thompson

Saygun, Ahmed Adnan [1907–1991]

Turkish composer.

İzmir-born Saygun studied music in Turkey and at the age of twenty won a competition for a state scholarship to study in France. He was a member of the first generation of Turkish composers—known as "The Five"—who sought to add harmonic substructures to Turkish folk songs, which are pure melodies. Saygun and his colleagues also composed symphonies incorporating folk music. In 1934 Saygun composed the first important Turkish national opera, *Feridun,* based on a Perso–Turkish legend. Saygun also composed the operas *Kerem,* whose libretto narrated the love affair of a Christian girl and a Muslim boy, and *Köroğlu* (The Son of the Blind Man), whose libretto tells the story of a chivalrous outlaw. Other compositions by Saygun include an oratorio, *Yunus Emre,* two string quartets, and piano concertos. His works have been performed in Paris, Moscow, New York, and Washington, D.C. Saygun also contributed to the training of the next generation of Turkish composers.

BIBLIOGRAPHY

AND, METIN. "Opera and Ballet in Modern Turkey." In *The Transformation of Turkish Culture: The Atatürk Legacy,* ed. by Günsel Renda and C. Max Kortepeter. Princeton, N.J., 1986.

ORANSAY, GÜLTEKIN. "Music in the Republican Era." In *The Transformation of Turkish Culture: The Atatürk Legacy,* ed. by Günsel Renda and C. Max Kortepeter. Princeton, N.J., 1986.

David Waldner

Sayyab, Badr Shakir al- [1926–1964]

One of the first Iraqi poets to write Arabic free verse.

Born in Jaykur, Iraq, and educated in Basra and Baghdad, al-Sayyab wrote one of the earliest poems of *al-shi'r al-hurr* (roughly, free verse). His was the first modernist attempt to develop complex, anti-traditional modes to explore the human condition, metaphysics, and social and political issues, as well as his own experience and feelings, in sharp contrast to the poetry that had dominated previous decades. Constructing a text as a closely interwoven whole, he embodies the organic nature of the quest for modernization in the Arab world.

Al-Sayyab remained closer to the spirit and tone of classical Arabic poetry than other *al-ruwwad* (pioneers) of al-shi'r al-hurr, even when using modern techniques or myth and symbolism. Those poems that appear ambiguous use myth or symbolic treatment of contemporary political situations.

Highly ideological (for many years a Marxist), al-Sayyab wrote more confessional and intimate poetry during his final illness. His life reads like a tale of political involvement and struggle, imprisonment, and suffering. The poet Adonis, a well-known scholar of Arabic literature, described al-Sayyab's poetry as "a point of meeting between two worlds, one retreating, the other advancing—emerging out of the future."

BIBLIOGRAPHY

KHOURI, MOUNAH, and HAMID ALGAR, eds. *An Anthology of Modern Arabic Poetry.* Berkeley, Calif., 1974.

Kamal Abu-Deeb

Sayyad, Parviz [1937–]

Iranian actor and director.

Sayyad was born in Lahijan. In 1975, he established the Little Theater of Tehran, where contemporary Western and traditional Iranian plays were performed. Sayyad is best known for the character of Samad, a simple provincial boy awestruck by the advances of modernity, who is perhaps the most popular television and cinematic personage in Iran.

BIBLIOGRAPHY

CHELKOWSKI, PETER. "Popular Entertainment, Media and Social Change in Twentieth-Century Iran." In *Cambridge History of Iran,* vol. 7. Cambridge, U.K., 1991.

Neguin Yavari

Sayyid

An Arabic word that literally means "master," "chieftain," or "lord."

In pre-Islamic Arabia *sayyid* (pl., *sada* or *asyad*) was used to refer to the preeminent leader of a clan or tribe. Early in the Muslim era, however, "sayyid" became an honorific title for all those who could claim genealogical descent from the clan of the prophet Muhammad (i.e., the Banu Hashim). This category basically included direct descendants of Muhammad himself—through the marriage of his daughter Fatima to his cousin Ali—as well as any other scions either of Ali or of Muhammad's two uncles, Abu Talib and Abbas. Over time, the title was restricted to Muhammad's direct descendants through his grandsons (by Fatima and Ali), Hasan and Husayn. A notable exception to this restriction is in the popular attribution of the title "sayyid" (frequently in the colloquial form, *sid* or *sidi*) to a wide variety of holy persons and other Muslim culture heroes. In Mecca and the surrounding Hijaz region of the Arabian peninsula, the custom developed of applying the title almost exclusively to descendants of Husayn, whereas the title "sharif" was reserved for the descendants of Hasan. In many traditional settings male sayyids often wear the distinctive green or black turban that has customarily marked sayyids and their families for public veneration. Although in most areas sayyids represent a relatively elite minority, in South Asia and Yemen they comprise significant social classes of Muslims. Throughout history many Muslim rulers have claimed sayyid status for themselves and their dynasties. Mulay Hassan II of Morocco and Hussein ibn Talal of Jordan are two contemporary monarchs who bear the distinction of sayyid.

Scott Alexander

Sayyid, Ahmad Lutfi al-   [1872–1963]

Egyptian author, editor, and educational leader.

Born to a landowning family in Daqhaliya province, he was educated at the Cairo Law School, where he founded Egypt's first law review. Upon graduating in 1894, he became a deputy public prosecutor. He later joined the palace-based secret society that became the basis for the National party. Egypt's ruler, Khedive Abbas Hilmi II, advised him to spend a year in Geneva to acquire Swiss nationality, so that he would be protected by the capitulations from Egypt's press law and thus be allowed to edit a nationalist newspaper. While living abroad, he came under the influence of Muhammad Abduh, the Muslim reformer, and decided to distance himself from the khedive. He returned to Egypt to work as a public prosecutor but resigned because of his growing dissatisfaction with Britain's rule. He opened a private law practice and defended the peasants who were tried in the DINSHAWAY INCIDENT. When a group of Egyptian liberals founded *al-Jarida* in 1907, they made him its editor. Its shareholders formed the Umma party as a counterforce to the khedive and the nationalists, and Lutfi was its main spokesman. His editorials favored individual rights and constitutional liberties against Abbas's autocratic pretensions, as well as against the ties of pan-Islam to the Ottoman Empire. Instead, he focused on building a strong Egyptian patriotism based on education and a sense of self-worth. He resigned after Britain declared its protectorate over Egypt in 1914. He became one of the early members of the Wafd (delegation) in 1919, but then distanced himself from party politics. From 1923 to 1941, he served as rector of Cairo University. He translated Aristotle's *Nicomachean Ethics* into Arabic and later reissued some of his editorials from *al-Jarida*. A champion of reason, he preferred a life of scholarship to a political career. Known as *Ustadh al-Jil* (Professor of the Generation), Lutfi al-Sayyid's influence on Egypt's intellectuals has been immense.

BIBLIOGRAPHY

AHMED, JAMAL M. *Intellectual Origins of Egyptian Nationalism.* London, 1960.

AL-SAYYID, AFAF LUTFI. *Egypt and Cromer.* London, 1968.

AL-SAYYID, AHMAD LUTFI. *Qissat Hayati* (The Story of My Life). Cairo, 1963.

WENDELL, CHARLES. *The Evolution of the Egyptian National Image from its Origins to Ahmad Lutfi al-Sayyid.* Berkeley, Calif., 1972.

Arthur Goldschmidt, Jr.

Sayyid, Jalal al-   [?–1992]

Syrian politician and dissident.

Jalal al-Sayyid was born in Dayr al-Zawr to a tribal family. During the Shishakli regime, al-Sayyid's brother Sa'id, was governor of Homs. In 1947, al-Sayyid participated in the founding meeting of the BA'TH party, and he was elected a member of the executive committee. In August 1949, he was elected a deputy. Later, members of the Ba'th party accused him of being feudal and reactionary. He opposed the merging of the Arab Socialist and Ba'th parties and refused party orders to leave Syria. He attended the Homs congress that included all those factions opposed to the Shishakli regime. He was jailed and then freed following the coup d'état that overthrew the Shishakli government. In 1954, al-Sayyid dissolved the Ba'th section in Dayr al-Zawr in order to reorganize it following the clashes between Ba'thists and Syrian nationalists. In 1955, he offered his resignation from the Ba'th party.

George E. Irani

Sayyida Zaynab Mosque

Modern structure honoring the Islamic saint.

The mosque of Sayyida Zaynab, a modern structure built on a venerable and revered site, honors one of the great Islamic saints of Cairo. Sayyida Zaynab was a historical person, most frequently identified as either the sister of Sayyidna Husayn or the companion of Sayyida Nafisa. The *mawlid* (feast day) of Sayyida Zaynab is one of the most colorful in Cairo, drawing thousands to celebrate her putative birthday.

Raymond William Baker

Sayyidna Husayn Mosque

A neo-Gothic structure just north of al-Azhar in the old bazaar quarter of Cairo.

Sayyidna Husayn mosque, which honors the Prophet's grandson, was built in 1792. Standing so close to al-Azhar and amid the beloved old quarters of the city, the mosque exerts a special hold on the imagination of Egyptians.

Raymond William Baker

Schistosomiasis

A disease of humans marked by blood loss and tissue damage.

Also known as bilharzia, schistosomiasis is spread by a snail that hosts the blood fluke (worm) that causes the disease. Water-related development programs, partic-

ularly large-scale irrigation projects like the Aswan High Dam, have created environments in which these snails flourish, resulting in a rapid spread of the disease, which previously had been limited in scope. Efforts to combat the disease have not yet succeeded because the chemicals that are used to kill the snails are prohibitively expensive. The medication that treats the disease can only be administered under close medical supervision, making it unsuitable for mass use. Next to malaria, it is probably humanity's most serious parasitic infection.

BIBLIOGRAPHY

WELSH, BRIAN W., and PAVEL BUTORIN. *Dictionary of Development.* New York, 1990.

David Waldner

Science and Technology

With the notable exception of Israel, science and technology in the Middle East is at an embryonic stage, especially when compared to the West. Whether and how it develops will depend largely on politics and economics in each country and in the area.

The science and technology systems in most Middle Eastern countries are, with two exceptions, similar to those in other Third World countries. Israel, whose system is akin to that of industrial countries, is the

Biotechnician in Bahrain, 1995. (BAPCO)

major exception. The other is Afghanistan, which has not yet established a scientific infrastructure.

Most Middle Eastern countries are primarily interested in applying science and technology for development. Some have sought to acquire capabilities in defense technologies but have been only partially successful. Israel alone has succeeded in applying technology for developmental and military purposes.

With the exception of Israel, information on professional manpower and science-related institutions in all countries is limited.

Manpower Development. Governments of the region have long recognized the importance of professional manpower to national development and have consequently devoted considerable efforts and resources to the provision of higher education. During the early 1950s, most countries except for Egypt and Israel suffered from shortages of professional manpower. These shortages have today been overcome everywhere in the region except Afghanistan.

Substantial numbers of engineers and scientists are now available. The Arab countries are in the lead, with a total of some 600,000 engineers. The figures on research and development (R&D) scientific manpower, though incomplete and fragmentary, are as follows: Egypt (1986), 21,000; Iran (1985), 3,200; Israel (1984), 20,000; Turkey (1985), 11,300. These countries also had a substantial number of university professors: Egypt (1988), 33,000; Algeria (1988), 14,000; Morocco (1989), 7,000; Iraq (1986), 4,600; Saudi Arabia (1988), 10,000; Syria (1986), 5,000; Iran (1988), 14,000; Turkey (1989), 31,000.

Graduate level education and postdoctoral specialization in the basic and applied sciences are still dependent on foreign study.

Despite large numbers of scientists and engineers, the science and technology systems in most countries suffer from a lack of articulation: higher education is not integrated with demand. Moreover, continuing and distance education is still underdeveloped. Consequently, there is an inability to adapt and upgrade manpower skills in an efficient and cost-effective manner.

Israel, by contrast, depends heavily on educated immigrants. Its universities are of high quality, and effective systems of continuing and distance education have been introduced.

Research & Development. R&D in Israel is at the same level as those of leading industrial countries. It publishes about ten thousand papers a year in referred journals surveyed by the Institute of Scientific Information (ISI) in Philadelphia. Its per capita publication output compares favorably with that of the United States, and the profile of its publications is similar to that of other industrial countries.

Israeli researchers circulate in and receive funding and support from European and American research establishments. A considerable proportion of Israeli R&D is directed toward weapons systems; but Israel also has strong research programs in most scientific and technological fields of relevance to its economy. It devotes about 3 percent of its gross national product (GNP) to R&D, and currently has about fifty thousand research scientists. Its heavy emphasis on military technology is, however, causing serious economic problems as a result of the current collapse of the world demand for weaponry.

The scientific output of the Arab countries can be compared favorably with that of Brazil and India, the leading Third World countries. During the 1980s, the number of scientific publications per million inhabitants was eighteen (Brazil), sixteen (India), and fifteen (the Arab world). The per capita output of the Arab countries is some 2 percent that of industrial countries. In 1990, there were more than five thousand publications from seven hundred Arab institutions. Half of these were from twelve institutions, eleven of which were universities. Other institutions involved in publishing were hospitals and agricultural research stations.

R&D in the Arab countries is overwhelmingly of an applied nature. Thirty-eight percent of publications are in medicine; 20 percent in agriculture; 17 percent in engineering; 17 percent in the basic sciences; and 8 percent in economics and management. Even work that is classified as basic science is often of an applied nature. The three leading countries in order of research output are Egypt (37 percent), Saudi Arabia (20 percent), and Kuwait (12 percent). In 1990, Kuwaiti output had started to approach that of European countries.

Publications from Iran and Turkey are on a more limited scale; their output in 1990 was 161 and 1300 respectively. The number of publishing institutions was 80 (Iran) and 155 (Turkey).

The profile of publications from Iran and Turkey, like that in the Arab countries, emphasizes traditional and applied fields such as medicine and agriculture; the proportion of publications in the basic sciences, molecular biology, information sciences, and other advanced areas is far below international levels.

The exact funding of R&D in the Arab world, Iran, and Turkey is not accurately known; it is estimated, however, to be below 1.0 percent (probably closer to 0.5 percent) of GNP throughout the region.

Institutional Framework. The capacity to apply science and technology is dependent on the prevailing institutional framework rather than on the actual number of professionals. Most of the countries have some form of institution to manage science and technology: ministries of science and technology or directorates, attached to the ministry of higher education, of planning, or to the prime minister, which are responsible for different aspects of science and technology.

But the pervasive nature of science and technology is still not recognized, and these institutions are generally bureaucratic and inflexible; they tend to regard science and technology as being restricted to R&D and manpower.

Once again, Israel is the exception; it has established an effective and comprehensive system of science policy planning and management.

The Application of Science and Technology. Some of the instruments through which science and technology are developed and applied are: consulting and contracting organizations, agricultural research stations, extension programs, hospitals, industrial firms, testing laboratories, information services, and others.

Most countries have organizations to provide these services that vary in competence and efficiency. A brief description follows of two strategic types of organizations.

Consulting organizations are critical instruments for planning and designing new projects and for adapting and transferring technology. A substantial number of state-run and private consulting firms have been established throughout the region. In fact, one of the largest international consulting firms in the Third World is Lebanese [Dar al-Hanadasa (Shair & Partners)]. Large public-sector consulting firms are found in most countries of the region.

Consulting firms are heavily oriented toward civil engineering technologies, with the result that the region is still dependent on the importation of consulting services in industrial technology.

Contracting organizations bring together ideas, plans, materials, equipment, labor, and financing to produce the desired products within an agreed schedule and cost. The largest contracting firms in the region are in Turkey, whose government has provided them with the necessary financial, risk cover, and diplomatic support.

There are around 100,000 Arab contracting firms, but the Arab countries still depend on foreign firms for 50 percent of their requirements. This is largely due to the absence of appropriate public policies. The leading Arab contracting companies are privately owned and based in Lebanon and Saudi Arabia.

National Science Policies. Israel is the only country in the region with the capacity to design and implement science and technology policies. In the rest of the region, national, regional, and international organizations have sought to promote the development of capabilities in science policy formation, but the results have been limited. This is due to the prevalence of preindustrial political cultures, which have made science policy formation difficult, if not impossible.

As of the mid-1990s there were increasing indications that Turkey would soon acquire an industrial political economy. When it does so, it will be capable of formulating and implementing science policies.

The colonial legacy of the region has led to the virtual elimination of intersectoral linkages and has resulted in the vertical integration of the components of a fragmented economy into foreign sources of technology. This situation has prevented the acquisition and accumulation of technological experiences, which in turn has reduced the chances of a transition to an industrial political economy.

The combination of underutilized capabilities and unexpected developments could lead the way to technology change. For example, the heavy bombing of Iraq, coupled with the stringent economic blockade, has forced the mobilization of Iraq's considerable capabilities in science and technology, which had previously been marginalized. A massive reconstruction of the country has consequently taken place. The same example applied to Iran during the 1980s.

Different countries in the region may discover how to mobilize their considerable professional scientific and technological manpower after other alternatives are no longer available. These challenges could induce changes in the political culture, which in turn could result in new attitudes toward science and technology.

BIBLIOGRAPHY

ALESCO. *Strategy for the Development of Science and Technology in the Arab World.* Tunis, 1987. English version available.
INSTITUTE OF SCIENTIFIC INFORMATION. *Science Citation Index.* Philadelphia, 1970–1991 (monthly).
OECD. *Main Science and Technology Indicators.* Paris, 1992 (biannual).
UNESCO. *UNESCO's Yearbook.* Paris, 1970–1991 (annual).
ZAHLAN, A. B. *The Arab Construction Industry: Acquiring Technological Capacity.* London, 1991.
———. *Science and Science Policy in the Arab World.* London, 1980.

Antoine Benjamin Zahlan

Scouts

Worldwide youth movement that began in England in the early 1900s; it now has affiliates in virtually every country.

Except for Afghanistan, all Middle Eastern countries have scouting associations, affiliated with the World Organization of the Scout Movement. The oldest are in Lebanon (founded 1912), Syria (1913), Egypt (1918), Iraq (1921), Tunisia (1933), and Algeria (1934). The region's office of the World Scout Bureau is in Cairo, Egypt, for all Arab countries; in Geneva, Switzerland, for Turkey; and in Manila, Philippines, for Iran. In Israel, the Girl's section belong to the Asia–Pacific scout region (Manila); the Boy's to the European (Geneva). Most countries have separate Boy Scouts and Girl Scout/Guide organizations.

As a Youth Movement in the Middle East, scouting revolves around camping and community service, including desert reclamation, medical aid, traffic control, tree planting, construction, helping pilgrims to Mecca, literacy activities, and disaster relief. Self-sufficiency and good citizenship are the goals, with volunteerism and outdoor activities stressed for health and positive attitudes toward society.

In 1990, the largest scout associations were in Iran (105,515), Egypt (73,275), Algeria (66,585), Tunisia (26,120), Israel (29,600), and Turkey (21,750). Total regional membership is some 450,000.

BIBLIOGRAPHY

BOY SCOUTS OF AMERICA, EXTERNAL COMMUNICATIONS OFFICE. *Fact Sheets.* Irving, Tex., 1992.

Guilain P. Denoeux

Sebastatsi, Mekhitar [1676–1749]

Armenian clergyman.

Sebastatsi was born in Sebastia (now Sivas). He was educated in the monastery of Surp Nshan (St. Mark) from 1685 to 1691. Thereafter he studied at a number of Armenian monasteries, including Echmiadzin, and in 1699 was ordained a celibate priest in the Armenian Apostolic Church. After his appeal to establish a new fraternal order rejected by the Armenian patriarchate of Constantinople (now Istanbul), Sebastatsi and his followers converted to Roman Catholicism and took refuge in Venice, where in 1717 the Senate allotted the island of San Lazzaro as the site of their monastery.

Once settled, Sebastatsi produced works that revived learning in the Armenian language: *Kerakanu-*

tiun grabari lezvi haykazan seri (Grammar for the classical language of the Armenian race; 1730), *Bargirk haykaznian lezvi* (Lexicon of the Armenian language; 2 vols., 1749–1769), and *Durn kerakanutian ashkharhabar lezvi hayots sharadretsial tajkakanav lezvav* (Gateway to the grammar of the vernacular language of the Armenians written in the Turkish language; 1727).

Of equal significance was Sebastatsi's training of a school of followers who formed the Mekhitarian Order. In Venice, and at a second branch established in Vienna (1811), the Mekhitarians established schools, promoted education, and published in the Armenian language.

The Mekhitarians continued to flourish in the twentieth century, with educational institutions in Armenian communities from the Middle East to the United States. Outside of Armenia and the Armenian patriarchate of Jerusalem, the manuscript collections of the Mekhitarian monasteries in Venice and Vienna are the largest in the world, and their vast libraries of Armenian works have made their monasteries centers of scholarly research. The Mehkitarians have been instrumental in providing Western scholars access to Armenian civilization.

BIBLIOGRAPHY

ADALIAN, ROUBEN P. *From Humanism to Rationalism: Armenian Scholarship in the Nineteenth Century.* Atlanta, Ga., 1992.

Rouben P. Adalian

Sebastiani, Horace [1772–1851]

French general.

Sebastiani was one of Napoléon Bonaparte's most trusted lieutenants. He traveled to Egypt and Syria in 1802/03 and reported favorably on the feasibility of a French reconquest. In 1806, Sebastiani became French ambassador in Constantinople (now Istanbul) and negotiated an informal alliance against Russia with the Ottoman sultan, Selim III. The resulting conflict between Russia and the Ottoman Empire saw a radical increase in French power in Constantinople that undermined the authority of Selim III and thus paved the way for his deposition in 1807. As French foreign minister in 1832, Sebastiani was unable to halt the conflict between Sultan Mahmud II and Muhammad Ali. Seven years later, serving as ambassador in London, Sebastiani made a futile attempt to alert his government to Lord Palmerston's determination to humble Muhammad Ali. Having rejected Sebastiani's warnings, the French cabinet watched as an English coalition defeated Egypt without the aid of France. This diplomatic humiliation brought down the government of Adolphe Thiers and severely weakened French influence in the Middle East for years to come.

BIBLIOGRAPHY

ANDERSON, M. S. *The Eastern Question*. London, 1966.
LEWIS, BERNARD. *The Emergence of Modern Turkey*. New York, 1968.

Zachary Karabell

Sebbar, Leila   [1941–   ]

Algerian novelist and essayist.

Leila Sebbar was born on 9 November 1941 in Aflou, Algeria, to a French mother and an Algerian father. She lives in Paris and writes in French.

Sebbar deals with a variety of topics, from psychology to fiction. Her novels often center the events around a young woman called Shérazade, a name very close to that of the heroine of the *Thousand and One Nights*. She is the backbone of three novels: *Shérazade, 17 Ans, Brune, Frisée, les Yeux Verts* (1980), *Les Carnets de Shérazade* (1985), and *Le Fou de Shérazade* (1991). Sebbar used the connection between the two heroines to establish the contrast between the old and the new generations of Algerian women.

Sebbar has also an interest in the Beur, the second generation of Maghribi youth who were born and raised in France and who have not integrated yet into French society. She often expresses their frustration in her novels. Her book *Parle Mon Fils, Parle à Ta Mère* (1984), a moving plea of a mother seeking to communicate with her son, is an illustration of the absence of dialogue between two generations who do not speak the same language.

Although she is the product of two cultures experienced on two levels, linguistic and social, Sebbar manages to remain outside her novels. Her detachment gives her a better perspective on her characters. It is a characteristic that clearly separates her works from those of young members of the Beur generation, who remain very central to their novels.

Sebbar's writings thus far have focused on the problems of emigration and the torments of life in exile. The latter is central to *Lettres Parisiennes, Autopsie de l'Exil* (1986), a correspondence with Nancy Huston.

BIBLIOGRAPHY

BAMIA, AIDA. "The North African Novel: Achievements and Prospects." In *Mundus Arabicus*, vol. 5. Ed. by Issa Boullata. Cambridge, Mass., 1992.

Aida A. Bamia

Secret Army Organization

A movement of French colons and renegade army officers that sought to block Algeria's independence.

The Secret Army Organization (Organisation Armée Secrète; OAS) was created in February 1961 under the leadership of COLON activists Pierre Lagaillarde and Jean-Jacques Susini. Its military leadership was provided by Generals Raoul Salan, Marie-André Zeller, Edmond Jouhaud, and—for a short time—Maurice Challe.

In April 1961, under Challe's leadership, the OAS attempted a coup in Algiers that appeared for a short time to threaten the metropolitan government as well. When the coup failed, the movement adopted a policy of undermining government authority by bombings and by assassinations of officials, of liberal intellectuals, and prominent Muslim leaders. As the Evian negotiations proceeded, the organization switched to a campaign of terror against Muslims in general, and finally, after France agreed to independence, to a "scorched earth" policy of massive destruction of infrastructure. On June 17, 1962, the OAS signed a cease-fire with the Front de Libération Nationale (FLN: National Liberation Front).

[*See also:* Algerian War of Independence]

BIBLIOGRAPHY

HORNE, ALISTAIRE. *A Savage War of Peace: Algeria, 1954–1962*. London, 1985.

John Ruedy

Security Council Resolutions 242 and 338

Resolutions designed to bring about a peaceful solution to the Arab–Israel conflict.

After the Arab–Israel War of 1967, the United Nations adopted, on 22 November, a resolution calling for a solution to the conflict based on the concept of "territory for peace." It emphasized the "inadmissibility of the acquisition of territory by war and the need for a just and lasting peace . . . ," and affirmed "withdrawal of Israeli armed forces from territories of the recent conflict" and "the termination of all . . . states of belligerency and respect for and acknowledgment of the sovereignty, teritorial integrity and political independence of every state in the area."

Interpretations regarding the extent of withdrawal have varied. The Arab position is that the resolution requires Israel's unconditional withdrawal from all the conquered territories. (Until 1988, the PLO rejected the resolution because it called for a settlement to the "refugee problem" and ignored Palestinian national rights.) In Israel, the Labor party's position was that withdrawal should take into account Israel's security needs, and the Likud bloc claimed that withdrawal from Sinai satisfied the terms of the resolution. The U.S. position, which had wide international support, is that withdrawal should take place with only minor border adjustments.

Security Council resolution 338, passed on 22 October 1973, called for immediate cease-fire, implementation of resolution 242, and negotiations between the parties. It also provided the basis for the disengagement agreements between Egypt and Israel (1974–1975) and Syria and Israel (1974).

Both resolutions have been the basis of all U.S. peace initiatives since 1967, including the Rogers Plan, the Camp David Accords, the Reagan Plan, and the Madrid Conference.

BIBLIOGRAPHY

QUANDT, WILLIAM B. *Decade of Decisions: American Policy Toward the Arab–Israeli Conflict, 1967–1976.* Berkeley, Calif., 1977.
SMITH, CHARLES D. *Palestine and the Arab–Israeli Conflict.* New York, 1992.

Philip Mattar

Seeb, Treaty of

See Sib, Treaty of

Sefaretname

A Turkish diplomatic report.

When an Ottoman ambassador or envoy sent to a foreign country by the sultan returned to Istanbul, he presented a *sefaretname* (report) providing information on the situation of the country, the work he accomplished there, and personal observations. The earliest such reports date to the late 1600s.

BIBLIOGRAPHY

Türk Ansiklopedisi. Ankara, 1981.

David Waldner

Sefriou, Ahmad [1915–]

Moroccan novelist and short story writer.

Sefriou was born in Fez, Morocco. He studied at the Mulay Idris college in Fez, receiving a predominantly French education. He subsequently held posts at the Moroccan Office of Arts and Crafts, the Batha Museum in Fez, and the Office of Historic Monuments in Rabat.

Sefriou is greatly interested in his country's folklore, as is obvious in his writings. *Le Jardin des Sortilèges ou Le Parfum des Légendes* (Paris, 1989; The Garden Sorcery or the Perfume of Legends) is essentially a book of folktales; other works, such as *Le Chapelet d'Ambre* (Paris, 1949; The Amber Rosary) and *La Boîte à Merveille* (Paris, 1954; The Magic Box) portray traditional Moroccan life and customs, which Sefriou appears to cherish. Although written while Morocco was a French colony, Sefriou's books seem to ignore this foreign presence. His preoccupation with the portrayal of his country's traditions is probably an affirmation of what appeared to be a threatened identity.

Sefriou's approach is that of an ethnologist revealing his society's customs and traditions and his religion's (Islam's) dictates. His novel *La Maison de Servitude* (Algiers, 1973; The House of Slavery) gives the reader a glimpse of traditional life in the city of Fez and of teaching at the Qarawiyyin. The style of the novel is very descriptive, with special attention paid to details, and Sefriou makes an effort to use Arabic terms in many instances, thus adding an element of local color to his writings. His concern for the preservation of his culture is not unconditional and blind, however. He believes in the evolution of societies and the inevitability—and the benefit—of change.

Aida A. Bamia

Sehbal

Ottoman Turkish magazine.

Founded by Hüseyin Sadeddin Arel, *Sehbal*'s first issue appeared on March 14, 1909; the last issue, on July 23, 1914. The first Ottoman publication to appear in a magazine format, *Sehbal* was a mass-circulation, family-oriented magazine. Alongside treatment of issues of daily life were regular columns on literature and music.

David Waldner

Şeker Ahmet [1841–c. 1906]

Ottoman Turkish painter.

Ahmet Ali Paşa, known as Şeker Ahmet Paşa, was born and educated in the Uskudar district of Istanbul. While a student at the medical school, his talent for painting drew the attention of Sultan Abdülaziz, who sent him to Paris where he studied the academic painting of the period with French artists Boulanger and Gérôme. In 1870, he displayed his work in a Parisian exhibition, and in 1871, he returned to Istanbul. Şeker Ahmet Paşa organized and participated in a number of exhibitions in Istanbul and won many Ottoman and foreign awards for his work. The highly finished quality of his paints and the static linearity of his renderings call to mind French academic painters such as Daubigny and Courbet. His series of landscapes of the gardens and parks of Istanbul, as well as a variety of still lifes, reflects the conscious efforts of Turkish artists to develop Western techniques of painting.

BIBLIOGRAPHY

RENDA, GÜNSEL, and C. MAX KORTEPETER, eds. *The Transformation of Turkish Culture: The Atatürk Legacy.* Princeton, N.J., 1986.

David Waldner

Şekip, Mehmet

Foreign minister in the Ottoman government of Lebanon.

Mehmet Şekip (also known as Shakib Efendi) was sent in 1845 by the Ottoman Empire, under pressure from the European powers, to end sectarian fighting in Lebanon. Before he accepted the assignment, he made it clear that a revision of the 1842 system of the double qa'immaqamate was necessary, and he called on the diplomatic envoys of the European powers to cease interfering in the internal affairs of Lebanon. His first action in Lebanon was to arrest leaders of both warring factions.

His revisions of the system of the double qa'immaqamate produced the "system of Shakib Efendi." According to the revisions, the QA'IMMAQAM would be assisted by a council representing Lebanon's various sectarian communities, and he himself would appoint members of the council. The council was given financial (tax collecting) and judicial responsibilities that formerly had been handled by the feudal landlords. Upon his return to Istanbul, the sectarian leaders resumed their bickering.

BIBLIOGRAPHY

AL-HAKIM, YUSUL. *Memoirs.*
SALIBI, KAMAL. *A Modern History of Lebanon.*

As'ad AbuKhalil

Selçuk, Munir Nurettin [1899–1981]

Turkish singer and composer.

One of the most skillful and famous Turkish singers of the twentieth century, Selçuk was born in Istanbul during the Ottoman Empire, the son of an official in the Imperial Council. His aptitude for music and his beautiful voice became apparent when he was still a child, and he then began to take music lessons from the foremost teachers of the time.

He gave his first public concert at the age of eighteen. Throughout the 1920s, he continued to study music, including a period of piano study in Paris, and his first recordings date from this decade. Beginning in 1942, he served on the board of directors of the Istanbul Conservatory and became its chief in 1953. He composed more than one hundred pieces and was a founder of the Eastern Music Group, which was led by Ali Rifat Çagetay.

BIBLIOGRAPHY

Türk Ansiklopedisi. Ankara, 1981.
Yeni Türk Ansiklopedisi. Istanbul, 1985.

David Waldner

Self-Denying Protocol

A multilateral agreement of 1860 that assured safety to Christians in Lebanon.

In the midst of a civil war in Lebanon, the mass killing of Christians was instigated by Druze and Muslims in the summer of 1860. France for some time had taken a particular interest in the Maronite community of Lebanon, and in response to the human suffering, Napoléon III decided to intervene to protect the Maronites. However, Great Britain had no desire to see French troops in Syria and moved to forestall unilateral French intervention. Insisting that the problem was an internal matter to be resolved by the Ottoman sultan, Great Britain called on the European powers to issue the Self-Denying Protocol of August 3–5, 1860, which was signed by Great Britain, France, Prussia, Austria, Russia, and the Ottoman Empire. It declared that the powers had no territorial ambitions in the Ottoman Empire and that their sole concern was the restoration of order in Lebanon in such a way as to guarantee the future security of the Christian communities. Within the year, a settlement had been achieved.

BIBLIOGRAPHY

HUREWITZ, J. C., ed. *The Middle East and North Africa in World Politics.* New Haven, Conn., 1975.

Zachary Karabell

Selim III   [1761–1808]

Twenty-eighth Ottoman sultan, 1789–1807.

The son of Mustafa III, Selim was allowed by his uncle Abdülhamit I, an unusually free and liberal upbringing, on the assumption that he would succeed to the throne. Wars against Russia during the reigns of his father and uncle convinced Selim of the need to modernize the Ottoman army, and while still a prince he sought advice and assistance from King Louis XVI of France for this purpose.

When Selim succeeded his uncle in April 1789, the Ottoman Empire was again at war with Russia and Austria. Selim's first act, in May, was to convene a special assembly of leading statesmen to discuss the empire's military and financial problems, and to request detailed reports on how to proceed with reforms. The resulting New Order program accelerated and formalized the piecemeal military and educational Europeanization started earlier. A new army corps was formed, with a separate financial bureau to administer earmarked revenues to support the effort. Schools to train officers for the army and navy in the European manner were given new impetus. Another extension of a process begun earlier was in diplomatic relations with European powers. Ambassadors had been sent to leading capitals to gather information on European politics and international relations, and to study recent military and technological advances; in 1792 the Ottoman government established permanent embassies in London, Paris, Berlin, Vienna, and St. Petersburg so that the empire could be better informed about European relations and present its concerns directly.

With Europe increasingly preoccupied with French Revolutionary wars, Selim turned his attention to internal political problems, using his new troops to suppress provincial notables who controlled large areas of the empire's territories. They had some initial success, but from 1797 the empire was embroiled in the European war when France took an active interest in the eastern Mediterranean, culminating in Napoleon's invasion of Egypt in 1798. The Ottoman Empire was thus forced to accept support from Britain and Russia against its traditional ally France. After Britain's navy and Selim's army turned Napoleon back from Palestine, France left Egypt in 1801, and Britain followed soon thereafter. Nevertheless, full Ottoman control could not be restored; the vice commander of the New Order army in Egypt, Muhammad Ali, eventually gained power.

In Arabia, Wahhabi doctrine had taken hold, and its Sa'udi champion rejected Selim's position as caliph of the Sunni Muslim community. In the Balkans, Russia's influence was growing, both in the Danubian principalities and in Serbia, where a revolt began in 1804. Since France's threat to the Ottoman territories had been lifted, Britain had assumed an active role in the eastern Mediterranean. After Napoleon's victories in central Europe, Selim, wishing to balance the influences of Britain and Russia, atempted to revive the alliance with France, but Russia's advance into Moldavia and Wallachia in October 1806 and Britain's naval activity near Istanbul in January 1807 prevented it.

Beset by foreign engagements not of his choosing; unable to establish authority in the provinces, where political, religious, and ethnic uprisings challenged his rule; and alienating large segments of Istanbul's population by what seemed to be an overhasty attempt to Europeanize while European powers dominated the empire's policies, Selim was deposed in May 1807 after a popular insurrection supported by palace attendants and out-of-favor officials. A year later, when provincial forces loyal to Selim marched on the capital, he was killed to prevent a countercoup.

Though a Europeanizing reformer, Selim was educated in the classical Islamic-Ottoman culture. He was a distinguished poet and a talented composer. He tried to regenerate the power of his empire through a European-style army, but in his political behavior he was a typical sultan. He helped develop policy and direction, but left government in the hands of viziers. To keep factionalism in check, he changed viziers and other statesmen frequently. His greatest misfortune was that his empire no longer could set its own course and go at its own pace. In the last decade of his rule, Selim found himself responding to foreign threats from rapidly shifting directions, desperately trying to keep in check external and internal forces that proved to be beyond his control.

BIBLIOGRAPHY

ALDERSON, A. D. *The Structure of the Ottoman Dynasty.* Oxford, 1956.

SHAW, STANFORD J. *Between Old and New: The Ottoman Empire under Selim III, 1789–1807.* Cambridge, U.K., 1971.

I. Metin Kunt

Semites

Members of a linguistic family; the term does not refer to religious, ethnic, or racial identification.

A Semite is a member of a group of peoples of southwestern Asia, chiefly represented by Jews and Arabs, who speak a Semitic language, any one of an Afro–Asiatic language family that includes Arabic, Aramaic, Amharic, and Hebrew.

BIBLIOGRAPHY

ZIRING, LAWRENCE. *The Middle East Political Dictionary.* Santa Barbara, Calif., 1984.

David Waldner

Semitic Languages

A group of languages, previously categorized as the Semito-Hamitic family, that are now described as a branch of the Afro-Asiatic linguistic family.

Hebrew, Aramaic, Syriac, and Ugaritic are derived from the Northwest Semitic group; Arabic and the Ethiopic languages belong to the South Semitic branch. The character-defining feature of Semitic languages is the system of consonant roots. Most words are triliteral (three consonants separated by vowels), though bi- and quadriliterals are also common. Each root represents a distinct meaning; variations from that root are derived by set patterns of vocalization, less important consonants, and prefixes or suffixes. The root sense of the verb is modified to express intensification, causation, reciprocity, etc., by vowel changes or prefixes. All members of the family have two genders, masculine and feminine, and, with the exception of Ethiopic languages, the adjective follows the noun and agrees with it in gender. Nominal sentences are ordered subject-verb-object, while verbal sentences are verb-subject-object.

BIBLIOGRAPHY

CAMPBELL, GEORGE L. *Compendium of the World's Languages.* London, 1991.

David Waldner

Sened-i İttifak

"Deed of agreement" agreed upon by Ottoman provincial magnates (ayans and derebeys), 1808.

In the fall of 1808, Grand Vizier Bayrakdar Mustafa Pasha called a conference in Istanbul. Bayrakdar had led the revolt that ousted Sultan Mustafa IV in July of that year and installed Sultan Mahmud II. He desired to restore various of the reforms of Selim III, who had been deposed in 1807, but the essence of the Sened-i İttifak was formal government recognition of the status and autonomy of the provincial magnates. Mahmud II signed the agreement reluctantly, then worked during his reign to annul its impact and undermine the magnates.

BIBLIOGRAPHY

LEWIS, BERNARD. *The Emergence of Modern Turkey.* New York, 1961.

Richard W. Bulliet

Sepehri, Sohrab   [1928–1980]

Iranian poet and painter.

Sepehri was born in Kashan and graduated from Tehran University's Faculty of Fine Arts. He founded a school of poetry resembling that of the French symbolists. Although commentators place him within the tradition of Iranian poetry, he created totally new metaphors in his verse. Sepehri's most famous piece, "Seda-ye Pa-ye Ab" (The Sound of the Water's Footsteps, 1965), is an autobiographical narrative verse that has been called a masterpiece of contemporary Persian poetry.

BIBLIOGRAPHY

KARIMI-HAKKAK, AHMAD. *An Anthology of Modern Persian Poetry.* Boulder, Colo., 1978.

Pardis Minuchehr

Sephardim

Jews whose roots are in the medieval Iberian peninsula.

The term *Sepharad* appears for the first time in the biblical book of Obadiah (verse 20), probably in reference to the city of Sardis in Asia Minor. *Sepharad* was initially used to designate Spain in the first century, and its identity with Iberia was widely accepted by the eighth century. The self-designation of Moses Maimonides, the twelfth-century philosopher and halakhist, as Sephardic (*ha-Sepharadi*) was accepted as denoting a Spanish Jew.

Sephardim constitute one of the two main branches of world Jewry. Throughout the Middle Ages they and the Jews of the rest of the Mediterranean constituted a majority of world Jewry. They had arrived in Spain at the time of the dispersion of Jews throughout the Roman Empire in ancient times, developing unique customs, outlook, language, and lore while living among both Muslims and Christians in medieval times. Under the influence of medieval Islam, Sephardim integrated the sciences, philosophy, Hebraic lore, and halakhah in new and dynamic forms. In close correspondence with Jewish legal authorities in Baghdad, Sephardic scholarship developed an independent legal voice by the tenth century. Sephardic creativity was especially noteworthy in poetry, where Arabic motifs and linguistic forms were deftly adapted to create a new body of literature in Hebrew. Sephardic Jews also were distinguished courtiers and statesmen in Spain until 1492.

Sephardic history is marked by alternating periods of fierce persecution and benign toleration under Muslims and Christians. With the progressive reconquest of Spain by Christian forces after the twelfth century, Sephardim confronted aggressive proselytizing, religious disputations, and periodic forced conversions. As a result of these efforts to undermine Judaism, Sephardim became split between forced converts and adherents to Judaism. Known as *conversos* and Marranos, the converts to Christianity presented a challenge to the Roman Catholic Church and the Spanish populace. Many attempted to become sincere Christians, and many tried heroically to maintain their Judaism in secrecy. Crypto-Judaism constituted a religious affront to the church, tantamount to heresy. Thus in 1481, an inquisition was established in Spain to ferret out secret Jews. It continued to prosecute them for many generations after Jews had been banished from Iberia.

In 1492 the Jews were expelled from Spain. A large number went to Portugal, where they were forcibly converted in 1497. Many of these forced converts eventually found their way to the Netherlands and the New World. Others found asylum in the Ottoman Empire, Italy, and North Africa, establishing new centers of Sephardic civilization in the Balkans, Anatolia, and Palestine. The Sephardic exiles tended to preserve medieval Castilian in the form they had spoken it in Spain (their language, known as Ladino, was medieval Spanish written in Hebrew characters), cherishing their customs, traditions, and folklore in their new lands of dispersion.

The Ladino-speaking centers of Jewish culture continued into the twentieth century. The last strongholds of Ladino were destroyed by the Nazis in 1943. Contemporary Sephardic communities exist on all continents, the largest ones located today in Israel, France, and the United States. Their traditional language has died out and their customs are becoming a preserve of the elderly as the younger generations undergo progressive assimilation to the Ashkenazic majorities among whom they live.

Jane Gerber

Serasker

Highest Ottoman military rank in the nineteenth century.

Equivalent to commander in chief of the military forces, the office of serasker was created in 1826. The serasker became the virtual minister of war under 1830s reforms, and he headed police and fire-fighting forces in Constantinople (now Istanbul) until 1845. The man responsible for extending the serasker's power over all of the Ottoman military corps was Mehmet Husrev, commander of the new Mansure army and serasker from 1827 to 1836. The serasker controlled his own treasury, which in the 1830s was by far the largest in the Ottoman government. Under Husrev's leadership, the seraskerate established its own weapons, clothing, and food industries to ensure provisions.

Beginning in the 1850s, the seraskerate developed its own school system. Under Abdülhamit II, who took the title of commander in chief, the serasker's power was diminished. The office and department were formally renamed minister of war and Ministry of War in the early twentieth century.

BIBLIOGRAPHY

Lewis, Bernard. *The Emergence of Modern Turkey*. New York, 1961.

Shaw, Stanford J., and Ezel Kural Shaw. *History of the Ottoman Empire and Modern Turkey*. Vol. 2. New York, 1977.

Elizabeth Thompson

Serbs

A Slavic people who migrated to the Balkans in the sixth and seventh centuries and accepted Christianity in the ninth century.

Today, over eight million Serbs live in and around Serbia, which is bounded by Hungary, Romania,

Bulgaria, Macedonia, Albania, Bosnia, and Croatia. Serbo-Croatian, which belongs to the South Slavic languages, is spoken by Serbs, Croats, Montenegrins, and Muslims. When used by Serbs, it is designated as Serbian and written in Cyrillic script. This feature, and their membership in the Eastern Orthodox faith, distinguishes the Serbs from the closely related Slovenes and Croats. The overwhelming majority of Serbs in Serbia make their livelihood from agriculture and industry.

The Serbs' historical heroes include Czar Stephen Dushan, who created a mighty empire encompassing much of the Balkan peninsula in the mid-fourteenth century and whose empire was later crushed by the Turks at the historic Battle of Kosovo in 1389. In the modern period, Karageorge (Black George) led a rebellion against the Turks starting in 1804, and Milos Obrenovic led another revolt in 1815; both provided dynasties that would rule over Serbia until the end of World War II.

BIBLIOGRAPHY

SINGLETON, FRED. *A Short History of the Yugoslav Peoples.* New York, 1985.

John Micgiel

Seri, Dan-Benaya [1935–]

Israeli author.

Seri was born in Jerusalem. His first novel, *Grandma Sultana's Salty Biscuits* (1980), was acclaimed for its originality in weaving folk motifs, psychological depth, and surrealism into a poetic prose rich in language and detail. His second book, *Birds of Shade* (1987), includes four novellas, one of which, "Siman-Tov's Thousand Wives," was made into a film.

Seri's works are set in Jerusalem and focus on its ethnic, Sephardic Jewish communities. He creates bizarre plots of sexual perversion stemming from cultural mores, customs, and taboos, as well as individual eccentricity. The fictitious community featured in these works is oblivious to the surrounding world, lives by its folk traditions and lusts, and is controlled by the intensity of a pseudological progression of events. The gallery of characters created by Seri appears in all of his books, forming a fantastic–realistic world of consistent anomalies. His prose style is saturated with biblical and Talmudic references, often used out of their original context and meaning, thus producing a cunning modernistic irony.

Mishael, the protagonist of Seri's recent novel *Mishael* (1992), is a lonely widower who discovers that he is pregnant. As his body grotesquely transforms to that of a woman, Mishael sets out to find himself a new wife, all the while confronting his own sexual identity and the harassment of his community. The novel suggests childhood traumas and guilt as the grounds for this predicament, yet the hero's acceptance of the unnatural as reality is its main strength.

Zvia Ginor

Setif

City southwest of Constantine in northeastern Algeria.

Setif is located at the site of the ancient Roman city of Sitifis. Near Setif in 1152 the Almohads defeated the Banu Hilal tribe. The city declined during the Ottoman Empire. During France's colonial administration, the city was the site of bloody riots and retributions (the SETIF REVOLT) in May 1945, which galvanized Algerian nationalism. The estimated population in 1983 was 187,000.

BIBLIOGRAPHY

ABUN-NASR, JAMIL M. *A History of the Maghrib in the Islamic Period.* Cambridge, U.K., 1987.

Phillip C. Naylor.

Setif Revolt

One of the most violent incidents in the history of French colonialism in Algeria.

The May 1945 revolt in the city of Setif, Algeria, was caused by the deportation proceedings of Messali Hadj, the rising expectations for reform, and the agitations of nationalists. After the start of a parade celebrating Europe's victory over fascism, Muslims demonstrated carrying nationalist placards. This provoked the police, leading to rioting and the deaths of 103 Europeans. French retribution probably caused between 5,000 and 10,000 Muslim deaths (although some contend that the fatalities were in the tens of thousands).

This event convinced many younger nationalists that violence was the only recourse to French colonialism as disclosed by the 1947 formation of the Organisation Spéciale (OS) and in 1954 the Front de Libération Nationale (FLN).

BIBLIOGRAPHY

AGERON, CHARLES-ROBERT. *Histoire de l'Algérie contemporaine: De l'insurrection de 1871 au déclenchement de la guerre de libération (1954).* Paris, 1979.

Phillip C. Naylor

Settlement Policy, Israel

Policy that resulted in a Jewish state in 1948 and that remains an inflammatory issue in the Arab world.

Settlement policy is a subject of scope and importance to the history of Zionism and to the development of its concepts and values. It is basic to understanding both the pioneering Jewish society of the late nineteenth and early twentieth centuries in Palestine and the emergence of the ARAB–ISRAEL CONFLICT.

In the broad sense, "settlement of Jews in the Land of Israel (Eretz Yisrael)" is the purpose of Zionism and the way to realize its aims—reestablishing Jews in their biblical homeland, providing them with a refuge from persecution, and creating a spiritual center for them. Immigration (ALIYAH) and settlement are the two concepts that have been interrelated since the nineteenth-century beginnings of Zionism. Through aliyah (literally, an ascent) that is fulfilled by settlement, a new Jewish society is being created by Diaspora Jews.

Chief among the Zionist ideals for the new society was an agricultural base, and land was purchased for farm communities from Ottoman and Arab landowners. As Jewish settlers came into Palestine, both urban and rural lifestyles were assumed, but by the 1930s eve of partition, agricultural settlements determined the borders of Jewish presence in western Palestine (since attempts at land purchases and settlement in Transjordan had not been successful). Consequently, hardly any Jewish settlement existed in the area that after 1948 became the West Bank (of the Jordan).

During the British mandate over Palestine (1922–1948), the Arabs viewed Jewish land purchases as the main instrument of Jewish domination, the means of evicting Arab fellahin (mainly tenant farmers) from their land. Zionist settlers complained that the mandatory government failed to implement Clause 11 of the 1922 League of Nations mandate, which stated that it would place state lands at the disposal of Jewish settlers to promote concentrations of Jewish settlements.

During the Ottoman Empire, 43 Jewish settlements had been established in Palestine, with a population of about 14,000. By 1948, some 291 Jewish agricultural settlements existed. From 1949 to 1953, some 300 new settlements were founded (mainly by immigrants to the new State of Israel). Locations followed Zionist principles of dispersing the population throughout the country—to areas that had never been farmed or to those from which Arabs had fled or been expelled.

Following the 1967 Arab–Israel War, in which Israel captured territory in the Gaza Strip, the Sinai peninsula, the Golan Heights, and the West Bank, settlements were used by the Israeli government to create a Jewish presence in these territories and to enhance security at the borders. Israelis who supported the ALLON PLAN, which reflected the Labor party's position, advocated keeping territories considered vital for defense purposes, such as the Jordan valley, but foresaw Israel's eventual withdrawal from the rest of the West Bank. First drafted following the 1967 War and reconsidered in the 1970s, the Allon Plan was never implemented. Between 1967 and 1977, the official Israeli view was, nevertheless, that those captured territories would in time be exchanged for durable peace agreements with the Arabs.

In the prestate period, the Revisionists—the forerunners of Likud party members—had not viewed agricultural and strategic settlements as effective political instruments for creating the Jewish state. After the 1977 elections, however, Menachem Begin and the newly installed Likud party adopted and greatly intensified the Labor party's emphasis on the efficacy of settlements. In making additional Jewish settlements their major national goal, they were joined by such religious Zionist groups as Gush Emunim (Bloc of the Faithful), whose members attached biblical significance to the retention of what was the whole of ancient Judea and Samaria, now the West Bank. In 1982, the evacuation of the Sinai and the Rafa salient, which concluded the first phase of the Camp David peace process, was attended by fierce debates among Israelis and Jews worldwide. Many political conservatives perceived the evacuation as an unacceptable retreat from the Zionist principle that no Jewish settlement should ever be abandoned.

From 1967 to 1977, twenty settlements were established on the West Bank and the Golan Heights, and in the Gaza area, with a total population of 3,867 Jews. By 1992, in the West Bank alone there were 117 settlements, populated by 107,000 Jews. Unlike the Labor party, which had avoided establishing settlements in areas heavily populated by Arabs, the Likud government deliberately placed the new settlements in the main hilly areas of the West Bank where most Arabs lived. The government appropriated as much as 60 percent of the land of the West Bank and over 30 percent of the land in the Gaza Strip for settlements. By making the Jews in these settlements answerable only to Jewish law, it subverted the recognition of the land as "occupied" territory.

The increased number of Jewish settlements in these occupied territories brought Israel unfavorable international attention and troubled its relations with the United States. In 1992, the United States refused to extend a $10 billion loan guarantee, which Israel needed to accommodate a great influx of Russian immigrants, until Israel agreed to freeze the construction of settlements in the West Bank and the Gaza area. Internally, the issue of the settlements divided Israelis and was the major focus of national politics. Not only did critics see the creation of new settlements as a chief obstacle in the peace process, but they also objected to the diversion of resources that were used to help subsidize the settlers. Billions of dollars were invested for Jewish settlements in the occupied territories between 1967 and 1992. Upon regaining power in the 1992 elections, the Labor party entered into peace negotiations with the Palestine Liberation Organization (PLO) and greatly curtailed allocation of resources to the existing settlements, freezing most work on new settlements.

BIBLIOGRAPHY

BEIN, ALEX. History of the Jewish Settlement in Israel. 5th ed., 1976. In Hebrew.
BEIN, ALEX, with Ruth Perlmann. Immigration and Settlement in the State of Israel. Tel Aviv, 1982. In Hebrew.
GVATI, CHAIM. A Century of Settlement: A History of the Jewish Agricultural Settlement in Eretz Israel. 2 vols. Tel Aviv, 1982. In Hebrew.
TESSLER, MARK. A History of the Israeli-Palestinian Conflict. Urbana, Ill. 1994.

Yaacov Shavit

Seven Sisters

Name given to the cartel of major oil companies that dominated the production and distribution of oil from 1930 to 1970.

The "sisters" were Standard Oil of New Jersey (Exxon), British Petroleum, ROYAL DUTCH SHELL, Chevron, Texaco, MOBIL, and GULF OIL. They lost control of oil reserves in the Middle East in the 1960s and 1970s, when petroleum resources were nationalized by the producing countries. Chevron and Gulf merged in 1986, so now there are six sisters. In the 1990s the sisters are still very important in distribution and refining, and in exploration for new sources, often in joint ventures with the members of the Organization of Petroloeum Exporting Countries (OPEC).

[*See also:* Arabian American Oil Company.]

BIBLIOGRAPHY

SAMPSON, ANTHONY. The Seven Sisters: The Great Oil Companies and the World They Shaped. New York, 1975.

Jean-François Seznec

Şevket, Mahmut   [1856–1913]

Ottoman general and grand vizier.

Born in Baghdad the son of a provincial government official, Mahmut Şevket, known as Şevket Paşa completed his studies in Constantinople (now Istanbul), where he entered military service. As part of a special commission for military purchases and training, he was sent to Germany for nine years. He was promoted to the rank of general in 1901. Between 1905 and 1909, he held several posts in Rumelia, achieving minor successes in easing tension in the region.

A year after the Young Turk revolution, Şevket Paşa achieved new prominence as commander of the Hareket Ordusu (operations army) that marched on Constantinople in April 1909, putting down the counterrevolution. In the new post of inspector general of Constantinople, he led the brutal represssion and punishment of the rebels under martial law for the next two years. In 1910, he became minister of war and advocated withdrawal of the military from politics. When the COMMITTEE OF UNION AND PROGRESS (CUP) seized power in January 1913, it appointed him grand vizier. Six months later, he was assassinated by CUP opponents. His murder introduced a new period of violent repression by the CUP.

BIBLIOGRAPHY

LEWIS, BERNARD. The Emergence of Modern Turkey. New York, 1961.
SHAW, STANFORD J., and EZEL KURAL SHAW. History of the Ottoman Empire and Modern Turkey. Vol. 2. New York, 1977.

Elizabeth Thompson

Sèvres, Treaty of

Peace treaty signed by Britain, France, and the Ottoman Empire after World War I.

World War I ended in the Middle East with the signing of the Mudros armistice by the Ottoman Empire on October 30, 1918; but the Middle East was only a small concern of the overall peace negotiations held in France in 1919—German issues took precedence.

Each nation and group came with its own agenda. British Prime Minister David Lloyd George, while mouthing all the proper slogans about goodwill to Middle Eastern peoples, was there to advance the interests of the British Empire. These included British-controlled sea and land routes to India and assurance that no other power be given important strategic areas. French President Georges Clemenceau, compensating for heavy French troop losses, adamantly adhered to each wartime agreement signed by the Allies that would give France a hold on Syria and southern Anatolia. He also hoped for dominance over the Turkish Straits and perhaps over what would become Turkey. U.S. President Woodrow Wilson came with his Fourteen Points.

In addition to the big three, representatives of other concerned nations and groups came to the peace negotiations, including the Hijazis, Armenians, Greeks, Italians, and Zionists. No permanent decision were made in 1919 in this atmosphere of claims and counterclaims.

At the end of 1919, British troops in Syria were replaced by French troops, giving the Arabs the impression that the SYKES–PICOT AGREEMENT would be upheld. In Palestine, anti-Jewish riots broke out. The Arab Syrian Congress elected Faisal ibn Husayn as king of Syria and his brother Abdullah ibn Husayn as king of Iraq and tensions rose in Iraq and Egypt. Britain realized that a treaty for the Middle East could no longer be postponed and in April 1920 met with France in San Remo, Italy, to forge an agreement on their points of difference. This prepared the way for a peace settlement with the Ottoman Empire—and the Treaty of Sèvres was signed on August 10, 1920.

By this treaty, the Ottoman sultan recognized that his Arab provinces were cut off from his empire. Control over the Straits went to an international commission. Arabia was recognized as independent and a British protectorate over Egypt was acknowledged. Syria and Iraq became provisionally independent under the newly created mandate system—with Syria to be under the French and to include Alexandretta, Aleppo, Damascus, and Beirut; France could deal with King Faisal as it wished. The state of Iraq was formed under British tutelage, with the province of Mosul attached to those of Baghdad and Basra. Palestine, including both sides of the Jordan river, became a British mandate as well, and the (pro-Zionist) BALFOUR DECLARATION of 1917 was written into it. Germany's shares of the Turkish petroleum Company went to France, and Britain got oil-

pipeline transit rights across Syria. Britain and France immediately moved into their respective spheres, although the League of Nations mandates did not become effective until 1923.

The Treaty of Sèvres, imposed on the Ottoman government, was never ratified—because of internal Turkish affairs—namely the rise to power of Mustafa Kemal Atatürk and the overthrow of the Ottoman sultan. Thus the treaty became obsolete and final arrangements were put off until the Treaty of LAUSANNE, signed in 1923.

BIBLIOGRAPHY

HUREWITZ, J. C., ed. *The Middle East and North Africa in World Politics, A Documentary Record.* London, 1979.
LEWIS, BERNARD. *The Emergence of Modern Turkey.* New York, 1961; 2nd ed., London, 1968.

Sara Reguer

Seyfiyye

Military bureaucracy in the Ottoman Empire.

The Seyfiyye, literally "men of the sword," was an autonomous hierarchy of military personnel comprising the sometimes competing forces of the army and navy. After the 1826 destruction of the janissaries, the *ağa* was replaced by the *serasker* (commander in chief), who eventually unified all branches of the military except the navy under a single hierarchy.

BIBLIOGRAPHY

SHAW, STANFORD J. *History of the Ottoman Empire and Modern Turkey,* vol. 1. Cambridge, U.K., 1976.
SHAW, STANFORD J., and EZEL KURAL SHAW. *History of the Ottoman Empire and Modern Turkey,* vol. 2. Cambridge, U.K., 1977.

Elizabeth Thompson

Sfar, Bashir   [c. 1865–1919]

Tunisian journalist.

From an aristocratic family of Tunis, Bashir Sfar was one of four editors of Tunisia's news periodical *Al-Hadira* (The Capital). Sfar was a leader of the reformist Young Tunisian movement, which brought together classically trained Tunisians from the Zaytuna mosque and modernly trained Tunisians from Sadiqi College in the middle years of the French protectorate. This was a precursor to the movement for independence from France.

BIBLIOGRAPHY

GUEZMIR, KHALED. *Jeunes Tunisiens*. Tunis, 1986.

Laurence Michalak

Sfar, Tahar   [1903–   ]

Tunisian nationalist.

One of the early and most vocal leaders of the DES-TOUR movement for nationalism, Sfar (like Habib Bourguiba, who became president of Tunisia after independence in 1956) was educated at the Sadiqi College and in France. In 1934, Sfar played a central role in the formation of the new Neo-Destour political party. In the late 1930s, faced with increasingly repressive measures by the French colonial administration (France held a protectorate from 1881), and disillusioned with the militant stance adopted by Bourguiba and others, Sfar effectively withdrew from politics.

BIBLIOGRAPHY

LEJRI, MOHAMED SALAH. "L'Evolution du Mouvement National Tunisien." Ph.D. diss. Lausanne, 1975.
MOORE, HENRY CLEMENT. *Tunisia since Independence*. Berkeley, Calif., 1965.

Matthew S. Gordon

Sfax

Tunisian seaport on the northeast coast of the Gulf of Gabès.

Sfax (also Sfaqes or Safaqis) was a Phoenician trading center before it was settled in the eighth century by Arab invaders spreading Islam; they built a mosque in the mid-ninth century. It continued as an important seaport for the Mediterranean olive oil trade and was one of the few Tunisian towns to resist the French occupation after the protectorate of 1881, thus suffering bombardment. After Tunisia became independent in 1956, Sfax became the center of a governorate and the second-largest Tunisian city, with a population of some 232,000 (projected for 1984).

Today it has a medical school, one of three appellate courts, a large prison, the regional radio station, an international airport and an air-force base, and a busy port that handles mainly phosphates and olive oil.

BIBLIOGRAPHY

Encyclopaedia of Islam, 1st ed.
Tunisia: A Country Survey. Washington, D.C., 1988.

Matthew S. Gordon

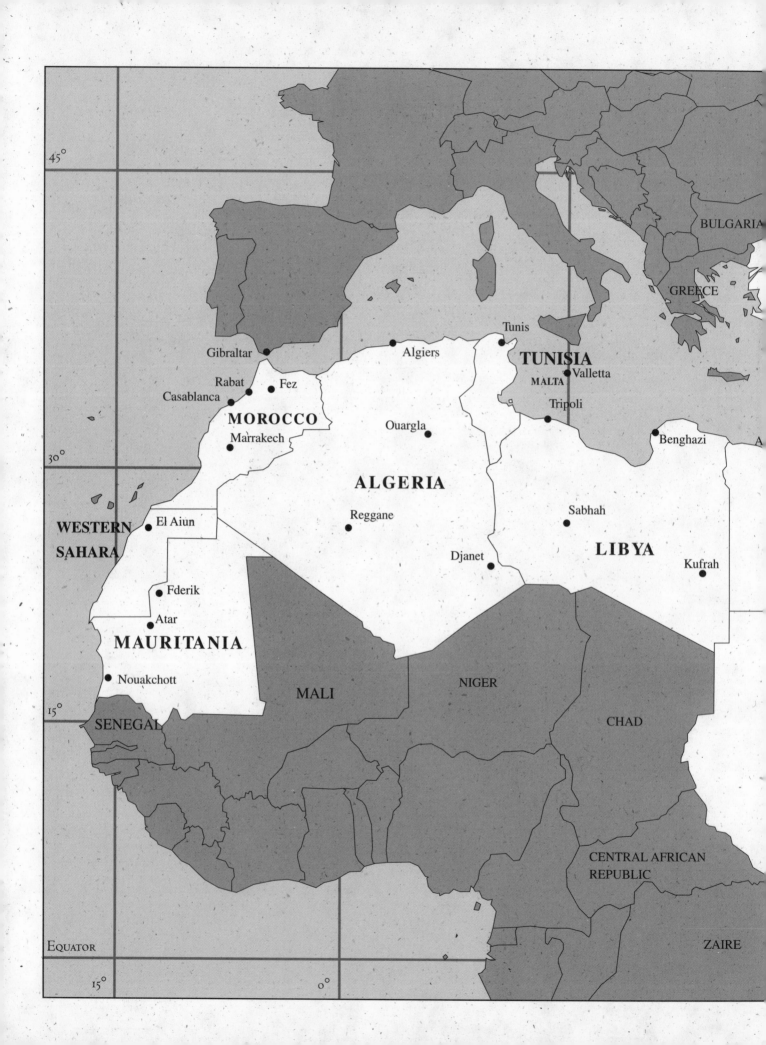